≡9 A:

CAPITAL MARKETS
AND COMPANY LAW

Capital Markets and Company Law

Edited by

Klaus J. Hopt, Hamburg, and Eddy Wymeersch, Gent

OXFORD
UNIVERSITY PRESS

OXFORD
UNIVERSITY PRESS

Great Clarendon Street, Oxford OX2 6DP

Oxford University Press is a department of the University of Oxford.
It furthers the University's objective of excellence in research, scholarship,
and education by publishing worldwide in

Oxford New York

Auckland Bangkok Buenos Aires Cape Town Chennai
Dar es Salaam Delhi Hong Kong Istanbul Karachi Kolkata
Kuala Lumpur Madrid Melbourne Mexico City Mumbai Nairobi
São Paulo Shanghai Taipei Tokyo Toronto

Oxford is a registered trade mark of Oxford University Press
in the UK and in certain other countries

Published in the United States
by Oxford University Press Inc., New York

British Library Cataloguing in Publication Data

Data available

Library of Congress Cataloging in Publication Data

Data available

ISBN 0-19-925558-X

1 3 5 7 9 10 8 6 4 2

Typeset by Hope Services (Abingdon) Ltd
Printed in Great Britain
on acid-free paper by
T. J. International Ltd., Padstow, Cornwall

Preface

'Capital markets and company law' is a connection that is not self-evident for many traditional European company lawyers and company law professors, at least in continental Europe. For decades company law was an area for itself, centered on the public company as an organization, concentrating on the structure of this organization and the relations between its various organs and shareholders, proud of its professionalism between theory and practice, and very much self-sufficient. Things have changed dramatically, though much later in Europe than in the United States. Capital market law has been emerging in all European countries, with the extensively developed U.S. American securities regulation serving for some as the ultimate model, while for others it is a perspective to be feared and—though probably impossible—avoided. The harmonization efforts of the European Union have contributed to the growth of a large body of harmonized law in the field of European company law, which has lagged far behind European stock exchange and capital market law, though lately there have been signs that it may be catching up. Today, company law and capital market law are widely recognized as two distinct but closely related areas that influence each other and partly overlap.

The functional interrelationship between both company law and capital market law is best illustrated by the recent phenomenon of the corporate governance movement, which has taught us that internal corporate governance—much of which is company law—and external corporate governance—in particular the pressures of the capital markets, including the market of corporate control—supplement each other and to a certain degree can even substitute for deficiencies in the other. Therefore, corporate governance and shareholder value and the corporate governance recommendations make up a good part of this book (expressly in parts IV and VI, but also concerning disclosure in part III, the role of the institutional investor in part V, and in relation to conflicts of interest in part VII).

Still, recent developments point beyond a mere interrelationship between company law and capital market law. This book is named *Capital Markets and Company Law* because the markets themselves, in particular the international securities markets, increasingly influence company law, national as well as European and international. The inverse relationship—the *La Porta et al.* thesis that company law is relevant for the capital and financial markets—has also been observed and is hotly debated, both on an empirical and a theoretical level, by *Coffee* and others. It is represented by a contribution on tunneling in part VIII. But this is not in the foreground of this book.

The internationalization of the securities markets due to increasingly momentous cross-border investment—which is only likely to accelerate since the introduction of the Euro—will strengthen even further the influence exercised by these markets on the rules and practices that govern the companies whose securities are quoted there. Most of these rules—whether rules of company law or of securities regulation—continue to be embedded in national legal systems and hence still present sometimes wide discrepancies. Yet the markets increasingly affect these rules and practices. These include not only the securities markets, but also strongly the market for corporate charters, based on competition between regulations, and further other competitive phenomena related to the role of the accountants or lawyers in company transactions.

In effect, as national rules are increasingly exposed to competition from other jurisdictions, they are being bent, either toward greater flexibility or toward solutions that have already been adopted in other jurisdictions. The same applies to rules that have been harmonized within the framework of the European Union and for which a need for updating is increasingly felt. A greater need for flexibility is felt especially with respect to rules related to the securities markets. Rules that originally were thought to protect investors—like legal capital—are being challenged by new practices where the protection flows from the effects of the efficient functioning of the market. Market influences can be enhanced by meaningful disclosure and the pressure of institutional investors, as shown in parts III and V of the book.

However, regulatory competition does not exist in all quarters. A deficit continues to exist, particularly in the field of cross-border transactions or relations. States continue to fence off their markets under the cloak of investor protection. For the longer term, one should ask to what extent regulations can continue to strike a balance between local interests and the need for opening up the local market.

An issue raised in many of the chapters and highlighted in the last two parts, IX and X, of the book is the tension between harmonization by directive and harmonization by the markets, between a top-down approach and a bottom-up drive for more comparable regulation, between convergence and divergence or path dependence.

This book goes back to an international conference held in Siena on April 30–31, 2000, which in turn was a follow-up to the symposium held at the Max Planck Institute for Foreign Private and Private International Law in Hamburg in 1997 (Hopt, Kanda, Roe, Wymeersch, and Prigge, (eds.) *Comparative Corporate Governanc: The State of the Art and Emerging Research*, OUP 1998). Corporate governance remained a key topic in both the Siena conference and in this new book that has grown out of the discussions there. A number of the participants in the Siena conference also participated in the Hamburg symposium, and several more specific topics—in particular, disclosure, accounting and auditing, the market for corporate control, and institutional investors—were revisited and taken further. The emphasis of the new book is somewhat less on economics (though part I of the book is filled with facts and figures and there is quite a lot of economic input and arguments in the remainder of the book) and less on American law, since the influence of the capital market on company law may be better observed by lawyers and may be a phenomenon particularly affecting Europe, where the capital markets have long lagged behind America. However, the aim of the two books is similar: namely, to provide a broad and sometimes broadly divergent picture of the field, the state of the art, and the emerging research of capital market and company law.

This new book is the product of continuous collaboration between the two editors that dates back to the early 1990s (Hopt and Wymeersch, (eds.) *European Insider Dealing*, London 1991, and *idem, European Takeovers*, London 1992). It was made possible by the contributions and cooperativeness of a large international and interdisciplinary network of colleagues working in the same field, many of whom have become friends. To our great satisfaction, these are being continually joined by many younger colleagues, among them some of our own academic disciples.

Special thanks are also due to Professor *Guido Ferrarini* of the University of Genoa and Professor *Marco Belli* of the University of Siena who facilitated the conference planning, and to Siena University for effectively taking care of the very efficient organization of the conference.

Further thanks are due to *Nicole Kransfeld* and *Sonja Spuesens* of Ghent University who were very proficient in offering effective support in the preparation of the conference, and to *Sofie Dejonghe* of Ghent University for editing the manuscripts.

The second editor would also like to thank the Max Planck Foundation for allowing him to fund this conference with the proceeds of the Max Planck Award for International Cooperation 1998.

October 2002
K.J. Hopt, Hamburg
E. Wymeersch, Ghent/Brussels

Contents

Figures

Figures

Tables

Tables

J.C. Coffee, Jr. (Chapter 33)

Cases

The Contributors

Yakov Amihud

Yakov Amihud is Ira Rennert Professor of Entrepreneurial Finance at the Stern School of Business, New York University. He has published more than 80 research articles in professional journals and in books. His research focuses on the effects of securities markets' design and trading methods on securities price behaviour, and the effects of liquidity on asset pricing. He served as a consultant on these subjects to leading securities markets. His research work also includes the evaluation of corporate financial policies and restructuring, mergers and acquisitions, managerial objectives, dividend policy, and topics in law and finance. He has edited and co-edited five books on topics such as LBOs, bank M&As, international finance, and securities market design.

Heinz-Dieter Assmann

Professor of Private, Commercial and Business Law, Comparative Law and Jurisprudence, University of Tübingen Faculty of Law, 1986 et seq. Born 1951. Dr. iur., Frankfurt/M., 1980; LL.M., Center for Study of Financial Institutions, University of Pennsylvania Law School, Philadelphia/USA, 1981; Attorney-at-Law, Frankfurt/M., 1984–85; Professor of Law, University of Heidelberg Faculty of Law, 1985–86. Managing Director of the Juristisches Seminar of the University of Tübingen, 1988 et seq. Editor in chief of the monthly law journal *"Die Aktiengesellschaft"*, 1993 et seq. Visiting Professor: University of Tokyo (1994), Chuo University, Tokyo (1995), University of Chicago Law School (Max Rheinstein Visiting Professor of Law, 1997); Member of the board of the German national committee of comparative law (Gesellschaft für Rechtsvergleichung), 1996 et seq.

Matthias Bank

Prof. Dr. Matthias Bank is Professor for Banking and Finance at the University of Innsbruck. He studied Economics and Business Administration at the University of Giessen and the University of Mannheim. He received his Ph.D. in finance from University of Erlangen-Nuernberg in 1997 and finished his habilitation in 2001. He teaches courses in investment and finance and advanced courses in banking theory and market microstructure. Prof. Banks research covers several topics like the design of financial institutions, market microstructure issues, and manipulation in stock and futures markets. He published several articles in academic and professional journals and is author of two books.

Marco Becht

Marco Becht is an Associate Professor of Economics and Finance at the Université Libre de Bruxelles and the Executive Director of the European Corporate Governance Institute (ECGI). He graduated from the London School of Economics and Political Science (LSE) and holds a Ph.D. in economics from the European University Institute (EUI) in Florence. Becht's research focuses on corporate governance and empirical corporate finance. He is a Resident Fellow at the European Center for Advanced Research in Economics and Statistics (ECARES) and a Research Associate of the Centre for Economic Policy Research (CEPR). He is the scientific adviser of the corporate governance committee of APCIMS-EASD (Association of Private Client Investment Managers and Stockbrokers—European Association of Securities Dealers). Previously he worked at the Centro de Estudios Monetarios y Financieros (CEMFI) in Madrid and the European Commission's Directorate for Industry (DG III). Publications include: 'Corporate Governance and Control' (with P. Bolton and A. Roell), 'Handbook of the Economics of Finance 2002' (forthcoming), 'The Control of Corporate Europe' (with C. Mayer), 2001, Oxford University Press, 'European Corporate Governance: Trading off Liquidity against Control', European Economic Review, 1999.

Michael Blair

Michael Blair QC is in independent practice at the Bar of England and Wales, specializing in financial services. He was previously the General Counsel to the U.K. Financial Services Authority from 1998–2000, and before that to the Securities and Investments Board from 1987. He is a member of the U.K. Competition Commission Appeal Tribunal, and is the Chairman of the U.K. Review Body on Doctors' and Dentists' Remuneration. Recent publications include *Blackstone's Guide to the Financial Services and Markets Act* 2000 (general editor) and *Butterworths Financial Regulation Service* (Editor in chief).

John C. Coffee, Jr.

B.A., Amherst, 1966; LL.B., Yale, 1969; LL.M. (in taxation), New York University, 1976. Following graduation from law school, was a Reginald Heber Smith fellow for one year, doing poverty law litigation in New York City. Corporate lawyer with Cravath, Swaine & Moore, 1970–76. From 1976 until coming to Columbia in 1980, was a professor at Georgetown University Law Center. Visiting professor at Stanford University Law School, the University of Virginia Law School, and the University of Michigan Law School. Adolf A. Berle Professor of Law, Columbia University Law School. Reporter for the American Bar Association for its Model Standards on Sentencing Alternatives and Procedures and for the American Law Institute's Principles of Corporate Governance. Member, National Academy of Sciences panel studying empirical research on sentencing; the National Research Council's Standing Committee on Law and Justice; and the Advisory Panel on Environmental Sentencing Guidelines to the United States Sentencing Commission. Currently member of the SEC's Advisory Committee on the Capital Formation and Regulatory Processes; the Subcouncil on Capital Markets of the United States Competitiveness Policy Council; and the Legal Advisory Board to the National Association of Securities Dealers (NASD); and has recently served as a member of the Legal Advisory Committee to the board of directors of the New York Stock Exchange. Former chairperson of the Section on Business Associations of the Association of American Law Schools. Fellow of the American Academy of Arts and Sciences; listed by the National Law Journal as one of "The 100 Most Influential Lawyers in the United States". Publications include *Cases and Materials on Securities Regulation* (with Jennings, Marsh, and Seligman, 8th edn., 1998); *Knights, Raiders and Targets: The Impact of the Hostile Takeover* (with Lowenstein and Rose-Ackerman, 1988); *Cases and Materials on Corporations* (with Choper and Gilson, 4th edn., 1995); *Business Organization and Finance* (with Klein, 6th edn., 1995). Principal interests are corporations, securities regulation, class actions, criminal law, and "white-collar" crime.

Paul Davies

Paul Davies is the Cassel Professor of Commercial Law at the London School of Economics and Political Science. He has held this post since 1998, having previously been Professor of the Law of the Enterprise at the University of Oxford. He is author of *Introduction to Company Law* (2002) and the editor of the 6th edition of *Gower's Principles of Modern Company Law* and one of the editors of *Palmer's Company Law*. He was a member of the Steering Group of the Company Law Review carried out under the auspices of the Department of Trade and Industry in the U.K. between 1998 and 2001. He is a contributor to many international symposia on company law, especially but not exclusively, in the area of corporate governance. He was elected a Fellow of the British Academy in 2000.

Werner F. Ebke

Born in 1951. Rechtsreferendar, University of Muenster, 1977; LL.M., University of California School of Law (Boalt Hall), 1978; Dr. iur., University of Muenster, 1983; Habilitation, University of Muenster, 1987. Werner F. Ebke is Professor of Law and holds the Business and Tax Law Chair at the University of Konstanz, Germany; he is also Global Professor of Law at New York University. From 1983 until joining the Konstanz Law Faculty in 1988, he was a professor at the Southern Methodist University School of Law in Dallas, Texas. He has been a Visiting Professor at the University of Illinois, Urbana-Champaign, the University of Florida at Gainesville, the University of Houston Law Center, the University of Lyon, France, the University of St. Gallen, Switzerland, and Chuo University, Tokyo, Japan, and is a Permanent Visiting Professor of Law at the University of Lucerne, Switzerland. Werner F. Ebke has published extensively in the areas of German, European, U.S. American and international company law, comparative corporate govern-ance, securities regulation, financial accounting and auditing, conflicts of laws, professional liability and European Union law. He received the prestigious Max Planck Research Award (with Detlev F. Vagts, Harvard Law School) and the Prestasi Brokers Award, Rand Afrikaanse Universiteit, Johannesburg, South Africa. He is a member of the New York Bar and the American Law Institute.

Laurent Faugérolas

Paris Bar, 1989. University of Law Bordeaux, 1988 (Ph.D. 1988 magna cum laude, thesis 1989). MBA ISA (HEC Group), 1986. Institut d'Etudes Politiques, Bordeaux, 1982.

Editorial board of the Dictionnaire Joly *Bourse et Produits Financiers*. Vice Chairman of the French branch of "Plan International", a not-for-profit organization. Numerous articles on com-pany law and corporate finance. *Les Offres Publiques (Take-over Bids)*, a book jointly published with Professor Thierry Bonneau (Panthéon-Assas), EFE éd.1999. Specialized in take-overs, M&A, IPOs and global offering. Advised Total in connection with its take-over on Elf Aquitaine and on PetroFina; Renault with respect to its acquisition of an interest in Nissan; advised the underwriters for the first issuance of tracking stocks in Europe (Alcatel, fall 2000); merger between Lyonnaise des Eaux and Compagnie de Suez; advised numerous IPOs and dual listings on the Premier and Nouveau Marches of Paris EuroNext; restructuring of the Euro Disney share capital in 1994.

Eilís Ferran

Eilís Ferran is a Reader in Corporate Law and Financial Regulation at the University of Cambridge and Director of the Cambridge University Centre for Corporate and Commercial Law (3CL). She is the author of numerous articles and books on company law and regulation, including *Company Law and Corporate Finance* (OUP, 1999). In 1999 she was a Special Adviser to the U.K. Parliamentary Joint Committee on Financial Services and Markets and between 2000 and 2001 she was a Special Adviser to the U.K. Parliamentary Select Committee on Education and Employment. She is a mem-ber of the Law Society's Company Law Committee.

Guido A. Ferrarini

Guido A. Ferrarini graduated from the Genoa Law School in 1972, and obtained an LL.M. from Yale Law School in 1978. He is Professor of Law at the University of Genoa and Director, Centre for Law and Finance.

He is Honorary Professor at the Faculty of Laws at the University College of London and is the author of various books and articles in the fields of financial law, corporate law, and business law.

He is member of the Advisory Committee of the Italian Securities Commission (*Consob*), Rome, member of the Board of Trustees of the International Accounting Standards Committee (IASC), London, member of the Board of Directors of the European Corporate Governance Institute, Brussels, and member of the Board of Directors of Telecom Italia S.p.A., Milan. He is co-editor of the Rivista delle Società and is advisor for the Corporate Governance Committee of the Italian Stock Exchange, Milan and advisor for the Financial Markets Act Drafting Committee ("Draghi Committee"), Italian Treasury Ministry, Rome (1997–1998).

Kenneth Garbade

Kenneth Garbade (B.S. (physics and history), California Institute of Technology, 1968; PhD., Princeton University, 1975) is a vice president of the Federal Reserve Bank of New York in the Capital Markets function. He is the author of *Securities Markets* (McGraw-Hill, 1982), *Fixed Income Analytics* (MIT Press, 1996), and *Pricing Corporate Securities as Contingent Claims* (MIT Press, 2001). He was formerly professor of economics and finance at New York University and managing director at Bankers Trust Company.

José M. Garrido

José M. Garrido (Madrid, 1965), LL. B., University of Alcalá (Spain), 1989; LL. M., University of London (1991); LL. D., University of Bologna (Italy) (1993).

Visiting Researcher at the Universities of Oxford, Cambridge and Harvard. Visiting Professor at the University of Paris-XII. Lecturer of Commercial and Corporate Law, University of Vigo (Spain) (1994–2001); Senior Professor of Commercial and Corporate Law (University of Castilla-La Mancha, Spain) (2001). Professor Garrido has written extensively on Insolvency Law, Corporate Law, and Securities Regulation, among other fields within the wider area of Commercial Law. He is one of the members of the Group of Experts appointed to explore the possibilities of resuming the EU's initiative of a Take-over Directive.

Wolfgang Gerke

Professor Dr. Wolfgang Gerke, born on February 3, 1944, is a full professor of Banking and Finance at the University of Erlangen, Nuremberg (Germany). He is also research professor of the Mannheim-based ZEW Zentrum für Europäische Wirtschaftsforschung (Central Institute for European Economic Research).

Following his university studies in Saarbrücken, his doctor's degree and his qualification as an academic lecturer (Habilitation) at Frankfurt University in 1972 and 1978, respectively, he was appointed full professor of Banking and Finance at the Universities of Passau (1978–1981) and Mannheim (1981–1992). He was offered full professorships at the Universities of Saarbrücken, Linz (Austria), Münster and Frankfurt. He is one of the editors of the German economic journal *DBW- Die Betriebswirtschaft*. His research focuses on issues relating to capital market, banking, stock exchange, set-up financing and financing of small caps as is also evidenced in his publications. Professor Gerke is a member of the Federal Treasury Expert Commission on Stock Exchange Issues.

Zohar Goshen

Professor of Law, Faculty of Law, Hebrew University of Jerusalem. Visiting Professor of Law, Columbia Law School, 1998, 2001; Yale Law School, fall 1999. Professor at the Global Law School Program, NYU Law School, 2000. Law Clerk, Supreme Court of Israel, The Honorable Chief Justice Meir Shamgar, 1986–87. Chairperson—the Disciplinary Court of Securities Advisers and Portfolio Managers, 1997–2000. Director (for public interests), Israel's Discount Bank, 1997–2002 (state appointed). Director of the Israeli Securities Authority (Israel's SEC), 1995–1997. Areas of Teaching and Research: Corporate and Securities Law; Corporate Finance; and Antitrust.

Peter Hommelhoff

Born in Hamburg in 1942. Law studies at the Free University of Berlin, moving from there to Tübingen and Freiburg. He obtained his doctorate at the University of Freiburg in 1973 and qualified for professorship at the University of Bochum in 1981. Also in 1981 he accepted the Chair of Civil Law/Commercial and Business Law at the University of Bielefeld. In 1983 he was appointed judge (in secondary office) at the Regional Appeal Court. In Bielefeld Hommelhoff was Dean of the Faculty of Law.

In 1990 Peter Hommelhoff was given the Chair of Civil Law/Commercial and Business Law and Comparative Law at the University of Heidelberg. Since 1992 he has been spokesman for the long-term collaborative research project "Company Organization and Company Activity according to German, European and International Law". In 1997 he became acting editor of the *Zeitschrift für Unternehmens- und Gesellschaftsrecht* (Corporation Law Journal), joined the Administrative Council of the University of Heidelberg and received the Max Planck Research Prize for international cooperation. Elected rector of the University of Heidelberg in 2001.

Klaus J. Hopt

Director at the Max Planck Institute for Private Law, Hamburg—1974–1995 prof. of law in Tuebingen, Florence, Bern, Munich—*Professional:* Judge Court of Appeals Stuttgart 1981–85; member of the German Takeover Commission 1995–2001, of the Deputation of the Deutscher Juristentag 2000–, of the High Level Group of Company Law Experts, European Commission 2001–02, of the Takeover Advisory Board 2002–; vice-president of the German Research Council (Deutsche Forschungsgemeinschaft) 2002–; expert for the German Parliament, various German Ministries, German Central Bank, European Commission, Bulgaria and World Bank—*Visiting prof.:* U. of Pennsylvania, EUI Florence, Paris I (Sorbonne), Kyoto U., U. Libre de Bruxelles, Geneva, Tokyo U., U. of Chicago, New York U., Harvard, Tilburg/The Netherlands (Anton Philips Chair), Paris II.—*Author: Kapitalanlegerschutz im Recht der Banken* 1975; *Legal Harmonization and the Business Enterprise* 1988 (with Buxbaum); Baumbach-Hopt, *Handelsgesetzbuch 30th ed.* 2000; *Corporate Group Law for Europe* 2000 (with Forum Europaeum).—*(Co-)Ed. Inter alia: (Comparative Corporate Governance* 1998 (Oxford U. P.); *RabelsZ, Zeitschrift für Unternehmensund Gesellschaftsrecht.—Honors:* Dr. iur. h.c. mult. (U. Libre de Bruxelles 1997, U. Catholique de Louvain 1997, U. de Paris V René Descartes 2000).

Simon Johnson

Simon Johnson is an Associate Professor at the Sloan School of Management, MIT. He is also a Faculty Research Fellow in the NBER research groups on corporate finance and international macroeconomics, a member of the International Advisory Board of CASE in Warsaw, and a non-resident scholar at the Asian Institute for Corporate Governance of Korea University.

In 2000–2001 Professor Johnson was a member of the US Securities and Exchange Commission's Advisory Committee on Market Information. His assessment of the need for continuing strong market regulation is published as part of the final report of that committee.

Professor Johnson's research focuses on the institutions that support or prevent growth. Most of his work deals with emerging markets, and draws on extensive fieldwork in Eastern Europe, the former Soviet Union, East Asia, and Latin America. Recent papers have appeared or are forthcoming in the *American Economic Review,* the *Quarterly Journal of Economics,* the *Journal of Financial Economics,* and the *Journal of Law, Economics and Organization.* He regularly uses these research findings, in association with the Brattle Group, to provide advice on emerging markets.

Marcel Kahan

Marcel Kahan is Professor of Law at the New York University School of Law. His main areas of teaching and research are corporate governance, securities fraud, and bondholder rights. He has written over 30 articles for law reviews, finance journals, and professional publications. One of his articles, "Do Bondholders Lose From Junk Bond Covenant Changes" (with Bruce Tuckman) was awarded the Merton Miller Prize for the best paper submitted to the *Journal of Business,* and three others have been selected as among the best corporate and securities articles by the *Corporate Practice Commentator.* Professor Kahan has been Visiting Professor at Harvard Law School, Columbia Law School, and the Hebrew University. He is a member of the Board of Directors of the Centre for Law and Business at New York University (1997–present) and of the Board of Directors of the American Law and Economics Association (2000–present).

Christian Kirchner

Dr. iur. Dr. rer.pol. Christian Kirchner, LL.M. (Harvard). Professor of German, European and International Civil- and Business Law and New Institutional Economics.

Academic background: Banking apprenticeship. Study of law and economics at Tübingen, Frankfurt am Main, at M.I.T. and Harvard University, (LL.M 1972). Dr. iur 1974. Dr. rer. pol. 1977. Research work in Japan. Habilitation (postdoctoral lecturing qualification) 1982. Tutor in Hanover, Berlin and Heidelberg. Assistant Professor 1977–1983. Professor at Hanover since 1984. Professor at the Humboldt University of Berlin since 1993. Current research emphasis: Competition Law, Corporation Law, Accounting Law, European Community Law, Law and Economics, New Institutional Economics.

Friedrich Kübler

Dr. iur. Friedrich Kübler, M.A. (hon.), received his legal education in Tübingen, Lausanne, Reading/Berks. and Bonn. He taught as a lecturer in Tübingen, Paris and at Harvard Law School and as a Professor in Giessen, Konstanz and Frankfurt. He is now a Professor emeritus in Frankfurt and continues to be a Professor of Law at the University of Pennsylvania. He is of Counsel with Clifford Chance Pünder in Frankfurt am Main.

Rafael La Porta

Rafael La Porta is an associate professor of Economics at Harvard. Dr. La Porta's research focuses on institutions that support or prevent growth. His most recent work deals with corporate govern-ance, contract enforcement, and the regulation of new business enterprises.

Florencio López-de-Silanes

Prof. Florencio López-de-Silanes specializes in International Corporate Finance and Financial Markets, Corporate Governance and Legal Reform, Privatization and Deregulation. He is a found-ing member of the Blue Ribbon Panel on Corporate Governance in Russia and the Committee on Best Corporate Practices in Mexico. He has helped international companies in their efforts to improve their corporate governance practices and has acted as an advisor to stock market commis-sions in several countries. Professor López-de-Silanes has also been an advisor to the governments of Russia, Peru, Malaysia, Egypt, Yemen, Colombia, Costa Rica and Mexico on issues of financial markets' regulation, corporate and bankruptcy law reform, industrial policy and privatization. More recently, he has worked as a consultant to the International Monetary Fund and to the World Bank on issues of corporate governance. Prof. López-de-Silanes is also the director of Yale University's International Institute of Corporate Governance, carrying out research, teaching exec-utives and regulators and providing policy advice on the relevance of investor protection for the reduction of the cost of capital, the development of capital markets and economic growth. His main publications fall in the areas of corporate finance, legal reform of financial markets, corporate and bankruptcy law, privatization, and trade and industrial policy particularly with respect to NAFTA. He received Harvard's Wells Prize for the Best Dissertation in Economics (1995), the National Award of Law and Economics of the National Association of Law and Economics in Mexico (1996), the Brattle Prize for distinguished paper in the Journal of Finance of the American Finance Association (1999), and the Jensen Prize for the best papers published in the Journal of Financial Economics in the Areas of Corporate Finance and Organizations (2000). He graduated with highest honors from Instituto Tecnológico Autónomo de México, and he has a Masters and a Ph.D. in Economics from Harvard University. Prior to joining the Yale University faculty, he was a professor at Harvard University from 1994 to 2001.

Marcus Lutter

Born in Munich in 1930. Law studies in Munich, Paris, and Freiburg. Professor at the Ruhr University from 1966. Professor at the University of Bonn in 1980, where he became Director of the "Instituts für Handels- und Wirtschaftrecht". Professor Emeritus University of Bonn since 1996. Founder of the "Zentrums für Europäisches Wirtschaftsrecht". Professor Lutter's research focuses on Corporate law and the Law of Company Groups.

Peter Nobel

Prof. Dr. Peter Nobel is attorney at law, managing partner of Nobel & Hug, attorneys at law, in Zurich, Professor for Private, Trade, and Commercial Law at the University of St. Gallen, and member of the Swiss Federal Banking Commission. He is editor-in-chief of Swiss Commercial Law Review and author of various textbooks and articles. He is a board member of various corporations.

Ben Pettet

Ben Pettet (b. 1955) read law at University College London and graduated with LL.B. (Honours) in 1976. In 1977 he was called to the Bar at Gray's Inn, where he was also awarded the Band Scholarship. He has practised as a barrister. He has been visiting adjunct Professor at Pace University, New York on their London programme and has taught part-time at St Edmund Hall, Oxford, and Robinson College, Cambridge. He has been editor of the Current Legal Problems Annual Review. He is currently a Senior Lecturer in Laws at UCL.

His research interests span Company Law, Securities Regulation/Capital Markets Law, Corporate Finance Law, and Comparative Law. He has numerous publications in these fields, the most recent of which is his new book: *Company Law* (Harlow, U.K.: Pearson Education Ltd, 2001).

Stefan Prigge

Stefan Prigge is Research and Teaching Assistant at the Chair of Banking and Finance, at the University of Hamburg in Germany. Born in 1966, he finished his studies in Economics at the University of Hamburg in 1992 and became Dr. rer. pol. at the same University in 1996. He was Research Associate at the Max Planck Institute for Foreign Private and Private International Law (Hamburg) from 1996 to 1998. Publications: *Zentralbank, Aktienkurssturz und Systemkrise* [*Central Bank, Stock Market Crash, and Systemic Crisis*] (Wiesbaden 1997), *Corporate Governance in Germany* (in Hopt et al., see below); co-author: *Corporate Governance in Germany* (with H. Schmidt, J. Drukarczyk et al.) (Baden-Baden 1997); co-editor: Comparative Corporate Governance—The State of the Art and Emerging Research (with. K.J. Hopt, H. Kanda, M.J. Roe, and E. Wymeersch) (Oxford 1998), *Wolfgang Stützel—Moderne Konzepte für Finanzmärkte, Beschäftigung und Wirtschaftsverfassung* [Wolfgang Stützel—Modern Concepts for Financial Markets, Employment, and Constitution of the Economy] (with H. Schmidt and E. Ketzel) (Tübingen 2001); further articles.

Uriel Procaccia

Dr. Uriel Procaccia is the Wachtell, Lipton, Rosen and Katz Professor of Corporate Law and Securities at the Hebrew University in Jerusalem. He is the author of the draft Companies Regulation Bill, which was later adopted as the Israeli Corporate Code of 1999, a former dean of the Hebrew University Law School, and a frequent visiting professor in numerous European and American Universities.

Jonathan Rickford

Jonathan Rickford is an English solicitor and consultant on regulatory policy. He is a member of the U.K. Competition Commission and Special Adviser to the U.K. Department of Trade and Industry on Company Law. He was the project director of the U.K. Company Law Review from 1998 to 2001.

   He was The Solicitor (General Counsel), Director of Regulation and Director of Strategy with British Telecommunications plc between 1987 and 1996 and The Solicitor to the Department of Trade and Industry between 1984 and 1987 and Head of Company Law in that department from 1979 to 1982. He also taught law at the University of California at Berkeley and the London School of Economics from 1968 to 1972.

Angel Rojo

Angel Rojo (Oviedo, 1947), LL. B. University of Oviedo (Spain), ; LL. D. University of Bologna (Italy). Visiting Researcher at the University of Freiburg (Germany). Senior Professor of Commercial and Corporate Law, Universidad Autónoma de Madrid (since 1991). Doctor *honoris causa* in several Universities. Professor Rojo is a permanent Member of the General Commission for Codification of Laws of the Kingdom of Spain, and responsible for the drafting of major statutes in the field of Spanish corporate and commercial law. Professor Rojo has written highly prestigious books and articles on almost all the key topics included in commercial law. He is also a practicing lawyer.

Guido Rossi

Professor of Company Law at the L. Bocconi University in Milan. LL.M. (Harvard Law School, 1953). Former President of Consob (Italian Stock Exchange Supervisory Body, 1981–1982). Co-editor of the following Law Reviews: "*Rivista delle Società*" and "*Banca, borsa e titoli di credito*". Author of many books and articles on corporate law, securities law, antitrust law and bankruptcy law.

Uzi Segal

Dr. Uzi Segal is Professor of Economics at the University of Western Ontario and Visiting Professor of Economics at Boston College. Professor Segal specializes in Economic Theory, especially in the areas of Justice and Social Choice. He is a frequent visitor in numerous European and American Universities.

Andrei Shleifer

Andrei Shleifer is a Professor of Economics at Harvard University and past editor of the Quarterly Journal of Economics. He was educated at Harvard and MIT, and previously taught at Princeton and the University of Chicago. He has published over 100 articles in the areas of financial economics, corporate governance, economic growth, and problems of transition from socialism. Shleifer is a recipient of several National Science Foundation Grants, a Sloan Fellowship, a prestigious Young

Presidential Investigator Award in Economics, and, in 1999, the John Bates Clark Medal awarded every two years by the American Economic Association to the best American economist under the age of 40.

Max Steiger

Max Steiger was a research assistant for Banking and Finance at the University of Erlangen-Nuremberg and the Centre for European Economic Studies in Mannheim. He studied Economics and Business Administration at the University of Mannheim. He received his Ph.D. in finance from the University of Erlangen-Nuremberg in 2000. He published articles on corporate governance and market microstructure in academic and professional journals. Currently, he is an executive assistant to the board of managing directors of Deutsche Bank AG, Frankfurt, covering strategic issues and developments in the capital markets and financial services industry.

Christiaan Timmermans

C.W.A. (Christiaan) Timmermans is judge at the Court of Justice of the European Communities since October 7, 2000. He studied law at Leiden University (doctor's degree 1973) in The Netherlands and served as référendaire (law clerk) at the Court of Justice of the European Communities (1966–1969). After having worked for the European Commission between 1969 and 1977, he became Professor of European Law at Groningen University (The Netherlands) (1977–1989). From 1989 to 2000 he was Deputy Director General of the EC Commission's Legal Service. He was also Visiting Professor at the Europa Instituut of Amsterdam (1978–1989); Visiting Fellow at the Centre for European Studies of the University of Cambridge (1994–1996); Visiting Lecturer at the Law School of Fordham University, New York (1996). Since 1999 he is part-time Professor of European Law at the University of Amsterdam. Author of books and articles on issues of European Law and national Business Law and Company Law.

Lutgart Van den Berghe

Doctor in economics, Ghent University. She is an executive director of the Vlerick Leuven Gent Management School and chairman of the Competence Centre 'Entrepreneurship, Governance and Strategy'. She is a part-time professor at Ghent University (domain of corporate governance) and functions as academic director of the Belgian Directors' Institute.

Christoph Van der Elst

Professor of Corporate Governance and Commercial Law, Financial Law Institute, Ghent University (Belgium); lecturer in company law, University of Utrecht (The Netherlands); Scientific Advisor, Belgian High Council for Economic Professions. Research fellow Financial Law Institute, 1995–2001; Ph.D. in Economics, Ghent University, 2001; J.D. Ghent University, 1995; Economics, Ghent University, 1991; Publications in corporate governance, company law, and commercial law.

Karel Van Hulle

Karel Van Hulle is Head of Unit for Financial Reporting and Company Law at the European Commission (Directorate-General "Internal Market"), which he joined in 1984 after having served eight years with the Belgian Commission on Banking and Finance. He chairs the meetings of the Accounting Directives' Contact Committee, the Committee on Auditing and the Accounting Advisory Forum. He has represented the EU in the Accounting Working Groups at the UN, UNCTAD and at the OECD and he represents the European Commission within IASC.

Since 1998, Mr. Van Hulle has also been made responsible for company law matters, which includes issues such as take-over bids and corporate governance.

Mr. Van Hulle is a lawyer by training. A part-time lecturer at the KULeuven, he is a member of the Executive Committee of the European Accounting Association and was nominated Distinguished International Lecturer in Accounting by the American Accounting Association in 1990.

Jaap Winter

Jaap Winter studied law in Groningen, the Netherlands and obtained a Ph.D. degree in 1992 on a dissertation on the Financing of Groups of Companies. He is partner at De Brauw Blackstone Westbroek in Amsterdam. From 1997 until 2002 he was senior legal advisor of Unilever. Jaap Winter is part-time professor of International Company Law at the Erasmus University of Rotterdam, the Netherlands. He is chairman of the Group of High Level Experts on Company Law set up by the European Commission in September 2001 and chairman of the Group of Experts on Cross-border Voting in Europe set up by the Dutch government in January 2002.

Eddy Wymeersch

Eddy Wymeersch is Professor of Commercial Law, University of Ghent, Belgium, where he is teaching company law, securities regulation and banking law. Consultant to EC Commission, World Bank and IFC; member of the corporate governance commission of the Brussels Stock Exchange and chairman of the SLIM working party (Simpler Legislation for the Internal Market) on the First and Second Directive. He also acts as adviser to the Belgian Government, inter alia as member of the Legislative Branch of the Council of State. He is a member of the board of the National Bank of Belgium and the Belgian Corporate Governance Commission. He was Chairman of the Board of Brussels International Airport Company (BIAC) and adviser on governance issues to several listed Belgian companies. At present, Chairman of the Banking and Finance Commission. He has published extensively on securities regulation, companies law, especially groups of companies, and corporate governance in the Belgian, European, and comparative perspective.

Part I:

Facts and Figures

1

The Equity Markets, Ownership Structures and Control: Towards an International Harmonization?

CHRISTOPH VAN DER ELST

Abstract

This paper provides an overview of the evolution of the equity markets and ownership structures in the nineties. Data on the equity markets show that the primary distinction between market-oriented and network-oriented systems must be readjusted. In some network-oriented countries equity markets became broader and more valuable. It seems that firms in network-oriented countries are seeking external capital without opting into legal systems that are more protective of minorities.

Existing ownership structures are relatively stable and adjusting slowly. The importance of the non-financial sector is diminishing in most European countries while foreign shareholders and institutional investors extend their stakes. These trends do not indicate that control in most European countries has shifted towards the markets: the non-financial sector still holds most of the large stakes and controls a significant number of small and large stock exchange listed companies in continental Europe.

This new evidence has important consequences for the existing research on the influence of legal aspects of external finance. Not only the ownership concentration but also the nature of the shareholding concentration must be added to those models.

Contents

Figures and Tables

A. Introduction

Since the publication of "The Modern Corporation and Private Property" by Berle and Means, a large literature on the separation of ownership and control has emerged. Commentators have identified two broad types of systems. The bank-oriented model is characterized by the concentration of shareholder power with banks and families and to a lesser extent the government. A market for corporate control has not been developed. The market-oriented system is characterized by large and liquid equity markets without powerful shareholders and a developed market for corporate control.

Japan and Germany are identified as bank-based systems where companies raise most of their finance from banks that have close, long-term relationships with their customers. The banks tend to hold considerable equity portfolios themselves and often name representatives to the board. The ownership is highly concentrated and that has a relative illiquid equity market as a negative consequence. Take-overs are negotiated and the market for corporate control plays an insignificant role. Block-ownership facilitates control of management and limits executive compensation.

In a market-based system, like the U.K. and the U.S., the relations between companies and investors are at arm's length. Investors are interested in short-term returns. Equity markets are very liquid and the market for corporate con-

Table 1: Bank-based and Market-based Governance Systems

Governance system	Bank-based system	Market-based system
Ownership	Concentrated	Diffuse
Board	Two tier or one tier	One tier
Equity markets	Illiquid	Very liquid
Take-over market	Minor role	Major role
Executive compensation	Moderate	High
Banking system	Universal	Fragmented

trol is highly developed. Table 1 gives an overview of the main differences between both systems.

In more recent studies the qualification of the systems has been redefined. Four groups of well-developed industrialized countries are identified: besides the market-based system a network-oriented system with three subsystems is introduced.[1] The latter contains Germanic countries, Latin countries, and Japan. The main characteristics of the three subsystems are identified in Table 2.

The differences between these systems are a result of the legal and regulatory environment. First, constraints on large investors arise from differences in company and bankruptcy law, portfolio regulation of financial institutions, tax laws, insider trading laws, disclosure rules, and antitrust law. An example illustrates this thesis: initial public offerings represent a major turning point in the life of a company and frequently need a change of the company's legal status.[2] In Germany, for instance, the legal requirements for employee representation on the supervisory board of the "*Aktiengesellschaft*", discourages the selling of financial instruments on the market.[3]

Secondly, the rules on corporate finance of companies differ. Equity issuance and trading in equity are in some countries subject to a variety of taxes: loans and internal finance have a competitive advantage over equity finance.[4]

---

[1] Other studies differentiate between the insider and the outsider systems, the former prevalent in Europe (except for the U.K.), Korea, Japan, etc., the latter in the U.S. and the U.K. (See M. Maher and T. Andersson, *Corporate Performance: Effects on Firm Performance and Economic Growth* (1999), paper presented at Tilburg University Law and Economics Conference on "Convergence and Diversity in Corporate Governance Regimes and Capital Markets", Eindhoven, November 4–5, 1999, 13–28).

[2] E.V. Ferran, *Company Law and Corporate Finance* (Oxford 1999) 72.

[3] S. Prowse, *Corporate Governance in an International Perspective* (1994) Basle, Bank for International Settlements, Economic paper no. 41, July 1994, 27–28.

[4] ibid. 25.

Table 2: Characteristics of the Network Oriented Systems

	Germanic	Latin	Japan
Ownership	Moderate/high	High	Moderate/low
Board	Two tier	In general one tier	De facto one tier
Importance of equity markets	Moderate/high	Moderate	High
Take-over market	Minor role	Minor role	Minor role
Perf.-dependant exec. Compensation	Low	Moderate	Low
Time horizon of economic Relationships	Long term	Long term	Long term

Based on J. Weimer and J. Pape, 'A Taxonomy of Systems of Corporate Governance' (1999) *Corporate Governance—An International Review* 154.

The complex ownership patterns caused by these differences in regulations are documented in most studies by aggregate figures on the distribution of ownership. These figures reveal nothing about the concentration of ownership, or about the identity of the large shareholders. The data contain no information on the evolution of the ownership patterns. This study presents new material on the ownership, the identity of the large shareholders, and recent developments of equity financing and ownership structures.

This study is structured as follows. Part one gives an overview of the developments and importance of the equity markets. First some general data on the evolution of the number of stock exchange listed companies, the market capitalization, the size of the listed companies, and the ratio market capitalization to GDP are presented. Secondly, equity issues are studied. The evolution of the number and the value of the initial public offerings indicates the convergence of some network-oriented and market-oriented countries. Equity issues of listed companies show a different pattern.

Part two starts with an analysis of the evolution of the shareholdings of different classes of investors. Section two describes the identity of important minority shareholders in four European countries. The third section of part two analyses recent data on major shareholdings: the voting block of the largest shareholder of different classes of companies is examined. Next, the class to which the majority shareholder belongs is identified. Finally, section five analyses the liquidity of the stock market and the importance of the different classes of investors. Part three concludes.

B. Equity Markets

I. General Data

1. Number of Companies

In all countries the structure of corporate sectors can be described as follows. A large number of small companies are privately owned by individuals, families and partners. The number of companies set up as a public company varies quite substantially in the different European countries. In the U.K., Germany, Austria, and the Netherlands only a small number of companies are public companies. In France, Belgium, Sweden, Spain, and Switzerland the number is much larger.[5]

In all countries only a small proportion of those public companies are listed. Table 3 gives an overview of the evolution of the number of stock exchange listed

Table 3: Evolution of the Number of Stock Exchange Listed Companies (1990–1999)

	1990	1993	1996	1999	growth 1990–99
Network-oriented					
Belgium	182	159	136	140	–23.1%
France	443	726	686	968**	118.5%
Germany	548	568	579	1,043	90.3%
Italy	257	242	244	247	–3.9%
Netherlands	222	239	217	233	5.0%
Spain	429	404*	357	718	67.4%
Japan (Tokyo)	1,627	1,667	1,766	1,892	16.3%
Market-oriented					
U.K.	1,946	1,927	2,339	2,292	17.8%
U.S. NYSE	1,774	1,945	2,476	2,631	48.3%
U.S. Nasdaq	3,876	4,310	5,167	4,829	24.6%
U.S. Amex	789	814	688	650***	–17.5%

*: 1992; **: Marché libre excluded; ***: 1998

Source: FIBV, FESE, Bourse de Paris, Italian, Belgian, and Tokyo Stock Exchanges, Nasdaq, and NYSE.

[5] See for some figures E. Wymeersch, 'A Status Report on Corporate Governance in Some Continental European States' in K. Hopt, H. Kanda, M. Roe, E. Wymeersch, and S. Prigge (eds.), *Comparative Corporate Governance—The State of the Art and Emerging Research* (Oxford 1998) 1049.

companies in the different European countries, Japan, and the U.S. In France, Germany, and Spain the number of companies has risen substantially. Among other possibilities, this seems to indicate that financing by public issues of equity became more important in these countries. This phenomenon took place in the second half of the nineties, whereas in the first half the number of listed companies remained unchanged in Germany and Spain.

One should take note that the definition is crucial: some stock exchanges only include those companies listed on the official market while other stock exchanges also include those companies listed on other markets; some countries, like Spain, include the investment funds in the figures, etc.

2. Market Capitalization

The development of the financial markets is not only measured by the number of stock exchange listed companies but also by the intensity of the use of the securities markets, measured by market capitalization and by the relationship between market capitalization and GDP.

Table 4 indicates that during the nineties the differences between the market-based system and the network-based system diminished while other differences

Table 4: Market Capitalization of Stock Exchanges (1990–1999)

In bill. $	1990	1993	1996	1999	growth 90–99
Network-oriented					
Belgium	65.4	78.2	119.1	187.3	186.4%
France	311.7	455.5	587.0	1508.8	384.1%
Germany	355.3	460.8	664.9	1437.7	304.7%
Italy	148.8	145.3	256.6	731.1	391.3%
Netherlands	119.8	182.6	375.4	697.9	482.6%
Spain	111.4	118.9	241.0	432.6	288.3%
Japan	2928.5	2906.3	3011.2	4200.0	43.4%
Market-oriented					
U.K.	850.0	1150.6	1642.6	2966.0	248.9%
U.S. (NYSE)	2692.1	4213.0	6842.0	11564.0	329.6%
U.S. (Nasdaq)	310.8	791.7	1511.8	4226.2	1259.8%

Source: FIBV, FESE, Bourse de Paris, Italian, Belgian, and Tokyo Stock Exchanges, Nasdaq and NYSE.

emerged. The equity markets of the U.S., Germany, France, and the Netherlands grew much more than the markets in Japan, Belgium and the U.K.

The patterns of growth of the different equity markets diverged: the market capitalization of individual companies listed on Nasdaq rose significantly. The same pattern, although to a lesser extent, could be found in Italy, the Netherlands, and Belgium, while in Spain, Germany, and France the growth was driven by new listings (Table 5).[6] In the latter countries the average individual capitalization of a stock exchange listed company only doubled during the nineties, while in the former the growth reached between 272% in Belgium, and 991% for Nasdaq listed companies.

3. Size of Listed Companies by Market Capitalization

In the beginning of the nineties only very large companies were listed on the NYSE and in Japan, while on Nasdaq and to a lesser extent in Spain and Belgium small companies raised equity capital in the public market. In 1999, on average, the largest companies could not only be found at the NYSE, but also at the Italian and the Dutch stock exchange. Companies listed in France, Belgium, Germany, and the U.K. had on average the same size. The difference between the London Stock Exchange and the other large continental European Exchanges diminished significantly.

Some say that in larger companies, where the shareholding is already dispersed, shareholders will not resist new equity issues, whereas companies in the hands of a few individuals will use their right of first refusal if the issue is not on a pre-emptive base and the proprietors do not possess the capital to subscribe the issue. Part 2 will examine whether the evolution of the differences of the size of companies influences the capital structure. This study will also show to what extent ownership structure diverges from voting control.

4. Capitalization to GDP

As Table 6 shows, equity finance by the public market was insignificant in Italy, Sweden, France, Germany, Belgium, and Spain in 1975. In those countries the market capitalization of quoted companies was less than 15% of GDP. By 1990 this pattern had not substantially changed: market capitalization figures rose quicker than GDP but except for Sweden the percentages of those countries were lower in 1990 than those for the U.K. and U.S. in 1975. Since 1990 the picture has changed substantially. In Switzerland and the Netherlands the stock markets are in 1999 at least as important as in the U.S., while even in France the

---

[6] For a more detailed analysis, cf. below, Table 7.

Table 5: Evolution of the Average Market Capitalization of Listed Companies
          (1990–1999)

In mln. $	1990	1993	1996	1999	growth 90–99
Network-oriented					
Belgium	359.3	491.8	875.7	1337.8	272.3%
France	703.6	627.4	855.7	1558.7	121.5%
Germany	648.4	811.3	1148.4	1378.5	112.6%
Italy	579.0	600.4	1051.6	2959.8	411.2%
Netherlands	539.6	764.0	1730.0	2995.3	455.0%
Spain	259.7	294.3	675.1	602.5	132.0%
Japan	1799.9	1743.4	1705.1	2285.1	27.0%
Market-oriented					
U.K.	436.8	597.1	702.3	1294.1	196.3%
U.S. (NYSE)	1517.5	2166.1	2763.3	4395.3	189.6%
U.S. (Nasdaq)	80.2	183.7	292.6	875.2	991.4%

Source: own calculations based on data of FIBV, FESE, Bourse de Paris, Italian, Belgian, and
Tokyo Stock Exchanges, Nasdaq, and NYSE.

market capitalization became higher than GDP. In the second half of last decade
the ratio market capitalization to GDP rose significantly in Germany, Italy, and
Spain.

II. Equity Financing

1. Initial Public Offerings

Another aspect of convergence between countries of the network-oriented and
market-oriented system is illustrated in Table 7. During recent years there have
been many new listings on most markets. The growth has been unevenly spread:
large markets like the NYSE were growing at a lower percentage rate than
smaller markets like France. The primary market of Belgium and Italy is lagging
behind.

The emergence and survival of new firms is affected by the possibility and cost
of obtaining finance. Some say that in a network-oriented system new firms may
find it very hard to obtain equity finance. In a market-oriented system external
funding is more important. So, a way of measuring the convergence of countries

Table 6: Evolution of Market Capitalization as Percentage of GDP (1990–1999)

	1975	1980	1985	1990	1994	1996	1998	1999
Network-oriented								
Belgium	15%	8%	26%	33%	36%	44%	97.5%	75.4%
France	10%	8%	15%	26%	34%	38%	67.8%	105.3%
Germany	12%	9%	29%	22%	24%	28%	50.6%	68.1%
Italy	5%	6%	14%	14%	18%	21%	47.9%	62.4%
Japan	28%	36%	71%	99%	77%	66%	64.5%	102.5%
Netherlands	21%	17%	47%	42%	67%	95%	157.6%	177.3%
Spain		8%	12%	23%	25%	33%	71.9%	72.6%
Sweden	3%	10%	37%	40%	66%	95%	122.3%	156.3%
Switzerland	30%	42%	91%	69%	109%	136%	259.4%	267.5%
Market-oriented								
U.K.	37%	38%	77%	87%	114%	142%	167.3%	198.0%
U.S.	48%	50%	57%	56%	75%	114%	157.0%	181.1%

Source: own calculations based on data of FIBV, FESE, Bourse de Paris, Italian, Belgian, and Tokyo Stock Exchanges, Nasdaq, NYSE, and OECD.

belonging to those two different groups is to compare the volume of equity finance raised by initial public offerings. In order to compare those figures between countries the ratio between the market value of the initial public offerings and GDP was calculated in Table 8.

The figures no longer confirm one of the differences between market-oriented and network-oriented systems. Between 1990 and 1997, US and UK companies raised on average each year 1% of GDP as equity capital.[7] During that same period continental European companies raised on average only a small fraction of GDP as equity. The percentage is substantially higher in years in which a large privatization took place, such as Deutsche Telekom in 1996.

In 1998 and 1999 the funding by equity in network-oriented systems is as high or higher as in the network oriented system. Especially in Spain, Germany, and Italy the 1999 initial public offerings raised more equity than those in the U.K. In 1998 the highest percentages can be found in France and Spain. The 1999 figure for Spain includes the important initial public offerings of REE and TPI. In Italy more than 60% of the value of the 1999 equity issues resulted from the privatization of Enel.

[7] Except between 1990 and 1992, where U.S. companies raised on average 0.51% of GDP as equity capital.

Table 7: Number of Initial Public Offerings During the Nineties

	1990–92	1993–95	1996	1997	1998	1999	Total	Total new/ total 1990
Network-oriented								
Belgium	5	4	8	13	19	24	73	40.1%
France	58	83	57	82	226	75	581	131.2%
Germany	51	39	20	35	67	168	380	69.3%
Italy	18	26	15	13	21	31	124	48.2%
Netherlands	14	22	6	15	22	17	96	43.2%
Spain	102	78	11	43	111	10*	355	82.8%
Market-oriented								
U.K.	386	540	345	217	169	198	1855	95.3%
NYSE	465	527	219	210	162	49	1632	62.0%
Nasdaq	772	1328	598	453	437	485	4073	84.3%
Amex	185	240	92	91	92	11	711	

Source: FIBV, FESE, Bourse de Paris, Italian, Belgian, and Tokyo Stock Exchanges, Nasdaq, and NYSE.

The figures for the Netherlands are difficult to compare. Since 1990 equity financing has become a major source of finance. Between 1963 and 1989 the issue of equity was almost zero.[8] A major part of the issues in the nineties are due to privatization—DSM, KPN, Postbank—and the reduction of stakes by the government—ING, KLM. Still, in 1999 the initial public offerings of UPC, Versatel, Libertel, KPNQuest, and Foxkids raised more than 3% of GDP as equity capital.

2. Other Equity Issues

Data on the equity financing by stock exchange listed companies is presented in Table 9. Again, the highest figures can be found in the Netherlands where each year listed companies raise equity equal to more than 3% of GDP. There seems no clear explanation for the major differences of equity financing in the Netherlands and the other countries. It is an open question whether the specific organization of ownership and control of Dutch companies can explain this difference in equity financing.

---

[8] L. Scholtens, 'De veranderende rol van de beurs in de samenleving' [1999] *Ondernemingsrecht* 446.

Table 8: Equity Raised by Initial Public Offerings as Percentage of GDP (1990–1999)

	1990–92 avg.	1993–95 avg.	1996	1997	1998	1999	1990–99 avg.
Network-oriented							
Belgium	0.04%	0.09%	0.46%	0.25%	0.52%	0.64%	0.23%
France	0.23%	0.21%	0.09%	0.65%	1.12%	0.49%	0.41%
Germany	0.10%	0.11%	0.65%	0.15%	0.20%	0.91%	0.25%
Italy	0.18%	0.51%	0.19%	0.09%	0.19%	2.22%	0.51%
Netherlands	2.37%	2.31%	1.12%	2.40%	4.43%	7.41%	2.94%
Spain	0.15%	0.20%	0.20%	0.22%	1.14%	4.23%	0.65%
Market-oriented							
U.K.	0.93%	1.00%	1.29%	0.93%	0.82%	0.58%	0.89%
U.S.	0.51%	0.88%	1.13%	0.89%	0.82%	1.14%	0.81%

Source: own calculations based on data of FIBV, FESE, Bourse de Paris, Italian, Belgian, and Tokyo Stock Exchanges, Nasdaq, NYSE, and OECD.

French, Spanish, and Belgian companies, although all belonging to the Latin network-oriented system, tap the market differently. The data show that external financing by Belgian companies is limited while French and Spanish companies raise on average almost as much equity through new equity issuance as U.S. listed companies. Note that the 1999 average of Spain is highly influenced by the capital increase of Repsol.

Italian companies do not frequently issue new shares. The average for Italian listed companies is, like for the Belgian companies, lagging behind the other network-oriented countries. The 1999 figure is rather exceptional: 90% of the equity raising is directly linked with the take-over of Telecom by Olivetti and Tecnost.

German listed companies raise even less equity capital. One possible explanation could be that after the flotation of the company the founders of German, and also Italian and Belgian companies, do not want to dilute their stakes.

French companies can raise equity without losing control. Double voting rights are a major factor in the French corporate governance system. Those aspects are examined in Part three of this study.

A possible explanation of the differences between France and other network-oriented countries could be that the one-share one-vote principle in the latter countries reduces the attractiveness of raising equity capital. Further research is necessary to conclude whether these findings are in line with the view of La Porta

Table 9: Equity Raised by Already Listed Companies as Percentage of GDP (1990–1999) (share buy-backs excluded)

	1990–92 avg.	1993–95 avg.	1996	1997	1998	1999	1990–99 avg.
Network-oriented							
Belgium	0.18%	0.30%	0.68%	0.47%	0.66%	0.30%	0.36%
France	0.62%	1.12%	0.80%	0.86%	1.12%	1.39%	0.94%
Germany	0.62%	0.68%	0.19%	0.29%	0.92%	0.40%	0.57%
Italy	0.43%	0.83%	0.18%	0.43%	0.81%	1.88%	0.71%
Netherlands	1.87%	3.29%	2.47%	3.04%	6.71%	7.67%	3.54%
Spain	0.86%	—	0.68%	0.40%	1.07%	4.57%	0.93%
Market-oriented							
U.K.	1.36%	1.67%	1.21%	0.84%	0.80%	1.07%	1.30%
U.S.	0.54%	1.13%	1.87%	2.04%	1.61%	1.10%	1.16%

Source: own calculations based on data of FIBV, FESE, Bourse de Paris, Italian, Belgian, and Tokyo Stock Exchanges, Nasdaq, NYSE, and OECD.

et al.[9] They concluded that the German equity market is broader than those belonging to the French legal system. They argue that the German law system offers better protection for minority shareholders. La Porta et al. found that in countries where this protection is better, equity markets are broader.

III. Preliminary Conclusion

The importance of the stock market for equity financing has risen substantially in all countries. The second half of the 1990s are characterized by a large number of initial public offerings and equity issues by listed companies. This was not only the case in countries belonging to the market-based system, but also in countries belonging to the network-oriented economies.

The patterns of growth converged: some differences between network-oriented systems and market-oriented systems have disappeared. However, other differences between network-oriented countries have emerged. The equity markets as measured by market capitalization to GDP and by equity financing no longer is a discriminating variable.

[9] R. La Porta, F. Lopez-de-Silanes, A. Shleifer, and R. Vishny, 'Legal Determinants of External Finance' [1999] *Journal of Finance* 1131–1150.

C. Evolution of Ownership and Control in the Nineties

I. Introduction

At the end of the eighties and in the beginning of the nineties the ownership structure was analysed by the portfolio composition of the different classes of shareholders.[10] This information was used to explain, among other things, the existence or absence of an active market for corporate control: when the individuals own a large portion of the shares, the degree of concentration will be low and mechanisms to influence managerial decision-making will be absent.[11] While this can be the case for the U.S. and to a lesser extent the U.K., that conclusion cannot be drawn for Europe.

The first study that considered the concentration of ownership and the identity of the large shareholders in Europe was published by Franks and Mayer.[12] They observed that the pattern of ownership as described by Berle and Means are by no means universal. In most European countries ownership is concentrated. In 1990, almost 85% of the German and 80% of the French large listed non-financial companies had at least one shareholder with 25% of the shares.

The study of Franks and Mayer was expanded by La Porta, Lopez-de-Silanes, and Shleifer who identified for 27 wealthy economies the ultimate controlling shareholders of the 20 largest and 10 medium-sized firms in 1995.[13] They classify a company as a controlled firm when a shareholder's direct and indirect voting rights exceed 20%. The main results of their research are presented in Table 10.

As Table 10 shows, less than 25% of the companies in Belgium, Italy, the Netherlands, Sweden, and Spain have no major shareholder. Families, the state, or trusts in the Netherlands, are the most important shareholders.[14] The number of German, French, and Swiss companies having the same classes of major shareholders is also significant. The typical Berle and Means corporation can be found in the U.S., the U.K., and in Japan.

[10] See e.g., Centre for European Policy Studies, *Corporate Governance in Europe* (1995) Brussels, 12–15; G. Gelauff and C. Den Broeder, *Governance of Stakeholder Relationships: the German and Dutch Experience* (Hague 1996) Central Plan Bureau, 54–56.

[11] J. Weimer and J. Pape, 'A Taxonomy of Systems of Corporate Governance' [1999] *Corporate Governance—An International Review* 156.

[12] J. Franks and C. Mayer, 'Corporate Ownership and Control in the U.K., Germany and France' [1997] *Journal of Applied Corporate Finance*, reprinted in D. Chew (ed.), *Studies in International Corporate Finance and Governance Systems* (Oxford 1997) 281.

[13] R. La Porta, F. Lopez-de-Silanes, and A. Shleifer, 'Corporate Ownership Around the World' [1999] *Journal of Finance* 471–517.

[14] In Belgium the widely held financial companies also have an important role. It is not clear which companies are included: it could be that Paribas, who controlled several listed Belgian companies, is included in this figure.

Table 10: Control of Large and Medium Publicly Traded Firms in 11 Countries

	Widely held (no shareh. >20%)	Family	State	Widely Held Financial	Widely Held Comp.	Miscel-laneous	Number of comp.
Belgium	10.0%	46.7%	13.3%	23.3%		6.7%	30
France	40.0%	30.0%	16.7%	10.0%		3.3%	30
Germany	36.7%	20.0%	23.3%	16.7%	3.3%		30
Italy	13.3%	30.0%	30.0%	3.3%	6.7%	16.7%	30
Netherlands	23.3%	20.0%	6.7%		10.0%	40.0%	30
Spain	23.3%	20.0%	26.7%	20.0%	10.0%		30
Switzerland	56.7%	36.7%		3.3%		3.3%	30
Sweden	20.0%	50.0%	13.3%	10.0%		6.7%	30
U.K.	86.7%	13.3%					30
U.S.	83.3%	16.7%					30
Japan	70.0%	6.7%	3.3%			20.0%	30

R. La Porta, F. Lopez-de-Silanes, and A. Shleifer, 'Corporate Ownership Around the World' (1999) *Journal of Finance* 492–494, Tables 2 and 3.

The authors of the study explain those differences in voting structure by the poor legal protection of minority shareholders in the former states. Only radical legal reforms that give shareholders explicit rights to prevent expropriation could change this ownership structure.

The European Corporate Governance Network analysed the voting structures in nine OECD countries.[15] Again, this database only contains data on one specific year. The composition of the database and the methodology differed substantially between the different countries. This hampers international comparison. The concentration of voting blocks is very high in Austria, Germany, Italy, the Netherlands, Spain, and Belgium. In other countries, like France and the U.K., they found a lower concentration. However, for those countries only a relatively small number or only the largest companies were included in the database.

[15] For an overview see M. Becht and A. Roell, 'Blockholdings in Europe: an International Comparison' [1999] *European Economic Review* 1049–1056.

II. Data Collection

1. Major Shareholdings

This study is based on a new database of ownership and voting structure of companies from six European countries: Belgium, Germany, France, Spain, Italy, and the U.K. All those countries had to implement the Council Directive 88/627/EEC of December 12, 1988 on the information to be published when a major holding in a listed company is acquired or disposed of.[16]

Natural persons and legal entities in public or private law who acquire, dispose or hold, directly or through intermediaries, holdings in companies whose shares are officially listed on a stock exchange in a Member State that reaches, exceeds or falls below 10%, 20%, $\frac{1}{3}$, 50% or $\frac{2}{3}$, must inform the company and the competent authority of the proportion of the voting rights he holds.[17] The threshold of 20% and $\frac{1}{3}$ does not need to be applied where the Member States apply the single threshold of 25%. The declarations must be disclosed to the public not more than nine calendar days after the receipt by the company.[18]

Articles 6 and 7 explain which voting rights should be attributed to the declarant: the most important attributions are the voting rights belonging to subsidiaries, concert parties, nominees and trustees, and deposited shares.

Table 11 lists the laws that implemented the Directive in the different European States. In most Member States the implementation of the Directive created difficulties which cannot be discussed in this study.[19]

The Directive imposes only minimum standards and all Member States require the disclosure at thresholds other than the ones imposed by the Directive.

In France and Germany the law states that crossing the 5% threshold must be notified. The latter uses the 25% exemption. This erodes the reliability of the data.

In Belgium and Spain every multiple of 5% must be declared. In the former the articles of association of a company can implement a threshold of 3%. About $\frac{1}{4}$ of all listed companies include in their bylaws the 3% threshold.

---

[16] Council Directive (EEC) 88/627 on the information to be published when a major holding in a listed company is acquired or disposed of [1988] O.J. L348, 62–65.

[17] Articles 1, 4, 5 and 6 of the Directive.

[18] Article 10 of the Directive.

[19] See, for Germany, M. Becht and E. Boehmer, *Transparency of Ownership and Control in Germany* (1998) Universität Osnabrück, Working Paper no. 69, 91 pages; for Belgium, F. De Bauw, 'La déclaration des participations importantes dans les sociétés cotées en bourse (Loi du 2 mars 1989 et arrêté royal du 10 mai 1989)' [1990] *Tijdschrift voor Belgisch Handelsrecht* 306–307; for the U.K., read Davies: "the basic principle is easy enough to state, though its detailed implementation has led to some horrendously complex rules" in (P. Davies, *Gower's Principles of Modern Company Law* 6th edn. (London 1997) 486; for the Netherlands: S. Perrick, 'De nieuwe Wet Melding Zeggenschap' [1997] *Ondernemingsrecht* 97. In the Netherlands, due to the different calculation of the numerator and the denominator, declarations of more than 100% frequently occur.

In the U.K. and in Italy each fluctuation exceeding a 1% level must be disclosed, from 3% on in the former and from 2% on in the latter. The 1998 reform in Italy confirmed the 2% threshold. The Consob had to provide other thresholds. The Consob regulation provides that a disclosure is due when the relevant holding crosses the thresholds of 5%, 7.5%, and all the multiples of 5%.[20]

In the U.K. directors must disclose every share they hold in the company.[21] Those data are included in the analysis.

Although article 10 of the Directive explicitly requires the company or the competent authority to disclose the notifications to the public, the Member

Table 11: Implementation of the Major Shareholdings Directive in the Member States

Belgium	Loi relative à la publicité des participations importantes dans les sociétés cotées en bourse et réglementant les offres publiques d'acquisitions—Wet op de openbaarmaking van belangrijke deelnemingen in ter beurze genoteerde vennootschappen en tot reglementering van de openbare overnamebiedingen	March 2, 1989
France	Loi No 89–531. Sécurité et transparence du marché financier, changing or introducing articles 356–1 and following of the Loi No 66–537 du 24 juillet 1966 sur les sociétés commerciales	August 2, 1989
Germany	Wertpapierhandelsgesetz[22]	July 24, 1994
Italy	Artt. 1/5 up to 1/5-bis legge No 216/74 modified by legge 149/92[23]	June 7, 1974
Spain	Real decreto 377/1991 sobre comunicacion de participaciones significativas en sociedades cotizadas y de adquisiciones por estas de acciones propias	March 15, 1991
U.K.	Disclosure of Interest in Shares (Amendment) Regulations 1993 (SI 1993/1819) changing Companies Act 1985, s. 198 et seq.	Sept 18, 1993

[20] M. Bianchi, M. Bianco, and L. Enriques, *Pyramidal Groups and The Separation between Ownership and Control in Italy* (1998) paper presented at the European Corporate Governance Network Conference "Ownership and Control: A European Perspective", Milan, November 4–5, 1998, 10.

[21] Companies Act 1985, s. 324.

[22] Substantially changed in 1998 by *Gesetz über den Wertpapierhandel in der Fassung der Bekanntmachung vom 9 September 1998* (*BGBl* I s. 2708).

[23] Significantly changed in 1998 by *legge No. 58/1998 and Regolamento di attuazione degli articoli 120, comma 4 e 122, comma 2, del decreto legislativo 24 Febbraio 1998, No. 58, in materia di communicazione delle partecipazioni rilevanti e di trasparenza dei patti parasociali (Adottato dalla Consob con delibera No. 11715 del 24 Novembre 1998).*

States complied in a substantially different manner. Therefore the data on corporate ownership are often difficult to assemble. In addition, the presentation of the notifications differs throughout the Member States, making the analysis even more complicated. For some countries it was necessary to use the information stored in other databases. Table 12 gives an overview of the source of the data used in this study.

The databases of the *Bundesaufsichtsamt für den Wertpapierhandel* (Germany), the *Commissione Nazionale per le Societa' e la Borsa* (Italy), and the *Comision Nacional del Mercado de Valores* (Spain) are updated regularly or each time a declaration is notified, so a print-out of the data of all companies at the end of 1999 was made.

For the U.K. no recent public data are available without charge. Reliable public databases could not be found. Recently, Goergen and Renneboog have stated: "The London Stock Exchange (LSE) covers the changes in an on-line Regulatory News Service but does not store any information. These LSE data are collected and stored by Extel Financial, which cannot make data accessible electronically but publishes a Weekly Official Intelligence Report. Copies of the hardcopy notifications have been available since 1992 at substantial cost (for this information £15,000 is charged)."[24]

2. Voting Rights—Voting Blocks

In some countries, Belgium for example, the notified stakes reveal not only the real but also the potential voting rights. The databases of other countries, like Spain, do not contain information on the potential voting rights. Therefore only real voting rights are included in the analysis.

The analysis focuses on voting blocks, which for most companies coincide with group blocks.

3. Capitalization

Capitalization figures of each company were delivered by the national stock exchanges. For U.K. companies, the author has used the market capitalization published in the financial pages of the Financial Times. The market capitalization of German companies was found in Börse Online-Statistik.

---

[24] M. Goergen and L. Renneboog, *Strong Managers and Passive Institutional Investors in the U.K.* (1998) paper presented at the European Corporate Governance Network Conference "Ownership and Control: A European Perspective", Milan, November 4–5, 1998, n. 21.

Table 12: Sources of Information

Belgium	1990 data: Annual reports of companies; Memento der Effecten; 1999 data: Notifications published by the Brussels stock exchange in the financial newspapers "Financieel-Economische Tijd" and the "Echo de la Bourse" and annual reports of companies
France	1990 data: J. Franks and C. Mayer, 'Corporate Ownership and control in the U.K., Germany and France' (1997) *Journal of Applied Corporate Finance*, reprinted in D. Chew, *Studies in International Corporate Finance and Governance Systems*, D. Chew (ed.), (Oxford 1997) 281–296; 1996 data: Dafsa, Des Liens Financiers, 2 volumes, 1998, 2,436 pages (capital rights); 1999 data: Annual reports of companies (voting and capital rights); Database Bourse de Paris at *http://www.bourse-de-paris/fr/frnews7/fsg710.htm* ("déclarations de franchissement de seuil"and "conventions d'actionnaires")
Germany	1990 data: J. Franks and C. Mayer, 'Corporate Ownership and control in the U.K., Germany and France'(1997) *Journal of Applied Corporate Finance*, reprinted in D. Chew (ed.) *Studies in International Corporate Finance and Governance Systems* (Oxford 1997) 281–296; 1999 data: Hoppenstedt Aktienführer 2000/ Bundesaufsichtsamt für den Wertpapierhandel—Datenbank für bedeutenden Stimmrechtanteile: *http://www.bawe.de/db_site.htm*
Italy	1992 data: Commissione Nazionale per le Societa' e la Borsa, Bollettino. 1999 data: Commissione Nazionale per le Societa' e la Borsa database consulted at *http://www.consob.it/trasparenza_soc_quot/assprop/attuale/menu.htm*
Spain	1999 data: Database of the Comision Nacional del Mercado de Valores *http://www.cnmv.es/english/queries/reg_ofi_ent_emisoras/reg_ofi_ent_emi.htm*
U.K.	1994 data: *Crawford's Directory of City Connections* (London 1995) 1,160 pages.
Stoxx 50	1998/1999 data: Hoppenstedt Aktienführer 2000/ Annual reports of companies

III. Methodology

1. Classification of the Shareholders

Some hypotheses have been made to classify shareholders in nine different classes: Individuals, non-financial companies, public authorities, foundations, banks, insurance companies, pension funds, investment funds, and foreign shareholders.

Usually, consolidated figures are used for analysis. As information on "acting in concert" was not available in all the Member States due to the use of different databases, this analysis was made as if no concert action takes place. For Italy and Belgium, data on the blockholding of the concert parties are available. Those data are added but not integrated in the model.

a. Individuals, Non-financial Companies, and Foundations

Individuals who notify their shareholdings are often families. If the latter declares their stake as a group, the consolidated figure is used. If each member of the family declares a stake, the different notifications are not summed up. From a point of view of "control" this means that the figures are at the bottom end. The same method is applied when the founding shareholders of the firm are mentioned. Especially for recent German initial public offerings the data seem to indicate that control has shifted to the markets, while it seems reasonable to assume that the founding members still control the company.

In some cases it was difficult to differentiate between families and non-financial companies. Families often use holding companies as an investment vehicle to control indirectly a variety of listed companies. This is especially the case in Belgium, Italy, and France. When the data indicate who controls the holding company—like the French notifications—the stakes are counted as family controlled stakes. In the other cases, where the control chain was less clear, the direct stake was mentioned as a non-financial company stake. Belgium and Italy are famous for their pyramid structures. This implies that the figures for some Member States are underestimating the real influence of families in listed companies.

Individuals also include employee ownership. The number of declarations of this class is very small. In some French cases the stakes of employees are managed by a fund manager. Those figures are included in the "investment fund" figure.

For the U.K. only the aggregated number of shares of the board of directors is available. In a significant number of cases the board "controls" the company. However, it is not known whether the members are acting in concert. Therefore, the board of directors is mentioned as a separate class in the table on majority shareholders.

About the structure of foundations no information is available. Therefore this class is kept separate.

b. Public Authorities

This class includes not only the national government but also local communities and cities. For Spain it was not possible to identify the government as "ultimate shareholder". Therefore, it is reasonable to assume that the Spanish data under-estimate the influence of the government.

c. Banks and Insurance Companies

The globalization of the financial sector created large financial groups offering a wide range of financial services including insurance. The Dutch-Belgian Fortis group offers insurance services but, after the take-over of the largest Belgian bank, Generale Bank, the banking activity became more important than the insurance services. If financial groups are offering all services, the main histori-cal activity was used to determine the class. In the case of Fortis group, these were insurance services.

d. Investment Funds, Pension Funds and "Other Financial"

Those three classes rarely declare major shareholdings in listed companies. Only if thresholds are beneath 5%, like in Italy and in some Belgian companies, some stakes are notified.[25] In the U.K. the stakes of pension and investment funds are generally managed by fund managers. The relationship between the latter and other entities like custodians is rather unclear.[26] Voting rights belonging to these entities were therefore mentioned as "other financial".

---

[25] In the U.K., only stakes of more than 5% are mentioned in *Crawford's Directory*.

[26] See G. Stapledon and J. Bates, *Enhancing Efficiency in Corporate Governance: How Recognizing the Nature of Modern Shareholding Can Lead to a Simplified Voting Process* (1999) paper presented at Tilburg University Law and Economics Conference on "Convergence and Diversity in Corporate Governance Regimes and Capital Markets", Eindhoven, November 4–5, 1999, 42 pages.

e. Foreign Shareholders

Foreign shareholders are not specified in detail. All classes are summed up. In some cases the determination of the nationality of the shareholder was rather tricky. This is especially the case when a major shareholder has a foreign majority parent, like AGF in France or Cobepa in Belgium. The stakes belonging to the latter controlled by a foreign shareholder are treated as if they belong to a "national" shareholder. This method is preferred, as not all "ultimate" shareholders are known.

2. Free Float

The sum of all stakes is never 100%. The other stakes are unidentified. In continental European companies, with their typical large stable shareholders, only the unidentified stakes—the free float—are traded on the market. This explains the illiquid continental markets.

3. Averages and Medians

To compute the concentration and distribution of blockholder stakes, different aggregation methods can be used. In this model the mean and the total ownership of the notified voting rights is calculated as follows:

Mean = $(\sum \text{PCTL}_i) / N$;
with PCTL = percentage of voting rights of the largest identified shareholder;
i = firm belonging to the population;
N = population of companies.
Total ownership of class j of shareholders = $\sum (\text{PCT}_{ij} * V_i)$;
with PCT = percentage of voting rights of an identified shareholder;
j = class to which the shareholder belongs (i.e. individual, non-financial company, public authority, foundation, bank, insurance company, investment fund, pension fund, other identified financial);
V_i= market capitalization of company i.
The total value of class j of shareholders is presented as a percentage of the market capitalization of all companies.

4. Portfolio Composition

Section four starts with a descriptive analysis of the evolution of the national ownership structure of listed companies. These figures are based on the portfolios of the different classes of investors. Except for Belgium, for which the author has made his own calculations, the figures stem from different sources.[27] The data are for 1990 and 1998 except for Italy: 1991–1997, Spain: 1992–1998; the Netherlands: 1990–1996, and Japan; 1990–1999.

IV. Analysis

1. Evolution of the Shareholdings of Different Classes of Investors

a. Domestic Non-financial Sector

General. At the beginning of the last decade the non-financial sector holds more than 60% of the shares in continental European companies. Foreign share-holders dominate in the Netherlands.[28] In the U.S. and Japan, the non-financial and the financial sector equally divide the shareholdings in listed companies, while in the U.K. ownership is institutionalized. By the end of the decade, the influence of the non-financial sector has decreased, most significantly in France and Spain. In the U.K. less than 20% of the shares are held by the domestic non-financial sector. Only in Italy and in Belgium are more than 50% of the shares owned by the domestic non-financial sector. The latter still has major holding companies controlling—directly or indirectly—stock exchange listed companies. In the former families, coalitions, and groups controlled by families extend their shareholdings.

Table 13 shows that the ownership structure is diverging in the network-oriented countries. The influence of the foreign investors increases in France and

---

[27] Germany: 1990: H. Hansen, 'Die Beteiligungsverhältnisse am deutschen Aktienmarkt' [1996] *Die Aktiengesellschaft* R88; 1998: DAI, *Privater Aktienbesitz in Deutschland: Aufwärtstrend setzt sich fort* (1999) 5.

France: 1990: FESE, *Shareownership Structure in Europe* (1995); 1998: M. Chocron, H. Grandjean, and L. Marchand, 'Les Marchés des Capitaux' [1999] *Bulletin de la Banque de France* May 46;

Italy: 1991: FESE, *Shareownership Structure in Europe* (1995); 1997: DAI, *DAI-Factbook 1999* (1999) 08.7 Italien;

Spain: 1992: FESE, *Shareownership Structure in Europe* (1995) 1998: BOLSA DE MADRID, *Rivista*, Diciembre 1999, 60;

Belgium: 1990: C Van Hulle, 'Bedrijfsfinanciering in België: waar naartoe?' [1998] *Tijdschrift voor Economie en Management* 1, 80; 1998: own research;

Netherlands: 1990 and 1996: Peeters rapport (1998) 42;

U.S.: 1990: DAI, *DAI-Factbook 1999* (1999) 08.7 USA; 1998: New York Stock Exchange;

U.K.: 1990: DAI, *DAI-Factbook 1999* (1999) 08.7 GB 2; 1997: Office for National Statistics, *Share Ownership: A Report on the Ownership of Shares at 31st of December 1997* (1999) London;

Japan: 1990: DAI, *DAI-Factbook 1999* (1999) 08.7 Japan 1; 1999: Tokyo Stock Exchange Shareownership Study 1999.

[28] Though no voting rights were attached to the ("certificates" of) shares.

Table 13: Non-financial Sector

	Germany	France	Italy	Spain	Belgium	Netherl.	US	UK	Japan
1990									
Individuals	16.9%	37.6%	21.8%	35.2%	28%	n.a.	50.8%	20.3%	20.5%
Companies	41.6%	22.8%	20.6%	10.7%	n.a.	n.a.	0.0%	2.8%	29.5%
Public									
authorities	3.6%	5.9%	27.6%	16.6%	n.a.	n.a.	0.0%	2.0%	0.2%
1998									
Individuals	15.0%	11.1%	52.9%	34.6%	17.7%	n.a.	41.9%	16.7%	19.0%
Companies	30.5%	17.7%	15.8%	5.5%	43.8%	n.a.	0.0%	1.4%	24.6%
Public									
authorities	1.9%	n.a.	8.1%	0.6%	3.9/%	n.a.	0.0%	0.1%	0.2%

n.a.: not available.
Source: see n. 27.

Spain but remains unchanged in Italy and Belgium. In Germany the financial sector has significantly raised its shareholdings.

Individuals. The trend of the declining importance of the individuals, which started as early as the fifties, continued in the nineties. In continental Europe, with the exception of the Southern European countries, individual investors own less than 20% of the shares. In France, due to different privatization laws, individual share ownership was vigorously promoted in the past. As the data show, those measures have failed. The study of the French National Bank shows that only 11% of the shares are owned by individuals. However, this study is oriented towards larger companies.

It seems reasonable to assume that individuals in the U.S., where institutional investors are well established and ownership taken separately, is widely dispersed, hold smaller stakes than individuals in European countries.

Non-financial companies. Ownership by non-financial companies is particularly striking in Belgium and to a lesser extent in Germany and Japan. One can find the explanation in the group phenomenon related to a high degree of concentration of ownership. The difference between the former and the two latter countries lies in the organization of those groups. Belgium is famous for its shareholding cascades—pyramids, a phenomenon that is somewhat transformed during the last decade but still remains the most important organization structure. In Japan, the Keiretsu is organized as a web of cross-shareholdings. The Keiretsu system tends to be restructured in programmes that cover many years. In Germany, a country where group law is well developed, the number of listed companies with non-financial shareholders holding a (super) majority has decreased.

In Anglo-Saxon countries non-financial companies do not hold stakes in other companies. For the Netherlands, no figures are available.

Public authorities.   The influence of the theory of Keynes on European public policy in the sixties and the seventies, and in some countries in the eighties, has disappeared completely in the nineties. As a consequence of privatization, the government is no longer a major shareholder. The process is still continuing in Italy and in France. In the latter no data are available for 1998, although stakes in terms of capital owned by the government are far below its voting power.[29]

b. The Financial Sector

The evolution of the importance of the financial sector shows a mixed picture. The sector substantially raised its shareholdings in Germany, France, and the U.S. In Italy and the U.K. these investors were selling. Financial institutions remained important shareholders in Japan and to a lesser extent in Spain and the Netherlands.

These trends have no one-dimensional explanation. They must be seen as a consequence of the differentiation of portfolios by the individual classes of institutional investors. This will be discussed in the following paragraphs.

Table 14 gives detailed information on the ownership of the different financial classes.

Banks.   Banks are, together with non-financial companies, the most important shareholders of Japanese companies. This was the case in 1990 and the picture has not changed in 1999. The figures of Germany show the same pattern, although the overall influence of banks as direct shareholders is smaller in Germany as compared to Japan.[30]

In Spain and Italy the consolidation in the financial sector reduced the number of listed banks and insurance companies. These companies frequently had banks as major shareholders.

In all the other countries, banks keep only small stakes.

---

[29] Cf. n. 41.

[30] Though the proxy voting system grants banks the majority of the votes at general meetings of most large stock exchange listed companies. For an analysis see T. Baums and C. Fraune, 'Institutionelle Anleger und Publikumsgesellschaft: Eine empirische Untersuchung' [1995] *Die Aktiengesellschaft* 97–112.

Table 14: Ownership of the Different Domestic Financial Classes

	Germany	France	Italy	Spain	Belgium	Netherl.	US	UK	Japan
1990									
Banks	10.3%	4.0%	10.5%	16.6%	—	0.6%	5.4%	0.7%	23.2%
Insurance comp.	11.2%	7.4%	3.5%	3.0%	—	—	5.0%	20.4%	15.7%
Pension funds	—	—	—	—	—	—	24.2%	31.6%	0.9%
Investment funds	4.3%	—	7.8%	1.0%	—	1.5%	7.1%	7.7%	3.7%
1998									
Banks	10.3%	—	7.7%	11.7%	0.8%	0.8%	3.4%	0.6%	22.6%
Insurance comp.	13.7%	—	2.7%	2.8%	5.8%	—	6.0%	21.6%	14.1%
Pension funds	—	—	—	—	1.2%	—	24.0%	21.7%	4.7%
Investment funds	12.9%	—	—	7.4%	8.3%	1.1%	16.3%	9.0%	1.6%

Source: see n. 27.

Insurance companies. The data in Table 14 show that the policy of most British insurance companies is to invest in British companies. This policy intensified even more in the second half of the nineties. The insurance companies are the most important shareholders of British companies. In Germany and Japan, insurance companies have large share stakes in listed companies but the evolution is different: only German insurance companies have expanded their shareholdings. However, some say that new German tax rules could cause a significant decrease in the shareholdings of insurance companies.[31]

In other countries the importance of insurance companies is rather small, although some large French insurance companies like AXA still belong to the group of large companies with cross-shareholdings ("GAS" or "Groupe actionnaire stable").

Investment funds. During the last decade the number and size of investment funds has exploded. These funds already hold more than 10% of the shares of stock exchange listed companies in the U.S. and Germany. Only in Japan and the Netherlands is the importance of this class of investors lagging behind.

[31] T. Major, 'Allianz Enjoys Profit Rise in Spite of Winter Storms' [2000] *Financial Times* February 17, 2000, 26.

Investment funds are a major force in the recent developments of the financial markets, investor relations, and corporate governance.

Pension funds.   The last major class is the pension funds. Data on the evolution of their portfolios of shares are only available for Japan, the U.K., and the U.S.

Due to changes in the law, inter alia the 1995 reform, the importance of U.K. pension funds as shareholders has decreased significantly.

During the last decade, U.S. pension funds held approximately ¼ of all shares of U.S. listed companies. In other countries, like Japan, pension funds slowly started investing in listed companies.

Although no figures are available, some say Dutch pension funds are decreasing their portfolios in Dutch companies since 1998. In 1990 the ownership of Dutch insurance companies and pension funds was estimated at 19%, in 1996 at 20.4%.

c. Foreign Ownership

Trends of globalization, liberalization, and internationalization result in a diversification of portfolios of investors. Foreign ownership is rising in all countries except in Belgium (Figure 1). Two reasons explain the diminishing importance of foreign shareholders in Belgian companies. First, companies with major foreign shareholders were taken over and de-listed and secondly, the Brussels stock exchange is rather illiquid, thus deterring foreign institutional investors.

In the Netherlands foreign shareholders own more than 40% of all shares, though this percentage was even higher in the beginning of the last decade. In Spain and France, foreign shareholders own already more than 35% of all shares. In the latter a recent study shows that in 10 companies of the CAC-40 foreign shareholders own more than 50% of the shares. In Totalfina more than 75% of the shares are owned by foreign shareholders.[32]

2. Analysis of the Evolution of Major Shareholders in Four European Countries

Franks and Mayer have studied the large shareholdings in three European countries in 1990. They used 25% blockholdings to show the differences between the U.K., France, and Germany. The data of the Franks and Mayer study have been compared with our data.

---

[32] A. Tricornot and J.B. Jacquin, 'En France les étrangers ont investi la place' [1999] *L'Expansion,* November 4, 1999, 46.

Figure 1: Ownership of Foreign Shareholders
Source: see n. 27.

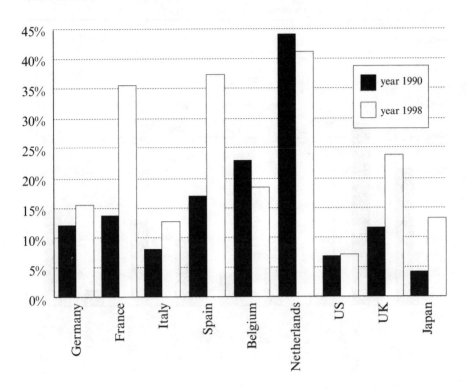

a. Germany

Franks and Mayer's study indicated that in Germany in 1990, 85% of the German firms had at least one shareholder owning more than 25% of the shares (Figure 2). Families and non-financial companies hold more than 20%, respectively more than 27% of those share blocks. Trusts and institutional investors are sometimes large shareholders, though banks actually come far down the list. Their major influence stems from the proxy votes they exercise on behalf of dispersed shareholders.

This pattern has significantly changed in 1999. An analysis of more than 500 German non-financial companies shows that more companies are widely held (25.7%). Due to initial public offerings families own a stake of more than 25% in 39.9% of the companies. As no "action in concert" is included the total number of widely held companies is probably lower and the number of family controlled firms higher. One should take note that some of the differences are probably due to the different population for 1990 and 1999.

Figure 2: Percentage of Companies with Share Stakes in Excess of 25% in 171 (1990) and 501 (1999) German Industrial and Commercial Companies
Source: own research based on data sources in Table 12.

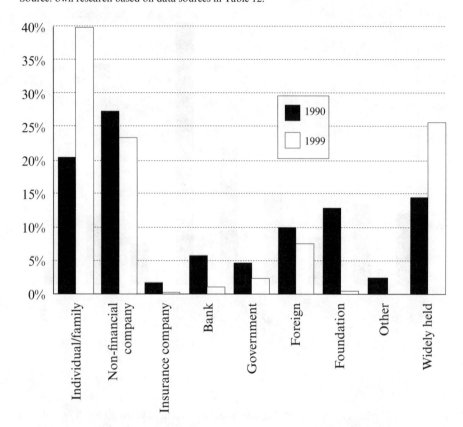

The importance of all the other classes has significantly diminished. In 23.4% of the companies a non-financial company has a stake of more than 25%. Large stakes of banks have diminished to 1.2%.

b. France

As in Germany, Franks and Mayer found that other French companies and to a lesser extent French families, have the largest proportion of large shareholdings; 21.4% of the companies do not have one shareholder with more than 25% of the shares (Figure 3).[33] More so than in Germany, the government, banks,

---

[33] However, when all the percentages in the study of Franks and Mayer are summed, the result is 105.5%.

Figure 3: Percentage of Companies with Share Stakes in Excess of 25% in 155 (1990) and 150 (1999) French Industrial and Commercial Companies

Source: own research based on data sources in Table 12.

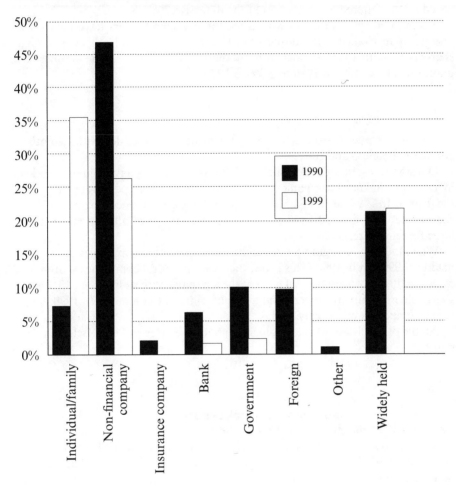

and foreign shareholders hold large stakes. This is due to the existence of double voting rights. Analysis of 156 companies in 1999 shows that 68% have a regime of double voting rights.[34]

Recent research of the voting blocks of 150 non-financial French companies shows that the German and French pattern of ownership does not differ

---

[34] In some companies the regime of double voting rights is different for ordinary and extraordinary general meetings.

substantially. The majority of the companies has one large shareholder, mostly a family or another non-financial company. Between 22% and 26% of the companies is widely held. Further research must show whether these data are influenced by the different composition of the database.

The number of companies with large foreign shareholders have developed differently in France and Germany. In France more than 11% have a foreign shareholder with a voting block of more than 25%, in Germany the number has diminished from 10% in 1990 to 7.5% in 1999.

c. Belgium

The analysis made by Franks and Mayer was further expanded with two other countries: Belgium and Italy.

During the last decade, Belgian families and individuals have sold their stakes in listed non-financial companies to other non-financial companies controlled by the former. In 1999 the number of companies having another company as a large shareholder is almost 50% (Figure 4). Approximately $\frac{1}{4}$ of all companies has a large foreign shareholder.

When looking at Figure 6 one might think that more companies are widely held in 1999 than in 1990. This is not the case. In several companies shareholders are acting in concert. Only 11.1% of the companies are widely held, 13% have shareholders acting in concert who are controlling the company. In 1990, 9.6% of the companies was widely held.

All the other classes of shareholders do not have large stakes in Belgian companies.

d. Italy

In Italy, several major developments took place during the last decade. Between 1992 and 1999 the number of family controlled firms increased by 7% from 29.4% to 36.8% while the number of firms having a non-financial company as a large shareholder decreased by 6% from 32.7% to 26.9% (Figure 5). The number of foreign controlled companies almost doubled from 5.9% to 11%. As in Belgium, there are very few companies widely held. Their number has decreased from 18.3% to 15.4%.

3. The Largest Shareholder of Stock Exchange Listed Companies

a. All Companies

The third section of this paper analyses recent figures on major shareholdings. The study focuses on the voting blocks in European companies. Becht's study

Figure 4: Percentage of Companies with Share Stakes in Excess of 25% in 136 (1990) and
135 (1999) Belgian Industrial and Commercial Companies
Source: own research based on data sources in Table 12.

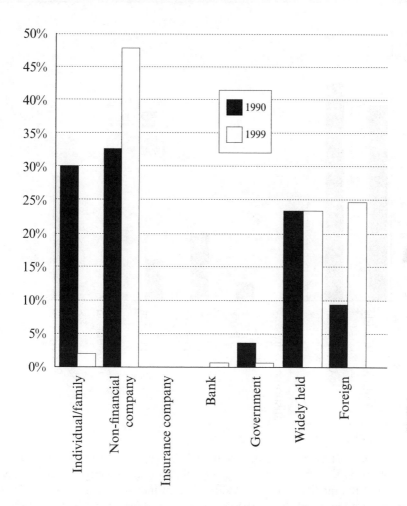

enables us to compare our figures with the largest voting blocks in U.S. companies. Becht has studied the largest shareholder of 6,559 U.S. companies.[35]

The average voting block of the largest shareholder of a U.S. company is 22.7%
(Figure 6). However, this percentage is significantly influenced by some majority

[35] M. Becht, *Beneficial Ownership of Listed Companies in the United States* (1998) paper presented at the European Corporate Governance Network Conference "Ownership and Control: A
European Perspective", Milan, November 4–5, 1998, 16 pages.

Figure 5: Percentage of Companies with Share Stakes in Excess of 25% in 153 (1992) and 182 (1999) Italian Industrial and Commercial Companies.
Source: own research based on data sources in Table 12.

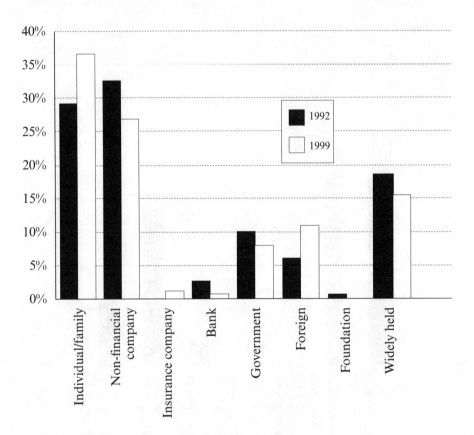

shareholdings. The median value is only 15.1%. These results are comparable with those of the U.K., where the average shareholding of the largest shareholder is 22.5%, and the median value 16.6%. In all Continental European countries the average voting block of the largest shareholder is at least twice as high: 36.6% in Spain, 41.7% in Belgium, 46.1% in Germany, 48.1% in Italy, and 52.0% in France. The median is even higher in France, Germany, and Italy. In some countries only non-voting stock is traded on the stock market, while the voting shares are held by one identified shareholder. This explains the maximum figure of 100%.

Less than 10% of continental European companies have no shareholder with more than 10% of the voting rights (Table 15). In the U.K., this ownership structure is dominant: 25% of all listed companies belong to this class.

Table 15: Number of Companies with no Shareholder Holding More than 10% of the Votes

Belgium 1999	Italy 1999	Spain 1999	Germany 1999	France 1999	U.K. 1994	U.S. 1996
8	13	26	39	12	333	1961
5.7%	5.6%	10.7%	7.2%	7.5%	25.0%	29.9%

Source: see note 35 and own research based on data sources in Table 12.

b. Index Listed Companies

Index listed companies are, on average, the largest listed companies. Harold Demsetz argued that those companies have a wide ownership.[36] Figure 7 indicates that in Europe one shareholder even controls some of the largest national stock exchange listed companies: some shareholders hold up to 70% of the votes.

On average large companies have one shareholder with a voting block of 24.8% (DAX) to 41.6 % (MIB). Due to the take-over of Telecom Italia and the introduction of Enel, the average of the latter went up from 35.5% in 1998 to more than 41% in 1999.

The situation is somewhat different for companies included in the international STOXX index. The voting structure of 45 companies is analysed. Dutch companies are not included due to the unclear voting right structure.[37] Only four companies have a majority shareholder; 11% of the companies have a "de facto" controlling shareholder with a voting block of more than 30%. The median of the largest voting block is only 6.6%. The capital concentration is even lower: AB Industrivärden has 26.4% of the voting rights of Ericsson but only 2.3% of the capital. Nokiterra Oy controls 16.1% of the voting rights of Nokia with 5.3% of the capital rights.

c. Newly Listed Companies

Analysis of the shareholder structure of the companies that went public in 1999 shows that the pattern of concentration of voting rights is not changing (Figure 8). The largest shareholder holds on average a voting block of more than 50% in Italy and France and almost 50% in Belgium. In Spain and Germany the largest

---

[36] H. Demsetz, *Ownership, Control, and the Firm* (Oxford 1988) 203–204.

[37] *"Stichtingen"* and *"Administratiekantoren"* sometimes own all the potential voting rights, diluting the actual voting rights.

Figure 6: Voting Block of the Largest Shareholder in Stock Exchange Listed Companies (1999)

Note: for the number of included companies see Table 16.

Source: own research based on data sources in Table 12.

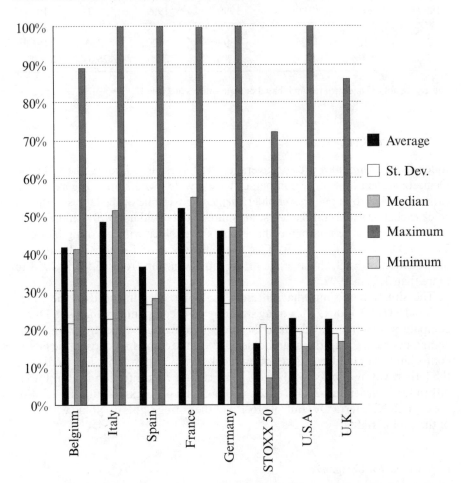

voting block is on average 40%. Those figures do not include parties acting in concert.

d. Other Listed Companies

The concentration of voting rights is even higher in the other stock exchange listed companies (Figure 9). In France and Germany the median and the aver-

Figure 7: Voting Block of the Largest Shareholder in National Index Listed Companies
Number of companies included: Belgium: 20; Italy: 30; Spain: 35; France: 38; Germany: 30; STOXX: 45.
Source: own research based on data sources in Table 12.

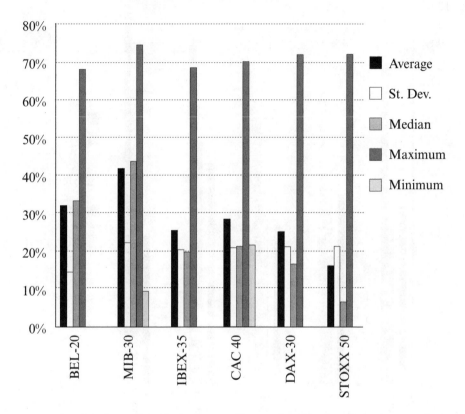

age voting block, and in Italy the median-voting block, of the largest share-holder exceeds 50%. Although the average in Belgian companies is somewhat lower at 44%, Belgian companies are controlled by concerting parties.

The largest shareholder of Spanish companies controls a smaller voting block: the median voting block reaches 29%.

4. Majority Shareholders—Market for Corporate Control

The fourth section of this study analyses the recent situation of the "control market" in several European countries. The structure of voting blocks is a determinant factor for the way the control market is organized. In all countries there is an active private market for corporate control: controlling stakes are privately

Figure 8: Voting Block of the Largest Shareholder in Newly Listed Companies
Number of companies included: Belgium: 11; Italy: 20; Spain: 10; Germany: 123; France: 13.
Source: own research based on data sources in Table 12.

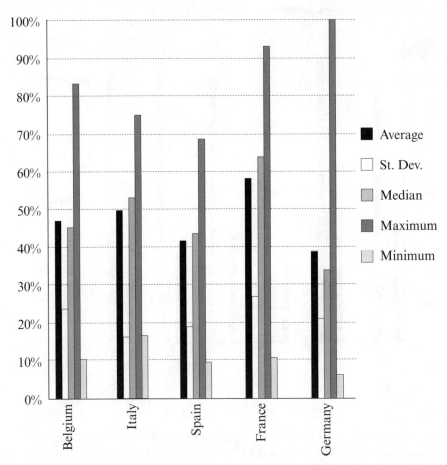

negotiated and afterwards, dependent on the regulatory environment, a mandatory take-over bid takes place.

In Belgium and Italy, where more than 62% and 69% of the stock exchange listed companies are controlled by one shareholder or a group acting in concert (Table 16), take-overs only occur after private negotiations. To a lesser extent this is also the case for France and Germany. In all countries exceptions exist: Telecom Italia, Mannesmann, Société Générale, Paribas, Generale Bank, to name but a few. Nevertheless, a huge majority of the cases the stock exchange does not decide the take-over contest.

Figure 9: Voting Block of the Largest Shareholder in Other Listed Companies
Number of companies: Belgium: 105; Italy: 186; Spain: 165; Germany: 389; France: 111.
Source: own research based on data sources in Table 12.

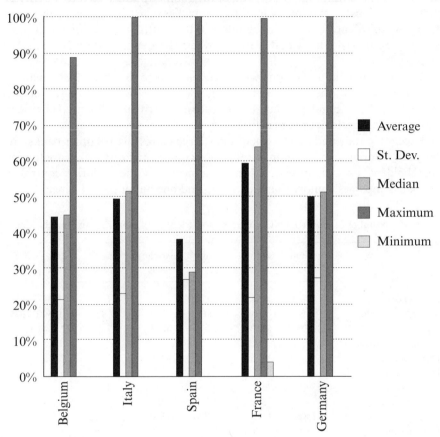

In the U.S. and the U.K. only 10% to 12% of the companies are controlled by a majority shareholder. In those countries, markets decide a control contest and a hostile take-over market has been developed.[38]

[38] However, the number of hostile take-overs is limited:

Number of hostile take-overs

	1990	1991	1992	1993	1994	1995	1996	1997	1998
U.S.	7	2	3	1	12	17	24	5	7
U.K.	15	14	5	7	3	12	6	7	4

Source: A. Von Buddenbrock, 'Abwehrstrategien gegen feindliche Übernahme' in DAI (ed.) *Die Übernahme börsennotierten Unternehmen* (Frankfurt am Main 1999) 278–279.

The identity of the majority shareholders does not differ substantially between different European countries: founding family members or board members (especially after a buy-out) control the company either directly (U.K.) or indirectly through a pyramid of holding companies (like in Belgium, France, and Italy). As the identity of the shareholders of the controlling non-financial companies in Spain is not known, it is unclear whether the same pattern exists in that country.

The German situation is somewhat different: due to the absence of a mandatory take-over bid, the absence of a squeeze-out rule[39] and the well-developed group law, a large number of companies with a majority non-financial company as shareholder is stock exchange listed.

Except for Italy and Spain, where some large banks control other banks, the only other important class of investors who acquired majority stakes are foreign shareholders. Foreign investors control almost ⅓ of the majority controlled Belgian companies,[40] more than ⅕ in Spain, and one out of six in France.

Table 16: Number of Controlled Companies and Identity of Controlling Shareholder

	Belgium 1999	Italy 1999	Spain 1999	Germany 1999	France 1999	UK 1994	US 1996
Number of comp.	140	234	242	542	160	1333	6559
Majority controlled	55	145	66	263	92	166	675
%	39.3%	62.0%	27.3%	48.5%	57.5%	12.5%	10.3%
Majority controlled by:							
Individual/family	—	35.2%	30.3%	44.9%	43.5%	1.2%	
Board of directors	—	—	—	—	—	76.5%	
Non-fin. comp.	63.6%	29.0%	24.2%	34.6%	33.7%	8.4%	
Insurance comp.	—	3.4%	3.0%	2.7%	—	0.6%	
Bank	1.8%	11.0%	19.7%	3.8%	3.3%	2.4%	
Government	3.6%	7.6%		2.3%	2.2%	—	
Foreign	30.9%	12.4%	21.2%	11.0%	17.4%	6.6%	
Foundation	—	1.4%	1.5%	0.8%	—	—	
Other	—	—	—	—	—	4.2%	
Total	100%	100%	100%	100%	100%	100%	
concerted exercise of voting > 50%	62.1%	69.5%					

Source: own research based on data sources in Table 12; U.S.: see n. 35.

[39] For an analysis of the recent developments of German company law see U. Noack, *Entwicklungen im Aktienrecht 1999/2000* (Frankfurt am Main 1999) 49 pages.

[40] Their indirect influence is even larger.

Not only is the number of controlled companies much higher in the network-oriented countries, but the number of companies that has a shareholder holding a voting block of more than 25% is also higher (Table 17/Figure 10). Less than 25% of the companies in Belgium, Italy, France, and Germany have no major shareholder. In the Netherlands and Spain the number is 43.8% and 57.9%. In the U.K. and the U.S. however, the numbers are 67.5% and 69.0%.

Table 17: Voting Concentration in Europe and the U.S.—Stake of the Largest Shareholder

	Bel.** 1999	It. 1999	Fr. 1999	Germ. 1999	Sp. 1999	Neth.* 1998	U.K.*** 1994	U.S. 1996
Over 50%	62.1%	62.0%	57.5%	48.5%	27.3%	19.5%	12.5%	10.3%
25% to 50%	25.7%	17.9%	21.9%	26.6%	28.9%	22.6%	20.1%	20.7%
10% to 25%	6.4%	14.5%	13.1%	17.7%	33.1%	34.0%	42.5%	39.1%
less than 10%	5.7%	5.6%	7.5%	7.2%	10.7%	23.9%	25.0%	29.9%

Note:
*: It is not clear whether the figures are capital or voting blocks;
**: Stake of the parties acting in concert;
***: The figures include the summed stakes of the board of directors.

Source: own research based on data sources in Table 12; Neth.: own calculations based on Monitoring Commissie Corporate Governance, *Monitoring Corporate Governance in Nederland* (1998) bijlage 3, 31–36; U.S.: see n. 35.

5. Liquidity of the Market—Capitalization of Notified Stakes

In the previous sections we analysed the evolution of the portfolio composition of different classes of investors and the position of the largest shareholder of stock exchange listed companies. The implementation of the major shareholdings Directive allows for a more detailed comparison of voting structures.

As more than 80% of the market value of all stock listed companies of six countries are included in the analysis, we argue that the sample is representative of the total market (Table 17).

For France the voting structure of 16.6% of all companies is included, a bias towards large companies as the analysed companies stand for 83.8% of market capitalization.

In Spain more than 50% of all companies are investment funds (SIM or SIM-CAV). These companies are excluded from the analysis.

In Table 18 the value of all the declared voting stakes of each class of investors is summed up. The value of the "not known" stakes indicates the liquidity of the

Figure 10: Voting Concentration in Europe and the U.S.—Stake of the Largest Shareholder
Source: see Table 17.

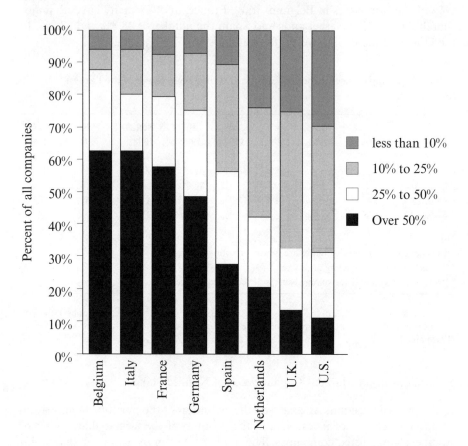

stock market.[41] The U.K. stock market is the most liquid: stakes larger than 5% only count for 14.4% of the value of all stakes. The Italian stock exchange is the most illiquid. Only 46.5% of the market capitalization is not identified. One should note that all stakes above 2% are included in the Italian figures while the U.K. figures only include stakes above 5%. Still, the value of the stakes between 2% and 5%—for Italian, French, and some German companies—is relatively small.

[41] Except for France where the liquidity can be significantly higher due to the use of double voting rights. Analysis of the 1996 capital rights show that the aggregate difference is rather small (own research):   *cont opposite/*

In Belgium more than 74% of the value of all declared stakes belongs to other companies. This is due to Belgian holding companies that control a large number of Belgian stock exchange listed companies. In Italy and France, two other network-oriented countries, a large number of large stakes belongs to non-financial companies.

Due to, inter alia, the recent explosion of public offerings of young German companies, the total market value of the declared stakes of the class "individuals" reaches more than 8%. In France the individual shareholders hold more than 7.5% of the total market value. Double voting rights and voting blocks attributed to this class of investors explain this high figure. A number of voting blocks are attributed to this class of investors for Italy. In the U.K. the board of directors holds significant stakes in a large number of stock exchange listed companies. The overwhelming majority of market value of the declared stakes of individuals belongs to the members of the board of directors.[42]

In France, Germany, and Italy, the government still holds approximately 10% of the market capitalization. Deutsche Telekom in Germany, France Telecom in France, and Enel in Italy highly influence these results. Those figures cast doubt on the reliability of the portfolio figures in Table 13.[43]

	Voting rights	Capital rights
	1999	1996
Non-Fin. Sector	**33.40%**	**36.36%**
of which:		
Companies	16.58%	26.33%
Individuals	7.58%	3.69%
Public authorities	9.24%	6.34%
Financial sector	**2.63%**	**4.81%**
of which:		
Banks	1.55%	2.01%
Insurance comp.	0.98%	2.73%
Pension funds		0.01%
Investment funds	0.10%	0.06%
Foreign	**6.62%**	**4.47%**
not identified	**57.35%**	**54.33%**
Total	100%	100%
Companies	160	679
Of all companies	16.65%	86.61%
Of capitalization	83.79%	90.61%

[42] Board members are seldom legal entities in the U.K.

[43] In 1998 the value of the declared government stakes was 8.1% of total market value in Italy.

Banks play an important role as shareholder in Spain, Germany, and Italy. In these countries the notified stakes of this class of investors represents more than 5% of the total market value. In Spain and Italy the importance of financial stock exchange listed companies in which banks hold large stakes explains the high percentage. In Germany, the *Großbanken* and some *Landesbanken* own large stakes in non-financial companies.

Allianz and Munchener Rück in Germany and Generali in Italy own large voting blocks in other large stock exchange listed companies, in general financial companies. In Germany, the cross-shareholdings between Allianz, Deutsche

Table 18: Value of the Identified Voting Stakes

	Belgium 1999	Italy 1999	Spain 1999	Germany 1999	France 1999	U.K. 1994
Non-Fin. sector	**41.76%**	**39.17%**	**12.88%**	**27.87%**	**33.40%**	**4.43%**
of which:						
companies	37.71%	21.40%	10.05%	6.37%	16.58%	0.84%
individuals	0.69%	5.59%	2.78%	8.23%	7.58%	2.99%
Public authorities	3.35%	9.86%		12.73%	9.24%	0.60%
Foundations		2.32%	0.05%	0.55%		
Financial sector	**0.74%**	**8.81%**	**9.95%**	**11.00%**	**2.63%**	**7.24%**
of which:						
Banks	0.10%	5.90%	9.62%	5.01%	1.55%	0.67%
Insurance comp.	0.63%	2.72%	0.33%	5.98%	0.98%	1.46%
Pension funds		0.00%	0.00%			
Investment funds	0.01%	0.19%		0.00%	0.10%	
Identified financial						5.11%
Foreign	**7.24%**	**5.53%**	**10.00%**	**3.83%**	**6.62%**	**2.92%**
Not identified	**50.27%**	**46.49%**	**67.17%**	**57.29%**	**57.35%**	**85.41%**
Total	100%	100%	100%	100%	100%	100%
companies	140	234	209	542	160	1333
of all companies	100%	94.74%	81.32%	51.97%	16.65%	76.30%
of capitalization	100%	97.96%	93.51%	95.13%	83.79%	93.48%

Source: own research based on data sources in table 12, FIBV, FESE, Bourse de Paris, Italian, and Belgian Stock Exchanges.

Bank, Dresdner Bank, and Munchener Rück, which substantially contribute to the percentage of this class of investors, still exist.

Insurance companies in other countries, especially in the U.K., have a diversified portfolio and do not have to declare major shareholdings. In the U.K. only 1.5% of the market value of the London Stock Exchange are notified stakes of more than 5%, whereas their total portfolio is estimated at 23.5%.

Our data show that other financial institutions like pension funds and investment funds do not acquire large stakes in stock exchange listed companies. In the U.K. allocation of the voting blocks was not always possible.[44] Moreover, fund managers frequently hold the voting rights not only for pension funds but also for investment funds and insurance companies. Therefore, an additional class, "identified financial", was created, indicating that the identity of the shareholder is known but the classification could not take place.

The last important class, "foreign shareholders", acquired significant stakes in Spanish, Belgian, French, and Italian companies. The policy of foreign shareholders towards Spanish, Italian, and French companies differs somewhat from the one towards Belgian companies. As mentioned higher, some large French and also Spanish and Italian companies have a majority of foreign shareholders. Individually those shareholders hold significant though not controlling stakes. In Belgium foreign shareholders control directly or indirectly large and small stock exchange listed companies.

Germany does not have the same number of large foreign shareholders. It is an open question whether the different legal culture—the rules on *Mitbestimmung* among other things—can explain the absence of foreign shareholders.

D. Conclusion

The objective of this study was to use information on equity markets and ownership structures to examine some characteristics of different governance systems.

In the nineties it is not only equity markets in market-oriented systems that facilitate equity finance, some markets in network-oriented systems provide a new environment of sources of equity. The number of initial public offerings in 1999 was almost as high in Germany as in the U.K. Since 1997, French listed companies raised more equity than British companies. In Sweden, Switzerland, the Netherlands, and France the ratio of market capitalization to GDP exceeds 100%.

---

[44] See G. Stapledon and J. Bates, *Enhancing Efficiency in Corporate Governance: How Recognizing the Nature of Modern Shareholding Can Lead to a Simplified Voting Process* (1999) paper presented at Tilburg University Law and Economics Conference on "Convergence and Diversity in Corporate Governance Regimes and Capital Markets", Eindhoven, November 4–5, 1999, 42 pages.

Dividing systems of corporate governance into market-oriented and network-oriented for comparative purposes is an oversimplification, rendered out-of-date by recent market developments.

The developments of the equity markets in some network-oriented systems do not enhance a dispersed ownership. In continental European countries the blockholder system with powerful controlling families, holding companies, and other non-financial companies is maintained. In 1999 share blocks in excess of 25% are for 63% in hands of the former classes in Germany, for 63% in France and for 64% in Italy. Voting blocks in excess of 50% can be found in 48% of the German companies, 57% of the French companies and 62% of the Italian companies. The average voting block of the largest shareholder exceeds 40% in France, Germany, Italy, and Belgium. On average, less than 10% of the companies have a dispersed ownership in these countries. Even in the largest companies the average voting block is substantially higher than in the U.S. and the U.K.

This new evidence has important consequences for the existing research on the influence of legal aspects of external finance. First, not only the ownership concentration but also the nature of different classes of shareholders must be analysed in future research. Secondly, the monitoring capacity of the different classes of large shareholders must be reflected in studies on the interaction of law and economics.

2

Recent Developments in the Market for Markets for Financial Instruments

STEFAN PRIGGE

Abstract

Some of the most far-reaching changes in the financial markets currently occur in the structure of the market for markets for financial instruments itself. This chapter first highlights some of the most prominent recent evidence. In the subsequent analysis, demand side, supply side, and governance aspects are dealt with. On the demand side, banks and security houses may currently be in a powerful position due to their role as switchmen with respect to order routing. However, investors, institutional as well as individual, are empowered at the expense of access intermediaries as opener, i.e. less intermediated, trading platforms become more realistic. On the supply side, the interplay of IT, regulation, and the tremendous growth in market volume increased the competitiveness in the market for markets significantly, in particular by lowering market entry barriers. The governance analysis claims that, until now, traditional exchanges and their emerging competitors differ not that much as one might think at first sight. Almost all of them are still member and customer controlled entities (MCCEs). However, since increasing competition unevenly affects the parties connected to an MCCE, power shifts can be observed. Significant steps towards an outside owned and controlled entity (OOCE) are still very rare. Such steps would include trading platform suppliers going public with a substantial free float. In summary, we seem to be at the beginning of the transformation of the market for markets to a much more competitive sector, which, until now, only has affected a few trading objects. Seen this way, for the future we should expect the emergence of a deeply differentiated range of products and services in response to the great diversity of preferences among the customers.

Contents

A.   Introduction
B.   Evidence
C.   Analysis
D.   Conclusion and Outlook

Figures

A. Introduction

Some of the most far-reaching changes in the financial markets currently occur in the structure of the market for markets for financial instruments itself. In 1996, Pagano and Steil wrote: "As the market for trading services becomes increasingly contestable, European exchanges will be forced to react by widening access, reducing fees, hiving off ancillary services, expanding their product range, and instituting new and cheaper modes of transacting. In order to do this, they may first have to undergo painful organizational restructuring, generally involving the dilution of member-firm control and increasing the direct influence of issuers and investors".[1a] This was a very good prognosis. Although development has gained much momentum since then, it seems that we are still at an early stage of this process.

The speed of change is high and seems to accelerate further. This conclusion emerges when one looks at the different stages of this paper: it was delivered to the conference organizers in early March 2000. As the conference took place at the end of March 2000, Euronext had entered the scene. Since then (at the time of writing in October 2000), Deutsche Börse and London Stock Exchange announced and buried their iX concept, and Tradepoint and Swiss Exchange announced their virt-x project, to name only the most significant incidents. Another one and a half years later (in April 2002), the scenery has changed significantly once again: Among other things, the three major European stock exchanges are listed companies, the Liffe is part of Euronext, and Deutsche Börse is building its vertical silo structure. This chapter will not attempt to be a comprehensive diary of the developments in the market for markets. Instead, it will describe in the first part most of the major incidents in 1999 and 2000, taking mainly a European perspective. In the second part, some basic patterns in the development will be sketched more abstractly.[1b] Fortunately, these considerations have passed successfully the test of time so far; they are not outdated by the development in the real world.[1c]

[1a] M. Pagano and B. Steil, 'Equity Trading I: The Evolution of European Trading Systems' in B. Steil (ed.) *The European Equity Markets. The State of the Union and an Agenda for the Millennium* (London, 1996) 1–58, at 50.

[1b] For the beginnings of competition in Europe at about 1985 and the development thereafter, see M. Pagano and B. Steil, 'Equity Trading I: The Evolution of European Trading Systems' in B. Steil (ed.), *The European Equity Markets. The State of the Union and an Agenda for the Millennium* (London 1996) 1–58, at 4–25 and passim.

[1c] For a shorter and more recent (as of October 2001) analysis, see S. Prigge, 'Basic Trends in the Recent Developments in the Market for Markets for Financial Instruments' [2001] 3 *Capco Institute Journal of Financial Transformation* 35–44.

B. Evidence

I. Trading[2]

1. Definitions

In the discussion of the emerging rivals amongst the traditional exchanges, such as Tradepoint, BrokerTec, or EuroMTS discussed below, the term Electronic Communications Network (ECN) is often used. There is no generally accepted definition of an ECN. Domowitz and Steil state that "an exchange or trading system is analogous to a communications network, with a set of rules defining what messages can be sent over the network, who can send them, and how they translate into trades".[2a] Seen this way, every electronic trading facility seems to be an ECN, be it an exchange, taken as a legal quality, or not. In the current discussion the term ECN seems to be mainly used for the group of electronic trading systems challenging the traditional exchanges. Consequently, Tradepoint, a regulated market, is called an ECN.

In this chapter, the following scheme for trading facilities will be used: a regulated market is an exchange. The established exchanges are called traditional exchanges, their rivals ECNs ("E" seems permissible since they all appear to offer electronic trading facilities).[3]

2. Tradepoint as a Challenger to Traditional Spot Stock Exchanges (Excluding virt-x)[4]

Tradepoint is a London-based, electronic stock exchange. It is a recognized investment exchange and has been designated a regulated market throughout Europe under the ISD (Investment Services Directive). Moreover, the SEC allowed U.S. firms a direct membership in Tradepoint with regard to trading in U.K. and European equities in spring 1999 and July 2000 respectively.[5] As of

---

[2] An integration of market microstructure aspects is beyond the scope of this chapter.

[2a] I. Domowitz and B. Steil, 'Automation, Trading Costs and the Structure of the Securities Trading Industry' *Brookings-Wharton Papers on Financial Services* (1999) 34–81 and 89–92, at 36.

[3] In a more refined approach one could label the traditional exchanges' rivals Alternative Trading Systems (ATSs) and distinguish several categories of ATSs; for such approaches see Deutsche Börse, 'Catalysts of Change' *Deutsche Börse Vision & Money* (no. 13, 2000) 69–73.

[4] With respect to pan-European equities trading, there are currently two hot spots: blue chips and stocks of high-growth companies. The latter are dealt with below under B.II, since for this group of companies listing regime and secondary market aspects are more closely connected.

[5] According to Tradepoint, it is the first time the SEC allowed U.S. firms direct membership of a non-U.S. stock exchange; Tradepoint, 'Press Release: U.S. Members Gain Direct Access to

January 2000, Tradepoint had 150 members coming from the EU countries, Switzerland, Hong Kong, and the U.S.[6]

Trading in listed U.K. equities (currently over 2,000) started in 1995. Tradepoint Financial Networks plc is itself a listed stock company, the shares of which are traded on the AIM segment of its domestic rival London Stock Exchange. This feature is a major distinction to almost all other regulated markets. Prior to 1999, shares were held by venture capital company Apax and dispersed owners. Despite some features very attractive to the important group of wholesale traders, such as anonymity and a central counterparty, Tradepoint never gained a share significantly exceeding 1% of total London-based trading in these equities. Consequently, Tradepoint was never able to generate profits and, therefore, seemed to be on its way out of business.

The status of Tradepoint in the market for trading facilities completely changed in July 1999:[7] At that time, a consortium led by the Reuter's subsidiary Instinet, a more than 30 year old trading platform, injected £14 million into Tradepoint, buying 70 million new shares which represent 54% of the company. The original members of the consortium were Instinet, Morgan Stanley Dean Witter, J.P. Morgan, Archipelago (an ECN), and American Century (a U.S. investment fund company). Other major players in the international financial markets have joined the consortium since then. In September 2000, Tradepoint's ownership structure was as follows (see Figures 1 and 2).

The attraction of Tradepoint to these prominent new owners and the prevalent public attention is not due to its status as a trading facility for U.K. equities. It stems from its potential to become the first pan-European market for blue chips. In July 2000, Tradepoint started its trading facility for the approximately 230 continental European equities that constitute the major European indices.[8]

European Equity Trading for the First Time' (July 5, 2000, visited September 13, 2000) http://www.tradepoint.co.U.K./pr990323.html.

However, this permit requires that trading volume on Tradepoint does not exceed 10% in British shares; 'SEC läßt Tradepoint-Terminals zu', *Börsen-Zeitung* March 24, 1999, 4.

[6] Tradepoint, 'Introduction and Background' (visited September 13, 2000), http://www. tradepoint.co.uk/exch_intro.html.

[7] Announced in May; 'Brokerage Firms in U.S. Invest in Tradepoint', *Wall Street Journal Europe* May 7, 1999, 20. For the status of Tradepoint after its reviving see also the interview with Instinet's CEO, Doug Atkin, in A. Currie, 'A Pioneer under Pressure' [1999] *Euromoney* (November) 79–82.

[8] Tradepoint, 'Press Release: Tradepoint to Launch First Integrated Pan-European Stock Exchange for Blue Chip Stocks on 10 July' (April 26, 2000, visited September 13, 2000) http://www.tradepoint.co.uk/pr000426.html.These indices include: FTSE EuroTop 300, MSCI Euro Index, MSCI Pan-Euro Index, DJ Stoxx 50, DJ Euro Stoxx 50, Dax 30, CAC 40, and MIB 30. Additional stocks are to be added at a later date.

The largest trading houses among the consortium's members are reported to have promised to direct trading volume with preference on Tradepoint's pan-European platform. By so doing they support Tradepoint's goal to become the leading trading facility for European blue chips by the end of 2001; 'Tradepoint macht mit Blue-Chip-Markt ernst', *Börsen-Zeitung* February 11, 2000, 3.

Figure 1: Total Holdings in Tradepoint

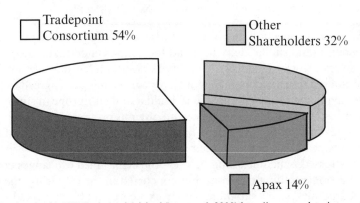

Source: Tradepoint 'A UK Exchange' (visited January 6, 2000) http://www.tradepoint.co.uk/exch2.
html.

Figure 2: Holdings in Tradepoint Consortium

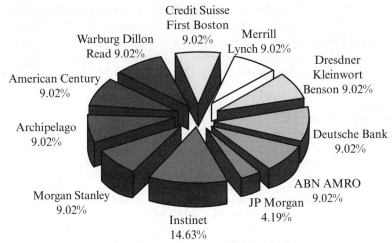

Source: Tradepoint 'A UK Exchange' (visited January 6, 2000) http://www.tradepoint.co.uk/exch2.
html.

This replicates the opportunities available in the national markets—easy access
to trading all shares representing the underlying stocks of major index derivatives—on a European scale.[9]

[9] Moreover, Tradepoint intends to trade securities uniting equities in baskets which represent
pan-European sectoral indices; Tradepoint, 'European Stocks on Tradepoint—An Introduction'
(visited January 18, 2000) http://www.tradepoint.co.uk/eurostocks1.html.

3. The Ever-changing Alliances Between Traditional European Spot Stock Exchanges (before projects such as Euronext, iX, and virt-x)[10]

There is a close connection, in both substance and timing, between the activities at Tradepoint (and similar activities) and the actions undertaken by traditional European spot stock exchanges.[11] In May 1999, only a few days before the consortium entered into Tradepoint, eight European exchanges[12] agreed to form an alliance having the principal purpose to build a unified European stock market. In September 1999, after there had been no obvious progress for several months, rumors said that major investment banks were about to build a platform for trading European blue chips on their own.[13] Only a few days later—in a meeting, they stressed, scheduled long before—the eight allied exchanges could not agree on a single trading platform, but concurred in the following: the current domestic trading systems should remain in existence, but be connected via interfaces to build a virtual European exchange. Trading of 300 to 600 European equities should commence in November 2000; the market model should comprise a central counterparty and ensure anonymity.[14]

Deutsche Börse AG started an initiative in December 1999. Although Deutsche Börse CEO Seifert stated that he does not want to jeopardize the alliance of eight[15]—and the fellow exchanges commented that in their view the alliance had not failed yet[16]—Deutsche Börse's announcement to significantly alter its structure can well be interpreted as an indication that the cooperation between the allied exchanges did not work satisfactorily. The exchange's plans,

---

[10] Similar stories could be told for traditional derivatives exchanges; see, for instance, the cooperation among CBOT and Eurex below (text accompanying nn. 61ff).

[11] For a comprehensive list of global mergers and alliances of automated exchanges, see I. Domowitz and B. Steil, 'Automation, Trading Costs, and the Structure of the Securities Trading Industry' [1999] *Brookings-Wharton Papers on Financial Services* 34–81 and 89–92, at 45.

[12] Somehow, this alliance of eight was an enlargement of the alliance between Deutsche Börse AG and London Stock Exchange upon which both surprisingly agreed in 1998. The exchanges in Madrid, Paris, Zurich, Milan, Amsterdam, and Brussels joined in ("2+6"). The story of the many preceding alliances and counter alliances will not be told here.

[13] According to press reports, Goldman Sachs, J.P. Morgan, and Merrill Lynch were the driving forces of this initiative. As to the trading platform, no final decision was said to be taken yet, but several options were available: e.g. Tradepoint, an extension of BrokerTec (see below text accompanying nn. 40ff) on spot equity trading, or one of the many ECNs (see below text accompanying nn. 51ff) of which several investment banks had bought stakes in; see, e.g. 'U.S.-Investmentbanken planen eigene Börsen in Europa' *Handelsblatt* September 13, 1999, 1; 'Spekulationen um Plattform für mögliche Europa-Börse' *Handelsblatt* September 14, 1999, 29.

[14] See, for example, 'Die acht Börsen einigen sich auf virtuelle Eurobörse—Start November 2000' *Börsen-Zeitung* September 24, 1999 1; 'Die Acht votieren für ordergetriebenes System' *Börsen-Zeitung* September 24, 1999, 3.

[15] 'Deutsche Boerse Has Bold Plans' *Wall Street Journal Europe* December 21, 1999, 15, 25.

[16] 'Die Kooperationsbörsen geben sich gelassen' *Börsen-Zeitung* 7.12.99, 3.

approved by the supervisory board, consisted, among other things, of the following items: participation of major international market participants in the exchange's capital[17]—with a share of about 50%[18]—and boards, development of a spot market for European blue chips (within the framework of the alliance of eight), development of a central counterparty, and development and, possibly, sale of ECNs. To reflect the denationalization, Deutsche Börse intended to rename itself Euroboard.[19] Moreover, Deutsche Börse/Euroboard planned to make an IPO at the *Neuer Markt* in summer 2000.[20] Just a few days before the extraordinary general meeting, this plan was abandoned in favor of iX.[21]

4. The Acceleration in the Race for a Pan-European Spot Trading Facility for Blue Chips in 2000

In the year 2000, the pace of the race for a pan-European spot trading facility for blue chips increased significantly. Beforehand, there was mainly the rivalry between the traditional exchanges and Tradepoint. Tradepoint is also part in one of the new partnerships and constellations which emerged—and partly disappeared again—in the course of this year: Jiway, Euronext, virt-x, and iX.

In February, Jiway surprisingly entered the market. London-based Jiway Ltd. is owned by the Swedish OM Gruppen[22] (60%) and Morgan Stanley Dean Witter (40%). By autumn 2000 they intend to provide a platform that allows online cross-border transactions of 6,000 European and U.S. shares, i.e. all

---

[17] Current shareholding structure of Deutsche Börse AG (before IPO): Deutsche Bank 14.1%, *Regionalbörsen* (regional stock exchanges) 10.09%, Dresdner Bank 7.65%, HypoVereinsbank 6.60%, Commerzbank 6.38%, *Kursmakler* (specialists) 5.06%, UBS 4.30%, ING/BHF Bank 3.70%, *Freimakler* (traders) 2.98%, DG Bank 2.84%, Hauck & Aufhäuser 2.30%, SGZ-Bank 2.03%, WestLB 1.90%, other banks 30.07%; according to 'Eigner der Deutschen Börse legen sich nicht fest' *Börsen-Zeitung* August 25, 2000, 3. Deutsche Börse AG does not publish its ownership structure in such detail.

[18] 'Deutsche Boerse Chief Plans Makeover' *Wall Street Journal Europe* January 7, 2000, 15, 26.

[19] For Deutsche Börse's plans see, for example, 'Deutsche Börse wird europäisch' *Deutsche Börse Reporter* (December 1999) 1 and 'Deutsche Boerse Has Bold Plans' *Wall Street Journal Europe* December 21, 1999, 15, 25 and 'Deutsche Boerse Chief Plans Makeover' *Wall Street Journal Europe* January 7, 2000, 15, 26.

[20] A general meeting was scheduled for May 4, 2000; 'Aufsichtsrat billigt Börsengang der Börse. Ab 2. Juni Aktienhandel bis 20 Uhr' *Börsen-Zeitung* February 29, 2000, 1 and 'Deutsche Boerse Plans to Go Public' *Wall Street Journal Europe* February 29, 2000, 15, 20. Listing regulations at the *Neuer Markt* require, inter alia, a free float of at least 20% of the shares.

[21] See below text accompanying n. 30.

[22] OM started in 1985 as the first for-profit exchange (options on Swedish stocks). OM has been listed since 1987. In 1998 it merged with the Stockholm Stock Exchange. Besides running exchanges OM Gruppen AB is also a major supplier of trading system technology. Its customers include, inter alia, the American Stock Exchange and the Milan Stock Exchange; 'Vorreiter der modernen Börsen' *Börsen-Zeitung* August 29, 2000, 4 and 'OM Gruppen sind der beimliche Star in Europa' *Börsen-Zeitung* September 23, 2000, 3.

shares listed in the London, Paris, Frankfurt, Swiss, Swedish, and Dutch markets, and also the top 150 shares on Nyse and Nasdaq. They claim to guarantee a price at least equal to the quote at the domestic market.[23] Jiway expects cost savings from eliminating the need for membership at local exchanges and from the introduction of a central counterparty and netting.[24] Jiway aims at the individual investor. It has applied to the Financial Services Authority to become a recognized investment exchange.[25]

In March 2000, the Euronext project was publicly announced. Euronext is the merger of Paris Bourse, Amsterdam Exchanges, and Brussels Exchanges. The holding company Euronext NV is a Dutch stock corporation. Paris Bourse is weighted with a 60% participation in Euronext, Amsterdam Exchanges with 32%, and Brussels Exchanges with 8%. Trading of equities[26] will take place on a single integrated trading platform with a single set of trading rules, but under three jurisdictions (depending on where the company is listed and where the market participant is located, respectively). More than 1,300 companies will have their stocks listed on Euronext, among which are about 25% of the companies that constitute the MSCI European index.[27] Clearing will follow a single-jurisdiction concept: French Clearnet S.A. will provide a central counterparty and allow for netting.[28] Completion of the exchange of shares from the incumbent exchanges to the new holding happened in late September and the implementation of the French trading system NST on all Euronext trading platforms is expected by summer 2001.[29]

At the beginning of May 2000, the iX Intermezzo began. It should last for four months. After the announcement of Euronext the general public eagerly

---

[23] To assess this guarantee it should be taken into account that a quote is not the actual price. Depending on the market model, placing an order in the market may initiate a second stage of price competition (best bid and best ask being the result of the first stage): market participants' competition for the incoming order may result in a price within the bid-ask-spread (price improvement); on price improvement see, for example, H. Schmidt, O. Oesterhelweg, and K. Treske, 'Der Strukturwandel im Börsenwesen: Wettbewerbstheoretische Überlegungen und Trends im Ausland als Leitbilder für den Finanzplatz Deutschland' [1997] 30 *Kredit und Kapital* 369–411, at 392–5 and H. Schmidt and A. Küster Simic, 'Kursverbesserung und Orderbuchtransparenz' [1999] 116 *Sparkasse* 524–32.

[24] Clearing and settlement are part of the competitive attack of Jiway; on clearing and settlement see below text accompanying nn. 92ff.

[25] Jiway 'Company' and 'Concept' [2000] (visited September 14, 2000) http://www.jiway.com/. and 'Morgan Stanley and OM Group Launch Online Trade Venture' *Wall Street Journal Europe* February 4, 2000, 13, 18.

[26] There will also be trading platforms for bonds, derivatives, and commodities.

[27] 'Midsize Bourses Draw Attention in Wake of Merger' *Wall Street Journal Europe* March 21, 2000, 13, 18.

[28] For details see Euronext 'Comprehensive Paper' (2000, visited September 14, 2000) http://www.aex.nl/aex.asp?url=compr.

[29] '"Das ist der erste Schritt"' *Börsen-Zeitung* September 9, 2000, 4.

anticipated the reaction of the London Stock Exchange and Deutsche Börse. They disclosed their intention to join as equals in iX (international Exchanges).[30] Blue chips were intended to be traded in London whereas growth companies would be traded in Frankfurt; however, this clause seemed to be vague. The German Xetra system was chosen as trading platform. At a later stage, Nasdaq was planned to enter iX. The merger was criticized both in the U.K. and in Germany from the very beginning. Each place suspected it would be the loser in this game of give and take: the decision to make Xetra the common trading system raised strong resistance. Complicated and controversial legal issues evolved. And, perhaps most importantly, clearing and settlement, which is the decisive issue for the large market participants who are the driving forces behind the race for a pan-European trading platform for blue chips (see below text accompanying notes 106ff), remained almost unmentioned in the iX agreement. It remains highly doubtful whether the general meetings of LSE and Deutsche Börse scheduled for September 14 would have seen 75% majorities for the merger. However, a few days before this date OM Gruppen launched a bid for the LSE, which the LSE declared hostile. One can think of several motives for OM: OM, as a major supplier of trading systems, wanted to promote its systems as against the rival Xetra system. On a more destructive line of reasoning, one could suspect OM of aiming at activating the City Code with its lengthy procedures to support the start of its Jiway project in October/November. Be that as it may, it is certain that not only the general meetings were cancelled, but that the LSE turned down the whole iX project in September. OM Gruppen's bid is still pending while writing this chapter. With respect to the analysis below in section C, which, *inter alia*, takes a closer look at the role of major global banks and investment companies, it should be noted that in the iX case the LSE was advised by Merrill Lynch and Deutsche Börse by Goldman Sachs.[31]

On July 10, Tradepoint not only opened its pan-European trading platform, it also announced virt-x. Virt-x is a market for pan-European blue-chip trading created by the Swiss Exchange and Tradepoint. It is intended to be a London based Recognized Investment Exchange under the supervision of the Financial Services Authority. Trading is due to start in the first quarter of 2001. Traded objects are those stocks that comprise the major pan-European indices. The London Clearing House will act as a central counterparty enabling anonymity. A netting option should be added soon.[32] Provision of these features implies that virt-x mainly hopes to attract institutional investors and other wholesale traders.

---

[30] In a way, this meant the way back from the alliance of eight exchanges to the 1998 cooperation between the London Stock Exchange and Deutsche Börse.

[31] 'The Jilted Exchange' *The Economist* June 24, 2000, 105.

[32] For details see virt-x, 'Service Offering—Management Summary' (2000, visited September 14, 2000) http://www.virt-x.com/contents/mgmt_summary.pdf.

Tradepoint will be renamed in virt-x. Hence virt-x plc will be publicly quoted in the London AIM. The Swiss Exchange and the Tradepoint consortium will each hold 38% in virt-x.[33] The consortium's members promised to trade through virt-x if it delivers the announced benefits.[34]

To sum up the current status: Tradepoint has realized a pan-European platform for blue chips, and virt-X (with Tradepoint) and Euronext work on the realization of their projects. LSE and Deutsche Börse have to redefine their strategies, with the former exchange being the object of a hostile bid. Other potential competitors for a pan-European platform for blue chips may be Easdaq, Nasdaq, and Cantor Fitzgerald;[35] however, what is known about their intentions is still quite vague.

5. Bond Trading: the BrokerTec Attack, the EuroMTS Expansion, and Eurex-Bonds

In most countries, bonds are mostly traded off-exchange,[36] moreover, bond trading is considered to possess substantial potential for the improvement of efficiency.[37] In the bond market, too—especially with respect to spot trading—there are numerous initiatives to change this situation for the most important bonds.[38] A selection will be introduced below.[39] One of these is BrokerTec. BrokerTec Global LLC was launched in June 1999 by a group of seven major banks and security houses comprising Goldman Sachs, Morgan Stanley Dean Witter, Merrill Lynch, Credit Suisse, Lehman Brothers, Salomon Smith Barney

---

[33] 'Schweizer Börse bricht aus Isolation aus' *Börsen-Zeitung* July 11, 2000, 5.

[34] 'The X Files' *The Economist* July 15, 2000, 88.

[35] On Easdaq and Nasdaq see below in B.II. According to John Hilley, chairman and CEO of Nasdaq International, Nasdaq's top priority in Europe is becoming the dominant pan-European platform for high-growth companies; trading of blue chips is of the second order; K. Astbury, 'Europa and her Competing Bulls' [2000] *Euromoney* February 121–6. Cantor Fitzgerald plans to offer trading of U.S. and European shares on its platform "e-speed" by the end of 2000; 'Deutsche Bank setzt im Bondhandel aufs Internet' *Handelsblatt* February 10, 2000, 43.

[36] In the U.S., see, for example, 'E-Bonds, Licensed to Kill' *The Economist* January 15, 2000, 79f, and in Germany, see, for example, Deutsche Bundesbank *Der Markt für deutsche Bundeswertpapiere* 3rd edn. (Frankfurt am Main 2000).

[37] For this view, cf., for example, 'E-Bonds, Licensed to Kill' *The Economist* January 15, 2000, 79f for the situation in the U.S.

[38] According to a recent questionnaire of Greenwich Associates among the 250 U.S. institutional investors most active in fixed-income securities, the majority of which soon expects the emergence of equity-trading-like structures for the most important bonds; 'Online Bond Trading Catches on with Large Fixed-Income Investors' *Wall Street Journal Interactive* February 9, 2000, 13, 18.

[39] For a brief survey see J. Rutter, 'New Adventures in Credit Trading' [March 2, 2000] 1 *Credit* 24–32.

(Citigroup), and Deutsche Bank.[40] Its goal is to create a global bond trading and clearing platform for both spot and forward trading. A good case in point for the analysis below is the way BrokerTec launched the derivative wing of its initiative: in July 1999, it sent a letter to leading derivatives exchanges and clearing houses, and also to some software houses, to ask for their participation in the construction of a unified global trading and clearing platform, starting with bond derivatives. In the manner of an ultimatum, the addressees were given only about 14 days to reply and five weeks to send in their proposals.[41] According to a BrokerTec member, the 20 to 25 responses they had received confirmed interest in BrokerTec's project.[42] BrokerTec is still advancing its plan: in December 1999, it bought the trading platform from a subsidiary of the Swedish OM Gruppen.[43] Spot trading in U.S., Belgian, French, and German government bonds started in the summer of 2000. BrokerTec offers a central counterparty and netting.[44] It intends to begin trading of U.S. Treasury bond futures in the first half of 2001.[45]

EuroMTS has its roots in a trading facility for Italian government bonds. In April 1999, it developed into a trading platform for French, German, and Italian government bonds.[46] As of September 2000, it provides electronic trading facilities for government bonds of eight Eurozone countries (Austria, Belgium, France, Germany, Italy, the Netherlands, Portugal, and Spain) and of Finland, has started trading in German *Pfandbriefe*, and intends to expand to Japan.[47] Since there is only wholesale trading among top market participants, so far no central counterparty has been installed except for the new repo trading facility.[48] Shareholders of London-based EuroMTS Ltd. are Italy SpA, the original core,

[40] 'BrokerTec Fiddles While Others' Systems Catch Fire' *Wall Street Journal Europe* October 27, 1999, 25. Since then, ABN Amro, Banco Santander Central Hispano, Barclays Capital, Dresdner Bank, and UBS Warburg have joined the group; 'BrokerTec geht an den Start' *Börsen-Zeitung* June 27, 2000, 8.

[41] Banken setzen Terminbörsen unter Druck *Börsen-Zeitung* July 16, 1999, 5 and Allmächtige Investmentbanken setzen Börsen zu *Börsen-Zeitung* December 31, 1999, 24.

[42] 'BrokerTec Fiddles while others' Systems Catch Fire' *Wall Street Journal Europe* October 27, 1999, 25.

[43] 'OM erhält Zuschlag für BrokerTec-Plattform' *Börsen-Zeitung* December 18, 1999, 7.

[44] 'Bond-Trading Service Joins a Parade of New Launches' *Wall Street Journal Europe* July 4, 2000, 24.

[45] BrokerTec, 'About BrokerTec' (2000, visited September 15, 2000), *http://209.176.0.42/AboutBtec/AboutBtecIndex.html.*

[46] 'EuroMTS übertrifft die Erwartungen' *Börsen-Zeitung* April 15, 2000, 3.

[47] 'MTS to Create Electronic System for Japan's Bonds' *Wall Street Journal Europe* December 17, 1999, 20 and 'Electronic Trading May Boost Pfandbriefe Market' *Wall Street Journal Europe* January 14, 2000, 18.

[48] 'Vom Siegeszug des elektronischen Bondhandels' *Börsen-Zeitung* May 22, 1999, 5 and 'London Clearing House ordnet OTC-Märkte' *Börsen-Zeitung* December 15, 1999, 3.

and 24 major banks and investment banks, including J.P. Morgan, Paribas, Warburg Dillon Read, Deutsche Bank, Morgan Stanley Dean Witter, ABN Amro, Cabato Holding, Credit Suisse First Boston, and Salomon Smith Barney.[49]

In October 2000, trading on Eurex-Bonds started. Spot, basis (i.e. simultaneous spot and forward trade), and repo transactions in German government bonds are the premier services offered. Eurex-Bonds GmbH is a joint venture of the Eurex exchange (70% share in capital) and 11 investment banks (ABN Amro, Barclays, BBVA, BNP Paribas, Caboto, Commerzbank, Deutsche Bank, Dresdner Bank, Goldman Sachs, Morgan Stanley Dean Witter, and West LB), who each hold a 3% stake. However, the banks hold 70% of the votes and Eurex 30%. Eurex-Bonds is not an exchange, but an ECN. A central counterparty will be offered in November, a netting facility will be available later. Eurex-Bonds wants to expand trading on other countries' government bonds and corporate bonds.[50]

6. The Emergence of Electronic Communications Networks (ECNs)

With respect to spot trading in equities, Tradepoint and Jiway currently are the only serious publicly announced ECNs for European blue chips.[51] ECNs are essentially a U.S. phenomenon. This is usually attributed to the more advanced automation of traditional exchanges in Europe.[52] Until now, most ECNs offer their services to wholesale traders. They account for about 33% of dealings in Nasdaq shares,[53] among the largest are Instinet (13.2%) and Island (11.5%).[54] ECNs' share in Nyse equities amounted to only 5% in March 2000. However, since then the SEC granted ECNs access to the Intermarket Trading System (ITS). Moreover, Nyse Rule 390, restricting Nyse members' ability to trade Nyse

[49] 'MTS to Create Electronic System for Japan's Bonds' *Wall Street Journal Europe* December 17, 1999, 20.

[50] 'Eurex-Bonds soll Finanzplatz stärken' *Handelsblatt* July 7, 2000, 46 and 'Eurex-Bonds nimmt den Handel auf' *Handelsblatt* October 6, 2000, 45, and '"Eurex-Bonds bietet mehr als die Konkurrenz"' *Börsen-Zeitung* September 7, 2000, 3.

[51] However, Easdaq with its status of a regulated market could be another appropriate vehicle to build such a market.

[52] See, for example, B. Steil in J.C. Louis, 'Crossing Networks Oust the Middlemen in Europe' [1999] *Wall Street & Technology* (Electronic Trading Supplement, November 1999) 25 or A.K. Achleitner 'Competition' [2000] 13 *Deutsche Börse Vision & Money* 43.

[53] 'FSA Solicits Market Opinion on Regulation' *Wall Street Journal Europe* January 24, 2000,16); data most probably as of the end of 1999.

[54] C. McEachern, 'ECNs Mull Linking Order Books to Bolster After-Hours Liquidity' [1999] *Wall Street & Technology* (Electronic Trading Supplement, November 1999) 33; data most probably as of fall 1999.

equities elsewhere, was abandoned. In August, the ECN Archipelago opened its customer's electronic access to Nyse-listed stocks. Consequently, ECNs' share in Nyse equities is expected to rise.[55]

An essential feature in order to understand the current upheaval in the market for trading facilities is the ECNs' ownership structure. It highlights in particular the significant impact of major investment banks.[56] The following figure, published in September 1999, provides instructive examples:[57]

Figure 3: Investment Banks' Stakes in Electronic Trading Facilities

Credit Suisse First Boston

Tradeweb	Dealer-investor on-line bond trading system
BrokerTec	Inter-dealer bond and futures broking system
EuroMTS	European government bond trading system
Tradepoint	Electronic stock exchange, based in London, 4.87% stake

---

[55] 'SEC ermöglicht ECN Zugang zur Nyse' *Börsen-Zeitung* March 21, 2000, 4 and, 'Archipelago öffnet New York Stock Exchange' *Handelsblatt* August 10, 2000, 39.
This article concentrates on competition in European equities trading. For additional information on competition in the U.S., see, eg E. Benhamou and T. Serval, *On the Competition between ECNs, Stock Markets and Market Maker* (Paper, December 1999); C. Nickson, 'Back to the Buttonwood Tree' [2000] *Euromoney* (June) 41–7; O. Oesterhelweg, *Anlegerorientierte Handelsverfahren für den deutschen Aktienmarkt* (Wiesbaden 1998), and H.R. Stoll, 'Market Fragmentation' [2001] 57/4 *Financial Analysts Journal* 16–20 (commenting on the debate whether fragmentation calls for a national central limit order book; the debate was particularly vivid when representatives of major market participants and exchanges testified before the Senate Banking Committee in March; see 'Major Broker-Dealers Propose a Sea Change in U.S. Markets' *Wall Street Journal Europe* March 1, 2000, 13, 18. and 'U.S. Exchanges, Securities Firms Debate Structure' *Wall Street Journal Europe* March 2, 2000, 18).

[56] That it is really the big names that are active can be seen by taking a look at rankings such as those by 'Polling a Market in Transition' *Euromoney* (September 1999) 145–52 for financing or I. Walter, 'The Asset Management Industry in Europe: Competitive Structure and Performance under EMU' in J. Dermine and P. Hillison (eds.) *European Capital Markets with a Single Currency* 265–309 (Oxford 1999) and J. Wrighton, 'America's Largest Overseas Investors' [1999] 24 *Institutional Investor* 85f for asset management. To facilitate interpretation of this table, and the banks and security houses mentioned at other places in this chapter, the top ranks of Euromoney's poll of the polls for 1999—a kind of a meta-ranking summarizing several rankings on capital raising, trading, advisory, and risk management—are reproduced: 1. Deutsche Bank, 2. Merrill Lynch, 3. Morgan Stanley Dean Witter, 4. Warburg Dillon Read, 5. Citigroup, 6. Goldman Sachs, 7. J.P. Morgan, 8. ABN Amro, 9. Chase Manhattan, 10. Credit Suisse First Boston, 11. Lehman Brothers, 12. HSBC Group, 13. Dresdner Kleinwort Benson, 14. BNP Paribas.

[57] See also E. Benhamou and T. Serval, *On the Competition between ECNs, Stock Markets and Market Maker* (Paper, December 1999) 11; C. Nickson, 'Back to the Buttonwood Tree' [2000] *Euromoney* (June) 43, and 'Bank Initiatives in Electronic Trading' *Risk* 13/3 (2000) (Electronic Trading Special Report) 22–4.

Figure 3: *cont.*

Goldman Sachs

Hull Group	Options trading, full stock acquisition
Wit Capital	Retail on-line investment bank, 20% stake
Archipelago	ECN, 25% ownership
Optimark	Alternative trading system, minority stake (undisclosed)
Brut	ECN, 10% stake
Primex Trading	Alternative trading system, joint venture with Merrill Lynch and Madoff Securities
Strike	ECN, 5% stake through Hull Group
BrokerTec	Inter-dealer bond and futures broking system; one of seven founder members
EuroMTS	One of 24 banks in the inter-dealer bond broker for the European market
Tradeweb	Dealer-investor on-line bond trading system. Goldman is one of four banks in initial consortium
Easdaq	European stock exchange, minority interest

J.P. Morgan

Archipelago	ECN, minority stake
Tradepoint	Electronic stock exchange, based in London, 2.26% stake

Lehman Brothers

Strike	ECN, minority stake
BrokerTec	Inter-dealer bond and futures broking system; one of seven founder members
EuroMTS	One of 24 banks in the inter-dealer bond broker for the European market

Merrill Lynch

Direct Markets	Merrill's e-commerce division; Merrill is the only investment bank to have created such a division
BrokerTec	Inter-dealer bond and futures broking system; one of seven founder members
Primex Trading	Alternative trading system, joint venture with Goldman Sachs and Madoff Securities
Tradepoint	Electronic stock exchange, based in London, 4.87% stake

Morgan Stanley Dean Witter

Tradepoint	Electronic stock exchange, based in London, 4.87% stake
Easdaq	European stock exchange, 2.5% interest
Brut	ECN, minority interest
Eclipse	ECN pushing after-hours trading, minority interest

Salomon Smith Barney/Citigroup

Strike	ECN, minority stake
BrokerTec	Inter-dealer bond and futures broking system; one of seven founder members
Tradeweb	Dealer-investor on-line bond trading system

Source: A. Currie, 'The New Battleground' [2000] *Euromoney* (September) 53–66, at 64, data most probably as of summer 1999, stakes in Tradepoint as of September 2000.

A recent initiative in Germany can be mentioned here: In May 2000, Consors, one of Germany's major online-brokers, announced that it was buying a 10 to 25% stake in the Berliner Börse AG and setting up an electronic trading facility.[58] Moreover, Consors declared that it was to buy a major participation in one of the largest order book keepers and most active market participant in Berlin. For example, Consors appears to intend to collect its customers' orders and to

[58] The Berliner Börse had demutualized into a stock corporation just a few days before the announcement.

route them to Berlin where there is a good probability that the Consors subsidiary will be the transaction partner.[59] However, Consors has not yet succeeded in convincing other brokers to join. Participation of other brokers would enhance the platform's liquidity. Possibly, other brokers hesitate because they want to avoid so close a collaboration, which may turn into dependency, with a competitor.

7. The Trend Towards Electronic Trading

For the trading objects under discussion there seems to be a clear trend towards electronic trading. All major new competitors entered the market for markets with an electronic trading facility. Moreover, among the traditional exchanges, prominent former supporters of floor trading try develop electronic platforms, either to complement or to substitute their incumbent system.[60] Often these initiatives were forced by prior heavy losses in market share against electronic competitors, e.g., the Liffe against Eurex with respect to the Bund future. Although there was no direct competition in a particular trading object, the CBOT's replacement as the world largest derivatives exchange by the Eurex is a good symbol for this process. The Liffe fostered its electronic LiffeConnect system and the CBOT its electronic trading system labeled Project A. In many instances, these changes in the market model were accompanied by severe conflicts among the incumbent members who had the decision-making power.

A good case in point is the erratic history of the cooperation between Eurex and CBOT. One major feature of a cooperation would be the move of the former open outcry market CBOT towards electronic trading. A first attempt to cooperate in late 1998 upset the CBOT: In December 1998, the members replaced their pro-cooperation chairman, Patrick Arbor, by David Brennan, who was said to be a supporter of floor trading.[61] In January 1999, the CBOT members decided by 450 to 390 votes not to cooperate with Eurex.[62] Only five months later, after losses in market shares that could not be ignored, a second poll brought a 750 to 126 majority for a cooperation.[63] A joint venture called

---

[59] 'Online-Börse soll Privatanleger locken' *Handelsblatt* May 30, 2000, 33 and 'Francionis kleine Revolution' *Handelsblatt* May 30, 2000, 14.

[60] See I. Domowitz and B. Steil 'Automation, Trading Costs, and the Structure of the Securities Trading Industry' [1999] *Brookings-Wharton Papers on Financial Services* 34–81, 89–92, at 42, for a list of exchanges moving to automated auction trading in 1997/8 that enumerates such prominent names as CBOT, CME, Liffe, LSE, and MATIF.

[61] 'CBOT wählt Patrick Arbor ab. Fragezeichen hinter Eurex-Allianz' *Börsen-Zeitung* December 11, 1998, 1.

[62] 'CBOT votiert gegen Eurex-Allianz. Franke: Project A keine Alternative' *Börsen-Zeitung* January 29, 1999, 1.

[63] 'Börsenriesen bilden Allianz' *Handelsblatt* June 26, 1999, 29.

a/c/e (alliance/cbot/eurex) was set up, in which each exchange holds a 50% stake. In August 2000, the Project A trading platform was turned off. Instead, the electronic trading platform a/c/e, which builds on Eurex technology, went live. This platform serves as an electronic trading device within the CBOT, but it also offers CBOT's and Eurex's members the opportunity to trade the other exchange's products, provided they have acquired the membership status in the exchange. During the first weeks of operation the electronic platform gained a remarkably high share in total CBOT volume, possibly hinting at a future decline of floor trading at the CBOT.[64]

8. Changes in the Governance Structures of Traditional Exchanges

The traditional exchanges seemingly regard their governance structure as not being appropriate for their current needs. One major trend is the demutualization of exchanges, which includes the possibility to detach ownership from membership.[65] Domowitz and Steil[66] enumerate in their list of exchange demutualizations, inter alia, Stockholm Stock Exchange (1993), Helsinki Stock Exchange (1995), Copenhagen Stock Exchange (1996), Amsterdam Exchanges (1997), Borsa Italiana (1997), Australian Stock Exchange (1998), Stock Exchange of Singapore (1999), and SIMEX (1999). The Frankfurt Stock Exchange (1991) may be added. The building blocks of Euronext, Paris Bourse, Amsterdam Exchanges, and Brussels Exchanges, are stock corporations, as is the new holding Euronext.[67]

This movement is still gaining momentum since at the time of writing some of the most important exchanges are considering demutualization plans: The London Stock Exchange changed into a stock corporation in March 2000.[68] At the beginning of the year 2000, the NASD board approved a two-stage demutualization of Nasdaq, which designates stakes to the large Wall Street houses (30–32%), smaller trading and market making firms (25%), the largest listed

---

[64] 'CBOT und Eurex wollen globalen Standard setzen' *Börsen-Zeitung* August 16, 2000, 3 and 'Finanzpackett des CBOT vor dem Aus' *Börsen-Zeitung* September 8, 2000, 3.

[65] The issue of self regulation, which is of major importance in cases of demutualization of entities which currently serve, inter alia, as self regulatory bodies, is not dealt with in this chapter; on this topic, see, for instance, G. Ferrarini, 'Stock Exchange Governance in the European Union' in M. Balling, E. Hennessey, and R. O'Brien (eds.), *Corporate Governance, Financial Markets and Global Convergence* (Dordrecht 1998) 139–60, passim and J. Köndgen, 'Ownership and Corporate Governance of Stock Exchanges' [1998] 154 *Journal of Institutional and Theoretical Economics* 224–51, at 242 and passim.

[66] See above, n. 60, at 53.

[67] Euronext 'Comprehensive Paper' (2000, visited September 14, 2000) http://www.aex.nl/aex.asp?url=compr, 5.

[68] 'Moderne Besitzstruktur für die LSE' *Börsen-Zeitung* March 16, 2000, 3.

companies (16.5%), and institutional investors (5%). NASD will hold a 22% block. A great majority of the members approved this plan in April 2000.[69] The Nyse also intends to demutualize, but due to difficulties in this process had to postpone this project.[70]

Moreover, demutualization is often accompanied by an announcement of a change in the exchange's goal: It turns from service for the members to profit maximization for the owners, see, e.g., the intentions of LSE, Nasdaq, and CME.[71] Euronext writes in its self-description about its three founding exchanges "All three had been demutualised at an earlier stage and were therefore no longer member-driven organizations. . ."[71a] The Swiss Exchange will indirectly, via virt-x, be connected with a ". . . commercially run publicly quoted company".[72]

Only few traditional exchanges are already listed themselves, e.g., the Australian Stock Exchange.[73] According to its designated CEO, Théodore, Euronext is intended to be listed until mid-2001.[74] Via virt-x the Swiss Exchange will be partly listed in the London AIM. This feature is closely linked to the goal of market value maximization. In addition, going public changes the governance environment of the respective entity significantly. At the time of writing this is being experienced by the LSE: On July 24, 2000, off exchange trading in LSE stocks began.[75] Only a few weeks later the LSE became object of a take-over bid by OM Gruppen in connection with the iX intermezzo.

The transition to a new market model is often accompanied by a change in the governance structure. In addition to the evidence on the cooperation between

---

[69] 'Nasdaq-Demutualisierung ist beschlossene Sache' *Börsen-Zeitung* January 6, 2000, 3 and 'Nasdaq-Umstrukturierung beschlossen' *Börsen-Zeitung* April 15, 2000, 5; 'NASD Sells Spinoff to Members' *Wall Street Journal Europe* February 8, 2000, 28.

[70] 'Nyse verschiebt den Börsengang' *Börsen-Zeitung* September 4, 1999, 4.

[71] 'London Stock Exchange plant Umwandlung in Aktiengesellschaft' *Börsen-Zeitung* July 31, 1999, 1, 'Nasdaq-Umstrukturierung beschlossen' *Börsen-Zeitung* April 15, 2000, 5, and W. Falloon, 'Chicago Merc Files Share Offer Plans' [2000] 13/2 *Risk* 6.

[71a] Euronext, 'Comprehensive Paper' (2000, visited September 14, 2000) http://www. aex.nl/aex.asp?url=compr), 5.

[72] virt-x, 'Service Offering—Management Summary' (2000, visited September 14, 2000) http://www.virt-x.com/contents/mgmt_summary.pdf, 2.

[73] The shares of Amsterdam Exchanges are currently traded on Reuters and were planned to be listed in 2002; G. Ferrarini, 'Stock Exchange Governance in the European Union' in M. Balling, E. Hennessey, and R. O'Brien (eds.) *Corporate Governance, Financial Markets and Global Convergence* (Dordrecht 1998) 139–60, at 141f, 146f and C. Di Noia, 'The Stock-Exchange Industry: Network Effects, Implicit Mergers, and Corporate Governance' (March 1999, Consob Studie Ricerche no. 33) 15. The Stockholm Stock Exchange is indirectly listed as a part of OM Gruppen AB; 'Vorreiter der modernen Börsen' *Börsen-Zeitung* August 29, 2000, 4 and 'Exchange in Stockholm Becomes Success Story' *Wall Street Journal Europe* May 16, 2000, 13, 24.

[74] 'Börsenchef: Euronext bleibt für alle offen' *Handelsblatt* August 15, 2000, 31.

[75] 'LSE-Anteile erstmals gehandelt' *Börsen-Zeitung* July 25, 2000, 4.

Eurex and CBOT above (text accompanying notes 61ff), the story of the CBOT can be continued: the conflict between floor and electronic trading supporters is mirrored in the present discussion about the future governance structure of the CBOT: in January 2000, the board of the CBOT proposed to divide the mutual, mainly floor-based exchange into two profit-oriented parts, one for floor trading and one for electronic trading (eCBOT). Members would receive shares of both trading parts; in a second step, the shares of the electronic trading division were intended to become publicly tradable and independent of the CBOT.[76] In summer the CBOT changed its plan in that eCBOT would remain a subsidiary of the CBOT.[77] It will be interesting to observe how the partly conflicting interests of floor and computer traders are reflected in the governance structure.

II. Listing (and the Race for a Pan-European Spot Trading Facility for High-growth Stocks)

Trading facilities aim at attracting business. Besides creating attractive trading, clearing and settlement, or other features, they can use the list of available trading objects as an additional feature to gain market share. With respect to spot equities trading, one option is to trade the shares of companies whose shares are already listed elsewhere. A second alternative is to offer such an attractive listing regime so as to become the market place where companies prefer to be listed. However, there is no fixed connection in the sense that the market with the most attractive listing regime is somehow automatically the major secondary market because—after the IPO—all competing market places can turn to option one, in case they have a suitable market segment. So the challenge is to tailor market segments in a way that they satisfy the preferences of issuers and investors better than any competing segment and that is good enough to encourage both parties to do business at all.

Since 1996 or 1997, being the preferred market for high-growth companies in Europe has gained a substantial attraction. So far there are two main actors in Europe: Euro.NM and Easdaq.[78] Euro.NM is a cooperation of the "new market" segments of the traditional exchanges in Belgium, France, Germany, Italy, and the Netherlands.[79] Trading started in 1996 as it did on Easdaq. Easdaq is

---

[76] W. Falloon, 'Old Option Threatens CBOT Restructuring' [2000] 13/2 *Risk* 46f.

[77] 'CBoT ändert Restrukturierungsplan' *Börsen-Zeitung* September 2, 2000, 5.

[78] For recent brief portraits of these markets as well as of Nasdaq Europe and techMARK (U.K.), see K. Astbury, 'Europa and her Competing Bulls' [2000] *Euromoney* (February) 121–6.

[79] However, in July 2000 Deutsche Börse announced that it will leave Euro.NM; 'Deutsche Börse aus Euro.NM ausgetreten' *Börsen-Zeitung* July 21, 2000, 3. This comes as no surprise since the new markets of the Euronext exchanges are also part of Euro.NM.

recognized as a regulated market in Belgium. There are about 100 shareholders, mainly banks, security houses, and venture capitalists.[80]

Both competitors strive to become the leading pan-European exchange for growth stocks. So far Euro.NM in general and the German *Neuer Markt* in particular are in the lead. On Euro.NM, as of the end of July 2000, 497 companies were listed with a market capitalization of €241.7 billion,[81] with a clear dominance of the *Neuer Markt* with more than 300 companies listed. On Easdaq, as of September 2000, 62 companies were listed with a market capitalization of €53.7 billion.[82] Moreover, the *Neuer Markt* attracts more and more foreign companies[83] and appears to have developed into an international market.

This situation made Easdaq change its strategy in summer 1999: it decided to implement a dual trading facility, i.e. no longer are only shares of those companies eligible for trading that made their initial listing on Easdaq, but also shares of other companies from adequate business sectors that are listed on other markets.[84] As of September 2000, there is dual trading in 83 stocks, the majority of which is listed on Nasdaq.[85] Another feature is dual listing: companies that are already listed on a regulated market in Europe, Israel, or the U.S. can be listed on Easdaq without issuing prospectus, provided that no capital is raised.[86] In addition, in the course of 1999, it raised capital and attracted new prominent shareholders, among which are Morgan Stanley Dean Witter, Goldman Sachs, and Tradepoint.[87] As a result, many shareholders of Tradepoint also hold a stake in Easdaq.[88]

Easdaq's initiative, most probably, was also caused by NASD's announcement to build a Nasdaq Europe in London, which should start in late 2000.[89]

---

[80] 'Easdaq mit erweitertem Aktionärskreis' *Börsen-Zeitung* April 29, 1999, 4.

[81] Euro.NM, 'Euro.NM Market Statistics' (visited September 18, 2000) http://www.euronm.com/index2.html and 'Easdaq führt 50 US-Aktien ins Dual Trading ein' *Börsen-Zeitung* September 5, 2000, 9.

[82] Easdaq, 'Easdaq Weekly Factsheet' (Issue 178, 4.-8. September 2000) (visited September 18, 2000) http://www.easdaq.com/pdf_files/week_factsheet/Week_report_Issue.pdf.

[83] As of January 2000, more than 10% of the companies came from abroad.

[84] 'Easdaq rüstet Handelsplattform auf' *Börsen-Zeitung* June 23, 1999, 3.

[85] 'Easdaq führt 50 US-Aktien ins Dual Trading ein' *Börsen-Zeitung* September 5, 2000, 9.

[86] 'Die Easdaq macht sich fein für den Privatanleger' *Börsen-Zeitung* February 8, 2000, 4.

[87] 'Easdaq plant Expansionsschub im Frühjahr' *Handelsblatt* November 1, 1999, 33.

[88] 'Easdaq erweitert Aktionärskreis' *Börsen-Zeitung* October 29, 1999, 4; for further information on Easdaq's structure, see G. Ferrarini, 'Stock Exchange Governance in the European Union' in M. Balling, E. Hennessey, and R. O'Brien (eds.) *Corporate Governance, Financial Markets and Global Convergence* (Dordrecht 1998) 139–60, at 152.

[89] 'Nasdaq plant europäischen Ableger in London' *Handelsblatt* November 8, 1999, 49. NASD also expands to Japan where its rival to the Mothers (Market of the High-Growth and Emerging Stocks) segment of the Tokyo Stock Exchange started in June 2000; 'Nasdaq Japan startet ruhigen Handel' *Handelsblatt* June 20, 2000, 46. As of September 2000, 12 companies are listed on Nasdaq

Temporarily, Nasdaq's participation in the iX project had been the European leg in its expansion plan. It is to be expected that iX's failure does not mean the end of NASD's plans for Europe.

But despite the *Neuer Markt's* success as a listing regime, its organizers, the Deutsche Börse, had to learn that other places can gain substantial shares in secondary market trading if investors' preferences are not fully satisfied: Before Deutsche Börse extended trading hours and reduced the minimum lot to one in spring 1998, the *Regionalbörsen*, in particular those in Stuttgart and Berlin, which offered these features, were able to attract about 70% of trading volume in *Neuer Markt* stocks. Afterwards, the *Neuer Markt* was able to expand its share to about 60%.[90] And in September 1998, Deutsche Börse revised its decision to abandon Frankfurt floor trading in *Neuer Markt* stocks as soon as these equities were tradable on Xetra because they feared a renewed significant loss in market share to the floor trading at the *Regionalbörsen*.[91] This example illustrates both the loose connections between the share in initial listing volume and in secondary market trading volume, and the large impact the features of a trading facility may have on the share in trading volume.

III. Clearing and Settlement

Clearing and settlement comprises those activities after a trade is agreed upon.[92] It is a business of its own, but is also closely connected to the market models of trading facilities and, consequently, to its competitiveness. During the last two years, major changes in this field concentrated on Europe.[93] With its 15 national and two international (Euroclear and Cedel) suppliers of these services[94] it is said to be "overly fragmented"[95] and to offer substantial potential for the

---

Japan; Nasdaq Japan 'Listed Companies' (visited September 18, 2000) http://www.nasdaq-japan.com/e/e_index.html.

[90] 'Xetra über alles' *Börsen-Zeitung* July 29, 1998, 1.

[91] 'Aktien bleiben auf dem Frankfurter Parkett' *Handelsblatt* September 2, 1999, 25.

[92] For a short, profound treatment of this field, see B. Bernanke, 'Clearing and Settlement during the Crash' [1990] 3 *Review of Financial Studies* 133–51.

[93] For a recent report, see European Central Bank 'Consolidation in the Securities Settlement Industry' [2000] *ECB Monthly Bulletin* (February) 53–9.

[94] As of May 1999; 'Deutsche Börse und Cedel planen europäisches Clearing-Haus' *Börsen-Zeitung* May 13, 1999, 1. The ECB counts 21 domestic and two international central securities depositories in the 11 countries of the Eurozone as of 1997; European Central Bank, 'Consolidation in the Securities Settlement Industry' [2000] *ECB Monthly Bulletin* (February) 53–9, at 53f.

[95] European Central Bank, 'Consolidation in the Securities Settlement Industry' [2000] *ECB Monthly Bulletin* (February) 53–9, at 56.

enhancement of efficiency.[96] The European Central Bank states that the clearing and settlement industry is in a process of consolidation, transforming it from locally protected institutions to competitors in a cross-border context.[97] At the top of the market participants' wish list is a central counterparty.[98] Besides reducing counterparty risk, a central counterparty has the interesting feature of being the key for netting positions.[99] Trades of a market participant in one instrument undertaken within a certain period of time, e.g. a day, could be netted. Thereby, firstly, the funds necessary for this transaction volume would be dramatically reduced. And secondly, the number and volume of transactions to be settled would significantly decrease.[100] The latter is particularly expensive for cross-border transactions. One cost driver in this field is the variety of data processing systems.[101] From this perspective, a unified European clearing and settlement would be the optimum.

In May 1999, Deutsche Börse Clearing (DBC), a subsidiary of Deutsche Börse, and Cedel made an advance in this direction: they merged to become Clearstream.[102] However, their efforts to attract other major European players did not succeed. Instead, in November 1999, French Sicovam/Clearnet, by can-

---

[96] As an example for this kind of statement, see Deutsche Börse, 'Catalysts of Change' [2000] 13 *Deutsche Börse Vision & Money* 12–9, at 15, 19. There are estimates that more than a billion Euro per annum could be saved; 'Banken setzen Terminbörsen unter Druck' *Börsen-Zeitung* July 16, 1999, 5. Another estimate says that clearing and settlement costs in Europe are 10 times those in the U.S.; 'Brussels Exchanges Mulls Alliance' *Wall Street Journal Europe* February 17, 2000, 15, 20.

[97] European Central Bank, 'Consolidation in the Securities Settlement Industry' [2000] *ECB Monthly Bulletin* (February) 53–9, at 55f.

[98] This refers mainly to spot markets.

[99] Deutsche Börse's CEO Seifert estimates that netting all transactions in regulated and unregulated European bond markets would save €3 billion; 'Seifert: Eurex Clearing bis Mitte 2000 zum Nettinghaus Europas ausbauen' *Börsen-Zeitung* December 23, 1999, 1.

[100] However, it should be noted that, at least for payment systems, there is a trend towards real time gross settlement systems, e.g. ECB's TARGET, to achieve early finality of transactions. To keep counterparty risk bearable for the central counterparty, the introduction of a central counterparty and netting must be accompanied by appropriate measures, such as capital standards for the participants, and initial and variation margining in deposits, to ensure integrity before the transactions in the financial instruments are netted and settled. However, the partly offsetting effects of open positions in different financial instruments decrease the aggregate amount of margins when the positions are held vis-à-vis a single central counterparty.

[101] For illustration purposes it can be mentioned that Deutsche Bank is member of 15 stock exchanges and 15 derivatives exchanges; 'Die börsennotierte Börse' *Börsen-Zeitung* January 29, 2000, 1. Since usually each exchange has its individual clearing and settlement procedures, it is no surprise that global market participants see a major cost saving potential in this field. Moreover, bypassing the necessity to become a member of so many exchanges should be an attractive feature of concepts like Jiway's.

[102] 'Deutsche Börse und Cedel planen europäisches Clearing-Haus' *Börsen-Zeitung* May 13, 1999, 1 and 'Cedel und DBC heißen jetzt Clearstream' *Börsen-Zeitung* January 20, 2000, 3.

celling its memorandum of understanding to cooperate with DBC and Cedel, teamed up with Euroclear.[103]

The prospect of missing the opportunity of a major consolidation in European back office activities, i.e. a merger of Cedel, DBC, and Euroclear, caused the foundation of the European Securities Industry Users' Group in spring 1999. There were 14 members: ABN Amro, Banque Bruxelles Lambert, Banque Paribas, Barclays Bank, Chase Manhattan, Citigroup, Credit Suisse Group, Fortis Bank, HSBC Holding, Merrill Lynch, Morgan Stanley Dean Witter, Nomura International, UBS, and Deutsche Bank. They joined shortly after Cedel and DBC had announced their plans. The group renamed itself European Securities Forum (ESF) in April 2000 and currently consists of about 24 major European and U.S. banks. The influential core group comprises Citibank Salomon Smith Barney, Deutsche Bank, Goldman Sachs, Morgan Stanley Dean Witter, and UBS Warburg.[104] The group tries to "encourage" the market participants to supply an efficient infrastructure in European securities markets.[105] Although ESF has put pressure on Euroclear and Clearstream to merge, this has not happened yet.[106] The slow progress prompted the ESF in October 2000 to start a new initiative.[107] It seems that ESF wants to replicate the BrokerTec approach (see above text accompanying notes 40ff): until the end of 2000 the group wants to develop a concept for a single European central counterparty. Then it intends to send its specifications to current and potential future suppliers of netting, clearing, and settlement services, inviting them to present their offers.[108]

Among the European stock trading places, Tradepoint already offers a central counterparty. Jiway, Euronext, and virt-x announced that they would offer this feature, too. A quotation in a virt-x paper nicely demonstrates the ESF's influence on the path Europe's trading platforms and back-offices are taking: virtue-x has shaped its clearing and settlement ". . . along the lines suggested by the European Securities Forum".[109] The silence on this subject was considered a major weakness in the iX project. Another option in the further development

---

[103] 'Sicovam/Clearnet wechseln ins Euroclear-Lager' *Börsen-Zeitung* November 24, 1999, 3.

[104] 'Pen Kent, übernehmen Sie!' *Börsen-Zeitung* October 19, 2000, 3.

[105] 'Banken fordern Verschiebung der Cedel/DBC-Fusion' *Börsen-Zeitung* July 10, 1999, 'Tauziehen um Clearing-Allianz' *Börsen-Zeitung* July 14, 1999, 3 and 'Pen Kent wird Antreiber für effiziente Euro-Börsen' *Börsen-Zeitung* April 11, 2000, 8.

[106] 'The X Files' *The Economist* July 15, 2000, 88.

[107] 'Group of Banks Plan European Counterparty' *Wall Street Journal Europe* October 18, 2000, 13.

[108] 'Global Player machen Druck auf Clearer' *Börsen-Zeitung* October 21, 2000, 5.

[109] virt-x, 'Service Offering—Management Summary (2000, visited September 14, 2000) http://www.virt-x.com/contents/mgmt-summary.pdf, 7. Note that six out of 11 members of the Tradepoint (the root of virt-x) consortium were also early participants in the ESF.

could be that derivatives markets, which usually already possess an advanced clearing and settlement facility, enlarge their business to spot trading. At least Liffe[110] and the Eurex[111] seem to consider this option: in October, the Eurex started its bond spot-trading platform Eurex-Bonds (see above text accompanying note 50). And the Liffe announced that it intends to start trading of an innovative product called Universal Stock Futures in January 2001.[112] Universal Stock Futures are futures on individual stocks. Since futures and underlyings share a close and determined relation, these futures—traded, cleared, and settled on the derivatives exchanges' infrastructure—may develop into a serious challenger in the competition for pan-European equities trading.

C. Analysis

Two parallels come to one's mind when looking at the developments in the securities markets: first, the advances in IT that have already shaken other business sectors more appropriate for e-commerce, e.g. the book retail business, now have reached the securities markets. However, the other business sectors were mainly those in which there was competition before e-business emerged. This leads to the second parallel: the impressive speed and force with which the power of competition strikes market structure and incumbent market participants as soon as deregulation becomes effective in markets shielded from competition for decades. Power shifts from producers to consumers. The consumers' preferences become the decisive feature. A well-differentiated supply emerges. In addition, a dramatically improved price-service ratio is to be expected.[113] Traditional exchanges were not hit by such a deregulatory strike at a certain date, instead, competitive pressure grew eventually. However, it met structures that had developed over centuries in an environment with, at best, moderate competition.

Having this picture and the evidence presented above in mind, one can structure the analysis along the following lines: what is the role played by the markets' customers (demand side of competition)? Is market entry nowadays easier and more attractive than before (supply side of competition)? Is the governance structure of suppliers an important aspect in competition?

[110] 'Liffe könnte Kassaprodukte handeln' *Börsen-Zeitung* July 22, 1999, 4.

[111] 'Deutsche Boerse Plans Eurex Expansion' *Wall Street Journal Europe* January 5, 2000, 14.

[112] The Liffe mentioned 15 European and U.S. stocks as underlyings; 'Liffe lanciert Aktien-Futures als Weltneuheit' *Börsen-Zeitung* September 21, 2000, 3.

[113] A good case in point is the lively market for long distance calls in Germany since deregulation in 1998.

I. Demand Side Aspects

What are the consumers' preferences? Don't they all want the same thing, i.e. trade a certain trading object at the lowest transaction cost possible? This is too simple a view. As long distance telephone calls have turned into a differentiated good the same can be expected with respect to securities trading. According to the two goods hypothesis,[114] the transaction of an asset consists of both the asset, which is homogeneous, and the transaction service. The "second good" may be, for example, immediacy, market depth, transparency, anonymity, or investor protection.[115] The preferences for the latter may differ for the parties involved.[116] The offered price-service ratio contributes to the transaction costs and may be reflected in quotes and prices.[117]

Who are the customers of trading services whose preferences might shape markets' structure? To keep the following discussion brief, only three groups should be distinguished:[118] private (retail) investors, asset managers and institutional investors (wholesale investors), and the group of security houses, banks, etc.

1. Private Investors

According to an estimation of the Securities and Investment Authority, the retail market will account for 50% of total equity trading volume in the U.S. in 2002.[119] In Europe, the number of online accounts (and with it the volume of trading) is expected to increase strongly.[120] But already today private investors

---

[114] H. Schmidt and S. Prigge, 'Börsenkursbildung' in W. Gerke and M. Steiner (eds.), *Handwörterbuch für das Bank- und Finanzwesen* 3rd edn. (Stuttgart 2001) 391–402.

[115] To illustrate, in one situation an investor prefers intermediacy, whereas in the next he wants to minimize market impact. The same holds for other transaction features such as trading of a basket versus trading a single object, or trading a bloc versus trading a retail amount.

[116] One implication of this hypothesis is that quotes and prices of a particular asset at a certain point of time may differ because they also reflect a second, individual component, the transaction service, besides the price for the pure asset.

[117] Price and transaction cost must not necessarily be explicit amounts. For example, if the level of investor protection offered is lower than the required one, the investor may transform this gap into an implied transaction cost; see Schmidt and Prigge, above, n. 114 for details.

[118] This is, of course, a gross oversimplification, but a more detailed structure is beyond the scope of this chapter. For a far more refined investor classification, see O. Oesterhelweg, *Anlegerorientierte Handelsverfahren für den deutschen Aktienmarkt* (Wiesbaden 1998).

[119] As cited by A. Currie, 'The New Battleground' [1999] *Euromoney* (September) 53–66, at 53, 60.

[120] According to a study by Forrester Research of January 2000, the number of accounts will develop as follows: 1999: 1.3 million, 2000: 1.9 million, 2001: 2.9 million, and 2004: 14 million; as quoted in Wall Street Journal Europe, 'Morgan Stanley and OM Group Launch Online Trade Venture' *Wall Street Journal Europe* February 4, 2000, 18.

are a strong force: for example, in the U.S., Island, one of the most successful ECNs, aims at servicing private investors, and Instinet, currently focused on institutional investors, plans to provide access to private investors.[121] Turning to Europe, the retail-investing sector is reported to have grown most notably in Germany.[122]

This assessment is in line with the fight for market share in *Neuer Markt* stocks between Deutsche Börse and some *Regionalbörsen* described above.[123] A second case in point is the initiative of Consors announced in May 2000 (see above text accompanying notes 58f). Consors is one of Germany's major online brokers and therefore may serve as an indicator for the importance of private investors. The growing importance of private investors in Germany is also witnessed by Deutsche Börse's announcements in September and October 2000, i.e. after the failure of iX, to consider private investors' preferences more strongly.[124] For Europe in general, Easdaq's increasing interest in private investors[125] and the announced strategy of Jiway (see above text accompanying note 22ff) can be mentioned. In summary, there are a lot of signs indicating that private investors are a growing power. Hence, their preferences can be expected to gain weight.

2. Asset Managers/Institutional Investors

Asset Managers are significant customers of trading services.[126] Asset management is also a global market in which competitiveness has increased. The decisive feature of an asset manager for his customers is his performance. As one alternative, he can try to outperform his competitors by means of superior asset selection. However, active asset selection is on the decline because it rarely man-

---

[121] Deutsche Börse, 'Catalysts of Change' [2000] 13 *Deutsche Börse Vision & Money* 12–9, at 15, 19.

[122] A. Currie, 'The New Battleground' [1999] *Euromoney* (September) 53–66, at 66.

[123] See text accompanying nn. 90f; H. Schmidt, 'Regionalbörsen und spezielle Handelsplattformen für Europa' in D. Hummel and R.-E. Breuer (eds.), *Handbuch Europäischer Kapitalmarkt* (Wiesbaden, 2001) 392–409, at 405f.

[124] 'Deutsche Börse droht, in Felder der Banken einzudringen' *Börsen-Zeitung* October 17, 2000, 1 and 'Frankfurt zielt nun auf Privatanleger' *Handelsblatt* September 22, 2000, 38. Among other things the opening of a second Xetra system is to be considered. It should contain features closer to individual investors' preferences; 'Pläne für das Ende des Parketts' *Handelsblatt* October 4, 2000, 45.

[125] 'Die Easdaq macht sich fein für den Privatanleger' *Börsen-Zeitung* February 8, 2000, 4.

[126] To give an impression: as of 1996, global total assets under management are estimated to amount to U.S.$30 trillion (I. Walter, 'The Asset Management Industry in Europe: Competitive Structure and Performance under EMU' in J. Dermine and P. Hillison (eds.), *European Capital Markets with a Single Currency* (Oxford 1999) 265–309, at 265, and past growth rates have been impressive (H. Blommestein, 'Impact of Institutional Investors on Financial Markets' in *Institutional Investors in the New Financial Landscape* (OECD Proceedings, 1998) 29–106, at 30f).

ages to beat passive portfolio management. Consequently, the latter is on the rise, i.e. the focus in asset management shifts to cost containment.[127] Besides management costs, trading costs are a major component. Thus, asset managers are more and more aware of the importance trading costs possess for their market position.[128] Consequently, this powerful group passes this pressure on to the other parties involved in transaction execution, such as their brokerages.[129] The emergence of execution cost rankings for brokerage firms, investment managers, and exchanges underlines the growing transparency and competitiveness in this field.[130]

Both groups, individual and institutional investors, are, of course, interested in buying attractive price and service combinations. However, it is quite probable that asset managers demand trading services that differ from those services private investors ask for.[131] Heterogeneous preferences can be supposed. Thus, the diversity (with respect to trading service) of trading facilities for a certain asset, which is emerging in response, is evidence of the empowerment of customers.[132]

3. Security Houses et al.

Security houses et al. are different from the two parties above in that they are part of both the supply and demand side. They are customers of trading services when they trade for their own account and when they offer asset management services, as they often do. In the latter case, they are subject to the fierce

---

[127] T. Booth and J. Wrighton 'Down, but not out' [1999] 24 *Institutional Investor* 45–50.

[128] See, for example, H. Schmidt, O. Oesterhelweg, and K. Treske, 'Der Strukturwandel im Börsenwesen: Wettbewerbstheoretische Überlegungen und Trends im Ausland als Leitbilder für den Finanzplatz Deutschland' [1997] 30 *Kredit und Kapital* 369–411, at 373f 376); P. Arlman, 'European Equity Markets after the Euro: Competition and Cooperation across New Frontiers' [1999] 2 *International Finance* 139–48, at 144; D. Cushing, 'Comment [to Domowitz/Steil]' [1999] *Brookings-Wharton Papers on Financial Services* 82–8, at 87, and I. Domowitz and B. Steil, 'Automation, Trading Costs, and the Structure of the Securities Trading Industry' [1999] *Brookings-Wharton Papers on Financial Services* (1999) 34–81, 89–92, at 62f.

[129] J. Schack, 'Cost Containment' [1999] 24 *Institutional Investor* 97–101, at 101.

[130] For details see Schack, above, n. 129.

[131] This should not imply that each of both market participant groups shares homogeneous trading services needs. For a survey of inquiries in institutional investors' preferences see P. Gomber, *Elektronische Handelssysteme* (Heidelberg 2000) 79–85.

[132] Clientele-specific market segmentation is expected, for example, by L. Harris, 'Consolidation, Fragmentation, Segmentation and Regulation' [1993] 2/5 *Financial Markets, Institutions & Instruments* 1–28, and W. Gerke and H.-W. Rapp, 'Strukturveränderungen im internationalen Börsenwesen' [1994] 54 *Die Betriebswirtschaft* 5–23, at 21, and H. Schmidt, O. Oesterhelweg, and K. Treske, 'Der Strukturwandel im Börsenwesen: Wettbewerbstheoretische Überlegungen und Trends im Ausland als Leitbilder für den Finanzplatz Deutschland' [1997] 30 *Kredit und Kapital* 369–411.

competition mentioned above so that they should also be interested in prices that are as low as possible for given transactions. In the former situation—trading for their own account—their interest should be the same, although somewhat weaker. This is because, on the one hand, lower transaction costs increase their return. On the other hand, there is an offsetting return coming from overpriced transaction services which, however, they have to share with other parties connected to the trading facility.

As suppliers of transaction services to private investors and asset managers they are exposed to increasing pressure. If customer preferences remain unsatisfied or transaction services are overpriced, now—due to significantly lowered entry barriers (see below section C.II)—(new) competitors will not hesitate to make use of this opportunity. Consequently, security houses et al. are interested in the creation of trading facilities that are attractive for customers, but also for themselves. The latter may lead to fierce fights among the parties connected to a trading facility for the decreasing total of monopoly rents (see below section C.III). These parties are not only in danger of losing part of their rent, but of being kicked out of business by a change of the market model.

At the moment, security houses et al. seem to be in a good position to pass most of the pressure on to the other parties connected to the trading platform because they possess an eminent position as switchmen for a large share of the order flow.[133] If the other parties connected to traditional exchanges, such as dealers or market makers, are not willing to follow the switchmen's lead to their satisfaction, the latter are in a good position to set up competing trading platforms, either in collaboration with other switchmen, e.g. Tradepoint, or alone with an internal trading system, e.g. Deutsche Bank's *Autobahn*.[134]

However, their actions also allow the conclusion that security houses sense the danger of being circumvented by private and institutional investors transacting directly with each other. Automation and IT allow institutional and private investors remote access to trading facilities,[135] thus, opening the alternative, or

---

[133] B. Rudolph and H. Röhrl, 'Grundfragen der Börsenorganisation aus ökonomischer Sicht' in K.J. Hopt, B. Rudolph, and H. Baum (eds.), *Börsenreform. Eine ökonomische, rechtsvergleichende und rechtspolitische Untersuchung* (Stuttgart 1997) 143–285, at 251f.

[134] *Autobahn* is a trading system for European government bonds. As of summer 2000, more than 1,500 institutional customers of Deutsche Bank use this trading facility; 'Deutsche Bank startet 24-h-Handel' *Handelsblatt* June 30, 2000, 45.

Professor Pagano particularly stressed the dual character of security houses—being both users and competitors of trading facilities—during the discussion in Siena.

[135] This development may also be augmented by the legislators when they facilitate cross-border remote access (and membership) as happened with the ISD. See, for example, M. Tison, *The Investment Services Directive and Its Implementation in the EU Member States* (Financial Law Institute Working Paper Series, no. 1999–17, Ghent, November 1999) 28–35 and passim.

threat, of an open(er) trading facility.[136] So called crossing networks[137] for fund managers, such as ITG Europe's Posit or E-Crossnet, do already exist. They offer, or plan to offer, trading in U.K. and Continental European stocks.[138] The London Stock Exchange was said to be thinking of allowing institutional investors direct market access,[139] asset managers are already members of Tradepoint.[140]

II. Supply Side Aspects

On the supply side, the evidence presented above revealed the following trends: there seems to be no doubt that competition in the market for markets did increase. Moreover, electronic trading is on the rise: the new market entrants do offer it, and the traditional exchanges try to supply it, too.

Domowitz and Steil's view fits nicely with the evidence. They claim that contestability in the market for markets did increase markedly in recent years and that this is mainly owed to automation.[141] During the long period of time before, the market for markets was much smaller due to fewer trading objects and much lower turnover per trading object. Without advanced IT, existing

---

[136] For the concept of an open trading facility, see text accompanying note 149; H. Schmidt, 'Regionalbörsen und spezielle Handelsplattformen für Europa' in D. Hummel and R.-E. Breuer (eds.), *Handbuch Europäischer Kapitalmarkt* (Wiesbaden, 2001) 397–409. For this train of thought, see also C. Di Noia, 'Competition and Integration among Stock Exchanges in Europe: Network Effects, Implicit Mergers, and Remote Access' [2001] 7/1 *European Financial Management* 39–72, at 51, and I. Domowitz and B. Steil, 'Automation, Trading Costs, and the Structure of the Securities Trading Industry' [1999] *Brookings-Wharton Papers on Financial Services* 34–81, 84–92, at 62f.

[137] Crossing networks can be seen as a subgroup of ECNs following a certain market model. They exist in a symbiotic relation with exchanges because they offer no price discovery and depend in this respect on the exchanges; J.C. Louis, 'Crossing Networks Oust the Middlemen in Europe' [1999] *Wall Street & Technology* (Electronic Trading Supplement, November 24–6, at 25.

[138] J.C. Louis, 'Crossing Networks Oust the Middlemen in Europe' [1999], see above n. 137 and Deutsche Börse, 'Catalysts of Change' [2000] 13 *Deutsche Börse Vision & Money* 12–9. Customer group and trading objects make these two crossing networks rivals to the traditional exchanges' and Tradepoint's efforts to create a market for European blue chips. ITG Europe's current trading volume in U.K. equities amounts to 10% of LSE volume. ITG Europe announced that, by the end of this March equities from Belgium, Germany, France, Italy, the Netherlands, Switzerland, Spain, and the U.K., ie, those markets formerly connected in the alliance of eight, can be traded on Posit Europe; 'Paneuropäisches Aktien-Crossing startet im März' *Börsen-Zeitung* February 18, 2000, 3.

[139] 'Londoner Börse plant neue Initiativen' *Börsen-Zeitung* August 26, 1999, 4.

[140] H. Schmidt, 'Der Strukturwandel im Börsenwesen' Dritter Zwischenbericht, Hamburg, February 1996; Tradepoint, 'Member List' (visited February 17, 2000) http://www.tradepoint. co.uk/.

[141] I. Domowitz and B. Steil, 'Automation, Trading Costs, and the Structure of the Securities Trading Industry' *Brookings-Wharton Papers on Financial Services* (1999) 34–81, 89–92, at passim. This view is supported, for instance, by H.R. Stoll, 'Organization of the Stock Market: Competition or Fragmentation?' [1993] 5/4 *Journal of Applied Corporate Finance* 90 and P. Gomber, *Elektronische Handelssysteme* (Heidelberg 2000) 59.

floor exchanges enjoyed network externalities in that they occupied the position of liquidity pools.[142] Development costs for automated trading systems were high. Besides other factors—regulation could be mentioned as another example—these features created high market entry barriers, which protected the incumbents from severe competition.

The situation changed dramatically during recent years: now, the market, i.e. turnover, is much bigger and thus more attractive for suppliers. Development costs for an automated trading platform decreased significantly and are now lower than for a floor-based platform.[143] The costs of operating automated facilities also decreased significantly. Moreover, the costs of access diminished due to remote access and membership. A major factor with respect to these latter aspects were changes in regulation which allowed remote access and membership within the EU and between the U.S. and the EU.[144] Information on prices and quotes for one asset at different markets is easily available. This weakens the anti-competition effect of the network externality and fosters the development of a landscape of numerous trading platforms for a particular asset, which specialize in satisfying the preferences of different trading clienteles.[145]

So far, the notion of increased competition among trading platforms was quite general. However, the options of security houses et al. to react, which were discussed in the previous section,[146] hinted at the fact that a trading platform is

---

[142] O. Hart and J. Moore, 'The Governance of Exchanges: Members' Cooperatives versus Outside Ownership' [1996] 12/4 *Oxford Review of Economic Policy* 53–69, at 55, call liquidity (they use the term market depth) the "key asset of an exchange".

[143] For the purpose of this discussion it is sufficient to distinguish only between floor and automated trading. In reality, however, floor trading is highly computer-supported, too, so that these trading forms may be much more similar than first thought.

[144] I. Domowitz and B. Steil, 'Automation, Trading Costs, and the Structure of the Securities Trading Industry' [1999] *Brookings-Wharton Papers on Financial Services* 34–81, 89–92, at 4 and K. Lannoo, 'Does Europe Need an SEC? Securities Market Regulation in the EU' (European Capital Markets Institute, Madrid, November 1999) 26f.

[145] It can be taken for granted that demand for tools that improve the grasp of market places for a particular asset increases with the number of market places. So it can be expected that private suppliers will provide this service. In the literature, there is controversy as to whether such a market-based linkage of market places is sufficient or whether an authority should be involved. This is because in such linkages price priority is secured, but secondary priorities such as time of order or order size are not. In particular, disregard of time priority may decrease the flow of limit orders and, as a consequence, may reduce liquidity in the complete network of market places. This problem leads Y. Amihud and H. Mendelson, 'A New Approach to the Regulation of Trading Across Securities Markets' [1996] 71 *New York University Law Review* 1411–66, to call for regulatory interference to improve control for multiple listing. H.R. Stoll, 'Market Fragmentation' [2001] 57/4 *Financial Analysts Journal* 16–20 supports market linkage by competition between professional market linkers because a linking mechanism provided by an authority would suffer from property rights problems. See also L. Harris, 'Consolidation, Fragmentation, Segmentation and Regulation' [1993] 2/5 *Financial Markets, Institutions & Instruments* 1–28 and B. Rudolph and H. Röhrl, 'Grundfragen der Börsenorganisation aus ökonomischer Sicht' in K.J. Hopt, B. Rudolph and H. Baum (eds.),

not a monolith. A transaction can be interpreted as a chain of services. To name but a few: perhaps an access intermediary is necessary because the investor is not allowed to enter the market himself. Or the market model requires the participation of a special intermediary, such as a market maker, in each transaction.[147] Competitive pressure affects the service chains unevenly. For example, its parts experience different effects, and the structure and even existence of the chain as such become questionable.[148] These aspects are dealt with in greater detail in the section below.

III. Governance Aspects

If the impression were right that we see a transformation from supply monopoly to a competitive market for markets, it would come as no surprise if the governance structures of the monopoly era were no longer optimal. At first sight, the fact that most of the challenging trading platforms are organized as corporations, whereas many traditional exchanges—though many heading for the corporate form—are still co-operatives, seems to be a decisive difference. To be sure, the internal structures of both differ markedly, as do the ways they can raise capital or change membership and ownership structure respectively. However, here the argument is put forth that the characteristics which distinguish significantly among trading facility suppliers are first and foremost the issue of who owns and controls the facility and, secondly, for those facilities being organized as a stock corporation, whether they are publicly quoted and have a significantly free float. If this argument is true, the seemingly great differences between traditional and new trading facility suppliers are only of minor significance.

Following Hart and Moore,[148a] one can label a certain governance structure *outside ownership*: "Under outside ownership, the people who have control over the firm, and take decisions on the firm's behalf, are typically not the same people who buy and use the firm's product". The goal of an *outside owned and controlled entity (OOCE)* is most probably maximizing its market value. The opposite could be called *member and customer controlled entity (MCCE)*. The parties connected to the MCCE may also have an interest in the market value

Börsenreform. Eine ökonomische, rechtsvergleichende und rechtspolitische Untersuchung (Stuttgart 1997) 143–285, on this issue which will not be dealt with more extensively here. I thank Professor Amihud for drawing my attention to this point.

[146] See text accompanying n. 133ff.

[147] See also the discussion of privileges below (text accompanying n. 149ff).

[148] Rudolph/Röhrl, see above, n. 145, 224ff, partition the transaction process in several stages of intermediation and analyse the effects of competition in this environment.

[148a] O. Hart and J. Moore, 'The Governance of Exchanges: Members' Cooperatives versus Outside Ownership' (1996) 12/4 *Oxford Review of Economic Policy* 53–69, at 56.

which, e.g. may be reflected in the prices for member seats. But also of enormous importance are the returns the parties generate from their status as, for example, market maker or security house with heavy trading activity at this exchange. It cannot be taken for granted that the parties connected to an MCCE have homogenous interests, instead, conflicts are to be expected. The usual means to cope with conflicts in a listed stock corporation—Hirschman's exit and voice—cannot fully be applied in an MCCE. There, superior power of some connected parties—the power may stem from various sources—may direct an MCCE's decisions. Another option is to compromise at the expense of parties not involved in the decision and without opportunity to oppose.

Prior to competition, most traditional exchanges occupied the status of a quasi-monopoly. Consequently, in case of conflicts, the last option offered an easy way out. In such an environment many privileges for connected parties can emerge. Privileges are understood as those features of a trading facility that differ from the benchmark of an *open* trading facility. There, no special parties exist, everybody who wants to trade places his order directly in the market.[149] Such privileges include, for example, the necessity to have the price determined by a specialist, the privilege for market makers that only they can place offers, or the necessity for investors to instruct a privileged party (access intermediary) because they have no direct access to the market themselves. This construction gives the privileged party preferred access to information (which may be particularly valuable in the case of transactions of large investors), the same is true for the privilege to inspect the order book.[150] This is not to say that privileges were formerly, or are now, necessarily attached to inefficiencies or monopoly rents in favour of the privileged parties. However, Pirrong finds some empirical evidence in support of the conjecture that exchange members earn monopoly rents.[151] In

---

[149] For this view, see H. Schmidt and A. Küster Simic, 'Zur Theorie der Geld-Brief-Spanne auf Anlegerauktionsmärkten: Der Einfluss der Orderbuchtransparenz auf die Abschlussunsicherheit' *Kredit und Kapital* (Sonderheft 15: Neue finanzielle Arrangements: Märkte im Umbruch, 2000) 137–72, at 141, reviving a concept of Göppert from the 1930s. I. Domowitz and B. Steil ('Automation, Trading Costs, and the Structure of the Securities Trading Industry' [1999] *Brookings-Wharton Papers on Financial Services* 34–81, 89–92, at 80) term this kind of market a non-intermediated market.

[150] For these examples, see M. Pagano and B. Steil, 'Equity Trading I: The Evolution of European Trading Systems' in B. Steil (ed.), *The European Equity Markets. The State of the Union and an Agenda for the Millennium* (London 1996) 1–58, at 41, B. Rudolph and H. Röhrl see above, n. 145, 225; I. Domowitz and B. Steil, see above, n. 149, 50; A. Currie, 'The New Battleground' [1999] *Euromoney* (September) 53–66, at 54, and H. Schmidt, 'Regionalbörsen und spezielle Handelsplattformen für Europa' in D. Hummel and R.-E. Breuer (eds.) *Handbuch Europäischer Kapitalmarkt* (Wiesbaden, 2001) 397–409.

[151] Using seat prices and balance sheet data, Pirrong calculates q-values for several major U.S. exchanges for the years 1986–95. In comparison with other industries, q-values of the same order can be found for companies that occupy a dominant market position due to regulation or other circumstances. Unfortunately, his calculations end in 1995. It would be interesting to see the development

traditional exchanges control of the entity's policy used to lie with the privileged parties.

Now, the environment is much more competitive since market entry has become easier and customers have become more powerful (see above sections C.I and C.II). The resulting pressure towards more efficient trading facilities affects, of course, the privileges.[152] For example, granting remote access may impair the position of incumbent members; fees may have to be reduced, possibly unevenly among MCCE parties; or the introduction of a new market model may erode a member group's position or even rationalize it away. Put more generally, in a surrounding with more competitive pricing and, presumably, lower profits, conflicts and heterogeneity[153] among the parties connected to an MCCE rise, whereas privileges—as a rent generating device—are in the process of vanishing as an easy way to overcome such conflicts.

New competitors, such as Tradepoint or BrokerTec, may be corporations, but most importantly they are also MCCEs. However, their principals are much more homogeneous. The principals are banks and security houses, i.e. parties "who buy and use the firm's product". Currently, they are probably the most powerful group among the parties connected to an MCCE due to their position as switchmen (access intermediaries) with respect to order routing.[154] However, they are themselves driven by powerful forces.[155] The introduction of crossing systems can be interpreted as being forced by the customers to move somewhat from an MCCE to an OOCE structure.[156]

---

of the q-values during a period of increasing competition. C. Pirrong, 'The Organization of Financial Exchange Markets: Theory and Evidence' (1999) 2 *Journal of Financial Markets* 329–57, at 349–53.

[152] See M. Pagano and B. Steil, 'Equity Trading I: The Evolution of European Trading Systems' in B. Steil (ed.), *The European Equity Markets. The State of the Union and an Agenda for the Millennium* (London 1996) 1–58, at 40, for a similar reasoning. See H. Hansmann, *The Ownership of Enterprise* (Cambridge 1996) 97 and passim for the importance of the members' homogeneity for the functioning of an enterprise.

[153] For increasing heterogeneity, see C Di Noia, 'The Stock-Exchange Industry: Network Effects, Implicit Mergers, and Corporate Governance' (March 1999, Consob Studie Ricerche no. 33) 57f.

[154] R. Lee (*What Is an Exchange? The Automation, Management, and Regulation of Financial Markets* (Oxford 1998) 20) points out: "Some of an exchange's members may also be its competitors, and these participants are likely to pursue different goals than those followed by non-competitors". For example, as the position of being a (potential) competitor for the exchange develops unevenly among the parties connected to an MCCE exchange, heterogeneity and differences in power among them increase.

[155] This situation is sometimes also described as the power of the order flow providers; see Philip DaFeo, CEO of the Pacific Exchange, as quoted in 'Welche Börse dem Privatanleger nutzt' *Börsen-Zeitung* October 18, 2000, 3. But the order flow providers seem to be aware of the fact that their power is only borrowed from the actual orderers.

[156] See above text accompanying n. 135ff.

Due to increased competitive pressure from the demand side and dramatically lowered market entry barriers on the supply side, exit has become a serious option for some MCCE parties. This leads to new, more homogeneous MCCEs[157] which partly only serve as a threatening gesture. In these cases, exit and voice are clear complements. Those parties connected to MCCEs who now have an improved and comparably superior opportunity to exit gain power (voice) in the traditional MCCEs. This is the general pattern of action and reaction in the market for markets between the competitors and within the traditional exchanges described above in section B.[158] In the latter case (within the traditional exchanges), as part of the reaction, a redistribution of privileges takes

---

[157] It seems plausible that the principals of these MCCEs are more homogenous; however, conflicts are to be expected there, too, since they are competitors in other fields, such as asset management services. An indication of conflicts may be that in EuroMTS, early 2000, two of the 29 participating banks tried to crash the system by bombarding it with odd quotes; 'EuroMTS Says Members Adhere to Market Rules' *Wall Street Journal Europe* February 22, 2000, 1. The tension, arising from being competitors in many fields, but at the same time being collaborators in the integral field of shaping and providing trading platforms, may have induced many banks and security houses to foster the development of in-house trading facilities, like Deutsche Bank's *Autobahn*; 'Deutsche Bank setzt im Bondhandel aufs Internet' *Handelsblatt* February 10, 2000, 43. These systems may be the starting point of another, paralleling course of development, i.e. the supply of in-house trading facilities as part of a vertical integrated service chain by individual banks and security houses.

[158] The traditional exchanges are well aware of this fact: Deutsche Börse's CEO Werner Seifert, with respect to Tradepoint: "We're there with our seven partners [in the alliance of eight European exchanges] trying to do everything so that no one thinks about bringing Tradepoint to life"; 'Deutsche Boerse Has Bold Plans' *Wall Street Journal Europe* December 21, 1999,15. And Liffe's CEO, Hugh Freedberg, explains that the electronic trading systems are the result of the frustration that developed during recent years among the market participants in reaction to the lack of flexibility of the traditional exchanges. Today, the traditional exchanges consider how they can offer the major participants services that generate added value; 'Elektronik soll der Liffe neue Impulse geben' *Handelsblatt* July 8, 1999, 47.

As a view "from the other side", read the statement of Duncan Niederauer, managing director and head of electronic trading for equities of Goldman Sachs: ". . .we would like to see the market structure in the U.S. substantially altered. I'm confident the NYSE and Nasdaq can both adapt, but we need to have other options if their organizational constraints prove insurmountable. ECNs could become less relevant if the primary exchanges innovate, but ECNs could also substantially alter the course of market structure if the exchanges choose not to"; A. Currie, 'The New Battleground' [1999] *Euromoney* (September) 53–66, at 66.

That most major security houses have a stake in more than one ECN is regarded as a hedge to be on the right side if one of these systems emerges as the future's dominant platform; so, for example, Instinet's Doug Atkin in A. Currie, 'A Pioneer under Pressure' [1999] *Euromoney* (November) 79–82, at 80 and J. Schmerken, 'ECN Portals Serve up a Menu of Appetizing Choice' *Wall Street & Technology* (Electronic Trading Supplement, November 1999) 10–4, at 12. But it may also serve to keep the emerging platforms in check. Moreover, multiple participation in trading facilities make a security house less vulnerable towards its fellows, which remain competitors, irrespective of cooperation in some field. Professor Pagano raised this point during the discussion in Siena.

place in favour of those groups who have gained power.[159] However, it is far from clear that a relative gain in privileges comes along with an absolute gain in privileges—at least as a gain in excess returns derived from privileges: increasing contestability within an environment should diminish such opportunities and the total amount of rents.[160]

This interpretation of the evidence is compatible with the results Hart and Moore derive from their model: a co-operative structure becomes less appropriate when heterogeneity among its members and competitiveness increase. But we are still far away from their alternative model, outside ownership.

So far, it has been argued that the characteristic of being a co-operative or a stock corporation is not as decisive as one might think,[161] and that a far more significant distinction is whether we have an OOCE or an MCCE. Seen this way, the changes in governance structures in the global market for markets are much smaller than the changes in other respects, e.g. the market model. The recent developments at the London Stock Exchange provide a good illustration: The LSE transformed into a stock corporation and its equities are traded OTC. Nevertheless, when the shareholders discussed the pros and cons of iX and OM Gruppen's bid, the effect on LSE's market value played, at best, a minor role. The debate focused on the deals' consequences for LSE's members' business activities. The overwhelming majority of LSE's shareholders still are members

---

[159] See, for example, the painful struggle within the CBOT briefly described above (text accompanying nn. 61ff and 76ff). In the case of the formerly planned change of Deutsche Börse into Euroboard, it goes without saying that offering major banks and security houses a significant stake and say in Euroboard would have meant, at the same time, a loss in power for the other parties.

[160] Several observers state that there is an international trend towards disintermediation, ie towards a reduction in privileges; see, for example, A. Gruber and A. Grünbichler, 'Electronic Communication Network. Börsen der Zukunft?' [2000] 48 *Österreichisches Bankarchiv* 769–74, at 772 and H. Schmidt and A. Küster Simic, 'Zur Theorie der Geld-Brief-Spanne auf Anlegerauktionsmärkten: Der Einfluss der Orderbuchtransparenz auf die Abschlussungssicherheit' *Kredit und Kapital* (Sonderheft 15: Neue finanzielle Arrangements: Märkte im Umbruch, 2000) 137–72, at 137–42. It would be an ambitious though worthwhile a task to analyse the relation between the power of the parties connected with an MCCE and their relative share in privileges, their individual profits derived from those privileges, and the total size of excess returns, during the course of time spent within an increasingly competitive environment. However, this exercise goes far beyond the scope of this chapter, the brief sketches have to suffice. For some examples of the nexus between competition and the amount of privileges, see H. Schmidt, 'Regionalbörsen und spezielle Handelsplattformen für Europa' in D. Hummel and R.-E. Breuer (eds.), *Handbuch Europäischer Kapitalmarkt* (Wiesbaden, 2001) 397–409, at 406f; this train of thought is generally also supported by B. Rudolph and H. Röhrl, 'Grundfragen der Börsenorganisation aus ökonomischer Sicht' in K.J. Hopt, B. Rudolph, and H. Baum (eds.), *Börsenreform. Eine ökonomische, rechtsvergleichende und rechtspolitische Untersuchung* (Stuttgart 1997) 143–285, at 160f.

[161] Sharing the view of M. Pagano and B. Steil, 'Equity Trading I: The Evolution of European Trading Systems' in B. Steil (ed.), *The European Equity Markets. The State of the Union and an Agenda for the Millennium* (London 1996) 1–50, at 42 and B. Rudolph and H. Röhrl, see above n. 160, 243f, but in contrast to J. Mues, *Die Börse als Unternehmen. Modell einer privatrechtlichen Börsenorganisation* (Baden-Baden 1999) 115–23, particularly 115f.

and act as such. If the LSE had moved significantly from an MCCE towards an OOCE, the share price would have had much more weight. But these events proved that the LSE still is an MCCE.

The incorporation of a trading facility supplier would be a more far-reaching event if it were accompanied by an IPO. First, simply because it would provide the opportunity for real outsiders to buy shares. Secondly, with the size of the stake initially offered to the public increases the incentive for the pre-IPO shareholders to signal credibly that the listed corporation will follow a market value maximizing policy. Otherwise, the pre-IPO shareholders would suffer from a grave reduction in the proceeds of the issue. This disadvantage increases, of course, with the size of the stake offered as does the significance of the countervailing power of other post-IPO, share market-related governance mechanisms.[162] Consequently, the issuance of a non-trivial stake would force the pre-IPO shareholders to conduct a market value maximizing policy, which is difficult to reconcile with privileges generating excess returns. An IPO with large free float could be a real emancipation from the major MCCE parties.

Thus, as long as not undertaken in connection with an IPO of the type described above, it is not certain that the announcements of several traditional exchanges, that their demutualization goes along with a shift to the goal of market value maximization, can be taken at face value. Moreover, the advantages of an IPO for the current incumbents are not clear. The easier access to capital is not very strong an argument since the currently most important incumbents should be able to finance expansion themselves or at least to arrange for a private placement. Other motives for an IPO include making use of the valuation function of the stock market, which, in particular in connection with improved fungibility, allows a smoother exit of former incumbents. The existence of a market valuation may mitigate the problem of different time horizons among the connected parties.[163] Pursuing a single (market value maximization) instead of several entity goals could lessen the agency problems between the platform's managers and their principals.[164] In addition, mergers and acquisitions could be made easier by using shares as transaction currency.[165]

---

[162] See M.E. Blume, J.J. Siegel and D. Rottenberg, *Revolution on Wall Street. The Rise and Decline of the New York Stock Exchange* (New York 1993) 46, for a brief sketch.

[163] R. Lee, *What Is an Exchange? The Automation, Management, and Regulation of Financial Markets* (Oxford 1998) 15f.

[164] ibid., 27f.

[165] As an *pro memoria* item for future governance research, an analysis paralleling the stimulating design of S. Kole and K. Lehn, 'Deregulation, the Evolution of Corporate Governance Structure, and Survival' [1997] 87 *American Economic Review Papers and Proceedings* 421–5, and 'Deregulation and the Adaptation of Corporate Governance Structure: The Case of the U.S. Airline Industry' [1999] 52 *Journal of Financial Economics* 79–117, should be suggested: They execute a dynamic analysis of governance structures in the U.S. airline industry, which was heavily deregulated in 1978. Kole and Lehn find that surviving incumbent market participants changed their

D. Conclusion and Outlook

Exchanges have been shielded from almost all competition for decades or even centuries. Now, they find themselves in an increasingly competitive environment. This development is gaining more and more momentum. The interplay between supply and demand side factors has made the market for markets attractive to new suppliers. The consumers are empowered at the expense of the suppliers. On the supply side, this causes conflict on several fronts: competition between old and new suppliers, conflicts within the group of old suppliers, and where one group connected to the old suppliers is also a major player at the new suppliers.

This group of access intermediaries is currently in a powerful position. However, their initiatives may also be due to the feeling that realization of open(er) trading platforms, to which institutional and individual investors[166] have direct, i.e. non-intermediated, access, is about to become a serious threat. But at the moment, this group is gaining ground within the changing governance structure of the established exchanges because they are in a position to pose a credible threat to create new suppliers, i.e. to exit. However, the new trading platforms do not differ that much in structure from the established exchanges since they are still mainly member and customer controlled entities (MCCEs), though more homogeneous.

Future development is hard to prognosticate. One should not simply extrapolate the current trend towards more open trading facilities and OOCE (outside owned and controlled entity) structures. Until now, competition and resulting structural change have only taken hold of the small subset of trading objects with the highest turnover, such as blue chips, fancy growth companies, and benchmark bonds. Most probably, these trading objects are most suitable for rationalization.

---

governance structures more significantly after deregulation than those incumbent competitors who had to leave the market. Surviving incumbent market participants differ in their governance structures from competitors who entered the market after deregulation. However, the former moved more strongly towards the new entrants' structures than did the failing incumbent market participants. In the case of the market for markets, there was no single event like a deregulation act to cause fiercer competition. Nevertheless, it may be instructive to execute a dynamic analysis of the governance structures of trading platforms, which contrasts traditional exchanges as of the early 90s, failing and surviving traditional exchanges at some future date, and ECNs at that future date.

[166] The expected rise of the individual investor should not be accompanied by a significant decline of institutional investors, if there is any at all, because standard economic theory suggests that there may be specialization advantages. However, the increasing availability of the option to hold and trade financial instruments directly to individual investors—either already existing or provided by market observers keen to enter the market in case of unsatisfied preferences—limits the leeway of institutional investors not to act in the beneficiaries' interest.

According to general economics, in an ideal market with full competition suppliers offer a deeply differentiated range of products and services in response to the great diversity of preferences among the customers. Applied to the topic under discussion—where we have a range of very different trading objects and investors—with competition spreading further a great diversity in the supplied products and services could be expected. In this case, we should find trading platforms which are more open and also those with significant intermediation, trading facilities which are organized more towards an MCCE structure and also those organized more towards an OOCE structure, facilities with different market models, etc. Some of these structures may resemble those of today, however, in the former case they would be the result of competition and, therefore, ideally, the optimal solution to satisfy the customers' preferences with respect to the transaction service. In this imagined world, there would be a great variety of trading facilities as far as the heterogeneous good of a transaction is concerned. Due to gigantic advances in IT, the coherence of the pricing of the homogeneous good, the pure trading object, would be ensured by adapter-like trading devices,[167] offsetting most of the liquidity pool externality that formerly had been a major force in trade centralization. In such an environment first mover advantages still should be attractive, but of a truly temporary and contestable nature.[168]

It will also be interesting to observe future development with respect to the following issues: if the relationship between major security houses and investment banks on the one side and traditional exchanges, in which these institutions have a major say, becomes ever more competitive, will we see a divorce?[169] For

---

[167] Adapters are briefly discussed in I. Domowitz and B. Steil, 'Automation, Trading Costs, and the Structure of the Securities Trading Industry' [1999] *Brookings-Wharton Papers on Financial Services* 34–81, 89–92, at 42f. See also the short discussion of market linkage in n. 145.

[168] The sketched possible future development would entail the chance to revive those market segments that are currently disregarded. For example, in Germany, those companies that are neither a blue chip nor a growth company find themselves neglected. This was true for those companies already listed in segments with low volume, low analyst coverage, and low public interest like the Mdax, the newly created Smax, or others. And those companies of this type interested in going public faced difficulties in obtaining a satisfactory valuation level or even preferred to abandon their already started IPO. This happened in Germany in 1999 and 2000, years with record numbers and volumes of IPOs; 'Das neue Jahr verspricht zu viel' *Börsenzeitung* December 31, 1999, 6 for 1999. Probably, market segments appropriate for those companies will remain national. This expectation is shared by Josef Nägel, head of the Neuer Markt, and Tim Ward, head of business development, LSE/techMARK; K. Astbury, 'Europa and her Competing Bulls' [2000] *Euromoney* (February) 121–6, at 124, 126.

[169] The competitive element of the relationship is increasingly felt. Rolf-E. Breuer, CEO of Deutsche Bank and chairman of Deutsche Börse's supervisory board, stated: "In the future, there will not only be competition among exchanges, but also increasingly between exchanges and banks" (author's translation); 'In einer virtuellen Welt ist der Kunde König' *Börsenzeitung*, September 23, 2000, B. 1. In October 2000, Volker Potthoff, a member of Deutsche Börse's management board, declared: 'As the exchange's customers (banks) are active in entities which are competitors of the exchange, the exchange thinks about granting private investors direct access to the

example, will security houses and investment banks give up their influential role in the governance structure of traditional exchanges, and how will their withdrawal from their (future) competitors be organized? A related issue concerns the observation that several security houses and investment banks hold stakes in most of the ECNs. Possibly, this structure is, inter alia,[170] due to the natural monopolistic feature of trading facilities, which may still shape the perspective of the acting parties. In this case a cooperative structure is appropriate. However, if the natural monopolistic feature of trading facilities is vanishing, so does the rationale for cooperative structures and joint ventures. Instead, trading platforms with none (the divorce just mentioned above) or only one security house or investment bank involved (internal systems) should emerge.

The chain that constitutes a securities transaction consists of many parts. The statements above dealt with trading and some preceding links in the chain. But the question of whether we will see a segregation of the parts of the chain, which were formerly vertically integrated, may be even more important for trading and subsequent parts, in particular clearing and settlement. Will we see competition among vertically integrated suppliers such as Deutsche Börse plans to become, or will we witness competition on each stage of a securities transaction among stand-alone suppliers, or both? There is no necessity that the development with respect to trading facilities must parallel the development with respect to netting, clearing, and settlement.

There are many questions and only vague expectations. It will be exciting to watch and analyse the emerging structures in the market for markets.

exchange, i.e. to bypass the banks as access intermediaries'; 'Deutsche Börse droht, in Felder der Banken einzudringen' *Börsen-Zeitung* October 17, 2000, 1.

[170] Other causes were mentioned above; see text accompanying n. 158.

3

European Disclosure for the New Millennium

MARCO BECHT

Abstract

"Imagine a system that is easy to use, easy to file into and compatible with off the shelf word processing packages. Imagine a system that could accept graphics, tables and charts. Imagine a system in which John and Jane Q. Public could access a complete library of disclosure material in their home as easily as the most highly paid Wall Street analysts.

How do we get there? What is the best, the fastest, the cheapest way of providing that service? It is now possible to let in the light at almost the speed of light. Your ideas and your suggestions will help us attain that goal."
Arthur Levitt, Chairman of the Securities and Exchange Commission, Opening Statement at the EDGAR Technology Conference, Washington DC on August 14, 1995

"The Council shall, acting unanimously on a proposal from the Commission and after consulting the European Parliament and the Economic and Social Committee, issue directives for the approximation of such laws, regulations or administrative provisions of the Member States as directly affect the establishment or functioning of the common market."
Treaty establishing the European Community, Article 94 (ex Article 100).

Contents

A. Introduction

Disclosure is widely recognized as a crucial prerequisite for the functioning of equity markets. A disclosure system for stock markets that seek to attract listings and investors from the European Union as a whole must provide useful, accurate, and timely information, irrespective of geographic location in a language investors understand. The system must be efficient and adaptable to changing needs. In this chapter I argue that our current systems do not meet these requirements.

In terms of content, European disclosure is inadequate. Shareholders are invited to appoint board members without knowing their experience or background. Shareholders vote on stock option plans without knowing the level of basic remuneration and the details of the plan. Related party transactions are often carried out in the dark.

In terms of working, we operate 15 disclosure systems based on company law combined with 15 systems of securities regulation, more than 15 stock market rulebooks, and 11 languages. Most systems are enshrined in inflexible laws that prescribe paper filing in obscure places. The securities commissions are mere executors of the letter of the law and do not have the autonomy to create and adapt their system according to the needs of companies, stock markets, and investors.

I propose to abolish paper filing, to scale down the disclosure requirements for listed companies based on company law, to replace and enhance them with securities regulation, to create a European disclosure authority, to make this authority only accountable to the European Parliament and to allow the authority to formulate standards and to design forms. Otherwise, in the new Millennium European markets will continue to lack pan-European disclosure standards or, (fortunately) de facto European standards will be set on other shores.

B. Where Europe Falls Short

The disclosure provisions in current European directives fall well short of international standards. U.S. SEC Form 20-F is becoming the de facto disclosure standard for European bluechips, particularly its non-financial disclosure sections.[1]

The IOSCO standard on the disclosure of non-financial information in cross-listings (IDSs) is imposing a standard at the level of the U.S. SEC's Form 20–F on cross-listings with non-EU countries more generally. Under the standard, EU registered companies listing in Poland comply with higher disclosure standards than companies with a cross-border listing inside the Union (at least as long as Poland does not join the Union).

As a rule, shareholders are not provided with the equivalent of a proxy statement. Agendas of annual meetings are published in accordance with company law and (typically) do not explain the items shareholders are supposed to vote on.

Crucial items are virtually absent from European non-financial disclosure standards, for example the ownership of cash-flow rights, detailed group and control structures, board remuneration, stock options, related party transactions, conflicts of interest, and anti-take-over provisions.

---

[1] See http://www.law.uc.edu/CCL/34forms/form20–F.html.

C. Why the Existing European Directives Do Not Work

(1) Many Directives are the result of accidents, not of careful planning (e.g. the Large Holdings Directive, 88/627/EEC).

(2) Directives are not the appropriate legal instruments for implementing disclosure regulation. The process from proposal (by the European Commission) to adoption to implementation is too slow and reform is even slower. European securities regulation should use the same instruments as merger regulation—Regulations, not Directives.

(3) Unlike the U.S. SEC, most competent authorities in Europe do not have the power to make rules and create forms (like Form 20–F, 10K, 14A, etc. in the U.S.).

(4) The existing systems mainly rely on company registers. This is impractical, slow and expensive.

    (a) Company register filings must be made on paper.

    (b) Access to hard copies is often difficult and/or expensive, despite the provision that "a copy of the whole or any part of the documents or particulars . . . must be obtainable by application in writing at a price not exceeding the administrative cost thereof" (68/151/EEC, art. 3–3).

    (c) Access at administrative cost only applies to hard copies. The fees for electronic access can be much higher.

    (d) For electronic access, the register often does not guarantee the accuracy of the retrieved information.

    (e) In many countries, there are too many registers (e.g. in Germany with approximately 720).

    (f) Most companies' websites do not display the company register name, place, and registration number.

    (g) Company stationery does not have to provide the address, telephone number or e-mail address of the company register.

(5) Most Member States have opted to implement paper-filing systems that favour selected local financial newspapers. These papers are often expensive and they are not necessarily circulated throughout the Union.

(6) Many documents are filed in a language investors at large and regulators do not readily understand.

    (a) Company law provides for disclosure in the official language(s) at the place of incorporation.

    (b) Securities regulation provides for disclosure "in the official language or languages, or in one of the official languages, or in another language provided that in the member state in question the official language or languages or such other language is or are customary in the sphere of finance and accepted by the competent authorities" (79/279/EEC, 88/627/EEC, 82/121/EEC).

(7) Enforcement is too lax because the regulators and market authorities have to waste too much time with the administration of paper filings.

(8) If the Investment Services Directive worked as intended, disclosure and supervision chaos would result. For example, a German registered company is listed on a Greek market but not on a German market. Its company law driven disclosure must be in German while its securities regulation driven disclosure must be in Greek. The German documents could be filed in the register of the city of *Giessen*, the Greek disclosure is filed in a Greek newspaper. Good news is published voluntarily on Bloomberg or Yahoo! in English. The competent authority for the Greek disclosure is the *Bundesaufsichtsamt für den Wertpapierhandel* in Frankfurt. The market makers could sit in France and Italy and most of the trading comes from an online broker in the Netherlands, with clients from all over the World. The French, Italian, and Dutch authorities would supervise them respectively.

D. Electronic Filing

Europe has not adopted mandatory electronic filing. The mere attempt to create a European electronic filing system would make the shortcomings of the current system painfully visible.

(1) Electronic filing must be compulsory, otherwise "bad news" might be disclosed through the paper route.

(2) Most existing attempts are electronic versions of the paper; e.g. SOPHIE in France that contains facsimiles of thick hard copy documents.

(3) True electronic filing uses standard, machine-readable forms that can be processed automatically by value added service providers and/or sophisticated users, allowing for cross-reference searches and other computer aided analysis.

(4) We now understand that network markets often generate powerful monopolies. There is a strong case for regulating and monitoring such monopolies.

E. Conclusion

If European securities markets want to succeed in the new Millennium, European politicians must accept that global investors, like airline pilots, communicate in only one language, English.

There are good reasons to believe that disclosure standards are associated with sizeable externalities and network effects. Disclosure is one of the areas where "harmonization" (standard setting) by one European authority is preferable to mutual recognition (competition between disclosure standards).

We must create a European disclosure authority. We must create a European, mandatory electronic filing system that is accessible from the internet free of charge.

The European disclosure authority must be given a clear mission: to ensure effective disclosure by all companies listed in the Union and for the benefit of all European investors, irrespective of their geographic location. To achieve this, the new authority must be able to formulate and reformulate its own disclosure rules and forms, while remaining democratically accountable.

We must create European disclosure standards and forms that are competitive and compatible with similar SEC standards, for example Form 20-F. The SEC has the task to develop standards that best serve U.S. investors, not European companies and investors. The European Union must adopt international standards like IOSCO's IDSs and participate constructively and pro-actively in the development of such standards.

We must recognize that closely held companies and companies with large numbers of shareholders have different agency conflicts and hence different disclosure requirements. Existing Directives must be consolidated, co-ordinated, brought up-to-date and preferably replaced by regulation.

Europe needs stronger and more integrated stock markets to (partially) capitalize its pension systems. The suggested improvements in European disclosure are essential for pension reform. The demographic clock is irreversible.

Part II:

Legal Capital

4

The Rules of Capital Under Pressure of the Securities Markets

FRIEDRICH KÜBLER

Abstract

This chapter compares the European corporate law systems, which have retained mandatory capital requirements, with the Corporation Statutes of the States in the U.S., where
these rules have been largely eliminated. Its main purpose is to explore the reasons for this
divergence. This chapter discusses some of the prevailing theories explaining the rules on
capital as an element of a specific "culture" or as the product of "path dependence". It
suggests a different approach by arguing that the emergence as well as the elimination of
rules on capital can be traced to changes in financial markets.

Contents

A. Introduction

Rules on the capital of companies emerged in the U.S. as well as in Europe in the
second half of the nineteenth century. They are generally viewed as a reaction to
the "separation of liability". Once the creditors of the corporation can no longer
look to shareholders for repayment, they should be protected by the imposition
of "legal capital" requirements upon the corporate entity which is now the only
debtor.[1]

In spite of this common origin further development has been divergent: today
the rules on capital in the U.S. differ considerably from those in Europe. They differ to some extent between American States and much more so between major
European countries like the U.K. and Germany. This is particularly interesting as
the EC at an early stage engaged in an ambitious programme of harmonization of

---

[1] For the history see B. Manning and J.J. Hanks, *Legal Capital* 3rd edn. (Westbury N.Y. 1990)
21; F. Kübler, *Aktie Unternehmensfinanzierung und Kapitalmarkt* (Cologne 1989) 18; M. Bauer,
*Gläubigerschutz durch eine formelle Nennkapitalziffer—Kapitalgesellschaftsrechtliche Notwendigkeit
oder überholtes Konzept?* (Frankfurt 1995) 133.

company law[2] and picked rules on capital as a primary playing field for this exercise.[3]

The main purpose of this paper is to explore the reasons for this divergence. The prevailing European view has been that rules on capital are rooted in a specific "culture"[4] or "philosophy".[5] A more modern and theoretically sophisticated approach may see them as the product of "path dependence":[6] the pre-existing rules and structures persist, as a major change would have undesirable consequences or will face opposition by powerful interest groups. Another explanation would be that rules on capital are primarily determined by economic conditions, that is by the—changing—features of securities as well as other financial markets; in this perspective rules will be amended whenever market changes render them inefficient.[7] There is no reason to assume that these explanations are mutually exclusive; it may well be that there are some elements of "path dependence" which are able to slow down the adaptation of legal rules and structures to changing economic conditions, but do not have the strength which would be necessary to bar in the long run any move to more efficient laws and legal institutions.

From a European perspective this is more than a mere exercise in social theory. It may well be that it is not only the continental system of corporate government which raises agency costs[8] but also that the rules on capital have become a costly burden for the operation of incorporated business activities. If this proves to be true, Europe is faced with the question whether it is a reasonable and worthwhile agenda to push for amendment or even elimination of the existing legal framework.

In part two of this chapter I present the basic aspects of the different capital regimes. In part three the rules on capital are viewed as part of their respective

---

[2] K.J. Hopt and R.M. Buxbaum, *Legal Harmonization and the Business Enterprise* (Berlin/ New York 1988) 167.

[3] See the Second Company Law Council Directive (EEC) 77/91 [1976] O.J. L26/1; in the following: the "2nd Directive".

[4] H. Wiedemann, *Gesellschaftsrecht Bd. 1* (München 1980) 558.

[5] M. Lutter, 'Das überholte Thesaurierungsgebot bei Eintragung einer Kapitalgesellschaft im Handelsregister' [1989] *Neue Juristische Wochenschrift* 2649.

[6] L.A. Bebchuk and M. Roe, 'A Theory of Path Dependence in Corporate Ownership and Governance' [1999] 52 Stanford Law Review 127; R.H. Schmidt and G. Spindler, *Path Dependence, Corporate Governance and Complementarity—A Comment on Bebchuk and Roe* (1998) Working Paper Series: Finance & Accounting no. 27, Universität Frankfurt am Main, Fachbereich Wirtschaftswissenschaften.

[7] H. Demsetz, 'The Structure of Ownership and the Theory of the Firm' [1983] 26 *Journal of Law and Economics* 375; R.S. Karmel, 'Is it Time for a Federal Corporation Law?' [1991] 57 Brooklyn Law Review 55, 90.

[8] See M. Roe, *Political Preconditions to Separating Ownership from Corporate Control* (typoscript 1999) *http://cep.lse.ac.uk/fmg/events/seminars/99–00/roe.htm.*

corporate systems in order to identify elements of path dependence. Part four explores the impact of financial markets as a factor of legal change. In Part five I try to come to some—preliminary—conclusions. The size of this chapter does not allow for an examination and discussion of all the relevant details; my observations have to be restricted to the more fundamental aspects.

B. Some Characteristics of Legal Capital Regimes

The following comparative analysis[9] has to keep in mind some of the basic features of the legal systems involved. In the U.S. nearly all of the relevant rules have been and continue to be State law; the impact of the Federal Government has always been and is still minimal.[10] The statutes deal basically with the corporation as a single legal institution comprising its public as well as its closed form. In Europe, the Second Directive is based on the distinction between a public and a private company; it applies only to the stock corporation,[11] which is designed for the public distribution of its shares, and not to the practically important institution of a limited liability company.[12] The Member States on the continent tend to have the same or very similar rules for both forms of a company. But Great Britain is different: the public company is subject to the requirements imposed by the Second Directive, while the private company continues to reflect a much less rigid approach,[13] again more similar to the American than the continental European attitude.

The rules are generally distinguished by their purpose: they may relate to the raising of capital (see I below) or they may have been enacted in order to ensure that capital is maintained (see II below). This distinction may again relate to the explicit or implied policies behind these rules (see III below). They burden companies and shareholders with costs (see IV below).

---

[9] For a more comprehensive presentation and additional information see Manning and Hanks (above, n. 1) 180; Bauer, above, n. 1, 110; Klose-Mokroß, *Gläubigerschutz im Kapitalgesellschaftsrecht am Beispiel der Lehre von der verdeckten Sacheinlage* (Frankfurt am Main, Berlin, Bern, Bruxelles, New York, Oxford, Wien 1997) 57; J. Wüstemann, *Generally accepted accounting principles. Zur Bedeutung und Systembildung der Rechnungsregeln der USA* (Berlin 1999) 45.

[10] For the issues discussed in this paper the most important involvement of a Federal agency is to be found in the influence the SEC exercises on the development of accounting standards.

[11] *Société anonyme* (France), *Aktiengesellschaft* (Germany).

[12] *Société a responabilité limiteé* (France) *GmbH* (Germany). Only the U.K. is similar to the U.S.; see P. Davies, 'Legal Capital in Private Companies in Great Britain' [1998] *Die Aktiengesellschaft* 346.

[13] ibid.

I. Formation of the Company and Raising of Capital

Article 6, para. 1 of the Second Directive requires the Member States to allow incorporation only if the charter (the articles of incorporation) provides for a specific amount of capital that has been subscribed by the founders; the minimum amount is 25,000 euro. This "stated" capital is divided into shares. Traditionally shares could be issued only at par value or more. Article 8, para. 1 of the Second Directive allows no par shares, but they too may not be issued for less than "their accountable par"; the consideration for all the shares is not allowed to be less than the amount of capital stated in the articles of incorporation. The American States following the Revised Model Business Corporation Act (RMBCA) require much less: in the articles of incorporation the company has to be authorized to issue a stated number of shares; the registration occurs without regard to the subscription and the consideration is to be determined by the board.[14]

The difference between the U.S. and the European system is still more obvious when the consideration for the shares to be issued is to be paid by items other than cash. The RMBCA allows any sort of property right, including "services performed, contracts for services to be performed, or other securities of the corporation".[15] The Second Directive is much more restrictive; it does not admit obligations "to perform work or supply services".[16] Under the RMBCA it is for the board of the corporation to determine if the consideration received for the share is adequate; any consideration which conforms to this determination is full payment of the stock.[17] By contrast, the Second Directive requires a "report" by one or more independent experts appointed by "an administrative or judicial authority";[18] the report has to describe each of the assets forming the consideration, explain the methods of valuation used and state that the value of the contribution in kind is at least equal to the amount fixed in the articles of incorporation.[19] In order to prevent the avoidance of these provisions, during the next two years certain transactions between the corporation and one of the founders have to be approved by the shareholders meeting and be examined by an independent expert. German courts view fully valid claims against a well-capitalized corporation as "disguised contributions in kind". If the prescribed procedure has not been followed and the company becomes insolvent later on,

---

[14] §§ 6.01 and 6.21 RMBCA.

[15] § 6.21(b).

[16] Article 7.

[17] § 6.21(c).

[18] Article 10, para. 1; in most Member States this is a court, see, e.g. § 33, para. 3 German Stock Corporation Act.

[19] Article 10, para. 2.

the consequences for the contributing shareholders are serious: the trustee in bankruptcy, on behalf of the creditors, can ask for full payment in cash; the shareholder is left with a—mostly unenforceable—restitution claim against the insolvent corporation.[20]

II. Maintenance of Capital

Every reasonably developed corporate law system regulates distributions to shareholders. The least restrictive provisions are again to be found in the U.S.; they mark the most recent developments. The RMBCA allows the payment of dividends as long as they do not interfere with the solvency or the liquidity of the corporation;[21] the distribution is not permitted if after the payment the corporation would be unable "to pay its debts as they come due" or its liabilities would exceed its assets. Delaware law still views the consideration paid for the shares which have been issued as "capital", but the board of the corporation has the discretion to qualify these contributions as surplus (which may be distributed to shareholders).[22] At the same time, the statute allows "nimble dividends" which can be paid out of current earnings even if this affects the capital of the corporation. Therefore, for the RMBCA as well as for the Delaware Statute, "capital" is no longer a barrier for the distribution of dividends to shareholders. By contrast, the Second Directive prohibits any payment to shareholders which would affect the "subscribed capital", and it allows the Member States to impose additional reserve requirements which further restrict the amount available for dividend payments.[23] Germany requires the corporation to use at least 5% of annual earnings in order to build up a "legal reserve" of at least 10% of the stated capital, which can only be used in order to make up for losses.[24]

Liquid assets are transferred from the company to its shareholders whenever the company repurchases its own shares. American corporate law, in principle, allows these buybacks;[25] they are generally subject to the same restrictions as dividends[26] and the power to make an offer for the corporation's own shares is

---

[20] BGHZ 110, 47, 52 (IBH/Lemmerz); for details see Klose-Mokroß, above, n. 9, 11; U. Hüffer, *Aktiengesetz, Kommentar* 3rd edn. (München 1999), § 27, Rn 9ff; F. Kübler, *Gesellschaftsrecht* 5th edn. (Heidelberg 1998), § 15, I4.c).

[21] § 6.40.

[22] § 154 Delaware General Corporation Law.

[23] Article 15, para. 1.

[24] s. 150 German Stock Corporation Act.

[25] The most elegant provision is § 6.31 (a) RMBCA: "A corporation may acquire its own shares and shares so acquired constitute authorised but unissued shares"; this resolves all the problems of "treasury stock".

[26] See § 1.40(b) RMBCA.

given to the board. The Second Directive again is much more restrictive: it requires authorization by the general meeting of shareholders and it limits the buyback transaction to shares representing not more than 10% of the subscribed capital.[27] This reflects the traditional European attitude that in general prohibits the repurchase of shares and allows exceptions only for very limited purposes.

A final element of the capital maintenance regime is provided by accounting rules.[28] In the German tradition accounting has been governed by the principles of "prudence", "imparity" and "realization". They allow building up "hidden reserves" and thus containing distributions to shareholders by consistently under-stating the value of assets and overstating the value of liabilities. A balance sheet that is determined by these standards may distort the financial situation of the com-pany, but it is meant to support the policy objective behind the rules on capital.

III. The Policies Behind Rules on Capital

There can be no doubt that the primary goal of rules on capital is the protection of creditors. First of all legal capital is meant to provide a "cushion" which will help creditors to be repaid even if the company has suffered substantial losses. And there is a second purpose of equal importance: to reduce the moral hazard resulting from the limitation of shareholders' liability.[29] As the corporation approaches the brink of insolvency or illiquidity there is a growing incentive for managers and controlling shareholders to engage in very risky activities. If they succeed they have saved their positions, if they fail they are not worse off than without the dangerous operations; they would have lost anyhow. Thus the rules on capital should prevent them from gambling to the detriment of creditors. It is much less clear whether these objectives are really achieved by the existing rules. The doubts can be explained by comparing rules on corporate capital with the capital adequacy requirements imposed upon banks. They serve essentially the same purpose, but the banking rules are much more demanding:[30] they oblige the tailoring of the amount of capital according to risk and the restora-tion of what has been lost.[31] This difference indicates the basic weakness of the

---

[27] Article 19, para. 1.

[28] R. Walz, 'Ökonomische und soziologische Unternehmensleitbilder vor den Toren des Gesellschaftsrechts' [1996] *Die Aktiengesellschaft* 161; F. Kübler, 'Institutioneller Gläubigerschutz oder Kapitalmarkttransparenz?' [1995] *Zeitschrift für das gesamte Handelsrecht und Wirtschafts-recht* 159, 550.

[29] This is very well explained by Davies, n. 11, above, at 349.

[30] The capital adequacy rules for banks serve the additional purpose to contain systemic risk and protect the payment system; this explains why they set a higher standard.

[31] The capital adequacy rules are more and more often amended and each time they become more complex; this indicates some of the regulatory difficulties legislators are facing where they want to reduce depositor or creditor risks by capital requirements.

corporate capital regime: the original capitalization can be—and often is—insufficient; and whenever creditors are looking for satisfaction from the assets of the corporation there is nothing left as the capital has been absorbed by losses. Very much the same is true for undisclosed reserves: whenever they are needed they are gone.[32]

Occasionally it is assumed that rules on capital also protect shareholders. It has been argued that the prohibition to issue stock below par protects existing stockholders against watering down the value of their shares by issuing stock below par.[33] A similar argument has been made in the context of the repurchase of stock by the company: the general prohibition prevents the majority from absorbing liquid assets to the detriment of minority shareholders.[34] In both cases protection could be provided by the enforcement of fiduciary duties. In addition the rules on capital have been defended by the observation that newly formed companies could rapidly run into insolvency if unavoidable start-up losses would not be absorbed by a mandated legal capital.[35] This observation raises the question how far the individual assessment of entrepreneurial risks should be substituted by mandatory rules enacted by government.

Finally some of the rules could also benefit management. This is obvious for accounting standards that grant discretion to make use of undisclosed reserves: they allow management first to hide profits and then to use hidden reserves in order to cover up later losses. But under certain circumstances the system as a whole can serve the interests of management: it helps to use corporate profits for self-financing and thus to escape competition on the capital market.

IV. The Cost of Rules on Capital

Rules on raising as well as rules on maintenance of capital do have a price, although it will not be easy to assess its importance. Again this chapter does not allow for more than a few observations.

The rules on raising of capital slow down the process of forming a company and of increasing its capital by issuing new shares. This is particularly obvious where shareholders are asked to contribute consideration in kind:[36] the evaluation

[32] This is concluded from insolvency statistics; see E. Strobl, 'IASC-Richtlinien und Gläubigerschutzbestimmungen nach deutschem Recht' in *Festschrift für Hermann Clemm* (München 1996) 389, 408.

[33] M.S. Spolidoro, 'The *Legal Capital and the Raising of Funds through the Issuance of Securities in Italy*' [1998] *Die Aktiengesellschaft* 363, 365.

[34] Argument and references in O. Peltzer, 'Die Neuregelung des Erwerbs eigener Aktien im Lichte historischer Erfahrungen' [1998] Wertpapier-Mitteilungen 324.

[35] M. Lutter, 'Gesetzliches Garantiekapital als Problem europäischer und deutscher Rechtspolitik' [1998] D*ie Aktiengesellschaft* 375, 376.

[36] See above, I.

by the founders has to be examined by an independent expert, his report again has to be inspected by the court before the corporation or the amendment of its legal capital will be registered. Neither the incorporation nor the new shares will be legally valid before they have been inserted into the commercial register. But even a cash contribution can involve complications: in Germany the applicants have to show that the money paid in is "definitively at the unrestricted disposition of the managing board";[37] in case of a wire transfer this has to be confirmed by the bank of the (future) company. As the bank can be held liable for any incorrect statement, it may be reluctant to confirm and/or will insist on being compensated for issuing a standby letter of credit.[38] For these reasons it is to be assumed that the procedure imposed by the rules on capital will burden the founders and/or the company with additional costs in time as well as in money. The rules on maintenance of capital restrict the freedom to make distributions to shareholders. This is most obvious for the regulation of corporate repurchases: rules allowing the acquisition by the company of its own shares only for specific purposes or only up to 10% of its stated capital either restrict its strategic choices or require the creation and issuance of new shares, thus imposing upon the company the costs of raising capital, which have been briefly explained in the preceding paragraph. In addition, there are purposes of a corporate repurchase that cannot be achieved by generating and issuing new stock. This appears to be particularly true for the "signalling" function of a fixed-price tender offer by the corporation for a percentage of its outstanding shares. There appears to be persuasive empirical evidence that the signal of such a buyback operation in most cases triggers a lasting increase in the price of the stock.[39] In addition the repurchase can serve to reduce liquidity by other means than distribution of dividends, or to stabilize an increasingly volatile stock market. After the October 19, 1987 market break, stock prices of companies that had already announced a repurchase programme or who immediately reacted by such an offer, had been less affected by the dramatic decline.[40] On the other hand, an accounting system which reserves a large amount of discretion to man-

---

[37] § 37, para. 1 sent. 2 German Stock Corporation Act.

[38] See § 37, para. 1 sent. 3 and 4. An interesting case is BGHZ 96, 231, 242ff (WestLB). Here the bank had required the applicant to use part of the cash contributions to repay a loan made by the bank to the applicant; the court held that the confirmation by the bank was not correct as the money was no longer at the disposition of the company.

[39] T. Vermaelen, 'Common Stock Repurchases and Market Signaling—An Empirical Study' [1981] 9 *Journal of Financial Economics* 139, 154; A. Ofer and A. Thakor, 'A Theory of Stock Price Responses to Alternative Cash Disbursement Methods—Stock Repurchases and Dividends' [1987] 42 *Journal of Finance* 365, 366; D.S. Lee, W.H. Michelson, and M.M. Partch, 'Managers' Trading Around Stock Repurchases' [1992] 47 *Journal of Finance* 1947; R. Comment and G. Jarrell, 'The Relative Signaling Power of Dutch-Auction and Fixed-Price Self-Tender Offers and Open Market Repurchases' [1991] 46 *Journal of Finance* 1243, 1253.

[40] U.S. Securities and Exchange Commission, The October 1987 Market Break, A Report by the Division of Market Regulation (1988) 6–1.

agement may involve lower costs than the implementation of standards like IAS or U.S. GAAP, which serve the primary purpose of improving market transparency.[41]

C. Rules on Capital as Elements of Legal Capital Regimes

At first glance the Europeans appear to be as happy with their rules on capital as the Americans are for no longer having to deal with them. In the U.S. I have not found any recent publication or other voice arguing that such rules should be reintroduced. In Europe most of the EC Member States share rather strong convictions that the system fixed by the Second Directive should not be amended.[42] Only the U.K. takes a different view, but its corporate law is much closer to the American model than to the systems on the European continent. This raises the question if and to what extent rules on capital are "path dependent" in the sense explained by Bebchuk and Roe.[43] For a—preliminary— answer I shall briefly summarize the American (see I below) and the continental European (see II below) systems and then examine how far the obvious stability of the European rules can be explained by reasons of efficiency (see III below) and/or interest group politics (see IV below).

I. Major Elements of the U.S. System

Not only American scholars, but increasingly also legislators and courts perceive the corporation as a network of contracts.[44] The contractual relationship can be implied and at the same time be imperfect. This is particularly true for shareholders: they bear the long term residual risk of success or failure. For this reason they retain the power to control and run the company for their own benefit. Accounting standards are designed to provide them with the information necessarily to control management and to make investment decisions. Many corporations have dispersed ownership,[45] but directors and managers are bound

---

[41] For example: it is much easier and less expensive to account for a balance sheet item by its historical costs than to use a "marking-to-market" approach which would provide much more accurate information.

[42] For Italy see Spolidoro, above, n. 33, 364; for Spain, A. Rojo, 'Unternehmensfinanzierung und gesetzliches Garantiekapital in Spanien' [1998] *Die Aktiengesellschaft* 358, 399. For the prevailing German view see Lutter, above, n. 35, 375.

[43] See n. 6.

[44] M.C. Jensen and W.H. Meckling, 'Theory of the Firm: Managerial Behaviour, Agency Costs, and Ownership Structure' [1976] 3 *Journal of Financial Economics* 301; F.H. Easterbrook and D.R. Fischel, *The Economic Structure of Corporate Law* (Cambridge 1991) 1.

[45] See Roe, above, n. 8.

by enforceable fiduciary duties. Investors regularly contribute equity; this reduces the importance of debt. Creditors are not seen as a homogeneous group. Contract creditors are able to manage risk by insisting on perfect contracts; they are expected to contribute to monitoring management.[46] Tort creditors can be protected by insurance and by disregard of the corporate entity.[47] Firms can decide where to incorporate. This has encouraged the States to enter into a race by offering favourable laws; and legislative competition has been an important factor in the gradual elimination of rules on capital.[48] Today it appears to be generally agreed that this is a welcome effect.

II. Major Elements of the European Model

The legal systems on the continent tend to view the corporation as an institution that has to be shaped by mandatory rules as it has to resolve conflicting claims made by the various "stakeholders" who contribute to the output of the firm. Creditors are stakeholders. They are seen as a homogeneous group; all of them are to be protected by the same rules on capital and by an accounting practice that allows the undisclosed formation and dissolution of reserves. The market for equity is underdeveloped; debt financing and self-financing are the most important sources of corporate funds, but creditors are not expected to partici-pate in the monitoring of management.[49] There are few truly public corpora-tions: even listed companies tend to have some form of concentrated ownership. There is no or very little of a market for corporate control. The rules on capital are mandatory. For this and other reasons legislative competition is viewed as undesirable,[50] and the harmonization of corporate law—including rules on capital—is and remains an important objective of EC policy.[51]

---

[46] M. McDaniel, 'Bondholders and Corporate Governance' [1986] 41 The Business Lawyer 413; A.J. Triantis and R.J. Daniels, 'The Role of Debt in Interactive Corporate Governance' [1995] 83 California Law Review 1073.

[47] R. Posner, 'The Rights of Creditors of Affiliated Corporations' [1976] 43 Chicago Law Review 499, 505; R. Meiners, J. Mofsky, and R. Tollison, 'Piercing the Veil of Limited Liability' [1979] 4 Delaware Journal of Corporation Law 351, 364; F.H. Easterbrook and D.R. Fischel, 'Limited Liability and the Corporation' [1985] 52 Chicago Law Review 89, 107.

[48] Bauer, above, n. 1, 129.

[49] This is an important aspect of the discussion of the "power of banks" in corporate govern-ance.

[50] And in most of the Member States excluded by the application of the "seat theory" which does not allow re-incorporation in a more favourable legal environment.

[51] C. Timmermanns, 'Die europäische Rechtsangleichung im Gesellschaftsrecht' [1984] 48 *Rabels Zeitschrift für ausländisches und internationales Privatrecht* 1, 14; H. Merkt, 'Das europäische Gesellschaftsrecht und die Idee des "Wettbewerbs der Gesetzgeber"' [1995] *Rabels Zeitschrift für ausländisches und internationales Privatrecht* 545, 567.

III. Path Dependence for Reasons of Efficiency

For the following it is assumed that a return of the American system to a regime of legal capital would imply high costs and little benefits and therefore clearly be inefficient. The question to be asked is if there are reasons of efficiency which prevent European systems gradually abandoning their rules on capital and thus converging with the American model. There are several points to be considered.

As long as equity markets are weak and firms depend on debt and self-financing, rules on capital are useful as they require or at least allow the restriction of distributions to shareholders: as long as shareholders are not expected to make regular and significant contributions to the company there is no need for attractive dividends. Self-financing is additionally served by accounting standards that allow management to hide profits by discretionary evaluation of assets and liabilities. But there appear to exist interdependencies: as long as accounting remains untransparent and rules on capital restrict distributions, investment in equity is not attractive and the stock market will remain weak.

Prohibitions of, or far reaching restrictions on, corporate repurchases can be viewed as equally supportive for a system relying to a large extent on self-financing. And there is little need for buy-backs of own shares. As long as the company cannot expect to raise funds by issuing stock, the management has no incentive to "signal" to the market its impression that the stock is currently undervalued.[52] And as long as there is no credible threat of an unfriendly take-over, the management has no incentive to have the company acquire its own shares in order to reduce liquidity.[53] For a corporate system that relies on self-financing, a high amount of liquidity is very desirable.[54] In sum: if there is no practical use for stock repurchases there is no harm in not admitting them. There may be even some benefits to be derived from such a rigid attitude, as there is no need for rules designed to prevent manipulation and abuses in buy-back operations.[55]

Another aspect is transaction costs. As far as creditors cannot rely on the "cushion" provided by legal capital they are expected to look for themselves; for this reason they will have to make contractual arrangements in covenants and

---

[52] See text and references to n. 39.

[53] A corporation with considerable liquid assets can be an attractive take-over target as the liquidity can be used to finance the tender offer.

[54] This aspect is emphasized by the use of pension commitments as a tool of corporate finance. It enables the firm to retain a part of the salaries owed to its employees and to use these funds for long term investments. As the commitment is a liability, the retained funds can neither be taxed nor distributed to shareholders.

[55] See, e.g. Rules 10b–6, 10b–7 and 10b–8 Securities Exchange Act; their purpose and reach is explained by L. Loss, *Fundamentals of Securities Regulation* (Boston, 1983), 998; L. Loss and J. Seligman, *Securities Regulation,* vol. 9 3rd edn. (Boston, 1992) 4018.

trust indentures and similar instruments. They can stipulate not only for collateral or the personal liability of major shareholders but also for restrictions imposed upon the financial management of the debtor corporation. The contract can provide for the limitation of distributions to shareholders similar to legal rules on capital. One could therefore argue that a mandatory legal regime could save the parties a lot of contracting. But this is persuasive only as long as it can be assumed that the legal capital regime is in fact able to grant creditors a satisfactory amount of certainty that they will be repaid out of corporate funds.

A similar observation can be made for involuntary creditors, in particular the victims of a tort for which the corporation can be held liable. Limited liability allows shareholders to shift the risk for potentially profitable but also potentially dangerous operations to outsiders. Legal capital is designed to absorb these risks and to reduce moral hazard. A system without rules on capital can achieve the same result by allowing tort victims to disregard the corporate entity and to recover directly from shareholders.[56] This requires the legal system to have adopted a theory of "piercing the corporate veil".[57] But this conclusion rests upon two assumptions: that the rules on capital in fact reach at least most of the critical cases, and that the costs for the legal capital regime[58] are lower than the aggregate expenses for all court proceedings.

Finally, persistence may be induced by the costs of legislative abolition of the legal capital regime. Even if it is true that a system like the American is less burdensome than a legal capital regime as the one imposed by the Second Directive, it may well be that the benefits achieved by the move to a more market-oriented model would be inferior to the costs of making the necessary changes. This may not be very likely if one looks at the long-term effects, but a cost-benefit analysis of this aspect will be particularly difficult.

IV. The Impact of Interest Groups

For the following it is assumed that the abolition of rules on capital would promote the transition to a more efficient corporate system. The question to be answered is whether desirable changes will not occur, as they will be blocked by influential interest groups. A first group to be examined is creditors. But even if it is assumed that all creditors have the same interests they cannot be viewed as a politically homogeneous group. In fact, several groups of creditors have to be

---

[56] See references in n. 47.

[57] Civil law systems have been much slower to do so; for the German adoption of the American experience see R. Serick, *Rechtsform und Realität juristischer Personen* (1955); U. Drobnig, *Haftungsdurchgriff bei Personengesellschaften* (Frankfurt/Berlin 1959); E. Rehbinder, *Konzernaußenrecht und allgemeines Privatrecht* (1969).

[58] See above, C.IV.

distinguished. Whenever they lobby for protection by legal provisions they do not appeal to look to corporate law but to rules that are more closely tailored to their specific interests. This is true for employees[59] as well as for service creditors (like the plumber who is called to repair a leaking pipe).[60] Banks are a particularly interesting group of creditors. Traditionally they have been in favour of the legal capital regime; but this seems to be no longer true.[61] This can be explained by changes in the lending market. As long as the spread between interest rates paid on deposits and received from loans was high, banks were interested to retain a system of corporate finance that had to rely on debt to a large extent. Since the spread has considerably narrowed and risks of long term lending have increased, banks have become more interested in the fee-earning securities business and thus favour a more market-oriented corporate system.

Employees (including managers) are not only creditors of the firm. They have a strong interest in the financial stability of the enterprise as a condition for retaining their jobs.[62] For this reason they prefer the traditional European system as it provides more incentives for low growth stability than for the taking of risks in order to enhance shareholder value. This may change where compensation is linked to performance and where golden parachutes facilitate mergers and take-overs.

Legal change may also be blocked by a lack of interest of legislators. The scarce resources of rule making are largely absorbed by the need to satisfy important constituencies. As long as there are no pressures law reform may be blocked even if everybody is convinced that it would improve the framework of economic activity. That is to say, as long as there are no vested and organized interests that would prefer a more market-oriented corporate system substantial amendments of the existing laws should not be expected.

D. The Impact of Financial Markets' Pressures for Change

This part of the chapter is designed to identify developments in financial markets pressing for changes in the traditional legal capital regime. The most important evidence can be gained from the American experience. In the U.S., rules on

---

[59] Klose-Mokroß, above, n. 9, 146.

[60] In 1993 Germany introduced a § 648a into its Civil Code (*BGB*) giving service creditors a claim for security (by collateral, surety or guarantee).

[61] See B. Walter, 'Gesetzliches Garantiekapital und Kreditentscheidung der Banken' [1998] *Die Aktiengesellschaft* 1998, 370: in this article the CEO of Dresdner Bank explains that the traditional rules on capital have become a burden for the lending business.

[62] The intensity of this interest again depends from the framework conditions. It is lower in an American-type flexible labour market as it is easier to find a new job. It is higher in a German-type market, which provides a high degree of job security as it is much more difficult to find new employment.

capital—similar to those in Europe—had been established by courts[63] as well as by legislation.[64] In a long process of more or less incremental steps the original system has been thoroughly transformed. I have never found a comprehensive historical description or analysis of this process; thus the chapter is limited to a few of the most important aspects.

I. The Growing Importance of Equity Financing

To the extent that debt and self-financing are replaced by equity as the primary source of corporate funds, rules on capital are felt to be a burden: they slow down the formation of new companies,[65] they impede the raising of capital,[66] they prevent distributions that would encourage the public to invest in stock.[67] These circumstances help to explain why American law has moved away from its former legal capital regime. And there are some more specific aspects to be taken into consideration:

Rules like article 7 of the Second Directive, which does not allow obligations "to perform work or supply services" to be used as consideration for the acquisition of newly issued stock,[68] generates obvious problems for the financing of high tech start-up companies. It hinders the innovative entrepreneurs in the use of their creative input as capital and thus may prevent them from adopting the corporate form as an instrument to attract venture capital investors. Therefore it is hardly surprising that the RMBCA allows "services performed" and "contracts for service to be performed" to be used as consideration for shares.[69]

At the same time the growing importance of equity affects accounting standards. The traditional function to contain distributions to shareholders is not eliminated but it is increasingly subordinated to the goal of transparency; financial statements are designed to provide investment information to the financial markets, that is: to potential buyers of shares and of debt securities. This is another transformation that appears to be motivated by economic incentives;

---

[63] *Wood v. Dummer*, National Reporter System, United States Series, The Federal Cases Comprising Cases Argued and Determined in the Circuit and District Courts of the U.S., Book 30 (1897) 435; *Sawyer v. Hoag*, 84 U.S. 610 (1873).

[64] See Manning and Hanks, above, n. 1, 21.

[65] See above, C.IVa.

[66] See above, C.IVa.

[67] See above, C.IVb.

[68] See above, n. 16.

[69] § 6.21(b).

there is persuasive evidence that the cost of capital declines with improved transparency.[70]

Another relevant aspect is the liberalization of stock repurchases. It can be viewed as a final step towards a very easy and flexible regime of corporate finance. Rules on "par value", "stated capital" and "legally required reserves" are repealed; they are replaced by the much simpler regime of an authorized capital which allows the board to issue stock and to buy it back from the market whenever such a measure serves shareholder value. The board is bound by fiduciary principles; they allow to sanction abusive practices but do not block useful transactions.

II. The Transformation of Debt Markets

Rules on capital are designed to eliminate or at least to reduce risk for all creditors and to put them all into the same boat: once the corporation is insolvent, they have to share the "cushion" provided by the stated capital. This is to say: they are all faced with the same amount of risk. Where creditor protection is left to contracting, risk can be differentiated and priced. "Junk bonds" are a good example: the creditor is entitled to a risk premium, that is to a (considerably) higher rate of interest for accepting higher risk by allowing the subordination of his claims to those of other creditors. This form of lending requires technical skills and may involve higher transaction costs, but if it works, it offers considerable advantages for both sides. Creditors are able to tailor loans to their specific ability to bear risk, and this will reduce the funding costs for the debtor companies. Once such a technique of pricing risk is used, rules on capital operate as a restriction of the freedom to contract, as they burden all creditors with risk-reducing costs, which at least some creditors would prefer to avoid in order to bargain for a higher return.

By reducing risk for all creditors, rules on capital are designed to resolve a problem of information costs: as far as creditors are able to rely upon the "safety cushion" of stated capital they do not have to investigate the liquidity and future solvency of the debtor corporation. But these costs are considerably lowered by the emergence of markets that offer financial information for creditors. The most obvious example is the "rating" of debt instruments by highly specialized agencies like Standard and Poor's or Moody's primarily for institutional

---

[70] D.W. Diamond and R. Verrechia, 'Disclosure, Liquidity, and the Costs of Capital' [1991] 46 *Journal of Finance*, 1325; Bartov and Botnar, 'Alternative Accounting Methods, Information Asymmetry and Liquidity: Theory and Evidence' [1996] 71 *The Accounting Review* 397 (1996); C.A. Botosan, 'Disclosure Level and the Cost of Equity Capital' [1997] *The Accounting Review* 72; C. Leuz and R. Verrechia, *The Economic Consequences of Increased Disclosure* (typescript 1999; in the author's files).

investors. This market is quite efficient. In order to avoid a less favourable rating, debtors are pressed to give the agency all the information that is asked for. The agencies are normally selected by the institutional investors; their success depends upon their reputation for being fully informed and for giving reliable forecasts.[71] By providing more transparency at lower costs rating allows the refinement of the pricing of risk in a way that is superior to the traditional mechanism of legal capital; this is another reason why rules on capital become obsolete.

Finally, credit risk can be diversified and re-allocated by securitization. There are many forms that are being increasingly used. Large syndicated loans are sliced into equal pieces that are traded between the participating banks. A company in need of debt financing will replace the traditional bank loan by issuing commercial paper or similar notes. Smaller claims like receivables are bundled to a pool that serves as the special purpose vehicle for issuing asset backed securities to institutional investors. In each case, securitization creates a trading market for debt instruments that reflects current information as to the liquidity of corporate debtors. This is another reason why rules on capital become increasingly obsolete.[72]

III. New Contractual Techniques of Creditor Protection

The Common as well as the Civil law has for a long time provided creditors with instruments like pledges, mortgages, and sureties, which can be used to reduce the risk that a (corporate) debtor will be unable to perform. But in more recent times new and much more sophisticated instruments have been created and are increasingly used.[73] Trade creditors are routinely stipulating retention of title, banks have refined the use of receivables as collateral and there are many contractual forms—sureties, guarantees, standby letters of credit, performance bonds—which allow liability to shift back to the shareholders. These new opportunities have contributed in several ways to the erosion of the stated capital regime. On the one hand their proliferation demonstrates that creditors have lost the confidence that they will be protected by rules on capital. At the same time they provide much better protection by enabling creditors to seek satisfaction from specific assets. But this means that these assets are no longer available for the protection of all other creditors. And this is normally not reflected in the financial documents of the company; most of these protective devices are off-balance sheet

---

[71] This is explained in greater detail in F. Kübler, *Rechtsfragen des Rating, in: Bankrechtstag 1996* (Berlin, New York 1997) S, 115, 118.

[72] And remember: as they do not report losses, they have never been very good in providing transparency of the debtor company.

[73] This is explained in details by Klose-Mokroß, above, n. 9, 93.

items. This helps to explain the fact that in most corporate bankruptcies there are no assets at all left for the—partial—satisfaction of unprotected creditors. That is to say: the use of the more advanced techniques of collateralization continues to devaluate the protection of creditors by traditional rules of capital. This obviously increases the problem for involuntary creditors such as the victims of a tort, as they are unable to rely on any form of contracting. As far as they are not protected by (liability) insurance they have to look for compensation from shareholders and/or managers. In this respect it appears unavoidable that legal systems continue to adopt and to refine remedies that disregard the corporate entity and the separation of liability it provides for shareholders.

IV. The Intensity of the Pressures for Change

The growth of the equity market, new forms of debt financing, and new instruments of creditor protection have continued to diminish the economic utility of rules on capital. In the U.S. this has led to the elimination of these rules; in Europe they still exist. It has to be asked whether there are other factors than path dependence to explain this divergence. There are at least two aspects to be mentioned. The first is time: in the U.S. the pressure for change started to work decades before this happened in Europe. This is particularly obvious for the growth of equity markets. But the new instruments of debt financing have been engineered in the U.S. and have only later and often slowly been adopted in Europe; this is true for securitization as well as for rating or for the establishment of trading markets for debt securities. The other explanation could be legislative competition. It appears that it has accelerated the elimination of rules on capital in the U.S. and that the Second Directive has at least contributed to blocking such a process in Europe.[74] But the elimination of legislative competition by European harmonization of the basic rules on capital can again be viewed as an element contributing to path dependence.

E. Where Will, Where Should Europe Go?

I. Repeal of the Second Directive or Extension to Limited Liability Companies?

It should be remembered that the approach adopted by the Second Directive is not very consistent: the European rules on capital apply only to stock

---

[74] This is assumed by D. Charny, 'Competition among Jurisdictions in Formulating Corporate Law Rules: An American Perspective on the "Race to the Bottom" in the European Communities' [1991] 32 Harvard International Law Journal 423, 455. But he thinks that creditors continue to derive benefits from the persistence of capitalization requirements in Europe.

corporations and not to limited liability companies, although both present at least the same amount of risk for creditors. There are initiatives to create a "European Private Company".[75] Such an enterprise will be faced with the question whether European legislation should provide for rules on capital or whether this should be left to the Member States. If the second alternative prevails, the question should be asked why the Second Directive is not repealed. The answer to both questions will depend upon how rules on capital have to be viewed: are they predominantly path dependent or will they be able to change under the pressures of the securities market?

II. The Example of the U.S.

Part C of the analysis shows that the (continental) European corporate law model contains elements that are likely to block the elimination of rules on capital. But Part D illustrates the increasing pressures exercised by markets. In order to determine which of these countervailing forces is likely to prevail, it may be useful to look to the American example. There the development started from a regime that certainly has never been the same as what we still see in Europe, but it had been much closer to the European model than it is today. Therefore the important lesson may be that the American system has gone a long way from being a much more rigid to a much more flexible regime of corporate finance; and that this change has been promoted primarily by the pressures of the securities and other financial markets.

III. Normative Change in Europe

At the same time it should be perceived that the European model is no longer as self-contained and waterproof as it has been only a few years ago. There are obvious signs that legislators, regulators, and courts have started to react to the impact of financial markets.

This happens on the national level. Most Member States have adopted doctrines that allow in specific cases to disregard the corporate entity and to hold shareholders liable with their private estates.[76] Germany has amended its stock corporation statute by introducing no par shares as an alternative to the traditional par value system.[77] Even if this change has been inspired by the need to

---

[75] EU-Commission (eds.) *Proposition pour une société fermée européenne* (Brussels 1997); Hommelhoff and Helms, 'Weiter auf dem Weg zur Europäischen Privatgesellschaft' [1999] *GmbH-Rundschau* 53.

[76] See references in n. 57.

[77] § 8 German Stock Corporation Act.

make it easier to translate the stated capital of stock corporations and limited liability companies from the denomination in DM into the new currency of the Euro and even it this does not (yet) affect the capitalization requirement it can and should be read as another sign of the beginning of change. The relaxation of the German rules on share repurchases[78] should be understood in the same way: the result is certainly not satisfactory, but the reform is a first step to a less rigid legal framework.[79]

The changes on the European level occur at a somewhat slower rate, but they may be or at least become considerably more important. First of all the Commission of the EC has indicated that it is no longer satisfied with the accounting regime that has been established by the Fourth and the Seventh Corporate Law Directives.[80] The "new strategy" favours international harmonization by adopting the principles stated by the International Accounting Standards Committee (IASC); and this implies the need for amendments of the Fourth and the Seventh Directive in order to make the existing framework compatible with IASC. In addition the Commission has established a working group—chaired by Professor Wymeersch—in order to explore how far the "SLIM"-programme[81] of the Commission can be extended to corporate law. The working group has made several recommendations aiming at the deregulation of the Second Directive;[82] they include:

(1) the abolition of the requirement of an external audit of contributions in kind as consideration for stock;[83]

(2) the elimination of the rule that a corporation may not repurchase more than 10% of its common stock.[84]

Finally, the European Court of Justice has decided the "Centros" case.[85] A Danish business had been newly incorporated as a British "private limited company" in the U.K. in order to continue operations in Denmark through a branch; thus the shareholders were no longer forced to comply with the much more demanding Danish rules on capital. The Danish authorities refused to register the branch as the re-incorporation served the purpose of circumventing the Danish capitalization requirements. The European Court of Justice held that

---

[78] § 71 no. 8 German Stock Corporation Act.

[79] For discussion see C. Escher-Weingart and F. Kübler, 'Erwerb eigener Aktien' [1998] 162 *Zeitschrift für das gesamte Handelsrecht und Wirtschaftsrecht* 537, 542; 555.

[80] K. Van Hulle, 'Die Zukunft der europäischen Rechnungslegung im Rahmen einer sich ändernden internationalen Rechnungslegung' [1998] *Die Wirtschaftsprüfung* 138.

[81] SLIM is an abbreviation for "Simpler Legislation for the Internal Market".

[82] This is reported by H.W. Neye, 'SLIM-Schlankheitskur für EG-Gesellschaftsrecht' [1999] *Zeitschrift für Wirtschaftsrecht* 1944.

[83] See above, C.Ib.

[84] See above, C.IIb.

[85] Case C-212/97, *Centros Ltd v. Erhvervs- og Selskabsstyrelsen* [1999] E.C.R. I-1459.

such a decision conflicts with the freedom of establishment granted by Article 43 of the EC Treaty: if the U.K.—following the incorporation doctrine[86]—allows a firm that operates in Denmark to incorporate in England, Denmark has to respect such a solution. The decision has been criticized for undermining the national rules on capital.[87] But this is exactly what should be seen as its beneficial effect.

IV. Conclusion

The evidence examined in this chapter appears to favour the conclusion that the existing rules on capital will not resist the pressures of the securities and other financial markets. But there are substantial elements of path dependence; they prove to be stronger in Member States with less developed markets. This allows the further conclusion that legal change, which is under way, will be slow, cumbersome, and incremental. Repealing major elements of the Second Directive would allow Member States like the U.K. and—in my view—Germany to adapt their corporate statutes to the increasing pressures of globalized markets; at the same time Member States like Italy and Spain could retain their rules on capital as long as they think it is useful and appropriate, although they might face some erosion of their capital regimes under the "Centros" ruling. At least for the Member States like the U.K. and Germany such a change would be the more beneficial the earlier it comes. As the financial markets of other Member States will continue to move in a similar direction, there are good reasons to assume that they too will be better off—at least in the long run.

---

[86] See above, D.I.

[87] See, e.g. P. Kindler, 'Niederlassungsfreiheit für Scheinauslandsgesellschaften' [1999] *Neue Juristische Wochenschrift* 1993; P. Ulmer, 'Inländische Zweigniederlassungen von Kapitalgesellschaften mit fiktivem Auslandssitz' [1999] *Juristenzeitung* 662, 664 (pleading for European harmonization of rules on capital for limited liability companies).

5

Legal Capital Rules and Modern Securities Markets—the Case for Reform, as Illustrated by the U.K. Equity Markets

EILÍS FERRAN

Abstract

This chapter looks at the appropriate role for general company law in protecting the interests of investors in a modern environment where powerful external controls can be exerted through the capital, and other, markets. Using legal capital rules that apply to new shares as the specific example around which to base the discussion, it considers the interplay between state intervention and self-regulation by markets participants. Pre-emption rights, which in the U.K. are governed both by statute and by guidelines developed by institutional investors, are examined closely. Institutional investors in the U.K. continue to value pre-emption rights. As well as their function as a mechanism for preventing value transfers from existing to new investors, pre-emption rights are regarded as playing an important corporate governance role in disciplining underperforming management. Contrary to the view that has commended itself to the Company Law Review Steering Group which has made proposals to government for the reform of U.K. company law, this chapter suggests that so long as pre-emption rights continue to be viewed by the market as being important in terms of corporate governance or for other reasons, then those requirements can be imposed on companies through the market and that statutory underpinning in the form of additional specific rules may not be necessary.

Contents

A. Introduction

Traditional explanations of the objectives that mandatory legal capital rules seek to achieve emphasize the goals of investor protection. "Investor protection" is a multi-faceted concept with characteristics that can only be teased out fully through careful and detailed analysis. Whilst it is obvious that the interests of creditors and the reasons why they may require protection will differ from those of shareholders, it is equally clear that identity of interests between creditors or between shareholders should not be assumed since they are not homogenous groupings. Yet drawing a basic distinction between creditors and shareholders is helpful, if only as a starting point, in the process of identifying a degree of commonality of interests between broadly-defined groups of investors and in putting the spotlight firmly onto the eventualities that groups of investors may reasonably be expected to seek protection against. This, in turn, then provides the base from which to pose the question that is central to this chapter, namely, the appropriate role for general company law in protecting the interests of investors in a modern environment where powerful external controls can be exerted through the capital, and other, markets.[1] For reasons of space, the emphasis here is on the position of shareholders but the existence of highly competitive, informed, and sophisticated debt and derivatives markets means that the issues discussed are equally relevant to the creditor-protection function of rules on legal capital.[2]

Leaving aside special cases where persons may hold shares as a way of expressing their support in a non-financial sense for a particular enterprise or venture,[3] the general common interest of shareholders lies in ensuring the value of their investment: they will expect those who are responsible for managing the company's affairs to refrain from conduct that erodes the value of their investment and they will look to the managers to adopt policies that maximize capital growth; further, they will want to curb opportunities for management to exploit their position at the expense of the shareholders or to engage in risky activities that are otherwise detrimental to their position. Company law has traditionally protected these shareholder interests in a variety of ways, principally through vesting in them the constitutional power to decide upon certain matters, including changes to the company's capital structure and its voluntary winding up, making them in substance the beneficiaries of directors' duties (although these duties are mediated through the company and can only be enforced by the company or, in limited circumstances, by individual shareholders acting on the company's behalf) and by imposing disclosure and audit requirements. Arguments in favour of the inclusion of some shareholder-protection provisions within the general framework of company law are familiar and need not be examined at

---

[1] See, e.g., the references in the OECD's 'General Principles of Company Law for Transition Economies', published at [1999] 24 Journal of Corporation Law 190, to the need for mandatory law where outside controls through the market may not yet be sufficiently developed.

[2] The rules on legal capital and creditor interests are discussed further in J. Armour, 'Share Capital and Creditor Protection: Efficient Rules for a Modern Company Law' [2000] 63 Michigan Law Review 355. See also E.V. Ferran, 'Creditors' Interests and "Core" Company Law' [1999] 20 Company Lawyer 314; L. Enriques and J.R. Macey, 'Creditors versus Capital Formation: The Case Against the European Legal Capital Rules' (2001) 86 Cornell Law Review 1166.

[3] For example, fans of a sporting club who may hold shares in the club's holding company as one element of their support for the club: B.R. Cheffins, 'Playing the Stock Market: "Going Public" and Professional Sports Teams' [1999] 24 Journal of Corporation Law 641.

length here.[4] In principle, it is open to all investors, whether they be providers of debt or equity finance, to seek to protect their interests through formal contracts but, unlike debt, ordinary shares are open-ended investments and a contract that sought to deal with all of the events that might occur whilst the investment was extant, would be both costly to produce and likely to be incomplete since it would be beyond the competence of even the most sophisticated (and expensive) corporate lawyers to devise a contract that anticipated every event in the life of a company. The likely complexity of the bargaining process provides at least a prima facie case for regulatory intervention to reduce transaction costs:[5] "standard terms" within the framework of company law relieve the parties from having to use costly and time-consuming contractual mechanisms to protect their interests or, at least, allow them to restrict their contractual bargaining to the matters that are of particular importance to them with company law then filling in any gaps that may remain.[6] Another relevant consideration is that many investors may lack the information, skill, or resources to be able to bargain effectively. So long as the interests of these investors coincide with those who are better able to protect themselves through market forces, there may be no cause for concern; but such identity of interests cannot always be assumed. Accordingly, the justification for intervention to redress inequalities in bargaining power is also relevant.[7]

Yet, acceptance of the proposition that there is *a* role for prescriptive requirements to protect shareholder interests does not preclude a critical examination of existing law with a view to establishing whether it imposes requirements that are inherently excessive or redundant in modern conditions or which create harmful effects, say with regard to the competitiveness of a national legal system law in the market for incorporations of new business, that are not outweighed by the benefits provided.[8] The absence of a competitive market is one justification for the imposition of mandatory regulation[9] so where a market has become highly developed and is dominated by professional and sophisticated investors, as is the case with the U.K. equity markets, it is appropriate to re-examine the

---

[4] See, e.g. B.R. Cheffins, *Company Law: Theory, Structure and Operation* (Oxford 1997) 65–69.

[5] A. Ogus, *Regulation: Legal Form and Economic Theory* (Oxford 1994) 17–18; *Company Directors: Regulating Conflicts of Interests and Formulating a Statement of Duties* (Law Commission Consultation Paper no. 153) (1998) para. 3.14.

[6] S. Deakin and A. Hughes, 'Economic Efficiency and the Proceduralisation of Company Law' [1999] Company Financial and Insolvency Law Review 169, 176–180 (arguing that contractual incompleteness results in company law performing a larger role than gap-filling).

[7] S. Breyer, 'Typical Justifications for Regulation' in R. Baldwin, C. Scott, and C. Hood (eds.), *A Reader on Regulation* (Oxford 1998) 79.

[8] Generally, A. Ogus, *Regulation: Legal Form and Economic Theory* (Oxford 1994).

[9] G.J. Benston and G.G. Kaufman, 'The Appropriate Role of Bank Regulation' [1996] 106 *Economic Journal* 688.

existing law and to ask a variety of related questions. A suitable starting point is to look at the operation of existing law and to consider whether it successfully achieves the particular investor-protection goals for which it was enacted. If it does not, then this suggests that reform may be needed. If, for example, the requirements in the companies legislation on a particular matter do not reflect what major investors actually want with the result that costly efforts have to be made to get round them, there is a manifest failure of the law as a mechanism to reduce transaction costs.

Consideration should at least be given to bringing the statutory requirements more closely into line with investor preferences. But the more radical question—is this law needed at all?—must also be asked. If investor preferences are clear and they can be imposed effectively on companies through the operation of normal market forces, perhaps supported by listing or[10] stock exchange requirements,[11] there may be no strong case for companies legislation to include its own set of standard terms in a non-waivable form or in a form that can only be waived by following a time-consuming and expensive process. Instead the options may be (i) to repeal statutory requirements entirely, (ii) to convert them to opt in provisions—a menu from which investors can choose,[12] (iii) to make opting out easier, for example for by lengthening the period of the opt out or by reducing the requisite majority of shareholder votes needed for that purpose.

Also, the possibility of some type of intermediate form of regulation lying somewhere between the extremities of detailed rules set out in legislation and complete deregulation should also be considered. Taking for these purposes a simple definition of regulation as meaning principles or rules that aim to change or direct the behaviour of entities or individuals that are subject to it,[13] from the perspective of English law it can readily be seen that the concept of regulation can embrace not only rules and standards contained in statute and case law but also codes made by public authorities under a statutory power (the codes made

[10] As from May 2000 in the U.K. admission to the Official List and admission to trading on a stock exchange have been separated. Listing is the responsibility of the Financial Services Authority in its role as U.K. Listing Authority whilst admission to dealings is the responsibility of the relevant stock exchange.

[11] Generally on regulation by exchanges see R. Romano, 'Empowering Investors: A Market Approach to Securities Regulation' [1998] 107 Yale Law Journal 2359, 2399–2401; P.G. Mahoney, 'The Exchange as Regulator' (1997) 83 Virginia Law Review 1453; A.R. Palmiter, 'Toward Disclosure Choice in Securities Offerings' [1999] Columbia Business Law Review 1; A.C. Pritchard, 'Markets as Monitors: A Proposal to Replace Class Actions with Exchanges as Securities Fraud Enforcers' [1999] 85 Virginia Law Review 925; S.J. Choi and A.T. Guzmán, 'Portable Reciprocity: Rethinking the International Reach of Securities Regulation' [1998] 71 Southern California Law Review 903.

[12] R. Romano, 'Empowering Investors: A Market Approach to Securities Regulation' [1998] 107 Yale Law Journal 2359, 2362.

[13] D. Llewellyn, 'The Case for Financial Regulation' [1999] 1 *Journal of International Financial Markets* 153.

by the U.K.'s Financial Services Authority under the Financial Services and Markets Act 2000 are an obvious example) and rules that an association imposes on its members and which may be subject to court-based enforcement through the law of contract (such as requirements for admission to trading which may be imposed by a stock exchange on applicant companies). It can also include rules that are established by a particular group or agency and which are observed in practice even though they are not directly enforceable by court-based legal mechanisms. Institutional investor guidelines that companies adhere to for reputational reasons[14] spring to mind here. So too do corporate governance codes. The U.K.'s *Combined Code* enjoys a peculiar status in that it is a voluntary code, supported by a disclosure requirement under the *Listing Rules*, which are now the responsibility of the Financial Services Authority as the U.K.'s competent authority for listing matters.[15] Companies that do not comply with the *Combined Code* risk seeing investor dissatisfaction being reflected in the share price and they may find it harder to raise new capital; and for their directors there are reputational risks in behaving in this way. However, the only legal obligation on companies is the contractual obligation under the *Listing Rules* to disclose compliance or to explain non-compliance.

Market-driven codes of conduct or sets of guidelines that are endorsed by major investors and hence followed in practice by companies in order to protect their commercial position[16] have the advantage of being closely attuned to market expectations. They can be applied in a flexible way to particular circumstances[17]

---

[14] A. Shleifer and R.W. Vishny, 'A Survey of Corporate Governance' [1997] 52 *Journal of Finance* 737, 749.

[15] The London Stock Exchange performed this role historically but the Financial Services Authority assumed responsibility with effect from 1 May 2000.

[16] These are sometimes referred to as "soft law". On the use, and variety of, meaning of the term "soft law" (especially in the context of international law): C.M. Chinkin, 'The Challenge of Soft Law: Development and Change in International Law' [1989] International and Comparative Law Quarterly 850; A.E. Boyle, 'Some Reflections on the Relationship of Treaties and Soft Law' [1999] International and Comparative Law Quarterly 901. Its use is not confined to international law: see, e.g. J. Kenner, 'EC law; Employment; Social Policy The EC Employment Title and the "Third Way": Making Soft Law Work?' [1999] 15(1) International Journal of Comparative Labour Law and Industrial Relations 33.

[17] In the U.K., the Pre-emption Group has for a number of years published an annual review of the operation of the Pre-emption Guidelines which set out the circumstances in which institutional investors can be expected to vote in favour of disapplication of pre-emption rights. These Guidelines are helpful to companies because they give a prior indication of the likely attitude of institutional shareholders to any proposal regarding a new share issue; but as guidelines rather than rules they can be applied flexibly. The annual reviews indicate that non pre-emptive issues falling outside the Guidelines will be supported by the institutions where circumstances—such as volatile market conditions—justify this course of action. Another situation where institutional investors may support a non pre-emptive issue that is outside the Guidelines is where it is an international offering made to enhance the issuer's international position and to broaden its market: 'Freepages' International Offering: the NASDAQ Factor' (1997) VIII (5) Practical Law for Companies 8.

and the process of changing them in response to new developments is likely to be far speedier than the equivalent process for amending a statutory requirement. The possible use of market-based regulatory mechanisms as an alternative to statutory regulation has been mentioned positively by those responsible for the ongoing review of company law in the U.K. in the context of its wider discussion about reform being driven by a presumption against regulation.[18] As has been remarked elsewhere,[19] this preference by U.K. company law policy-makers for non-statutory regulation and, indeed, the growth in practice in the 1990s in the use of codes that are not legally enforceable, especially in the area of corporate governance,[20] seems to be in sharp contrast to the developments in the related field of U.K. financial regulation where the trend has been in the opposite direction, away from self-regulation and towards a comprehensive statutory regulatory framework with powerful enforcement mechanisms.[21] However, the U.K.'s preference for self-regulation of the corporate sector should not be overstated. Despite the initial apparent zeal for a 'hands-off' approach, as the company law reform proposals have evolved, it is become clear that many prescriptive legal rules will remain, particularly in relation to directors' duties.

A familiar criticism of non-statutory, or private, regulation is that flexibility and adaptability may be achieved at the expense of certainty and predictability. Another is that it may result in plethora of overlapping, yet different and possibly even conflicting, requirements and/or in gaps in the scope of regulation.[22] Whether ostracism by the market is an effective enforcement mechanism is also

---

[18] *Modern Company Law for a Competitive Economy. The Strategic Framework* (Company Law Review Steering Group Consultation Document) (February 1999) paras 2.21–2.23; *Modern Company Law for a Competitive Economy. Developing the Framework* (Company Law Review Steering Group Consultation Document) (March 2000) paras 3.119–3.121.

[19] E. Wymeersch, *Company Law in the 21st Century* (1999) 3 International and Comparative Corporate Law Journal 331.

[20] See the codes emanating from the work of the Cadbury (financial aspects of corporate governance), Greenbury (directors' remuneration), Hampel (corporate governance) and Turnbull (internal controls) Committees.

[21] The case for public sector regulation in addition to, or partly in place of, self-regulation is made in C. Goodhart, P. Hartmann, D. Llewellyn, L. Rojas-Suárez, and S. Weisbrod, *Financial Regulation: Why, How and Where Now* (London/New York 1998) Ch. 1. See also C. Briault, *The Rationale for a Single National Financial Services Regulator* (FSA Occasional Paper Series 2) (May 1999); D. Llewellyn, *The Economic Rationale for Financial Regulation* (FSA Occasional Paper Series 1) (April 1999).

[22] The Hampel Committee was itself sensitive to this potential problem. It was its initiative that led to the consolidation of the Cadbury, Greenbury, and Hampel requirements into the Combined Code annexed to the Listing Rules. Combined Code, para. E.1.1. calls upon institutional investors to endeavour to eliminate unnecessary variations in their corporate governance and performance criteria for the companies in which they invest.

debated.[23] In the context of market-driven regulatory standards that reflect the expectations of a particular group, the potentially damaging effect of observance of those standards on those with different interests is another potential cause for concern. Mechanisms for checking the potential misuse of power thus also require attention.

In broad terms, the task is to devise a regulatory structure that is, to borrow a phrase, "enough but not excessive".[24] There is potentially much to be said for a combined or mixed regulatory system that allows the market to regulate itself wherever it can do so effectively but which supplements and reinforces market-based regulation with suitable legal standards and appropriate legal court-based enforcement mechanisms. In this context it is important to recognize that the line between state and market regulation can often become blurred and that the state can exert powerful influence over the content of market-based regulation by endorsing the use of codes or other regulatory devices which are then adhered to in practice because of market perception that failure to do so may result in more interventionist regulation in the form of statutory requirements.[25]

Part B contains an assessment of current English statutory law, and under-lying EC directive requirements, relating to new share issues. These aspects of the regulation of legal capital are singled out for particular examination because they are matters where, in the U.K., regulation through institutional investor guidelines is already well-developed and thus the question whether underpinning of market requirements by statutory regulation is still necessary or desirable is directly in point.

Particular attention is paid to pre-emption requirements. Institutional investors in the U.K. continue to value pre-emption rights.[26] Recent research commissioned as part of the on-going general review of company law[27] indicates that for investors the importance of pre-emption rights lies not only in their function as a mechanism for preventing value transfers from existing to new

---

[23] F. La Porta, F. Lopez-de-Silanes, A. Shleifer, and R.W. Vishny, 'Law and Finance' [1998] 106 *Journal of Political Economy* 1113; F. Modigliani and E. Perotti, 'Security Markets Versus Bank Finance: Legal Enforcement and Investor Protection' (2000) 1 *International Review of Finance* 81.

[24] The source is *Company Directors: Regulating Conflicts of Interests and Formulating a Statement of Duties* (Law Commission Consultation Paper no. 153) (1998) para. 2.17.

[25] A. Ogus, 'Re-thinking Self-Regulation' [1995] 15 Oxford Journal of Legal Studies 97.

[26] B.S. Black and J.C. Coffee, 'Hail Britannia? Institutional Investor Behavior Under Limited Regulation' [1994] 92 Michigan Law Review 1997; G.P. Stapledon, *Institutional Shareholders and Corporate Governance* (Oxford 1996) Ch. 4.

[27] *Modern Company Law for a Competitive Economy. Developing the Framework* (Company Law Review Steering Group Consultation Document) (March 2000) paras 3.160 and 4.162; J. Franks and C. Mayer, *Governance as a Source of Managerial Discipline* (Paper prepared for the Company Law Review, Committee E on Corporate Governance) (2000) http://www.dti.gov.uk/cld/franksreport.pdf.

investors but also in their corporate governance role: pre-emption rights force management in need of additional equity finance to go back to their existing shareholders for it or for permission to obtain it from other sources and this is seen to be a significant discipline on underperforming managers. Yet the undoubted preference for pre-emption rights should not be allowed to obscure the fact that the existing pre-emption provisions in the English companies legislation, and in the Second Directive, are open to criticism. The essence of the criticism is that the statutory pre-emption rights procedure is not in accord with market preferences with the result that it is common practice for companies to disapply the legislation in order to make pre-emptive offers of securities in a different way from that which the legislation prescribes. Thus what happens in practice is that the market regulates itself outside the statutory regime. From this an obvious question to ask is whether the statutory regime can be reformed so as better to reflect investor preferences. But whether a statutory regime is needed at all, or whether opting out of it should be made easier, are also relevant questions.

Part C of the chapter looks at underwriting. Underwriting practices in the U.K. have attracted the attention of competition authorities in recent years. At one point it appeared that statutory intervention to remove anti-competitive practices (which impacted adversely on smaller investors) was being considered but the eventual response was in the form of an agreed statement of "best practice" published by the Bank of England and supported by other influential bodies. This recent chain of events is recounted briefly here as an illustration of the sensitive deployment of market-based regulatory techniques in relation to the control of sophisticated securities and capital markets. Finally, Part D draws some conclusions.

B. Statutory Framework of English Law on New Share Issues

I. Authorized Share Capital

The Companies Act 1985 contains three main provisions that directly regulate the process of increasing share capital. First, under section 121 of the Companies Act 1985 increases in authorized share capital must be approved by the shareholders in general meeting. The form of the resolution required for this purpose is for companies to determine themselves by a provision in their articles; it is usual for articles to specify an ordinary resolution, which requires a simple majority of those voting. The authorized share capital requirement is the oldest statutory method of regulating share issues in the English companies legislation but it is limited in its effect in that it only enables shareholders to exert a degree of control over the preliminary stage of the process and does not allow them to control the actual issue of shares or, in particular, the identity of the persons to whom the new shares are offered. Additional layers of regulation added to the companies legislation at a later date,[28] namely, the requirement for shareholders to authorize the actual allotment of shares and pre-emption rights, seek to achieve the same broad effect of vesting control over share issues in the shareholders but the newer requirements are directed at what may be regarded as the most important aspects of the process, namely, how many shares can be issued at any time and to whom.[29] Also, the concept of authorized share capital can be seriously misleading in that a statement of a company's authorized share capital gives no indication whatsoever of the finance that a company has raised by allotting shares: thus the common description of many U.K. private companies as "£100 capital" companies is often wrong since only a fraction of the stated authorized share capital of £100 may actually have been issued and the amount paid or payable in respect of the issued shares may be a nominal amount such as £1. That the authorized share capital requirement is an anachronism has been recognized by the review bodies and its abolition has been recommended, although this has encountered some opposition.[30] This proposal could be implemented without change at the European level because the Second Directive does not require Member States to impose authorized share capital requirements.

[28] By the Companies Act 1980, ss. 14 and 17.

[29] There is a possible technical advantage to shareholders with regard to the remedies available for non-compliance with the authorized share capital requirement as opposed to the more modern provisions. An allotment of shares in excess of the authorized share capital is thought to be void (*Bank of Hindustan China and Japan Ltd v. Alison* (1871) L.R. 6 C.P. 222; *Re A Company, ex p. Shooter* [1990] B.C.L.C. 384 at 389), whereas the validity of an allotment is unaffected by the fact that the directors may have acted without the authority required by the Companies Act 1985, s. 80 or in breach of the statutory pre-emption requirements under the Companies Act 1985, s. 89: Companies Act 1985, s. 80(10) and s. 92. Yet whether general shareholder interests are well served by disgruntled shareholders being able to obtain a remedy to the effect that a share issue is void, with all the disruption to the market that this could entail where the shares are publicly traded, is questionable (see *Re Thundercrest Ltd* [1994] B.C.C. 857 at 863). In any case where a breach of s. 80 or s. 89 is not merely technical but is part of a scheme in which directors abuse their position, the breach of duty on their part may provide a separate ground for the setting aside of the allotment: *Re Thundercrest Ltd* [1994] B.C.C. 857. If the breach of the statutory requirements results from a mistake that too may be a ground on which the issue may be avoided: *Re Cleveland Trust plc* [1991] B.C.C. 33.

[30] *Company Formation and Capital Maintenance* (Company Law Review Steering Group Consultation Document) (October 1999). The Law Society Company Law Reform Committee has raised some objections to the proposal to withdraw the authorized share capital requirement, including that it could remove controls over directors attaching special rights to shares and could thus be used in ways seriously prejudicial to existing shareholders' interests: *Company Law Reform: Capital Maintenance* (Jan. 2000) (no. 389). The Committee's point is an important one but it does not, it is suggested, provide a convincing case for the retention of the authorized share capital requirement since the directors' power to issue preference shares or other classes of shares with special rights could presumably be controlled through appropriate provisions in articles or, possibly, in s. 80 authorities.

II. Authority to Allot Share Capital

The second statutory requirement regulating share issues is section 80 of the Companies Act 1985. This section prohibits directors from allotting relevant securities,[31] such as shares, unless they are authorized to do so either by the shareholders in general meeting or by the company's articles. The maximum amount of shares that may be allotted under the authority and its expiry date must be stated in the authorizing article or resolution.[32] The expiry date of a section 80 authority must be not more than five years from the date of the authorising resolution or the date of incorporation where the authority is contained in articles at the time of incorporation.[33] A section 80 authority may be renewed for further periods not exceeding five years by the passing of an ordinary resolution to that effect[34] and it may be revoked or varied, also by ordinary resolution.[35] A section 80 authority can be specific or general and conditional or unconditional.[36]

Section 80 implements into English law article 25 of the Second Company Law Directive, although the directive applies only to public companies whereas section 80 is generally applicable. It enables the shareholders to exercise direct control over share allotments but, subject to the mandatory requirement relating to the maximum duration of the authority, leaves it up to the shareholders to determine how much control they want to exert or, conversely, how much flexibility they wish to give to the directors in terms of the amount of shares that can be allotted and other conditions that must be satisfied. The evidence from practice relating to public companies is that institutional investors are concerned to exercise control over the amount of the capital that can be allotted by linking it to the company's existing capital structure: in particular, the Association of British Insurers, the representative body for one major group of institutional investor, takes the view that the maximum amount of capital in respect of which a section 80 authority is in place from time to time (other than that which is reserved for issue in connection with contractual conversion rights or options) should not exceed the lesser of the company's authorized (but unissued) share capital and one-third of the issued equity capital at the time the authority is

---

[31] The term 'relevant securities' is defined by s. 80(2) and means (a) shares in the company other than shares shown in the memorandum as having been taken by the subscribers to it or shares allotted in pursuance of an employees' share scheme, and (b) any right to subscribe for, or to convert any security into, shares in the company (other than shares so allotted).

[32] Companies Act 1985, s. 80(4).

[33] ibid.

[34] Companies Act 1985, s. 80(5).

[35] Companies Act 1985, s. 80(4). An ordinary resolution suffices even where the authorization is in the articles: Companies Act 1985, s. 80(8)

[36] Companies Act 1985, s. 80(3).

given.[37] Otherwise, however, detailed conditions are not usually imposed. Overall, although criticisms about technical aspects of the section, such as the fact that the requirement to state an "amount" appears to preclude the use of a formula, are occasionally voiced, there appears to be little dissatisfaction with the operation of section 80 in relation to public companies. There is no apparent pressure to return to the pre-1980 deregulated position in which shareholders had no direct control mechanism over the allotment of authorized shares and a challenge depended on showing that the allotment had been made in breach of directors' duties. For private companies (which are not subject to the Second Directive), a more relaxed regime has been available since 1990 under which a section 80 authority can be given for a fixed period of more than five years or for an indefinite period.[38] Opting out of the general scheme and into the more relaxed regime requires the consent of all of those who are entitled to vote on the matter[39] and for this reason it is reasonable to assume that it is of most relevance to companies with only a few shareholders.

III. Pre-emption Rights

Pre-emption rights are enshrined in the Companies Act 1985, s. 89. This provision implements the Second Company Law Directive, article 29 into domestic law. The Second Directive is intended to safeguard the rights of shareholders and third parties.[40] It seeks to provide a minimum level of protection for shareholders and creditors of public companies in all Member States.[41] Issues of new shares for non-cash consideration are not within the scope of article 29. It is open to Member States in their domestic legislation to require issues of new shares for

---

[37] *Directors' Power to Allot Shares* (ABI) (May 1995) (available via the ABI's Institutional Voting Information Service, http://www.ivis.computasoft/ivis/ivisweb.nsf).

[38] Companies Act 1985, s. 80A, inserted by the Companies Act 1989, s. 115(1) as from April 1, 1990. *Modern Company Law for a Competitive Economy. Developing the Framework* (Company Law Review Steering Group Consultation Document) (March 2000) paras 7.28–7.32 put forward the suggestion that s. 80 should cease to apply to private companies.

[39] Companies Act 1985, s. 80A(1) (specifying the requirement for an elective resolution) and Companies Act 1985, s. 379A (defining an elective resolution).

[40] Second Directive, preamble, second recital; Joined Cases C-19/90 and C-20/90 *Karella* and *Karellas* [1991] E.C.R. I-2691, judgement of May 30, 19991, para. 30. See generally E. Werlauff, 'Common European Company Law: Status 1998 (2). The Background to Harmonization, Disclosure, Capital, etc.' [1998] 9 European Business Law Review 210, 212–213.

[41] Case-381/89 *Sindesmos Melon Tis Eleftheras Evangelikis Ekklisias* [1992] E.C.R. I-2111, judgment of March 24, 1992, para. 32; Case C-441/93 *Panagis Pafitis* [1996] E.C.R. I-1347, judgment March 12, 1996, para. 38; Case C-42/95 *Siemens AG/Nold* [1996] I-6017, judgment of November 19, 1996, para. 13.

non-cash consideration to be done on a pre-emptive basis;[42] but the Companies Act 1985 does not extend pre-emption rights in this way.

In broad terms section 89 of the Companies Act 1985 obliges a company which is proposing to allot equity securities, such as ordinary shares,[43] to offer the opportunity to acquire those shares first to holders of the company's existing relevant shares in proportion to their existing holdings.[44] The offer must be made in writing to all existing shareholders[45] and it must be kept open for at least 21 clear days.[46] The procedural requirements regarding the sending of offer letters to shareholders are modified in relation to overseas shareholders to permit, instead, the making of the offer to them by means of an advertisement in the London Gazette.[47] This modification is intended to relieve the issuing company of the burden of complying with the securities laws of the countries in which shareholders are resident and which could be triggered by the making of an offer in those jurisdictions. Only to a limited extent does domestic law, and the underlying European law that it implements, follow the now-standard approach in the U.S.A. of treating pre-emption rights as optional.[48] Under section 95 of the Companies Act 1985, public companies can opt out of pre-emption rights for a maximum period of five years. Private companies (which are not within the scope of the Second Directive in any event) can opt out entirely.[49] Public company opt-outs must be made by a provision in the articles or by a special resolution, that is a resolution passed by a majority of at least 75% of the votes cast.[50]

In some technical respects, such as the requirement to make the offer in writing, it can readily be seen that English law, as influenced by the Second Directive,

[42] Case C-42/95 *Siemens AG/Nold* [1996] E.C.R. I-6017, judgment of November 19, 1996.

[43] The term 'equity securities' is defined by Companies Act 1985, s. 94(2). It means relevant shares (other than subscriber shares and bonus shares) or rights to subscribe for, or to convert securities, into relevant shares. The term 'relevant shares' is, in turn, defined by s. 94(5) as being shares other than shares carrying rights to participate in capital and dividend distributions only up to a specified amount and shares allotted pursuant to an employee's share scheme. The definition excludes typically drafted preference shares from pre-emption right entitlements but preference shares that are fully participating as regards capital and/or dividends are included. Also excluded are warrants and convertibles.

[44] See Companies Act 1985, s. 94(5) (discussed in previous note) for the definition of 'relevant shares'. The holders of shares allotted under an employee' share scheme (relevant employee shares) also benefit from pre-emption rights: s. 89(1).

[45] Companies Act 1985, s. 90(2). The minimum period in the Second Directive is 14 days: art. 29.3.

[46] Companies Act 1985, s. 90(6).

[47] Companies Act 1985, s. 90(5).

[48] R.C. Clark, *Corporate Law* (Boston: Little Brown, 1986) 719; W.A. Klein and J.C. Coffee, *Business Organization and Finance* 7th edn. (New York: Foundation Press, 2000) 220–221.

[49] Companies Act 1985, s. 91.

[50] Companies Act 1985, s. 95.

is rather prescriptive and a potential hindrance to the efficient operation of elec-
tronically-driven securities markets.[51] Yet, whilst facilitating the use of modern
methods of communications is clearly an essential component of a reform
process, any review of pre-emption rights should also be conducted at a more
fundamental level. There follows an attempt to identify the underlying investor-
protection purposes of pre-emption rights and to consider whether, or to what
extent, the law, as presently framed and as operated in practice, achieves those
goals. In summary, the conclusion drawn is that statutory pre-emption rights do
seek to protect some legitimate interests of shareholders but that as a "standard
form" transaction cost saving device, they are defective because the prescribed
requirements are often less attractive to investors than alternative pre-emption
requirements that have been developed by the market. The poor "fit" of the
statutory terms means that parties have to go through the process of opting out
of these terms at regular intervals. Although the processing of opting out may
not be particularly complicated or costly, since all that it requires is a routine resolution passed at the AGM or another general meeting, a system of company
law that aspires to be truly "modern" should not retain formalities that do not
secure a real benefit. It is suggested that there is a strong case for removing pre-
emption rights from the realm of statutory regulation and allowing the market
to regulate this matter instead. Alternatively, opting out could be made easier,
such as by lengthening the permissible duration of an opt-out. If either of these

---

[51] There is some doubt on whether electronic forms of communication satisfy statutory requirements for "writing": *Corporate Action Standardisation* CREST publication (May 1996); V. Knapp,
'CREST: Impact on Corporate Transaction' [1996] 7 (10) P.L.C. 23; (1997) 12 (11) Butterworths
Journal of International Banking and Financial Law 552. The requirement for the offer to be made
in writing stems from the Second Directive, art 29.3 which states that where a company's shares are
registered (as is the case under English law, for the moment, for shares trading within CREST) all
shareholders must be informed in writing of the pre-emptive offer. The English Law Commission has
advised that emails and website trading generally will satisfy statutory requirements for "writing"
but that electronic data interchange will not: *Electronic Commerce: Formal Requirements in
Commercial Transactions: Advice From the Law Commission* (Law Commission Paper, December
2001). The Law Commission notes that this view is not universally held but hopes that by publishing its advice it can promote a consensus. The Commission suggests that if absolute certainty is
required in particular circumstances, context-specific legislation should be passed for that purpose.
Note the Electronic Communications Act 2000, s. 8, which authorizes the Secretary of State to modify legislation so as to facilitate the use of electronic forms of communication.
  Article 29.3 also states that the minimum offer period must be 14 days. Even without changes at
the European level, there is thus scope for the offer period for a Companies Act 1985, s. 89 pre-
emptive offer to be reduced. In 1999 the possibility of reducing the s. 89 offer period (which would
reduce the period when underwriters of the issue are "on risk" and hence lead to possible savings in
underwriting costs) was referred to the Company Law Review Steering Group by the U.K.'s competition authorities: Underwriting Services for Share Offers: A Report on the Supply in the U.K.
(Monopolies and Mergers (now Competition) Commission) (Cm. 4168) (February 1999). The
Steering Group has recommended that the period should stay at 21 days but with power for the
Secretary of State to reduce the period to not less than 14 days: *Modern Company Law for a
Competitive Economy. Final Report* (July 2001) para. 7.31.

suggestions were to be taken up, it seems unlikely that the corporate governance disciplining effect of pre-emption rights would be lost since the market could impose its own requirements, with the advantage that those requirements could be fine-tuned and adjusted from time to time to reflect changing market conditions. But, although the balance of power between the management and the general body of shareholders in a company might not be significantly affected by removing, or reducing, statutory regulation of pre-emption rights, there is also the separate issue of regulating potential conflicts of interest between groups of investors. Complete coincidence of interest between major investors that are able, through their market dominance, to impose pre-emption requirements on corporate management and smaller investors should not necessarily be assumed.

a. Dilution of Voting Control

One justification for pre-emption rights is to prevent dilution of shareholders' voting control and in the view of some commentators, this is their principal function.[52] Thus, for example, an Advocate-General to the European Court of Justice has described the shareholders' right to retain unchanged their proportional share of the their holding in the capital as being a right that is inherent in being a shareholder.[53] This view of pre-emptive rights as being an integral part of being a shareholder has some historical support[54] but it is noteworthy that specific pre-emption rights only became part of English company law as a result of implementation of the Second Directive.[55] Prior to that, new share issues were more lightly regulated, with a requirement for shareholders to approve increases to authorized share capital and directors' fiduciary duties being the principal control mechanisms.

Evidence from practice indicates that major institutional investors in the U.K. attach importance to the principle that their proportionate share of, as they see it, the ownership of the company should not be diluted without their consent.[56] The ability of shareholders to exercise control over management by using the voting rights attached to their shares has been emphasized in recent

[52] "Pre-emptive rights are designed principally to protect existing stockholders from the dilution in voting control attendant upon the issuance of new stock"—L.E. Mitchell, L.A. Cunningham, and L.D. Solomon, *Corporate Finance and Governance* 2nd edn. (Durham N.C.: Academic Press 1996) 841.

[53] *Siemens AG/Nold* [1996] E.C.R. I-6017, opinion of September 19, 1996, para. 15.

[54] R.W. Hamilton, *The Law of Corporations* (West Publishing 4th edn, 1996) 173.

[55] By the Companies Act 1980, s. 17. See further P.G. Xuereb, 'Corporate Management and the Statutory Right of Pre-emption: A Comparative Review' (1988) 37 International and Comparative Law Quarterly 397.

[56] *ABI/NAPF Joint Position Paper on Pre-emption, Cost of Capital and Underwriting* (July 1996) para. 1.1.

years. The explanation for this may lie in the growing domination of the U.K. equity markets by institutions[57] since in a market dominated by professionals the opportunity for any one dissatisfied investor to 'beat the market' by selling at a competitive rate is likely to be much reduced. In some circumstances the size of their holdings may mean that institutions are, in practical terms, locked into their investments. Where the ability to exit a company by selling its shares becomes restricted, investors can reasonably be expected to pay more attention to exerting control by actively participating in the internal decision-making process and exercising the rights attaching to their shares.[58] The idea that voting control is of marginal significance or that it does not provide justification for the imposition of pre-emption rights since investors that are concerned about holding an investment in a certain proportion of the share capital can always acquire shares in the market to maintain their holding,[59] is not in line with the prevailing view.

Yet it is important to note that statutory pre-emption rights do not provide an absolute guarantee against dilution and that in some circumstances, or for some investors, the protection afforded by pre-emption rights against dilution can be illusory. At a formal level, pre-emption rights provide a shareholder with an offer that it is free to accept or reject but in substance this structure may have a coercive effect.[60] Existing shareholders who do not want to invest or who do not have the funds to invest will find their voting rights diluted against their will yet so far as laws on pre-emption are concerned they are powerless to stop this. It is open to a shareholder whose holding is diluted by a pre-emptive offer that is made in conformity with the requirements of the Companies Act 1985, s. 89 to

---

[57] Final Report of the Committee on Corporate Governance (January 1998) (Hampel Committee Report) para. 5.1 notes that 60% is held by U.K. institutions, around 20% by foreign, mainly institutional, owners and the remaining 20% or so by private individuals. The DTI also estimates that around 80% lies in institutional hands: *Shareholder Communications at the Annual General Meeting* (Consultative Document) (April 1996) para. 1.7. It has also been estimated that, on the basis of January 1996 data on the ownership of the shares of the largest 300 companies, on average their 20 largest institutional shareholders accounted for between one third and one half of their share capital: M. Gaved, *Institutional Investors and Corporate Governance* (Foundation for Business Responsibilities Issues Paper no. 3) (March 1998).

[58] J.C. Coffee, 'Liquidity Versus Control: The Institutional Investor as Corporate Monitor' [1991] 91 Columbia Law Review 1277, 1288–1289; Hampel Committee Report para. 5.3; Sir Adrian Cadbury, *Board Focus: The Governance Debate* (London: Egorv Zehnder International 1997) 28 quoting Georg Siemens, founder of Deutsche Bank: 'if you cannot sell, you must care'.

[59] 'Pre-emption Rights' [1987] 27 *Bank of England Quarterly Bulletin* 545, 547.

[60] This was expressly recognized by the European Court of Justice in Joined Cases C-19/90 and C-20/90 *Karella* and *Karellas* [1991] E.C.R. I-2691 where, at para. 26 of the judgment, the Court said of an increase in a company's capital that it would "have the effect either of obliging the original shareholders to increase their contributions to the capital or of imposing on them the addition of new shareholders, thus reducing their involvement in the decision-taking power of the company". See also *City Capital Associates v. Interco Inc* 551 A. 2d. 787 (Del Ch 1988).

apply to court for relief on the grounds that the affairs of the company are being managed in an unfairly prejudicial manner.[61] Some cases argued on this ground have succeeded but, significantly, they have tended to involve private companies and to be situations where the disputed rights issue was just one element of the breakdown in the personal relationships between the operators of the business.[62]

Mutual Life Insurance Co of New York v. The Rank Organization Ltd[63] was an attempt to use general shareholder remedies provided by the companies legislation[64] to challenge a public company rights issue made in conformity with legal requirements but which had a dilutive effect on shareholders resident in the United States and Canada. In accordance with established U.K. market practice, the statutory pre-emption rights had been disapplied by special resolution so as to exclude U.S. and Canadian resident shareholders from the offer of securities and to permit the company instead to pay them a cash equivalent. The court rejected the shareholders' claim and amongst the reasons for this rejection was a specific statement to the effect that no shareholder had the right to expect his fractional interest in the company to remain constant forever. Although the directors of the company were required to act fairly as between groups of shareholders with different interests, this did not require parity of treatment.[65] The *Mutual Life* decision was followed in *Re BSB Holdings Ltd (No. 2)*[66] where, again, a shareholder failed in its attempts to challenge a complex capital reorganization that included a rights issue.

These cases clearly reject the notion that all shareholders have an inviolable right not be diluted against their will and recognize that in some circumstances the broader corporate interest in raising capital on the most favourable terms can be allowed to override these individual shareholder interests. Also despite the emphasis that is sometimes placed upon it, the reality, as the facts of *Mutual Life* itself demonstrate, is that even investors do not treat prevention of dilution as a sacrosanct principle: there, the U.K.-based shareholders were content to vote for dilution of their North American counterparts.[67] Thus, from the

---

[61] *Shareholder Remedies A Consultation Paper* (Law Commission Consultation Paper no. 142) (1996) paras 9.36–9.38.

[62] *Re a Company (No. 007623 of 1984)* [1985] B.C.L.C. 80, ChD ((1986) 2 B.C.C. 99, 453 ChD is a report of the full hearing of the case and [1986] B.C.L.C. 430, CA is a report of the hearing on appeal (sub nom *Re Cumana Ltd)*); *Re a Company (No. 007623 of 1984)* [1986] B.C.L.C. 362, ChD.

[63] [1985] B.C.L.C. 11, ChD.

[64] The claim was brought under the Companies Act 1985, s. 14 which creates a statutory contract between a company and its members. The views expressed by the court would seem to be equally applicable to a claim brought under Companies Act 1985, s. 459.

[65] Second Directive, art. 42 enshrines the principle of equality of treatment of shareholders in the same position and requires Member States to implement the directive consistently with this principle.

[66] [1996] 1 B.C.L.C. 155, ChD.

[67] This raises the issue of potential conflicts of interest between groups of shareholders, a point that is developed later in this chapter.

perspective of English law and practice, it can be seen that the anti-dilution principle, by itself, is not an entirely convincing explanation for the importance that is commonly attached to pre-emption rights; alternative reasons must be sought.

b. Preventing Value Transfers From Existing Shareholders to New Investors

The other main conventional justification for pre-emption rights is that they are necessary to prevent the transfer of value from existing shareholders to new investors.[68] In order to assist with the marketing of an issue, new shares are typically offered at a discount to the prevailing market price.[69] If the discount element involved in a new issue of shares is not offered to existing shareholders this can result in erosion in the value of their investment.[70] Yet, the point about pre-emption rights providing imperfect protection in that they only achieve the desired effect in favour of shareholders who take up their rights is as relevant here as it was in relation to their function as an anti-dilution mechanism: the formally voluntary offer may be coercive in its effect because shareholders may be forced to take up their rights in order to maintain their financial position. Nothing in the Companies Act 1985, or in the underlying Second Directive, mitigates the potential for this form of practical coercion.

Happily, however, established market practice and, in the case of listed securities, listing requirements[71] in this instance fill in the gap in the statutory regime. The *Listing Rules* require pre-emptive offers to be made on a renounceable basis so as to allow existing shareholders who do not want to invest further in the company to safeguard their financial position by trading their rights to acquire the new shares at a discount price.[72] Also, "lazy" shareholders are protected by the

---

[68] An early analysis of this argument is provided in H.S. Drinker, 'The Pre-emptive Right of Shareholders to Subscribe New Shares' [1930] 43 Harvard Law Review 586. A more recent expression of the anti-transfer of value justification for pre-emption rights is contained in the *ABI/NAPF Joint Position Paper on Pre-emption, Cost of Capital and Underwriting* (July 1996).

[69] Or, more precisely, a discount greater than is necessary to reflect the increased number of shares in the market as a result of the issue. Recent judicial analysis of the process of fixing the issue price and marketing of securities is provided in *County Ltd v. Girozentrale Securities* [1996] 3 All E.R. 834, CA. It is not a breach of directors' duties to issue shares at a discount to the market price with a view to ensuring the success of the issue: *Shearer v. Bercain* [1980] 3 All E.R. 295, ChD, 307.

[70] Worked examples supporting this point can be found in *Guidance on Share Issuing Good Practice for Listed Companies* (Bank of England) (October 1999), Technical Annex, and in E.V. Ferran, *Company Law and Corporate Finance* (Oxford 1999) Ch. 18.

[71] para. 4.16.

[72] Again, worked examples showing the operation of the nil-paid rights market can be found in *Guidance on Share Issuing Good Practice for Listed Companies* (Bank of England) (October 1999), Technical Annex, and in E.V. Ferran, *Company Law and Corporate Finance* (Oxford 1999) Ch. 18. These examples simplify the position by ignoring such matters as the tax consequences of selling

requirement[73] for the company to sell the entitlements of shareholders who do not take up their rights or trade them in the nil-paid market, and to remit the cash proceeds to those shareholders.

There is no evident pressure for these protective measures to be hard-coated by incorporation into positive statutory law, and such a move would clearly run counter to current deregulatory trends. Rather, the evidence from the capital markets is of a shift in the opposite direction with the emergence of the open offer, which is a variant on the traditional rights issue structure.[74] An open offer is a pre-emptive offer of new securities to existing shareholders in proportion to their existing holdings. It differs from a rights issue in that the minimum offer period is only 15 business days. Also the offer is not made by means of a renounceable letter and no arrangements are made to sell for the benefit of shareholders shares representing entitlements that have not been taken up. These requirements governing open offers are set out in the *Listing Rules*. The *Listing Rules* further specify that an open offer of equity securities of a class already listed may not normally[75] be made if the offer price is to be at a discount of more than 10% to the middle market price of the securities at the time when the terms of the offer are announced. This is a protective measure that helps to restrict the extent of the erosion of value of the investments of those shareholders that do not take up their rights.

Since the structure of an open offer is different from that envisaged by the requirements of the companies legislation on pre-emption, the Companies Act 1985, s. 89 must be disapplied before an open offer can be made. It is now common practice for disapplication resolutions to contain wording authorizing open offers. Major institutional investors have not raised formal objections to the use of open offers[76] but this is not surprising given that they tend to take up their rights anyway. The categories of investor who lose out more if a company raises capital by means of an open offer rather than a rights issue are smaller and pri-

nil-paid rights instead of investing in the new securities. In fact an investor's position can be seriously affected by the capital gains tax consequences of selling nil-paid rights. This point has been drawn to the attention of HM Treasury by the U.K.'s competition authorities with the suggestion that CGT rules might be suitably modified: *Underwriting Services for Share Offers: A Report on the Supply in the U.K.* (Monopolies and Mergers (now Competition) Commission) (Cm. 4168) (February 1999).

[73] para. 4.19. This requirement only applies where the cash proceeds are above £3.

[74] A. McCrum, 'Equity Funding: Stagecoach's Open Offer and International Offering' [1999] (X) 10 Practical Law for Companies 9.

[75] The use of an open offer outside these circumstances may be sanctioned where the issuer is in severe financial difficulties or there are other exceptional circumstances.

[76] Although it is reported in C.J. Millerchip, 'British Land Placing and Open Offer' [1995] 6(3) Practical Law for Companies 6, 8 that the ABI has indicated that it would be concerned if there was to be a concerted move towards the use of open offers as opposed to rights issues for larger equity capital raising.

vate shareholders who may lack the resources to take up their rights or lack the financial sophistication to appreciate the consequences of failing to do so.

c. Options for Reform: Status Quo, Deregulation, or Re-regulation of Pre-emption Rights?

In the U.K. there has been a dialogue, stretching back over many years, between companies and institutional investors about the disapplication of pre-emption rights. Broadly speaking, the argument from the corporate side is that it is an unduly short-term perspective to focus on the transfer of value resulting from the discount element in a new issue of securities and that the longer term financial interests of a company and its shareholders may be better served by allowing it more flexibility in the methods of raising capital. As well as broadening a company's investor base, alternative methods of offering securities may involve lower discounts than are expected in traditionally-structured rights, which will impact on the number of shares that the company needs to issue to raise the desired amount of finance and hence impact on dividends per share and other accounting ratios unless historical data on these matters are adjusted to reflect the larger number of shares in issue.[77] One particular point that is made is that a rights issue can involve higher underwriting costs than other types of offer of securities. Recent market innovations in underwriting structures, examined in Part C of this chapter, seek to address concerns about underwriting costs. With regard to the more general aspects of the discussion, the settled compromise, as set out in Pre-emption Guidelines agreed between representatives of listed companies, institutional investors, and the London Stock Exchange and in operation in the U.K. equity markets since 1987, is that institutional investors will support resolutions to disapply the Companies Act 1985, s. 89 in two cases: first, they will sanction disapplication for non-pre-emptive offers but only where the amount of shares that can be allotted in this way is limited; and second, as discussed already, they will vote in favour where the disapplication is to allow the company to make allotments that are not fully in conformity with statutory pre-emption rights because, for example, they exclude overseas shareholders or are in the form of an open offer. The U.K. Company Law Review Steering Group appears to be disinclined to support radical reform of the statutory pre-emption

---

[77] But note that it is now widely recognized that the impact of an increased number of shares in issue should be reflected in adjustments to ratios such as earnings per share and dividend per share so as to ensure that there is no substantive change in distribution or other financial policy: *Financial Reporting Standard* 14 (ASB) (October 1998); *ABI/NAPF Joint Position Paper on Pre-emption, Cost of Capital and Underwriting* (July 1996), para. 2.1; *Guidance on Share Issuing Good Practice for Listed Companies* (Bank of England) (October 1999) para. 21.

regime in the Companies Act 1985.[78] The reason given for this is that recent evidence suggests that pre-emption requirements have an important disciplinary effect on underperforming management by limiting their access to equity.[79] The Steering Group does not wish to dilute any such disciplinary effect. Yet it is debatable whether evidence about the importance that the market attaches to pre-emption rights necessarily points to the conclusion that those rights have to be retained in statutory form. Instead, it can be argued that the evidence supports an entirely different conclusion, namely, that so long as pre-emption rights continue to be viewed by the market as being important in terms of corporate governance or for other reasons, then those requirements can be imposed on companies through the market and that statutory underpinning in the form of additional specific rules is not required.

If statutory protection of pre-emption rights were to be withdrawn altogether, that would create theoretical opportunities for management to act in ways prejudicial to the interests of shareholders generally by issuing shares on a non-pre-emptive basis, thereby diluting existing shareholder interests and eroding the value of their investment. Although managerial decisions about methods of raising finance must be made in accordance with fiduciary duties,[80] factors such as difficulties in establishing standing to bring claims alleging breach of fiduciary duties[81] and the reluctance of the courts to second-guess business decisions,[82] limit the impact of these duties as a mechanism for controlling managerial power. Also, although it may not be to liking of its existing shareholders and therefore perhaps commercially unwise, it is debatable whether a managerial decision to raise finance by a non-pre-emptive issue of securities would be held to be in breach of fiduciary duty where the decision is based on the commercial advantages of the favoured issue structure on such matters as underwriting and other ancillary costs, but where for existing shareholders it has a dilutive and

[78] *Modern Company Law for a Competitive Economy. Developing the Framework* (Company Law Review Steering Group Consultation Document) (March 2000) paras 3.160 and 4.162. See also *Final Report* (July 2001) para. 7.31.

[79] J. Franks and C. Mayer, *Governance as a Source of Managerial Discipline* (Paper prepared for the Company Law Review, Committee E on Corporate Governance) (2000) *http://www.dti.gov.uk/cld/franksreport.pdf*).

[80] *Hogg v. Cramphorn Ltd* [1967] Ch. 254, ChD; *Bamford v. Bamford* [1970] Ch. 212, CA; *Howard Smith Ltd v. Ampol Petroleum Ltd* [1974] A.C. 821, PC.

[81] Difficulties in enforcing duties within the corporate context have been examined by the English Law Commission at length in its work on shareholder remedies: Consultation Paper no. 142 and Report no. 246 (1997). A dilutive share issue made in breach of fiduciary duties could be challenged as amounting to unfairly prejudicial conduct: *Re DR Chemicals Ltd* [1989] B.C.L.C. 383, ChD. Although the scope of the unfair prejudice remedy may have been reduced by the decision of the House of Lords in *O'Neill v. Phillips* [1999] 2 All E.R. 961, it is still possible to apply for relief under s. 459 where powers are used "in a manner which equity would regard as contrary to good faith" (at 967 per Lord Hoffmann).

[82] *Howard Smith Ltd v. Ampol Petroleum Ltd* [1974] A.C. 821, PC.

value-eroding effect. Under English law, the office of director does not carry with it any direct fiduciary duties to shareholders.[83] Therefore, such a decision would only be open to challenge in ordinary circumstances if it could be shown to be in breach of the directors' duty, owed to the company, to act in the interests of the company. This is unlikely. Although the English courts, and legislature, have not provided an entirely clear statement of how directors should resolve tensions between short and longer term considerations in exercising their powers, it is widely considered[84] that directors discharge their duties if they are guided by what they genuinely believe to be interests of the shareholders in the longer term. On this basis, there would be no breach in the suggested circumstances.

Yet, based on current U.K. market practice, it does not seem unreasonable to suggest that the concerns and issues mentioned in the last paragraph would remain of largely theoretical interest only if specific statutory underpinning for pre-emption rights were to be withdrawn for companies whose shares are actively traded in the securities market. In that event, given their strong preference for pre-emption rights, it is likely that institutional investors would impose their own equivalent pre-emption requirements and that commercial pressures would mean that companies would abide by them in the ordinary course of events. This suggestion is supported by the evidence provided by the market-based regulation of shares issues for non-cash consideration: although such issues fall outside the scope of statutory regulation, they are, in effect, subject to

---

[83] This is established in *Percival v. Wright* [1902] 2 Ch. 421 and is confirmed by more recent authorities: *Re Chez Nico (Restaurants) Ltd* [1991] B.C.C. 763; *Platt v. Platt* [1999] All E.R. (D) 818; *Penskin v. Anderson* [2001] B.C.C. 874, [2001] 1 B.C.L.C. 372. However, this does not preclude duties to shareholders arising in particular circumstances such as where there is an assumption of responsibility by directors to shareholders so as to give rise to a duty of care in tort (*Dawson International plc v. Coats Paton plc* (1988) 4 B.C.C. 305 at 314, Court of Session) or where there are special facts demonstrating a relationship of particular trust and confidence vested in the directors by the shareholders giving rise to fiduciary obligations: *Coleman v. Myers* [1977] 2 N.Z.L.R. 225, NZ SC and CA.

[84] The Company Law Review Steering Group (the body directing the current wide-ranging review of company law in the U.K.) recognizes that directors have a duty to build appropriate long-term relationships but acknowledges that there is case for making the true character of the duty more explicit: *Modern Company Law for a Competitive Economy. The Strategic Framework* (Company Law Review Steering Group Consultation Document) (February 1999), Ch. 5.1; *Modern Company Law for a Competitive Economy. Developing the Framework* (Company Law Review Steering Group Consultation Document) (March 2000), Ch. 2. See also The Final Report of the Committee on Corporate Governance (1998) (the Hampel Committee Report) para. 1.16; P. Goldenberg, 'Shareholders v. Stakeholders: The Bogus Argument' [1998] 19 Company Lawyer 34, 36–37; L.C.B. Gower, 'Corporate Control: The Battle for the Berkeley' [1955] 68 Harvard Law Review 1176 considering The Savoy Hotel Limited and the Berkeley Hotel Company Limited: Investigation under Section 165(b) of the Companies Act 1948: Report of Mr. E. Milner Holland, QC (HMSO, 1954) which includes the summary of an argument from Counsel that the 'Company' [means] the present and future members of the Company and that the board should conduct the company's business upon the footing that it would be continued as a going concern and accordingly should balance a long-term view against short-term interests of present members.

pre-emption requirements because of investor guidelines requiring issuers to give existing shareholders the right to "claw back" the new shares.[85] To the extent that there is concern about the limitations of market-based forms of regulation—ultimately the managers of a company could choose to ignore market requirements or guidelines reflecting investor expectations regarding pre-emption rights—then, if such actions were to be motivated by considerations other than the securing of corporate benefits, clearly stated directors' duties coupled with an effective enforcement regime (matters that are also on the U.K.'s reform agenda) would supplement and, arguably, adequately reinforce the market requirements.

Whilst deregulation of statutory requirements relating to pre-emption may not disrupt significantly the corporate governance control mechanisms operating between management and shareholders, it is also necessary to consider the position between different groups of investors. Deregulatory reform agenda that promote a shift towards market-based control and regulation need to be sensitive to possible market imperfections and one such imperfection is that not all participants in a market may have identical interests. If more opting out by shareholders is to be sanctioned, or regulation though statutory requirements is to be withdrawn altogether, the possibility of conflicts of interest between groups of shareholders should not be overlooked. Notwithstanding general deregulatory goals, careful consideration may need to be given to possible minority-protection mechanisms that should be built into the regulatory framework. It is possible to think of equity financing structures that could impact differently on different groups of investors. For example, an open offer, which is essentially a rights issue stripped of the traditional protections for shareholders who do not take up their rights, may, in broad terms, be expected to affect adversely at least some smaller shareholders who lack the financial resources to invest in the new shares or the financial acumen to appreciate the consequences of failing to do so; larger, institutional investors are unlikely to experience such difficulties. The potential for conflict of interests between investors becomes even more serious in companies that are dominated by a few shareholders, a rare situation in U.K. publicly quoted companies where, collectively, major institutions may dominate but no one institution is likely to hold a controlling stake but more common in other Continental jurisdictions. In such cases, the structure of a new issue may be largely driven by the personal preferences of the controlling shareholders and these may diverge significantly from the interests of other shareholders and perhaps also from the corporate interest in raising finance on the best terms commercially available.

Present day English company law does not restrict significantly the power of majority shareholders. Shareholders do not owe fiduciary duties to each other.

---

[85] ABI Guideline, *Shareholders' Pre-emption Rights and Vendor Placings.*

Exceptionally, the court may strike down shareholder actions on the grounds of "fraud on the minority", that is where the majority has used its power to oppress the minority but it is clear from the cases that where a decision of the shareholders secures commercial benefits for the company this will be sufficient to insulate it from effective challenge, regardless of the motives of the individual shareholders who voted in favour of it.[86] Even in respect of decisions that are neutral so far as the company's commercial interests are concerned (and in the context of this discussion, such situations are likely to be very rare since it will usually be possible to argue that there are corporate advantages in making an issue otherwise than on a fully pre-emptive basis with built in protections against value erosion), the English courts do not lightly intervene. In particular, the framework of English company law does not contain a clear rule to the effect that absence of a positive corporate benefit is itself sufficient to allow the court to strike down a decision that has a discriminatory effect on some shareholders.[87] Moreover, the concept of "fraud on the minority" is one that was developed by the courts largely to deal with shareholder resolutions that had a discriminatory effect. Where shareholders are able to impose their views simply through the operation of market forces, the English courts seem effectively powerless to intervene to check the exercise of majority power.[88]

So would statutory deregulation of equity financing procedures in favour of market-based regulation require new forms of legal control on majority shareholder power to be put in place? At least in the U.K. context, the answer to this question would seem to be no. First, such a development would not fit easily with the traditional reluctance of the courts to become embroiled in internal disputes involving companies with publicly traded shares. Secondly, for many investors the prospect of having to commence proceedings in order to obtain relief is likely to be unappealing; they are more likely to favour preventative measures. Thirdly, it would open up the possibility of disruptive and damaging litigation by maverick shareholders. Lastly, vesting such a power in the court could be an excessive response to a limited potential problem, at least so far the U.K. markets are concerned, and could be unduly restrictive to the proper

[86] P.L. Davies, *Gower's Principles of Modern Company Law* 6th edn. (London 1997) Ch. 26.

[87] It has been suggested that the legitimacy of the exercise of majority power should be judged by reference to its impact on the "individual hypothetical member" (*Greenhalgh v. Arderne Cinemas Ltd* [1951] Ch. 286 at 292). The test of the individual hypothetical member is, however, not one that can easily be applied and there is much force in the comment that this "member" is "one of the imaginary characters of company law who could safely be declared redundant": D.D. Prentice, 'Alteration of Articles—Expropriation of Shares' [1996] 112 L.Q.R. 194 (discussing *Gambotto v. WCP Ltd* [1995] 182 C.L.R. 432, H Ct (Aust) where the court sought to formulate a more workable test).

[88] Such conduct would not fall within the Companies Act 1985, s. 459 because that relates to unfair prejudice in the conduct of the company's affairs; in the circumstances envisaged, the powerful shareholders would be acting in their own interests: *Re Astec (BSR) plc* [1999] B.C.C. 59.

operation of a company's business. Although this chapter has highlighted the potential for conflicts of interests between groups of shareholders, very often such interests will in reality coincide: reverting back briefly to the open offer example mentioned earlier, the interests of major institutional investors in portfolio diversification should ensure that they monitor the use of issue structures that require shareholders to invest in the new securities in order to avoid value erosion. Although there are no formal institutional investor guidelines on open offers as yet, in this context it is relevant to note that the Association of British Insurers' has indicated that it would be concerned if transactions representing more than around 15% of existing issued capital or discounts above 7.5% did not make adequate provision for the protection of shareholders.[89]

To the extent that there is the potential for conflicts of interest, a looser form of intervention, say by means of a voluntary code that is not driven solely by the self-interest of a particular group, may be more appropriate than enhanced judicial control. The inclusion of suitable provisions in the conditions that must be satisfied by listed companies is an obvious possibility. But as well as the Financial Services Authority, in its role as U.K. listing authority, other agencies may also play a role in the development of regulation, as is illustrated by the recent intervention of the Bank of England in the area of underwriting commissions. Here, in what may in time be seen to be a classic example of soft lawmaking, that is the development of standards that are adhered to in practice even though they are not supported by sanctions enforceable through the courts or tribunals, the Bank has lent its authority to the development of innovative practices in the underwriting market. Concern about the lack of competition in the underwriting market formed the background to the Bank's intervention. Market failure in the form of anti-competitive practices provides at least a prima facie case for regulatory intervention in the public interest.[90] The Bank's intervention in this matter can be viewed as responsive regulation, that is, regulation that is responsive to market structures and to the behaviour of those who operate within it.[91] Although a low-level, "light touch" form of regulation, it is underpinned by the possibility of statutory intervention to correct market failure should the less intrusive method prove ineffective; this implicit threat provides a powerful incentive towards practical compliance.

---

[89] A. McCrum, 'Equity Funding: Stagecoach's Open Offer and International Offering' [1999] (X) 10 Practical Law for Companies 9.

[90] A. Ogus, *Regulation: Legal Form and Economic Theory* (Oxford 1994) 30–33.

[91] Generally, I. Ayres and J. Braithwaite, *Responsive Regulation—Transcending the Deregulation Debate* (Oxford 1992).

C. The Regulation of Underwriting Commissions, Underwriting Structures, and Share Issuing Good Practice

For many years underwriting commissions on rights issues in the U.K. market were fixed at the fairly standard level of two % of the proceeds of the issue. The bulk of this (1.25%) went to the sub-underwriters. Underwriting commissions at these levels were tolerated by the investment committees of the Association of British Insurers and the National Association of Pension Funds and were well within the limits on lawful commissions out of capital prescribed by the Companies Act 1985. Section 97 of that Act allows a commission to be paid provided payment is authorized by the company's articles and the amount paid does not exceed the amount or rate authorized by the articles or 10% of the issue price, whichever is the less.

However, in the 1990s, the Office of Fair Trading began to scrutinize the established underwriting practices in the U.K. markets on competition grounds. This review first came into prominence in November 1994 when the OFT published a research report which it had commissioned and which concluded that the fees charged by sub-underwriters greatly exceeded the value of the insurance of the success of the issue which they provided [92] The report made the point that some institutional investors were major participants in sub-underwriting activity and had thus the opportunity to earn significant fees from the company. The authors drew the conclusion that those who were at risk of losing out in the standard underwriting market processes were the issuing company's private investors and smaller institutions which were unable to participate in sub-underwriting. In the context of this chapter, this is an example of the already identified problem of potentially conflicting interests between groups of shareholders.

Over the following few years, there were a number of further OFT publications that continued to express dissatisfaction with market processes with regard to underwriting.[93] This dissatisfaction culminated in November 1997 with the matter of underwriting commissions being referred to the Competition

---

[92] P. Marsh, *Underwriting of Rights Issues: A Study of the Returns Earned by Sub-Underwriters from U.K. Rights Issues*, OFT Research Paper no. 6, November 1994. Previous research dating back to 1963 pointed towards the same conclusion: see Chapter 2 of the Marsh Research Paper. See also F. Breedon and I. Twinn, 'The Valuation of Sub-Underwriting Agreements for U.K. Rights Issues' [1996] 36 *Bank of England Quarterly Bulletin* 193.

[93] *Underwriting of Equity Issues*, Report by the Director General of Fair Trading, (March 1995) announcing a two year monitoring period; *Underwriting of Equity Issues OFT Report* (December 1996) containing a survey showing little evidence of change in market practices; OFT Press Release (July 1997) indicating dissatisfaction at the absence of vigorous competition in the underwriting market.

Commission[94] for investigation. The Commission's Report, published in February 1999,[95] found that complex monopoly situations existed in established underwriting practice and that the standard practice operated against the public interest. However, it refrained from recommending direct statutory intervention. Instead, it made a number of suggestions for changes in regulatory practice, including a recommendation that the Bank of England should publish guidance for companies on share-issuing good practice. The Bank's paper was duly published in October 1999.[96] The Bank encouraged companies to consider using a competitive tender process to set commission rates rather than the standard commission rates mentioned earlier and also to examine the possibility of arranging underwriting at a negotiated (as opposed to the standard) fee as an alternative to tendering for issues. Competitive tendering underwriting processes had, in fact, become a feature of the U.K. markets even prior to the publication of the Bank's paper. The scrutiny of established practices by the competition authorities might have acted as a catalyst for the development of these innovative structures designed to reduce underwriting costs.[97] In line with earlier publications from the competition authorities, the Bank of England's paper also suggested that in particular circumstances a deep discounted issue that is not underwritten might be a more cost effective way of meeting the objectives of the issue. This recommendation was based on the analysis of underwriting fees as being a direct cost to the issuer unlike the level of discount which is not a cost to the issuer and which does not affect shareholder wealth so long as protection against value erosion is in place. The Bank's paper acknowledged that companies might be reluctant to employ deep discount issue structures because past U.K. practice had been for their use to be largely confined to companies in financial difficulties; but commented that "there is no reason in principle why a deep discounted issue should be associated with a market perception of weakness on the part of the issuer". That market sentiment is moving in favour of deeply discounted issues is demonstrated by the structure of a rights issue by the Pearson Group in July 2000, the first major rights issue for some time. The new shares were offered at a heavily discounted price and although the issue was underwritten the fees charged by the underwriters amounted to just 0.5%, as opposed to the 2% that had historically been the market norm. Press coverage suggested that the company would have dispensed altogether with underwriting but for concerns raised by the

[94] Then known as the Monopolies and Mergers Commission.

[95] *Underwriting Services for Share Offers: A Report on the Supply in the U.K.* (Cm. 4168) (February 1999).

[96] *Guidance on Share Issuing Good Practice for Listed Companies* (Bank of England) (October 1999) (available at www.bankofengland.co.uk/shareissuing.htm)

[97] R. Hinkley, D. Hunter, M. Whittell, and M. Ziff, *Current Issues in Equity Finance* (London: Association of Corporate Treasurers 1988), 34–35.

U.S. vendor of the business that was to be acquired by Pearson using the proceeds of the issue as consideration.[98]

The appropriate regulatory strategy in given circumstances will depend on a range of factors, including the nature of the market that is to be regulated and its historical background, institutional framework and cultural context. The Bank of England's intervention in respect of underwriting commissions is an example of a regulatory technique—inviting the market to regulate itself with the implicit threat of an escalation in direct regulation by the state should that invitation be declined—that may, perhaps, be especially familiar in the U.K. context. There are many similar examples that could be cited but, for present purposes, reference to the Bank of England's (now disbanded) regulation of the new issues markets by the operation of an informal queuing system based on notification to the Bank may suffice. This type of "public authority assisted" self-regulation may not be entirely suitable for export to markets that do not share the same range of historical and other references as the U.K. and in particular circumstances, this approach may fall below the "minimal sufficiency principle" of regulation that others have described.[99] The recent Bank of England intervention with regard to underwriting is mentioned here simply to illustrate the point that in discussing the possible reform of rules that are presently imposed by statute, the choice should not be presented in stark terms: regulation v. deregulation. Rather, the point at issue is more often likely to be the choice of the appropriate regulatory response from the range of options that may be available. In this regard, the concept of "regulation" itself should be broadly interpreted as including control mechanisms, like market-based codes of practice, that may not be the product of direct state intervention, albeit that, in some instances, the state may indirectly influence their development.[100]

D. Conclusion

This chapter has used the specific example of pre-emption rights to examine the case for simplifying or reducing prescriptive company law requirements that may have become excessive in view of the maturity and sophistication of modern financial markets. It is an example that suggested itself because, in the U.K., investor preferences are well known and it is possible to identify both advantages and possible dangers in shifting more firmly towards a market-based regulatory system. In principle, other aspects of the rules on legal capital, such as the ban

---

[98] 'Pearson Undermines a Moribund Tradition' *Guardian* August 1, 2000.

[99] I. Ayres and J. Braithwaite, *Responsive Regulation—Transcending the Deregulation Debate* (Oxford 1992), 19.

[100] R. Baldwin, C. Scott, and C. Hood, *A Reader on Regulation* (Oxford 1998), 2–4.

on the giving of financial assistance, are susceptible to the same analysis.[101] The absolute[102] nature of the ban on the giving of financial assistance by public companies means that there is no established practice from which to gauge whether the statutory requirements broadly reflect equity investor preferences; though it seems reasonable to suggest that they can hardly be pleased about the expenditure that U.K. companies are reported to incur annually in obtaining legal advice on financial assistance[103] and that they would welcome at least some clarification of the statutory requirements.

Since the Second Directive is a barrier to the type of full-scale reform that might otherwise recommend itself, it is clearly essential that debate about reforming legal capital rules should take place at the European level as well as in the national context and that it should be treated as an element of a wider reform agenda rather than being tackled in a piecemeal fashion.[104] Recent U.K. companies legislation unhappily provides many examples of fragmentary law reform measures that were enacted in response to specific problems or immediate difficulties but which failed to achieve their intended effect[105] or which have never been brought into force because it was discovered after enactment that they did not work or would cause more problems than they solved.[106] Law reform is a

---

[101] Though the role of the law in protecting creditor, as well as shareholder, interests would then come more sharply into focus; the area of pre-emption rights is an unusual aspect of the rules on legal capital because it is a largely neutral topic so far as creditor interests are concerned. See E.V. Ferran, 'Creditors' Interests and "Core" Company Law' [1999] 20 Company Lawyer 314 for an analysis of the creditor-protection role of the ban on financial assistance and an assessment of proposals to reduce this role—i.e. to allow financial assistance with shareholder approval so long as the company providing the assistance is and will remain solvent (*Modern Company Law for a Competitive Economy. The Strategic Framework* (Company Law Review Steering Group Consultation Document) (February 1999) paras 5.4.20–25 and *Modern Company Law for a Competitive Economy. Company Formation and Capital Maintenance* (October 1999) paras 3.41–3.48. *Modern Company Law for a Competitive Economy. Developing the Framework* (Company Law Review Steering Group Consultation Document) (March 2000) paras 7.16–7.25 and *Final Report* (July 2001) para. 10.6 recommend the abolition of the ban on the giving of financial assistance by private companies.

[102] Subject to the exceptions provided by the Companies Act 1985, ss. 153–4. These provisions do not allow for shareholders to authorize the giving of financial assistance. Such a regime exists only for private companies (s. 155ff).

[103] *Modern Company Law for a Competitive Economy. The Strategic Framework* (Company Law Review Steering Group Consultation Document) (February 1999) para. 5.4.22 estimates that the cost to companies is some £20 million per annum. There is some anecdotal evidence that this may be an under-estimate.

[104] The work of the Company Law SLIM Working Group on The Simplification of the First and Second Company Law Directives (October 1999) is relevant here, although its proposals are somewhat modest. However, the High Level Group of Experts established by the European Commission in 2001 to define new priorities for the broader future development of company law in the European Union are working on a more ambitious set of proposals.

[105] For example, Companies Act 1985, s. 3A (general commercial company object).

[106] For example, Companies Act 1989, Pt. IV (company charges).

political process and any new legal rules that eventually emerge will inevitably be shaped by the pressures that are brought to bear on that process by powerful interest groups, who may see disadvantages to themselves in proposed reforms or who may be otherwise unwilling to embrace change. Also, the history of EC company law tells us clearly that divergences in Member States' markets and legal systems are likely to result in a slow pace of change at that level. But recognition of the fact that practical pressures may later whittle it down does not diminish, indeed may even reinforce, the importance of setting an ambitious reform agenda that is not necessarily captured by existing norms. Arguing from the specific examples considered in this chapter to a more general conclusion it is suggested that a strong case can be made for radical overhaul of the Second Directive with a view to restricting its scope and thereby allowing Member States to adapt their laws to modern market conditions and to opening up opportunities for market-based regulation assisted by sensitive intervention by regulatory agencies in appropriate circumstances.

6

Legal Capital Rules and the Structure of Corporate Law: Some Observations on the Differences Between European and U.S. Approaches

MARCEL KAHAN

Abstract

Legal capital rules are just one element of the general legal regime of creditor protection. Even though the rules on legal capital in the United States are extremely lax, fraudulent transfer law addresses, in a more general way, the very issue addressed by legal capital rules: distributions by companies to shareholders which harm creditors. Unlike legal capital rules, however, fraudulent conveyance law uses flexible standards, rather than fixed accounting figures, to distinguish permissible from impermissible distributions. Such standards are more sensible than the one-size-fits-all approach of legal capital rules in addressing this complex issue. A similar standard-based approach is used in the U.S. to limit the ability of corporate boards to issue shares for improper purposes. In this area, as well, the high quality of the judicial system in the U.S. and the relative infrequency in which the issue arises probably makes a standard-based approach preferable, at least for the U.S.

This commentary will address the two papers, by Professors Friedrich Kübler[1] and Eilis Ferran,[2] presented at the conference on the Rules on Capital under the Pressure of the Securities Markets.

Contents

A. Minimum Legal Capital Rules

Professor Kübler's chapter examines the minimum legal capital rules embedded in the various company laws in the U.S. and in the Member States of the European Union. He argues that there are major differences between the approach typically taken in the U.S. and the one prevailing in continental

---

[1] F. Kübler, 'The Rules of Capital under the Pressure of the Securities Markets', see above, Chapter 4.

[2] E.V. Ferran, 'Legal Capital Rules and Modern Securities Markets—The Case for Reform, as Illustrated by the U.K. Equity Markets', see above, Chapter 5.

Europe. To oversimplify, the U.S. rules are lax, while the European rules impose some meaningful constraints. Under the pressures of the securities market, Professor Kübler suggests, the European rules will, over time, become more like those in the U.S.[3]

I agree with Professor Kübler's assessment, both with respect to the present state and the future direction of the legal capital rules. In my commentary, I want to take a step back from Professor Kübler's analysis and look at the rules on capital from a broader perspective. First, I want to argue that legal capital rules should not be analyzed by themselves, but should be seen as an element of the general legal regime of creditor protection. Secondly, I want to ask how a regime for creditor protection should be designed; what role, if any, the rules on legal capital should play in it; and how we should view the pressure of securities markets to relax these rules.

One of the main thrusts of legal capital rules is to limit the ability of companies to make distributions to their shareholders when doing so would be harmful to the company's creditors. Legal capital rules create such limits by establishing minimum legal capital requirements. Distributions that would result in companies having less than the required minimum are prohibited. As Professor Kübler notes correctly, the primary goal of these rules is the protection of creditors.[4]

Since the rules on legal capital in the U.S. are extremely lax, one may be tempted to conclude that there is little legal protection for creditors in the U.S. This conclusion, however, would be mistaken. The law in the U.S. contains an extensive set of rules addressing, in a more general way, "distributions"—through dividends, share repurchases, or self-dealing transactions—by companies to shareholders which harm creditors. These rules fall under the heading of "fraudulent transfer law" and basically prohibit transfers by any person if two conditions are satisfied. First, the person does not receive "reasonably equivalent value". Secondly, the person is left, after the transfer, insolvent or with unreasonably small capital. Having intent to defraud is not required to violate these provisions.[5]

Fraudulent transfer laws are generally applicable, rather than specifically designed for corporations. Corporate distributions, however, raise some specific issues under fraudulent transfer law. In particular, if a corporation pays a dividend or repurchases its shares, does it receive reasonably equivalent value?

---

[3] See Kübler chapter, above n. 1.

[4] See Kübler chapter, above n. 1.

[5] See Uniform Fraudulent Transfer Act, § 4 (prohibiting transfers without receiving reasonably equivalent value when debtor was engaged in business for which remaining assets were unreasonably small); § 5 (prohibiting transfers without receiving reasonably equivalent value when debtor is insolvent).

The answer that most courts have given to this question is: "no".[6] Thus, in the U.S., *any* dividend and *any* sums a company pays to repurchase its shares is a fraudulent transfer *if* the company, after paying the dividend or repurchasing its shares, is left insolvent or with unreasonably small capital. Although the relevant threshold—"insolvency" and "unreasonably small capital"—is an imprecise standard, rather than a precise accounting figure, the thrust of these elements of fraudulent transfer law is obviously the same as the thrust of the legal rules on capital: to limit the ability of a company to channel cash to shareholders when its creditworthiness is impaired. Viewed in this light, I think, the difference between the U.S. and the Europe in the overall legal regime protecting creditors against distribution to shareholders is not as stark as Professor Kübler suggests.

Taking a further step back and asking how a legal regime of creditor protection ought to be designed, I think there is much to be said for the "fraudulent transfer" approach over the "legal capital" approach. This is especially true if one believes that the rules on creditor protection should not be entirely left to contractual arrangements.

Substantively, the "fraudulent transfer" approach differs from the "legal capital" approach in that it applies to all entities, not just corporations, and in that the threshold of when "distributions" are prohibited takes into account features that are company specific. In both respects, the "fraudulent transfer" approach is sensible. In particular, assessing the proper amount of capital for a firm is an extremely complex task that does not lend itself to a one-size-fits-all rule-oriented regime where the legislature imposes uniform "one size fits all" quantitative thresholds for all (or large subsets of) corporations.

One should also note that, within the U.S. system, the "fraudulent transfer" approach is *not* subject to the same competitive pressures that a "legal capital" approach would be. The rules on legal capital are part of the law on corporations, and the rules that apply to a corporation are principally those of its State of incorporation.[7] In the U.S., corporations, by choosing where to incorporate, can thus choose between legal capital rules of 50 different States. Moreover, they can, by changing their State of incorporation, opt out of one legal capital regime and into another *without* having to obtain the approval of, or having to give notice to, their creditors.[8]

Academics debate whether the competitive pressures that such a system produces are desirable or undesirable from the perspective of shareholders.[9] But

[6] See, e.g. *U.S. v. Gleneagles Investment Co, Inc* 565 F. Supp. 556 (MD Pa 1983).

[7] See, e.g. E.F. Scoles and P. Hay, *Hornbook on Conflict of Laws* 3rd edn. (St Paul 1999) § 23.2.

[8] See, e.g., Del Code Ann tit 8, § 252 (requiring approval of board of directors and shareholders for a merger into a foreign corporation).

[9] See, e.g., W.L. Cary, 'Federalism and Corporate Law: Reflections upon Delaware' [1974] 83 Yale Law Journal 663, 666 (competitive pressures undesirable); R. Romano, 'Law as a Product:

it is an altogether different question whether such a system results in optimal creditor protection. Even if one favours a regime of creditor protection that consists largely of default rules, it is unclear why the choice of rules that govern the internal affairs of the corporation (traditional corporate law) should be bundled with the choice of rules that govern the protection of creditors. And it would seem odd to permit shareholders and directors, by having the company reincorporate, to modify the applicable creditor-protective rules unilaterally. In other words, the present system is unlikely to result in *corporate law* rules that provide optimal *creditor* protection.

Fraudulent transfer law, however, is not part of the law of incorporations and the State law that controls is not the one of the State where the corporation is incorporated.[10] Thus the competitive pressures that are present with respect to corporation law are absent. If mandatory or quasi-mandatory creditor protection rules are desirable, this choice of law approach seems more sensible for the U.S. and, post *Centros*,[11] for Europe as well. But even if contractual freedom should reign supreme in the area of creditor protection, there are substantial arguments in favour of a modified fraudulent transfer approach, where parties select the applicable legal regime contractually, over a "legal capital" approach.

B. The Power to Issue New Shares

Let me also make some brief comments on Professor Ferran's paper, which looks at an entirely different set of capital rules: those constraining the power of directors of public companies to issue new shares. In the U.K., shareholders are permitted to, and do, grant directors the right to issue, over the next year, shares in an amount up to 5%, if made on a non-preemptive basis, or up 33%, if made on a preemptive basis.[12]

In the U.S., corporate law fiduciary duties limit the ability of boards to issue shares for improper purposes.[13] (In addition, stock exchange rules require shareholder approval for share issuance that exceeds 20% of the company's outstanding shares.)[14] Preemptive rights are rare. In the U.K., Professor Ferran tells

Some Pieces of the Incorporation Puzzle' [1989] 1 *Journal of Law, Economics & Organizations* 225 (competitive pressures desirable).

[10] T.H. Day, 'Solution for Conflict of Laws Governing Fraudulent Transfers: Apply the Law That Was Enacted to Benefit the Creditors' [1993] 48 Business Lawyer 889 (noting that situs of transferred property is most significant factor in determining applicable law).

[11] *Centros Ltd v. Erhvervs- og Selskabsstyrelsen* [1992] 2 Common Market Law Review 551.

[12] See Ferran chapter, above, n. 2.

[13] See generally *Schnell v. Chris-Craft Indus Inc* 285 A, 2d 437 (Del 1971) (board of directors may not exercise its powers for inequitable purposes).

[14] See, e.g., New York Stock Exchange Listed Company Manual § 312.03; NASD Manual § 4310(c)(25)(H)(i) (relating to Nasdaq SmallCap issuers) and § 4460(i)(1) (relating to Nasdaq National Market issuers).

us, fiduciary duties are weak, and restrictions on directors' powers therefore need to be stronger.[15]

The pattern of regulation here thus resembles the one for shareholder distributions with respect to creditor protection. The U.S. adopts a more imprecise, standard-like, ex post, adjudicatory approach (fiduciary duties for share issuance; an "unreasonably small capital" threshold for shareholder distributions). The U.K. adopts a more precise, rule-like, ex ante, regulatory approach (quantitative thresholds).

Which approach is preferable? The answer is not self-evident. Indeed, different approaches may be preferable in different countries. Two factors, however, may be important in choosing between regulation via standards and regulation via rules. The first is the quality of the judicial system. The approach in U.S. relies more on competent judges, who are needed to distinguish accurately share issuance that ought to be deemed fiduciary duty breaches from those that do not. Delaware's corporate judiciary, in particular, enjoys a reputation for its expertise and high quality.[16] The second factor is the frequency with which the issue arises.[17] The more often share issuance arguably run afoul of fiduciary duties, the more costly is the U.S. approach of ex post review and the more efficient becomes an ex ante regulatory approach.

In fact, relatively few cases have arisen in the U.S. where directors of public corporations have been accused of breaching their fiduciary duties by approving an issuance of shares. While this does not conclusively establish that abusive share issuance are rare in the U.S., it creates a prima facie case that the system of ex post regulation is, for the U.S., the superior one.

[15] See Ferran chapter, above, n. 2.

[16] See E. Kamar, 'A Regulatory Competition Theory of Indeterminacy in Corporate Law' [1998] 98 Columbia Law Review 1908 (arguing that quality of Delaware judiciary is more important in system where laws are standard based).

[17] See L. Kaplow, 'Rules versus Standards: An Economic Analysis' [1992] 42 Duke Law Journal 557.

Part III:

Disclosure and Accounting

7

Financial Disclosure and Accounting

KAREL VAN HULLE[1]

Abstract

This chapter describes the development of the accounting harmonization in the EU from a minimum amount of harmonization based upon the principle of equivalence for all limited liability companies, to a more sophisticated harmonization for listed companies based upon one single set of accounting standards. As it proved impossible to increase the level of harmonization on the basis of the Accounting Directives, the Commission proposed in 1995 to allow global players to prepare their consolidated accounts on the basis of International Accounting Standards (IAS). This chapter describes how this worked in practice and how the Commission—in close co-operation with Member States—did its utmost best to ensure a coherence between the Directives and IAS. Finally, the chapter sets out the new policy whereby all listed EU companies will be required to prepare their consolidated accounts on the basis of IAS by 2005. The chapter concludes by insisting on the need for a closer co-operation between interested parties in the EU on accounting issues. Such co-operation will now be possible within the European Financial Reporting Advisory Group (EFRAG), which will provide technical expertise to the Commission.

Contents

A. Introduction

Harmonization of accounting rules within the EU has not been an easy matter. Harmonization is carried out through the Accounting Directives,[2] which were

---

[1] The views expressed in this chapter are attributable only to the author.

[2] Fourth Council Directive (EEC) 78/660 on the annual accounts of certain types of companies [1978] O.J. L222/11; Seventh Council Directive (EEC) 83/349 on consolidated accounts [1983] O.J. L193/1; Eighth Council Directive (EEC) 84/253 on the approval of persons responsible for carrying out the statutory audits of accounting documents [1984] O.J. L126/20; Council Directive (EEC) 86/635 on the annual accounts and consolidated accounts of banks and other financial institutions [1986] O.J. L372/1; Council Directive (EEC) 91/674 on the annual accounts and consolidated accounts of insurance undertakings [1991] O.J. L374.

not intended to develop a new system of accounting but tried to make an acceptable compromise between the different accounting traditions that existed (and continue to exist) in Member States. Important features of the Directives are that they apply to all limited liability companies and that they do not contain any specific rules for listed companies or for companies having made a public issue of securities.

As a result of the implementation of the Accounting Directives, the quality of the financial information published by companies in Member States has considerably improved. However, it must be admitted that financial statements produced by companies from different Member States are still not readily comparable. This is a direct consequence of the large number of options in the Accounting Directives, but also results from the fact that many important accounting issues are not dealt with in the Directives.

It is interesting to note that the continued existence of important differences between the financial information provided by companies in Member States has never been seriously criticized. Apparently, market players were satisfied with the minimum level of harmonization introduced by the Directives. The only problem that arose in practice was related to the lack of disclosure of financial statements in certain Member States. This was felt to be harmful from the point of view of competition.

Things began to change in the beginning of the nineties, when an increasing number of major European companies had to turn to the capital markets in order to satisfy their need for capital. The markets required those companies to provide information that was more extensive and sometimes also different from the information they had to prepare on the basis of their national legislation based upon the Accounting Directives. Producing different sets of financial statements—one required by the Directives and another imposed by the capital markets—is confusing and burdensome. This is the reason why the Commission published a Communication in 1995,[3] in which it proposed to Member States to permit global players to prepare their consolidated financial statements on the basis of International Accounting Standards (IAS), provided these standards are in conformity with the Accounting Directives.

Since the introduction of the Euro on January 1, 1999,[4] pressure has been mounting in European financial markets to have a more harmonized framework for financial reporting. In its 1999 Communication on Financial Services,[5] the Commission therefore announced that it would come forward as soon as possi-

---

[3] Communication of the European Commission on '*Accounting Harmonization: A New Strategy vis-à-vis International Harmonisation*', COM 95(508).

[4] For the accounting aspects relating to the introduction of the Euro, see European Commission, *Accounting for the introduction of the Euro*, XV/7002/97.

[5] Communication of the European Commission on '*Financial Services: Implementing the Framework for Financial Markets: Action plan*', COM (1999) 232.

ble with proposals that would give a direct option to companies to prepare their financial statements in accordance with IAS, always under the condition that there are no conflicts with the Accounting Directives. In order to ensure that conflicts between the Directives and IAS are kept to a minimum, the Accounting Directives would be amended in order to adapt them to international accounting developments and to the needs of the Single Market.

On June 13, 2000, the Commission adopted a new Communication on the EU Financial Reporting Strategy,[6] in which it is proposed that all listed EU companies prepare their consolidated financial statements in accordance with IAS at the latest in 2005. The Communication announced that the Commission would introduce a formal proposal before the end of 2000. IAS will be introduced into the EU legal environment after endorsement by a mechanism to be set up at EU level. This mechanism will comprise a technical and a political level. Furthermore, a proposal to amend the Accounting Directives was introduced by the Commission in May 2002. The intention is to remove as far as possible conflicts between the Directives and IAS and to adapt the Directives to changes that have taken place in the area of financial reporting since their adoption. On February 13, 2001, the Commission adopted a proposal for a Regulation on the application of IAS.[7] This proposal introduces the requirement for all listed EU companies and for all EU companies whose securities are offered to the public to prepare their consolidated financial statements for each financial year on or after 1 January 2005 in conformity with the IAS adopted by the EU endorsement mechanism. The proposal also provides the framework for setting up an Accounting Regulatory Committee that will decide on the adoption of IAS for use within the EU.

This chapter describes how the Commission's new Accounting Strategy was developed and what its possible consequences will be for the future of accounting harmonization in the EU.

B. Alternative Solutions Considered in Developing the 1995 Accounting Strategy

When the Commission was faced in the early nineties with the question of how to solve the problem of global players that were looking for capital on international capital markets and that had to produce two different sets of financial statements, it considered a number of possible solutions.

---

[6] Communication of the European Commission on '*EU Financial Reporting Strategy: the Way Forward*', COM (2000) 359.

[7] Proposal for a Regulation of the European Parliament and of the Council on the application of international accounting standards, COM (2001) 80.

I. Conclusion of a Mutual Recognition Agreement with the U.S.

The real problem for European global players is the access to the U.S. capital market. A solution would therefore consist of obtaining an agreement with the U.S. on the mutual recognition of accounts. The Commission has attempted to initiate such discussions, but has found little interest on the American side. Accounts prepared by U.S. companies under U.S. GAAP are in fact already recognized in all Member States. This is not the case in the U.S. for accounts prepared by European companies in accordance with the Accounting Directives. Furthermore, the Directives themselves do not provide a sufficiently detailed set of standards to meet U.S. requirements and there are important differences between Member States as a result of the many options included in the Directives. For the Commission, it became quickly clear that the obtaining of a mutual recognition agreement with the U.S. was not a realistic proposition.

II. Exclusion of Global Players from the Scope of Application of the Directives

Another solution that was examined by the Commission was the exclusion of large listed companies from the scope of application of the Accounting Directives. These companies would then be free to follow other rules. Although this solution appeared attractive at first sight, it quickly turned out to be a thorny issue because an answer had to be given to a number of difficult questions, such as the scope of the exclusion (all listed companies, certain listed companies, companies with important non-EU shareholdings, etc.) and the rules that the excluded companies would then have to apply (international accounting standards, U.S. standards or both). Further problems related to the need to amend a number of Directives and to the inevitable consequence of abandoning the homogeneous approach to accounting harmonization.

III. An Update of the Accounting Directives

Because one of the problems is that the Accounting Directives are not sufficiently detailed, a solution would have consisted of updating the Directives, to include technical solutions for the various accounting issues that have not yet been dealt with. This would have required an amendment of the Directives. It would have been difficult to agree on the issues that should have been covered in such a revision. Furthermore, some Member States would certainly have tried to renegotiate those parts of the Directives they did not like. The preparation and negotiation of such an important revision of the Directives would have taken a long time and new issues would probably have arisen by the time the amendments had been fully adopted and implemented in Member States.

IV. Creation of a European Accounting Standards Board

Another option considered by the Commission was the creation of a European Accounting Standard Setting Board. Such a body would have provided the EU with the possibility of adopting common solutions for the many technical problems arising in the accounting field. However, setting up such a body (which would have required legislation) and developing a comprehensive set of European accounting standards would have taken a great deal of time. In addition, there was the fear that such a solution would eventually result in the creation of an additional layer of standards between national standards and international standards.

C. Characteristics of the 1995 Accounting Strategy

In developing a new accounting strategy, the Commission paid particular attention to respecting the principles of subsidiarity and proportionality enshrined in the Maastricht Treaty. New legislation or amendments to existing legislation at EU level should be avoided as far as possible.

The creation of an additional layer of standards on top of those already existing or in preparation should be avoided. There is no need to develop European standards for the sake of having European standards when other solutions are equally satisfactory.

It was also clear that a more flexible framework was needed, which could respond rapidly to current and future developments. Unless the framework adopted at European level can be changed without too many difficulties, there is a risk that the solutions adopted are cast in stone. If these solutions no longer correspond with today's needs, it is difficult to justify their existence.

Finally, it was important for the proposed approach to provide legal certainty and to ensure the respect for Community law.

After lengthy discussions with Member States and interested parties, the Commission published in November 1995 a Communication "Accounting Harmonization: a New Strategy vis-à-vis International Harmonization", in which a new approach to accounting harmonization is proposed. The Commission suggests in its Communication that it put its weight behind the international harmonization process that is already well under way in the International Accounting Standards Committee (IASC). Global players in Europe should be allowed to prepare only one set of financial statements, preferably prepared in accordance with International Accounting Standards and possibly with a distinction between annual and consolidated accounts.

In the Commission's opinion, the production of two sets of financial statements is not only costly but also confusing. The publication of different figures in different environments undermines the investor's confidence in the published financial information. It is therefore of utmost importance that European companies can satisfy differing requirements by producing only one set of financial statements.

The Commission clearly prefers a solution whereby large European companies seeking capital on international capital markets can produce their financial statements on the basis of International Accounting Standards (IAS). The preference for IAS is justified by the fact that only the IASC is producing results that have a clear prospect of recognition in the international capital markets within a timeframe that corresponds with the urgency of the problem. Through the agreement with the International Organization of Securities Commissions (IOSCO) there is a real possibility that the major global securities regulators will accept in the not too distant future financial statement based upon an agreed set of IAS.

The preference expressed in favour of IAS means at the same time that the Commission does not advocate the preparation of financial statements by European companies on the basis of U.S. GAAP. American standards are developed without any European input. They are designed to satisfy the needs of the American capital market and are not necessarily suitable in a European context. The Commission is however aware of the fact that a growing number of large European companies prepare their financial statements on the basis of U.S. GAAP. This is particularly the case for those European companies that are listed on the New York Stock Exchange. To the extent that the financial statements prepared by these companies are also in conformity with the Accounting Directives, there is strictly speaking no problem from a European point of view. Nevertheless, the Commission believes that this can only be a next best solution and that preference should be given to a solution that is more international.

The preparation of financial statements in accordance with IAS means for many companies in Europe that they must distinguish between annual accounts and consolidated accounts. This pragmatic solution is indeed needed for those companies that are based in Member States where there is a close linkage between accounting and taxation. In most instances, consolidated accounts have the advantage of not being the basis upon which the distributable or taxable profit is based. The application by a parent undertaking of different accounting policies in its parent entity accounts and its consolidated accounts is possible in those Member States which have introduced the option provided for in article 29(2) of the Seventh Directive. The use of different valuation rules is possible on condition that the rules are in conformity with the Fourth Directive.

In its Communication, the Commission makes it quite clear that its option in favour of IAS implies that the EU participates more actively in the work of the International Accounting Standards Committee.

D. Examination of the Conformity Between IAS and the Accounting Directives

The preparation of consolidated financial statements on the basis of IAS is only possible to the extent that there are no conflicts between IAS and the Accounting Directives. It was therefore important for the Commission to examine with Member States to what extent conflicts exist. In order to do this, a Task Force was set up composed of experts from the Commission and Member States. The Task Force concluded that there were in 1996 no major conflicts between IAS and the Accounting Directives. As a result, it was possible for a European company to prepare its consolidated accounts in conformity with IAS without being in conflict with the Accounting Directives.

The findings of this Task Force were endorsed by the Contact Committee on the Accounting Directives, which is chaired by the Commission and is composed of those representatives of the Member States who are directly responsible at national level for accounting matters. The findings were published by the Commission in 1996.[8]

I. Interpretation of the Conclusions of the Contact Committee on the Conformity Between IAS and the Accounting Directives

The Contact Committee has since 1996 also examined all IAS that were adopted since that time. Separate positions have been published on IAS 1,[9] on IAS 12,[10] on IAS 35, IAS 36, IAS 37, IAS 38, IAS 22 (revised 1998), IAS 16 (revised 1998), IAS 28 (revised 1998), IAS 31 (revised 1998),[11] IAS 19,[12] IAS

[8] Contact Committee on the Accounting Directives, *An Examination of the Conformity Between the International Accounting Standards and the European Accounting Directives*, European Commission, Office for Official Publications of the European Communities, Luxembourg, 1996, 22 pages.

[9] European Commission, Directorate-General XV, *Examination of the Conformity Between IAS 1 and the European Accounting Directives*, Brussels, XV/7030/98.

[10] European Commission, Directorate-General XV, *Examination of the Conformity Between IAS 12 and the European Accounting Directives,* Brussels, XV/7012/97.

[11] European Commission, Directorate-General XV, *Examination of the Conformity Between IAS 35, IAS 36, IAS 37, IAS 38, IAS 22 (revised 1998), IAS 16 (revised 1998), IAS 28 (revised 1998), IAS 31 (revised 1998) and the European Accounting Directives*, Brussels, XV/6010/99.

[12] European Commission, Directorate-General XV, *Examination of the Conformity Between IAS 19 (revised 1998) and the European Accounting Directives*, Brussels, XV/6020/99.

32,[13] and IAS 40.[14] No separate position has been published on IAS 41 (Agriculture) because the issue covered in that standard is not dealt with in the Accounting Directives. It is the intention to bring all these position papers together into one single document now that IASC has completed its core set of standards and that a new IASC Board has been nominated.

In order to give immediate guidance to companies that wanted to prepare their financial statements over the financial year 1998 in accordance with IAS, the Commission published a position paper in April 1999[15] in which it indicated to what extent problems could arise in relation with the IAS that had already entered into force. The main conclusion of this document is that there are at present no major conflicts between IAS and the Accounting Directives. A similar document has been prepared for financial statements for the financial year starting on or after 1 January 1999.[16]

The only conflict identified in the document relates to the exclusion from the scope of the consolidation of certain subsidiaries. This problem is dealt with in IAS 27 and in article 14(1) of the Seventh Directive. Article 14(1) of the Seventh Directive states that an undertaking must be excluded from the consolidated accounts when its inclusion would be incompatible with the true and fair view principle. In contrast, IAS 27 only provides for exclusion from consolidation when control is intended to be temporary or where the subsidiary operates under severe long-term restrictions.

However, the Commission observes that whilst there seems to be a textual conflict between IAS 27 and the Directive, it is doubtful whether this will have any effect in practice. For example, while IAS 27 does not allow for the exclusion from consolidation of a subsidiary on the grounds of different activities, it is a matter of judgment as to whether the consolidation of enterprises that undertake different activities would be incompatible with the true and fair view principle. In fact, current thinking is that such undertakings should be consolidated, with the appropriate segmental information being given in the notes to the accounts in order to explain the performance of the individual operations. The Contact Committee failed to see any case where article 14 would actually require the exclusion of an undertaking from consolidation. It must however be

[13] European Commission, Directorate-General XV, *Examination of the Conformity Between IAS 32 (revised 1998) and the European Accounting Directives*, Brussels, XV/6026/99.

[14] European Commission, Directorate-General Internal Market, *Examination of the Conformity Between IAS 40 and the European Accounting Directives*, Brussels, MARKT/6904/01.

[15] European Commission, Directorate-General XV, *Examination of the Conformity Between IAS in Issue and Applicable to Accounting Periods Beginning Before 1 July 1998 and the European Accounting Directives*, Brussels, XV/6005/99.

[16] European Commission, Directorate-General Internal Market, *Examination of the Conformity Between IAS in Issue and Applicable to Accounting Periods Beginning Before 1 July 1999 and the European Accounting Directives*, Brussels, XV/6003/2000.

observed that this examination does not extend to the area of financial conglomerates.

Views differ on the question whether a bank should be allowed to consolidate an insurance subsidiary or vice versa.

This latest examination of the conformity between IAS in issue and applicable to accounting periods beginning before July 1, 1999 and the European Accounting Directives also includes all applicable interpretations of the Standing Interpretations Committee.[17] The Commission has published a separate position paper concerning the conformity between SIC-16 and the European Accounting Directives.[18] This interpretation deals with the difficult question of the acquisition by a company of its own shares. The paper concludes that there is no conflict with the Directives. However, it also pointed out that, in Member States where purchases of own shares for trading purposes are allowed and the shares are dealt with by the company like any other security, capitalization is considered appropriate and consistent with the balance sheet layout requirements in the Fourth Directive. Although SIC-16 does not allow such treatment, it is considered more appropriate than to deduct the shares from equity.

Since the publication of the last conformity document, which dealt with IAS in issue and applicable to accounting periods beginning before July 1, 1999, IAS 37 on Provisions, Contingent Liabilities, and Contingent Assets has entered into effect. This standard creates a conflict with the prudence principle to be found in Article 31(1)(c)(bb) of the Fourth Directive, where a restructuring is announced after the balance sheet date but before the financial statements are formally prepared. In that case, the Fourth Directive would require companies to create a provision in order to cover the future liability, whilst IAS 37 would not allow this because the announcement took place after the end of the financial year.

The examination by the Contact Committee does not contain a value judgment on IAS as such. IAS clearly contains requirements that go beyond what is necessary and they do not contain certain elements that are imposed by the Directives. Rather than examine which set of rules is the better one, the Contact Committee asked itself the question to what extent a hypothetical European company that wants to prepare its financial statements in accordance with IAS can do so without being in conflict with the Accounting Directives. There was a presumption that a European company that wants to apply IAS will be prepared to conform to all the requirements, even with those that it might find too burdensome. At the same time, it is clear that those requirements imposed by the

---

[17] All these analyses can be found on the Commission's website at *http://europa.eu.int/comm/internal_market/en/company/index.htm*

[18] European Commission, Directorate-General XV, *Examination of the Conformity Between SIC-16 and the European Accounting Directives*, Brussels, XV/6035/99.

Accounting Directives that go beyond what is required by IAS must equally be complied with.

The absence of any value judgment is important because it shows the commitment of the EU towards international harmonization. This is very different from a similar study undertaken in 1996 by the Financial Accounting Standards Board which concluded that there are no less than 255 differences between IAS and U.S. GAAP, implying that much still needs to be done before IAS will reach the high quality level of U.S. GAAP.[19]

There are at present no major conflicts between IAS and the Accounting Directives. This does not mean that there are no conflicts with national law. The Accounting Directives contain an important number of options. It may well be that national law has chosen an option that is not allowed under IAS. For instance, whilst IAS 38 requires the capitalization of development costs, national law may prohibit such capitalization. As the Fourth Directive makes the capitalization of research and development costs a Member State option, there is no problem from a European point of view.

In the same way, it is presumed that where the Accounting Directives give an option to companies, companies will apply that option that is in conformity with IAS. For instance, whilst article 35(3)(b) of the Fourth Directive allows companies to apply direct costing in the case of inventory, IAS 2 requires full costing.

The absence of major conflicts also results from the fact that IAS contains a number of options. Companies can select those options that are in conformity with the Accounting Directives. For instance, companies do not have to value their investments at the higher market value at the balance sheet date. They can opt for the valuation at the lower of cost or market, which is in conformity with the Fourth Directive. There are a number of other issues where it is important to read the conclusions arrived at by the Contact Committee, which point out which accounting treatment provided for in a particular IAS should be followed in order to ensure compatibility with the Accounting Directives.

II. Possible Solutions at Member State Level

The Contact Committee has only looked into possible conflicts between the Accounting Directives and IAS. It has not examined to what extent the application of IAS is possible under national law. Theoretically speaking, two possibilities exist for opening up the national accounting environment to companies wishing to apply IAS.

One solution could consist of the introduction into national law of those accounting options that are available under the Accounting Directives but have

---

[19] Financial Accounting Standards Board, *The IASC-U.S. Comparison Project: A Report on the Similarities and Differences between IASC Standards and U.S. GAAP,* Norwalk, 1996.

not yet been implemented. The adaptation of national law would then allow companies to comply both with the Directives and with IAS.

As an example, one could refer to the question of capitalization of development costs. Some Member States do not allow development costs to be capitalized. IAS 38 requires this. The Fourth Directive allows Member States to permit or to require the capitalization of development costs. If a Member State that presently prohibits the capitalization of development costs would decide to amend its national legislation to bring it in line with IAS 38, it could perfectly well do so, without coming into conflict with the Fourth Directive on this point.

Denmark has decided to take this route: the present accounting legislation is being rewritten so as to make it both IASC and EU compatible and at the same time more user-friendly. This solution was also discussed in France and in Germany. In both countries, a debate has taken place on whether new options should be introduced into the law so as to make it possible for companies to comply both with IAS and with the Accounting Directives. The situation in these countries is different from that in Denmark because in France and in Germany there is a close linkage between accounting and taxation. This makes it impossible to adopt IAS as the basis for financial reporting by all companies. Whilst the introduction of new accounting options would make it more difficult to compare the accounts of companies at national level, it would have the advantage of providing legal certainty and of preventing national law from becoming outdated.

A second solution would be to exclude certain companies from the application of national law and to allow them to apply a different set of rules, such as IAS, which is more acceptable to international capital markets. The implementation of this solution immediately raises two questions: which companies should be excluded from the application of national law and which alternative set of rules should be allowed. Both questions have been discussed at length, particularly in Austria, Belgium, Finland, France, Germany, Italy, and Luxembourg. In all cases, the exemption only applies to consolidated accounts because these accounts are normally used in an international environment and have no direct tax or profit distribution consequences.

On the first issue, the debate focused on whether the exclusion should only apply to those companies that have an international vocation, i.e. those companies that are listed on a foreign capital market, or are preparing a listing on a foreign capital market, or whether all listed companies should be allowed to claim the exemption. While France, Germany, and Italy have in the end decided to apply the exemption to all listed companies, Belgium has opted for the first approach with some changes. Companies with important activity abroad or companies (such as oil companies) operating in a sector where a specific set of accounting rules (such as U.S. GAAP) is used may also claim the exemption.

On the second issue, problems have arisen with those companies that were already applying U.S. GAAP. These companies wanted to continue to do so and did not favour a solution that would only have allowed the application of IAS. As Parliaments were often involved in the debate, there was a lot of discussion about U.S. supremacy. Preference seems to have gone towards a solution that would still allow Europe to have some say in the process. The French law, for instance, allows the application of U.S. GAAP until December 31, 2002 (the time at which the IASC-IOSCO agreement would normally have entered into effect). Similarly, in Germany, the exemption only applies until the financial year 2004. In Belgium, it was decided to leave the matter for the moment in the hands of the government and the supervisory authorities, which may grant an exemption. It is understood that a law might be enacted as soon as the situation has become clearer at international and at European level.

Whichever solution is chosen, there can be no doubt that the application of an alternative set of rules is only possible to the extent that there are no conflicts with the Directives. Member States can indeed exempt a company from the application of national law. They cannot do so from the application of Community law.

It will therefore be very important in practice to examine to what extent the foreign rules (primarily IAS or U.S. GAAP) contain provisions that are in conflict with the Accounting Directives. Companies will not be able to apply those rules and if they were to do so, the auditors would have to qualify the accounts.

In order to deal with this problem, France (Law of April 6, 1998) has set up a special Committee (*Comité de Réglementation Comptable*) that must screen the foreign rules. This Committee will also examine to what extent the foreign rules comply with Community law. In practice, the system has not yet become operational in France because it is not always clear to what extent conflicts exist with Community Law.

In Italy, the Law of February 6, 1998 empowers the government to identify the accounting rules which listed companies may be allowed to apply. The Law states explicitly that the government, in co-operation with the Supervisory Authorities, can only identify accounting rules that are in conformity with the Accounting Directives.

In Belgium, the Commission for Banking and Finance or the Minister of Economic Affairs may allow companies listed on international capital markets or with an international vocation to depart from the accounting rules prescribed by Belgian law, on the condition that these rules are in conformity with the Accounting Directives. The auditor must specifically confirm in his report the compliance with the mandatory provisions of the Accounting Directives. In Germany, the *Kapitalaufnahmeerleichterungsgesetz* of February 13, 1998 allows listed companies to depart from the German accounting rules on consolidation and to apply internationally recognized accounting principles on condition that the consolidated accounts are in conformity with the Accounting Directives. The question to what extent foreign accounting rules are in conformity with the Accounting Directives is entirely left to companies and their auditors. The auditor must confirm in his report that the conditions for the exemption have been satisfied, which implies that the company does not apply accounting rules that are contrary to the Accounting Directives. In order to assist companies and their auditors in answering this question, an Accounting Standards Committee (*Deutsches Rechnungslegungs Standards Committee*) has been set up, which— besides giving some guidance on accounting matters in Germany—can assist companies and their auditors in assessing to what extent the application of foreign rules and particularly of IAS or U.S. GAAP is creating problems in the local environment. The DRSC has recently published a standard dealing specifically with the question of the conformity assessment between the Directives and IAS or U.S. GAAP.

III. The New Role of the Contact Committee as regards IASC

In order to ensure conformity between the two sets of rules, the Contact Committee on the Accounting Directives is closely monitoring the work of IASC. Since 1991, the Commission has been an observer on the Board of the IASC. A representative from the Commission attends the Board meetings without voting rights. The representative does not speak on behalf of all Member States because there is no official mandate to do so. In addition, the Commission participates in a number of Steering Committees. Here also, the Commission representative does not have voting rights and does not represent as such Member States. A Commission representative also attends the meetings of the Standing Interpretations Committee in an observer capacity.

In order to help the Commission observer in carrying out his task, two initiatives have been taken as a result of the New Accounting Strategy. A special Technical Subcommittee has been set up under the Contact Committee on the Accounting Directives. This Technical Subcommittee meets three to four times a year and discusses the various papers, draft statements of principles, and exposure drafts published by the IASC. In practice, the Technical Subcommittee meets prior to each IASC Board meeting. On the basis of the discussions in the Technical Subcommittee, the Commission sends its comments to the IASC. These comments do not necessarily reflect the unanimous position of Member States but they certainly express the majority position. The second initiative taken consists in the appointment of a technical adviser, who accompanies the Commission representative to his meetings within IASC. This technical adviser, a technical partner of Ernst & Young in London, was selected on the basis of a public tender procedure. His main role is to help the Commission in the technical formulation of positions to be defended within IASC.

IV. The Need for Legal Certainty

It is of utmost importance that there is legal certainty. Position papers are therefore published at regular intervals by the Commission services on the basis of discussions within the Contact Committee. These papers clearly state those areas where conflicts exist. In practice, all IAS and Interpretations by the SIC are screened for their conformity with the Accounting Directives.

The option in favour of IAS can only be made real if the IASC refrains from adopting solutions that are clearly in conflict with the Accounting Directives. The European Board members have a particular responsibility in this respect. If solutions are adopted that are not acceptable in a European context, companies that have opted for IAS will be forced to comply with the Accounting Directives and to prepare a reconciliation statement that shows the differences between the figures arrived at on the basis of the Accounting Directives and the figures that would have resulted from a full application of IAS. This is burdensome and should be avoided.

One potential major conflict, concerning IAS 1 "Presentation of Financial Statements" could be avoided. Originally, this standard did not recognize the overriding character of the true and fair view principle. This has now been corrected in the final standard. Against considerable opposition from the U.S., but also from Australia and Canada, the Board adopted a solution that requires companies in exceptional circumstances to depart from an IAS in order to show a true and fair view. It is important that on this point the Board has agreed to give priority to professional judgment rather than to support the so-called cookbook approach.

Of course, one should remain flexible. The worst thing would be to insist on solutions that do no longer meet the needs of today's environment. This is the reason why the Commission has announced in its Communication on a New Accounting Strategy that it will not hesitate to propose changes in the Accounting Directives, where such changes appear necessary, notably in order to avoid conflicts with IAS.

The area in which conflicts are most likely to occur in the near future is that of the recognition and measurement of financial instruments. After discussions with Member States in the Contact Committee, the Commission has recently proposed an amendment to the Fourth Directive and Seventh Directives that introduces fair value accounting for certain financial assets and liabilities.[20] This amendment is necessary because the Directives are based on the principle of his-

---

[20] Proposal for a Directive of the European Parliament and of the Council amending Directives 78/660/EEC and 83/349/EEC as regards the valuation rules for the annual and consolidated accounts of certain types of companies, COM (2000) 80 of February 24, 2000.

torical cost and there is a growing tendency in Member States to mark to market certain items, such as marketable securities.

The issue of fair value accounting has become more urgent since the adoption by the Board of IASC of IAS 39 "Financial Instruments: Recognition and Measurement" in December 1998. The proposal does not apply to banks or insurance companies. Rather than enter into a detailed description of the rules to be followed in fair valuing financial assets and liabilities, the proposal requires Member States to allow or require all or certain companies to fair value certain financial assets and liabilities. The proposal should therefore be seen as an enabling exercise allowing Member States to permit companies to comply with IAS without being in conflict with the Accounting Directives.

The adoption of the New Accounting Strategy in 1995 has made it possible to agree on a number of questions that had remained on the table for many years. Because a decision had to be made about the conformity of certain IAS with the Directives, Member States were forced to give a clear indication as to whether certain accounting solutions were covered by the existing text of the Directives. The Contact Committee, for instance, indicated that the inclusion of positive exchange differences on monetary items in the profit and loss account was not contrary to the prudence principle contained in Article 31 of the Fourth Directive. This statement means that Member States can no longer argue that there is a conflict with the Directive. Another question is whether Member States must allow this accounting treatment. In order to clarify the meaning of a number of provisions in the Accounting Directives, the Commission has published in January 1998 an Interpretative Communication concerning certain Articles in the Fourth and Seventh Council Directives on Accounting.[21] This Communication aims to give guidance to bodies responsible for setting accounting standards in the Member States, to accounting professionals, and to users and preparers of accounts. The views expressed in this Communication are based upon discussions that were held within the framework of the Contact Committee on the Accounting Directives and the Accounting Advisory Forum. They do not necessarily represent the unanimous position of all Member States. However, by publishing these interpretations, the Commission hopes to contribute to creating more legal certainty.

Particularly important is the reminder in the Communication that the consolidated balance sheet and profit and loss account must be drawn up in accordance with the layouts prescribed by the Accounting Directives and that no valuation methods can be applied that are in conflict with those allowed under these Directives. This is an important message to those companies that want to prepare their accounts in conformity with IAS or U.S. GAAP.

[21] O.J. C16 of January 20, 1998.

E. Towards a Mandatory Application of IAS

On June 13, 2000, the Commission published its Communication "EU Financial Reporting Strategy: the Way Forward" in which it is proposed to move harmonization a step further. Whilst the 1995 Communication was looking primarily at the situation of European global players going to international capital markets, this Communication looks into the requirements that need to be put in place in order to allow a European capital market to come about. There is general agreement that Europe has the potential of creating a capital market that can match that in the U.S. However, we are not there yet. Many things will have to improve in order to bring about an efficient capital market at European level. Financial reporting plays an important part in this. There needs to be more disclosure and more comparability. The main ideas announced in the Communication are now translated into an official Commission proposal, i.e. the Proposal for a Regulation of the European Parliament and of the Council on the application of international accounting standards, which was issued on February 13, 2001.

I. Requirement for Listed EU Companies to Apply IAS

Comparability of financial information, which is an essential feature of an efficient capital market, requires the use of the same standards by all market players. This is the reason why the Commission is now proposing to introduce a requirement for all listed companies to prepare their consolidated financial statements in conformity with IAS by 2005 at the latest. The same requirement will apply to all companies preparing a public offer prospectus (Article 4 of the Proposed Regulation). This proposal is far-reaching (it will directly affect some 7,000 companies in the EU) and elevates IAS to a higher level than they have at present.

Unlisted companies planning to make an initial public offering of their securities might also wish to use IAS. The Commission therefore proposes that Member States be permitted either to require or to allow unlisted companies to publish their financial statements in accordance with the same set of standards as those for listed companies. More specifically for unlisted financial institutions and insurance companies, Member States may wish to extend the requirement to apply IAS to facilitate sector wide comparability and to ensure efficient and effective supervision.

Because of the need for comparability, the Commission decided not to allow companies to choose between national standards, IAS or U.S. GAAP. In the same way, the Commission decided that all listed EU companies should apply the same rules and that there should not be specific exemptions for small listed companies.

In order to ensure that the requirement to apply IAS will enter into effect at the same time in all Member States, the requirement is introduced through a Regulation rather than through a Directive. A Regulation has direct effect and does not require specific implementation by Member States. This avoids delays in transposition and reduces the risk of national variations.

II. The Exercise of Public Oversight

IASC is a private organization. It would not be wise to delegate accounting standard setting unconditionally and irrevocably to a private organization over which the EU has no influence. In addition, it is important to create legal certainty by identifying the standards that listed companies will have to apply in the future. This is the reason why the Commission proposes the creation of an endorsement mechanism at EU level. This endorsement mechanism will also examine whether the standards adopted by the IASC conform to EU public policy concerns. The IAS used in the EU will be the standards endorsed by this mechanism. The endorsement mechanism will have a technical and a political component.

As far as the technical component is concerned, the Commission has asked the European Federation of Accountants (FEE) to examine the possibility for setting up a technical structure at EU level that would combine the main parties that are interested in financial information, i.e. users and preparers as well as the accounting profession and the accounting standard setters. Negotiations are far advanced and will lead to the creation of a private sector body, named EFRAG "European Financial Reporting Advisory Group". A technical committee, composed of highly qualified experts, will be set up. It will provide technical expertise concerning the use of IAS within the European legal environment. It will participate actively in the international accounting standard setting process and organize the co-ordination within the EU of views concerning IAS. The Commission will be represented in this committee in an observer capacity.

As for the political component, this matter is dealt with in the Accounting Regulation. A regulatory committee, the Accounting Regulatory Committee, will be set up. This Committee will operate under established comitology rules. The Committee will be chaired by the Commission and composed of representatives of the Member States. It will adopt or reject IAS on the basis of a proposal made by the Commission. In accordance with the normal comitology procedure, the European Parliament will be informed about the work of the Accounting Regulatory Committee. The European Parliament can also intervene if it considers that the Commission has exceeded its powers.

III. Enforcement

Introducing a set of uniform accounting standards for listed EU companies is one thing, making sure that the standards are effectively complied with is quite another matter. Enforcement in the field of financial reporting in the EU is weak as compared with enforcement in the U.S. Problems will further increase if companies are allowed to apply other than national standards. There is therefore a need for more effective enforcement. Securities regulators in Europe are worried that in the absence of an effective enforcement mechanism, Europe could end up finding itself in a similar situation as the U.S. in the early thirties. Lack of guidance on standards to be applied and lack of supervision on the way the standards are being applied might well undermine the confidence in the expanding European capital market. This must be avoided at all costs.

Enforcement comprises a cascade of different elements including clear accounting standards, timely interpretations and implementation guidance, statutory audit, monitoring by supervisors, and effective sanctions. The endorsement mechanism should take care of the first two elements. On statutory audit, there is the work of the EU Committee on Auditing that was set up in 1998 as a result of the Commission Communication on Statutory Audit.[22] This Committee, which is chaired by the Commission and composed of representatives of Member States and of the accounting profession, is discussing a number of issues that aim at establishing an equivalent and high level of statutory audit quality throughout the EU. These issues relate to the identification of the auditing standards that should be applied, the contents of the audit report, audit quality assurance, and the independence of the statutory auditor.

Securities supervisors also have a crucial role in ensuring that listed companies comply with financial reporting requirements. There is clearly a major interest in ensuring accurate and consistent application of accounting standards in the securities markets that they oversee. The Forum of European Securities Commissions is discussing ways and means to improve the present situation. It has set up a specific Accounting Group that will closely monitor the work of the endorsement mechanism at EU level and that will also discuss enforcement issues. The securities supervisors should develop and implement a common approach to enforcement. Such an approach would establish a level playing field and avoid the danger of regulatory arbitrage.

---

[22] Communication of the European Commission on 'Statutory Audit in the European Union: the way forward', O.J. C143 of May 8, 1998.

F. Concluding Remarks

The 2000 Communication and the Proposed Accounting Regulation make it clear that the EU has opted in favour of IAS as a means to improve comparability of financial statements for listed EU companies.

However, most companies in the EU are unlisted and although Member States have the possibility to allow or require the application of IAS for unlisted companies as well, it is clear that most unlisted companies will be hesitant to adopt a reporting framework that is very detailed and complicated. For the large majority of companies within the EU, the Accounting Directives will still remain relevant. However, they need to be modernised and made IAS compatible as far as possible. This is a major challenge. After extensive consultations with Member States, the Commission introduced a formal proposal in May 2002.

The Commission has opted for a regime whereby all limited liability companies will remain subject to the Accounting Directives. Listed companies will have to apply IAS to the extent that there are no conflicts with the Accounting Directives. The removal of conflicts can be done by appropriate amendments to the Directives. It can also take place by exempting those companies that apply IAS from certain provisions of the Directives. Companies need to be in a position to move from one reporting system (Accounting Directives as implemented by national law) to another (endorsed IAS) without being unduly hindered.

The Commission has declared its support for the work of IASC. Meanwhile, IASC has adopted a new structure that is radically different from that which existed before. The new structure is a mirror image of that which exists in the U.S. Just like FASB, the new Board of IASC, which is now called IASB (International Accounting Standards Board), is primarily composed of full-time members. These members were appointed by the Board of Trustees on January 25, 2001. The Board does no longer comprise observers so that the Commission is removed from the Board in the same way as IOSCO, the Basle Committee, and China. Although there are now five European Board members out of a total of 14 members, there is no specific European representation on the Board so that it is not certain that a European perspective will be defended within the new Board. These are important changes that have caused worries both with the Commission and with Member States. Given the EU's choice in favour of IAS, it is important that the EU as such is represented in an appropriate manner within IASC. This is also the explicit wish of the European Parliament that was expressed in a letter sent by the Chairperson of the Economic and Monetary Committee to Commissioner Bolkestein, who holds responsibility for the Internal Market.

Much of the support IASC has received during the last couple of years is related to the hope that IOSCO might at some stage publicly endorse IAS so that financial statements prepared on the basis of IAS would be acceptable to securities regulators around the world. IOSCO adopted last year a resolution that supported the IASC's core set of standards although a number of reservations were made. The main stumbling block is the SEC, which has published a Concept Release in 1999, through which it has opened the debate in the U.S. on the acceptability of IAS for listings within the U.S. The tone of this document is very critical towards anything that differs from the U.S. regulatory scene. The SEC also broadens the debate to include auditing, corporate governance, and enforcement. It remains to be seen whether the SEC will find enough support for opening up the U.S. market for standards which are not directly or indirectly based upon U.S. GAAP. Because the SEC has expressed support for the new structure of IASC and because two members of FASB are now included in the Board of IASC, it is hoped that this will result in more convergence between IAS and U.S. GAAP.

The success of IASC will to a large extent depend upon developments within the EU. If a European capital market is developed on the basis of IAS, there will be a valid alternative to U.S. GAAP and IAS will become operational in practice. The increased harmonization that will result from this for listed companies throughout Europe will have a positive impact upon harmonization for other companies.

The restructuring of the IASC in 2001 and the creation of a new International Accounting Standards Board (IASB) with full-time members has certainly been influenced by developments in the EU. The announcement by the EU that IAS will be the reporting framework for consolidated financial statements of listed EU companies from 2005 onwards has greatly increased the importance of IAS. Greater involvement of the US in the work of the IASB should also contribute to convergence between IAS and U.S. GAAP. Meanwhile, the EU has delivered on its promise: on 7 June 2002, the Council of Ministers adopted the Commission's proposal for a Regulation[23] on the application of IAS, after this proposal already received an overwhelming support in the European Parliament on 12 March 2002.

---

[23] Regulation (EC) No 1606/2002 of the European Parliament and of the Council of 19 July 2002 on the application of international accounting standards (2002) O.J. L243/1.

8

The Impact of Transparency Regulation on Company Law

WERNER F. EBKE

Abstract

Transparency rules have gained increasing attention, both in theory and practice, as a means for monitoring corporations and their managers. This chapter will explore the current and the possible future impact of transparency regulation on corporate governance. The author argues that transparency is not just a fashionable word, but rather a relevant and valuable legal, economic, and political concept that will shape corporate law, corporate legal scholarship, and corporate practice in the years ahead. The author concludes that those who believe that corporate governance will function just as well as without transparency carry a heavy burden of persuasion.

Contents

A. Introduction
B. In Search of Answers
C. Conclusions

A. Introduction

This chapter will explore the current and the possible future impact of transparency regulation on the law of business associations. In some ways the question is part of a very old debate concerning the separation of ownership and control in public corporations. However, the modern corporate governance debate in both the U.S. and the EU does give that old question a new twist. Traditionally, the discussion revolved around the question of what significance structural and organizational transparency has for the monitoring of corporate management.[1] Several comparative studies have revealed a gradual convergence of the management and monitoring structures employed on both sides of the Atlantic.[2] In recent years, financial, capital market, and social transparency rules have gained increasing attention, both in theory and practice, as a means

---

[1] D.F. Vagts, 'Reforming the "Modern" Corporation: Perspectives from the German' [1966] 80 Harvard Law Review 23; M.A. Eisenberg, *The Structure of the Corporation: A Legal Analysis* (Toronto 1976).

[2] See, e.g. M.J. Roe, 'Some Differences in Corporate Structure in Germany, Japan, and the United States' [1993] 102 Yale Law Journal 1927.

for monitoring corporations and their managers.[3] Legal comparison has begun to study the interaction of the various transparency rules and their impact on corporate governance in different legal traditions.[4] Yet, it is still largely unsettled whether the various corporate governance systems are moving more towards a transparency-driven approach to the monitoring of corporate managers or whether structural and organizational arrangements for corporate control will ultimately prevail.

Moreover, transparency is also part of two more recent debates that are linked to, but distinct from, the corporate governance issue. The first debate concerns the role that transparency rules may play in the European Union in overcoming the current stagnation of the process of company law harmonization from 'the top down' by means of European legislation.[5] Should the promulgation of European transparency rules be seen as a viable alternative to company law harmonization? To what extent, if any, can European transparency legislation substitute, or at least effectively supplement, company-law based monitoring mechanisms and devices that vary widely from one Member State to another? Are there any adverse or semi-adverse consequences likely to flow from more far-reaching European transparency requirements?

The second debate concerns the increasing significance of global financial transparency. This debate relates to the role of U.S Generally Accepted Accounting Principles (U.S. GAAP) and International Accounting Standards (IAS) as a means to improve the efficiency of capital formation in light of the mandate for investor protection.[6] While seven of the 15 EU Member States now permit parent companies and internationally operating companies to employ foreign or international accounting principles (in lieu of the principles required by the law of the corporation's State of incorporation),[7] 'bridging the

---

[3] See, e.g. B. Grossfeld and W.F. Ebke, 'Controlling the Modern Corporation: A Comparative View of Corporate Power in the United States and Europe' [1978] 26 American Journal of Comparative Law 397.

[4] See, e.g. W.F. Ebke, 'Unternehmenskontrolle durch Gesellschafter und Markt' in O. Sandrock and W. Jäger (eds.) *Internationale Unternehmenskontrolle und Unternehmenskultur* (Tübingen 1994) 7; B. Grossfeld and W.F. Ebke, 'Probleme der Unternehmensverfassung in rechtshistorischer und rechtsvergleichender Sicht' Part I [1977] 22 *Die Aktiengesellschaft* 57, Part II, [1977] 22 *Die Aktiengesellschaft* 92; A. Conard, 'The Supervision of Corporate Management: A Comparison of Developments in European Community and United States Law' [1984] 82 Michigan Law Review 1459.

[5] W.F. Ebke, 'Company Law and the European Union: Centralized versus Decentralized Lawmaking?' [1997] 31 International Lawyer 961; P. Behrens, 'Krisensymptome in der Gesellschaftsrechtsangleichung' in U. Immenga, W. Möschel, and D. Reuter (eds.) *Festschrift in Honor of Ernst-Joachim Mestmäcker* (Baden-Baden 1996) 831.

[6] W.F. Ebke, 'Rechnungslegung und Prüfung im Umbruch' [special issue June 1997] 36 *Mitteilungen der Wirtschaftsprüferkammer* 12.

[7] W.F. Ebke, 'Die Internationalisierung der Rechnungslegung, Revision und Publizität und die Schweiz' [2000] 119 *Zeitschrift für Schweizerisches Recht* 39, 59.

GAAP'[8] appears to be an almost insurmountable obstacle in some other countries, including the U.S.[9] In addition, the question arises whether the principles underlying the global financial reporting framework should be set nationally (e.g. by legislation, governmental agencies or private standard-setting bodies) or by international or supranational standard-setters.[10] Furthermore, different opinions exist as to the present and future objectives of financial accounting and reporting.

B. In Search of Answers

The answers to these and other related questions are organized as follows: Part I will briefly review the meaning of transparency. Part II will highlight various aspects of structural transparency and their impact on the law of corporations. Part III will provide a series of examples to illustrate how organizational transparency affects the law of corporations. Part IV will discuss the impact of financial transparency and make the case for international, as opposed to national, financial accounting principles and disclosure requirements for listed companies and 'global players'. Part V will address the question of whether, in the European Union, transparency legislation is a viable alternative to the harmonization of company law. Part VI will review how social transparency will change the governance of corporations.

I. The Meaning of Transparency

Transparency is not just a fashionable word.[11] It is an 'eleventh commandment' of Western democracies.[12] Democratic societies insist generally on openness and

---

[8] E.M. Sherbet, 'Bridging the GAAP: Accounting Standards for Foreign SEC Registrants' [1995] 29 International Lawyer 875. See also J.D. Cox, 'Rethinking U.S. Securities Laws in the Shadow of International Regulatory Competition' [1992] 55 Law & Contemporary Problems 157, 157; M.B. Fox, 'Securities Disclosure in a Globalizing Market: Who Should Regulate Whom' [1997] 95 Michigan Law Review 2498.

[9] On 16 February 2000, the Securities and Exchange Commission (SEC) issued a Concept Release on International Accounting Standards, 17 CFR pts 230 and 240 (2000). The Release solicits input about the quality of the International Accounting Standards (IAS) of the London-based International Accounting Standards Committee (IASC). The SEC's request for comments is, however, seen by some as 'a shrewd ploy by the SEC chief'. His hope, some say, is to bolster his stand against the IAS by building support from U.S. companies. See M. McNamee, 'Can the SEC Make Foreign Companies Play by its Rules?' [2000] *Business Week* at 46 (March 6, 2000).

[10] W.F. Eke, 'Accounting, Auditing and Global Financial Markets' in T. Baums, K.J. Hopt, and N. Horn (eds.) *Corporations, Capital Markets and Business in the Law. Liber Amicorum Richard M. Buxbaum* (The Hague 2000) 113.

[11] B. Vesterdorf, 'Transparency—Not Just A Vogue Word' [1999] 22 Fordham International Law Journal 902.

[12] L. Lowenstein, 'Financial Transparency and Corporate Governance: You Manage What You Measure' [1996] 96 Columbia Law Review 1335, 1342.

transparency through all three branches of government. In the European Union, too, transparency is recognized as a fundamental principle.[13] Democratic societies do require openness and transparency as part of the public's unquestioned (if sometimes exaggerated) 'right to know'.[14] Transparency also plays an increasingly important role in the context of (public) corporations. Most studies on transparency in the context of public corporations begin with a reference to leading writers of the early 1900s such as Louis D. Brandeis, a progressive author and eventually an influential Supreme Court Justice,[15] Felix Frankfurter who helped select the draftsmen of the federal securities laws and who was instrumental in shepherding the Securities Act of 1933 through Congress,[16] and, of course, Columbia professors Adolph A. Berle and Gardiner C. Means who first recognized the separation of ownership and control in the large modern corporation.[17] As Professor Steve Thel has pointed out correctly, disclosure was not an end in itself for Brandeis, but a means to an end—breaking up the untoward concentration of economic power in the hands of the 'money monopoly'.[18] Berle and Means discussed the concept of disclosure predominantly in the context of corporate power and a lack of accountability to shareholders and the public.

The separation of ownership and control was not a conscious choice. Nobody ever made a decision that companies would work better if they separated ownership and control. Rather, it was an almost inevitable consequence of the technological and procedural changes made in order to meet the needs of a rapidly changing economy.[19] We know now that the phenomenon of separation of ownership and control is by no means confined to corporations. Rather, similar developments can be observed in other business associations, including cooperative societies (*Genossenschaften*).[20] However, in the past and current debates about management and control, the corporation has been the centre of attention.[21] This should not come as a surprise in view of the fact that the corporate form is so appealing, so essential. The limited liability for investors, the free transferability of investor interests, the legal personality (entity-attributable

[13] L.J. Brinkhorst, 'Transparency in the European Union' [1999] 22 Fordham International Law Journal 128; C. Timmermanns, 'Subsidiarity and Transparency' [1999] 22 Fordham International Law Journal 106.

[14] Lowenstein, above, n. 12, 1342.

[15] L.D. Brandeis, *Other People's Money and how Bankers Use It* (Boston 1914).

[16] See J. Seligman, *The Transformation of Wall Street* 2nd edn. (New York 1995) 57, 78.

[17] A.A. Berle and G.C. Means, *The Modern Corporation and Private Property* (New York 1932).

[18] See S. Thel, 'The Original Conception of Section 10(b) of the Securities Exchange Act' [1990] 42 Stanford Law Review 385, 405–06 and n. 90.

[19] R.A. Monks and N. Minow, *Watching the Watchers; Corporate Governance for the 21st Century* (Cambridge 1996) 101.

[20] B. Grossfeld, *Genossenschaft und Eigentum* (Tübingen 1975).

[21] This chapter will focus primarily on public corporations.

powers, life span, and purpose), and centralized management have contributed to the vitality and the appeal of the corporate form and facilitated the accumulation of capital, resources, and influence.[22] Today, corporations exercise vast power in all democratic societies. Legislators, judges, and academics better accept it as a fact and move on from there.

It is equally true that most shareholders of large corporations do not participate in the activities by which their 'property' is managed and by which the corporation affects its shareholders, third parties (e.g. employees, creditors, and consumers) and the public at large, both nationally and internationally. It is indisputable that shareholders of public corporations have largely been unable, and sometimes also unwilling, to exercise the responsibilities of ownership of corporations. Shareholders of modern public corporations typically vote with management or sell their shares ('Wall Street rule'). The proxy systems that have developed in both the U.S. and the EU Member States have not succeeded in making shareholders an influential element in the decision-making processes and the monitoring of corporate management. Electronic shareholder voting, which several corporations in the U.S. and in Europe have begun to implement and which is already specifically permitted by some corporation laws,[23] may induce some shareholders to participate more actively in corporate governance.[24] Yet it is questionable whether the availability of on-line voting will solve the basic problem of the rational ignorance of shareholders.

The rapid growth of institutional shareholdings has not changed the situation much. Empirical and other research has shown that institutional investors are equally reluctant, both in the U.S. and the European Union, to be active monitors of the companies they invest in.[25] Monitoring or taking board seats is viewed by institutional investors as only one possible way of maximizing performance and will continue to have to compete with the alternative strategies of sale, whether in the market or to a bidder, or of passivity (i.e. waiting for other pressures on unsuccessful management to take effect).

Not surprisingly, therefore, corporate management has become more and more powerful. However, power without accountability invites abuse, in

---

[22] See Grossfeld and Ebke, above, n. 4, 22 *Die Aktiengesellschaft* 63–64; R.C. Clark, *Corporate Law* (New York 1986) 2.

[23] See, e.g. Va Code Ann Section 13.1–847 (Repl. Vol. 1999).

[24] G.P. Kobler, 'Shareholder Voting Over the Internet: A Proposal for Increasing Shareholder Participation in Corporate Governance' [1998] 49 Alabama Law Review 673.

[25] See, e.g. T. Baums, R.M. Buxbaum, and K.J. Hopt (eds.), *Institutional Investors and Corporate Governance* (Berlin/New York 1994); B. Black, 'Agents Watching Agents: The Promise of Institutional Investor Voice' [1992] 39 University of California at Los Angeles Law Review 811; Symposium, 'The Institutional Investor's Goals for Corporate Law in the Twenty-First Century' [2000] 25 Delaware Journal of Corporation Law 35; R. Romano, 'Less is More: Making Institutional Investor Activism a Valuable Mechanism of Corporate Governance' [2000] 18 Yale Journal on Regulation 174.

government as well as in business. Therefore, the single major challenge addressed by corporate governance is how to grant managers the necessary discretionary power over the conduct of the business and affairs of the corporation while holding them accountable for the use of that power. Academics, judges, legislators, shareholders, managers, board advisors, and even directors themselves continue to disagree as to how corporate executives can be monitored efficiently and effectively. And, indeed, there are no easy answers.

In this situation, comparative legal research may be particularly helpful. While one may not find final solutions abroad for one's own corporate governance problems at home, the comparative method may help to better understand existing models and available options. A thorough comparative analysis is particularly essential in multi-jurisdictional legal systems such as the EU and the U.S.[26] Moreover, transnational comparative legal studies provide interesting insights into the close interaction between a country's legal tradition and corporate culture on the one hand and corporate governance on the other.[27] A closer look reveals that all corporate governance systems in the EU and the U.S. build, more or less, on structural, organizational, financial, capital market, and social transparency to influence corporate governance and corporate behaviour.

II. Structural Transparency

While some countries, in particular the U.S., rely heavily on financial transparency, individual incentives (including stock options, stock compensation, and performance-based management compensation), the disclosure of potential conflicts of interests, and the private enforcement of breaches of fiduciary duties, many continental legal systems have traditionally relied more heavily on structural mechanisms (board of outside directors, external auditors, and labour representatives on the board) to ensure that corporate power is exercised not only in the best interest of the corporation and its shareholders but also of society at large.[28]

---

[26] W.F. Ebke, 'Die Zukunft der Rechtsetzung in multijurisdiktionalen Rechtsordnungen—Wettbewerb der Rechtsordnungen oder zentrale Regelvorgabe: am Beispiel des Gesellschafts- und Unternehmensrechts' [special issue no. 28, 1999] 118 *Zeitschrift für Schweizerisches Recht* 106.

[27] For a more detailed exposition of this view, see Ebke, above, n. 4, 14–21; R.J. Gilson, 'Globalizing Corporate Governance: Convergence of Form or Function', [2001] 49 American Journal of Comparative Law 329; J.C. Coffee, 'The Future as History: The Prospects for Global Convergence in Corporate Governance and Its Implications' [1999] 93 Northwestern University Law Review 641.

[28] B. Grossfeld, 'Management and Control of Marketable Share Companies' [1973] 13 International Encyclopedia of Comparative Law Ch. 4.

1. Board Structures

Corporate boards of directors are a ready example in support of this proposition. Obviously, boards are a crucial part of the corporate structure.

a. The Basic Models

Legal systems have different views, however, as to the mechanisms and structures used to keep executives accountable to the directors as well as the mechanisms and structures used to keep the directors accountable to the shareholders. Over the past 40 years or so, the structure of the board of directors of European and American companies has been cogently analysed in enormous depth by both lawyers and economists. More recent research shows that three basic models have gained widespread acceptance: the unitary board model including both management and supervisory roles, the unitary board model including inside and outside (and sometimes independent) directors, and the two-tier or dual board model. The latter two models recognize a need for a special link between those who provide the capital (the shareholders) and those who use the capital to create value (the managers), and that this link's primary role is to monitor management on behalf of the shareholders. Proponents of the two models mentioned disagree, however, as to whether there needs to be a sharp separation of executive and monitoring functions.

b. Sharp Separation versus Flexibility

Despite much criticism, many Western European countries (e.g. Austria, Germany, Denmark, France, and The Netherlands) have opted for the two-tier board model, although in some countries (e.g. France) the two-tier board model is not mandatory. The separation of management and control is not a formality and certainly not one about titles and compensation. It is a question of power and, equally important, of *structural transparency*. The two-tier system of management and control has the advantage of clearly separating from each other the management of the corporation by the executive board and the supervision exerted by the supervisory board.[29] The legislators of the countries mentioned favour a clear (even though not always clean cut) separation of the roles because they believe it will lead to more objective oversight and evaluation of the corporation's executives and create an environment of greater accountability. Even those who favour the American-style unitary board system concede that the major advantage of the two-tier model is, 'that it achieves the separation of those

---

[29] Grossfeld, above, n. 28, 10 and n. 50.

who manage from those who monitor in a particularly sharp manner, and therefore results in extreme organizational transparency'.[30] This transparency is, of course, needed in certain countries (e.g. Germany) to effectuate a system of labour representation (*unternehmerische Mitbestimmung*) on the board that is designed to integrate employee representatives into the corporation's monitoring system and decision-making processes.

Needless to say, the two-tier system is far from being perfect, but it is in many respects much better than its reputation in various academic and other circles. The outside directors' (*Aufsichtsrat*) ability to oversee management (*Vorstand*) is, no doubt, undermined by the fact that many outside directors are unable to devote sufficient time or resources to the job. And in some cases the outside directors may even lack the competence and professionalism that it takes to monitor management effectively. To what extent the lack of competence and professionalism can be offset by the representatives of institutional investors and large banks on the board is still unclear and would seem to depend upon the individual circumstances of each corporation.

Of course, a separation of executive and monitoring functions can be achieved even without a sharp and formal separation of management and control.[31] Many American corporations have, as Melvin A. Eisenberg quite properly noted almost 25 years ago, already adopted 'working structures strikingly similar to the two-tier system'.[32] Yet, structural transparency does seem to have its advantages. While there has not been much empirical work, at least one study found that in the U.S. companies with separate CEO and chairmen consistently outperform those companies that combine the roles.[33] For these and other reasons, some commentators have recommended that a company should not permit a single individual to serve as both its CEO and chairperson of its board of directors. Alternatively, if a company allows a single individual to serve as its CEO and chair, Harvard Business School professors Jay Lorsch and Martin Lipton, among others, have asserted that a company's board of directors should select a senior independent director to lead the independent directors.[34] It should also be noted that the two-tier board system may have a positive impact on the solution of numerous other corporate governance issues such as the nomination and election of directors, management compensation, interlocking directorates, and the appointment and remuneration of the corporation's independent auditor.

[30] Eisenberg, above, n. 1, 183.

[31] ibid., 183.

[32] ibid., 180.

[33] P.L. Rechner and D.R. Dalton, 'CEO Duality and Organizational Performance: A Longitudinal Analysis' [1991] 12 *Strategic Management Journal* 155.

[34] For details, see C.E. Bagley and R.H. Kopples, 'Leader of the Pack: A Proposal for Disclosure of Board Leadership' [1997] 34 San Diego Law Review 149.

2. Independent Auditors

The statutory audit is an essential element of the system of corporate governance and transparency, both in the EU and in the U.S.

a. Role

The role of the statutory auditor is to examine periodically the financial statements of the audited company and to express an opinion as to the truth and fairness of the views expressed in the financial statements that are prepared by the executives of the company.[35] Unlike their counterparts in the U.S., the corporation laws of all EU Member States now require medium-sized and large corporations, and even unincorporated business associations (e.g. limited partnerships with a sole corporate general partner[36]) to have their annual, though not their quarterly and other interim, financial statements audited by independent accountants. In the U.S., federal securities laws finally broke the silence of the State corporation laws by requiring companies falling in the ambit of the Securities Exchange Act of 1934 to include in their annual report (Form 10–K) audited and certified financial statements. In addition, certain industries (e.g. banks and insurance companies) are subject to statutory audit requirements. Yet, the number of companies subject to a statutorily required audit remains to be significantly lower in the U.S. than in the EU—a fact the legal, economic, and political consequences of which have never been analysed properly.[37] Moreover, the scope of an audit varies widely from one country to another. In some European countries (e.g. Germany) auditors are now required by law to examine, and to express an opinion on, the management's report on the company's state of affairs (*Lagebericht*) and the effectiveness of the risk management system that corporations are required to install in order to protect investors.[38]

b. Position

Auditors were for many years regarded in some European countries (e.g. Belgium, France, Germany, and Switzerland) as being an 'officer' of the

---

[35] W.F. Ebke, 'In Search of Alternatives: Comparative Reflections on Corporate Governance and the Independent Auditor's Responsibilities' [1984] 79 Northwestern University Law Review 663, 672.

[36] For details, see W.F. Ebke, 'Commentary' in K. Schmidt (ed.), Münchener *Kommentar zum HGB* (München 2000) § 316 annot .3.

[37] It should be noted, however, that both in the U.S. and in Europe banks and other creditors often insist that the debtor submit audited and certified financial statements as a condition for granting a loan or delivering goods or services.

[38] Ebke, above, n. 36, § 317 annot. 59.

corporation to be audited.[39] This view cannot be reconciled, however, with the requirement that the auditor be independent of both executives and supervisors.[40] Independence requires a sharp structural separation of the auditor from the corporation's executives and supervisors. Fortunately, the need for those structural safeguards is recognized more and more in Western Europe. Thus, for example, in Germany[41] and Switzerland,[42] courts have expressly rejected the view that the auditor is an 'officer' of the audited corporation. This view is in line with the law or at least prevailing views of legal commentators in many other countries according to which the auditor is an independent external expert[43] or, in the words of the U.S. Supreme Court, a 'public watch-dog', rather than part of the company's *internal* monitoring system.[44]

c. Independence

Structural transparency would improve if auditors were as independent in fact as they are in theory. While independent of their clients in many respects, accountants are still under pressure to 'cheerlead' for their clients, not least because a modern accounting firm sells a variety of non-audit services in addition to the basic audit function. Those services typically produce more revenue than auditing services. As the statutory audit function is key to all systems of corporate governance and transparency models, the mechanisms and devices for ensuring the independence of auditors and the objectivity of their work product, both in fact and in appearance, will require a thoughtful discussion of a great number of independence issues. These issues include, but are not limited to, the question of a mandatory rotation of the statutory auditor,[45] the possible personal, financial, and other links between the auditor and his client, the relationship between the auditor's fees from a particular client and the total revenues of the auditor's firm, multidisciplinary legal practices and the compatibility of non-audit services and statutory audits. The recent decision of the German Supreme Court in *Allweiler* illustrates the importance of the availability of clear and

---

[39] ibid., § 316 annot. 26–27.

[40] ibid.

[41] See, e.g. [1987] BayObLGZ 297, 308; cf. [1980] 76 BGHZ 338, 342 (1980) ('wie ein Gesellschaftsorgan'). But see [1995] 16 BGHZ 17.

[42] BG, [1998] AJP/PJA 1235. A similar view was also expressed by the drafting committee of the proposed Swiss law on accounting and auditing. For details, see Ebke, above, n. 7, 74–75.

[43] For details and references, see Ebke, above, n. 36, § 316 annot. 23.

[44] *United States v. Arthur Young & Co* 465 U.S. 805, 817–18 (1984).

[45] The German legislature recently decided against a mandatory *external* rotation of the independent auditor, but requires that the actual auditor be replaced by the accounting firm after a certain number of years. For details, see Ebke, above, n. 36, § 319 annot. 50–51.

unambiguous rules concerning the dividing line between audit services and non-audit services.[46]

d. Appointment and Compensation

Given the importance of the auditor's independence, the power to select, nominate, and appoint the auditor and to negotiate his fees is a particularly crucial matter. In most countries, the external auditor is elected by the corporation's general meeting of shareholders. Given the inactivity of most shareholders and the lack of efficient proxy systems, the distribution of the powers to select, nominate and appoint the auditor and to negotiate his fees becomes a central issue. Corporate governance systems that are based on the two-tier board model or a formal separation of management and supervisory functions have the characteristics essential to ensure the necessary transparency if the selection, nomination, and appointment processes and the negotiation of the auditor's fees are left to the supervisors rather than the managers. The same considerations apply in corporate governance systems with a unitary board all members of which are outsiders or independent, respectively. In such a model, a clear and transparent separation of management, supervisory, and audit functions is ensured if only outside and/or independent board members have the power to select, nominate, and appoint the statutory auditor and negotiate the auditor's fees. In countries that prefer a unitary board structure which includes both management and supervisory functions, the power to select, nominate, and appoint the external auditor and to negotiate the auditor's fees should be delegated to an audit committee consisting exclusively of outside and/or independent directors (NYSE rule).

e. Removal

Equally important is the question of whether shareholders have a right to remove the auditor. In some countries (e.g. the U.S. and Switzerland), the statutory auditor's engagement may be terminated at will by the client.[47] The

---

[46] [1996] 135 BGHZ 260. The German Supreme Court reversed the decision of the Court of Appeals (*Oberlandesgericht*) of Karlsruhe, [1995] 50 *Betriebs-Berater* 2644, and, in effect, upheld the decision of the District Court (*Landgericht*) of Konstanz, [1995] 34 *Mitteilungen der Wirtschaftsprüferkammer* 102. For details of this seminal case, see, e.g. W.F. Ebke, 'Case Note' [1998] 37 *Mitteilungen der Wirtschaftsprüferkammer* 76; P. Hommelhoff, 'Abschlussprüfung und Abschlussberatung' [1997] *Zeitschrift für Unternehmens- und Gesellschaftsrecht* 550; N. Neumann, 'Abschlussprüfung und Beratung nach der Allweiler-Entscheidung des BGH' [1998] 19 *Zeitschrift für Wirtschaftsrecht* 1338; V. Röhricht, 'Beratung und Abschlußprüfung' [1998] 51 *Die Wirtschaftsprüfung* 153.

[47] For details, see, e.g. Ebke, above, n. 7, 81–82.

termination triggers, of course, far-reaching reporting requirements on the part of the auditor (e.g. Form 8–K). In Germany by contrast, it is relatively difficult to remove an auditor once he has been appointed.[48] The engagement can only be terminated in exceptional cases. While shareholders, too, have the right to remove an auditor, two German district courts have held that the appointed auditor can only be removed by shareholders holding at least 10% of the audited company's outstanding shares of stock. Relying on section 318(1) of the Commercial Code (*Handelsgesetzbuch*), the District Courts of Cologne[49] and Munich[50] dismissed the shareholders' action that claimed that the auditor was not independent for lack of impartiality. Both courts expressly refused to grant the shareholder-plaintiffs the right to set aside the general meeting's election of the auditor. Under section 243(1) of the German Corporation Code (*Aktiengesetz*), an action to set aside a majority decision of the general meeting of shareholders (*Anfechtungsklage*) may be brought by each shareholder regardless of the number of shares held by him. The courts argued, inter alia, that, by imposing a 10% threshold, the legislature intended to protect both the auditor and the company against unwarranted removal proceedings that, like strike suits, may have a nuisance value.[51] Of course, under German law, certain facts (e.g. a financial interest of the auditor in the client company or the preparation by the auditor of the financial statements to be audited) render the auditor's appointment void *ipso iure*. Thus in such a case there is no need for shareholder actions to remove the auditor.

f. Liability

The question of what role the law of civil liability of the auditor can or should play in regard to corporate governance is of increasing importance. How the legal responsibilities of those who are to prepare financial statements (i.e. management) and those who are to examine them for the benefit of the shareholders and the financial markets (i.e. independent auditors) should legally be defined is a matter of controversy, both nationally and internationally. In countries with a developed market economy there is, however, a general consensus that criminal law should not play a major role in this respect.[52] Ethical and other professional

---

[48] For details, see Ebke, above, n. 36, § 318 annot. 32–51.

[49] LG Cologne [1997] 42 *Die Aktiengesellschaft* 431 ('*KHD*').

[50] LG Munich [2000] 45 *Die Aktiengesellschaft* 235 ('*Bayerische HypoVereinsbank*').

[51] For further details, see W.F. Ebke and A.-V. Jurisch, 'Der unerwünschte Abschlussprüfer: Ersetzungsverfahren (§ 318 Abs 3 HGB) versus Anfechtungsklage (§ 243 Abs 1 AktG)' [2000] 45 *Die Aktiengesellschaft* 208.

[52] See, e.g., M.I. Steinberg, 'Emerging Capital Markets: Proposals and Recommendations for Implementation' [1996] 30 International Lawyer 715, 723–25.

standards as well as the law of civil liability are considered in most market economies to be better suited to provide the necessary legal protection.

Most industrialized countries leave the task of developing principles and rules of auditor's liability to the courts rather than the legislature.[53] This is particularly true with respect to the auditor's liability to parties other than his client (third-party liability). Most legislatures confine themselves to an occasional, selective intervention in the complex web of relevant liability rules and principles. New legal developments are rarely initiated by legislatures. Legislatures usually only react to judicial and other developments of the pertinent laws if the developments are viewed as undesirable.[54] Comparative research suggests that in shaping the law of the independent auditor's civil liability, legal systems have had a far-reaching impact on each other, even across boundaries of different legal traditions.[55] Many legal as well as economic studies have concluded, however, that an even-handed approach to the liability issue is needed to best serve the interest of the audited company, the auditor, third parties, and the financial markets.[56]

g. Reform Efforts

The role, position, and liability of independent auditors are the subject of intense discussions in various circles. In 1996, the Commission of the European Union published a Green Paper on 'The Role, the Position and the Liability of Auditors in the European Union'.[57] In its Green Paper, the EU Commission has pointed out several areas that may lend themselves to improvement and further action at EU level. The Green Paper is intended to raise the awareness of all interested parties in the issues at stake and to elicit comments. The Green Paper is based on a study that was carried out by the Maastricht Accounting and Auditing Research Centre (MARC).[58] Many of the issues raised in the Green

---

[53] W.F. Ebke, *Die Haftung der Wirtschaftsprüfenden, rechts- und steuerberatenden Berufe in rechtsvergleichender Sicht* (Heidelberg 1996) 1–2.

[54] An example in support of this proposition is a recent law adopted by the State of New Jersey. See NJ Stat Ann § 2A:53A-25 (West Supp 1997). This law overturns the New Jersey's Supreme Court's decision in *Rosenblum, Inc v. Adler*, 461 A 2d 138 (NJ 1983). The Private Securities Litigation Reform Act of December 22, 1995, and the 1998 revision of § 323 of the German Commercial Code are other recent examples. For a more detailed exposition of this view, see Ebke, above, n. 7, 86–87.

[55] W.F. Ebke and D. Struckmeier, *The Civil Liability of Corporate Auditors: An International Perspective* (London 1994)

[56] Ebke, above, n. 36, § 323 annot. 138–141.

[57] O.J. EC C321 at 1 (October 28, 1996).

[58] *Final Report of a Study on the Role, Position and Liability of the Statutory Auditor within the European Union* (European Commission ed. 1996) Office for Official Publications of the European Communities, Luxembourg.

Paper were discussed in great depth at a conference held in Brussels, Belgium, on December 5–6, 1996.[59] Following the conference, the EU Commission launched a comparative law study to inquire into the different auditor liability regimes within the EU.[60] The study was conducted by a law firm in Paris, France. The study was presented to the EU Commission in March 2000 and is still under review by the EU Commission and various professional organizations.

Meanwhile, several EU Member States have taken steps to strengthen the position and the role of the statutory auditor within the corporate governance system. Thus, for example, in 1998 the German legislature enacted the Law on Control and Transparency in the Area of Enterprises (*KonTraG*).[61] This statute aims, inter alia, at enhancing the role and the position of the auditor vis-à-vis the managing board (*Vorstand*).[62] In addition, under a new amendment to the German Law on Accountants (*Wirtschaftsprüferordnung*) which entered into effect on 1 January 2001, a mandatory peer review (*Qualitätskontrollverfahren*) of statutory auditors will be required in Germany no later than December 31, 2005, adding substantial transparency. Accountants and accounting firms that audit listed corporations are required to be reviewed by their peers no later than December 31, 2002. Similar developments can be observed outside the EU. Thus, for example, in the U.S., the independence issue is presently under close scrutiny by the Securities and Exchange Commission. In Switzerland, too, the position and role of the statutory auditor (*Revisionsstelle*) is under review by the legislature.[63] The Annual Meeting of the Swiss Lawyers Association (*Schweizerischer Juristenverein*) held on September 29–30, 2000, in St. Gallen, Switzerland, addressed the independence issue as well.

III. Organizational Transparency

Structural transparency alone would be insufficient, however, to hold management accountable to both the corporation and the shareholders. Structural transparency rules need to be supplemented by organizational transparency

---

[59] The papers presented at the conference are published in *Act of the Conference on the Role, the Position and the Liability of the Statutory Auditor within the European Union* (European Commission ed. 1997).

[60] See *Communication from the Commission on the Statutory Audit in the European Union: The Way Forward*, O.J. C143 at 12, 15 para. 3.15 (May 8, 1998).

[61] BGBl 1998 I 786.

[62] For details, see, e.g. P. Hommelhoff, 'Die neue Position des Abschlußprüfers im Kraftfeld der aktienrechtlichen Organisationsverfassung' Part I (1998) 53 *Betriebs-Berater* 2567, Part II (1998) 53 *Betriebs-Berater* 2625.

[63] For details of the provisions on auditing in the proposed law on financial accounting and auditing, see Ebke, above, n. 7, 68–90.

rules that require transparency in the context of the internal affairs of large public corporations.

1. Basic Documents

Legislatures have had little theoretical difficulty with permitting shareholders to inspect their corporation's books and records (subject sometimes, however, to certain qualifications).[64] Similarly, corporation laws agree, in principle, that basic documents, especially information about the persons who are authorized to bind the corporation, should be made available to shareholders and others. Thus, for example, the expressed rationale of the transparency requirements of the First Directive is that 'the basic documents of the company should be disclosed in order that third parties may be able to ascertain their contents and other information concerning the company, especially particulars of the persons who are authorized to bind the company'.[65] Article 6 of the First Directive requires Member States to provide appropriate penalties for failure to disclose financial statements and for the omission of prescribed details from commercial documents to be filed with the competent agency or court. In *Verband deutscher Daihatsu-Händler eV v. Daihatsu Deutschland GmbH*[66] and *Commission v. Germany*,[67] the European Court of Justice provided some guidance as to the type of penalty required by article 6 of the First Directive. In March of 2000, Germany brought its laws in line with the Court's rulings.[68]

2. The Breakthrough: *Centros*

The significance of transparency vis-à-vis third parties was stressed in the recent *Centros* decision of the European Court of Justice.[69] In this decision, the Court

---

[64] See, e.g. § 16.02 RMBCA.

[65] First Council Directive (EEC) on co-ordination and safeguards which, for the protection of the interests of members and others, are required by Member States of companies within the meaning of the second paragraph of article 58 of the Treaty, with a view to making such safeguards equivalent throughout the Community [1968] O.J. L065/8.

[66] Case C-97/96 *Verband deutscher Daihatsu-Händler eV v. Daihatsu Deutschland GmbH* [1997] E.C.R. I-6843. For a brief, yet thoughtful discussion of this case, see V. Edwards, *EC Company Law* (Oxford 1999) 26–27.

[67] Case C-191/95 *Commission v. Germany* [1998] E.C.R. I-5449. For details of this case, see A. Gehringer, 'Anmerkung' [1999] 10 *Europäisches Wirtschafts- und Steuerrecht* 65.

[68] BGBl 2000 I 154. For details of the new statute which implements a directive of the European Union, see, e.g. C. Luttermann, 'Das Kapitalgesellschaften und Co-Richtlinie-Gesetz"[2000] 21 *Zeitschrift für Wirtschaftsrecht* 517; D. Zimmer and T. Eckhold, 'Das Kapitalgesellschaften & Co-Richtlinie-Gesetz' [2000] 53 *Neue Juristische Wochenschrift* 136.

[69] Case C-212/97 *Centros* [1999] E.C.R. I-1459. For details of this highly controversial decision, see, e.g. R.M. Buxbaum, 'Back to the Future? From Centros to the Überlagerungstheorie' in

emphasized the role of disclosure in regard to the right of a company duly formed under the laws of a Member State to establish a branch in another Member State. The Danish Trade and Companies Board (*Erhvervs- og Selskabsstyrelsen*) had refused to register the branch of Centros Ltd., an English private limited company, in Denmark on the grounds, inter alia, that Centros, which did not do any business in the U.K., was in fact seeking to establish in Denmark, not a branch, but a principal establishment, thereby circumventing Denmark's minimum capital requirements. Noticing that the company in question was holding itself out correctly as an English company rather than a company governed by Danish law, the Court emphasized that the company's creditors were on notice that it was subject to laws different from those which govern the formation of private limited liability companies in Denmark.

The Court pointed out that creditors can 'refer to certain rules of Community law that protect them', such as the Fourth Council Directive on financial accounting and disclosure[70] and the Eleventh Council Directive concerning disclosure requirements relating to branches.[71] Thus, in the Court's opinion, creditor protection does not necessarily depend upon traditional 'safeguards' such as minimum capital requirements or piercing the corporate veil, but can also be effectuated by means of full and fair disclosure of relevant facts.[72] This holding of the European Court of Justice is, in my view, a major breakthrough in terms of corporate transparency the significance of which for the harmonization of the EU Member States' laws of business associations cannot be overestimated.[73]

K. Berger, W.F. Ebke, S. Elsing, B. Grossfeld, and G. Kühne (eds.), *Festschrift für Otto Sandrock* (Heidelberg 2000) 149; W.F. Ebke, 'Das Schicksal der Sitztheorie nach dem Centros-Urteil des EuGH' [1999] 54 *Juristenzeitung* 656; H. Merkt, 'Das Centros-Urteil des Europäischen Gerichtshofs—Konsequenzen für den nationalen Gesetzgeber' [2000] 2 *VGR* 111; W.-H. Roth, 'Case C-212/97—Centros Ltd v Erhvervs- og Selskabsstyrelsen, Judgement of 9 March 1999' [2000] 37 Common Market Law Review 147; O. Sandrock, 'Centros: Ein Etappensieg für die Überlagerungstheorie' [1999] 54 *Betriebs-Berater* 1337; E. Wymeersch, 'Centros: A Landmark Decision in European Company Law' in T. Baums, K.J. Hopt, and N. Horn (eds.), *Corporations, Capital Markets and Business in the Law. Liber Amicorum Richard M. Buxbaum* (The Hague 2000) 629.

[70] Fourth Council Directive (EEC) 78/660 on the annual accounts of certain types of companies [1978] O.J. L222/11.

[71] Eleventh Council Directive (EEC) 89/666 concerning disclosure requirements in respect of branches opened in a Member State by certain types of company governed by the law of another State [1989] O.J. L395/36.

[72] The Court's observation can easily be reconciled with its reference to the protection of consumers by means of disclosure in the *German Beer* case. See Case 178/84—*Commission v. Germany* [1987] E.C.R. 1227. In this case, the Court held that Germany was not entitled to block the importation of foreign beer that was not brewed in accordance with the German law on beer purity (*Reinheitsgebot*), but may allow beer brewed in accordance with this law to be labelled accordingly to adequately inform and, thereby, to protect consumers.

[73] For a more detailed exposition of this view, see W.F. Ebke, 'Centros—Some Realities and Some Mysteries' [2000] 49 American Journal of Comparative Law 623.

3. Conflicts of Interests

Organizational transparency works particularly well with respect to various conflict-of-interests transactions, including corporate opportunity transactions[74] and even interlocking directorates.[75] But transparency has proved to work equally well in the case of stock option grants and in the area of executive and director compensation.[76] Compensation is one of the most sensitive and complex tasks facing the board and the corporation, because by definition, no member of the board can view the issue without conflicts of interests. Pay according to performance is just as important with executives as it is with supervisors. As with executive compensation, the important question in director remuneration is not 'how much', but 'how'. Of course, the assumption of risk should be rewarded. It is often said that directors are paid far too much for what they do, but not nearly enough for what they ought to do. To link their own wealth to the performance of the company is a desirable step. But unless carefully designed, stock related compensation (in the form of stock options and/or outright grants) for directors could encourage measures that attempt to engineer a short-term increase in the stock price at the sacrifice of long-term viability of the company. An interesting legislative initiative recently enacted in Michigan permits corporations incorporated there to designate an independent director, meeting certain criteria, for special compensation, rights and responsibilities, including determinations of indemnification, transactions that raise questions of conflicts of interests, and derivative litigation.

4. Duty of Care and Loyalty

A corporate governance system that relies heavily upon organizational transparency necessitates a shift in thinking about fiduciary duties. Most jurisdictions describe the director as having two duties, the duty of care and the duty of loyalty.[77] Yet a web of legal duties, no matter how closely knit and how well

---

[74] F. Kübler, 'Erwerbschancen und Organpflichten' in W. Hadding, U. Immenga, H.-J. Mertens, K. Pleyer, U.H. Schneider (eds.), *Festschrift für Winfried Werner* (Berlin / New York 1984) 437.

[75] W.F. Ebke, 'Interlocking Directorates' [1990] 19 *Zeitschrift für Unternehmens- und Gesellschaftsrecht* 50; J. Wells, 'Multiple Directorships; the Fiduciary Duties and Conflicts of Interest That Arise When One Individual Serves More Than One Corporation' [2000] 33 John Marshall Law Review 561.

[76] See, e.g. T. Götze, *Aktienoptionen für Vorstandsmitglieder und Aktionärsschutz* (Baden-Baden 2001); K. Deutschmann, *Vergütungshalber gewährte Aktienoptionen im deutschen und U.S.-amerikanischen Steuerrecht* (Baden-Baden 2000).

[77] Ebke, above, n. 4, 31–32. See also generally T.E. Abeltshauser, *Leitungshaftung im Kapitalgesellschaftsrecht* (Cologne 1998).

defined, will not suffice in and of itself. To be effective, the substantive rules need to be accompanied by enabling and facilitating procedural rules, including rules relating to derivative lawsuits.[78] The legal cost rules, too, would have to be shaped in a way to make it viable for shareholders to enforce the management's duties of care and loyalty. For the approach to be even-handed, a director's conduct would have to be judged, however, according to the business judgment rule.

5. Voting

In theory, directors are elected by their constituency. Most corporate lawyers will agree, however, that the electoral process has not been an effective mechanism for assuring that directors represent the interests of the shareholders. Except for the rare case of a proxy contest, where those trying for control of the company nominate (and finance) a competing slate of directors, there is no chance of the nominees not being elected. Shareholders' abstention carries little weight in large corporations. Moreover, the electoral system can be manipulated, in some countries, to reduce the efficacy of shareholder voting rights by adopting a staggered (or classified) board structure. While staggered boards may be contrary to shareholder interests as the adoption of a staggered board can result in a loss of share value, they also serve to protect the board from the company's shareholders by protecting directors from raiders. The voting system of course, gives rise to a whole new set of issues, including the contents of proxy statements and related documents that have to be disclosed to the shareholders. While these issues have been discussed on a comparative basis and in enormous depth, it is fair to say that we are far from having solved them in any legal system.

IV. Financial Transparency

Financial accounting and disclosure were adopted to restore trust and confidence in the financial markets and to make the financial markets fair and efficient. Financial transparency gives substance to shareholders' rights by providing the information essential to their exercise. But quite apart from these intended benefits, financial accounting and disclosure have been a most efficient and effective mechanism for inducing managers to manage responsibly. Almost

---

[78] P. Ulmer, 'Die Aktionärsklage als Instrument zur Kontrolle des Vorstands- und Aufsichtsratshandels' [1999] 163 *Zeitschrift für das gesamte Handelsrecht und Wirtschaftsrecht* 290; M. Becker, *Verwaltungskontrolle durch Gesellschafterrechte* (Tübingen 1997) 598–623. The leading comparative treatise on this subject is B. Grossfeld, *Aktiengesellschaft, Unternehmenskonzentration und Kleinaktionär* (Tübingen 1968).

unnoticed, reliable financial accounting and disclosure have become a corporate governance tool of the first order.[79]

1. National Approaches

State corporation laws in the U.S. traditionally did not deal with financial accounting and disclosure, and American lawyers may find it somewhat unusual to discuss financial transparency in the context of the law of corporations. However, today section 16.20(a) RMBCA expressly provides that a corporation shall furnish its shareholders with annual financial statements, which may be consolidated or combined statements of the corporation and one or more of its subsidiaries, that include a balance sheet as of the end of the fiscal year, an income statement for that year, and a statement of changes in shareholders' equity for the year unless that information appears elsewhere in the financial statements. Needless to say, financial accounting and disclosure requirements of the SEC and the stock exchanges (e.g. the New York Stock Exchange) as well as the financial accounting standards developed by the Financial Accounting Standards Board (FASB) and others have offset greatly the traditional silence of State corporation laws.[80] Although mandatory financial disclosure has become an established feature of U.S. capital markets since 1933, aspects of it are still controversial.[81] Moreover, some commentators have called into question the inevitability of *federal* regulation of disclosure. Thus, for example, Professor Roberta Romano recently suggested that federal regulation of securities disclosure should be replaced by a 'menu approach to securities regulation under which firms elect whether to be covered by federal law or by the securities law of a specified state'.[82]

In the EU, financial accounting and disclosure are regulated primarily by the First,[83] the Fourth[84] and the Seventh[85] Company Law Directives. The European law of financial accounting has been criticized for not requiring reporting of

[79] Grossfeld and Ebke, above, n. 3, 422; Lowenstein, above, n. 12, 1336.

[80] Lowenstein, above, n. 12, 1336.

[81] For an overview of the debate on the need for mandatory financial disclosure under the securities laws, see J. Seligmann, 'The Historical Need for a Mandatory Corporate Disclosure System' [1983] 9 Journal of Corporation Law 1. Two other classic works setting out the parameters of this debate are F.H. Easterbrook and D.R. Fischel, 'Mandatory Disclosure and the Protein of Investors' [1984] 70 Virginia Law Review 669, and J.C. Coffee, 'Market Failure and the Economic Case for a Mandatory Disclosure System' [1984] 70 Virginia Law Review 717.

[82] R. Romano, 'Empowering Investors: A Market Approach to Securities Regulation' [1998] 107 Yale Law Journal 2359, 2362.

[83] See above, n. 65.

[84] See above, n. 70.

[85] Seventh Council Directive (EEC) 83/349 on consolidated accounts [1983] O.J. L193/1.

segment data and cash flows. The lack of a mandate for interim reports is also viewed critically by some. Thereby is too often overlooked, however, that many EU Member States do require segment reporting and cash flow statements by certain companies (e.g. listed companies or groups of affiliated companies), even though they are not required to do so under European law. Interim reports are often published on a voluntary basis. Most importantly, ad hoc disclosure is now the rule in the EU. Needless to say, there is some concern about the quality of some of the traditional European accounting principles that are considered to be no longer appropriate for globally operating enterprises. However, since the pronouncement of its 'new strategy' in 1995,[86] the EU Commission has worked hard to modernize European accounting principles and to bring them in line with the International Accounting Standards (IAS).[87] On June 13, 2000, the EU Commission formally announced that from the year 2005 on all European groups of affiliated companies would be required to use International Accounting Standards. Moreover, Member States will be permitted to make International Accounting Standards available to other companies as well.[88] While this step is a salutary one, financial analysts tend to be less concerned about even fundamentally different accounting principles because their tools and methods seem to make it possible to overcome limitations, if any, resulting from any given set of financial accounting principles.

2. Internationalization of Financial Transparency

Corporate financial transparency has become an international issue. Amid an outcry from the New York Stock Exchange (NYSE), investment bankers and various interest groups, the U.S. continues to require foreign issuers to use U.S. GAAP, either directly or by means of 'reconciliation', as a precondition to listing their stocks in the U.S. (a classic case in support of the proposition that markets are making law!).[89] Financial and capital markets are, no doubt, global. Why should financial accounting principles for companies taking advantage of the global financial and capital markets be national? Of course, many will find it difficult to give up their own system of financial accounting (which, as every lawyer and accountant knows, is the best in the world) and apply (unknown) foreign or international accounting principles and disclosure requirements instead.

---

[86] See COM (1995) 508 (final). For details, see K. Van Hulle, 'International Harmonization of Accounting Principles: A European Perspective' [special issue June 1997] 36 *Mitteilungen der Wirtschaftsprüferkammer* 44.

[87] For details, see Ebke, above, n. 7, 51–52.

[88] COM (2000) 359 (final).

[89] For details, see Ebke, above, n. 10, 115–17.

Yet what makes lawyers and accountants think that their own financial accounting principles and disclosure requirements are uniquely accurate, when the London-based International Accounting Standards Committee (IASC) is refining its accounting standards so energetically? What makes European lawyers and accountants think that European GAAP are 'more preferable' than U.S. GAAP when one recalls that, in February 2000, the EU Commission published a draft directive concerning fair-value accounting for certain complex financial instruments[90] and that similar principles are already generally accepted in the U.S. and under IAS 39?[91] Conversely, what makes American lawyers and accountants think that U.S. GAAP are 'better' than IAS when the FASB is trying to limit, for example, the availability of 'pooling of interest' accounting in mergers and the IAS almost completely bar the pooling method in mergers.[92]

There is room for movement from both directions. From the point of view of globally operating companies, a policy of openness towards international standards of accounting has significant advantages, particularly if the IAS are directed towards the information needs of the financial and capital markets.[93] One of the central concerns of commercial enterprises today is enhancing, through excellent long-term management, corporate profit and shareholder gain[94] and global competitiveness. A shareholder-value and market-oriented approach to financial transparency requires financial accounting principles that serve the information needs of the financial and capital markets and suffice to fulfil the demands of international rating agencies and financial analysts. Most of the IAS do meet these requirements; those that do not meet them need to be refined in a concerted action by all concerned to achieve a set of internationally accepted principles of accounting that will facilitate the international flow of capital and relevant financial information.

It is sometimes said that the U.S. is in a better position than many European countries to 'modernize' its financial accounting principles because the U.S. is not burdened by a requirement that tax accounting must conform to financial accounting.[95] Thereby is too often overlooked, however, that thus far the

---

[90] COM (2000) 80 (final). For details, see, e.g. P. Scharf, 'Bilanzierung von Finanzinstrumenten nach dem Vorschlag der EG-Kommission: Ein Vergleich mit IAS 39' [2000] 56 *Der Betrieb* 629; M. Hommel and T. Berndt, 'Neue Entwicklungen in der Jahresabschlussrichtlinie: Bewertung zum Fair Value' [2000] 55 *Betriebs-Berater* 1184.

[91] See Ebke, above, n. 7, 52 and 54. For details, see S. Siegel, 'The Coming Revolution in Accounting: The Emergence of Fair Value as the Fundamental Principle of GAAP' 36 *Mitteilungen der Wirtschaftsprüferkammer* 81 [special issue June 1997].

[92] Ebke, above, n. 7, 55.

[93] Ebke, above, n. 10, 124.

[94] Cf. s. 2.01(a) of the ALI Principles of Corporate Governance: Analysis and Recommendations (1992).

[95] See Lowenstein, above, n. 12, 1335, 1341. For an excellent comparative analysis of the relationship between financial and tax accounting in Germany and in the U.S., see H.J. Lischer and

internationalization of financial accounting affects primarily the consolidated accounting of parent companies (*Konzerne*) and that consolidated financial statements are, as a general rule, not relevant for income tax purposes in most European countries because the group of affiliated companies as a whole is not considered to be a taxable person.[96] For this reason, Germany and six other EU Member States had little theoretical difficulty exempting parent companies from preparing their consolidated financial statements on the basis of financial accounting principles other than their national GAAP (e.g. IAS or U.S. GAAP).[97] Of course, the 'tax-must-conform-to-book' rule (*Massgeblichkeitsgrundsatz*) needs to be reconsidered (and probably be abolished) if financial accounting principles based on shareholder value and fair values are to be applied to taxable persons as well.[98]

3. Electronic Distribution of Business Information

The growth of the Internet as a medium for delivering business reporting information has altered the way information flows from companies to investors and creditors. That structure will continue to change as companies bring new technologies to the process and as information users find new ways to gather and analyse information. On January 31, 2000, the FASB published a report on Electronic Distribution of Business Reporting Information.[99] The objectives of this study were to survey the state of reporting business information over the internet and to identify notable practices. A second report dealt with the redundancies between SEC and FASB reporting requirements, thus pointing the way to eliminating overlap and duplication. Other countries will have to address similar issues of transparency by means of the new information technology.

V. European Transparency Rules

What role can transparency play in the EU in the development of a European law of business associations and capital market law at a time when the process of company law harmonization from 'the top down' by means of European leg-

P.N. Märkl, 'Conformity between Financial Accounting and Tax Accounting in the United States and Germany' 81 [special issue June 1997] 36 *Mitteilungen der Wirtschaftsprüferkammer.*

[96] Ebke, above, n. 7, 58.

[97] See text accompanying n. 7.

[98] See, e.g. F.D. Broer, *Massgeblichkeit und Internationalisierung der Rechnungslegung* (Baden-Baden 2001); P. Spori, 'Differenzierte Massgeblichkeit bei getreuer Darstellung' [2000] 69 *Archiv für Schweizerisches Abgabenrecht* 105; Ebke, above, n. 6, 19–20.

[99] www.rutgers.edu/Accounting/raw/fasb/brrppg.html.

islation has proved to be more and more difficult?[100] Should the promulgation of European transparency rules be seen as a viable alternative to company law harmonization? To what extent, if any, can European transparency legislation substitute, or at least effectively supplement, structural and organizational monitoring devices that vary widely from one Member State to another? Are there any adverse or semi-adverse consequences likely to flow from more far-reaching European transparency requirements?

These questions are part of the broader and extremely complex issue of whether harmonization of company law in the EU is possible or even desirable? The company law harmonization programme of the EU has not only slowed down, but has come to a virtual standstill. The Fifth Company Law Directive was put to rest in 1991. In May 1999, the proposed Statute of a European Company was voted down by Spain. The German Justice Minister's recent plea for a 'uniform' European corporation law[101] can hardly be reconciled with the position Germany and many other EU Member States have been taking over the past 40 years or so with respect to the approximation of the law of business associations. Also, the question remains, how much uniformity of company law do we need and how much diversity is desirable?

However, almost unnoticed, the EU Commission has already shifted its focus. Rather than focusing on traditional company law harmonization, the EU is increasingly proposing financial and capital market transparency rules dealing, for example, with such important subjects as fair value accounting, insider trading, and tender offers. Financial transparency and capital market legislation will not obviate most substantive corporate law rules, neither at EU nor at Member State level.[102] But such legislation can supplement existing and future substantive rules concerning the structure and organization of the corporation. In the light of the past experience, the development of structural and organisational transparency rules should be left to a private body, such as a European Law Institute (ELI).[103]

---

[100] Ebke, above, n. 5, 962; W.F. Ebke, 'Unternehmensrecht und Binnenmarkt: E pluribus unum? [1998] *RabelsZ* 195.

[101] H. Däubler-Gmeling, *Frankfurter Allgemeine Zeitung* at 15 (13 August 1999) ('We need a uniform company law faster than we thought').

[102] Ebke, above, n. 4, 34. J. Köndgen, 'Die Relevanz der ökonomischen Theorie der Unternehmung für rechtswissenschaftliche Fragestellungen—ein Problemkatalog' in C. Ott and H.-B. Schäfer (eds.), *Ökonomische Analyse des Unternehmensrechts* (Tübingen 1993) 133. See also C.J. Müller-Schatz, 'Über die Notwendigkeit gesellschaftsrechtlicher Aufsichtsregeln' [1988] 129 *Zeitschrift für Schweizerisches Recht* 191; R.M. Buxbaum and K.J. Hopt, 'Legal Harmonization and the Business Enterprise Revisited' in R.M. Buxbaum, G. Hertig, A. Hirsch, and K.J. Hopt (eds.), *European Business Law. Legal and Economic Analyses on Integration and Harmonization* (Berlin 1991) 391, 402–04.

[103] For a detailed exposition of the role of a European Law Institute (ELI), see W.F. Ebke, 'Unternehmensrechtsangleichung in der Europäischen Union: Brauchen wir ein European Law Institute?' in U. Hübner and W.F. Ebke (eds.), *Festschrift für Bernhard Grossfeld* (Heidelberg 1999) 199.

VI. Corporate Social Transparency

The foregoing discussion has thrown some light on the significance of financial transparency in the modern corporate world. At present, there is clearly more financial transparency than corporate social transparency, both in the U.S. and in the EU. The term corporate social transparency commonly refers to disclosure of information about a reporting company's products, the countries in which a company does business, and the labour and environmental effects of a company's operations in its home country and around the world. Other types of social disclosure may include information on the use of corporate resources for public-welfare, humanitarian, educational, and philanthropic purposes,[104] political contributions[105] or the effects of using a company's products on consumer health and safety.[106] Consistent, periodic disclosure of such information in a standard format would, in the opinion of some commentators, help to create 'social transparency' in the financial markets comparable to the financial transparency that now exists.

Such proposals are less revolutionary than it may appear at first glance as some federal statutes in the U.S. and the laws of many EU Member States require companies of a certain size and in certain industries to submit compliance reports to the government on an annual basis. In the U.S., some companies have made this information available on their Web page, but not yet in the SEC's EDGAR database. In an article for the Harvard Law Review, Professor Cynthia Williams has illustrated that the SEC has the statutory authority in fashioning proxy disclosure to require disclosure either to promote the public interest or to protect investors.[107] Thus social transparency of companies is not a question of legislative power, but of political, economic, and social expediency.

If it is true that managers 'manage what they measure', then measuring social and environmental effects in a consistent, comparable way could act as an impetus for management to reduce those impacts that shareholders could interpret as negative. Of course, there is the fear that disclosure relating to social and envi-

---

[104] F. Stevelman Kahn, 'Pandora's Box: Managerial Discretion and the Problem of Corporate Philanthropy' [1997] 44 UCLA Law Review 579.

[105] In the U.S., it is unlawful, under the Foreign Corrupt Practices Act, for any reporting company or its officers or directors to give money to foreign government officials or political parties in efforts to influence the decision of such foreign government officials. See § 30A, 15 USC § 78dd-1 (1994). The Federal Election Campaign Act of 1971 regulates corporate and individual campaign contributions and provides for public disclosure, by candidate, of funding sources. See 2 USC §§ 441a–441g (1994). Similar laws exist in various European countries.

[106] See, e.g. Regulations Restricting the Sale and Distribution of Cigarettes and Smokeless Tobacco Products to Protect Children and Adolescents, 60 *Fed Reg* 41, 314–15 (1995).

[107] C.A. Williams, 'The Securities and Exchange Commission and Corporate Social Transparency' [1999] 112 Harvard Law Review 1197.

ronmental matters could interfere with the functioning of the market by introducing non-financial variables into investors' investment decisions. However, expanded social disclosure could also be a mechanism to permit shareholders to impose greater accountability on the corporate exercise of power. It is important to notice that the accounting profession, both in Europe and in the U.S., has been developing social audit procedures and disclosure formats since the late 1970s.[108] Obviously, the creation of socially transparent markets must be premised on generally (preferably internationally) accepted social accounting principles and auditing standards if social transparency is to produce a true and fair appraisal of the social effects, both positive and negative, created by public corporations in their pursuit of economic returns.

C. Conclusions

In the 1950s, many corporate lawyers felt that their job had been done and that they had no questions left to answer. As Bails Manning put it in 1962: 'Corporation law, as a field of intellectual effort, is dead in the United States'.[109] Twenty-five years later, however, the take-over era turned Manning's statement on its head. The creation of financial investments to finance take-overs of any company, of virtually any size, presented directors with the most demanding challenges in corporate history. Another 20 years later, directors of European companies are facing similarly demanding challenges. In view of the current developments it is fair to expect that corporate law will continue to be one of the most exciting areas of intellectual endeavour, with transparency playing an increasingly important role in corporate governance. Transparency is not just a fashionable word. It is a relevant and valuable legal, economic, and political concept that will shape corporate law, corporate legal scholarship, and corporate practice in the years ahead. Those who believe that corporate governance will function just as well without transparency carry a heavy burden of persuasion.

[108] See R. Gray, D. Owen, and C. Adams, *Accounting and Accountability* (London/New York 1996) 32–35.

[109] B. Manning, 'The Shareholder Appraisal Remedy: An Essay for Frank Coker' [1962] 72 Yale Law Journal 223, 245.

9

Audit Within the Framework of Corporate Governance

PETER NOBEL

Abstract

Corporate governance as a main issue of the more recent academic, and mainly Stock Exchange orientated, discussion has focused extensively on the functions of the board of directors. At its core, however, corporate governance is concerned with shareholder value in a market economy or beyond, with an emphasis on long-term wealth creation, leadership, and control.

Although differences in cultural traditions and legal systems have led to varying models for corporate governance, today's globalization of capital markets is calling increasingly for the acceptance of uniform principles. On an international level, numerous reports have been published—*inter alia*, the Cadbury Report and the related Code of Best Practice from the Cadbury Committee (U.K.), the Hampel Report (U.K.), the Rapport Viénot (France), the Millstein Report (prepared for the OECD), and the OECD Principles of Corporate Governance. European Stock Exchanges have also elaborated Codes of Corporate Governance, especially with regard to the scope of disclosure and transparency.

These codes need to deal more intensively with a topic, which, until now, has only arisen in a secondary form: the role and function of the independent external audit. The significance of this topic is tied to the willingness of the investing public to invest in corporations. Investors must be able to put their faith in issuers' financial statements: independent auditors play a key role here by ensuring that financial information disclosed by issuers is reliable. The Enron debacle has very much accentuated the importance of this issue.

The importance of the independent audit is already set out in the abovementioned principles as well as in European and American legislation (the latter having recently passed new regulations modernizing its rules in this area). Still lacking, however, particularly on an international level, is the demand for a more efficient, external, independent control and the development of a definitive response to the ensuing question of the status of the external audit and the function of the external auditor. The need to elaborate on the principles developed thus far and thereby to strengthen the concept of the independent external audit, particularly in the light of its significance within the corporate governance framework, remains as a crucial task for the future. As noted by Arthur Levitt Jr. during his tenure as chairman of the Securities & Exchange Commission,

> In what other profession is it one's duty to tell the customer when he's wrong? . . . .
> What other profession is enshrined in our nation's securities laws to serve no interest but the public's? What other profession so directly holds the key to public confidence—the life force of our markets? . . . . Alas, it has become clear that the perceived value of the audit is being put at risk.[1]

Following Enron, the relevance of this statement as well as Levitt's efforts, in general, to strengthen the enforcement of securities laws and require far greater disclosure from companies can be fully appreciated.

---

[1] Statement of Arthur B. Levitt before the annual meeting of accounting-industry trade group in Las Vegas, *The Economist*, October 18, 2000, p. 99.

Contents

A. Corporate Governance

Corporate governance is an internationally debated interdisciplinary concept with many characteristics.[2] Underlying its definition is a conviction that active shareholder participation in the governing of a corporation will enhance its ability to create wealth. The concept has origins in the U.S. and Britain; in the U.S. it can be traced to the 'agency theory,' which views shareholders as owners and directors as their agents, and it reflects the fear that corporate managers will steal investor money and use it wrongly.

At its core, corporate governance concentrates on shareholder value in a market economy or beyond, with a main focus upon long-term wealth creation, organized firm leadership and control.[3] Among other things, the concept includes aspects of a functional balanced interplay of structure, competence, and control.[4]

Corporate governance is characterized by a country's institutional and legal framework as well as its economic and business culture. Due to differences in the various legal systems, institutional conditions, and traditions, there is still no internationally valid universal model for corporate governance. Today's globalization of the capital markets is, however, calling increasingly for the creation

[2] P. Nobel, *Corporate Governance: der Brückenschlag vom Aktionariat zum Management* INDEX 1998, 8.

[3] U. Schneider and C. Strenger, 'Die "Corporate Governance-Grundsätze" der Grundsatzkommission Corporate Governance' [2000] 3 *Die Aktiengesellschaft* 106.

[4] P. Böckli, 'Corporate Governance: Der Stand der Dinge nach den Berichten "Hampel", "Viénot" und "OECD" sowie dem deutschen "KonTraG" ' [1999] 1 *Südtiroler Wirtschaftszeitung* 3.

and acceptance of uniform basic principles, which include corporate governance.

I think that shareholder primacy is prevailing in the sense that the creation of
wealth will benefit customers, employees, managers, and shareholders, but I
doubt that we have already arrived at the end of the history of corporate law.

The recent and intensively conducted academic, as well as practice-oriented,
debate over corporate governance has led to the publication of a significant
number of reports on an international level. Here, I will only mention the
following: the Cadbury Report of 1992, with the accompanying Code of Best
Practices of the English Cadbury Committees; the English Greenbury and
Hampel Reports of 1995 and 1998; the French Rapports Viénot I and II of 1995
and 1999; the 'Statement on Corporate Governance' of the American Business
Roundtable of 1997; the Millstein Report of 1998 and the (thereupon based)
OECD principles of Corporate Governance of 1999; the Berlin Initiative Group
German Code of Corporate Governance[5]; the Corporate Governance Principles
of the European Association of Securities Dealers (EASD)[6]; and, finally, the
Paper of the German *Grundsatzkommission* for Corporate Governance of
Spring 2000. Also of relevance here is the German Law of 1998 on control and
transparency (*KonTraG*), and the more recent German Corporate Governance
Code ('Deutscher Corporate Governance Kodex', February 26, 2002).
Numerous publications from countries as diverse as Australia and India supplement this list.[7] Also noteworthy here are the numerous Codes which have been
elaborated in all the European countries.[8] This chapter will examine the status
of the audit within the structure of corporate governance, particularly in light of
the principles emanating from the above mentioned reports. The current international discussion on corporate governance places an emphasis upon management, boards of directors, and their competencies: The call for responsible
corporate leadership has led to an increasing demand for independent audit
committees which is already reflected in the basic principles. The need for elaboration of these principles and, thereby, for strengthening the concept of the
independent external audit, particularly in the light of its significance within the
corporate governance framework, is a basic premise of this chapter.

---

[5] *German Code of Corporate Governance* (*GCCG*), Berlin Initiative Group German Code of
Corporate Governance (Berlin June 6, 2000), www.gccg.de

[6] EASD, European Association of Securities Dealers, *Corporate Governance Principles and
Recommendations* (May 2000).

[7] An updated overview can be found at www.ecgn.ulb.ac.be.

[8] See 'Comparative Study of Corporate Governance Codes Relevant to the European Union
and Its Member States', Final Report and Annexes I–III, January 2002, http://europe.eu.int/
comm/internal_market/en/company/company/news/corp-gov-codes-rpt-part 1_en.pdf.

B. The OECD Principles of Corporate Governance

In May 1999, the OECD published basic principles on corporate governance, which are based principally on the Millstein Report. The OECD presumes that the private sector, and not the legislature, has the main responsibility for the design of such principles or standards.[9] The OECD report and the principles issued thus far follow the Anglo-American train of thought regarding corporate governance in that two aspects are always cited: the leadership of the corporation and the alignment of interests of the corporation's shareholders and stakeholders.[10] The main focus of the OECD principles is clearly on shareholder value and the monistic board system with basic principles encompassing, e.g. protection of stakeholders and of shareholder rights, equal treatment of shareholders, disclosure, and transparency. All of the latter are directed at corporate leadership. This approach, which concentrates mainly on the board of directors, has already been considered in the discussion of the Cadbury Report of 1992. The boards 'must be free to drive their companies forward but must exercise that freedom within a framework of effective accountability. This is the essence of any system of good corporate governance'.

C. Code of Best Practices of the German *Grundsatzkommission* on Corporate Governance and the German Corporate Governance Code

In spring 1999, a representative German commission (*Grundsatzkommission*) examined various notions of the publicly listed German firms and published a uniform catalogue of basic principles.[11] These principles do not contain a legislative proposal; rather, they encompass rules and corresponding responsibilities to which corporate executive boards, supervisory boards (i.e., board of directors), and management should commit themselves.[12] The commission interprets the stakeholder interest mentioned in the OECD report as an international recognition of the German principles of worker participation and dualistic leadership. They stress that the published principles concentrate basically on the duties of the executive board (management body) and the supervisory board (governing body) and the division of their competencies. In contrast to the

---

[9] P. Hommelhoff, *Die OECD-Principles on Corporate Governance—ihre Chancen und Risiken aus dem Blickwinkel der deutschen Corporate Governance-Bewegung*, These No. 2.

[10] P. Böckli, 'Corporate Governance: Der Stand der Dinge nach den Berichten "Hampel", "Viénot" und "OECD" sowie dem deutschen "KonTraG"' [1999] 1 *Südtiroler Wirtschaftszeitung* 9.

[11] U. Schneider and C. Strenger, 'Die "Corporate Governance-Grundsätze" der Grundsatzkommission Corporate Governance' [2000] 3 *Die Aktiengesellschaft* 109.

[12] ibid.

system of the uniform bodies found in the Anglo-American system, the German principles focus on dualistic systems with supervisory and executive boards.[13]

Also noteworthy here is the recently published German Corporate Governance Code ('Deutscher Corporate Governance Kodex'): Developed by German business, this Code contains statutory regulations for the management and supervision of German listed companies together with national and international standards for 'good and responsible governance'. In essence, it is aimed at increasing the transparency of Germany's corporate governance rules for both national and international investors and thereby fortifying confidence in corporate management. As presented on February 26, 2002, the Code is based on current German statutes; following the anticipated enactment of the German Transparency and Disclosure Law (currently a bill: 'Transparenz- und Publizitätsgesetzes' dated February 6, 2002), legislative modifications will be accommodated in the Code's first revision.[14]

D. Stock Market Development of Corporate Governance Codes

It is worth noting at this point that almost all stock markets are developing codes of corporate governance, with particular regard to questions of information disclosure and transparency. Thus, the *Comitato per la Corporate Governance delle Società Quotate 1999* for the Italian stock market has published a Code of Conduct as well as an accompanying report, and, likewise, the London Stock Exchange has published a 'Combined Code'. Codes such as these are basically similar to the already mentioned Cadbury, Greenbury, and Hampel[15] Reports in their content; but they especially stress questions regarding transparency and disclosure of information as well as the need for extended internal controls. Moreover, the Combined Code has mandated the creation of audit committees for the U.K. In Switzerland, the new corporate law which entered into force on July 1, 1992, bears many similarities to the Cadbury and Hampel Reports.[16]

E. The Increased Function of the Audit

Before taking a closer look at the some of the relevant corporate governance principles, it is important to consider briefly the increased function of the audit from an international perspective.

---

[13] Böckli, see above, n. 10, 6.

[14] www.Corporate-Governance-Code.de/eng/download/CorGov_Endfassung_E.pdf.

[15] Böckli, see above, n. 10, 11.

[16] See also Comparative Study of Corporate Governance Codes Relevant to the European Union and Its Member States, above, n. 8.

The globalization of the capital market requires the application of generalized principles to the corporate judgment. The procurement of capital depends upon the willingness of the investing public to trust and to invest in corporations. The independent auditor increasingly plays a key role in the creation of that necessary trust.

The rapid development of the information and communication technology and, in particular, the development of the electronic trading platforms will change the manner by which transactions are carried out as well as the way in which financial information is transferred. Company reporting over accounting has also changed: through Internet reporting, investor access to information has been facilitated and the analysis and comparison of information improved. Increasingly, investors want their decisions to be compatible with a basic continuum of standardized corporate information derived from finance and non-finance information. In addition, regular corporate reporting on accounts plays a fundamental part in the guarantee of transparency for investor protection and contributes to the general stability of the market.[17]

Today's auditors review financial statements according to the internationally recognized principles of U.S. GAAP and IAS. These same basic principles will be increasingly recommended for general application by international organizations such as the International Organization of Securities Commissions (IOSCO) or the EU.[18]

In response to Enron, the EU has published a paper outlining measures to avoid similar events in Europe with an emphasis, inter alia, on policy issues in the areas of financial reporting, statutory audit, corporate governance and transparency. With regard to reporting, the paper calls for early adoption and enforcement of the proposed EU Regulation on IAS so that these standards will become mandatory for all publicly traded EU companies by 2005.[19]

The financial statements issued according to these international accounting standards are reviewed by auditors. It is their task to ensure that these statements correspond to the international standards, render a 'true and fair' view, and are free of materially false statements. Of course, it is not the task of the auditors to issue the financial statements on their own or to take on the responsibility of guaranteeing, absolutely, the accuracy of the published figures.

[17] EU COM(2000) 359; July 13, 2000; 3.

[18] Communication of the Commission to the Council and the EU Parliament, July 13, 2000; COM(2000) 359; 1.

[19] The paper, 'A First Response to Enron Related Policy Issues' is available on the internet at www.europa.eu.int/comm/internal_market/en/company/index.htm. The IAS regulation was endorsed by the European Parliament and the Council (IP/02/417, IP/01/200 and MEMO/01/40). On 31 May 2002, the EU Council of Ministers and the European Parliament adopted a 'Directive to Modernize the EU Accounting Rules'. The Directive forms part of the Financial Services Action Plan (IP/00/1269). On 7 June 2002, the EU Council of Ministers agreed to the adoption of the IAS by all listed EU companies by 2005.

Through the audit, the auditor takes on a responsibility to all those interested in the corporation. The audit is the only independent instance where the corporation is required to present its results with information upon which outsiders can rely for their decisions. Thus, today, independent auditors are increasingly assuming the role of a public confidant. This quasi-public position of trust is stressed heavily in the U.S.A. In spring 2000, the SEC published an extensive, and very important, report about the role of the external auditor and the question of its independence. The report has caused a heated debate and has already proved to have had an impact on those concerned. Among other things, it was noted in the report that:

> Independent auditors have an important public trust function. Every day, millions of people invest their savings in our securities markets in reliance on financial statements prepared by public companies and audited by independent auditors. Investors must be able to put faith in issuers' financial statements. The federal securities laws make independent auditors 'gate-keepers' to the public securities markets. By certifying the public report that collectively depicts a corporation's financial status, the independent auditor assumes a public responsibility transcending any employment relationship with the client and owes ultimate allegiance to the corporation's creditors and stockholders, as well as to the investing public.[20]

The EU has been developing a three pronged strategy on auditing since 1998 dealing with external quality assurance, auditor independence, and auditing standards. According to the above mentioned EU paper responding to Enron, a Recommendation on auditor independence will soon be issued by the Commission requiring, in essence, that the auditor 'demonstrate (and document) that none of his actions compromise his independence'. This Recommendation will also indicate areas where non-audit services to the audit client are prohibited because of the potential risk to auditor independence. The Enron debacle has also strengthened EU recognition of the need to enhance supervision of the audit profession. A Communication on future priorities for auditing strategy will be presented by the Commission to the European Parliament and Council before the end of 2002.[21]

F. Focus on the Demands of Management

As mentioned at the outset of this chapter, the extensive international debate concerning corporate governance has, until now, heavily emphasized the demands placed upon the corporation's management and board of directors, as well as the questions concerning the competence of these bodies. Thus, existing codes mainly establish, without exception, principles for the responsibility and

---

[20] SEC, Proposed Rule: *Revision of the SEC Commission's Auditor Independence Requirements*, June 2000 17 CFR Parts 210 and 240; www.sec.gov/rules/proposed/34_42994.htm,2.

[21] www.europea.eu.int/comm/internal_market/en/company/index.htm, 4.

tasks of the bodies, underscore their information and disclosure duties, deal with compensation questions, and contain rules governing conflicts of interest and transactions in which a person acts as a representative or proxy for both parties. Until now, the focus of these principles has been upon the realization of a responsible corporate leadership.

The concept of responsible control systems has mostly been viewed as an internal control problem resulting in a demand for the creation of independent audit committees as sub-committees of the administrative board (board of directors). This is similarly called for by the Hampel report, referring to the suggestions of the Cadbury Report, which is concerned with the creation of audit committees occupied by directors that do not participate in management and are responsible to the board:

> We support the Cadbury recommendation (Report 4.35(a) and (b)) that all listed companies should establish an audit committee, composed of non-executive directors, as a committee of, and responsible to, the board.[22]

With regard to the tasks of such committees, it is further provided:

> The duties of the audit committee include keeping under review the scope and results of the audit and its cost-effectiveness, and the independence and objectivity of the auditors.[23]

The abovementioned German corporate governance principles of the *Grundsatzkommission* also foster the creation of the audit committee as part of the supervisory board. The latter should evaluate the audit report of the auditor and report to the supervisory board on the accompanying financial statement, with particular consideration given to the future development of the corporation.[24]

The creation of audit committees received strong support from the American Blue Ribbon Committee, which has called for a stronger independence and a higher qualification for members of the said committees.

All reports or codes emphasize that, in the interests of the corporation and the shareholders, the audit committee should be composed of directors, independent of management, who should be elected in a manner open and transparent to the shareholders.[25]

The relevance of the external independent control, the external audit, has, until now, been given little recognition in the published principles, but it is up to the external auditors 'to feed' the audit committees.

---

[22] Hampel Report, 2.21, 21.

[23] ibid.

[24] *Grundsatzkommission* Corporate Governance, *Corporate Governance Grundsätze für börsennotierte Gesellschaften* July 2000, 8.

[25] Exemplary, *Code of Conduct*, Borsa Italiana 5.6, 14.

G. The New Perspective: External Audit as Part of Corporate Governance

The external audit has already been introduced into the corporate governance debate, however, its importance within the corporate structure has not been given sufficient attention. Moreover, as evidenced by the principles elaborated upon below, the precise role of the external auditor has not yet been agreed upon.

As previously stated, the importance of the external audit has, until recently, only had a subordinate connection with the debate concerning the formation of external audit committees. Currently, however, the audit is increasingly granted the position and task of a public trust function in the public debate. Due to this, it should also be given a higher and more independent significance within the framework of the principles of corporate governance. Thus, the 1998 EU Commission has stated:

> The role of the auditor must be seen in connection with the corporate management. Generally, a consensus exists regarding the possibility of strengthening the position of the external auditor within the structure of the corporation (unofficial translation).[26]

One basis for this increased importance of the external audit is the actual discussion concerning the independence of the auditor vis à vis its client.

The Cadbury report deals with the significance of the audit in detail in sections 5.1 to 5.35. With regard to its function as an independent monitoring mechanism, it is noted:

> The annual audit is one of the cornerstones of Corporate Governance. . . . The audit provides an external and objective check on the way in which the financial statements have been prepared and presented, and it is an essential part of the checks and balances required. The question is not whether there should be an audit, but how to ensure its objectivity and effectiveness.[27]

The 1998 Hampel Report stresses the importance of a more detailed external audit which is elaborated upon in its section 6, 'Accountability and Audit'. Regarding auditor independence, it is stated:

> Everyone concerned accepts the principle that auditors must be objective and thus remain independent from company management. Statutory provisions, auditing standards and professional guidance all aim to ensure that this principle is applied in practice. We are confident that those concerned will keep these safeguards under close scrutiny and will bring in any improvements which are necessary. . .[28]

---

[26] Communication of the Commission concerning the Audit in the EU, future plans in Official Journal, C143 of (0805/1998) 0012.

[27] Cadbury Report, 5.1.

[28] Hampel Report, III, 6.8 (See generally, Hampel Report; III, 6.5–6.9, 50ff).

Another related aspect of significance here is the audit committee's role in the maintenance of auditor independence and objectivity:

> The audit committee is an essential safeguard of auditor independence and objectivity; we suggest that it should keep under review the overall financial relationship between the company and the auditors. In particular, the audit committee should have a key role where the auditors also supply a substantial volume of non-audit services to the client . . .[29]

Also, in the Millstein Report, perspective 16, the following position was observed:

> Policy makers and regulators should encourage sound audit practices, which include board selection of, and reliance on, an independent auditor.[30]

In the OECD principles, IV.C, it is stated:

> An annual audit should be conducted by an independent auditor in order to provide an external and objective assurance on the way in which financial statements have been prepared and presented.

And, the German *Grundsatzkommission* made the following statement in their corporate governance principles:[31]

> The supervisory board selects and assigns the auditor for the annual statement of accounts.

To ensure the independence of the auditor, particular attention is given to the following:

> —that the assigned auditor did not, in the previous 5 years, generate more than 30% of his total turnover from the audit and the consulting of the corporation or from companies in which the corporation participates with more than 20%, and that this is not anticipated for the ongoing year.
> —that no auditor will be engaged for the audit if he or she has in the past 10 years issued the audit certificate or has signed the consolidated accounts in more than 6 cases.
> —that there is no conflict of interest existing between the auditor and the company.

The supervisory board can also set up their own standards regarding the more important points which further the legal standing and the scope of the audit. The awarding of the contract also includes the agreement on the audit fee. All members of the supervisory board receive the audit reports in good time for the conferences which are held in the presence of the auditors.

The Berlin Initiative Group German Code of Corporate Governance, an undertaking of the Economics and Management Faculty of the Technical University of Berlin, has recently proposed guidelines for corporate leadership and supervision with a section on the annual audit[32] which pays particular attention to the role of auditor independence and neutrality:

[29] Hampel Report, III, 6.9.

[30] Millstein Report, perspective 16, 23.

[31] *Grundsatzkommission* Corporate Governance, *Corporate Governance Grundsätze für börsennotierte Gesellschaften* (July 2000) 9.

[32] *German Code of Corporate Governance* (*GCCG*), s. 2, Annual Audit, see above, n. 5, 33–4.

The auditor is an independent guarantor of open disclosure for the reference groups of the company, and in addition to that, is a supportive partner to the Supervisory Board in the supervisory process. He controls separate parts of Management Board dealings but is also available to the Management Board as advisor.

With regard to the connection between auditor independence and control, it is noted:

The independence of the auditor is essential for a consistent and reliable control. Hence, the auditor takes all reasonable steps to safeguard his neutrality. Before anything else, he ensures that the extent of the mandate for audit as well as any additional business relationships with the company to be audited (for example, consultancy contracts) does not affect his economic independence.

A provision for ensuring such independence and neutrality suggests:

The Supervisory Board should also take into consideration, on the recommendation for the appointment of the auditor, whether the work of the auditor should undergo evaluation by an expert third party at regular intervals (peer review).[33]

Finally, another more recent and noteworthy set of corporate governance principles addressing the external audit has been elaborated by the European Association of Securities Dealers (EASD). Pursuant to their 'Corporate Governance Principles and Recommendations', Principle VIII, which deals with disclosure, emphasizes obtaining 'independent verification and certification of the existence of appropriate controls'.[34] With regard to external auditors, it is provided that they 'should be independent and free from conflicting interests which, if they exist, must be disclosed [and that] the external auditors' responsibilities towards shareholders are without prejudice to their additional duties of informing the board of their findings with regard to internal controls and other verifications'. Finally, it is recommended that external auditors attend shareholder meetings 'to which they report on and request at relevant board and committee meetings'.[35]

Although relatively young, the Codes of corporate governance are already in need of a development of their perspectives. In this respect, they have to deal more intensively with a topic, which, until now, has only arisen in a secondary form: still lacking is the demand for a more efficient, external, independent control and the development of a definitive response to the ensuing question of the status of the external audit and the exact function of the external auditor.

[33] ibid., ss. 2.1, 2.6 and 2.7, (respectively).

[34] EASD, European Association of Securities Dealers, *Corporate Governance Principles and Recommendations* (May 2000) 8.

[35] ibid., 21.

H. The Independent Audit in Europe

Increasing emphasis is being placed on the importance of an independent audit in Europe. In Germany, corresponding audit rules found in HGB § 316–324, have been strengthened by the *KontTraG* (laws on control and transparency in the corporate area). Article 2 para. 8 *KonTraG* adds two new requirements to the catalogue of § 319 HGB, which is the article that sets forth the auditor independence standards: first, an auditor is no longer considered as independent if in the previous five years, he generated more than 30% of his total annual income from the audit and the consulting of the corporation or from companies with which the corporation is related (this was 50% before the *KonTraG*). Secondly, an auditor's independence is seen as impaired if, in the case of auditing a publicly listed corporation, the auditor has in the last 10 years issued the audit certificate in more than six cases.

In Switzerland, regulations concerning independence can be found in the '*OR*' (obligations law) '*BankG*',(banking law) '*AFG*', (investment fund law) '*BEHG*', (stock exchange and securities trading law); also in the draft for the '*RRG*' (accounting laws) and in the respective ordinances and directives of the *Treuhandkammer* (Swiss Institute of Certified Accountants and Tax Consultants). An increased tendency towards independence can already be seen in the new '*RRG*'. Foreign pressure will soon lead to heightened demands for the same. On the EU level, the principle of independence is postulated in the Fifth and Eighth Directives, the concept is, however, not defined in detail and, thus, a more concrete delineation is up to the individual Member States.

The Directive is concerned principally with the harmonization of the technical requirements of the auditor; however, it also contains the demands for the honesty and independence of the auditor.

In 1998, the EU expressed the opinion that the existing requirements for auditor independence in EU law would be sufficient for all demands and that a simple further development by practice would be enough.

Currently, the EU has changed its mind and is in the process of revising its accounting standards to conform to modern developments. The Commission wants to present modernization proposals before the end of the year 2002. In connection with this, they will also be forced to consider the increasing importance of the external independent audit, as is currently being requested by the U.S.A. The Commission has also already indicated that the list of authoritative criteria for the audit, the development of standards for the professional ethics, and the development of a system to insure quality will be aimed at in order to create a framework for high quality.[36]

---

[36] Communication of the EU Commission of June 13, 2000; COM (2000) 359, no. 27.

Nowadays, it cannot be doubted that the accounting and the audit are part of the laws about capital markets and that the further development of rules concerning these subjects are very closely connected to the efforts to create an internal financial market for the EU.

I. Consequence: Increased Demands for Independence

Behind this 'public watchdog' function,[37] the auditor is expected to maintain a high level of independence from the client. Auditors should not only be factually independent from the audited corporation; they should also appear as such in the eyes of a critical outsider. This requirement of an 'independence in fact and appearance' is not only generally recognized but made more especially concrete via pressure exerted by the American SEC supervisory authorities.

J. Development of the 'Big Five' Audit Firms

The development of the 'Big Five',[37a] the five largest and leading accounting firms in the world, plays an important role within the debate. In recent years, the 'Big Five' have broadened their field of activity. Their original activity, the actual accounting, is no longer particularly significant and not really interesting financially. Today, the 'Big Five' earn 50% of their income in the management/consulting field, which was only 13% in 1981.[38] But, the traditional audit work still gives the corporations the ideal opportunity to offer other and more lucrative services in the consulting area to their audit clients.

Today the scope of services of the large audit companies includes the implementation of computer systems, the design of E-Commerce solutions, the outsourcing of the entire human resource division, or even active portfolio care or legal representation. An extensive threat to the objectivity of the audit company results from the many-sided contractual relations or involvement between the audited firms on the one hand and the audit companies, acting simultaneously as adviser and auditor, on the other. It follows logically that the SEC raises the legitimate question in its report of how an auditor should be able to objectively and independently audit a company whose leadership powers are recruited by its own auditing firm and /or whose EDV system or E-commerce entrance is implemented through its own corporation.

---

[37] SEC, Proposed Rule: *Revision of the SEC Commission's Auditor Independence Requirements* (June 2000) 5.

[37a] These were at the time of writing, E&Y, PwC, Deloitte and Touche, KPMG, and Arthur Andersen.

[38] SEC, Proposed Rule: *Revision of the SEC Commission's Auditor Independence Requirements* (June 2000) 8.

K. Demands of the SEC (Securities and Exchange Commission)

An intensified attention is given to the independence of the auditor in the U.S.A., where the professional organization and the ISB (Independent Standards Board) have taken over the further development of the independence principles. The SEC has long made clear that its auditor independence rules prohibit an auditor from certifying the financial statements of a client if the auditor works for a firm that has an attorney-client relationship with the same client ('no advocacy').[39]

The leadership in this area is in the SEC under its chairman, Arthur Levitt, whose goal, *inter alia*, has been to improve the quality of investor information flows, particularly to more recent participants in the financial market who happen to be 'ordinary members of the public'.[40] In a recent speech before the annual meeting of the accounting-industry trade group in Las Vegas, Mr. Levitt, appealing to member virtue, stated:

> In what other profession is it one's duty to tell the customer when he's wrong? . . . What other profession is enshrined in our nation's securities laws to serve no interest but the public's? What other profession so directly holds the key to public confidence—the life force of our markets? . . .Alas, it has become clear that the perceived value of the audit is being put at risk.[41]

In spring 2000, the SEC proposed new regulations and announced them at a public hearing; recently, it has conducted several open hearings. In its report on the new rulings, the SEC underlines the public function of the audit and its responsibility for the functioning of the capital market.

Following extensive discussions, the SEC approved a final proposal to Modernize the Rules Governing the Independence of the Accounting Profession on 15 November 2000.[42] The final proposal takes account of some of the criticism raised by the 'Big Five' in the public hearings, especially the alternative proposals formulated and presented by PWC and Ernst & Young.

---

[39] Letter of Harvey J. Goldschmid, Chief Council, SEC, et al. to Philip S. Anderson, Esq, President ABA, July 12, 1999, in Discussion Memorandum, Legal Services, Independent Standards Board; see also, Model Rule 5.4; American Bar Association.

[40] *The Economist*, October 18 2000, 99.

[41] ibid., 100.

[42] The Commission's Proposal to Modernize the Rules Governing the Independence of the Accounting Profession, November 15, 2000; www.sec.gov/news/extra/faqaud.htm. (It should be noted that since the delivery of this paper for the occasion of the First European Conference on Corporate Governance in November 2000, the SEC issued its 'final rule' for the revision of the Commission's auditor independence requirements, which entered into force in February 2001. Although similar, in most respects, to the original proposal, the final rule is somewhat less stringent: it can be accessed at http://www.sec.gov/rules/final/33-7919.htm: another important US development concerning, inter alia, auditor independence is the recently enacted Sarbanes-Oxley Act of 2002, H.R.3763; 107th Congress at http://news.findlaw.com/hdocs/docs/gwbush/sarbanesoxley 072302.pdf.)

The SEC formulated its demand for independence in four principles that are incorporated into a preliminary note purported for use as a general guidance in measuring auditor independence.[43] The principles elicit when an auditor is not independent and illustrate situations where the SEC has determined that 'reasonable investors would agree' that an auditor's independence has been impaired. These are when the auditor:

—has a mutual or conflicting interest with the audit client;
—audits his own firm's work;
—functions as management or an employee of the audit client; or
—acts as an advocate for the audit client.

Additionally, the SEC listed some relationships between auditor and client, which might impair the auditor's independence. These include:

—financial relationships;
—employment relationships;
—business relationships.

Regarding General Standards for Auditor Independence, it is stated that 'an auditor's independence is impaired either when the accountant is not independent "in fact" or when, in light of all relevant facts and circumstances, a reasonable investor would conclude that the auditor would not be capable of acting without bias'.[44]

Beyond the questions of whether the scope of financial or personnel associations between auditors, their relatives, or other connected persons and those who are audited, or related persons, are permitted, there is a further and important concern underlying the new SEC rules. Primarily, the rules deal with the scope of non-audit services, especially the consulting services that might be offered by the auditor to an audit client without impairment of independence. Here, the SEC has clearly taken into consideration drawing a line and prohibiting auditors from offering any non-audit service to audit clients. The proposals presented for public hearing did not consider such a radical solution; the final proposals set a narrow boundary for the future permissible service area of the auditing firms. In particular, there will be a limitation placed on the overflow of lucrative consulting services.

According to the SEC rules, future auditing firms may no longer provide the following services because, through such services, their independence as auditing firms is impaired:

—bookkeeping services;
—financial information systems design and implementation;

[43] Proposed Rule § 210.2–01(b), SEC Report, 70.

[44] The Commission's Proposal to Modernize the Rules Governing the Independence of the Accounting Profession, November 15, 2000, www.sec.gov/news/extra/audfact.htm, 1–2.

—appraisal or valuation services, fairness opinions, or contribution-in-kind reports;
—actuarial services;
—a complete internal audit outsourcing;
—management functions;
—human resources;
—broker-dealer, investment adviser, or investment banking services;
—legal services.

Contrary to its first proposal, the SEC allows for the provision of IT consulting services and Internal Audit Services in its final rule, under certain circumstances:

> The auditor cannot operate or supervise the operation of the client's IT systems, but he will be allowed to provide IT consulting services provided that the management:
>
> (1) acknowledges to the auditor and audit committee management's responsibility for the client's system of internal controls,
> (2) identifies a person within management to make all management decisions with respect to the project,
> (3) makes all significant decisions with respect to the IT project,
> (4) evaluates the adequacy and results of the project, and
> (5) does not rely on the accountant's work as the primary basis for determining the adequacy of its financial reporting system.[45]

Concerning Internal Audit Services, it is stated that '[a]n audit firm would be allowed to perform up to 40% (measured in terms of hours) of an audit client's internal audit work'.[46]

Also new is the Proxy Disclosure Requirement, pursuant to which '[c]ompanies would disclose in their annual proxy statements, IT consulting and all other services provided by their auditors during the last fiscal year [and would] also state whether the audit committee has considered whether the provision of the non-audit services is compatible with maintaining the auditor's independence'.[47]

The intensified pace of the SEC has placed pressure on the 'Big Five' firms. Significant effects are already obvious: Ernst & Young, for example, has already sold their consulting area to Cap Gemini and PWC has tried to sell their consulting division to Hewlett-Packard, a plan that was abandoned by HP on November 13, 2000. Even KPMG, which heavily opposed the new SEC rules in the public hearings, has published plans for an international restructuring.[48]

---

[45] The Commission's Proposal to Modernize the Rules Governing the Independence of the Accounting Profession, November 15, 2000, www.sec.gov/news/extra/faqaud.htm, 3.

[46] ibid., 3.

[47] ibid., 5.

[48] *Financial Times*, September 18, 2000.

L. The Independent Auditor as the Basic Principle of Corporate Governance

The structure of the corporate governance principles requires elaboration to meet the demands for a strong independent external audit. Although the external audit has always been a part of corporate governance, its past treatment lacked sufficient consideration and importance. The time has come for this topic to be given the intensified attention it has long deserved.

APPENDIX

The Commission's Proposal to Modernize the Rules Governing the Independence of the Accounting Profession
(SEC Fact Sheet, Nov. 15, 2000; http://www.sec.gov/news/extra/faqaud.htm; see also Final Rule: Revision of the Commission's Auditor Independence Requirements, n. 42, above.)[49]

The Commission will consider the adoption of rules that modernize the requirements for auditor independence. Primarily in three areas:
(1) investments by auditors or their family members in audit clients;
(2) employment relationships between auditors or their family members and audit clients; and
(3) the scope of services provided by audit firms to their audit clients.
The rules would significantly reduce the number of audit firm employees and their family members whose investments in, or employment with, audit clients would impair an auditor's independence.

They would also identify certain non-audit services that, if provided to an audit client, would impair an auditor's independence. The proposals would not extend to services provided to non-audit clients.

A limited exception would be provided to an accounting firm for inadvertent independence violations if the firm has quality controls in place and the violation is corrected promptly.

Companies would disclose in their annual proxy statements certain information about *non-audit services* provided by their auditors during the last fiscal year.

---

[49] See SEC, 'Revision of the Commission's Auditor Independence', Release Nos. 33-7919, 34-43602, 35-27279, IC-24744, IA-1911, FR-56, File No. S7-13-00, 27 December 2000, *CCH SEC Docket*, vol. 73 No. 15, 1917 at http://www.sec.gov/rules/final.shtml. Another revision is taking place at the time of writing, see 'Proposed Rule; Strengthening the Commission's Requirements Regarding Auditor Independence', Release Nos. 33-8154, 34-46934, 35-27610, IC-25838, IA-2688, FR-64, 2 December 2002 at http://www.sec.gov/rules/proposed/35-8154htm.

Four Principles

The proposed release articulated four principles by which to measure an auditor's independence. An accountant is not independent when the accountant
(1) has a mutual or conflicting interest with the audit client,
(2) audits his or her own firm's work,
(3) functions as management or an employee of the audit client, or
(4) acts as an advocate for the audit client.
Many commentators expressed concern that the principles may cast too wide a net and affect services that would not impair an auditor's independence. The staff, accordingly, has recommended to the Commission that the four principles be taken out of the rule itself and be incorporated into a preliminary note and used as general guidance.

Financial Relationships

The adopted rules in the area of financial relationships would be similar to the proposed rules. They would narrow significantly the circle of people whose investments trigger independence concerns. Today, many partners in firms that do not work on the audit of a client, as well as their *spouses and families,* are restricted from investing in a firm's audit clients. The rules the Commission considers today would limit such restrictions to principally those who work on the audit or can influence the audit.

Employment Relationships

Adopted substantially as proposed, the employment relationship rules would greatly narrow the scope of people within audit firms whose families would be affected by the employment restrictions necessary to maintain independence. The rules also identify the positions, namely those in which a person can influence the audit client's accounting records or financial statements, which would impair an auditor's independence if held by a 'close family member' of the auditor.

Business Relationships

Consistent with existing rules, independence would be impaired if the accountant or any covered person has a direct or material indirect business relationship with the audit client, other than providing professional services.

General Standard for Auditor Independence

The rule is based on the widely endorsed principle that an auditor must be independent in fact and appearance. While some commentators stated that an appearance-related standard departs from current Commission rule, the Commission, courts, and the profession have long recognized the importance of the appearance of independence.

The staff, however, was mindful of the concern that an appearance standard would be subjectively applied. The final rule articulates that an auditor's independence is impaired either when the accountant is not independent 'in fact' or when, in light of all relevant facts and circumstances a reasonable investor would conclude that the auditor would not be capable of acting without bias. The objective 'reasonable investor' standard is a common construct in securities laws.

Non-Audit Services

The rules identify nine non-audit services that are deemed inconsistent with an auditor's independence. Seven of the nine services are already restricted by the A1CPA, SECPS, or SEC. As such, much of the Commission's rule proposal sought to codify existing restrictions. Commentators expressed concern that the proposal went beyond the scope of the current prohibitions. In response, the rules the staff recommends the Commission adopt today would closely track the current language found in the existing prohibitions.

Bookkeeping or Other Services Related to the Audit Client's Accounting Records or Financial Statements. Paralleling closely the current prohibition on bookkeeping, an audit firm could not maintain or prepare the audit client's accounting records or prepare the audit client's financial statements that are either filed with the Commission or form the basis of financial statements filed with the Commission. Exceptions include providing services in emergency situations, provided the accountant does not undertake any managerial actions or make any managerial decisions. Exceptions also include bookkeeping for foreign divisions or subsidiaries of an audit client, provided certain conditions exist.

Financial Information Systems Design and Implementation. The auditor cannot operate or supervise the operation of the client's IT systems. However, the auditor could provide IT consulting services provided certain criteria are met. These criteria include that management: (1) acknowledges to the auditor and audit committee management's responsibility for the client's system of internal controls, (2) identifies a person within management to make all management decisions with respect to the project, (3) makes all the significant decisions with respect to the IT project, (4) evaluates the adequacy and results of the project, and (5) does not rely on the accountant's work as the primary basis for determining the adequacy of its financial reporting system.

The issuer would also disclose the total amount of fees for IT services received from its auditor. The prohibition does not include services an accountant performs in connection with the assessment, design, and implementation of internal accounting controls and risk management controls.

Appraisal or Valuation Services or Fairness Opinions. The final rule would not ban all valuation and appraisal services. Its restrictions apply only where it is reasonably likely that the results of any valuation or appraisal would be material to the financial statements, or where the accountant would audit the results.

Actuarial Services. Closely tracking the SECPS prohibition on actuarial services, actuarial-oriented advisory services would be limited only when they involve the determination of insurance company policy reserves and related accounts. Certain types of actuarial services could be performed if the audit client uses its own actuaries or third party actuaries to provide management with the primary actuarial capabilities, management accepts responsibility for actuarial methods and assumptions, and the accountant does not render actuarial services to an audit client on a continuous basis.

Internal Audit Services. An audit firm would be allowed to perform up to 40% (measured in terms of hours) of an audit client's internal audit work. The rule would not restrict internal audit services regarding operational internal audits unrelated to accounting controls, financial systems, or financial statements. The rule would provide an exception for smaller businesses by excluding companies with less than $200 million in assets. Providing any internal audit services for an audit client, however, would be contingent on management taking responsibility for and making all management decisions concerning the internal audit function.

Management Functions. Consistent with current SEC rules, an auditor's independence would be impaired when the accountant acts, temporarily or permanently, as a director, officer, or employee of an audit client, or performs any decision-making, supervisory, or ongoing monitoring function for the audit client.

Human Resources. Closely paralleling the SECPS rules, an auditor would not be able to recruit, act as a negotiator on the audit client's behalf, develop employee testing or evaluation programmes, or recommend, or advise that the audit client hire, a specific candidate for a specific job. An accounting firm could, upon request by the audit client, interview candidates and advise the audit client on the candidate's competence for financial accounting, administrative, or control positions.

Broker-Dealer Services. Consistent with current AWPA rules, an auditor could not serve as a broker-dealer, promoter, or underwriter of an audit client's securities.

Legal Services. An auditor could not provide any service to an audit client under circumstances in which the person providing the service must be admitted to practice before the courts of a U.S. jurisdiction.

Affiliate Provisions

The proposed rule contained a definition of an 'affiliate of an accounting firm' that many commentators felt might affect accounting firms' joint ventures with companies that are not their audit clients and the continuation of small firm alliances—relationships that traditionally have not been thought to impair an accountant's independence. After considering these comments, the staff has recommended that the definition in the proposed rule not be adopted. Instead, the Commission would continue to analyze these situations under existing guidance.

An 'affiliate' of an audit client would be defined to be any entity that can significantly influence, or is significantly influenced by, the audit client, provided the equity investment is material to the entity or the audit client. 'Significant influence' generally is presumed when the investor owns 20% or more of the voting stock of the investee. The significant influence test is *used* because under GAM it is the trigger that causes the earnings and losses of one company to be reflected in the financial statements of another company.

Contingent Fee Arrangements

The rules reiterate that an accountant cannot provide any service to an audit client that involves a contingent fee.

Quality Controls

The rules provide a limited exception from independence violations to the accounting firm, if certain factors are present:
—The individual did not know the circumstances giving rise to his or her violation.
—The violation was corrected promptly once the violation became apparent.
—The firm has quality controls in place that provide reasonable assurance that the firm and its employees maintain their independence. For the largest public accounting firms, the basic controls must include, among others, written independence policies and procedures, automated systems to identify financial relationships that may impair independence, training, internal inspection and testing, and a disciplinary mechanism for enforcement.

Proxy Disclosure Requirement

Companies would disclose in their annual proxy statements the fees for audit, IT consulting and all other services provided by their auditors during the past fiscal year.

Companies will also state whether the audit committee has considered whether the provision of the non-audit services is compatible with maintaining the auditor's independence.

Lastly, the registrant would be required to disclose the percentage hours worked on the audit engagement by persons other than the accountant's full time employees, if that figure exceeded 50%. This requirement responds to recent moves by some accounting firms to sell their practices to financial services companies. The partners or employees often become employees of the financial services firm. The accounting firm then leases assets, namely auditors, back from those companies to complete audit engagements. In such cases, most of the auditors who work on an audit are employed elsewhere unbeknownst to the public.

Part IV:

Corporate Governance and Shareholder Value

10

Shareholder Value and the Modernization of European Corporate Law

GUIDO FERRARINI

Abstract

In this chapter, I argue that the shareholder value concept is a useful yardstick by which to measure the responsiveness of corporate law and practice to the needs of capital markets. I analyse, in particular, some of the corporate law institutions and practices that offer an organizational setting for the wealth creation process, focusing on the board of directors, take-overs, and share buy-backs. The general question that I ask is whether European corporate law is sufficiently responsive to the needs of shareholder value creation. I answer that question by reference to a number of aspects of European corporate law and indicate avenues for future research.

Contents

A. Introduction

In this chapter, I argue that the shareholder value concept appears as a useful yardstick by which to measure the responsiveness of corporate law and practice to the needs of capital markets; it also offers a wider perspective than that provided by a pure agency costs approach. The concept of shareholder value appears to offer the rationale for law reforms in different areas, such as executive compensation, take-over defences, and financial restructurings, which represent a promising field for research in European corporate governance.

I analyse, in particular, some of the corporate law institutions and practices that offer an organizational setting for the shareholder wealth creation process, focusing on the board of directors, take-overs, and share buy-backs. The focus on wealth maximization is consistent with recent "law and finance" research that analyses corporate law from an investor protection perspective, concentrating on shareholders and creditors' rights, and their enforcement.[1] This chapter is

---

[1] See R. La Porta, F. Lopez-de-Silanes, A. Shleifer, and R.W. Vishny, 'Law and Finance' [1998] 106 *Journal of Political Economy* 1113.

concerned with rules that promote shareholder value creation,[2] and not necessarily coincide with those directed to reduce agency costs.[3] The general question
that I ask is whether European corporate law is sufficiently responsive to the
needs of shareholder value creation[4]. I try to answer that question by reference
to a number of aspects of European corporate law and to indicate avenues for
future research.

This chapter is organized as follows. Firstly, the shareholder value approach
is analysed and the convergence of the legal systems toward a shareholder model
of corporate law is examined.[5] Secondly, the legal duties of managers with respect
to shareholder value creation are considered, looking at the European best practices. Moreover, the controls and incentives applicable to managers are examined
from the internal governance viewpoint, focusing on the board of directors' role
in corporate strategy formulation and in the selection, monitoring, and remuneration of management. Thirdly, the market for corporate control is discussed with
regard to the defensive arsenal available to targets in the American and European
jurisdictions, and the use and limits of defensive measures and alternative
arrangements. The monitoring function of the market for corporate control is
widely acknowledged,[6] as is the fact that take-overs generally enhance corporate

---

[2] The rules on boards of directors are studied from a performance perspective in empirical works
of finance: for a review, see K. Lohn and L.W. Senbet, 'Corporate Governance and Board
Effectiveness' [1998] 22 *Journal of Banking & Finance* 371 at 380; see para. II below.

[3] One of the central issues in corporate governance discussion is the agency costs' problem,
which derives from the separation of ownership and control, and refers to the "difficulties financiers
have in assuring that their funds are not expropriated or wasted on unattractive projects": see
A. Shleifer and R.W. Vishny, 'A Survey of Corporate Governance' [1997] 52 *Journal of Finance* 737,
741. Corporate law provides ways to minimize such costs and indemnify the damaged investors.
More than shareholder value creation, it is the reduction of managerial opportunism that is central
to this area of the law. Indeed, the major problem dealt with by corporate law is "how to keep managers accountable to their other-directed duties while nonetheless allowing them great discretionary
power over appropriate matters" (R.C. Clark, *Corporate Law* (New York 1986) 33–34.

[4] Corporate law is concerned with shareholder value creation, despite the fact that the corporation's purpose is traditionally defined as profit maximization that does not necessarily coincide with
shareholder wealth maximization. American law and finance scholars tend to consider profit maximization as equivalent to shareholder value maximization: see F.H. Easterbrook and D.R. Fischel,
The Economic Structure of Corporate Law (Harvard 1991) 36; R. Romano, *The Genius of American
Corporate Law* (Washington DC 1993) 2. Finance theory, however, makes a distinction between the
two concepts (see, e.g. S.A. Ross, R. Westerfield. and B. Jordan, *Fundamentals of Corporate Finance*
5th edn. (New York 2000) 9), as reflected by the shareholder value literature: see, e.g. A. Rappaport,
Creating Shareholder Value 2nd edn. (New York/London 1998) 13; see also n. 11. As to British law,
see P. Davies (below, Chapter 11), arguing that company law facilitates but does not require or guarantee the maximization of shareholder value.

[5] On this convergence, see H. Hansmann and R. Kraakman, *The End of History for Corporate
Law*, [2001] 89 *Georgetown Law Journal* 439–468.

[6] H. Manne, 'Mergers and the Market for Corporate Control' [1965] 73 *Journal of Political
Economy* 110; F.H. Easterbrook and D.R. Fischel, above, n. 4, 171.

value: "since targets gain and bidders do not lose, the evidence suggests that take-overs create value".[7] Fourthly, financial restructurings are approached from a law and finance perspective, focusing on share repurchases and the rules on financial assistance. I argue that the design of corporate law structure should be such as to reduce the cost of equity capital and provide techniques for financial restructuring (spin-offs, debt-financed recapitalizations, leveraged buy-outs, etc.), which promote shareholder value creation.[8]

B. Finance Theory and Corporate Law

I. The Shareholder Value Approach

If we adopt a corporate manager's standpoint and ask what a good financial management decision is, the answer given by a standard finance textbook is straightforward: "the goal of financial management is to maximize the current value per share of the existing stock".[9] This statement requires some explanation. Clearly, firms should be managed so as to make money or "add value" for their owners. The problem is defining this objective adequately. Reference to profit maximization is frequent, but lacks precision. First of all, it is not clear whether we should refer to short-term, long-term or average profits.[10] Furthermore, accounting earnings fail to measure changes in the economic value of the firm.[11] Under the economic model of valuation, share prices are

[7] M.C. Jensen and R.S. Ruback, 'The Market for Corporate Control' [1983] 11 *Journal of Financial Economics* 5, 22.

[8] "The great mystery is how merely changing the financial or ownership structure can enhance the value of assets residing on the other side of the balance sheet": G.B. Stewart, *The Quest for Value. The EVA Management Guide* (1990), 9.

[9] Ross, Westerfield, and Jordan, above, n. 4, 11. Consequently, the object of corporate finance as a field of study is defined by saying that "we need to learn how to identify those investments and financing arrangements that favourably impact the value of the stock". In other words, corporate finance is "the study of the relationship between business decisions and the value of the stock in the business".

[10] ibid. 9. If we refer to short-term profits, then actions such as deferring maintenance will tend to increase profits, but are not necessarily desirable. If we refer to long-term profits, then it is not clear what the appropriate trade-off is between current and future profits.

[11] See Rappaport, above, n. 4, 14–20. There are three important reasons why earnings fail to measure changes in the economic value of a firm: (i) alternative accounting methods may be employed (prominent examples are the differences that arise from last-in, first-out (LIFO) and first-in, first-out (FIFO) approaches to computing cost of sales, various methods of computing depreciation, and purchase versus pooling-of-interests accounting for mergers and acquisitions); (ii) investment requirements are excluded (to move from earnings to cash flow, two adjustments are needed: firstly, the depreciation must be added back to earnings; secondly, capital expenditures must be deducted from earnings); (iii) time value of money is ignored for earnings calculation (whereas the economic value of an investment is the discounted value of the anticipated cash flows). Rappaport concludes that, in light of these differences "it should come as no surprise that *earnings growth does not necessarily lead to the creation of economic value for shareholders*" (18).

determined by investors looking at "about just two things: the cash to be generated over the life of a business and the risk of the cash receipts".[12] The appropriate goal for a firm, therefore, is to maximize the *current* value of the stock. The criterion is unambiguous and does not pose any short-term versus long-term issue.[13]

Looking at corporate practice, the shareholder value philosophy has gained widespread acceptance in the U.S. Until the early eighties, management thinking was largely governed by a short-term earnings orientation.[14] Subsequently, corporate raiders provided an incentive for managers to focus on creating value. In the nineties, similar results were determined by institutional investors who demanded long-term value creation.[15] Furthermore, with the globalization of both competition and capital markets along with the wave of privatizations, shareholder value has been capturing the attention of executives in the U.K., Continental Europe, Australia, and even Japan.[16]

Creating value is complex. The crucial rule is offered by the theory of finance and is incorporated in the "net present value" approach to the capital budgeting decision (i.e. the process of planning a firm's long-term investments): "an investment should be accepted if the net present value is positive and rejected if it is negative".[17] If there is no market price for the investment—as often happens— its net present value (NPV) needs to be estimated. The future cash flows from the investment have to be estimated, in the first place.[18] Their present value must then be calculated through a procedure called the discounted cash flow (DCF) valuation.[19] If the result is negative, the investment in question is not a good one and should not be undertaken.[20]

Cash flows should be estimated both after taxes and after all reinvestment needs have been met, but before interest and principal payments on debt (as the

---

[12] See Stewart, above, n. 8, 22, who adds: "The accounting model relies on two distinct financial statements—an income statement and balance sheet—whereas the economic model uses only one: sources and uses of cash" (24).

[13] Ross, Westerfield and Jordan, above, n. 4, 11.

[14] Rappaport, above, n. 4, 14–20.

[15] ibid. 2. See B. Holmstrom and S.N. Kaplan, *Corporate Governance and Merger Activity in the U.S.: Making Sense of the 1980s and 1990s* [2001] 15 *Journal of Economic Perspectives* 121, arguing that corporate governance in the 1980s was dominated by intense merger activity distinguished by the prevalence of LBOs and hostility, whereas internal corporate governance mechanisms appear to have played a larger role in the 1990s.

[16] ibid.

[17] Ross, Westerfield and Jordan, above, n. 4, 247.

[18] See T. Copeland, T. Koller, and J. Murrin, *Valuation. Measuring and Managing the Value of Companies* 2nd edn. (New York 1996) 135.

[19] Ross, Westerfield, and Jordan, above, n. 4, 246, and Chapters 5 and 6.

[20] ibid. 247, where it is specified: "in the unlikely event that the net present value turned out to be exactly zero, we would be indifferent between taking the investment and not taking it".

firm's cash flows are directed to both its equity and debt investors).[21] The expected cash flows need to be discounted back at a rate that reflects the cost of financing the investment. The relevant concept is that of overall cost of capital, including both the cost of equity and the cost of debt.[22] An equivalent concept is that of required return. If the cost of capital (or required return) for an investment is 10%, the NPV is positive only if the investment's return exceeds 10%.[23]

From the applied finance perspective, other criteria have been developed to assist managers in the difficult task of creating value.[24] One of the most popular is defined as economic value added (EVA), which is operating profits less the cost of all of the capital employed to produce them.[25] Management should focus on maximizing EVA, which "will increase if operating profits can be made to grow without tying up any more capital, if new capital can be invested in projects that will earn more than the full cost of the capital and if capital can be diverted or liquidated from business activities that do not provide adequate returns".[26] In essence, EVA does not depart from conventional valuation analysis.[27] The net present value prescription is simply restated as follows: "accept all investment opportunities which will produce a positive discounted EVA".[28]

[21] See A. Damodaran, *Value Creation and Enhancement: Back to the Future,* Columbia University Finance Department Working Paper (1999) (FIN-99-018), 4–5, suggesting the following formula: EBIT (1-tax rate)—(Capital Expenditures—Depreciation)—Change in non-cash working capital = Free Cash Flow to the Firm. The author comments that "the difference between capital expenditures and depreciation (net capital expenditures) and the increase in the non-cash working capital represent the reinvestments made by the firm to generate future or contemporaneous growth".

[22] See Ross, Westerfield, and Jordan, above, n. 4, 418, referring to the weighted average cost of capital (WACC), which is calculated on the basis of the respective weights of equity and debt (if total value is V, the former is E/V, the latter is D/V, and V = E + D), the cost of equity (R_E) and the cost of debt (R_D) after taxes (T_C is the corporate tax rate). Consequently: WACC = (E/V) × R_E + (D/V) × R_D × (1–T_C).

[23] ibid., 419.

[24] For a critical overview, see Damodaran, above, n. 21, arguing that the traditional discounted cash flow model can be complex, as the number of inputs increases, and that it is very difficult to tie management compensation systems to this model. "In this environment, new mechanisms for measuring value that are simple to estimate and use, do not depend too heavily on market movements, and do not require a lot of estimation, find a ready market" (30–31).

[25] Another is "cash flow return on investment" (CFROI), which measures the percentage return made by a firm on its existing investments: ibid. 31.

[26] Stewart, above, n. 8, 3.

[27] Damodaran, above, n. 21, arguing that there is little that is new or unique in these competing measures, and while they might be simpler than traditional discounted cash flow valuation, the simplicity comes at a cost.

[28] See Stewart, above, n. 8, 3.

II. Shareholders and Stakeholders

An important question, which has been widely discussed by economists and lawyers, in connection with the creation of shareholder value, is whether corporate managers should exclusively maximize shareholder return or balance the interests of all stakeholders.[29]

1. The Anglo-American Model

An idea popular in the U.S. until the early eighties held that corporations should be "socially responsible" institutions managed in the public interest.[30] Today, the prevailing opinion is that management's primary goal should be to maximize value for shareholders. One reason is that managers should be held accountable to someone: "a manager told to serve two masters (a little for the equity holders, a little for the community) has been freed of both and is answerable to neither".[31] Another reason is that maximizing profits for equity investors assists the other "constituencies" automatically. In a market economy, successful firms provide jobs for workers, goods for consumers, and prosperity for stockholders. Wealthy firms provide better working conditions and social wealth, including cleaner environments.[32]

Shareholders have governance rights because they are the residual claimants and have the best incentives to reduce agency costs, being those who gain the most from efficient production.[33] According to a recent American view, firms

[29] Rappaport, above, n. 14, 5; J. Tirole, *Corporate Governance,* CEPR. Discussion Paper No. 2086 (1999) 36.

[30] M.M. Blair, *Ownership and Control. Rethinking Corporate Governance for the Twenty-First Century* (Washington DC 1995) 202. Hansmann and Kraakman, above, n. 5, 4, refer to a "manager-oriented model" of corporate law and argue that at the core of it "was the belief that professional corporate managers could serve as disinterested technocratic fiduciaries who would guide business corporations in ways that would serve the general public interest". They find in the corporate social responsibility literature of the 1950s (M. Dodd, J.K. Galbraith, and A. Berle) "an embodiment of these views".

[31] Easterbrook and Fischel, above, n. 4, 38; Tirole, above, n. 29, 5: shareholder value provides more focus and sharper incentives to managers; it also prevents deadlock in decision-making.

[32] Easterbrook and Fischel, above, n. 4, 38.

[33] R.J. Gilson and M.J. Roe, "Understanding the Japanese Keiretsu: Overlaps between Corporate Governance and Industrial Organization" [1993] 102 Yale Law Journal 871, at 887; Blair, above, n. 30, 227, arguing, however, that the goal of good corporate governance should be to maximise the wealth creating potential of the corporation as a whole, rather than just to maximize value for shareholders; these two goals differ whenever some participants in the enterprise other than shareholders make special investments in physical assets, organizational capabilities, or skills whose value is tied to the success of that enterprise: see at 275; see also Tirole, above, n. 29, 43, noting that shareholder value leaves scope for important externalities and some distasteful implications.

should maximize stockholder value subject to a "good citizen" constraint, i.e. they should try to minimize social costs even in the absence of a legal obligation to do so.[34] In fact, companies that establish a reputation for being "good corporate citizens" can use it to their benefit. Ultimately, companies will become more socially responsible if it is "in their best interests economically to not create social costs".[35]

2. The German Model

The elements for analysis appear to be different in Continental Europe, particularly if we consider the German governance model. This model is characterized by co-operation and long-term relationships among stakeholders in the firm.[36] The concept of the "interest of the company as a whole" is "a key concept of German corporate culture".[37] Klaus Hopt makes a sharp distinction between the German and U.S. models by saying: "Maximization of shareholders' wealth has hardly ever been the objective of German stock corporations, certainly not in companies with dispersed ownership or regarding payment of dividends".[38] The German model is more oriented to the enterprise than to the corporation, as reflected by "the discussion on *Aktiengesellschaft* versus *Aktienunternehmen* and *Gesellschaftsrecht* versus *Unternehmensrecht*".[39] The two models are also compared by saying that the Anglo-American model reflects a "shareholder society", whereas the German model corresponds to a "stakeholder society", and that their relevant features derive more from differences in national institutions than in managerial objectives.[40]

---

[34] For an account of this view, see A. Damodaran, *Applied Corporate Finance* (London 1999) 29. This view substantially reflects the ALI Principles of Corporate Governance, below, n. 74.

[35] ibid., arguing that firms that are perceived as socially irresponsible could lose customers and profits, and that investors might avoid buying stock in these companies: "as an example, many college and state pension plans in the United States have started reducing or eliminating their holdings of tobacco stocks to reflect their concerns about the health effects of the product".

[36] For an overview, G.M. Gelauff and G. den Broeder, *Governance of Stakeholder Relationships. The German and Dutch Experience*, SUERF Studies no. 1 (1997) 26.

[37] E.R. Schneider-Lenné, "Corporate Control in Germany" [1992] 8 *Oxford Review of Economic Policy* 11.

[38] K. Hopt, 'Labour Representation on Corporate Boards: Impacts and Problems for Corporate Governance and Economic Integration in Europe' in R.M. Buxbaum et al. (eds.), *European Economic and Business Law* (Berlin / New York 1996) 269.

[39] ibid., arguing that labour co-determination has contributed to this outlook of the German system, without being a decisive factor.

[40] See Gelauff and Den Broeder, above, n. 36, 36, arguing that under German institutions it is rational for managers to take the interests of stakeholders into account and to invest in long term relationships; see also J. Kay, *The Business of Economics* (Oxford 1996) 112, suggesting that some aspects of the German "trusteeship model" of corporate governance offer advantages with respect

In this scenario, little room seems to be left for shareholder value. However, changes are under way also in the German governance model, as a consequence of globalization and the new role of the securities markets in the financing of enterprises. According to a recent comparative study, "perhaps the most dramatic manifestation of a changing corporate landscape has been the sudden emergence of a distinctly Anglo-Saxon concept: the need for senior company officers to concentrate on the creation of what most in Germany refer to simply as 'sharcholder value'".[41] Indeed, the use of the term has become fashionable and corporate managers pay more than lip service to the interests of shareholders.[42] On the doctrinal level, efforts have been made to host the shareholder value concept in the corporate law structure.[43] This reflects a more general trend towards a greater shareholder focus in corporate governance and reform,[44] as also witnessed by the 1998 Law on the Control and Transparency in Business (*KonTraGesetz*).[45]

3. Mixed Models

These models are characterized by the concurrence of the institutional and the contractual views of the corporation, and also by a growing shift from the former to the latter view.[46] In France, the corporate governance best practices are

to the "agency model" prevailing in the U.S. and the U.K. and should be adopted to build a new model of corporate governance.

[41] T.J. André, 'Cultural Hegemony: the Exportation of Anglo-Saxon Corporate Governance Ideologies to Germany' [1998] 73 Tulane Law Review 69, at 109.

[42] Several indicia of the consideration given to shareholder value are offered, such as the establishment of investor relations departments by listed companies; corporate restructurings and downsizing; increasing use of the services of American investment banks: ibid., 110. Of course, no cultural revolution is to be expected. On the one hand, the concept of shareholder value is hardly self-defining and may serve different purposes; on the other, some are sceptical of the Anglo-Saxon challenge to the German consensus mentality which is represented by the concept at issue; see ibid., 112–115, reporting that much of the debate in Germany has focused on the "excesses" of a concept believed to be imported wholesale from the U.S.

[43] P.O. Mülbert, 'Shareholder Value aus rechtlicher Sicht' [1997] *Zeitschrift für Unternehmens- und Gesellschaftsrecht* 129, at 141; A. Werder, 'Shareholder Value-Ansatz als (einzige) Richtschnur des Vorstandhandelns?' [1998] *Zeitschrift für Unternehmens- und Gesellschaftsrecht* 69, 74.

[44] H. Schmidt et al., *Corporate Governance in Germany*, HWWA (1997) 235. See, more recently, the Recommendations of the German Government Panel on Corporate Governance (Baums Report, July 2001) at http://otto-schmidt.de/corporate_governance.htm, on which T. Baums, *Company Law Reform in Germany*, J.W. Goethe-Universität, Frankfurt a.M., Institut für Bankrecht, Working Paper no. 100.

[45] U. Seibert, 'Control and Transparency in Business (*KonTraG*). Corporate Governance Reform in Germany', http://www.bmj.bund.de/misc/e_kont.htm, including among the Parliament's aims "that the law should actively keep pace with public companies as they gear up to the requirements and expectations of international financial markets. This also means that corporate strategy needs to be more strongly oriented towards shareholder value".

[46] See P. Didier, 'La théorie contractualiste de la société' [2000] *Revue des Sociétés* 95.

increasingly focused on the shareholders' interests,[47] even if the "corporation as a firm" conception has not entirely been abandoned (see II below). A mixed view of the company appears to be still dominant: "la société présente à la fois des caractères contractuels et des caractères institutionnels" ("the company presents, at the same time, contractual and institutional characters"),[48] as reflected by the discussion on the *intérêt social* and its relationship with the *intérêt commun*.[49] However, in the case of listed companies, it is the *intérêt du marché*, which prevails over the company's interest.[50]

In Italy, the institutional theory of the corporation was dominant in the first half of the last century, under the influence of the German model, and was then adhered to by the Supreme Court.[51] However, this theory was vigorously opposed by the legal writers in the Fifties and Sixties, so that a contractual view of the corporation is prevalent today.[52] The company's interest is identified with the shareholders' common interest, which is defined as the objective and hypothetical interest of the average member.[53] This interest is also correlated with the goal of profit maximization, representing the ultimate corporate aim.[54]

[47] See the study by COB, *Création de Valeur Actionnariale et Communication Financière* (2000) at http:// www.cob.fr, arguing that the shareholders' role is gaining importance in terms of remuneration and power in modern economic and social systems, and that the consideration of the total costs of capital is also a stable acquisition of these systems. See also Pirovano, 'La "boussole" de la société. Intérêt commun, intérêt social, intérêt de l'entreprise' [1997] *Recueil Dalloz* 189.

[48] P.H. Bissara, 'L'intérêt social' [1999] *Revue des Sociétés* 5, at 6.

[49] ibid., 24, stating that the two concepts are identical, because the shareholders have made a contract to form the corporation and only the continual prosperity of the common enterprise, to which their company is dedicated, can generate the expected profits and increase the shares' value. See also M. Cozian and A. Viandier, *Droit des sociétés* 11th edn. (Paris 1998) 175.

[50] ibid., 29.

[51] See, e.g. Cass (Italian), June 20, 1958, no. 2148 (1959) *I Giur it*, 1, c 204; Cass (Italian), October 25, 1958, no. 3471 (1959) *I Giur it*, 1, c. 869. Both judgments define the company's interest as a superior interest, distinct from that of the individual members.

[52] See F, Ascarelli, 'L'interesse sociale dell'art 2441 cod civile' [1956] *Rivista delle società* 93; L. Mengoni, 'Appunti per una revisione della teoria sul conflitto di interessi nelle deliberazioni di assemblea della società per azioni' [1956] *Rivista delle società* 434; A. Mignoli, 'L'interesse sociale' [1958] *Rivista delle società* 725; P.G. Jaeger, *L'interesse sociale* (Milan 1964). For an overview, see P.G. Jaeger and F. Denozza, *Appunti di diritto commerciale*. I. *Impresa e società*, 2nd edn. (Milan 1992) 215; for a different approach, F. Galgano, *Diritto Commerciale. Le Società*, (Bologna 1998/99) 153, concluding that neither the institutional nor the contractual theories accurately reflect the Italian law.

[53] L.C.B. Gower's definition of the company's interest as that of the 'hypothetical average member' who presumably has no personal interest apart from those as member, is approved by Mignoli, above, n. 52, 748 (with reference to L.C.B. Gower, *The Principles of Modern Company Law* 2nd edn. (London 1957) 520) who defines the company's interest as the 'lowest common denominator' uniting shareholders since the company formation until its dissolution.

[54] See Mignoli, above, n. 52, 748. See also P.G. Jaeger, 'L'interesse sociale rivisitato (quarant'anni dopo)' [2000] I *Giur Comm* 795; P. Ferro-Luzzi 'Riflessioni sul gruppo (non creditizio)' [2001] *Riv Dir Comm* 14, both emphasizing the role of shareholder value in the analysis of the company's interest.

However, not all the theories elaborated under the contractual view of the corporation are alike and some reach results similar to those obtainable under the institutional approach to the corporation.[55]

C. European Best Practices

European corporate governance made significant progress during the 1990s; amongst its achievements, the national codes of best practice deserve particular attention. In this section I analyse the role of shareholder value in internal corporate governance, the relationship between shareholders and stakeholders in the European codes, and the executive remuneration best practices in view of shareholder welfare maximization.

I. Corporate Governance Codes

The publication in 1992 of the Cadbury Report in the U.K. was a watershed to be followed by the Viénot and Peters Reports in France (1995) and the Netherlands (1997).[56] In 1998, the Cardon Report was issued in Belgium and the Olivencia Report in Spain, whilst the Hampel Report led to the London Stock Exchange's Combined Code. In 1999, a new Viénot Report was issued in France and a report (including a best practice code) was published in Italy under the auspices of *Borsa Italiana* (Preda Report).[57] The widely held view that companies' self-regulation is a distinctive feature of common law systems needs reassessment: codes of best practice have an increasingly important role in the governance of continental European listed companies.[58] The reasons for this are well known, and include the role played by institutional investors in modern equity markets and competition between national financial systems.[59]

The Hampel Report (1998) emphasized the role of shareholder value, stating, "the importance of corporate governance lies in its contribution both to business

[55] See Jaeger, above, n. 52, 116, who criticizes the theories which define the company's interest either as the interest of the legal person, or as including the interests of workers and other stakeholders, or simply those of future shareholders.

[56] These reports, and the others subsequently referred to in the text, can be found at the site of the European Corporate Governance Institute: http://www.ecgi.org/codes/menu_europe.htm

[57] On the Preda Report see, from a comparative perspective, G. Ferrarini, 'Corporate Governance Codes: A Path to Uniformity?' [1999] *Euredia* 475. After completion of this chapter, a German Corporate Governance Code was adopted by the Cromme Commision (February 2002) as recommended by the Baums Report, above, n. 44.

[58] See, however, for a critical view, G. Rossi, below, Chapter 21.

[59] For an evaluation of self-regulation in the U.K., see B.R. Cheffins, *Company Law. Theory, Structure and Operation* (Oxford 1997) 364; for an assessment of the U.K. best practices, see J. Rickford, below, Chapter 20, and the comments by B. Pettet, below, Chapter 22.

prosperity and accountability. In the U.K. the latter has preoccupied much public debate over the past few years. We would wish to see the balance corrected".[60] In a similar vein, Ira Millstein argued that boardroom behaviour is critical, as the "professional board" is an active monitoring organization that participates with management in formulating corporate strategy in the interests of shareholders, develops appropriate incentives for management and other employees and judges the performance of management against the strategic plan.[61] This is reflected by the definitions of the board's responsibilities and key functions offered by the OECD Principles of Corporate Governance, para. V, and some continental codes.[62] However, proof of the link between board governance and performance is difficult to pin down. Some empirical studies have tried to link one or at most a few elements of board structure (number of independent directors, board size, etc.) to measures of corporate performance (such as stock price) or to a single corporate event (CEO replacement, response to take-over bids, etc.).[63] Their results have been defined as "inconclusive " or "ambivalent", but do not disprove a link between board activism and increased investor returns.[64] A recent study has attempted to establish a correlation between board independence[65] and corporate performance measured on the basis of "economic value added" (EVA), i.e. the company's ability to create wealth for shareholders.[66] This study demonstrates "a substantial and statistically significant correlation between an active, independent board and superior corporate performance", without proving causation.[67]

---

[60] Hampel Report, at 7. In the Committee's opinion, "public companies are now among the most accountable organisations in society", but the board's first responsibility is to enhance the prosperity of the business over time. Accountability requires appropriate rules and regulations, in which disclosure is the most important element. However, "it is dangerous to encourage the belief that rules and regulations about structure will deliver success".

[61] I. Millstein, 'The Professional Board' [1995] 50 Business Lawyer 1427, 1433–39.

[62] Cardon Report, para. I; Olivencia Report, para. I; Preda Report, para .I.

[63] For a review, see S. Bhagat and B.S. Black, 'The Uncertain Relationship Between Board Composition and Firm performance' [1999] 54 Business Lawyer 921.

[64] I. Millstein and P. MacAvoy, 'The Active Board of Directors and Performance of the Large Publicly Held Corporation' [1998] 98 Columbia Law Review 1283, at 1296–1297.

[65] Assessed on the basis of indicia for the behaviour of professional boards, such as independent board leadership, periodic meetings of the independent directors, formal rules for the relationship between the board and management: ibid., 1299. A different study by Bhagat and Black, above, n. 63, has considered the recent trend towards supermajority-independent boards and concluded that there is no convincing evidence that increasing board independence will improve firm performance.

[66] See Millstein and MacAvoy, above, n. 64, 1303.

[67] ibid. 1318, where the comment: "It might be inferred that managers willing to assume the risks associated with a professional board are better able to generate higher returns to shareholders. On the other hand, why do so? It seems to us less than likely that good corporate governance is a luxury of firms that are performing extraordinarily well".

With respect to European corporate governance codes, it will be interesting to see whether a similar correlation exists once the principles concerning the board's structure and independent directors have been implemented on a large scale. However, the differences in ownership structure between continental European and Anglo-American listed companies should also be taken into account,[68] as already acknowledged by recent reports.[69] Presumably, the proportion of independent directors vis-à-vis other directors will reflect a company's ownership structure.[70] It is possible, however, that the number of independent directors will increase once the new concept has been assimilated and a sufficient number of professional directors have established a reputation for this role.[71]

---

[68] The ownership structure of European companies is highly concentrated: see E. Wymeersch, 'A Status Report on Corporate Governance Rules and Practices in Some Continental European States' in Hopt et al. (eds.), *Comparative Corporate Governance. The State of the Art and Emerging Research* (Berlin/New York 1998) 1152. A recent study on large shareholding in Europe shows that in several countries the median largest voting stake in listed companies is over 50%, suggesting that voting control by a large blockholder is the rule rather than the exception. In Italy, out of a number of 216 listed companies, the median largest voting block is 54.53%, similar to Austria (52%), Belgium (50.6%) and Germany (52.1%). In the U.K., by contrast, a sample of 250 listed companies shows a modest median value of 9.9%, whereas in the U.S. over 50% of companies have a largest shareholder who holds less than 5% of the shares. See M. Becht and A. Röell, 'Blockholdings in Europe: An International Comparison' [1999] 43 *European Economic Review* 1049, who preview the findings of research on large shareholding in Europe carried out by the European Corporate Governance Institute (http://www.ecgi.org); F. Barca and M. Becht (eds.) *The Control of Corporate Europe* (Oxford 2002). For a broader perspective, see R. La Porta, F. Lopez-de-Silanes and A. Shleifer, 'Corporate Ownership around the World' [1999] *Journal of Finance* 471, who use data on ownership structures of large corporations in 27 wealthy economies and find that, except in economies with very good shareholder protection, very few of these firms are widely held. Concentration helps to solve the agency problem created by dispersed shareholders, but gives rise to a different problem as concentrated voting and management power can be abused to the detriment of the minority shareholders: A. Shleifer and R.W. Vishny, above, n. 3 at 740.

[69] See, e.g. the Preda Report, which specifies that the role of independent directors may vary with reference to the ownership structure of corporations. In the case of concentrated ownership, emphasis is put on the protection of minority shareholders, even though the independent directors' role with reference to the shareholders in general is also highlighted. As stated in the second Viénot Report (1999), para. II, "la présence d'administrateurs réellement indépendants en nombre suffisant dans les Conseils d'administration et dans les comités du Conseil est un élément essentiel de la garantie de la prise en compte de l'intérêt de l'ensemble des actionnaires dans les décisions de la société" ("the presence in the Board of directors and in the Board's committees of a sufficient number of directors who are really independent is essential to guarantee that the interests of the shareholders as a whole are taken into account in the company's resolutions").

[70] If there are controlling shareholders, some of the outside directors will be connected with them and monitor the company's management on their behalf: see the Viénot Report (1995), para. II. 2, and the Olivencia Report, para. 2.2. If the shareholders are dispersed, an Anglo-American type of board consisting of a majority of independent directors will result.

[71] This appears to be the case in France. After noting the increasing number of independent directors in French listed companies, the second Viénot Report recommends that the boards of such companies include at least one third of independent directors: see Part 3, para. II, also stating that the audit and nomination committees should comprise at least one third of independent directors,

II. Profit Maximization and Stakeholder Protection

The corporate governance codes analyse the relationship between shareholder value, profit maximization, and stakeholder protection. The Hampel Report follows the "in the long run" perspective that reconciles the goal of shareholder value maximization with a more broadly defined goal of social responsibility for corporations.[72] The shareholders are interested in a company's sustained prosperity and the directors can pursue the objective of long-term shareholder value successfully by developing and sustaining stakeholder relationships.[73] Similarly, the ALI Principles of Corporate Governance make reference to "long-run profitability and shareholder gain", justifying "an orientation toward lawful, ethical, and public spirited activity". The long-term profitability of the corporation generally depends on meeting the fair expectations of stakeholders and short-term profits can be properly subordinated to this goal.[74] The Italian and Spanish Reports follow a similar approach.[75] The OECD Principles also adhere to a "long run" view of wealth maximization, but emphasize the recognition of "the rights of stakeholders as established by law" (to limit the impact of stakeholder protection on corporate law and directors' duties, considering the concurring regulation of stakeholders' relationships, such as those with workers).[76]

The Viénot Report (1995) favours an "enterprise" view of the corporation,[77] whilst minimizing the differences from the Anglo-Saxon shareholder value approach: "il s'agit là de nuances plutôt que de conceptions absolument différentes" ("these are nuances rather than absolute conceptual differences").[78]

whereas the remuneration committee should have a majority of the same. This number is higher than that recommended by the first Report, suggesting a minimum of two independent directors for each board: see para. II.2; see also para. III.3 on the board's committees, providing that at least one member of the audit committee should be an independent director. Four years have been enough to change the French attitude towards independent directors and move the best practice in this area towards the British model.

[72] This perspective is examined by Blair, n. 30 above, 216, with reference to the U.S. discussion. As to British law, see P. Davies, below, Chapter 11, who analyses also the Company Law Review proposals, where the primacy of the shareholders' interests is asserted.

[73] Hampel Report, para. 1.18.

[74] American Law Institute, *Principles of Corporate Governance: Analysis and Recommendation*, para. 2.01 (1994).

[75] Preda Report, para. 4; Olivencia Report, para. 1.3; see also the board of directors' model regulation referred to the Spanish corporate governance code, arts. 6 (shareholder value creation) and 7 (other interests).

[76] See Principle No. III (the role of stakeholders in corporate governance). The relevant comment states, inter alia: "It is, therefore, in the long-term interest of corporations to foster wealth-creating co-operation among stakeholders".

[77] For a critical approach, see P.H. Bissara, 'L'intérêt social' [1999] *Revue des sociétés* 5.

[78] Viénot Report (1995), para. 1, specifying that the company's interest does not mean ignoring the market, but is a standard for the directors' conduct that transcends their particular interests.

Viénot defines the "intérêt social" as the " intérêt supérieur" of the "personne morale", i.e. of the enterprise pursuing its own goals, which are different from those of the shareholders, employees, creditors, suppliers and clients. These goals reflect the common interest in the prosperity of the enterprise.[79] The second Viénot Report smoothes the differences from the Anglo-Saxon approach by focusing on shareholders' interests and referring, e.g. to a periodic self-assessment by the board of directors and to the appointment of truly independent directors.[80]

Difficulty in the doctrinal debate on corporate goals is posed in Germany by the relationship between the company law and the enterprise law perspectives. Under the former perspective, the management and supervisory boards should pursue the goal of the company as an association, i.e. profit maximization.[81] Under the latter perspective, the interests of the company's enterprise should also be furthered by the management and supervisory boards, but the nature of those interests and their relationship with profit maximization are disputed.[82] Conflicting criteria have been developed by the authors, who have often suggested that the company should pursue not only profit maximization in the interests of investors, but also the welfare of other stakeholders.[83] These theories have been critically examined in the light of the formation and spirit of the 1965 Stock Corporation Law (*Aktiengesetz*) and the argument has recently been developed that under this law the company stays in the foreground and pursues the goal of long-term profit maximization in the shareholders' interests.[84]

Furthermore, the relationship between shareholder value and profit maximization has been explored with particular reference to cases in which the two concepts do not coincide.[85] An example is offered by the destination of surplus cash flow when the company cannot invest the same at a rate of return sufficient to add economic value. Whereas the profit maximization perspective appears to be neutral on this matter, the shareholder value approach may require that free-

---

[79] Viénot Report (1995), para. 1.

[80] Viénot Report (1999), para. II; see also Bissara, above, n. 77.

[81] See H. Wiedemann, *Gesellschaftsrecht* (München 1980) I 338, 626. See also German Panel on Corporate Governance 'Corporate Governance Rules for Quoted German Companies' (July 2000) for references to the corporate interest (para. 1.a) and long-term corporate value creation (para. 3.a).

[82] See, e.g. F. Kübler, *Gesellschaftsrecht* 5th edn. (Heidelberg 1998) 224; K. Schmidt, *Gesellschaftsrecht* 2nd edn. (Cologne 1991) 675.

[83] For a review, see Mülbert, above, n. 43, 141.

[84] ibid., 142. See, however, K. Hopt, 'Common Principles of Corporate Governance in Europe?' in B. Markesinis (ed.) *The Coming Together of the Common Law and the Civil Law* (Oxford 2000) 105, 119, arguing that the recent discussion on shareholder value has been carried on at a rather theoretical level and has not changed the traditional view that the corporate aims should include the interests of shareholders, the interests of creditors, and those of the employees.

[85] Mülbert, above n. 43, 156.

cash-flow is distributed to shareholders.[86] In order to reconcile the two goals from a company law perspective, it has been suggested that it is in a listed company's interests to have good relations with the capital market by implementing a shareholder value approach.[87] Therefore, in the absence of value adding investment projects, the directors could comply with the profit maximization goal simply by recommending the distribution of free-cash-flow to shareholders.

III. Executive Compensation

The Greenbury Report (1995) was the first in Europe to set out best practices in the field of directors' remuneration. Its recommendations were substantially followed by the Hampel Report and the Combined Code, and some of its basic principles have been incorporated in the continental codes. These recommendations and principles reflect the main international concerns relating to the level of executive pay, the procedure for its determination, and the disclosure of the same.

First, "the level of remuneration should be sufficient to attract and retain the directors needed to run the company successfully, but companies should avoid paying more than is necessary for this purpose" (see Section 1.B.1. of the Combined Code). The optimal level of remuneration will be largely determined by the market that is increasingly global.[88] Furthermore, "a proportion of executive directors' remuneration should be structured as to link the rewards to corporate and individual performance" (*ibid.*). As recognized by the corporate governance literature, incentive contracts with managers are a way to reduce agency costs by aligning the managers' interests with those of investors.[89]

The link to company performance can be established through annual bonuses, stock option schemes, or long-term incentive plans. From a shareholder value perspective, a truly effective incentive system is one that "makes managers think like and act like owners".[90] Therefore, in judging the

---

[86] See, e.g. Stewart, above n. 26, 137, 481; for some policy implications, M.C. Jensen, 'Agency Costs of Free Cash Flow, Corporate Finance and Take-overs' (1986) 76 *American Economic Review* 323 (the problem is how to motivate managers to disgorge the cash rather than investing it below the cost of capital or wasting it in organisational inefficiencies).

[87] See Mülbert, above, n. 43, 161.

[88] Hampel Report, para. 4.3. On the managerial labour market, see E.F. Fama, 'Agency Problems and the Theory of the Firm' [1980] 88 *Journal of Political Economy* 288.

[89] See Shleifer and Vishny, above, n. 3, 744.

[90] A. Ehrbar, *EVA. The Real Key to Creating Wealth* (New York 1998) 95, specifying that compensation plans typically have four objectives: (i) to align management and shareholders interests; (ii) to provide sufficient leverage, as measured by the variability of potential rewards; (iii) to limit retention risk, i.e. the risk that managers will leave for a better offer; (iv) to keep shareholder costs at a reasonable level.

performance of managers, the focus should be on value added measured by one of the usual standards, such as net return on investment or EVA.[91] If stock options are granted, their value is related directly to shareholder returns, providing managers with strong economic incentives.[92]

Secondly, the procedure for fixing executive remuneration should be formal and transparent, and a remuneration committee should be set up by the board of directors to avoid potential conflicts of interest (see Section B.2 of the Combined Code). As shown by the U.S. experience, "the more serious problem with high-powered incentive contracts is that they create enormous opportunities for self-dealing for the managers, especially if these contracts are negotiated with poorly motivated boards of directors rather than with large investors".[93] This explains why remuneration committees should consist exclusively of "independent" directors (see Section B.2.2 of the Combined Code), a requirement that has not been followed by some continental Codes,[94] presumably on the (rather weak) assumption that "strong" owners are better at controlling executive pay than professional directors. Furthermore, shareholders should be invited specifically to approve all new long-term incentive schemes (see Section B.3.4. of the Combined Code), and the issue has also been raised whether directors should be generally accountable to shareholders with respect to executive remuneration.[95]

Thirdly, the company's annual report should contain a statement of remuneration policy and details of the remuneration of each director (Section B.3 of the Combined Code). Also, in continental Europe a trend is emerging which requires disclosure of executive pay in the annual accounts,[96] but there is still some resistance to full disclosure of individual remunerations, as shown by the

---

[91] See R.A. Brealey and S.C. Myers, *Principles of Corporate Finance* 6th edn. (New York 2000) 326; Ehrbar (above n. 90) 106 ("two characteristics of EVA bonus plans . . . are crucial to their effectiveness as a corporate governance mechanism: Managers know that the only way they can make themselves better off is by creating more wealth for shareholders, and they also know that they will share in any wealth they do create").

[92] See Rappaport, above, n. 14, 113, highlighting the shortcomings of conventional stock option plans which do not meet the "superior performance" test.

[93] Shleifer and Vishny, above n. 3, 745.

[94] See, e.g. the Preda Report, art. 8.1 (the majority of the committee will consist of non-executive directors); see, however, the second Viénot Report, Part III, para. II (the majority of the committee will consist of independent directors).

[95] See the DTI Consultative Document on Directors' Remuneration, July 1999, Ch. 7, stating, inter alia, that it may be appropriate for the board to discuss aspects of directors' remuneration with investors, and that the dialogue between the board and investors is more likely to be effective if it is underpinned by a framework which facilitates voting on resolutions relating to directors' remuneration at company meetings.

[96] See, e.g. the Italian Securities Commission (*Consob*) Regulation no. 11791, Encl 3C.

second Viénot Report rejecting the Anglo-Saxon requirement of detailed information.[97]

IV. Assessment

Apart from these and other divergences, which either reflect variations amongst the national legal systems or are attributable to path-dependency, the European codes of best practice substantially contribute to uniformity in the corporate law field, particularly from the shareholder value perspective. First of all, the principle of shareholder value creation is recognized and the board of directors should implement this principle in formulating the company's strategies and in selecting and remunerating executives. A "professional" board is generally linked with good performance, even if proof of causation has not yet been offered. Furthermore, the continental codes try to reconcile shareholder value maximization and stakeholder protection from a "long run" perspective, similar to that followed by the Anglo-American best practice. The German model offers an exception, but the shareholder value approach is also receiving wide recognition in the field of public companies. Following the Greenbury Report in the U.K., the executive remuneration model is becoming uniform as to compensation structure and level, and the board of directors' activity is organized so as to minimize potential conflicts of interest.

Some general issues deserve further comment, such as the role of self-regulation and that of corporate law. The best practice codes provide a frame of reference to the board of directors, who are free to adhere to the relevant principles or not, provided that adequate disclosure is offered. The capital markets ultimately assess the board's functioning and performance, and the share prices incorporate information as to the quality of governance.[98] Institutional investors may find in the national codes guidance as to the best practices in the countries in which they invest, and a few of them use their own codes as a parameter for assessment of the issuers.[99]

Management's acceptance of the shareholder value principle is also requested by investors in systems traditionally classified as stakeholder societies. It is not enough for managers to declare the acceptance of this principle, but evidence must be given of its implementation, e.g. through stock option plans and other incentive agreements. On the whole, market discipline is breaking new grounds in continental Europe, as an essential supplement to corporate law, and the

---

[97] See the second part of the second Viénot Report, recommending detailed, but not individual disclosure of executive pay.

[98] For similar comments, see Easterbrook and Fischel, above, n. 13, 17.

[99] See, e.g. the CALPERS' Corporate Governance Principles: http://www.calpers-governance.org/principles/default.asp

codes of best practice play an important role with respect to directors and investors.

At the same time, corporate law assures the enforcement of fiduciary duties. The courts specify these duties, particularly in cases of director liability.[100] However, the business judgment rule in practice restricts the duty of care enforcement. In fact, the courts avoid interfering with business decisions when the directors are thought to have exercised an honest judgment in good faith in the pursuit of corporate interests.[101] Also the issue of shareholder value maximization, albeit central in the field of fiduciary duties, tends to be covered by the business judgment rule and is rarely addressed by the courts[102] (except for cases relating to take-over defences: see III below). This is generally approved for at least two reasons.

First, judges lack the professional expertise to take business decisions in lieu of directors. Secondly (and perhaps most importantly), the perspective of an extensive judicial review of business decisions would discourage risk taking by the boards of directors, contrary to the interest of investors who can easily reduce firm-specific risks through diversification.[103] Furthermore, corporate law provides the executive compensation mechanisms necessary to align the managers' interests with those of the owners. These mechanisms have been subject to sweeping changes in continental Europe. Traditionally, the law was only concerned with facilitating employee participation in company capital, as witnessed by article 41 of the Second Company Law Directive, providing that Member States may derogate from various provisions (including Article 29 on pre-emption rights) to the extent required "to encourage the participation of employees, or other groups of persons defined by national law, in the capital undertakings". However, value creation needs are best satisfied by incentive agreements with the firm's executives, including stock-option plans, which are obviously different from the participation schemes offered to employees.

---

[100] The fiduciary principle is a rule for completing incomplete bargains in a contractual structure: see Easterbrook and Fischel, above, n. 13, 92.

[101] See W.T. Allen, 'The Corporate Director's Fiduciary Duty of Care and the Business Judgement Rule Under U.S. Corporate Law' in K. Hopt et al., *Comparative Corporate Governance. The State of the Art and Emerging Research* (Berlin/New York 1998) 307, 322.

[102] See M.J. Roe, *The Quality of Corporate Law Argument and its Limits*, Columbia Law School, The Centre for Law and Economic Studies, Working Paper no. 186 (15 February 2001) http://papers.ssrn.com/paper.taf?abstract_id=260582, arguing at 4 that one of the limits to the 'quality-of-corporate-law argument' in the analysis of the separation of share ownership from corporate control is the following: 'A good core of corporate law—that attacks and destroys insider thievery— is not enough to induce separation. Managerial agency costs of another sort must also be contained—costs that come from dissipating shareholder value—and corporate law as conventionally understood does little directly to contain these managerial agency costs'.

[103] Allen, above, n. 101, quoting the author's judicial opinion in *Gagliardi v. TriFoods Int'l Inc* 683 A.2d 1049, 1052 (Del Ch 1996).

The national legal systems tend to follow the European directive model, but some have removed the main barriers to the introduction of stock-option plans for managers. French legislation, for instance, was modified in various stages to host the new compensation mechanisms. At the beginning, managers were excluded from share offers to employees (made possible by a 1970 law), but since 1987 stock-option plans have become generally available to joint-stock companies.[104] However, directors as such are not admitted to these incentive schemes, which require the beneficiary to be bound by a labour agreement.[105] Consequently, an executive director can benefit from a stock-option plan because of his or her position as general manager (*PDG*) or simply as a manager of the company. Similar treatment is applicable to management stock options in Italy.[106] In Germany, on the contrary, the stock-corporation law was modified in 1998 (see the new para. 192 (2) No. 3 *Aktiengesetz*) so as to allow new share offers not only to the employees, but also to the members of the management committee (not of the supervisory board).[107]

D. Take-over Defences

I. General

Take-overs can create value.[108] As shown by Jensen and Ruback almost 20 years ago, shareholders of target firms realize large positive abnormal returns in completed take-overs, whilst statistically significant but small positive returns are realized by bidders.[109] Take-over defences can contribute to the value creating process, but can also hinder the target's acquisition by bidders. In this section, I intend to examine such defences and the main rules applicable to them from a comparative perspective, and assess the role played by the shareholder value concept in this area.

[104] See R. Vatinet, 'Le clair-obscur des *stock options* à la française' [1997] *Revue des sociétés*.

[105] Cozian and Viandier, above, n. 49, 346.

[106] See C. Acerbi, 'Osservazioni sulle *stock options* e sull'azionariato dei dipendenti' [1998] *Rivista delle Società* 1193, 1253.

[107] See K. Kühnberger and M. Kessler, 'Stock option incentives—betriebswirtschaftliche und rechtliche Probleme eines anreizkompatiblen Vergütungssystems' [1999] *Die Aktiengesellschaft* 453, 459.

[108] For an overview of the theories explaining value maximization in take-overs, see R. Romano, 'A Guide to Take-overs: Theory, Evidence and Regulation' in K. Hopt and E. Wymeersch (eds.), *European Take-overs. Law and Practice* (London 1992) 4.

[109] M.C. Jensen and R.S. Ruback, 'The Market for Corporate Control. The Scientific Evidence' [1983] 11 *Journal of Financial Economics* 5, at 22; from another perspective, take-overs serve as a control mechanism that limits managerial departures from maximization of shareholder wealth (ibid., 29). For an updated discussion, see J. Weston, K. Chung, and J. Siu, *Take-overs, Restructuring, and Corporate Governance* 2nd edn. (Englewood 1998) 124.

Shareholders in tender offers are faced with a dilemma: "acting independently each shareholder maximizes his wealth by tendering, although all target shareholders are better off if nobody tenders until they receive a larger fraction of the take-over gains".[110] Take-over defences can help to solve this co-ordination problem by enhancing the bargaining power of target management versus bidders. Defensive measures, however, give rise to a conflict of interest problem, as managers might entrench themselves instead of maximising shareholder wealth.[111] The core question, therefore, appears to be one of internal governance: should managers or shareholders take the final decision as to take-over defences? This section will try to outline the American approach to poison pills and post-bid defences and the European trends in the same area, and to compare the two approaches, focusing on core governance issues.

II. American Defences

In the U.S., defensive tactics are a matter within the business discretion of the target's directors and officers.[112] As stated with reference to poison pills, they were originally intended to act as a means of allowing the board to fulfil its responsibility of maximizing value for the shareholders.[113] However, "a corporation does not have unbridled discretion to defeat any perceived threat by any Draconian means available".[114] A distinction is made between defensive tactics that benefit shareholders and those that merely protect management. In order for the business judgment rule to apply, the board must demonstrate that the take-over represented a threat to corporate policy and existence.[115] Moreover, the defensive measure must be "reasonable in relation to the threat posed".[116] This is an "intermediate standard" (with respect to the business judgment rule originally invoked by the courts) requiring a "proportionality review" in order to decide whether a defensive response is warranted.[117]

---

[110] Jensen and Ruback, above, n. 109, at 31.

[111] This has led some authors to recommend a passivity rule for management: see, e.g. F.H. Easterbrook and D.R. Fischel, 'The Proper Role of Target's Management in Responding to a Tender Offer' [1981] 94 Harvard Law Review 1161. For a recent contribution, see L.A. Bebchuk and A. Ferrell, 'Federalism and Corporate Law: the Race to Protect Managers from Take-overs' [1999] Columbia Law Review 1168, 1193.

[112] Clark, above, n. 3, 581.

[113] J.R. Macey, 'The Legality and Utility of the Shareholder Rights Bylaw' [1998] 26 Hofstra Law Review 835, 837.

[114] *Unocal Corp v. Mesa Petroleum Co*, 493 A.2d 946 (Del 1985).

[115] See *Cheff v. Mathes*, 41 Del Ch 494, 199 A.2d 548 (S Ct 1964).

[116] *Unocal Corp v. Mesa Petroleum Co*, above, n. 114.

[117] See R. Gilson and R. Kraakman, 'Delaware's Intermediate Standard for Defensive Tactics: Is There Substance to Proportionality Review? [1989] 44 Business Lawyer 247.

The validity of poison pills has been recognized in a way consistent with this standard. In *Moran v. Household International*,[118] the Delaware Supreme Court found that a "flip-over" plan was a reasonable protection against a two-tier tender offer. The Court also implied that the board's power to redeem the plan in case of a favourable offer might be essential for the validity of a poison pill. As a result, the proportionality review is deferred from the time the pill is adopted to the time an offer is made and the board declines to redeem the pill.[119] However, many argue that a board can now use the poison pill to implement a "just say no" defence against a take-over[120]. The basis for this argument is represented by two recent cases (concerning defences other than the poison pill). In *Paramount Communications Inc. v. Time Inc.*,[121] the Delaware Supreme Court held that a defensive measure that precluded Time's shareholders from accepting Paramount's tender offer and receiving a control premium in the immediately foreseeable future was not disproportionate. This was because the board of directors is empowered to make "the selection of a time frame for the achievement of corporate goals" and is "not obliged to abandon a deliberately conceived corporate plan [such as the Time tender offer for Warner] for a short-term shareholder profit unless there is clearly no basis to sustain the corporate strategy".[122] In *Unitrin Inc. v. American General Corp.*,[123] the Delaware Supreme Court accepted the target's argument that a stock repurchase programme was justified by the risk that the target's shareholders might accept an inadequate offer because of "ignorance or mistaken belief" regarding the board's assessment of the long-term value of the target's stock.[124] The same Court seemed to widen further the latitude within which the directors can act when faced with a hostile bid by stating that, "if the board of directors' defensive response is not draconian (preclusive or coercive) and is within a 'range of reasonableness', a court must not substitute its judgment for the board's".[125]

[118] *Moran v. Household International*, 500 A.2d 1346 (Del 1985).

[119] See J. Choper, J. Coffee, and R. Gilson, *Cases and Materials on Corporations* 4th edn. (New York 1995) 916.

[120] See J.N. Gordon, 'Mergers and Acquisitions: "Just Say Never?" Poison Pills, and Shareholder-Adopted Bylaws: an Essay for Warren Buffett' [1997] 19 Cardozo Law Review 511, at 522, noting that perhaps the most important unresolved question in American corporate law concerns the ultimate power of the board of a Delaware corporation to block an unwanted take-over bid.

[121] *Paramount Communications, Inc v. Time Inc*, 571 A.2d 1140 (Del 1989).

[122] ibid., at 1154.

[123] *Unitrin, Inc v. American General Corp*, 651 A.2d 1361.

[124] ibid., 1385.

[125] ibid., 1388. As a result, the "just say no" question is apt to receive a positive answer and a bidder facing the target's board refusal to redeem the pill is left with the possibility of starting a proxy fight to substitute the managers: see Gordon, above, n. 20 at 527, quoting the first and only post-Unitrin case directly to address the question, *Moore Corp Ltd. v. Wallace Computer Services*, 907 F. Supp. 1545 (D Del 1995).

III. European Defences

Take-over defences in Europe offer two broad scenarios. In the U.K., pre-bid defences are allowed in principle, but rarely used;[126] post-bid defences are subject to shareholders' approval under the City Code.[127] In continental Europe, relatively high barriers to take-overs exist or are created in practice,[128] whereas post-bid defences are subject to different national regimes waiting to be harmonized under the Thirteenth Take-overs Directive, once adopted.[129] These two broad scenarios reflect the different corporate governance systems and capital market structures in continental Europe and the U.K. In addition, both scenarios appear to be different from that prevailing in the U.S., as is shown by the fact that poison pills are not used in Europe and that pre-bid defences, when adopted (as they often are on the continent), are designed more to create barriers to take-overs than to increase shareholder value through a successful acquisition of the target. In this section, I focus on post-bid defences and their treatment under the proposed Thirteenth Directive (which was, however, rejected by the European Parliament on July 4, 2001).

In the EU, the regulation of post-bid defences has been, to some extent, de facto harmonized,[130] whereas legal harmonization through the adoption of a Take-overs Directive has encountered new difficulties, as will be shown below. The regulatory model prevailing in European countries, with the notable exception of Germany, appears to be that embodied by General Principle no. 7 of the City Code, stating: "At no time after a bona fide offer has been communicated to the board of the offeree company, or after the board of the offeree company

---

[126] See P.L. Davies, 'The Regulation of Defensive Tactics in the United Kingdom and the United States' in K. Hopt and E. Wymeersch (eds.), above, n. 108, 195, 205; T. Jenkinson and C. Mayer, *Hostile Take-overs. Defence, Attack and Corporate Governance* (London 1994) 18.

[127] See General Principle 7 and Rule 21 ('Restrictions on Frustrating Action') of The City Code on Take-overs and Mergers.

[128] See Chapter 8 ('Defensive Measures: the Continental Approach') of Hopt and Wymeersch, above, n. 108, 217, and in particular the contributions by Schaafsma (The Netherlands), Simont (Belgium) and Maier-Raimer (Germany). See, more recently, the Report of the High Level Group of Company Law Experts on Issues Related to Takeover Bids (Brussels, 10 January 2002) at http://europa.eu.int/comm/internal_market/en/company/news/hlg01-2002.pdf.

[129] See N.J. Clausen and K.E. Sørensen, 'The Regulation of Take-over Bids in Europe: the Impact of the Proposed 13th Company Law Directive on the Present Regulation in EU Member States' [1999] 1 International and Comparative Corporate Law Journal 169, at 206.

[130] See K. Hopt, 'The Duties of the Directors of the Target Company in Hostile Take-overs—German and European Perspectives' in G. Ferrarini, K. Hopt, and E. Wymeersch (eds.), *Capital Markets in the Age of the Euro. Cross-Border Transactions, Listed Companies and Regulation* (The Hague, London, New York 2002), 401, stating that "in Europe in the last few years take-over laws and codes have been enacted in many countries. Most of these are patterned on the British City Code and include just like it a prohibition of frustrating action or in other terms a requirement of neutrality of the board of the target company".

has reason to believe that a bona fide offer might be imminent, may any action be taken by the board of the offeree company in relation to the affairs of the company, without the approval of the shareholders in general meeting, which could effectively result in any bona fide offer being frustrated or in the shareholders being denied an opportunity to decide on its merits".[131] This principle is specified by rule 21 on "frustrating action", which includes defensive measures.[132] The following actions are mentioned by rule 21: issuance of shares, options in respect of shares and securities carrying rights of conversion into or subscription for shares; sell, dispose or acquire assets of a material amount; making contracts otherwise than in the ordinary course of business. Similar rules have been adopted in Austria,[133] Ireland,[134] Italy,[135] Portugal,[136] Spain,[137] and Switzerland.[138]

In Germany, the Take-over Code of 1997 included a rule of neutrality (article 19) similar to the British rule on frustrating action; however, this was a voluntary Code and was adopted by only 63% of the listed companies.[139] Anyhow, the new German Take-over Law[140] provides that the management board cannot take frustrating actions, except for those which have been approved by the supervisory board (para. 33(1)). If the general meeting authorizes the management board to take frustrating measures subject to the competence of that meeting, the authorisation cannot last for more than eighteen months (para. 33(2)).[141] In France, the law states only that the securities regulator (COB) must be notified of the target's acts other than those accomplished in the ordinary course of business; a rule that is clearly "milder" than those adopted in countries following the British model.[142]

The common position adopted by the Council on June 19, 2000 with a view to the adoption of a directive on take-over bids included a "managerial

---

[131] See, for a commentary, D. Pudge, 'Conduct during the Offer; Timing and Revision; and Restrictions Following Offers' in M. Button and S. Bolton (eds.), *A Practitioner's Guide to the City Code on Take-overs and Mergers* (London 2001) 179.

[132] See, e.g. G. Stedman, *Take-overs* (London 1993) 395.

[133] See para. 12 of the Law on Take-over Bids (*Übernahmegesetz*) of 1999.

[134] See rule 21 of the Irish Take-over Rules (1997).

[135] See art. 104 of the Consolidated Financial Services Act.

[136] See art. 1822, Investment Securities Code (*Código dos valores mobiliàrios*).

[137] See art. 14, Royal Decree 1197, July 26, 1991, on the regulation of take-over bids.

[138] See art. 29, para. 2, Federal Act on Stock Exchanges and Securities Trading of 1995. Also, in Belgium there is a rule of neutrality of the target's board; however, some defensive measures are permitted: see Arts. 8, 14, 15, *Arreté Royal* concerning take-over bids of 1989.

[139] Hopt, above, n. 130, 396.

[140] The German Take-over Law was approved on December 20, 2001 and entered into force at the beginning of this year.

[141] ibid., para. I.1.c).

[142] ibid., para. I.2; see Article 3, COB Regulation No. 89-03 (1989).

passivity" rule clearly influenced by the City Code. Article 9(1)(a) of the common position provided that the target's board of directors "should abstain from any action which may result in the frustration of the offer" unless authorised by the shareholders' general meeting. This rule closely resembles General Principle no. 7 of the City Code. Defensive measures are typically included in the concept of frustrating action. Article 9(1)(a) referred to one in particular, identified as the "issuing of shares which may result in a lasting impediment to the offeror to obtain control over the offeree company". Clearly, this specification did not limit the scope of the rule, which was general in character and focused on the key concept of "frustration" of the offer.[143]

Article 9 is one of the Directive's provisions that have encountered criticism from the European Parliament in its second reading.[144] The legislative resolution adopted by the Parliament on the Council's common position amended article 9(1)(a) by adding two specifications. The first referred to the time from which the passivity rule is applicable to the target company. The proposed wording was similar to that used by rule 21 of the City Code, as it made reference not only to the official information about the bid, but also to "the time when, by whatever means, the existence of a bid becomes known". This amendment was accepted by the Commission, who agreed to extend the application of the "principle of neutrality" from the time when, by whatever means, the existence of a bid becomes known to the managers of the offeree company.[145] The second amendment represented a significant departure from the British model, as it specified that not only the prior authorization of the target's general meeting, but also that of the "supervisory board (if any)" would justify a frustrating action by the target. This would have introduced discrimination between companies depending on whether they have either a one-tier or a two-tier governance system (which would generally depend on the applicable corporate law). However, it is submitted that there are no reasons to differentiate on the basis of the internal governance structure, contrary to what is provided for by the recent German Take-over Law.[146] The "managerial passivity" rule implies that only the target shareholders have the right incentives to decide upon the defensive

---

[143] See N.J. Clausen and K.E. Sørensen, 'The Regulation of Take-over Bids in Europe: the Impact of the Proposed 13th Company Law Directive on the Present Regulation in EU Member States' [1999] 1 International and Comparative Corporate Law Journal 169, 207.

[144] See the European Parliament legislative resolution of December 13, 2000 on the Council common position for adopting a directive of the European Parliament and of the Council on company law concerning take-over bids (8129/1/2000—C5-0327/2000—1995/0341 (COD)), Prov Ed 298.924.

[145] See Commission Opinion pursuant to art. 251(2)(c) of the EC Treaty on the European Parliament's amendments to the Council's common position regarding the proposal for a directive concerning take-over bids, Brussels, February 12, 2001, COM(2001) 77 final, 1995/0341 (COD), 4.

[146] See above, n. 140, and the accompanying text.

measures proposed by the management; therefore, the supervisory board could not be a proper substitute for the general meeting.[147] For similar reasons, the Commission rejected the second amendment[148] and also a third amendment proposed by the European Parliament.[149]

The Council and the Parliament's positions in respect of frustrating actions were so different that conciliation appeared to be almost impossible.[150] In fact, the compromise agreed as a result of the conciliation procedure kept the target's duty to consult shareholders before adopting defensive measures, as proposed by the Commission in article 9 of the Directive. However, three additional elements were agreed: (i) a longer period for Member States to implement the Directive (four years plus an additional year for article 9); (ii) informational safeguards for employees in the target company; (iii) further analysis of three controversial issues, such as the "equitable price" in mandatory bids, the majority shareholders' right to acquire the shares of the minority shareholders ("squeeze-out"), and the equal treatment of shareholders.[151] However, the proposed text was finally rejected by the European Parliament at its second reading.

IV. Comparison

Differences among the national markets for corporate control are a reflection of diversified ownership structures of listed companies. Diffuse ownership is

---

[147] See K. Hopt, above, n. 130, 407, arguing that "even a qualified majority of the supervisory board cannot achieve the legitimacy of a general shareholder meeting".

[148] See Commission Opinion, above, n. 145, 6.

[149] The Parliament's legislative resolution amended article 9 by adding a new paragraph 2, which would have allowed the target's board to take different courses of action in some cases. Firstly, the supervisory authorities could "in conformity with national law, adopt guidelines as to the permissibility of any other defensive measures" (art. 9(2)(a)). In addition, the Member States could grant the supervisory authorities powers to authorise or forbid the adoption of defensive measures by a company (art. 9(2)(b)). Article 9(2)(d) specified, however, that the defensive measures authorized by the general meeting could not be forbidden by the competent supervisory authority. All this would have placed the regulators in an unprecedented role with respect to defensive measures. If the European Parliament's aim were to introduce rules closer to those applicable in the U.S. (as argued by Mr. Klaus-Heiner Lehne, Rapporteur to the Committee on Legal Affairs and the Internal Market of the European Parliament; see the Draft Recommendation for Second Reading on the Council Common Position, Provisional Edition 294.900, 17/20 (Explanatory Statement)), the rules just mentioned would have gone in the wrong direction by substituting the courts for regulators.

[150] The political discussion was also a reflection of opposing views amongst academics: see C. Kirchner and R.W. Painter, 'Towards a European Modified Business Judgment Rule for Take-over Law' (2000) 1 *Business Organisation Law Review* 353; P.O. Mülbert and M. Birke, 'In Defence of Passivity—on the Proper Role of a Target's Management in Response to a Hostile Tender Offer' [2000] 1 European Business Organization Law Review 445.

[151] See 'Take-overs Directive compromise agreed by Conciliation Committee, Luxembourg, 5–6 June 2001', http://europa.eu.int/comm/internal_market/en/company/company/news/o1–216.htm.

common in the U.S. and the U.K., whereas it is an exception in continental Europe. Structural barriers to take-overs are frequent on the continent of Europe, but rare across the Atlantic and in the U.K. Technical barriers (such as cross-shareholdings, pyramidal groups, etc.) are also rare in the U.K. and the U.S. (with the exception of non-voting shares and other departures from the one share–one vote idea), whilst they are still important in continental Europe.

1. Pre-bid Barriers or Tactics?

The very concept of a "barrier" shows the peculiar European attitude towards pre-bid defences, aimed at immunizing companies from take-overs. The American terminology (defensive "tactics" or "strategies" and the like) implies that defences are aimed either at improving the bid terms or frustrate the offer, if it is not wealth maximizing. Shark-repellents and poison pills are usually justified as reducing the coercion produced by take-over bids on target share-holders. The paradigm is offered by a two-tier bid creating a prisoner's dilemma for target shareholders, who fear to be frozen-out in the following merger if the tender offer is successful. But also one-tier bids can throw the offerees into a similar dilemma, if the bid price does not reflect the target's value and the share-holders accept the offer out of fear of being left with low-value minority shares, if the bidder gains control of the target.[152]

In Europe, the mandatory bid rules in force at the national level tend to exclude coercive two-tier bids, as they either require a bid for all the sharehold-ings or admit a partial bid upon the condition that it is approved by the major-ity of the relevant holdings.[153] However, bids for all the shares can also create pressure to tender and the mandatory bid rules do not solve this problem, as they lead "neither to the acquisition of more shares by the bidder nor to a higher premium".[154] A comparison with the American experience, therefore, shows that despite the non-recurrence in Europe of two-tier bids of a coercive

[152] See L.A. Bebchuk, 'Toward Undistorted Choice and Equal Treatment in Corporate Take-overs' [1985] 98 Harvard Law Review 1693, at 1696, 1717, arguing however that "allowing obstruc-tive tactics . . . is a very costly and inadequate method of dealing with the problem of distorted choice" (at 1743).

[153] This is the partial bids treatment adopted by the City Code on Take-overs and Mergers, Rule 36 (requiring approval by the City Panel and the shareholders holding over 50% of the voting rights). On the pressure to tender reduction operated by this rule, see Bebchuk, above, n. 152, 1796.

[154] M. Burkart, D. Gromb, and F. Panunzi, 'Why Higher Take-over Premia Protect Minority Shareholders' [1998] 106 *Journal of Political Economy* 172, at 187, who add: "The shortcoming of the MBR [mandatory bid rule] is its lack of coercion. It does not require the bidder to buy all shares, but merely those shares tendered. This obligation is vacuous since it remains still at the bid-der's discretion how many shares will actually be tendered". On the pressure to tender in all-shares offers, see Bebchuk, above, n. 152, 1717, 1796 (with reference to the British Code on Take-overs and Mergers).

nature,[155] the target shareholders may need protection against the pressure to tender generated by all-shares offers, notwithstanding the adoption of mandatory bid rules at the Member States' level. This is what defensive tactics can provide, by allowing the target to bargain with the bidder about the terms of the offer.

However, a defensive arsenal of the American type is still unknown in Europe. Poison pills are not used and would probably violate either corporate law principles or stock exchange regulations and companies' best practices.[156] In particular, the national rules implementing the Second Company Law Directive would create barriers against the use of poison pills. For instance, the rules on capital formation would make it difficult to issue securities at a discount in order to dilute the capital of the bidder. Furthermore, the rules on shareholders' equal treatment and pre-emptive rights would forbid the bidder's discrimination as to the issuance of shares that is determined by the poison pill.[157] In addition, the rules on shares' issuance, as well as those provided for by the Third Company Law Directive on mergers of public companies, would be an obstacle to the recognition of "flip-over rights", i.e. the target shareholders' rights to subscribe the bidder's shares at a discount, so as to dilute its capital.[158] The "flip-in rights" would also be difficult to admit, as they entitle the target shareholders to resell their shares to the issuer and would therefore be subject to the limits on share repurchases foreseen by the Second Directive. In any case, the poison pill's success in the U.S. is connected with the fact that the board of directors has full discretion in the issuance of new shares. In Europe, on the other hand, a decision to increase a company's capital must ultimately rest with shareholders, so that it would be easily defeated if motivated by anti-take-over purposes.

---

[155] It should also be noted that cash-out mergers are not allowed by European law, as harmonized under the Third Company Law Directive (see arts 3(1) and 4(1) allowing a cash payment not exceeding 10% of the nominal value of the shares issued for the merger).

[156] See P. Davies, 'The Regulation of Defensive Tactics in the United Kingdom and the United States' in K. Hopt and E. Wymeersch (eds.), *European Take-overs. Law and Practice* (London 1992) 195, 205.

[157] Also in the U.S., several decisions have invalidated planned poison pills on the grounds that state law does not permit a corporation to discriminate amongst shareholders of the same class: see J.H. Choper, J.C. Coffee and R.J. Gilson, *Cases and Materials on Corporations* 4th edn. (New York 1995) 904.

[158] In the U.S., the question "why is the asserted right to convert target shares into bidder shares legally enforceable?" is answered as follows: "If there is a merger between the target and the bidder, the answer probably is that the surviving firm by operation of law assumes the liabilities of the merging firm, which here include the obligation to honour the conversion privilege. However, where the 'flip-over' provision is triggered by some other condition (as it usually can be in the current version of the pill), it is far from clear that the bidder is liable simply because the target provides that a 'flip-over' right exists. For example, if the 'flip-over' is triggered by a sale of some assets between the bidder and the target, the legal status of the 'flip-over' would seem uncertain. Still it possesses a deterrent threat" (ibid., 902).

Shark repellents could be more easily accepted within the European corporate and capital market law setting, and to some extent they are already used (at least as far as super-majorities are concerned). The recourse to "fair price" provisions, for instance, could help to improve the bid terms and obtain better protection for the target shareholders.[159] However, these provisions should be analysed from the mandatory bid perspective in order to ascertain whether and to what extent the relevant rules can be either derogated or supplemented to improve investor protection in the case of a bid.

2. Post-bid Resistance: Powers and Instruments

The comparative analysis of post-bid defences highlights the diversity of internal governance structures, which in turn reflects more basic differences in the allocation of powers between directors and shareholders in American and European corporations.[160] In the U.S., boards of directors have been able to adopt the poison pill under their general authority to issue shares and to decide upon the pill's redemption under their responsibility of maximizing value for the shareholders. The same holds for the generality of pre-bid defences. In Europe, in contrast, a preference has emerged for an allocation of powers to the shareholders' meeting, along with the British model.

The distance between the two legal systems in the present area is shown by the academic discussion concerning recent attempts made by shareholder activists in the U.S. to limit the power of the board through the adoption of bylaws requiring the directors to redeem the pill in certain circumstances.[161] The question has been asked, in this respect, whether shareholders have such power of initiative and, in order to answer it positively, the need has been felt to develop a doctrinal analysis of the allocation of powers between the board and the shareholders, asking in particular "to what extent can shareholders give the board mandatory instructions through the medium of by-law amendments".[162] On the other hand, these actions by American shareholders may show that even there a reallocation

[159] "Fair price amendments" provide an "exception to a supermajority vote requirement for a second-step transaction where the price to be paid minority shareholders exceeds a specified amount which may be greater than the price paid in the initial tender offer": see R.J. Gilson and B.S. Black, *The Law and Finance of Corporate Acquisitions* 2nd edn. (New York 1995) 738.

[160] The question why the U.S. state legislatures have adopted a more pro-target management view is considered by P. Davies, below, Chapter 11.

[161] See Macey, above, n. 113, 861.

[162] J. Coffee, 'The Bylaw Battlefield: Can Institutions Change the Outcome of Corporate Control Contests?' [1997] 51 University of Miami Law Review 605, at 606.

of powers between directors and shareholders could take place in the not too distant future.[163]

However, the British approach also needs critical assessment, particularly from the shareholder voting perspective. The allocation of powers to the shareholders' meeting generates well-known collective action problems, such as widespread shareholders' rational apathy and free riding.[164] These problems may be reduced by the presence of institutional investors in the company's capital and also by the fact that decisions on defensive strategies are apt to increase the shares' value in a short time, by determining an improvement of the bid terms. Therefore, even assuming a sceptical attitude towards institutional shareholders' activism, an exception should be made with reference to their participation to post-bid defences, in light of the short-term profits that such conduct might generate.[165]

A different problem is created by block-holders if they own a minority stake of the share capital sufficient to participate in the control of the target. If the private benefits of control are relatively high (as happens in countries where investor protection is not yet fully developed[166]), the target block-holders might resist the take-over for reasons other than shareholder value maximisation. The outcome (if the block-holders' vote prevails, also as a consequence of the other shareholders' apathy) could be similar to that obtained in the U.S. when managers resist a take-over mainly for entrenchment purposes.

Furthermore, the comparison between the American and the European legal systems shows a substantial diversity as to the range of defensive tools available. This appears to be an effect of the different characteristics of corporate law, which is more enabling in the U.S. and less concerned about creditors' protection than in Europe.[167] The Second European Directive, for instance, severely restricts the repurchase of the company's own shares, thus narrowing the scope of buy-backs as defensive measures.[168] The same Directive provides for

---

[163] A preference for the British system is expressed by Bebchuk and Ferrel, above, n. 111, 1193, arguing that it is an example of "regulation that both addresses possible defects in the take-over process and ensures that shareholders, not management, have the ultimate say on whether a take-over proceeds".

[164] See Clark, above, n. 3.

[165] See J.R. Macey, 'Institutional Investors and Corporate Monitoring: A Demand Side Perspective in a Comparative View' in K. Hopt *et al.*, above, n. 101, 903, at 916: Institutional investors do not seem to be engaging in the continuous monitoring that demands active involvement; like other investors, they appear to rely on market forces, particularly on the market for corporate control.

[166] See L. Zingales, 'The Value of the Voting Right: a Study of the Milan Stock Exchange' [1994] 7 *Review of Financial Studies*, 125.

[167] See, among others, W.J. Carney, 'The Political Economy of Competition for Corporate Charters' [1997] Journal of Legal Studies 303, 318.

[168] For a critical analysis of the Second Directive, see Kübler, above, Chapter 4.

pre-emptive rights in the case of an increase of the company's capital, making it difficult for the target to allot shares to a friendly party in the event of a hostile bid.[169] As argued for the U.K. (but the comment could be extended to Europe in general), "it is clear that companies have relatively few defences available in the event of a hostile bid. Target companies are typically limited to financial announcements (such as updated dividends and profit forecasts); disposals or revaluations of assets; appeals to various regulators, or finding a white knight".[170]

3. Defences versus Market Rules

The relevance of the comments made above with respect to the limited exportability of American defences varies according to whether the analysis is applied to continental Europe or the U.K. In the continent, both structural and technical barriers make take-overs difficult, so that the question of the target defence often does not arise. In the U.K., the ownership structure of many listed companies is similar to that prevailing in the U.S. and there is an active market for corporate control, thereby raising the question why defensive strategies are rarely used. An answer could also help to predict possible developments in continental Europe, particularly if the number of diffuse ownership companies increases.

The limited use of take-over defences in the U.K. is due not only to technical difficulties created by company law (mainly as a reflection of the European directives), but also to the influence of institutional investors who oppose the use of excessive discretion by the managers. Moreover, the City Code on Take-overs and Mergers contains rules that can be regarded as substitutes for American defences from the viewpoint of shareholder value enhancement. First, rule 10 of the City Code provides: "It must be a condition of any offer for voting equity share capital which, if accepted in full, would result in the offeror holding shares carrying over 50% of the voting rights of the offeree company that the offer will not become or be declared unconditional as to acceptances unless the offeror has acquired or agreed to acquire (either pursuant to the offer or otherwise) shares carrying over 50% of the voting rights . . .". The rationale for this rule is to exercise pressure on the bid's price, as the supply curve is upward sloping, i.e. "the supply of shares is increasing in the bid price".[171] As empirical evidence seems to indicate, "the number of shares supplied in a tender offer indeed increases with

---

[169] See Davies, above, n. 126, 206.

[170] Jenkinson and Mayer, above, n. 126, 24.

[171] M. Burkart, D. Gromb, and F. Panunzi, 'Why Higher Take-over Premia Protect Minority Shareholders' [1998] 106 *Journal of Political Economy* 172, 181.

the bid premium".[172] Therefore, Rule 10 qualifies the requirement for a total offer, as not only should a bid concern all the target's shares (as shown, a contrario, by Rule 36 on partial bids[173]), but the bidder should offer a price sufficient to obtain the majority of the voting rights.

Secondly, rule 31.4 provides: "After an offer has become or is declared unconditional as to acceptances, the offer must remain open for acceptances for not less than 14 days after the date on which it would otherwise have expired . . .". The rationale for this rule seems to be to avoid the pressure to tender typical of take-over bids.[174] Those who are willing to accept shall tender their shares before the bid's expiry; the others can wait, as they shall benefit from an extension of the bid's term if the same becomes unconditional as to acceptances. As argued by Bebchuk, "the requirement turns the 'first round' into the equivalent of an approval vote, because a shareholder's decision whether to tender in that round matters only in the event that his decision proves pivotal for the bid's fate. To express a preference for the bid's success, a shareholder has to tender his shares in the first round; to express a preference for the bid's failure, he has to hold out in that round".[175]

Thirdly, rule 36.5 (concerning "partial offers") states: "Any offer which could result in the offeror holding shares carrying 30% or more of the voting rights of a company must normally be conditional, not only on the specified number of acceptances being received, but also on approval of the offer, normally signified by means of a separate box on the form of acceptance, being given by shareholders holding over 50% of the voting rights not held by the offeror and persons acting in concert with it. . .". This rule appears to address and attempt to solve the "prisoner's dilemma" facing target shareholders, who should otherwise accept a sub-optimal price or take the risk of being left in a minority position (if the bid succeeds).[176]

---

[172] ibid. 182, citing J. Hirschleifer, "Mergers and Acquisitions: Strategic and Informational Issues" in R.A. Jarrow, V. Maksimovik, and W.T. Ziemba (eds.), *Handbook in Operations Research and Management Science*, Vol. 9 *Finance* (Amsterdam 1995).

[173] Rule 36.1 states: "The Panel's consent is required for any partial offer. In the case of an offer which could not result in the offeror holding shares carrying 30% or more of the voting rights of a company, consent will normally be granted".

[174] See Bebchuk, n. 152 above at 1797.

[175] ibid., 1798, who adds: "The problem is that expressing a preference for the bid's success might involve extra transaction costs in comparison to expressing a preference for the bid's failure".

[176] ibid., 1800, arguing, however, "the problems posed by partial bids and bids for all shares are essentially the same".

E. Financial Restructurings

I. General

Finance theory and practice show that "most of the time financial restructurings do change the way corporations are run and do create new, enduring values".[177] As argued by Jensen, the evidence from LBOs and leveraged restructurings "has demonstrated dramatically that leverage, payout policy and ownership structure . . . affect organizational efficiency, cash flow, and hence value. Such organizational changes show that these effects are especially important in low-growth or declining firms where the agency costs of free cash flow are large".[178] Share repurchases and leveraged recapitalizations can reduce these costs and contribute to value creation.[179] Leveraged acquisitions also assure investors that surplus cash flow will not be wasted[180] and offer "an incentive structure for realizing value (improving operating performance) in 'undervalued' companies".[181]

Corporate finance rules, therefore, should facilitate the various types of financial restructurings in order to enhance shareholder wealth creation. Existing limits to share repurchases and leveraged buy-outs should be carefully examined and their rationale should be confronted with the value enhancing effects of financial restructurings. A similar study would be clearly outside the confines of this paper, as it would require an in-depth analysis of the rules on capital, share repurchases, and financial assistance included in the Second Company Law Directive and the national laws implementing the same.[182] In this section, in order to illustrate a European de-regulatory trend in this area motivated by shareholder value considerations, I will briefly consider the French and German law reforms concerning share repurchases and a recent proposal for the revision of the second company law directive.

---

[177] Stewart, above, n. 8, 479.

[178] M.C. Jensen, 'The Modern Industrial Revolution, Exit, and the Failure of Internal Control Systems' [1993] 48 *Journal of Finance* 18, 868.

[179] See, for an updated discussion, J. Weston, K. Chung, and J. Siu, *Take-overs, Restructuring, and Corporate Governance* 2nd edn. (Englewood 1998) 257, 371; leveraged recapitalizations involve a relatively large issue of debt that is used for the payment of a relatively large cash dividend or for the repurchase of common shares.

[180] Stewart, above, n. 8, 492.

[181] G.P. Baker and G.D. Smith, *The New Financial Capitalists. Kohlberg Kravis Roberts and the Creation of Corporate Value* (Cambridge 1998) xii, 44. See, in particular, S. Kaplan, 'The Effects of Management Buyouts on Operating Performance and Value' [1998] 24 *Journal of Financial Economics* 217.

[182] See the chapters by F. Kübler, above, Chapter 4 and E.V. Ferran, above, Chapter 5.

II. Recent Reforms

Both the French and German law reforms concerning share repurchases were enacted in 1998. In France, share buy-backs were forbidden by the 1966 law on commercial companies. However, the company could buy its own shares for one of the following purposes: (i) to annul the same and execute a capital reduction decided upon by the shareholders' general meeting; (ii) to transfer its shares to the employees within either a profit-sharing or a share-option scheme; (iii) to stabilize the share price (if the company was listed). This regime appeared to be too restrictive, as extensively shown by the Esambert Report published in January 1998.[183]

The Esambert Report posited that share repurchases are motivated by shareholder value creation and argued that the exceptions contemplated by French law were insufficient for a dynamic financial management. On the one hand, the mechanisms of the share capital's reduction were too rigid and burdensome; on the other hand, the rules concerning share repurchases for stabilization purposes were inadequate from a capital restructuring perspective.[184] At the same time, comparative law shows that in the U.S. "le capital social peut fluctuer de manière assez souple" (the legal capital may fluctuate in a rather light way) and share repurchases are frequent and respond to multiple goals. British companies are also relatively free to purchase their own shares, albeit within the limits fixed by the Second Company Law Directive and the Stock Exchange rules.[185] The Esambert Report concluded by recommending a reformulation of the French rules on share repurchases, to the extent allowed by the European Directive: the principle should be one of liberty and the procedural requirements should be simplified.

This recommendation was brought forward by article 41 of the law of July 2, 1998, liberalizing share repurchases. Under the new regime, the shareholders' general meeting can fix the goals of share buy-backs and the company can purchase and resell its own shares, annul the same under a simplified procedure, use the shares for stock options, etc. Such liberalization is balanced by increased transparency and specific rules to be followed in order to carry out the relevant transactions.[186] The reform has been successful, according to a recent report by the *Commission des Opérations de Bourse*, concluding that the new rules have

---

[183] See the *Report sur le rachat par les Sociétés de leurs propres actions* written for *COB* by Mr. Bernard Esambert at http://www.cob.fr/frset.asp?rbrq=doc.

[184] ibid., 13.

[185] ibid., 16.

[186] See *COB, Rachat par les Sociétés de leurs propres actions: bilan et propositions,* (January 2000) at http://www.cob.fr/frset.asp?rbrq=actu, 5.

stimulated many transactions and have determined an increase of the shareholders' benefits per share and of the share prices in the short-term.[187]

A similar reform was introduced in Germany by the *KonTraG* of 1998. Also in Germany share repurchases were allowed in exceptional circumstances provided for by para. 71(1) *AktG,* such as an acquisition made to avert severe and imminent damage to the company (no. 1), to offer shares to the employees (no. 2), to compensate shareholders in given circumstances (no. 3) or to redeem shares in order to execute a reduction of capital (no. 6). Only credit and financial institutions had some room for manoeuvre, being entitled to purchase their own shares for purposes of securities trading on the basis of a resolution of the shareholders' meeting (no. 7, introduced in 1994 by the second law for the promotion of financial markets). In 1998, article 1, no. 5(a) of the *KonTraG* modified para. 71(1) *AktG* by adding a new No. 8, which liberalizes, to some extent and within the limits foreseen by the second company law directive, the share buy-backs also for companies other than credit and financial institutions. However, the trade of own shares is forbidden (only credit and financial institutions are allowed to practice it under para. 71(1) no. 7). Interestingly, the German authors also explain this liberalization by reference to the shareholder value concept.[188]

III. European Developments

The national law reforms just mentioned had to comply with by the Second Directive rules on acquisition of own shares (art. 19), but also these rules are undergoing revision within the Simpler Legislation for the Single Market (SLIM) initiative.[189] A Company Law SLIM Working Group was created with a view to identifying where simpler legislation could replace the existing legislation in the field of the first and second company law directives.[190] As to article 19 of the Second Directive, the SLIM Group found that the 18-month time-limit on the general meeting's authorization for the share buy-back was too brief and proposed to extend it to five years. Furthermore, the SLIM Group deemed the limitation to 10 per cent of the subscribed capital[191] restrictive and unnecessary

---

[187] See *COB, Rachat par les Sociétés de leurs propres actions: bilan et propositions,* 11.

[188] See K. Martens, 'Erwerb und Veräusserung eigener Aktien im Börsenhandel' [1996] *Die Aktiengesellschaft* 337.

[189] The purpose of the SLIM initiative is not to harmonize, but to slim down regulation.

[190] The Working Group was made of Member States' representatives and experts in and users of company law, and was chaired by E. Wymeersch. See the Explanatory Memorandum and the Recommendations on the Simplification of the First and Second Company Law Directives (October 1999) at http://www.law.rug.ac.be/fli/index.html.

[191] See art. 19(1)(b), stating that "the nominal value or, in the absence thereof, the accountable par of the acquired shares, including shares previously acquired by the company and held by it, and shares acquired by a person acting in his own name but on the company's behalf, may not exceed 10 per cent of the subscribed capital".

if the company disposed of distributable assets. Consequently, it suggested to a reformulation of the rule by limiting the acquisition of own shares to the amount of distributable assets.[192] In this way, the creditors would be protected, without unnecessarily hindering the company's ability to adjust its capital structure according to the needs of shareholder wealth maximization.

The SLIM Group also reviewed article 23 of the Second Directive, which prohibits "financial assistance" by stating at its first paragraph: "A company may not advance funds, nor make loans, nor provide security, with a view to the acquisition of its shares by a third party". The SLIM group suggested reducing this prohibition to a minimum, either limiting financial assistance to the amount of distributable net assets or limiting the prohibition to the assistance for the subscription of newly issued shares.[193] The rationale for this proposal can be found in an essay written by Eddy Wymeersch shortly before.[194] Article 23 of the second directive derived from British law and "was conceived as an instrument akin to the rules on the repurchase of own shares, and hence as an instrument designed to protect the company's capital".[195] However, "the rule is based on a strange reasoning: while the directive does not forbid . . . a company to repurchase its own shares nor to grant loans to its shareholders, the combination of both transactions in one perspective . . . would result in an outright prohibition".[196] Furthermore, the financial assistance prohibition affects an area of corporate practice that is already subject to different rules, such as those on own shares, credit to shareholders and conflicts of interest. The outcome of all this is "hardly understandable" and deletion of article 23 is suggested.[197]

The field that would benefit mostly from the SLIM Group's proposal is that of leveraged acquisitions and, in particular, leveraged buy-outs. In the Member States the question has frequently been considered whether the financial assistance prohibition would also forbid either the distribution of dividends by the target or the merger of the target and the acquirer, when they provide the means to repay the loan contracted by the acquirer in order to finance its acquisition.[198] This issue is often analysed without critical consideration of the prohibition's

---

[192] See the Explanatory Memorandum, above, n. 190, 8.

[193] ibid.

[194] E. Wymeersch, 'Article 23 of the Second Company Law Directive: the Prohibition on Financial Assistance to Acquire Shares of the Company' in J. Basedow, K. Hopt, and H. Kötz (eds.), *Festschrift für Ulrich Drobnig* (Tübingen 1997) 725.

[195] ibid., 733.

[196] ibid., 741.

[197] ibid., 746.

[198] ibid., 736. This question was recently dealt with by the Milan Tribunal, judgment of May 13, 1999, in the case of *Bruni Pio v. Trenno SpA* (2000) *Le Società* 75, holding that LBO transactions are valid in principle, but may be fraudulently directed to avoid the financial assistance prohibition.

rationale and adequate analysis of the LBOs' value creating potential. Therefore, the proposed reform would probably stimulate the growth of leveraged acquisitions in Europe and enhance shareholder value, without affecting creditor protection.

F. Conclusions

I began this chapter with an analysis of the role of shareholder value in internal corporate governance. The European codes of best practice emphasize this role. They also analyse the relationship between shareholder value, profit maximization and stakeholder protection, following the "in the long run" perspective that reconciles the goal of shareholder value maximization with that of the social responsibility of corporations. Difficulty in the doctrinal debate is posed in Germany by the relationship between the company law and the enterprise law perspectives. However, according to a recent German view, the company stays in the foreground and pursues the goal of long-term profit maximization in the shareholders' interests. The European corporate governance codes also set out best practices in the field of directors' remuneration. Their recommendations and principles reflect the main international concerns relating to the level of executive pay, the procedure for its determination and the disclosure of the same.

On the whole, the European codes of best practice contribute to uniformity in the corporate law field, particularly from the shareholder value perspective. A "professional" board is generally linked with good performance, even though proof of causation has yet to be offered. The capital markets ultimately assess the board's functioning and performance, and the share prices incorporate information as to the quality of governance. Market discipline is breaking new grounds in continental Europe and is proving to be an essential supplement to corporate law. The issue of shareholder value maximization, however, tends to be covered by the business judgment rule and is rarely addressed by the courts. Nevertheless, executive compensation mechanisms are used to align the managers' interests with those of the owners and have been subject to sweeping changes as a result of legal reforms.

I moved on to examine take-over defences and the main rules applicable to them from a comparative perspective. Target shareholders are faced with a prisoner's dilemma. Take-over defences can help to solve the relevant co-ordination problem by enhancing the bargaining power of the target management. Defensive measures, however, give rise to a conflict of interest problem, as managers might entrench themselves instead of maximizing shareholder wealth. The core question appears to be one of internal governance: should managers or shareholders take the final decision as to take-over defences? The comparative analysis of post-bid defences highlights the diversity of internal governance structures, which in turn reflects more basic differences in the allocation of powers between directors and shareholders in American and European corporations.

The European approach, however, needs critical assessment from the shareholder voting perspective. The allocation of powers to the shareholders' meeting generates well-known collective action problems. Another problem is created by block-holders if they own a minority stake of the share capital sufficient to participate in the control of the target. If the private benefits of control are relatively high, the target block-holders might resist the take-over for reasons other than shareholder value maximization. Furthermore, comparison between the American and the European legal systems reveals a substantial diversity as to the range of defensive tools available; a reflection of the corporate finance rules included in the second company law directive. The modification of these rules (e.g. by liberalizing share buy-backs) will allow the European defensive arsenal to grow.

I then considered some aspects of financial restructurings. Share repurchases and leveraged recapitalizations can reduce the "costs of free cash-flow" and contribute to value creation. Leveraged acquisitions assure investors that surplus cash flow will not be wasted and offer an incentive structure for improving operating performance. Consequently, corporate finance rules should facilitate the various types of financial restructurings in order to enhance shareholder wealth creation.

A recent French report posited that share repurchases are motivated by shareholder value creation and argued that the exceptions contemplated by French law were insufficient to be compatible with a dynamic financial management. A reform of the law followed. Under the new regime, the shareholders' general meeting can fix the goals of share buy-backs that can be made for trading, investment, etc. Such liberalization is balanced by increased transparency and specific rules to be followed in order to carry out the relevant transactions. A similar reform was introduced in Germany by the *KonTraG* of 1998.

These reforms were conditioned by the second directive rules on the acquisition of own shares, which are, in turn, undergoing a revision within the Simpler Legislation for the Single Market initiative. The SLIM Working Group deemed that the 10% limit of subscribed capital is unnecessarily restrictive and suggested limiting the acquisition of own shares to the amount of distributable net assets. The SLIM Group also suggested reducing the prohibition of financial assistance to a minimum. The field that would mostly benefit from the SLIM Group's proposal is that of leveraged acquisitions and, in particular, LBOs.

On the whole, the shareholder value concept appears as a useful yardstick by which to measure the responsiveness of corporate law and practice to the needs of capital markets. It also offers the rationale for law reforms in different areas, which represent a promising field for further research in European corporate governance.

11

Shareholder Value, Company Law, and Securities Markets Law: A British View

PAUL DAVIES

Abstract

The argument in this chapter is that the move to shareholder value in the U.K. has been driven, on the legal front, not by changes in the law relating to directors' duties nor the rules on shareholders' appointment and removal rights, despite the central role one might expect such rules to play in determining how central management exercises the discretion vested in it. Rather, what has been important are changes in shareholder structure. These have operated at two levels. At the first level, they have permitted shareholders to extract some greater value from their traditional company law entitlements, especially in relation to the removal of under-performing management. At a second level, re-concentration of shareholdings in the hands of the institutions has permitted them to bring about changes in the rules and practices of the securities markets which are favourable to the promotion of shareholder value, notably in the areas of pre-emption rights and take-over bids.

Contents

Table

A. The Emergence of Shareholder Value

In 1956 C.A.R. Crosland published a book entitled *The Future of Socialism*.[1] Crosland had been an academic economist at Oxford, was at the time of writing Labour MP for Grimsby and was to be briefly a minister in the 1964 Labour government before an untimely death. He was the leading theorist on the reformist wing of the Labour Party. Besides setting out a positive agenda for the Party, the book was concerned to divert the Party away from some of its then current policy proposals. These proposals included ideas for further nationalization of industry and, less radically, proposals to place government or worker

---

[1] C.A.R. Crosland, *The Future of Socialism* (London 1956).

directors on the boards of large companies. Although Crosland conceded that 'In principle I can see little to be said for the present law',[2] which vested control rights in shareholders, nevertheless equally little valuable social change was to be expected from a reform of company law: 'It is easy to become bemused with con-stitution-making and legal formulae'.[3] This was because the 'functionless' share-holders were incapable of exercising the control rights that the law vested in them, as a result of the separation of management and ownership, and in any event did not desire to do so. In consequence 'the psychology and motivation of the top management class itself' had fundamentally changed as a result of its newfound independence from the firm's shareholders.[4] In this brave new man-agerialist world 'a change in the law, logical though it might be, would make no difference to the underlying reality. Despite the existing law, the shareholders have little power, and the government and the unions have much'.[5]

By contrast, the Hampel Committee on Corporate Governance, when it turned in 1998 to consider 'the aims of those who direct and control companies', was clear that: 'The single overriding objective shared by all listed companies, whatever their size or type of business, is the preservation and the greatest practical enhancement over time of their shareholders' investment'.[6] The pursuit of this objective might require the company to develop relationships with a number of non-shareholder groups but in doing so they must have regard to the overriding objective just identified.

Of course, it might be that these two very different views of managerial objec-tives and behaviour reflected different political standpoints, and rather than any actual changes in the factors constraining and directing the decisions of the cen-tralized management of large companies over the period between the 1950s and the end of the last century. However, this seems unlikely. Crosland, for example, quoted in his support the 1950s champions of shareholder value. He could do this because they shared his analysis of then prevailing situation, though of course they differed from him radically on the issue whether this situation was to be welcomed.[7] Equally, a notable contemporary critic of the status quo can share with Hampel the view that shareholder interests dominate management decision-making, whilst rejecting that Committee's assessment of the utility of such a situation.[8] This chapter will therefore take as its, admittedly not fully proved, starting point the proposition that, over the last half century or so, the

---

[2] C.A.R. Crosland, *The Future of Socialism* (London 1956), 265.

[3] ibid., 276.

[4] ibid., 15.

[5] ibid., 276.

[6] Committee on Corporate Governance, Final Report (London 1998), para. 1.16.

[7] Crosland, above, n. 1, 267–8.

[8] W. Hutton, *The State We're In* (London 1995) 156–7.

interests of shareholders have become central to the decision-making of centralized management in a way they were not at the beginning of the period. By
contrast the interests of other stakeholders, or even the freedom of management
to conduct the business in its own interest, have declined in potency. The issue
that the chapter seeks to address is the nature of the legal changes that have
contributed to this highly significant development.

B. Company Law: Constant Content and Changing Context

I. The Stability of Company Law

In seeking to address the issue posed at the end of the previous paragraph, one
comes up against an immediate paradox. One might imagine that an increase in
the power of shareholders as against management would be reflected in changes
in company law, since one of the central tasks of company law is to regulate the
principal-agent relationship between shareholders and the centralized management of large companies.[9] Yet, the re-emergence of shareholder influence
appears to have occurred against the backdrop of a remarkable stability over the
post-war period in the relevant company law provisions. That period may be
about to end with the recent publication of two important reports from the Law
Commissions (on shareholder remedies and directors' duties[10]) and with the
very recent proposals of the Company Law Review, established by the
Department of Trade and Industry.[11] Nevertheless, during the period with
which we are concerned company law remained largely unchanged in the relevant respects. In fact, the one significant change to the law, which will be discussed further below, appeared to go in the opposite direction from the
promotion of shareholder value.[12]

What are the aspects of company law most relevant to the promotion of
shareholder value on the part of centralized management? These may be seen as
being, on the one hand, the standards governing the exercise of discretion by
centralized management—mainly the law on directors' duties. In particular,
how far do these standards constrain management to place the shareholders'

---

[9] For the avoidance of doubt it should be stated that this chapter is concerned only with companies where centralized management is factually distinct from the shareholders.

[10] Law Commission (Law Com. no. 261) and Scottish Law Commission (Scot Law Com. no.
173), *Company Directors: Regulating Conflicts of Interest and Formulating a Statement of Duties*,
Cm. 4436, 1999; Law Commission (Law Com. no. 246), *Shareholder Remedies*, Cm. 3769, 1997.

[11] Company Law Reform Steering Group, *Modern Company Law: Final Report* (London:
Department of Trade and Industry, July 2001, Vol. I, Ch. 3 and Annex C). The consultation documents issued by the Company Law Review, the research commissioned by it and various other documents are available on its web-site: www.dti.gov.uk/cld/review.htm.

[12] See Section II(B) below, dealing with s. 309 of the Companies Act 1985.

interests first? On the other hand, the rules relating to the appointment and removal of the members of the board of directors are crucial. In whose hands do these powers lie? Directors' duties are still governed, substantially, by the common law, though with some statutory accretions, whilst shareholders' appointment powers have always been regulated principally through the Companies Acts and the articles of association of particular companies.

The common law moves forward only if litigation drives it, and yet litigation over the common law of directors' duties in the U.K. (in contrast to the U.S.) has always been relatively infrequent. English law has traditionally constrained very tightly the *locus standi* of individual or even minority groups of shareholders to bring derivative actions; and this has had a consequential impact upon the development of the substantive law.[13] Indeed, it can be maintained that the last fundamental review by the House of Lords of the law relating to directors' duties occurred as long ago as 1942.[14] As for the appointment and removal of board members, the centrepiece of the law relating in this area, the right of an ordinary majority of the shareholders to remove a director at any time, was added to the statute book in 1947. Thus, throughout the 'Crosland-Hampel' period, the shareholders' legal powers to remove the board remained a constant.

However, it may be entirely wrong to suppose that the rise of shareholder value required any change to substantive company law. Crosland did not deny that the company law of his period vested control rights in the shareholders; his argument was that in practice shareholders were unable to enforce the rights that company law conferred upon them because of the dispersion of shareholdings. If this argument is correct, then a change in the factual ability of shareholders to enforce their rights might explain the rise of shareholder value to its present position of prominence. The rest of this section will explore this hypothesis, which embodies two sub-propositions. The first is that the (unchanging) company law does embody a theory of shareholder control (Section II(B)); the second that a re-concentration of shareholdings has enabled shareholders actually to take advantage of the rights which company law has traditionally conferred upon them (Section II(C)).

[13] It is revealing that major developments in the law relating to the directors' duties of competence are currently occurring in statutory proceedings to disqualify directors on grounds of unfitness, where the litigation is brought by the State rather than the shareholder. See, for example, *Re Westmid Packing Services Ltd* [1998] 2 All E.R. 124; *Re Kaytech International plc* [1999] 2 B.C.L.C. 351, both decisions of the Court of Appeal.

[14] *Regal (Hastings) Ltd v. Gulliver* [1942] 1 All E.R. 378—and even then the official law reports did not get around to reporting the case until 1967! However, the Privy Council, on appeals from Commonwealth courts, has made one or two notable contributions; and the judicial membership of the HL and PC overlaps.

II. Company Law and Shareholder Control

It is argued in this section that at the level of professed principle the goal of shareholder value sits fairly comfortably within the traditional rules of company law. Let us look first at the rules conferring appointment and removal rights in relation to directors or controlling the exercise by directors of their discretion.

1. Appointment and Removal Rights

These rules are contained in the Companies Act and are clearly consistent with the dominance of shareholder value. Although the Act in fact has little to say about the appointment of directors, and the articles of association of most companies make it difficult for shareholders to propose their own candidates for board membership, as opposed to accepting or rejecting those put forward by the board itself,[15] nevertheless all this pales into insignificance in the light of the provisions of section 303 of the Companies Act 1985, which is the modern version of the provision introduced in the late 1940s. This section permits an ordinary majority of the shareholders at any time to dismiss all or any of the directors, without giving any reason, no matter what contrary provisions may be found in the company's articles or the director's contract of service, subject only to an obligation to pay compensation to any director whose contract is wrongfully terminated. This must be read together with the provisions of section 368 empowering the holders of 10% of shares carrying the voting rights to requisition a speedy meeting of the company.

Of course, the compensation payable for breach of directors' typically fixed-term contracts may be substantial and the prospect of paying it may chill the use of section 303. This has led both the statute and the corporate governance committees to promote limits on the length of directors' fixed-terms and on the length of contractual notice periods.[16] Nevertheless, sections 303 and 368, as they stand, are significant provisions in promoting the primacy of the shareholder interest. The U.K. rules contrast with those in most States of the U.S. where the opportunity to remove directors arises only annually and, in the case

---

[15] See Table A, art. 76 and P. Davies, 'The United Kingdom' in Th. Baums and E. Wymeersch (eds.), *Shareholder Voting Rights and Practices in Europe and the United States* (London 1999) 347.

[16] Shareholder approval is required by s. 319 of the Companies Act 1985 for directors' contracts which cannot be terminated by the company within a five-year period, whilst the Combined Code says that there is 'a strong case' for setting notice periods at no more than one year: Section 1.B.1.7. The Combined Code is part of the U.K. Listing Rules, now issued by the Financial Services Authority, and listed companies must either comply with the Code or explain to their shareholders the reasons for their non-compliance. The Company Law Review, above n. 11 at paras 6.12–6.14 has proposed to reduce the statutory period to one year (except in case of first appointments) but also to allow shareholders to give such approval in advance.

of companies with staggered boards, the whole board may be replaceable only over a number of years.[17] In the U.K., by contrast, control of the majority of the votes feeds through directly into control of the board. It seems to be mainly on the basis of these sections that Bob Monks, vice chairman of Hermes Lens asset managers, has characterized the U.K. as 'easily the world leader' in the accountability of management to investors.[18]

2. Rules and Standards Constraining the Exercise of Managerial Discretion

With regard to directors' duties, our concern is with the duties of loyalty, rather than of competence, and in particular with the question, whose interests must the directors promote, at least as far as the law 'in the books' is concerned? The formal answer to that question, as in so many European systems, is that the directors must promote the interests of 'the company'. However, English law seems to be tolerably clear that, as far as the common law is concerned, (i) the phrase 'the interests of the company' is meaningless unless 'the company' is identified with one or more groups of people involved in the company or affected by its actions;[19] and (ii) that 'the company' means the members (or shareholders),[20] at least so long as it is a going concern.[21]

However, the matter is not entirely free from doubt and there are those who have argued that the common law recognized a broader notion of 'the company' than just the shareholders (or members). If the common law required the duties to be owed to the shareholders, it has been asked, why did it not say so, instead of referring to 'the company' as the beneficiary of the duties? The answer, which has not convinced everyone, is that 'the company' is a way of referring to the shareholders collectively, for it is the shareholders as a whole, rather than individual shareholders to whom the directors owe their duties, at least in the standard case.[22] The minority view that shareholder value is *inconsistent* with the traditional common law was strengthened by the enactment in 1980 of the only significant statutory change to the relevant law during the period under consideration. This was the introduction of a requirement that directors 'have regard

---

[17] See M. Kahan, 'Jurisprudential and Transactional Developments in Take-overs' in Hopt et al. (eds.), *Comparative Corporate Governance* (Oxford 1998) 691.

[18] *Financial Times*, February 17, 2000, 18.

[19] See the crisp statement by the Law Commission, 'In reality [the company] has no interests of its own' (*Company Directors: Regulating Conflicts of Interest and Formulating a Statement of Duties*, Law Commission Consultation Paper no. 153, 1998) para. 11.21.

[20] J.E. Parkinson, *Corporate Power and Responsibility* (Oxford 1993) Ch. 3.

[21] The interests of the creditors are increasingly recognized within directors' common law duties if the company approaches insolvency, but the most powerful expression of this development is to be found within the Insolvency Act 1986 itself, notably s. 214 on wrongful trading.

[22] *Gower's Principles of Modern Company Law* (London 1997), 599–601.

in the performance of their functions [to] the interests of the interests of the company's employees in general, as well as to the interests of its members' (now section 309 of the Companies Act 1985). This provision is grist to the mill of the opponents of shareholder value who, today, are not those who argue for nationalization but those whose analysis of the company is based upon stakeholding theory, i.e. the importance to the efficient conduct of business of long-term relationships not only with suppliers of equity capital but also with suppliers of other inputs and with customers.[23] The section is a puzzling provision. At one level it was the only concrete outcome of the Committee of Inquiry on Industrial Democracy (the 'Bullock' Committee),[24] which reported in 1977, and yet it was introduced by a decidedly non-corporatist Conservative government. Ever since it was introduced, it has been debated whether it operates so as to put the interests of the employees on a par with those of the shareholders or whether it simply makes the point, as was probably already the law, that promotion of the interests of the members should be implemented by policies which recognize that shareholder benefit requires the interests of the workforce to be taken into account.[25] This issue has not been clearly resolved by the courts, partly because no special way for employees to enforce the duty, should they have thought it worth doing so, was created.[26]

However, the matter will be settled if the proposals of the Company Law Review are accepted by the legislature. These proposals are based on the primacy of the shareholder interest but re-state that interest in an 'inclusive' way. In its Final Report the Company Law Review[27] proposed to reformulate and embody in statute the central duty of loyalty in the following way:

A director of a company must in any given case—
    (a) act in the way he decides, in good faith, would be most likely to promote the success of the company for the benefit of its members as a whole . . .; and

[23] See S. Deakin and G. Slinger, 'Hostile Take-overs, Corporate Law and the Theory of the Firm' in S. Deakin and A. Cosh (eds.), *Enterprise and Community: New Directions in Corporate* (Oxford 1997); G. Kelly and J. Parkinson, 'The Conceptual Foundation of the Company: A Pluralist Approach' [1998] 2 Company Financial and Insolvency Law Review 174.

[24] Report of the Committee of Inquiry on Industrial Democracy, Cmnd. 6706, 1977.

[25] Parkinson, above, n. 20, 82–86.

[26] However, the section has been useful occasionally to boards seeking to repel attacks on their conduct by shareholders seeking to advance shareholder value arguments. Thus, in *Re Saul D Harrison & Sons plc* [1995] 1 B.C.L.C. 14, the directors of a barely profitable business ignored a golden opportunity to wind it up and distribute its assets to the shareholders when its premises were compulsorily purchased with full compensation. The Court of Appeal thought that s. 309 allowed the board to support its decision to continue trading at new premises by reference to the fact that keeping the business going would be of benefit to its employees, many of whom were long-serving and some of whom were educationally sub-normal.

[27] Above, n. 11.

(b) in deciding what would be most likely to promote that success, take account in good faith of all the material factors that it is practicable in the circumstances for him to identify.[28]

The most significant aspect of the CLR's proposal is that it makes it explicit that the shareholders' interests are central by replacing the phrase 'interests of the company' in the common law formulation with 'for the benefit of the members as a whole' in the proposed statutory version. Thus it renders untenable the minority view referred to above, and removes the ambiguities generated by the reference to 'the company' in the common law formulation. However, clarity is achieved in a way that stresses the inclusive nature of this duty to the shareholders through the requirement on directors to take into account "all material factors". In this way the document also solves the ambiguity problem generated by section 309 of the Act, mentioned above, which would presumably disappear from the statute book under the CLR's proposals.

The CLR's proposal can be seen as having emerged from a debate, exposed in its earlier consultative document,[29] which constituted a more generalized version of the arguments generated by section 309. Should the law be altered so as to make the interests of all stakeholders free-standing objects of the directors' attention, of equal status with those of the shareholders, or should the shareholders' interest be given primacy, but within a framework which recognized the significance of non-shareholder interests to the company's commercial success? In the terminology of the earlier document, was 'pluralism' or 'enlightened shareholder value' the better approach? The CLR in the end opts for the latter. The shareholders' interests constitute the ultimate touchstone of legality, but the 'circumstances' to which the directors are to have regard in promoting the success of the business for the benefit of its shareholders include the company's need to foster its business relationships, including those with its employees, suppliers, and customers; the impact of its operations on local communities and the environment; and the need to maintain a reputation for high standards of business conduct.[30] This 'inclusive' way of stating the duty removes, or should remove, any impression that promotion of the shareholders' interests requires riding roughshod over non-member interests. However, management is given a clear goal to work toward but is reminded and required to have regard, in the achievement of that goal, to the interests of other groups. The ultimate goal is the promotion of the shareholders' interest but the interests to be taken into account include all other groups likely to have a long-term relationship with the company or to be affected by its decisions.

---

[28] See n. 11, at 345, Principle 2.

[29] *Modern Company Law: The Strategic Framework*, Consultation Document (London: Department of Trade and Industry, February 1999) 33–55.

[30] Above, n. 28, Note 2 to Principle 2.

The CLR thus seeks to offer something to both the shareholder value and the stakeholder camps. Which is the bigger gainer? At a rhetorical level probably the former. The primacy of the members' interests is asserted. Although the phrase 'shareholder value' is not used, the words 'for the benefit of its members as a whole' probably come as close to it as is compatible with the structure of British company law. The reference needs to be to the 'members' rather than the 'shareholders' because one type of company which may be incorporated under the Companies Act does not issue shares.[31] More important, the proposal has to refer to the 'benefit' of the members rather than to 'shareholder value' because companies incorporated under the Companies Act may be used for both profit-making and non-profit-making activities.[32] In short, the specification of the objective of the company is a matter for the members. Nevertheless, it is clear that in the case of the company incorporated to carry on a profit-making business, the proposed formula uses shareholder value as the touchstone for the core directors' duty.

What ought to be welcomed by the stakeholder proponents is the endorsement by the proposed formula of their theories as to how companies generate value for shareholders, i.e. by building sustainable relations with the other specified groups. Indeed, at the level of the impact of the formula on the behaviour of companies, the stakeholder proponents seem likely to be the bigger gainers. As we shall see below, the features of the common law formula which make it such a weak tool in litigation have been retained in the CLR's proposals. However, the enforcement of the inclusive aspect of the duty is envisaged as occurring, not via litigation, but through an enhanced annual reporting requirement for companies. At least for large companies it is proposed that an Operating and Financial Review, based partly on existing non-mandatory Accounting Standards Board guidance, should become compulsory and, where relevant, the OFR would cover the company's handling of its relations with stakeholders. The success of this project will probably depend largely upon the ability of the accounting bodies to develop standards which prevent companies from taking refuge in merely self-serving statements and upon the skill of auditors in applying those standards. Nevertheless, sensitizing central management to the impact of its decisions on non-shareholder groups is more likely to be achieved, in my view, by regular, standardized reporting, which will facilitate the

---

[31] This is the company 'limited by guarantee', often used for not-for-profit activities. Thus my employer (LSE) is 'a charity and is incorporated in England as a company limited by guarantee under the Companies Acts (Reg. No. 70527)'. But companies limited by shares can also be used for not-for-profit activities.

[32] The CLR proposes for the future a separate form of incorporation, not under the general Companies Act, for charitable companies but not-for-profit companies which are not charitable would continue to use the general form of incorporation: above, n. 11, Ch. 9.

mobilization of public opinion by stakeholder representatives, than by occasional litigation based on subjectively conceived obligations.

One may conclude this section by stating that, in relation to both appointment and removal rights and the standards governing the exercise of directors' discretion, British law is, and has been throughout our period, compatible with the promotion of shareholder value. This is certainly the case in relation to removal rights; the majority view of the scope of directors' duties, as they are currently formulated, is also consistent with a shareholder value approach; and the CLR's proposals, if adopted, will make this compatibility explicit, whilst also suggesting that shareholder value is not inconsistent with fair dealing with the interests of other stakeholding groups.[33] Thus, the first leg of our hypothesis[34] is established. It was not the state of the law at the time when Crosland wrote which rendered shareholders impotent in large companies. Company law, in fact, gave primacy to their interests, but the mechanisms by which it attempted to promote the shareholders' interests were not ones of which shareholders were able effectively to avail themselves. This enables us to move forward to consider the second leg of the hypothesis: that a change has occurred in the dispersion of shareholdings that has mitigated the factual weakness of the shareholders. They are now able to make effective use of the tools which company law has always provided to them.

III. The Re-concentration of Shareholdings and the Utilization of Company Law

As we have seen, Crosland attributed the weakness of shareholders to the dispersion of shareholdings, which reduced the incentive of shareholders to use their control rights, as provided by company law, and generated instead an incentive to sell in the market if they were disappointed with the company's performance. Dispersed shareholdings were equated, in short, with a preference on the part of shareholders for 'exit' as against 'voice'. The re-concentration of shareholdings in the hands of a smaller number of larger shareholders holds out the prospect that the traditional internal governance rules of company law will recover their potency, because re-concentration substantially reduces shareholders' co-ordination problems. This supports the hypothesis that the significant change which occurred during the post-war period was not that company

---

[33] Whether, as far as non-shareholders, this is a too optimistic view is a question there is not space here to debate. For an adverse assessment of the CLR's proposals, as far as employees are concerned, see Wedderburn, 'Employee, Partnership and Company Law' (2002) 31 *Industrial Law Journal* 99. This analysis concentrates on the textual formulation of directors' duties and does not consider the value of the OFR.

[34] See above.

law was altered (in fact, it was not) but that changes outside the law significantly altered the practical significance of that law. Crosland's fundamental argument that shareholders neither wished nor were able to exercise their control rights would thus begin to appear less persuasive (as perhaps would his argument that there was not much social improvement to be gained by reviewing company law). If the 'functionless' shareholder in fact begins to function, we have to squarely face up to the issue, as the CLR does, of whether allocating control rights exclusively to shareholders is the best policy.

Table 1: Ownership of Listed U.K. Equities

Beneficial Owner	1963	1969	1975	1981	1989	1993	1997
Individuals	54	47.4	37.5	28.2	20.6	17.7	16.5
Insurance companies	10	12.2	15.9	20.5	18.6	20	23.5
Pension funds	6.4	9	16.8	26.7	30.6	31.3	22.1
Collective investment schemes	1.3	2.9	4.1	3.6	7.5	9.1	8.6
Banks	1.3	1.7	0.7	0.3	0.7	0.6	0.1
Others*	27	26.8	25	20.7	22	21.3	29.2

* In recent years this consists mainly of the category 'Rest of World' (in 1997: 24%). Unfortunately, this category is not broken down further.
Source: Office for National Statistics, *Share Ownership: A Report on the Ownership of Shares at 31 December 1997* (London: The Stationery Office, 1999) 8.

That shareholdings in the U.K. have become to some significant degree re-concentrated in recent decades is well established. Pressures on individuals, to make provision for retirement outside the wholly inadequate state system of support in old age, has resulted in the U.K. in an enormous flow of savings onto the stock market.[35] Also well known is the consequence of these flows in terms of patterns of shareholding, i.e. a decline in the proportion of shares held by individuals and a rise in the proportion held by institutional shareholders, especially pension funds and insurance companies. The most recent figures suggest that this is a process which has now run its course, partly because funds established in the post-war period have reached maturity and partly because new governmental solvency requirements are pushing managers towards a re-balancing of their investments in a manner which is more favourable to fixed-interest

[35] See P. Davies, 'Institutional Investors in the United Kingdom' in Baums, Buxbaum, and Hopt (eds.), *Institutional Investors and Corporate Governance* (Berlin/New York 1994) Ch. 9.

securities, whether governmental or corporate. Nevertheless, the change over the period with which we are concerned has been substantial.

Of course, re-concentration at the level of the market as a whole is less relevant for the use of internal accountability mechanisms than re-concentration at the level of individual companies, but research shows that re-concentration at the one level has flowed through into re-concentration at the other, especially if attention is focused on re-concentration of voting rights, rather than on ownership, i.e. on the fund managers who usually have the power to exercise the voting rights of a number of institutional shareholders. Relatively small coalitions of shareholders are able jointly to control shares which probably represent a majority of the votes likely to be cast at general meetings, at least outside the very largest companies quoted on the London Exchange.[36] This is a far cry from the 'Berle & Means company' which Crosland had in mind.

1. Re-concentration and Directors' Duties

Although the change in the levels of concentration of shareholdings in listed companies in the U.K. is well established, one still needs to ask the question: is the factual level of re-concentration so far achieved capable of restoring to shareholders the power to use the traditional control instruments of company law? There are reasons for being cautious about giving an unqualifiedly positive answer to the question, but the reasons for caution differ as between shareholders' removal rights and directors' duties. We therefore examine each separately, beginning with the latter.

As far as the enforcement of directors' duties by litigation is concerned, there is an important issue related to the formulation of the directors' core duty to promote the interests of the company which needs to be noticed before one turns to the question of how shareholders might organize themselves effectively to enforce the duty. There are good reasons to think that, in the case of this basic duty, a significant obstacle to greater litigation is the substantive formulation of the legal rule. The duty to act bona fide in the best interests of the company is a duty to act in what the directors think, not what a court may think, is in the best interests of the company.[37] This is the classic, subjective formulation of a duty designed to catch only egregious examples of failure to promote the shareholders' interests. Only if no reasonable director could possibly think that the challenged decision was in the shareholders' interests (or if the directors have rashly

---

[36] See G.P. Stapledon, *Institutional Shareholders and Corporate Governance* (Oxford 1996) 106–117; B. Black and J. Coffeee, 'Hail Britannia? Institutional Investor Behavior Under Limited Regulation' (1994) 92 Michigan Law Review 1997.

[37] *Re Smith & Fawcett* [1942] Ch. 304.

left evidence that they did not put the shareholders first)[38] will their action be subject to review by the courts. Nor does the law seek to specify a time frame over which the shareholders' interests should be maximized. The duty is owed, it has been said, to present and future members, an inelegant formulation which is open to the criticism that a duty cannot be owed to an unidentified class of people, but the purpose of this formula seems clear enough. Thus directorial action which appears contrary to the interests of the shareholders in the short term may be defended on the grounds that it will maximize their utility over the longer term and the legal rule does not purport to constrain the directors in favour of the former time-frame So, if 'short-termism' is a problem in the conduct of U.K. companies, then the fault does not lie with the way the law is formulated, though there is some evidence that it may lie, in part, with the way in which the law is perceived.[39]

It should be noted that these features of the basic duty of directors are substantially retained in the Company Law Review's reformulation of the duty, quoted above in sub-section (B). The core duty is still formulated subjectively so as to require the director to act in the way 'he decides, in good faith, would be most likely to promote the success of the company' and there is now an explicit requirement to take into account both the long-term and the short-term consequences of decisions. However, this latter duty and the duty to take into account the interests of other stakeholders now carry a small objective element since those consequences and those non-shareholder interests which are to be taken into consideration are those which 'a person of care and skill would consider relevant'. Of course, the whole of the law on directors' duties is not formulated on a subjective basis. When it comes to directors' duties to remain within the bounds set by the company's constitution or to avoid conflicts of interest, the duties are formulated objectively.[40] However, these duties catch only particular aspects of directors' conduct. A decision which does not directly further the personal interests of the directors is unlikely to be capable of challenge under the conflicts rule, if all that can be said of it is that another decision might have served the shareholders' interests better. The core legal duty remains a subjectively formulated one, which is in consequence of limited impact in practice.

Even if these problems relating to the substantive formulation of directors' duties were solved, there would remain the question of whether shareholders can effectively enforce them. It is true that the legal rule is that, where directors are alleged to be in breach of their duties to the company, the power to initiate

---

[38] *Re Holders Investment Trust* [1971] 1 W.L.R. 583; *Re W & M Roith* [1967] 1 W.L.R. 432; *Regentcrest plc v. Cohen* [2001] 2 BCLC 80.

[39] The CLR proposes a better formulation: the director should take into account "the likely consequences (short and long term) of the actions open to the director": above, n. 28, Note 1 to Principle 2.

[40] Gower, above, n. 22, 601–623.

litigation on the company's behalf (which articles of association normally vest exclusively in the board), is given also to the general meeting of shareholders.[41] In principle, therefore, the collective action problems which shareholders face when seeking to mobilize a majority in the general meeting in favour of litigation ought to be relevant and, by the same token, the re-concentration of shareholders ought to increase the likelihood of shareholders' decisions in favour of litigation. Alternatively, the shareholders might use, or threaten to use, the removal rights, discussed in the next sub-section, either to persuade the existing board to take legal action on behalf of the company or to install a new board that will initiate the litigation. Thus, if the problems relating to the substantive formulation of the law were resolved, there might open up the same debate about shareholders' decisions collectively to initiate litigation as has arisen in relation to their power to remove directors—and with the same explanation (see below) as to why this power is not utilised to the optimal extent.

However, it is possible to conceive of the right to initiate litigation on the company's behalf being delegated further within the company, to some subset of the shareholders as a whole (as in Germany) or even to the individual shareholder (as in the derivative action). The 'derivative action', which has been the main driver of litigation to enforce directors' duties in the U.S. By contrast, however, British company law is extremely reluctant to recognize further delegation within the shareholding body of the right to sue. The notorious 'rule in *Foss v. Harbottle*'[42] at present tightly constrains the locus standi of individual or minority shareholders to complain of breaches of duty by directors. The Law Commission has proposed reform by vesting discretion in a judge to determine whether it is in the best interests of the company to permit derivative action to proceed.[43] It is not evident that the proposals will produce a significantly higher level of enforcement of directors' duties. Although criticizing the obscurity of the present law, the Commission endorsed the policies underlying the current restrictive standing requirements.[44] If this attitude informs the exercise by the judges of their proposed discretion, significantly higher levels of litigation may not emerge.[45]

---

[41] Gower, above, n. 22, 658.

[42] *Foss v Harbottle* (1843) 2 Hare 461.

[43] Report no. 246, above, n. 10.

[44] ibid., para. 6.4.

[45] If suit is allowed, costs should not be a problem. Since 1975 it has been established that, if the minority shareholder can sue to enforce the company's rights, then the company, subject to appropriate safeguards, should pay for this benefit, even if the suit is ultimately unsuccessful: *Wallersteiner v. Moir (No. 2)* [1975] Q.B. 373. The new procedure proposed by the Commission will reflect this principle. Thus, difficulties in funding derivative actions seem not to explain, at least directly, the lesser role of derivative actions in the U.K., though the different funding mechanism may do so indirectly: throwing the cost onto the company may have reinforced British judges' reluctance to accept broad rules about standing for individual shareholders.

2. Re-concentration and Directors' Removal Rights

When one moves from the enforcement of directors' duties to the utilization of shareholders' removal rights, however, the re-concentration of shareholdings seems likely to be more significant. The right of an ordinary majority of shareholders to remove all or any of the directors at any time and for any reason is a strong rule, qualified only by the absence of a cap on the damages which a company may have to pay for breach of contract, a lack which the Combined Code has begun to address.[46] However, effective use of the section does require that shareholders be able to surmount their collective action problems. This has been recognized as a difficulty in the past, but it is a problem which re-concentration of shareholdings would seem directly to address. So, is it the case that shareholder value has found its main legal expression in greater use by shareholders of their removal rights as against directors?

The first point to makes is that it is wrong to test the impact of the removal right by establishing simply the extent to which it has been used. One needs to take into account as well the extent to which the threat of its use has been effectively deployed. There are good reasons connected with the costs of intervention why institutional shareholders should initially use their removal right as part of a private bargaining process with the incumbent management in which the shareholders seek in private a change of policy from the board or the resignation of its leading members.[47]

Research has indeed shown that the level of institutional utilization of—or of the threat to utilize—removal rights has increased in recent years. However, and this is the second point to be made, the level of that activity still seems to have fallen below its full potential and this has led influential critics to berate institutional shareholders for failing to extract full value from the rights which company law gives them.[48]

What is the explanation for the under-utilization? Although the long-standing removal right conferred upon a simple majority of the shareholders by the Companies Act has been given a new practical significance by the re-concentration of shareholdings, this new possibility for 'voice' has been added to, but has not replaced, the alternative exit strategy for institutional shareholders. For fund managers and institutional shareholders faced by an under-performing portfolio company, the revival of the removal right has created a choice between its exercise and the traditional exit strategy via a sale in the

---

[46] See sub-section (B) above.

[47] Stapledon, above, n. 36, 124–129.

[48] A notable critic has been J. Charkham, *Keeping Good Company* (Oxford 1995) 282–289. On levels of intervention see also the Company Law Review, *Developing the Framework* (London: DTF, March 2000).

market or to a take-over bidder. It seems likely that the shortfall in potential use of the removal right can be explained largely by the fact that, from the point of view of the fund manager, exit is the less costly choice than the exercise of voice in many cases, for example, where the institution can engineer a bid for the company. It should be remembered that pressures of competition for mandates among fund managers has made them highly cost-sensitive. Fund managers have an incentive not to join activist coalitions, both because they may then be able to free ride on the efforts of others and because it will often be uncertain whether, if they do join in, the costs of intervention will be outweighed by the subsequent increase in the company's share price. Finally, it needs to be borne in mind that, in the case of managers that are part of financial conglomerates, intervention raises conflicts of interest. Thus, a fund manager which has taken an activist stance as against the management of a particular company may find that it has prejudiced the chances of the corporate finance arm of the firm to obtain their kind of work from that company. It is perhaps not surprising that the most publicly activist institutions are those which do not suffer from such conflicts of interest because they are single function bodies.[49]

3. Conclusion

This section set out to explore the hypothesis that, in the absence of any significant relevant change in company law, the rise to prominence of shareholder value was to be explained by reference to changes in the factual context in which company law operated, changes brought about, in particular, by a re-concentration of shareholdings. The first leg of this hypothesis is well supported: British company law is based upon the idea of investor control and so allocates control rights to shareholders. The second leg of the hypothesis was that the change in factual context enabled shareholders to exercise the control rights which company law gave them in a way which they previously they had been unable to do. Re-concentration of shareholdings turned out to be a less significant fact in relation to both the enforcement of directors' duties and the removal of directors than might have been expected. So we are left still searching for a complete explanation for the rise of shareholder value in a context of unchanging company law. The operation of traditional company law in a new factual context may constitute part of the explanation for the rise in shareholder value but not the whole of it.

[49] Company Law Review, *Developing the Framework*, 252–257; Black and Coffee, above, n. 36, 2055–2074.

C. Securities Markets Law and Shareholder Value

In the previous section we assumed that the re-concentration of shareholdings would have its main impact on corporate governance through intervention on the part of institutional shareholders in the affairs of their portfolio companies, such intervention taking the form of the shareholders using their company law entitlements to replace or reform under-performing management. This assumption can be queried on two grounds. First, intervention could also operate not at the level of individual companies but at the level of companies (or, at least, listed companies) as a whole and could occur indirectly rather than directly. By this is meant that institutional shareholders, via their trade associations, could seek to influence the bodies which set the rules which govern the ways companies operate. Such activity need not be instead of, but rather in addition to, intervention at individual company level, but the attractions of the more generalized form of intervention are clear. It is cheaper because the costs of intervention are spread over a large number of companies (all the companies governed by the relevant rules) and the free rider problem is reduced or even eliminated because the intervention is effected via the institutional investors' trade associations (Association of British Insurers, National Association of Pension Funds, Institutional Shareholders Committee, etc).[50]

Secondly, such intervention in rule setting may concentrate, not on company law, but on the rules governing the operation of the securities markets. It is easy to see why institutional shareholders should find it easier to influence securities market than company law rules. Company law rules are set, at least currently, through the normal legislative process where the institutional investors would be only one among a number of powerful influences on the ultimate shape of the legislation. Considerable parts of securities market law, however, have been devolved to regulators which are closer to the market participants, notably the Stock Exchange and, now, the Financial Services Authority, for the listing rules and the City Panel on Take-overs and Mergers for the rules on take-overs. It is likely that institutional shareholders will have greater influence over rule setting of this type than over the general legislative process. Indeed, it could be said to have been one of the objectives of delegating rule setting in this area that those close to the market should have more influence over the process.

In this section of the chapter, therefore, attention shifts from company law to securities markets law[51] and the role of institutional shareholders in the reform of the latter set of rules. The first contrast with company law that emerges is that

---

[50] Membership of the trade associations is broadly based.

[51] The exact line between these two sets of rules is, of course, indistinct. See the discussion of pre-emption rights (on issue) below. The EU rules on this matter are to be found in the second Company Law Directive, but they are arguably more a part of securities law than company law.

securities market law did undergo profound changes in respects relevant to the issue of shareholder value in the period between Crosland and Hampel. Two areas of change seem to have been particularly pertinent to the rise of shareholder value, and we shall now examine them in turn.

I. Pre-emption Rights on Issue

Franks and Mayer[52] report a strong linkage between turnover of executive directors and the provision of new equity finance. Why does a company's need to raise new equity finance give its shareholders, especially the institutions, an effective opportunity to apply pressure to the company's management? There is, of course, the general need for the company to submit to the scrutiny of the securities market in such a case. A company will be able to sell its shares on terms that are more attractive to it if it can demonstrate a track record of promoting shareholder value. Pre-emption rights,[53] it will be argued below, reinforce the value-enhancing impact of the market by binding the company to the promises explicitly and implicitly made at the time of a share issue—or, at least, make it more difficult for the company to adopt a particular financing technique which would undermine such promises. Even before statutory pre-emption rights were introduced into British law by means of the second EC Directive,[54] the Stock Exchange rules, reflecting institutional investor preferences, included pre-emption rights. Moreover, despite the statutory changes of 1980, the Companies Act rules continue to be relatively unimportant since they apply only to equity issues for cash and may be disapplied by vote of the shareholders for periods of up to five years.

Disapplication resolutions have become routine items on the agenda for the annual general meetings of listed companies. Much more important in practice are the Pre-Emption Group guidelines,[55] which indicate the circumstances in which institutional shareholders will vote in favour of disapplication resolutions, even when these conform to the requirements of the Companies Act.

The Pre-Emption Group Guidelines, which are essentially the result of bargaining between the institutional shareholders and companies and their advisers, under the aegis of the Exchange, indicate that institutional shareholders will

---

[52] 'Governance as a source of managerial discipline', available on the CLR web site, above, n. 11. See also Stapledon, above, n. 36, 129–130.

[53] The obligation of an issuer to offer new shares pro rata to the existing shareholders.

[54] Second Council Directive (EEC) 77/91 on Co-ordinating the Safeguards on Formation of Public Limited Companies and the Maintenance and Alteration of their Capital, with a view to making such safeguards equivalent [1976] O.J. L26/1, art. 29.

[55] Monopolies and Mergers Commission, *Underwriting Services for Share Offers* (London, The Stationery Office, Cm. 4168, 1999), para. 3.14.

accept waiver of their statutory rights if the company (a) restricts the new shares to be issued for cash to 5% of the issued ordinary shares in any one year and 7.5% over any rolling period of three years, and (b) restricts the discount on any issue to 5%.[56] In addition, the Association of British Insurers has issued guidelines for vendor placings (where the company does not formally issue its shares for cash and so is not caught by the statutory rules, but the shares are in effect so issued because the vendor to the company immediately places in the market the shares received in exchange for its assets). In this case the guidelines are that the discount must be restricted to 5% and the consideration must not exceed 10% of the shares in issue.[57] Neither of these sets of guidelines prevents the company from seeking *ad hoc* approval for issues that do not conform to the guidelines.

The main objective of these rules is, of course, to protect the existing shareholders from the dilution of their existing positions in the company, either control dilution or, more likely, financial dilution, since in the case of discounted non-pre-emptive issues the cost of the discount is borne by the existing shareholders. However, it seems likely that the pre-emption rules also have governance consequences by increasing the reliance of the management on the current shareholders. This may occur both positively and negatively. Positively, management is put in a position in which it must actively solicit shareholder support for issues that do not conform to the guidelines. Negatively, the guidelines make it difficult for management to pursue a strategy of issuing deeply discounted shares to new investors as part of an implicit bargain whereby the new investors will support the incumbent management against existing shareholders. Although the statutory pre-emption rule and the guidelines have been criticized for raising the cost of capital, the guidelines have survived a competition law challenge,[58] and have been positively commended by the Company Law Review on corporate governance grounds.[59]

II. Take-over Regulation and Shareholder Value (and some Anglo-American Contrasts)

The second area of securities market law that is relevant to this chapter is regulation of the market in corporate control. These rules link back to our discussion above of the shareholders' removal rights, for the alternative, often available to institutional shareholders contemplating the removal of incumbent manage-

---

[56] ibid., Appendix 3.1 for the full text of the Guidelines.

[57] ibid., para. 3.28.

[58] ibid., paras 2.161–2.165.

[59] '. . . the rule has an important disciplinary effect on under-performing management by limiting their access to equity. We would not wish to dilute any such disciplinary effect.': CLR, above, n. 48, para. 4.165. See also Franks and Meyer, above, n. 52.

ment under their company law powers, is to accept a bid from an offeror (per-haps found by or on behalf of the institutions themselves) which, after obtaining control, will do that job in place of the current shareholders. In contrast to the static company law (at least in the area of control rights), take-over regulation in the U.K. underwent a very big change in its regulatory structure during the post-war period. This was the introduction in 1968 of the first City Code on Take-overs and Mergers and its subsequent development by the City Panel on Take-overs and Mergers.[60] Although now a substantial and sophisticated body of rules,[61] the Code is founded upon two central ideas, both of which are apt to promote the idea of shareholder value, viewed from the perspective of the share-holders of the target company. The two principles are: equal treatment of target shareholders (designed to deal with acquirer opportunism) and the 'non-frustration' rule designed to place the decision on the fate of the bid exclusively in the hands of the shareholders of the target company and to reduce the target management to an information-providing and persuading role. It is the second idea which mainly concerns us here and which provides the contrast with take-over rules in the U.S. It is to be found in General Principle 7[62] of the City Code and is given more concrete expression in Rules 21 and 37. These constitute a tough set of provisions, because they focus on the effects of board action, not target management's bona fides or purposes. If the effect of a proposed move by target management is to frustrate a bid, then shareholder approval is required and that consent must be given in the face of the offer and not as a general per-mission in advance of the bid. Thus, the City Code deals with the acute conflict of interest which target management faces in a take-over bid by shifting the deci-sion over the success of the offer out of the hands of the target board and into the hands of the target shareholders.

Although it is common in some quarters to lump together British and U.S. corporate law and take-over regulation, there is a distinct contrast in this area between what British and U.S. rules require. U.S. take-over rules (predomi-nantly in this respect the province of state corporations laws) do not sideline tar-get management. Rather, the target board is put in a position of considerable influence (though not one of invulnerability) and can control to a substantial

---

[60] The current edition of the Code is the seventh: The City Code on Take-overs and Mergers and the Rules Governing Substantial Acquisitions of Shares (London: Panel on Take-overs and Mergers, 7th edn, May 2002).

[61] The Code contains 10 General Principles and 38 rules, the rules in some cases being accom-panied by extensive Notes.

[62] 'At no time after a bona fide offer has been communicated to the board of the offeree com-pany, or after the board of the offeree company has reason to believe that a bona fide offer might be imminent, may any action be taken by the board of the offeree company in relation to the affairs of the company, without the approval of the shareholders in general meeting, which could effectively result in any bona fide offer being frustrated or in the shareholders being denied an opportunity to decide on its merits'.

degree the issues of whether the bid is put to the shareholders of the target at all and, if so, on what terms. By holding it to be consistent with directors' fiduciary duties for boards of potential targets, first, to adopt without shareholder approval a poison pill defence and, second, in the face of an actual offer to refuse to redeem the pill (again whether or not the shareholders approve), provided this is done in the bona fide belief that it is necessary to protect the integrity of the business strategy which the board has put in place, the U.S. rules are clearly less responsive to the conflicts of interest to which target boards are subject in hostile bids and more responsive to the argument that setting business strategy is the preserve of centralized management rather than of the shareholders.[63] The board is not invulnerable because the above provisions do not protect the incumbents from a proxy contest at the next annual general meeting in which the shareholders seek to replace them by a set of directors who are more open to bid approaches; and this knowledge will no doubt feed back into the board's decision whether or not to redeem the pill. Nevertheless, the poison pill (together with anti-take-over statutes)[64] does give a determined management the inestimable advantage of time to prepare its position against the bid.

What are the rationales for the U.S. approach? As already hinted, one might be that the decision on a bid and its potential change of business strategy is one more appropriately taken by the board of the target than its shareholders. This is not, however, persuasive. The decision which the bid presents to the target company is at least as akin to an investment decision which shareholders make when they decide to buy or sell shares in a particular company as it is to management decisions which are allocated to the board. In other words, shareholders may be as expert in taking this class of decisions as directors and, given their infrequency and importance to the shareholders, one can expect that shareholders will appropriately inform themselves about the decision that has to be taken.

Alternatively, it might be argued that the board of the target should control the bid process in order to protect target shareholders against bidder opportunism (principally the various forms of pressure to tender). This may seem a more plausible argument where take-over regulation is embedded in the common law of directors' duties, as it is in the relevant respects in the U.S., rather than in customized take-over code, as is increasingly the European norm. Where there is a fully developed code, such as the City Code, it is possible to deal separately with the issues of target management conflict of interest and acquirer opportunism, rather than relaxing the rules on the former in order to address the latter set of issues. As noted above, the City Code's second 'big idea' is equality

[63] See Kahan, above, n. 17.

[64] For a selection of such provisions see C.R. O'Kelley, Jr and R.B. Thompson, *Corporations and other Business Associations: Selected Statutes, Rules and Forms* (New York 1998) 349–391. For a critique see L.A. Bebchuk and A. Ferrell, 'Federalism and Corporate Law: The Race to Protect Managers from Take-overs' (1999) 99 Columbia Law Review 1168.

of treatment of the target shareholders, which principle is aimed at controlling bidder opportunism. Thus, the two fundamental principles of the Code aim, separately, at the control of bidder and target management opportunism as against the target shareholders.

The third possible rationale is that protection of the position of the incumbent management is seen as a proxy for the protection of non-shareholder interests affected by the take-over. This rationale is supported by the presence of con-stituency statutes in many U.S. States, which, at least in the context of take-over bids, permit the incumbent board to abandon their exclusive consideration of the interests of the shareholders and to give equal consideration to a wide range of additional interests.[65] Take-over rules which respond to the conflicts of inter-est of incumbent management by placing the decision on the offer with the tar-get shareholders, as the City Code does, find it difficult to give any substantial recognition to the interests of stakeholders other than target shareholders, because there is no longer a corporate decision-making process into which consideration of such stakeholder interests can be built. The actual take-over transaction is effected by private treaty between bidder and the shareholders individually.

Nevertheless, it can be questioned whether the U.S. rules do more than per-mit the entrenchment of target management under the guise of protecting target shareholders against bidder opportunism or protecting the interests of non-shareholder groups. Probably, effective stakeholder protection requires general corporate mechanisms for building their interests into the governance of the company (as with the employee interest in large German companies), which mechanisms continue to operate into the bid situation, rather than ad hoc amendments to the principle of shareholder control which are triggered only when a take-over is in prospect.

It is an interesting question why British and U.S. take-over regulation has developed in such different ways. In a recent article Bebchuk and Roe have linked anti-take-over rules, such as those to be found in the U.S., with histori-cally diffuse ownership structures. The argument is essentially one grounded in political theory. If shareholdings are diffuse, shareholders will be no match for the influence of managers in the political process and the result will be rules which discourage take-over bids, especially hostile ones: 'Professional managers are clearly a much more powerful group in a country with diffuse ownership (such as the United States) than in one with concentrated ownership (such as Germany)'.[66] The implication would seem to be that the pro-shareholder British rules result from a higher degree of shareholding concentration in the U.K. and

[65] O'Kelley, Jr and Thompson, above, n. 64, 345–348.

[66] L.A. Bebchuk and M.J. Roe, 'A Theory of Path Dependence in Corporate Ownership and Governance' (1999) 52 Stanford Law Review 127, 158.

thus a greater influence wielded by shareholders in the rule-making process in the U.K.

There are a number of difficulties with these propositions, two of which relate to the statistics on shareholder concentration in the U.S. and the U.K. and the third, more fundamentally, to the nature of the alleged link between shareholder concentration and pro-shareholder take-over regulation. First, it is not clear that at the level of the individual company, which is the level to which Bebchuk and Roe seem to refer, British shareholdings remained concentrated in family hands until a later period than in the U.S. It has indeed been argued by Chandler that this was the case and that family ownership in the U.K. ceased to be an important feature of British shareholding structures only in the 1980s.[67] However, there is work by others which supports the thesis that family ownership had ceased to be significant in the U.K. by the Second World War or shortly thereafter.[68] If the latter argument were correct, then the concentration of ownership at the individual firm level would seem a poor explanation for the pro-shareholder orientation of the City Code.

Secondly, given that Bebchuk and Roe's analysis concentrates on the respective influence of professional managers and shareholders on the rule-setting process for the market in corporate control, it is far from clear that it is the level of shareholder concentration at individual company level which is the crucial determining factor, as against shareholder concentration at the aggregate level (level of the whole economy). Governments and other rule-setters might well be influenced by the views of an important set of providers of funds to companies via the securities markets, irrespective of the extent to which they held controlling blocks in particular portfolio companies. Indeed, if there were a large number of families, each with a holding confined to a particular company (or group of companies), whereas the non-controlling institutional holdings were in the hands of relatively few institutional shareholders, the latter might be more successful that the former in the political process because they could co-ordinate their actions more effectively. Whatever the truth about the levels of family holdings in the U.K. before the 1980s, we have already seen from Table 1[69] that when the City Code was introduced institutional shareholders held about 20% of the equity shares of companies listed on the London Stock Exchange and this could be the basis for effective lobbying of the rule-setters, even if these aggregate holdings rarely translated into individual institutions holding controlling blocks in portfolio companies.

---

[67] A.D. Chandler, *Scale and Scope: the Dynamics of Industrial Capitalism* (Cambridge 1990).

[68] The empirical evidence is carefully assessed by B.R. Cheffins, 'Putting Britain on the Roe Map: the Emergence of the Berle-Means Corporation in the United Kingdom' (2000), available on http://papers.ssrn.com/paper.taf?abstract_id=218655.

[69] See above.

However, this second argument might be thought to be supportive of the Bebchuk and Roe proposition, albeit in an amended form. The explanatory factor is, indeed, the level of shareholder concentration, and Bebchuk and Roe were mistaken only in looking at concentration at individual firm level rather than at the aggregate level. Even if it is true to say that family ownership had ceased to be a dominant feature of shareholding in the U.K. by the Second World War, one could argue that there was substituted for family ownership a growing concentration of shareholdings in the hands of institutional shareholders. By the 1960s this had reached the point where those shareholders were able to influence significantly the drafting of the City Code of 1968 and its subsequent amendments.

Nevertheless, this point does not fully get Bebchuk and Roe out of the woods, because the levels of aggregate institutional shareholdings do not appear to have been significantly higher in the U.K. than in the U.S. in the post-war period.[70] So it may be that it is not simply the aggregate level of institutional shareholding which is important but that level coupled with the respective skills of institutional shareholders and professional managers in co-ordinating their views through their trade associations in the lobbying process for new rules and also on the nature of the legislative processes they were aiming to influence. As Bebchuk and Ferrell point out in a contemporaneous article,[71] the British procedure for producing a set of take-over rules (via the City Panel) gave institutional shareholders in the U.K. an advantage over the representatives of management because the rule-making process was delegated by Government to the City institutions, led by the Bank of England. U.K. regulation 'is not imposed from the outside by a detached governmental body but rather by a group that has strong connections to the interested parties' and that that group 'gave less weight to managerial interests because of the close connection at least some of them had with the interests of shareholders.' By contrast, the constituency statutes of the U.S. are the product of state legislatures, which are not so much 'detached governmental bodies' but vehicles for the expression of particularist local interests of the type likely to suffer in hostile bids. They are thus relatively fertile grounds for lobbyists in the managerial cause.[72]

The third difficulty with the Bebchuk and Roe argument is its implication that the higher the degree of concentration of shareholdings, the higher the level of

---

[70] See H. Garten, 'Institutional Investors and the New Financial Order' (1992) 44 Rutgers Law Review at 607–612.

[71] Bebchuk and Ferrell, above, n. 64, 1192–3.

[72] See R.J. Gilson, 'The Political Ecology of Take-overs: Thoughts on Harmonizing the European Corporate Governance Environment' in K. Hopt and E. Wymeersch (eds.), *European Take-overs: Law and Practice* (London 1992) 49–50; G. Miller, 'Political Structure and Corporate Governance: Some Points of Contrast between the United States and England' [1998] Columbia Business Law Review 70–75.

shareholder interest in take-over rules which facilitate hostile bids. See, for example, their contrast between the U.S. and Germany in the quotation above. However, Germany has traditionally been noted as a country where both share-holdings are highly concentrated in family hands and where management is even more deeply entrenched by the relevant take-over law than is the case in the U.S.[73] The explanation is probably that, where shareholdings are highly concentrated, the controlling shareholder has little interest in promoting take-over regulation that sidelines management if a bid is made. In such a case, the board is likely to consist of the nominees of the majority shareholder and will do what that shareholder wants, and thus rules formally shifting the decision on the bid into the hands of the shareholder are unnecessary. To put the matter another way, if the bidder deals with the directors in such a case, it is in effect dealing with the majority shareholder and hostile bids, whereby the bidder appeals over the heads of the incumbent board to the shareholders of the target, are beside the point. Thus, controlling shareholders have little interest in the first fundamental principle that underlies the City Code.

However, if controlling shareholders view the first principle behind the Code with indifference, they may regard its second principle (shareholder equality) with positive alarm. If block-holders, whether they be families groups or other commercial corporations, see their interests as lying in their ability to continue to extract the private benefits of control from the company in which they are invested and have confidence that, should they wish to dispose of their shares at some indeterminate time in the future, they will be able to obtain a good price in a friendly deal, they may see the equality principle as a threat to their position. If, in order to deal with bidder opportunism as against target company sharehold-ers, the take-over regulation contains a mandatory bid rule, then the impact of that rule may be to deprive block-holders of the ability to realize a premium for control when they eventually sell out. Whether that consequence follows will depend upon how the mandatory bid rule fixes the price to be offered in the required bid. If that price, as in the British Code, is fixed at the price paid by the acquirer for the controlling block, then all premiums for the sellers of large blocks will be eliminated. If, however, the price rule allows for some discount from the highest price paid to acquire the controlling shares, there may be scope for dif-ferential pricing which preserves at least a part of the block-holder's premium.[74]

---

[73] The successful bid by Vodaphone for Mannesmann was much commented on precisely because so few hostile bids for German companies have succeeded. The new German law on take-overs (*Gesetz zur Regelung von öffentlichen Angeboten zum Erwerb vobn Wertpapieren und von Unternehmensübernahmen* of December 20, 2001) still gives management the possibility of putting powerful anti-take-over defences in place, at least where shareholder approval has been obtained in advance of the bid. See especially § 33.

[74] See, for example, the *Loi fédérale sur les bourses et le commerce des valeurs mobilières*, art. 32(4) (Switzerland). This sets the price in the mandatory bid at not less than three-quarters of the

This may demonstrate that large block-holders may wield sufficient political influence to preserve some of the private advantages of control under take-over regulation, but one still lacks a positive reason for such controlling shareholders to seek take-over regulation.[75]

Overall, the relationship between levels of share concentration, whether at individual firm or aggregate level, and attitudes towards facilitating take-over bids, especially hostile bids, turns out to be complex. At either end of the spectrum, that is, where shareholdings are highly dispersed or highly concentrated, there may be significant opposition to such regulation. In the former case the opposition may be effectively promoted by incumbent management, which fear for their jobs, whilst the highly dispersed shareholders are incapable of mounting effective opposition to the managerial arguments. In the latter the opposition may come from large shareholders that fear for their sale premiums and do not need regulation to foster hostile bids. It is perhaps only at intermediate levels of shareholding concentration that rules promoting hostile bids are obviously in the shareholder interest. At such levels, the shareholders have no control premium to sacrifice to the equality principle whereas their ability to use the traditional control devices of company law as against the incumbent management is so set about with potential difficulties that they see value in adding to their armoury the additional weapon of the hostile bid and side-lining incumbent management in the bid process.

Whatever the explanation for the stance taken by the City Code, it seems clear that its provisions facilitating hostile bids provide a major incentive to the management of British companies to maintain a high price for its shares on the stock market. This is true not only defensively, i.e. a company whose securities are highly priced does not provide an attractive target for potential bidders. A high share price also provides a currency with which the management can launch bids, either because potential offerees will find paper offers by such a bidder attractive or because a company with a high share price will find it easier to raise the cash with which to make a cash offer or to provide a cash alternative to a paper offer. This statement of the incentives on the management of companies to promote shareholder value (defined in terms of a high stock price) should not lead, however, to the conclusion that the take-over threat operates across the board to produce this result. First, the incentive to the managements of potential bidders to maximise share price may bring about only a partial alignment of the interests of bidder shareholders and management. Whereas the gains in take-

price paid for the controlling block, provided that the price shall be not less than the market price for the shares when the mandatory bid is made.

[75] British institutional shareholders, not being in general controlling shareholders, would not object to the equality principle. However, the tough equality rule embodied in the City Code is another piece of evidence that controlling family shareholders were not influential in the U.K. by the 1960s.

overs to target shareholders are well established, the empirical evidence about the gains to bidder shareholders shows these are quite modest or even negative.[76] This may suggest that the mechanisms for aligning management and share-holder interests in the choice of bid targets or in the decision about how much to pay for a target are not fully efficient. Indeed, it is a feature of most take-over codes that they do not address principal/agent problems as between bidder management and bidder shareholders but leave them to the general corporate law, which, as we have seen,[77] is rather ineffective. There may be a case for bigger shareholder input into the decision by the bidder's management to launch a bid.[78]

Secondly, turning to take-over targets, although targets tend to be moderately under-performing companies, there is evidence that the worst performing companies are under-represented among take-over targets.[79] It was pointed out some time ago that truly bad performance might be an effective take-over defence,[80] because the process of turning around such companies would be too daunting for potential bidders. On this basis, the scope for the take-over threat to promote shareholder value at the bottom of the performance table would seem to depend on how quickly the market picks up the beginnings of under-performance and how quick is the company's descent from under-performance to an economic condition which provides its own shelter from take-over bids.

D. Conclusion

The argument in this chapter has been that the move to shareholder value in the U.K. has not been driven, on the legal front, by changes in the law relating to directors' duties nor the rules on shareholders' appointment and removal rights, despite the central role one might expect such rules to play in determining how central management exercises the discretion vested in it. Rather, what has been important are changes in shareholder structure. These have operated at two levels. At the first level, they have permitted shareholders to extract some greater value from their traditional company law entitlements, especially in relation to the removal of under-performing management. At a second level, re-concentration of

[76] G.A. Jarrell, J.A. Brickley, and J.M. Netter, 'The Market for Corporate Control: the Empirical Evidence since 1980' (1988) 2 *Journal of Economic Perspectives* 49.

[77] Above, Section II.

[78] The Listing Rules of the Financial Services Authority require approval of bidder shareholders where the target represents more than 25% of the assets, profits, turnover, market capitalization, or gross capital of the bidder: Listing Rules, paras 10.4, 5 and 37.

[79] Franks and Meyer, above, n. 52.

[80] J.C. Coffee, 'Regulating the Market for Corporate Control' (1984) 84 Columbia Law Review 1146, Part II.

shareholdings in the hands of the institutions has permitted them to bring about changes in the rules and practices of the securities markets which are favourable to the promotion of shareholder value, notably in the areas of pre-emption rights and take-over bids. One conclusion from this analysis is that those who oppose putting shareholder value centre-stage in managerial objectives would do better, as far as listed companies in the U.K. are concerned, to concentrate on reform of securities market law rather than core company law, despite the apparent direct relevance of the latter to this issue.

12

Corporate Governance in Germany

KLAUS J. HOPT

Abstract

Six systemic elements of corporate governance can be found in the international discussion: the board, labour co-determination and labour markets, financial intermediaries, stock exchange and capital markets, the market for corporate control, and disclosure and auditing. German corporate governance makes use of all six of these elements, but not enough. Highlights for internal corporate governance reform concern: shareholder activism (large, institutional and private), further improvements of the two-tier board system (more flexible labour co-determination, improved internal risk monitoring system, a better flow of information from the management board to the supervisory board and from the latter to the auditors and back) and the auditors and accounting (independence of auditors, group accounts, quarterly reports). Highlights for reform as to external corporate governance concern the stock exchange, the capital markets, and in particular the market for corporate control. In Germany there is a vivid discussion on the role of binding law and codes of conduct, on enforcement by self-control and external control, and on the systemic responsibility of the auditing profession.

Contents

A. Introduction

An American study by renowned economists from Harvard has attracted a great deal of attention worldwide.[1] The study claims to have empirical proof of a correlation between the development of financial markets and the economy on

---

[1] La Porta et al. in several publications, e.g. R. La Porta, F. Lopez-de-Silanes, A. Shleifer, and R. Vishny, 'Legal Determinants of External Finance' [1997] 52 *Journal of Finance* 1131; also 'Law and Finance' [1998] 106 *Journal of Political Economy* 1113; also 'Investor Protection and Corporate Governance' [2000] 58 *Journal of Financial Economics* 3; R. La Porta, F. Lopez-de-Silanes and A. Shleifer, 'Corporate Ownership Around the World' [1999] 54 *Journal of Finance* 471; A. Shleifer and R. Vishny, 'A Survey of Corporate Governance' [1997] 52 *Journal of Finance* 73. Cf. the critical remarks by E. Berglöf and E.-L. Von Thadden, 'The Changing Corporate Governance Paradigm:

the one hand, and the degree of investor protection and corporate governance implemented in a country on the other. In this ranking, Germany does not do so well: its position is in the lower ranks. France and Germany's southern neighbours in Europe are even worse off, but this cannot be a consolation. When this is discussed with American observers from academia and business, statements such as those set forth in the following paragraph arise. And, whether they are correct or are merely prejudice, they are still alarming.

These observers say that the German capital market is still clearly underdeveloped on an international scale. They claim that Germany still does not have a take-over law and no practice of hostile take-over bids. According to them, Vodafon versus Mannesmann was just an isolated case. The supervisory board in the German two-tier system is clearly inferior to the American unitary board. German auditors cannot compensate for this, particularly since there are doubts about their independence, and they are not supervised by a body with competencies and enforcement powers such as those of the SEC. The German accounting law, which gives precedence to the protection of creditors over the protection of shareholders, cannot compete with the IAS, and even less with U.S. GAAP. The shareholders are the real owners of the company, but where is shareholder value in Germany? The German universal banks are not on the same level as the American investment banks. Bank participation in industry and bank representatives sitting on supervisory boards happens frequently in Germany. However, it is often unproductive and even detrimental. And this is particularly true for the reciprocal and even circular participations, which are typical of German corporate governance and make it a closed insider system. The German Stock Corporation Act is very cumbersome and needs deregulation. These observers even say that mandatory capital, rigid pre-emptive rights, a complicated German law of groups (*Konzernrecht*), and in particular labour co-determination, are fossils from another age. They are a source of wonder for Americans and a reason for them to be glad about their own competitive system.

Can we discard these judgments as prejudice, or is the German system of corporate governance really so bad? As usual, the truth lies somewhere in the mid-

Paradigm: Implications for Developing and Transition Economies' in S. Cohen and G. Boyd (eds.), *Corporate Governance and Globalization* (Cheltenham 2000) 275, 280ff.

For an American view on German corporate governance, see, e.g. E.B. Rock, 'America's Fascination with German Corporate Governance' [1995] *Die Aktiengesellschaft* 291; T.J. André, 'Cultural Hegemony: The Exportation of Anglo-Saxon Corporate Governance Ideologies to Germany' [1998] 77 *Tulane Law Review* 29; D. Charny, 'The German Corporate Governance System' [1998] *Columbia Business Law Review* 145; J. Gordon,' Deutsche Telekom, German Corporate Governance, and the Transition Costs of Capitalism' [1998] *Columbia Business Law Review* 185; M.J. Roe, 'German Codetermination and German Securities Markets' [1998] *Columbia Business Law Review* 167; A.R. Oquendo, 'Breaking on Through to the Other Side: Understanding Continental European Corporate Governance' (2001) 22 *University of Pennsylvania Journal of International Economic Law* 975.

dle. But what is then the justified core of such assessments, and where are improvements possible? This question concerns the entire system as well as many of its individual parts, and therefore it cannot be dealt with in an exhaustive way. What we can do, however, is try—in the light of modern international, law, and economics discussions—to address the most important areas that make for the quality of a corporate governance system, and to refer to a number of potential improvements.[2] We must pay particular attention to the role of the auditors, which the German legislators have entrusted with the role of partner of the supervisory board.[3]

B. Systemic Elements of Corporate Governance in the International Discussion and the Use of these Elements in the German System

I. Six Systemic Elements of Corporate Governance in the International Discussion

In modern comparative corporate governance theory—and this is the internationally established term—the systemic elements of corporate governance are the following:
(1) the board (management board and supervisory board);
(2) labour co-determination and labour markets;
(3) the financial intermediaries;
(4) stock exchange and capital markets;
(5) the market for corporate control, i.e. take-over bids;
(6) disclosure and auditing.
These elements can be found in different combinations and intensity in the various national corporate governance systems. The given combination of these elements in a single country has developed through that country's history and makes up for the national peculiarity of a system. In modern theory, this is referred to as path dependence. I will briefly discuss each of these six elements and its importance for the German system. This is purely a survey and a comparative introduction and does not yet contain personal assessments. For details of corporate governance in the triad of the U.S., Germany and Western Europe, and Japan, and for the economic and legal theory of corporate governance, I

---

[2] IDW, 'Fortentwicklung der Unternehmensüberwachung in Deutschland' *IDW-Fachnachrichten* 6/2000, 229ff; idem, Stellungnahme des IDW zum Fragenkatalog der Regierungskommission 'Corporate Governance': Unternehmensführung—Unternehmenskontrolle—Modernisierung des Aktienrechts, *IDW-Fachnachrichten* 10/2000, 521.

[3] W. Schruff, 'Unternehmensüberwachung und Abschlußprüfer', in Institut der Wirtschaftsprüfer (IDW), ed., *Kapitalmarktorientierte Unternehmensüberwachung—Chancen und Risiken* (Duesseldorf 2001), 149.

refer to the book on 'Comparative Corporate Governance' prepared at the Hamburg Max Planck Institute for Private Law.[4]

1. The Board (Management Board and Supervisory Board)

The core of any system of corporate governance is the management and control body of a company. In the German system, the shareholders have delegated the day-to-day management to the management board and have entrusted the monitoring to the supervisory board. This separation of task between two organs— which is mandatory—is more than a hundred years old,[5] and has never been seriously questioned in any reforms of corporate law in Germany. Nonetheless, from a comparative perspective, this 'two-tier system' is a rather special path. In the Anglo-American law systems but also in Switzerland and many other countries, there is only one organ—the board—for management and monitoring. It is common knowledge that a quite controversial debate is going on internationally on the pros and cons of the two systems.[6]

2. Labour Co-determination and Labour Markets

The workforce influences corporate decision-making and governance internally as well as through the labour market. This influence assumes a special importance if it is exercised within the supervisory organ or even the management of the company, as is the case in Germany, where representatives of the workforce and the unions sit and vote in the supervisory board. The German and Dutch parity or quasi-parity labour co-determination has remained a unique feature[7]

---

[4] Cf. K.J. Hopt, H. Kanda, M.J. Roe, E. Wymeersch, and S. Prigge (eds.), *Comparative Corporate Governance—The State of the Art and Emerging Research* (Oxford 1998). See also K. Keasey, S. Thompson, and M. Wright (eds.), *Corporate Governance: Economic and Financial Issues* (Oxford, 1997); ibid. (eds.), *Corporate Governance, 4 vols* (Cheltenham1999) (reprints).

[5] K.J. Hopt, 'Ideelle und wirtschaftliche Grundlagen der Aktien-, Bank- und Börsenrechtsentwicklung im 19. Jahrhundert' in H. Coing and W. Wilhelm (eds.), *Wissenschaft und Kodifikation im 19. Jahrhundert, vol. V, Geld und Banken* (Frankfurt 1980) 128, 152ff.

[6] See K.J. Hopt in 'The German Two-Tier Board (Aufsichtsrat), A German View on Corporate Governance' in K.J. Hopt and E. Wymeersch (eds.), *Comparative Corporate Governance—Essays and Materials* (Berlin, New York 1997) 3; ibid. 'The German Two-Tier Board: Experience, Theories, Reforms' in K.J. Hopt, H. Kanda, M.J. Roe, E. Wymeersch, and S. Prigge, see n. 4 above, 277; see most recently M. Lutter, 'Corporate Governance rechtsvergleichend—die deutsche Sicht' and P. Davies, 'Comparative Corporate Governance—an English and Market Perspective' in 'Symposium "Corporate Governance—European Perspectives", For the 60th Birthday of Klaus J. Hopt' *Zeitschrift für Unternehmens- und Gesellschaftsrecht* 2001, 224, 268, English version in *International and Comparative Corporate Law Journal* 2 (2000) Issue 4.

[7] Korn/Ferry International, *Board Meeting in Session*, European Board of Directors Study, London 1996.

that has not motivated other countries to follow suit. Interestingly enough, in the Netherlands, full labour co-determination does not apply to the multi-national companies, which might shy away from incorporating in the Netherlands.[8] In other European countries, there is parity only on a one-third basis. In Anglo-American countries, any kind of boardroom co-determination is strictly rejected, both by industry and trade unions as well as by economic theory.[9] The controversy has now also affected German economics and has led to a theoretical discussion[10] in which critics and proponents are equally represented. Enterprise practice, however, has come to an arrangement with labour co-determination.

3. Financial Intermediaries

The influence of German banks on companies—particularly the large banks such as the Deutsche Bank, Dresdner Bank, Commerzbank, and Westdeutsche Landesbank Girozentrale—is by far more important than in other countries such as the U.S. and Great Britain. This is true even though concentration in the German banking sector is rather minor compared to concentration in various neighbouring countries; the market share held by private banks in Germany is only 26%.[11] The critics, in particular, find fault with the combination of lending,

---

[8] As to Germany, see H. Oetker, 'Mitbestimmungsgesetz' in K.J. Hopt and H. Wiedemann (eds.), *Großkommentar Aktiengesetz* 4th edn. (Berlin/New York 1999) Pt. 12; as to the Netherlands, see A.F.M. Dorresteijn, 'Corporate Governance Issues in the Netherlands: The Legal Structure for Large Companies' in E. Wymeersch (ed.), *Further Perspectives in Financial Integration in Europe* (Berlin/New York 1994) 209, 214. The development in Europe is described by K.J. Hopt, 'Labor Representation on Corporate Boards: Impacts and Problems for Corporate Governance and Economic Integration in Europe' [1994] 14 *International Review of Law and Economics* 203; for a longer German version, see 'Arbeitnehmervertretung im Aufsichtsrat—Auswirkungen der Mitbestimmung auf corporate governance und wirtschaftliche Integration in Europa' in *Festschrift für Ulrich Everling*, vol. I (Baden-Baden 1995) 475.

[9] As to the discussion, cf. for the one side E. Gerum and H. Wagner, 'Economics of Labor Co-determination in View of Corporate Governance', for the other M.J. Roe, 'German Co-Determination and German Securities Markets', both in: Hopt, Kanda, Roe, Wymeersch, and Prigge, above, n. 4, 341 and 361. As to the path dependency of labour co-determination, see K.J. Hopt, *Zeitschrift für Unternehmens- und Gesellschaftsrecht* 2000, 779, 798ff; for an English version, see ibid., 'Common Principles of Corporate Governance in Europe?' in B.S. Markesinis (ed.), *The Clifford Chance Millennium Lectures, The Coming Together of the Common Law and the Civil Law* (Oxford 2000) 105. See also the defence from a legal point of view by C. Windbichler and G. Bachmann, 'Corporate Governance und Mitbestimmung als "wirtschaftlicher ordre public" ' in *Festschrift für Gerold Bezzenberger* (Berlin 2000) 797.

[10] A good survey on the economic arguments is given by D. Sadowski, J. Junkes, and S. Lindenthal, *Zeitschrift für Unternehmens- und Gesellschaftsrecht* 2001, 110.

[11] Monopolies Commission, Thirteenth Main Report 1998/1999, Bundestags-Drucksache 14/4002 of August 16, 2000, no. 123: The public sector as a whole has a market share of 50% of the business of all credit institutions (public credit institutions: 36%, public credit institutions with

bank participation, chair, and seats on many supervisory boards, and the 'depository vote,' i.e. banks voting their clients' stock.[12] In addition, there is the influence that the banks exercise through their investment company subsidiaries.[13] On the other hand, the U.S., after many attempts, has abandoned its system of functional separation under the Glass-Steagall Act[14] and, in Germany, the major universal banks, i.e. the Deutsche Bank and others, are undergoing rapid changes to catch up internationally and keep up with the American investment banks.

4. Stock Exchange and Capital Markets

Compared to the U.S. and Great Britain, stock exchanges and capital markets in Germany have long been clearly underdeveloped.[15] Only in recent years have we seen clear rethinking. There are now (before the recent crisis) 15 million shareholders in Germany, a number that not too long ago nobody would have envisaged. The number of listed companies and generally of stock corporations has increased considerably. New exchange market segments such as the New Market have been quite successfully introduced, notwithstanding the dramatic stock price decline and many irregularities that we see at present in this market segment. International techniques of issuing and placement, such as book building and auctions, have also taken a firm hold in Germany.[16] Anglo-American contract and auditing techniques, such as due diligence in cases of mergers and acquisitions, have now been firmly established. The discussion of shareholder value is also fully underway in Germany.[17] Good corporate governance is said

special tasks: 14%), the private banks have a market share of 26%, and the private credit co-operative societies have roughly 15%.

[12] See P.O. Mülbert, 'Empfehlen sich gesetzliche Regelungen zur Einschränkung des Einflusses der Kreditinstitute auf Aktiengesellschaften? *Gutachten E zum 61. Deutschen Juristentag*, Karlsruhe 1996; K.J. Hopt, 'Corporate Governance und deutsche Universalbanken' in D. Feddersen, P. Hommelhoff, and U.H. Schneider (eds.) *Corporate Governance* (Cologne 1996) 243.

[13] T.H. Baums and E. Theissen, 'Banken, bankeigene Kapitalanlagegesellschaften und Aktienemissionen' [1999] *Zeitschrift für Bankrecht und Bankwirtschaft* 125.

[14] Gramm-Leach-Bliley Act (GLBA), November 12, 1999, cf. J.R. Barth, D. Brumbaugh, and J.A. Wilcox, 'The Repeal of Glass-Steagall and the Advent of Broad Banking' [2000] 14 *Journal of Economic Perspectives* 191; M. Gruson, 'Die Reform des Trennbanksystems in den USA' [2000] *Zeitschrift für Bankrecht und Bankwirtschaft* 153; Hoffmann, *Zeitschrift für Wirtschafts- und Bankrecht (WM)* 2000, 1773.

[15] K.J. Hopt and H. Baum, 'Börsenrechtsreform in Deutschland' in K.J. Hopt, B. Rudolph, and H. Baum (eds.) *Börsenreform* (Stuttgart, 1997) 287; ibid., *Zeitschrift für Wirtschafts- und Bankrecht (WM)* Sonderbeilage 4/1997, 1.

[16] M. Hoffmann-Becking, 'Neue Formen der Aktienemission' in *Festschrift für Lieberknecht* (Munich 1997) 25; W. Groß, 'Bookbuilding' [1998] 162 *Zeitschrift für das gesamte Handelsrecht und Wirtschaftsrecht* 318.

[17] P.O. Mülbert, [1997] *Zeitschrift für Unternehmens- und Gesellschaftsrecht* 129; F. Kübler, 'Shareholder Value: Eine Herausforderung für das Deutsche Recht?' in *Festschrift für Zöllner*

to be rewarded by the stock exchange, with stock prices that are up to 20% higher.[18]

5. The Market for Corporate Control

Until recently there has not been a functioning market for corporate control in Germany.[19] Hostile take-overs in particular have so far been almost unknown. The cases of Krupp versus Thyssen in 1997 and Vodafone versus Mannesmann in 1999/2000 are still individual cases, yet they clearly signal a tidal change. In line with that, Germany did not have a legal framework for take-overs until 2002. It is true that the German Take-over Code of 1995, as amended in 1998 and administered by the German Take-over Commission in Frankfurt, did provide a basis for 95 procedures of cases, of which 87 were voluntary and 13 mandatory.[20] This is a good record. Nevertheless, a considerable number of companies, among them some major ones, had failed to submit voluntarily to the Take-over Code. As a consequence, this code was not a substitute for a legal regulation, and the new German Take-over Act has been in force since January 1, 2002.[21]

6. Disclosure and Auditing

In corporate governance, disclosure and auditing have played an outstanding role in Germany as well as internationally.[22] Company disclosure, which takes various forms, grants reliable information to the players in the market, particularly when it is audited. It is a more market-compatible intervention than

(Cologne 1998) 321; see also K.J. Hopt, 'Gemeinsame Grundsätze der Corporate Governance in Europa?—Überlegungen zum Einfluß der Wertpapiermärkte auf Unternehmen und ihre Regulierung und zum Zusammenwachsen von common law und civil law im Gesellschafts- und Kapitalmarktrecht' [2000] *Zeitschrift für Unternehmens- und Gesellschaftsrecht* 779, 798ff.

[18] C. Strenger, 'Einflußmöglichkeiten professioneller Anleger auf die Unternehmen', in IDW (ed.), *Kapitalmarktorientierte Unternehmensüberwachung—Chancen und Risiken* (Duesseldorf 2000), 65.

[19] As to the relationship between European and German take-over law, see K.J. Hopt, [1997] 161 *Zeitschrift für das gesamte Handelsrecht und Wirtschaftsrecht*, 368.

[20] H. Loehr (chairman of the German Take-over Commission), 'Der Übernahmekodex— Aktuelle Situation und Ausblick', Press conference on June 13, 2000. For details, see German Take-over Commission, *Drei Jahre Übernahmekodex* (Frankfurt 1999).

[21] Federal Gazette of December 20, 2001, vol. 1, p. 3822. Cf. also Börsensachverständigen-kommission, 'Standpunkte zur künftigen Regelung von Unternehmensübernahmen' Frankfurt, February 1999; K.J. Hopt, 'Auf dem Weg zum deutschen Übernahmegesetz, Überlegungen zum Richtlinienentwurf 1997, zum Übernahmekodex (1997) und zum SPD-Entwurf 1997' in *Festschrift für Zöllner* (Cologne et al. 1998) 253, 263ff, 266ff.

[22] H. Merkt, *Die Publizität von Unternehmen* (Tübingen 2000).

substantive, mandatory legal provisions. The periodic disclosure by annual accounts as regulated in the third book of the German Commercial Code is still the core of all kinds of company disclosure.[23] Yet the German Securities Trading Act of 1995 (WpHG) introduced instant disclosure, the 'disclosure ad hoc' (section 15 of the WpHG). This kind of disclosure has since developed rapidly, a rather surprising scenario since it was previously embodied in section 44 a of the Stock Exchange Act where it had been fully dormant.[24] The duties under § 21 WpHG to notify and disclose changes of voting interests in listed companies must also be mentioned. They are important because they start at the threshold of 5% of the voting rights, in contrast to the antiquated regulations of the Stock Corporation Act that set the threshold at 25% of the voting rights.[25]

II. Basic Premises in the Evaluation of the German System and its Development and Reform

The discussion surrounding the German system of corporate governance is highly controversial. In view of competition that threatens to test many acquired rights and positions, this can hardly be surprising. In this discussion a great many general statements have been made and a host of specific proposals have been opposed, some in a rather misleading if not deceptive way. In such a discussion it is indispensable to be certain of one's own basic assessments and to disclose them right at the beginning.

1. No System Change and no Comprehensive Reform of the Stock Corporation Act

In the debate on the stock corporation and bank law reform of 1998, some demanded the introduction of far-reaching changes to the German system of corporate governance. One of the catchwords was dismantling the 'power of the banks'. This system change was rejected by the Parliament under the government of the Christian Democrats with the approval of the German Lawyers Association (*Deutscher Juristentag*)[26] and many legal and economic

---

[23] Cf. the commentaries on the German Commercial Code, e.g., A. Baumbach and K.J. Hopt, *HGB* 30th edn. (Munich 2000) s. 238ff; W.D. Budde and H. Clemm et al., *Beck'scher Bilanz-Kommentar* 4th edn. (Munich 1999).

[24] Bundesaufsichtsamt für den Wertpapierhandel (BAWe), Annual Report 1999, 27ff; there are many legal controversies, cf. K.J. Hopt [1995] 159 *Zeitschrift für das gesamte Handelsrecht und Wirtschaftsrecht* 135, 146ff; *Insider Regulation and Timely Disclosure, Forum Internationale*, no. 21, The Hague 1996.

[25] H.D. Assmann and U.H. Schneider (eds), *Wertpapierhandelsgesetz* 2nd edn. (Cologne 1999) s. 21ff; C. Windbichler in K.J. Hopt and H. Wiedemann, *Großkomm. AktG*, see above n. 8 (1999) Pt. 10, s. 20.

[26] Resolutions of the 61st Deutscher Juristentag Karlsruhe 1996, s. E.

experts.[27] This basic assessment is still valid today despite spectacular failures such as Holzmann. The reforms introduced by the Act of 1998 were in force for the first time for the business year beginning after December 31, 1998. Therefore they have still not been tested in practice. Hasty changes of these rules would be amiss. What is needed is a careful analysis of individual weak points.

There is also no immediate need for a comprehensive reform of the German Stock Corporation Act, apart from some modernization inter alia concerning modern techniques of communications as just enacted. It is not quite clear whether the Governmental Commission on Corporate Governance sees and plans this in a different way. According to its questionnaire, which deals with problems which vary greatly in nature and importance, this cannot be ruled out altogether.[28] A rapid legislative solution without sufficient preparation and broad discussion, as is happening in German civil procedural law despite the protest of many judges and practising lawyers and as is planned in the German law of obligations, can backfire. A fundamental reform of stock corporation law during this or the next parliamentary term would also not be a responsible act in view of the scarce legislative resources and the grave need for fundamental structural reforms of much of the backward-looking German social welfare, retirement pension, and labour legislation.

The reform of the accounting law is much more important. Here major changes are to be expected.[29] These are driven mainly by the international financial markets, to which the European Union cannot close its eyes. The European Commission has summed up its own views in an important statement of June 2000 dealing with the accounting strategy in the European Union and the agenda of reform.[30] In addition to this reform, German corporate governance definitely needs major reforms in the area of stock exchange and capital market law, and certainly most of all in the field of take-overs.

---

[27] Cf. the contributions in 'Die Aktienrechtsreform 1997', *Die Aktiengesellschaft,* Special Issue August 1997.

[28] In the meantime the Report has been published: T. Baums, ed., *Bericht der Regierungskommission Corporate Governance* (Cologne 2001). It contains many reform suggestions, both major and minor. In the light of this report the government plans to come up with several reforming Acts, partly before the end of this legislative period, partly during the next one. The report is sound, though more fundamental problems like labour co-determination and the board size have not been treated. The report is discussed extensively in: P. Hommelhoff et al. (eds.), *Corporate Governance, Gemeinschaftssymposion der Zeitschriften ZHR/ZGR,* Heidelberg 2002, general report by K.J. Hopt, 27–67.

[29] Cf. the contributions to the symposium held by the *Zeitschrift für Unternehmens- und Gesellschaftsrecht* on January 14/15, 2000 in Kronberg/Taunus on 'Bilanzrecht, Gesellschaftsrecht, Kapitalmarktrecht', *Zeitschrift für Unternehmens- und Gesellschaftsrecht* [2000] 535–778.

[30] European Commission, *Mitteilung an den Rat und das Europäische Parlament, Rechnungslegungsstrategie der EU: Künftiges Vorgehen,* Brussels, June 13, 2000, COM (2000) 359 fin. See below, C.III.2, 3.

2. The Case Against Too Much Regulation and Juridification

Typically, politicians react too late and then come out with laws and bureaucracies. We should caution against this. Too much regulation and juridification is bound to result in inflexibility and the paralysis of initiative and the market forces. On the contrary, what is needed is deregulation, also in the field of stock corporation and stock exchange law. To be sure, deregulation does not just mean repealing norms; it can accompany partial re-regulation. Re-regulation can be necessary, because deregulation of too broad or unnecessary provisions makes room for provisions that aim more accurately at the regulatory problems.[31] In this process, it is important to check carefully whether instead of mandatory legal regulation the same effect can be achieved by decentralized, voluntary self-regulation. This is true on the European level as well as on the Member State level. Let us look at just one example: the Institute of German Auditors (IDW) has asked for better qualification of the members of the supervisory boards.[32] This is justified. But the legislators of the 1997 Act saw correctly that legislative measures dealing with this were not needed. As of 2001 the German Corporate Governance Code deals with many of these questions on a disclose-or-explain basis.

3. The Role of Liability

Rules on liability are necessary. But liability is only one part of corporate governance, and a rather small one at that. It must not be overdone or it will paralyse initiative and a necessary willingness to take risks. This applies to management boards, which need the freedom of the business judgment rule,[33] as well as to auditors, who must not be exposed to an unforeseeable third-party liability.[34]

[31] As to the problem of juridification, see generally F. Kübler (ed.), *Verrechtlichung von Wirtschaft, Arbeit und sozialer Solidarität, Vergleichende Analysen* (Baden-Baden 1984); G. Teubner (ed.), *Juridification of Social Spheres, A Comparative Analysis in the Areas of Labor, Corporate, Antitrust and Social Welfare Law* (Berlin/New York 1987). On regulation, see A.I. Ogus, *Regulation, Legal Form and Economic Theory* (Oxford 1994) and J. Basedow, K.J. Hopt, T. Kono, H. Baum (eds.), *Transsectoral Issues of Regulation (Banking, Capital Market, Insurance, and Telecommunications Regulation)*, Max Planck conference at Ringberg Castle, Tegernsee, Oct. 24–27, 2001 (forthcoming, Kluwer Law International).

[32] IDW, see above, n. 2, *IDW-Fachnachrichten* 6/2000, 229, 230.

[33] Cf. K.J. Hopt, 'Die Haftung von Vorstand und Aufsichtsrat—Zugleich ein Beitrag zur corporate governance-Debatte' in *Festschrift für Mestmäcker* (Baden-Baden 1996), 909; W. Goette, 'Leitung, Aufsicht, Haftung—zur Rolle der Rechtsprechung bei der Sicherung einer modernen Unternehmensführung' in K. Geiß, K. Nehm, H.E. Brandner, and H. Hagen (eds.), *Festschrift aus Anlaß des fünfzigjährigen Bestehens von Bundesgerichtshof, Bundesanwaltschaft und Rechtsanwaltschaft beim Bundesgerichtshof* (Cologne 2000) 123.

[34] Cf. briefly, below, C.III.1.

The dangers of detrimental defence strategies against exaggerated liability are well known. In the medical field, we are suffering from defensive medicine, and we do not wish to have defensive auditing.

4. Responsibility of the Auditors Between Internal and External Corporate Governance

On the part of the public, there is a tendency to expect too much from the auditors (the 'expectation gap') and to hold them primarily responsible for failures in the system of corporate governance. Yet one must first turn to internal corporate governance and hold the shareholders themselves and the supervisory board primarily responsible, and only afterwards the auditors who co-operate with the supervisory board. The auditors, however, must live up to this systemic responsibility that, though it comes in second, is by no means less important. Effective external corporate governance by the stock exchanges, the capital market, and a functioning market for corporate control must supplement internal corporate governance.

So much for the German system of corporate governance and its various elements. Let us now turn to the reform debate and throw some light on a number of possible developments and improvements of the system. In doing this, I am following the international discussion in distinguishing between internal corporate governance[35]—i.e. within the corporation itself (by the shareholders, the supervisory board, and, though they are between internal and external control, by the auditors, see below Part C)—and external corporate governance—i.e. on the market (stock exchange and capital markets, market for corporate control, and enforcement, see below Part D).

C. Highlights for Reform: Internal Corporate Governance

I. Shareholder Activism

1. Large Shareholders

One basic difference between Germany and the U.S. and some other countries is the fact that in Germany there are many large shareholders and relatively few public corporations in widespread shareholding without blockholders. This

---

[35] On the distinction made between internal control and external control, see with further references K.J. Hopt, 'Corporate Governance: Aufsichtsrat oder Markt?—Überlegungen zu einem internationalen und interdisziplinären Thema' in P. Hommelhoff, H. Rowedder, and P. Ulmer (eds.) *Max Hachenburg, Third Memorial Lecture 1998* (Heidelberg 2000) 9, 24ff, 39ff.

difference in the ownership structure[36] has the consequence that the realities of control and the needs for protection in Germany are typically different from those in the U.S. This is bound to have effects on corporate governance and the debate in public, in legislation, and in economic and legal theory. In the U.S., the focus is first on the protection of shareholders against management. In American legal and economic theory, this relationship between the shareholders and the board is the paradigm for a principal agent conflict. In Germany, however, and more generally in continental Europe, we concentrate on the protection of minority shareholders and on the principal agent conflict between the minority and the majority. Reversibly, the danger of abuse of minority rights and, thus, the protection of the majority against rapacious minority shareholders are practical realities in Germany and therefore a topic for lively debate.[37]

2. Institutional Shareholders

In the U.S. and Great Britain, and in a number of other countries with better-developed stock exchange and capital markets, it is the institutional investors who are the decisive players of public companies,[38] a phenomenon that is still less marked in Germany, though it is gradually on the rise.[39] It suffices to refer here to the California Pension Fund CalPERS and the surprisingly high influence it has had with its calls on international corporate governance in various European countries, including Germany.[40] Smaller neighbouring countries, such as Austria, tell us that Austrian management boards feel as if they were being summoned to the U.S. to render account to the institutional investors. It is a difficult proposition, indeed, for European board members to get used to the

---

[36] On these problems there is extensive economic research, e.g., European Corporate Governance Network (ECGN), *The Separation of Ownership and Control: A Survey of 7 European Countries, Preliminary Report to the European Commission* vols 1–4, Brussels 1997, http://www.ecgn.ulb.ac.be/; J. Franks and C. Mayer, 'Corporate Ownership and Control in the U.K., Germany and France' [1996/97] 9 *Journal of Applied Corporate Finance* 30; R. La Porta, F. Lopez-de-Silanes, and A. Shleifer, 'Corporate Ownership Around the World' [1999] 54 *Journal of Finance* 471; W.R. Emmons and F.A. Schmid, 'Corporate Governance and Corporate Performance' in S. Cohen and G. Boyd (eds.), *Corporate Governance and Globalization* (Cheltenham 2000), 59, 76ff; E. Lehmann, J. Weigand, Does the Governed Corporation Perform Better? Governance Structures and Corporate Performance in Germany, *European Finance Review* 2000, 157.

[37] M. Lutter, 'Zur Abwehr räuberischer Aktionäre' in *Festschrift 40 Jahre Der Betrieb* (Stuttgart, 1988) This was the topic debated on the 63rd Deutscher Juristentag 2000 in Leipzig, cf. below, n. 42.

[38] T. Baums, R.M. Buxbaum, and K.J. Hopt (eds.) *Institutional Investors and Corporate Governance* (Berlin/New York, 1994).

[39] C. Strenger, 'Einflußmöglichkeiten professioneller Anleger auf die Unternehmen', see above, n. 18.

[40] CalPERS, International Corporate Governance, German Market Principles, 1999.

fact that only performance and shareholder value count there. If performance is unsatisfactory, institutional investors do not necessarily react within the corporation itself. Apart from some exceptions, that are quite popular but possibly overemphasized, all is still done according to the venerable Wall Street rule, i.e. voting by your feet, as it is called, by selling the stock. Whether this will change in the U.S. and, after the usual lag, also in Europe, remains to be seen. It is a quite fascinating development to follow.

3. Private Shareholders

Next to the large shareholders and the institutional investors, private investors must not be overlooked.[41] They, too, are integrated into the company monitoring by their shareholder rights, including their shareholders' rights to sue. The latter was the topic of the German Lawyers' Association Conference (*Deutscher Juristentag*) held in September 2000 in Leipzig: 'Is it recommended to proceed to an amendment of the corporate law rules on voidability of shareholder resolutions and on the liability of a board, in particular as to the rights of minority shareholders to sue?'[42] The right of the individual shareholder to bring an action to set aside a resolution of the shareholders' meeting for violation of the law was unanimously considered as indispensable.[43] This resolution was in reaction to certain proposals to restrict this right by requiring a minimum number of shares and/or a minimum duration of shareholding in parallel to the German law on board liability.[44] Instead, a clear majority recommended, in addition to further improvements, that legislators broaden the application of the District Court proceedings under section 306 of the Stock Corporation Act in which the amount of the compensation and the consideration due to minority shareholders in

---

[41] See the comparative view by K.J. Hopt, 'Shareholder Rights and Remedies: A View from Germany and the Continent' [1997] Company Financial and Insolvency Law Review 261.

[42] Th. Baums, *Empfiehlt sich eine Neuregelung des aktienrechtlichen Anfechtungs- und Organhaftungsrechts, insbesondere der Klagemöglichkeiten von Aktionären?, Gutachten F zum 63. Deutschen Juristentag*, Leipzig 2000; reports by N. Götz, R. Marsch-Barner, and K. Schmidt. The choice of the topic was mainly influenced by the member of the Deputation Peter Ulmer, who had treated the topic earlier and was followed in most parts by Th. Baums; see P. Ulmer, 'Die Aktionärsklage als Instrument zur Kontrolle des Vorstands- und Aufsichtsratshandelns' [1999] 163 *Zeitschrift für das gesamte Handelsrecht und Wirtschaftsrecht* 290. The earlier debate at the symposium held by the *Zeitschrift für das gesamte Handelsrecht und Wirtschaftsrecht* had been far more critical as to these theses, cf. the discussion report by L. Schnorr [1999] 163 *Zeitschrift für das gesamte Handelsrecht und Wirtschaftsrecht* 377 and the critical reports by G. Krieger and E. Sünner [1999] 163 *Zeitschrift für das gesamte Handelsrecht und Wirtschaftsrecht* 343 and 364. The proposals made by Th. Baums are also critically reviewed by Schwarz,[2000] *Zeitschrift für Rechtspolitik* 330.

[43] Resolutions of the 63rd Deutscher Juristentag Leipzig 2000, Section E. Business Law, I.1.C.a).

[44] ibid., I.7.a. b.

corporate groups is determined.[45] In particular, they recommended against giving the individual shareholder a right to enjoin the management from acts which
supposedly are against the law or against the articles of association. Instead, the
standing should depend on whether the plaintiff can make the case that the competence of the general assembly of shareholders has been infringed upon by the
board.[46] As to liability of the board, it was recommended that the business judgment rule be laid down expressly in section 93 pars. 2 of the Stock Corporation
Act.[47] Furthermore, there was agreement that the requirements for bringing a
suit in liability according to section 147 of the Stock Corporation Act are too
restrictive and should be reformed. In particular, it was held that the threshold
requirements should be lowered: shares that amount to 1% of the stated capital
of the corporation or that amount to a price of 100,000 Euro on the stock
exchange or on the market should suffice to give standing.[48] It was also held that
in order to avoid unnecessary, clearly unfounded, and blackmail suits, an
express admission by the trial court should be necessary and facts purporting to
find the suspicion of bad faith or other grave violations of the law or the articles
of association by the board member sued should be substantiated.[49] Only a
minority, though a strong one, was in favour of a right of the individual shareholder to sue ('actio pro socio'). The minority[50] pointed in vain to the fact that
such an individual shareholder right to sue exists in the U.S,[51] Switzerland, other
countries, and even in the German law of groups. Finally, a resolution was
adopted in favour of a fundamental reform of the special audit according to
sections 142 et seq. of the Stock Corporation Act.[52] Such a reform should deal
adequately with the problems posed by confidentiality and by the need to extend
the special audit beyond the single corporation to members of the group of
companies. The requirements and procedural provisions for the special audit

---

[45] Resolutions of the 63rd Deutscher Juristentag Leipzig 2000, I.11.a.

[46] ibid., II.1.a, b.B.

[47] ibid., III.1, following P. Ulmer, [1999] 163 *Zeitschrift für das gesamte Handelsrecht und
Wirtschaftsrecht* 290 (299). On the business judgment rule, see Hopt and Goette, above, n. 33.

[48] ibid., III.3.B.a, 4.b, c.

[49] ibid., III.5.a, b aa.

[50] ibid., III.2; surprisingly enough this view has been shared by Deutsche Schutzvereinigung für
Wertpapierbesitz e.V. (DSW*)*, *Reformvorschläge zum Anfechtungs- und Organhaftungsrecht*
(Düsseldorf 2000) II 2. In favor of an individual shareholder right to sue (but after a review proce-
dure by the district court), e.g., M. Becker, *Verwaltungskontrolle durch Gesellschafterrechte*
(Tübingen 1997) 529ff; M. Lutter [1995] 159 *Zeitschrift für das gesamte Handelsrecht und
Wirtschaftsrecht* 287, 306; ibid. [2000] *Juristenzeitung* 837, 841; W. Bayer [2000] *Neue Juristische
Wochenschrift* 2609, 2618ff.

[51] Cf. J.C. Coffee, 'Class Action Accountability: Reconciling Exit, Voice, and Loyalty in
Representative Litigation' [2000] 100 *Columbia Law Review* 370.

[52] s. 309 para. 4, 310 para. 4, 317 para. 4, 318 para. 4 of the German Stock Corporation Act.

and the liability suit according to section 147 should be harmonized as far as possible.[53]

II. Further Improvements Concerning the Board

1. Board System, Labour Co-determination

The separation between management and supervisory board is a key decision of the German legislators that goes back far into the nineteenth century and, according to the overwhelming view in German practice and legal theory, has clear merits and should not be questioned. This assessment is not called into doubt by the debate on improving board performance[54] and by the many legislative reforms of the law of the supervisory board.[55] In particular, it can be noted that even under the one-tier board system of the U.S. and Great Britain, the functions of management and of monitoring tend to be separated. This is done by appealing to outside directors, also called independent directors, who have specific competencies and tasks in situations of conflicts of interest and when other critical decisions have to be made.[56] The most important advantage of the one-tier system, it is said, is that these outside directors are on the management board itself and do not form a separate organ like the supervisory board; they thus have direct access to information, management, and monitoring of the corporation.[57] One disadvantage, as we see from the German side, is that all members of the board have been integrated into decisions that may have

[53] ibid. at III.9 (proposal by Hommelhoff). This view is shared by DSW, see above, n. 50, II 3. On the special audit, see Forum Europaeum Konzernrecht, [1998] *Zeitschrift für Unternehmens- und Gesellschaftsrecht* 672, 715ff and H. Fleischer, [2000] *Recht der Internationalen Wirtschaft* 809, each with many comparative law references. On the experiments made with the special audit in the Netherlands, see most recently J. Gernoth and M. Meinema [2000] *Recht der Internationalen Wirtschaft* 844. This view is endorsed by the High Level Group of Experts on Company Law in its *Second Report for the European Commission*, Brussels, November 2002.

[54] The debate on the 'problem of the board' was already raging at the turn of the nineteenth to the twentieth century; cf. R. Passow, 'Die Entstehung des Aufsichtsrats der Aktiengesellschaft' [1909] 64 *Zeitschrift für das gesamte Handelsrecht und Wirtschaftsrecht* 27.

[55] The most important recent reform was instituted by the Reform Act of 1998 ('*KonTraG*'); cf. M. Lutter [1995] 159 *Zeitschrift für das gesamte Handelsrecht und Wirtschaftsrecht* 287; 'Die Aktienrechtsreform 1997' *Die Aktiengesellschaft Sonderheft* August 1997.

[56] E.g. The Combined Code, Principles of Good Governance and Code of Best Practice, May 2000, as to board balance: Principles A.3, Code A.3.2. See also the comparative law view by E. Wymeersch, 'A Status Report on Corporate Governance Rules and Practices in Some Continental European Countries' in Hopt, Kanda, Roe, Wymeersch, and Prigge (eds.), see above, n. 4, 1045, 1098ff. Yet there is empirical research that dampens expectations that are too high; cf. S. Bhagat and B.S. Black, 'The Relationship Between Board Composition and Firm Performance' in Hopt, Kanda, Roe, Wymeersch, and Prigge (eds.), see above, n. 4, 281.

[57] Davies, see above, n. 6.

been incorrect. And there is no institutional distance between those board members who do the day-to-day management and those board members who monitor management. Thus, the information flow from the management board to the supervisory board must function and should be further improved, but a system change to the one-tier board system in the Anglo-American style does not seem warranted.

What should be considered, however, is granting companies an option between the two-tier and the one-tier system, as is done in France since quite some time, more recently in Italy and now also in the Statute for the European Company. This has also been recommended by the High Level Group of Company Law Experts in its *Second Report for the European Commission* of November 2002. It would then be up to companies that were not sufficiently large to form only one organ, and in major or international companies to entrust the monitoring to a specific organ. If this option were available, tradition and path dependency would certainly influence few German corporations to make use of it and choose the one-tier board system. But this is not the decisive point. In France also, most companies have remained with the traditional French system of the administrative board and a strong PDG (*président directeur général*). But quite a number of major and international companies have decided in favour of the two-tier board system. This is the case for around 20% of the companies forming the CAC 40—that would correspond to the German DAX Index—such as AXA, Peugeot, Printemps, and Paribas.[58]

It would be beyond the scope of this chapter to examine in more detail the difficult question of German labour co-determination on the supervisory board.[59] In a lengthy study by the Commission on Co-determination of the Bertelsmann Foundation and the Hans Böckler Foundation,[60] the interested parties represented on that Commission, employers as well as trade unions, ultimately spoke in favour of the status quo ante. This is hardly surprising in view of the patrons of the study and the composition of the Commission. Unofficially it is said that the debate within the Commission was at times fierce and the pressure to come

---

[58] M. Cozian, A. Viandier, and F. Deboissy, *Droit des sociétés* 13th edn. (Paris 2000) 780; P. Le Cannu, 'Pour une évolution du droit des sociétés anonymes avec directoire et conseil de surveillance' [2000] *Bulletin Joly Sociétés* 483.

[59] A trade union view is given by R. Köstler, 'Anforderungen der Arbeitnehmer an eine effektive Unternehmensüberwachung', in IDW, ed., *Kapitalmarktorientierte Unternehmensüberwachung—Chancen und Risiken* (Duesseldorf 2001), 105; for a view from industry and banks, see M. Endres, 'Organisation der Unternehmensleitung aus der Sicht der Praxis' [1999] 163 *Zeitschrift für das gesamte Handelsrecht und Wirtschaftsrecht* 441, 454ff: the supervisory board is forced by law to have too many members and labour co-determination is considered by foreign enterprises as rather burdensome.

[60] Bertelsmann Stiftung and Hans-Böckler-Stiftung (eds), *Mitbestimmung und neue Unternehmenskulturen—Bilanz und Perspektiven* (Report by the Commission on Labour Co-determination) (Gütersloh 1998).

up with a compromise was overwhelming. While this fact diminishes the scientific weight of the study, is also shows that in Germany both sides, industry and labour, have been able to come to an arrangement with the existing system. It would, therefore, not be wise to set labour co-determination, i.e. boardroom co-determination, on the reform agenda, simply for political reasons. Nevertheless, there are still pleas for reform: some, such as the proponents of industry and banks, advocate for less co-determination; others even agitate for more co-determination, i.e. full parity co-determination, such as some proponents of trade unions and of the socialist movement. As seen from the point of economic theory, however, the assessment is still highly controversial. The institutional economic argument is that co-determination models would prevail on the market if they really involved economic advantages for the company. In this view, the very fact that a mandatory legal provision is needed makes this kind of labour co-determination economically implausible. On the other hand, there has been practical experience in Germany that co-determination makes a contribution to stabilizing cooperation between investors and employees. It may possibly even serve as an early warning system of social conflicts. However that may be, this is a clear case of path dependency.[61] Whether this special German solution will live up to international competition on a medium- or even long-term basis remains to be seen.

2. The Monitoring System According to Section 91 Para. 2 of the Stock Corporation Act

One of the major tasks of inside corporate governance is the installation and constant improvement of suitable monitoring systems by the management board (section 91 para. 2 of the Stock Corporation Act) and its control by the supervisory board and to a limited extent, i.e. in case of officially listed companies (section 318 para. 4 of the Commercial Code) by auditors. Section 91 para. 2 is of recent origin. It was introduced by the board reform of 1998. It reads: 'The management board shall take suitable measures, in particular establish a monitoring system, for the early recognition of developments endangering the future existence of the company'. This provision has given rise to sharp criticism in the legal world.[62] This is not entirely without justification, both in relation to the codification as such and also to the wording of the provision. On substance,

---

[61] K.J. Hopt, 'Gemeinsame Grundsätze der Corporate Governance in Europa?' [2000] *Zeitschrift für Unternehmens- und Gesellschaftsrecht* 779, 800ff, with many references to both positions concerning the debate, the view taken there is the middle way.

[62] E.g. U. Hüffer, *AktG* (4th edn. Munich 1999) s. 91 comment 5 with further references. The legislative history is reported by U. Seibert, 'Die Entstehung des § 91 Abs 2 AktG im KonTraG—"Risikomanagement" oder "Frühwarnsystem"?' in *Festschrift für Bezzenberger* (Berlin/New York 2000) 427.

however, there is no question that internal controlling and the assessment of its establishment and its good functioning by the supervisory board and the auditors are absolutely necessary, in spite of the difficulty that this assessment gives rise to.[63] This is also evident by the experience in Great Britain, where the board and the auditors are facing similar problems. The Turnbull Report,[64] which has now been integrated by the London Stock Exchange in the Combined Code, had no inhibition against prescribing many details of such a 'sound system of internal control to safeguard shareholders' investment and the company's assets'.[65]

Wide experience involving section 91 para. 2 of the Stock Corporation Act is not yet available. The set norm must be tested by the daily experience. Its content will be concretized in time by practical involvement, legal writings, and court decisions. The Institute of German Auditors (IDW) at present is working on an auditing standard as to internal monitoring systems.[66] It remains to be seen whether the requirement of a monitoring system in a legal sense can be extended toward a general risk management that is well known in management science and auditing practice and takes many different shapes.[67]

3. Functioning Flow of Information from the Management Board to the Supervisory Board

It is also important to secure sufficient flow of information from the management board to the supervisory board according to sections 90 para. 1 and 111 para. 2 of the Stock Corporation Act. An important part of this information duty is the information to be given by the management board to the supervisory board concerning the follow-up of entrepreneurial planning, i.e. the reporting should be extended to how the entrepreneurial planning is later actually exe-

---

[63] P. Hommelhoff and D. Mattheus, 'Corporate Governance nach dem KonTraG' [1998] *Die Aktiengesellschaft* 249, 251; D. Mattheus, 'Die gewandelte Rolle des Wirtschaftsprüfers als Partner des Aufsichtsrates nach dem KonTraG' [1999] *Zeitschrift für Unternehmens- und Gesellschaftsrecht* 682, 702ff; A. Baumbach and K.J. Hopt, *HGB* (30th edn. Munich 2000) s. 317 comment 9, 10 with further references. See in general C. Orth, *Abschlussprüfung und Corporate Governance* (Wiesbaden 2000).

[64] The Institute of Chartered Accountants, *Internal Control, Guidance for Directors on the Combined Code* (September 1999) (chairman: Nigel Turnbull), with 47 sections and an appendix: Assessing the effectiveness of the company's risk and control processes. Cf. R. Smerdon, 'Turnbull: An Opportunity for Lawyers or Just Another Box for Ticking?' [2000] International Company and Commercial Law Review 248.

[65] Combined Code, Principles D.2.

[66] IDW Prüfungsstandard: *Die Prüfung des Risikofrüherkennungssystems nach § 317 Abs. 4 HGB* (IDW PS 340), as of September 11, 2000. See on this problem D. Dörner, 'Beurteilung von Unternehmensrisiken im Rahmen der Abschlußprüfung', in IDW, ed., *Kapitalmarktorientierte Unternehmensüberwachung—Chancen und Risiken* (Dusseldorf 2001), 229.

[67] Hüffer, see above, n. 62, s. 91 comment 9, gives a negative answer.

cuted within the company and what deviations have arisen as compared to the plan.[68] The need to give and the right to ask for such information must also be extended to subsidiaries in a group of companies. This group-wide reporting must be generally applicable, not only within the limits set by the Federal Civil Court (*Bundesgerichtshof*) in its famous *Holzmüller* case.[69] Furthermore, it has been suggested that certain parts of the management board's reporting to the supervisory board should be included in the legally prescribed auditing. Again, the Turnbull Report and the Combined Code have shown that the problems arising in the U.K. are quite similar.[70]

4. Improvement of the Communication Between the Supervisory Board and the Auditors

Just as the flow of information from the management board to the supervisory board must function, the communication between the supervisory board and auditors must also be in order. The quality of internal corporate governance is determined by the weakest link. Therefore, this communication between auditors and supervisory board needs to be further improved. This has long been called for and was part of the proposals made in the debate on board reform in 1998.[71] On the other hand, one must realize that communication presupposes that the supervisory board is able to understand and evaluate the information. Accordingly, the profile of the German supervisory board members must be improved. More professionalization and basic instruction in reading the balance sheets is necessary. Last but not least, the international dimension of the company's business should be mirrored at least to a certain degree in the composition of the board. Up to now German boards have contained very few foreigners. Of course, none of these requirements is the business of the legislators; instead, they need to be handled flexibly according to the needs of the company and the pressures of the market.

[68] This proposal and the one mentioned in the following sentence have become law and have been introduced into the Stock Corporation Act by the Transparency and Disclosure Act 2002.

[69] BGHZ 83, 122 = Neue Juristische Wochenschrift 1982, 1703; cf. the critical view by D. Joost [1999] 163 *Zeitschrift für das gesamte Handelsrecht und Wirtschaftsrecht* 164.

[70] The Institute of Chartered Accountants, Internal Control, see above, n. 64; on groups of companies in particular, see s. 14, 41.

[71] K.H. Forster [1999] *Die Aktiengesellschaft* 193; D. Dörner, [2000] *Der Betrieb* 101; R. Ludewig, 'Kassel KonTraG—Aufsichtsrat und Abschlussprüfer—Gedanken zur Kooperation und Anderem' [2000] *Der Betrieb* 634; S. Schmidt [2000] *Die Wirtschaftsprüfung* 799, 805.

III. Auditors and Accounting

1. Auditors

In the current discussion on company monitoring and the reform of accounting and auditing law, some are calling for obligatory external rotation of auditors. Such a rotation would have the advantage of more independence of the auditors. Yet this is bought at the expense of considerable disadvantage, particularly the time needed for getting to know the company. Practical experience shows that this can take considerable time in large enterprises, groups of companies, enterprises with e-business, and in particular enterprises that are struggling. As a result, monitoring by auditors may be hampered in the most critical cases, candidates, and times. Up to now, neither practical experience nor theory has shown a clear way out of this dilemma. A mandatory external rotation of auditors can, therefore, not be recommended at this time, but should be studied further.[72]

Similar difficulties and disputes exist as to whether simultaneous auditing and advisory services should be separated as a matter of mandatory law.[73] In the U.S., the SEC has now enforced a reform in the face of fierce resistance by the profession. It remains to be seen what the consequences will be for the quality of reporting and auditing. The interference by such a law with the present structure of the auditing business is, of course, fundamental. In my view, such far-reaching legal prohibitions in order to avoid conflict of interest should be regarded with suspicion. This view is based both on the theoretical conviction that legislative interference with market structure needs clear justification, and on practical experience of the American bank separation system under Glass Steagall, which has finally been changed to allow American banks to act, to a certain degree, as universal banks. Therefore, mandatory separation is not suitable as a model for Germany before the practical consequences have been studied. However, mandatory disclosure of the consulting fees to the supervisory board, though not to the general assembly of the shareholders, is a reform proposal that could be acceptable in Germany. But this cautionary view as to mandatory separation does not mean that the U.S.-American development should be considered irrelevant for Germany, in particular after the Enron crisis and the Sarbanes-Oxley Act of July 2002. As in any case of movement and reform in the U.S., we in Europe have to watch very carefully to see what this means for us, in particular whether this may have an effect upon, or even spill over to, Europe. This effect of osmosis and influence, whether by professional

---

[72] External rotation is rejected on economic grounds by B. Arruñada and C. Paz-Ares, 'Mandatory Rotation of Company Auditors: A Critical Examination' [1997] 17 *International Review of Law and Economics* 31.

[73] cf. e.g. B. Arruñada, 'The Provision of Non-Audit Services by Auditors, Let the Market Evolve and Decide' [1999] 19 *International Review of Law and Economics* 513.

imitation or by the forces of the markets, is unfortunately often overlooked in Germany and elsewhere by politicians as well as business leaders. However, it would be outright negligence to ignore it.

Another question is whether and to what degree the auditor can be held responsible for uncovering irregularities.[74] This question is of considerable practical importance, but nonetheless rather difficult to answer. Even before Enron the US-American SEC requested the Panel on Audit Effectiveness to give its view on this issue.[75] The recommendations of the panel were viewed rather critically in Germany as to their content, their reach and their suitability for detecting irregularities.[76] And rightly so, because this could change the character of auditing toward a so-called control of embezzlement, i.e. from a sample audit as has been standard up to now, to the presumption that there might be fraud and embezzlement on the part of the company and its management. Such a change of audit might also have a considerable impact in the field of auditors' liability. However, the auditing profession should not close its eyes to the fact that the general public holds the auditors responsible for undiscovered irregularities, at least gross ones, no matter whether there is a legal responsibility or not. Therefore, it is in the very interest of the profession to look for ways and means that extend the probability of discovering irregularities in the course of auditing as far as is feasible. This is even more true after Enron.

The auditing profession has proposed that the auditor should be obliged to inform the organ that selects the auditor of his auditing fees. It is expected that this would help to set up more appropriate auditing fees.[77] According to a further proposal of the auditing profession, in cases of bankruptcy[78] the auditors should have the right and the duty to disclose the auditing reports made during the last three years to the parties of the proceedings.[79] This way, the profession hopes to be in a better position to defend itself in those spectacular difficulties and failures of enterprises where, as a matter of course, auditors are criticized by those involved as well as by the press and the general public for having audited negligently or even having been complaisant in auditing, and rendering their

---

[74] D. Mertin, 'Die Verantwortung der Abschlußprüfers für die Aufdeckung von Fraud', in IDW, ed., *Kapitalmarktorientierte Unternehmensüberwachung—Chancen und Risiken* (Dusseldorf 2001), 259.

[75] For details, see S. Schmidt [2000] *Die Wirtschaftsprüfung* 793.

[76] S. Schmidt [2000] *Die Wirtschaftsprüfung* 793, 710.

[77] IDW, above, n. 2, l, FN-IDW 10/2000, 521, 526. The remuneration of the auditor is usually fixed by the management board and not by the supervisory board. Since the auditor is the partner of the supervisory board and also commissions the auditor to audit (s. 111 para. 2 sentence 3 of the Stock Corporation Act), this task should be taken over by the supervisory board. This could also be laid down in the act.

[78] Cf. H.-J. Früh, 'Die Beratung der Unternehmen vor und in der Insolvenz', in IDW, ed., *Kapitalmarktorientierte Unternehmensüberwachung—Chancen und Risiken* (Dusseldorf 2001), 293.

[79] IDW, above, n. 2, *FN-IDW* 10/2000, 521, 526ff.

certification of the financial statement, for reasons of conflicts of interest, for aiming at maintaining the auditing mandate for the next time, or for other reasons. It is clear that in such cases the auditors who are bound by professional secrecy are indeed in a dilemma. Under exceptional circumstances disclosure might be legitimate even under the present law, namely according to the principle of protecting one's own legitimate interests laid down in section 193 of the Penal Act.[80] Yet it would certainly be preferable to implement this by law or regulation.

The question of liability of auditors has been the subject of much debate in recent years. This debate has amounted to an amendment of section 323 of the Commercial Code of 1998, which had a ridiculously low ceiling of 250,000 euro for auditors' liability in the case of mandatory annual accounts. The reform was certainly long overdue. The upper limits of liability have been moderately increased to 1 million euro for each single case of auditing, and to 4 million euro for listed companies.[81] Whether this is sufficient is questionable in the light of international experience, which shows that such ceilings do not exist in most other countries. Third-party liability of auditors is even more controversial.[82] Legislators have refrained from becoming involved in this since the auditing profession, which had originally pushed the enactment of such a provision, began to wonder whether it might not be counterproductive. In the meantime, a landmark decision of the Federal Civil Court (*Bundesgerichtshof*) has shed some light on this, though it has by no means solved the problem in its entirety. These solutions found by legislators and courts cannot, of course, satisfy all parties concerned. It is clear that the discussion on auditor liability will continue.[83]

2. Group Accounts

Group accounts must be internationalized steadily.[84] This cannot be questioned any longer, at least since Daimler-Benz had to render a transformation account

[80] There is a similar problem for bank secrecy, see A. Baumbach and K.J. Hopt, *HGB* 30th edn. (Munich 2000) 7 *Bankgeschäfte* comment A/10 with further references.

[81] For details, see ibid., § 323 comment 9.

[82] BGHZ 138, 257; H. Zugehör, 'Berufliche "Dritthaftung"' [2000] *Neue Juristische Wochenschrift* 1601.

[83] References on the debate can be found in A. Baumbach and K.J. Hopt, see above, n. 23, s. 323 comment 8.

[84] Cf. European Commission, *Rechnungslegungsstrategie der EU: Künftiges Vorgehen*, June 13, 2000, see above, n. 30; P. Hommelhoff, 'Europäisches Bilanzrecht im Aufbruch' [1998] 62 *Rabels Zeitschrift für ausländisches und internationales Privatrecht* 381; C.P. Claussen, 'Konzernabschluß versus Einzelabschluß der Muttergesellschaft'; J. Hennrichs, 'Ausbau der Konzernrechnungslegung im Lichte internationaler Entwicklungen' and W. Busse von Colbe, 'Ausbau der Konzernrechnungslegung im Lichte internationaler Entwicklungen' [2000] *Zeitschrift für Unternehmens- und Gesellschaftsrecht* 604, 627 and 651; IDW, see above, n. 2, FN-IDW 10/2000,

leading over from German group accounts to group accounts under the U.S. Generally Accepted Accounting Principles (U.S. GAAP) in 1993 in order to have its stock listed at the New York Stock Exchange. Even without mandatory law, the 'preparers' of the accounts have no choice in the long run since they are forced to render international accounts by the admission conditions of the international stock exchanges—the New York Stock Exchange has 390 foreign listings—and by the 'users', i.e. the American institutional investors and other international shareholders. Furthermore Section 292a of the German Commercial Code, which allows for group accounts to be set up according to standards other than German group accounting principles, is only of a temporary nature and its validity is questionable under constitutional law.[85] This internationalization could proceed in such a way that framework principles are laid down in the Commercial Code, i.e. the group account law of the Commercial Code is rendered compatible with international demands. Not all of this can be laid down in the Code itself. At least some concretization will still be necessary and will have to be done by the German Accounting Standards Committee (*DRSC*).[86] At this time, it is not yet clear where the line should be drawn between principles and their concretization, or between legislation and regulation. Further questions exist, e.g. whether the group accounts would need to be formally approved. Such a requirement would give the supervisory board the option to ask the general assembly of shareholders in specific cases to approve not only the normal annual financial statement, but also the consolidated financial statement of the group.[87]

Development in Europe is moving toward the introduction of the International Accounting Standards (IAS). The European Commission decided to ask all listed EU companies to submit their group accounts according to the IAS principles. This will be mandatory from 2005 on. The Member States have an option to extend the mandatory application of the IAS also to companies that are not listed and to single accounts.[88] This means that listed companies from 2005 on can no longer render their group accounts according to U.S. GAAP instead of IAS. This is bound to lead to conflicts of European companies with US-American regulatory agencies, in particular with the SEC, as well as with the demands of the American and possibly also international capital markets. One way out would be

521ff; M. Künnemann, 'Die Internationalisierung des Konzernabschlusses', in IDW, ed., *Kapitalmarktorientierte Unternehmensüberwachung—Chancen und Risiken* (Duesseldorf 2001), 179.

[85] P. Kirchhoff [2000] *Zeitschrift für Unternehmens- und Gesellschaftsrecht* 681; contra M. Henssler and C. Slota, *Neue Zeitschrift fuer Gesellschaftsrecht* 1999, 1133 (1139).

[86] References on the controversy concerning the DRSC can be found in A. Baumbach and K.J. Hopt, see above, n. 23, s. 342 comment 1.

[87] IDW, see above, n. 2, *FN-IDW* 10/2000, 521, 525ff.

[88] European Commission, *Rechnungslegungsstrategie der EU: Künftiges Vorgehen*, June 13, 2000, see above, n. 30, no. 16(7); K. Van Hulle, 'Die Reform des europäischen Bilanzrecht: Stand, Ziele und Perspektiven Bilanzrecht, Gesellschaftsrecht, Kapitalmarktrecht' [2000] *Zeitschrift für Unternehmens- und Gesellschaftsrecht* 537, 541ff.

to approximate the IAS and the U.S. GAAP, or at least to try to come to certain solutions of reciprocal recognition. The International Accounting Standard Committee (IASC) made a big step forward by completing certain core standards, which in May 2000 were recommended conditionally by the IOSCO. The condition was that some of these core standards should be amended by 2001. Yet in any case the only solution is compromise. This compromise should be carefully prepared by professionals. A certain tolerance of the American side is necessary, otherwise international co-operation is simply not feasible.

3. Single Accounts

While group accounts are in the forefront of attention and discussion, the single accounts of independent enterprises should not be forgotten. The single account must also be rendered more meaningful. In this respect, one must keep in mind the different aims of single accounts and group accounts. One of the functions of the single account is to keep a certain capital, minimum capital or stated capital, within the company for creditor protection.[89] It determines the maximum dividends payable by the company to its shareholders. In Germany in particular, the meaningfulness of the single account usefulness is impaired by the 'principle of relevance' of the individual account for the tax account and, in exceptional cases, also vice versa. It follows that, quite apart from the relationship between group accounts and single accounts, clear separation of the company's individual account and its tax account is on the reform agenda, though the Federal Court of Finance and occasionally also the legislators have already made exceptions to the principle of mutual relevance.[90] The development of an independent accounting law for tax purposes would have other advantages as well, e.g. this would free the Member State legislators from being bound by European law and from the threat of interference from the European Court of Justice.

However, the single account and the group account should not drift too far apart. Of course, it is difficult to say how this aim can be reached in view of the different interests of the large, internationally active companies on the one side and the many small companies that are basically sticking to national markets on

---

[89] The German principle of prudence and its relationship with European accounting law are treated by P. Hommelhoff, 'Europäisches Bilanzrecht im Aufbruch' [1998] 62 *Rabels Zeitschrift für ausländisches und internationales Privatrecht* 381, 386. An economic critique of the principle of prudence was presented recently by W. Sprißler, 'Gläubigerschutz durch Kapitalerhaltung?', in IDW, ed., *Kapitalmarktorientierte Unternehmensüberwachung—Chancen und Risiken* (Dusseldorf 2001), 85; L. Enriques and J.R. Macey, 'Creditors Versus Capital Formation: The Case Against the European Legal Capital Rules' (2001) 86 *Cornell L. Rev.* 1165. In defense of the minimum capital in accounting law for protective reasons, cf. W. Schön, 'Gesellschafter-, Gläubiger- und Anlegerschutz im Europäische Bilanzrecht' [2000] *Zeitschrift für Unternehmens- und Gesellschaftsrecht* 706, 725ff.

[90] J. Schulze-Osterloh, 'Handels- und Steuerbilanz' [2000] *Zeitschrift für Unternehmens- und Gesellschaftsrecht* 594.

the other side. Yet a significant number of proposals have been made by the IDW and others as to many of these issues, e.g. reducing the many options for accounting and valuation in accordance with the principle of neutrality as to tax consequences, broadening the principle of continuity of the accounts, and extending the information requirements in the notes to the balance sheet and the profit and loss statement. This matter is beyond the scope of this chapter.

4. Quarterly Reporting by Listed Enterprises

Quarterly reporting by all listed enterprises would improve enterprise disclosure and serve the interests of investors and markets.[91] This is not a task for the legislators, however, and should be left to the stock exchanges. Competition between stock exchanges will by itself lead to correct admission requirements, i.e. those demanded by the users for the various market segments. The best example for this is the introduction of the New Market in Frankfurt some time ago, where sub-annual interim reports are demanded as a condition for listing; these are requested as proof of quality, without a specific legal basis. There is a general tendency towards shorter reporting intervals. In the future there might be monthly reports, and one day even the possibility of looking into accounts daily via the Internet. Some enterprises report that this would already be technically possible today. It would make sense to require a limited review of the interim reports by an auditor—i.e. not a full audit concluded by a certification, but only a limited audit concluded by a negative statement.

In the long run, one can expect that the accounts will vary depending on whether the company's stock is listed or not.[92] This is in line with the observation that for some time now, specific law for listed companies is in the process of being formed, partly by national legislators—e.g. in Italy—and partly as a result of the pressures of the international markets.[93]

D. Highlights for Reform: External Corporate Governance

I. Stock Exchange and Capital Markets

1. Stock Exchange Law Reform

In Germany, a fundamental reform of stock exchange law is long overdue. This has been explained extensively—from an economic as well as a legal

---

[91] IDW, see above, n. 2, *FN-IDW* 10/2000, 521, 522ff.

[92] B. Pellens and R.U. Fülbier, 'Differenzierung der Rechnungslegungsregulierung nach Börsenzulassung' [2000] *Zeitschrift für Unternehmens- und Gesellschaftsrecht* 572.

[93] P. Hommelhoff, 'Anlegerinformationen im Aktien-, Bilanz- und Kapitalmarktrecht' [2000] *Zeitschrift für Unternehmens- und Gesellschaftsrecht* 748, 769ff argues for having special rules for corporations that are active on the capital market.

and comparative perspective—in the opinion rendered by the Hamburg Max Planck Institute at the request of the Federal Ministry of Finance.[94] The 30 recommendations developed there have been published widely, e.g. in the German banking law review 'Wertpapier-Mitteilungen',[95] and need not be presented here in detail. The difficulties that arose later in the failed merger of the German Stock Exchange and London Stock Exchanges have illustrated impressively how urgent this reform is.[96] One proposal made was to soften the requirement of a public law structure of stock exchanges in Germany by giving them the option of having the structure of a private company limited by shares. If a stock exchange has the form of a private stock corporation, it would have the currency, i.e. its own shares, necessary for the making of or responding to international take-over bids, since cash payment offers in this range of size are difficult. The need for reform is also obvious when looking at supervision and international supervisory co-operation—even though, contrary to the view held by some, such an international co-operation, while difficult, would already be possible right now, both in practical and in legal terms.[97] The hope that the process of internationalization by itself would quickly lead to optimal solutions while legislators stand by idly, may be fallacious. Yet in the longer run, international competition of sites and states will have its way and lead to reform, even against the resistance from different camps and interests. The Fourth Financial Market Promotion Act which has just been enacted in June 2002 has dealt with a number of stock exchange problems, but for time reasons has not gone further. In September 2002 the German Lawyers' Association (Deutscher Juristentag Berlin) has come forward with the urgent plea for far-reaching reforms of stock exchange and capital market law. It remains to be seen whether and how far German legislators will dare to tackle fundamental stock exchange law reform in the forthcoming Fifth Financial Market Promotion Act 2003.

---

[94] K.J. Hopt, B. Rudolph, and H. Baum (eds.), *Börsenreform, Eine ökonomische, rechtsvergleichende und rechtspolitische Untersuchung* (Stuttgart, 1997), summary in K.J. Hopt and H. Baum, *WM Sonderbeilage* 4/1997 (comparative law) and the thorough contributions by H.J. Hellwig, 'Möglichkeiten einer Börsenreform zur Stärkung des deutschen Kapitalmarktes' [1999] *Zeitschrift für Unternehmens- und Gesellschaftsrecht* 781 and CP Claussen, [2000] *Zeitschrift für Bankrecht und Bankwirtschaft* 1; see also Opitz [1997] ÖBA 848; W. Gerke, 'Eine ökonomische, rechtsvergleichende und rechtspolitische Untersuchung' [1998] *Zeitschrift für betriebswirtschaftliche Forschung* 1167; V. Potthoff, [1998] *Zeitschrift für Wirtschafts- und Bankrecht* 154; G. Müller, [1999] *Kredit und Kapital* 322; cf. further the German Monopolies Commission, *Ordnungspolitische Leitlinien für ein funktionsfähiges Finanzsystem* [Sondergutachten 1998] comments 69ff (26). See also the legal opinion written at the request of the regional stock exchanges by T. Baums and U. Segna, *Börsenreform* 1998.

[95] Published also in [1997] *Zeitschrift für Wirtschafts- und Bankrecht* 1637.

[96] Cf. the contradicting opinions by Kümpel and H. Hammen, and U.H. Schneider and U. Burgard [2000] *Zeitschrift für Wirtschafts- und Bankrecht* -Sonderbeilage 3/2000, 3 and 24, and by E. Schwark (2000) *Zeitschrift für Wirtschafts- und Bankrecht* (WM) 2517.

[97] The problems of transborder securities supervision are dealt with by E. Kurth [2000] *Zeitschrift für Wirtschafts- und Bankrecht* (WM) 1521.

2. Further Development of Capital Market Law in the EU

The further development of capital market law is an important part of the European Commission's agenda. The Commission rightly intends to further modernize and partially harmonize the capital market law in the European Union. By 1999 it had already presented an activity framework for financial services.[98] In the meantime this plan has been carried further. The planned measures include the mutual recognition of the stock exchange prospectuses; the financing of newcomer enterprises that are not yet listed and the creation of legal rules for specialized risk capital funds; corporate governance; further development of the accounting and disclosure obligations; the development of a common understanding of the role of the auditor at law in view of making reliable information available to the investors and the capital markets within the European Union; the abolition of restrictions of investment for investment funds; equal conditions of competition for similar financial products; the elaboration of a so-called charter for supervisory agencies; the overhauling of the European Union's bank capital requirements in parallel to those recommended by the Basel Committee on Banking Supervision; the examination of the questions arising from the existence or formation of financial conglomerates; and the filling of legal lacunae in the area of payment and settlement systems for securities.

There is also considerable need in Germany for reform in the field of capital market law, e.g. as far as manipulation of stock markets is concerned.[99] The Forum of European Securities Commissions (FESCO) has presented a proposal that is intended to be the basis for a directive of the European Commission.[100] The Federal Supervisory Office for Securities Trading *(BAWe)* was involved in

[98] European Commission, *Umsetzung des Finanzmarktrahmens: Aktionsplan*, Brussels, May 11, 1999, COM (1999) 232 fin, reprinted in [1999] *Zeitschrift für Bankrecht und Bankwirtschaft* 254ff; European Commission, *Financial Services Priorities and Progress Third Report*, Brussels, November 8, 2000, COM(2000) 692/2 final; *Initial Report of the Committee of Wise Men on the Regulation of European Securities Markets*, Brussels, November 9, 2000 (*Lamfalussy* Committee); J. Mogg, 'Looking Ahead to the Next Century: EU Priorities for Financial Services' [1999] *Euredia* 9; K.J. Hopt, 'Europäisches Kapitalmarktrecht—Rückblick und Ausblick' in S. Grundmann (ed.), *Systembildung und Systemlücken in Kerngebieten des Europäischen Privatrechts* (Tübingen 2000) 307 (326ff); Federation of European Stock Exchanges (FESE), *Report and Recommendations on European Regulatory Structures*, Brussels, September 2000.

[99] References to books and journals concerning the problems of illegal manipulation and legal price maintenance (*Kurspflege*) can be found in A. Baumbach and K.J. Hopt, *HGB* 30th edn. (Munich 2000) 14 BörsG § 88 comment 1; see in particular U. Lenzen, 'Unerlaubte Eingriffe in die Börsenkursbildung' [2000]; ibid., [2000] *Zeitschrift für Bankrecht und Bankwirtschaft* 1131; K. Schäfer, [1999] *Zeitschrift für Bankrecht und Bankwirtschaft* 1345; M. Weber [2000] *Neue Zeitschrift für Gesellschaftsrecht* 113; from an international viewpoint, cf. C. Altendorfer, 'Kursmanipulationen am Wertpapiermarkt: Ein rechtsvergleichender Blick auf den Sanktionenbereich' in J. Aicher, S. Kalss, and M. Oppitz (eds.), *Grundfragen des neuen Börserechts* (Vienna 1998) 207.

[100] FESCO, *Market Abuse* (Paris June 19, 2000).

the work of harmonizing the relevant rules under the FESCO proposals.[101] In the meantime the European Commission has come up with a draft directive on insider dealing and market manipulation (market abuse)[102] which with certain changes has good chances to be adopted. German legislators took up some of these points, in particular stock price manipulation, when enacting the Fourth Financial Markets Promotion Act in June 2002.[103]

II. The Thirteenth Directive and the German Take-over Act

1. The Common Standpoint of the Thirteenth Directive and its Future After the Resolution of the European Parliament

The market for corporate control can only be mentioned very briefly since the discussion on take-overs is long-standing and in an advanced state. The Common Standpoint on the Thirteenth Directive concerning take-over bids as of June 2000 must be considered to be a reasonable compromise.[104] Yet the European Parliament in its legislative resolution dated December 13, 2000, has come up with a whole range of far-reaching modifications of the Common Standpoint, in toto twenty, including more rights for labour, a cash offer alternative, freedom for the board to take defensive action provided the supervisory organ[105] is in agreement, and a squeeze-out cash by the bidder who has reached 95 per cent of the voting stock. The most critical issues are the consideration to be offered in the mandatory bid, including a cash alternative, and the watering down of the duty of the board to refrain from frustrating action. Surprisingly enough, the highly controversial question as to which supervisory office should be competent for supervising international take-overs has not been taken up again by the European Parliament, even though Mr. Klaus-Heiner Lehne, the reporter of the legal affairs committee, had announced the unraveling of the

---

[101] FESCO, *Stabilization and Allotment, A European Supervisory Approach*, Consultative Paper (Paris September 15, 2000). Cf. K.J. Hopt/I. Waschkeit, 'Stabilisation and Allotment—A European Supervisory Approach'—Stellungnahme zum FESCO-Konsultationsdokument vom 15.9.2000, *2d Festschrift für Werner Lorenz*, Munich 2001, 147.

[102] European Commission, May 30, 2001 COM(2001) 281 final.

[103] See also the recommendations made in the Max Planck study that have been developed for the Federal Ministry of Finance, Hopt/Baum in: Hopt/Rudolph/Baum, *loc.cit.*, 287 (438 et seq.). Major points of this study have been taken up by the legislators (cf. the acknowledgment in the draft Act 172).

[104] Common Standpoint of the Council as of 19.6.2000, reprinted in *AG* 2000, 296. Cf. *Krause, NZG* 2000, 905; *Neye, AG* 2000, 289; *Pötzsch/Möller, WM Sonderbeil* 2/2000, 4 et eq.; *Hopt*, Auf dem Weg zum deutschen Übernahmegesetz—Gemeinsamer Standpunkt des Rates zur 13. Richtlinie und Diskussionsentwurf des Übernahmegesetzes, *Festschrift für Koppensteiner*, Vienna 2001, 61.

[105] This is not the supervisory board though the text is somewhat misleading.

complicated compromise reached. Under this compromise, competences are split between the supervisory bodies of the target and of the bidder, the former being entrusted with supervising the company law issues including neutrality of the board, and the latter with supervising the capital market issues.

Difficult negotiations led to the adoption of a joint text by the Conciliation Committee on 6 June 2000.[106] Yet when this text was presented to the European Parliament, it failed to obtain the required majority in the Plenary session on July 4, 2001. 273 members voted in favour and 273 members voted against the compromise text. The European Commission reacted by calling a High Level Group of Company Law Experts to make recommendations how to meet the demands of the Parliament and national governments, in particular Germany. It asked the Group to consider the following three issues:

—How to ensure the existence of a level playing field in the European Union concerning the equal treatment of shareholders across Member States;

—The definition of the notion of an 'equitable price' to be paid to minority shareholders;

—The right for a majority shareholder to buy out minority shareholders ('squeeze-out right').

The Group presented its recommendations in a report of January 10, 2002.[107] As to equal treatment it stated two principles: shareholder decision-making after announcement of the bid and proportionality between risk and control after the announcement of the bid. Its recommendation to introduce a break-through right after completion of the bid seemed to please Mr. Lehne, but scared national governments, in particular Germany and Sweden. The European Commission has announced to present a new draft in October 2002, though it is not yet sure how it would look like. It certainly will not go all the way the Group has recommended. While adopting the break-through rule for many take-over defenses, the European Commission will spare out double voting rights that are common in France and multiple voting rights that are common in Sweden. It hopes by this to get the necessary support by the European Council. Yet it is doubtful whether the European Parliament will accept this compromise for lack of a level playing field.

It is difficult to make a prognosis about the final outcome. The positions of the national governments, the European Parliament and the European Commission are very difficult to reconcile. In the worst case, the whole directive might fail to be adopted. This would be a real drawback for the European

---

[106] Joint text of the directive on company law concerning takeover bids, approved by the Conciliation Committee, Brussels, 19 June 2001, Document PE-CONS 3629/1/01 Rev 1.

[107] Report on Issues Related to Takeover Bids, Report of the High Level Group of Company Law Experts, Brussels, 10 January 2002, European Commission.

Commission, not only as to take-over regulation, but more generally for European company and capital market law harmonization.[108, 109]

2. The German Take-over Act as of December 2001

Since the fate of the Thirteenth Directive was uncertain, Germany has quickly promoted the preparatory work on its own planned Take-over Act. The need for Germany to be competitive as a financial market simply did not allow to wait any longer for the Thirteenth Directive. The Federal Ministry of Finance submitted a first draft for discussion in June 2000. Because of quite a number of critiques that were brought forward, the draft was revised.[110] The official ministerial draft bill was submitted by July 2001, and the Act was adopted in Parliament in December 2001. The Act has been in force since January 1, 2002.[111]

As to the content of the German act, the disclosure provisions, the mandatory bid and the procedure meet the common European standard. Yet the unambiguous obligation of both boards not to take frustrating actions against the bid that was still contained in the discussion draft was dropped at the intervention of the Chancellor himself on the suggestion of the Volkswagen company. While the prohibition for the board to take defensive action is still mentioned in the act, it is watered down by two highly controversial provisions. One provision allows the shareholders' meeting to permit the boards to take defensive actions within the next eighteen months. Furthermore the board by itself may, without needing the consent of the shareholders' meeting, take those actions that a board of a company that was not subject to a bid would have taken. The exact reach of the second provision is unclear. The first reactions of the jurisprudence give widely different interpretations to it. It remains to be seen how the courts will decide once a case comes up. In sum, the German take-over act, at least as to the prohibition of frustrating actions, is not up to the common European standard for takeovers.[112]

---

[108] Cf. more generally *Hopt*, Company Law in the European Union: Harmonisation and/or Subsidiarity?, (1999) 1 *International and Comparative Corporate Law Journal* 41.

[109] On harmonization of European company law, see *Habersack*, *Europäisches Gesellschaftsrecht* (Munich 1999), 96; *Steding*, *NZG* 2000, 913; *Wiesner*, *ZIP* 2000, 1792; *Wouters*, European Company Law: Quo vadis? *Common Market L. Rev.* 37 (2000) 257.

[110] Cf. *Pötzsch/Möller*, WM Sonderbeil 2/2000; *Land/Hasselbach*, *DB* 2000, 1747; *Hopt*, loc. cit., *Festschrift für Koppensteiner* (Vienna 2001), 61.

[111] See above, n. 21. *Federal Gazette* of December 20, 2001, vol. I, 3822. For a detailed analysis of the new act see K.J. Hopt. 'Grundsatz- und Praxisprobleme nach dem Wertpapiererwerbs- und Übernahmegesetz', (2002) 166 *Zeitschrift für das gesamte Handelsrecht und Wirtschaftsrecht* 375.

[112] Cf. as to this standard *Hopt*, Verhaltenspflichten des Vorstands der Zielgesellschaft bei feindlichen Übernahmen—Zur aktien- und übernahmerechtlichen Rechtslage in Deutschland und Europa—, in: *Festschrift für Lutter* (Cologne 2000), 1361.

III. Law, Codes, and Enforcement

1. Binding Law and Codes of Conduct

The corporate governance system in Germany is based heavily on mandatory law. Mandatory law is indeed indispensable in many ways. The tradition in Germany is quite different in this respect from, e.g. the British one, though even there the recent Financial Services and Markets Act 2000 is a big step in the direction of regulation and juridification. In Germany, the experiences with the Insider Trading Guidelines and even with the more recent German Take-over Code are not comfortable. While the latter has never reached broad acceptance, the Take-over Code of the Panel on Take-overs and Mergers has been applied throughout the City and even to foreign enterprises in thousands of cases. Some German companies, including large ones, have shown very little understanding for the Take-over Code and its consequences, for the industry as well as for the German system. This attitude must be considered shortsighted and, from an international perspective, even outright provincial. The consequences were obvious. This was already the case with the German Insider Trading Guidelines, and it has now become the case also with the German Take-over Act, which as of January 1, 2002 has replaced the German Take-over Code and is not only mandatory, but more far reaching in all respects. The signs of the times are international indeed. The German auditing profession and its professional representation at the IDW have understood this tide and are working hard to meet its challenges.

Codes of conduct that follow the British example and the example of many other countries are a good complement to mandatory law, provided they are meaningful, concrete, and respectful of the needs and possibilities of reality.[113] The Cadbury Report has set the standard. Together with two later reports, the Hampel Report and the Turnbull Report, it is now the basis for the Combined Code of the London Stock Exchange and is practically binding for listed companies.[114] The Codes of the OECD,[115] Principles of Corporate Governance of the European Association of Securities Dealers in Brussels,[116] and the German Code on Corporate Governance as of 2001[117] should also be mentioned here. The differences among all of them are considerable.

---

[113] Cf. most recently P. Hommelhoff, 'Chancen und Risiken der OECD Principles für das deutsche Gesellchafts-und Unternehmensrecht' in Symposium "Corporate Governance—European Perspectives", For the 60th Birthday of Klaus J. Hopt *ZGR* 2001, 238.

[114] The Combined Code, Principles of Good Governance and Code of Best Practice, May 2000.

[115] OECD, *Principles of Corporate Governance*, May 26/27, 1999, OECD *Financial Market Trends* no. 73, June 1999, 129ff.

[116] European Association of Securities Dealers (EASD), *Corporate Governance, Principles and Recommendations*, Brussels, May 2000.

[117] *Deutscher Corporate Governance Kodex (German Code of Corporate Governance)* as of February 26, 2002, reprinted also in *ZIP* 2002, 452 and *AG* 2002, 236.

2. Enforcement by Self-control

Corporate governance measures are useless without enforcement. Enforcement is therefore a key topic. This is undisputed in the legal and auditing profession, in theory as well as practice. The question that remains is how to enforce and whom to entrust with the enforcement. There is a good case for trying enforcement by self-control first.[118] Peer review dates back 25 years in the U.S. The German auditing profession has called for its introduction in Germany, and German legislators have enacted a reform Act on the Auditors Profession, which provides for such a review.[119] Yet peer review has its inherent limits. This is often misunderstood in public discussion. Peer review is a review of the system, and can by no means amount to one more audit.

Therefore, the IDW has proposed the introduction of an independent private supervisory body in Germany similar to the British Financial Reporting Review Panel.[120] Such a body would be composed of members of the various groups concerned and would be independent from and have its place beside peer review. The experiences gathered from the German Accounting Standards Committee in Berlin, which was formed according to section 342 of the Commercial Code, would be taken into consideration. The formation of such a body could be an important measure that would help to create and justify confidence. It is important to see that this would not amount to doubling the peer review. But the task of the panel would be to step in if there is a public discussion on the accuracy of a specific audit, or if a complaint has been made to the panel that a specific certificate of audit is unlawful. Peer review concentrates on the auditor, while the panel would concentrate on the specific audit.

---

[118] K.J. Hopt, 'Self-Regulation in Banking and Finance—Practice and Theory in Germany', in *La Déontologie bancaire et financière/The Ethical Standards in Banking & Finance* (Brussels 1998) 53.

[119] Draft Act, Wirtschaftsprüferordnungs-Änderungsgesetz (WPOÄG). Cf. P. Marks and S. Schmidt, 'Externe . . . Änderungsgesetzes (WPOÄG) [2000] *Die Wirtschaftsprüfung* 409; K.U. Marten and A. Köhler, 'WPO-Novelle. . . von Wirtschaftsprüfern in Deutschland' [2000] *Betriebs-Berater* 867; R.J. Niehus, 'Der Peer Review-Beirat . . . Oversight Board' [2000] *Die Wirtschaftsprüfung* 457 and 'Düsseldorf Peer Review in der deutschen Abschlussprüfung—Ein Berufsstand kontrolliert sich' [2000] *Der Betrieb* 1133; M.R. Theisen, 'Das Peer Review System in der Wirtschaftsprüfung aus der Sicht der Öffentlichkeit', in IDW, ed., *Kapitalmarktorientierte Unternehmensüberwachung—Chancen und Risiken* (Duesseldorf 2001), 461. On the discussion in the U.S., cf. S. Schmidt, 'Empfehlungen des Panels on Audit Effectiveness zur Verbesserung der Qualität der Abschlußprüfung' [2000] *Die Wirtschaftsprüfung* 793, 807ff.

[120] Cf. IDW, see above, n. 2, *FN-IDW* 6/2000, 229 (230); F.C. Janssen, 'Überlegungen zur Sicherung einer ordnungsmäßigen Rechnungslegung in Deutschland', in IDW, ed., *Kapitalmarktorientierte Unternehmensüberwachung—Chancen und Risiken* (Duesseldorf 2001), 301.

3. Enforcement by External Control

Enforcement by self-control must be supplemented by external control. This is true in the international context. At any rate, this corresponds to the German tradition. Yet self-control may have an impact on the necessity and the extent of external control. The introduction of a body entrusted with supervising markets or banks as well as companies is not even considered in Germany.[121] On the other hand, turning the German Federal Supervisory Office for Securities Trading (*BAWe*, since May 1st, 2002 united with the credit and insurance supervisory offices and renamed: German Office for Financial Services Supervision, *BAFin*) into a body with the competence and the powers to fully supervise the capital markets as in most of the other western industrialized states is indispensable.[122] Up to now its competencies have been restricted, because the supervision of stock exchanges was reserved to the ministerial supervisory bodies at the level of the state in which the stock exchange has its seat. Also, the competencies are enumerative and comprise only insider trading, including instant disclosure ('ad hoc disclosure'), the enforcement of the notification and publication obligations on changes of voting interests in listed companies, and the rules of conduct for investment firms stemming from the Investment Services Directive of the European Union, since January 1st 2002 also public take-overs. These restrictions are outdated. The question of whether there should be a role—and if so, which role—for the Federal Supervisory Office for Securities Trading toward auditors and accounting has started to be debated in Germany only recently,[123] a state of affairs that is quite different in the U.S. and other countries. The international discussion has gone further and deals now with a far more difficult and highly controversial question, namely whether a European banking and securities supervisory body (instead of, or in addition to, the national supervisory bodies) might make sense.[124] This is an issue that must be discussed further, even though a European answer is still unrealistic. This for political reasons, but may also be because supervision at the national level, i.e. on the scene, might be more efficient. On the national level there is a discussion as to whether one single financial markets supervisory body is preferable to having separate supervisory bodies. In Switzerland and at least some other

---

[121] References on the earlier discussion can be found in: K.J. Hopt, *Der Kapitalanlegerschutz im Recht der Banken* (Munich 1975) 526ff.

[122] K.J. Hopt and H. Baum in Hopt, Rudolph, and Baum, see above, n. 15, 287, 445ff.

[123] E.g. J. Henrichs, [2000] *Zeitschrift für Unternehmens- und Gesellschaftsrecht* 627, 648ff.

[124] G. Hertig, 'Regulatory Competition for EU Financial Services' [2000] *Journal of International Economic Law* 349, 373ff; R. Lee, 'Supervising EU Capital Markets: Do We Need a European SEC' in R.M. Buxbaum, G. Hertig, A. Hirsch, and K.J. Hopt, *European Economic and Business Law* (Berlin/New York 1996), 187 (European SEC); K. Lenaerts and A. Verhoeven, 'Towards a Legal Framework for Executive Rule-Making in the EU? The Contribution of the New Comitology Decision' [2000] 37 *Common Market Law Review* 645.

countries, bank supervision and securities and exchange supervision are concentrated in one supervisory body. For Switzerland, a governmental commission has just proposed an integrated financial market supervisory commission that would combine the functions until now held by the Swiss Banking Commission and the Swiss Federal Agency for Private Insurances.[125]

4. The Systemic Responsibility of the Auditing Profession

In summary, corporate governance in Germany is not in such a bad state as the American statements mentioned at the beginning might make us believe. But it is definitely in need of improvement. These improvements can no longer be left to the discretion of the responsible parties,[126] be it the Parliament, the judges, the companies, or the auditing profession. The global competition of capital markets and of sites and states simply does not permit this.

Jürgen Schrempp, the chairman of the board of Daimler-Chrysler, recently said at the Overseas Club in Hamburg: 'In a global village, the shortcomings and mistakes of governmental regulations are disclosed mercilessly. Industrial nations cannot profit from the advantages of the world economy and, at the same time, do without internal reforms'.[127] The German board and auditing reform of 1998 and the reform discussion that has been outlined in this chapter assign major influence and responsibility to the auditors as partners to the supervisory board. It can be stated without exaggeration that keeping the supervisory board system under the challenge of the Anglo-American unitary board system and, more generally, maintaining the German system of corporate governance in competition with other world-wide competing corporate governance systems will depend to an important degree on the auditors meeting the expectations of the German legislators and public as laid down in the 1998 Act. This implies that the auditing profession carries a high measure of responsibility.

[125] Expertengruppe Finanzmarktaufsicht, *Finanzmarktregulierung und -aufsicht in der Schweiz (Banken, Versicherungen, Allfinanz und Finanzkonglomerate, andere Finanzdienstleistungen)*, Final Report, Bern, November 2000 (*Zufferey*-Commission).

[126] E. Wymeersch, 'Globalization of Shareholdings and Corporate Governance' in Symposium "Corporate Governance—European Perspectives", For the 60th Birthday of Klaus J. Hopt, [2001] *Zeitschrift für Unternehmens- und Gesellschaftsrecht*, 294.

[127] J. Schrempp, Lecture given in the Übersee-Club Hamburg, May 7, 1999, in *Reden zum Übersee-Tag* (Hamburg, 1999), 68, 74.

E. Conclusion: 20 Theses

I. Systemic Elements of Corporate Governance in the International Discussion and the Use of these Elements in the German System

1. Six Systemic Elements of Corporate Governance in the International Discussion

In modern comparative corporate governance theory, the systemic elements of corporate governance are the following: a) the board (management board and supervisory board); b) labour co-determination and labour markets; c) financial intermediaries; d) stock exchange and capital markets; e) the market for corporate control; and f) disclosure and auditing.

2. Basic Premises in the Evaluation of the German System and its Development and Reform

There is no reason for changing the German system of corporate governance or for comprehensively reforming the German Stock Corporation Act. This does not exclude a number of specific reform measures.

There is a case against too much regulation and juridification. It leads to inflexibility and paralyses the forces of the market.

Liability is part of corporate governance, but it must not paralyse personal initiative and lead to risk aversion.

As regards the public there is a tendency to ask too much of the auditors ('expectation gap') and to hold them primarily responsible for failures in the system of corporate governance. Yet one must first turn to internal corporate governance, and to hold the shareholders themselves and the supervisory board primarily responsible, and only afterwards the auditors, who are to co-operate with the supervisory board. Effective external corporate governance by the stock exchanges, the capital market, and a functioning market for corporate control must supplement internal corporate governance.

II. Highlights for Reform: Internal Corporate Governance

1. Shareholder Activism

Large shareholders are typical for Germany. This is quite different from the U.S. The institutional shareholders have an important role to play. Their number and relevance are increasing in Germany also. But the private shareholders also have their part to play in internal corporate governance. They exercise it by their shareholder rights (including shareholder rights to sue, see German Lawyers Association Biannual Meeting 2000 in Leipzig).

2. Further Improvements Concerning the Board

Giving up the German two-tier board system in favour of the Anglo-American one-tier board is not the solution. Yet giving enterprises an option to choose between the two-tier and the one-tier board system as in France, Italy and under the new regime for the European Company would have advantages. Giving up the German labour co-determination is also not opportune at the moment ('path dependency').

One of the major tasks of inside corporate governance is the installation and constant improvement of suitable monitoring systems by the management board (section 91 para. 2 of the Stock Corporation Act) and its check by the supervisory board and to a limited extent, i.e. in case of officially listed companies (section 318 para. 4 of the Commercial Code) by auditors.

It is furthermore decisive to have a functioning flow of information from the management board to the supervisory board. This is particularly true for the enterprise planning and its implementation. The duties of the management board to inform the supervisory board and the rights of the latter to be informed must extend also to subsidiaries.

The communication between the supervisory board and the auditors must be further improved.

3. Auditors and Accounting

Mandatory external rotation of auditors cannot yet be recommended. As to the question of mandatory separation between auditing and consulting, the U.S.-American development must be watched carefully because of its possible influence on Europe.

Group accounts must be steadily internationalized. Section 292a of the German Commercial Code is only of a temporary nature and its validity is doubtful under constitutional law. In Europe, accounting is developing toward the International Accounting Standards (IAS). A conflict between these standards and the U.S. GAAP should be avoided as far as possible but cannot be excluded.

The single accounts must become even more meaningful. Single accounts and group accounts should not deviate too much from each other.

Quarterly reporting by listed enterprises is necessary, but it should be left to the stock exchanges and the markets rather than the legislators.

III. Highlights for Reform: External Corporate Governance

1. Stock Exchange and Capital Markets

A fundamental reform of German stock exchange law is long overdue. The international competition of sites and states will finally have its way even against resistance from different camps and interests. The difficulties that have arisen in the failed merger of the German Stock Exchange and the London Stock Exchanges have illustrated once more how urgent this reform is. The modernization and partial harmonization of the capital market law in the European Union must be carried further.

2. The Thirteenth Directive and the German Take-over Act

The Common Standpoint of the Thirteenth Directive on Take-overs is a reasonable compromise. The vote of the European Parliament unravelling this compromise endangers the enactment of the Directive altogether. In view of this Germany was not able to wait for the enactment of the Directive, but came up with the German Take-over Act of 2002. The mandatory bid requirement and the duty to refrain from frustrating action belong to the European minimum standard for take-over laws. The duty to refrain from frustrating action does not prevent the management board from evaluating the bid and stating clearly if it thinks it's not in the best interest of the shareholders of the target.

3. Law, Codes, and Enforcement

Not all corporate governance reforms in Germany need legislative intervention and mandatory laws. Codes of conduct that follow the British example and the example of many other countries are a good complement, provided they are meaningful, concrete, and respectful of the needs and possibilities of the practice.

Even the best reform measures are of no avail if they are not well enforced. Enforcement can and should first be by self-control. The recent introduction of the peer review by German legislators—initiated by the auditing profession and its professional body, the Institute of German Auditors (IDW)—is to be welcomed. The Institute's proposal of establishing an independent private supervision body similar to the British Financial Reporting Review Panel merits great attention.

Enforcement by self-control must be supplemented by external control. In any case, this corresponds to the German tradition. Yet self-control may have an impact on the necessity and the extent of external control. The introduction of a body entrusted with supervising markets or banks as well as companies is not even considered in Germany. On the other hand, turning the German Federal Supervisory Office for Securities Trading into a body with the competence and the powers to fully supervise the capital markets as in most of the other western industrialized states is indispensable. The question which role the Federal Supervisory Office for Securities Trading should have toward auditors and accounting and whether a European supervisory body (instead of or in addition to the national supervisory bodies) makes sense, must be discussed further.

In the global competition of sites and states, the better system of corporate governance has an edge. The German legislators who enacted the German Reform Act of 1998 (board and auditors law reform) have entrusted the auditing profession with the role of partner of the supervisory board. This is a responsibility for the whole system of corporate governance that the auditing profession must meet actively to prevent the system as well as the profession from suffering harm.

13

Impact of Take-overs and their Regulation on French Company Law and Practice

LAURENT FAUGÉROLAS*

Contents

A. Introduction

When a tender offer is launched, it gives rise to an exceptional situation in the life of a company by putting divergent interests face to face. On the one hand, there is the interest of the target, which is naturally to pursue its business in order to make profits. On the other hand, there is the interest of the market, which views a tender offer as a capitalistic, or even speculative operation. From the latter vantage point, the shareholders, regardless of their stake in the share capital of the target company, have to benefit from the operation at least as if no offer had been launched.

In accordance with the *Code Monétaire et Financier* (French Securities Law Code), the regulating of tender offers falls within the scope of the *Conseil des Marchés Financiers* (Financial Markets Board), (known as the *CMF*) under the control of the *Commission des opérations de bourse* (called the *COB*), which is the French stock exchange commission. Within the scope of this legal framework, the *CMF* has drafted regulations (the *Règlement Général*), including Title V devoted to the rules governing tender offers.

The unique feature of the French system lies in the fact that the task of regulating and overseeing the tender offer process in the French stock exchange is entrusted to the *CMF*, a professional body. The latter supervises the implementation of the rules it has adopted. Beyond this paradox, however, it is obvious that stock exchange regulations tend to develop autonomously, as the system governing tender offers illustrates.

The fundamental principles governing French company law are theoretically applicable during a take-over period. Even though the *Code de Commerce*

* Avocat au Barreau de Paris, Partner, Willkie Farr & Gallagher.

(French Company Law Code) already provided for certain specific features in the event of a tender offer, the question of imposing a system of exceptions when a tender offer is launched has never been addressed. Yet today there are some manifest divergences between the rules stated by company law and the regulations covering tender offers.

Among these divergences, the question of complying with company interest during the tender offer period appears particularly interesting insofar as it involves a conflict between two different uses of the notion: the interests of the shareholders and the market, and those of the firm.

Company interest is a fundamental notion under French company law; it may be considered as the mutual interest of the shareholders concerning the proper operation of the company. This notion, which is omnipresent in the *Code de Commerce*, guides all the principles of French company law.

A tender offer period gives rise to an exceptional situation in which the interests of the shareholders may diverge from those of the company's management, turning the application of the rules of French company law, based on co-operation among the players to ensure the durability of the company, into a complex issue.

Thus the study of the impact of tender offer regulations in France on company law and their practice must be carried out from the standpoint of this fundamental notion of company interest, which will allow us to emphasize the difficulty for both the initiator and the target company in reconciling their conflicting interests.

B. Launching a Tender Offer and Complying with Company Interest

The study of the impact of regulating tender offers on company law and their practice requires a brief review of the fundamental mechanisms of French company law. It is mainly governed by the principle of company interest, which is very much present in the *Code de Commerce* on commercial companies, as well as by case law and legal doctrine. A short overview of the principles of French company law will allow us to underscore the possible divergences between the rules of company law and those governing tender offers on the French stock market.

I. Company Interest, the Fundamental Principles of French Company Law

Company law is designed to organize the relationship of shareholders into a specific social structure. It is thus contractual by nature, as article 1832 of the French Civil Code attests:

A company is made up of two or more persons who agree by contract to grant to a joint enterprise property or their industry in view of sharing the profits or taking advantage of the saving that may result from it . . .

Thus, numerous principles of contract law also govern company law. For example, the prohibition against unilaterally increasing a shareholder's commitments is similar to the prohibition against aggravating a debtor's debt to a company or a third party against his will. Similarly, the company cannot provide for the exclusion of a shareholder, in accordance with article 1134 of the French Civil Code, which stipulates that legally formed agreements cannot be revoked except by mutual consent of those that concluded them.

A company is therefore a contract by which several persons decide to become associated and agree upon their relationship and the method of operating of their group, in the form of bylaws adapted to their needs.

Nevertheless, there is a principle that limits the contractual scope and explains certain restrictions imposed by the law of July 24, 1966, namely, company interest. The notion of company interest has not been clearly defined either by legislators or by the courts. It is, however, a fundamental concept of French company law, in the sense that it is the source of most of the rules of company law. It explains, for example, the power given to the majority to impose its decisions, as well as the right of a judge to intervene in the course of company life, for example against majority or minority abuses, to name temporary directors, or to order a valuation to be carried out, etc.

Indeed, company interest is understood to mean the mutual interest of the shareholders. It refers to the consensual character of the company contract. In this sense, a resolution adopted by the shareholders in view of satisfying their interests will be in conformity with the interests of the company, because it has been adopted collectively.

In a limited liability company, the most prevalent form of companies listed on the stock exchange, the shareholders make contributions, in exchange for which they obtain rights in the company, particularly the right to share the profits, the right to vote, and the right to withdraw from the company. Their interest in sharing the profits is linked implicitly to the company's enrichment, and to enable this enrichment, they enjoy the possibility of taking part in approving decisions by voting at the annual meeting. Thus, if a disagreement persists, they must be able to withdraw from the capital.

Moreover, the company's prosperity leads to the enrichment of both company assets and shareholder assets, in such a way that the interests of the latter coincide with those of the company. In some situations, however, it will be necessary to choose between these interests when they have become divergent. In this case, the notion of majority takes on its full meaning. Indeed, it is possible to postulate that in every instance, the company interest will be that which the shareholders have decided to satisfy, and the decision will be valid only because it was made in accordance with the procedures defined by law or by the bylaws from a contractual point of view.

Complying with company interest becomes one of the decisive stakes within the scope of a tender offer. Indeed, a tender offer creates an exceptional situation in the life of the company, in which the interests of the social bodies meet in a face-to-face conflict. Yet there is no question in the *Code de Commerce* of applying a system of exceptions to this particular situation affecting the target. Rather, in this case traditional principles of company law, though adapted, are applied. It is therefore legitimate to be interested in finding out whether the fundamental principles governing company law are applied during the tender offer period.

II. Tender Offer Regulations from the Standpoint of the Notion of Company Interest

Stock market regulations have developed gradually in a slightly different direction, being highly favourable to tender offers, which are perceived as energizing and animating factors of the markets. Hence, it appeared essential to encourage the negotiation of the shares of target companies, particularly from the viewpoint of the principles that gradually grew out of this market practice. Thus, the transparency and security of transactions, the principles of competition and the free play of bidding, or yet again, the equal treatment of shareholders were all established as veritable dogmas.

In its regulation no. 89-03, the *COB* laid down the overreaching principles that are to guide the actions of both the initiator and the target during a tender offer. Indeed, in article 3, the regulation provided that "during a tender offer, the initiator and the target company must ensure that their acts, decisions and declarations do not result in compromising the company interest and the equal treatment or information of the shareholders of the companies concerned". Regulation no. 89-03 has been modified and replaced recently by regulation no. 2002-04. Please note that such change has not affected the foregoing principle.

It would therefore seem that the principles of company law would apply during a tender offer. It is possible, however, to detect a number of divergences between stock exchange regulations relating to tender offers and company law concerning the situation of both shareholders and management.

Shareholders of public companies have only a limited number of prerogatives. They mainly enjoy two recognized rights: the right to sell their shares and to vote on the direction to be followed by company management at annual meetings. At the same time, both of these rights are affected by the launching of a tender offer.

As far as the shareholders' right to sell their shares is concerned, their prerogatives are restricted due to the fact that some types of transfer are prohibited during a tender offer or strictly controlled by special procedures, such as the price guarantee aimed at organizing the transfer of a majority of shares. Moreover, questions have been raised as to the validity of commitments made by a shareholder to offer his shares in a tender offer that must later be registered by the beneficiary of the commitment. Indeed, it is quite common that the offerer will attempt to ensure the success of the operation by means of concluding such agreements with certain shareholders. The *COB* has refused to validate these commitments, however, when they carry a risk of impeding the free play of competition and bidding. In this case, the debtor that does not contribute his shares to the tender offer cannot be held contractually liable, despite an obvious violation of his commitment, which is contrary to the fundamental principles of contract and tort law. In this instance, stock market regulations prevail and impose their requirements.

The shareholders' right to decide is also affected by the launching of a tender offer. Thus the decision to transform a limited liability company into a limited partnership with shares, carries with it the obligation for the shareholder(s) with controlling interest in the company to launch a buyout and therefore to buy back the shares of minority shareholders. Similarly, if the *CMF* deems it necessary, the majority shareholder will be required to file a buyout plan when it proposes at an extraordinary general meeting several major changes in the by-laws, particularly provisions pertaining to the legal form of the company, the terms of sale, and transfer of share capital and the rights relating thereto.

In both of these hypotheses, the prerogative offered to the minority shareholders, is a total exception to majority rule in company law. These adjustments to the rules that prevail in the absence of a tender offer make it possible to strengthen the protection of minority shareholders.

The question of carrying out capital increases during a tender offer also illustrates the exceptional nature of the tender offer situation. Indeed, the *Code de Commerce* provides for the right of a shareholders' meeting to delegate to the board of directors the authority to conduct a capital increase. The *Code Monétaire et Financier* restricted this right. The delegation of authority to the board of directors is indeed suspended during a take-over bid or share exchange, unless the shareholders' meeting has expressly authorized a capital increase prior to the tender offer for a period not to exceed one year, provided the increase is not reserved. Aside from the fact that these restrictions reduce the means of the target company to counter-attack against the offer, particularly by reserving the capital increase to a white knight, it would seem that the decision-making powers of the shareholders' meeting are also affected thereby. Indeed, the shareholders' meeting is no longer free to make decisions that could weigh on the outcome of the tender offer. Market rules consider, in fact, that the right to respond to the offer belongs to each shareholder, rather than coming under the scope of the shareholders' meeting. Hence, there is a real contradiction with the principles of company law stated above.

The shareholders' meeting is not, however, the only body that sees its operations disturbed during the tender offer period. Management action also appears to be paralysed by the launching of a tender offer. Aside from their obligation not to compromise company interest or equal treatment and information given to shareholders, which is required at all times in the life of the company, the management powers of senior executives are sharply restricted during a tender offer period. Indeed, *COB* regulation no. 2002-04 states:

> If the target company and persons acting in concert with it wish to perform actions other than those related to the management of ordinary operations, with the exception of actions expressly authorized by the shareholders' meetings called during the tender offer, the management of the target company shall inform the *COB* so that the latter may ensure that the public is informed and make known, if applicable, its opinion.

At first glance, this rule does not prohibit acts other than those of ordinary management, but simply stipulates the obligation to inform the *COB* of such acts. The stated principle is tantamount, however, to prohibiting the top management of the target company from performing any acts that go beyond ordinary management. This interpretation has been strengthened, moreover, by article 5 of the European directive that requires the top management, unless otherwise authorized by the shareholders' meeting, to refrain from "deciding to carry out operations of a nature other than that of ordinary operations concluded under normal conditions".

The company thus sees its general operations impeded. The top management must restrict itself to managing ordinary business, until the results have been made public. Consequently, several months can go by without the target being able to pursue its activity normally. Moreover, this prohibition extends to the whole group, which can also prove to be contrary to company interest by considerably impeding the target company's strategy. Thus, in the recent examples of tender offers, it is possible to mention the fact that the bid launched by Banque Nationale de Paris to take over Société Générale and Paribas was aimed at preventing Société Générale from completing its projects, particularly to oppose the merger planned with Paribas.

Regulating tender offers also lays down terms that are exceptions to the principles of company law, often in the sense of reducing the target company's room to manoeuvre. Indeed, it is based primarily on the principles governing stock exchange regulations that attest to the specific features of tender offer law. Among the justifications put forward to explain the exceptional nature of the regulations governing tender offers is the idea that a company that wishes to gain access to the stock markets must go along with the requirement to adjust some of its operating rules.

C. Adapting the Principle of Company Interest to Comply with the Specific Features of Stock Market Law

It is necessary to go beyond the mere observation of divergences and sometimes even incompatibilities between company law and tender offer regulations, and to present the specific features of the regulations governing tender offers.

I. The Impact on Regulating Tender Offers from Listed Companies

1. Underlying Principles of Tender Offer Regulations

The *CMF* drafted new regulations in 1998 concerning tender offers and amended them again in 2000. These regulations are more or less in line, however, with the previous ones and the principles underlying the regulations have not changed. Tender offer regulations are therefore organized in such a way as to ensure the equal rights of the shareholders and market transparency. The *CMF* intended to stipulate expressly in its regulations the principles underlying them. These principles consist of equal shareholder rights and market transparency and integrity as well as fairness in transactions and competition. Going beyond a mere declaration of intention, the *CMF* clearly intended to specify and clarify the essential principles that were to govern tender offers, so that these principles could serve as an autonomous source of *CMF* decisions in the future.

2. Tender Offer Regulations

Mandatory tender offers were set up in France mainly in order to protect minority shareholders, by allowing them to sell their shares in the event of significant changes affecting the company's shareholder structure. They are therefore quite exceptional measures, which have no equivalent in companies that are not listed on the stock exchange. A tender offer must be made in all cases where the ownership threshold of one third of the voting rights or shares held in the capital of a company admitted to trading on a regulated market is exceeded, or whenever a person acting alone or in concert, already holding between $\frac{1}{3}$ and 50% of company shares or voting rights, increases his stake by more than 2% in less than 12 consecutive months.

Exceptions to the foregoing rules are provided for, particularly for situations that, in fact, do not require launching a tender offer, either because the offer procedure is deemed to be inappropriate, or because it would serve no purpose with regard to the objectives pursued, as the protection of minority shareholders can be ensured by other means.

3. Particular Features of Tender Offer Regulations

Special tender offer procedures have been provided for the event that, within the listed company, there is already a shareholder acting alone or in concert holding a majority of voting rights or capital. These procedures are applied when the majority shareholder decides to sell its shares. Once again, there is no equivalent procedure for unlisted companies.

a. *Garantie de Cours*

The aim of the *garantie de cours* (standing market offer) is to allow minority shareholders to withdraw from the company at the same price as the one offered to the majority shareholder for the transfer of his block of shares. This regulation, as provided for in the *Règlement Général* of the *CMF*, presents undeniable advantages compared to a tender offer, such as the absence of bidding, price modulation, flexibility and rapidity of transaction, etc. Like the majority shareholder, minority shareholders may thus benefit from the valuation linked to premium control. A special procedure has thus been provided for, which requires the buyer to accept any sales proposal from a minority shareholder for a period not to exceed 10 market days, at the price at which the transfer of the majority stake is to be or has already been paid. Article 5-4-3 of the new *Règlement Général* of the *CMF* provides for a return to mandatory tender offers in specific cases. Transactions that meet the criteria of *garantie de cours* but are combined with related items likely to affect the equality between the price paid for the majority block and the price offered to the other shareholders may be governed by tender offer regulations. In this case, the problem lies in defining what we mean by "related" items. The new *Règlement Général* of the *CMF* also authorizes a return to mandatory tender offers when the block(s) are acquired from persons who did not previously hold, either alone or jointly, a majority of the company voting rights.

b. The Buyout

The buyout is designed to give minority shareholders the right to transfer their shares to majority shareholders under certain circumstances, particularly in the case of a majority stakeholder with at least 95% of company voting rights and in the event of major modifications of the target. The *CMF* has given itself the power clearly to require a buyout by the majority shareholder when this procedure is deemed to be legitimate.

4. Recent Reforms

The current trend at the *CMF* since 1997 has been to allow target companies to better resist hostile take-over bids. Thus, the 1997 reforms, aimed either at extending the minimum offer period (up to 35 market days in the case of a hostile take-over bid), or at lowering the threshold for statements of intention, were intended for this purpose. Similarly, article 5-2-9 of the *Règlement Général* of the *CMF* formulates a very special case of an exception to the principle of offer irrevocability. Thus, the initiator may terminate its offer if, during the offer period, the target company adopts measures leading to definite, immediate modifications of its substance or if the offer becomes irrelevant. This provision therefore seems to leave a certain amount of room to manoeuvre to targets of hostile take-over bids, particularly to take defence measures intended to discourage the initiator. Recent market battles, notably the one pitting Elf Aquitaine against TotalFina, testify to this. In reaction to the TotalFina take-over bid, Elf first adopted a "pacman" defence by initiating, in turn, a bid to take-over Total. In the end, TotalFina raised the bidding through an exchange offer that was favourably received by the board of directors of Elf Aquitaine. Nevertheless, Elf could not withdraw under the current state of tender offer regulations, and it was on the basis of article 5–2–9 that the *CMF* authorized it to withdraw.

It appears from these examples that the *CMF* has acquired more definite power from the new regulations and now disposes of a broader margin of assessment based on less rigid criteria.

II. Comparing Company Law with Tender Offer Regulations

The multiplication of hostile take-over bids in France since the summer of 1997 has once again raised the question of the means of action available to the target company during a hostile take-over bid. Indeed, the room to manoeuvre for a target company whose top management has to restrict itself to carrying out only ordinary management acts is reduced during a tender offer. The regulation rules out, moreover, the possibility for the target company to oppose the initiator of a tender offer with a right of first refusal for the target aimed at preventing the initiator from acquiring the target company's shares. More generally, current regulations governing tender offers are based on the principle according to which any defences that absolutely prevent the launching of a tender offer are prohibited. From this standpoint, numerous acts of senior executives, which would incidentally be lawful during the normal course of the life of a company, are affected and restricted during a tender offer period.

1. Preventive Self-defence Measures Accepted by Company Law

Numerous preventive strategies have been implemented by listed companies to cope with possible hostile take-over bids. The question of their validity, however, is at the very core of the conflict between company law and stock exchange regulations. Indeed, while these measures are lawful from the stand-point of company law, they contravene, however, certain principles of stock exchange regulations.

This is the case for alarm systems and the *identification of the assailants* in particular: such as the possibility of the company demanding of shareholders to register their shares by name beyond a certain holding threshold, or the obliga-tion to notify the stock exchange authorities should the thresholds of voting rights exceed $\frac{1}{20}$, $\frac{1}{10}$, $\frac{1}{5}$, $\frac{1}{3}$, $\frac{1}{2}$ or $\frac{2}{3}$, thresholds which can be lowered in the articles of incorporation to 0.5%, or the obligation to make a statement (*déclaration d'intention*) for shareholders exceeding the thresholds of $\frac{1}{10}$ and $\frac{1}{5}$. These measures are accepted completely by both company law and stock exchange regulations.

Next, there are measures intended to *reinforce the power of leading sharehold-ers*. The by-laws may thus provide for *double voting rights* in favour of shares for which registration in the name of one shareholder has been justified for at least two years. Shareholders frequently use this advantage by holding their shares through the intermediary of a holding company that is not listed on the stock exchange. Company by-laws can also set up a statutory levelling-off of voting rights, and can even prohibit a shareholder from holding a number of shares exceeding a pre-determined threshold. Such a measure cannot, however, be maintained in the event of a successful tender offer and the *COB* (French stock exchange commission) has ruled that these bylaw restrictions become automat-ically obsolete as soon as a shareholder reaches a certain shareholding threshold at the outcome of a tender offer.

Similarly, the traditional solutions of *concentrating power*, particularly through holding companies or shareholders' agreements, seldom exist in com-panies open to take-over bids, as their shareholder structure is by nature extremely fragmented. The hostile position taken by the *COB* towards *poison pill* procedures eliminates any interest in them. In 1998, in the *Bénédictine* case, the *COB* deemed that the company had to refrain from implementing any clause that would grant to a third party an option on the most advantageous assets of the company or allow the third party to suddenly break off a contractual rela-tion with the company in the event of a change of majority holding, specifying that "this type of clause was designed to impede tender offers and therefore the normal operation of the market". This clear-cut position of the COB has numer-ous consequences, since the target will not be free to dispose of major or strate-gic assets during the tender offer period. The commercial partners of the target company will not be able to provide for a withdrawal clause in the event of a change of the controlling shareholder, or in any case, take advantage of it during a tender offer period. Stock exchange regulations appear in this case to be particularly restrictive. These limitations may ultimately be harmful at one point or another to the target company. These operations will indeed be suspended throughout the tender offer. Yet, in some cases, operations must be carried out quickly; an interruption linked to a tender offer could well be damaging for the company. Moreover, it is always possible that the offerer draws out the offer period, and delaying tactics have been widely used by some, particularly with a view to putting pressure on the target company.

With regard to the possibility for a limited liability company (*société anonyme*) to transform itself into a limited partnership with shares (called "SCA", *société en commandite par actions*), stock exchange regulations once again set limits on company law. Indeed, protecting the interests of minority shareholders in listed companies has led to implementing, in some cases, the possibility for shareholders to withdraw through a buyout. The transformation of a limited liability company into a limited partnership with shares is indeed one of the cases for launching a buyout. Thus, the right to transform a limited liability company into a limited partnership with shares is highly conditional and often limited by the consequent obligation to register a buyout. In this case, stock exchange regulations are added to the terms provided for by company law, and above all restrict the exercise of this right. Again with regard to a buyout, we would note the new powers recognized as belonging to the *CMF* since it can now require the filing of a buyout after major structural changes have occurred in a listed company. This control was given to the *CMF* in order to allow minority shareholders to withdraw from the company. Yet, these are again exceptional measures as far as company law is concerned, for which majority rule is authoritative. Incidentally, one might say more generally that the measures specific for listed companies aimed at protecting the interests of minority shareholders are always, in one way or another, exceptions to the principle of the majority.

2. Means of Action During a Tender Offer Period

a. Issuing Capital During a Tender Offer

Since 1994, there has no longer been any doubt as to the possibility of using authorizations for capital increases given by the shareholders' meeting to the board of directors during a tender offer period, provided that these authorizations refer expressly to the offer period, that the issue is not reserved and, naturally, that company interest is complied with. This right is not as advantageous as it might appear, however: the impossibility of carrying out a reserved capital increase forces top management to choose between two rather unattractive options, either to maintain preferential subscription rights, which are by nature transferable for the benefit of the assailant, and merely shift the purpose of the offer to the preferential subscription rights, or to eliminate them, which opens up even wider share acquisition possibilities to the offerer. In all of these cases, the rights of the target company have been affected, since the company is denied its right to issue shares to an individual beneficiary.

b. Extraordinary Meeting of Shareholders During a Tender Offer

Article 5-2-2 of the *Règlement Général* of the *CMF* provides that the length of the tender offer period must be from 25 to 35 market days in the case of a hostile take-over bid, and that the initiator of a tender offer has the right to initiate the withdrawal of one's offer, with the agreement of the *CMF*, in the event that the target company adopts measures of definite and immediate application which would modify its substance or if the offer becomes irrelevant. However this does not make sense unless we admit the right of the target company to defend itself by taking steps that exceed ordinary management actions. Thus operations such as capital increases and reductions, exceptional dividend distributions, mergers, strategic asset acquisition or disposal would be lawful. The COB regulation 89-03, replaced by regulation 2002–04, seemed to be trying to limit the company that is the target of a tender offer to carrying out only ordinary management actions. This is indeed the majority interpretation adopted by the doctrine, given that any operation outside of this scope is subject to the control of the *COB*.

Recent decisions, particularly in the cases of Rallye-Promodès or BNP-Société Générale-Paribas, have shown that some defensive measures, which would undoubtedly have been considered unlawful previously, have been accepted. Thus the right to use share subscription forms of which the market was aware has been recognized, along with the right to use a block of treasury stock shares, even during a tender offer. These authorizations may indicate a tendency towards softening stock market regulations in favour of complying with the principles of company law.

However, the new regulation no. 2002-04 of the *COB* provides that the target company may repurchase its own shares during an offer period when the offer is paid entirely in cash, only in connection with an existing share purchase programme (*programme de rachat*), with the express authorization of the shareholders' meeting and provided such programme has already been implemented. In all of these cases, one must avoid a system that would, by its effect, make a competing tender offer inoperative, and therefore prevent any take-over by another initiator. The principle of free competition is given wide preference in this instance compared to the traditional rules of company law. If counter-attack mechanisms have been somewhat improved in recent years, the principles of giving free play to bidding and to competition, equal treatment of shareholders, etc. largely prevail, as we have seen, whenever there is a conflict between company law and stock exchange regulations.

D. Conclusion

The comparison of the fundamental principles of French company law with French tender offer regulations allows us to underscore the prevalence of the latter during tender offers. Indeed, the provisions of the *Code de Commerce* retreat in the face of the requirements of stock market mechanisms, especially tender offers, regardless of their nature. The issue is thus to determine whether these exceptions to the *Code de Commerce* are such as to affect adversely the interest of the target company. The most striking example is prohibiting the top management of a public company targeted by a take-over bid from carrying out any acts other than those of ordinary management. This provision was set up, in particular, so that the target company could not modify its legal form or its substance during the tender offer, either to make the take-over more difficult or to cause the initiator to lose interest in the target company. The outcome of this principle may nevertheless be to paralyse the target company, especially as the total tender offer period may be extended if all the available possibilities of recourse are used. This case raises the question of pursuing company interest as the sole purpose of company management, especially if company interest is assimilated to shareholder interest.

In public companies, these shareholders are mainly investors, in the sense that their primary objective is speculative and financial. They are not partners in the traditional sense of the term, in other words their stake in the capital of the company is not connected to any *intuitu personae*. Moreover, the prerogatives of the minority shareholders of a public company are restricted: their participation in the life of the company is reduced insofar as their access to information resulting from legal obligations is often insufficient. Furthermore, they do not have certain rights such as the right to have a resolution put on the agenda of a shareholders' meeting, unless they are able to rally enough shareholders to represent 5% of company share capital to ask written questions, request a management assessment, or disclaim the competence of the statutory auditor.

Consequently, the genuine prerogative of a shareholder of a public company, in his capacity as owner of his shares, is that of being free to transfer them. This prerogative takes on its full significance during a tender offer period, since it is by contributing to the offer or, on the contrary, by abstaining from it, that the shareholder can decide the outcome. The primacy of market regulations over company law during the tender offer period illustrates the need to first and fore-most protect the interests of the shareholders.

Finally, stock market regulations have developed autonomously, particularly as regards tender offers. The tender offer system is thus established and con-trolled by a sole authority and implements specific mechanisms which differ from the principles governing company law, even if the fundamental principles of the latter, particularly compliance with company interest, continue to be extremely important.

14

Shareholder Value: A New Standard for Company Conduct

CHRISTIAN KIRCHNER

Contents

A. Introductory Remarks

The chapters by Guido Ferrarini and Paul Davies are both discussing *one* problem but from different perspectives. Whereas the Ferrarini chapter chooses an economic approach and puts corporate law issues into the framework of finance theory, the Davies chapter starts with a common law perspective and then re-conceptualizes the problem as an issue of capital market law. Thus both chapters end up with an analysis that show certain similarities. If I should try to grossly simplify the line of arguments of both papers, I would state that company law today is more or less inconclusive as far as "shareholder value" is concerned, whereas capital market law is the decisive factor for the definition of the shareholder value concept.

Both chapters are too complex to be reviewed here in detail. I would rather try to highlight what I believe are the essential arguments and to criticize those arguments that in my view should be clarified. In order to be able to do this, I shall first outline the analytical framework and then put the discussion of the two chapters into this framework.

B. Incentives and Sanctions for Shareholders and Stakeholders

Legal rules and provisions constitute constraints and incentives for the actors who are the addressees of those rules and provisions. Those addressees are individual actors who try to attain their individual goals, as managers, employees, shareholders, creditors, and so on. Company law defines the powers of certain actors who have to take decisions that affect the enterprise, thus creating incentives and constraints for these actors. *Governance structure* is nothing else than a set of rules that contain incentives and constraints for managers, employees, shareholders and creditors. When we ask which decisions managers should take this is nothing else than putting together two different questions:

(1) Which decisions will be rewarded by special earnings (incentive rules)?
(2) Which decisions will (with a certain probability) lead to extra-costs (sanctions)?

If we look to shareholders' decisions we will find a different problem: being the residual claimants, shareholders are interested in receiving a better return on their investment in a specific enterprise than they could otherwise achieve. Thus they are interested in finding managers who are successful in attaining their (the shareholders') goals. The so-called agency-problem is only one part of the problem; minimizing agency costs does not help investors if their agents have no capabilities and incentives to raise return on investment. Shareholders must be interested in writing intelligent contracts with managers, finding a good mix between incentives, and reducing agency costs. Company law is more or less an attempt to write standard contract terms for those relational contracts. The shareholders may either try to improve the given contracts if the results are unsatisfactory; or they may sell their shares and contracts to others. This exit option as such is an implicit contract clause and works as a constraint for managers. But the exit option contains a specific problem: the collective action problem. The total group of shareholders may reach a better result, i.e. a better price for their contract if they are able to co-ordinate their individual decisions.

Where are the stakeholders and the creditors in this picture? The stakeholders are contract parties of the company; those contracts are concluded between managers and stakeholders. These contracts lead to agency-problems in the relationship between managers and shareholders. The same is true for contracts between managers and creditors. If rules of mandatory law provide that managers' decisions (not only those directly concerning the contracts at stake) take into account stakeholders' interests, those rules do not directly improve the position of stakeholders. They do not get better contractual conditions (one could argue that not taking into account stakeholders' interests constitutes a breach of contract, but at present this line of argument has not been developed). On the other side it is evident that the agency-relationship between shareholders and managers has been affected if managers may evade civil liability by arguing that a decision that is not in the best interest of shareholders may be justified by stakeholders' interests. The controversy over stakeholder or shareholder concepts in company law thus boils down to a specific defence for managers in derivative actions by shareholders against managers.

C. Profit Maximization Versus Shareholder Value Maximization

Ferrarini asks whether corporate law is concerned with shareholder value creation and distinguishes between profit maximization and shareholder value maximization. Is this really a question that has to be answered by corporate law as such or rather by specific provisions written into contracts between shareholders and managers? Shareholders would easily find out that "profit maximization" is a very vague term and that "shareholder value maximization" is not much better. For the purpose of attacking managers' decisions in derivative actions these terms are not too helpful for shareholders. All the attempts to define short-term or long-term profit maximization are futile as long as this cannot be reformulated as an argument in a derivative action against managers. The effective constraints for managers' discretionary power flowing from abstract definitions of the ultimate goals of a business enterprise are negligible. The effective incentives and constraints are being provided by contracts between managers and shareholders and exit options for shareholders.

The various corporate governance codes analysed in the Ferrarini chapter are nice compromises between the more or less victorious shareholder concept and the desire to not totally neglect the stakeholder concept. The two essential issues at stake are *executive compensation* and *fiduciary duties*. The first issue is more a matter of intelligent contracts between managers and shareholders (there may be agency problems if those compensation plans are concluded between managers and employees because they may lead to a dilution of shareholders' property rights).

Fiduciary duties are a key issue because a broad definition of management goals leads automatically to rising agency costs. If this is realized by investors it will have a negative impact on the value of the shares. Shareholders may make use of the exit option. The extra agency costs are then reflected in the lower market price. The effect on shareholders is neutral with the exception of those shareholders that have not correctly anticipated the effect of that definition of fiduciary duties. The price will have to be paid by those actors with less favourable exit options; i.e. part of the labour force. Fiduciary duties will be more important when it comes to defence strategies of target companies in takeover bids. I shall come to that problem later.

If we focus on the pure company law perspective we find out that the theoretical discussion of shareholder versus stakeholder concept is of less importance than we might have expected. It dwindles down to cases of fiduciary duties in derivative actions against managers. Actions against managers turn out to be nothing else than instruments for disciplining managers. And both chapters argue correctly that today there are other and more potent disciplining methods. They have to do with the exit option for shareholders. With the change of ownership structures, which are analysed in the Davies chapter, equity owners today are in a position to exert pressure on managers by using the exit option. This is especially true for institutional investors. I would like to add two arguments to those that the Ferrarini and Davies chapters are putting forward:

(1) Institutional investors have changed. Managers of those institutions have come under pressure from their own constituency to make their decisions on the basis of expected return on investment. And they can do this better in a world of international competition of capital markets with enhanced transparency.

(2) Today there is no longer a clear dividing line between equity holders and certain types of creditors who can make use of clauses in long-term credit contracts (relational contracts) to exercise control over managers.

Thus it seems to be no longer necessary to put the burden of protecting creditors on accounting law viewed as part of company law. The overall impression then is that today it is futile to put too much stress on the distinction between various concepts of shareholder value or stakeholder protection. In a globalizing world those actors who are winners are those who have better exit options. These are shareholders, certain groups of creditors, and last but not least certain groups of employees. Employees who have a high market value, i.e. whose investment in human capital is not too specific, today have a real exit option and are no longer interested in life-long positions with one employer. Before looking into the normative issue of whether or not it might be prudent to make use of a stakeholder concept in corporate law in order to protect stakeholders, we have to turn to the role of capital market law and its functions for strengthening the shareholder perspective vis-à-vis the stakeholder perspective.

D. Defence Measures of Target Companies in Take-over Bids

First I would like to mention that I am in agreement with both chapters as far as the growing importance of capital market law vis-à-vis corporate law is concerned. Both chapters clearly demonstrate that the shareholders' position is automatically strengthened if there are functioning capital markets where investors can exercise their exit option either individually or collectively. Here too I would like to add the growing importance of international credit markets because certain types of creditors are in a better position compared with that of shareholders. My critical remarks on the capital market argumentation of both papers refer to the discussion of defence measures of managers of target companies in take-over bids. Both papers stress the importance of a neutrality rule for target company managers along the line of the London City code, which has more or less been incorporated in article 8 of the draft take-over directive (Thirteenth directive) of the European Union. The Ferrarini chapter mentions the differences between such a new European neutrality rule and the U.S. modified business judgment rule as being developed by the courts of Delaware. Ferrarini supposes that the neutrality rule leads to a transfer of powers of managers to shareholders. But the chapter does not address the collective-action problem properly. If defence measures have to be adopted by a general shareholders' meeting, this cannot lead to an effective transfer of powers to shareholders under the specific conditions of the present rules on shareholder meetings in continental European corporate law. Those shareholder meetings are not effective instruments for quickly responding to hostile take-over bids. The decision-taking procedure is much too time-consuming. If we neutralize the target company's management under those circumstances we have a serious collective-action problem. Even those defence strategies, that are in the best interest of the target company and its shareholders, cannot be brought into action. Thus the concept of a strict neutrality rule should be given up and be substituted by a so-called European modified business judgment rule which allows for defence strategies of the target company's management which are in the best interest of the target company—and its shareholders. But the burden of proof that those activities are in the best interests of the company is shifted to the management if a majority of shareholders of the target company rejects those measures by electronic vote. Such a European business judgment rule should be incorporated into the new European take-over law, thus bringing about a convergence between the European and the American position.

To sum up I agree with Ferrarini and Davies that corporate law is no longer the most important factor in defining actual standards for company conduct, i.e. conduct of managers. It is the *variety* of exit options of different groups of actors that actually forces managers to look to shareholder value as a guiding principle. It is the quality of take-over law which is the essential factor today in shifting the weight from the stakeholder to the shareholder perspective. But if it comes to take-over law we should be careful not to totally subdue stakeholders' to shareholders' interests. A modified business judgment rule could serve that purpose. And do not forget: if we want to better protect stakeholders' interests we should apply labour law; but we have to take into consideration the price.

15

Shareholder Value: A New Standard for Company Conduct

MICHAEL BLAIR

Abstract

This short contribution analyses the underlying purpose of the high-level obligations laid on directors by the general law of corporations in England and Wales, together with a short addition on the further duties of financial companies under the U.K. system of financial regulation. To the question "What are the directors of a company supposed to try to achieve?" the answer given is that, with the benefit of enlightened self interest, and a sense of appropriate civic responsibility, the concept of maximizing shareholder value is indeed a dominant concept for describing, motivating, and evaluating company conduct.

Contents

Introduction

The title for this topic, and the contributions by the two authors, Professors Ferrarini and Davies, lead me to conclude that the central, rock-bottom, issue relevant to this agenda item is a question, and a pair of answers to it.

The question is "What are the directors of a company supposed to try to achieve?" And the answers are two-fold:

(a) 'to maximize the benefits for the "company" (as properly defined for this purpose)'; and

(b) 'to comply with the legal standards of carefulness and of fair and open conduct expected of them'.

I perhaps need not spend too long to justify the question, since the answering of it is the harder of the two tasks. Suffice it to say that a discussion about standards for company conduct has to relate to the governing mind of the company, which is taken to be its board. And conduct on its own is a concept without much substance without the enlivening addition of the purpose towards which the conduct is aimed.

A. The First Part of the Answer

Classic corporate theory in all developed communities starts from the proposition that the directors owe a duty to the company, and that that is the fundamental duty to which they are subject. The answer I offer, therefore, is at one level fairly obvious. "Maximizing benefits" and "for the company" are unlikely to be contentious at this level, save among those who would wish the directors to owe obligations quite outside the corporate context. My answer to those critics is to ask them to await the analysis I give to answer b).

If then it is agreed that the directors have to maximize benefits for the company, subsidiary questions or greater interest arise, that is:
1. What is the company for this purpose?
2. What is the nature of the benefits to be maximized?
3. Over what period is the matter to be approached?
These three subsidiary questions can perhaps be described as "Who?", "What?", and "When?"

I. Who?

The "Who?" question has been exhaustively analysed in the U.K. in particular in the Company Law Review's Steering Group's Strategic Framework Paper of February 1999. In that paper a distinction was drawn between "the enlightened shareholder value" approach, based on the existing principles of British company law, and a "pluralist" approach under which directors would be required to balance shareholders' interest with those of others committed to it, such as employees and suppliers. The latter approach is typified as the stakeholder approach. In the result the "shareholder" approach was selected the true aim, or at any rate was the predominant aim in the Final Report of 2001.

II. What?

As Professor Ferrarini has observed, the U.S. theorists tend to regard maximization of shareholder wealth as equivalent to the maximization of company profit. In a market with no imperfections, and with rational and socially acceptable behaviour on all sides, this approach might well hold the field, worldwide.

But those limiting conditions seem not to prevail in all developed economies, or, indeed, in many of them. Even in the U.S., markets have on occasion been described as over valued, or unduly volatile ("irrational exuberance"). Recent experience in the European markets in relation to Internet companies, many of which had a substantial following in the markets, even though they had not yet declared any profits, tends to indicate that there are fashions and trends in our markets which extend well beyond pure, rational, economics as known in the university lecture rooms.

Market volatility in the U.K. has increased considerably since 1996. In part this may be because the market makers, with their capability for smoothing supply and demand, have moved out to let in the order driven system. In part, as well, it may be because of structural changes in our economy, which are leading to consequential changes in stock market composition and appeal. Over time, with the increased access to technology that now surrounds us, the markets should become more mature, and more able to measure rationally the prospect of early gain, and the basis for assured long-term growth.

Even then, however, there is likely to be some non-financial assessment and some personal and indeed political preference in terms of achieving benefits. I leave aside shareholder benefits like discount on cross-Channel travel, and, indeed, the "following" effect induced on potential shareholders, as on consumers, by successful advertising and public relations. Recent interest in ethical investment, and in health and environmental issues such as deep sea oil and tobacco, show the effect on directors of these wider perceived benefits for the shareholders and their preferences.

III. When?

I have covered some of the ground in dealing with II. above. Over the last ten years or so, there has been, in the U.K., a sporadic but continuous debate on the short term/long term issues affecting stock market investment. There is no room for a full analysis here, but there are signs that institutional preferences are beginning to acquire a somewhat longer term approach, and that pure short-termism may recede somewhat in comparison with the long term benefits of growth.

In part this is because of attempts to mobilize more fully the powers of institutional voting. In part, too, it is because of the increasing focus of investment in the stock market upon longer term gains for the purposes of personal pension and retirement (in 2000 over half the money managed by members of the then existing (London) Institutional Fund Managers Association was associated with long term retirement in one way or another). Thirdly, the pressure on margins and on expenses in fund management (induced in part by greater transparency required by the regulators) has made the cost of frequent fund switching more visible and relatively more significant. While a reduction in Stamp Duty on equity transactions (if it were ever to come about) might have an opposite effect, by making switches cheaper to effect, that probably would not outweigh the forces tending to reinforce the longer term view.

B. The Second Half of the Answer

The answer I give, in the second place, to the question about directors' proper motivation is that they should comply with the legal standards properly expected of them. In this context, there are two areas of current interest that I would like to highlight. I might have wished to add a third, that is some observations on the U.K. Listing Rules, and the so called Combined Code which is embedded within them, but that subject has been fully covered elsewhere.

My two topics therefore are:
(1) The duties expected of company directors as a matter of law, and,
(2) For companies in the financial services sector, some remarks about the recent regulatory requirements on senior management arrangements, systems and control.

C. Topic 1: Companies' Duties

As well as the work of the Company Law Review, referred to above, I ought to draw attention to the two Law Commissions' input into company law reform (there are two Commissions, one for England and Wales and the other for Scotland).

One of the main results of that effort is the report of the Law Commissions of September 1999 on Company Directors: Regulating Conflicts of Interests and Formulating a Statement of Duties. While some of the substance of that report relates to some special elements and details of British company law, some of the recommendations are of very considerable worldwide interest. In particular, the Commissions recommended the introduction of a statutory statement of the principal duties which a director owes to the company. And they recommend that the basis on which a director should be judged as having complied with that duty should contain a dual standard, that is a universal standard of care expected of everyone, coupled with a subjective additional level of responsibility for those who could reasonably be expected to comply with a higher quality level.

The draft statement proposed by the Law Commissions is annexed hereto (pages 185–186 of Cm 4436). The Commissions recommend that that statement should be made available to all directors on taking office, and that new directors should sign a form acknowledging that they had read it. The obligations themselves should not be exhaustive: that is, it should be made plain that a director is subject to other duties not reflected expressly in the statement. So far, the report has not been implemented, but may well feature in the Bill which is expected to carry the Company Law Review reform of U.K. company law into effect before long.

D. Topic 2: Senior Management Arrangements, System, and Controls in the Financial Services Sector

My final topic concerns those companies which are concerned with the provision of financial services in the U.K. and which, therefore, fall under the aegis of the Financial Services Authority, under the Financial Services and Markets Act 2000. Since the U.K. is a major world player in the financial services field, I hope that these remarks are not out of place, even though the financial sector in the U.K. is variously estimated at only between 8% and 20% of the economy.

In pursuing its objectives, the FSA is required to have regard to the responsibilities of those who manage the affairs of authorised persons (section 2(3)(b) of the Act). The regulation of these institutions hereafter will be carried on at the level of the firm itself, and other requirements also impinge directly on the senior managers as individuals.

The FSA has made new law in the form of rules and principles, in those areas. That concerning the firms themselves is in the FSA's Sourcebook on Systems and Controls, while that concerning the specific responsibilities of individual directors is in the Sourcebook on Approved Persons. Both are, of course, relevant to a discussion on company law, but that about the firms themselves is perhaps the more important of the two.

The key elements of the new requirements on firms' senior management systems are:

(a) first, an obligation on firms to require them to take reasonable care to establish and maintain a clear and appropriate apportionment of *responsibilities* among directors and senior managers. The purpose is to ensure that individual responsibilities are clear and that the business and affairs of the firm can be adequately monitored and controlled by top management: and

(b) secondly, an obligation is laid on firms to take reasonable care to ensure that appropriate *systems and controls* are established and maintained.

This formulation, naturally enough, does not deal directly with maximizing benefits, or with shareholder values. However, the relationship is not that remote. These requirements themselves derive their intellectual basis from the Barings case in the U.K., where the problems of inadequate systems and controls were such that the shareholders' funds and the value of the equity in a long established and highly respectable London investment house were completely lost.

These new requirements are intended to add some value to the parallel but less specific requirements of company law. Even in listed companies, which have the Combined Code, further value is discernible, though it is plain that the two can be looked at similarly. In considering whether firms have complied with the FSA systems and control requirements, due credit is to be given for those who comply with corresponding provisions in the Combined Code and the relevant guidance.

E. Conclusion

I conclude that, with the benefit of enlightened self interest, and a sense of appropriate civic responsibility, the concept of maximizing shareholder value is indeed a dominant concept for describing, motivating, and evaluating company conduct.

APPENDIX

DRAFT STATEMENT OF DIRECTORS' DUTIES

General

(1) The law imposes duties on directors. If a person does not comply with his duties as a director he may be liable to civil or criminal proceedings and he may be disqualified from acting as a director.

(2) Set out below there is a summary of the main duties of a director to his company. It is not a complete statement of a director's duties, and the law may change anyway. If a person is not clear about his duties as a director in any situation he should seek advice.

Loyalty

(3) A director must act in good faith in what he considers to be the interests of the company.

Obedience

(4) A director must act in accordance with the company's constitution (such as the articles of association) and must exercise his powers only for the purposes allowed by law.

No secret profits

(5) A director must not use the company's property, information, or opportunities for his own or anyone else's benefit unless he is allowed to by the company's constitution or the use has been disclosed to the company in general meeting and the company has consented to it.

Independence

(6) A director must not agree to restrict his power to exercise an independent judgment. But if he considers in good faith that it is in the interests of the company for a transaction to be entered into and carried into effect, he may restrict his power to exercise an independent judgment by agreeing to act in a particular way to achieve this.

Conflict of interest

(7) If there is a conflict between an interest or duty of a director and an interest of the company in any transaction, he must account to the company for any benefit he receives from the transaction. This applies whether or not the company sets aside the transaction. But he does not have to account for the benefit if he is allowed to have the interest or duty by the company's constitution or the interest or duty has been disclosed to and approved by the company in general meeting.

Care, skill, and diligence

(8) A director owes the company a duty to exercise the care, skill and diligence, which would be exercised in the same circumstances by a reasonable person having both
(a) the knowledge and experience that may reasonably be expected of a person in the same position as the director, and
(b) the knowledge and experience which the director has.

Interests of employees, etc.

(9) A director must have regard to the interests of the company's employees in general and its members.

Fairness

(10) A director must act fairly as between different members.

Effect of this statement

(11) The law stating the duties of directors is not affected by this statement or by the fact that, by signing this document, a director acknowledges that he has read the statement.

Part V:

The Institutional Investor

16

The Changing Role of Institutional Investors—A German Perspective

WOLFGANG GERKE, MATTHIAS BANK, AND MAX STEIGER[1]

Abstract

This chapter examines the future role of institutional investors in Germany and the way they will influence the German financial market taking into account the latest developments of information technology. Increasing market transparency will considerably decrease margins in asset management and increase the share of indexed assets of institutional investors. This is one of the reasons why institutional investors will considerably increase the volatility of the markets. They will also increasingly influence the existing stock exchange structures compared to today. As far as the companies are concerned there will be less incentives for institutional investors to exert active influence. This will be done passively or indirectly via codes of best practice or other standards specified by public institutions, interest groups or other important market players. Furthermore the continental European financial systems will become more and more market-oriented under the pressure of institutional investors. In the course of an increasing market orientation, the continental European universal banks will concentrate either on investment banking/asset management/finance of venture capital or on commercial banking.

Contents

Tables

A. Introduction

Two of the most prominent trends in the international capital markets of recent years are the increasing importance of institutional investors and the fast

---

[1] Prof. Dr. Wolfgang Gerke, Prof. Dr. Matthias Bank, Professor for Banking and Finance, University Innsbruck, Dr. Max Steiger, Deutsche Bank AG, Frankfurt/Main. We thank Jörg Fleischer for helpful comments and discussions.

development of information technology. Although both movements have proceeded relatively independently from each other so far, a stronger link is beginning to emerge. Information technology will substantially influence the competition between institutional investors for clients' funds. On the one hand, investors can accurately choose institutional investors due to generally agreed Performance Presentation Standards. However, if their portfolio managers miss chosen benchmarks, well-informed private investors switch to more successful funds.[2] On the other hand, private investors increasingly tend to avoid institutional investors by using direct brokers via the Internet (make-or-buy-option), due to reduced information and transaction costs. Although institutional investors are at present experiencing a large inflow of funds, the consequences of changing investment behaviour of private investors remain to be seen. In any case, this make-or-buy-option increases the competition that institutional investors are exposed to.

Information technology influences indirectly the asset side of institutional investors. They urge providers of trading systems and government authorities to improve basic economic and legal conditions on the world's financial markets in order to obtain low trading costs and high liquidity. In addition, an increasing number of institutional investors are concerned with systematic corporate governance activities in order to achieve an improved return on the managed funds.

There are basically two ways for institutional investors to increase shareholder value: they can sell their stocks and switch to investments with higher expected returns (exit strategy), or they can directly influence the management by means of active corporate governance (voice strategy).[3]

The following is a discussion on the future role institutional investors will play in connection with the changed basic conditions of information technology. Special attention will be paid to European and German conditions.[4] In the fol-

---

[2] See M. Gruber, 'Another puzzle: the growth in actively managed mutual funds' [1996] 51 *Journal of Finance* 783–810.

[3] See J.C. Coffee, 'Liquidity versus Control: The Institutional Investor as Corporate Monitor' [1991] 91 Columbia Law Review 6 1277–1368; A. Bhide 'The Hidden Costs of Stock Market Liquidity' [1993] 34 *Journal of Financial Economics*, 31–51; P. Bolton and E.-L. Von Thadden, 'Blocks, Liquidity and Corporate Control' [1998] 53 *Journal of Finance* 1 1–25; E. Maug, 'Large Shareholders as Monitors: Is there a Trade-Off between Liquidity and Control? [1998] 53 *Journal of Finance* 1 65–98; C. Kahn and A. Winton, 'Ownership Structure, Speculation and Shareholder Intervention' [1998] 53 *Journal of Finance* 1 99–129; M. Becht, 'European Corporate Governance: Trading off Liquidity against Control' [1999] 43 *European Economic Review* 1071–1083, as well as M. Steiger, *Institutionelle Investoren im Spannungsfeld zwischen Aktienmarktliquidität und Corporate Governance* (Baden-Baden 2000). Direct exertion of influence can also be seen in the European stock markets, see K. Lannoo, 'A European Perspective on Corporate Governance' [1999] 37 No. 2 *Journal of Common Market Studies* 269–294.

[4] For a description of the situation in Spain and a more pessimistic view of the future role of institutional investors as it is expressed in our chapter see A. Rojo and J.M. Garrido, *Institutional*

lowing part, we first describe the growing influence of institutional investors on the financial markets. In part C, we describe the influence of information technology on the environment of institutional investors; based on this we develop concrete theses on the changing role of institutional investors in part D.

B. Institutionalization of the Investment Process

The institutionalization[5] of the investment process, where professional market investors manage private savings, is a global trend.[6] As there is no common definition of institutionalization, the various studies include different institutions. This makes it difficult to compare the results, especially on an international basis. We use three characteristics to identify institutional investors: first, they are independent legal entities; secondly, their core business is the professional management of assets on behalf of their clients and thirdly, institutional investors manage an outstandingly high amount of funds.[7] However, with respect to the third characteristic one must take into account that due to their diversification strategies institutional investors generally hold less than 1–3 % of the share capital of an individual company.[8]

According to our characteristics, institutional investors in Germany are private insurance companies, pension funds, capital investment companies (*Kapitalanlagegesellschaften*), non-financial companies, foundations, public authorities, as well as banks.[9] Social security companies as well as investment management companies, associations, and central banks are, however, not considered to be institutional investors.[10]

International comparisons of the institutional investors' influence on capital markets and corporate governance are mostly based on pension funds (of

---

Investors and Corporate Governance: Solution or Problem? (Ch. 18 below). For the continental systems of corporate governance they argue that the main problem is the concentration of power in the hand of banks, which leads to inefficient governance outcomes.

[5] See W. Gerke and M. Steiger, *Einfluss der Kapitalmärkte auf die Corporate-Governance-Strukturen in Europa*, in *Handbuch Europäischer Kapitalmärkte* (Wiesbaden 2000).

[6] See H.J. Blommenstein and K. Biltoft, 'Trends, Structural Changes and Prospects in OECD Capital Markets' in OECD (ed.), *The New Financial Landscape: Forces Shaping the Revolution in Banking, Risk Management and Capital Markets* (Paris 1995) 293.

[7] See D. Schiereck, 'Institutionelle Investoren' in *Sparkasse*, 109 Jg, Nr 8 (1992) 393.

[8] Exceptions to the rule are venture capital corporations that mostly hold more than 25% per financed company without, however, renouncing on diversification.

[9] See International Monetary Fund (IMF), 'International Capital Markets: Developments, Prospects, and Policy Issues' in *World Economic and Financial Surveys* (Washington DC 1995) 165. Although venture capital corporations are not considered institutional investors they feature the most important characteristics of such investors.

[10] See D. Schiereck, 'Institutionelle Investoren' in *Sparkasse*, 109 Jg, Nr 8 (1992) 393.

importance mainly in Anglo-Saxon countries), on private insurance companies, and on capital investment companies with their respective national attributes.[11] Universal banks, which are typical for continental Europe, occupy a special position as far as corporate governance is concerned. They are direct investors although they often also act as providers of corporate debt, members of the supervisory boards, and authorized representatives of their customers at general meetings. Hence, banks need to be analysed separately.[12] In many continental European countries, non-financial enterprises own cross-shareholdings that enable them to strongly influence the corporate governance of the respective companies. These companies are, however, themselves subject to active corporate governance by pension and investment funds so that they will be treated as objects of corporate governance. In addition to this, non-financial companies generally hold stakes of over 10% in other companies for strategic reasons and in addition to a mere increase in value[13]. All other institutions mentioned are of no major importance as far as corporate governance is concerned.

I. Growth and Structure of Managed Assets

There are many reasons for the institutionalization of investment in Europe: Anglo-Saxon funds increase their stakes in European companies in order to improve their return/risk patterns by way of international diversification.[14] Technological progress in information transmission and processing increases the international expertise of institutional investors. Increasing professionalism in selecting and trading shares and the simplified international securities transactions boost the integration of the global capital markets.[15] In view of the problems of the public old-age pension scheme, European investment companies increasingly manage to convince small investors of the long-term superiority of

---

[11] See OECD, *Institutional Investors—Statistical Yearbook 1999* (Paris 1999).

[12] For Germany see, e.g. J. Edwards and K. Fischer, *Banks, Finance and Investment in Germany* (Cambridge 1994); M. Nibler, *Bank Control and Corporate Performance in Germany: The Evidence* in University of Cambridge, Faculty of Economics and Politics, Research Paper Series, No. 48, 1995; F. Seger, *Banken, Erfolg und Finanzierung: Eine Analyse für deutsche Industrieunternehmen* (Wiesbaden 1997) and D. Neuberger, 'Anteilsbesitz von Banken: Wohlfahrtsverlust oder Wohlfahrtsgewinn?' in *Universität Rostock, Lehrstuhl für Volkswirtschaftslehre—Geld und Kapital,* Working Paper, 1996.

[13] For an analysis of the benefits of different ownership structures see M. Pagano and A. Roell, 'The Choice of Stock Ownership structure: Agency Costs, Monitoring, and the Decision to go Public' [1998] *Quarterly Journal of Economics* 187–225.

[14] See The Conference Board, 'Institutional Patterns of Institutional Investment' in *Institutional Investment Report*, Vol. 2, No. 3 (Washington DC 1999) 33 and 44.

[15] See International Monetary Fund (IMF), 'International Capital Markets: Developments, Prospects, and Policy Issues' in *World Economic and Financial Surveys* (Washington DC 1995) 65.

an investment in mutual funds.[16] Funds enable even private investors with relatively small savings to engage in diversified economy-wide investments to ensure their old-age provision.[17]

This trend results in the increasing concentration of stock capital with institutional investors. The portfolios of private insurance companies, investment companies, and pension funds of the OECD-countries amounted to approx. U.S. $26 trillion (see Table 1) by the end of 1997. The increase of assets managed by institutional investors in Germany between 1990 and 1997 is outstanding among OECD-countries and should be highlighted. Asset allocation structure of the institutional investors of the individual Member States of the EU differs considerably. While the share of stocks of the portfolios of institutional investors relevant for corporate governance reached 40% or 67%, respectively, in the U.S. and Great Britain in 1996, investments in bonds and loans traditionally dominate in continental European countries so that the equity weighting in the portfolios reaches from 6% in Spain, Hungary and Iceland to approx. 14% in Germany and Italy, to about 26% in France, Belgium, Finland, and the Netherlands.[18] These figures show that the connection between the progressive institutionalization and the increase in the managed stock capital implicitly suggested in the public discussion does not exist in all of the European capital markets.

II. Changes in the German Old-Age Pension Scheme

We expect an above-average increase in institutionally managed assets in Germany as a reform of the existing old-age pension scheme is unavoidable due to demographic changes. The level of provision generally considered to be necessary is no longer guaranteed by the existing pension scheme. The pay-as-you-go-system of the public old-age insurance is to be complemented by a mandatory, privately managed pension system according to the level premium system. Defined contribution systems need to be incorporated into companies' pension funds as an additional possibility of organized corporate pension schemes. In the future, it should be possible to outsource defined benefit plans together with the accompanying assets without any tax losses. We finally demand that beneficiaries of corporate or private old-age provisions should be

---

[16] See P. Davis, *Pension Funds—Retirement-Income Security, and Capital Markets, An International Perspective* (Oxford 1995) and K. Lannoo, 'A European Perspective on Corporate Governance' [1999] 37 No. 2 *Journal of Common Market Studies* 269–294.

[17] See W. Gerke, 'Der Finanzplatz Deutschland braucht Innovation statt Reaktion' [1995] *Zeitschrift für das gesamte Kreditwesen* 14–24.

[18] See OECD, *Institutional Investors—Statistical Yearbook 1999* (Paris 1999) 32–33.

Table 1: Growth of Assets Managed by Institutional Investors (all figures in U.S.
          $ billion)

	1990	1997	Growth in % p.a. (in U.S. $)	Growth in % p.a. (in national currency)
U.S.A.	6,875.7	15,867.5	12.7%	12.7%
Great Britain	1,116.8	2,226.9*	10.4%	12.4%
France	655.7	1,263.2	9.8%	12.3%
Germany	599.0	1,201.9	10.5%	13.3%
Japan	2,427.9	3,154.7	3.8%	3.3%
The Netherlands	378.3	667.8	8.5%	11.3%
Total	12,053.4	24,382.0	10.5%	
Total of all OECD-countries*	13,768.2	26,001.2	9.5%	

Source: OECD (1999) 20, 32–34, and own calculations. *As of 1996.

taxed on receipt regardless of the method of organization as is international common practice.[19]

The realization of the reforms demanded by us will further boost the development of institutional investors. Even if our suggestions will not be followed in detail, the German old-age pension scheme will give way to the pressure of the market. The German financial system will therefore develop considerably faster than expected from a bank-oriented to a more market-oriented system. Savings will then be invested increasingly by institutional investors in the international stock and bond markets instead of entering the balance sheets of banks as bank deposits as was the case so far. Direct financing via capital markets instead of bank loans will therefore become more attractive to capital-seeking companies.

III. Changes in Shareholder Structures

A further result of the institutionalization is the change that can be observed in the shareholder structures (see Table 2). On the one hand, the share of stocks directly held by private households is constantly decreasing, and on the other

[19] These recommendations are to be found in the *BMF* (*Bundesministerium der Finanzen*), *Bericht des Arbeitskreises "Betriebliche Pensionsfonds"* (Bonn 1998).

hand, an increase in the share of stocks held by insurance companies, pension, and investment funds can be observed. Money is shifted from private to institutional investors. Due to this fact, a constantly declining number of investors hold an ever-increasing share of the outstanding shares of public limited companies.[20] Nevertheless, if one ignores the non-financial institutions, the pension, and mutual funds only hold a low percentage in public limited companies due to reasons of diversification and index tracking. They are therefore considered to be minority shareholders.[21] Among other things, it depends on the ownership structure of public limited companies as to what extent the right to control the management as well as the right to vote are exercised.[22]

Table 2: Ownership Structure of Selected Industrial Nations (percentage of total shares outstanding)

Country	Year	Private Households	Companies	Government	Banks	Insurances/ Pensions*	Investment funds	Foreign trade
France	1977	41%	20%	3%	24%	n.a.	n.a.	12%
	1992	34%	21%	2%	23%	n.a.	n.a.	20%
	1995	19.4%	58%	3.4%	4%	2%	2%	11.2%
Germany	1970	28%	41%	11%	11%	n.a.	n.a.	8%
	1993	17%	39%	3.0%	29%	n.a.	n.a.	12%
	1995	14.6%	42.1%	4.3%	10.3%	12.4%	7.6%	8.7%
Great Britain	1969	50%	5%	3%	36%	n.a.	n.a.	7%
	1993	19%	2%	1%	62%	n.a.	n.a.	16%
	1995	29.6%	4.1%	0.2%	2.3%	39.7%	10.4%	13.7%
Japan	1970	40%	23%	0%	35%	n.a.	n.a.	3%
	1993	20%	28%	1%	42%	n.a.	n.a.	8%
	1995	22.2%	31.2%	0.5%	13.3%	10.8%	11.7%	10.3%
USA	1981	51%	15%	0%	28%	n.a.	n.a.	6%
	1993	48%	9%	0%	37%	n.a.	n.a.	6%
	1995	36.4%	15%	0%	0.2%	31.3%	13%	4.2%

Source: Deutsches Aktieninstitut (1998) 08.6-4. (*Insurances/Pension funds)

[20] See R. La Porta, F. Lopez-de-Silanes and A. Schleifer, 'Corporate Ownership Around the World' [1999] 54 No. 2 *Journal of Finance* 471–517 for an international and European Corporate Governance Network, *The Separation of Ownership and Control: A Survey of 7 European Countries—Preliminary Report* (Brussels 1997), for a European comparison.

[21] See A. Shleifer and R. Vishny, 'Large Shareholders and Corporate Control' [1986] 94 *Journal of Political Economy* 461–488 and H. Demsetz and K. Lehn, 'The Structure of Corporate Ownership: Causes and Consequences' [1985] 93 No. 6 *Journal of Political Economy* 1155–1177.

[22] In Germany, e.g. there is a high share of concentrated ownership that complicates the potential influence of minority shareholders on corporate governance. See M. Steiger, *Institutionelle*

IV. Changed Basic Conditions in the Investment Process

In recent years, the growing importance of institutional investors has led to a stronger consideration of their requirements by legislation. This includes the global adaptation of accounting standards and regulations of investor protection that closely match the American model. In addition, institutional investors increasingly are in a position to indirectly force the financed companies to act in certain ways by applying the so-called Codes of Best Practice in corporate governance. This includes the introduction of more informative accounting standards and the acceptance of take-over codes.

On the other hand, institutional investors have to publish more detailed and standardized reports. Such performance and presentation standards (PPS) were developed by professional organizations of the investment community (such as AIMR or *DVFA*).[23] PPS especially emphasize the presentation of total return on the basis of composites including all transaction and management costs, according to which an institutional investor has to report the return of all managed assets of one class (e.g. shares) for a period of at least five years or from the date the fund was first issued, whichever is shorter. This creates a high degree of transparency when competing for clients' funds.

C. Impact of Technological Changes on Institutional Investors

The development of information technology,[24] for instance through the Internet, and the pressure on authorities of individual countries, has resulted in significant changes in the financial markets in recent years.[25] Outstanding developments include:

- access to information for professional and private market participants at low cost,
- widening and broadening of available public information,
- reduction of the costs of market access by increasing automation and computerization of order handling of the entire process of stock market transactions,

Investoren im Spannungsfeld zwischen Aktienmarktliquidität und Corporate Governance (Baden-Baden 2000).

[23] See AIMR Performance and Presentation Handbook (1997). AIMR is the acronym for Association for Investment Management and Research, and *DVFA* stands for *Deutsche Vereinigung für Finanzanalyse und Anlageberatung.*

[24] An ever increasing amount of data can be transferred by a constantly growing quantity of communication media (PC, mobile phone, cable TV). Quality is thereby increasing while the cost per information unit is falling.

[25] Company law will also be affected. See, e.g. E. Wymeersch, *Company Law in the 21st Century,* Working Paper 1999–14, Financial Law Institute, University Gent, October 1999 for examples of the impact of electronic data transmission on company law.

• deregulation and reduction of bureaucratic barriers of individual countries, supported by the introduction of the European domestic market and the Euro. Seen from the point of view of the neo-classic capital market theory all these developments indicate a direction that implies a higher degree of capital market efficiency.[26]

The analysis of the technological changes leads to our first thesis:

Thesis 1: the technological development of the provision of information and of the network of trading platforms brings the real capital markets closer and closer to the conditions of a perfect capital market. Decreasing information costs are the cause for the change from a competition of quality to a pure price competition.

Although real markets will never show perfectly all the mentioned characteristics, the described change of the general setting of the financial markets causes a reduction in friction and market deficiencies as well as a cut in information costs, a process still far from completion. The costs of running financial markets are slumping. Indications for this are the efforts of the European stock exchanges to create a pan-European platform for the most liquid stocks in order to reduce the explicit and implicit transaction costs, the participation of large banks in the ECN "Tradepoint", the increasing direct competition on the North American continent between NYSE, NASDAQ and the evolving Electronic Communication Networks (ECN) and the abolition of the separation of investment and commercial banking in the U.S. The integration of handling processes via the Internet—so-called business-to-business (B2B) applications—will, in the future, eliminate remaining frictions in order processing. This process is well advanced in the financial services sector in particular.

Institutional investors operating on a global level have helped to initiate this trend and at the same time are directly adversely affected. Concerning investments, they demand that stock exchanges, banks, and public authorities create conditions that help cut the costs of portfolio management. Due to the high competition for clients' funds, they are forced to pass favourable conditions to their clients. Competition and falling margins on the liability side force institutional investors to fully utilize all potential for productivity increases, broaden their basis for commissions by purchasing other finance companies and pass on cost reductions to their customers.

---

[26] A perfect capital market is generally described as follows: no market friction and therefore no transaction costs as a precondition for perfect liquidity, no information costs and therefore homogeneous information for all market participants and no market deficiencies such as taxes, regulations or restrictions for short sales. See, e.g. T.E. Copeland and J.F. Weston, *Financial Theory and Corporate Policy* 3rd edn. (Reading, Mass 1988) 194.

D. The Future Role of Institutional Investors

In the past, institutional investors in continental Europe largely promoted the harmonization of the general framework on the capital markets of the most important industrial nations. Although perfect harmonization has not yet been achieved, the national authorities and the commission of the EC make efforts to harmonize the capital market. Gaps in the general framework often were bridged by private standards set by the institutional investors. In general, the menacing potential of institutional investors seems to be credible. Countries like Austria, whose corporate governance system has not yet been adapted to the international customs in a sufficient way, are avoided by globally operating institutional investors to the disadvantage of the real sector of local economies.[27]

We expect the trend of the worldwide harmonization of the general framework at the financial markets to be continued given the pressure of the institutional investors. As a result, the continental European financial markets in particular will change from a more bank-oriented corporate governance structure to a market-oriented corporate governance system. In Europe, a growing percentage of savings will also be at the disposal of the non-financial companies via share and bond markets and no longer via bank loans. Institutional investors already globally play the central role in putting the capital to its best-possible use.[28]

In spite of the expected growing market shares of institutional investors, we doubt that they would play an even more active role in corporate governance in the future. As will be shown below, we expect a more passive role of the institutional investors in setting external standards for financed companies (indirect voice) accompanied by an exit option becoming cheaper by growing liquidity at the secondary markets. All above mentioned aspects will be discussed below and put into concrete hypotheses about the future role of institutional investors.

I. Institutional Investors as Market Participants

Due to large net inflows of capital and the processing of new information, institutional investors as a group have a high need of transaction. This need can be satisfied by official stock exchanges or recently by electronic communication networks (ECN).[29] Due to the mutual interest in low transaction costs, anonymity,

---

[27] See 'Xetra hat Erwartungen nicht erfüllt' *Handelsblatt* of December 29, 1999, No. 253, 35. However, a company like Volkswagen AG, too, where the government still has a say in the corporate governance structure, suffers from a reduction of institutional investors value.

[28] See Part B.I.

[29] ECNs are proprietary trading systems that do not have the status of a stock exchange with corresponding regulations concerning fair market prices or independent trade and market supervision.

a low level of regulations, and a lack of adaptability by official stock exchanges, institutional investors have an increasing need for ECNs as an alternative for transaction.[30] From the onset, ECNs have been designed for institutional investors by their operators. Quality-wise, ECNs are looking for competition with established stock exchanges not only by lowering transaction costs but also by using state-of-the-art settlement systems, lengthening trading sessions, enabling smaller tick sizes and guaranteeing high liquidity. These advantages are accompanied by potential shortcomings such as additional fragmentation of liquidity, lack of immediacy, a higher risk of manipulation due to a non-existent trading and market supervision, and uncertainties about system capacities.[31]

From a legislative point of view, institutional investors are not particularly worthy of being protected given their professionalism and their willingness to participate in ECNs. They are able to estimate and bear the special risks of trading via ECNs. Also, institutional investors always have the possibility of managing their transactions via official stock exchanges. The status of a stock exchange that is obliged to respect all regulations should only be imposed if the operators are planning to give access to private investors meriting protection.[32] Consequently, ECNs can be qualified as an institution similar to a stock exchange[33] without need for special regulation.[34] This argument leads to our second thesis:

Thesis 2: in the future, institutional investors will strongly influence the structures of existing stock exchanges reinforcing their demand for alternative possibilities of trade, e.g. via ECNs. There is no need for a special regulation of alternative trading systems in the stock exchange legislation, as long as a qualified pricing is guaranteed at the stock exchanges and private investors are not admitted.

[30] Approximately 82% of the U.S. fund managers use one or several ECNs. See Greenwich Associates, *Worldwide Institutional Brokerage: Changing Scene*, Equity Report, November 1998.

[31] See R. Dornau, *Alternative Handelssysteme in den USA und in Europa*, Working Paper, December 1999.

[32] See Regulation ATS of SEC. See Securities and Exchange Commission, Regulation of Exchanges and Alternative Trading Systems, Release No. 34-40760, File No. S7-12-98, November 12, 98.

[33] See K.J. Hopt and H. Baum, 'Börsenrechtsreform in Deutschland' in K.J. Hopt, B. Rudolph and H. Baum (eds.), *Börsenreform* (Stuttgart 1997) 287–466 for a discussion of potential stock exchange definitions and a corresponding reform of the German law governing stock exchange transactions. The authors plead for qualifying alternative trade systems as institutions similar to stock exchanges. They thus do not fall within the scope of the German Stock Exchange Act, but can be regulated separately, e.g. in the course of the Securities Trading Law (*Wertpapierhandelsgesetz*).

[34] However, there could be a problem if ECNs reach a certain relative size in comparison to the volumes at the official stock exchanges. This makes qualified pricing more and more difficult or even impossible with the decrease of turnover volume. An ECN should qualify automatically as a stock exchange when it generates a certain total share of the total turnover of all stock exchanges and all institutions similar to stock exchanges.

The above-mentioned fragmentation of liquidity due to an increasing number of trading systems and longer trading session makes pricing in the capital markets more vulnerable to non-information-based price fluctuations. The "privatiza-tion" of trading activities via proprietary trading systems can, all other things equal, lead to higher volatility at public stock exchanges.[35] From an economic point of view, there is the risk of an undesirable development as higher volatility increases the cost of risk. Further technological developments and high trans-parency standards may also be a reason for an increase in price volatility in the capital markets. First, an increasing availability of homogenous information and homogenous interpretations can lead to a correlated behaviour (herding) of institutional investors.[36] Due to their high market share and the high impact on the market of institutional investors as a result, there is a risk of overreaction and excess volatility.[37] Secondly, the increasing benchmark orientation and the easy comparability of institutional portfolios create incentives to imitate competitors' behaviour. When competing for clients' funds, it is often more important to achieve an average portfolio (pooling) as to take the risk of performing below average (separation). The incentive is even stronger the less the institutional investor is investing in information acquisition.[38] From the point of view of each separate institutional investor, a collective irrational behaviour of all other institutional investors is little detrimental. Thirdly, increasing investments in index products results in institutional investors investing completely price-insensitively in the selected benchmarks. From their point of view, the price is completely irrelevant, because their individual success in investing is not the basis for their management performance. Therefore, increasing indexing can lead to the fact that the connection between prices and intrinsic values is loos-ened up and that over- or under-reactions become more likely. Thus there is an incentive for institutional investors to manipulate market prices. Therefore, such manipulations should be explicitly prohibited by regulation. Let us assume that

[35] The fragmentation of the order flow increases the probability of liquidity-induced, erratic price fluctuations.

[36] See J. Lakonishok, A. Shleifer, and R. Vishny, 'The Impact of Institutional Trading on Stock Prices' [1992] 32 *Journal of Financial Economics* 23–43. J.R. Nofsinger and R.W. Sias, 'Herding and Feedback Trading by Institutional and Individual Investors' [1999] 54 *Journal of Finance* 2263–2295, document a strong positive correlation between changes of the portfolio of institutional investors (institutional ownership) and returns, measured in the same period of time. Their result is consistent with institutional herding.

[37] The overreaction can turn out stronger if the liquidity is distributed to several trading systems. See above.

[38] See D.S. Scharfstein and J. Stein, 'Herd Behavior and Investment' [1990] 80 *American Economic Review* 465–479, J. Lakonishok, A. Shleifer, R.H. Thaler, and R.W. Vishny, 'Window Dressing by Pension Fund Managers' [1991] 81 *American Economic Review Papers and Proceedings*, 227–231 and J. Lakonishok, A. Shleifer, and R.W. Vishny, 'Contrarian investment, Extrapolation, and Risk' [1994] 49 *Journal of Finance* 1541–1578.

a capital investment company offers both actively and passively managed funds at the same time. Then there might be an incentive that both funds trade securities via the stock exchange and that the share prices move in the desired direction from the actively managed fund's point of view. This manipulation technique is called order matching. This will obviously not harm anybody directly, because the passively managed fund always achieves the indexed return on investment. Let us further assume that the share price is €50 and the index 100. Now, both funds are positioning "matched orders" for a share price of €55. The share price jumps to €55 and therefore the index climbs to 101 when we assume that the rate of the share in the index is 10%. After that, the share price and the index drop back to €50 and 100, respectively. Now, the actively managed fund again buys at €50 and has made a 10% trading profit. The passively managed fund has only followed the index development. It is interesting to see that nobody is directly harmed by this order matching.

This argument leads to our third and fourth theses:

Thesis 3: the rising institutionalization will increase the volatility in the capital markets. A more and more homogenized information set increases the probability of a correlated behaviour of institutional investors leading to price over- and under-reactions (excess volatility).

Thesis 4: the increasing transparency, benchmark orientation, and indexing are reinforcing the incentives for institutional investors to imitate the competitors' behaviour and to invest in a price-insensitive way. This leads to a high probability of over- and under-reactions in the capital markets (excess volatility).

Where the transparency of the capital markets is increasing, passive investment strategies help institutional investors to reduce transaction costs. In such an environment, it is becoming difficult to an increasing extent for all investors to achieve advantages in information and to make use of them in a profitable way with an active investment strategy.

Therefore, a major part of institutional investors' funds has already been invested in indexed portfolios. In this case, the performance of the managed assets develops parallel to the selected indices. Such a passive investment strategy saves management resources and reduces transaction costs. An institutional investor does not have to face the risk of performing worse than the benchmark. The principal (e.g. private investor) avoids an additional agency risk, because it is possible for institutional investors to follow up incompatible goals. A possible way of reducing the agency risk could be the diversification of the money managers in order to attain an average level of competence or to detrimental self-interests. However, such a strategy also avoids the systematic achievement of excess returns on investment due to talented portfolio managers.

In comparison to a portfolio actively managed by many independent portfolio managers, a passive index tracking strategy shows a lower variance with the
same expected return (after transaction costs). This will make rationally acting
institutional investors offer more index-oriented strategies. Otherwise, they run
the risk of investors switching directly into index certificates. This argument
leads to our fifth thesis:

Thesis 5: increasing market transparency will severely reduce the margins in
asset management and will increase the share of indexed investments of institutional investors.

II. Corporate Governance Efforts of Institutional Investors

In order to acquire new clients' funds for global asset management, institutional
investors have to achieve a performance that is equal to or even higher than the
benchmark return. Hence, many Anglo-Saxon pension and investment funds
claim to follow a so-called shareholder activism within the scope of a corporate
governance strategy. Consequently, their major objective is the maximization of
the shareholder value.[39] Efficient corporate governance is necessary to create a
higher corporate value in the long run.[40] Institutional investors hereby implicitly
assume the following relationships:
• the actions of the management influence the performance of the company,
• the corporate governance system influences the basic framework guiding the
  management decisions,
• an efficiently organized corporate governance reduces the agency costs promoting the harmonization of the managers' and shareholders' objectives,
• it is also assumed that the improved performance of some companies as a
  result of this will lead to higher welfare of the entire economy.[41]
The assumption that corporate governance influences the performance of a company was one reason for the acquisition of companies in the U.S. in the 1980s.
In many cases of hostile take-overs, the buyers paid a premium compared to the
actual market value assuming that a higher company value would be achieved
by changing the composition of the board and the management, respectively.[42]

[39] See California Public Employees' Retirement System (CalPERS), *Why Corporate Governance
Today?* (Sacramento 1999) 1.

[40] See C. Strenger, 'Corporate Governance: Die Erwartungen professioneller Investoren' [1999]
12 *Die Bank* 822–825.

[41] See M.M. Blair, *Ownership and Control—Rethinking Corporate Governance for the Twenty-
First Century* (Washington DC 1995) 6–11, and OECD, *OECD Principles of Corporate Governance*
(Paris 1999) (www.oecd.org.daf/governance) 15.

[42] See, e.g. M.C. Jensen and R.S. Ruback, 'The Market for Corporate Control: The Scientific
Evidence' [1983] 11 *Journal of Financial Economics* 5–50, M.C. Jensen, 'Takeovers: Their Causes and

Contrary to the widespread opinion that there is a clear relationship of cause and effect between corporate governance and company performance, we believe that the influences of highly competitive product and financial markets already force an optimization of performance. However, taking a positive relationship between cause and effect as a basis, one must examine which forms of corporate governance have a major influence from the institutional investors' point of view.

Since the end of the 1980s, the Anglo-Saxon institutional investors in particular have been more concerned with the subject of corporate governance. They have to achieve a higher return on investment for their investors due to a better performance of the companies. Several empirical studies investigate to what extent a strategy of active company control applied by institutional investors in the U.S. leads to improved company results. The Californian public pension fund CalPERS (California Public Employees' Retirement System) is the pioneer of shareholder activism.[43] CalPERS, furthermore, tries to achieve a return on investments above the index performance by active trading. This might be a successful strategy because empirical studies indicate that the stock markets especially are far from efficient.[44]

It is remarkable that mainly public pension funds appear as active advocates of improved corporate governance.[45] The numerous private pension funds, e.g. those of the major U.S. industrial and service companies, have rarely appeared as active investors in public so far. The reason for this could be the potential clash of interests that these private pension funds are exposed to, as is the case for insurance and capital investment companies. Too much criticism of corporate governance and the performance of other companies could possibly endanger potential business relationships. There is an objection to the commitment of

Consequences' [1988] 2 *Journal of Economic Perspectives*, 1, 21–48, L. Herzel, 'Are Institutional Investors a Likely Substitute for the Takeover Market?' in A.W. Sametz and J.L. Bicksler (eds.), *Institutional Investing: Challenges and Responsibilities of the 21st Century* (Homewood 1991) 128–137 and W.H. Mikkelson and M.M. Partch, 'The Decline of Takeovers and Disciplinary Managerial Turnover' [1997] 44 *Journal of Financial Economics* 205–228.

[43] See California Public Employees' Retirement System (CalPERS), *Why Corporate Governance Today?* (Sacramento 1999) 1.

[44] See E.F. Fama and K. French, 'The Cross-Section of Expected Stock Returns' [1992] 47 *Journal of Finance* 427–465 and E.F. Fama and K. French, 'Common Risk Factors in the Returns on Stocks and Bonds' [1993] 33 *Journal of Financial Economics* 3–56 on the significance of corporate betas. A theory to explain the irrational actions of many investors has been found by the relatively new field of research of behavioural finance. See, e.g. D. Kahneman and A. Tversky, 'Prospect Theory: An Analysis of Decision Under Risk' [1979] 47 *Econometrica* 263–291, W. De Bondt and R.H. Thaler, 'Does the Stock Market Overreact?' [1985] 40 *Journal of Finance* 793–805 and M. Unser, *Behavioral Finance am Aktienmarkt—Empirische Analysen zum Risikoverhalten individueller Anleger* (Bad Soden im Taunus 1999), with further indications.

[45] See D. Del Guercio and J. Hawkins, The Motivation and Impact of Pension Fund Activism' [1999] 52 *Journal of Financial Economics* 293–340.

the public pension funds because politicians who can exert influence on the funds do not always prefer a performance maximizing strategy.[46] Furthermore, the public pension funds would be controlled by managers aiming at a high publicity that will support their political or private-sector careers without taking into exclusive consideration the interests of the persons entitled to a pension.[47] Due to the broad selection of pension funds, periods, and endogenous success factors empirical studies have not yet shown a positive relationship of cause and effect between the active requirement of improved corporate governance by institutional investors and the performance of companies.[48] In the resume of the empirical studies investigated by Black (1997), he concludes that shareholder activism in the American fashion has only a minor influence on the performance of companies.[49] Karpoff (1998) gives a comprehensive and highly differentiated overview of 20 different studies that investigate the existence of a relationship of cause and effect. According to these studies, the contradictory results can be explained by different ways of defining and evaluating the success of shareholder activism. Karpoff summarizes that the institutional investors are only effecting minor changes in the governance structures and thus only exert a minor influence on shareholder value.[50]

In general, shareholder activism can be shown by active participation during general meetings, voting behaviour, and personal conversations (one-on-ones) between the institutional investors and the management. The reasons for the increased efforts of U.S. investors can be found in the growing institutionalization of the share markets and the pressure of the institutional investors to replicate market-wide indices in the asset management. On the other hand, the numerous activities of companies and different U.S. states to protect company acquisitions resulted in the market for company control not working as efficiently as at the beginning of the 1980s. Therefore, Karpoff argues that an improvement of return on investment can only be achieved by shareholder activism.[51]

---

[46] See R. Romano, 'Public Pension Fund Activism in Corporate Governance Reconsidered' [1993] 93 No. 4 Columbia Law Review 795ff.

[47] See K.J. Murphy and K. Van Nuys, *Governance, Behavior, and Performance of State and Corporative Pension Funds*, Harvard Business School, Discussion Paper, 1994.

[48] See Council of Institutional Investors (CII), *Does Ownership Add Value?, A Collection of 100 Empirical Studies* (Washington DC 1994) for an overview of the results of 101 empirical studies on shareholder activism and other corporate governance subjects.

[49] See B.S. Black, *Shareholder Activism and Corporate Governance in the United States*, Columbia University, Discussion Paper, 1997, 2.

[50] See J.M. Karpoff, *The Impact of Shareholder Activism on Target Companies, A Survey of Empirical Findings*, Working Paper, University of Washington, 1998, 24.

[51] See J.M. Karpoff, *The Impact of Shareholder Activism on Target Companies, A Survey of Empirical Findings*, Working Paper, University of Washington, 1998, 3.

The question arises which incentives lead to shareholder activism. Some theses represented in academic literature doubt that this increasingly important group of shareholders is interested in taking care of the corporate governance of companies, as—due to the liquidity of secondary markets and the possible sale of the share position at any time—there is a more attractive alternative at least for major public limited companies. The doubts about the efficiency of the shareholder activism to increase the returns on investment are additionally nourished by the contradictory results of empirical studies on the validity of a positive causal connection between shareholder activism and company performance. The general consideration of both strategies (exit versus voice) from the institutional investors' point of view is the main subject of numerous theoretical and empirical studies.[52]

The link between liquidity in the stock markets and corporate control has already been shown by Demetz (1968). According to him, a concentration of the possession of shares, considered as a necessary but not sufficient condition for efficient corporate governance, is causing a reduction of potential buyers and sellers in the market. This means a reduced liquidity in the secondary market. The trade-off between liquidity and control is an application of the generalized theory of Hirschman (1970). Consequently, all members of an institution have the choice between "exit" and "voice", that means between liquidity serving to get rid of an investment any time (exit) and corporate governance serving to increase the return on investment (voice). Those companies ignoring the value orientation of the company management in the course of the globalization of goods and factor markets will be punished with higher cost of capital due to lower share prices. The "exit" as menace or execution of penalty is traditionally considered a passive and anonymous strategy,[53] where, as a rule, no dialogue takes place with the companies concerned.

Activities of institutional investors called shareholder activism represent another type of this consideration within the scope of the corporate governance.

---

[52] See J.C. Coffee, 'Liquidity versus Control: The Institutional Investor as Corporate Monitor' [1991] 6 Columbia Law Review 1277–1368, A. Bhide, 'The Hidden Costs of Stock Market Liquidity' [1993] 34 *Journal of Financial Economics,* 31–51, P. Bolton and E.-L. Von Thadden, 'Blocks, Liquidity, and Corporate Control' [1998] 53 *Journal of Finance* 1–25, E. Maug, 'Large Shareholders as Monitors: Is There a Trade-Off between Liquidity and Control?' [1998] 53 *The Journal of Finance* 65–98, C. Kahn and A. Winton, 'Ownership Structure, Speculation and Shareholder Intervention' [1998] 53 *The Journal of Finance* 99–129, M. Becht, 'European Corporate Governance: Trading off Liquidity against Control' [1999] 43 *European Economic Review* 1071–1083, and M. Steiger, *Institutionelle Investoren im Spannungsfeld zwischen Aktienmarktliquidität und Corporate Governance* (Baden-Baden 2000).

[53] See B.S. Black, *Shareholder Activism and Corporate Governance in the United States,* Columbia University, Discussion Paper, 1997, 526ff, and J.P. Hawley and A.T. Williams, *Corporate Governance in the United States: The Rise of Fiduciary Capitalism—A Review of the Literature,* Graduate Business Programs, Saint Mary's College of California, Discussion Paper, 1996, 49.

The companies in the portfolio are supervised. A long-term "relationship investing" strategy is implemented to achieve changes for the purposes of the shareholders.[54] The sale of major share positions held by institutional investors is often not possible because of illiquid secondary markets or the objective to track indices.[55] Following a voice strategy, institutional investors frequently come into direct contact with companies in the course of investor relations. The group of financial analysts shows the highest frequency of contacts. The analysts can be differentiated into the so-called "sell side" and "buy side" analysts.[56] Employees of brokerage houses and investment banks are considered as sell side analysts. Institutional investors, e.g. of an insurance company, an investment company, or an equity trading department of a commercial bank, are buy side analysts. When preparing a survey, there is a vivid exchange of views between analysts and companies. The financial analysts are in charge of giving buy, hold, or sell recommendations for the stocks that they analyze. We were in a position to prove empirically that the influence of such recommendations on the development of share prices is significant at least for sell recommendations in the German market.[57] That means that the analyst's recommendations may have a substantial impact on the companies' cost of capital. Therefore, by maintaining good investor relationships, the companies provide this target group with actual information that is important for evaluation. From the institutional investor's point of view, personal conversations with the board members have the most leverage in terms of influence.[58] It is true that the rules that are applied globally to avoid insider trading complicate the dissemination of information that is relevant to the evaluation during those one-on-one meetings. However, taking into consideration the free riding related to active corporate governance, many institutional investors achieve economic advantages as regards information during these personal conversations. Hence, the managers may give detailed interpretations of public information in a legal way. Furthermore, in these one-on-ones, they obtain a better impression of the competencies and the abilities of the management.

[54] See L.A. Gordon and J. Pound, 'Information, Ownership Structure and Shareholder Voting: Evidence from Shareholder-Sponsored Corporate Governance Proposals' [1993] 48 *Journal of Finance* 697–718 and S.L. Gilland and L.T. Starks, *Shareholder Activism and Institutional Investors: The Effects of Corporate-Governance-Related Proposals*, University of Texas, Department of Finance, Working Paper, 1996.

[55] See R.H. Koppes and M.L. Reilly, 'An Ounce of Prevention: Meeting the Fiduciary Duty to Monitor an Index Fund Through Relationship Investing' [1995] 20 The Journal of Corporation Law 413–449.

[56] See W. Paul, 'Investor Relations-Management—demonstriert am Beispiel der BASF' [1991] 10 *Zeitschrift für betriebswirtschaftliche Forschung* 923–945, 933.

[57] See W. Gerke and M. Oerke, 'Marktbeeinflussung durch Analystenempfehlungen' [1998] 1 *Zeitschrift für Betriebswirtschaft* 187–200.

[58] See M. Steiger, *Institutionelle Investoren im Spannungsfeld zwischen Aktienmarktliquidität und Corporate Governance* (Baden-Baden 2000) for Germany.

Due to the significance of personal conversations and conferences of analysts, the SEC proposed new regulations at the end of 1999, the so-called Regulation FD which should actually be a matter of course in view of the fair treatment of all groups of investors. In this respect, the American capital market followed the German practice.[59] The widely spread practice of exclusively passing on important information to the securities analysts of major brokerage houses in advance is prohibited in Germany. The Internet could be used to solve the problem of a fair disclosure of information. Transmitting analyst conferences in the Internet is a cost-efficient way of guaranteeing that the public will be informed at the same time as the analysts and that all investors have equal opportunities. This, of course, makes it increasingly difficult to achieve information advantages which in turn reduces the incentive for an active discussion with the companies. This leads to our sixth thesis:

Thesis 6: in the future, institutional investors will have little direct influence (direct voice) on companies, because technically efficient markets leave no room for sufficient return on investment in comparison to the cost of exerting influence.

Exerting direct influence on the management, all shareholders benefit from the positive effects of shareholder activism and the corresponding costs are borne by the active shareholder. The high competitive pressure among institutional investors and the high degree of transparency is a strong incentive for free riding on the efforts of others. In the future, institutional investors will be less and less in a position to privatize at least part of the additional returns of shareholder activism.

The investment branch is already today taking the consequences of this dilemma. The formulation of so-called "codes-of-best-practice" is one possibility to exert indirect control (indirect voice). Such codes represent public goods, as nobody can be excluded from using them as a basis for their own investment policy.[60] From the point of view of information economy, codes are a simple and transparent benchmark for investors to guarantee a minimum quality. From the investor's point of view, they can be interpreted as self-selection strategy showing the quality of the companies to be financed. Companies that do not accept

---

[59] "The all-too-common practice of selectively disseminating material information is a disservice to investors and undermines the fundamental principle of fairness" (Arthur Levitt, president of the SEC).

[60] Even supranational institutions are participating in the development of such codes. In 1999, the OECD, for example, published a paper describing the principles of a "good" corporate governance. See OECD, *OECD Principles of Corporate Governance* (Paris 1999) (www.oecd.org.daf/ governance). These principles can serve institutional investors as a guideline. A Code of Best Practice, especially for German companies, was published recently. See German Panel on Corporate Governance, *Corporate Governance Rules for German Companies* (Frankfurt/Main January 2000) (www.corgov.de).

or that abuse the code regulations will be "punished" by increasing cost of capital. Therefore, those codes are an efficient possibility to exert indirect influence on companies seeking capital. These reflections lead to our seventh thesis:

Thesis 7: in the future, institutional investors will exert more indirect influence (indirect voice) on companies seeking capital via external standards (e.g. codes of best practice).

Direct influence on the part of institutional investors is moreover not likely due to the fact that no detailed suggestions for operating or strategic decisions can be expected because of a lack of specialization of portfolio managers in relevant cases.[61] The production of such information is very expensive due to a lack of specialized knowledge. As a rule, the exertion of influence is limited to a plausibility check as regards shareholder value goals and a comparison with the peer group. Here, it must be taken into consideration that the compliance with external standards is likely to be a credible signal for the plausibility of actions taken by the management.

However, such direct exertion of influence by the major banks is repeatedly found in Germany. They exert direct influence, e.g. by positioning managers in financed companies to manage crises. For example, due to their major stake in Philipp Holzmann AG, Deutsche Bank was able to appoint the Chairman of the Board. The failure of the management with respect to Holzmann shows that active exertion of influence by banks does not necessarily lead to better results. One must have in mind that the stake of banks is much higher than the average stake held by other institutional investors like pension funds.

III. Harmonization of International Regulatory Settings Forced by Institutional Investors

In the wake of globalization and increasing convergence of capital markets, the Anglo-Saxon and continental European system of corporate finance and control is changing only slowly. Meanwhile, only the increase of the shareholder value is followed as a common corporate objective. [62]

One of the most important factors of internationally observed corporate governance systems is the structure of the respective national corporate finance

---

[61] See E.F. Fama and M.C. Jensen, 'Organizational Forms and Investment Decisions' [1985] 10 *Journal of Financial Economics*, 101–119 and E.F. Fama and M.C. Jensen, 'Separation of Ownership and Control' [1983] 26 *Journal of Law and Economics* 301–325.

[62] See Th. Baums, *Corporate Governance Systems in Europe—Differences and Tendencies of Convergence*, Universität Osnabrück, Institut für Handels- und Wirtschaftsrecht; Discussion Paper, No. 8, 1996, 6–14.

system. The different financing portions of equity and debt result in important implications for corporate control that is mainly realized either by the providers of equity or debt.[63] This also results in national differences in specific ways equity and/or debt is raised by companies. The Anglo-Saxon financial system is more market-oriented while the continental European one is more bank-oriented.[64] In bank-oriented systems such as Germany, the banks hold a central position in corporate finance and control. The borrowing terms are negotiated individually and bilaterally between the borrower and the financial institution. At the same time, banks exert corporate governance. This may lead to conflict of interests. The market-oriented systems, however, take care of the capital market financing on the contract terms specified by the debt holders; banks play a minor role with respect to the classic long-term debt financing.[65] Where Germany was seen as a bank-oriented system in the past and the U.S. as a market-oriented one,[66] Germany is progressively approaching the market-oriented system.[67]

The difference between market-oriented and bank-oriented finance systems is less significant if all sources of corporate capital on both sides of the Atlantic are taken into account.[68] Internal financing structures dominate not only in countries considered to be market-oriented such as the U.S. and Great Britain, but also in countries classified as bank-oriented.[69] Based on the clear dominance of

[63] Whereby, due to the different laws, providers of debt can only react to deficits in the corporate control, whereas providers of equity can act.

[64] See C. Mayer, 'Financial Systems and Corporate Governance: A Review of the International Evidence' [1997] 154 *Journal of Institutional and Theoretical Economics*, 144–176 and E.A. Berglöf, 'A Note on the Typology of Financial Systems' in K.J. Hopt and E. Wymeersch (eds), *Comparative Corporate Governance—Essays and Materials* (Berlin/New York 1997) 151–164.

[65] See M. Hellwig, 'Banking, Financial Intermediation and Corporate Finance' in A. Giovanni and C. Mayer (eds.), *European Financial Integration* (Cambridge 1990) 35–63, and F. Allen, 'Stock Markets and Resource Allocation' in C. Mayer and X. Vives (eds.), *Capital Markets and Financial Intermediation* (Cambridge 1993) 81–116.

[66] See F. Allen and D. Gale, *A Welfare Comparison of Intermediaries and Financial Markets in Germany and the U.S.*, The Wharton School, University of Pennsylvania; Discussion Paper, No. 12, 1994, 1–13.

[67] See, e.g. W. Gerke and G. Pfeufer, 'Finanzintermediation' in W. Gerke and M. Steiner (eds.), *Handwörterbuch des Bank- und Finanzwesens* 2nd edn. (Stuttgart 1995) col. 727–735, col. 733–734, and M. Bank, *Gestaltung von Finanzierungsbeziehungen* (Wiesbaden 1998) 289ff.

[68] See J. Edwards and K. Fischer, *Banks, Finance and Investment in Germany* (Cambridge 1994) who doubt the strong role of the German banks.

[69] See R.H. Schmidt and M. Tyrell, 'Financial Systems, Corporate Finance and Corporate Governance' [1997] 3 *European Financial Management* 333–361, 337ff; W. Gerke et al., *Probleme deutscher mittelständischer Unternehmen beim Zugang zum Kapitalmarkt, Analyse und wirtschaftspolitische Schlußfolgerungen, Schriftenreihe des ZEW* (Baden-Baden 1995) 26ff; S.M. Fazzari, G. Hubbard, and B.C. Petersen, 'Financing Constraints and Corporate Investment' in *Bookings Papers on Economic Activity* (Vol. 1 1988) 141–195 and C. Mayer, 'Financial Systems, Corporate Finance, and Economic Development' in G. Hubbard (ed.), *Asymmetric Information, Corporate Finance, and Investment* (Chicago/London 1990) 307–332.

internal finance, companies seeking independence from external capital seem to be anxious to limit the banks' possibilities of co-determination regardless of the prevailing financial system.[70] The role of the providers of capital is most important when cash flows are exhausted and new funds have to be brought in from outside.[71]

An international comparison of corporate governance structures can be carried out on the basis of the formal and informal network of relationships among shareholders, a representative committee of the shareholders and the company management.[72] The remainder of this part only discusses the most important patterns of this relationship network.[73] The international differences become obvious considering the so-called outsider-versus-insider systems displaying the special features of the ownership and control structures.[74]

The Anglo-Saxon outsider system is based on relatively liquid secondary markets. It shows a widely fragmented ownership of shareholder groups and comprises a larger distance between investors and management (at arm's length relationship). To control agency conflicts caused by the separation of ownership and management an active market for mergers and acquisitions emerged which reached its first peak at the end of the 1980s.[75] In contrast to this, less illiquid securities markets and closer links between providers of capital and management

---

[70] In this context, the idea that the financial system, be it market-oriented or bank-oriented, can exert an important control function over the company must be modified. See M. Hellwig, 'Unternehmensfinanzierung, Unternehmenskontrolle und Ressourcenallokation: Was leistet das Finanzsystem?' in B. Gahlen, H. Hesse, and H.J. Ramser (eds.), *Wirtschaftswissenschaftliches Seminar Ottobeuren* (Tübingen 1997) 211–252, 228.

[71] See J. Franks, C. Mayer, and L. Renneboog, *Who Disciplines Bad Management?*, London Business School, University of Oxford and Tilburg University, Discussion Paper, 1998.

[72] See M.J. Roe, *Comparative Corporate Governance*, Columbia Law School, Discussion Paper, 1997, 2.

[73] For international comparisons of the different corporate governance systems, see M.J. Rubach and T.C. Sebora, 'Comparative Corporate Governance: Competitive Implications of an Emerging Convergence' [1998] 33 *Journal of World Business*, No. 2, K.J. Hopt and E. Wymeersch, *Comparative Corporate Governance: Essays and Materials* (Berlin/New York 1997); M.J. Roe, *Comparative Corporate Governance*, Columbia Law School, Discussion Paper, 1997; C. Mayer, 'Financial Systems and Corporate Governance: A Review of the International Evidence' [1998] 154 *Journal of Institutional and Theoretical Economics* 144–176; K. Kojima, *Corporate Governance: An International Comparison*, RIEB Kobe University, Discussion Paper, No. 34, 1995; M.J. Roe, 'Some Difference in Corporate Governance in Germany, Japan and America' in Th. Baums, R.M. Buxbaum and K.J. Hopt (eds.), *Institutional Investors and Corporate Governance* (Berlin/New York 1994) 23–88 and S. Prowse, 'Corporate Governance in an International Perspective: A Survey of Corporate Control Mechanisms Among Large Firms in the United States, the United Kingdom, Japan and Germany' in Bank for International Settlements (ed.), *BIS Economic Papers* (Basel 1994).

[74] See C. Mayer, 'Financial Systems and Corporate Governance: A Review of the International Evidence' [1998] 154 *Journal of Institutional and Theoretical Economics*, 146–149.

[75] See J. Franks and C. Mayer, 'Ownership and Control' in H. Siebert (ed.), *Trends in Business Organization: Do Participation and Cooperation Increase Competitiveness?* (Tübingen 1995) 171–195, 164, who defeat the thesis that hostile takeovers exert a disciplinary influence.

are characteristics of the continental European insider system alongside concentrated share ownership.[76] It is typical of these insider systems that corporate control is exerted by one single investor, e.g. a family or another company or a dominating provider of debt (e.g. by the so-called "Hausbank" in Germany).[77] Intervention in the course of the corporate governance process is effected by either changing the senior management initiated by the majority shareholder or by rationing or recalling debt.[78] The German universal banks play a special role on an international comparison. Besides their function as the most important provider of debt of a company, they exert additional influence on many companies by way of participations or by taking seats on the supervisory board, and especially by exerting proxy voting rights at general meetings on behalf of the shareholders. This multiple possibility of intervention not only as shareholders but also as providers of capital is the basis for the increasing criticism of the so-called "power of the banks".[79]

In the case of the Anglo-Saxon corporate governance systems, the role of the banks is limited due to laws and regulations. As the banks mainly provide the companies with only short-term debt and as long-term capital is raised via the capital market, the influence of the banks is small.[80] Investors do not usually intervene directly within the company, but often through external control mechanisms, e.g. the market for corporate control, or by court decisions.[81] The market for corporate control can lead to an increase in market efficiency for the

[76] See E. Berglöf, 'A Note on the Typology of Financial Systems' in K.J. Hopt, and E. Wymeersch (eds.), *Comparative Corporate Governance—Essays and Materials* (Berlin/New York 1997) 151–164, 159–164, and M.J. Roe, Comparative Corporate Governance, Columbia Law School, Discussion Paper, 1997.

[77] See J. Franks and C. Mayer, 'Ownership and Control' in H. Siebert (ed.), *Trends in Business Organization: Do Participation and Cooperation Increase Competitiveness?* (Tübingen 1995), 184.

[78] See M. Harris and A. Raviv, 'Capital Structure and the Informational Role of Debt' [1990] 45 *Journal of Finance* 321–349.

[79] See M. Adams, 'Begrenzung der Bankenmacht—Sind die Vorschläge der Bundesregierung zur Reform des Aktienrechts ausreichend?' in Bundestagsfraktion Bündnis 90/DIE GRÜNEN (ed.), *Das deutsche Bankensystem—Innovationsbremse oder Erfolgsgarant?* Dokumentation der Veranstaltung am 5 März 1997 in Bonn (Bonn 1997) 22–29; P. Mülbert, 'Begrenzung der Bankenmacht—Sind die Vorschläge der Bundesregierung zur Reform des Aktienrechts ausreichend?' in Bundestagsfraktion Bündnis 90/DIE GRÜNEN (ed.), *Das deutsche Bankensystem—Innovationsbremse oder Erfolgsgarant?* Dokumentation der Veranstaltung am 5 März 1997 in Bonn (Bonn 1997) 61–68; Th. Baums, 'Vollmachtstimmrecht der Banken—Ja oder Nein?' [1996] 1 *Die Aktiengesellschaft* 11–26 and M. Weber, 'Die Macht der Banken—ein Kommunikationsproblem?' in International Bankers Forum eV (ed.), *Der Weg der Banken ins 21. Jahrhundert* (Wiesbaden 1996) 439–450.

[80] See OECD, 'Eigentumsverhältnisse, Kontrolle und Entscheidungsprozesse in deutschen Unternehmen' in *OECD-Wirtschaftsberichte* (Germany 1995) 94–145, 19.

[81] See E. Berglöf, 'A Note on the Typology of Financial Systems' in K.J. Hopt and E. Wymeersch (eds.), *Comparative Corporate Governance—Essays and Materials* (Berlin/New York 1997) 151–164, 155.

purposes of the shareholders and may strengthen their position by limiting the scope for disadvantaging the shareholders due to the high percentage of internal financing.[82] The shareholders are compensated by distributions in form of an acquisition premium for the currently inefficient corporate governance structures. In the U.S., however, the boom of hostile take-overs led to expensive defence strategies of the management under attack[83] and, in some cases, to a redistribution of the material and immaterial assets between the different entitled groups (employers, management, debt holders, and revenue department).[84]

Due to the numerous differences between the two basic systems of corporate finance and corporate governance, the academic discussion focuses on the systems' possible convergence and superiority.[85] On the one hand, the globalization of capital markets can induce a convergence of the systems.[86] The internationalization of institutional investors ensures that national standards of an efficient corporate governance are converted into national law in the form of codes of best practice drawn up under private law, as was the case with the law for control and transparency in the company sector (*KonTraG*) in Germany in May 1998.[87] Also, the efforts towards mutual acceptance of the universally accepted accounting standards, U.S.-GAAP and IAS, lead to an increasing harmonization of market standards with respect to the transparency of accounting procedures. The pursued conversion of the take-over regulations in the 13th EC guideline can be considered as another incentive towards the convergence of the systems, where the most essential items of the so called "City Code" (British take-over code) are to be adapted. All these developments are further evidence

[82] See S.J. Grossman and O.D. Hart, 'Takeover Bids, the Free-Rider Problem, and the Theory of the Corporation' [1980] 11 *Bell Journal of Economics* 42–64.

[83] See A. Shleifer and R.W. Vishny, 'Large Shareholders and Corporate Control' [1986] 94 *Journal of Political Economy* 461–488.

[84] See M. Hellwig, 'Unternehmensfinanzierung, Unternehmenskontrolle und Ressourcenallokation: Was leistet das Finanzsystem?' in B. Gahlen, H. Hesse, and H.J. Ramser (eds.), *Wirtschaftswissenschaftliches Seminar Ottobeuren* (Tübingen 1997) 211–252, 218.

[85] See J.C. Coffee, *The Future as History: The Prospects for Global Convergence in Corporate Governance and its Implications,* Law and Economics Studies, Columbia University School of Law, Working Paper No. 144; M. Balling, E. Hennessy, and R. O'Brien, 'Corporate Governance, Financial Markets and Global Convergence' [1998] 33 *Financial and Monetary Policy Studies* 199–262; M.J. Rubach and T.C. Sebora, 'Comparative Corporate Governance: Competitive Implications of an Emerging Convergence' [1998] 33 *Journal of World Business* 2; M.J. Roe, *Comparative Corporate Governance,* Columbia Law School, Discussion Paper, 1997; R.H. Schmidt and M. Tyrell, 'Financial Systems, Corporate Finance and Corporate Governance' [1997] 3 *European Financial Management* 333–361 and Th. Baums, *Corporate Governance Systems in Europe—Differences and Tendencies of Convergence,* Universität Osnabrück, Institut für Handels- und Wirtschaftsrecht; Discussion Paper, No. 8, 1996.

[86] See M.J. Roe, *Comparative Corporate Governance*, Columbia Law School, Discussion Paper, 1997, 11.

[87] Attempts to further reduce the influence of German banks by restricting proxy votes and increase the efficiency of supervisory boards have recently been made in Germany.

of the convergence of the conceptions of a perfect and integrated global capital market.

Most of the highly developed countries are already on the way to install efficient corporate governance systems. The role of major investors and the legal protection of minority shareholders are thus accentuated differently.[88] None of the systems displays a clear superiority as yet.[89] Due to a different general framework, such as the political system and the historical development of the social rights or the nations themselves, it is difficult to compare the systems.[90] The discussion about the adaptation of the elements of one system through the respective competing financial and control system is always revived when the economic success alternates between both systems.[91] This leads to our eighth thesis:

Thesis 8: in the future, the international general settings will progressively be brought into line due to pressure exerted by the institutional investors. The continental European financial systems will increasingly become market-oriented.

IV. The Role of Universal Banks as Institutional Investors

Recently, the general settings for banks in the leading industrialized countries have changed considerably. The Gramm-Leach-Bliley-Act passed in the U.S. abolished the so-called Glass/Steagall-Act that provided a strict separation of

[88] See A. Shleifer and R.W. Vishny, 'A Survey of Corporate Governance' [1997] 52 *Journal of Finance* 737–783, 739.

[89] See S.N. Kaplan, 'Corporate Governance and Corporate Performance: A Comparison of Japan, Germany, and the U.S.' [1996] 9 *Journal of Applied Corporate Finance* 86–93 and S. Prowse, 'Corporate Governance in an International Perspective: A Survey of Corporate Control Mechanisms Among Large Firms in the United States, the United Kingdom, Japan and Germany' in Bank for International Settlements (ed.) *BIS Economic Papers* (Basel 1994).

[90] On the other hand, the different historical interrelations in countries themselves exert influence on the respective system of corporate finance and corporate control, see, e.g. R. La Porta, F. Lopez-de-Silanes, A. Schleifer, and R.W. Vishny, 'Legal Determinants of External Finance' [1997] 52 *Journal of Finance* 1131–1150.

[91] See M.J. Roe, 'Mutual Funds in the Boardroom' [1993] 5 *Journal of Applied Corporate Finance* 56–61, J.P. Charkham, 'A Larger Role for Institutional Investors' in N. Dimsdale and M. Prevezer (eds.), *Capital Markets and Corporate Governance* (Oxford 1994) 99–110; O.G. Lambsdorff, 'Die Überwachungstätigkeit des Aufsichtsrats: Verbesserungsmöglichkeiten de lege lata und de lege ferenda' in D. Feddersen, P. Hommelhoff, and U.H. Schneider (eds.), *Corporate Governance—Optimierung der Unternehmensführung und der Unternehmenskontrolle im deutschen und amerikanischen Aktienrecht* (Cologne 1996) 217–233 and R.M. Buxbaum, 'Die Leitung von Gesellschaften: Strukturelle Reformen im amerikanischen und deutschen Gesellschaftsrecht' in D. Feddersen, P. Hommelhoff and U.H. Schneider (eds.), *Corporate Governance: Optimierung der Unternehmensführung und der Unternehmenskontrolle im deutschen und amerikanischen Aktienrecht* (Cologne 1996) 65–93.

commercial and investment banking.[92] Although this strict separation had crumbled in recent years,[93] U.S. banks are now able to operate in all banking business areas at the same time (Universal Banking). In continental Europe, on the other hand, a trend can be seen towards a voluntary separation of commercial and investment banking. For European universal banks there are growing potential conflicts because of their role both as providers of debt as well as shareholders of the same companies. Here traditional structures prove increasingly unsuitable for solving the conflict of interests emerging in universal banks. Within grown structures it is difficult to set up so-called firewalls between individual business units and control them by compliance departments. Seen from this point of view, the formation of universal banks in the U.S. is less loaded with conflicts of interest. When integrating independent structures, firewalls and compliance rules can be implemented more efficiently. Nevertheless, an efficient integration management has to be set up to generate synergies.

Due to the squeeze on the interest margin of German banks and due to the requests of the bank supervisory authority for high equity capital, the loan business is regarded more and more as a complimentary product to off-balance-sheet operations. German banks instead attempt to develop their asset management and investment banking departments.

Foreign investors mainly criticize the German financial system for its cross holdings in non-financial companies and the substantial equity holdings of the big German banks in the most important listed German companies. This network is called "Germany Inc. (Deutschland AG)".[94] It has—at least so far—helped to avoid unfriendly take-overs of major firms by foreign companies.[95] But even unfriendly take-overs within Germany itself hardly exist. The first spectacular attempt was the take-over conflict between Krupp/Hoesch AG and Thyssen AG. The unfriendly take-over bid failed, but a friendly merger of both companies has meanwhile taken place.

---

[92] See D. Kuckelkorn, 'Neue Ära für Amerikas Banken' *Börsenzeitung,* October 29, 1999.

[93] This concerns in particular the formation of Citigroup which emerged from Citibank (commercial bank), The Travellers Group (insurance) and Salomon Smith Barney (investment banking).

[94] A further characteristic of "Deutschland AG" is the co-determination legally implemented in the corporate governance system which allows workers and trade unions to influence management decisions. Seen from this point of view, the German corporate governance system can be called a stakeholder system which is based on the consent of all stakeholders. This system does not increase added value and suppresses the shareholder value idea. Neither the banks providing both equity and debt nor the members of the Board or the employees (trade unions) have ever been motivated to question or change the existing company structures.

[95] An example is the unsuccessful takeover attempt of the German Continental AG by the Italian company Pirelli. With regard to the finally successful Mannesmann/Vodafone acquisition it should be noted that Mannesmann neither had a concentrated ownership structure nor were any of the major banks large shareholders. Mannesmann was not part of the so-called "Deutschland AG".

The big German banks play a decisive role in this connection. Their role both as shareholders and providers of debt causes a conflict of interests especially due to the fact that their main objective is to secure their position as providers of debt. Although a thorough restructuring of the German companies would have emphasized the shareholder value it would at the same time have led to a loss in influence. For tax reasons, the banks would not have wanted to increase restructuring profits in the form of hidden reserves, as taxes on earnings would have run into billions of Euros. In addition to this, German banks have not yet developed an internationally comparable competence in the mergers and acquisitions sector. They are currently trying to catch up by investing heavily into human resources. Why then should German banks try and bring about a restructuring of the economy at the beginning of the new millennium if there is no sufficient management competence in investment banking and no sufficiently developed capital market, assuming that high tax payments and finally a loss of power and influence were to be expected?

Against this backdrop, it is even surprising that the big German banks are aiming voluntarily at separating gradually from industrial holdings. The real reason may be the tough competition introduced into Germany by foreign investment banks in the 1990s. Apart from this, the German stock market underwent a rapid development over recent years. The Initial Public Offering of Deutsche Telekom in 1996 and the subsequent seasoned offering in 1999 and the development of the Neuer Markt as a source of venture capital and as an attractive exit possibility for venture capitalists is transforming the stock market into a serious alternative to debt financing via the banking system. In addition to this, companies are issuing corporate bonds to replace bank lending and reduce the dependence on key relationship banks. Accordingly, German big banks invest heavily in investment banking competence in order to prevent this profitable business area from being lost entirely to Anglo-Saxon players. A decisive step towards dissolving the *Deutschland AG* has already been realized by implementing a tax reform. The tax reform allows the tax-free sale of industrial holdings so that the main reason for banks to stick to their industrial holdings no longer exists. It is to be expected that the competence in the merger and acquisition sector will be used to enter this profitable business area. A further impetus comes from the successful take-over of Mannesmann AG by Vodafone/Airtouch with a take-over volume of about DEM 400 billion.

Taking all this into account, a further development can be observed in German big banks. Legally and organizationally independent venture capital companies are increasingly being founded by these banks. As institutional investors, they provide promising small and mid-sized businesses with equity capital. In order to realize synergies, banks form financial holding companies with specialized individual companies. Young companies are to be made marketable and accompanied when going public. Apart from the prospect of capital gains, initial public offerings are expected to generate revenues. There is also the possibility to act as designated sponsor[96] in the secondary market and to take part in secondary offerings. If restructuring is required, the investment banking division of the financial holding company can be consulted. In effect, the entire capital market life cycle of a company is covered. These arguments lead to our ninth thesis:

Thesis 9: due to conflicts of interest, the German universal banks will concentrate either on investment banking/asset management/financing of venture capital or on commercial banking and reduce their shareholdings. The socio-politically disputed Deutschland AG is starting to dissolve. The planned tax law reform will boost this trend.

E. Conclusions

In the past, the German financial market already followed structural U.S. developments with a delay of two to eight years. Remarkable is the professionalization of the investment processes through the appearance of institutional investors and the high growth rates in managed funds. In the past years, institutional investors have managed to change the legal and informal basic conditions in their favour mainly in Anglo-Saxon countries.[97] In continental Europe, this development took place only in part and was mostly restricted to high growth rates of investment funds. Institutional investors in Germany were either minor subsidiaries of universal banks, which focus on lending and deposit business, or insurance companies with highly conservative investment methods due to legal regulations or a lack of competition. The legal regulations concerning the public and companies' pension scheme prevented the emergence of pension funds. The underdeveloped German stock market was not least a result of this constellation. The banking and insurance industry was not very interested in changing the status quo so that legal basic conditions remained unchanged for a long time.

The European unification with the formation of the domestic market and the increased activity of U.S. investment banks and pension funds have put the German legislative and the interest groups under pressure. The development is one-dimensional as the rules of the financial markets that are dominated by the U.S. are increasingly being accepted in continental Europe. Due to this and their political and economic predominance, the U.S. holds an actual monopoly

---

[96] Designated sponsors provide liquidity in the German trading system XETRA.

[97] This concerns in particular the takeover regulations of Anglo-Saxon countries. A further example is the establishment of alternative trading systems (ECNs). The introduction of ERISA (Employment Retirement Income Security Act) in the U.S. in 1974 and the so called 401k-plans boosted the development of pension schemes.

through the stipulation of accounting standards and the institutional organization of the capital markets. The increasing shift of power towards institutional investors as a group that apparently make their investment decisions on grounds of hard economic arguments and performance prospects[98] at the same time increases their responsibility for global economic development. Seen from today's point of view, it is, however, not clear whether the institutional investors are aware of this increase in responsibility and in which way undesirable developments can be countered. The evolving completion of the global capital markets made possible by a progressing technologization and harmonization of regulations in line with U.S. standards are likely to reduce the role of institutional investors to mere portfolio management for a competitive management fee.

To summarize, we see the future role of institutional investors and further developments in the following areas especially:

- As far as the competition for clients' funds is concerned, the increasing technologization will produce a degree of transparency that increasingly pushes institutional investors into the role of price takers (liability side). Increasing market transparency will considerably decrease margins in asset management and increase the share of indexed assets of institutional investors.
- In the future, institutional investors will influence the existing stock exchange structures even more in order to create an environment that favours their needs.
- In the future, institutional investors will considerably increase the volatility of the markets. This is partly due to a more correlated behaviour as information is becoming more and more homogeneous, and partly due to the increasing percentage of indexed portfolios.
- There will be fewer incentives to exert active influence on the companies for institutional investors.
- In the future, institutional investors will passively or indirectly influence companies via codes of best practice or other standards specified by public institutions (e.g. OECD), interest groups (e.g. AIMR) or other important market players (e.g. CalPERS).
- The continental European financial systems will become more and more market-oriented under the pressure of institutional investors.
- In the course of an increasing market orientation, the continental European universal banks will concentrate either on investment banking/asset management/finance of venture capital or on commercial banking.

---

[98] It is questionable whether the decisions are rational. It cannot be excluded that in certain situations institutional investors and private investors do not act entirely rationally. An example is the so-called herd instinct of portfolio managers where the decision of the competitor merely is copied, resulting in a common reaction of all portfolio managers on the entire market. A correlated behaviour of portfolio managers can, however, also be attributed to an identical and correct interpretation of new information. In this case, the behaviour would be rational.

17

Cross-border Voting in Europe[1]

JAAP W. WINTER

Abstract

This paper investigates the difficulties in the cross-border exercise of voting rights by shareholders. The difficulties arise as a result of differences in the company laws, securities laws, and securities systems in the Member States of the European Union, which have all been set up decades ago to serve national purposes. In addition there are uncertainties in the rules of private international law governing these securities systems. These differences cause serious problems where shares are increasingly held through cross-border chains of intermediaries from investors to custodian and depository banks, national and international clearing organizations and regional or global custodians. As a result the author concludes that Europe is in need of a new legal and practical infrastructure which would facilitate cross-border voting by shareholders. The consolidating stock exchanges and clearing markets will increase the necessity of such an infrastructure, but will in itself not provide this infrastructure. Legislation, on a European scale, is required. In devising a new system, Europe should look at the U.S., where a number of these problems have been overcome in the past. With the knowledge of hindsight, Europe could probably even improve on the U.S. system.

Contents

Figures

[1] Translated from inaugural lecture held at Erasmus University Rotterdam on April 14, 2000.

A. The Growing Significance of Market-oriented Systems of Corporate Governance in Europe

The predominant system of corporate governance in Europe, apart from the U.K., traditionally has been a control-oriented system in which large share-holders (families, banks, companies holding cross-participations) exercise actual control over the management of companies. Market-oriented systems of corporate governance, in which the share-ownership is widely dispersed, shareholders are not interested in exercising control ('rational apathy'), and ownership and control as a result have been separated, were the exception.[2]

In today's 'New Economy' economies are experiencing prolonged growth, driven by technological innovations and the related global integration of major economic sectors such as energy, information and communication, pharmaceuticals, and the car industry. In such an environment market-oriented systems of corporate governance undeniably become more important. Companies in these sectors that want to compete on a global scale need liquid stock markets to be able to finance substantial investments and acquisitions of and mergers with other players on those markets.[3] They will have to adapt their corporate governance regimes towards the market-oriented system if they want to gain actual access to those markets.[4] The same development can be seen for companies that take the step from a national scale to a European scale.

These developments are being strengthened by the growing importance attached to institutional investors in Europe. Historically, pension funds and investment companies have played a subordinated role in Europe. To an increasing extent savings are being placed in investment funds and pensions are being financed with capital coverage systems.[5] The funds that are obtained are being

---

[2] See for general discussions of the various types of corporate governance systems and the prospects of convergence between them J.C. Coffee, 'The Future as History: the Prospects for Global Convergence in Corporate Governance and its Implications' [1999] 93 Northwestern University Law Review 641–707; W.W. Bratton and J.A. McCahery, 'Comparative Corporate Governance and the Theory of the Firm: the Case against Global Cross Reference' [1999] Columbia Journal of Transnational Law 223.

[3] This type of acquisition/merger on a global scale is financed solely with new shares. Vodafone offers Vodafone shares to Mannesmann shareholders, America On Line offers AOL shares to Time Warner shareholders, DaimlerBenz and Chrysler offer DaimlerChrysler shares to DaimlerBenz and Chrysler shareholders. This way, no real price is paid for the acquisition. What is mainly at stake is whether the parts that the two groups of shareholders acquire in the combined company are in relation to the value of the two component parts.

[4] Coffee points particularly to these developments that lead to a gradual process of convergence, 'stealth convergence', of corporate governance systems in the direction of the market-oriented system without formal company law necessarily converging as well, see above, n. 2, 705. See also C. Doyle, 'Mannesmann is just the beginning' *The Wall Street Journal*, February 11, 2000, 8.

[5] Coffee, see above, n. 2, 671.

invested more and more on the stock markets, where superb returns on investment can be achieved.[6]

From an institutional point of view, too, a lot of work has been done over the past ten years to improve the quality of the European securities markets. A great many European directives have been introduced, mainly aimed at guaranteeing greater transparency and disclosure on securities markets, for example as regards the notification of substantial holdings in publicly listed companies and changes in such holdings,[7] the information that has to be provided during a flotation and the periodic disclosure of information by listed companies,[8] and to combat insider trading.[9] These directives are intended to protect the position of investors on securities markets. Another important development is the establishment of the Thirteenth Directive relating to company law in respect of public offers for shares. The draft directive contained two key elements: (1) the obligation to make an offer for all shares upon acquisition of a controlling interest in a listed company and (2) a prohibition for the board to put up defensive devices after the announcement of a public offer. Both elements are aimed at allowing the stock market to decide on the acquisition of control in listed companies. The draft directive was rejected by the European Parliament in 2001. It is expected that the Commission will publish a revised draft of the directive in 2002 following the recommendations of the High Level Group of Company Law Experts of January 2002.[10]

In 1999 the European Commission drew up a Financial Services Action Plan that includes proposals for achieving an efficient financial market in Europe.[11] High on the agenda is a directive that is aimed at abolishing national constraints on cross-border investments by pension funds. Due to the further integration of the underlying economic markets for goods, services and information, the interest of investors is shifting from investments in national stock markets towards

---

[6] For Dutch pension funds that have a relatively high percentage of their investments in shares, a total return of up to 25% is estimated for 1999, *Het Financieele Dagblad*, January 14, 2000. For an enumeration of the growing investments of pension funds in various countries see B. Asher, 'The Development of a Global Securities Market' in F. Oditah (ed.), *The Future for the Global Securities Market* (Oxford 1996) 17.

[7] Council Directive (EEC) 88/627 on the information to be published when a major holding in a listed company is acquired or disposed of [1988] O.J. L129/43.

[8] Council Directive (EEC) 89/298 co-ordinating the requirements for the drawing-up, scrutiny and distribution of the prospectus to be published when transferable securities are offered to the public [1989] O.J. L124/8 and Council Directive (EEC) 82/121 on information to be published on a regular basis by companies the shares of which have been admitted to official stock-exchange listing [1982] O.J. L3/99/23.

[9] Council Directive (EEC) 89/592 co-ordinating regulations on insider dealing [1989] O.J. L334/30.

[10] See for the report of the High Level group (http://europa.eu.int/comm/internal_market/en/company/company/news/02-24.htm).

[11] Financial Services: Implementing the Framework for Financial Markets: Action Plan, 1999.

investments in different economic sectors within one single European market.[12] The introduction of the Euro has brought an enormous stimulus to this cross-border investment because it has in any event eliminated the foreign exchange risk on investment in other EMU member countries.

As yet, however, a truly uniform European stock market does not exist. The stock markets in Europe, together with the related systems for the settlement of securities transactions and giral dealings in securities are organized on a national basis. All the directives I have just mentioned do not create a single, uniform market but harmonize national stock markets, each having their own competent and supervisory authorities, and leave the Member States discretion in the way the directives are implemented. In 1999, eight European stock exchanges have started consultations to assess whether they can establish a pan-European stock exchange for the 300 biggest European companies. The separate financial interests of the stock exchanges, notably the investments they have made in their own computerized trading systems and certainly also the fragmented systems for the settlement of securities transactions, are currently preventing them from actually establishing a pan-European stock exchange.[13] Provisionally the plans are limited to setting up a communal trading platform that will enable the affiliated stockbrokers to trade on all stock exchanges. Very recently the Amsterdam, Brussels, and Paris exchanges have announced to merge into a new exchange, EURONEXT.[14]

Where all this will lead to in due course is difficult to predict. The securities industry is changing very rapidly. The discussions between the original eight stock exchanges do not seem to be progressing smoothly.[15] No one knows exactly what the consequences of modern information and communication technology will be or whether fully electronic stock exchanges will become com-

[12] Dutch pension funds are investing an increasingly bigger part of their capital abroad, see *Het Financieele Dagblad*, January 11, 2000, 19, 'Pensioenvermogen vloeit het land uit' [Pension capital flows out of the country]. On the subject of the need for a drastic realignment of pension systems in Europe see the report of the European Round Table of February 2000: European Pensions—An Appeal for Reform, available via http://www.frdb.org/english/news/pensions.htm. See also *Het Financieele Dagblad*, February 16, 2000, 8.

[13] See *Het Financieele Dagblad*, February 16, 2000, 13 and 19, 'Integreren moet van achteren' [Integration has to start from the back].

[14] According to the press release of the three exchanges, taken from http://www. euronext.com/lang.html on March 20, 2000, EURONEXT will combine the stock, bond, and derivatives markets of the three. EURONEXT will set up a single clearing organization and wishes to come to use a single settlement organization as well. For this Euroclear is the first choice, according to the press release.

[15] *Deutsche Börse*, one of the participants, is apparently taking its own separate route under the name 'Euro Board', *Het Financieele Dagblad*, February 9, 2000, 15, 'Beursalliantie sterft stille dood' [Stock exchange alliance dies a quiet death].

petitors of traditional stock exchanges.[16] For the time being, however, it seems that national stock markets will continue to form the basis in Europe and that there will be increasing integration between those markets as traders will make trades direct on the various markets and investors will want to invest on those various markets.

B. Cross-border Voting

Within the development of a European market-oriented system of corporate governance there is one important aspect which to date has not received any attention at all: the cross-border exercise of voting rights by shareholders. In the European Commission's Financial Services Action Plan no attention is devoted to this aspect.[17] It is specifically the European fragmentation of national stock markets with national systems for the settlement of securities transactions and for giral securities trading, combined with the differences in securities legislation and company law in European countries, that makes cross-border voting by shareholders extremely difficult and brings risks for the decision-making process within companies. I shall argue that efficient and structural cross-border voting is not possible without the intervention of the European legislator.

Let me eliminate one possible counter-argument straight away. People might say: "In view of the rational apathy of shareholders, does it really matter if shareholders in a market-oriented system of corporate governance cannot exercise voting rights? Apparently they themselves are not sitting and waiting for that?"[18] However, as a result of the corporate governance debate, greater value has been attached to the voting right of shareholders, specifically in a market-oriented system of corporate governance. Partly, this results from the realization that the market for corporate control does not work at all in many cases (for instance in the Netherlands) and, where it does work, it does not always lead to

---

[16] It may be the case that a truly pan-European electronic stock exchange such as Tradepoint, which is now being set up by a number of big stockbrokers, will ultimately offer investors and traders the biggest economies of scale and time savings and hence yield cost benefits, see *Het Financieele Dagblad*, February 16, 2000, 19, 'Tradepoint leunt op banken voor succes' [Tradepoint pressurises banks for success]. The Swedish stock exchange has meanwhile announced that it wants to set up an electronic stock exchange together with Morgan Stanley Dean Witter under the name *Jiway*, on which 6,000 European *and* American stocks will be traded, at dramatically lower costs for investors, *Financial Times*, February 9, 2000, 14: 'Brave new world beckons for Europe's day traders'. The traditional stock exchanges will be forced by these electronic competitors to lower their costs.

[17] Nor is any reference made to cross-border voting rights in the report of the Committee on Economic and Monetary Affairs of the European Parliament about the Financial Services Action Plan, report dated March 1, 2000, A5-0059/2000.

[18] An argument somewhat along these lines is made by J.N. Druey.

efficient results.[19] In addition, the exit option is not always available or attractive to investors. Particularly institutional investors with relatively big holdings experience difficulties in selling their shares. In any event they take their losses when they sell: in many cases the market will already have anticipated the problems, which means that selling will no longer be attractive.[20] The selling of shares is made even more difficult due to the fact that many investors nowadays base a large part of their shareholdings on the tracking of specific share indexes, such as the AEX, the S&P 500, the Eurostoxx 50, etc. To avoid deviating too much from the index they have to hold shares in at least the companies that have the heaviest weightings in that index, regardless of their performances. Pulling out when things take a turn for the worse is then no longer possible.[21]

The market is therefore not a perfect mechanism for control of the management of publicly listed companies. In consequence, a need also exists within the market-oriented system of corporate governance for internal control by shareholders that explicitly ask the management to render account of its actions and who participate actively in decision-making at the meeting of shareholders. The right to vote is therefore certainly important for shareholders, especially in that it allows them to bring influence to bear on crucial decisions relating to the company (strategic decisions such as merger or sale of major subsidiaries) and to replace the management where there is cause to.[22] In the corporate governance reports that have been published in various countries in recent years, it is mainly institutional investors who are urged to make actual use of their voting right.[23] Some countries

---

[19] It is dubious, for instance, whether the wave of hostile takeovers in the U.S. in the 1980s, many of which were financed with junk bonds and left industry saddled with enormous debt, ultimately had a positive result, cf. M.A. Sargent and D.R. Honabach, *Proxy Rules Handbook* (New York 1998) 1–5ff.

[20] T. Baums and R. Schmitz, *Shareholder Voting in Germany*, 4, paper available at http://www.uni-frankfurt.de/fb01/baums/arbeitsp.htm.

[21] How important this 'index tracking' has meanwhile become was reflected by the scenes that took place when the AEX index was realigned in February 2000. A number of stocks dropped out of the AEX, a number of others were included in it and the weighting in the index was modified for all stocks. Investors wanted to bring their portfolios into line with these changes. This led to massive buy and sell orders and caused chaotic share price movements on the final trading day before the new index was due to take effect. See *NRC Handelsblad*, February 19, 2000, 15, 'Chaotische koersen bij nieuwe AEX' and 'Vaarwel efficiënte effectenmarkt'; *Het Financieele Dagblad*, February 19, 2000, 1, 'Nieuwe weging AEX-index haalt beurs hard onderuit'.

[22] cf KN Schacht, 'Institutional Investors and Shareholder Activism' in *Meetings of Shareholders* (1999), available at http://www.ascs.org/newslt9.html, Supplement, 5-8 and 5-9.

[23] Peters Committee, 19–20 Hampel Committee, recommendation 34: "We believe that institutional investors have a responsibility to their clients to make considered use of their votes; and we strongly recommend institutional investors of all kinds, wherever practicable, to vote the shares under their control. But we do not recommend that voting should be compulsory".

even make it obligatory for certain institutional investors to exercise the voting right attached to their investments.[24]

Efficient possibilities of exercising the voting right are also regarded as an essential element of corporate governance in the OECD Recommendations on Corporate Governance.[25] In the light of these developments Dutch companies that want to attract investors on a European and worldwide scale will find it difficult to maintain oligarchic arrangements and anti-take-over constructions that withhold the voting right from investors. The Dutch cabinet would also like to see shareholders being allowed to exercise their voting right, at least "in peacetime". A recent proposal submitted to the Parliament provides that holders of non-voting depository receipts of shares should have the right to exercise voting rights in peacetime.[26] If they are not to make themselves vulnerable to the risks of absenteeism, companies will have to try to get larger numbers of shareholders actively involved in the decision-making at the shareholders' meeting. To that extent their interest coincides with the growing need felt by shareholders to exercise their voting right. This is the rationale for the establishment of the Shareholders Communication Channel in the Netherlands, which in 2002 will for the first time give shareholders the opportunity to use voting forms that have been sent to them to cast their votes by proxy, without being present themselves at the meeting.[27] In the U.K. and Germany there are also signs that a start is slowly being made on involving the ultimate shareholders more directly in the

[24] The French Act of March 25, 1997 makes it mandatory for pension funds to vote on the shares that they hold. The Act is still awaiting an implementing decree, which the present French government provisionally does not seem to be willing to issue. The French government does not seem to be an advocate of the formation of pension funds, cf Y Guyon, 'Questionnaire with respect to Shareholders' Votes in General Meetings' in *Shareholder Voting Rights and Practices in Europe and the United States* (2000) 15–16. In the U.S., pension funds that are covered by the Employee Retirement Income Security Act (ERISA) are obliged to exercise their voting right, cf. M. Klausner, J. Elfenbein, report in Th. Baums and E. Wymeersch (eds.), *Shareholder Voting Rights and Practices in Europe and the United States* 12. In Italy an Act was introduced in 1998 that obliges investment funds to exercise their voting right, cf P. Marchetti, G. Carcano, and F. Ghezzi, 'Shareholder Voting in Italy' in *Shareholder Voting Rights and Practices in Europe and the United States*, ibid., 25–26. For the role played by institutional investors in corporate governance, see P.L. Davies, 'Institutional Investors as Corporate Monitors in the U.K.' in K.J. Hopt and E. Wymeersch, *Comparative Corporate Governance* (Berlin/New York 1997) 47–66 and G. McCormack, 'Institutional Shareholders and the Promotion of Good Corporate Governance' in B.A.K. Rider (ed.), *The Realm of Company Law* (London 1998) 131–160.

[25] Sections A and C3, 26 and Schacht, see above, n. 22.

[26] TK 28719. As to the feasibility of the distinction between "wartime" and "peacetime", all sorts of questions can be asked; see for example J.W. Winter, 'Oorlog en vrede' *Ondernemingsrecht* 1999/8, 203; P.J. Dortmond in his speech to the Nijmegen congress in 1999, in an article by Honée, 16–17.

[27] For background details about the Communication Channel see J.W. Winter, 'Stemmen op afstand via het Communicatiekanaal Aandeelhouders' in *Corporate Governance voor juristen* vol. 30 in the series "Uitgaven vanwege het Instituut voor Ondernemingsrecht te Groningen" (Groningen 1998) 81–103.

decision-making.[28] Given the increasing level of cross-border investment *proxy voting* is the only realistic possibility for shareholders to be given a more structured involvement in the decision-making at the shareholders' meeting. For investors it is physically impossible to actually attend shareholders' meetings in the various countries. This certainly applies to institutional investors who hold shares in large numbers of companies. A further complication here is that the annual general meetings are usually concentrated in the period from March through to May, so that meetings of different companies in which investments are held may take place on the same day.[29] Proxy voting makes it possible to take part in the decision-making at the shareholders' meetings of a large number of companies. For shareholders abroad proxy voting is in fact the only possibility of participating in the company's decision-making.

C. Shareholding in a World of Giral Securities

The voting right traditionally accrues to shareholders, i.e. to those who can prove to the company that they hold title to certain shares issued by the com-

---

[28] In the U.K. proxy solicitation has long taken place amongst the 'members' of the company, i.e. the shareholders that are registered in the share register. The London Stock Exchange prescribes this for publicly listed companies, Yellow Book, chapters 9.26, 13.28 and 13.29. To an increasing extent, however, the actual shareholders are hidden behind 'nominees', such as custodians and brokers who are registered in the share register on behalf of their clients. The introduction of CREST, a new electronic settlement system for securities transactions in the U.K., has strengthened this development. The great majority of the 'pooled accounts' within CREST are held by custodians and brokers on behalf of their combined clientele. For more about CREST and the various accounts within it, see J. Benjamin, *The Law of Global Custody* (London 1996) 171–190. In the United Kingdom a project will be started this year in which about 150 publicly listed companies will participate. Its aim is to enable the investors behind the brokers and custodians to exercise their voting right directly. In Germany banks have traditionally voted on the basis of the '*Depotstimmrecht*' on behalf of the clients who have deposited shares with them, mostly without specifically asking those investors for instructions. The possibilities of doing that have meanwhile been limited as a result of the introduction of the *Kontroll- und TransparenzGesetz* in 1998. For example, banks are no longer allowed to use proxies that contain no instructions from their clients in cases where the banks themselves hold 5% or more in a company's capital and wish to exercise the voting rights attaching thereto, s. 135(1) AktG, cf. P. Bavelaar [1998] 'Corporate Governance in Duitsland Reform des Aktiengesetzes, *De Naamloze Vennootschap* 83; Baums, Schmitz, see above, n. 20. From my contacts with German publicly listed companies I understand that efforts are being made to ensure that clients give their banks specific instructions for each meeting.

[29] Fortunately, the situation is not as extreme as it is in Japan. There, it is the custom for the annual shareholders' meetings of some 90% of the publicly listed companies to be organized on the same day. The colourful argument for this practice is that it protects the management of Japanese companies against the unwanted presence of Japanese gangsters who would otherwise disrupt the shareholders' meetings, see C. Arnold, 'Shareholder Voting in the EU. Voting Abroad: Practical Experiences' in *Shareholder Voting Rights and Practices in Europe and the U.S.*, see above, n. 24, 5.

pany. Only shareholders shall have voting rights, states article 2: 118 para. 1 of the Dutch Civil Code sternly. This is a basic rule in company law worldwide.[30]

However, as a result of the way in which shares are held in the modern world of securities, it is extremely complicated to ascertain who is the actual shareholder. In many cases it turns out that the ultimate investor is in legal terms not a shareholder in the company.

Originally investors, at least on the European continent, held shares in the form of bearer certificates. The classic form was a mantle and dividend sheet with separate dividend coupons, which was held by the investor himself. Transfer of ownership was effected by placing the bearer certificate in the possession of the acquirer, cf. article 3: 93 Civil Code. With the increase in stock market trading, the printing of bearer certificates, the custody of bearer certificates on behalf of clients[31] and the physical transfer of ownership after stock exchange transactions became ever more expensive and cumbersome. Besides, bearer certificates ran the risk of being stolen, after which the thief could then cause ownership to pass to a third party who had acquired the bearer certificates in good faith, cf. article 3: 86 Civil Code.[32]

The securities industry therefore has an interest in ensuring that the physical certificates are reduced as much as possible or even eliminated entirely. The first step taken towards achieving this was to *immobilize* the securities.[33] Nowadays the physical certificates are held almost exclusively by professional custody firms, and no longer by individual investors. These custody firms in turn place the certificates in the custody of a central giral institution, which in the Netherlands is called Necigef. Instead of physically holding their own certificates, the investors hold a securities account with their bank or stockbroker (from now on I will refer to these as 'banks' for brevity's sake), in which the number of shares they have placed in custody are administered. The banks are affiliated institutions of Necigef. The transfer of ownership of shares takes place by crediting them in the name of the acquirer in the relevant section of the administration of the affiliated institution, article 17 of the Giral Securities Trading Act (*Wge*), who will then be considered to be joint owner of the collective pool of

---

[30] See the various contributions in *Shareholder Voting Rights and Practices in Europe and the United States*, see above, n. 24. This basic principle also applies in countries where a distinction is made between legal owners and beneficial owners, such as the U.S. and the U.K. In those countries the legal owner, the person who is registered in the share register, has the voting right. In principle, the beneficial owner has no voting right. For more details about the U.S., see below.

[31] To ensure that investors who have placed bearer certificates in the custody of banks continue to hold title to those shares and would not be affected by a possible bankruptcy of the bank, the banks should hold the certificates on an individualised basis for each client, HR (The Netherlands) January 12, 1968 NJ 1968, 274 (*Teixeira de Mattos*).

[32] R. Goode, 'The Nature and Transfer of Rights in Dematerialised and Immobilized Securities' in F. Oditah (ed.), *The Future for the Global Securities Market* (Oxford 1996) 110.

[33] ibid., 110–112; J. Benjamin, *The Law of Global Custody* (1996) see above, n. 28, 13.

securities deposited with the institution. Article 15 *Wge* makes it clear that the joint owner of a collective deposit is entitled to exercise the voting right on shares up to the amount for which he is joint owner in the collective pool. The affiliated institution must, upon so being requested, give the joint owner the possibility of exercising that voting right. In other European countries similar giral securities systems have been developed.

A more far-reaching method of reducing physical certificates is to issue what are known as *globals*.[34] All securities of the same class are—upon issue or in the event of a subsequent change in those securities as a result of a split or a consolidation—embodied in one single bearer certificate which is deposited with the central institution. Separate certificates are no longer available. Although this may not be in conformity with article 26 *Wge*, which gives the joint owner the right to demand at all times the delivery of all the securities of which he is joint owner,[35] it has meanwhile become the most common way in which securities are issued in the Netherlands.[36]

The most far-reaching method is the complete *dematerialization* of shares: they are no longer embodied in any form of physical certificate at all. In France,[37] Finland, and Greece publicly listed shares are by definition dematerialized.[38] Another variant of dematerialization is now being applied in Germany. There, the biggest publicly listed companies are converting their bearer shares into registered shares, for which no share certificates are (need to be) issued.[39]

[34] *The Law of Global Custody* (1996), 13ff; F. Christie and H. Dosanjh, 'The Practical Elements of Settlement and Custody' in F. Oditah (ed.), *The Future for the Global Securities Market* (Oxford 1996) 133.

[35] For further details see J.W. Winter, 'Voetbalaandelen' [1998] *Tijdschrift voor Ondernemingsrecht* 191–192; for a different view see M.A. Blom, 'Dematerialisatie van effecten en ontwikkelingen rond de Wge' in *Onderneming en Effecten* (1998), 191–195.

[36] The AEX and Necigef are also bringing some slight pressure to bear to induce publicly listed companies to convert their existing K certificates (where still extant) and CF certificates into globals, see the AEX publication *Global Note, Op weg naar dematerialisatie* (July 1999).

[37] Art. 94 II of Loi no. 81-1160 of 30 December 1981 and art. 1 Décret no. 83-359 of May 2, 1983, see *Code des Sociétés* (Paris, Dalloz edn 1999) 975ff.

[38] For Finland and Greece see H. Toiviainen, 'Shareholder voting in the EU, Country Report Finland' in *Shareholder Voting Rights and Practices in Europe and the U.S.*, see above, n. 24, 11 and in the same book N. Georgekopoulos, 'Shareholder Voting in Greek Company Law' at 3. Since 1995 Belgium has offered companies the possibility of issuing securities without any underlying documents at all. However, the dematerialisation legislation is awaiting implementing decrees which have still not been forthcoming, cf. C. Sunt, 'Dematerialisatie van vennootschapseffecten' [1996] 9 *N.F.M.* 243–251; M. Tison, 'De uitgifte van gedematerialiseerde vennootschapseffecten, bemerkingen bij de wet van 7 april 1995' in H. Braeckmans (ed.), *Het gewijzigde vennootschapsrecht 1995* (Antwerp 1996) 229–261.

[39] U. Noack, 'Die Namensaktie—Dornröschen erwacht' [1999] 25 *Betriebs-Berater* 1306–1310. In Sweden and Finland publicly listed companies have registered shares only. The share register of companies listed in those countries is held on their behalf by a central institution, which also settles the transactions on the stock exchange, see R. Skog, 'Shareholder representation and proxy voting in Swedish listed companies' in *Shareholder Voting Rights and Practices in Europe and the U.S.*, see above, n. 24, 5 and H. Toiviainen, see above, n. 38, 11.

The same possibility will perhaps also be available in the Netherlands in the foreseeable future. Although the Giral Securities Trading Act is not explicitly opposed to the giral processing of registered shares, it is solely aimed at the custody of bearer certificates.[40] At this moment work is being done on an amendment to the *Wge* to enable the giral processing of registered shares.

Shareholding in a giral securities world means in fact that a bank administers a number of shares in a securities account in the name of the investor. These are referred to as *computerized securities*.[41] The company that has issued the shares does have a problem, or at least a concern. It can no longer demand the submission of a bearer certificate as proof that a person is a shareholder if such person wants to attend the shareholders' meeting and vote. Companies still do stipulate that such a deposit should be made,[42] but the reality of the situation is that an investor can only show that a certain number of shares are administered in his securities account. The company must be able to rely on that. In the explanatory memorandum to the *Wge* it was stated at the time that issuing institutions must not be compelled to accept declarations concerning joint ownership from affiliated institutions. The development was left to be determined by actual practice.[43] Meanwhile the practice is that a realistic alternative to such declarations no longer exists. The law has to acknowledge this reality, in the sense that the company must also be able to rely on the accuracy of such declarations, except of course where it is aware of their inaccuracy. If resolutions have been adopted at a shareholders' meeting, for example, it must not be possible for them to be subsequently overturned if a voting right is found to have been exercised by persons in respect of whom affiliated institutions have wrongly stated that they were (at the relevant moment) joint owners. It is possible to defend the argument that this is already valid law, resulting in particular from article 3: 36 Civil Code, but it would be good if this could be confirmed explicitly in the law as part of the proposed amendment to the *Wge*. [44]

D. Chains of Intermediaries

In today's practice the investor invests more and more often via one or more intermediaries. I shall use the term 'investor' below to refer to the person who holds the shares in a securities account for himself and not for others who in turn

---

[40] See *Explanatory Memorandum on the draft Wge*, Schuurman and Jordens, *Nederlandse Wetgeving* vol. 169, XXVIII–XXIX; see also M.A. Blom, see above, n. 35, 200–201.

[41] Benjamin, see above, n. 28, 12ff.

[42] See Art. 2: 117 para. 2 Civil Code.

[43] Schuurman and Jordens, see above, n. 40, 24.

[44] In Belgium and France it is indeed the case that the entitlement to shares is proved by a declaration from the bank that administers the securities account in which the shares are registered.

hold a securities account with him. I will refer to those who administer securities accounts for others as 'intermediaries'. I will give two examples of intermediaries, which I will base on Dutch investors in a Dutch company. Amongst private investors the *leasing of shares* is very popular.[45] In the case of share leasing the full economic interest in the shares is with the investor and not with the lease company. For technical financial reasons, however, the investor is not formally a shareholder but only acquires the shares after expiry of the lease period. In the interim period the lease company is the shareholder. The lease company holds the securities in a securities account with an affiliated institution and is thus the joint owner. As joint owner the lease company is entitled to the shares, even though it holds them for the account of underlying parties.[46] As joint owner it can exercise the voting right pursuant to article 15 *Wge*. As far as I have been able to ascertain, the conditions set by share leasing companies do not contain a provision to the effect that the investor has an entitlement towards the lease company to exercise the voting right on the underlying shares, for example by instructing the lease company to exercise the voting right in a certain way or to receive a proxy from the lease company so that the investor can exercise the voting right himself.[47] Such a right would fit in well with the nature of the lease construction. As far as the company is concerned, however, it is still the lease company—as joint owner of a collective deposit with an affiliated institution—that is authorized to exercise the voting right.

A second example. Private and institutional investors often contract out part of their investment portfolio to asset managers.[48] In part, these investments are invested in investment funds administered by the asset manager and including shares of various different companies. The chain becomes even one link longer if the investment fund is not administered by the legal person managing the capital on behalf of the client/investor, but—as is so often the case—by an affiliated legal person. Investment funds exist in all shapes and sizes. Investment funds usually have a custodian, a manager and participants. Sometimes the

---

[45] In recent years Dutch private investors have invested around 3.5 billion euro in share lease constructions, with more than 2.6 billion euro invested in market leader Legio-Lease, see *Het Financieele Dagblad*, December 24, 1999, 22, 'Nipo: aandelenlease schiet omhoog'.

[46] HR (The Netherlands) 23 September 1994 NJ 1996, 461 (*KasAs-Drying*).

[47] To ensure that the investor's capital rights are protected, the lease conditions sometimes do contain the provision that the shares registered in a collective pool in the name of the lease company are pledged to the client/investor as security for his claims against the lease company. In that case, however, it is not stipulated that the voting right is also transferred to the client/pledgee.

[48] Stapledon and Bates write that 80% of the U.K. pension schemes use solely external asset managers; only 12% use only their own, internal asset managers, 'Enhancing Efficiency in Corporate Governance: How Recognizing the Nature of Modern Shareholding Can Lead to a Simplified Voting Process' (Tilburg collection) 11. Figures are not known for the Netherlands, but the trend here, too, seems to be that pension funds contract out the management of their investments to professional external asset managers.

fund's capital is jointly owned by the participants, sometimes the custodian is designated as the legal owner, and in many cases it is not clear who holds title to the underlying shares. It would cause friction if an individual investor in the fund could lay claim to the right to exercise the voting right in respect of the underlying shares. The investor does not have an individual interest in those shares but only a collective interest together with the other participants in the fund. The exercise of the voting right seems to fit best within the role of the fund manager, though he is not in fact the owner of the underlying shares.[49] To exercise the voting right he would need a proxy from the custodian or from the combined participants.

Asset managers can also invest in shares for clients on an individual basis. To the extent that the asset manager is not himself an institution that is affiliated to Necigef, he will often—for reasons of efficiency—keep a securities account in his own name with an affiliated institution, in which the investments of all of the asset manager's clients are administered jointly. Such accounts are also known as *omnibus accounts*.[50] As holder of that securities account, the asset manager is the person who holds title to the shares, even though he is holding them for underlying parties. As joint owner the asset manager is authorized to exercise the voting right. The ultimate investor is not authorized towards the company to exercise the voting right. Whether the investor must be given the opportunity to exercise the voting right depends on the legal relationship between the asset manager and the investor.[51]

E. Cross-border Shareholdings

The chain of intermediaries becomes even longer and the situation more unclear in case of cross-border shareholdings, in other words if an investor with a securities account in one country holds shares issued by a company in another country. I shall take a Dutch publicly listed company as my starting point. All sorts of separate chains of intermediaries are possible, sometimes downstream of the chains I have just described and sometimes intertwined with them.

---

[49] S.E. Eisma and C.A.E. Uniken Venema, *Eigendom ten titel van beheer naar komend recht, Preadvies van de Vereniging Handelsrecht* (1990) 122ff.

[50] Stapledon and Bates, see above, n. 48, 15; J.W. Winter, 'Stemmen op afstand via het Communicatiekanaal Aandeelhouders', see above, n. 27, 99.

[51] In the U.K. the National Association of Pension Funds published a report in 1999 which focuses specifically on this problem for pension funds that contract out their investments to asset managers, *Report of the Committee of Inquiry into U.K. Vote Execution* (July 1999 (also known as the Newbold Report, after its chairman). Stapledon and Bates propose that, with regard to these comparatively permanent chains of intermediaries, it should be stipulated in the Companies Act that the formal shareholder can notify the company that the information and voting forms must be sent to a specific ultimate investor who takes the place of the formal shareholder, see above, n. 48, 25.

Figure 1: Possible Chains of Legal Relationships Between the Company and the Ultimate Investor

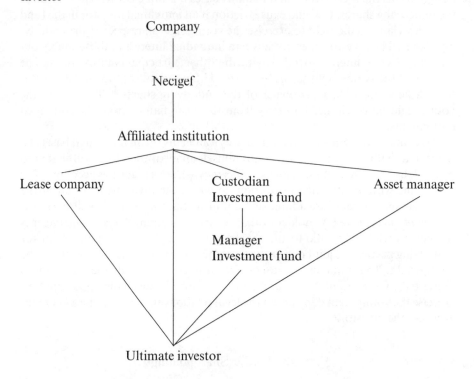

The first possibility is that the bearer certificates are in the custody of foreign banks. Some banks in Switzerland, Germany, and the U.K. store the bearer certificates issued by Dutch companies. The investor in Switzerland then holds a securities account with the Swiss bank that holds the certificates.

This variant no longer occurs very often. In Europe, alongside the national immobilization described earlier, an international immobilization of securities has taken place. Most foreign banks have had their stocks of bearer certificates transferred to custody businesses in the country of issue. A Spanish bank, for example, will normally hold an omnibus account with an affiliated institution of Necigef, in which the shares that the Spanish bank originally held on behalf of its clients are administered in the name of the Spanish bank.

In recent years the central giral institutions in Europe, such as Necigef, have started entering into alliances with each other, specifically to facilitate the cross-border settlement of securities transactions. Pursuant to article 2 para. 1(f) of the Decree for the implementation of article 4 *Wge*, foreign central giral institutions can be admitted as an affiliated institution of Necigef. In the jargon these institutions are known as CSDs, which stands for Central Securities Depositories.[52] Conversely, Necigef can also hold accounts with foreign CSDs, article 35(b) *Wge*.[53] In this chain, for instance, the French CSD Sicovam is an affiliated institution of Necigef. French banks in turn are affiliated institutions of Sicovam. French investors hold securities accounts with a French bank.

In addition to national CSDs, two international clearinghouses are active in Europe, Euroclear and Cedel. The latter was recently amalgamated with Deutsche Börse Clearing, the German CSD. They now work together under the name Clearstream.[54] These international clearinghouses handle the clearing and settlement of international securities transactions for banks and stockbrokers, i.e. they handle the transfer of ownership of and payment for the securities. Banks and stockbrokers are affiliated as Participants to Euroclear and as Customers to Cedel. Euroclear and Cedel form the links between, say, a Finnish, German, or Italian bank and the Dutch giral system.[55] As a rule they keep securities accounts for this purpose with affiliated institutions in national giral systems.[56] These again are omnibus accounts, in which Euroclear and Cedel hold shares in their own name for the benefit of their underlying Participants and Customers. Euroclear and Cedel also hold securities accounts with each other. Recently Euroclear and Cedel were admitted as affiliated institutions of Necigef. They no longer need to maintain securities accounts with an affiliated institution of Necigef, as they themselves are direct joint owners of the giral deposit that is held by Necigef. The Participants and Customers of Euroclear and Cedel do not hold shares for themselves via these clearing houses, but for their underlying clients. In some cases those are the investors. But in many cases Participants and Customers are in turn intermediate links in a much longer chain that ultimately leads to the investor and they play the role of, say, custodian of an investment fund or that of an asset manager. The securities accounts of the Participants and

[52] F. Christie and H. Dosanjh, see above, n. 34, 131. In the meantime Deutsche Börse Clearing AG in Germany, CREST Company in the U.K., Sicovam in France, CIK in Belgium, SIS in Switzerland, APK in Finland, and ÖKB in Austria have been admitted as an affiliated institution of Necigef.

[53] H.L.E. Verhagen, 'De girale levering van effecten in het internationale privaatrecht' in *Onderneming en Effecten* (1998), 244. See also C.W. Le Rutte, 'Internationale levering van effecten?' in M.J.G.C. Raaijmakers, R. van Rooij, and A.J.S.M. Tervoort (eds.) *Ondernemingsrecht in internationaal perspectief* (NGB collection 1995) 230ff.

[54] There are reports that Euroclear and Clearstream are meanwhile also holding talks about a merger, *Het Financieele Dagblad*, February 5, 2000.

[55] For a description of the Euroclear system, which is based in Brussels and which is subject to Belgian law, see H.L.E. Verhagen, see above, n. 53, 247ff. A description of the Cedel system, which largely corresponds to the Euroclear system but is subject to the law of Luxembourg, is given by Christie and Dosanjh, see above, n. 34, 131ff.

[56] Christie and Dosanjh, see above, n. 34, 134.

Customers with Euroclear and Cedel are thus again omnibus accounts in which they hold shares in their own names for the benefit of their combined clients.

Another common international practice nowadays is that the simple holding of giral securities and the settlement of securities transactions is contracted out by professional parties to third parties specialised in this work. Instead of maintaining relationships with various custodians in the countries in which they invest, investors often prefer to enter into a relationship with a *global custodian*. A global custodian maintains relationships with custodians and clearing houses in a number of countries and handles the settlement of securities transactions for its clients in those countries.[57] It is customary for global custodians to hold shares for their clients in omnibus accounts in the global custodian's name with local custodians, for example with an affiliated institution within the *Wge* system. The global custodian who maintains the omnibus account is entitled as joint owner to exercise the voting right. Global custodians also all hold accounts with Euroclear and Cedel.

The reality is of course much more varied than the diagram shows. But what the diagram is in any event intended to show is that various chains of intermediaries are possible between an investor and the company, depending on the way in which the various intermediaries have established their connections with other intermediate links. In practice it is not possible to make an accurate step-by-step trace of the route between the chain of intermediaries and the company for certain shares held by an investor. For each intermediary there are various possible and parallel links with intermediaries higher up in the chain. In respect of certain securities an Italian bank may maintain a relationship with a global custodian, who in turn holds the securities on its behalf with Euroclear or with Cedel or with an affiliated institution. The Italian bank can also hold securities directly with Euroclear or Cedel. The Italian bank does not keep a record for each individual investor of the chain of intermediaries via which the shares are held on his behalf, nor does it know which routes those chains take downstream of the link with which it has a relationship. The same applies to the subsequent links in the chain. As a result there is no clear-cut answer to the question of which chain of intermediaries holds certain securities on behalf of a specific ultimate investor.[58]

F. Voting Rights in Cross-border Chains of Intermediaries

Who in the various chains is entitled to exercise the voting right related to the shares? If the links in the chain are established in different countries, then the first question that arises is: according to the law of which country should you

---

[57] Benjamin, see above, n. 28, 1ff.

[58] J.R. Rogers, 'Of Normalcy and Anomaly: Thoughts on Choice of Law for the Indirect Holding System' [1998] *Journal of International Banking and Financial Law*, Special Supplement, 50.

Figure 2: A Diagram of Some Possible Chains of Intermediaries

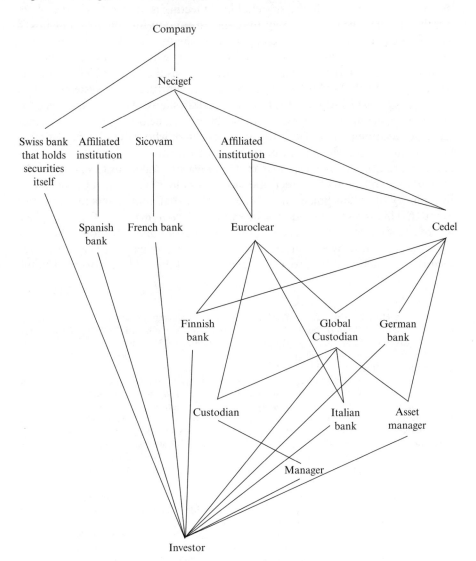

assess who is entitled to vote? The applicable law as regards the person to whom the voting right accrues in the shareholders' meeting is the *lex societatis*, or the law that governs the legal status of the company and its internal relationships.[59] As I have already said, national company law usually rules that the voting right accrues to the shareholder.[60] The question then is who—in these cross-border chains leading from the company to the investor—is the shareholder and on the basis of which law should this be determined. In giral securities systems we can no longer say that someone is the holder of certain shares. The securities account holder has a claim under property law to shares that he holds jointly with other securities account holders. Basically, the question of who is the shareholder must be reformulated as: who has the property-law entitlement to shares? In the international literature consensus exists that, as regards giral securities systems, the property-law position of the securities account holder is governed by the law of the country of establishment of the intermediary that administers the securities account. This is also referred to as the *law of the intermediary*. The only place where proof exists of the investor's position is in the administration of his securities account held by his intermediary. The rule originally applied to bearer securities, namely that the property-law position of the holder is governed by the

---

[59] H. van Houtte, 'The Law Applicable to Securities Transactions: Choice of Law Issues' in F. Oditah (ed.) *The Future for the Global Securities Market* (Oxford 1996) 69–70; P. Vlas, *Rechtspersonen*, vol. 9, Praktijkreeks IPR, (Kluwer, Deventer 1993) 91; see also art. 12 para. 4 and art. 13 para. 2 of the draft bill for the *Wet conflictenrecht goederenrecht* of the Dutch State Commission for Internationaal Private Law, report to the Minister of Justice, November 1998, 59, 62. However, it is not always clear which law is the *lex societatis*. Some countries, including the Netherlands and the U.K., apply the *incorporation doctrine*. The *lex societatis* is in that case the law of the country in which the company is incorporated. Other countries, such as France and Germany, take as their basis the principle of the actual headquarters, the *siège réel*. The *lex societatis* is then the law of the country in which the legal person has its actual registered office, cf. Van Houtte, see above, same note, 70–71; Vlas, see above, same note, 4ff. For details of both systems and the significance of the *Centros* decision of the European Court of Justice, see H. De Wulf, 'Centros: vrijheid van vestiging zonder race to the bottom' [1999] 12 *Ondernemingsrecht* 318–324 and the commentary by J.N. Schutte-Veenstra on the ECJ's decision, in [1999] 8 *Ondernemingsrecht* 227–229.

[60] There is, however, a further complication here in that the voting right may in a limited number of cases accrue to a person other than the shareholder. In the Netherlands, for example, the pledgee and usufructuary of shares may have the voting right related thereto, see art. 2: 88 and 89 para. 3 Civil Code. In the case of shares that form part of the giral securities trading system the attachment of the right of pledge and usufruct takes place by entering the shares in the name of the pledgee/usufructuary if this is a party other than the affiliated institution itself, arts. 20 and 23 *Wge*. As a result the shares are removed from the account of the shareholder. In such as case, however, it remains unclear whether the voting right has also been transferred to the pledgee/usufructuary or whether it has remained with the shareholder. Both are possible and in the giral system no record is kept of this. In foreign giral systems similar complications may occur. In the remainder of this chapter I shall disregard this for the sake of simplicity, though I am aware that the question is important given the extensive provision of collateral on giral securities portfolios in modern financial trading.

law of the country in which the certificates are physically located, the *lex situs*,[61] no longer works in modern international giral securities systems. In case of the chains of intermediaries in various countries that I described a moment ago, it is not possible to ascertain the precise location in which bearer certificates are held for a specific securities account holder. In practice those certificates may be held at various links in the chain, and there will be no marker attached to show what entitlements exist for certain investors. In the case of fully dematerialized securities no certificates are stored anywhere at all. It is therefore agreed that in the giral securities system the *lex situs* is the place where the relevant administration is located, regardless of where the underlying certificates are.[62]

The referral rule of the law of the intermediary is laid down in the European Finality Directive. This directive is aimed at limiting the "system risk" that arises if a party in a giral payment or securities system does not fulfil its obligations, and it stipulates that the property-law position of the holder of collateral rights to giral securities is governed by the law of the Member State in which the securities account is held.[63] This provision has meanwhile been introduced in the Netherlands in article 212f of the Bankruptcy Act.[64] The State Commission for

[61] See art. 13 of the draft bill for the *Wet Conflictenrecht Goederenrecht* [Act on the conflict of laws, property law], see above, n. 59, 62.

[62] See, for example, Benjamin, *The Law of Global Custody*, see above, n. 28, at 84–85. The question as to the applicable law in the case of giral securities deposits has been frequently discussed in international legal literature, but against a different background than the determination of the entitlement to vote. In financial trading, notably within the framework of derivatives transactions, it is customary for parties to transfer or pledge entire securities portfolios as collateral for the fulfilment of their obligations. Those securities portfolios are kept in giral form and may consist of various classes of securities that have been issued by companies and institutions in various countries. In many publications the question is asked which country's law should be applied to assess the property-law aspects of those collateral transactions. Cf. Verhagen, see above, n. 53, 250; R. Potok, 'Rapporteur's summary' [1998] *Journal of International Banking and Financial Law* Special Supplement, 5. This special supplement was devoted entirely to this question and contained contributions by R. Potok and M. Moshinsky on Cross-border Collateral: 'a Conceptual Framework for Choice of Law Situations'; M. Moshinsky 'Securities held through a Securities Custodian—Conflict of Law Issues'; R. Goode 'Security Entitlements as Collateral and the Conflict of Laws'; J. Benjamin 'Recharacterisation Risk and Conflict of Laws'; Fentiman 'Cross-border Securities Collateral: Redefining Recharacterisation Risk'; and the previously mentioned contribution by Rogers 'Of Normalcy and Anomaly: Thoughts on Choice of Law for the Indirect Holding System'. From now on I shall refer to this special supplement as the 'Oxford Colloquium'. See also J. Benjamin, 'Immobilized Securities: where are they?' [1998] *International Journal of Banking and Financial Law*, 85–87 and L.L. De Ghenghi and B. Servaes, 'Collateral held in the Euroclear System: a Legal Overview' [1999] *International Journal of Banking and Financial Law*, March, 83–90; R. Potok, 'Article 9 (2) European Union Finality Directive' [1999] *Journal of International Banking and Financial Law*, July–August, 279–281.

[63] Art. 9 para. 2 of the directive on the definitive character of the settlement of payments and securities transactions in payment and settlement systems, 98/26/EC.

[64] For a description of this provision see Verhagen, see above, n. 53, 254–255; R. Potok, 'Article 9(2) European Finality Directive' [1999] *International Journal of Banking and Financial Law*, July–August, 279–281. For the changes made in the Bankruptcy Act to implement the directive, see

international private law has linked up with this. Article 14 of the draft bill for the *Wet conflictenrecht goederenrecht* [Act on the conflict of laws, property law] states that the property-law regime that is applicable to rights for the delivery and giral transfer of securities as against, in brief, a giral intermediary is governed by the law of the state in which that intermediary is established, or that of the office of that intermediary where the securities account is kept.[65]

Apart from the Finality Directive, which specifically declares that the law of the intermediary is applicable to collateral rights in respect of giral securities, it is not established fact that all European countries will in fact generally apply this referral rule to the property-law position with regard to giral shares. However, for the sake of convenience, let us assume that this is the case. The question then is what this means for determining the entitlement to vote on shares by holders of securities accounts. I assume that the relevant legal system will grant the holder of the securities account the entitlement to exercise the rights attaching to the securities that are administered in the account, as is explicitly done by article 15 *Wge* in the Netherlands.[66]

J.B. Huizink, 'Een uitzondering op de 00.00-uur regel' [1999] 1 *Tijdschrift voor Insolventierecht* 13–18.

[65] See above, n. 59, 68. For further details about this provision see Blom, see above, n. 35. In this approach it should be recognized that the right that the account holder has and transfers or gives as collateral is a claim to securities as against the intermediary with whom he holds an account and a claim that can be exercised solely against this party. Piggy-backing to an intermediary higher up in the chain is not possible. The emphasis lies on the claim against the relevant intermediary, not on the co-ownership rights to the underlying securities, which rights have been more or less diluted via the chain of intermediaries. Also along the same lines is section 8–503 of the American Uniform Commercial Code, see p. 419 below. Blom mainly emphasizes the co-ownership character of the claim against the intermediary in the *Wge* system and comparable foreign systems, a claim that has a knock-on effect in higher links in the chain. The suggestion made by this approach is that also the intermediaries located higher up in the chain and perhaps even the issuing company must accept the co-ownership claim of the foreign securities account holder, which would render the system enormously complicated. The State Commission therefore rejects this approach, see above, n. 59, 66–67.

[66] As far as I can judge, this claim is more often implicit rather than explicit. The German *Depotgesetz*, for instance, does not contain a provision that is comparable to art. 15 *Wge*. The entitlement to vote is apparently derived from the co-ownership "*nach Bruchteilen*" [according to fractions] that arises when securities are placed in "*Sammelverwahrung*" [in collective custody], cf. para. 6 *DepotG*, and from the regulations in the *AktienGesetz* which make it obligatory for "*Kreditinstituten*" to pass on information from the company to "*Aktionäre*" [shareholders], cf. para. 125(1) and 128(1) AktG. For Belgium it is implicit in Art. 11 of the KB [Royal Decree] of 10 November 1967 and Art. 74 para. 1(2) *Vennootschapswet* [Companies Act], as amended by the act of 7 April 1995, which provides that, for the exercise of associative rights to securities that have been introduced into a giral system or have been dematerialized in some other way, companies must make do with a "declaration from the affiliated institution that establishes that the shares registered in the name of the owner or his intermediary are unavailable until the date of the general meeting". The same system applies in France. The shareholder who holds a securities account and who wishes to be admitted to the meeting of shareholders should submit a declaration from his bank stating that the shares cannot be placed at the holder's disposal up to and including the date of the meeting, cf. 'Mémento Pratique Francis Lefebvre' [1998] *Droit des Affairs, Sociétés Commerciales* n. 1841.

As we have seen, the links in the cross-border chains from the company to the investor are often established in different countries. If the law of the intermediary is applied, then a number of legal systems will be applicable in those chains, and each system will grant a property-law claim to the shares, coupled with a claim to exercise the voting right attaching to them. In this way a paradoxical accumulation of claims to exercise voting rights is created in the chain. Everyone in the chain can lay claim to exercise the voting right! For the company it is impossible to ascertain whom it has to recognize as being entitled to vote.

The application of different legal systems to the various links in the chain can lead not only to a cumulating of claims to voting right, but also to outright collision of claims. Under the Dutch Giral Securities Trading Act (*Wge*) the holder of an account with an affiliated institution holds title as joint owner to the shares, even where he himself is also an intermediary and holds the shares for underlying parties.[67] According to Dutch law the company must therefore recognize the joint owner in the Dutch affiliated institution as the person who holds title and who is therefore authorized to exercise the voting right on the shares, such to the exclusion of the underlying parties. In the chain in which the Spanish bank holds a securities account with an affiliated institution in the Netherlands, that Spanish bank is authorized to exercise the voting right, and this authority is specifically not granted to the investor who holds the account with that bank. According to Spanish law, the investor will probably have such a claim. Similar collisions may also occur in the other chains.

I am not aware of any rule of national law or international private law that can provide the company with a definite solution on how it has to handle these cumulative and sometimes conflicting claims to voting right. In the light of that uncertainty it seems wise for a Dutch company to abide by the rules of the Giral Securities Trading Act: the joint owner is authorized, underlying parties are not. If the validity of decision-making at the shareholders' meeting is ever contested due to the incorrect attribution of the voting right, then such a dispute will have to take place before a Dutch judge (article 2: 15 Civil Code) who will have to apply Dutch international private law. Perhaps the Dutch judge, failing a decisive link-up with another country, may be inclined to apply Dutch law, as the law of the country in which the company is established. The consequence is that, to the extent that the underlying parties have a claim to exercise voting rights in accordance with the law that is applicable to their property-law position, they can only make this claim valid if they have a written power of attorney from the person who, as a joint owner, holds title to the shares under the terms of the *Wge*. The power of attorney could be given to the nearest intermediary in the chain, who in turn gives a sub-power of attorney to the next intermediary

---

[67] See n. 46 above.

and so on, until it reaches the investor. In this way the voting right trickles downwards through the chain. But this does not lead to a satisfactory result for the company and the ultimate investor. Actual ignorance of the exact chain from the investor to the company and the cumulative and conflicting claims in the part of the chain outside the Netherlands mean that it is impossible to establish with certainty which party would have to provide the power of attorney to the relevant investor. Apart from the actual complications in ascertaining what the relevant chain looks like and in collecting the required powers of attorney in good time, it can never be established with certainty that the investor with a written power of attorney or a chain of powers of attorney is lawfully participating in the decision-making at the meeting. In fact, the system is a blind alley.[68]

G. Are Registered Shares a Solution?

Perhaps registered shares offer a solution. In international private law it is assumed that the property-law regime of a registered share is governed by the law that is applicable to the company that issued the share. This is also laid down in article 12 of the draft bill for the Act on conflict of laws, property law.[69] The complication of cumulative or conflicting claims to voting right on the basis of different legal systems in the chain of intermediaries does not seem to occur.[70] In the case of registered shares the rule generally is that the person who is considered to be the shareholder is the person who is registered in the share register. This applies, for example, in the U.K., in which only registered shares exist, and in Germany where—as mentioned—the biggest publicly listed companies are converting their bearer shares into registered shares.[71] In practice, however,

---

[68] The solution given by Stapledon and Bates, see above, n. 48, 25, whereby the formal shareholder notifies the company that the information and voting forms have to be sent to a specific ultimate investor who takes the place of the formal shareholder, does not work in situations in which it is not clear what the chain is between the ultimate investor and the formal shareholder and this chain may be subject to constant change. The solution is unsuitable for cross-border holdings of shares.

[69] See above, n. 59,12.

[70] However, the question that does arise is what the applicable law should be if registered shares are held via collective giral securities deposits, as is the case in Germany. The *lex societatis* may then conflict with the law of the intermediary. Blom assumes that the law of the intermediary as a referral rule also applies if registered shares are held via collective giral securities deposits, see above, n. 35, 381.

[71] Section 361 Companies Act and section 67, para. 2 AktG. In the Netherlands that rule does not exist as such. The shareholder is the person who has acquired the shares upon their issue by the company or by virtue of a valid transfer of ownership. Registration in the share register is not a constitutive element for a valid transfer. Nonetheless, publicly listed companies that keep their share register properly up to date will take the persons registered in it as their basis. If persons other than those registered in the register believe they are shareholders, they will have to prove their right as against the company.

many of the ultimate investors are not themselves included in the share register, but are to be found behind parties who are included in the register on their behalf.[72] In this way a chain of powers of attorney from the formal shareholder to the investor or a chain of voting instructions in the opposite direction is still needed to allow the investor to participate lawfully in the voting at the shareholders' meeting.

In terms of cross-border situations the problems are not solved by registered shares either; in fact they become even bigger. That is the case, for instance, with the German companies that recently converted their bearer shares into registered shares. In the share register of these companies the holders of securities accounts with German banks are registered directly. Deutsche Börse Clearing handles the electronic settlement of stock exchange transactions in these shares as well as the subsequent entry of shares in the acquirer's name in the company's share register.[73] The company can thus see from day to day who its shareholders are.[74] For the purposes of cross-border securities transactions DBC has set up links with foreign CSDs, including Necigef. These foreign CSDs are included in the share register of the relevant German companies. Under German law, therefore, Necigef is a shareholder in companies such as Deutsche Bank, Siemens and Deutsche Telekom.[75] Necigef has sent out a circular to affiliated

---

[72] For the resulting loss of voting rights for private shareholders see the consultative report by the DTI and the Treasury, Private Shareholders: Corporate Governance Rights, 1996; see also P. Davies, 'General Meetings and Voting in the U.K.' in *Shareholders Voting Rights and Practices in Europe and the United States*, see above, n. 24.

[73] This process takes place in phases, from the "*Freier Meldebestand*" to the "*Zugewiesener Meldebestand*" and ultimately registration in the "*Aktienbuch*", the share register. For the seller it takes place in the exact reverse order. See Cascade RS, 'Namensaktien' (Registered Shares) in *Giroversammlungverwahrung*, a publication of Deutsche Börse Clearing AG. For the renewed interest in registered shares in Germany see also U. Noack, see above, n. 39.

[74] Deutsche Börse Clearing is selling the "registered shares" product specifically with a view to the investor relations activities of listed companies. German banks are apparently not as hesitant as Dutch banks about making information about their clients available to the company.

[75] Illustrative in this respect is the advertisement published by Deutsche Telekom AG in *Het Financieele Dagblad* of January 13, 2000. In that advertisement Deutsche Telekom states: "After the conversion a share register will have to be kept in which the shareholders of Deutsche Telekom AG are registered, together with a mention of their surname, first name, occupation (the mention of the shareholder's occupation is indeed compulsory in accordance with section 67, para. 1 AktG, JWW), address and the number of shares of Deutsche Telekom AG that they have in their possession. For the shares held in deposit by German banks the registration of the shares in the name of the owners takes place directly. Due to the technical infrastructure of the central securities depositories in other European countries it is not automatically possible to register the shares in the name of the actual owners. The intention is that, instead of the foreign shareholders, the relevant depository bank or central depository custodian will be registered in the share register of Deutsche Telekom. Shareholders who have a deposit outside the Federal Republic of Germany and who wish to be registered in the share register of Deutsche Telekom AG can contact their depository bank for this purpose. The particulars can then be passed on via the relevant central depository manager to Deutsche Telekom AG for the purpose of registration by hand in the electronic share register". The

institutions following the conversion by German companies of their shares into registered shares.[76] In that circular Necigef states "that for the time being no facilities will be made available for the issue of documents entitling admittance to shareholders' meetings, or for the exercise of voting rights. For good order's sake we would inform you that Necigef will refrain from exercising the voting right acquired by virtue of registration in the relevant share register." Dutch investors are no longer shareholders in German companies, but in addition they are not given the opportunity, either via voting proxies or voting instructions to Necigef, to exercise the voting right in respect of the shares that they hold.[77] To the extent that Necigef or another foreign CSD might offer facilities to joint owners in their giral systems to exercise the voting right, there still remains the problem of cumulative and sometimes conflicting claims to exercise that voting right in the international chain of intermediaries from the link of the foreign CSD through to the investor. As from the link of the foreign CSD which is registered in the share register, the applicable law is again the law of the intermediary as the referral rule, with all the attendant complications.[78]

H. Further Complications

To make the fog that shrouds shareholder status and voting rights in European giral securities systems slightly more impenetrable than it already is, let me point

significance of the latter is slightly beyond my grasp. I have the impression that the foreign investor who takes this route will not be able to sell his shares direct on the stock exchange. For a detailed explanation of the system and its consequences for shareholders see also the announcement by Siemens AG in the editorial section of *Wertpapier-Mitteilungen* of June 26, 1999.

[76] Circular 1076 of August 12, 1999.

[77] An even clearer example is offered by the Finnish situation. It is mandatory for Finnish publicly listed shares to be dematerialised. The holders of these shares are registered in the share registers, which are administered for the publicly listed companies by a central institution bearing the fine-sounding name '*Arvopaperikeskus*'. Shareholders in Finland have to be registered in this company's share register. Shareholders outside Finland need not be registered themselves in the register, the shares are allowed to be registered in the name of a nominee. This is what happens in most cases. The foreign investor holds a securities account with his own bank. This bank, or more probably another intermediary higher up in the chain, will be registered in the Finnish share register as nominee for the ultimate investor. Under Finnish law, however, the consequence is that neither the nominee nor the ultimate investor is allowed to exercise the voting right on the shares. The only ones recognized as entitled to vote are the owners of shares who are registered in the share register. A nominee is apparently not regarded in Finland as the owner of the shares. Cross-border voting is thus rendered effectively impossible, cf. H. Toiviainen, see above, n. 38,10. I understand that a similar rule applies in Sweden, but then without making a distinction between Swedish and foreign shareholders. The ultimate investor behind a nominee who is registered in the share register will himself have to be registered in the share register in good time in order to be able to exercise his rights, cf. R. Skog, see above, n. 40, 5–6.

[78] This is the view of the State Commission, see above, n. 59, 68. See also Blom, above, n. 35, 382.

to a complication that arises from the differences between the national systems for the clearing and settlement of securities transactions. After a securities transaction has been effectuated on the stock exchange, it has to be settled: the seller should deliver the shares that have been sold and receive the selling price, whilst the buyer should pay and receive the shares. Despite the modern technology that is used, this settlement process takes time. But in one country the settlement of securities transactions takes more time than in another. In the U.K. securities transactions are settled within a period of five days after the transaction. After five days the buyer is registered in the share register and thus becomes the shareholder. This is referred to as T+5 (transaction plus 5). The AEX in the Netherlands applies a T+3-system. In Germany transactions are settled at T+2.[79] These differences in settlement moments may mean that in case of cross-border transactions, e.g. a share sale from the U.K. to Germany, there may be two investors in the U.K. and Germany who at the same moment are regarded as the persons with an entitlement to the same shares. In the U.K. the shares are only debited from the seller at T+5, in Germany they have already been credited to the buyer at T+2. In case of a transaction in the opposite direction the outcome may be that for a period of three days no one is regarded as having entitlement to the shares. If the interim period comprises the day that determines shareholder status and thus gives the entitlement to exercise the voting rights, this may lead to a double voting right for various parties in respect of the same shares, or to the actual removal of the voting right from both parties in respect of those shares. Theoretically, it is even conceivable that a shareholder could acquire a double voting right for himself by having shares booked from a U.K. register to a German securities account shortly before the moment that is decisive for the entitlement to exercise the voting right. I have on occasion raised this point during conversations with bank staff. The reaction in most cases was one of resounding silence.

CSDs and intermediaries which are confronted with differing settlement times in cross-border transactions are faced with the problem that their books do not tally during the period between the moment they have to deliver shares (by crediting them to the securities account of their affiliated institution/client) and the moment those shares are delivered to them (by being credited to their own securities account). To solve this problem they borrow shares from some clients who hold securities accounts with them in order to bridge over the period. Similarly, other market parties such as global custodians and asset managers who regularly have obligations to deliver without having the actual shares in their possession borrow shares from account holders to cover these *short positions*. The borrowing of securities, or *securities lending*, is the oil that lubricates the stock market. One estimate has it that some 5 to 10% of the total number of

---

[79] See the publication about Cascade RS by DBC, see n. 73 above.

securities transactions every day involves *securities lending*.[80] To enable the borrowing of securities, intermediaries enter into securities lending agreements with each other and with institutional investors. These investors are willing, in return for a fee, to loan out their securities temporarily to the person who administers the securities account, provided that sufficient guarantee is given that the securities will be returned. In this way they can increase the return on their portfolio. The practice is that on the basis of such an agreement the borrower is entitled to loan the shares at any moment. Intermediaries enter into securities lending agreements with a large number of clients. Which agreements they use from day to day is fairly arbitrary. Their systems automatically debit shares from the accounts of clients. As a result the lender loses his property-law claim to the shares,[81] yet without this being preceded by a transaction by that lender. Instead, the lender has a contractual claim against the borrower that the shares will be delivered back to him, and that claim—if all is properly arranged—will be covered by collateral security. The lender does not know that shares are being borrowed from his securities account. He is only informed of that afterwards. If the moment that is decisive for the entitlement to vote at the general meeting lies in the period when the shares have been lent out, the lender will lose his voting right as a result of the securities loan. As securities lending operations take place daily on a large scale, the result is continuously extensive and unpredictable fluctuations in voting right exist in the giral securities system. The voting right in respect of shares "sloshes around", as it were, throughout the giral system. It is not clear whether the lack of voting rights is always registered at a given moment in the securities systems.[82] My impression is that many institutional investors are in any event not aware of this consequence of their securities lending operations. If they wish to be certain that they can exercise the voting right on all the shares they hold at any given moment, they must include a clause in the securities lending agreements to the effect that no securities will be lent at moments that are decisive for the voting right on the shares that they hold, or alternatively that the borrower will deliver the borrowed shares back in good time or will vote on them in line with the lender's instructions.[83] I do not hold any high hopes as to the practical workability of such agreements.

---

[80] This estimate is given in the Newbold Report in the U.K., see above, n. 51, 19. With this in mind, the G-30 recommended in its 1995 recommendations on clearing and settlement of securities transactions that "securities lending and borrowing should be encouraged as a method of expediting the settlement of securities transactions", see Le Rûtte, n.53, above, 244.

[81] This involves "user loan" agreements, in which the borrower becomes the person entitled to the loaned securities and is obliged to return the same quantity of securities to the lender.

[82] The Newbold Report points out that the transfer of ownership that results from the securities lending is often not processed immediately in the share register of U.K. companies, which means that it is not clear to the parties who in fact has the voting right, see above, n. 51, 19.

[83] The Newbold Report recommends the latter particularly for pension funds, ibid., 19.

I. Depositing, Blocking, and Registering

Let me add one further complication to the list. The company law regulations that determine whether shareholders are entitled to vote also differ in several essential respects from one country to the next. I shall limit myself to the company-law regulations that are linked to the moment and the way in which investors, whether or not with cross-border shareholdings, have to hold shares if they are to be entitled to vote at the general meeting.[84]

In most countries the principle is that only those persons have voting rights who are shareholders at the moment of the shareholders' meeting.[85] In the case of bearer shares the problem that originally existed was how it was possible to establish in practice that the persons wishing to attend the meeting were really shareholders at that moment. Basically, they would have to take the physical certificates along with them to the meeting to prove their shareholder status. To prevent this, many countries prescribe, or at least companies are given the possibility to prescribe, that the holders of bearer shares should deposit their shares by a certain time prior to the meeting with the company or with a bank designated by the company. The latest day on which the shares have to be deposited varies from five,[86] three to six,[87] seven,[88] to ten days[89] before the meeting. This implies that the shareholder must in any event hold title to the shares not only at the moment of the meeting, but also as much as three to ten days beforehand if he is to be able to vote at the meeting. Implicitly or explicitly, it is then assumed that the shares remain blocked during this period up to and including the meeting, so that it is certain that the shareholder is still entitled to the shares at the time of the meeting. The exact consequences of this blocking of shares in the various countries are not entirely clear. Sometimes blocking seems to mean that transfer of shares via stock exchange transactions is no longer possible at all.[90]

[84] There are even more company-law regulations that hamper proxy voting by shareholders. Many countries offer the possibility of imposing restrictions on voting rights. Shares with no voting rights also occur, with the Dutch certification of shares basically being a disguised example of that. In France the possibility exists of double voting rights for loyal shareholders. The "one share one vote" principle is not a generally accepted principle in European company law. Similarly, a short period between the convocation for the meeting and the meeting itself, as is possible in many countries, makes effective proxy voting difficult. For an overview of further problems see Arnold, see above, n. 29, 4ff.

[85] This is the case, for example, in France, Italy, Spain, Germany, Belgium, Greece, and Switzerland, see the various country reports in *Shareholder Rights and Practices in Europe and the U.S.* cf n. 24.

[86] France, Italy, and Spain, see the reports referred to in the previous footnote.

[87] Belgium, see the report referred to in n. 85.

[88] Netherlands, see art. 2: 117 para. 3 Civil Code.

[89] Germany, see the report referred to in n. 85.

[90] In this respect see Guyon for France, see above, n. 24, 5.

In other cases it is assumed that transfer is possible but the consequences of this in the relationship with the company are not clear. In many cases neither the seller nor the buyer can vote on the shares that have been transferred.[91]

Whatever the case may be, the depositing and blocking of shares dates from a time when shareholders themselves still held physical certificates or could ask their bank to deliver such certificates. In the current times of immobilized and dematerialized securities trading such regulations no longer work. Physical depositing has not taken place for ages. Banks merely provide declarations about the number of shares registered in the name of their clients.[92] Especially practices such as securities lending, which can be initiated and settled fairly automatically in electronic systems, undermine the blocking regulation. The reality is that the blocking of shares that have been 'deposited' often hardly takes place at all in practice.[93] For investors the blocking of shares, in so far as it is actually complied with, is an extremely constraining measure. During the period when the shares are deposited, they lose the possibility of selling their shares and hence the ability to respond to market developments. For many investors the blocking of shares as a precondition for taking part in the decision-making at the general meeting is therefore unacceptable.[94] If, in the case of proxy voting, larger numbers of shareholders are given the opportunity of participating in the decision-making, then the blocking of shares might even have a seriously adverse impact on stock exchange trading.[95]

In the Netherlands this was the reason, specifically with a view to proxy voting via the Shareholders Communication Channel, for the introduction in article 2: 119 Civil Code of the possibility for a company to set a registration date, which is not allowed to be more than seven days prior to the meeting. The shareholders on the registration date are entitled to vote at the meeting, even if they dispose of their shares after that date and prior to the meeting. This prevents

---

[91] See for Germany Baums and Schmitz, see above n. 20, 9 and for Spain A.J.T. Hermida, 'Shareholder Voting in Spain' in Shareholder *Rights and Practices in Europe and the U.S.*, see above, n. 24, 9. This is also the situation in the Netherlands. The banks give an implicit or explicit undertaking to the company to block the deposited shares up to and including the meeting. If blocked shares are transferred after commencement of the deposit period, then the seller will lose his right to vote, whilst the acquirer will in fact no longer be able to meet the deposit requirements. The directors of the company can therefore also deny the acquirer access to the meeting, cf Asser-Maeijer 2-III, 333–334.

[92] See p. 397 above for the question whether companies should be able to rely on such declarations.

[93] German banks generally allow transactions to be performed up to 24 hours before the meeting, despite the assumed blocking. The idea is that the seller then loses his voting right and the acquirer receives the voting right. In the case of stock exchange transactions, however, it is no longer possible to track the resultant shift in the voting right, cf. Baums and Schmitz, see above, n. 20, 9.

[94] Arnold, see above, n. 29, 6.

[95] Winter, 'Stemmen op afstand via het Communicatiekanaal Aandeelhouders', see above, n. 27, 91.

their shares from having to be blocked up to and including the meeting and makes it possible for bigger numbers of shareholders to take part via proxy voting in the decision-making at the general meeting.[96] Similar *record date* systems exist in Sweden and Finland, where the registration date is set at ten and five days prior to the day of the meeting respectively.[97] A registration date shortly before the meeting does encourage proxy voting, but is still not ideal. Such a 'short' registration date makes it necessary for companies to ascertain twice who their shareholders are: the first time to establish which shareholders have to be sent the annual documents together with voting forms, the second time to check whether they still hold shares and, if so, how many they hold on the registration date. The result is that shareholders, if they wish to take part in proxy voting, have to hold their shares as from a moment prior to the convocation up to and including the registration date. For many investors this 'voluntary blocking' is an obstacle to proxy voting. The changing composition of the groups of shareholders in the first check and in the second check also creates complications, for instance in the case of omnibus accounts (those are precisely the accounts in which the underlying holders are foreign investors) and as regards the possibility for shareholders to react to the documents sent out by the company.[98] These problems are solved if the registration date that determines the entitlement to vote is set well before the meeting, i.e. prior to the convocation for the meeting. Companies then only need to establish once who their shareholders are. These shareholders receive voting forms and are entitled to vote, regardless of whether they sell their shares after the registration date. A second check just before the meeting is not needed. Nor is there a need for shareholders to hold onto their shares until just before the meeting to ensure that their votes count. This is the American record date system.[99] In none of the European countries is such a 'long' registration date possible. When submitting the draft registration date bill, the Minister of Justice announced that work will be done on a parliamentary bill that will in due course enable a registration date to be set at a much earlier time, prior to the convocation for the meeting.[100]

---

[96] On the subject of the Registration Date Act see M.J. van Ginneken, 'De registratiedatum in Nederland' [1999] 15 *Ondernemingsrecht* 404–410 and M. van Olffen, 'Het wetsvoorstel registratiedatum voor de uitoefening van stem- en vergaderrechten' in S.C.J.J. Kortmann, N.E.D. Faber, and J.A.M. Strens-Meulemeester (eds.) *Vertegenwoordiging en tussenpersonen* (Kluwer Deventer 1999) 147–160.

[97] See the contributions by Skog and Toiviainen in the collection *Shareholder Voting Rights and Practices in Europe and the U.S.* (see above, n. 24).

[98] For more about these problems see Winter, Stemmen op afstand via het Communicatiekanaal Aandeelhouders, see above, n. 27, 99–101 and Van Ginneken, see above, n. 96, 407–408.

[99] See p. 421 below.

[100] TK 26 668 n. 3, 4.

J. An Unsatisfactory Situation

For the company wishing to allow its shareholders in Europe to take part in proxy voting, all these complications create a risk: the decision-making at the general meeting may subsequently prove to have been invalid in that parties took part in the decision-making who were not shareholders or were not entitled to cast votes by virtue of a valid power of attorney or chain of powers of attorney. Unlike the situation where shareholders have to attend the meeting in person in order to vote—something that is done by only a very small number of foreign shareholders—this risk in the case of proxy voting potentially relates to a large number of shareholders with cross-border holdings of shares. As a result the validity of the decision-making can really be jeopardised if structural mistakes are possible on a large scale.

This realization will prevent prudent publicly listed companies from creating facilities for shareholders for cross-border proxy voting. For the investor the situation is likewise unsatisfactory. The answer to the question whether he is entitled to the voting right but also the validity of a power of attorney or voting instructions that he has given will depend on circumstances elsewhere in the chain that are completely unknown to him and that he cannot influence. Nor will his direct contact in the chain, the bank with which he holds securities, normally be able to really help him to find out what needs to be done to allow him to take part lawfully in the decision-making. It is simply a matter of waiting to see whether his votes will really be counted as valid. The practical and legal differences between the national systems also increase the risk that investors and intermediaries who have to complete certain formalities to exercise their vote or cause it to be exercised may make mistakes. Because of all this effective and structural cross-border proxy voting by shareholders is not possible in Europe at this moment.

K. E-voting

Just like companies that seek the appreciation of investors are nowadays forced to explain what investments they are planning to make in the internet and how much money they will, at least for the time being, be losing on those investments, so must I, too, at least ask the question of whether the modern information and communication technology can (help to) solve the problems I have just outlined. The fundamental problem, viz. that in the present-day cross-border giral securities world it is practically unfeasible and in many cases also really impossible to establish who the company's shareholders are who are entitled to vote, can in my view not be solved by using modern technology. Technology has ensured that the cross-border holding of shares in a giral, computerized form is nowadays comparatively simple. The law in Europe has lagged behind this development and is not yet able to regulate in an orderly fashion the consequences that this has for the exercise of voting rights. It is not technology but the law that has to solve this problem.

Nevertheless the application of information and communication technology will make proxy voting by shareholders much more efficient. Publicly listed companies can make their annual documents available to shareholders electronically by publishing them on their website. The investor who has access to internet can consult the annual documents direct, without the mediation of intermediaries, immediately after they have been published on the website, regardless of where his computer is installed. This makes it unnecessary for physical documents to be sent by post, which in cross-border chains also involves sending them from one link to the next. Direct access via the internet gives the investor much more time to assimilate the information and to consider how he will cast his vote.

Proxy voting could also take place completely electronically, in which case we would call it *e-voting*. Shareholders can make it known how they wish to vote by accessing a special section of the company's website, where they can vote interactively on the agenda items by clicking the mouse a few times. It is also possible to vote by telephone, in the same way that we order cinema tickets today.[101] In both forms of electronic voting, access can be restricted to those who, as the persons with title to the shares, have received an access code from banks. This electronic voting saves a great deal of time and costs.[102]

Lastly, the organization of the general meeting can also be radically changed. It is already possible to organize shareholders' meeting in which shareholders can participate interactively via satellite links or webcash.[103] The possibilities of organizing a *net meeting* via internet in which pictures, the spoken word, text and graphics can be integrated no longer seem so far away.[104] These possibilities also offer very different perspectives. Proxy voting by shareholders results in a record of how shareholders have voted or how they will cause their votes to be cast

---

[101] Both forms of electronic voting are meanwhile applied in the U.S., see 'P.L. Rosch, The Electronic Proxy Vote: Is Shareholder Communication Coming of Age?' [1996] *Professional Administrator*, 2–4.

[102] The American business ADP, which in fact carries out the proxy solicitation for the vast majority of American companies, charges companies costs of $0.35 for each voting form received and processed, $0.18 for each telephone vote processed and $0.03 for each internet vote processed. The total saving if the company also sends out its proxy materials solely electronically amounts to around $8 per shareholder, see the brochure of J.P. Morgan, *Internet Voting and Electronic Delivery of Shareholder Communications*, March 2000, 4.

[103] A.F.M. Dorresteijn, 'Stemmen op afstand en de electronische snelweg' *WPNR* 6385 (2000) 18.

[104] U. Noack, 'Moderne Kommunikationsformen vor den Toren des Unternehmensrechts' [1998] 3 *Zeitschrift für Unternehmens- und Gesellschaftsrecht* 601.

during the general meeting.[105] This record could also be drawn up separate from a formal meeting at which shareholders actually get together. Voting and the meeting itself could be formally decoupled. Shareholders' meetings can be organized to exchange information between the company and the shareholders who feel a need for it. This can be integrated with the present practice of investor relations meetings to which publicly listed companies normally only invite limited groups of shareholders and analysts at the moment.[106] Voting on formal resolutions is then organized separately via electronic procedures for proxy voting.[107] However, the law in Europe has not yet reached that stage. Company law in the EU Member States prescribes that the general meeting is to be held at a certain place at which shareholders physically meet either in person or represented by others.[108] Proxy voting therefore usually requires the granting of a power of attorney to a person who casts votes at the meeting on behalf of the various shareholders. In most cases that power of attorney has to be in writing.[109] In some countries it is possible for shareholders to vote directly by mail without attending the meeting or authorising someone to attend on their behalf.[110] In such cases, too, the vote has to be cast in written form. Electronic voting or authorizing a representative to vote on your behalf is not possible in Europe at the moment.

L. Shareholder Voting in the U.S.

Before I make suggestions for several building-blocks for a European solution at the end of this paper, it is good to take a look at what the situation is like in the U.S., where proxy voting has for decades formed an integral part of the corporate governance of publicly listed companies.

American company law, which incidentally is state and not federal law, recognises only registered shares.[111] Normally these are embodied in the form of

---

[105] Cf. P.J. Dortmond, *Stemovereenkomsten rondom de eeuwwisseling*, inaugural lecture Leiden 2000, 15.

[106] For the problems relating to the provision of information to limited groups of shareholders and analysts see S.E. Eisma, *Investor Relations*, inaugural lecture Leiden, 1998.

[107] For more details see speech by Judith Hanratty, Company Secretary of BP Amoco, during a seminar organized by Pensions & Investment Research Consultants (PIRC) in London. A summary of the speech can be found on the website of BP Amoco www/bpamoco.com/speeches, visited on January 21, 2000.

[108] Cf. art. 2:116 Civil Code; similarly, for Germany see s. 121 AktG, and for Sweden Ch. 9, s. 10 Companies Act.

[109] Cf. art. 2: 117 para. 1 Civil Code; for Germany s. 134 AktG; for Sweden Ch. 9, s. 2, para. 1 Companies Act.

[110] In France the possibility of this *"vote par correspondence"* has existed since 1983, see art. D. 131-1 and following, in Belgium since 1991, art. 74 para. 4 Vennootschapswet, and in Italy for publicly listed companies since 1998, art. 127 TU.

[111] Klausner and Elfenbein, see above, n. 24, 5.

share certificates. For their transfer the requirement is that the seller returns his certificate to the company, which then issues a new certificate registered in the name of the acquirer. The person to whom a share certificate has been issued is registered in the share register and by virtue of that is allowed to vote.[112] Given the increasing volume of stock exchange trading, this physical settlement of share transactions became very problematical in the 1960s. Since then the *indirect holding system* has been developed. Nowadays, according to information from the Depository Trust Company (DTC), approximately 95% of all American securities are held by the DTC via its *nominee* Cede & Co.[113] Cede & Co is registered on behalf of the DTC in the share register of American publicly listed companies and is thus the *registered owner* of almost all shares in issue. Apart from the DTC there are normally only a very small number of private shareholders directly registered in the share register. The DTC is the central institution of the national giral securities system to which American custodians, brokers and banks are affiliated. Stock market transactions in the U.S. are settled via this giral system of the DTC. The investors hold shares in a securities account with a bank or broker. The latter can also be direct account holders with the DTC, but in most cases there is a chain of intermediaries from the ultimate investor through to the DTC. Transfers of shares after stock exchange transactions are processed in the books of the institutions that are affiliated to the DTC, but not in the share register of the company. The investor is not a registered owner and cannot exercise rights direct as against the company. He is only a *beneficial owner*.

The indirect holding system of the DTC is governed by the provisions of Part 5 of article 8 of the Uniform Commercial Code. These provisions set uniform rules for giral securities systems in the American states which have included article 8 UCC in their legislation, such as New York, where the DTC is established.[114] By virtue of section 8-501 the person who acquires shares in a securities account with a *securities intermediary*[115] receives a *security entitlement* as against the securities intermediary. The security entitlement as against a securities intermediary also comprises his security entitlement as against a higher intermediary in the chain with whom the first intermediary holds a securities account, and so on. The financial assets that the securities intermediary holds for the holders of entitlements do not form part of his capital and are not subject to claims by

---

[112] R.F. Franklin, J.A. Finkelstein and G.P. Williams, 'Meetings of Stockholders' (1999 Supplement), para. 9.5, 9-8; see also s. 219(c) Delaware General Corporation Law.

[113] See the website of the DTC www.dtc.org, Business We Serve, 2, visited on February 27, 2000.

[114] A.B. Strauss, 'Comment: Reviewing revised article 8 of the Uniform Commercial Code' [1998] The Wayne Law Review, winter, 226.

[115] A securities intermediary is every clearing agency and every party which has as its business the administering of securities accounts for others and which acts in such capacity, s. 8-102(a)(14) UCC.

creditors of the securities intermediary, section 8-503(a). The holder of a security entitlement can only exercise rights against the securities intermediary, section 8-503(c),[116] not against other links higher in the chain. The transfer and provision of collateral on a security entitlement is governed by the law of the American state in which the securities intermediary is established, section 8-110(b), and in this case, too, the law of the intermediary applies.

Although under American company law the investor does not have an entitlement against the company to exercise the voting right, he can in fact exercise the voting right on the basis of American securities law. Section 14(b) of the Securities and Exchange Act of 1934 obliges banks, brokers, custodians, and the like to send on proxy material to the clients for whose account they hold shares. This applies only to beneficial owners who have no objections to their name and address data being made known to the company, the *non-objecting beneficial owners* or *NOBOs*. The company has the right to inspect the NOBO list of any bank or broker.[117] A similar obligation to send on proxy material is imposed by the New York Stock Exchange on its members, rule 451 NYSE Listing Rules. Companies listed on the New York Stock Exchange are obliged to give their shareholders, both registered and beneficial owners, the opportunity of voting by proxy, sections 402.04 and 05 NYSE Listing Rules.[118] Lastly, section 8-506 UCC requires the securities intermediary to exercise the rights attaching to the assets to which a security entitlement of a securities account holder relates, if the latter instructs him to do so. The securities intermediary can do this by giving the securities account holder a direct opportunity to exercise those rights, or by exercising the rights himself in accordance with the instructions of the securities account holder, section 8-506(2).[119] In practice companies send voting forms to the shareholders that are included in the share register. Cede & Co as nominee for the DTC then issues an *omnibus proxy* in which it grants proxy to its affiliated institutions to vote on as many shares as each of them holds with the DTC. On behalf of these institutions specialized *proxy services* companies, of which ADP is by far the biggest[120] and which are given direct access to the computer data of those institutions, search to find the persons who hold securities accounts

[116] Section 8-503(d) gives a number of exceptions to this rule for very specific cases.

[117] Section 14(a)-13(a)(1)(ii)(A) Securities and Exchange Act 1934.

[118] There is one exception to this provision, i.e. "where applicable law precludes or makes virtually impossible the solicitation of proxies in the U.S." By virtue of this exception foreign companies that are listed on the NYSE do not need to carry out proxy solicitation in the U.S. if their own law precludes proxy solicitation or makes it practically impossible.

[119] The NYSE Listing Rules oblige its members to refrain in a great many cases from exercising the voting right themselves without instructions from the client, section 402.08 NYSE Listing Rules.

[120] ADP Proxy Services does this for the great majority of the American banks, brokers and custodians. On behalf of the Dutch Shareholders Communication Channel this same business handles the despatch of information and voting forms to securities account holders with affiliated institutions and the processing of voting forms that have been returned.

with them and then send them the information from the company and the voting forms. Sometimes they are investors, in other cases the chain of intermediaries passes via custodians, banks and brokers in the various states until it reaches the investor. The proxy services companies also process the voting forms that have been returned and pass on to the company the final result of the votes exercised by the beneficial owners. All beneficial owners thus ultimately vote by virtue of a proxy from the registered owner Cede & Co.[121]

American company law applies the system of a long record date. Solely those who are shareholders on the record date are entitled to attend the meeting and vote. According to the law of most states the record date can be between 50 or 60 days before the meeting. If the company's articles of association do not make provision for a specific record date, then according to the law it is normally the day prior to the day of convocation.[122] The person who acquires shares after the record date cannot claim the exercise of voting rights as against the company, but may under certain circumstances demand from the seller who was the owner on the record date that such seller should grant him proxy or should vote in accordance with his instructions.[123] This rule applies to registered owners. American experts whom I consulted on this told me that they were not aware of any cases in which beneficial owners had acquired shares via the stock exchange after the record date and wanted to claim the entitlement to exercise the voting right. In practice the record date is accepted by them as a given fact. The long record date in the U.S. obviates the problems that can form an obstacle to proxy voting in the event of a short record date. As far as I am aware, only the U.S. and Canada apply such a long record date.[124] However, this does present problems in, say, the transatlantic situation in which a Dutch company is listed on the NYSE and wants to allow its American shareholders to vote via proxy voting. For a meeting of such a company a sort of record date is often set in the U.S. that will in any event make it possible to establish the persons to whom the information from the company and, where required, the voting forms can be sent. American investors and their brokers and banks, however, assume that the shareholders, both registered and beneficial, are actually entitled to vote on the record date. No adjustment is made in the event that the shares are subsequently sold. Under Dutch company law, however, it is only those persons who are shareholders on a record date shortly before the meeting who are entitled to vote. This does not constitute a problem provided that on the Dutch record date,

---

[121] Franklin, Finkelstein, and Williams, see above, n. 112, paras 10.7, 10-12–10-14 and the diagram on 10-31.

[122] e.g. s. 213(a) Delaware General Corporation Law.

[123] Franklin, Finkelstein and Williams, see above, n. 112, paras 9.5, 9-11–9-12.

[124] For Canada see Winter, 'Stemmen op afstand via het Communicatiekanaal Aandeelhouders', see above, n. 27, 101.

which is shortly before the meeting, Cede & Co, acting for the DTC as registered owner, holds at least as many shares as correspond to the number of proxy votes. As not everyone will vote by proxy, this will normally be the case. The fact that Cede & Co issues voting proxies to investors who are no longer beneficial owners on the record date shortly before the meeting is under Dutch law immaterial as regards the validity of those votes.[125] One area where a problem does exist, though, is the case in which the beneficial owner, having sent in a voting form for the record date in the Netherlands, might then transfer his shareholding to a securities account with a Dutch bank from which he can validly request admittance to the meeting and can vote at the meeting. In that way he can vote twice on his shares.[126] As far as I know, the securities systems in the U.S. and the Netherlands are at the moment not equipped to prevent this happening.

American company law and securities law meanwhile permits the electronic transmission of information from the company to shareholders and also allow electronic proxy voting by shareholders.[127] Telephone and web-based voting is already widely applied in the U.S.[128] ADP reports that for 1,000 American

[125] DaimlerChrysler AG, which issued 'global shares' after the merger, i.e. registered shares that have the same form and characteristics in Germany and the U.S., does have a problem. The share register of DaimlerChrysler AG is now held in part in the U.S. and all securities account holders in that part are included in the DTC system. Via an electronic link between the DTC and DBC changes resulting from stock exchange transactions on the NYSE are passed on each day to the German custodian of the share register of DaimlerChrysler AG. The securities account holders in the U.S. are not beneficial owners, yet under German law they are actually the registered shareholders who are directly entitled to the voting right. Since Germany does not apply a record date but solely allows those who are shareholders at the time of the meeting to exercise the voting right, it is necessary for checks to be made to be made up to the meeting to establish whether securities account holders in the U.S. (and in Germany) have sold their shares and thus lost their voting right. In a letter dated September 3, 1998 the NYSE asked its members to monitor the positions of securities account holders in DaimlerChrysler AG until the meeting and to remove the voting proxies of investors who have sold their shares. This process has to be monitored by the Bank of New York as transfer agent of DaimlerChrysler in New York and by ADP; see M. Schell, M.L. Wolff, and G.A. Gnaedig, 'DaimlerChrysler: Global Shares for a Global Market' [1999] *The Mergers & Acquisitions Lawyer*, January, 1–8. People in the securities industry New York whom I talked to about this very much doubt whether this process will and can work in practice.

[126] This problem can be formally reasoned away. The beneficial owner Y who, after having filled in a voting form, has his shares transferred to a securities account in the Netherlands, does not vote twice on the same shares. In itself, his transfer leads to a reduction in the number of shares held by the DTC (Cede & Co) in the share register. On the assumption that not all beneficial owners will vote by proxy the DTC will on the short record date hold more shares than are needed for the votes cast by beneficial owners via proxy solicitation. The proxy votes that are counted for Y in America are in fact votes on shares that are held by other persons in America as beneficial owners and on which they do not exercise a voting right. It would only become a formal problem if all beneficial owners were to fill in voting forms and if some of them subsequently caused their shares to be transferred.

[127] See the SEC Release 34–36345 (1995) Use of Electronic Media for Delivery Purposes and s. 212(c)(2) Delaware General Corporation Law.

[128] Klausner and Elfenbein, see above, n. 24, 9–11. ADP has set up a separate website for this, www.adp.com, which investors can access using numerical codes.

publicly listed companies 6% of the proxy votes were cast via the internet or by telephone in 1999. Expectations are that this proportion will double in 2000 and show further strong growth thereafter.[129]

M. Building Blocks for a European Solution

The American system offers prospects for a European solution. One great advantage of the U.S. system compared to the European one is that in America there is only one giral securities system in operation. Within that system the securities holdings of investors are determined in an unambiguous way. Crediting and debiting of securities takes place on the basis of uniform operational agreements. This eliminates the complications that arise from different clearing and settlement practices, which cuts out at least one of the causes of mistakes when establishing the entitlement to vote. It would be good if a similar uniform giral securities system could be created in Europe. Whether that will happen will depend on market developments, on the competition between the existing and new national and international trading, clearing and settlement systems in Europe. Those developments will not be driven primarily by the interest of shareholders in being able to exercise their voting rights, but by the financial interests of stock exchanges, clearing organizations, banks, and investors. Whether this will eventually lead to a single European clearing and settlement organization is impossible to predict. The outcome might also be the creation of a number of major clearing and settlement *hubs*, which process the main international flows of securities transactions, via national CSDs that settle transactions at a national level. One thing is certain: the world of securities clearing and settlement in Europe will undergo a drastic change in the near future. It is the market that determines these developments; European legislators have no role to play in this area. And yet European legislation can contribute a great deal towards helping to make cross-border proxy voting possible in practice. In both securities law and company law the existing rules, originally drawn up for national markets, can be harmonized. If we believe that cross-border voting is important for companies and their shareholders, then the obstacles that I have been describing must be cleared away over the short term. To start with securities law, I would advocate a European directive that sets out rules for giral securities systems comparable with those in article 8 of the American Uniform Commercial Code. The directive would have to determine the character of the claim by the holder of a securities account as against the intermediary who administers the account and should also make it clear that the law of the intermediary determines the law that governs the property-law aspects of that claim.

---

[129] See the brochure by J.P. Morgan, *Internet voting and electronic delivery of shareholder communications,* March 2000, 2.

In addition, the directive would have to rule that the issuing institution is allowed to rely on the correctness of a declaration by an intermediary who administers a securities account about the entitlement of a holder of that account. Lastly, and perhaps most importantly for proxy voting, the directive would have to stipulate that each intermediary who administers securities accounts for other parties is obliged to give such other parties the opportunity of exercising the rights attached to the securities administered in such accounts, or to exercise those himself on the instructions of such other parties. If there are no instructions the intermediary should not be able to exercise those rights. Such a provision would ensure that no cumulative or conflicting claims to voting rights arise within chains of intermediaries.

In themselves, such rules do not provide clarity about whom, within chains of intermediaries, is actually the shareholder and who is, in such capacity, entitled to vote. What is clear in this system is that the investor must in practice be able to exercise the voting right, but whether he does that as shareholder or as a proxy acting for another person cannot be clearly established. The Americans have found a pragmatic solution for this. The DTC, via its nominee Cede & Co, is registered as central institution of the giral system in the share register of companies. Solely Cede & Co is a genuine shareholder, all other parties in the giral system have a derived, beneficial right. The actual investors are never shareholders. If they vote, they do that on the basis of a proxy from Cede & Co. In Europe there is no need for us to follow this route which, albeit pragmatic, is perhaps also slightly too unimaginative. The challenge that we face is to do it better. As the German example shows, the holders of securities accounts with banks can be legally regarded as registered shareholders in the company. The drawback, however, is that this does not work outside of Germany's borders, as the link-up with foreign giral systems does not function effectively or in a uniform way, which means that only the foreign CSDs are registered in the share register. Basically, it should also be possible for investors abroad to be registered in the company's share register. We need to investigate the conditions that need to be applied to ensure that all investors in European giral securities systems can be regarded as shareholders of the company and can acquire an all-embracing right as a shareholder as against the company. I believe that such a system is certainly feasible, but it will require a much greater uniformity of national and international giral systems than currently exists in Europe.

Company law in the European Member States also needs to be harmonized. The proposal for a fifth European directive on company law contains a provision on proxy voting. This directive, the first draft of which was published as long ago as 1972, is aimed at setting harmonised rules on the structure of the public limited company as well as rules on the rights and obligations of its corporate bodies. The directive has never developed beyond the draft stage. Fundamental disagreement exists between the Member States about the way in which the management and supervision has to be regulated within the company. Article 28 of the draft sets out a few basic rules that a person has to comply with if he openly solicits proxies from shareholders and offers to appoint a representative for them. The provision prescribes, *inter alia*, the information that this person must cause to be sent to the shareholders, it states that he must request instructions and must indicate how the representative will vote in the event that the shareholder does not give any instructions, that he may only depart from the instructions under special circumstances, etc.[130] This provision needs to be studied closely once more and tightened up.[131]

An essential element for successful proxy voting is that companies must be able to set a long record date, prior to the convocation for the meeting. The draft fifth directive contains no provisions on this[132] and needs to be modified in this respect. A long record date would not only eliminate the present problems relating to the blocking of shares and the changing groups of shareholders, it would also bring Europe in line with America, which would mean that transatlantic proxy voting would encounter fewer problems. The draft fifth directive allows the convocation for the shareholders' meeting to be made using electronic communication media provided that all shares are registered and provided it is possible to establish that the convocation has been sent to every shareholder and to establish the date on which the convocation took place, article 24, para. 1(a). But shareholders can only give a written proxy for the purpose of voting, article 27 para. 3. Here, too, the directive must be modified to allow electronic and telephone voting. When doing that we should certainly also look at whether it is possible to decouple the formal procedure of voting by shareholders from a physical meeting of shareholders.

---

[130] For the text of this provision see *Losbladige Rechtspersonen, Aanverwante Stukken*, vol. 3, 'Europese Richtlijnen Vennootschapsrecht' [European Company Law Directives], Bijlage 5a, 26.

[131] The fact that provisions of this type are important was reflected by the commotion about the recent general meeting of Dordtsche Petroleum NV. This general meeting had to decide on a bid that had been made for the shares in Dordtsche by various parties, including the ABN Amro bank. A higher than usual majority vote was required if the resolutions were to be adopted. From the newspaper I gather that more than half of the private shareholders of Dordtsche had a securities account with ABN Amro. They received a letter from ABN Amro giving them the possibility of granting a proxy to vote in favour of the resolutions to be adopted. The possibility of granting a proxy to vote against was not offered to the shareholders. Nor, it seems, was the information provided to shareholders entirely objective, see *Het Financieele Dagblad*, March 4, 2000, 6, 'Kwalijke dubbelrol ABN Amro bij bod op Dordtsche' [ABN Amro plays undesirable dual role in bid for Dordtsche]. None of this has much to do with proxy voting as is being sought via the Shareholders Communication Channel.

[132] On the basis of Article 26, which rules that every shareholder who has fulfilled the formalities set by law or the articles of association is entitled to attend the general meeting (and may then vote), it seems that we have to deduce that only persons who are shareholders on the day of the meeting are allowed to vote.

It will not, I fear, be possible to achieve progress on these points for such time as they continue to form part of a draft for a fifth directive which, because of other issues, is being buried away as deeply as possible by the Member States. I would therefore advocate that the functioning of the shareholders' meeting and proxy voting by shareholders should be unlinked from the fifth directive and that these should over the short term be regulated in a separate directive, preferably in relation to the proposals that I mentioned in the area of securities law. The importance to companies and their shareholders of an efficient system of cross-border proxy voting in Europe and ultimately the importance to Europe of an effectively functioning market-oriented system of corporate governance justify an accelerated and sharply focused approach.

18

Institutional Investors and Corporate Governance: Solution or Problem?

JOSÉ M. GARRIDO AND ANGEL ROJO

Abstract

The rise of institutional investors is an undeniable fact in every developed stock market of the world. The purpose of this chapter is to explore the interaction between the growing importance of institutional investors and the debate on corporate governance, with special attention given to the Spanish legal environment. In the U.S., the phenomenal rise of institutional investing has led a significant part of academia to defend the role of institutional investors as a solution to the separation of ownership and control. It is submitted, however, that there remain significant differences between Anglo-American corporate governance systems and continental European systems. The presence of blockholders and especially the importance of banks present great difficulties for effective monitoring by institutional investors. As a matter of fact, dominance of institutional investors by credit institutions can even mean that institutional investors could add problems to the corporate governance system, instead of furnishing a solution.

In the final part of the chapter, some ways of action available to institutional investors in Spanish law are analysed. The fundamental requirements for a positive role of institutional investors in corporate governance, namely independence and accountability, would necessitate legal reform.

Contents

A. Introduction: the Debate on Corporate Governance

One of the most recurring topics in corporate law is the debate on corporate governance. Since the early twentieth century, when Thorstein Veblen published his fascinating works on the future of the corporation (*The Theory of Business Enterprise*; *The Engineers and the Price System*),[1] where he envisaged the control of a new kind of economic actors, the manager-engineers, and the early thirties,

---

[1] T. Veblen, *The Theory of Business Enterprise* (New York 1904); *The Engineers and the Price System* (New York 1924).

when Berle and Means's famous book (*The Modern Corporation and Private Property*) started to influence a whole line of scholarship,[2] the question of who exerts power within the corporation and how that power can be subjected by a system of checks and balances has been studied repeatedly from different points of view.

The initial formulation of the problem rests on the assumption that in the large corporation, a disorganized body of shareholders find themselves in a situation in which the cost of exerting their rights is higher than the benefit obtained. In this situation of "rational apathy",[3] corporate managers would control the company by taking advantage of shareholders' passivity. The centre of power moves from the shareholders' meeting to the board of directors. This poses an important "agency problem",[4] as the managers are able to act without restraint, and in furtherance of their personal objectives, instead of the corporation's. The situation of "power without responsibility", derived from the separation of ownership and control,[5] gives rise to conflicts of interest, scenarios where managers serve their own interests in complete or partial disregard of the proclaimed objective of maximizing the shareholders' (or the corporation's) benefits.[6]

After the characterization of the problem, there have been, roughly speaking, two main proposals for its solution. The first one is founded on the benefits of the "corporate control market". In a developed stock market, the performance of a company is immediately and perfectly reflected on its quotation.[7] A fraud-

---

[2] A. Berle and G. Means, *The Modern Corporation and Private Property* (New York 1932) It is interesting to place this book in context: see the exchange between Professors Berle and Dodd: E.M. Dodd, Jr, 'For Whom are Corporate Managers Trustees? [1932] 45 Harvard Law Review 1145; A. Berle, Jr, 'For Whom Corporate Managers *are* Trustees: A Note' [1932] 45 Harvard Law Review 1365. It is also interesting to notice that one of the contemporary criticisms made to Berle and Means was their omission of credit institutions in their analysis: see N.L. Meyers, Book Review [1933] 42 Yale Law Journal 997, 999.

[3] See B.S. Black, 'Shareholder Passivity Reexamined', 89 [1990] Michigan Law Review 520. Cf. A. Menéndez, 'El absentismo de los accionistas y el desequilibrio de poder en la sociedad anónima' in *Estudios De Castro* (Madrid 1976) II, 273; J. Duque, 'Absentismo del accionista y acciones sin voto', in *Estudios J.B. Vallet De Goytisolo*, VII, (Madrid 1988) 143.

[4] The term "agency problem" derives from the economic literature and by no means has a strict legal sense.

[5] See E.F. Fama and M.C. Jensen, 'Separation of Ownership and Control' [1983] 26 Journal of Law and Economics 301.

[6] See extensively M.J. Roe, *Strong Managers Weak Owners: The Political Roots of American Corporate Finance* (Princeton, 1994). See V. Brudney, 'Corporate Governance, Agency Costs, and the Rhetoric of Contract' [1985] 85 Columbia Law Review 1403.

[7] Of course, this depends on the force attached to the Efficient Capital Market Hypothesis (ECMH). A good introduction to this fundamental economic theory can be found in R.A. Brealey and S.C. Myers, *Principles of Corporate Finance* (4th edn. New York 1991) 287ff. On some of the implications for securities law, see I. Ayres, 'Back to Basics: Regulating How Corporations Speak to the Market' [1991] 77 Virginia Law Review 945; J.R. Macey and G.P. Miller, 'Good Finance,

ulent or negligent management would inevitably cause a significant decline in the company's stock quotation. The fundamentals of economic analysis suggest that the company would be more valuable in the hands of a competent management (highest valuing user) than in the hands of the present management. Therefore, if there are managers and financial entrepreneurs monitoring the markets, the companies badly or inadequately managed will be detected, and these entrepreneurs will offer a premium over the shares' listed price in order to acquire control of the company. In this way, the hostile take-over bid would work as a disciplinary device against incompetent or fraudulent managers.[8] The problem with this approach to corporate governance is that it demands a highly developed stock market and a favourable legal and cultural environment as regards the use of hostile take-overs. But even in the countries where these assumptions hold true, the elevated costs[9] associated with take-over bids make unrealistic the idea that managers live in fear of the threat of a hostile take-over.[10] Only in the most egregious cases does the corporate control market acts against extremely incompetent managers.[11]

The second proposal to the solution of the corporate governance problem reflects the economic changes in the structure of share ownership.[12] The emergence of important shareholders, able to channel huge financial resources belonging to vast numbers of persons, is probably one of the most important developments in the contemporary corporate scene.[13] These shareholders,

Bad Economics: An Analysis of the Fraud-on-the-Market Theory' [1990] 42 Stanford Law Review 1059.

[8] See L. Herzel, 'Boards of Directors versus Institutional Investors' in Th. Baums, R.M. Buxbaum, and K.J. Hopt (eds.), *Institutional Investors and Corporate Governance* (Berlin/New York 1994) 161. See B. Arruñada, *Control y regulación de la sociedad anónima* (Madrid 1990); J. García De Enterría, 'El control del poder societario en la gran empresa y la función disciplinar de las OPAs' [1993] *Revista de Derecho Bancario y Bursátil* 665. Instead, Zurita considers takeovers and institutional investors as competing or complementing mechanisms of efficiency (J. Zurita, 'Las instituciones de inversión colectiva y las ofertas públicas de adquisición de valores', in *La protección de los partícipes de los fondos de inversión* (Madrid 1997) 155.

[9] See R. Morck, A. Shleifer, and R.W. Vishny, 'Alternative Mechanisms for Corporate Control' [1989] 79 *American Economic Review* 842.

[10] See J.N. Gordon, 'Institutions as Relational Investors: A New Look at Cumulative Voting' [1994] 94 Columbia Law Review 124; J.C. Coffee, 'Regulating the Market for Corporate Control: A Critical Assessment of the Tender Offer's Role in Corporate Governance' [1984] 84 Columbia Law Review 1145.

[11] See J. Pound, 'The Rise of the Political Model of Corporate Governance and Corporate Control' [1993] 68 New York University Law Review 1003; P. Davies, 'Institutional Investors as Corporate Monitors in the United Kingdom' in K.J. Hopt, H. Kanda, M.J. Roe, E. Wymeersch, and S. Prigge (eds.), *Comparative Corporate Governance* (Berlin/New York 1997) 47.

[12] See B.S. Black, 'Shareholder Passivity Reexamined' [1990] 89 Michigan Law Review 520.

[13] This was already predicted by A. Berle, *Power Without Property* (New York 1959) 53ff. See R.C. Clark, 'The Four Stages of Capitalism: Reflections on Investment Management Treatises' [1981] 94 Harvard Law Review 561.

known as "institutional investors" would supposedly furnish a solution to the corporate governance problem.[14] Given the fact that rational apathy is linked to the negligible percentage of shares owned by most individuals, the important amount of shares in the hands of institutional investors would allow these to exert a remarkable influence in the company and to monitor the managers' behaviour. The "atomization" of shareholders that gave rise to the "managers' revolution" could be reversed through the intelligent use of the powers awarded to the institutional investor. The problem of separation of ownership and control could be mitigated when taking into account that important shareholders do exist, and that their active role would serve as a limit to the abuse of power by corporate managers.[15]

Nevertheless, the idea that institutional investors represent the proper balance against the unrestricted power of managers seems to face considerable difficulty in practice.[16] Only a few institutional investors have decided to take an active role in the corporate life of the companies where they invest.[17] For the most part, involvement in the corporation is just an obstacle for the most obvious solution to a corporate governance problem: sale of the shares (which is popularly known as "Wall Street Rule", or "Vote with your feet"). So, in the classic dilemma between "exit" and "voice",[18] institutional investors have favoured the first solution. Or, in the words of Professor Coffee, the alternative between liquidity and control is decided mostly in favour of preserving liquidity.[19] The lack of incentives for adopting an active stance against the managers' abuses or incompetence is almost self-evident.

In spite of the adverse circumstances, corporate scholars continue viewing in the institutional investors some kind of solution to corporate governance problems, suggesting, in some cases, appropriate regulatory reforms in order to increase the monitoring potential of these investors.

[14] See B.S. Black, 'Shareholder Passivity Reexamined', see above, n. 12, 520ff; J. Pound, 'The Rise of the Political Model of Corporate Governance and Corporate Control', see above, n. 11, 1003ff; J.M. De Paz Arias, 'Los inversores institucionales como medio de resolución del conflicto de intereses entre administradores y accionistas en la sociedad abierta' [1995] *Revista de Derecho Bancario y Bursátil* 857.

[15] See B.S. Black, 'Shareholder Passivity Reexamined', see above, n. 12, 520ff; B.S. Black, 'Agents Watching Agents: The Promise of Institutional Investor Voice' [1992] 39 UCLA Law Review 811; J.N. Gordon, 'Institutions as Relational Investors: A New Look at Cumulative Voting', see above, n. 10, 124ff.

[16] See E.B. Rock, 'The Logic and (Uncertain) Significance of Institutional Shareholder Activism' [1991] 79 Go Law Journal 445.

[17] The best example is CalPERS. There are other instances, such as TIIA-CREF, the Wisconsin Public Retirement Fund, Lens, or EA. But these are islands of activism in an ocean of passivity.

[18] The dilemma has been aptly characterized by A.O. Hirschman, *Exit, Voice, and Loyalty: Responses to Decline in Firms, Organizations, and States* (Cambridge 1970).

[19] See J.C. Coffee, 'Liquidity versus Control: The Institutional Investor as Corporate Monitor' [1991] 91 Columbia Law Review 1277.

B. Corporate Governance Models

The debate on corporate governance has been considerably enlarged by comparative corporate studies.[20] The realization, by U.S. scholars, that there are very different models of corporate governance has brought about several consequences. On a first level, there is what has been termed a "fascination" for other corporate governance models, specially the German model.[21] On a second level, this fascination is justly criticized, as it ignores fundamental differences among the systems, and the difficulties of importing or exporting rules of law or corporate practices that are alien to a given country.[22]

The comparative studies on corporate governance are far from useless, though. Thanks to these studies, it is possible to identify the major differences in the corporate law systems and in the techniques used to solve governance problems.

The systems of corporate governance can be roughly classified according to the importance of the role played by the stock market.[23] In the Anglo-Saxon system of corporate governance, the stock market is the main source of financing. Therefore, there is a well-developed stock market, and share ownership is widely spread. To this economic data, one may add a relevant legal fact: direction of the company is within the competence of the board of directors, subject only to the control of the shareholders' meeting.

[20] See R.M. Buxbaum, 'Comparative Aspects of Institutional Investment and Corporate Governance' in Th. Baums, R.M. Buxbaum, and K.J. Hopt (eds.), *Institutional Investors and Corporate Governance* (Berlin/New York 1994) 3.

[21] See E.B. Rock, 'America's Fascination with German Corporate Governance' [1995] *Die Aktiengesellschaft* 291; Some admiration for the German system of corporate governance can be found in Roe (M.J. Roe, 'Some Differences in Corporate Structure in Germany, Japan, and the United States' [1993] 102 Yale Law Journal 1927; M.J. Roe, 'Some Differences in Corporate Governance in Germany, Japan and America' in Th. Baums, R.M. Buxbaum, and K.J. Hopt (eds.), *Institutional Investors and Corporate Governance* (Berlin/New York 1994) 23).

[22] See J.C. Coffee, 'Liquidity versus Control: The Institutional Investor as Corporate Monitor', see above, n. 19, 1277ff. In fact, corporate law can only be studied in connection with the social and economic characteristics of a system: see A. Rojo, 'La sociedad anónima como problema' [1988] *Revista de Derecho Mercantil* 7, published in English as 'The Typology of Companies' in R.R. Drury and P.G. Xuereb (eds.), *European Company Laws. A Comparative Approach* (Darmouth 1991) 41ff; R.C. Clark, 'The Interdisciplinary Study of Legal Evolution' [1981] 90 Yale Law Journal 1238; R.C. Clark, 'Contracts, Elites, and Traditions in the Making of Corporate Law' [1989] 89 Columbia Law Review 1703. Of course, as Professor Coffee has put it, *"Law matters"* (J.C. Coffee, 'The Future as History: The Prospects for Global Convergence in Corporate Governance and Its Implications' [1999] 93 Northwestern University Law Review 641.

[23] See R.J. Rajan and L. Zingales, 'What Do We Know about Capital Structure? Some Evidence from International Data' [1995] 50 *Journal of Finance* 1421, where a distinction is made between "market systems" and "bank systems", although primarily referred to corporate finance. On the determinants of differences in corporate ownership, see H. Demetz and K. Lehn, 'The Structure of Corporate Ownership: Causes and Consequences' [1985] 93 *Journal of Political Economy* 1155.

On the other hand, there is the continental system of corporate governance.[24] In this system, the role of the stock market is secondary, as most of the companies are financed through bank loans. There are major shareholdings in the hands of a few economic actors. That is why the system is often referred to as "blockholder system", or "network system".[25] Banks play a paramount role in this corporate governance system. They possess significant shareholdings in most of the large companies and, moreover, they are the main providers of finance. In some of the continental models, there are organs whose function is to control the managers—as in the well-known German system; in others, the corporate structure is very similar to that of the Anglo-Saxon companies.[26]

It is clear, therefore, that there are significant differences between these two systems. To be sure, there is a clear convergence of the models, whereby banks will perhaps play a more important role in the U.S. corporate scene in the future, and probably blockholdings will be more than occasional; and, on the other hand, stock markets are becoming the main source of financing for the largest European companies. It is quite likely that the Anglo-Saxon system will emerge triumphant from the collision with the continental system, but the final outcome is still uncertain. In recent years, the European stock exchanges are becoming increasingly important, due to a number of reasons among which the deregulation of the economy and the privatization of important companies are especially notable. It seems that the continental corporate governance models are evolving towards the Anglo-Saxon pattern and that problems and solutions will become gradually similar to those experienced and tried in the U.S. and in Britain. This is the likely future of the European stock markets,[27] although it is impossible to tell whether any given factor could reverse the trend.

[24] Of course, there is also the highly peculiar Japanese model, based on the *keiretsu* structure (See E. Berghof and E. Perotti, 'The Governance Structure of the Japanese Financial Keiretsu' [1994] 36 *Journal of Financial Economics* 259; M.J. Roe, 'Some Differences in Corporate Structure in Germany, Japan, and the United States', see above, n. 21, 1927ff; S. Kaplan and B. Minton, 'Appointments of Outsiders to Japanese Boards: Determinants and Implications for Managers' [1994] 36 *Journal of Financial Economics* 225; J.K. Kang and A. Shivdasani, 'Firm Performance, Corporate Governance, and Top Executive Turnover in Japan' [1995] 38 *Journal of Financial Economics* 29.

[25] See E. Wymeersch, 'Institutional Investors, Financial Groups and their Impact on Corporate Governance in Belgium' in Th. Baums, R.M. Buxbaum, and K.J. Hopt (eds.), *Institutional Investors and Corporate Governance* (Berlin/New York 1994) 347, with interesting comments on the Belgian system.

[26] See M. Trías Sagnier, *Los inversores institucionales y el gobierno de las grandes sociedades* (Madrid 1998) 24, where the author remarks the similarity between the financial tenets of the German and Spanish model of corporate governance, and the similarities between the Anglo-Saxon structure of the corporation and the Spanish legal system.

[27] W. Gerke, M. Bank, and M. Steiger, '*The Changing Role of Institutional Investors—a German perspective*', unpublished paper, 2000.

The implications of the differences between the two basic systems of corporate governance are extremely interesting. Taking into account the descriptions of the two systems, it is clear that the problem of the separation of ownership and control is remarkably intense in the Anglo-Saxon system, but in the continental system that problem presents a different intensity and nature. Disperse ownership of shares requires a well-developed stock market, and that element is absolutely necessary for a situation of separation of ownership and control to arise. From this follows that the problem of separation of ownership and control, the fundamental problem of corporate governance in the Anglo-Saxon literature, is highly idiosyncratic, i.e. requires a set of facts, features, and circumstances that have only developed in full in a certain number of legal systems.

In the continental models, managers are subject to the monitoring of blockholders and financial institutions. As a matter of fact, financial institutions tend to occupy seats in the board of the large corporations, so they have a first-hand knowledge of the company situation and they are able to control the actions undertaken by managers. In this way, managers have considerably less power and are accountable for the misuse of that power. But the fundamental corporate governance problem in the continental system lies with the exercise of power by blockholders.

The existence of large blocks of shares avoids the problem of separation of ownership and control. But the concentration of ownership and control ("a mixed blessing") has its own problems: the development of a stock exchange calls for new minority shareholders, and these shareholders may find, to their disappointment, that their interests are not taken into account, but only those of the blockholders.

The problem can be more intense where the blockholders are financial institutions. It is well known that banks are major shareholders in large companies, that at the same time they are the main providers of finance, and, what is more, those banks frequently act as representatives of the private shareholders whose shares are deposited with or administered by the credit institutions. Traditionally, it was considered that this concentration of power could lead to an effective control of managers by banks. But the fact that banks have power to control the managers does not necessarily imply that banks are good monitors[28]: financial institutions often find themselves involved in conflicts of

---

[28] See J. Charkham, *Keeping Good Company: A Study of Corporate Governance in Five Countries* (Oxford 1994) 36. As a matter of fact, in the context of a network system such as the Swiss, it has been said that the company general meeting is an "organ for acclamation", and that the role of banks as shareholders and as proxies for shareholders has a direct relation to that unfortunate development (see P. Schmitt, *Das Verhältnis zwischen Generalversammlung und Verwaltung in der Aktiengesellschaft* (Zürich 1991) 9, 97ff). The control of institutional investors by banks could only worsen this situation.

interests, as their position as creditors and providers of finance frequently clashes against their role as shareholders.[29]

The prevailing power of important blockholders has an obvious victim: the small shareholder. The interests of small investors are ignored, so these refrain from a more active participation in the stock market. Besides, historical inadequacies in securities regulation have not allowed a full development of protective measures in favour of minority shareholders and of small investors in general.

This rough analysis reveals that the situation in different corporate governance systems can be relatively diverse. Its logical consequence is that solutions for one system are not necessarily valid solutions for other systems. In a nutshell, this applies, generally, to corporate governance issues, and especially to the role of institutional investors.

C. Institutional Investors and Corporate Governance Models

As it has been said before, the active role of institutional investors is contemplated as one of the possible solutions to corporate governance problems. But, first, it will be necessary to define precisely the corporate governance problem that is meant to be solved: where the problem is that of disperse ownership of shares, it is clear that institutional investors can mitigate that problem, at least in theory. The emergence of a category of investors that aggregate the investments of a large number of individuals could help to find a solution to the problem of the rational apathy of small shareholders. Certainly, if the justification for shareholder passivity is that the small size of the investment does not justify the costs of monitoring and controlling the managers, this justification is less evident for institutional investors. Although institutional investors' shareholdings may widely vary in size, in a number of cases the amount of money invested in a company is remarkably high. In the view of some legal and economic theorists, the amount of the investment would justify the necessary costs incurred in monitoring the management.[30] Besides, the percentage of shares held by institutional investors would allow the use of several legal measures against an incompetent

---

[29] There is also the problem of the monitoring and control of the banks themselves. Central banks do not control the corporate practices of financial institutions, and, curiously, it is in European banks where corporate problems approximate those of the large American corporation with dispersed ownership. In banks, managers are able to assert control with remarkably small shareholdings, and have an important mechanism of controlling the proxy machinery (F. San Sebastián, *El gobierno de las sociedades cotizadas y su control* (Madrid, undated) 120–121. Cf. R. Stulz, 'Managerial Control of Voting Rights' [1988] 20 *Journal of Financial Economics* 25). Maybe it is correct to assert that "banks control themselves" (J. Charkham, *Keeping Good Company: A Study of Corporate Governance in Five Countries*, see above, n. 28, 36).

[30] J. Pound, 'The Rise of the Political Model of Corporate Governance and Corporate Control, see above, n. 11, 1041.

or fraudulent management, and would give a great deal of leverage in the negotiations with the managers. The result of all this would be a higher level of management's responsibility and accountability, which in turn would benefit all shareholders.

But this is more theory than reality. In practice, most institutional shareholders adopt a passive attitude towards corporate management, and towards corporate activity in general.[31] It can be said that, in most cases, the behaviour of institutional investors replicates that of small shareholders. The reasons for the "rational apathy" of institutional investors are several: first, there is clearly a "free rider" problem.[32] If a given institutional investor engages in monitoring the corporate managers, it will bear the whole cost of that activity, whereas the rest of institutional investors and individual shareholders will benefit from that activity. So, the most likely outcome is that none of the institutional investors will monitor the managers' behaviour. There is a second question to be taken into account: institutional investors tend to favour "exit" over "voice" as the strategy to be adopted in the event of a severe corporate crisis. It is easier for an institutional investor to sell its shares in the company rather than taking an active role in the solution to the crisis. The liquidity and interconnections of the markets are increasing, so selling the shares is an option even for large shareholders. On the other hand, the costs of taking an active role can be enormously high, and the percentage of shares held by an institutional investor will normally be insufficient to compensate for those costs. Besides, the more involved an institutional investor becomes in a company, the more difficult will be for that investor to leave the company. So, institutional investors avoid commitment and prefer to leave "an open door", in case it is necessary to exit the company. Finally, it can be said that institutional investors tend to mirror each other's movements, so that the sale of shares by an institutional investor can easily cause a "herd" effect.[33] Institutional investors usually leave a company when it runs into a difficult situation, and the high volume of the transactions involved increases the market's volatility.[34] The rest of the shareholders will hardly benefit from it.

---

[31] See L. Enriques, 'L'attivismo delle investitori istituzionali negli Stati Uniti: una rassegna degli studi empirici' [1998] *Revista delle Società* 1998, 592.

[32] See S. Levmore, 'Monitors and Freeriders in Commercial and Corporate Settings' [1982] 92 Yale Law Journal 49.

[33] See D.S. Sharfstein and J.C. Stein, 'Herd Behavior and Investment' [1990] 80 *American Economic Review* 465; J.R. Nofsinger and R.W. Sias, 'Herding and Feedback Trading by Institutional and Individual Investors' [1999] 54 *Journal of Finance* 2263; R. Wermers, 'Mutual Fund Herding and the Impact on Stock Prices' [1999] 54 *Journal of Finance* 581.

[34] See E. Gliozzi, 'Società per azioni e mercati finanziari' [1999] *Rivista Trimestrale di Diritto e Processuale Civile* 759. On the other hand, J. Lakonishok, A. Shleifer, and R.W. Vishny, 'The Impact of Institutional Trading on Stock Prices' [1992] 32 *Journal of Financial Economics* 23, consider that movements in prices caused by the activity of institutional investors are favourable for the market, as they reflect a better information than that of the average investor.

Comparing the behaviour of institutional investors to that of private share-holders, then, it is apparent that there are many similarities between them.[35] The problem becomes how to bring about a greater involvement on the part of the institutional investors. It is submitted that a more active role by institutional investors demands a host of regulatory measures, and that even if those measures were implemented, a solution is not guaranteed for the corporate governance problems derived from a situation of separation of ownership from control. In all corporate governance systems, there are advocates of institutional investor activism as a solution to the monitoring problem in large companies, but equally common to all systems is the hard fact that most institutional investors adopt a passive attitude. The idea of implementing rules providing for the compulsory exercise of voting rights by institutional investors has had just a limited impact. Only U.S. private pension funds are required by law to vote their shares,[36] but in practice this obligation is unenforceable. In some European countries, there have been recommendations indicating the usefulness of exercising the voting rights, but not a legal obligation (as in England[37]). In France, the obligation to vote has been introduced,[38] but it has not been implemented so far, and the enforceability of the provision will be a problem, as it is in the U.S. In Italy there is great controversy as to the existence of an obligation to vote the shares, but most of the commentators are contrary to the existence of such an obligation.[39] The same can be said of German law.[40] So, the vast majority of legal systems recognize implicitly that institutional investors can legitimately adopt a passive attitude in the companies where they invest, and private investors do no have a cause of action based solely on that fact.

Institutional investor activism has a different connotation in the context of continental corporate governance systems. In the continental systems, dispersion of share ownership is not the main corporate governance problem. As a

---

[35] On the trading preferences of institutional investors, see E.G. Falkenstein, 'Preferences for Stock Characteristics as Revealed by Mutual Fund Portfolio Holdings' [1996] 51 *Journal of Finance* 111; M.J. Gruber, 'Another Puzzle: The Growth in Actively Managed Mutual Funds' [1996] 51 *Journal of Finance* 783.

[36] This derives from ERISA, § 404(a)(1)(A) and (B), as interpreted by the DOL (DOL Guidelines).

[37] See *Cadbury Report*, paras 6.11.2 and 6.12; *Hampel Report*, paras 5.7–5.10.

[38] See art 58 loi no. 96/597 (July 2, 1996).

[39] See art. 40 D Lgs no. 58 (24.2.1998). See R. Costi, 'Risparmio gestito e governo societario nel TU della Finanza' in *Atti del convegno ABI su TU della Finanza, Banche, Mercati, Gestione del Risparmio* (Rome 1998); A. Zizzi, in C. Rabitti Bedogni (ed.), *Il testo unico della intermediazione finanziaria* (Milano 1998) 309ff.

[40] In German law, it is recognized that the managers have the right to vote, and that they have fiduciary duties, but there is no obligation to vote (see KAGG, September 9, 1998, § 9; and § 37j; see T. Paul and R.H. Päsler, *Das deutsche Investmentrecht—German Investment Law* (Frankfurt am Main 1999)).

matter of fact, there are important shareholdings even in the largest companies, and many of the substantial shareholdings belong to financial institutions.[41] In this regard, the emergence of the institutional investors could be a positive development, as these could act as a *counterpower* to the influence of blockholders. It is apparent that the rise of the stock markets in the continental systems owes a great deal to the role of institutional investors, the vehicle through which many individuals have first approached the stock exchanges.

But institutional investors are far from constituting a solution to the corporate governance problem in the continental systems. First of all, it must be remarked that the holdings of institutional investors can mean a fundamental difference in a system of disperse ownership, but in a blockholder system, the holdings of institutional investors are, almost by definition, too small to give them a decisive influence over the company. Secondly, it should also be remarked that most institutional investors are controlled by financial institutions, so, where the blockholders are precisely these financial institutions, institutional investors do not help to solve the corporate governance problem; on the contrary, they can add to the problem of blockholder control.

The point is that the differences in the structure of the corporate governance systems determine differences in the nature of corporate governance problems and in the available solutions to them. In the case of the continental systems of corporate governance, regulatory changes are even more necessary, because otherwise institutional investors do not help in solving corporate governance problems, but tend to aggravate them instead. In other words, if institutional investors are able to help in the solution of corporate governance problems, they need to be active *and* independent. Otherwise, there is a potential for additional damage to minority shareholders.

D. The Role of the Institutional Investors: the Spanish Case

In this section, we explore the role of the institutional investors in a continental corporate governance system, including some ideas that could improve the

---

[41] Although the data present rich differences, the existence of large blocks of shares is a common feature in the continental markets: see P. Bolton and E.L. Von Thadden, 'Blocks, Liquidity and Corporate Control' [1998] 53 *Journal of Finance* 1; M. Becht and A. Röell, 'Blockholdings in Europe: An International Comparison' [1999] 43 *European Economical Review* 1049; M. Bianco and P. Casavola, 'Italian Corporate Governance: Effects on Financial Structure and Firm Performance' [1999] 43 *European Economical Review* 1057; M. Becht, 'European Corporate Governance: Trading off Liquidity against Control' [1999] 43 *European Economical Review* 107. A. Shleifer and R.W. Vishny, 'A Survey of Corporate Governance' [1997] 52 *Journal of Finance* 737, consider that the existence of large shareholders is very positive for corporate governance, although they recognize that "large investors represent their own interests" (at 758). In an earlier work (A. Shleifer and R.W. Vishny, 'Large Shareholders and Corporate Control' [1986] 94 *Journal of Political Economics* 461), the authors had identified fundamental divergences of interests between small and large shareholders, as common wisdom holds.

present situation. The analysis is centred on the Spanish system of institutional investing, but many of the findings and conclusions can easily be extended to other continental systems.

One of the most important changes experienced in the Spanish financial system during the last years is the reform of the stock exchanges. Nowadays, the access to financing through the stock markets has spread widely. Besides, a series of privatization issues, a crisis of the public model of social security, and a relative economic bonanza, have caused an unprecedented expansion in the ownership of shares.

In this expansion of the stock market, institutional investors have played a major role. A great number of Spanish citizens have placed funds in collective investment schemes, and the opening of the economic system has also attracted a great number of foreign institutional investors.

The question posed is the role of the emerging institutional shareholders in the problems of corporate governance. To study the question, we start with a description of the situation of institutional investing in Spain, from an economic and from a legal point of view, including the complex typology of institutional investors in the Spanish legal system. After that, we shall deal with the legal problems of institutional investors when trying to engage in what is called "shareholder activism". The conclusion of the analysis is that the institutional investors can only play a minor role in the solution to the corporate governance problem, although there are some measures that can increase the involvement of these investors in the running of the company, and create checks and balances to the power of blockholders.

In the Spanish stock market, most of shareholdings are held by institutional investors, in a wide sense. It is possible to distinguish between traditional institutional investors, such as banks and insurance companies, and the modern forms of institutional investors, identified with the various types of collective investment schemes. These are institutional investors in the narrow sense, and, unless specified, we refer only to them when we use the expression "institutional investors".

The typology of institutional investors in Spanish law is relatively complex,[42] but similar to that of the other European Union Member States. Basically, there

---

[42] See M. Trías Sagnier, *Los inversores institucionales y el gobierno de las grandes sociedades*, see above n. 26, 90ff; J.M. Michavila, 'Principios institucionales de los planes y fondos de pensiones' [1989] *Revista de Derecho Bancario y Bursátil* 341; I. Farrando, 'La inversión a través de instituciones de inversión colectiva' [1993] *Revista de Derecho Bancario y Bursátil* 681; F. De Roda, 'Las instituciones de inversión colectiva en España' [1991] *Papeles de economía española* 158; J.F. Sanz, 'La inversión colectiva' [1991] *Actualidad financiera* N 11, T-37; A.J. Tapia Hermida, 'Institutional Investors and Corporate Control in Spanish Perspective' in Th. Baums, R.M. Buxbaum and K.J. Hopt (eds.), *Institutional Investors and Corporate Governance* (Berlin/New York 1994) 399; A.J. Tapia Hermida, *Sociedades y fondos de inversión y fondos de titulización* (Madrid 1998); A. Roncero 'Los inversores institucionales y el denominado "gobierno corporativo"' in G. Esteban (ed.), *El gobierno de las sociedades cotizadas* (Madrid 1999) 665 ff.

are two types of institutional investors: those based on a trust-like structure (pension funds,[43] investment funds)[44] and those based on a corporate structure (investment companies).[45] What is important to note is that most of the managing companies are owned by financial institutions.[46]

Institutional investors are subject to a complex regulation, whatever their legal structure. Although most of the rules refer to purely financial aspects, some of them affect their investment practices and corporate behaviour. In this regard, the most important rule is the one that establishes that institutional investors can only hold, as a maximum, 5% of the securities issued by a company.[47] This rule, a consequence of the implementation of EU Directives, greatly limits the possibilities of shareholder activism by institutional investors, but it is logical in the context of a system that has given absolute priority to the need of diversifying risk. This is still the case even under Directive 2001/108, which relaxes the diversification requirements for investment funds in a limited way.[48]

---

[43] Pension funds are regulated by the 1987 Act, and a royal decree (RD September 30 1988). See R. La Casa, *Los fondos de pensiones* (Madrid 1997)

[44] Investment funds, and the rest of institutional investing schemes (including funds of funds), apart from pension funds, are regulated by the Act on Collective Investment Institutions (*Ley de Instituciones de Inversión Colectiva*, (*LIIC*) Ley 46/1984, succesively reformed). A Royal Decree (RD 291/1992, s. 7.1a) has defined for some purposes the concept of "institutional investors" without any strict legal criteria, but rather making the term "institutional" equivalent to "professional".

[45] These investment companies can use a fixed capital structure (SIM) or a variable capital structure (SIMCAV). See B. Rico Arévalo, 'Las sociedades de inversión mobiliaria de capital variable como sociedades anónimas especiales' [1998] *Revista de Derecho Bancario y Bursátil* 1023.

[46] See A. Roncero, 'Los inversores institucionales y el denominado "gobierno corporativo" ', see above, n. 43, 678.

[47] See art. 4.2 LIIC. See F. Rodríguez Artigas, 'Instituciones de inversión colectiva (sociedades y fondos de inversión)' [1989] *Revista de Derecho Bancario y Bursátil* 527; ibid., 'Entidades del mercado de inversión colectiva. Sociedades y fondos de inversión' in A. Alonso Ureba and J. Martinez-Simancas (eds.), *Instituciones del mercado financiero*, VI, (Madrid 1999) 3487; M.F. Generoso Hermoso, M.P. Dopazo Fraquio, M.D. Ortega López, M.J. Muñoz Fernández and A. Muñoz Fernández, *Fondos de inversión mobiliarios e inmobiliarios* (Madrid 1992). This percentage is considered in Spanish law a substantial participation (see M.S. Flores Doña, *Participaciones significativas en sociedades anónimas* (Madrid 1995)), so that institutional investors try not to reach that ceiling in order to avoid the obligation of communicating the acquisition of the shares. See also M.E. Fernandez-Villarán, 'Las limitaciones legales a la gestión y la normativa sobre la valoración de activos de las IICs', in *La protección de los partícipes de los fondos de inversión* (Madrid 1997) 97. This rule applies also to pension funds (s 34.4°, RD 1307/1988, September 30, 1988): see J.E. Cachón Blanco, 'Fondos de pensiones y sus entidades gestoras' in A. Alonso Ureba and J Martinez-Simancas (eds), *Instituciones del mercado financiero*, VI (Madrid 1999) 3591. The same regulation exists in many of the other countries of the European Union, such as Germany (see § 89 KAAG 1998).

[48] This has been the way in which the Spanish Parliament has implemented the EU Directive on UCITS (Council Directive (EEC) 85/611 on the coordination of laws, regulations, and administrative provisions relating to undertakings for collective investment in transferable securities [1985]. O.J L375/3), that demands that these investment schemes must be unable to exert control of the

I. The Attitude of Institutional Investors

For the most part, it can be argued that institutional investors have replicated the private investors' behaviour. Institutional investors tend to base their investment decisions on performance in the stock exchange, but they show little or no interest in monitoring management,[49] in showing up at the shareholders' meeting, and, generally speaking, in taking an active role in the company. Indexing is becoming the most used technique in institutional investing, and it clearly implies a passive attitude. There are no cases of Spanish institutional investors that consistently take an active role in the companies where they invest. So, intervention by institutional investors is, at its best, piecemeal, and limited only to the most egregious cases of corporate abuse. Foreign institutional investors—particularly U.S. investors—have been known to play an active role, but only through informal contacts with members of the board of directors.

II. The Possibilities of Corporate Action by Institutional Investors

The fact that institutional investors have adopted a passive attitude does not imply that there are no legal means to take corporate action. Spanish corporate law offers some opportunities that could be used by institutional investors.[50]

First of all, Spanish law recognizes a system of "proportional" voting for the election of the board of directors.[51] This system is functionally similar to the system of cumulative voting of some U.S. jurisdictions, although the legal technique is different.[52] A minority shareholder can elect a member of the board

companies where they invest (s. 25). The proposed reforms to the UCITS Directive seek a flexibilisation of the diversification requirements in order to make possible investment techniques such as indexing (see Proposal 98/C 272/08, and Proposal 98/C 280/08).

[49] See P. Davies, 'Institutional Investors as Corporate Monitors in the United Kingdom', see above, n. 11, 47ff, who points to the fact that institutional investors are inadequate monitors because they lack the means for the task.

[50] In a recent study, R. La Porta, F. Lopez-De-Silanes, and A. Shleifer, 'Corporate Ownership Around the World' [1999] 54 *Journal of Finance* 471, place Spanish corporate law together with other "anti-director" systems, such as the U.S. system or the English system. This label, referred to the content of minority shareholders' rights, is relatively misleading, as practice shows that some possibilities of corporate action are more theoretical than real.

[51] See art. 137 LSA. This system is also regulated by the Royal Decree 821/1991.

[52] The system of cumulative voting, also used in several U.S. jurisdictions, is one of the ways proposed by some scholars in order to gain influence in the board of directors (See S. Bhagat and J.A. Brickley, 'Cumulative Voting: The Value of Minority Shareholder Voting Rights' [1984] 27 *Journal of Law and Economics* [1984] 339; cf. R.J. Gilson and R. Kraakman, 'Reinventing the Outside Director: An Agenda for Institutional Investors' [1991] 43 Stanford Law Review 863, although there may be problems in having a direct presence in the board (see J.N. Gordon, 'Shareholder Initiative: A Social Choice and Game Theoretic Approach to Corporate Law' [1991] 60 University of Cincinnati Law Review 347).

if the fraction of shares it holds is equivalent to the result of dividing the total company capital by the seats in the board. An example will illustrate this: in a company where the board is composed of 20 directors, a shareholder in possession of a 5% of the capital is entitled to elect one director (100/20 = 5).[53] It could be the case that the number of directors was lower than 20, in which case a single institutional investor would be unable to elect a member of the board. But a coalition of several institutional investors could possibly elect a director in most cases.[54]

Institutional investors can also use the range of minority protection rights. Apart from being able to sue the directors—the regime of derivative actions is particularly permissive[55]—a minority shareholder in possession of 5% of the capital can call a extraordinary shareholders' meeting, in which it is always possible to ask for a vote to force the directors to resign. To do this, the minority shareholder (or shareholders) must ask the directors to call a meeting; if they refuse to call a meeting, then the minority shareholder should file a petition to a judge, who will effectively call the shareholders' meeting.[56] Every shareholder can also use its information rights, whereby can acquire knowledge of important data regarding the activities and financial state of the company.[57]

Outside the strictly legal rules, institutional investors can also exert influence on the company managers through informal meetings with them. This lobbying is probably the course of action most favoured by many institutional investors.[58]

[53] For the different working of the cumulative voting system, see A.T. Cole, 'Legal and Mathematical Aspects of Cumulative Voting' [1950] 2 *SCLQ* 225. The system of proportional voting has some pitfalls, and is not widely used in practice. The main flaw is that it is unclear whether the majority can force the resignation of the director elected by the minority: see A. Rojo, 'Comentario a STS 2.3.1977' [1977] *Revista de Derecho Privado*, 468; F. Martínez Sanz, *La representación proporcional de la minoría en el consejo de administración de la sociedad anónima*, (Madrid 1992); G. Alcover, 'Representación proporcional de la minoría y principio mayoritario' [1994] *RdS* 83. There is also uncertainty as to the process of grouping the shares necessary to exercise the right.

[54] See F. San Sebastián, *El gobierno de las sociedades cotizadas y su control*, see above, n. 29, 88. Coalitions can play a very important role in corporate governance (See J.C. Coffee, 'Unstable Coalitions: Corporate Governance as a Multi-player Game' [1990] 78 Georgetown Law Journal 1495; G. Rossi, 'Le diverse prospettive dei sindacati azionari nelle società quotate e in quelle non quotate' [1991] *Revista delle Società* 1353; F. Vicent Chulià, 'Licitud, eficacia y organización de los sindicatos de voto' in *Estudios J Girón* (Madrid 1991) 1207; A. Pérez Moriones, *Los sindicatos de voto para la junta general de sociedad anónima* (Valencia 1996)).

[55] Although a greater judiciary involvement in corporate governance could be desirable (see J.C. Coffee, 'The Mandatory/Enabling Balance in Corporate Law: An Essay on the Judicial Role' [1989] 89 Columbia Law Review 1618), the position of judges in traditional civil law countries (and in many common law countries) is contrary to adopting an interventionist attitude in corporate life.

[56] Arts 100 and 101 LSA. See J.C. Riera, 'La Junta general de accionistas convocada judicialmente'[1988] *Revista de Derecho Privado* 15ff.

[57] Art. 112 LSA.

[58] See J. Pound, 'The Rise of the Political Model of Corporate Governance and Corporate Control', see above, n. 11, 1003ff; F. San Sebastián, *El gobierno de las sociedades cotizadas y su*

III. The Risks of Corporate Action by Institutional Investors

Institutional investors have to consider that there are risks in their taking an active role in corporate governance, even where that active role is only informal.

Participation in the board of directors can cause several problems. Even if a director representing institutional investors performs a non-executive role, the dreaded question of personal liability can arise, although there are no reported cases of listed companies where this liability has been applied. But there are other possible risks as well: the main one is that, through the member of the board, institutional investors have access to price sensitive information and commit insider trading.[59] This is also a risk associated with the practice of having informal contacts with the company managers.

The problems of taking an active role in the shareholders' meeting are diverse, but significant nonetheless. The question of the existence of fiduciary duties towards the minority shareholders is particularly obscure in Spanish law, but it is not totally impossible that institutional investors could face liability for voting in favour of blockholders' proposals in the general meeting. This is one of the facts taken into account by institutional investors. Moreover, the vote of the institutional investors can constitute a crime in egregious cases: the Criminal Code includes an offence, called "abuse of majority", whereby the shareholders forming a majority can face severe criminal sanctions for improper use of their vote.[60]

IV. Some Ideas for the Regulation of Institutional Investors

There are some interesting ideas being debated on the regulation of institutional investors. Most of them deal with the rules relating to minority shareholders' participation in the company.[61] In our view, there are some appealing ideas that

control, see above, n. 21, 88; P. Davies, 'Institutional Investors as Corporate Monitors in the United Kingdom', see above, n. 11, 47ff; B.S. Black and J.C. Coffee, 'Hail Britannia? Institutional Investor Behaviour Under Limited Regulation' [1994] 92 Michigan Law Review 1997.

[59] See J.M. De Paz Arias, 'Los inversores institucionales como medio de resolución del conflicto de intereses entre administradores y accionistas en la sociedad abierta', see above, n. 14, 857 ff; R. Weigmann, 'I fondi mobiliari come azionisti' [1987] *Revista delle Società* 1987, 1089. See art. 285 and 286 of the Spanish Criminal Code. See M. Bajo, 'Uso de información privilegiada' in *Empresa y derecho penal (II)* (Madrid 1998) 121.

[60] See art. 291 of the Spanish Criminal Code. See J. García De Enterría, *Los delitos societarios. Un enfoque mercantil* (Madrid 1996); C. López, 'La protección de los partícipes en un fondo de inversión y el nuevo Código penal' in *La protección de los partícipes de los fondos de inversión* (Madrid 1997) 217ff, 240–241.

[61] A related topic is the regulation of shareholders' associations, that are playing an increasingly important role in some countries, such as France (see A.J. Tapia Hermida, 'Los accionistas y el gobierno de las sociedades cotizadas. Observaciones a la vista de algunas crisis financieras recientes' in *Estudios A. Menéndez* (Madrid 1996) II, 2543; R. Torino, 'L'istituzionalizzazione delle minoranze azionarie. Le associazioni di azionisti in Francia e in Italia' [1998] *Revista delle Società* 603).

could increase the institutional investors' active role in the conduct of corporate affairs,[62] but there are far more important questions to be dealt with, especially the *independence* of institutional shareholders and their *responsibility* towards private investors.[63] Indeed, the overriding impulse of regulation must be directed towards ensuring the independence of judgment of institutional investors and their accountability to private investors.

As to the participation in the board of directors, the system of "proportional" voting should be reformed in order to ensure that the director designed with the vote of the institutional shareholders cannot be removed by the decision of the majority. The Olivencia Code of best practice recommends such as the Olivencia Code of best practice, recommend that public corporations form a board in which there must be present a number of independent directors and "propri-etary" directors (*consejeros dominicales*).[64] Independent directors are supposed to defend the interests of small private shareholders,[65] whereas "proprietary" directors represent the interests of the main company shareholders. Institutional investors may find in these types of directors a good vehicle for the protection of their rights and for the obtaining of information regarding the company. The overall idea of the Olivencia code is to transform the board into a monitoring organ, able to control the management.[66] This goal requires the institutional investors' cooperation.

[62] Some authors consider that the limit of the percentage of shares in a company that can be held by an institutional investor (5%) should be modified, in order to give institutional investors greater possibilities of control (See M. Trías Sagnier, *Los inversores institucionales y el gobierno de las grandes sociedades*, see above, n. 26, 301; cf. A. Roncero, 'Los inversores institucionales y el denominado "gob-ierno corporativo"', see above, n. 42, 697ff). This modification would probably constitute a violation of the EU Directive on Collective Investment Schemes, if it gives the possibility of exerting control in the company. See V. Allegri, 'Il fondo comune come azionista: l'esercizio del diritto di voto'[1988] *Revista delle Società* 790. Moreover, the real problem is the separation from the credit institutions. If institutional investors are not independent from banks, the problems can be even more severe.

[63] It is true that many of the envisaged reforms in the European systems do not provide for a bet-ter protection of the small shareholders, but of the institutional investors themselves: see G. Visentini, 'Osservazioni sulla recente disciplina delle società azionarie e del mercato mobiliare' [1998] *Revista delle Società* 172; See E. Gliozzi, 'Società per azioni e mercati finanziari, see above, n. 34, 759ff.

[64] See M. Olivencia, 'Managers' Revolution/Independents' Counter-revolution (Ensayo sobre una nueva fase en la evolución de la sociedad anónima)' in *Estudios A Menéndez*, (Madrid 1996) II, 2173; G. Esteban, 'La renovación de la estructura de la administración en el marco del debate sobre el gobierno corporativo' in G. Esteban (ed.), *El gobierno de las sociedades cotizadas* (Madrid 1999) 137.

[65] The idea of the independent director as a solution to the corporate governance problem was analysed with scepticism by V. Brudney, 'The Independent Director—Heavenly City or Potemkin Village?' [1982] 95 Harvard Law Review 597.

[66] See M.M. Sánchez Álvarez, 'El Código Olivencia y la responsabilidad de los miembros del Consejo de Administración' [1999] *RdS* 133. It is unclear that the board can really perform an effec-tive monitoring function: see R. Morck, A. Shleifer and R.W. Vishny, 'Alternative Mechanisms for Corporate Control', see above, n. 9, 842ff.

Regarding the role of the institutional investors in the shareholders' meeting, there are some interesting ideas: first, it is desirable that the concept of minority shareholder, for the purpose of determining some minority shareholders' rights, be specified in a different way. Instead of relying on a fixed percentage—5%, at present—the amount of shares necessary to constitute a minority should be made dependent on the total company capital. It is well known that 5% is too high a percentage in a large public company,[67] and it is not often that even institutional investors reach that percentage in listed companies. The amount of shares necessary to exercise minority rights would substantially decrease in the largest companies.[68]

Besides, the very content of minority rights should be redefined. In particular, minority shareholders should be able to introduce topics for discussion and vote in the shareholders' meeting.[69]

Proxy rules could be relaxed, in order to give institutional investors the opportunity to act as representatives of small private shareholders.[70] Nevertheless, this is a delicate matter, because restrictive proxy rules are one of the devices, albeit ineffective, designed to curtail excessive bank influence in shareholders' meetings.

An extraordinarily interesting idea consists of giving a "voting premium" to shareholders. Presently, some companies have introduced an "attendance premium", in order to foster assistance to the shareholders' meeting. Those shareholders that do attend the meeting are entitled to a small compensation. The idea is to introduce a compensation for voting, instead of a premium for attending the meeting. Notice that the premium is given to the shareholders that vote in favour or against the proposals made in the meeting, so that it does not limit the shareholders' fundamental right to vote freely. Only a wide construction of this right, i.e. understanding that the shareholder has a right to abstain, could be an obstacle to the implementation of this idea. That consideration aside, the voting

---

[67] See J. Juste, *Los derechos de la minoría en la sociedad anónima* (Pamplona 1995) 211–213.

[68] See E. Polo, 'Abuso o tiranía. Reflexiones sobre la dialectica entre mayoría y minoría en la sociedad anónima' in *Estudios A Menéndez* (Madrid 1996) II, 2284; C. Alonso Ledesma, 'El papel de la junta general en el gobierno corporativo de las sociedades de capital' in G. Esteban (ed.), *El gobierno de las sociedades cotizadas* (Madrid 1999) 615.

[69] This would be a very positive development (See M. Trías Sagnier, *Los inversores institucionales y el gobierno de las grandes sociedades*, see above, n. 26, 331), and would put Spanish law in line with other legal systems, as those of the U.S. (see Securities and Exchange Act, rules 14a-7, 14a-8, 14a-11), and of most European countries. This is a very important and powerful instrument in the hands of institutional investors: see L.A. Gordon and J. Pound, 'Information, Ownership Structure, and Shareholder Voting: Evidence from Shareholder-Sponsored Corporate Governance Proposals' [1993] 48 *Journal of Finance* 697.

[70] See M. Trías Sagnier, *Los inversores institucionales y el gobierno de las grandes sociedades*, see above, n. 26, 333; R. Costi, 'Il governo delle società quotate: tra ordinamento dei mercati e diritto delle società' [1998] *Diritto del commercio internazionale* 65.

premium could become a real incentive for an active role of institutional investors and even of small private shareholders.

Nevertheless, the problem in the continental systems of corporate governance is not only the institutional investors' passivity, but, as it was remarked before, the concentration of power in a few shareholders, what has been termed the "blockholder system". The fact that most institutional investors are controlled by credit institutions virtually eliminates the possibilities of a solution to corporate governance problems by the institutional investors' intervention, as credit institutions are often blockholders themselves, and in other cases have links to the controlling blockholders.[71]

The most important regulatory changes, therefore, should affect the structure of institutional investors, if these are to play a role in solving corporate governance problems. As a minimum, it would be necessary to introduce an adequate regulation of conflicts of interest.[72] Institutional investors face frequent and intense conflicts of interest, as the interests of the participants may demand one course of action, whereas the interests of the controlling company—the financial institution—may demand a different one.[73] A regulation of fiduciary duties[74] and possible courses of action in conflict of interests situations is one of the most urgent measures to be taken in the regulation of institutional investors.[75] However, it would be also interesting to limit the influence of banks on

---

[71] See A.J. Tapia Hermida, 'Las sociedades gestoras de carteras' in A. Alonso Ureba and J. Martinez-Simancas (eds.), *Instituciones del mercado financiero*, VI (Madrid 1999) 3775 ff, 3779–3881.

[72] See M. Bianco and P. Casavola, 'Corporate governance in Italia: alcuni fatti e problemi aperti' [1996] *Revista delle Società* 426, who remark the conflicts of interest derived from the regulation of institutional investors. Presently, there is a rule on conflicts of interest in Spanish law (art. 52 LSRL), but it refers only to private companies, and its application to public companies is doubtful, to say the least. The Olivencia code of best practice contains also an abstain rule for conflicts of interest in public companies, but its enforcement will be extremely difficult.

[73] See R. Weigmann, 'I fondi mobiliari come azionisti', see above, n. 59, 1089ff; P. Davies, 'Institutional Investors as Corporate Monitors in the United Kingdom', see above, n. 11, 47ff; M. Bianchi and L. Enriques, *Corporate Governance in Italy After the 1998 Reform: What Role for Institutional Investors?*, [2001] CONSOB, Quaderni di Finanza no. 43, and also available at http://papers.ssrn.com/.

[74] Of course, it should be clear first whether the fund manager is in a fiduciary position vis-à-vis the private investor. That seems to be the most sensible solution (see A Sánchez Andrés, 'Para un catálogo de problemas "mayores" en materia de protección de los partícipes de un fondo de inversión' in *La protección de los partícipes de los fondos de inversión* (Madrid 1997) 9ff, 18), but the question is less clear in the light of the statutory wording.

[75] See *Report on Investment Management. Principles for the Regulation of Collective Investment Schemes and Explanatory Memorandum* (IOSCO) 1995, para. 6. In Spanish law, the refinement of fiduciary duties and conflicts of interests has been present in the academics' agenda for a long time: see M. Broseta, 'La sociedad gestora en los Fondos de Inversión Mobiliaria' in *Coloquio sobre el régimen de los Fondos de Inversión Mobiliaria* (Bilbao 1970) 211ff.

institutional investors through several restrictive measures—i.e. limits to the participation in managing companies.

It could also be considered that the law would favour institutional investors adopting a corporate structure. In this way, the interests of the participants are better protected, although this solution faces the formidable inconvenience of the trend towards specialized management in investment activities that justifies the dominant position of investment managers. Nevertheless, it must be remarked that the institutional investors based on a contractual scheme are more easily dominated by credit institutions—who are the main or sole share-holders of the managing companies—and the participants are left in a situation of confusion as to their rights. Systems of civil law ignore the trust structure.[76] So, instead of the relatively clear rules of strict liability of the trustee in Anglo-Saxon law, there are many difficulties in determining the standard of diligence of the fund manager in Spanish law.[77] If these regulatory problems are not solved, the agency problem inherent to corporate governance is merely shifted.[78]

E. Conclusion

The debated role of institutional investors must be analysed in different ways in the existing systems of corporate governance. In the Anglo-Saxon systems of corporate governance, where the main problem lies with the disperse ownership of shares, institutional investors are in a position to become efficient monitors of management.[79] Nevertheless, there are few incentives for the corporate action of

---

[76] The legal nature of investment funds is unclear: some authors refer to them as a type of "collective ownership" (see L. Fernandez Del Pozo and L. De Alarcon Elorrieta, 'Aproximación al estudio de nuevas categorias de cotitularidad jurídica: las comunidades funcionales y los fondos de gestión' [1989] *Revista Crítica de Derecho Inmobiliario* 617, but the situation is confusing: see J.R. Ustarroz Ugalde, 'La naturaleza jurídica de los fondos de pensiones' [1987] *Revista de Derecho Bancario y Bursátil* 581. Nevertheless, although the trust structure is practically ignored in Spanish law, it is recognized that the law should try to reach results "substantially equivalent" to those of the trust: see, for instance, J.M. Moreno-Luque, 'Notas para un estudio del contrato de participación en un fondo de inversión' in *La protección de los partícipes de los fondos de inversión* (Madrid 1997) 297ff, 313.

[77] See A.J. Tapia Hermida, "Los accionistas y el gobierno de las sociedades cotizadas. Observaciones a la vista de algunas crisis financieras recientes", see above, n. 42, 2543. There is a recent—but remote—possibility of indicting fund managers for fraudulent administration (arts 295 and 297 of the Spanish Criminal Code). See R.M. Mata Martín, 'Delitos societarios: administración desleal y demás figuras delictivas' in *Empresa y derecho penal (I)* (Madrid 1998) 337.

[78] See J.M. De Paz Arias, 'Los inversores institucionales como medio de resolución del conflicto de intereses entre administradores y accionistas en la sociedad abierta', see above, n. 14, 857ff.

[79] Recent empirical studies suggest, rather, that institutional investors are poor monitors: see S. Wahal, 'Pension Fund Activism and Firm Performance' [1996] 31 *J. Fin Q. Analysis*, 1; M. Faccio and M.A. Laster, 'Do Occupational Pension Funds Monitor Companies in which they hold large stakes?' [2000] *Journal of Corporate Finance* 71.

institutional investors, so regulatory changes should be introduced if institutional investors are to take a more active role in the corporate scene.[80] For these reasons, it is doubtful that institutional investors are the answer to the corporate governance problem.[81]

In the continental systems of corporate governance, the main problem is the concentration of power in the hands of blockholders. It is true that the continental systems are evolving towards a greater importance of the stock markets, but the fact that institutional investors are subject to the control of the credit institutions only aggravates the corporate governance problem,[82] by placing more power in some of the more conspicuous blockholders. If institutional investors are to help in the solution of this problem in the continental system, it is essential that the independence from the credit institutions be guaranteed. Independent institutional investors can serve as a counterbalance to the power of financial institutions and other blockholders, at least from a theoretical point of view. Nevertheless, it is necessary that the rules allow opportunities for action to institutional investors, and give incentives to corporate activism. Besides, fund managers must be made accountable to the participants. Otherwise, institutional investing results in a severe "agency problem", of the kind that it was intended to avoid in the first place. To find adequate solutions, the issues of independence and accountability of institutional investors must be properly addressed; if not, what could be a solution could very well add to the problem.

---

[80] Even if these regulatory changes are introduced, it will be necessary to break the inertia provoked by the conditions in which institutional investors have developed (cf. M.J. Roe, 'Chaos and Evolution in Law and Economics' [1996] 109 Harvard Law Review 641).

[81] See T. Hadden, 'Corporate Governance by Institutional Investors? Some Problems from an International Perspective' in Th. Baums, R.M. Buxbaum, and K.J. Hopt (eds.), *Institutional Investors and Corporate Governance* (Berlin/NewYork 1994) 89; R. Romano, 'Public Pension Fund Activism in Corporate Governance Reconsidered' in Th. Baums, R.M. Buxbaum and K.J. Hopt (eds.), *Institutional Investors and Corporate Governance* (Berlin/New York 1994) 105; P. Davies, 'Institutional Investors as Corporate Monitors in the United Kingdom', see above, n. 11, 47ff.

[82] For these reasons, it has been adequately stated that a corporate governance reform must begin by the study of the particular features of each system, and that it is unwise to "import" a foreign system of corporate governance: see D. Preite, 'Investitori istituzionali e riforma del diritto delle società per azioni' [1993] *Revista delle Società* 476. See also W.W. Bratton and J.A. McCahery, 'Comparative Corporate Governance and the Theory of the Firm: The Case Against Global Cross Reference' [1999] 38 Columbia Journal of Transnational Law 213.

19

Optimism and Pessimism: Complementary Views on the Institutional Investors' Role in Corporate Governance

JOSÉ M. GARRIDO

Contents

A. Optimism and Pessimism?

In my role as commentator, I face an impossible conflict of interest, as the result of being co-author of one of the chapters I purport to discuss. Of course, my complimentary remarks are directed towards the other authors of the chapters, excluding myself, whereas my criticisms are to be understood mainly as self-criticisms.

It is hardly possible, and completely unnecessary, to compare the three chapters; and it is so because the methodology and scope of the three chapters are totally different. This should be borne in mind, as it is a very apt departing point in this field of analysis: there are numerous perspectives on the role of institutional investors in corporate governance, and each perspective gives a different view, pleasant or not, of one of the richest and talked-about developments in the stock markets and in company law.

The chapter by Professor Gerke, co-authored by Bank and Steiger, furnishes a very interesting view on the economic implications of the "rise and rise" of institutional investing, and the likely changes that will be introduced, presumably, in that archetypal model of continental corporate systems, the classic German "network" system.[1] Gerke, Bank, and Steiger affiliate themselves to the "convergence" thesis, whereby network systems will be increasingly replaced by market systems of corporate governance. They see the German universal bank

---

[1] The chapter is based on a series of "theses", in the best German tradition. There are other instances: see U. Schneider, 'Auf dem Weg in den Pensionkassenkorporativismus? (Zehn Thesen zu den Auswirkungen der zunehmenden Beteiligung institutioneller Anleger an den Publikumaktiengesellschaften)' [1990] *Die Aktiengesellschaft* 317.

system dissolving, under the pressure of the markets and of recent legal changes. The network system will be replaced, in the future, by a market system populated with large institutional investors, Internet trading systems, and an omnipresent volatility; a market where most of the institutional investors will "base" their investment decisions on indexing, and where these institutional investors will have renounced direct corporate activism. Instead, they will prefer to exert indirect influence, through the promotion of codes of best practice and the political pressure on the legislator.

A superficial reading of the paper by Gerke, Bank, and Steiger may give the impression of overt optimism about the future. But that connotation is not so clear. As good economists, they avoid a direct valuation of the likely changes introduced by the institutional investors' behaviour. And, most probably, their optimism is more directed to the change from a network governance system to a market-oriented system than to the specific role to be played in the future by institutional investors.

Professor Rojo and myself, instead, analyse the problems that plague institutional investors' activism from the perspective of the Spanish legal system—a less known and less important "network" system, but representative of a situation that is common elsewhere in Europe—and identify the main areas where improvements have to be made if institutional investors are really going to contribute to a major change in corporate governance. We found that a number of important legal changes have to be made, and, especially, that *independence* and *accountability* of institutional investors must form the cornerstone of a new system of corporate governance, in contrast with the present situation, where independence and accountability are by no means warranted.

So, in a broad sense, it is possible to speak of an "optimistic" theory on the role of institutional investors in corporate governance, and a "pessimistic" view, although, as it will be seen later, these two views are more complementary than conflicting. The third chapter, by Professor Winter, could be easily placed within the "pessimistic" view. Professor Winter introduces a very specific, technical and complex issue: the vote by foreign shareholders in European corporations ("crossborder voting"). Obviously, this issue affects in a direct way the possibilities of institutional investors' activism. From the very start of Professor Winter's chapter, it is possible to realize the magnitude of the obstacles that face institutional investors willing to take an active role in the companies where they invest.[2] The overall picture is a very bleak one: in the present state of affairs it is almost impossible for foreign institutional investors to exercise their voting rights in the companies incorporated in many of the EU Member States (in

---

[2] See C. Fraume, *Der Einfluss institutioneller Anleger in der Hauptversammlung* (Köln/Berlin/Bonn/München 1996) 104ff, on the disincentives for foreign institutional investors to take part in the general meeting.

Winter's words: "effective and structural cross-border proxy voting by share-holders is not possible in Europe at this moment"). The solution is, again, legal reform, and that reform should probably be spearheaded by an EU Directive.

These two views, the "optimistic" one and the "pessimistic" one, are held without connection to the authors' nationalities. At least, it is desirable to believe that. It is hardly possible to point at a particular reason why three German Professors would find very interesting possibilities in the role of institutional investors in a market-oriented system, whereas two Spanish Professors and a Dutch Professor are not so excited by that development. Even recognizing that Germany is experiencing rapid regulatory changes that affect the structure of its corporate governance system, most probably there is a more important and revealing reason for the different views. And the fact is that Professors Gerke, Bank, and Steiger are all economists; whereas Rojo, Winter, and myself are all lawyers. It is evident that in our chapters there is a professional bias: the economists identify new courses of action, avenues of development; the lawyers warn of the risks, signal the pitfalls, the holes in the legal fabric. So, maybe the "optimistic" and "pessimistic" views of the role of institutional investors in corporate governance correspond, somewhat, with the "economic" and the "legal" view of the topic,[3] and that the two views complement each other.[4]

B. A Word about Methodology

In the field of corporate governance in general, and on the role of institutional investors in particular, empirical studies are much needed and welcome.[5] Our discussions on the economic significance of institutions, or on the legal rules that affect them, should be underpinned by empirical studies that point to the facts behind the rules and the economic models. The problem is the lack of fundamental guidelines for this empirical research.

---

[3] Of course, there are 'pessimists' among the economists and 'optimists' among the legal academics (especially in the U.S.), but, as the text implies, the 'optimistic' and 'pessimistic' views broadly correspond to the approaches taken by economics and law, respectively: see, on the 'optimistic' side, specially C. Bathala, K.R. Moon, and R.P. Rao, 'Managerial Ownership, Debt Policy, and the Impact of Institutional Holdings: An Agency Perspective' [1994] 23 *Financial Management* 38; S.L. Nesbitt, 'Long-term Rewards from Shareholder Activism: A Study of the CalPERS Effect'[1994] *Journal of Applied Corporate Finance* 75–80; M.P. Smith, 'Shareholder Activism by Institutional Investors: Evidence from CalPERS' [1996] *Journal of Finance* 227; B.S. Black, 'Agents Watching Agents: The Promise of Institutional Investor Voice' [1992] 39 UCLA Law Review 811, 813–814.

[4] They can complement even if, as the saying goes, "the optimists believe that we live in the best possible world. The pessimists fear it is true".

[5] See M. Steiger, *Institutionelle Investoren im Spannungsfeld zwischen Aktienmarkt-liquidität und Corporate Governance* (Baden Baden 2000).

First, I would propose a unification of the concept of institutional investor. Strange as it may seem, the definition of the concept of "institutional investor" is an unsolved question. So, when an American specialist refers to institutional investors, he is very likely thinking about pension and investment funds, whereas an Englishman may have in mind insurance companies, and a German may think about banks. Of course, it is possible to say that all these institutions fall within the general concept of "institutional investor". As a matter of fact, there is a trend in securities regulation towards identification of the term "institutional investor" with "professional investor", as opposed to private or small investor.[6] Perhaps that terminology can be justified from a certain economic point of view, but it makes little sense in corporate law. Investors who own their shares and investors whose shares are subject to others' beneficial interests are fundamentally different realities. I suggest that we should concentrate on the analysis of pension funds, investment funds, and investment companies as institutional investors. Otherwise, if we do not agree over what an institutional investor is, obviously our differing views will become reciprocally incomprehensible.

A second, and more difficult question, is how to measure institutional investment. Obviously, the answer to the question is directly influenced by the solution to the problem of the concept of institutional investor. But there is more to it than just that. Sometimes, the available data are misleading. We have data on the percentage of shares held by institutional investors; or data on the money managed by institutional investors. But more data are necessary: especially, the percentage institutional investors devote to other investments apart from shares, and the investments made abroad (and, correspondingly, the number of shares held by foreign institutional investors). So, more data are needed, and more data discrimination. It is evident that the assets managed by institutional investors have grown in a dramatic way in recent years, and that is a universal trend. Nevertheless, it should be remarked that the growth in assets does not necessarily translate into a huge increase in share ownership, because recent data show that funds invest heavily in public and private debt, favouring these securities over shares. What is more, most data do not distinguish between investment shares held in national companies, and investment in "foreign" shares. If this is taken into account, together with Professor Winter's fundamental observation that foreign shareholders are almost forced not to vote, then the real weight of institutional investors is greatly diminished.

---

[6] This trend in evident in Spanish law, and also elsewhere, as in France: see H. De Vauplane and J.-P. Bornet, *Droit de la bourse* (Paris 1994) 121. The function of the concept of "professional investor", however, is related to the possibility of lifting some of the investor protection rules where the investors themselves are hardly in need of protection.

The third question is, by far, the most difficult one. How to measure institutional investors' influence?[7] The point is that the kinds of data that are really needed is hardly available. Data are needed on the voting pattern of institutional investors, including not only the number of votes, but also whether those votes were effectively cast, and whether the vote was in favour or against management proposals. As anyone can imagine, it is next to impossible to gain access to these data. In empirical research, the survey technique has been used to address this question. But surveys face severe limitations in this context, being inadequate as a technique for social research where the subjects of the survey are interested in its result—therefore, their answers are not "natural"—and where it is virtually impossible to check the truth or even the approximation to the truth of those answers. So, it is necessary to take all those surveys on institutional investors' influence with a pinch of salt.[8]

As for the benefits of institutional investors' activism, the question of the "causality link" has not been solved (i.e. whether stocks held by institutional investors perform better because of the activism, or were chosen by institutional investors because of their superior performance).[9] We are left in total bewilderment when we learn that, in fact, stocks held by institutional investors have a worse performance than the rest.[10]

Finally, there is the question of how to assess institutional investors' independence and accountability. Of course, the legal data may be clearly insufficient, and what is needed is knowledge of the real enforcement of the law. In all those cases where managed funds are dependent on credit institutions, it would be essential to discover whether there is any bias in the fund manager's investment decisions, and to check the existence of a coincidental pattern of voting between the managed fund and the credit institution. Of course, we all have tentative answers to these questions, but it would be tremendously helpful to see them confirmed by reality.

---

[7] See M. Steiger, *Institutionelle Investoren im Spannungsfeld zwischen Aktienmarkt-liquidität und Corporate Governance*, see above, n. 5, 75ff.

[8] See, for instance, G.R. Downes, E. Houminer, and R. Glenn Hubbard, *Institutional Investors and Corporate Performance* (Washington 1999)

[9] See E.B. Rock, 'America's Shifting Fascination with Comparative Corporate Governance' [1996] 74 Washington University Law Quarterly 367, 387 ("Do institutional investors improve corporate performance or, rather, do they choose to invest in firms with superior performance?"); and C.P. Himmelberg, R.G. Hubbard, and D.N. Palia, 'Understanding the Determinants of Managerial Ownership and the Link between Ownership and Performance' [1999] 53 *Journal of Financial Economics* 353.

[10] M. Faccio and M.A. Laster, 'Do Occupational Pension Funds Monitor Companies in which they hold large stakes?' [2000] *Journal of Corporate Finance* 71. See also S. Wahal, 'Pension Fund Activism and Firm Performance' [1996] 31 *Journal of Financial Quarterly Analysis*, 1.

C. The Present State of Institutional Investors' Activism

The chapter by Professors Gerke, Bank, and Steiger develops a number of theses on the likely future of corporate governance from the institutional investors' point of view. In substance, institutional investors will demand special facilities for trading, and this in turn will increase volatility. Institutional investors will favour exit over voice, and in the case where they will try to influence management, they will do so by means of informal contacts with the managers themselves. Institutional investors will also exert influence in order to improve corporate governance standards and make the main stock exchanges adopt codes of best practice.

From a legal point of view, we are forced to look at the present and at the past that has begotten this present. And precisely from this point of view, we conclude that that "future" is possibly so immediate as to deserve the name of "present".

The development of Internet Trading Systems, and other specialized platforms for trading, is increasing liquidity; and globalization as a whole is increasing the possibilities for institutional investing all over the world. As for the adoption of codes of best practice, it is a reality in most European markets. Volatility is also too real.[11] And "short-termism" is no longer a fancy term that refers to financial practices in the Anglo-Saxon markets, but is extending to other markets as well.[12]

The fact that all these developments are taking place does not mean that their implications should be disregarded. The transformation of continental network systems into corporate systems akin to those of Britain or the U.S. is the most important fact of all. There appears to be some agreement on the thesis that there is a convergence between blockholder systems and market systems, even if there are substantial differences as to how this convergence will be achieved.[13] But convergence can come about in different fashions and degrees, and convergence in economic terms does not guarantee that the same legal problems will be solved in the same way.

---

[11] E. Gliozzi, 'Societá per azioni e mercati finanziari' [1999] *Rivista Trimestrale di Diritto Processuale Civile* 759, 768.

[12] See T.L. Hazen, 'The Short-Term/Long-Term Dichotomy and Investment Theory: Implications for Securities Market Regulation and for Corporate Law' [1991] 70 North Carolina Law Review 137.

[13] On the controversy about convergence or non-convergence of corporate governance systems, see specially H. Hansmann and R. Kraakman, 'The End of History for Corporate Law" [2000] http://www.law.harvard.edu/programs/olin_center/; J.C. Coffee Jr, 'Convergence and Its Critics: What are the Preconditions to the Separation of Ownership and Control?' [2000] http://www. law.columbia.edu/lawec/; R.J. Gilson, 'Globalizing Corporate Governance: Convergence of Form or Function' [2000] http://www.law.columbia.edu/lawec/.

Anyway, it is clear that, for a long time, we will have to cope with the problems of blockholder-dominated companies in Europe. Convergence does not mean "identity". Important economic, social, and legal differences will persist. It is also clear that the process of convergence is being accelerated in some cases, as in Germany. But it is significant that the major changes experienced very recently in Germany are the product of direct legal intervention, and not of the market themselves.[14]

In the present state of affairs, we still have, by and large, European stock exchanges where most of the companies are controlled by a small number of blockholders. So, institutional investors dominate the market, but they do not dominate the companies. So what is the use of the ascent of institutional investing? There is an immediate answer to that, and it is that listed companies are greatly favoured by the rise of institutional investing, as they can find a solid investment base, where previously there was just a very thin market. That is something to be welcomed. But there are also problems: first, the protection of the beneficial owners of shares. There are very few and ineffective means of control of fund managers in continental European laws. Secondly, the aligning of fund managers with blockholders, or with credit institutions, which can be detrimental to the private investors' interests. Finally, Winter has noted the problems institutional investors face when trying to exercise their voting rights with respect of shares held in foreign countries.[15]

In the face of these circumstances, the behaviour of institutional investors can be characterized, generally, as "passive". The practice of indexing is becoming quite common, and there are very few instances of "activist" institutional investors in Europe. At best, institutional investors try to influence management though informal contacts. The well-known "free rider" problem faced by institutional investors means that most institutional investors are unlikely to take action where the benefits will be shared by all shareholders and the costs borne exclusively by the activists. So, in many ways, institutional investors are no

---

[14] See Th. Baums, 'Vollmachstimmrecht der Banken—Ja oder Nein?' [1996] *Die Aktiengesellschaft* 11; J. Esser, 'Bank Power in West Germany Revisited' [1990] 13 *Western European Politics* 17, 23; Th. Baums, 'Corporate Governance in Germany: The Role of the Banks' [1992] 40 American Journal of Comparative Law 503; Th. Baums and C. Fraune, 'Institutionelle Anleger und Publikumgesellschaft: Eine empirisiche Untersuchung' [1995] *Die Aktiengesellschaft* 97.

[15] Strikingly, those difficulties seem not to exist for U.S. institutional investors: see C.K. Brancato, *Institutional Investors and Corporate Governance* (Chicago/London/Singapore 1997) 128: according to Brancato, in 1995 U.S. institutional investors voted 72% of their shares abroad. But maybe this is a consequence of having to comply with the DOL guidelines that demand institutional investors' voting, although those rules only apply to private pension funds. Nevertheless, enforcement of the obligation to vote is almost non-existent, and much less for shares in foreign companies: see R.E. Benfield, Note and Comment: 'Curing American Managerial Myopia: Can the German System of Corporate Governance Help?' [1995] 17 Loyola of Los Angeles International and Comparative Law Journal 615, 640.

different from private investors.[16] All of them face a problem of collective action: whoever acts, acts for the benefit of the group, and the whole group reaps that potential benefit without sharing the costs.[17] And, as with individual shareholders, the activism of a few tends to be spectacular and is the object of disproportionate attention, but it is unlikely to challenge successfully the balance of power.[18] The consequence of all these circumstances is the relinquishing of the monitoring function. As a matter of fact, and, with a few exceptions, institutional investors have never claimed their role as "police shareholders".[19]

The small shareholdings of institutional investors, as compared to the blockholders', limit their possibilities,[20] even though some of these shareholdings are sufficiently large as to prevent "exit" in satisfactory economic terms, because the European markets are still considerably thin.[21] The problem is that, even in this case, it is more interesting for the institutional investor to side with management or with other blockholders and make the best of a bad situation. Because of this, it would not be realistic to assume that institutional investors do not experience the same temptations that managers and blockholders' experience, as there are serious possibilities that institutional investors align their positions with those of managers or blockholders, and not with the position of small minority shareholders.[22] It is also naïve to believe that institutional investors will stay in the company and fight to the last bullet in the name of small shareholders' interests.[23]

[16] Compare M. Useem, *Investor Capitalism* (New York 1996) 53ff and P. Montalenti, 'Corporate governance, raccomandazioni consob e prospettive di riforma' [1997] *Rivista delle Società* 713; G. Visentini, 'La teoria della personalità giuridica ed i problemi della società per azioni' [1999] *Rivista delle Società* 89, 127, n. 31. See also H. Garten, 'Institutional Investors and the New Financial Order' [1992] 44 Rutgers Law Review 585, 590ff.

[17] E.B. Rock, 'Controlling the Dark Side of Relational Investing' [1994] 15 Cardozo Law Review 987; G. McCormack, 'Institutional Investors and the Promotion of Good Corporate Governance' in B.A.K. Rider (ed.), *The Realm of Company Law* (London/The Hague/Boston 1998) 131, 150–151.

[18] W.W. Bratton and J.A. McCahery, 'Regulatory Competition, Regulatory Capture, and Corporate Self-regulation' [1995] 73 North Carolina Law Review 1861, 1906ff.

[19] In the U.S., as it has been noted, the situation is different, with a small but very active number of institutional investors engaged in corporate governance guerrilla warfare. R.S. Karmel, 'Stock Markets and the Globalization of Retirement Savings—Implications of Privatization of Government Pensions for Securities Regulators' [1999] 33 International Lawyer 955; T.C. Paefgen, 'Institutional Investors Ante Portas: A Comparative Analysis of an Emergent Force in Corporate America and Germany' [1992] 26 International Lawyer 327.

[20] L. Lowenstein, *Sense and Nonsense in Corporate Finance* (Reading (Mass) 1992) 216, "institutional investors own so many stocks, that none is important".

[21] See M.R. Wingerson and C.H. Dorn, 'Institutional Investors in the U.S. and the Repeal of Poison Pills: A Practitioner's Perspective' [1992] 92 Columbia Business Law Review 223, 227.

[22] G.P. Stapledon, *Institutional Shareholders and Corporate Governance* (Oxford 1996) 207.

[23] It is not possible to change institutional investors into venture capitalists (see R.A.G. Monks and N. Minow, *Watching the Watchers* (Cambridge 1996) 160; R.C. Pozen, 'Institutional Investors: The Reluctant Activists' [1994] *Harvard Business Review* January–February 1994, 140–149).

D. The Need for Reform

An "optimistic" view of the corporate governance system does not require any legal action. The market will evolve in the most appropriate way and the result will be the best possible one. The "pessimistic" view, on the other hand, places emphasis on the need of introducing legal reforms as a prerequisite for improvement of the present situation.

The foundation of a positive role of institutional investors in corporate governance is the strengthening of their independence and of their accountability. Only if fund managers are subject to a stricter legal regime than that applying to company directors,[24] will there be a slight chance that institutional investors contribute, in turn, to a more effective enforcement of directors' duties in listed companies.

A complete regulation of conflicts of interest within investment funds and investment companies,[25] an effective enforcement of insider trading sanctions, and, in general, an adequate prevention of abuses derived from unequal access to information and unequal influencing of management, are also factors that deserve careful attention.[26]

With those reforms in place, some positive developments on the part of institutional investors might be expected, and, most of all, no negative effects should exist. It is far more difficult to make such a statement on the present state of affairs. If institutional investors are to become important players and activists in European companies, sufficient attention must be paid to the risks derived from activism. The whole European regime of collective investment schemes is based on the idea of diversification. But diversification and monitoring are almost symmetrically opposing concepts.[27] Perhaps there should be two types of institutional investors, one tending towards diversification, possibly based on indexing, and a riskier type of "governance fund". Through these governance funds it should be easier to develop a monitoring function in companies[28]. And of

---

[24] See J. Charkham and A. Simpson, *Fair Shares* (Oxford 1998) 145ff.

[25] See J.A. Grundfest, 'Just Vote No: A Minimalist Strategy for Dealing with Barbarians Inside the Gates' [1993] 45 Stanford Law Review 857, 919; J. Pound, 'The Rise of the Political Model of Corporate Governance and Corporate Control' [1993] 68 New York University Law Review 1003, 1068. Without solving the issue of conflicts of interest, there is no real possibility of institutional investor activism: B.S. Black, 'Shareholder Passivity Reexamined' [1990] 89 Michigan Law Review 520.

[26] Institutional investors should be subject to stricter scrutiny and disclosure requirements: I.M. Millstein, 'Can Pension Funds Lead the Ownership Revolution?' [1991] *Harvard Business Review* May–June 1991, 166, 166–167.

[27] Cf. M.J. Roe, 'The Modern Corporation and Private Pensions' [1993] 41 UCLA Law Review 75.

[28] J.H. Matheson and B.A. Olson, 'Corporate Law and the Longterm Shareholder Model of Corporate Governance' [1992] 76 Minnesota Law Review 1313.

course, in any case, it is absolutely necessary that the obstacles to cross-border voting be removed. In this context, Winter's idea of a separate EU Directive dealing with proxy voting and rules for the general meeting seems particularly appropriate.

E. Conclusion: What Can We Realistically Expect from Institutional Investors?

Institutional investors present an unlikely solution to our corporate or stock exchange regulation problems.[29] They are merely the result of a given economic development, and their existence is basically explained in terms of larger concentration, economies of scale, investment opportunities in a globalized economy, and other concurring factors.

Having said that, it is important that we use institutional investors as a means to help solve those problems, instead of worsening them. So, it is submitted that instiutional investors have the opportunity of playing just a modest role as corporate actors, but it is hoped indeed that that role will be a positive one.

The crisis of modern corporate law is wider, and deeper; it is a crisis of the structure of the corporation, of the very idea of shareholder democracy.[30] The famous saying comparing the indifference of shareholders to that of sheep still holds true, with exceptions.[31]

Personally, I find it difficult to count myself among those who hold great expectations for institutional investors' activism. For one thing, institutional investors are essentially investors: they are not altruistic benefactors, nor they should be. The use of institutional investors as the ultimate solution, the *deus ex machina* in corporate law, is a worrying sign of intellectual exhaustion. If we have to rely on the disinterested action by institutional investors to solve all corporate governance problems, we are probably abandoning the prospect of a real solution to them. Instead, if we acknowledge the present problems in the regulation of companies and securities markets, we may find a proper role for institutional investors and a new equilibrium in corporate governance.

---

[29] See E.B. Rock, 'Controlling the Dark Side of Relational Investing' [1994] 15 Cardozo Law Review 987; R. Romano, 'Public Pension Fund Activism in Corporate Governance Reconsidered' [1993] 93 Columbia Law Review 795.

[30] See L.S. Sealy, *Company Law and Commercial Reality* (London 1984) 60: "the idea that shareholder democracy is a practicable concept, or that it is a good solution to any problem, has been shown time and again to be fallacious".

[31] R. Nader, M. Green, and J. Seligman, *Taming the Giant Corporation* (New York 1976) 129: "the monumental indifference of most shareholders is worse than that of sheep".

Part VI:

The Corporate Governance Recommendations

20

Do Good Governance Recommendations Change the Rules for the Board of Directors?

JONATHAN RICKFORD

Abstract

This chapter examines questions surrounding the relationship between "good governance recommendations", or "codes on corporate governance" and the law, addressing: the extent to which such recommendations have become formal or de facto rules; whether the results are beneficial; the extent to which such recommendations depend on other rules for their effectiveness; and the extent to which the phenomenon belongs to company or capital market regulation.

In the context of a utilitarian rationale, the origins and contents of the U.K., U.S., and a number of European and British Commonwealth codes are examined and evaluated; the mechanisms, legal and market led, for securing compliance and their effectiveness are discussed; and the political and economic effects and likely developments are considered.

It is argued that such codes need to be considered in the context of wider developments in capital markets and in particular in the capital structure of companies. The trends towards, and away from, "juridification" of such codes are examined and the conclusion reached that such codes are of growing significance as a new source of law of central importance for company lawyers.

Contents

A. Introduction—Proposed Agenda

This chapter[1] is tasked to address the question "Do good governance recommendations[2] change the rules for the board of directors?" The question can be taken as analytical—is the effect of the recommendations to change the formal rules by which the board operates?—or empirical—is the effect to change the way the board behaves in practice?

This in turn prompts other questions, which I propose to regard as implicit in the task—do such recommendations change the rules for, and the behaviour of, parties other than the directors, particularly shareholders?—are any such changes (whether in the behaviour of boards of directors or of shareholders) changes for the better? What do we mean by "better"? Are such changes the changes which good governance recommendations actually sought to bring about? Can such recommendations, operating alone, be expected to achieve these objectives, or are other interventions, particularly changes in the law, or in regulatory rules, or in the operation of the markets, necessary in order to bring about the appropriate change? And what indications are there of such legislative, or regulatory, or market, activity that is likely to bring such change about?

The subject also raises issues that are close to the main theme of this conference—i.e. the relationship between company, or corporations, law, and the law governing capital markets. Corporate governance is normally regarded in the U.K. as "the system by which companies are directed and controlled"[3]—a definition which appears to be widely accepted internationally.[4] While the regimes

---

[1] The author is the Project Director of the U.K. Government's Company Law Review, an independent review established by the Department of Trade and Industry (DTI), to review the whole of British company law and achieve a restatement in modern, accessible terms with a view to establishing a competitive legal infrastructure—see "Modern Company Law for a Competitive Economy", DTI March 1998. The chapter draws heavily on Review work; and is particularly indebted to Professor John Parkinson of Bristol University, chairman of the working group on directors, and to John Healey, formerly the secretary to the Hampel Committee on Corporate Governance (see below). Full review documentation is available on the DTI website: www.dti.gov.uk/cld/review.htm.

[2] The term "recommendations" raises a troublesome, but probably unimportant, semantic problem. The advisory or imperative language to be found in the various codes of practice and guidance documents on governance vary, both in imperative or hortatory strength, and in their formal and informal sanctions, from what may fairly be described as "recommendations" to something close to, or even actual, legally binding rules. What they have in common (broadly) is the behaviour addressed. I propose to use the words "recommendations", "guidance", "requirements", "codes" as seems most natural in context. The scope of this chapter, like the main codes, is limited to listed public companies.

[3] *Report of the Committee on Financial Aspects of Corporate Governance* 1992 ("Cadbury"), 2.5. Endorsed by the Committee on Corporate Governance 1998 ("Hampel"), 1.15.

[4] A valuable international comparative survey, heavily relied on below, of corporate governance recommendations and codes is H.J. Gregory and E.R. Forminard (Weil Gotshal & Manges LLP), *International Comparison of Board Best Practices*, July 1998, kindly provided to the Company Law

which we are considering are typically embodied in recommendations, there is already evidence of the familiar metamorphosis of such recommendations into "best practice", commonly accepted contractual rules and ultimately fully fledged public interest, mandatory legal or regulatory rules.

Legal and regulatory rules (whether mandatory or default contractual[5]) about the way in which companies are directed and controlled are of course the heartland of company law. Yet many of the pressures for systems of corporate governance originate from the capital markets and in particular from institutional investors[6] (though, in the U.K. and the U.S. at least, there have also been other influences at work, as we shall see below). We thus have company law being hammered out, but on a financial market anvil. This raises questions about appropriate mechanisms for development and perhaps implementation of the recommendations. So far in the U.K. the mechanisms employed have been those of capital market regulation. But there are proposals for change in this too.

In view of this initial exploration of the nature of the issues raised, it is proposed in this chapter to explore the following topics:

- the origin and rationale, character and content of the "recommendations". This may be familiar territory to some readers; it is proposed to visit the subject as summarily as possible, but in the belief that not all readers will be familiar with it; the main emphasis here (because of the limitations of the author) will be on the U.K. experience.
- the mechanism for compliance and the level of de facto compliance.
- the effects of compliance, economic and political.
- dependencies—the conditions required to make the recommendations effective.
- dynamics—what are the likely developments in this field (focusing again primarily on the U.K., but with an eye on global conditions and the pressures for harmonization)? I propose here to look both at the way in which good governance recommendations themselves can be expected to develop and at the extent to which other mechanisms, in particular legal intervention, may be expected to occupy the field.
- in the latter context particularly, there is a case for policy discussion—in what directions is it desirable for these processes to develop?

Review by the authors (hereinafter Weil Gotshal and Manges). There is also a useful conspectus of codes attached to the Commonwealth Association for Corporate Governance Guidelines—Principles for Corporate Governance in the Commonwealth, 1999 ("Commonwealth Guidelines"), www.cbc.to.

[5] By a "default contractual" rule is meant a rule which applies to create contractual relations but which can be displaced by alternative contractual provision by the parties.

[6] For an account of the process of development of the various sets of recommendations in the U.S. and the role in the process of the California Public Employees Retirement System ("CalPERS") see I.M. Millstein and P.W. MacAvoy, 'The Active Board of Directors and the Large Publicly Traded Corporation' [1998] Columbia Law Review 1282 ("Millstein and MacAvoy").

The key point of evaluative reference, in keeping with the current preoccupations of the author, will be on the potential of these phenomena to achieve beneficial results. It seems sensible therefore to begin briefly with an exploration of what is meant by that.

B. Cui Bono?

We have provided an answer to this question for the purposes of the U.K. review[7]—in our view the proper function of company law (within which we include good governance codes and recommendations for this purpose) is to provide the optimal conditions for generation of wealth and welfare, in the broadest sense. We believe that the best way of achieving this is, very briefly, to enable autonomous economic choices, individual and collective, in a climate of disclosure, with the minimum legal intervention necessary to protect externalities. Distributive justice (in favour of employees, for example) is not regarded as a function of company law, though it is likely to be an incidental effect of good company law systems in the terms defined.

In the context of governance we believe that the need is to examine all the institutions and players, including the classic preoccupations of company lawyers, directors, shareholders, and creditors, and the markets (particularly the capital markets and the market in corporate control), and to determine whether the pattern of rights and powers, legal and economic, provides the optimal balance of sanctions and incentives for wealth producing activity. This credo is probably not controversial. Its main importance may be the stress that it places on the context in which governance codes operate. Indeed, as we shall see below, the Governance Codes themselves recognize the importance of many factors other than the behaviours and processes of the company board. A related point is the importance of competition—not merely the familiar anti-trust preoccupation with competition in product markets (not our subject, though to my mind overwhelmingly the most important influence in favour of good governance, on directors, shareholders, and others), but also competition between companies in the field of internal governance systems, and jurisdictional competition between legal systems. The importance of flexibility of company governance systems, the need for room within them for variation and natural selection and their capacity to respond to change, technological, economic and social, is recognized as a key driver[8] in the U.K. review. It seems very appropriate that the theme of jurisdictional and institutional diversity which arises in this context should be

---

[7] See Company Law Review Steering Group, *Modern Company Law for a Competitive Economy, The Strategic Framework* (*"Strategic Framework"*), Chapter 2, DTI February 1999 and ibid., *Developing the Framework* (*"Developing the Framework"*), March 2000, 2.25, 2.26 and Ch. 3.

[8] See *Developing the Framework*, 2.6.

discussed in the venue for the delivery of this chapter—the city-state of Siena. If one asks what characterizes the key periods in which our Western civilization developed and established its most beneficial characteristics, then one settles on, I suggest, two periods in particular, Greece in the sixth and fifth century BC and fifteenth and sixteenth century Italy. Both periods were characterized by astonishing developments in thinking, political, philosophical and scientific,[9] culture and technology. Both were characterized by vigorous competition in all fields, including in systems of internal governance, between a number of small and diverse city-states. The analogy ought not to be pressed too far, but the concern that political and market pressures for national, regional, and global uniformity may inhibit such diversity is discussed below. In short, there are dangers in good governance recommendations becoming *too much* "the rule".

C. Origin and Rationale

Origins and rationale are important, for assessing the continuing desirability of measures and as one basis for assessing their effects. But some readers may be familiar with the origins and objectives of the U.K., U.S. and other codes of practice on corporate governance and may wish to move immediately to Part D of the chapter.

The growth in concern about corporate governance and the consequent codes of practice are often regarded as the result of pressures from capital markets and institutional investors, and their rationale as investor protection in response to market failures in control of the director/investor agency relationship. In fact the origins, at least in the U.K. and the U.S., appear to be more diverse.

I. U.K.

1. Cadbury—Scandals

The main begetter of British company law since its origin has been financial scandal and the British Act[10] can be read as a history book of such scandals since the first Act in 1855.[11] The initial stimulus for the first British codes on

---

[9] Siena's council members were surely ever conscious of these connections, with Ambrogio Lorenzetti's great fresco of the parable of good and bad governance ever looking down at them.

[10] Companies Act 1985, now including amendments made in 1989 and very minor amendments in 1996.

[11] Of course there have been other influences. The original imperative for Gladstone in 1844 was the need to find a standard form of incorporation with limited liability for major enterprises at the height of industrial development and "railway mania" The invention of the British private company limited by shares in 1907 was stimulated by jurisdictional competition from the French Societe en Commandite. A more recent influence has been EU harmonization, implemented in the 1980s.

corporate governance was no different. The main events which provoked the process, in the late 1980s and early '90s, were the accounting and systems failures which characterised the collapse of Polly Peck plc and the Bank of Credit and Commerce International and the comprehensive governance failures which led to the Maxwell scandal, involving the substantial collapse of the Daily Mirror newspaper and the plundering of the Mirror employees' pension fund by a dominant chairman/chief executive officer, unchecked by a supine and compliant board of directors and a body of investors, which included some major financial institutions. All had been warned that Maxwell "could not be relied on to exercise proper stewardship of a publicly quoted company" by government inspectors some 20 years before,[12] but continued to support him.

These events led to concern about the reputation of the London markets but also to widespread public and political concern. However, while earlier scandals in the late '70s and '80s produced a strong legislative reaction in the early Thatcher years,[13] by the '90s the Thatcher and Major governments had lost any taste for interventionist companies legislation and the natural inclination was to look to "the City", business, and the professions to develop codes of practice to respond to these problems. And they were keen to defend themselves.

There was also, and remains, a strong bias in British company law against legislative intervention in institutional and structural aspects of company governance. For example, there is no statutory demarcation of the relative roles of shareholders and directors, which are a matter for contract; and almost no regulation of the functions of the board.[14] The duties of individual board members and general constraints (if any) on the proprietary powers of shareholders are a matter for case law.

So the first code of practice on corporate governance in the U.K. was issued by the Committee on the Financial Aspects of Corporate Governance, chaired by Sir Adrian Cadbury, former chairman of Cadbury Schweppes plc, (Cadbury

---

[12] See *In re Pergamon Press Ltd* [1971] Ch. 388 and *Maxwell v. Department of Trade and Industry* [1974] Q.B. 523 CA.

[13] In 1980 insider dealing was criminally sanctioned for the first time; the Peachey Property scandal, for example, which involved directors' abuse of company assets, led to the establishment in 1981 of important criminal offences, particularly what are now ss. 320–322 of the Companies Act 1985 on directors' transactions with the company; the Guinness share ramping inquiry in the mid '80s led to strengthening of financial service legislation; and the professional governance system for accounting and audit was much strengthened, after the Dearing Report, by the Companies Act 1989.

[14] The board as such is hardly recognized in the Act. The default constitution ("Table A" of 1985), which is widely followed, confers on the directors all the powers of the company, subject to express contrary provision and to limited powers reserved to the shareholders by the Act. It also confers a power on shareholders to give directions to the directors by qualified majority. The Act requires that any director can be dismissed by shareholders by ordinary majority (s. 303). There is no reservation to directors of matters of everyday management—compare SEC proxy rules.

Committee) in 1992.[15] It covered guidance on the board's role, including in particular the need to ensure that the board is not dominated by one individual[16] and is structured and operated so as to maintain its independence; the functions and composition of the board, including the qualities required of non-executive directors; procedures for setting and disclosing directors' pay; the board's duties to present a balanced view of the company's performance in company reporting and elsewhere; and the board's obligation to establish and maintain effective internal controls and relationships with external auditors. The Code was addressed to listed companies but it was hoped that as many other companies as possible would seek to meet its requirements.[17] The traditional British reliance on disclosure manifested itself in the implementation of the Cadbury Code. The London Stock Exchange adopted in its Listing Rules[18] requirements that listed companies should report to shareholders in the annual report on their compliance with the Code and that this report should be audited.[19]

2. Greenbury—"Fat Cats"

The second stage in the development of good governance recommendations in the U.K. was the establishment in 1995 of the Study Group on Directors' Remuneration, chaired by Sir Richard Greenbury (the then chairman of Marks and Spencers plc, at that time a well regarded British retailer). The concern which led to the establishment of this group had less to do with governance and the operation of company boards and more with public and government disquiet about the levels of remuneration being awarded to directors, particularly those in privatized utility companies,[20] for doing, allegedly, much the same jobs as they had been doing in the nationalized companies.

---

[15] The Committee (like the two which followed—see below) was established and financed by the private sector, particularly the National Association of Pension Funds and the Association of British Insurers (which had themselves issued earlier guidance on good governance) but with Government encouragement. The membership was drawn from business, City institutions, and the professions.

[16] Cadbury Code 1.2. Cadbury did not advise that the chairman and chief executive roles be split.

[17] ibid., 3.1. Any attempt to apply governance codes to private and unlisted companies has been more or less explicitly abandoned.

[18] The listing rules offered a ready means of imposing the code on listed companies. They operated contractually as part of the agreement between the company and the exchange on admission and were effective as a result of the London Stock Exchange's de facto monopoly of listing in U.K. markets. However this has now changed—see below. The (wholly unrealistic and inappropriate) legal sanction for breach was de-listing of the company whose board was in breach; the real sanction was public and market opprobrium.

[19] Section 12.43—now replaced, see below.

[20] Particularly gas, water, and electricity network monopolies. Similar concerns were expressed about telecommunications (British Telecommunications plc) in the late '80s, but once service performance and competitive conditions improved criticism in this sector faded.

A key government concern was the discrediting of the flagship privatization policy that had been a major component of the Thatcher government's achievements since the early '80s. Business interests were concerned about the discrediting of the capitalist system in the eyes of the general public, epitomized in the sobriquet "fat cats". The motivation can thus be fairly described as primarily defensive and political.

The Code issued by Greenbury was essentially a comprehensive elaboration of the Cadbury Code about executive directors' remuneration, including provision for an independent remuneration committee of the board, composed entirely of independent non-executive directors, to review performance and set remuneration levels for executive directors (a remarkable removal of the responsibility of the board as a whole to set incentives and reward achievement), and an annual, audited remuneration report, in the name of that committee, setting out full details, in respect of each individual director, of all remuneration and perquisites.[21]

3. Hampel—Rationalization?

The third stage of U.K. good governance developments was the work of yet another Committee on Corporate Governance established in 1995 and chaired by Sir Ronald Hampel (then chairman of Imperial Chemical Industries plc).[22] Its task was to review the Cadbury and Greenbury codes and their operation, to propose amendments and, significantly, to extend the enquiry further by looking "afresh" into the role in governance of shareholders and auditors.[23] There were a number of concerns. Increasing transparency in relation to directors' remuneration seemed to be having little, if any, effect in checking of the rate of its increase, which in listed companies exceeded by a wide margin the rate of wage inflation in the economy as a whole. Indeed some believed that the effect of widespread publicity for directors' remuneration packages as a result of

---

[21] A further concern was with compensation packages on dismissal. The British Act sets a maximum notice period (and thus level of compensation for loss of office), without specific general meeting approval, of five years (1985 Act, s. 319). Greenbury, supported by Hampel, proposed a "normal" period of one year. Greenbury Report Ch. 7, Hampel Final Report 1998, 24. The British Law Commissions in their *Report on Directors' Duties and Conflicts of Interest* (hereinafter *Law Commissions—Directors*) proposed a reduction to three years, Law Com no. 261, Scot Law Com. no. 173, 1999, HMSO Cm. 4436. For current developments, see below.

[22] The initiative came from the Financial Reporting Council, the body recognized under the Companies Act as the source of authoritative accounting standards (through its subsidiary, the Accounting Standards Board) and for their enforcement (through the Financial Reporting and Review Panel). Other sponsors were the London Stock Exchange, the Confederation of British Industry, the Institute of Directors, the Consultative Committee of Accounting Bodies, the National Association of Pension Funds, and the Association of British Insurers.

[23] Committee on Corporate Governance ("Hampel"), Preliminary Report, August 1997, 1.7.

Greenbury had actually increased the "going rate", at least in less generous companies. Some believed (and still believe)[24] that one reason for the lack of restraint was that the levels of remuneration of fund managers too was very high; they were thus not well placed to carry the burden of asserting their control rights as shareholders to restrain the level of directors' remuneration.

A different concern was about the growing cost of compliance with corporate governance codes. Cadbury had produced a significant industry in training and developing company professionals, company secretaries, accountants, and others, in techniques of compliance, and had led to what Hampel described as "disproportionate" and "excessively detailed" disclosures, combined with "anodyne" statements of policy, on remuneration in annual reports.[25] It was argued by some that the proliferation of board committee meetings to monitor and police board operations was distracting boards from their main operational purpose, which in the British unitary board culture is to lead the high level strategy and monitor the operation of the business, and that the emphasis on disclosure was leading to perfunctory "box-ticking" and a preoccupation with process, rather than a focus on operational performance (in fact, it is of the essence of such codes, which cannot, because of their legal character, confer rights on third parties, to prescribe processes and disclosure rather than mandate operational behaviour—a point we shall explore further below).

There were hints of an adverse reaction of this kind to some of the results of the Cadbury and Greenbury recommendations in Hampel's preliminary report in May 1997. There was a concern to reassert the collective responsibility of the board—for example the report on remuneration should not in Hampel's view have been in the name of the remuneration committee.[26] The preoccupation with "box-ticking", or "boilerplate", perfunctory compliance with the existing codes, as opposed to a desirable, functionally useful, response to actual business needs led Hampel to suggest the restructuring of the existing codes in a new form. The new form was to consist first, of statements of "general principle", by reference to which boards were to declare their philosophy for governance, and second, illustrative guidance "developing" the principles and reflecting the earlier codes.[27] This distinction is reflected in the distinction in the implementing Combined Code between "principles" and "provisions"[28] (we shall return to this question of legislative form and business need when we consider the practical

---

[24] Evidence to the Company Law Review.

[25] Hampel Preliminary Report, 1.9, 4.15, 4.16.

[26] ibid., 2.12, retained in the Final Report 4.14.

[27] Hampel, Preliminary Report, Ch. 2, Final Report, Ch. 2.

[28] The principles remain as principles but the explanatory guidance has become "provisions"— see London Stock Exchange (now Financial Services Authority) Listing Rule 12.43A and Combined Code "appended to" the Rules, July 1998 (hereinafter Combined Code).

implementation and enforcement of the Code, below. It is relevant to the flexibility issues already mentioned).

The Hampel Committee was appointed under a Tory government which had begun with an increasingly confident neo-liberal laissez faire politico-economic policy and ended in a state of political debilitation, in which major initiatives were hard to achieve. But Hampel reported under a "New" Labour government, committed to modernization of the national constitutional and economic institutions. The press speculation that the Final Report represented a weakening of the earlier codes was rebutted by Hampel, who asserted that the new code was tougher and more onerous.[29] A significant tightening was indeed evident. New obligations on shareholder governance were included (requiring "considered exercise" of voting power and in "considered dialogue" with companies on disclosures), as were new obligations on companies—to communicate with shareholders in the annual general meeting and elsewhere; to engage in "effective dialogue" with shareholders;[30] and to strengthen the independent element on the board by the identification of a "lead" independent director. But on a number of key issues the final report remained less strict than many critics believed appropriate. These issues included the responsibility of the board as a whole, rather than the remuneration committee, for remuneration policy; the reservation of director appointment decisions, including the appointment of outside directors, to the board as a whole rather than to the nomination committee (subject of course to shareholder confirmation); and the continuing assertion of the defensibility of combining the role of chairman and chief executive. Hampel was also quite explicit about the inability of codes to restrain directors' remuneration and offended some by continuing to stress that there was no demonstrable connection between compliance with governance codes and business success.[31]

On March 4, 1998 the then Secretary of State for Trade and Industry, launching the Company Law Review,[32] welcomed the report, but said "Hampel is not the end of the story. Hampel has proposed a governance structure for business; and the Stock Exchange are working on a Combined Code (a consolidated version of Cadbury, Greenbury and Hampel recommendations to be incorporated in the London Stock Exchange listing rules). It is now for companies to show

---

[29] *Financial Times* January 29, 1998, 11.

[30] Final Report 2.13–2.17 and Pt. 5.

[31] Launching the Final Report Hampel said "My committee was criticized for saying there is no hard evidence to link business success to good governance. But the evidence from the U.S. is that when a company performs poorly, shareholder action, leading to a change of management, and not improved governance, is what has produced improved results"—*Financial Times* January 29, 1998, 11.

[32] See above, n. 1.

leadership in delivering best practice on the basis of that structure and code. I intend to work closely with business to help them to bring that about."

It was not difficult to discern a possibility, even a threat, of more interventionist action by government. In fact the terms of reference of the company law review included the need to examine the interoperation of the law and the code[33] and the later review consultation documents reopened a number of issues on the status and functioning of non-executive directors and board committees.[34] The government has also already reopened the issue of directors' remuneration and of political and charitable contributions with proposals that envisage the possibility of mandatory rules on shareholder involvement in decision making in these fields. Thus, in the terms of our title, a clear dynamic in the direction of transforming good governance recommendations into more formal rules was already evident in the U.K. in early 1998.

These developments and their likely implications are discussed in the context of reflections on the future of good governance recommendations in Part G of the paper below. But it seems sensible here to remind ourselves in a little detail of the essential content of the U.K. Combined Code, which now operates as the implementation of the bulk[35] of these various committee recommendations, before looking briefly at the origins and rationale for good governance recommendations in the U.S. and elsewhere.

The central recommendations concerned the operation of the board and to the participation of non-executive directors, and in particular independent non-executive directors, in board decision making and in the functioning of the three board committees concerned with governance, the audit committee, remuneration committee, and nomination committee. The key recommendations were that

- companies should be headed by "an effective board which should lead and control the company"[36];
- the posts of chairman and chief executive officer should "normally" be separate[37];

[33] The Review was "to consider the proper relationship between company law and non-statutory standards"—*Modern Company Law for a Competitive Economy*, DTI 1998, 5.2.

[34] Developing the Framework, 3.112–3.159. A further Review document "*Completing the Structure*", reaching firm views, was published in December 2000; see particularly 4.44–4.62 and now Final Report, DTI 2001, URN 01/942, adopting these proposals, but adding a number of other recommendations on, *inter alia*, directors' terms of employment and the role of institutional shareholders in Ch. 6.

[35] The parts of the Hampel report addressed to shareholders have not been fully implemented (see below), though the government has as part of pensions law introduced a measure requiring disclosure of voting policies by pension fund trustees.

[36] Combined Code, A.1.

[37] Combined Code, A.2—"there should be a clear division of responsibilities at the head of the company which will ensure a balance of power. . . A decision to combine the posts of chairman and chief executive should be publicly justified."

- At least a third of the board should consist of non-executive directors, a majority being "independent of management and free from any business or other relationship which could materially interfere with the exercise of their independent judgement".[38]
- There should normally be three board committees:
  - —a nomination committee,[39] composed of non-executive directors in the majority, but not necessarily independent ones, to examine and make recommendations to the full board on board appointments, executive and non-executive[40];
  - —a remuneration committee, entirely of independent non-executive directors, to determine the remuneration of all executive directors and make recommendations to the board on the framework of executive remuneration[41]; and
  - —an audit committee, composed of at least 3 directors, all non-executive and a majority independent, to review the scope, results and cost-effectiveness of the external audit and the relationship with the auditors.[42]
- Considerable stress is placed on the board's responsibilities to keep shareholders informed and engage in dialogue with them.[43] The board "should present a balanced and understandable assessment of the company's position *and prospects* [emphasis added]"[44]; and shareholders should receive proper information with notices of general meeting resolutions, e.g. biographical details of directors proposed for appointment.[45]

---

[38] Report 3.14, but the Combined Code merely requires " balance. such that no individual or group can dominate the board's decision making"—A.3.

[39] "unless the board is small"—Combined Code A.5.1. Hampel had actually recommended as a principle "a formal and transparent procedure" for board appointments, with a nomination committee making recommendations to the board being recognised as good practice—Final Report 2.7.

[40] Directors should be submitted for re-election by shareholders at least every three years—Combined Code A.6

[41] A "formal and transparent procedure" is required for setting remuneration with no director involved in determining his own. Remuneration should not be more than necessary to attract and retain directors, with performance related elements forming a significant proportion for executives. There are detailed provisions about incentive schemes and their approval by shareholders. There should be "an objective" of reducing directors' service contracts to one year's duration; longer periods to attract new directors should reduce once they are in office. Full disclosure is required, as demanded by Greenbury, but on behalf of the Board. General meeting approval is not required as a matter of course but the case for such endorsement of the policy should be considered each year—Combined Code, Part B.

[42] Combined Code, D.3.

[43] Combined Code, C.1, C.2.

[44] Combined Code, D.1.

[45] Combined Code, A.6.2.

- there should be an identified lead non-executive director who would be the point of contact for shareholders concerned about the operation of the company.[46]
- The system of internal controls, operational, financial and compliance, including risk management systems, should be reviewed at least annually and a report given to shareholders.[47] Guidance on this has been issued recently by the Institute of Chartered Accountants for England and Wales and endorsed by the Stock Exchange—compliance with the guidance will be regarded as compliance with the provision.[48] The guidance requires embedded, but dynamic and evolving, systems and processes of risk management, with the annual report covering changes, frequency of board assessment and identified failures.[49]

As well as these provisions on the operation of the board, Hampel, as we have noted, also made recommendations on dialogue with shareholders and behaviour of institutional investors. These are also included in the Combined Code. The main provisions are:[50]

—companies should be open to dialogue with institutional investors, and the annual general meeting used "constructively" to communicate with private investors;

—institutional investors should make "considered use" of their voting powers and be open to dialogue with companies;

—institutions should evaluate disclosures about governance, giving due weight to all factors drawn to their attention (a reflection of the enforcement or implementation mechanism and of the "normative" quality of the Code— see below);

—institutions should ensure their voting intentions are carried out (a reference to the complexity of ownership structures in institutional investment—see below).

This completes our review of the origins and history to date of the U.K. governance code. Before evaluating its effectiveness in practice it is proposed to turn very briefly to consider the position in the U.S. and elsewhere.

---

[46] Hampel, Final Report, 3.18, Combined Code, A.2.1.

[47] Combined Code, D.2.

[48] Internal Control—Guidance for Directors on Compliance with the Combined Code, widely known as the Turnbull Report, ICAEW September 1999, ISBN 1 84152 010 1 The Foreword to the Code declares the adoption by the Stock Exchange of the guidance as authoritative.

[49] Hampel rejected the argument for a public audit of this report, regarding the adequacy of such controls as a matter for directors—Final Report 6.12.

[50] Combined Code Part C and Section 2.

II. U.S.—Hegemony and Diffidence

The origin of the good governance movement in the U.S. appears rather different from that in the U.K. As ever, references to "Anglo-American" corporate law and practice tend to obscure important differences deriving from a still very different business culture. To generalize dangerously, to British eyes the U.S. business philosophy tends to place much more emphasis on the charismatic business leader, highly remunerated, highly professional, trained in the intellectual ferment of the business school, relied upon to deliver the success of the capitalist system.[51] While the focus in the U.K. has been on attracting capital, the focus in the U.S. has been on attracting managers, and this differentiation continues. Indeed in evidence to our Review one leading American international fund manager suggested that the pro-shareholder bias of the British system presents a key attraction to capital in the globalizing market. In this perspective U.S. governance culture looks more French than British.

Be this as it may, it seems reasonably clear that the more or less contemporaneous move in the U.S. towards more open and responsive board structures was prompted in part by the concerns of U.S. lawyers, which have a long history, at the lack of accountability of U.S. managers (one thinks of Berle and Means,[52] more recently Melvin Eisenberg[53] and the American Law Institute Principles of Corporate Governance[54]), in part by the failures of management, raiders and legislatures adequately to protect the interests of stock-holders in the merger mania years. But the most significant contribution seems to have come from a loss of confidence within corporate America itself as result of corporate commercial failures in the face of foreign, and particularly Japanese, competition. This was epitomized by the decline and rise of General Motors, punctuated by the forced resignation of its chief executive, Robert Stempel, in 1992 after he "lost control of his board".[55] The press comment at the time celebrated the victory of an independent board, but the reality was one of many years of board failure. In 1994 the GM board issued its Corporate Governance Guidelines on significant Board Issues, which have been perhaps the most significant set of

---

[51] Cf. the continuing differing approaches to the unified chairman/CEO—below, n. 59.

[52] *Modern Corporation and Private Property* (New York 1932) revised 1967.

[53] E.g. 'Structure of Corporation Law' [1989] Colorado Law Review 1461

[54] *Analysis and Recommendations* 1992.

[55] *Wall Street Journal*, October 23, 1992—quoted in R. Monks and N. Minow, *Watching the Watchers; Corporate Governance for the 21st Century* (Cambridge 1995) (hereinafter Monks and Minow), which gives an accessible account of the General Motors case and its implications for governance at pages 327–371. Shortly after the events at GM the chief executives of IBM and Westinghouse were also discharged, "because business as usual did not constitute acceptable performance" Millstein and MacAvoy, see above, n. 6, 1289.

guidelines, at least amongst those originating in the U.S.[56] Perhaps the main reason for the widespread influence of these guidelines was the initiative of the California Public Employees' Retirement System (CalPERS) Trustees, who circulated a copy of them to the 300 largest companies in America inviting comments, and then "graded" them, A+ to F, on their reply, publishing the results. The grades placed particular emphasis on the independent monitoring relationship between boards and executives.[57]

It may thus be fair to assert that while the impetus for corporate governance guidelines in the U.K. was prompted by systems failures and failures of shareholder control, as well as board failure, the impetus in the U.S. was poor commercial performance. But in both countries institutional investors rapidly dominated subsequent developments.

Whatever conclusions one draws about the origins of the codes in the two countries, there are important differences of content. While there is agreement about the importance of director independence, and about the need for independent audit, compensation, and nominating functions,[58] there is no preference in the U.S. for separation of chairman and CEO ("the board does not have a policy"—GM guideline No. 4, 1997) and the Business Round Table positively favours unification of the roles, as more efficient.[59] Nor is there any substantial compensating support for a designated lead independent director as stressed in the U.K. codes.[60] On the other hand, under the GM guidelines the board is to meet regularly in the absence of the executives to discuss their performance and to evaluate the CEO and outside directors are to screen and recommend candidates for board membership. The U.K. Code lacks any such provision. The overall impression is of a much more open and independent board structure, but much greater concentration of executive power, in the U.S. than the U.K. This may reflect the much greater prevalence in the U.S. of boards with only one or

[56] These were revised in 1994 and 1997. In addition to the ALI guidance other U.S. codes include the *Business Roundtable Guidelines on Corporate Governance*, 1997 (hereinafter BRT Code); the *CalPERS Corporate Governance Market Principles*, 1998 (hereinafter CalPERS Code); and the *Council of Institutional Investors Core Policies, Positions and Explanatory Notes*, 1998 (hereinafter CII Code).

[57] See Millstein and MacAvoy, see above, n. 6, 1290.

[58] These are endorsed by all the major U.S. codes—see Millstein and MacAvoy, above, n. 6, 1288–1289.

[59] Compare BRT 1997, 13—"the BRT believes that most corporations will continue to choose, and be well served by, unifying the positions of chairman and CEO. Such a structure provides a single leader with a single vision for the company and most BRT members believe that it results in more efficient organization".

[60] "... it is desirable for directors to have an understanding of how non-executive leadership ... is to be provided ... In some boards ... one strong figure might provide the natural leader ... Whether the board's understanding should be codified ... should be for individual boards to determine"—BRT, ibid.

two executive members, with operational management governed in a separate management board. The trends and implications are discussed in Part D, below.

III. OECD

The OECD Principles on Corporate Governance were agreed by OECD ministers in May 1999 and adopted shortly thereafter. They were developed as a set of agreed standards for developing and evaluating corporate governance systems in member and non-member countries. They are declared[61] to be "essential for the development of good governance practice" and "increasingly important for investment decisions of relevance to the increasingly international character of investment". While "there is no single model of good corporate governance. there are some common elements that underlay" it. But the subject is recognized as evolutionary and requiring a flexible framework for development.

There is little doubt that OECD member governments regarded this code as an opportunity to set out some principles which would be of relevance to developing and newly developed economies in the aftermath of the Asian economic crisis. A result of the breadth of this audience was the need to cover a wider ambit of governance rules than had been covered in the U.K. and U.S. codes and the many other similar codes that had emerged in Europe and in a number of British Commonwealth countries. The OECD principles thus cover in a superficial fashion most of the main topics of company law and include quite basic rules about the shareholder company relationship, such as the right to security of ownership in, and transfer of, shares, participation in control (including the rights of beneficial holders to ensure that custodians or nominees execute their wishes—a major issue in the U.K.—see below), accounting and disclosure, and the need for properly functioning markets, as well as board strategic and monitoring responsibilities, high board standards and board independence from management. By covering such a wide field the principles exposed some key areas on which Member States disagreed, particularly the division between the "shareholder value" philosophy of corporate purposes (the orthodox British and U.S. approach—in the U.S. at least in the ALI principles and in general company law, though not in anti-take-over statutes) and the stakeholder, or pluralist, view widely adopted in countries influenced by German principles of corporate governance. This delayed final agreement and required some careful drafting.[62]

There must be doubt generally whether the OECD principles in their present form will have any real influence in the developed world since they reflect a

---

[61] Drawn from OECD Principles, OECD 1999, Preamble.

[62] OECD Principles, Principle III.

widely accepted minimal level of accepted practice, but there are exceptions to this, for example:

- Principle I E requires that markets in corporate control should be allowed to function efficiently and transparently and that anti-take-over devices should not shield management from accountability; and
- Principle IV, on disclosure, requires disclosure of forward-looking information on commercial objectives and risks, stakeholder, community and environmental interests, and governance structures and policies.

The first of these, in spite of the curious drafting, seems likely to cause problems for some OECD jurisdictions. The second requires standards of reporting relevance conspicuously absent from, for example, many EU countries' accounting regimes.[63]

The World Bank was closely involved in the development of the OECD Principles; proposals have been made for IMF surveillance and periodic review. While the principles can scarcely be expected to have any influence on company boards in any of the countries of immediate concern to this conference, they constitute a point of reference for more open minded legislators and are already a minor, but real, influence on the U.K. approach, at least to disclosure—see below. There may well be pressure for the further development and implementation of the OECD code in due course.

IV. Other Jurisdictions

Space and time (and the author's competence) preclude a full examination of governance codes in other countries. Suffice it to say that in France the two Vienot Reports of 1995 and 1999, have had a widely recognized effect in opening up corporate governance (at least according to available English language assessments) and, after a shaky start, have begun to prise apart the extraordinary powers of the president-directeur general. The more familiar recommendations on board committees are increasingly adopted. Legislation on some aspects of board operation, including the setting of remuneration, appears to be imminent.[64] In a number of Commonwealth countries codes broadly similar[65] in content to the U.K. code have been adopted.[66] The Commonwealth itself developed

---

[63] Including the U.K., but for Company Law Review proposals see below.

[64] Source—*Davis Global Investors Annual Report 1999*—www.davisglobal.com ("Davis Global").

[65] But there are interesting contrasts—for example the Indian Code (see below, n. 66) recommends that for large companies, if the chairman/CEO offices are combined, the board should have at least 50% independent non-executive membership, and where they are separate, at least 30%.

[66] Canada—*Toronto Stock Exchange Guidelines for Improved Corporate Governance* (Dey Report), 1994; Australia—*Corporate Practices and Conduct* (Bosch Report) (sponsored by various Australian professional, financial, and business institutions) 1995; India—*Confederation of Indian*

a set of guidelines more or less contemporaneously with the OECD, as a result of a declaration at the Edinburgh Commonwealth summit in 1997. These are very similar to the OECD Principles, but go considerably further on stakeholder governance issues, requiring the board to identify stakeholders and develop policies for relationships with them. The "inclusive" approach to recognition of stakeholder relationships is advocated.[67]

In the Netherlands, the Peters Report[68] is interesting as a code which is clearly designed to improve openness of governance and responsiveness to investors, in the context of the globalization of the capital markets, but taking account of the need to adjust a corporate governance system based on two-tier boards and a pluralist philosophy to these market pressures. Striking statements in that context are—"There are no conceivable circumstances which can justify any relaxation of the principle that the management should be fully accountable to the providers of risk capital", and "The basic principle is that the Board of Directors and Supervisory Board should have the confidence of the shareholders' meeting... Boards cannot perform satisfactorily in the long run without that confidence".[69]

D. Mechanisms for, and Levels of, Compliance

This part of the chapter now seeks, at last, in the light of this description of the content of the various codes, to answer the question, whether corporate governance recommendations have become rules, first by examining the formal and informal pressures for compliance and then by considering actual compliance in practice.

Industry, Desirable Corporate Governance—a Code, 1998; Malaysia—*High Level Finance Committee Report on Corporate Governance*, Kuala Lumpur, 1999; Singapore—*Stock Exchange, Manual and Best Practices Code*, 1999; Hong Kong—*Stock Exchange of Hong Kong, Guide for Directors*, 1997; South Africa—*Institute of Directors of South Africa, Report on Corporate Governance* (King Report), 1994.

[67] *Commonwealth Guidelines*, Principle 8, Preface, 3.

[68] *Corporate Governance in the Netherlands—40 Recommendations*, 1997.

[69] Recommendations 5.1, 5.3. Other interesting recommendations are for: a limit of one ex-management board member on the supervisory board; board attendance at and dialogue with shareholders at the general meeting; and the supervisory board to report publicly on whether it has appointed nomination, audit, and remuneration committees—Recommendations 2.5, 5.1, 3.2. At the time of going to press a code adopting the "comply or explain" disclosure approach has been published and endorsed by the Government in Germany see German Federal Ministry of Justice Press Release No. 9, 26 February 2002; see www.corporate-governance-code.de/eng/news/presse-20020226.html.

I. The U.K. Combined Code—Norm-setting by Disclosure.

We have already noted that the U.K. Combined Code was incorporated in, or strictly speaking "annexed to" the rules for London Stock Exchange listing. The implications of this may be of some interest. The mechanism adopted was the insertion of a new listing rule[70] that imposed two disclosure requirements for inclusion in the statutory annual report:

*   the first requires the directors to provide a narrative account of how they have complied with the Code Principles, in a form which must enable shareholders to evaluate the mode of compliance, and to state whether or not they have complied with the more detailed Provisions and, where they have not, to give reasons.
*   secondly, a statement is required of the company's policy on remuneration of directors and a detailed account all forms of remuneration, director by director.

For obvious reasons, the first requirement could not apply to parts of the Code addressed to shareholders. These have no legal implementation, though they are recorded in the annex to the rules that contains the code. An audit report is required of compliance with specified, objectively verifiable parts of the Code and with the detailed requirements on disclosure of directors' remuneration.

The overall effect was one of mixed formal legal obligation and market enforcement. The Stock Exchange was to engage in spot checks to ensure that disclosure was being made, but made no attempt to verify its content. Auditors were to give a significant self-enforcing effect. But the main pressure for compliance was to come from institutional investors; as Sir Adrian Cadbury anticipated, "The Committee was looking to market regulation rather than strictly self-regulation to win board acceptance. . . Provided investors, analysts and lenders valued compliance with the Code, it would confer a market advantage on companies which complied. . . good corporate governance is increasingly being linked to good corporate performance and complying could be expected to add to a company's competitive edge". In answer to the question, "why not make compliance compulsory?", Sir Adrian responded that "it is hard to frame legislation which will frame governance standards".[71]

In fact the practical effect of requiring justification of departure from the Code norms is to create a regulatory presumption in favour of the Code rules or recommendations, including the more detailed Provisions, dischargeable by public explanation by reference to the particular circumstances of the company.

---

[70] Rule 12.43A. For transfer of authority to the Financial Services Authority for listing rules see below, n. 73.

[71] Sir A. Cadbury, Gresham College Special Lecture, *The Future for Governance—Rules of the Game*, May 1998.

This creates an incentive on boards to focus on the issues raised by the Code and to consider very carefully the implications of making an exception report. Addressing the Code is legally mandatory; the standard of rigour in doing so is subject to audit scrutiny on key points; and the sanction of opprobrium in failing to do so is likely to be substantial. In spite of Sir Adrian's suggestion that this is market enforcement, it seems substantially more rigorous. This can be tested by asking whether, in the absence of the listing rule, there would have been equally effective pressures for compliance from the market alone.

Similar techniques for securing compliance through disclosure have been adopted in a number of Commonwealth countries,[72] but similar codes in all other countries appear to be wholly advisory, though market enforcement and compliance is effective in some, see below. A particular difficulty has arisen in the U.K. with the changing status of the London Stock Exchange and proposals for the establishment of rival exchanges, in London. The demutualization of the London exchange and its re-establishment on a commercial footing made its continuing responsibility for public interest, as opposed to narrow exchange-related, enforcement functions unattractive commercially to the Exchange and hard to justify in principle. It was therefore announced in 1999 that the responsibility for these and many other parts of the listing rules would be transferred to the Financial Services Authority.[73] But the imminent possibility of U.K. based companies, to which good governance policies ought to be applied, obtaining a listing on markets beyond the territorial jurisdiction of that Authority raises questions about the appropriateness of listing rules, and perhaps even of that authority, as the competent body to exercise this jurisdiction. The use of capital market regulation to achieve these governance ends does not fit with the jurisdictional needs of the regime. This subject was addressed by the U.K. Review in the context of a detailed scrutiny of all the devolved and delegated regulatory functions relating to company law and a transfer of jurisdiction to the body responsible for reporting standards was proposed (see below).

---

[72] Australian Stock Exchange listing rule 4.10.3 requires an account of corporate governance policies by reference to the Bosch report; in Canada a similar requirement operates on the Toronto and Montreal Stock Exchanges in relation to the Dey Report; the Hong Kong Stock Exchange requires an account of compliance with the Exchange's best practice guidelines; similar provisions operate in South Africa in relation to the King Report; the Indian Code recommends that Stock Exchanges should progressively insist on an annual certificate of compliance by listed companies— see Weil, Gotshal and Manges, passim.

[73] See Consultative Paper, Transfer of the U.K. Listing Authority to the FSA, Financial Services Authority, December 1999, www.fsa.gov.uk., Financial Services and Markets Act 2000, Part VI, especially s. 96, and Financial Services Authority, The Listing Rules, May 2000, Rule 12.43A.

II. Market Mechanisms—the Growth of Governance Monitors

The result of the corporate governance movement in the U.K. has been a, not always welcome, sense, on the part of boards and institutional investors, of being under scrutiny. There is also a sense, how well justified we shall examine below, that there may be market advantage in investing in companies with open governance arrangements. This demand has created a market for advice to investors on company compliance with codes, and to the growth of businesses providing such services.

In 1999 the Company Law Review commissioned one such company, Pensions and Investment Research Consultants Ltd (PIRC) to provide a report on levels of compliance with the U.K. Code for the one year since Hampel reported. Rather high levels of compliance had been achieved on almost all aspects. For example, 93% of FTSE 100 companies had more than 33% of board directors who were non-executives, and even for SmallCap (i.e. smaller quoted companies outside the FTSE 350 index), companies, where non-executives are more difficult to find, the figure was already at 74%. Scores on these aspects have increased steadily since Cadbury reported; but disclosure of board consideration whether the remuneration report should be put to the general meeting was much lower, at 48% for FTSE 100, and 22% for SmallCap, companies.[74]

So there is convincing evidence that Code requirements are becoming "the rule" in the U.K. Similar services to global investors are creating an international norm between countries, which may be beginning to bite on legislators and local capital markets as well as on companies. For example, an American firm, Davis Global Advisors Inc., produces annual reports which compare not only the performance of companies but also of legislators in this field, using a complex scoring system.[75] This purports to show that the U.K. is "in first place" in governance standards, followed by the U.S. and France, but with Germany "catching up" as a result of recent legislation on reporting.[76] Criteria adopted include openness of corporate control markets and transparency standards, as well as the mainstream components of corporate governance codes.

III. Pressures for Uniformity

The growth of these services gives rise to some concerns. Davis Global notes that the U.K. scores "badly" on openness of boards (i.e. percentage of non-executive directors), scoring about half the level in the U.S. and at about the same level as

---

[74] PIRC, Compliance with the Combined Code, 1999, DTI website, above, n. 1.

[75] The annual report is available on www.davisglobal.com.

[76] *Gesetz zur Kontrolle und Transparenz im Unternehmensbereich (KonTraG)* 1998.

France. The U.K. pulls ahead because of its exceptionally open market in corporate control.

It may well be that there is an optimal balance of the various factors that go
to make up the corporate governance equation and that this will vary from one
country and politico-economic culture to another. Moreover, levels (as
reported, at least) of board openness may depend on the formal legal structure
of boards—countries with supervisory boards can score high on independent
board committees; even in the U.S. the prevalence of the division between the
board proper, with strategic and monitoring functions, and the management
board, charged with operations, makes the possibility of boards dominated by
non-executives much more feasible than in the U.K.. There is concern in the
U.K. that such a "split unitary" board may raise the risk of dominance of the
board by the CEO (or the CEO and one or two others), because of his sole access
to information, as compared with a board where there is wider communication
with a number of executives. Moreover, the movement in the U.S. towards more
open boards than in the U.K. is balanced by the retention in the U.S. of the combined CEO/chairman.[77] Can any reasonable comparative inference be drawn on
the balance between these two variables? Indeed, could it be that the combined
chairman/CEO is more of an asset, or less of a liability, in the U.S. than the
U.K., or, indeed, even vice versa? Again, the flexibility of the norm-based structure of the Combined Code will be lost if companies are simply scored on openness on the basis of whether or not they have a combined CEO/chairman
without consideration of the explanation offered and the real balance of power
within the organization.

But even more critical is the question whether compliance with such codes
does actually contribute to more effective economic performance by companies.
If not, then the whole governance movement can be castigated as a value
destroying exercise and the provision of advice by these kinds of services as a
delusion.

Even so, perhaps there are other desirable but non-economic, or not quanti-
tatively verifiable, benefits to be derived from the governance movement.

E. Economic and Political Effects

The growth and success of these service organizations looks on the face of it like
a legitimization of the governance movement by market forces. Yet Hampel said
confidently in his Preliminary Report that there was "no hard evidence to link
success to good governance" (Cadbury, as we have seen, had a different opinion.)

---

[77] See Davis Global Annual Report 1999, Analysis.

I. Evidence of Economic Benefit

Very extensive studies in this field have indeed produced inconclusive or contradictory results. There are arguments that governance preoccupations may actually distract directors from their proper strategic and operational concerns. There are also arguments that the effect of governance systems may vary according to context, as a result of exogenous sectoral or other factors, or that quantitative assessments of compliance with codes, rather than qualitative and behavioural examinations of the manner of compliance, are unlikely to establish correlationships between board processes and corporate performance.

The literature survey commissioned for the U.K. Review found a real lack of consensus on these questions.[78] A specific quantitative study by Franks and Mayer commissioned for the Review also found a poor co-relationship between board openness, in terms of numbers of non-executive directors on the board, and performance and managerial discipline in the U.K., as compared with the U.S.[79] The Millstein and MacAvoy study, for example,[80] in the U.S. seems to show a convincing co-relationship between board openness and corporate success.[81] But while it appears to show that openness and success are concomitant, it does not show a causal relationship.[82]

On the other hand, the Franks/Mayer study found a strong link in the U.K. between turnover of CEOs in underperforming companies and the presence of a non-executive chairman, suggesting that this component of the U.K. Code was having beneficial economic effects. While this was a criterion in the U.S. study, it is not clear how often it was present and, as we have noted, separation of chairman and chief executive posts is relatively uncommon in the U.S.

This evidence was a matter of concern to the U.K. Review. In the hope that the trends towards a better performance which seemed to be discernible in the research might be demonstrable by an updating report of the data, examining the performance of U.K. companies from 1994 to 1998, the Review

---

[78] *Empirical Evidence on Corporate Control*—J. Cook and S. Deakin ESRC Centre for Business Research, Cambridge 1999, 5–34, available in the DTI library.

[79] J. Franks and C. Mayer, *Governance as a Source of Management Discipline*, paper for the Company Law Review, DTI website, above, n. 1. This assesses effectiveness of managerial discipline by the correlationship between underperformance, turnover in management and the openness of boards.

[80] See above, n. 6.

[81] "Board openness" is determined by reference to the presence of any one or more of the following—independent board leadership (i.e. non-executive chair or lead director); separate periodic meetings of independent directors; and/or formal rules or guidelines on board/management relations. "Success" is determined by reference to relative economic value added.

[82] Millstein and MacAvoy also record numerous inconclusive or contrary studies, see above, n. 6, 1296–7.

commissioned a further report; but[83] the indications from it are still that in the U.K. non-executives do not perform a significant function in disciplining performance. The difference between the two jurisdictions may be explicable on the basis that in the U.K. there is a relatively high, and probably rather uniform, level of compliance with the Code. It may be that well and badly managed companies are scoring alike, whereas in the U.S. the tendency to adopt open structures may be characteristic of superior management skills. To infer that the level of non-executive participation in boards in the U.K. will, if increased, lead to improvements in performance seems as dangerous as to infer that greater separation of chairman and chief executive roles will have the same effect in the U.S.

Whatever the explanation for these apparent differences, the U.K. Review was faced with a problem—did the apparently relatively inferior performance of U.K. governance systems, as compared with the U.S., indicate that better rules, or practices, were required, or that governance requirements were not the way to better performance, or were the problems of empirical research in this area so severe that they should rely on an intuitive judgment that open governance systems are obviously better?[84]

II. Other Possible Effects

There are other, more political, and perhaps more cynical, lines of argument in favour of open corporate governance systems—that like transparency they legitimate corporate power. Some management may reluctantly bite the bullet on that basis.

Similarly, if the fashion is to favour investment in open managed companies then investment managers will follow, for defensive reasons. This will lead to a real reduction in the cost of capital for open managed companies; but the root cause of this will be the perceived, and not the actual, merits of good governance requirements.

Finally, there is much more convincing evidence that effective monitoring and interventionist policies by institutional investors are capable of adding value.[85] Open management systems are designed to facilitate such intervention. It seems evident that they will; but the fact remains that no quantitative evidence has been produced that they do.

---

[83] Updating survey by S. Letza and P. Hardwick, published on the DTI website, above, n. 1.

[84] Cf. Millstein and MacAvoy—"The search for econometric proof that an active and independent board matters to corporate performance may well be futile", see above, n. 6, 1298.

[85] For example, the studies of CalPERS investment strategy—see S.L. Nesbitt, *The CalPERS Effect—A Corporate Governance Update*, Wilshire Associates Inc, 1995. See too Monks and Minow, above, n. 55, at 514.

F. Dependencies

All this suggests that we would be ill advised to consider good governance codes in isolation. Their effectiveness in changing board behaviour is likely to depend on extraneous factors.

I. Shareholder and other communication

We have noticed the emphasis in the U.K. code on shareholder dialogue and transparency.

A further preoccupation is with the agency relationship between investors with control rights and the legal stockholder who is entitled to exercise them, which is becoming increasingly important in the era of electronic trading.[86] The effect of the chain of relationships between the professional counterparties, who operate as principals making title through electronic transfer systems and the beneficial owners of the relevant stocks is to divorce the companies invested in from their real owners, and to make the flow of information necessary for the exercise of control rights difficult or impossible.[87] New technology may help to solve these problems, but U.K. studies suggest that the problems are more deep seated.[88] In some countries the emphasis is on making the annual general meeting (AGM) more effective (see the Peters Committee recommendations above). In the U.K. there is growing recognition that while the AGM has not yet reached its "sell-by" date other means of communication are more important.[89]

Interestingly, both comprehensive disclosure and the need to secure effective control rights are major components of the OECD and Commonwealth Principles and, so far as disclosure is concerned, the need of boards to ensure adequate disclosure for stakeholders is explicitly recognized.[90]

II. Shareholder Motivation

Providing shareholders with the information and institutional mechanisms that enable them to intervene is not enough to ensure good governance. They must be motivated to do so. We have seen that while the U.K. Code purports to lay

---

[86] See *Developing the Framework*, 4.7–4.18, for proposals to reform U.K. law to facilitate company/beneficiary communication and influence.

[87] ibid.

[88] National Association of Pension Funds Committee of Inquiry into Vote Execution, London July 1999.

[89] *Developing the Framework*, 4.24–4.64.

[90] OECD Principles III D, IV A.6; Commonwealth Guidelines, Principle 6.

down rules on institutional shareholders in that regard, the mechanisms of implementation do not provide any formal or informal sanctioning support; the listing rules bind companies and indirectly their management, but have no effect in practice on shareholders. It is not entirely evident why this should be so— de-listing or otherwise penalizing a company in which investors have a stake and have failed to perform their duties of governance looks at first sight like a reasonable last resort sanction on the investors, at least no more absurd than as a sanction on directors. Where the institutional investor is itself listed the listing rules could also bite directly. But the duty properly to manage an investment is one which institutional shareholders owe in many cases to their investor clients, whose interests are not served by any such sanction. Disciplining institutions in this way is widely regarded as a step too far, perhaps not solely because the institutions have been the main supporters of the development of the codes in the first place.

There are other well-documented constraints on institutions exercising governance rights. The "free-rider" problem is well known—intervention is expensive and the benefits accrue to competitor investors. Close involvement in company management and information may disable an investor from dealing because of insider dealing concerns. In the U.K., where ownership is exceptionally diffuse,[91] effective intervention may require joint action by a number of institutions; this in turn may raise questions whether they constitute a group acting in concert, requiring notification to the Stock Exchange under the rules on disclosure of interests in shares of listed companies.[92] While perhaps not technically applicable, and not barring intervention even if applicable, such disclosure constitutes a substantial deterrent to intervention. This problem looks particularly important in the U.K. with its very diffuse structure of shareholding, but global developments suggest such structures are increasing.[93] These technical problems ought, in principle, to be soluble. A more fundamental problem is conflict of interest. Increasing concentration of financial institutions and diversity of shareholdings has led to a very high probability that in cases of corporate failure requiring intervention by institutional shareholders one of those whose participation in the intervention is needed will have a business relationship with the company invested in. For example, the institution or an associate may manage the company's pension fund, or be concerned in providing it with advice on corporate finance, or on mergers and acquisitions, or other market activity. The

---

[91] See Franks and Mayer, above, n. 79.

[92] Companies Act 1985 Part VI, implementing, in more stringent form (the initial threshold is 3%) the Council Directive (EEC) on the information to be published when a major holding in a listed company is acquired or disposed of [1988] O.J. L348/62.

[93] For evidence on the degree of concentration of shareholdings in the U.K. see Franks and Mayer, above, n. 79, and G Stapledon, *Analysis and Data on Share Ownership and Control in the U.K.*, a study for the Company Law Review, DTI website, above, n. 1.

result may be a conflict between the interests of the investing institution's share-holders, concerned to retain the business relationship, and their investment clients, concerned to maximize the value of their investments. The likely result of any such conflict will be for the investing institution to rely on sale of the shares, if trouble looms, rather than to invoke control rights. The extent to which such conflicts are a problem in practice is extremely difficult to determine. The U.K. Review received substantial evidence of increasingly frequent intervention by institutions operating in London in the management of a wide range of British companies, resulting in major changes of strategy and/or board control; but the information was inevitably provided in confidence.

To the extent that good governance provision depends on a healthy relationship between boards and shareholders all these matters are a source of concern.

G. Whither Good Governance Recommendations?

I. Strengthening the Code—Recommendations, or Rules, or Law?

The development of governance codes in the U.K. can be regarded as recognition of the deficiencies in a legal framework for governance which is so flexible that it leaves gaps in the framework of board and other governance processes. On this analysis one might expect the recommendations and norms emerging to be likely to graduate, as a result of public policy pressures, towards company law.

Whether this should indeed happen is an issue raised by the U.K. Review, but it focused on a limited number of areas where code rules were suggested as possibly fit for more substantial legal provision. The main area was the monitoring role of non-executive directors, where it was suggested that more substantial rules may be desirable:
- directly to define and prescribe the monitoring duties of non-executive directors;
- to tighten up the appointment process for such directors, to ensure their genuine independence from management;
- to require a separate consideration of, and report by, such directors on management quality and process;
- To require that the chairman and chief executive posts should be separated, and even that the chairman should be formally independent, so that former chief executives cannot be chairman.

In all these cases the question was raised whether the rules adopted should be regulatory or statutory.

The issue inevitably arises of whether the U.K. should adopt the two-tier board structure, but this was rejected, even as an option for companies[94] on the

---

[94] Though such an option may be inevitable with adoption of the European Company Statute.

ground that it would destroy the strengths of the single board approach and unnecessarily complicate the law.

We have noted the changing framework of implementation for the Code at the time when the U.K. Review proposals emerged in December 2000. Retention of the disclosure obligation for companies but with a more effective sanction was proposed. More effective means of securing exercise of governance responsibilities by institutional shareholders, secured by disclosure obligations, also emerged in the Final Report with implementation of the Code transferred to a Company Law and Reporting Commission with general oversight of company law. Ongoing oversight and development of the Code is already formally in the hands of the British Financial Reporting Council as a result of provisions of the Hampel Report itself and the Financial Services Authority, with wider sanctions powers,[95] is now responsible for listing rules.

A related question is provision for interpretation of the Code. In a recent widely publicized paper the English Law Society has argued that the current interstitial status of the Code (neither statute, nor subordinate legislation, nor regulatory rule, but merely ancillary guidance) means that there is no authoritative body to interpret it. Disclosure of non-compliance is mandatory and informal sanctions, at least, are severe, yet there is no authoritative means of determining what is required in marginal cases.

These considerations raise wide questions about the appropriate mechanism for development of flexible governance rules in this area. Similar questions about legislative and enforcement institutions arise in the closely related area of standards setting for company reporting and accounting. The rigid provisions of the British Act, with their criminal penalties, in part implementing the European Fourth, Seventh and Eighth Directives, are widely perceived to be an inappropriate regulatory mechanism in the area of financial and other reporting. The Review makes proposals for the devolution of this area (subject of course to the overriding binding constraints of the Directives) to a subordinate, more flexible, expert, and faster moving set of rule making and enforcement bodies.[96]

In short, while the governance codes may have demonstrated weaknesses in areas not governed by the British legislation, it by no means follows that legislation is the best response.

II. Strengthening the Legal Context

Whatever the outcome on the reform of the rules and guidance embodied in the Code, the Review has made major proposals that will strengthen the context within which that Code will operate. Largely independently of Code considera-

---

[95] Financial Services and Markets Act 2000, Part VI.

[96] *Developing the Framework*, 5.40–5.73. See now U.K. Review, Final Report, Ch. 5.

tions, proposals have been made on a range of areas that are of direct relevance. The most important are for:

- statutory codification of directors' fiduciary duties, including an explicit recognition of a company's dependence on its stakeholders;[97] this may fill, to some extent, the gap in U.K. law referred to above;
- a new forward-looking qualitative annual report by directors on the company's performance, strategy, dependencies, and impacts and on its governance systems;[98] here again the effect is to extend the transparency obligations of directors in fields covered at present only by the codes;
- a wider audit corresponding to this[99];
- better communication with shareholders in the context of the general meeting[100];
- enabling of direct communications between owners of control rights in the company and its board, to ensure more effective exercise of such rights;
- a mandatory requirement that the outstanding term on a director's service contract should not exceed one year, except for his first term, which should not exceed three.[101]

It will be evident that these proposals fall wholly or partly within the areas covered by the governance codes. Unlike such codes, they affect the substantial behavioural and transparency obligations of directors, imposing or facilitating new forms of relationship with shareholders. The proposal on duration of directors' contracts is a direct interference in the remuneration field. These ideas are likely, if accepted, to result in primary legislation.

III. Political Initiatives in the U.K.

While the U.K. Review, independent of government, pursued questions about strengthening the regime in the areas directly covered by the Code and in reforming areas which are very much part of the relevant context, and which in some cases overlap with Code provisions, the government had already picked up one area of direct concern and was clearly minded to engage in legislative activity, regardless of the review and of the Code. This was the area of directors' remuneration, where as we have seen, the Codes have had no, or even a damaging, effect on the outcome.

---

[97] *Developing the Framework*, 3.40. See now Final Report, Ch. 3 and Annex C.

[98] *Developing the Framework*, 5.74–5.101. See now Final Report, Chs. 3 and 8.

[99] *Developing the Framework*, Ch. 5; Final Report. Ch. 8.

[100] ibid., 4.24–4.64; Final Report, Ch. 7.

[101] *Developing the Framework*, 3.89, Annex A, 19–25, adopted and extended in Final Report, 6.10–6.14.

The U.K. government issued a consultative Document on this subject in July 1999 and firm proposals, with draft legislation, finally emerged in December 2001. These favoured a detailed annual remuneration report, with comparative performance statistics, to shareholders and annual advisory general meeting votes on the policy.[102] The main options set forward for reform had included:

- obliging listed companies to have a remuneration committee entirely composed of independent non-executive directors;
- amending the Code to ensure proper process within the committee;
- requiring detailed disclosure on the linkage of pay to performance;
- stronger disclosure of directors' service contracts;
- greater shareholder involvement, by requiring one or more of the following:
  —shareholder approval, by annual resolution, of the board committee's remuneration report itself—i.e. the actual rates and payments—or of a statement of remuneration policy; or
  —requiring all directors, or just the remuneration committee chairman, to stand for re-election annually; or
  —provision enabling shareholders to move a resolution on remuneration at the annual general meeting.

It is still not finally decided whether the U.K. government will require annual shareholder approval of remuneration policies. But the fact that government, so soon after the Code was adopted, made proposals of this kind is significant. First, the sanction of legislation is an evident secondary threat in the absence of compliance with the Code and its objectives. Secondly, government itself has made proposals that involve possibly strengthening the provisions of the Code. The origin of the Code may lie with the markets and practitioners; it is beginning, perhaps, to become government territory.[103]

H. Conclusion

The examination of the good governance code phenomenon seems to raise a number of themes of general interest. It is evident that these codes will not go away. They raise important theoretical and policy questions and the answers may be applicable more widely than the traditional subject matter of good

---

[102] Directors' Remuneration, DTI, 1999 URN 99/923 and URN 01/1400. As this volume went to press the British Parliament passed legislation requiring an annual report to shareholders on remuneration practice and policy, including an explanation of the relationship between pay and performance, and an annual advisory shareholder resolution thereon. This will come into force for financial years ending after 30th January 2002—SI 1986/2002, 1 August 2002.

[103] The U.K. government also introduced legislation requiring shareholder involvement in political contributions by companies. However, this appeared to be a matter of exclusively political significance. Political Parties, Elections and Referendums Bill—Bill 34 2000.

governance. They represent a new source of company law, opening up new techniques of concretization of legal norms and for their implementation.

Quis custodiet? Governance of the governance codes themselves is a major issue. Even if their importance is initially a market phenomenon, once the codes gain authority they will involve legislative, or rule making, interpretative, and increasingly adjudicative, functions. The related institutional issues are already emerging.

The style of the codes relates to their source and institutional context. The strength of non-legislative codes is their flexibility. The struggle is for a style which matches commercial reality and need, so that compliance is useful and fits a wide variety of contexts. Yet U.K. experience shows developing and conflicting pressures for greater formality and more robust institutions in the field. Regionalization and globalization of capital markets will also tend to militate against such flexibility and diversity.

Modern communications and electronic execution of commercial transactions may also have a similar straitjacket effect. They may lead too, to a divorce between effective governance by the risk takers and the efficient operation of capital markets. A new complex agency relationship, between custodian and ultimate investor, requires governance. Financial intermediaries may render true owners "absentee landlords". The Codes already address these issues, but more substantial provision looks necessary.

In sum, the relatively new good governance phenomenon may be regarded by some mainstream company lawyers as something apart. But good governance has always been at the heart of company law. The new codes appear to be of central importance.

21

Do Good Governance Recommendations Change the Rules for the Board of Directors?

GUIDO ROSSI

Abstract

This chapter examines the effects of corporate governance rules on the behaviour of the board of directors. After asserting that neither corporate laws nor securities regulations change original corporate structures, it asserts that path dependency and countries' political environment are the primary factors affecting corporate behaviour. Examining various codes of best practice, it explains that corporate governance rules lack a clear theory of the corporation, in addition to being vague and inconsistent. Furthermore whenever they are made a mandatory predicate, to listing the company on a stock exchange, their provisions are usually watered down, so that they are less demanding. Originally created for public companies in market-oriented systems, they can impede managers' ability to divert firm resources to their own private uses. However, they cannot be transplanted to other countries where ownership is not separated from corporate control. The chapter therefore concludes that assertions about the effects of corporate governance rules are part of a new mythology of company law.

Contents

A. Path Dependence and Corporate Governance

The rules for boards of directors are provided by statutes, although these rules are generally so vague that they leave the task of imposing duties on the directors to different external mechanisms, such as hostile take-overs and other corporate governance devices. But neither the statutes nor the corporate governance rules have a clear theory of the corporation. The basic purpose that both endeavour to attain is to avoid managerial shirking and to impede managers from diverting firm resources for their own private uses. But whenever one has to formulate a set of duties for directors and consequential liability provisions, the relevant considerations are often not clear or philosophically compatible. In addition, any reference to a "poor" or "good" performance as a basis for evaluating directors' behaviour or to inefficient management as an explanation for take-overs[1] seems unsatisfactory. Also, the assumption that in a properly functioning corporate governance system poorly performing management teams will be replaced is disputable.[2]

The market for corporate control and the replacement of management teams does not always depend on their poor performance, but basically on the structure of the market, i.e. on the diffuse existence of blockholders, on the activism of institutional investors, on the minority control of money lenders and banks, or on the degree to which shareholders' agreements for coalition-controlled companies support or oppose mergers or take-overs (which would result in changes in management).

Whether monitoring by large blockholders is superior to market-oriented systems is, however, highly questionable. Meanwhile, Professor Jeffrey Gordon is correct in suggesting that the problem of monitoring by banks or by equity representatives largely depends on a firm's capital structure in a particular economic environment.[3]

Furthermore, the condition of capital ownership, governance structures, and the economic environment depend on the past and reflect the initial structure of the economy. Therefore, one should not underestimate the deep rift existing between U.S. and European economic progress and development of industries. In the former, the original private and market-oriented accumulation of capital has led to the development of industries and economic progress, whereas in Europe, and in particular in Italy, such accumulation has been due, in the first instance, to state-owned enterprises and, to a much smaller extent, to family firms. The theory of path dependence in corporate ownership and governance is the only possible explanation for the persisting and important differences between market-oriented corporate structures and public firms with concentrated ownership.[4]

---

[1] R. Romano, 'A Guide to Takeovers: Theory, Evidence and Regulation' [1992] 9 Yale Journal on Regulation 129; J.R. Macey, 'Institutional Investors and Corporate Monitoring: A Demand-Side Perspective in a Comparative View' in K.J. Hopt, H. Kanda, M.J. Roe, and E. Wymeersch (eds.), *Comparative Corporate Governance* (Oxford 1998) 913–916.

[2] H.G. Manne, 'Mergers and the Market for Corporate Control' [1965] 73 *Journal of Political Economy* 110.

[3] J.N. Gordon, 'Deutsche Telekom, German Corporate Governance, and the Transition Costs of Capitalism' [1998] 185 Colorado Business Law Review 200. See J.C. Coffee, 'The Future as History: The Prospects for Global Convergence in Corporate Governance and its Implications' [1999] 93 Northwestern University Law Review 654–657.

[4] See L.A. Bebchuk and M.J. Roe, 'A Theory of Path Dependence in Corporate Ownership and Governance' [1999] 52 Stanford Law Review 127. "Controlling shareholders are common when investor protection is weak": L.A. Bebchuk, *A Rent-Protection Theory of Corporate Ownership and Control,* Working Paper 7203, *National Bureau of Economic Research,* July 1999, 1.

My first assumption is that neither competition nor globalization are powerful enough to create a real convergence, formal or functional,[5] of corporate laws and securities regulations. My second assumption is that corporate governance rules may converge but, for many reasons, they will have very little influence on corporate structures.[6]

The first assumption does not require specific evidence. One should in fact note that even the EU directives on corporate law and securities regulations, which have been applied to all Member States, have not changed the original corporate structures. The theory of path dependence looks virtually indisputable. The failure of the Italian 1998 reform of company law for listed companies,[7] in spite of many rules, demonstrates this point. The law granted minority shareholders more extensive powers and, in accordance with the underlying philosophy of the reform, which was to trigger institutional investors' activism, gave them powers in monitoring listed companies.[8] The existence of control blockholders (held by banks and families in most of public companies, and by the State in the half-realized privatization of the biggest holdings) and the co-ordination of shareholder agreements, interlocking directorships and conflicts of interest, leave only a very small number of listed companies that can be considered public companies (only 32 out of 240).[9]

B. Social Democracy, Public Firms, and Efficient Financial Markets

In a recent paper entitled 'Political Preconditions to Separating Ownership from Corporate Control',[10] Professor Mark J. Roe has argued that the core problems of the public firm cannot be resolved in a strong social democracy, because

---

[5] See R.J. Gilson, *Globalizing Corporate Governance: Convergence of Form or Function* (December 5, 1998) (unpublished manuscript, prepared for a Sloan Conference at Columbia Law School), J.C. Coffee, above, n. 3, at 649, n. 27.

[6] For a different opinion see F.H. Easterbrook and D.R. Fischel, *The Economic Structure of Corporate Law* (Cambridge 1991) 212–18; R.S. Karmel, 'Is it time for a Federal Corporation Law' [1991] Brooklyn Law Review 90; H. Demetz, 'The Structure of Ownership and the Theory of the Firm' [1983] 26 Journal of Law and Economics 75; H. Hansmann and R. Kraakman, *The End of History for Corporate Law* (Draft Paper, November 19, 1997, prepared for Sloan Conference at Columbia Law School) arguing that corporate governance rules have achieved a high degree of uniformity in the U.S., Europe, and Japan.

[7] *Testo Unico delle disposizioni in materia di intermediazione finanziaria*, DLgs 24 Febbraio 1998, n. 58, hereinafter TUF (1998).

[8] M. Bianchi and L. Enriques, *Has the 1998 Reform of Italian Listed Company Law Fostered Institutional Investor Activism?* (September 22, 1999) (unpublished manuscript).

[9] CONSOB, *Relazione per l'anno 1999*, Rome, March 31, 2000, 115.

[10] M.J. Roe, *Political Preconditions to Separating Ownership from Control: The Incompatibility of the American Public Firm with Social Democracy*, June 1999, Columbia Law School, The Centre for Law and Economic Studies.

agency costs are higher 'and the mechanisms that would control the agency are harder to implement'. The absence of a strong social democracy, where managers are not pressed to stabilize employment, would explain the presence in the U.S. of the widespread ownership in Berle-Means firms, and efficient financial markets.

Germany has been referred to as a typical social democracy, where, also through co-determination, managers and employees are allied and opposed to distant shareholders. Professor Mark Roe's paper deserves thorough examination and deep consideration, especially in its analysis of political factors as the almost exclusive prerequisites to the public corporation.

Considering the law governing corporations as the main factor influencing the organizational form of public firms, we should take note of the fact that the German *Aktiengezetz* of 1936, which has influenced not only the subsequent laws in Germany but also the Italian civil code, was founded on the famous basic principle, summarized some years before the law by German Jurist, R. Netter, who stated that ". . . *die Aktiengezellshaft habe drei Feinde: den Aktionär, die Steuerbehörde und den Arbeiter*" (Corporations have three enemies: shareholders, taxes and employees).[11] This is the basis of the so-called *Führerprinzip* of the law in favor of managers: any collusion between managers and employees seems to have been avoided.

There have been serious discussions for many decades among European scholars on the legal nature of corporations; the debate has been as wide-ranging as among American corporate scholars. European scholars fall into two categories: the followers of the contractual theory, who believe that the interest of the company coincides with shareholders' interests, and the followers of the institutional theory, who consider the interest of the "*Unternehemen an sich*" to be superior.[12] Both have deep political roots. In 1926, Lord J.M Keynes wrote (in an essay entitled "The End of *Laissez-Faire*"): "It is almost true to say that there is no class of persons in the Kingdom of whom the Governor of the Bank of England thinks less when he decides on his policy than his shareholders. Their rights, in excess of their conventional dividend, have already sunk to the neighbourhood of zero. But the same thing is partly true of many other big institutions. They are, as time goes on, socializing themselves".[13]

The two theories, however, coexist and have been used to support different and sometimes contradictory interpretations of the same law, even though

---

[11] R. Netter, 'Zur aktienrechtlichen Theorie des "Unternehmen an sich"' in *Festschrift für A. Pinner* (1931) 507.

[12] The famous Berle-Dodd debate (see A.A. Berle, 'Corporate Powers in Trust' [1931] 44 Harvard Law Review 1049; E.M. Dodd, 'For whom Are Corporate Managers Trustees' [1932] 45 Harvard Law Review 1145) in Europe has been more controversial and polemical.

[13] J.M. Keynes, *Essays in Persuasion* (New York 1931) 312–315.

governance rules have not changed companies' structures. Neither of them, however, have any relationship with social democracy.

The various generations of anti-take-over statutes, also in the U.S., favor incumbent employees and create a strong alliance between managers and employees to avoid corporate migration.[14] Notwithstanding those statutes, one cannot compare the relative levels of mobility in the workforces of the U.S and Europe, but this stems from different reasons that have nothing to do with social democracy.[15]

I would never maintain that law does not matter, but corporate law alone cannot create a legal system that will establish an environment in which securities markets can grow. Public agencies are the most important interpreters of such laws and in different countries they act on different assumptions about efficiency and authority. The SEC is no CONSOB or COB.

In any case, this perspective can shed new light on the 'Strong Convergence Thesis', as it has been proposed by Professor J.C. Coffee in his paper, "The Future as History".[16] The excessive emphasis on the protection of minority shareholders should also be reconsidered, because minority shareholders vary not only between common law and civil law systems, but even among the various countries of continental Europe. For many reasons, institutional investors, like pension funds, act now more like true owners and less like stock market investors, primarily because they recognize that ownership is less liquid than it used to be. As a result, interaction with corporate managers is much closer than it used to be.[17] But the majority of investors own too few shares to carry any influence with corporate managers and consequently, liquidity remains essential to them. Their position, as minority shareholders, requires a different kind of protection. For the institutional investors, which I consider to be like *insider minority shareholders*, protection should be based more on disclosure regulations and 'good' corporate governance rules. Meanwhile, stronger legal protection is necessary for common unsophisticated investors, to address important corporate transactions, such as mergers, acquisitions, take-overs, insider trading, spin-offs, and so on. This protection should be guaranteed by public agencies, like the SEC, CONSOB and COB. Finally, I believe that for investors who are not institutional and do not have any relationship with the corporate

---

[14] Easterbrook and Fischel, above, n. 6, 8.2.1.

[15] Coffee, above, n. 3, 655: "Why does corporate governance rank high on labour's agenda in Europe but not in the United States? . . . If employment prospects are brighter elsewhere, U.S. workers can migrate from New York to California at relatively low cost, but a German worker cannot as easily move to Italy or Great Britain. Language and culture are important constraints".

[16] Coffee, above, n. 3, 646.

[17] P.L. Bernstein, 'Stock Market Risk in a Post Keynesian World' [1998] 21 *Journal of Post Keynesian Economics* 15.

management, self-regulation rules are not enough, and their protection has to be guaranteed by the state through the intervention of a public authority.

Professor R. Romano maintains that state competition for securities regulation, in which state and federal regulators would stand on an equal regulatory footing, has the advantage that "no government entity can know better than market participants what regulations are in their interest, particularly as their requirements are continually changing as financial market conditions change".[18] The EU rules and Member States' securities regulations are often in the same position. However, one should always keep in mind that, if uninformed and unsophisticated investors are to be protected, statutes have to regulate the financial market, because, as Louis Loss wrote, in reference to the development of the statutes: 'In short, Congress did not take away from the citizen "his inalienable right to make a fool of himself". It simply attempted to prevent others from making a fool of him.[19] This is particularly true now that individual investors participating through the Internet are increasing in comparison to institutional investors (who have for many years taken the place of the millions of individuals in the market), giving rise to a new form of economy: "people's capitalism".[20]

It might be correct to declare that *law matters*, but as Professor Mark Roe has argued "good law may arise . . . but ownership may *still* not separate from control*, despite* good law, if the nation's political environment would make separation too costly for distant stockholders".[21] Therefore law matters, but it is not enough, because the main problems remain the corporate structure and path dependence.

When ownership is concentrated, and control is exercised directly or through coalitions, neither corporate law or securities regulation, no matter how good they may be, will modify the basic corporate structure. There will be no Berle-Means firm, and separation of ownership from control will become impossible because as in Italy, France, and Germany, it is concentrated in the same person: the manager-owner. Manager-owners, who possess minority stakes and interlocking directorships guaranteed through a system of holding companies and blocking shareholders' agreements sit on the majority of boards of directors of listed companies. Each one linked to the other, these manager-owners are ready to become a "white knight" if a hostile tender offer should occur. The glue that

---

[18] R. Romano, 'Empowering Investors: A Markets Approach to Securities Regulation', see above, n. 1, 149.

[19] L. Loss, *Fundamentals of Securities Regulation* (Boston 1983) 36.

[20] V. Perlo '"People's Capitalism" and Stock-Ownership' [1958] 48 *American Economical Review* 333, 347: 'The basic claim of "People Capitalism", that the rank and file of the population are becoming owners of the means of production in American industry, is without foundation in fact. The widespread diffusion of this theory signifies only the effectiveness of organised propaganda'.

[21] Roe, above, n. 10, 46.

binds manager–owners together consists of banks, and explaining their power as a political product of social democracy is rather tenuous. Italy, unlike Germany, has no co-determination, and what induces Italian firms to stay private, much more than in Germany, is the lack of a generally accepted disclosure culture, the existence of rules applicable only to listed companies, and the attitude of the controlling banks, rather than any other reason that could be related to, or inferred from, the inherent features of social democracy.

Whatever convergence might be foreseen, it will be difficult to change the current manager-owner structures into Berle-Means firms and the two patterns will coexist for a long period of time, despite uniform securities regulation dictated by the EU.

The theory of path dependence, as formulated by Lucian A. Bebchuk and Mark J. Roe, thus proves satisfactory. Most countries are imprisoned by their history.

C. Corporate Governance Rules Have No Clear Theory of Corporation

As it turns out, corporate governance rules are converging and becoming effective to a much larger extent, notwithstanding the fact that it is very hard to find clear principles in the incumbent flood of codes of best practice. All the corporate governance recommendations have been drafted as self-regulatory rules, but the inconsistent provisions of statutes and case law regarding the nature of the corporation can also be found in these rules: there is no resolution of questions about the appropriate constituents and concerns of corporations. In the founder of the family of codes of 'best practice', the "American Law Institute, Principles of Corporate Governance: Analysis and Recommendation" of 1994, hereinafter *Principles*, one cannot find, as Professor Lawrence E. Mitchell has pointed out, any "clear and coherent theory of the corporation".[22] Both section 2.01, on the objective of the corporation and section 6.02 of the *Principles*, on the role of shareholders and managers vis à vis the "unsolicited tender offers" do not consider the incumbent shareholders' interest exclusive or give management the opportunity to refer to non-shareholder constituencies, like stakeholders and even to the *society at large*.

---

[22] L.E. Mitchell, 'Private Law, Public Interest?: The ALI Principles of Corporate Governance' [1993] 61 George Washington Law Review 872. At 882: "The ALI, by its own admission, resolves (this) ambiguity by combining in section 2.01 a variety of inconsistent provisions found throughout the statutes and the case law without any apparent recognition of, or regard for, the fact that they often are predicated on philosophically incompatible positions. Instead of clarity and guidance, the ALI perpetuates the confusion. Another area in which this philosophical ambiguity is apparent is section 6.02. . . . Ultimately, by failing to address the fundamental issues of corporate law, the ALI has made no one happy".

It is not different in the British City Code on Take-over and Mergers, which imposes on directors the following rule: "It is the shareholders' interests taken as a whole, together with those of employees and creditors, which should be considered".[23]

The American Business Roundtable (BRT) Report of 1997 follows the same line, stating that: "It is in the long term interests of stockholders for a corporation to treat its employees well, to serve its customers well, to encourage its suppliers to continue to supply it, to honour its debts, and to have a reputation for civic responsibility. Thus, to manage the corporation in the long-term interests of the stockholders, management and the board of directors must take into account the interests of the corporation's other stakeholders". Many codes of best practice, like the Cadbury, Greenbury, Hampel, Peters, Cardon, Ruiz, Dey, etc., do not take a position on this question.

The OECD Principles of Corporate Governance cover a special area (see Section III in the first part of the Principles) for the role of stakeholders, maintaining that "the corporate governance framework should recognize the rights of stakeholders as established by law and encourage active co-operation between corporations and stakeholders in creating wealth, jobs, and the sustainability of financially sound enterprises".

However, the French Vienot Report is without any doubt the only code based on a definition of the corporate governance interest close to that of the '*Unternehmen an sich*': 'l'intérêt social peut ainsi se définir comme l'intérêt supérieur de la personne morale elle-même, c'est-à-dire de l'entreprise considérée comme un agent économique autonome, poursuivant ses fins propres, distinctes notamment de celles de ses actionnaires, de ses salariés, de ses créanciers dont le fisc, de ses fournisseurs et de ses clients, mais qui corrispondent à leur intérêt général commun, qui est d'assurer la prospérité et la continuité de l'entreprise'.

But this new definition, in the opinion of Philippe Bissara, is ready to surrender to the similarly vague term "market interest", which, however, should not be confused with shareholders' interest, nor should it have any reference to the rhetoric of the shareholders' value.[24] The confusion exists at a very high level.

When corporate governance rules become compulsory, they are somewhat less demanding. In order to have its securities traded on the market, any issuer has to enter into a listing agreement with NYSE, AMEX, or NASDAQ, which contains corporate governance provisions. Typically, these provisions may require the presence of at least two outside directors on the board, the existence

---

[23] *City Code on Take-overs and Mergers* 5th edn. (1996).

[24] P. Bissara, 'L'intérêt social' [1999] *Revue des sociétés* 5: 'L'intérêt du marché se substituerait-il à l'intérêt commun des actionnaires? En partie sans doute'.

of an audit committee, and provisions for an equal opportunity for the holders of shares of a target corporation to participate in a tender offer. Those rules represent a minimum standard, which is not going to have any influence on board of directors behavior and, therefore, can easily be disregarded.

Despite different approaches adopted by governance recommendations, one common and consistent criticism emerges: all of them lack a philosophically, politically, and doctrinally coherent corporate model. The consequence is absolutely devastating, both for the basic matter of management conduct and for the duties of directors, from the duty of loyalty to the duty of candor. These duties remain vague and courts are being left with the task of defining their content.

D. Corporate Governance Rules are Vague and Inconsistent

It appears to be extremely difficult to examine one by one the rules of all the codes of best practice in order to determine what could be considered a "good recommendation", and what would not be. Two general statements can, however, be declared consistent. The first one relates to the limited application of corporate governance rules, which can really be applied only to Berle-Means firms in Anglo-Saxon markets. On the other hand, wherever the model is that of managed corporations, where the CEOs are responsible for decision-making and the shareholders' only task is throwing out the boards if they perform poorly, corporate governance rules are of limited value or have no place at all. But, in the first case the pressure of institutional investors is already affecting the rules of the boards, even when good principles are not expressly adopted, and good governance recommendations are just a sort of written accepted restatement of other rules, already required by statutes or by public authorities. Furthermore, one should consider that the vague wording of such rules makes it easy for the corporations to subscribe to them, but to continue evading their core underlying philosophy. Ethical codes do not appear to have a very different destiny. Finally, I do not believe that compliance with such rules by a corporation constitutes the reason for investors to buy its shares.

In the case of managed corporations, there is no room to apply serious corporate governance rules. No independent director will be found in such a cultural environment, which is inherently prone to conflicts of interest. When participating on the board, the only way out for a director is to resign.

However, the problem of independent directors (or unrelated directors, in the words of the Canadian Dey Code) is going to be one of the most discussed issues of corporate governance. Not only are independent directors mandatory in listed corporations, but now there are rules in the U.S. requiring a large percentage (up to the majority, as some have suggested) of independent directors on

the boards of investment fund companies.[25] The necessity of including independent directors on boards is connected to the limits of interlocking directorship.
Some rules impose a maximum number of boards on which a director can participate. Service on too many boards can interfere with an individual's
ability to perform his responsibilities. Another problem is that the definition of
'independence' is generally very loose, and sometimes, like in section 3 of the
Italian corporate governance code, too vague and dependent solely on directors'
subjective judgment regarding the appropriate limits on their conduct relating to
economic ties they have with management or controlling shareholders. In practice, the vague and over-permissive nature of these rules does not prevent the
lawyers of controlling shareholders from considering themselves independent!

However, as stated in the Preamble of the OECD Principles of Corporate
Governance, there is no single model of good corporate governance. Therefore,
if the most relevant good rule of corporate governance is the presence of independent directors on the board, no common element can embrace the different
models of corporations. In chapter V, n. E, the same Principle is stated as follows: "The board should be able to exercise objective judgement on corporate
affairs independent, in particular, from management". There is no controversy
about the independence from management of independent directors. This rule
can be applied to a Berle-Means firm model, but not to the continental European
model, where boards and managers are very weak, and where very strong owners are controlling corporations, directly or through coalitions and shareholders'
agreements.

Some basic rules for disclosure and transparency may be self-evident and of
no consequence for the structure of the company. It has been pointed out that
shareholders' agreements or any other form of coalition, with other controlling
shareholders, individuals, family holdings, and cross-shareholdings, are the ultimate and real place where important decisions regarding the corporation are
made.[26] Those circumstances explain the minimal importance of the board of
directors in those companies. Boards act as institutional centers where the decisions are not made, but merely ratified. The relatively recent Italian reform on
listed companies (TUF, 1998) provides that shareholders' agreements shall be
null and void if not disclosed in a proper and detailed manner. I do not intend
to examine this unfortunate rule (art. 122), but I want to emphasize that the
disclosure of such agreements, which are already more or less well-known to the

---

[25] See S. Bhagat and B. Black, 'The Relationship Between Board Composition and Firm
Performance' in Hopt, see above, n. 1, 281; S. Bhagat and B. Black, *Board Independence and Long-
Term firm Performance*, Columbia Law Working Paper No. 143 and Stanford Law John M. Olin
Working Paper No. 188, February 2000, downloadable at http://papers.ssrn.com/sol13/papers.
cfm?abstract_id=133808.

[26] See G. Rossi, 'Concorrenza, mercati finanziari e diritto societario' [1999] 44 *Rivista delle
Società* 1305.

market, is absolutely useless. The important thing to be disclosed would be the decisions made at the level of the agreement, which is reached behind closed doors and secretly passed on to the directors and managers. Any rule of disclosure or transparency can be without effect or even abused if the target is wrong.

E. Corporate Governance and Tax Reform

Governance problems result from the separation of ownership and control. When the two are not separated, however, governance rules, if they exist, must be completely different from those applicable to the Berle-Means firm, and I do wonder whether they can be established by Codes of best practice or by corporate law.

One could find good evidence for this assumption in the fact that really good corporate governance rules are in fact imposed by statutes or public authorities, however not in the field of corporate law, but rather through laws that are not directly aimed at regulating corporate matters.

A recent significant example in which the DG.4 of the Brussels Commission imposed a good governance rule on Italian Insurance Companies is the case *Generali/Ina* (i.e. to eliminate interlocking directors).[27] It was thus introduced a rule which is absolutely new to the Italian boards of directors of listed companies, in which interlocking directors are commonly employed as a means to guarantee control of the circular blocked ownership of different companies, thereby impeding any market for corporate control. And it is not strange at all, if my thesis is correct, that the *Codice di autodisciplina* of the Italian Stock Exchange does not provide a limit for the number of directorships a single person can hold in listed companies. The role of passive advisors fulfilled by directors in the Italian boards is responsible for blocking the market of control and explains why interlocking directorships are common among listed companies.[28] Finally, all commentators who have analysed the recent German tax reform emphasize its relevance for corporate governance.[29]

The disposal by banks and others of their cross-holdings in big German corporations will no longer be subject to capital gains tax. This will transform German corporate structure, generating capital flows for investment in new businesses. The German financial market will become much more efficient, converging towards the structure of Anglo-Saxon corporations.[30] In fact, in

---

[27] Case COMP/M1712—*Generali/Ina*, January 12, 2000; SG (2000) D/100503.

[28] See S.P. Ferris, M. Jagannathan, and A.C. Pritchard, *Monitoring by Directors with Multiple Board Appointments: Corporate Performance and the Incidence of Securities Fraud,* University of Michigan, Paper 99-013.

[29] P. Stephens, 'Blind to the New Europe' *Financial Times*, February 4, 2000, 13.

[30] See Bebchuk and Roe, above, n. 4, 136.

January 2001 the German Panel on Corporate Governance published the "Code of Best Practice for German Corporate Governance", which contains the most extensive rules governing "conflicts of interest and own-account transactions". It is not, however, sufficiently clear what the distinction is between the interest of the company and that of the group to which the company belongs. This is a very controversial point in Germany and a pitfall for any good corporate governance rule.

F. Conclusion

Social, economic, legal, and political backgrounds are the real conditions upon which any system of corporate governance must be founded. Furthermore, attitudes and patterns of behaviour are much more important than any good recommendation. One should take note that the company laws of Japan and the U.K., or of Italy and Russia, are not too dissimilar in structure, but the results are polar opposites.

The asserted effect of rules of good corporate governance is a new form of mythology. It has gained a reputation of being the best of medicines (like disclosure, compared by Justice Brandeis, to sunshine) for the ills of corporations. It is not. It has to be appreciated that promulgating new rules for boards of directors is only helpful for countries in which Berle-Means firms are dominant and good rules can be implemented. If one considers that the nature of corporation is a nexus of contracts, one could assume that managers and directors are liable to the company and to the shareholders in the case of non-compliance with the rules of corporate governance that have been adopted. In other countries, with different legal tradition, history, and culture, corporate governance rules can be misleading, and the idea of transplanting governance principles to all countries can even be downright calamitous. As has already been said: "You can't expect to deliver thunderbolts from Mount Olympus".

22

Do Good Governance Recommendations Change the Rules for the Board of Directors?

BEN PETTET

Contents

A. Introduction

This chapter is presented as the "Discussion Report" to chapters written by Mr. Jonathan Rickford and Professor Guido Rossi. Both their chapters are expert and thoughtful and, intriguingly reach quite different conclusions. It is interesting at the outset to compare some lines from near the end of the chapters:

> *Mr. Rickford*: In sum, the relatively new good governance phenomenon may be regarded by some mainstream company lawyers as something apart. But good governance has always been at the heart of company law. The new codes appear to be of central importance.

> *Professor Rossi*: Corporate governance belongs to the new company mythology. It has gained the reputation of being the best of disinfectants [like disclosure, compared by Justice Brandeis, to sunshine] for the ills of corporations. It is not.

B. Mr. Jonathan Rickford's Chapter

Mr. Rickford argues in his chapter that some analysis of the origins and rationale of corporate governance codes is important for enabling a proper assessment of their desirability and effects. He is obviously quite right in this. Accordingly, he gives a detailed account of the history of the development of the U.K. corporate governance codes and an account of the development of codes in the U.S. and elsewhere. He makes the general observation that in the U.K. the impetus for corporate governance guidelines was prompted by systems failures[1] and the impetus in the U.S. came from poor commercial performance. In comparing the codes he concludes that the overall impression in the U.S. is of a much

---

[1] And failures of shareholder and board control.

more open and independent board structure, but greater concentration of executive power, than in the U.K. He also gives us a 'magic carpet' tour of many of the world's corporate governance codes.

I wish to take issue with two small points in this section, both relating to the origins of U.K. company regulation and, in view of the idea that I have developed below,[2] of considerable significance for an explanation of what has caused the phenomenon of the codes. The first point is Mr. Rickford's statement that 'The main begetter of British Company law since its origin has been financial scandal' where I feel that the emphasis is inappropriate. It is true that much of company law owes its existence to regulatory response to systems failures, but the main driving force for its existence has been and remains, surely, the facilitation of the entrepreneurial desire to use the structure of the firm and to acquire the benefits of incorporation and limited liability which usually go with it. From the earliest days of Royal charters of incorporation in the fifteenth century and later, the fundamental reason for the existence of rules under which incorporation is possible is to facilitate business.

The second point is his statement that the Cadbury Committee was "established and financed by the private sector, *particularly*[3] the National Association of Pension Funds. . .". This is obviously true, but I feel the emphasis is misplaced and that the main pressure for the setting up of the Cadbury Committee at that time came from the nation's audit firms who, as a result of litigation against them, were in fact finding that they were having to bear the financial burdens of the systems failures in corporate governance.[4] Both this and the previous point may seem perfunctory comments, but I feel that they are significant and endeavour to show why, below.[5]

Mr. Rickford moves on to consider the important question of whether corporate governance recommendations have become rules. He does this by examining the pressures for compliance and then considers actual compliance in practice. He observes that the practical effect of the Stock Exchange requirements for listed companies to justify departures from the Code is to create a regulatory presumption in favour of the Code which in turn creates a major incentive for boards to focus on the issues raised by the Code and to consider very carefully the implications of making an exception report. As he observes, addressing the Code is *legally* mandatory.[6] He then makes the important general

[2] At pp. 513–514.

[3] My emphasis.

[4] Mr. Rickford repeats the emphasis: 'Auditors give a significant self-enforcing effect. But the main pressure for compliance comes from institutional investors. . .'. and '. . .the institutions have been the main supporters of the developments of the codes in the first place.'

[5] At pp. 511–514.

[6] This presumably comes about partly by virtue of the company's contractual relationship with the listing authority for the listing of its shares.

observation that similar techniques for securing compliance through disclosure have been adopted in a number of Commonwealth countries but, "as far as I am aware, similar codes in all other countries are wholly advisory, though market enforcement is effective in some".

On the question of compliance in fact, he cites the findings of the PIRC report on current compliance and that scores have increased steadily since Cadbury reported, and concludes that there is convincing evidence that Code require-ments are becoming "the rule" for boards in the U.K.. In my view this conclu-sion is appropriate and is justified by the evidence he cites, and also to some extent by the findings of the Cadbury Monitoring Sub-Committee's Report in 1994. It has also become clear that in the U.K., the Codes have succeeded in creating a new business culture in which compliance matters are taken seriously. There are many examples of this, one such are the proposals by the Institute of Directors for directors to obtain a qualification of "Chartered Director".

Mr. Rickford expresses some justified concerns arising out of the growth of businesses providing governance monitoring services particularly when coun-tries are compared with each other. He observes that according to the Davis Global report the movement in the U.S. towards more open boards than in the U.K. is balanced by the retention in the U.S. of the combined CEO/chairman and then asks "Can any reasonable inference be drawn on the balance between these two variables? Indeed, could it be that the combined chairman/CEO is more of an asset, or less of a liability, in the U.S. than in the U.K., or, indeed, even vice versa?"

Mr. Rickford raises what he rightly calls the 'critical question' whether com-pliance with such codes does actually contribute to more effective economic per-formance by companies. If not, he observes, then "the whole governance movement can be castigated as a value destroying exercise and the provision of advice by [business services] as a delusion". He argues that studies have pro-duced "inconclusive or contradictory results" and that the literature revealed a "real lack of consensus". He cites a study by Millstein and MacAvoy, which showed that while board openness and corporate success are concomitant, it did not show a causal relationship. Mr. Rickford's conclusions are in the form of a series of questions: "Does the apparently relatively inferior performance of U.K. governance systems, as compared with the U.S., indicate that better rules, or practices, are required, or that governance requirements are not the way to bet-ter performance, or are the problems of empirical research in this area so severe that we should rely on an intuitive judgment that open governance systems are obviously better?" He also cites Millstein and MacAvoy's warning that "The search for econometric proof that an active and independent board matters to corporate performance may well be futile". From the tenor of Mr. Rickford's writing here, I would guess that his provisional conclusion is contained in his last question; and I would agree with him.

Mr. Rickford argues that the effectiveness of good governance codes in changing board behaviour is likely to depend on extraneous factors. In this context he discusses the need to provide shareholders with the information and the institutional mechanisms which enable them to ensure good governance, and also the need to motivate them to do so, possibly by the imposition of disclosure obligations. The relative lack of economic incentive for the institutions to get involved in corporate governance is something that I shall return to below.

There follows a discussion of what the future might hold for good governance recommendations. He considers the idea that code provisions might find their way into legislation, so that they represent a new source of company law. There is consideration of the problems of future interpretation of the Code in view of the fact that there is no authoritative body to interpret it, and overall the problem of the future development of the Code. No doubt appropriate solutions will be found for these matters in due course. There is also a discussion of law reform proposals that will strengthen the legal context in which the Code operates. Finally there is an account of the fact that in the area of director's remuneration where compliance has been low, the government is planning to do something about it, either by strengthening the Code or by legislation. Mr. Rickford feels this is 'significant' and that the "origin of the Code may lie with the markets and practitioners; it is beginning perhaps to become government territory." Even if no actual legislation emerges, this observation ties in well with his earlier point about the Code being a new source of company law.

Mr. Rickford summarizes his observations, and concludes with the very reasonable observation that "In sum, the relatively new good governance phenomenon may be regarded by some mainstream company lawyers as something apart. But good governance has always been at the heart of company law. The new codes appear to be of central importance".

C. Professor Guido Rossi's Chapter

Professor Rossi's paper takes a different approach by not looking at the effect of self-regulatory codes in particular, but rather by looking at the effect of corporate governance regimes as a whole, both statute and governance recommendations. In essence Professor Rossi is focusing on the effect which corporate governance regimes (statute and corporate governance rules) have on corporate structures. It appears to me that there are four main themes that he develops. I will comment on each of these in turn.

The first of these is that even if there is convergence on corporate laws and securities regulation, the rules will nevertheless have scant influence on corporate structures.[7] At the outset he takes the position that the divergences in corporate structures under different regimes is due to the historical background so that "capital ownership, governance structures, and economic environment depend on how they were at earlier times and reflect the structures that the economy had initially". He subscribes to the theory of path dependence[8] as the explanation for the continuing differences between the market-oriented corporate structures such as one would typically find in the U.S. and the public firms with concentrated ownership such as one would find in some European states, particularly Italy.[9]

He illustrates these ideas by reference to the fact that EU Directives on corporate law and securities regulation are applicable to all Member States, but that the corporate structures have not changed. This he ascribes, in the main, to the general absence of Berle and Means companies in Italy, France and Germany where control is concentrated in the same person: the manager-owner. He argues that these "manager-owners through possession of minority stakes and interlocking directorships, guaranteed through a system of holding companies and blocking shareholders' agreements, sit on the majority of boards of directors of listed companies. . .The binding glue are banks. . .it will be difficult to change the manager-owner structures into Berle-Means firms and the two patterns will coexist for a long period of time, despite uniform securities regulation dictated by the EU." Professor Rossi's conclusion on this: "Most countries are imprisoned by their history."

This seems basically correct as things are at the moment but I find myself wondering whether more time needs to elapse before we can reach a firm conclusion. Already, in the last year or so we have seen an extension of the concept of hostile take-over, into Germany (Vodafone/Mannesmann) and in Italy (Olivetti/Telecom Italia) and more of these can certainly be expected in the future. Such events might well produce different patterns of ownership and structure in the long run.

Another problem that Professor Rossi visits is the idea that corporate governance rules have no clear theory of corporation. Here, he is looking more closely at self-regulatory codes of governance and is arguing that they are defective on the important matter of whether the company is to be managed solely for the shareholders or whether it is to be managed also in the interests of the

---

[7] See the beginning of his chapter.

[8] L.A. Bebchuk and M.J. Roe, 'A Theory of Path Dependence in Corporate Ownership and Governance' [1999] 52 Stanford Law Review 127.

[9] It is perhaps worth observing that the U.K., although a European country, has corporate structures more resembling those of the U.S. than Italy.

corporation's other stakeholders, such as employees, debtors, and suppliers. He takes the view that "all of them lack a philosophically, politically, and doctrinally coherent corporate model."

This is no doubt true and it perhaps reflects the complexity of the task facing those who seek to balance, in a definitive way, the moral claims of the various participants in companies located in modern industrial democracies.

Professor Rossi considers the question of what constitutes a "'good' recommendation of codes of practice". He is pessimistic about the value of codes: ". . . [G]ood governance recommendations are just a sort of written accepted statement of other rules, already drafted by statutes or by public authorities. Furthermore, one should consider that the vague wording of such rules makes [it] easy for the corporations to subscribe to them, but continue to evade their core underlying philosophy. Ethical codes do not appear to have a very different destiny. Finally, I do not believe that the compliance with such rules by a corporation constitutes the reason for investors to buy its shares".

My own view, which is based mainly on my experience of the U.K. position is that they can make a useful contribution, both by filling in areas on which the statutes and case law are silent and overall by helping to create a culture of thoughtfulness in governance. Of course, as Professor Rossi observes, there will often be cases where the directors comply only on the surface. Professor Rossi's last sentence in the above quotation raises the important point as to whether the codes provide any economic benefit.[10]

In various places in his chapter, Professor Rossi develops the theme that codes of corporate governance really only have relevance for Berle and Means firms in Anglo-Saxon markets. For in countries where the model is that of the managed corporation (i.e. Italy, etc.) the CEOs are responsible for decision making and the only role of the shareholders is to remove boards if they perform poorly. In view of this Professor Rossi cautions against transplanting corporate governance rules to countries where Berle and Means firms are not present and is sceptical about its value in such backgrounds: "Corporate governance belongs to the new company mythology. It has gained the reputation of being the best of medicines [like disclosure, compared by Justice Brandeis, to sunshine] for the ills of corporations. It is not".

This is an important perspective which it is well for those of us from countries in which "Berle and Means" companies are a regular feature of the capital markets to bear in mind when we try to consider the value of corporate governance codes.

---

[10] Those issues are discussed above in relation to Mr Rickford's chapter, where similar points were raised.

D. Codes as Bargains to Alter the Legal Rule

I. Codes are a Market Response

Lastly, I myself would like to develop a perspective that occurred to me mainly in relation to the position of the audit firms in the U.K., but can, although to a lesser degree, be applied to institutional investors. The question initially involves an examination of what has provided the impetus for the adoption of corporate governance codes in the U.K., because I feel the answer to this bears considerably on one of the major themes of this book that is whether or not the capital markets are driving company law.

It is fairly clear that most of company law and securities regulation in the EU and U.S. has come from public (i.e. government intervention).[11] The idea, inherent in the Efficient Capital Markets Hypothesis, that markets themselves will require the supply of information and development of rules which align managers' behaviour to shareholder interests and that therefore public regulation is inappropriate, has not gained much credence among legislators and we find thoroughly entrenched systems of public regulation in the EU and the U.S. Thus in the context of companies, law tends to be 'top down'. However, the corporate codes seem to be presenting us with a different phenomenon; emanating from the lower levels. They are, surely, a market response in its truest sense, coming from the participants, as a set of demands made to corporate managers. It is interesting to examine why these demands have been made. This can be done by examining the engines that have been driving the adoption of governance codes.

II. The Engines Driving the Adoption of Codes

1. The Accountancy Profession

My own perspective of the setting up of the Cadbury Committee and the adoption of the subsequent report differed from that of Mr. Rickford,[12] for I have always had the impression that it was the accountancy bodies, representing the nation's auditors, rather than the investment institutions, who were the main agitators for reform of corporate governance by the end of the 1980s.[13] At that

---

[11] Although obviously participants in the commercial world often make representations for law reform.

[12] See above.

[13] Paragraph 2.1 of the Cadbury Report reflects this: '**Reasons for setting up the Committee** The Committee was set up in May 1991 by the Financial Reporting Council, The London Stock Exchange, and the accountancy profession to address financial aspects of corporate governance . . . Its sponsors were concerned at the perceived low level of confidence both in financial reporting and

time the accountancy firms had come to realise that they were in a hopelessly exposed position in a major corporate fraud if they had been the statutory auditors. They had found that when a company went into liquidation (or administration), the liquidator would cause the company to sue the statutory auditors for negligent performance of their audit contract.[14] They then realized that unless directors were candid with them and unless the top tier of governance organs worked reasonably well, they were in a position where in practice, owing to the size of the company, it would often be difficult to discover the fraud, but equally difficult to maintain that they were not at fault thereby. Operating as partnerships with joint and several liability of each partner the accountants were in an unenviable position. Their professional indemnity insurance policies often covered only a fraction of the liability that the litigation sought to cast upon them: the writ in the BCCI action against the auditors claimed £5.2 *billion*. Some audit firms were bankrupted. In addition to stirring the Cadbury pot, the accountants presented a list of demands and ideas to the Department of Trade and Industry seeking: an amendment of section 310 of the Companies Act 1985 so that they could put a cap on their liability into the audit contract;[15] an amendment to the law of joint and several liability so that the liability on each partner might be proportionate; a business vehicle which gave them limited liability without the need to comply with the reporting requirements of the Companies Act. Here then was the main engine for Cadbury.

2. Institutional Investors

It is true that to some extent the institutions have provided impetus for the corporate governance movement in the U.K. Some have been more active over the years than others. The "M & G letter" became famous among company secretaries and boards[16] and in the early 1980s the Prudential Assurance Company fought an expensive legal action against some directors who had allegedly committed breaches of duties. Although institutional investors clearly have a general

---

in the ability of auditors to provide the safeguards which the users of company reports sought and expected. The underlying factors were seen as the looseness of accounting standards, the absence of a clear framework for ensuring that directors kept under review the controls in their business, and competitive pressures both on companies and on auditors which made it difficult for auditors to stand up to demanding boards'.

[14] The liability that was causing the problems was contractual rather than the possibility of wide tortious liability. In the event, the *Caparo* case narrowed down the tortious liability, but this made little difference to the predicament of the audit firms, who were being made liable under their contracts.

[15] Section 310 prevented corporate officers from limiting their liability.

[16] Sent to companies in which the unit trust had a stake, it exhorted better performance with the implication that the stake would be sold if it was not forthcoming.

interest in well-run companies and clean markets the economic reality is that it is not in their interest to spend much time on getting involved in corporate governance. Their economic rewards come to them only if they do well in their perennial battle to outperform average returns. Their job is to pick the stocks, which are currently undervalued, by the market. This is overstated, but their economic incentive is not as sharp as that of the accountants, and it seems clear that the Cadbury Committee felt that the institutions needed to be prodded into action and accordingly devised the incentive of recommending that institutional investors should increase their policies on the use of voting rights.[17] My anecdotal impression is that there has been a great increase in institutional activity during the 1990s.

3. The Government

The government has liked the development of the corporate codes. It is getting a lot of regulation of the corporate sector very cheaply. Overall, its role has been that of an enthusiastic spectator rather than a driving force.[18]

4. The Corporate Governance Service "Industry"

In the wake of the Cadbury Report an industry has emerged which consists of people in various parts of the economy who derive a living, partially or wholly, from keeping alive the corporate governance debate, and from monitoring compliance with codes. While not instrumental in bringing about the setting up of the Cadbury Code, the influence of the corporate governance industry can nevertheless be detected at work ever since. The industry participants typically consist of publishers, academics, journalists, independent research firms, in-house compliance officers, and politicians. It is difficult to be precise about the extent of the influence of these people in ensuring that self-regulatory codes and their enforcement remains a live issue, and all that can probably be said is that they are a not insignificant element in driving the monitoring and development process of corporate governance mechanisms.

III. Bargaining Around the Allocation of Liability

In my view, what has been happening in the U.K. with regard to the adoption of corporate governance codes, can, to some extent, be understood as the process

---

[17] Cadbury Report, paras 6.9–6.12.

[18] Although in the area of directors' remuneration the politicians have made a point of showing more interest.

by which parties to a situation governed by a set of rules producing a particular outcome are bargaining with each other to produce a change in the outcome.

Thus the rule allocates liability and risk to audit firms by providing a weak legal regime[19] of corporate governance which permits directors to abuse their powers, and a tough regime for auditors based on contractual duty of care, which is difficult to discharge and operates as a kind of guarantee of the performance of the directors, which the shareholders and creditors can enforce via liquidation and administration proceedings. The audit firms could theoretically move into different business, but given their long term know-how, the transaction costs of abandoning their audit role would be high and so they are forced into trying to strike a better bargain with the boards under which the boards voluntarily agree to make a better job of compliance with their duties of care and good faith. Part of the bargain struck involves giving the auditors an enhanced influence in corporate governance by the establishment of a requirement for audit committees. By these means the auditors, who find that they have made a bad bargain, seek to bring whatever pressure they can, in order to get the other side to agree to modifications albeit through the adoption of self-regulatory "soft law".

To a lesser extent, the same holds true for institutional investors, both in the U.K. and probably elsewhere, who find that a weak legal regime is permitting corporate collapses and frauds which would not otherwise have occurred, and which damage the investments which they make on behalf of the investors who are clients of the institution. Since the fund managers are agents of the investors, their incentive to get involved in corporate governance as a general issue largely depends on the extent to which they will be rewarded by their investor clients for doing so or punished for not doing so. The likelihood of reward is scant and any improvements in corporate governance as a whole produce the free rider problem that they accrue equally to the benefit of competitors. The Cadbury Committee could see this, and tried to increase the likelihood of the punishment reaction by exhorting the institutions to account to the investors for their use of the votes attached to the shares in the fund;[20] thus flagging up the point that at that time, in many institutions, proxy forms went straight in the bin.[21]

IV. Conclusions

Given that for the accountancy profession in the U.K. the situation was really very serious, one would expect to find that quite a concrete result emerged. More

---

[19] Largely due to enforcement difficulties.

[20] Cadbury Report, para. 6.12.

[21] As regards the other 'engines', the government gets a boost for their espoused aim of having free and fair markets, and the ancillary service industry which has sprung up since 1991 thrives, and both can perhaps be seen as free riders in the overall process.

so than in other countries where the main pressures for the adoption of codes came from the investor institutions who as has been suggested are under less pressure to secure a result. The enforcement mechanisms adopted in the U.K. in terms of the Stock Exchange's quite rigorous requirement for a compliance statement perhaps do confirm this expectation, whereas in many other countries corporate governance codes have a status akin to guidance and are not dissimilar to codes of ethics. Similarly, one would expect to see a lessening of interest by the audit firms, if and when they manage to solve their problems by other means, such as higher levels of care, increased insurance cover, restructuring, caps on liability, etc. In this event one would come to see the now-quite-developed corporate governance movement sustained largely by the other engines, of institutional investors, government and ancillary service providers.

23

Do Good Governance Recommendations Change the Rules for the Board of Directors?

LUTGART VAN DEN BERGHE

Contents

Abstract

Opinions differ in respect to the drivers and effects of corporate governance recommendations. Independent monitoring is an essential instrument, while substance must prevail over form. Emphasis should be placed on changing the attitude and behaviour of business leaders.

It is clear that there is a tendency of migration from soft law and self-regulation to legislation. Consequently, the development process, content, and efficiency of such governance recommendations need more careful attention. Moreover, flexiblity and adaptability of these recommendations from a geographical, as well as a firm typology perspective, are essential for their effectiveness.

The fact that corporate governance covers a broad area has been proven again by the approach developed respectively by Jonathan Rickford and Guido Rossi. Moreover, their conclusions teach us, again, how opinions differ in respect to the drivers and effects of corporate governance recommendations.

I will not summarize of these two chapters, nor focus on all relevant questions raised by these two authors. In this respect, I can refer to the chapter by Ben Pettet. I will focus mainly on a number of elements that are of special interest, because I differ on these points, or hope to add some extra dimensions to the discussion.

A. The Chapter by Mr. Jonathan Rickford

I personally agree with most of the analysis presented by Jonathan Rickford; a few examples in this respect: the danger of migration from soft law and self-regulation to legislation, the need for flexibility, the need to focus the implementation and monitoring on substance over form, and the considerable differences between the U.K. versus the U.S. model of corporate governance. I would like to discuss some issues that either merit some comment or some extra dimensions.

I. Drivers Behind the Increased Attention for Corporate Governance in General and for Corporate Governance Recommendations More Specifically

I agree that the drivers are rather diversified and that 'commercial' considerations have also stimulated this whole movement to a large extent. However, I would like to add some extra dimensions to this discussion.

It is perhaps feasible to make the following categorization.

1. Negative or Defensive Drivers

Scandals, abuse of power, lack of economic performance, gaps, or deficiencies in the legal framework can all be considered as 'negative' drivers behind the construction of corporate governance recommendations. To put it differently, these recommendations should be regarded as a 'remedy' when things go wrong in business; they have to be seen as a medicine for all kinds of business diseases.

2. Positive or Offensive Drivers

No attention has been paid in the chapters of this Part to more offensive drivers; does this mean that corporate governance recommendations are only seen as a remedy (besides the commercial drivers, discussed below)? Or are potential positive drivers insufficiently taken into consideration? What could an offensive or positive driver look like? Think of the wish to set benchmarks for best practices, to stimulate the development of listing on the stock exchange as a modern (?) way of corporate finance, to motivate enterprises to become more transparent and appealing to foreign investors, etc. Comparative research of the corporate governance system in Belgium and the Netherlands[1] concluded that these countries have different governance systems, that favour other strategies: the Dutch systems favours external growth and expansion strategies, whereas the Belgian system leads to more focus on profitability and internal growth. Parallel research within a broader geographical scope[2] led to the conclusion that the Anglo-American governance system favours innovation and new ventures, whereas the continental European and the Japanese system are more suited to re-engineering and re-organization of mature industries.

---

[1] C. Van Hulle, '*Is het systeem van Corporate Governance belangrijk? Op zoek naar de impact van verschillen van modellen*', referaat Vlaams Wetenschappelijk Economisch Congress, KULeuven, 1998.

[2] L.G. Thomas III and G. Waring, 'Competing Capitalisms' [1999] 20 *Strategic Management Journal* 729–748.

3. Commercial Drivers

It is, to my knowledge, exceptional that attention is drawn to the many commercial drivers behind this whole corporate governance movement. I therefore agree completely with the statements made in this respect by Rickford and Pettet. I would like to summarize this important observation and add some extra dimensions for further discussion.

I agree with Pettet that the *auditors* are a very important driver; this not only holds for the Cadbury Code, but is also true for the new code developed on Internal Control and Risk Management. Where I differ to some degree is that this interest goes beyond only diminishing their liability. I think that this is also of interest to these professions, because it opens new markets for further consulting and services. To illustrate this statement, let me refer to the discussion of the Peters Report in the Netherlands. The Dutch business world was opposed to following the Cadbury recommendation to make the audit of the governance statements in the annual accounts obligatory. The main reason was the extra burden at the cost side, while it was doubtful whether auditors would be able to make such an evaluation, given that they are absent from board meetings most of the time.

Another market that has been created on the new corporate governance wave is *the market of advice and services to shareholders*. Not so much the institutional investors themselves, but firms servicing them, have fostered the attention on obligatory voting and other related issues. This can be illustrated by referring, e.g. to the establishment of firms like LENS.

Institutional investors, although often referred to as one of the main drivers behind this trend, have not played the same active role in all countries. Not only do geographical distinctions appear, but differences also exist within the group of institutional investors: the impact of large public pension funds in the U.S., like CalPERS or TIAA-CREF, and large private pension funds, like Hermes in the U.K., has been instrumental in fostering corporate governance recommendations. This has influenced other important pension funds, like ABP or PGGM in the Netherlands, to follow that same track. In other countries, with less important pension funds, like Belgium, their role has been far less prominent in fostering new corporate governance recommendations.

Many *other* organizations, that have stimulated the attention for corporate governance recommendations, can be found. Examples are institutions active in headhunting for (non-executive and especially for independent) directors, in education, and in networking for directors (like the Belgian Directors' Institute).

As long as these organizations limit their operation to commercial and marketing issues, I cannot see why this would hurt the business world. If there is a need for a certain service, or such a need has been created by market forces, this is the normal way of innovative entrepreneurship. Where things can go wrong, from a welfare and business perspective, is when such organizations start to lobby for extra regulation and government intervention to create new markets or make those new markets more sustainable. Let me refer in this respect to the efforts developed by the IoD in the U.K. to plead for obliging directors to acquire the degree of 'Chartered Director'.

II. What Causes the Need for Flexibility in Developing, Implementing, and Monitoring Corporate Governance Recommendations?

I fully agree with Rickford that corporate governance recommendations need to be flexible. Nevertheless, I think that flexibility as a concept, as well as the reasons behind the need for flexibility need some extra attention. Flexibility is necessary from different perspectives, perspectives that highlight at the same time the diversity this flexibility concept has to cover.

1. Adaptability from a Geographical Perspective

Based on our international research,[3] I do agree completely with Rossi, that corporate governance systems differ quite substantially from one country to another, and are good examples of the path dependency theory. Even in a globalizing world, it is impossible, for the time being, to set detailed standard rules to apply them on a worldwide base. Differentiation or flexibility is a must from a geographical perspective.

2. Adaptability from One Firm to Another

Even within a single country one has to distinguish different types of firms. Although most of the recommendations have been developed for listed firms, these types of firms are not the only ones who need corporate governance recommendations. On the contrary, the more firms are closed, the less market forces will force basic corporate governance principles to be obeyed. Moreover, the importance of listed corporations is not the same in all countries. Although listing has gained quite a substantial increase of attention, many companies still feel reluctant towards listing. Illustrative in this respect is the remark made by Rossi, in relation to the Italian reluctance towards 'opening up' and 'disclosure'. The Belgian business world shows remarkable resemblance to the Italian one (not only in this respect!).

---

[3] L. Van den Berghe (in collaboration with L. De Ridder), *International Standardization of Good Corporate Governance* (Boston 1999).

3. Adaptability Over Time, Within a Firm

In a volatile business climate, firms need to operate with great flexibility in order to react quickly to changes in their market environment. Corporate governance recommendations need to give the business firms this necessary flexibility.

4. Combining All These Remarks

One could summarize by stating that corporate governance recommendations need to be flexible, because they have to answer to very different business circumstances and needs. Referring to the 'negative' drivers listed above, one could say that the diseases differ greatly from one to another, and so should be the medicine. In consequence, all global and standard approaches will be condemned to stay at a rather general level, as regards what the basic rules will be, like the OECD principles, while their more detailed 'provisions' or 'recommendations' will be interpreted as explanatory guidance with a high degree of flexibility.

III. Who Will be Responsible for What Type of Monitoring?

As long as countries opt for soft law or self-regulation, the issue of monitoring needs special attention. Although some systems opt for the development of best practices to set the benchmark to be followed, most codes developed or supported by the stock exchange make these recommendations obligatory for listed companies. I therefore do not agree with the statement made by Rickford that the codes outside the U.K. are wholly advisory.

The question remains, to what extent are the stock exchange authorities themselves in a good position and willing to accept monitoring as their responsibility. This question deserves special attention, certainly in the light of the increasing market focus of these institutions. I would like to plead for an independent monitoring. The potential role of market players, like institutional investors, is weak in my opinion. They suffer from the 'free rider syndrome' and eventually from a possible conflict of interest. Moreover, the question needs to be raised to what extent investors can be considered as shareHOLDERS or, on the contrary, are more to be seen as shareTRADERS. The high volatility of shareholdership, certainly in open markets like the U.S., is increasingly leading to the second type of investors. The average holding period of shares in the U.S., as published by Business Week (September 20, 1999) is illustrative in this respect. How could such traders be interested in following up on the compliance with basic corporate governance recommendations?

The question of the optimal monitoring system also needs to look into the approach to be used. Hampel correctly warned for a pure 'box ticking approach'. The issues corporate governance has to tackle are so important but at the same time so complex, that a pure formal system can never make the necessary changes in practice. It is clear that substance must prevail over form, but the emphasis should be placed on changing the attitude and the behaviour of business leaders.

IV. Is the Attention Given to Corporate Governance Worthwhile?

Corporate governance recommendations (see Rickford) as well as corporate law (see Pettet) do need to facilitate entrepreneurship and economic welfare. This must be the ultimate test. This testing is, however, more easily said than done. We should not wonder why the scientific literature is so poor or contradictory in explaining this causality. Economic performance and entrepreneurship are very complex phenomena and are driven by so many different factors, that focusing on corporate governance issues alone can never lead to sufficient reliable insights. This is certainly true when focusing on a very limited number of corporate governance variables, like the distinction between the functions of CEO and chairman of the board, or on the number or relative importance of independent directors. This hypothesis can also be found in the recent analysis of Millstein & MacAvoy, a study mentioned in the chapter by Rickford. This does, however, not mean that scientific research is not valuable in this respect, on the contrary. But the usefulness of corporate governance recommendations, which cover a wide area of business practice, may not be judged on fragmented analysis. This is certainly the case when the analysis covers different types of firms that indeed need different corporate governance structures and practices (see above).

In this respect, we would like to refer to the statement made by Rickford, that an optimal set of corporate governance recommendations should be seen as depending upon the optimal balance or equilibrium, given the specific characteristics of a country (and also of a company). This statement proves again the value of the parallel drawn by Rossi with the 'path dependency theory'.

V. Who Can Benefit From Governance Recommendations?

Researchers in corporate governance, as well as organizations developing corporate governance recommendations, focus mainly on listed companies. This is certainly understating the usefulness of these recommendations for society. Recent research that I made on the governance for non-profit organizations, like co-operatives, or for governmental organizations, has proven that these institutions need to be given far more attention in this governance debate. The same holds for supranational as well as for non-governmental organizations (see my paper on the problems that occurred in the European Commission, the IOC, and the FIFA[4]). Rickford correctly raised the question as to what extent the institutional investors should not be subjected to a specific set of governance recommendations themselves, or to state it differently, they too should 'walk their talk'.

B. Some Open Questions

Before turning the attention to the paper of Rossi, I would like to ask some open questions for further discussion:

- To what extent can the European Market flourish without a European har- monization? Is there indeed no need for uniformity, as stated by Rickford, or will the integration of the financial markets oblige the European Commission to move a step further in the direction of harmonisation? The case of the merger between the French, Dutch, and Belgian Stock Exchanges could be an interesting factor to stimulate further harmonization.
- Rickford argued against the two-tier board. What arguments can be given to support this statement?
- The most recent developments in the U.K. suggest that firms should give a forward-looking disclosure on many business issues. How far can one go in forward-looking disclosure without hurting competitiveness or revealing com- petitive positions or strategies to competitors?

C. The Chapter by Professor Guido Rossi

In contrast to the chapter by Rickford, I cannot subscribe to a number of the conclusions reached by Rossi.

I. What Drives Corporate Structure?

Rossi states that, whatever corporate governance recommendations may be, they will have scant influence on corporate structure. I would like to differ on this point. Corporate governance recommendations are only indirect driving forces behind corporate structure. The main drivers certainly are corporate strategy (does a firm want to globalize or not, to merge or stay independent, etc.) and corporate finance (to what extent is external financing necessary, does the firm want to use the capital market or other sources of external financing, etc.).

---

[4] L. Van den Berghe, '*Could Corporate Governance Cure the Problems Faced by the European Commission, the IOC and the FIFA*', Working Paper Belgian Directors' Institute, Gent, 1999.

II. Are Corporate Governance Recommendations Only Relevant for Berle-Means Firms?

Here again, I would like to differ from the hypothesis, developed by Rossi. I agree that the impact of corporate governance recommendations will differ according to the type of firm. Where I no longer follow Rossi is when he states that corporate governance recommendations are only relevant for Berle-Means firms. In fact, his statement that 'different environments will necessitate a different set of recommendations' proves that this is not true. If corporate governance recommendations are sufficiently flexible (instead of rigid standards for a national economy or even global standards), tailoring to the specific needs of the firm and its environment will be possible. This will lead to more relevant and effective recommendations.

   As has been mentioned before, potential differentiation factors are numerous:
* The strategic and corporate finance choices (as mentioned before);
* The life cycle or the development cycle of the firm;
* The type of market environment or sector (e.g. difference between the new and the old economy, between the financial sector and the non-financial firms, etc.).

The many national corporate governance recommendations are developed within the basic local reference framework of the 'dominant firm type' in that market. This is one of the reasons why standardization is not possible on a national, or on an international level. If one looks for a standard approach, the type of firm criterion is certainly as important as the difference in national environment. On this point I agree completely with the statement made by Rossi, that one has to be wary of transplanting corporate governance rules to other countries. In fact my analysis of the different types of corporate governance systems and the different sets of recommendations has shown clearly that each type of firm has its own corporate governance challenges and potential problems, which need specific tailor-made solutions:
* In the managerial capitalism model, where managers have overwhelming influence on corporate governance structures and business decisions, the recommendations should look for countervailing powers, independent control and supervision, critical evaluation of executives' contracts and remuneration, etc.;
* In the reference shareholder model with large blockholders, pyramidal holding structures, etc., recommendations should mainly focus on protecting minority shareholders, preventing conflicts of interest, and stimulating that the strategy is developed with reference to the firm as a whole, not missing corporate opportunities, etc.;

- Although some of the recipes can be analogous, e.g. independent boards, their function will be rather different.

III. Are Corporate Governance Recommendations Ignoring the Theory of the Corporation?

I do not agree with the statement that corporate governance recommendations completely ignore the basic choices on the role of the firm in society. Let me refer in this respect to the distinction between (one of) the Belgian and the Dutch codes. The Peters Commission in the Netherlands opted for the corporation as an end in itself. This has consequences, e.g. for the definition of the role of the Supervisory Board and the type of board members. Every member of this board has to be independent and nobody can represent a specific stakeholder group. Moreover, all board members have to foster the welfare of the company as a whole and look after the interest of all stakeholders. On the contrary, the Belgian code, developed by the Banking and Finance Commission, recognizes implicitly the important influence of the reference shareholder and his interests. This is especially clear in categorizing the non-executive directors as three types, the independent directors, the directors representing the reference shareholder(s), and the other non-executive directors.

IV. What is the Value of these Governance Recommendations?

Rossi is rather pessimistic about the value of corporate governance recommendations. He states that these recommendations will have scant influence because they are easy to subscribe and because institutional investors are indifferent to the quality of governance. Both statements do not represent the business reality in a number of countries. Look in this respect, e.g. at the premium institutional investors are willing to pay for companies with better governance practice (McKinsey analysis[5]) or at the influence of the CalPERS black list in the U.S., the U.K., or France. The fierce resistance of some business circles to generalization of corporate governance recommendations, moreover, proves that these recommendations are not easy to implement for all types of firms. My own research in Belgium showed that foreign subsidiaries especially deviate to a considerable extent from the 'substance' of good corporate governance recommendations, whereas smaller and medium sized companies have more problems with coping with the more formalized approach, prescribed by corporate governance codes.

---

[5] F.R. Felton, A. Hudmund, and J. van Heeckeren, 'Putting a value on Board Governance' [1996] 4 *McKinsey Quarterly*, 170–175.

It is therefore of utmost importance to look at the factors that favour a higher value of these governance recommendations. One element in this respect certainly is the need for sufficient flexibility. Another important factor is to be found in a long-term stimulation of better governance attitude and behaviour. This factor can certainly not be guaranteed by formal recommendations (alone). This supposes a change in mentality, attitude, and even in culture. That such changes need time and effort is straightforward. The reference made to the Italian opposition against disclosure is a good example in this respect.

D. Some Remarks on the Comments Made by Pettet

One question that comes to mind is the following: to what extent are codes a response to market forces and is corporate law influenced by the developments on the capital markets?

In this respect, I would like to develop the following hypothesis. In the modern knowledge society, the business world is confronted with a 'raplex' environment (an environment with rapid and complex changes), with global players becoming more powerful than many of the states in which they have been incorporated; this creates the pressure for market driven de-/re-regulation and self-regulation.

Given this raplex environment, the legislator, the supervisory institutions, etc. all lag behind the fast changing business world; some examples in this respect can be found in the financial sector, which is the scene of global financial convergence :

- with legislation lagging behind (e.g. changes in the U.S. lagged behind the merger movement between Citibank and Travelers);
- with supervisory institutions still structured for specialized institutions (see, e.g. the creation of the Joint Forum to find an answer to the threats posed by financial convergence).

Part VII:

Conflicts of Interest

24

The Impact of Insider Trading Rules on Company Law

HEINZ-DIETER ASSMANN

Abstract

This study deals both with the impact of insider regulation on European and German company law and the impact of insider trading regulation, including disclosure requirements, on the corporate governance of a company that is subject to this regulation. In Europe the impact of the insider trading rules and the impact of the duty of timely disclosure on company law are almost exclusively dealt with in a rather narrow national context by attempting to interpret conflicting rules of company law and capital market law in a way that avoids or resolves such conflicts. In addition, much of the impact of insider trading regulation and the duty of timely disclosure has not been on company law as such but on corporate conduct, corporate organization and corporate governance, thus complementing company law rather than leading to conflicts with company law. Although it goes without saying that the development of company law through capital market regulation such as insider trading rules and timely disclosure requirements has led to tacit changes of each Member State's model of company law regulation, there is, at least in Europe, no clear concept of which way the development should be directed. Thus in Europe the impact of insider trading rules and the requirement of timely disclosure on company law has been and will continue to be dealt with on a piecemeal basis rather than by introducing fundamental changes in either company law or capital market law. However, to the extent that the relationship between company law and insider trading regulation is concerned, it is safe to say that this will not be different in other legal regimes of the world.

Abbreviations of German authorities and codes cited in the study

FSO Federal Supervisory Office for Securities Trading (*Bundesaufsichtsamt für den Wertpapierhandel*)
SCA Stock Corporation Act (*Aktiengesetz*)
STA Securities Trading Act (*Wertpapierhandelsgesetz*)

Contents

A. Introduction: the Issues and the Scope of the Study

The impact of insider trading regulation on company law has, to date, and to the author's knowledge, not been an issue of systematic research. This may be due to the fact that the regulation of insider trading is generally considered to fall under the more general heading of capital market regulation, i.e. the regulation of companies' behaviour in the capital markets. In other words, insider-trading regulation is not basically distinguished from other institutional arrangements. Nevertheless, it is obvious from the U.S. perspective of securities regulation that elements of capital market regulation—such as the disclosure rules of the Securities Act (SA) and the Securities Exchange Act (SEA)—may well have the effect of both regulating a company's conduct and influencing its internal organization, thus, being functionally equivalent to company law.[1] As a corollary, this study will not only focus on the impact of insider trading regulation on company law but will also discuss the extent to which insider trading regulation amounts to an equivalent to company law in respect of its effect of regulating a company's conduct, its organization, and even corporate governance. The extension of the study's scope, thus, becomes more pertinent when attention is drawn to the fact that insider trading regulation is regularly accompanied by disclosure rules in the form of timely disclosure requirements, the purpose of which—inter alia—is to reduce the risk of insider information being communicated and to prevent insider trading. In order to ensure compliance with these disclosure obligations, the organizational framework of listed companies has been subject to substantial change.

While this study will deal both with the impact of insider regulation on company law and the impact of insider trading regulation, including disclosure requirements, on a company's corporate governance we shall not deal with the impact of such rules and regulations on the companies' conduct in the marketplace, especially in the financial markets. As a consequence, the study will not develop upon the links between company law and capital market law as elements either of the broader concept of "the law of the enterprise" (*Unternehmensrecht*) or of efficient capital market regulation. More importantly, the study will not question the concepts underlying the distinction between company law and capital market law.

Moreover, one should be aware that this study is only to a limited extent based on information provided by "corporate insiders" on the impact of insider trading regulation and disclosure requirements. Rather, the majority of conclusions are drawn from mere observation, the writer's own research into the ramifications of company law and insider trading regulation, and sometimes speculation. As this inquiry is not, therefore, based on evidence proved by empirical study, it may be that it will provoke questions serving as blueprints for further empirical investigation.

---

[1] See R. Karmel, *Regulation by Prosecution* (New York 1982) 203ff; R.B. Stevenson, *Corporations and Information* (Baltimore 1980) 79ff, 91ff.

Finally, it should be noted that the study will concentrate on the author's German experience, i.e. on German stock company law (*Aktienrecht*) and German stock companies (*Aktiengesellschaften*). However, as both insider trading regulation and the law of the stock company has been the subject of harmonization within the European Union (EU) it may be assumed that most conclusions drawn from the author's German experience are basically valid at least for other Member States of the EU.

The 1994 insider trading regulations had a radical effect on capital market regulation in Germany and marks the introduction of genuine capital market law to replace the previous company law and stock exchange oriented scheme. The developments in German law therefore provide a suitable touchstone upon which to base a discussion of the issues in this study. On the other hand, it must be conceded that the three-tier model of corporate governance underlying German stock company law, including co-determination (e.g. under the Co-determination Act of 1976) in the supervisory board (*Aufsichtsrat*), is still a rather unique feature of German law.

B. Company and Capital Market Law

For an inquiry into the impact of insider trading regulation upon company law no detailed information on German stock company law is required.[2] However, as has just been noted, it should be kept in mind that stock company law in Germany is centred upon a three-tier model of corporate governance based on three necessary organs, i.e. the board of directors (*Vorstand*), the supervisory board (*Aufsichtsrat*), and the general meeting of the shareholders (*Hauptversammlung*). Moreover, it should be noted that in some more closely held corporations an advisory board is established to represent the interests of family or large block-shareholders both in dealing with the directors and in the general meeting. For an understanding of German company and capital market law it may also be helpful to know that until the 1990s capital market law was virtually identical to stock corporation law, stock exchange law, and banking law.[3] This was due to the fact that, from its introduction in the 1870s, the stock corporation was the only legal form that had access to the capital markets, i.e. the stock exchanges. The adoption of insider trading regulation in 1994 was the stepping stone for the introduction of genuine capital market regulation in Germany.

---

[2] For details see H.-D. Assmann, B. Lange, and R. Sethe, 'The Law of Business Associations' in W. Ebke and M. Finkin (eds.), *Introduction to German Law* (The Hague 1996) 137ff. For translation of the *Aktiengesesetz* into English see M. Peltzer and A.G. Hickinbotham, *German Stock Corporation Act and Co-Determination Act* (Cologne 1999).

[3] K.J. Hopt, 'Vom Aktien- und Börsenrecht zum Kapitalmarktrecht?' [1976] 140 *Zeitschrift für das gesamte Handels- und Wirtschaftsrecht* 201 (I); [1977] 141 *Zeitschrift für das gesamte Handels- und Wirtschaftsrecht* 389(II).

The German *insider trading regulation*[4] is part of the Securities Trading Act of 1994 (STA)[5]: Under Sec. 14 I STA a *primary insider is prohibited* (1) from acquiring or disposing of insider securities for his own account or for the account of a third party or on behalf of a third party by taking advantage of his knowledge of insider information, (2) from communicating or making available any insider information to another without authorization, and (3) from recommending to a third party, on the basis of his knowledge of any insider information, the acquisition or disposal of insider securities. Like a primary insider a secondary insider is also prohibited from taking advantage of insider information by acquiring or disposing of securities for his own account or for the account of a third party (Sec. 14 II STA). However, a *secondary insider* is not barred from disclosing insider information to any third party, or from recommending the purchase or sale of a transferable security on the basis of insider information.

A *primary insider* is defined as a person who:

(1) by virtue of his participation in the management or supervisory body or as general partner of the issuer or an undertaking affiliated with the issuer,

(2) by virtue of his holding in the capital of the issuer or of an undertaking affiliated with the issuer, or

(3) by virtue of the exercise of his profession or his activity (*Tätigkeit*)[6] or his duty, by destination (*bestimmungsgemäß*),[7]

has knowledge of *insider information*, i.e. of information which has not been made public relating either to one or several issuers of insider securities or to insider securities and which, if it were publicly known would be likely to have a significant effect upon the price of the insider securities (Sec. 13 I STA). Any person who does not receive insider information as a primary insider is considered a *secondary insider* (Sec. 14 II STA).

A person who violates the insider dealing prohibition is liable to imprisonment of up to five years or a fine (Sec. 38 I STA). The enforcement of the insider trading prohibition is assigned to the Federal Supervisory Office for Securities Trading (FSO, *Bundesaufsichtsamt für den Wertpapierhandel*).

---

[4] For greater detail see H.-D. Assmann in G. Wegen and H.-D. Assmann (eds.), *Insider Trading in Western Europe—Current Status* (London 1994)15ff.

[5] Principally, the translation of the STA follows U.R. Siebel, M. Prinz zu Löwenstein and R. Finney (eds.), *German Capital Market Law* (New York/Munich 1995). For another translation of the Securities Trading Act into English see *The Second Financial Market Promotion Law*, (Bank-Verlag, Cologne 1995) 16ff.

[6] As the term "Tätigkeit" does not require contractual relations between the parties to the communication of an insider information it is translated into "activity" rather than "employment".

[7] "By destination" ("*bestimmungsgemäß*") means that the information was intended to be communicated or to become known to such person.

As a preventive measure against violations of the insider trading prohibitions, Sec. 15 STA requires any issuer of transferable securities admitted to trading on a domestic stock exchange to publish promptly any new fact which has occurred in the issuer's field of activity and which is not publicly known if knowledge of such fact is likely to have a significant effect on the exchange price of the security ("timely disclosure").

C. The Impact of Insider Trading Regulations on Company Law, Corporate Organization, and Corporate Governance

I. General Observations

It is a general yet remarkable observation on the issue of the impact of insider trading regulation on company law that following the adoption of the STA and the insider trading prohibition in 1994 the majority of companies began to redefine, if not to say "reboot" themselves in order to comply with the new rules. There was hardly any internal transfer or communication of information or any transfer across the borders of a company that was not scrutinized for its compatibility with the insider trading regulations. The communication of information via long-established channels, for example, information being passed by directors to a pool of family shareholders prior to the information being made available to the company's supervisory board or its shareholders in general meeting, were suddenly challenged as being unlawful. It is reported that in some companies members of the supervisory board refused to receive insider information in the exercise of their duties, and required the directors to hire lawyers or other professionals to separate insider information from other information forwarded to the supervisory board. In merger and acquisition negotiations both bidder and target companies became increasingly confused about the legality of well-established techniques such as due diligence investigations, which potentially make insider information available. At the same time, the Supervisory Office for Securities Trading was confronted with a wave of publications allegedly required to comply with the duty of timely disclosure of non-public price-sensitive information (under Sec. 15 STA).

Without doubt, the legal uncertainties in applying the new insider trading provisions intensified the industry's nervousness. On the other hand, today, more than eight years after the adoption of the STA, a number of directors and officers of listed companies still have no clear idea about the impact of the insider trading prohibition on the execution of their duties and their company's business.

Today, the initial confusion caused by the introduction of the insider trading regulations in 1994 has subsided and in its place there is now a calmer appreciation of the duties arising from the insider trading prohibition and of the impact of insider trading regulation generally upon the conduct of a company's business. This study will go on to look at this development in detail and concludes these general remarks with two equally general observations: Firstly, the main impact of insider trading regulation for companies has been the radical restructuring of the flow of information within the company, between the organs of the company, and across the company's borders. There is yet another question, the answer to which requires *normative* analysis, to what extent the insider trading regulations actually call for a particular method of organizing transactions to be established and monitored by the directors of a company. The second observation is that company law and insider trading regulation produce conflicting duties, compliance with which calls for a broader concept of regulation which goes further than accepting the established rules that more recent legislation supersedes older legislation on the same point and that legislation which addresses a particular point of law should be applied in preference to more general principles.

II. Information Flow Within the Company

1. Authorized Communications

As has been outlined previously, primary insiders are, inter alia, prohibited from communicating or making available any insider information to another party without authorization. First, it should be recalled that the qualification of a person as a primary insider depends either upon his status as a member of the management or supervisory body or the acquisition of the insider information by exercise of his activity[8] or his duty including activities or duties as an employee of the company. Secondly, it must be concluded that the insider trading prohibition for primary insiders does not distinguish between communications within the company and communications across the company's borders. Thus, primary insiders (e.g. directors, officers, members of the supervisory board, or employees of the company) are barred from communicating insider information (e.g. to another director, officer, member of the supervisory board, or employee) except were such communication is authorized. It goes without saying that the communication must be authorized by the law and not by one of the parties to the communication or the company's constitution.

This raises the question of how one can determine whether the intra-company communication of insider information is authorized by law. There is no doubt that the answer to this question is crucial for the functioning of corporate governance, for the organization of a company, for the carrying on of its busi-

[8] See above, n. 6.

ness and, last but not least, for the performance of the company. Having regard to the wording of the EC Directive on insider dealing it is generally accepted that any communication of insider information must be considered as authorized if it is made in the normal exercise of the insider's employment, profession, or duties.[9] It is, today, also accepted that "normal" has to be broadly interpreted in order to allow the proper functioning of business institutions and must not be construed as "usual" or "required under the particular circumstances". A broad construction of "normal" is also justified by the fact that the insider information being communicated remains protected because the addressee himself becomes a primary insider upon the acquisition of the information.

Nevertheless, it cannot be denied that determining what may be regarded as a "normal" intra-company communication calls for a *normative* analysis considering, on the one hand, the policy behind insider trading regulation and, on the other hand, both the interests of the company and of the public in the effectiveness of corporate institutions. A *normative* analysis is also required in cases where duties to report imposed by (mandatory) provisions of company law are in conflict with the prohibition of unauthorized communications of insider information. However, this conflict may be resolved in favour of allowing such intra-firm communications if, again, one remembers that the information is protected because the addressee of the information himself becomes a primary insider.

2. Communications Within and Between the Management and Supervisory Bodies

When one applies the rules outlined above, communications of insider information, both within and between the management and supervisory bodies of a corporation, will generally be authorized. In light of the responsibilities of the members of the board of directors for the management of the company, the merits in applying this rule to communications between directors are clear. Similarly, by reason of the supervisory obligations of the supervisory board, the same applies to communications of insider information between the board of directors and members of the supervisory board.[10] There is no serious doubt that the members of the supervisory board must accept the acquisition of insider information as part of the information communicated to board members and

---

[9] See H.-D. Assmann and P. Cramer, in H.-D. Assmann and U.H. Schneider (eds.), *Wertpapierhandelsgesetz* (2nd edn. Cologne 1999) ß14 n 48. *Bundesrats-Drucksache* 793/93, of November 5, 1993, 47ff = *Bundesrats-Drucksache* 12/6679, of January 27, 1994, 47ff; Art. 3 lit a of Council Directive (EEC) 89/592 co-ordinating regulations on insider dealing [1989] O.J. L334, 31 (Insider Dealing Directive). For the development and the content of the Directive see K.J. Hopt, 'The European Insider Dealing Directive' in K.J. Hopt and E. Wymeersch (eds.), *European Insider Dealing* (London 1991) 129ff.

[10] For the reporting requirements of the board of directors to the supervisory board see s. 90 of the Stock Corporation Act.

cannot require the directors to filter out insider information. At the same time, the board of directors is not obliged to restrict communications of insider information to those necessary or even indispensable for the exercise of the obligations of the supervisory board. It goes without saying that communications between directors, between the board of directors and the supervisory board and between the members of the supervisory board must have some connection with the normal exercise of the employment and the duties of the parties to the communication if they are to qualify as authorized communications.

Having regard to the fact that under German law the supervisory board of listed companies is codetermined (e.g. under the Co-determination Act of 1976), suspicion naturally attaches to the situation where the board of directors report highly "sensitive" confidential information, if at all, exclusively to the representatives of shareholders. The question whether the board of directors is authorized to do this is a question of company law and not of insider trading law. However, to the knowledge of the author insider trading rules have at least not served to intensify the problem of selective communications between the board of directors and the members of the supervisory board. Rather, it is much more likely that the actual taking of decisions of the board of directors qualifying as insider information will be delayed as long as feasible, and that such decisions be disclosed to the public (Sec. 15 STA) and/or to the chairman of the supervisory board (Sec. 90 I s. 2nd SCA) prior to their communication to the members of the supervisory board. Finally it should be noted that while there is good reason to suspect that the adoption of insider trading regulation has to some extent had an impact on the flow of information between the board of directors and the supervisory board and, thus, on corporate governance, evidence on the issue is not yet available.

3. Communications Between the Board of Directors and the General Meeting

As a rule, the board of directors is not allowed to communicate insider information to the shareholders in a general meeting.[11] This rule is justified by the fact that the shareholders of a company have no greater right to receive insider information than the general public. It should also be noted that the communication of insider information to the general meeting may not be considered as a sufficiently broad disclosure (under Sec. 15 STA) to make the information publicly available.

Applying this rule a conflict may arise between the right to information of a shareholder in the general meeting (Sec. 131 I SCA) and the obligation of the

---

[11] See Assmann and Cramer, above, n. 9, §14, n. 49b; K.J. Hopt, 'Insider-Probleme' in H. Schimansky, H.J. Bunte, and H.J. Lwowski (eds.), *Bankrechts-Handbuch* (München 1997) §107 n. 39.

members of the board of directors not to impart insider information to the general meeting. Having regard to the directors' obligations to disclose timely non-public price-sensitive information (under Sec. 15 STA) this conflict should not arise in practice. However, by way of exception, such a conflict would arise if the board of directors fails to comply with its duty to disclose the insider information. Under German company law the issue, thus, is whether the board of directors can refuse to provide information under Sec. 131 III no. 5 SCA on the basis that the communication would render the management board criminally liable under the insider trading regulations. A number of doctrines have been proposed to resolve this conflict.[12] However, there is no prevailing opinion. The only issue which is not disputed is that the board of directors, if it is prepared to do so, may try to postpone the publication or communication of the information and exercise its obligation of timely disclosure before the information is provided to the shareholders in general meeting. This is not the place to discuss a peculiarity of German company law in detail and it must suffice to express the author's opinion that such a breach of the directors' duty should not entitle either an individual shareholder or the shareholders represented in the general meeting to acquire insider information prior to the insider information being disclosed to the public.

4. Communications Between the Board of Directors and Individual Shareholders (Including the Members of an Advisory Board and of "Family Pools")

In general, the policy of insider trading regulation to provide equal access to insider information prohibits privileged communications of insider information to individual shareholders, e.g. large block-shareholders, or particular groups of shareholders, e.g. shareholders represented in an advisory board. Although both the EC Insider Dealing Directive (art. 2 no. 1) and the STA (Sec. 13 I no. 2) take into account that a person may acquire insider information by virtue of his holding in the capital of the issuer this should not be construed as authorizing any communication of insider information from the board of directors to an individual shareholder merely by virtue of his holding in the capital of the company. While this seems to be broadly accepted, the exceptions to this general rule are controversial.

If there is any rule attached to the exemptions proposed in the literature it may be found in the principle of "institutional exemptions". This principle may be construed as authorizing exemptions from the general prohibition against the communication of insider information to individual shareholders if the communication is required for the proper functioning of either well established legal institutions (such as the proper functioning of stock companies) or transactions

---

[12] For details and further references see Assmann and Cramer, above, n. 9, §14, n. 50.

in the companies' shares through mergers or acquisitions. For example, communications of insider information to a shareholder are broadly considered to be authorized if the seller of a block of shares is required by the other party to the transaction to disclose all available information, including non-public information, provided that the transfer of information is in the interests of the company and the insider information is protected both by law and a penalty fixed by a contract with the addressee(s) of the information.[13]

However, it will come as no surprise that the general acceptance of "institutional exemptions" has not provided a definitive solution to the problem of identifying authorized communications to individual shareholders. Rather, the controversy has shifted to the discussion of the scope of "institutional exemptions". Today, one of the main areas of discussion is whether the board of directors is authorized to communicate insider information to the members of a pool of "family shareholders".[14] While communications to a non-mandatory advisory board are generally considered as unauthorized there is a widespread view that family enterprises would be prejudiced vis-à-vis large business corporations through insider dealing regulation if their boards of directors were to be barred by the insider trading rules from imparting insider information to the members of the family pool.[15] Assumed the information is—indeed—helpful or even necessary to arrive at a consensus between the family shareholders and, thus, its communication is in the interests of the company, would this be sufficient to set aside the right of other shareholders and of the public to equal access to insider information? The answer to this question depends on one's willingness to accept and protect institutions such as "family owned corporations". Thus, German lawyers seem to be increasingly inclined to give a positive answer to the question and not further curtail the few incentives for family owned enterprises in "going public",[16] although this is not the prevailing opinion.[17] In any case, insider information imparted to family pools would still be subject to the prohibitions imposed on primary insiders (Sec. 14 I STA; Art. 2 no. 1 and Art. 3 EC Insider Dealing Directive).

[13] See Assmann and Cramer, above, n. 9, §14, n. 88b with further references.

[14] For further references see Assmann and Cramer, above, n. 9, §14, n. 54b; K.J. Hopt, 'Familien- und Aktienpools unter dem Wertpapierhandelsgesetz' [1997] *Zeitschrift für Unternehmens- und Gesellschaftsrecht* 1ff.

[15] K.J. Hopt, 'Insider Regulation and Timely Disclosure' [1996] 21 *Forum International* 1, 9.

[16] K.J. Hopt, 'Grundsatz- und Praxisprobleme nach dem Wertpapierhandelsgesetz' [1995] 159 *Zeitschrift für Unternehmens- und Gesellschaftsrecht* 135, 146.

[17] See Assmann and Cramer, above, n. 9, §14, n. 54b.

5. Communications Between Connected Enterprises

The situation, however, may be different if an individual shareholder or the pool of "family shareholders" qualifies as a "controlling enterprise" under the German law of groups of companies (Sec. 15ff. SCA).[18] As this seems to be a German peculiarity the study will only comment briefly on the issue. Nevertheless, it seems to be worthwhile to draw attention to the impact of insider trading regulation upon the law of groups of companies in order to show that there is a clear trend in legal reasoning towards accepting institutional arrangements protected and regulated by company law rather than redefining them under the auspices of insider trading rules.

Although connected enterprises are legally separate entities (Sec. 15 SCA), communications of insider information both between controlling enterprises and dependent enterprises and between dependent enterprises, are generally considered as intra-firm communications. Thus, they are authorized if they are made in the normal course of communications required to enable the enterprises to meet their corporate responsibilities, their legal duties and/or their contractual obligations vis-à-vis each other and third parties.[19] The policy of this doctrine is that insider-trading rules should not be applied to usurp the regulatory function of the law of groups of companies. As a corollary, communications between the board of directors of the issuer and the pool of "family shareholders" should be considered as generally authorized if the family-pool qualifies as a dominant enterprise.

6. Communications Between Employees

Applying the same rule, communications of insider information between employees (including communications between directors and officers in their capacity as employees and other employees of the company) will also be considered as authorized if they are made within the normal course of the parties' employment, profession, or duties. As has been outlined previously, even communications of insider information that are not "necessary" or "indispensable" to the exercise of

---

[18] Section 15 STA reads: "Connected enterprises are legally separate enterprises which, in relation to each other, are majority owned and majority owning enterprises . . . dependent and controlling enterprises (ß17), members of a group of enterprises . . ., enterprises with cross shareholdings . . ., or parties to an enterprise agreement. . .". Section 17 I STA defines dependent and controlling enterprises as follows: "Dependant enterprises are legally separate enterprises over which another enterprise ("controlling enterprise") is able to exercise, directly or indirectly, a controlling influence".

[19] H.-D. Assmann in M. Lutter, E. Scheffler and U.H. Schneider (eds.), *Handbuch der Konzernfinanzierung* (Cologne 1998) n. 12.25, 12.27ff; Assmann and Cramer, above, n. 9, §14, n. 54d; Bundesaufsichtsamt für den Wertpapierhandel/Deutsche Börse, *Insiderhandelsverbot und Ad-hoc-Publizität nach dem Wertpapierhandelsgesetz* 2nd edn. (1998) 21.

an employee's employment or duty will be authorized. The purpose of this generally accepted broad interpretation of what should be considered as within the normal course of intra-firm communications is not to place undue demands on the organs, officers, and employees managing a company's business.

If and to what extent the insider trading rules require that the directors and officers of a company are subjected to organizational duties necessary to ensure that communications of insider information do not take place outside normal channels is yet another question and will be addressed later in this study.

III. Information Flow Across the Company's Borders

Setting aside mandatory reporting requirements, company law is rather liberal in regulating communications across the company's borders. Even under the German Stock Company Act, which consists to a large extent of mandatory rules, there are only a few regulations dealing indirectly with the issue. For example, under Sec. 93 I s. 2, 116 SCA, the members of the board of directors and members of the supervisory board must not disclose confidential information and trade secrets of the company. In theory at least, insider trading regulation and the duty of timely disclosure place new demands upon the organs and employees in managing communications across the company's borders. However, in practice the burdens imposed on cross-border communications prove to be rather moderate. Again, the rule that any communication of insider information must be considered as authorized if it is made in the normal exercise of the insider's and the addressee's employment, profession, or duties applies. The application of the rule in the case of cross-border communications is justified by the fact that the person to whom the insider information is imparted will himself become a primary insider and be subject to the insider trading prohibitions, thus largely protecting the insider information. Nevertheless, the requirement to restrict cross-border communications to what is legally considered as "normal" imposes a higher duty of care on the organs and the employees of the company. Moreover, timely disclosure requirements add to the burdens imposed on the internal regulation of cross border communications.

Obviously, the insider trading rules and duty of timely disclosure, by virtue of the restrictions which they have imposed upon traditional forms and methods of communications within the company and across its borders, have "caused considerable upheaval amongst the German business".[20] The "upheaval" may only to a small extent be attributed to the formal complications imposed on the disclosure of non-public price-sensitive information. Rather, the upheaval is a result of the effective ban imposed by the insider trading rules and the duty of timely disclosure, inter alia, on cross-border communications. It is reported that

---

[20] Hopt, above, n. 15, 10.

even today directors often fail to timely disclose insider information prior to the issue of press releases or briefings of financial analysts, and thus insider information is imparted to these persons in a non-authorized way. While the prohibition on communicating insider information to individual representatives of the public prior to their disclosure may be easily respected by imposing an obligation to keep the information secret, a conflict may nevertheless arise if the management is under a duty to disclose all facts available to it, e.g. when it has to file reports or issue prospectuses. In the normal course of business timely disclosure should be an appropriate means of handling the problem. However, the managers of companies, e.g. companies operating in the banking business, having obtained insider information without being legally authorized to disclose it in a timely manner, face greater difficulties in escaping the conflict. As a rule it is accepted today that the management may comply with these conflicting duties by refraining from reporting the insider information and by also making sure that the report is not untrue in the light of the insider information.[21]

Without doubt, communications to authorities such as the Federal Supervisory Offices or the Federal Cartel Office are authorized under the insider trading rules, even if the communication of the information is not required by law. The same can be said of communications to consultants of the firm or to individual members of the company's organs such as lawyers, accountants, and other persons performing professional services. However, to keep the number of insiders as low as possible, communication of insider information to professionals must only be considered as authorized if it can be reasonably expected that the information is relevant to the services being performed.

The ways in which cross-border communications by a company may take place are too numerous to go in to by way of a case-by-case analysis of communications authorized under the insider trading rules. Thus, it must instead suffice to conclude that on the one hand the application of insider trading rules has been sufficiently broad not to impose impediments to the ordinary exercise of business. However, on the other hand, under the insider trading regulations and as a result of the uncertainties surrounding the interpretation of the insider trading rules, communications across a company's borders have become an issue of law and, thus, more complicated.

IV. The Impact of Insider Trading Regulation on Directors' Duties

1. Duties to Refrain From Insider Trading

Today, it seems generally accepted that directors and other corporate fiduciaries owe a fiduciary duty to the company not to take advantage of insider

---

[21] See, Assmann and Cramer, above, n. 9, §14, n. 65 with further references.

information by acquiring or disposing of insider securities for their own account, for the account of a third party, or on behalf of a third party.[22] Moreover, as directors owe duties of due care to their company it should not be a matter for dispute that directors are also required to refrain from insider trading for the account of the company. Insider trading rules are, thus, adding to the growing number of statutes and regulations which, in general terms, define such duties of care.

While this may be easily accepted as a rule, its impact on the management of a company's business is rather extensive. Again, a few examples must suffice to illustrate its consequences. There are a number of complications arising from insider trading rules in relation to the adoption and the exercise of stock options schemes as incentives for management.[23] As a precautionary measure, both to avoid opportunities being given to the management whereby they may take advantage of insider information and to avoid the management being placed under suspicion of insider trading, such stock options provide for a waiting period to be observed by the management prior to the exercise of an option. While the stipulation of waiting periods started as "good practice" under the German insider trading rules it may, today, be considered as a mandatory requirement of German company law.

Unquestionably, transactions in the company's own securities are not generally exempted from insider trading rules or from the requirement of timely disclosure.[24] Thus, insider trading rules and the requirement of timely disclosure add to the directors' duties under company law (as they must be observed when repurchasing or reselling the company's own shares, making stock repurchase plans, for example) a far less flexible instrument of corporate finance than previously. Although the extent of the impact of insider trading rules on transactions in a company's own securities is still under dispute, it seems to be accepted in principle that the adoption of any plan to engage in transactions in the company's own shares may be considered as insider information, provided knowledge of such plan would be likely to have a significant effect on the price of the issuer's securities if it were made public.[25] The same may be said of

---

[22] Hopt, above, n. 15, 20. For the U.K. see P. Davies, *Gower's Principles of Modern Company Law* (London 1997) 444ff.

[23] For German law see Assmann and Cramer, above, n. 9, §14, n. 88bff with further references; J. Fürhoff, 'Insiderrechtliche Behandlung von Aktienoptionsprogrammen und Management Buy-Outs' [1997] *Die Aktiengesellschaft* 83; Bundesaufsichtsamt für den Wertpapierhandel, Schreiben of October 1, 1997: *Insiderrechtliche Behandlung von Aktienoptionsprogrammen für Führungskräfte.*

[24] E. Wymeersch, 'The Insider Trading Prohibition in the EC Member States: A Comparative Overview' in K.J. Hopt and E. Wymeersch (eds.), *European Insider Dealing* (London 1991) 65ff, 80ff.

[25] Assmann and Cramer, above, n. 9, §14, n. 27b; F.A. Schäfer, in F.A. Schäfer (ed.), *Wertpapierhandelsgesetz, Börsengesetz, Verkaufsprospektgesetz* (Stuttgart 1999) §14, n. 69; Wymeersch, above, n. 24, 80.

changes in and modifications of existing repurchase or reselling plans the details of which have previously been made public.

It is worth mentioning that prohibitions imposed on the directors' and officers' management of the company's business by insider rules may be considered as duties (of care) owed by the management to the company irrespective of whether or not one considers the prohibition on insider trading to be applicable to the company as a legal person in its own right. In most cases the observation that states refrain from imposing the insider trading prohibitions on legal persons must be attributed to the fact that they have framed the prohibition on insider trading in a criminal context and, at the same time, adhere to the principle that legal persons cannot be held criminally liable.[26] A related issue is the appropriate concept of liability under corporate law to sanction the management's breach of the duties imposed by the insider trading prohibition.[27]

2. Organizational Duties

While it seems that under the Anglo-American system of company law, directors' organizational duties are to a great extent incorporated within the directors' general duty of care, specific organizational duties have developed under the European tradition of company law. Although the organizational duties of directors have numerous forms and rationales under the company laws of the various Member States of the EU it is a fairly common feature that directors are required to organize the company in a way which guarantees compliance with legal obligations imposed upon the company, the company's management and the company's employees. Moreover, it is a common feature of both the Anglo-American and the European legal systems of company law that directors can be held liable for negligence for not supervising officers, inter alia, to ensure that they comply with their duties under company law and other statutes and regulations. At least in relation to European company law and insider trading regulation it may, thus, be concluded that directors owe a duty of care to organize and supervise the management of the company's business in a way which will prevent insider trading.

To comply with these organizational duties, companies acting as credit institutions have established "compliance divisions". This is, however, not strictly required under company law and insider trading regulation. Rather, the means by which the directors ensure that the company's officers and employees comply with the insider trading regulations are left to the directors' discretion, provided that they fulfil this purpose.

[26] For details see Wymeersch, above, n. 24, 76ff.

[27] For a detailed discussion under US company law see R.C. Clark, *Corporate Law* (Boston 1986) §8.2 and §8.5.

It is a peculiarity of German law that directors are held liable under the law of infractions (*Gesetzber Ordnungswidrigkeiten*) for breach of duty to supervise officers and employees who have failed to comply with obligations which are imposed on the company and which are punished criminally or with a fine (§130 Gesetz über Ordnungswidrigkeiten). However, this statute would only apply if the company as a legal person were subject to the insider trading prohibition. The answer to this question, as has already been noted, is a matter of German law.[28]

To conclude, there seems to be a broad consensus that the insider trading rules have had the result of placing directors under organizational duties of care whereby they are required to implement and monitor procedures for the prevention of insider trading by the company's management and employees. Hence, it may already be too late to raise the question, whether the gains achieved by requiring the directors of an issuer to help prevent insider trading are worth the costs of the organizational inflexibility which result from the directors' duty to introduce suitable internal measures capable of counteracting infringements of the insider trading prohibition. The alternative would be to restrict liability to the insider and leave preventative measures to the insider trading rules and the sanctions laid down in the law. It is, however, conceded that this alternative would be more attractive if the detection of insider trading was easier than it actually is.

V. Shareholders as Fiduciaries?

Under art. 2 no. 1, and art. 3 of the European Directive on Insider Dealing (and also under Sec. 13 I no. 2, 15 STA) any shareholder who by virtue of his holding in the capital of the issuer possesses insider information is prohibited from taking advantage of that information, from disclosing it to any third party (unless such disclosure is authorized), and from recommending a third party, on the basis of that information, to acquire or dispose of insider securities. While persons who acquire insider information on account of their shareholding in the company are, thus, treated as primary insiders, it must also be considered whether or not these shareholders also owe a fiduciary duty to the company and to the company's other shareholders to refrain from insider trading in the shares of the issuer.

Although there seems to be a clear trend towards generally accepting that shareholders do owe fiduciary duties, such duties are, however, restricted to shareholders holding a significant block of shares or exercising influence on the company's business. Thus it may be argued that shareholders that occupy a privileged status of this nature within the company are also under a duty to refrain

---

[28] See Assmann and Cramer, above, n. 9, §13 n. 4a.

from insider trading and from exploiting information that belongs to the company and the general public. However, small shareholders should not be treated differently if they have acquired the insider information "by virtue of their holding in the capital" of the company. In both cases the insider information has been acquired on a privileged basis and no distinction can therefore be drawn between large and small shareholders.[29]

VI. Corporate Governance

Initially, it is difficult to imagine how insider-trading rules can have an impact on corporate governance. The consequences of insider trading rules on corporate governance become, however, more obvious if insider trading regulation and the duty of timely disclosure as a preventive measure of insider trading are taken together. In this way, at least three effects of these regulations on corporate governance should be taken into consideration.

First, and with particular regard to the duty of timely disclosure, it is likely that decision-making by the board of directors concerning issues in relation to which the requirement of timely disclosure arises will be delayed until the latest possible date in order to keep the issues secret for as long as feasible. However, even if this hypothesis were correct, the impact of staggered decision-making on the management of a company's business is likely to be negligible. Delayed decision-making would, if anything, only increase the danger of trading taking place based on knowledge of non-public information, which information, even if not timely disclosed, will still be considered as insider information provided it would have a significant effect on the price of the insider securities if it were publicly known.

Secondly, at the time the insider trading rules and duty of timely disclosure were adopted in Germany it was also suggested that these regulations would have the effect of restricting, or at least delaying, communications to the supervisory board. However, this fear has, to date, not been confirmed.

Moreover, it was argued that the insider trading rules and duty of timely disclosure would require directors to disclose decisions of the board of directors prior to their communication to, and their discussion by, the members of the supervisory board, thus exerting pressure on the members of the supervisory board to approve the decisions taken by the board of directors. While there is an obvious danger that the free decision-making of the members of the supervisory board is seriously prejudiced if the board is put in the position of having to approve decisions of the board of directors already made public, the conflict between company law rules on the one hand and insider trading rules and timely disclosure rules on the other hand can be avoided by the proper interpretation

---

[29] Also Hopt, above, n. 15, 21.

and application of the latter. It is now generally accepted that, both under European law and German insider trading rules, decisions taken by the board of directors must be considered as insider information although they have yet to be approved by the supervisory board, provided that the public would consider the knowledge of the decision of the board of directors as price-sensitive information.[30] However, it is also accepted that the duty of timely disclosure does not require decisions taken by the board of directors to be made public prior to the decisions being approved by the supervisory board.[31] Thus, while the decision of the board of directors is protected as insider information, the free decision-making of the supervisory board is preserved.

Thirdly, the mandatory rules imposed by insider trading regulation and the duty of timely disclosure obviously have the effect of reducing the board of directors' flexibility in organizing the company and in managing the company's affairs. However, the loss of flexibility is outweighed by gains from both the improvement in the external controls on the management and the improved confidence of the shareholders and the public in having equal access to price-sensitive information. It is the task of the legislator now to maximize these gains by making the interplay between company law—providing for internal control mechanisms—and insider trading rules and timely disclosure rules—providing for external control mechanisms—more efficient.

While there seems to be a lack of internal control mechanisms under the U.S. legal system of company law and securities regulation, the European legal system of company law and securities regulation as developed in a series of pertinent EC directives is clearly biased in favouring internal control mechanisms with their basis in mandatory company law. However, it is obvious that the impact of insider trading rules and the duty of timely disclosure on company law is an issue that concerns the European and primarily the German legal system of company law rather than of the U.S. legal system. This is due to the fact that securities regulation is a more recent field of legislation in the EU which has from its inception (i.e. the Treaty of Rome of 1958) been preoccupied with perfecting the law governing stock companies as a system of mandatory rules.

D. Conclusion

In 1993, when the German Securities Trading Act was drafted, *inter alia*, to transpose the European Insider Trading Directive into national law, the Ministry of Justice invited a number of academics (selected by Marcus Lutter)

---

[30] See, e.g. H.-D. Assmann, in H.-D. Assmann and U.H. Schneider (eds.), *Wertpapierhandelsgesetz* 2nd edn. (Cologne 1999) §13 n. 36a with further references.

[31] See, e.g. Assmann, above, n. 30, §13 n. 36a; S. Kümpel, in Assmann and U.H. Schneider (eds.), *Wertpapierhandelsgesetz* 2nd edn. (Cologne 1999) §15 n. 48ff, 50a. Hopt, above, n. 15, 13.

to discuss the possible impacts of insider trading regulation and the duty of timely disclosure on the Stock Corporation Act, the result of the meeting was to propose a number of drafting changes which were only technical in nature. As a member of the group, it was my impression then that this was in fact all we were asked to consider. That is to say, the Ministry was not interested in the impact of insider trading and timely disclosure rules on corporate organization, the conduct of companies in the markets, on corporate governance, and on the capital markets as an instrument of corporate control. In actual fact, nobody was, at the time, in a position to foresee such impact and propose changes that would have required a radical restructuring of the system of company and capital market law. Leaving aside the fact that the discussion group had been in the dark about the topics to be discussed when it entered the discussion room, the author is hesitant to state that, were the same discussions to take place today, we would be in a better position to initiate changes in the system of corporate and capital market regulation. Although this study has highlighted some clear impacts of the insider trading rules and duty of timely disclosure on companies and corporate law, it is clear that in resolving these issues we are "path dependent", i.e. we are bound to respect traditional methods of law reform and work within the existing framework of company law. Moreover, in Europe competition between different legal regimes has now been replaced by the central decision making of the Commission as a monopolist and an addressee of lobbyism and the Member States have lost their autonomy in adopting new systems of regulation.

Thus in Europe the impacts of the insider trading rules and the duty of timely disclosure on company law are almost exclusively dealt with in a rather narrow national context by attempting to interpret conflicting rules of company law and capital market law in a way which avoids or resolves such conflicts. In addition, much of the impact of insider trading regulation and the duty of timely disclosure has not been on company law as such but on corporate conduct, corporate organization, and corporate governance, thus complementing company law rather than leading to conflicts with company law. Although it goes without saying that the development of company law through capital market regulation such as insider trading rules and timely disclosure requirements has led to tacit changes of each Member State's model of company law regulation there is, at least in Europe, no clear concept of which way the development should be directed. To conclude, in Europe the impact of insider trading rules and the requirement of timely disclosure on company law has been and will continue to be dealt with on a piecemeal basis rather than by introducing fundamental changes in either company law or capital market law. However, to the extent that the relationship between company law and insider trading regulation is concerned, it is safe to say that this will not be different in other legal regimes of the world.

An Institutional Innovation to Reduce the Agency Costs of Public Corporate Bonds: Changing the Role of the Trustee

YAKOV AMIHUD, KENNETH GARBADE, AND MARCEL KAHAN[1]

Abstract

This chapter proposes an innovation in the design of publicly registered corporate bonds: an entity, which we call a *supertrustee*, will be responsible for active monitoring of the borrower and for renegotiation and enforcement of the bond contract. In this, the supertrustee will have the responsibility and authority of a solitary private lender, such as a bank. The goal is to facilitate relatively inexpensive and non-opportunistic renegotiation and enforcement of bond covenants, thus enabling public debt to have more and tighter covenants that better control the behaviour of the firm without requiring that the firm sacrifice strategic flexibility. The result will be a reduction in the agency costs of public debt, in the same way that those costs are reduced in private lending, without impairing liquidity or diversifiability.

Contents

A. Executive Summary

Debt financing gives rise to conflicts of interest between creditors and stock-holders that are better controlled with private loans than publicly traded bonds.

[1] The authors would like to thank Bill Allen, Lucian Bebchuk, Bernie Black, John Coates, Tamar Frankel, Alon Harel, Louis Kaplow, Ehud Kamar, David Norris, Eric Otts, Ed Rock, George Triantis, Philipp V. Randow, and the participants at the Harvard Law School Law and Economics Workshop, the University of Pennsylvania Law School Law and Economics Workshop, and the Columbia Law School Conference on Alternative Corporate Governance for their helpful comments. We would also like to thank the Filomen D'Agostino and Max E. Greenberg Research Fund for their financial assistance. The views expressed are those of the authors and do not necessarily reflect the position of the Federal Reserve Bank of New York or the Federal Reserve System.

However, public debt has greater liquidity and diversifiability. We propose an institutional innovation—a "supertrustee"—that incorporates the desirable characteristics of private debt into public debt. In particular, the supertrustee will be responsible for active monitoring of the borrower and for renegotiation and enforcement of the bond contract.

Corporate managers, acting on behalf of shareholders, sometimes have incentives to undertake initiatives that would reduce the value of a firm's bonds. Creditors protect themselves with loan covenants that restrict the actions of the firm or that specify minimum operating characteristics whose breach triggers acceleration of a loan's maturity. However, covenants may prevent the firm from undertaking value-increasing projects, or the firm may inadvertently breach a covenant and trigger financial distress. The joint interests of creditors and shareholders may be better served with numerous, tight covenants that can be *waived or renegotiated* as the occasion demands.

Encumbering public bond indentures with many and tight covenants, with the intention of renegotiating them should the need arise at a later date, has two problems: renegotiation is costly when bondholdings are fluid and bondholders are dispersed (covenant changes require a time-consuming and expensive vote by the bondholders and individual bondholders have little incentive to acquire information and to negotiate with the issuer) and a firm may be apprehensive of bondholders acting opportunistically. For example, bondholders may demand compensation for agreeing to an amendment that far exceeds the uncompensated cost of the amendment. For these reasons, public corporate bonds typically have few and loose covenants.

Agency costs of debt are controlled more effectively with bank and privately placed loans, where ownership is neither fluid nor dispersed and where lenders negotiate non-opportunistically in order to promote a reputation that will enhance the flow of new business. (Bondholders do not care about their reputations because issuers cannot control the identity of their public creditors). On the other hand, private loans are inferior to public bonds in their liquidity and diversifiability.

We propose that a publicly registered corporate bond provide for a "supertrustee" to act on behalf of bondholders. The supertrustee will be charged with responsibility to monitor compliance with covenants and will be given exclusive authority to negotiate amendments and to decide what action to take in the event of a breach. By ameliorating the problems associated with the dispersion and fluidity of ownership, our proposal will allow public bonds to more closely resemble private loans, with more and tighter covenants, active monitoring and relatively inexpensive renegotiation. This will more effectively control agency costs while allowing an issuer to undertake projects that enhance the aggregate value of the firm. At the same time, because it is publicly traded, the debt will retain the benefits of liquidity and diversifiability.

The supertrustee is intended to emulate the behaviour of a solitary private creditor in monitoring compliance, in renegotiating covenants, and in deciding what action to take following breach. This behaviour can be elicited with incentives regarding liability, compensation, and appointment power.

The liability regime for the supertrustee should take account of the benefits to bondholders that flow from the supertrustee's reputation for non-opportunistic behaviour, i.e., enhancing the confidence of the issuer that tight covenants will not be enforced opportunistically. We recommend that the supertrustee's decisions be evaluated under a standard analogous to the "business judgment rule." This will allow the supertrustee the latitude needed to take account of the effect of its decisions on its own reputation.

The compensation of a supertrustee should be greater for bonds issued by companies with more complicated operating characteristics and for bonds with more complex covenants and bearing more credit risk, for which more intense monitoring is appropriate and more renegotiation is likely. Given the latitude in decision making available to the supertrustee, its compensation may also include incentives similar to executive stock options.

The supertrustee will be appointed initially by the borrower—thereby emulating the situation in the private credit markets where a borrower chooses its creditors. This will increase the sensitivity of the supertrustee to the cost of acquiring a reputation for opportunistic behaviour. The bond indenture may further provide for the bondholders to elect a replacement supertrustee—just as stockholders choose a board of directors. This will enhance the responsiveness of the supertrustee to creditor concerns.

We believe the proposed structure will be more desirable for debt issued by firms with greater inherent credit risk and in more volatile industries with significant intangible assets. The scheme will be more attractive for larger issues and for issuers with more public indebtedness because most of the costs of a supertrustee do not vary with the size of an issue or the number of issues. The scheme will also be more attractive for longer term bonds because there are temporal economies of scale in monitoring a company through time and because covenant protection and the ability to renegotiate covenants are both more valuable on longer term debt.

B. Introduction

Debt financing by a corporation gives rise to conflicts of interest between creditors and stockholders.[2] This costly conflict is better controlled in private loans extended by banks and institutional lenders than in publicly traded bonds.

---

[2] M.C. Jensen and W.H. Meckling, 'Theory of the Firm: Managerial Behaviour, Agency Costs and Ownership Structure' [1976] *Journal of Financial Economics* 305–360.

However, public debt has advantages not shared by private debt: greater liquidity and diversifiability. In this chapter, we propose an institutional innovation—a "supertrustee"—that incorporates the desirable characteristics of private debt into public debt.

Section C describes the nature of the agency costs of debt and how those costs are addressed in private loan agreements and public bond indentures. Section D presents our proposal, section E describes the duties of the supertrustee, and section F proposes incentives and rules to regulate its behaviour. In section G we discuss the companies that may choose to adopt this institutional innovation. Concluding comments are offered in section H.

C. The Agency Costs of Debt and Differences Between Private and Public Debt

Corporate directors and executive officers, acting in the best interests of shareholders and to maximize stock prices, sometimes undertake initiatives that reduce the value of a firm's bonds and even the aggregate value of the firm.[3] For example, the firm may choose a high-variance project that transfers wealth from bondholders to stockholders even if it has a negative net present value.[4]

Creditors protect themselves against the prospect of wealth transfers to stockholders with a variety of devices. Most prominently, limiting the maturity of a loan enables creditors to renegotiate the terms of the loan in light of the evolving characteristics of the firm.[5] However, short maturities may be unattractive to creditors who need to fund long dated liabilities and to companies financing the purchase of long-lived capital assets. Also, long-term debt saves the issuance costs of frequent rollover financing.

Creditor interests can also be protected with loan covenants that restrict the actions of the firm or that specify minimum operating characteristics whose breach triggers acceleration of a loan's maturity.[6] However, covenants are

[3] *Journal of Financial Economics* 305–360, s. 4.

[4] See also the leveraged re-capitalizations and special dividend payments of Colt Industries (*Wall Street Journal*, July 21, 1986 and July 24, 1986) and Quantum Chemical (*Wall Street Journal*, December 29, 1988) and the spin off of Marriott International by Marriott Corporation as originally proposed in 1992 (*Wall Street Journal*, October 6, 1992 and October 7, 1992 and R. Parrino, 'Spin-offs and Wealth Transfers: The Marriott Case' [1997] *Journal of Financial Economics* 241–274).

[5] M. Carey, S. Prowse, J. Rea, and G. Udell, 'The Economics of Private Placements: A New Look,' [1993] *Financial Markets, Institutions & Instruments* 40–41 and 45.

[6] C. Smith and J. Warner, 'On Financial Contracting' [1979] *Journal of Financial Economics* 129, 134 and 137. See also A. Kalay, 'Stockholder-Bondholder Conflict and Dividend Constraints' [1982] *Journal of Financial Economics* 211–233; R. Landau, *Corporate Trust Administration and Management* 4th edn. (New York 1992) 126–147; M. Kahan and B. Tuckman, 'Private versus Public Lending: Evidence from Covenants,' in J. Finnerty and M. Fridson (eds.), *The Yearbook of Fixed Income Investing* (Chicago 1993) and G. Triantis and R. Daniels, 'The Role of Debt in Interactive

costly.[7] They may prevent the firm from undertaking value-increasing projects, or the firm may inadvertently breach a covenant (such as a specified financial ratio), thereby triggering acceleration of maturity and provoking costly financial distress.[8] More generally, tight restrictive covenants and stringent minimum operating characteristics do not eliminate agency costs associated with debt financing. In many cases the joint interests of the firm's creditors and shareholders can be best served with numerous, tight covenants that can be *waived or renegotiated* as the occasion demands.[9] Thus, for example, high-risk investment opportunities that would benefit the firm as a whole do not have to be bypassed if managers can negotiate compensatory payments to creditors. Similarly, the firm can avoid costly bankruptcy if creditors can temporarily waive breaches of minimum operating characteristics.[10]

But encumbering public debt contracts with many and tight covenants, with the intention of renegotiating them should the need arise, has two problems. First, renegotiation of public bond covenants is costly when bondholdings are fluid and bondholders are dispersed.[11] Changes in covenants require a vote by the bondholders, which is time-consuming and expensive to administer. Moreover, individual bondholders have little incentive to acquire information and to negotiate with the issuer over the terms of a covenant waiver or amendment. Outside of unusual circumstances, there is also no committee or agent to represent bondholders in negotiations with the issuer. Given these costs and difficulties, renegotiation of the terms of publicly traded debt is largely infeasible as a practical matter.

Secondly, a borrowing firm may be apprehensive of bondholders acting opportunistically should it request a covenant amendment. For example, if interest rates have increased substantially since the bonds were issued, bondholders may refuse to waive a breach of a minimum operating characteristic in order to force redemption of the bonds at par—thus provoking costly distress. Or, bondholders may demand compensation for agreeing to a covenant

---

Corporate Governance' [1995] California Law Review 1073–1113. Typical covenants include constraints on dividend payments and the assumption of additional indebtedness, requirements for minimum liquidity and interest coverage ratios, and (more rarely) explicit constraints on asset sales, cash acquisitions and restructuring.

[7] See above, n. 2.

[8] See also Smith and Warner, above, n. 6, 129, 134 and 137.

[9] On the process and consequences of changes in bond indentures, see Kahan and Tuckman, above, n. 6. See also Carey, Prowse, Rea, and Udell, above, n. 5, 36 and 42, and Smith and Warner, above, n. 6.

[10] The creditors' right to decline to renew the waiver provides protection against acts that would transfer wealth from creditors to stockholders.

[11] See Carey et al., above, n. 5, 39 and 44; Landau, n. 6 above, 139 and Kahan and Tuckman, see above, n. 6.

amendment that far exceeds the uncompensated cost of the amendment.[12] The fluidity of ownership of public bonds accounts for the possibility of such opportunistic behaviour: bondholders do not care about their reputations because issuers cannot control the identity of their public creditors, so creditor reputation has no effect on future transactions.[13]

For the foregoing reasons, public corporate bonds typically have few and loose covenants.[14] Because public bondholders have limited protection against corporate initiatives that would transfer wealth to shareholders, they demand higher yields to compensate for prospective losses in value. The limited reduction of the agency costs of debt thus translates directly into a higher cost of credit and reduction in the scale and value of the firm's investments.

Agency costs of debt are controlled more effectively in bank debt and privately placed loans, where ownership is neither fluid nor dispersed. Single lender bank loans have more and tighter covenants than publicly traded bonds precisely because their provisions can be renegotiated and waived relatively easily, and because the borrower faces a counterparty who is informed about the affairs of the company and the industry in which it operates.[15] Lending banks negotiate in a non-opportunistic way because borrowers control whom they borrow from, so a bank has an incentive to develop a reputation that will enhance the flow of new business.[16]

Monitoring by lenders also reduces the agency costs of debt.[17] Banks actively monitor borrowing firms for compliance with the terms of their loan contracts and for acts that might lead to harmful consequences, thus possibly pre-empting such acts. On-site examinations and meetings with management are not unusual.[18] Similar behaviour is observed in private lending by insurance companies.[19] In public debt, this ancillary monitoring is absent because of the free rider problem. As a result, a borrowing firm's actions can go unchecked for a period of time before any harmful outcome is observed and by then it may be too late to avoid the costly consequences. The absence of monitoring by holders of public debt thus gives a firm greater leeway to engage in actions that induce

[12] See, for example, the prolonged struggle of Burlington Northern to amend covenants on public bonds issued in 1896 (*Wall Street Journal*, May 20, 1987, *Rievman v. Burlington Northern*, 618 F. Supp. 592 (SDNY, 1985), 644 F. Supp. 168 (SDNY, 1986), 118 F.R.D. 29 (SDNY, 1987)).

[13] Carey et al., above, n. 5, 44.

[14] ibid.

[15] ibid., at 28–32, 36–38 and 43, Kahan and Tuckman, above, n. 6. Syndicated bank loans with many co-creditors provide for representation of creditor banks by a syndicate manager.

[16] Carey et al., see above, n. 5, 44. The situation is similar with private placements (E. Zinbarg, 'The Private Placement Loan Agreement' [1975] *Financial Analysts Journal* 33–52).

[17] See above, n. 2.

[18] A. Saunders, *Financial Institutions Management* (Chicago 1994) 55–56.

[19] See Carey et al., see above, n. 5; Kahan and Tuckman, see n. 6 above.

wealth transfers from bondholders. Creditors demand commensurately higher yields on their public bonds.[20]

The foregoing discussion pointed out the advantages of private debt relative to public bonds in reducing the agency costs of debt. But private loans are inferior to public bonds in their liquidity and diversifiability. In general, investors require higher yields on investments in less liquid assets.[21] The ability to convert public bonds into cash quickly and cheaply is a valuable characteristic that, *ceteris paribus*, creditors are willing to pay for in the form of higher bond prices and lower yields. Additionally, the relatively small unit size of public bond issues—typically $1,000 principal value—facilitates diversification of idiosyncratic, firm-specific, risk, thus enabling portfolio allocations with better risk-return characteristics even for small investors. This increases the potential investor base for the bonds and reduces the required yield.[22]

Borrowers choosing between public bonds and private loans face a trade-off.[23] Public bonds have superior liquidity and are more easily diversified, but have relatively few and weak covenants with limited control of the agency costs of debt. Private loans better control the agency costs of debt through tighter covenants, renegotiation, and closer monitoring, but are illiquid and their size limits diversification by small investors. At present, both choices—public debt with loose covenants and lack of monitoring and private loans with limited liquidity and diversifiability—impose some costs. Our proposal is intended to combine the better features of each of these two types of debt.

D. The Proposal

This chapter proposes an institutional innovation in the structure of public bonds intended to emulate the advantages of private loans—active monitoring,

---

[20] However, Smith and Warner above, n. 6, 146) observe that bondholders can require that a firm be monitored by, for example, insurance companies.

[21] See K. Garbade, 'Analyzing the Structure of Treasury Yields: Duration, Coupon and Liquidity Effects' [1984] *Topics in Money and Securities Markets,* Bankers Trust Company, reprinted in K. Garbade, *Fixed Income Analytics* (Cambridge 1996); Y. Amihud and H. Mendelson, 'Asset Pricing and the Bid-Ask Spread' [1986] *Journal of Financial Economics* 223–249 and 'Liquidity, Maturity, and the Yield on U.S. Treasury Securities [1991] *Journal of Finance* 1411–1425; W. Silber, 'Discounts on Restricted Stock: The Impact of Illiquidity on Stock Prices' [1991] *Financial Analysts Journal* 60–64 and A. Kamara, 'Liquidity, Taxes, and Short-Term Treasury Yields' [1994] *Journal of Financial and Quantitative Analysis* 403–417.

[22] See R. Merton 'A Simple Model of Capital Market Equilibrium with Incomplete Information' [1987] *Journal of Finance* 483–510 and S. Mukherji, Y. Kim and M. Walker, 'The Effect of Stock Splits on the Ownership Structure of Firms' [1997] *Journal of Corporate Finance* 167–188.

[23] See Y. Amihud and H. Mendelson, 'Liquidity and Asset Prices: Financial Management Implications' [1988] *Financial Management* 5–15 on the trade-off between control and liquidity in publicly traded corporate claims.

tight covenants, and ease of re-contracting—while retaining the benefits of liquidity and ease of diversification.

We suggest that a publicly registered corporate bond provide for a "supertrustee" who will act on behalf of the dispersed and temporally changing bondholders. The supertrustee will be charged with responsibility to monitor the compliance of the borrower with the terms of the bond covenants and given exclusive authority to negotiate amendments to the covenants and to decide what action to take in the event of a breach of a covenant. By ameliorating the problems associated with the dispersion and fluidity of ownership of public debt, our proposal will allow the structure of public bond covenants to more closely resemble private loan agreements, with more and tighter covenants, active monitoring, and relatively inexpensive renegotiation. This will more effectively control the agency costs stemming from the conflict of interest between stockholders and bondholders while allowing an issuer to undertake projects that enhance the aggregate value of the firm. At the same time, because it is publicly traded, the debt will retain the benefits of liquidity and diversifiability.

The Trust Indenture Act of 1939 (hereafter, "the Act") presently requires appointment of a trustee for a publicly registered corporate bond.[24] However, the trustee contemplated by the Act has little responsibility to monitor compliance with bond covenants, no authority to renegotiate the terms of an indenture, and limited ability to choose what action to take following breach of a covenant.[25] The supertrustee that we propose would have substantially greater responsibilities and authority, including the authority to act independently of bondholders.

Our proposal is voluntary and market based. We do not propose to mandate the appointment of a supertrustee for all public bond issues but to allow appointment at the option of the issuer.[26] If the supertrustee is effective in reducing the agency costs of debt it will reduce the issuer's borrowing costs in two ways. First, tighter bond covenants and greater monitoring by the supertrustee will reduce the yield required by investors. Second, the ability to renegotiate the debt contract will reduce the likelihood that the firm will be forced to forgo value-increasing projects in the future.

---

[24] Smith and Warner, above, n. 6, 148–151) and Landau (see above n. 6) describe the duties and powers of a trustee. Section 304 of the Act specifies certain securities exempted from the provisions of the Act.

[25] Smith and Warner, above, n. 6, 150 (". . . while the trustee must act in good faith, his responsibilities often go no further unless there is a default.") and Landau, above, n. 6, 26, 69 (". . . duties of the trustee [prior to default] are largely administrative . . .") and 140 (". . . under the usual indenture [the trustee] has . . . no authority or right to give any . . . consent [to a change in the indenture] or waiver.").

[26] Similarly, the firm that issues the bond will specify, by contract, the rules under which the supertrustee operates, including its appointment and replacement and its compensation.

The costs of the supertrustee will be paid by the bond issuer in the same way that issuers pay rating agencies to rate their bonds. The firm issuing a bond will consider the costs and benefits of having a supertrustee appointed for the bond and will choose to have one appointed if the benefits exceed the costs. Importantly, a supertrustee perceived by investors as ineffective may suit the borrower but it will not bring about the expected reduction in the cost of borrowing and its benefits will not outweigh its costs.

E. Duties of the Supertrustee

The supertrustee is intended to emulate the behaviour of a solitary creditor on a private loan—such as a bank—in obtaining information about a borrower and assessing covenant compliance, in renegotiating the terms of the indenture and in deciding what action to take following breach of a covenant.

I. Monitoring

With respect to monitoring compliance with the bond indenture, the supertrustee will have access to non-public corporate documents, including financial statements and cash flow projections for subsidiaries and divisions. The supertrustee will also have access to the officers and directors of the firm and the firm's accountants—as well as communications between the firm and its accountants—if it requires additional information. On the basis of the information gathered, the supertrustee will be required to make an independent determination that the issuer is not in violation of any covenant.

The responsibility and authority of the supertrustee to monitor compliance differs sharply from the monitoring responsibilities of a conventional trustee.[27] The latter generally does not have access to non-public information and relies instead on public filings with the SEC, such as annual and quarterly reports.[28] More significantly, it does not have to assess compliance independently [29] but can rely on annual compliance certificates submitted by the company stating that it is not in violation of any covenants.[30]

[27] However, a conventional trustee does have substantial responsibility with respect to monitoring the release and substitution of property pledged as collateral for a mortgage bond (Landau, above, n. 6, 112–123).

[28] Landau, above, n. 6, 134 and Smith and Warner, above, n. 6, 143.

[29] Landau, above, n. 6, 70) observes that while ". . . it is usually provided that a trustee *may* [emphasis added] make independent investigations . . . of the performance by the obligor of its covenants . . . it is recommended that an express qualification be inserted [in the indenture] to the effect that the trustee is under no duty to do so".

[30] Compliance certificates are described by Smith and Warner, above, n. 6, 145–146. Compliance certificates for public bonds are conclusory. They merely state whether or not a covenant has been

II. Renegotiation

The supertrustee will be authorized to renegotiate the terms of a bond indenture independently of bondholder direction and without the need for approval by bondholders of its actions. This is a key element of our proposal because it eliminates the difficulty of the issuer negotiating indenture amendments with a fluid and dispersed group of creditors. We expect that lowering the cost of renegotiation of bond covenants will foster the inclusion of more and tighter covenants in public bond indentures, which will better control corporate behaviour and lower the agency costs presently associated with public debt.

We further anticipate that the supertrustee will be well informed about the nature of the issuer's business (as a result of its monitoring obligations) and able to identify the merits and dangers of any proposed change in the indenture. This is in sharp contrast to the present situation, where individual bondholders have little incentive, and the conventional trustee has no significant responsibility, to acquire information about the company and hence neither party is well prepared to negotiate covenant changes.

Some indenture amendments entail relaxing a restrictive covenant in return for the firm making a lump sum payment to creditors or raising the coupon rate on a bond. More extreme amendments involve extending the maturity of the bond, deferring interest payments, or forgiving part of the contractual payments (including interest rate reductions and forgiveness of principal repayments). Such amendments are not uncommon in private workouts of distressed debt and can be in the best interests of creditors if the alternative—forcing the firm to adhere to the original payment provisions—triggers a costly financial distress.[31]

Giving the supertrustee the power to approve changes in the core terms of a bond is not essential to our proposal and may be unacceptable to bondholders. Private loan agreements (which our proposal is intended to emulate) with multiple creditors provide that changes in core terms require the consent of every lender, whereas covenant changes require only the consent of a majority of lenders.[32] This suggests that creditors value the right to veto changes in core terms much more than they value the right to veto other covenant changes and that they would be reluctant to cede (to a supertrustee) power to approve changes in core terms. On the other hand, the cost of obtaining the consent of a

breached and do not provide any supporting information. A supertrustee, like a private creditor, would be authorized to request detailed calculations affirmatively demonstrating compliance with a covenant.

[31] S. Gilson, K. John and L. Lang, 'Troubled Debt Restructurings: An Empirical Study of Private Reorganization of Firms in Default' [1990] *Journal of Financial Economics* 315–353. See also C. Baldwin and S. Mason, 'The Resolution of Claims in Financial Distress: The Case of Massey Ferguson' [1983] *Journal of Finance* 505–516.

[32] M. Roe, 'The Voting Prohibition in Bond Workouts' [1987] Yale Law Journal 274.

limited number of co-creditors on a private loan is much lower than the cost of obtaining such consent from many dispersed corporate bondholders. Giving the supertrustee the authority to renegotiate core terms may be more valuable for public bonds than for private loans. Section 316(b) of the Trust Indenture Act presently *requires* unanimous approval of bondholders to changes in a bond's core terms.[33] The most extensive implementation of our proposal would there-fore require legislative changes to this provision.

The discretion we propose for the supertrustee to renegotiate indenture pro-visions on behalf of bondholders may be considered far reaching. However, stockholders delegate comparable discretionary authority to the board of direc-tors and grant the board wide latitude in making decisions that materially affect shareholder wealth. In addition, indenture trustees under English law presently have some discretion in renegotiating bond covenants and making modifications to indentures that (in the opinion of the trustee) are not materially prejudicial to the interests of bondholders.[34] However, as a matter of practice, a trustee under U.K. law does not typically exercise its power to make substantial permanent covenant changes or agree to changes in covenants in return for changes in the core terms of a bond. Our proposal goes beyond the discretion presently prac-ticed by English trustees. Additionally, a U.K. trustee does not have the signifi-cant monitoring obligations that we propose and hence may be less well informed than a supertrustee about the nature of a borrower's business. Finally, under our proposal the supertrustee's discretion to renegotiate the terms of the bond indenture would be limited by the contract that determines what it can change without bondholder consent—and this can vary from one bond indenture to another.

III. Enforcement

Upon breach of a covenant, the supertrustee will have the power to decide whether to waive the breach for a specified period of time, or to amend the indenture to relax the covenant or to accelerate the maturity of the bond. In the absence of a payment default it can exercise this power independently of bond-holders and even contrary to their express preferences.

The enforcement power of a supertrustee is substantially greater than the enforcement power of a conventional trustee. While the latter has authority to accelerate the maturity of a bond following a defined Event of Default, it shares that power with bondholders, who can independently declare a bond immedi-ately due and payable as well as reverse the decision of the trustee to accelerate

---

[33] ibid.

[34] We thank Phillip Randow, University of Osnabrueck and David Norris, Law Debenture Corporation plc, for information about U.K. practice.

maturity. A conventional trustee ordinarily has no authority to waive a breach of a covenant or to amend the indenture to relax a covenant.[35] In addition, holders of a majority of outstanding bonds can direct a conventional trustee to take actions that they specify.[36]

F. Incentive Structure of a Supertrusteeship

We remarked earlier that the supertrustee is intended to emulate the behaviour of a solitary private creditor in monitoring covenant compliance, in renegotiating the terms of the indenture and in deciding what action to take following breach of a covenant. This behaviour can be elicited with a variety of incentives regarding liability, compensation, and the power to appoint and replace the supertrustee.

I. Liability

In negotiating changes in a loan agreement and in enforcing the agreement, a private creditor takes account of the effect of its actions on the value of the loan *and also* on its reputation for non-opportunistic behaviour.[37] The latter element is an important aspect of the creditor's ability to attract future business and also accounts for the willingness of the borrower to agree to tight covenants when the loan is originated: a borrower would be reluctant to agree to tight restrictions on its decision-making and stringent limits on its operating characteristics if it did not have confidence that those restrictions and limits can be relaxed when it is in the best interests of shareholders and not contrary to the interests of the creditor.[38]

The supertrustee will have substantial powers and must be held accountable for its actions. However, the liability regime for the supertrustee should take account of the benefits to bondholders which flow from the supertrustee's reputation for non-opportunistic behaviour, i.e., enhancing the confidence of the issuer that if it agrees to tight covenants it can expect that those covenants will not be enforced opportunistically if it subsequently seeks a waiver or amendment. More particularly, the liability regime should not require that the supertrustee always make a decision that extracts the maximum immediate value for bondholders. The regime should also recognize that the anticipated *ex post* behaviour of the supertrustee affects *ex ante* the borrower's willingness to accept restrictive bond covenants.

---

[35] Landau, above, n. 6, 140.

[36] ibid., 140, 207.

[37] Carey et al., above, n. 5, 42–44.

[38] ibid., 42.

We recommend that the supertrustee's decisions be evaluated under a standard analogous to the "business judgment rule" applicable to decisions by a board of directors, so that bondholders can not sue a supertrustee if its judgment is viewed as being merely wrong or substantively unreasonable.[39] This will allow the supertrustee the latitude needed to take account of the effect of its decisions on its own reputation.

The Trust Indenture Act of 1939 specifies a much stricter regime of trustee liability. Following a default, section 315(c) of the Act prescribes that the indenture trustee must "use the same degree of care and skill [in exercising its enforcement powers] as a prudent man would exercise or use under the circumstances in the conduct of his own affairs".[40] The prudent man rule would almost certainly preclude a supertrustee from taking into account the effect of its decisions on its own reputation and almost certainly requires that a trustee act in the exclusive best interests of bondholders in a narrow sense. When applied to a supertrustee, this may not be in the best *ex ante* interests of the borrower and lenders.[41]

Section 315(d) of the Act provides more generally that the indenture trustee may not be relieved from liability for its own negligent actions or its own negligent failure to act.[42] However, this provision is modified by section 315(a) and (b), which provide that, prior to default, the trustee must fulfil only those (relatively few) duties set forth in the indenture and that the trustee may rely on compliance certificates provided by the company. Our proposal envisions substantial pre-default duties for the supertrustee and would not allow the supertrustee to rely on corporate compliance certificates. Because our proposal contemplates greater duties than those commonly found in indentures qualified under the Act, section 315(d) might be inconsistent with a business judgment standard for the supertrustee.[43]

[39] They should, however, be able to bring a claim if the supertrustee acts in bad faith or in the presence of a disabling conflict of interest. The supertrustee's interest in acting non-opportunistically should not, for this purpose, constitute a disabling conflict of interest.

[40] It is common practice for a trustee under the Act to consult with, and seek guidance from, bondholders following default, thereby avoiding any significant liability under the prudent man rule (Landau, above, n. 6, 207–208).

[41] Landau, above, n. 6, 53 observes that private placements (which are not subject to the provisions of the Act) that provide for a trustee usually do not impose a prudent man standard following default.

[42] ibid., 4, describes the reason for this prohibition on immunity provisions in a bond indenture.

[43] Exempting supertrustee bonds from the liability provisions of s. 315 does not necessarily require a legislative amendment to the Act. The Securities and Exchange Commission enjoys broad statutory authority to "exempt . . . any security or transaction . . . from any one or more provisions of [the Act], if and to the extent that such exemption is necessary or appropriate in the public interest and consistent with the protection of investors and the purposes fairly intended by" the Act.

II. Compensation

The compensation of a supertrustee should be commensurate with its duties and responsibilities. In broad terms, compensation should be greater for bonds with more complex covenants, for bonds issued by companies with more complicated and less transparent operating characteristics, and for bonds bearing more credit risk and for which more intense monitoring is appropriate and more renegotiation is likely to be needed.

Given the considerable latitude in decision making available to the supertrustee, its compensation may include incentives to encourage it to fulfil its duties effectively.[44] The incentives can be penalties for poor performance, bonuses for superior performance, or both. Such incentive compensation should be positively related to changes in bond values resulting from the supertrustee's actions but not to changes in value that stem from matters beyond the supertrustee's control, such as changes in the general level of interest rates. Thus compensation could be tied to changes in market values that result from variations in the bonds' credit risk. For example, the supertrustee could be compensated according to a schedule that simulates an option—similar to the stock options granted to corporate managers and directors—whose value varies inversely with the spread between the yield on the bonds and the yield on Treasury debt.[45]

III. Appointment and Replacement

The supertrustee can be appointed by bondholders—just as stockholders choose a board of directors—or by the borrower—thereby emulating the situation in the private credit markets where a borrower chooses its creditors. Because the borrower is the party that decides whether a public bond issue will have a supertrustee, it should also be the party that decides how the supertrustee will be appointed.

The choice between the two appointment schemes depends on whether, on balance, it is more desirable to enhance the incentive of the supertrustee to represent bondholder interests or whether it is more desirable to encourage non-

---

[44] However, bond-rating agencies perform their tasks without such incentive-based compensation. The economic interest of a rating agency in preserving its reputation suffices as an incentive for diligence.

[45] This scheme, however, imposes penalties and delivers bonuses for reasons that may be unrelated to the actions of the supertrustee, such as fluctuations in the business outlook for the industry in which the firm operates. A similar criticism can be directed at executive stock options.

opportunistic behaviour by the supertrustee.[46] Giving the borrower the power to appoint the supertrustee will increase the sensitivity of prospective supertrustees to the cost of acquiring a reputation for opportunistic behaviour in negotiating waivers and amendments to bond indentures.[47] This does not imply that a supertrustee selected by the borrower will be indifferent to creditor interests. Investors will not accept a lower rate of interest on a supertrustee bond if they do not have confidence that the supertrustee will act responsibly and the borrower will have no incentive to select such a supertrustee.

On the other hand, the responsiveness of the supertrustee to creditor concerns will be greater if bondholders have the power to elect a supertrustee after the bond has been issued. To reduce the borrower's anxiety that it may have to deal with an opportunistic supertrustee, the indenture might provide that if bondholders replace a supertrustee appointed by the borrower, they must elect the replacement from a list of candidates submitted by the borrower.

G. Who Might be a Supertrustee?

The supertrustee is a device to locate responsibility for monitoring, renegotiating, and enforcing a public bond indenture in a single entity. This enables borrowers and lenders to overcome the problems created by the dispersion and fluidity of public debt without sacrificing the liquidity and diversifiability of that debt. These benefits are not free, because the supertrustee will have to be compensated for the substantial responsibilities it undertakes. The supertrustee structure is economically efficient only if the added costs of a supertrustee are smaller than the benefits of (a) being able to issue debt at a lower rate of interest, and (b) avoiding inflexible constraints on future actions.

---

[46] Under either scheme, there should be an exception permitting prompt replacement of the supertrustee in cases where it grossly neglects to fulfil its duties, acts in bad faith, or becomes subject to a disabling conflict of interest. The replacement procedure should enable a material fraction of the bondholders (for example, 25%) to move to have a supertrustee replaced. As long as a greater percentage (perhaps a majority) of bondholders do not oppose replacement, the supertrustee should be removed upon a finding by a court or arbitrator that the supertrustee has acted in a proscribed manner.

[47] Protection of non-public information is another reason for the borrower's desire to control the identity of the supertrustee. A major task of the supertrustee will be to seek information from the borrower and monitor the borrower. In doing so, the supertrustee will have access to non-public information, as is the situation now with private lenders such as banks (A. Saunders, *Financial Institutions Management* (Chicago 1994) 55–56, E. Fama, 'What's Special About Banks' [1985] *Journal of Monetary Economics* 29–39 and C. James, 'Some Evidence on the Uniqueness of Bank Loans' [1987] *Journal of Financial Economics* 217–235). This activity is an important feature of financial intermediaries and a reason for their particular involvement in lending to information-problematic borrowers (see the discussion in Carey et al., above, n. 5, at 44), which can be emulated by the supertrustee.

We believe the supertrustee structure will be more desirable for debt issued by firms with greater inherent credit risk and less transparent operations and by firms in more volatile industries with significant intangible assets, such as entertainment and biotechnology.[48] In addition, because most of the costs of a supertrustee are fixed costs that do not vary with the size of an issue or the number of issues outstanding, the scheme will be relatively more attractive for larger bond issues and for issuers with more public indebtedness. The same supertrustee may be appointed to more than one bond issue of the same firm, and this would be economical because of economies of scale in the acquisition and use of information. Finally, the proposed scheme will be more attractive for longer-term bonds for two reasons. First, there are temporal economies of scale in monitoring a company through time because information acquired in past years reduces the cost of monitoring the company in future years. Secondly, covenant protection is relatively more valuable on longer-term debt, as is the ability to renegotiate restrictive covenants and stringent minimum operating characteristics.

H. Conclusions

This chapter has proposed an institutional innovation designed to lower the cost of credit obtained from issuing publicly traded bonds by reducing the agency costs of those bonds without impairing their liquidity or diversifiability. The proposal would focus responsibility for contract monitoring, renegotiation, and enforcement on a new entity, the supertrustee, and thereby seek to overcome the free rider problem associated with the dispersion of ownership of public debt. By emphasizing the economic significance of a supertrustee's reputation for responsible behaviour, the proposal would also reduce the incidence of opportunistic behaviour in contract renegotiation and enforcement associated with the fluidity of ownership of public debt.

Some readers may question the desirability of our proposal and wonder why, if it is so beneficial, somebody hasn't already tried it. We have two responses. First, every innovation has to start someplace. Secondly, it may be that the increasing emphasis on encouraging corporate directors and executive officers to act to maximize shareholder value has only recently tipped the balance of public debt contract design in favour of more elaborate devices to reduce the agency costs of that debt.

Other readers may question the feasibility of our proposal, arguing that it is complex and uncertain of outcome. Our response is that we are not proposing to mandate a new architecture of debt contracting but rather to expand the menu available to market participants. We would be surprised if the proposal were suitable for all but we do believe that some may find it appetizing.

---

[48] Carey et al., above, n. 5 characterize such firms as "information-problematic" borrowers.

26

The Impact of Insider Trading Rules on Company Law

ZOHAR GOSHEN[1]

Contents

A. Introduction
B. A Market View
C. A Company View

A. Introduction

It is my privilege to write a 'Discussion Report' to a thoughtful and illuminating paper with excellent analysis and presentation of the topic by Professor Heinz-Dieter Assmann. As I am no expert on German Law, however, I will limit myself to commenting on the overall project.

The analysis of *The impact of insider trading rules on company law* can take two different views. One form of analysis can take a *market view* in which the impact of insider trading rules on company law is examined through their influence on capital markets. A second approach can take a *company view* in which the impact of insider trading rules on company law is examined through their influence on the firm's governance structure and mode of operation. This is the view taken by Professor Assmann. These views, of course, do not exclude each other, as they reveal complementary aspects of the issue. However, to evaluate one of them it is important to present both views, as I will do next.

B. A Market View

One of the important goals of company law is to provide rules that will assist the parties involved in the firm's business to reduce "agency costs". Conflicts of interests create agency problems, and coping with them imposes agency costs (monitoring, bonding, and residual loss).[2] The main agency costs in the firm's business stem from three "agency problems", each of them resulting from conflicting interests. First, the agency problem between managers and shareholders,

---

[1] Professor of Law, The Hebrew University of Jerusalem. Visiting Professor of Law, Columbia Law School.

resulting from the separation of ownership and control (*the management problem*). Second, the agency problem between controlling shareholders and minority shareholders, resulting from the combination of *partial* ownership and control (*the control problem*). And third, the agency problem between creditors and shareholders, resulting, mainly, from the limited liability of shareholders (*the creditors problem*).

The severity of each agency problem depends on the economic and business structures in any given state. In a state where dispersed ownership is prevalent, such as the U.S., the management problem will be the major source of agency costs. In states where concentrated ownership is common, like in the EC, the control problem will dominate over the management problem as the source of agency costs. Although these two agency problems are different in nature, it is impossible to determine in the abstract which business structure leads to lower agency costs.

Given the *initial* difference in business structures, other factors will influence the overall agency costs. Among others: the quality of the judicial system in handling company law issues, the quality of the capital market, the quality of the market for corporate control, and the quality of institutional investors.[3] Thus, obviously, the challenge presented to company law in each state is different.

In states where capital markets are efficient, the market for corporate control is effective, and the judicial system is proficient, company law can be more elective in nature. It can rely on markets to exert pressure on the different players in the firm's business to avoid exploiting agency problems, and can leave more room for the parties to write their own contractual or institutional arrangements. On the other hand, in states where capital markets are inefficient, the market for corporate control is ineffective and the judicial system is not proficient, company law will have to cope with these realities. More mandatory arrangements will be included and clear rules will dominate over vague standards.[4]

Of course, accepting market realities and tailoring company law around them does not prevent a policy maker from trying to change and improve markets. It is here where the impact of insider trading rules can be seen. Restriction on insider trading is a crucial step necessary for the formation of an *efficient* and *liquid* capital market.[5]

---

[2] See, M.C. Jensen and W.J. Meckling, 'Theory of the Firm: Managerial Behavior, Agency Costs and Ownership Structure' (1976) 3 J. Fin. Econ. 305.

[3] Zohar Goshen, 'The Efficiency of Controlling Corporate Self-Dealing: Theory meets Reality', Cal. L. Rev. (forthcoming March 2003).

[4] See, e.g. B. Black and R. Kraakman, 'A Self Enforcing Model of Corporate Law' (1996) 109 Harv. L. Rev. 1911 (developing a "self-enforcing" model to drafting corporate law for emerging capitalist economies).

For markets to be efficient, information about the value of firms must be incorporated quickly and accurately into stock prices.[6] Calculating value, comparing it with market prices, and trading to capture the profits that can be gained from the deviations between price and value leads to incorporation of information into prices. This process involves two different tasks: *production of information*—searching for information that affects prices—and *pricing information*—analyzing information and trading based on discrepancies between price and value. Additionally, for markets to be liquid, there must exist sufficient trading to enable buyers and sellers to consummate transactions expeditiously. Liquidity is achieved on account of three principal reasons: portfolio adjustments, consumption/investment adjustments, and divergence of opinions.[7] These two roles of providing efficient pricing and liquidity can be performed either by "insiders"—who have access to inside information coupled with the knowledge and ability to evaluate information and to price it—or by "analysts" (i.e., a wide range of professional and institutional investors) who produce financial analytical work upon which they base their investment decisions.

However, "insiders" trading and "analysts" trading cannot coexist. The reason is the inability of analysts to receive normal return on their investment in information when insiders are trading. Investing in informed trading is a costly activity, and analysts who undertake such activity expect to achieve some extra return from their investment and trading to compensate for the additional cost of producing and analyzing information. But, when insider trading is permitted analysts are unable to capture deviations between price and value. Since insiders enjoy informational advantage, due to their proximity to the information, they will consistently beat the analysts. Unable to gain normal return on their investment in information, analysts will exit the market. Thus, permitting insider trading entrust the role of creating an efficient and liquid market in the hands of insiders. On the other hand, restricting (and effectively enforcing) insider trading will enable analysts to gain normal return on their investment in information, and thus will lead to the development of analysts' industry. Analysts working in a competitive information-market are better than insiders (who enjoy exclusivity over inside information) in providing an efficient and liquid capital market.[8]

One aspect of analysts' advantage over insiders has a direct effect on the company's performance. Reducing agency costs in the company setting requires,

---

[5] Zohar Goshen and Gideon Parchomovsky, 'On Insider Trading, Markets, and "Negative" Property Rights in Information' (2001) 87 Va. L. rev. 1229.

[6] For a comprehensive description of the processes by which markets attain efficiency, see, Ronald Gilson & Reiner Kraakman, 'The Mechanisms of Market Efficiency' (1984) 70 Va. L. Rev. 549.

[7] See, H.R. Stoll, 'Alternative Views of Market Making', in *Market Making and the Changing Structure of the Securities Industries*, 67, 68 (Amihud, Ho, & Schwartz, ed., Lex. Books, 1985).

[8] Goshen & Parchomovsky, above, n. 5.

among other things, monitoring agents. An inherent part of searching and pricing information is monitoring management performance. Insiders cannot perform this role effectively, due to the nature of the agency problem that they have to monitor (i.e., they have to monitor themselves). Analysts, on the other hand, will monitor the management, evaluate the performance of the company, and impound this information into the market price. Unlike individual shareholders, analysts are experts and enjoy economies of scale and scope in monitoring management. Moreover, analysts are repeat players vis-à-vis companies and their managers. These qualities allow analysts to effectively reduce agency costs.

Analysts have, as well, other indirect influence on the company. Efficient pricing leads to increased ownership of institutional investors and a more effective capital market. Institutional investors are more equipped and willing to use their voice within the firm, thereby further improving the quality and effectiveness of monitoring management.[9] A more remote effect of an efficient capital market is creating an appropriate climate for a greater degree of dispersed ownership. Dispersed ownership is the basis for the development of an effective market for corporate control. Again, institutional investors and a market for corporate control will further lead to a reduction in agency costs.

As agency costs are getting lower, company law can be more elective and greater reliance could be entrusted on market players. From this view restricting insider trading leads to the development of analysts' industry, which in turn leads to an efficient capital market. An efficient capital market reduces agency costs and changes the nature of the required company law. The market view, thus, points to the chain reaction that ties between insider trading rules and company law through markets.

C. A Company View

The rules restricting insider trading have a direct effect on the company's operation. As clearly explained and presented by Professor Assmann, the information flow within the company and outside of the company is affected. The degree of the effect is a direct function of the scope of the restrictions. The wider the scope of the restrictions, the greater the influence on the firm's governance structure and mode of operation.

Indeed, there is a tradeoff between the encumbrances on the firm's functioning and the gains from the restriction on insider trading. Finding the optimal tradeoff brings up the question: What should be the appropriate scope of the insider trading restrictions? The answer to this question is crucial for either

---

[9] See, Bernard S. Black, 'Agents Watching Agents: The Promise of Institutional Investors Voice' (1992) 39 UCLA L. Rev. 811.

determining the scope of the restrictions (interpretation of the law) or evaluating the efficiency of the restrictions. To answer this question, however, one should have a view regarding the goal served by the insider trading rules. This is the part that could supplement Professor Assmann's chapter.

There are several rationales[10] that could serve as the basis for the insider dealing restrictions: preventing unfair trading conditions; preventing misappropriation of company's property; protecting the mandatory disclosure requirements, and, as offered above, creating an analysts' market. Different rationales entail different scope for the insider trading restrictions, and a different measure for implementation ("an access theory", "fiduciary duties toward the source of information", and "fiduciary duties toward the investors in the market").

It is not clear to me what is the rationale adopted by the German law. But the questions are there: Is it legal to tip an analyst about a massive fraud performed within the firm?[11] Is "selective disclosure" legal?[12] Is "warehousing" legal?[13] Should an analyst's report, prepared of public information, be disclosed to the public as well? Therefore, it is important to clarify the rationale that the German Law is purporting to promote via the prohibition on insider trading. Determining the goal of the restriction on insider trading will allow determining whether and to what degree it is justified to encumber the information flow within the firm and out of it.

---

[10] See Jonathan R. Macey, *Insider Trading: Economics, Politics, and Policy* 7 (1991).

[11] *Dirks v. SEC* 463 U.S. 646, 654 (1983).

[12] Donald C. Langevoort, 'Investment Analysts and the Law of Insider Trading' (1990) 76 Va. L. Rev. 1023, 1034–36.

[13] *U.S. v. O'Hagen,* 117 S.Ct. 2199 (1997).

Part VIII:

Groups of Companies

27

Do We Need a Law on Groups of Companies?

EDDY WYMEERSCH

Abstract

Groups of companies is a subject that attracts wide attention, especially in Continental Europe, much less in the U.K. and the U.S. Groups, in essence, raise issues of conflicts of interest. Therefore the rules on conflicts have to be analysed: in most European states, these are dealt with in terms of prohibitions, procedures, and structures. More rarely general standards, such as "fiduciary duties" are used. Regulation often strives at eliminating the group conflicts by allowing or mandating exit for minority shareholders. These techniques are efficient in listed subsidiaries. Group law will remain important for taking care of other interests, especially creditors, or for unlisted subsidiaries.

Contents

Tables

A. Introduction

The fascination of Europeans, especially German lawyers, for the subject of groups of companies is often puzzling to North American academics. The reasons cannot be found in the prevalence of the group phenomenon in Europe: American companies are obviously not founding fewer subsidiaries than European ones, nor is the law less developed[1].

[1] See the voluminous collection by P. Blumberg: *The Law of Corporate Groups: Procedural Problems in the Law of Parent and Subsidiary Corporations* (Cambridge 1983); *The Law of Corporate Groups: Problems in the Bankruptcy or Reorganization of Parent and Subsidiary Corporations, Including the Law of Corporate Guaranties* (Cambridge 1985); *The Law of Corporate Groups: Tort, Contract, and other Common Law Problems in the Substantive Law of Parent and Subsidiary Corporations* (Cambridge 1987); *The Law of Corporate Groups: Problems of Parent and Subsidiary Corporations Under Statutory Law of General Application* (Cambridge 1989); *The Law of Corporate Groups : Problems of Parent and Subsidiary Corporations Under Statutory Law Specifically Applying Enterprise Principles* (Cambridge 1992).

One of the differences between the two systems is probably the prevalence of listed subsidiaries in Europe. Most English and to a lesser extent most American companies do not have controlling shareholders, although some may have important shareholders. But more significantly, in European companies, there are not only significant shareholders, but more important controlling shareholders, i.e. parent companies running the listed subsidiary as part of the group.

Empirical research undertaken at the Ghent University has indicated that in most of the continental European securities markets, companies are dominated by one or few shareholders, holding large blocks, often more than 50% of the shares. Most of the time these shareholders are other companies. We have not been able, for lack of workable criteria, to distinguish which companies are part of a larger group, or which are simply dominated by a single shareholder, the holding company in which the dominant partner has lodged his participation. In the larger companies, the former hypothesis would apply, while in smaller one, a single, dominating partner would be the usual scheme. Often these are "family owned" companies.

The following table[2] gives an insight in the structure of ownership in some of the European markets. It should be mentioned that at least in some states, this structure has changed in the last three to four years, due to the ongoing restructuring of industry in Europe. The figures are based on the analysis of the mandatory disclosure of significant holdings, disclosure that has been imposed pursuant to a 1988 European directive.[3]

The central issue underpinning the entire subject of corporate groups is that of conflicts of interest, in the broad sense. If the company itself, which is often described as a "nexus of contracts", inherently creates tension between divergent interests,[4] this is especially the case if the overall firm is organized over

---

[2] Source: C. Van der Elst, *Aandeelhouderschap van beursgenoteerde vennootschappen, Economisch-juridische analyse in België en in Europa* (Kluwer 2001). The tables indicate the number of controlled companies as a percentage of total number of listed companies, or of companies that have been analysed. All companies listed on the main market are included, except for the U.K. and the U.S.

[3] Council Directive (EEC) 88/627 on the information to be published when a major holding in a listed company is acquired or disposed of [1988] O.J. L 348/62.

[4] See F. Easterbrook and D. Fischel, *The Economic Structure of Corporate Law* (Cambridge 1991) 1–39; M.A. Eisenberg, "The Conception that the Corporation is a Nexus of Contracts, and the Dual Nature of the Firm" [1999] *Delaware Journal of Corporation Law*, 819,with references; R.C. Clark, "Agency Costs Versus Fiduciary Duties" in J. Pratt and R. Zeckhauser (eds.), *The Structure of Business* (Boston 1985) 55–69, also printed in L. Solomon, D. Schwartz, and J. Bauman, *Corporations. Law and Policy, Materials and Problems*, (2nd edn. St Paul 1988) 333ff; V. Brudney, "Corporate Governance, Agency Costs and the Rhetoric of Contract"[1985] Columbia Law Review 1403, especially 1409–10 and 1421–25; S. Cheung, "The Contractual Nature of the Firm" [1983] *Journal of Law, Economics and Organization* 6. This idea was already developed, although in different terms, by the Dutch Company law professor J.M.M. Maeijer, in the inaugaural address in 1964 *Het belangenconflict in de naamloze venootschap* (The Hague 1964). See also his renewed analysis of the matter: Maeijer, *25 jaar belangenconflict in de NV* (Tjeenk Willink-Zwolle 1989).

Table 1: Voting Concentration in Europe and the U.S.—Stake of the Largest Shareholder

	Belgium	Italy	France	Germany	Spain	Netherlands	U.K.	U.S.
	1999	1999	1999	1999	1999	1998	1994	1996
>50%	62.10%	62.0%	57.5%	48.5%	27.3%	19.5%	4.7%	10.3%
25% to 50%	25.70%	17.9%	21.9%	26.6%	28.9%	22.6%	16.3%	20.7%
10% to 25%	6.40%	14.5%	13.1%	17.7%	33.1%	34.0%	55.2%	39.1%
<10%	5.70%	5.6%	7.5%	7.2%	10.7%	23.9%	23.8%	29.9%
total no. companies	140	234	160	542	242	159	1,333	6,559

several legal entities each of which, being a separate legal entity, has its proper interest.

The frequency and intensity with which these conflicts may arise greatly intensify the agency and other problems that are encountered in the paradigm of the firm. The legal order shows a great distrust of these phenomena, evidenced by a considerable number of important court cases.[5] Therefore also, the securities markets put a negative evaluation on their shares often leading to a significant discount over the value of the underlying assets.

B. A Typology of Group Companies

Before further analysing the complex nature of these conflicting relationships, it seems useful to put down a typology of group companies. This typology will be useful as the conflict of interest shows up in substantially different terms and degrees, according to the intensity of the parent's domination, and according to the fields in which the conflict is likely to arise. Therefore the legal issues involved—and consequently the remedies found in the legal systems—will be function of said differences.

Group relations exist in a wide variety of forms.

---

[5] There have been some reporters on cases on groups of companies: See F.J.P. Van Den Ingh and L. Timmerman, *Jurisprudentie Concernrecht* (1993); cases in Belgian law are made available at the website of the Financial Law Institute (www.law.rug.ac.be/fli/) under the heading of Forum Europaeum. For Swiss law: Druey, J.N. and Vogel, A., *Das schweizerische Konzernrecht in der Praxis der Gerichte*, (Zürich, 1999).

I. The 100% Subsidiary

In the case of the 100% subsidiary, the interest of the parent and of the subsidiary are largely parallel, conflicting interests showing up only with regard to the position of the creditors. As long as their rights are recognized, the parent can freely decide what the subsidiary should do. In a European context, one could say that as long as the capital remains unimpaircd,[6] there is no compelling reason why the parent's influence should be restricted.

II. The Subsidiary With Minority Shareholders

Subsidiaries with minority shareholders create an additional set of issues in the conflicts nexus: whether these shareholders will have to be protected may depend on the conditions on which they agreed to join the company. In the absence of specific contractual conditions, the legal system may offer protection against the majority abusing its position, e.g. by offering withdrawal rights to the minority. In most legal systems, some form of protection of this type exists, whether the company is part of a group or not.[7]

III. Publicly Listed Companies

An additional layer of interests is added if the company has attracted public investors: by publicly calling on external financiers, the company has increased its exposure to investor protection issues. In this case, the matter transcends the level of private interests and becomes a subject of public policy, namely to safeguard reliability of the public securities markets and avoid the financial system becoming destabilized.[8] Once the shares are publicly traded the fiduciary duties of directors are intensified proportionately to the public confidence on which the

---

[6] The second company law directive contains the rule according to which impairment of the capital should lead to reorganisation measures: see art. 17, Second Council Directive (EEC) 77/91 on coordination of safeguards which, for the protection of the interests of members and others, are required by Member States of companies within the meaning of the second paragraph of Article 58 of the Treaty, in respect of the formation of public limited liability companies and the maintenance and alteration of their capital, with a view to making such safeguards equivalent [1976] O.J. L 026/1.

[7] See further art. 635ff Belgian Company Code. Similar provisions exist in Dutch and French law.

[8] This was the express rationale in the case holding that at least some part of the take-over regulation in Belgium is mandatory, as belonging to the rules of "public interest" (or "*ordre public*"), therefore leading to nullity of contracts violating the provision. See Cass (b) March 15, 1994 [1994–1995] *Arresten van het Hof van Cassatie* no. 114; [1994] *Revue Banque*, 258, with a comment by A. Bruyneel; [1995] *Tijdschrift voor Belgisch Handelsrecht* 15, comment by F. Glansdorff; [1995] *Tijdschrift voor Rechtspersoon en Vennootschap* 176, comment by H. Laga (*Wagons Lits*).

securities markets are founded. Market supervisors like to refer to the directors' duties "towards the markets".

Even in publicly listed companies, it frequently happens that one or several important shareholders exercise a significant, sometimes controlling influence. However, these shareholders should not all be treated as one and the same. A fundamental difference relates to the "private benefits" these shareholders can extract out of the company. Depending on the individual situation, there can be great differences.

If, as often happens after an initial public offering, the former owner remains an important shareholder, there is some likelihood that he will try to extract some private benefits from the company. However, the range of benefits and their amount remain limited: there may be some excess remuneration, or some management fees, an above market rent for the shareholder's real estate may have been stipulated, family members may be employed. But all in all, the over-all impact of these benefits probably will remain within reasonable limits.

IV. Holding Companies

If the parent company is heading a conglomerate, the situation is already more complex. Group management will usually underline the advantages of the "synergies" deriving from the functioning of the different group members. Although the business activities of the subsidiaries may be very different, the group will be managed more or less on an integrated basis. Transactions between group members will be frequent, and at conditions that have not been tested in the market. Group preferences will result, leading to cross subsidization of group entities. Transactions without apparent justification will allow funds legally to flow to the parent, or to other group entities: sweetheart deals, excessive rents, but also management fees are frequently found, or at least feared. Minority shareholders in the parent will experience difficulties obtaining a precise picture of the group's financial situation: consolidated financial statements will contribute to better understanding, but do not necessarily reflect the whole picture, e.g. due to the heterogeneity of the group. The precise flows of transactions between group companies remain hidden as a consequence of consolidation. Minority share-holders in the parent company fear that their grip on management of the group will slip away as they will have no direct access to the subsidiaries' assets.[9] Also, minority shareholders in other group entities fear that profits will be shifted away to other group companies, especially if the parent is holding a higher percentage in the latter. The phenomenon has been ably described by Rafael La

---

[9] This idea sustains some significant cases, in Germany (BGH, February 25, 1982, BGHZ, 83,122– *Holzmüller*) and in almost identical terms, in France (Cass (fr), January 24, 1995, [1995] *Revue des Sociétés* 46, comment by Jeantin; [1995] *Bulletin Joly Bourse* 321).

Porta, c.s., as "Tunnelling".[10] Distrust will be showing up: investors will shy away from the group, by reducing their investment in the subsidiaries and as a consequence by under-pricing the shares. This discount on the value of shares of listed subsidiaries as compared to the value of their underlying assets can easily be observed in the markets.

The following table gives a sample of the discounts that are characteristically found for shares of some Belgian holding companies. The "estimated value" usually refers to the management's valuation. Similar discounts can be found in other states.

Table 2: Sample of Discounts for Shares in Some Belgian Holding Companies

Company	Stock Price	Estimated value	Discount	Date
NPM	100	181.95	45.0%	9-3-00
Cobepa	53.8	93.9	42.7%	10-3-00
Gevaert	61.85	66.77	7.4%	31-12-98
GBL	228	501.07	54.5%	10-3-00
Gimv.	78.46	85.71	8.5%	29-2-00
Electrafina	119.7	179.68	33.4%	17-9-99
Ibel	60.73	84.54	28.2%	31-12-98
Mosane	117.7	166.46	29.3%	31-12-98
Sofina	46.6	57.48	18.9%	31-12-98
Solvac			25%	31-3-99

V. Parent and Subsidiary are Engaged in the Same Line of Business

A further layer of entanglement within the group occurs when parent and subsidiary are engaged in the same line of business. Here the parent competes with the subsidiary: as its interests in the listed subsidiary are only partial, the parent will normally give preference to its own interest, or to the interests of its other subsidiaries, which are fully owned or in which the parent holds a higher percentage. Apart form the traditional transactions mentioned in the previous case, the potential conflicts are numerous: business propositions may be diverted from the subsidiary; research initiatives and researchers transferred to other group entities, know how or even production facilities transferred, etc. In these cases the subject can be identified in terms of "corporate opportunities". In addition,

---

[10] See further the study by R. La Porta, also published in [2001] *American Economic Review* May 90/2, 22–27.

the parent may also impose "negative opportunities", forbidding the subsidiary to enter certain markets, e.g. in the case of a territorial subdivision of the product markets, or of certain fields of development, e.g. by centralizing research at the parent's level.

In each and any of these situations the fundamental legal issue is that of a conflict of interest between the parent and its subsidiary, and their respective outside investors. Depending on the financial condition of the group members, there may also be conflicts with the interest of the creditors of the single group members, and of the employees as well, especially if the employees are sharing in the subsidiary's profits, or are holding stock options in the subsidiary company.

VI. Companies With a State Interest

An additional dimension in this complex network of conflicting interests occurs when—mostly at the parent's level, but possibly also at the subsidiary's level—the state or one of its entities intervene, as is sometimes the case in Europe. The state's interest being situated at the macro level, additional conflicting interests may be at stake, opposing the company's interest to the general interest, or to the political interest. Examples are numerous: apart from direct political intervention, one could mention directives given by the state based on its employment policies, on tax considerations, on national prestige, and so on. Answers to this question have been diverse: some states have publicly declared that they would abstain from any intervention in the company's management,[11] others have preferred to divest their interest, privatizing for other, especially budgetary reasons. Divestiture as such has often led to better returns.

The problems are more acute if both parent and subsidiary are publicly held. The following developments will mainly deal with listed companies. However, they also occur in closely held groups, where minority shareholders are involved at the subsidiary level. These shareholders are supposed to have been able to fend for themselves upon entering the company: theoretically the law should not provide for any special protection. In practice this is often a meagre consolation: minority stakes arise not only at formation of the company, but often are the result of mergers that were approved without the minority's consent, or shares may have been inherited. Or the business may have changed causing the former family to be outwitted by a more powerful group. Should there be, in the general interest, a specific form of minority protection in closely held companies? The topic of minority protection in closely held groups is almost a separate one.[12]

---

[11] This was, e.g. expressly mentioned in the public offering prospectus of BP shares, in the days when the U.K. government held a significant block of shares in BP.

[12] See the rules on squeeze-out and on withdrawal as found in the Netherlands (art. 335ff NBW) and in Belgian company Acts (art. 636ff), see further below.

When the state, directly or indirectly, owns a significant part of the shares, and even more when it owns a majority, the sets of conflicting issues become even more acute. The state as a shareholder seldom is interested in the return on its investment. Usually it cannot fall back on a large reserve of trained business managers. Structurally, the interests of the state are opposed to those of the firm: instead of profit maximization, the state aims at reducing the company's profits, and hence it negatively affects its—internal and external—financing means. The state acts as a tax collector, as a price regulator, as a safeguard for diverse public policies, in many jurisdictions including employment policies: in these and many other cases the general interest will prevail over the investors' objective of profit maximization. If the shares are traded on the markets, they can be expected to present a significant discount, which normally will be deeper than the discount observed for listed subsidiaries of commercial firms.

In some cases, the state declares that it will in no way intervene in the firm's management: these firms have since been successfully privatized. See our paper on Shareholders' rights in cases of related parties transactions, in First South-East Europe Corporate Governance Roundtable at www.oecd.org./pdf./M. 00018000/M00018919.pdf (20–21 September 2001).

C. Conflicts of Interest

All legal systems in Europe have been struggling with conflict of interest issues. Most legislators have only dealt with the simple case of conflict arising when a transaction intervenes with one of the members of the board. More complicated are conflicts with dominant shareholders, whether between majority and minority shareholders, or—as is more frequently found in Europe—between a dominant group of companies and a subsidiary, listed or with minority shareholders. The specific case in which the state acts as a dominant shareholder has rarely been addressed.

I. The Fiduciary Rule

In general, one could distinguish two main approaches: the first deals with conflicts by enacting a general principle, especially a fiduciary rule. This is rarely found in the legislation; it may be underpinning certain decisions in case law. This approach has several advantages: by stating a vague principle, it aims at creative ambiguity. Parties feel insecure about their behaviour and try to find out where the limits of their liability may be situated. Being risk averse, they will normally tend to be overcautious and will set the criteria at a higher level than would have been adopted for an explicit rule. However, the efficiency of this approach hinges on the presence of sufficiently effective enforcement, both in terms of bringing the cases to light and having them judged by the courts. A sufficiently strong, motivated, and trained judiciary is one of the prerequisites of regulating conflicts of interest by way of general principle.

Examples of this first approach can be found in U.K. case law dealing— although obviously more cautiously than its American counterpart—with conflict issues on the basis of the general principle of the duty of loyalty, according to which company directors owe loyalty to the company and should act in its interest, the latter to be distinguished from the interest of the shareholders.[13] Scandinavian statutes[14] contain the provision that company directors should not act against the company's interest. As mentioned further, Belgian law might offer an opening in the same direction, while on the other hand case law has denied the existence of a general principle dealing with conflicts of interest in general.[15] In the other European states, there is the somewhat more vague principle based on the general criterion of "good faith". The case law has not developed a general concept similar to the "duty of loyalty".

Apart from legal systems adhering to a general principle of a fiduciary nature, there might be systems adopting other general rules with the same pre-emptive effect. German case law has developed an important body of precedents dealing with the so-called "de facto" groups in the context of GmbH groups, where the court has on the one hand stated a refined principle of group law, while on the other giving increasingly specific guidance on the parties' conduct when dealing with groups relations within the GmbH context. It should be mentioned that this body of law has developed outside the framework of the statutory rules on groups of companies, which only address AG groups.

One can only guess why the continental legal systems have not developed a generally formulated fiduciary duty in the public companies,[16] leading directors to be held to an overall duty of loyalty. Several explanations may be tried: some

[13] P. Davies, *Gower's Principles of Modern Company law* 6th edn. (London 1997) 599–600.

[14] But obviously also in the Scandinavian systems: see for the Swedish Companies Act, Ch. 8, §13, where it is stated that "the board or other representative of the company may not enter into legal transactions . . . which are likely to give an undue advantage to a shareholder or a third party to the detriment of the company or other shareholders". Compare the similar rule in s 58 of the Danish Companies Act, compare s. 63; also Ch. 8, s. 10 of the Finnish Companies Act

[15] See Court of Appeals of Brussels, 19 January 2001(*Tractebel*) [2001] 2 *Revue de Droit Commercial Belge* 108; [2001] 11 *Droit bancaire et financier* 121, with comment by D. Willermain.

[16] Notwithstanding legal writing where the existence of a duty of loyalty is often mentioned, more clearly between members of the company than as an obligation of the directors: see, e.g. D. Schmidt, *Les conflits d'intérêts dans la société anonyme* (Paris 1999) no. 16 and 66; compare in Belgium: also Ph Ernst, *Belangenconflicten in naamloze vennootschappen* (Antwerp 1997) and A. François, *Het vennootschapsbelang* (Antwerp 1999). It should, however, be noted that German case law recognizes the existence of a fiduciary duty (*Truepflicht*) in the *GmbH* and other companies based on personal relationships between shareholders, leading to a duty of loyalty: this duty of loyalty is held to govern the relationship of the members towards the company, and of the members among themselves.

jurisdictions state that directors owe no duties to the shareholders, but only to the company, as a legal entity.[17] However, in U.K. law too, the duty of loyalty is owed to the company, not to the shareholders individually.[18] The availability of explicit legal rules, such as outright prohibitions, or formal legal procedures, probably have played a role: once the rule or the procedure has been complied with, minorities would not have been able to challenge the transaction. The argument was expressly mentioned in a recent Brussels case.[19] Also once the formalities have been complied with, there will be less soul searching for the other directors, even if the transaction itself had not been in the best interest of the company.[20] These procedures are widely found in the Latin European states.[21] Under French law, and formerly also under Belgian law,[22] directors cannot be held liable provided the procedure has been accurately followed. However, the French procedure provides for an authorization by the general meeting of shareholders of any contract with conflicting interests.[23] No similar approval is provided for in Belgian, in Italian, or Spanish law.

In general, one could state that on the European continent, until recently, there was less sensitivity to issues of personal conflict of interest. This impression may be linked to the predominance of controlling, especially family holdings in many listed companies. Also, the existence of a closely knit social network linking most directors of large companies may have contributed to an implicit code of conduct preventing parties from entering into a transaction with personal interest, as different from group interests. As to the latter both case law and legal writing has shown a keen interest, not only in Germany but all over the continent.[24] A further explanation may be found in the fact that disloyal activities may be dealt with in other ways.

In at least some of the continental jurisdictions, disloyal conduct of directors essentially would fall under criminal provisions, which at least in some jurisdictions, are frequently invoked and effectively enforced. This is especially the case in France, with the rules on *"abus de biens sociaux"*, now also

---

[17] In this sense Schmidt, above, n. 16, 10ff.

[18] See above, n. 13, 599.

[19] See in the *Tractebel* case, mentioned in n. 15.

[20] See under the traditional Belgian rule, before it was modified in 1995: the criticism by J. Van Ryn, *Principes de droit commercial* (Brussels 1954) no. 600, 391.

[21] It would be presumptuous to refer here to traditional religious differences between the catholic south and the protestant north.

[22] Under Belgian law, the directors will be jointly liable if the transaction appears to have been "grossly" inequitable to the company. See art. 529, Companies Code.

[23] art. 101 L225–38 Commercial Code; the agreement will not be binding unless after the authorization has been granted.

[24] See for an overview of the numerous case law developments, the overview of group law edited by M. Lutter, *Konzernrecht im Ausland* ZGR Sonderheft (Berlin 1994) and by E. Wymeersch, *Groups of Companies in the EEC* (Berlin 1992).

introduced in Belgian law.[25] Similar rules exist in Dutch[26] and in German law.[27] In addition, Dutch law contains a very developed and frequently used judicial remedy, according to which the court can order an investigation in the company's affairs if a plaintiff [28] has made it likely that there can be "doubt about the proper management of the company".[29]

If the criminal procedures have been provided for, plaintiffs would prefer to file a complaint with the public prosecutor and have the disloyal director prosecuted by the state, in which case plaintiffs normally would be able to claim damages within the framework of the criminal procedure, without having to bear the expenses of a civil lawsuit.

The availability of alternative enforcement instruments is however not a very convincing argument. In the U.K., a large part of company law is enforced by the public authorities. The Department of Trade and Industry has extensive powers to investigate corporate misconduct be it under the Companies Act or the Insolvency Act. The FSA could step in under Financial Services Act. The DTI acts, on application of shareholders or on request of the secretary of state.[30] Both investor interest and creditor protection are within the DTI's remit. The number of investigations is significant, and is mainly influenced by the public attention paid to the alleged wrongdoing.[31]

As to remedies, it is worthwhile to mention that in the U.K. and in other jurisdictions, disloyal directors are disqualified from further taking part in business activities.[32] This disqualification is considered a very effective instrument in the U.K., where it is often applied. It is usually considered more effective than other enforcement mechanisms, also taking into account its preventive qualities or as a deterrent.

Civil remedies based on minority action usually are less effective, especially in the absence of a class action or of derivative suits, while the prohibition of contingent fees has reduced the willingness of the plaintiff bar to take on minority protection cases.

[25] Article 492 bis, Belgian Criminal Code.

[26] Compare art. 342 Dutch Criminal Code.

[27] § 823 II *BGB* juncto § 166 German Criminal Code.

[28] In this case, plaintiffs may be either shareholders, the advocate general in the public interest, the unions, or an association representing the employees: arts 345 and 347, Dutch Civil Code.

[29] Article 350(1) Civil Code. Among these, the existence of conflicting interest has been accepted by the court: OK 26 September 1991, NJ, 1992, 310 (VHS); OK 6 January 1994, NJ, 1995, 199 (Text Lite).

[30] ss. 431 and 432 Companies Act. See above, n. 13, 691. The Company Law Review Committee's final report (2001) advocates another form of reinforcement of the administrative support for regulating companies' conduct, by setting up a Company Law and Reporting Commission and a Reporting Review Panel, see for details: Final Report, vol. 1, Ch. 3 and 5.

[31] For figures see M. Farrar, *Company Law* (London 1998) 498.

[32] See, e.g. under Belgian law, RD no. 22 of October 24, 1934.

The absence of a general fiduciary duty in continental legal systems may be attributed to a variety of factors, none of which seems decisive.

II. Continental Systems

In most continental jurisdictions one finds specific statutory techniques dealing with conflicts of interest at the level of the board of directors. Three main techniques can be found.[33] First, there is the outright prohibition, e.g. on a director for taking out loans out of company funds.[34] These are rather rare, at least in general company law.

In a second series of jurisdictions the law would essentially prescribe a procedure, based on notice of the conflict to the board, approval by the board, the involved director abstaining from taking part in the decision, and some form of disclosure to the shareholders.

This approach is followed in most Latin European jurisdictions law, e.g. in French law where directors have to declare their conflicting interest, and where the transaction is finally submitted to the general meeting.[35] In Belgian law, the board may decide—and the director who finds himself in a conflict situation may take part in the vote—but the transaction and its terms must be disclosed to the general meeting.[36]

If the procedure has not been followed the directors may be held liable. In practice this does not occur frequently, as in most cases the majority shareholder will discharge the director from liability.

If the procedure has been followed, there would usually be no further risk of liability. Directors may therefore be able to enter into transactions that are detrimental to the company, provided their fellow directors agree. Even in the absence of having respected the formal rules, the risk of liability is limited, as mostly shareholders are not willing to sue, being often related to the director. Only in the case of bankruptcy is there an increased danger, the bankruptcy liquidator will often try to hold the directors liable for the damages caused by a breach of formal legal rules. The causal relationship may be difficult to prove.

This unsatisfactory situation has been adapted: in French law by providing for an approval of the general meeting, which reportedly is rather implicit, due

---

[33] For a more detailed subdivision, see Ernst, above, n. 16.

[34] E.g. § 89 *AktG*; also: ss. 330 to 342, U.K. Companies Act. Exemptions would normally apply to loans being made to holding or parent companies; art. L 225-43 Commercial Code.

[35] See for the details arts L 225-38 and L 225-40 Commercial Code.

[36] This only applies to closely held companies: without this rule, decision making in these companies would have been blocked if all directors have conflicts, what happens quite often in family companies. No comparable intervention applies under Spanish or Italian company law, see art. 2391 Italian Civil Code, calling for information to the auditing board (*collegio sindacale*).

to the numerous cases submitted to the general meeting and to the complexity of the contracts to be approved. Under Belgian law, directors may be held jointly liable if one of them has entered into a transaction that was "grossly detrimental" to the company.[37] In the latter case, one could consider this rule to constitute a step into the direction of a fiduciary duty, as the directors may be held liable even if the procedures had been fully complied with. The rules imply that directors should better closely monitor their fellow directors.

German and Dutch[38] law have no express provisions dealing with conflicts of interest: in both cases, if a conflict arises at the level of the management board, the matter is transferred for decision to the supervisory board. At the supervisory board, similar conflicts normally do not occur, as generally its members are not involved in actual decision making. However, governance recommendations insist on members of supervisory boards avoiding any conflict, or better any appearance of a conflict.[39]

III. Conflicts of Interest in Group Companies

1. General

The previous rules on conflicts of interest relate to personal conflicts of interest between a director and the company. Indirectly, these rules also relate to group relationships. There are several techniques to achieve that objective.

If the director has a significant interest in the party with whom the company is contracting, the rules on conflicts will apply as relating to indirect conflicts. Mere interlocking directorates will not suffice, except, as mentioned further, in the case of France.

In some jurisdictions, the parent can be held to the same duties as the director of its subsidiary if the parent acts as a "de facto" or "shadow" director.[40] This is expressly provided for in U.K. law, e.g. in the sections on loans to directors.[41] A similar rule is found in Belgian law.[42] In French law, it only relates to transactions of the company with another company of which a director is also a director, or

---

[37] See art. 529, Companies Code: the criterion is that of the "abusive financial advantage" (*"avantage financier abusif"*) that benefited one of the directors.

[38] Art. 146 Dutch Civil Code; §122 *AktG*.

[39] See Dutch Peters Code, June 1997, § 214.

[40] E.g. the provision cited by Gower-Davies, n. 13, 183, n. 37; compare Belgian law, art. 530 Companies Code.

[41] See U.K. company law, whereby it is expressly forbidden to make a loan to a director, or to a director of its holding company (s. 330(2) Companies Act). As a shadow director is to be treated as a director (s. 330(5) Companies Act). However, intra-group loans are exempted (s. 336). In French law, there is a similar prohibition: loans to directors are forbidden (art. L 225-43 Commercial Code).

[42] Art. 530 Companies Code.

involved in its management, or has a significant interest.[43] But it would not apply if there is no interlocking director between parent and subsidiary.

An interesting group related technique is found in Belgian law, where about two thirds of the listed companies are dominated by significant shareholders. Transactions between a Belgian listed company and its significant shareholder—not necessarily a parent—are subject to a procedure according to which the matter has to be submitted to a committee of the board, composed of three directors, that are "independent vis-à-vis the transaction", i.e. that have not previously been involved in the transaction. The committee is assisted by an independent expert. The committee's opinion is laid before the full board, which decides without being bound by the committee's opinion. However, the conclusion of the committee's opinion, and of the board's decision, are reprinted in the annual report. If the procedure has not been followed, the transaction may be annulled, e.g. on the demand of the receiver in bankruptcy, and directors may be held liable.

A recent Act[44] aims at reinforcing the rule by requiring directors to be fully independent and by imposing liability on directors if, although the procedure has been followed, it appears that the transaction was grossly detrimental to the company. This remedy would allow for correcting gross imbalances in intra-group transactions.

The rule's pre-emptive effect, which appears to be quite important, is based mainly on the objective assessment of the transaction, disclosure, and possibly liability. The rule can be considered as an important step in the development of a law on groups of companies. A group law issue that has come up in several jurisdictions relates to the position of the members of the board of directors that have been appointed by, or on the proposition of, the dominant shareholders. Should these directors be entitled to vote or act on matters involving the relationship with the parent company?

In Belgium this subject has been very controversial, especially in cases in which a parent company was bidding on the minority shares in its subsidiary. According to the take-over regulation the target's board is obliged to state its opinion on the merits of the bid.[45] It was litigated as to whether the board members that were de facto representing the parent company were entitled to express themselves. The tribunal of Brussels, in a first instance decision, declared that due to these directors' conflict of interest, it would be contrary to a general principle of law relating to conflicts of interest that these directors

---

[43] See art. L 225-38 Commercial Code.

[44] Law 2 August 2002, OJ 22 August 2002.

[45] On the basis of art. 15, R.D. November 8, 1989; this opinion should inform investors on the merits of the bid. It also contains the opinion of the employees, as expressed in the Work Council.

take part in the decision.[46] The decision was overruled by the Court of Appeal, who denied the existence of any general principle on conflicts of interest in company matters.[47]

2. German Group Law

Apart from Portugal,[48] Germany is the only European state that has introduced formal regulation on the law of company groups. Without entering into the details of this complex regulatory system, one could summarize, for the present purposes at least, the system as follows.

German legislation only deals with companies limited by shares that are part of a group.[49] The basic idea underlying German group law is that if a company—listed or not—is dominated by another, it should either be run in its own interest, whereby the parent may not cause any harm to the subsidiary, or if not, the subsidiary should be indemnified by the parent. If the parent is not willing to indemnify the subsidiary for the negative effects of group dominance, it should opt for the legal regime of the "contractual group" under which such dominance is fully permitted, and minority shareholders obtain either an indemnity or a dividend guarantee.

This idea is further detailed in the central technique of German law on "de facto" groups. In these groups, the dominating company should not use its influence so as to cause harm to the dominated one, and if this occurs any negative impact should be set off, during the same accounting year or at least in the following year.[50] Practically, this aim is achieved by requiring the managing board of the subsidiary to draw up a list of pro and cons, of profits and losses, stating all transactions, but also all measures that have been taken at the demand or in the interest of the parent, including the opportunities which were denied to the subsidiary.[51] The balance of these charges and advantages must be listed by the board and checked by the auditor. The subsidiary has a right of action for

---

[46] Commerce Tribunal, Brussels, October 26, 1999, for an extensive analysis see J.M. Gollier, 'L'OPA volontaire de l'actionnaire majoritaire. Commentaires des affaires Tractebel et Cobepa' [2001] *Revue Pratique des Sociétés* no. 6831, 5.

[47] Brussels, see above, n. 15.

[48] Portuguese Companies Act, arts 488–508. Croatia has also introduced rules on groups of companies that are quite similar to the German ones. See: the studies by K. Hopt and K. Pistor, C. Jessel-Holst, P. Hommelhoff and E. Wymeersch on Groups in Transition Economies, in [2001] 2 European Business Organization Law Review 1ff.

[49] For the definition of group relationships see, §§ 15ff *AktG* "Uniform management" or "*einheitlicher Leitung*" is the essential criterion according to German company law.

[50] § 311 *AktG*.

[51] § 312 *AktG*. Although there is no explicit legal provision dealing with corporate opportunities, a comparable duty certainly exists.

obtaining compensation for the difference. The parent company and the management of the subsidiary may be held liable for not effectively claiming to be indemnified for the negative balance.

However, group management may decide to rid itself of this cumbersome procedure by entering into a contractual arrangement with the subsidiary: this is the "domination agreement", according to which the subsidiary submits itself to the decisions of the parent and, although remaining a separate entity, is bound to obey the parent's orders. Specific measures are enacted to protect creditors. Minority shareholders have the right to leave the company at a certain price fixed by the tribunal, to be paid in cash or in shares of the parent.

To summarize, at least in theory, group influence is recognized but should not be used to harm the subsidiary. Even if this harm is fairly limited, it should be set-off against the parent. If the parent cannot guarantee the subsidiary to be treated fairly, it should buy out the minority, possibly making them an offer to become shareholders of the parent.

As was ably stated by Hommelhoff and Druey,[52] the German system is far from satisfactory. It is based on a valid theoretical concept—that of balancing the profits and losses—but is unworkable in practice.

Although several attempts have been made, the EU has not succeeded in convincing the other Member States to introduce formal rules on substantive group law.[53] In the meantime, a substantial body of case law has developed in each of the states, indicating that the issues underlying the German scheme are met in all jurisdictions but are solved in different ways.

In most European states, there are ample rules of group law: labour law, but also intellectual property law, contract law, and competition law have been affected by the group phenomenon, not to mention accounting[54] and prudential supervision,[55] for which detailed rules, including European directives, have been enacted. According to the prevailing European opinion, all fields of the legal system have been affected by the group phenomenon.

One of the central issues affecting groups of companies is the criterion of permissible group influence: is the subsidiary allowed to take account of the presence and even of the interest of the group, or should it be managed exclusively in its own interest? The answer to this question may be affecting issues of

---

[52] P. Hommelhoff and J.N. Druey, "Empfiehlt es sich, dass Recht faktische Unternehmensverbindungen neu zu regeln?" [1992] 59 *Deutscher Juristentag*.

[53] This is the so-called "ninth company law directive", which has never formally been submitted by the Commission.

[54] Seventh Council Directive (EEC) 83/349 based on the Article 54(3)(g) of the Treaty on consolidated accounts [1983] O.J. L193/1.

[55] See the European Parliament and Council Directive (EC) 98/78 on the supplementary supervision of insurance undertakings in an insurance group [1998] O.J. L330/5.

group liability, directors' liability, permissible intra-group transactions, and also the validity of pre-insolvency transactions, while even in criminal cases it has been considered decisive. It affects the liability of the group vis à vis third parties, especially creditors, and the relationship of the group towards minority shareholders as well.

3. The U.K. Approach

As mentioned above the statutory provision of German *AG* group law is based on the assumption that each company should be managed on its own, and that group synergies should not cause harm to the subsidiary, while if such harm occurs, redress has to be offered to the subsidiary. This concept does not deny the advantages of the group structure, but aims at preventing its functioning from harming the interests of both creditors and minority shareholders.

A similar approach is followed in the U.K., at least in the self-regulatory instruments as applicable in the London markets. Two instruments should be discussed here: the rules applicable to companies upon their listing on the market, and the rule on mandatory bids as enacted in the City Code on take-overs and mergers. Both instruments are based on the idea that there should be no dominant shareholder in listed companies, and if there is, he should abstain from using his influence, or be obliged, once the 30% threshold is crossed, to take over all the outstanding shares. In both cases, the rules are self-regulatory, in the sense that their violation would not result in invalidating the transactions, or give rise to specific liabilities, but would lead to "administrative" sanctions, embedded in the functioning of the market.[56]

According to the Listing Rules as applied by the London Stock Exchange under the previous regulatory scheme, companies applying for listing were obliged to meet the following requirement if they appeared to have a dominant shareholder. The basic idea behind these rules is the elimination of the influence of the controlling shareholder, defined at a 30% threshold, while at the same time avoiding the parent to build up a stronger influence in the subsidiary.

According to the Listing Rules:

3.13 The applicant (for listing) must be capable at all times of operating and making decisions independently of any controlling shareholder and all transactions and relationships in the future between the applicant and any controlling shareholder must be at arm's length and on a normal commercial basis. The applicant must also demonstrate that the composition of its board is such that all significant decisions are taken by directors of whom the majority are independent of any controlling shareholder. Where potential conflicts exist . . . the applicant

---

[56] Under the Financial Services and Markets Act 2000, s. 72, the FSA is in charge of applying the listing conditions previously administered by the London Stock Exchange. It is open to discussion whether and to what extent this change in legal status will affect the remedies in case of violation.

must demonstrate that arrangements are in place to avoid detriment to the general body of shareholders of the applicant. . .

These principles are detailed in the Relationship Agreement between the Exchange and the listed company. In several clauses of this agreement the independence of the company is further guaranteed. So, e.g. is it stated that:

- In order to insure the independence of the board, the controlling shareholder shall not appoint more than five out of 12 directors, while three must be "independent directors" and two executives,
- Furthermore, the removal of directors—other than those appointed by the controlling shareholder—is subject to a board decision with a two-thirds majority,
- on issuance of additional shares, the controlling shareholder shall insure that the investors can have the opportunity to acquire additional shares so as to maintain their voting percentage,
- while the controlling shareholder promises to refrain from entering into competition with the listed company, or from hiring management of the listed company.

The City Code on Take-over and Mergers provides in para 9.1 that an offer for all outstanding shares shall be made by "any person who acquires, whether by a series of transactions over a period of time or not, shares which (taken together with shares held or acquired by persons acting in concert with him) carry 30% or more of the voting rights of a company".

While the first rule aims at preventing the dominant shareholder from exercising any influence on the company and hence the negative effect of group membership, the second prevents group influence from coming into being by offering an exit to those shareholders that fear that they will be harmed by said influence. In both cases the underlying philosophy is that group influence is potentially detrimental to investors, and therefore should be avoided.

4. The Rozenblum Doctrine

A different opinion is followed in most other European jurisdictions, and even in Germany for the de facto *GmbH* groups. In these systems, group influence is accepted, and both creditors and minority shareholders will have to abide by group influence, unless certain boundaries have been crossed.

The benchmark case is the French Supreme Court case known as the *Rozenblum* case.[57] It relates to a criminal prosecution for *"abus de biens*

---

[57] Cass (fr) 4 February 1985 [1985] *Dalloz* 478, with comment by D. Ohl; [1985] *Revue des Sociétés* 648, comment by Jeandidier; [1985] *Gazette du Palais* I 377, comment by J.P. Marchi; Cass (fr) February 13, 1989, [1989] *Revue des Sociétés* 692, with comment by B. Bouloc; Cass (fr) 4 September 1996 [1997] *Revue des Sociétés* 365, comment by B. Bouloc. There have been several other cases with the same holding.

sociaux". As the director of a number of unrelated companies, all of which were controlled by Mr. Rozenblum and his associate, the defendant Rozenblum was prosecuted for having siphoned away assets between the different companies, to sustain those that were making losses. According to the court, whether these transfers were permissible should be judged by the following criterion:

> the financial assistance given by the "de iure" or "de facto" directors of a company to other group companies in which they held a direct or indirect interest, should be supported by an economic social or financial common interest, to be evaluated in the light of a policy developed with regard to the group as a whole and should not be devoid of any return or disrupt the balance of the mutual obligations of the companies involved, nor exceed the financial capacity of the company that is supporting the burden.

Belgian case law is based on the same criterion, but allows for an even greater flexibility, at least with respect to the definition of the group.[58] In contrast to the French law, it does not require the different group companies to be linked by an overall plan based on an economic, financial, social, etc. network of interdependent interests, but defines the group in terms of a parent-subsidiary relationship, and thus on mere control.

By comparison to the German approach, the French rule is much more flexible and allows a lower degree of protection to minority shareholders, and to creditors as well. In fact one could over-summarize by stating that according to the mentioned German technique, harming the subsidiary is forbidden, except to the extent that it can be set-off, while the opposite is true in France, where no group transaction is forbidden, provided there is some "quid pro quo".

German case law on de facto *GmbH* groups also deserves separate mention, as it imposes a stricter liability in case of qualified dominance of the company by its shareholder.[59] Numerous cases have been rendered with respect to the liability of the shareholder of a *GmbH*, who had exercised what was considered "excessive influence" on the company. If the shareholder acted as an entrepreneur, and not merely in a private capacity, and provided the company is under his total dependence—and not simply controlling it—he will be held to compensate the losses of the company, leading over time to joint liability.[60] The rule is based on the idea that by putting a company with limited liability in between himself and his creditors, the owner will not be allowed to shift the business risk to his creditors.

---

[58] See for an analysis of the cases, the chapter on Belgian group law in E. Wymeersch (ed.) *Groups of Companies in the EEC* (Berlin 1993).

[59] See for an overview U. Immenga, in the chapter on German group law, in Wymeersch (ed.) above, n. 55; also M. Lutter and W. Zöllner, "Das Recht der verbundenen Unternehmen in Deutschland" in *I Gruppi di Società, Giuffrè* (Milan 1996) vol. 1, 217–244. The literature on German group law is too plentiful to be cited here.

[60] For further details, see W. Zöllner in A. Baumbach and A. Hueck, *GmbHGesetz, Gmbh-Konzernrecht* Schluszanhang, 80ff.

Under Dutch law, and under French and Belgian law as well, it would be accepted that the group interest may be taken into account in managing the subsidiary, although the latter's interest may not entirely be sacrificed to the group.[61] Although there is a wider variety of opinion, the same criterion would, it seems, be followed in Dutch law as well.[62]

The *Rozenblum* criterion, as it has been framed by the French court in the context of a criminal case, is often considered very lax: by not specifying any time frame within which the set-off has to take place, and limiting the review to gross unbalances, the rule allows very wide discretion to group management to act to the detriment of the subsidiary. Therefore, although the *Rozenblum* criterion may be useful for streamlining relations within a closely owned group, it seems unfit to determine relationships when listed companies are involved. In practice, in some states other safeguards have been introduced, leading de facto, and under the fear of reputation damage, to arms' length conditions for intra group transactions.[63]

IV. Minority Protection in Case of Take-overs: the Mandatory Bid Rule

The issue of minority protection is receiving renewed attention in the context of take-over bids, more particularly under the form of the "mandatory bids". The link with the groups of companies discussion deserves some explanation.

In most continental European systems, listed companies have a controlling or dominant shareholder. As a consequence, control in these companies usually changes, not by public tender offer, but as a consequence of a private sale of shares, leading to a change in control. In these transactions, the former controlling shareholder usually receives a considerable control premium. In the 1970s, the markets got upset by the sheer amount of these premiums, which were considered predatory vis-à-vis the minority shareholders. Therefore, a concept was developed whereby in case of a sale of control, the acquirer should bid for all the target 's shares, whether or not at the price paid for the control block. The obligation to bid for all shares upon a change of control was an important part of the failed Thirteenth Company Law Directive, which attempted to harmonize take-over rules in Europe.[64] In fact the rule is already applied in a majority of the

---

[61] See François, above, n. 16, 707.

[62] See S.M. Bartman and A.F.M. Dorresteijn, *Van het concern* (Gouda-Quint 2000) 111ff; more restrictive, L. Timmerman, "Twee opvattingen over concernrecht" [1994] *Tijdschrift voor vennootschappen, verenigingen en stichtingen* 179, 2.

[63] See the Belgian rule mentioned above (art. 524 Companies Code). One should not omit the influence of the tax rules, especially on transfer pricing.

[64] If, as is the Commission's intention, a new directive will be tabled, it is very likely that the mandatory bid rule will be included.

states.[65] It provides for a mandatory bid in case of a change of control. If an exchange bid is proposed, a cash alternative should be provided for.

As far as groups are concerned, the mandatory bid rule serves as a potent minority protection device, as it allows minority shareholders to exit the company, often at favourable conditions. As to its practical outcome, the rule is comparable to the one mentioned above under German group law.

The underlying rationale of the rule—as applied on the European continent—is akin to group of companies issues and rationale. The acquisition of a controlling stake in another company very often leads to the inclusion of that company in a larger group. The control premium can be explained, to some extent at least, on the basis of the likelihood of private benefits that the acquirer expects to extract from the acquired company, a typical group issue. Rather than running the risk of being confronted with disgruntled investors, the acquirer will prefer to bid for all the outstanding shares. Therefore the mandatory bid has been described as a form of protection upon entry into the group. This type of protection is the more necessary as usually the target will be the subject of a very thorough reorganization, raising numerous questions of parent subsidiary conflicts and corporate opportunities. If the minority shareholders would have been obliged to remain, it is likely that they would be complaining about the radical changes the bidder is imposing. Therefore, it is preferable to allow the shareholders to tender their shares, for cash, or as happens more frequently these days, in exchange for shares of the parent. In the latter case, the additional shares will contribute to the parent's market liquidity.

The mandatory bid rule has certain drawbacks.[66] It leads to a systematic withdrawal of listed companies from the stock exchange list, resulting in an undeniable anaemia in the smaller states' markets.[67] As the target companies

---

[65] For an overview: J.M. Nelissen Grade, 'Het openbaar bod: zes jaar ervaring' in *De Regulering van het beursapparaat* (1997) 110. Belgium practised the rule by way of recommendation since the mid sixties; it was laid down in the law in 1989. France introduced it in the seventies, to be more strictly re-regulated several times, last in 1998 (art. 5.5.1 of the *Règlement général du CMF*). Italy introduced the principle in 1992 and re-regulated it in 1998: see R. Weigmann in G.E. Colombo and G.B. Portale (eds.) *Trattato delle società per Azioni* (Torino 1993) Vol. 10, Pt. II, 400ff. Spain and Portugal have similar regulations; while Switzerland first experimented with a voluntary regulation, that was finally put into the law effective January 1, 1999. Austria and Sweden more recently adhered to similar regulation. See for the discussion: R. Skog, *Does Sweden need a Mandatory Bid Rule? A Critical Analysis*, Corporate Governance Forum, 1995, Stockholm. Finally, Germany has adopted a similar rule, with a 30% threshold (2002 Take-over Law).

[66] The economic justification of the rule was criticized in American economic writing: see L. Bebchuk, "Efficient and Inefficient Sales of Corporate Control" [1994] *The Quarterly Journal of Economics* 957–993; also M Kahan, "Sales of corporate control"[1993] *The Journal of Law, Economics and Organization* 369–379.

[67] This undeniably was the case in Belgium, where 12,47% in 1999 and 18,16% in 1998 of the market capitalization disappeared from the exchange (source: Fortis Bank, *De Belgische financiële markten in 1999* (Brussels 2000) 60).

have to be taken over in full, this has led to an accelerated transfer of companies into the hands of large, mostly foreign bidders. Companies in small states may complain about this bias in favour of the larger companies, mostly established in the larger states, as only these are able to offer the more attractive conditions—according to the directive: with a cash alternative—to motivate investors to tender their shares. Usually the rule is being described as a minority protection rule: this is but one side of the coin. Often it appears that the rule strengthens the negotiating position of the "de facto" controlling shareholder.[68]

It cannot be denied that, once introduced in the legal system, the rule is a vital factor in structuring control transactions, but also in the market valuation of shares as, depending on the circumstances and the applicable regulations, share prices will include the expected control premium. As the share price includes the expected control premium, the mandatory bid becomes an indispensable part of the valuation process, and creates its own justification.

It is useful to mention that take-over regulation normally contains a squeeze out feature: once the bidder has acquired a certain percentage of the shares, he is obliged to reopen the bid and to allow the remaining shareholders to tender their shares, at the same conditions. Often, shareholders are pressed to tender under the threat of a de-listing of the shares, or under the prospect of seeing dividends for the coming years severely cut back. In practice most shareholders seem to accept the bidder's offer.

V. Squeeze-out Provisions

Apart from regular take-over bids, and from mandatory bids, there is an increasing number of listed companies going private, whether as a consequence of the parent bidding for the subsidiary's minority shares—often in exchange for the parents' shares,—or by having the company itself bidding for its own shares, followed by a technical reduction of its legal capital. Only in rare cases does one witness the same result being achieved by way of a management buy-out.

In both cases the result is similar: group problems are being solved by eliminating minority shareholders, at least at the level of the subsidiary company.

Depending on the factual situations, the squeeze-out provisions that are found in several of the Member States, play a support role in the development of wholly owned groups. Due to historical circumstances, there is a decreasing

---

[68] See on the subject: E. Wymeersch, 'The Mandatory Bid, A Critical View' in K.J. Hopt and E. Wymeersch (eds.) *European Takeovers—Law and Practice* (London 1992) 351; for further crticicm, see in the Netherlands L. Timmerman, 'Tegen het verplichte bod' in Instituut voor Ondernemingsrecht (ed) *Corporate governance voor juristen* (Groningen 1998) 105; or a different view: H.J. De Kluiver, 'Voor het verplichte bod' [1998] *Ondernemingsrecht*, 253; in Sweden: R. Skog, 'Does Sweden Need a Mandatory Bid Rule? A Critical Analysis' [1995] Corporate Governance Forum.

number of companies with only a small percentage of their shares effectively publicly distributed. Trading is very thin, and prices volatile. These companies often consider going private, and apply for de-listing.

Traditional squeeze-out provisions are found in different European states. The remedy has often been used in France,[69] in the Netherlands[70] and is now being tested in Belgium.[71] It has been introduced in Germany.[72]

In France the squeeze-out works both ways: not only can the company apply for acquiring the shares of the remaining 5% shareholders, but those shareholders can also demand their shares to be taken over by the group owning the majority of the shares.[73] The rules only apply to listed companies.

The *Conseil des Marchés Financiers* or *CMF* is in charge of applying the procedure: it will grant the application if the market in the shares has become too illiquid. The *CMF* will appreciate whether the price offered is "not likely to harm the interest of the minority shareholders.[74] The procedure is being used very frequently and has led to the elimination of a considerable number of illiquid shares from the securities markets. It only applies to shares that have once been listed on a regulated market.[75] One should mention that the obligation relates not only to a traditional squeeze-out situation in which the trading liquidity has become marginal, but includes cases in which the company will be substantially changed, both in terms of its legal structure and with respect to its business. A change of the company's legal form (especially into that of the *société en commandite par actions*[76]) also triggers the obligation to bid. Also, the merger of a subsidiary into its parent, or the transfer of substantially all the assets to a third party would trigger the obligation for the controlling shareholder to offer the other shareholders to tender their shares.[77]

---

[69] For details, see A. Viandier, *OPA, OPE et autres offres publiques* (Paris 1999) 2549, listing all transactions for the period between January 1996 and May 1998.

[70] Article 94a and 201a NBW, applicable to both listed and unlisted companies.

[71] See art. 513 Companies Code and art. 45ff RD of 8 November 1989.

[72] See Wertpapier- und Übernahmegesetz, of 20 December 2001. See 4th *Kapitalmarktförderungsgesetz,* the draft of which is published at www.bundes finanzministerium.de

[73] Article 5-6-1 of the *Règlement du Conseil des marchés financiers*; it has several times been decided that the mere fact that the conditions of the rule have been met, does not suffice to entitle the minority shareholder to demand the acquisition of his shares: the *CMF* will grant the application if it appreciates that the share market has dried up so that the shareholder cannot transfer his share under normal price and time conditions.

[74] Paris 18 April 1991 [1991] *Revue des Sociétés* 765, comment by D. Carreau and D. Martin.

[75] See for details on the procedure: A. Viandier, *OPA, OPE et autres offres publiques* (Paris 1999) 2511, 417.

[76] As in the latter, the management, often another company, has been irrevocably appointed, which is contrary to the SA rules, where board members can be revoked without notice (*ad nutum*).

[77] See for further details: A. Viandier, n. 74, at no. 2590, p. 434, who raises doubts as to the validity of this regulation.

An additional remedy applicable only to Dutch and Belgian unlisted companies should be mentioned as it points into the same direction. The Dutch legislator[78,79] has introduced rules allowing oppressed shareholders in unlisted companies—e.g. subsidiaries of groups—to be bought out by the other shareholders that are the cause of their grief. A first rule allows a 30% or more shareholder to apply to the court for an order whereby the other shareholders will be mandated to tender their shares at the price fixed by the court. The remedy can only be granted to a plaintiff provided he can produce evidence of "serious reasons" (*justes motifs, gegronde redenen*), mainly referring to oppression or unacceptable conduct by the other, presumably majority shareholders.

A minority shareholder may, on the other hand, apply to court for having his shares taken over by the other shareholders, if he can prove "serious reasons", especially oppressive conduct on the part of the defendants. In both cases, there are ample procedural safeguards. The procedures have been applied numerous times since their introduction into the law in 1995.

The benefits of these rules have been denied to shareholders of listed companies as these were supposed to enjoy sufficiently flexible exit rights on the markets.

All these squeeze-out techniques point to the same direction: to offer an exit to minorities and, for listed companies, to ensure that the markets do not trade shares of companies that are essentially majority owned and dominated. In both cases, the ultimate aim is to overcome the minority's oppression, i.e. as deriving from group relations.

Actual practice also goes in the same direction. In Belgium especially, there have been numerous cases in which companies were fully taken over by their dominant—not necessarily 50 +% shareholder—by offering shares of the parent in exchange. The motives for these transactions lie regularly in group considerations: group management prefers to have its hands free in restructuring and integrating the formerly listed subsidiary, thereby avoiding any criticism from the minority shareholders and from the markets. At the same time, exchanging the subsidiary shares against the parent's increases the liquidity of the investment.[80]

---

[78] art. 2. 335 NBW.

[79] art. 635, Companies Code; for an analysis of the cases, see H. Braeckmans, "Gedwongen overdracht en overneming van aandelen: nieuwe rechtspraak" [1998] *N.F.M.* 211; H. Braeckmans, "De uitsluiting en uittreding van aandeelhouders" [2000–2001] *Rechtskundig Weekblad* 1361; M. Pottier and M. De Roeck, "Le divorce entre actionnaires" [1998] *Revue de Droit Commercial Belge* 556ff.

[80] Further motives relate to inclusion in market indexes: if the relative turnover of the shares does not exceed a certain percentage, say 20%, the share will not qualify for one of the leading indexes. In at least one case, the squeeze-out was motivated by the need to avoid valuation of the parent's portfolio at the—highly depressed—market price of the few remaining shares of the subsidiary. Attention should also be paid to insider issues.

These share for share exchanges have been made possible by a changed attitude of the parent's controlling shareholders with respect to the dilution of their control holdings: formerly they would have refused additional external financing to avoid their block being diluted; presently they have abandoned this approach by preferring a more liquid, but legally less influential investment in the parent company. It should be further analysed whether this changed ownership structure can be related to their change of perception of the role of control in large listed companies.

D. Conclusion

The final outcome of the foregoing analysis is that there are fundamentally two approaches to deal with the position of minority shareholders in listed companies that are dominated by other companies.

One is to try to master the influence the parent exercises on its listed subsidiary by a whole range of techniques, going from rules on groups of companies to specific case law on abuse of control. Most of these techniques can be applied across the board, whether the subsidiary company is listed or not.

On the other hand, there is the much simpler and much more radical technique whereby the minority is allowed, or urged, to leave the subsidiary, for cash, or in exchange for shares of the parent. The latter approach is evidenced in a series of rules the conditions of which differ greatly but which have the same outcome. These relate to mandatory bids, appraisal rights and squeeze-out remedies. For reasons of valuation, these techniques will be most effective if the shares are listed.

It seems likely that in the longer term these rules and practices will transform a great number of listed subsidiary companies into wholly owned subsidiaries. The development will result in less listed companies with a greater capitalization, and more liquidity. These changes take place under market pressure, but also because the markets allow the developments to take place. Conceptually, the development might lead to rendering the need for a law on groups of companies superfluous, at least as far as this case of minority shareholder protection is concerned.

Regulations could monitor and steer this development towards closer integration of listed companies within the group. In fact, these developments are already under way. It is likely that a future take-over directive will render a full take-over upon change of control in listed companies mandatory all over Europe. Regulators could decrease the threshold as from which mandatory bids become compulsory, thereby freezing a number of existing holdings, or triggering more rapidly the bid obligation. But in any case, all outstanding shares will be the subject of the bid.

Also, conditions for allowing squeeze-out remedies could be lowered: it is subject to discussion whether even under the 95% threshold, many listed companies have a sufficient number of shares on the market to justify regular trading. The new rules for inclusion in the indexes—which use a criterion based on turnover, not on market capitalization—point in the same direction.

In the past, European exchanges have allowed shares being listed, although only a small percentage was effectively placed in the market. The minimum requirement for "admission to official listing" has been fixed at 25%.[81] In practice, however, this condition did not apply to listing on "new markets" or other small company markets. One could imagine that upon listing, companies would have to guarantee that within a stated period of time the majority of their shares would be put on the markets.

More efficient and better updated systems of disclosure of significant holdings[82] could render the market structure more transparent. Better and more reliable information on ownership concentration would contribute to companies that organize a market for their securities to insure that it is sufficiently deep and liquid to stir institutional interest.

The final outcome of these developments might be that the proper functioning of the securities markets and the role played essentially by large investors might contribute to put pressure on the existence of groups, at least of those in which minority investors are present at the level of the subsidiary.

The foregoing analysis naturally leads to the question whether there is a future for group law. The answer is clearly yes in general but not necessarily for listed group companies.

Group law largely extends beyond the boundaries of minority protection. It raises numerous other issues, as were mentioned above. Many of these relate to parent-subsidiary relations, with or without minority shareholders.

Even for listed groups there always will remain issues of group law, especially of creditor protection, that are not dealt with by eliminating minority interests.

Thirdly, focusing on minority protection, its seems likely that there will continue to be listed companies with controlling shareholders. Even recently listed companies appear to have controlling shareholders. There are good arguments, at least for the new ventures to maintain during their initial period, some stable shareholder.[83] Furthermore, unless one would oblige all existing controlling

---

[81] See Schedule A, § 4, First Council Directive (EEC) 79/267 on the coordination of laws, regulations and administrative provisions relating to the taking up and pursuit of the business of direct life assurance [1979] O.J. L063/1.

[82] The present system, implementing the 1988 EU directive on major shareholdings, presents grave defects at the level of implementation in the Member States, making any analysis very haphazard.

[83] In this sense see C. Mayer, *Ownership matters* February 10, 2000, Brussels lecture for the Leo Goldschmidt Chair.

shareholders to divest themselves of their blocks—which is utterly unrealistic, and probably even unconstitutional—the pursuance of the presently existing control positions will have to be taken into account. Therefore, it seems reasonable to assume that in the longer term also, there will remain a need for group law, probably less for listed companies but mainly, but not exclusively, for unlisted ones.

What are the issues that in a future group law would have to be dealt with? We will limit ourselves to questions of group law relating to listed companies.

According to the analysis undertaken above, group law is mainly about questions of conflicts of interest. This is also what the present techniques are attempting to do. However, these techniques have some major drawbacks. Although they may be useful in unlisted group context, they are not likely to sustain investors' confidence. Most are extremely heavy to handle, inefficient, and rather non-transparent. Markets are not able to assess the extent of the effects of group influence on the company's results. Rarely do the existing techniques intervene *ex ante*, while *ex post* redress is of no interest to the markets. All this undermines markets' confidence in the company's correct functioning.

An interesting outline for a law on groups has been prepared by the Forum Europaeum, a group of mainly university professors and practitioners from all over Europe.[84] The final report of the Forum proposes several remedies that, apart from the mandatory bid, and mandatory withdrawal rights, could contribute to a better solution to present group problems. However, being applicable to all groups, listed or not, these proposals might need further refinement as far as listed companies are concerned: the proposed standard for permissible group conduct—the *Rozenblum* standard—may be too lenient in the context of listed companies.

Some have pointed to the beneficial effects of having a general fiduciary standard, whereby directors adapt their conduct to a generally formulated duty of loyalty. Supported by strict enforcement in the courts this approach could render directors' conduct more apprehensive of the consequences of breaches of their duty of loyalty.

Although useful as an additional tool, it seems doubtful whether this should be the main line of regulating group conduct in Europe, especially on the continent where little familiarity exists with fiduciary duties, and the resulting duty of loyalty. Looking at the absence of case law in adjacent fields and the rarity of

---

[84] Forum Europaeum, "Konzernrecht für Europa" [1998] *Zeitschrift für Unternehmens- und Gesellschaftsrecht* 72; in English: "Corporate Group Law for Europe" Corporate Governance Forum, Stockholm, 2000, 111. For an analysis, see K.J. Hopt, *Common Principles of Corporate Governance in Europe?*, paper prepared for the Millennium Conference in London, April 7, 2000, published in B.S. Markesinis (ed.), *The Coming Together of the Common Law and the Civil Law* (Oxford 2000).

court decisions inflicting civil remedies on directors, the prospects for this approach seem too weak to be recommended.

Modern corporate governance techniques, as presently being developed in several European states might contribute to a better *ex ante* solution of the problem. An efficient mechanism should be based on the following premises:

- transparent decision making allowing for an *ex ante* check on conflicts of interest transactions;
- objective assessment by independent directors both of the financial conditions of the transaction, and of its business justification;
- external reporting, allowing third parties, including the markets to judge the impact of the transaction;
- effective sanctions *ex post*, if necessary.

One could imagine several methods to achieve these objectives.

So, for example, does the Belgian regulation attempt to ensure that intra-group transactions take place at objective conditions, without any group bias? This regulation has not solved, however, the issue of corporate opportunities, which most of the time cannot be tackled except at the level of the parent company. It has been proposed that the board of the subsidiary should state in its annual report the opportunities that, according to its knowledge, have been diverted, as well as the "negative opportunities", i.e. the orders given by the parent restricting the subsidiary's field of activity.

Group law is entering new fields of development under the influence of the securities markets. As far as listed subsidiaries are concerned, there is a tendency for controlling shareholders to take over the minority shares in their subsidiaries. Several legal instruments sustain this development, which also corresponds to the expectations of the markets.

Generally, the securities markets take a negative attitude to the presence of controlling shareholders. Listed companies that do not follow the former line of action will increasingly be confronted with additional regulations, some attempting to eliminate group influence, others guaranteeing their decisions being taken independently and without interference of the controlling shareholder. They may prefer to simply buy out the minority. The answer to the question in the title is: yes, we need a law on groups of companies in Europe.

Impact of the Financial Markets on Issues of Group Law

PETER HOMMELHOFF

At first glance, this subject seems tailor-made only for German and Portuguese corporate lawyers. That is because they are the only ones within the European Union who know codified corporate group law. Outside the Union, codified corporate group law is also rarely found: in Brazil, Croatia, Slovenia, and Taiwan. Studies by the *Forum Europaeum Corporate Group Law* have shown that non-codified versions of corporate group law are much more widespread: that is wherever the instruments of normal corporate law, insolvency law, or even criminal law have been adapted and developed in order to overcome specific problems of corporate group law. Let me remind you of the French "*Rozenblum*" doctrine.

The fact is that we do find widespread corporate group law, but not simply as a codified special subject. This may justify the issues I propose to address in this chapter. Admittedly, the following reflections are to a large extent based on a German point of view.

This chapter is divided into four parts. First of all, the investor's information concerning the corporate group will be taken into consideration. Afterwards, the conflict between corporate group entry protection and corporate group existence protection will be dealt with. The third part is dedicated to the wholly owned company as the model in take-over law. And finally, in the fourth part, the consequences for stock-listed subsidiaries and the protection of its stock-holders will be scrutinized.

A.

According to the traditional understanding of the European legislator, accountancy law is part of corporate law. What is more, accountancy law and capital market law overlap in many and various ways. From this point of view, the question whether the financial markets influence corporate group law can be answered easily with an unreserved "yes".

I. In the field of corporate group accountancy law (i.e. the accountancy of a corporate group), the international capital markets have set a revolution in motion. In Germany, stock-listed parent companies no longer need to give an account under German and European law. They can, instead, submit an annual report under international rules. In practice, that means that parent companies can replace the present group report under the Commercial Code (§ 292a German Commercial Code) with a report under U.S. GAAP or under IAS. The purpose of granting German companies discretion like this is to make it easier for them to be admitted to the New York Stock Exchange. What is more, international investors with an eye on the Frankfurt security markets can be provided with information instruments they are familiar with. Thus the newly imported discretion pertaining to corporate group reports serves to unlock the international capital markets, and strengthens the German financial market.

This revolution was triggered by pressure from the international capital markets, which the German legislator wanted to take into account. As for issues of content, this revolution introduces into German accountancy law accounting standards that are merely investor-related. However, corporate group accountancy law has not only introduced changes pertaining to content. It has also and mainly adapted the legal sources of corporate accountancy law: statutory provisions are replaced by guidelines developed and approved by circles of specialists, *standard setting bodies*. In Germany, a private accounting committee, the *German Accounting Standard Committee (GASC),* has made it its task (which is protected by law, § 342 German Commercial Code), among other things, to develop recommendations with regard to the application of principles concerning corporate group accounting. The first set of principles, in particular those concerning segmentation of the corporate group report and those concerning capital flow calculation were discussed and have been published officially. Therefore, the de-codification and re-privatization of the corporate group report is profoundly revolutionary.

II. Clearly weaker than in the field of corporate group accounting and less radical are the impulses of the financial markets with regard to the transparency of holding status. In company law it originally only included the obligation of an enterprise to announce the acquisition of more than 25 or 50% of a corporation's capital. This announcing obligation aims to "better inform the shareholders, the creditors, and the public about planned and current corporate group connections and to make more visible the power structure within the corporation which is frequently not recognisable for the corporation's management itself". The transparency of holding status based on corporate law is an instrument of corporate group entry protection codified in the German Corporation Act: those who might later be in danger will be able to recognize an up-coming threat at an early stage.

From a capital market perspective, these publicity instruments based on corporate law were insufficient in two respects. With 25%, the first threshold was much too high. The intervals were just as insufficient. Moreover, not everybody was obliged to make an announcement. This duty was reserved for enterprises. From this the EC Council of Ministers drew consequences for stock-listed corporations in the Transparency Directive. The German legislator later transferred and harmonized these consequences with the publicity obligations based on corporate law.

In order to inform the company concerned as well as the Federal Supervisory Office for Securities Trading about substantial changes in the company's holding status, every stockholder reaching, exceeding, or falling below 5, 10, 25, 50 or 75% of the voting rights in a stock-listed corporation, has to inform the corporation and the supervisory office accordingly. These capital market law publicity obligations go beyond those based on corporate law and, in this way, improve the corporate group entry protection.

B.

Corporate group entry protection by capital market law is also one of the keywords that the German corporate lawyer connects with the take-over directive project, namely with the mandatory bid in accordance with article 5 of the recent proposal version of 2001 (which was finally rejected). In Germany, the project of a national Take-over Act has been realized recently in the face of strong political pressure. However, it is still difficult to predict to what extent this project relates to corporate group entry protection by capital market law. The reason is that up to now nothing but some basic items (in particular regarding the question of a mandatory cash offer) has been presented in connection with the German mandatory bid. Therefore, I will continue by focusing on the last directive proposal, even though the joint text which had been approved by the Conciliation Committee was finally rejected by the European Parliament. That is because the take-over directive did not fail (temporarily) due to different opinions with regard to the mandatory bid, at least in essence.

I. In Germany emphatic protest was raised against the directive proposal in its initial versions of 1989 and 1990. The *Bundestag* in particular had turned down the mandatory bid intended to be imposed on everyone who would surpass the $33\frac{1}{3}$% threshold. The reason given was that such a provision would lead to many wholly owned subsidiaries, a tendency which was not wanted. Further, such a provision was supposed to prevent the collection of capital from many small investors. Indeed, Germany is not exactly renowned for a remarkable number of group-related or dependent subsidiaries listed at its stock exchange: *Deutsche Lufthansa*, *Telekom*, and *Schmalbach Lubeca* or *Infineon*, the semi-conductor subsidiary of *Siemens* and *Fujitsu*, may be mentioned here as examples. But it was not only with regard to the capital market that the model of a wholly owned company caused headaches in Germany. Some people were afraid that an extended corporate group *entry* protection could lead to an unwanted result.

The necessity to establish additional corporate group *existence* protection was supposed to get out of focus. This fear therefore pertained mainly to the protection of the outstanding stockholders and the creditors in group-dependent subsidiaries. It was about the issue of whether the existence of a mandatory bid as an instrument of corporate group entry protection could induce the European and national legislators to protect all the stockholders making no use of the offer and staying within the then group-connected company. One wanted to protect those shareholders from gross abusing conduct by the parent company. To a certain extent these fears were intensified by doubts about whether a corporate group entry protection based on capital market law could push out the corporate group existence protection. This would have the consequence that in Germany the traditional corporate group law (which is based on the *Marleasing* doctrine) could come into conflict with Community law.

The reaction of the EU Commission to the German fears was a revision of the directive proposals in June 1996 and November 1997. In the case of control acquisition the Member States were required to provide for a mandatory bid or (as it said) "other appropriate and at least equivalent precautions for the protection of the minority shareholders in the target corporation". As a result, under Community law Germany was able to maintain the traditional corporate group law complete with corporate group existence protection. Germany could even take advantage of not being forced to transfer the mandatory bid into its national law, but this on a particular pre-condition: the protective effect of German corporate group law had to keep track with that of the mandatory bid. And that's what Klaus Hopt had considerable doubts about. However, this compromise suggestion has not been adopted in any later directive proposal version. That is all well and good, but from a German perspective the question of whether the corporate group existence protection in stock-listed corporations will fall victim to the European capital market law arises once again.

II. To this extent the relevant provisions were to be found in article 5 paras. 3 and 4 of the directive proposal of 2001. Para. 3 aims at protection of the outstanding shareholders in the case of an enterprise agreement and at inclusion, while para. 4 leaves space for the system of compensation of disadvantages in the provisions of § 311 et seq. of the German Corporation Act.

1. Contrary to what the opinion might be on first glance, the opening clause of para. 3 did not comprise the order that the compensation and paying-off claims of the outstanding stockholders under §§ 304/305 of the German Corporation Act would have come to an end one year after the transposition date of article 15 of the directive. Instead, para. 3 took some of the pressure with regard to time off Germany: for the transposition of the mandatory bid based on Community law, the German legislator should be given one more year of grace without being forced

to repeal the provisions of §§ 304/305 of the German Corporation Act. Additionally, it follows indirectly from this that Community law was willing to accept the fundamental existence of agreement and inclusion groups. Thus, there was no cause for being afraid that capital market law could have a destructive influence.

2. The aim of enabling continuation with the old law was expressed in para. 4 with particular clarity. Beyond the outsider protection of §§ 304/305 of the German Corporation Act, it created room for other provisions for outsider protection, in particular §§ 311 et seq. of the German Corporation Act with its system of compensation of disadvantages in a practical corporate group and in case of dependency. However, this authorization to continue with the old law (and also to establish new regulation in addition to the mandatory bid) was limited: the other instruments of investor protection should only be accepted insofar as it would not hinder the normal course of the (mandatory) bid. It was the aim that the mandatory bid based on capital market law must not be restricted in its effectiveness by other mechanisms of protection. This applies to the bid procedure as well as to the bid itself. In any event, it is not clear in which ways the German system of compensation of disadvantages in §§ 311 et seq. of the Corporation Act, or the reporting and examination procedure that the German legislator has wrapped around it should be able to restrict the mandatory bid based on capital market law: neither the information included in the mandatory bid (article 6 paras. 2 and 3 take-over directive proposal) nor the calculation of the compensation (article 5 para. 1) will suffer from the system of compensation of disadvantages. Therefore, fears that capital market law could have a destructive influence are just as unfounded as fears pertaining to the law of the practical corporate group discussed earlier.

III. From a German perspective, the relationship between corporate group entry protection and corporate group existence protection in stock-listed corporations can be realized as soon as the take-over directive comes into force: The at present still informatory entry protection by transparency of holding status will be substantially strengthened under capital market law, if there is a mandatory bid. But this will not affect the traditional corporate group existence protection. Admittedly, the EU has not espoused the cause of traditional corporate group existence protection, but the Member States are given leeway to maintain their traditional protective instruments or to create new ones. This can be done through measures taken by the national legislators, the courts, or the stock exchange authorities. But these mechanisms of a corporate group existence protection must not affect the mandatory bid based on community law.

C.

In view of the question giving rise to this discussion, "Impact of the Financial Markets on Issues of Group Law", it has to be determined whether the directive proposal was still adhering to the model of a wholly owned company and whether this had an effect on its separate provisions.

I. The analysis of single provisions of the directive proposal in particular makes it clear that the proposal was indeed aware of the phenomenon of the stock-listed subsidiary and fully accepted it.

1. First of all, this follows mainly from legislative self-restraint. Because of this, the legislators wanted to exclude all controlling shares from the mandatory bid, which already existed once the directive would have been put into force. The legal basis for this self-restraint was article 5 para. 1 of the directive proposal. This provision comprised only stock acquisitions made after the directive had been put in force. The result is that corporation group connections that were in existence would already have been excluded from the obligation of launching a bid. Thus Germany needs not offer repurchase to the outstanding *Telekom* stockholders.

Similarly, *Siemens* and *Fujitsu* need not offer repurchase of the *Infineon* stock; they would not need to do so even if the directive had been in force when the *Infineon* shares were placed. That is because even if the directive had been in force when the *Infineon* shares were placed, *Infineon*'s parent corporations would not have *acquired* their shares within the meaning of article 5, but would have sold shares they had *held* till then. This analysis is of general importance for the practice of companies to go public gradually, in several stages. As the Federal Government sold its *Lufthansa* shares step by step via stock exchange to the investing public, there will be no change in the future: under the take-over directive it will remain possible to introduce an up to then wholly owned company step by step to the capital market. The directive will neither force swamping of the financial markets with an oversupply of shares, nor will it waive the specific confidence that might for the investors result from the fact that the up to now parent corporation (like *Siemens* and *Fujitsu*) still has a share in the corporation even after going public.

2. After all, stock-listed subsidiaries are in accordance with the regulation concept of the European legislators. This finds additional expression in the release from the mandatory bid provided for in article 5 para. 2 of the directive proposal. According to this provision, the bidder who has launched a voluntary take-over bid to the target's stockholders but did not acquire all outstanding shares would not need to submit another offer: whoever did not accept the

voluntary bid, cannot hope for another one. Speculation is excluded. From a German perspective, this release is aimed at stock-listed subsidiaries.

Finally, in this context the up to now missing "squeeze out" must be dealt with. Under EU law the bidder has no chance to exclude those stockholders who want to stay in the target corporation in spite of a take-over bid against their free will. This, moreover, becomes apparent from the fact that the take-over directive is not at all oriented to the model of a wholly owned company.

II. But if this is the way it is, then one directive guideline concerning the offer documents, i.e. the content of the offer, is gaining particular importance: the bidder's intentions with regard to the future business policy and future obligations of the target corporation; its employees, and its management, including possible material changes of employment conditions (article 6 para. 3(h) of the directive proposal).

This offer information has no relevance for those stockholders of the target that are willing to accept the offer and to leave the corporation. However, for the other group of shareholders who are willing to stay in the corporation in spite of the take-over bid, the offer information has significant relevance. The information about the target's business activity is, in other words, apart from the information concerning compensation (article 6 para. 3(d) of the directive proposal), the most important criterion for the single stockholder when making his decision about whether or not to leave the corporation. Before obtaining this information, the stockholder will not be able to make a decision "fully informed about the situation" (article 6 para. 2 Take-over Directive).

Therefore, the directive will in the case of every take-over bid, be it voluntary or mandatory, grant the shareholder a real (not just a formal) choice. And, inversely, this applies to the bidder in the case of a mandatory offer: the bidder remains at liberty to convince as many stockholders as possible to stay in the corporation—for instance by allocating particularly attractive business activities within the corporate group, or by legal and real mechanisms determined to validate the target and subsidiary's relative independence within the corporate group.

Compared to the current German law, this concept of the directive brings a particular gain: up to now the outstanding stockholders had to put up with the inclusion of their corporation into a practical corporate group without protest and without the opportunity to leave the corporation. Besides, they could only hope that the system of compensation of disadvantages would work effectively in their corporation. Under the directive, the situation is quite different: the outstanding stockholders are freed from their passive roles as martyrs, and they are granted an active choice. Doing this forces the parent corporation that wants to keep its subsidiary stock-listed to use the appropriate measures in order to encourage the outstanding subsidiary stockholders to stay. This is another important contribution a corporate group entry protection by capital market law could make.

III. In conclusion, therefore, it can be said that the capital markets and the law that might come up with the take-over directive persistently influence the traditional law of practical corporate groups for stock-listed subsidiaries.

D.

The conclusion that the take-over directive will, if it is realized, not only recognize and accept stock-listed subsidiaries, but will to a certain extent also be aimed at those corporations, has certain implications for perfecting the traditional law.

I. The most important consequence is to be found in the field of accountancy. Neither the German nor the European accountancy law can cope with the special information needs of the outstanding stockholders in their capacity as investors in a stock-listed subsidiary: their well and woe does not depend simply on the success and failure of the markets where the corporation's activities are to be found. The kind of duties the parent corporation allocates to the subsidiary and the subsidiary's own business chances which are kept intact by the parent are important factors, too. But current accountancy law has up to now made a stepchild out of the special situation of the subsidiary. There is no differentiation between subsidiaries outside a corporate group and those that are dependent within such group. The only place to describe the specific group situation is in the situation report of the subsidiary (§ 289 German Commercial Code); but for this report the current content-oriented guidelines under the Fourth Directive and under national law are much too general to guarantee the necessary specific information for investors in group subsidiaries.

It follows that, with regard to this kind of information, capital markets *must* influence corporate group law. However, the appeal for regulation is not directed at the European legislators. The focus is, as has been mentioned before, at the moment completely upon private "legislators," the *standard setting bodies*. Therefore, those committees should be obliged to provide for adequate investors' information within group-dependent subsidiaries. As long as the European legislators do not face such duty, it should be performed by those national legislators that want to strengthen their countries as financial places, and therefore especially the German legislator.

II. Particularly the German legislators should face an additional duty then; namely the duty to cautiously reform the traditional law of compensation of disadvantages in §§ 311 et seq. German Corporation Code with the aim of increasing its *acceptance* among the investors. As future take-over law is willing to guarantee investors' protection by granting stockholders the choice to stay in the target corporation under acceptable conditions, the German legislators must improve the corporate group existence protection. What is needed is a drastic improvement that enables investors in subsidiaries to put their trust in this law. Therefore, the legislator should not place responsibility for those investors' interests totally on the involved group corporations. In the long run, the capital market will not get by without a minimum legal ceiling of protection of interests and confidence in favour of the subsidiary's investors. The *Bundestag* is obliged and bound to formulate policy in connection with the questions raised by financial markets and group law. The German Lawyers Conference suggested some plan of action some years ago, but was turned down by a large majority. The race for passing new take-over law cannot be run without a warm-up of reform. Beyond any reasonable doubt: *The financial markets really do influence corporate group law, and they have to.*

29

Tunneling

SIMON JOHNSON, RAFAEL LA PORTA, FLORENCIO LOPEZ-DE-SILANES, AND
ANDREI SHLEIFER*

Contents

The emerging markets crisis of 1997–1998 offers many instances of looting of firms by their controlling shareholders. Assets were transferred out of companies, profits syphoned off to escape creditors, and troubled firms in a group propped up using loan guarantees by other listed group members. Johnson et al.[1] show that countries whose legal systems restrict such looting of firms more effectively had milder financial crises in 1997–1998. In this chapter, we use the term tunneling, coined originally to characterize the expropriation of minority shareholders in the Czech Republic (as in removing assets through an underground tunnel), to describe the transfer of assets and profits out of firms for the benefit of those who control them.

We take on several questions about tunneling. Does it occur only in emerging markets, with their generally poor law enforcement, or does it also happen in developed countries? Is it possible to tunnel a company legally? What forms does legal tunneling take? Finally, *how* does the law in countries with good law enforcement accommodate tunneling?

These questions bear on recent research showing that legal protection of minority shareholders and creditors is an empirically significant determinant of financial development across countries.[2] This research also shows that company law in civil law countries, especially French civil law countries, is less

* Sloan School of Management at MIT, Harvard Department of Economics, Yale School of Management, and Harvard Department of Economics, respectively. We are grateful to Pietro Busnardo, Mario Gamboa, James Reynolds, and Joshua Schuler for excellent research assistance, to Luca Enriques, Ed Glaeser, Oliver Hart, Bengt Holmstrom, David Laibson, and Mark Ramseyer for helpful comments, to Theodor Baums, Klaus Hopt, Chizu Nakajima, Dominique Schmidt, Ekkerhard Wenger, and Eddy Wymeersch for help with understanding some legal issues, and to the National Science Foundation for financial support.

[1] Simon Johnson, Peter Boone, Alasdair Breach, and Eric Friedman. "Corporate Governance in the Asian Financial Crisis." *Journal of Financial Economics*, 2000, 58, pp. 141–186.

[2] Rafael La Porta, Florencio Lopez-de-Silanes, Andrei Shleifer, and Robert W. Vishny. "Legal determinants of external finance." *Journal of Finance*, 1997, *52*, 1131–1150.

protective of minority shareholders than that in common law countries.[3] In this chapter, we focus specifically on the legal treatment of minority shareholders in different legal systems with respect to tunneling.

Using well-known cases from France, Italy, and Belgium, we show how legal tunneling happens in developed civil law countries. We focus on French civil law countries, although cases from German civil law countries indicate similar problems. We present three judicial decisions, which legal experts and textbooks view as indicative of situations in the respective countries, where courts allowed substantial expropriation of minority shareholders. Courts did so not through neglect or incompetence, but using specific legal logic. By focusing on advanced market economies, and on tunneling which was explicitly blessed by courts, we show that tunneling occurs in countries with effective law enforcement and not just in emerging markets.

A. How the Courts Allow Tunneling

We use the term tunneling narrowly to refer to the transfer of resources out of a company to its controlling shareholder (who is typically also a top manager). Most public companies in Western and Eastern Europe, Asia, and Latin America have such controlling shareholders.[4] As we use the term, tunneling does not cover other agency problems, such as incompetent management, placement of relatives in executive positions, excessive or insufficient investment, or resistance to value-increasing take-overs.

Tunneling comes in two forms. First, a controlling shareholder can simply transfer resources from the firm for his own benefit through self-dealing transactions. Such transactions include outright theft or fraud, which are illegal everywhere (though often go undetected or unpunished), but also asset sales, contracts such as transfer pricing advantageous to the controlling shareholder, excessive executive compensation, loan guarantees, expropriation of corporate opportunities, and so on. Second, the controlling shareholder can increase his share of the firm without transferring any assets through dilutive share issues, minority freezeouts, insider trading, creeping acquisitions, or other financial transactions that discriminate against minorities. Here we focus primarily on the first kind of tunneling, but mention the second at the end.

The laws of most countries prohibit certain kinds of tunneling. In assessing conduct, courts generally use two broad principles, which appear in all major legal systems. The first is duty of care, which in this context refers to the

---

[3] Rafael La Porta, Florencio Lopez-de-Silanes, Andrei Schiefer, and Robert W. Vishny. "Law and Finance." *Journal of Political Economy*, 1998, *106*, 1113–1155.

[4] Rafael La Porta, Florencio Lopez-de-Silanes, and Andrei Shleifer. "Corporate Ownership around the World." *Journal of Finance*, 2001, *54*, 471–517.

responsibilities of corporate directors (and applies to controlling shareholders in so far as they also serve as directors). The duty of care, derived from the Roman concept of *mandatum*, requires a director to act as a reasonable, prudent, or rational person would act in his position. In most countries, courts implement the duty of care using the "business judgment rule," which gives directors the benefit of the doubt when conflicts of interest are absent unless the plaintiffs demonstrate willfulness or negligence on the directors' part. In the U.S., for example, courts rely on the business judgment rule to protect transactions that provide nonmonetary benefits to insiders at the expense of outside shareholders (e.g., empire building), decisions on executive compensation that are approved by a majority of disinterested shareholders, and most take-over defenses. Not surprisingly, these are the areas where the abuse of minority shareholders in the U.S. is perceived to be significant.

The second general principle is the duty of loyalty, or fiduciary duty, which addresses specifically situations with conflict of interest. This duty requires that insiders do not profit at the expense of shareholders, or of the corporation as the case may be, depending on whom they legally owe loyalty to. The duty of care may allow a transaction that benefits insiders at the expense of outside share-holders unless the latter can show that it does not have a legitimate business pur-pose and that its sole intent is expropriation. The duty of loyalty, in contrast, may statutorily rule out such self-serving conduct or invite the court to examine its fairness.

In common law countries, the duties of loyalty and care are associated with very different standards of proof. "In the case of duty of care, there must be a requirement for exercising a certain amount of care and when a director fails to exercise such care, he is considered guilty of negligence, whereas in the case of fiduciary duty, the very fact that the interests of a director are in conflict with those of the company itself constitutes the basis for liability, and if the interests of the company are prejudiced as a result of such conflict, liability for breach of fiduciary duty arises . . .".[5]

A further obstacle for a plaintiff attempting to prevail under the duty of care is the absence of a simple rule (e.g., maximize profits) to characterize the behav-ior of a "rational" manager. In the U.S., the Delaware Supreme Court held that directors resisting a hostile take-over bid are protected by the business judgment rule if they show a threat to the "corporation" by considering the impact on ". . . creditors, customers, employees, and perhaps even the community generally" (*Unocal Corp.* v. *Mesa Petroleum Co.*). The interests of stakeholders play an even larger role in some Continental European countries (e.g., Germany) where insiders are not only allowed to take into account the interests

---

[5] Mitsuko Akabori Shibuya, "Fiduciary Duty of Directors-Fairness in Regulation of Corporate Dealings with Directors," *Law in Japan: An Annual*, 1972, 5(97), 115–131 at 127.

614   *Simon Johnson, Rafael La Porta, Florencio Lopez-de-Silanes, and Andrei Shleifer*

of stakeholders but *must* do so. In fact, in many Continental European countries the interests of stakeholders are allowed to weigh in even in standard self-dealing cases. Of course, shareholders are less likely to obtain remedy where conflicts of interests are assessed through the lens of stakeholders.

There is another important difference between civil and common law countries. Regulating self-dealing behavior involves a basic trade-off between legal predictability and fairness. Civil law countries emphasize the predictability of the law and rely on statutory rules to govern self-dealing behavior. They do so even though the formal statutory rules that are consistent with legal certainty may invite insiders to creatively structure unfair transactions so as to conform to the letter of the law. In contrast, common law countries emphasize the notion of fairness and, as a result, the ". . . general fiduciary duty of loyalty is a residual concept that can include situations that no one has foreseen and categorized. The general duty permits, and in fact has led to, a continuous evolution in corporate law".[6] Precisely because the common law notion of fiduciary duty is associated with a high level of judicial discretion to assess the terms of transactions and to make rules, it is at odds with the civil law emphasis on legal certainty. As a consequence, while civil law courts in developed countries can stop outright theft and fraud through the application of statutes, they find it more difficult to stop self-dealing transactions with a plausible business purpose.

A clear example of the reluctance of courts in civil law countries to broadly apply the principle of fairness to corporate directors comes from Japan. After the war, the Americans introduced the concept of the duty of loyalty of directors into Japanese corporate law. However, "in considering whether there has been a conflict of interest, the Japanese courts have shied away from attempting any detailed analysis of the case . . . While it is clear that the American draftsman intended to import into Japanese law principles that would be recognized by any common law lawyer as involving essentially fiduciary standards, this is certainly not the way in which the Japanese judiciary has proceeded. Their approach has been very much on the basis of commercial law and fair dealing rather than the need to eschew breaches of stewardship. Consequently, the law in Japan is very much more formal and, therefore, inflexible than in its common law counterparts".[7]

In sum, courts in civil law countries may accommodate more tunneling than courts in common law countries because of: 1) a narrower application of the duty of loyalty largely to transactions with no business purpose, 2) a higher standard of proof in conflict of interest situations, 3) a greater responsiveness to stakeholder interests, and 4) a greater reliance on statutes rather than fairness to regulate self-dealing transactions.

    [6] Robert C. Clark *Corporate Law*, Boston: Little, Brown, 1986.
    [7] Chizu Nakajima, *Conflicts of Interest and Duty: A Comparative Analysis in Anglo-Japanese Law*. London, U.K.: Kluwer Law International, 1999 p. 51.

B. Cases on Tunneling

In this section, we discuss several well-known cases of tunneling in Western European countries, which are generally taken by legal scholars as indicative of how the courts see the law.

1. *SARL Peronnet* (Corporate Opportunities).[8] SAICO, a minority shareholder of SARL Peronnet, a French company controlled by the Peronnet family, sued the directors from the Peronnet family. The Peronnet family established a new company, SCI, solely owned by family members. SCI bought some land and took out a loan to build a warehouse. SCI then leased the warehouse to SARL Peronnet, which expanded its business, and used the proceeds to repay the loan. The plaintiff argued that the Peronnet family expropriated the corporate opportunity of SARL Peronnet (namely to build a warehouse), and thereby benefited itself at the expense of minority shareholders.

The court ruled against SAICO, on two grounds. First, it held that the decision by Peronnet to pay SCI to warehouse its products was not against the social interest, as evidenced by the fact that sales of SARL Peronnet expanded during this period. Second, the court held that SARL Peronnet's expansion had benefited SAICO as well. It could thus be argued that the decision to build a warehouse through SCI was not taken with the *sole* intention of benefitting the majority shareholders (i.e., the Peronnet family), and had a legitimate business purpose. Under French law, this was sufficient to rule against SAICO. The court took no interest in the questions of whether the creation of SCI, and the prices it charged SARL Peronnet for the use of the warehouse, were fair to SAICO and other minority shareholders. The court took a very particular interpretation of the effect of the deal on the minority shareholders of SARL Peronnet: as long as they have not suffered an actual loss, the business judgment rule protected the Peronnet family. In the U.S. and the U.K., courts would be very suspicious of the conduct of the Peronnet family unless it could demonstrate that it closely mimicked an arms-length transaction through an independent valuation of the lease and/or approval by independent directors.

2. *Marcilli* (Transfer Pricing).[9] Marcilli, an Italian machinery maker, was 51% owned by its controlling shareholder, Sarcem, a Swiss machinery maker, and 49% owned by two minority shareholders, Mr. Anguissola and Mr. Mignani (the plaintiffs), who sat on the board. Mr. Bonello, the President and CEO of Sarcem, also became President of Marcilli in 1982. Shortly afterwards, the plaintiffs resigned from the board, and sued Sarcem. They demanded a court

[8] D Schmidt, *Les Conflits d'Intérêts dans la Societé Anonyme*. Paris: Librairie Duchemin, 1999.
[9] Lorenzo Stanghellini, "Corporate Governance in Italy: Strong Owners, Faithful Managers. An Assessment and Proposal for Reform." *Indiana International and Comparative Law Review*, 1997, 6, pp. 91.

inspection and intervention, since the absence of derivative suits made it impossible for minority shareholders to seek damages without the consent of Sarcem. The plaintiffs alleged that Sarcem, among other things: i) precluded Marcilli from exporting its products directly, requiring that they only be sold through Sarcem; ii) charged too high a markup for Marcilli products it resold, compromising Marcilli's market share and pocketing short term profits; iii) sold and exhibited Marcilli products under its own trademark; iv) overcharged Marcilli for the services it provided such as costs of participating in international fairs; and v) did not pay Marcilli for its goods on time.

The court declined to appoint a judicial investigator since it found that the influence exerted by the majority shareholder was consistent with a *group* policy, and therefore a well-defined and explicit business discipline could not be excluded. In deciding for Sarcem, the court focused on the duty of care, with two further twists favoring the defendant. First, the duty of Mr. Bonello, Marcilli's President, was to the group including Sarcem rather than to the shareholders of Marcilli. Second, since the issues involved day-to-day business transactions as opposed to explicit board decisions, none of the statutory rules governing conflicts of interest kicked in, since these rules only apply to resolutions of collective organs (shareholders' meetings or boards of directors). Again, no fairness test was used, and the court sanctioned tunneling from a company to its controlling shareholder through transfer pricing.

3. *Flambo and Barro* (The Plunder of Barro).[10] A French firm, Flambo, was the controlling shareholder in a Belgian company, Barro. Several significant minority shareholders of Barro (the plaintiffs) sued Flambo arguing that it literally stripped Barro of its assets, and demanded judicial intervention and remedies. The plaintiffs argued that Flambo: i) tried to pledge Barro (i.e., the whole company) as collateral to guarantee Flambo's debt; ii) forced Barro to acquire all of the new shares of Flambo in a capital increase; iii) withdrew a substantial sum from Barro's accounts without subsequent repayment; iv) diverted an important contract with Rank Xerox from Barro to Flambo; and v) made use of the utilities belonging to Barro without paying for them.

Since Belgium has no statutory rules relating to intergroup transactions, the court relied on the business judgment rule, and held that Flambo's conduct was consistent with the interest of the group as a whole. The court pointed out that, in principle, it was not objectionable for a subsidiary to support its parent as long as the subsidiary itself was not in danger of bankruptcy. Fairness to the minority shareholders of Barro did not come up in the ruling and while the court disallowed Flambo to continue transferring resources from Barro without judicial review, it did not propose any remedies for past expropriation or even a

---

[10] Eddy Wymeersch, 1993, *Groups of Companies in the EEC: A Survey Report to the Commission on the Law Relating to Corporate Groups in Various Member States.* Berlin: W. De Gruyter.

change in Barro's board. As in the previous case, the court took a broad view of the interests of the group rather than the subsidiary company, and therefore (up to a limit) saw no problem with the tunneling of resources out of a subsidiary to the controlling shareholder.

In addition to tunneling assets, profits, or corporate opportunities, the controlling shareholder can expropriate minority shareholders through financial transactions, such as diluting their stakes through a closed subscription to new shares. Such transactions are relatively common in emerging markets, such as Russia. In Western Europe, the forms of financial expropriation are subtler. In one German case, a company avoided honoring its minority shareholders' preemptive right to a new issue of equity by raising capital in kind. In another famous case, Volkswagen, the controlling (75%) shareholder of Audi, bought out a small equity stake of a minority shareholder in Audi for DM 145 per share. The price was based on a valuation provided by VW. Two weeks later, VW bought out a very large (14%) stake in Audi from the British-Israeli Bank for DM 220 per share. The German Supreme Court refused to hear the complaint from the small shareholder on the grounds that the controlling shareholder did not owe any duties of good faith or loyalty to the minority shareholders. The court also agreed that VW was under no obligation to reveal its negotiations with the British-Israeli Bank because such a revelation might have negatively affected the valuation of VW's shares.

C. Conclusion

In this chapter, we use legal cases to establish four propositions. First, even in developed countries, tunneling—the diversion of corporate resources from the corporation (or its minority shareholders) to the controlling shareholder—can be substantial.

Second, much of the tunneling is legal, i.e. consistent with both the statutes and the basic principles followed by judges. Although some tunneling (especially in emerging markets) takes the form of theft or fraud, legal tunneling takes place in developed countries as well.

Third, such legal tunneling takes a variety of forms, including expropriation of corporate opportunities from a firm by its controlling shareholder, transfer pricing favoring the controlling shareholder, transfer of assets from a firm to its controlling shareholder at non-market prices, loan guarantees using the firm's assets as collateral, and so on. Tunneling can also take the form of financial as opposed to real transactions—dilution of minorities being the leading example.

Finally, we identified some potential differences between civil and common law countries in how courts approach tunneling cases. In civil law countries, the expropriation of minority shareholders by the controlling shareholder in a transaction with a plausible business purpose is often seen as consistent with directors' duties, especially if the controlling shareholder is another firm in the group. Self-dealing transactions are assessed in light of their conformity with statutes and not on the basis of their fairness to minorities. In contrast, fairness to minority shareholders as a broad principle going beyond statutes is central to the analysis of self-dealing transactions by common law courts, and the burden of proof in such cases is favorable to outside shareholders. (Perhaps the reason that pyramidal group structures are relatively rare in the U.S. and the U.K. is that many transactions inside a group would be challenged on fairness grounds by minority shareholders of subsidiaries, who would get a receptive hearing in court.)

These findings are broadly consistent with a growing body of research suggesting that civil law countries are less protective of minority shareholders than are common law countries. Moreover, these findings suggest yet again that it is the laws themselves, and the ways in which the courts apply them, that matter for real outcomes, including the extent of tunneling. The earlier research (e.g., La Porta et al.[11] and Glaeser, Johnson, and Shleifer[12]) has focused on statutes in describing the differences in legal systems. Here we find that, in addition, the application of general principles such as the duty of care and the duty of loyalty by courts may influence how firms in different countries organize and finance themselves.

One can argue, of course, that while these elements of legal systems have stunted the development of stock markets in advanced civil law countries, they have not had a major effect on economic development as these countries have found substitute mechanisms of limiting expropriation and financing firms. This is surely true to some extent. Two points, however, are worth stressing. First, in recent years, the advanced civil law countries — encouraged in part by a technology boom and in part by the flow of funds from foreign investors — have found it attractive to promote stock market financing for new firms via legal reform. The creation of Neuer Markt in Germany and Nouveau Marché in France, with their greater protection of minority shareholders, illustrates this policy. Second, for less developed countries, including those that suffered from the Asian crisis, the failure of the legal system may be very costly precisely because it accommodates vast amounts of tunneling. Using legal reform to reduce tunneling is then a crucial element of promoting financial and economic development.

---

[11] See n. 3.

[12] Edward L. Glaeser, Simon Johnson and Andrei Shleifer. "Coase v. The Coasians," Quarterly Journal of Economics, 2001, 116, pp. 853–899.

30

The Impact of Financial Markets on Issues of Group Law

MARCUS LUTTER

Statement

The influence and the importance of the capital markets and their laws on the groups of companies is extraordinarily great. In this regard, one need only consider group accounting, the duties to inform shareholders about developments in the group, both on a regular basis and on special occasions, and last but not least, the take-over rules. All of this has been covered extensively in the chapters by Eddy Wymeersch and Peter Hommelhoff and need not be repeated here.

In relation to the impact of the financial markets on issues of group law, Hommelhoff's reference to the difference between wholly owned subsidiaries and partly owned subsidiaries seems to be of particular importance. Are the latter listed on an exchange? The mother company has reason enough to act as dutiful leader of the subsidiary. Is the membership of the subsidiary in the group not economically viable, is it even detrimental to the subsidiary? Its stock price will slump and its minority shareholders will leave. Here, the capital markets exercise a highly disciplinary influence and I could almost imagine that the further minority protection provided by the sections 311 et seq. of the German Stock Company Act are only necessary, if at all, as a sort of threat. I therefore view the regulatory and disciplinary force of the capital markets as being much stronger than Eddy Wymeersch perceives them to be: it cannot be in the interest of the mother company to harm itself through falling stock prices of the subsidiary. This is even more true if the shares of the mother company are also listed, because the decreasing price of the subsidiary's shares will most certainly have a negative impact on the mother company's shares.

A totally different matter is the legal and factual situation in the wholly owned subsidiary. As part of the group it is integrated into group accounting and the capital markets' information system. And, of course, the information rights of the mother company's shareholders also extend to the affairs of the subsidiary. But the capital markets and their laws have no kind of influence on this constellation. And this is no wonder because the subsidiary is not listed. From the mother company's perspective, the group is just *a form of organization*. The wholly owned subsidiary is just a part of *one* enterprise, represented by the mother and her shares. Whether Avantis has 10, 50 or 500 wholly owned subsidiaries makes no difference for the market of Avantis' shares: the market exerts no influence on this question of organization, but it applauds or criticizes the group and its management as a whole through the market of the mother company's shares.

Here, only the well-known problem of the protection of creditors of the subsidiary remains. The market provides no answer to it. And therefore, legal rules, which are known throughout the world, are required. The most commonly known is the piercing of the corporate veil doctrine of U.S. law.

This leaves the comparatively rare cases of subsidiaries that are *not* wholly owned and whose shares are *not* publicly traded, in which the minority has thus no means to vote with its feet. Law and practice of the capital market do not and cannot have an impact on this situation. The protection of the minority in the subsidiary has to be provided by the law and its enforcement. This can entail difficulties in the management of the group, e.g. if the subsidiary supplies certain items to the mother company: this can lead to endless discussions with the minority about investments and fair prices and the mother company can ultimately be forced to make a very enticing take-over offer to the minority.

Under the aspect of good corporate governance such a model is therefore less advisable. And if I am correctly informed, U.S. companies try to avoid it wherever possible.

Part IX:

Harmonization of Company Law

31

Harmonization in the Future of Company Law in Europe

CHRISTIAAN TIMMERMANS

Abstract

The European Community and Company law: the ambitious start, the mediocre achievements, the much more modest approach of the present. The reason for this downgrading of ambitions: completion of the internal market which appears to function without further harmonization of company law. The general attitude towards (detailed) harmonization has also become more sceptical in connection with the drive for subsidiarity. Member States apparently have not been sufficiently afraid of competition between company law systems to prefer harmonization by law to harmonization through the market. At any rate, they are still able to protect themselves against the import of less strict company statutes by applying the real seat approach, or by adopting special rules with regard to pseudo-foreign companies. However, the judgment of the ECJ of March 9, 1999 in case C-212/97, *Centros*, might change this. According to *Centros*, the pseudo-foreign company is to be regarded as a fully legitimate exercise of the right of establishment under the EC Treaty. Without taking explicit position as to the real seat approach and without overturning the earlier *Daily Mail* judgment (Case 81/87), Centros has potentially far-reaching consequences for the treatment of foreign companies within the framework of the company law system of the host country of a branch. If these consequences were to be confirmed by subsequent case law of the ECJ this might (but not necessarily will) give a new impetus to EC harmonization of national company law systems.

Contents

A. Introduction

In 1988 I attended a Conference in Lugano organized by Professors Alain Hirsch and Gérard Hertig to discuss with a small group of specialists the results of the research project of Professors Richard Buxbaum and Klaus Hopt on Legal Harmonization and the Business Enterprise.[1] It became one of the most

---

[1] R.M. Buxbaum and K.J. Hopt, *Legal Harmonization and the Business Enterprise—Corporate and Capital Market Law Harmonization Policy in Europe and the USA.* (Berlin/New York 1988)

stimulating colloquia I have ever attended.[2] On that occasion I presented a paper on the possible consequences for EC-harmonization in the field of company law of a then recent judgment of the European Court of Justice in a case related to a pseudo-foreign company (*Segers*, Case 79/85 judgment of July 10, 1986).[3] One of the reasons to accept Professor Eddy Wymeersch's invitation for the Siena Conference has been that recently the Court of Justice has decided a new case on that issue but this time more fully reasoned and therefore with a possibly larger impact than the Segers case (*Centros*, Case C-212/97 judgment of March 9, 1999).

Before discussing the *Centros* case, I shall first briefly comment on where we stand with the EC activities in the field of company law.

B. The European Community and Company Law

The subject has been extensively analysed in academic writing, including by some eminent experts attending the Siena Conference (Klaus Hopt, Marcus Lutter, Eddy Wymeersch).[4] Let me just recall some of the basic aspects and discuss recent developments.

The legal base for harmonization of company law is still the former article 54(3)(g), now article 44 para. 2(g) of the EC Treaty. Its wording has been left unchanged by the Maastricht Treaty of 1992 and the Amsterdam Treaty of 1997. Only the decision-making procedure has been amended, to become the so-called co-decision procedure. According to this Article of the Treaty the Community legislator is under a duty to co-ordinate "to the necessary extent the safeguards which, for the protection of the interests of members and others, are required by Member States of companies or firms . . . with a view to making such safeguards equivalent throughout the Community".

The Hallstein Commission during the mid-sixties read this article as a clear instruction to harmonize basic rules of national company law systems, that is rules on public and private companies. It launched an ambitious programme for that purpose. The First Harmonization Directive of March 9, 1968 covered accordingly all limited liability companies (disclosure, nullity, and validity of

[2] R.M. Buxbaum, G. Hertig, A. Hirsch and K.J. Hopt (eds.), *European Business Law, Legal and Economic Analyses on Integration and Harmonization* (Berlin/New York 1991).

[3] Case 79/85, *Segers* [1986] E.C.R. I-2375.

[4] For literature with further references see V. Edwards, *EC Company Law* (Oxford 1999); K.J. Hopt, 'Company Law in the European Union : Harmonization and/or Subsidiarity ?' [1999] International and Comparative Corporate Law Journal 41; M. Lutter, *Europäisches Unternehmensrecht* 2nd edn. (Berlin/New York 1994); J. Wouters, 'European company law : Quo Vadis ?' [2000] Common Market Law Review 257; E. Wymeersch, 'Unternehmensrecht in Europa—Perspektiven einer Harmonisierung, in 40 Jahre Römische Verträge' *Schriften des Rechtszentrums für europäische und internationale Zusammenarbeit*, vol. 9, 1998, 187.

obligations).[5] Immediately afterwards aspirations were downgraded. Priority was given to harmonization for the public company, the firm intention being, once harmonization for the public was completed, to continue harmonization for the private companies. An exception was made for accounting rules and rules on annual and consolidated accounts, where the global approach of covering all limited liability companies was maintained.

What followed is well known. Two specific directives were enacted on public companies during the second half of the seventies (capital protection, internal mergers) followed by a directive on splitting (scission) in the early eighties.[6] The accounting directives were finalized, later on amended and completed by the Eleventh Directive.[7] On private companies very little was achieved. Apart from the First Directive just mentioned and of course the important accounting rules, only the Twelfth Directive regarding the one member company can be mentioned.[8] Harmonization regarding the private company has never been seriously pursued. There are no formal Commission proposals (albeit that the European Commission's White Paper of 1985 on the completion of the internal market announced proposals for that purpose). These intentions have not materialized. Apparently, the aspirations of the Commission, in comparison with its original programme from the sixties, have drastically changed and become much more modest.

Of course, as far as public companies are concerned, the discussions on the proposed Fifth Directive were for a long time suspended,[9] priority having been

---

[5] First Council Directive (EEC) 68/151 on coordination of safeguards which, for the protection of the interests of members and others, are required by Member States of companies within the meaning of the second paragraph of article 58 of the Treaty, with a view to making such safeguards equivalent throughout the Community [1968] O.J. L065/8.

[6] Second Council Directive (EEC) 77/91on coordination of safeguards which, for the protection of the interests of members and others, are required by Member States of companies within the meaning of the second paragraph of article 58 of the Treaty, in respect of the formation of public limited liability companies and alteration of their capital, with a view to making such safeguards equivalent [1976] O.J. L026/1; Third Council Directive (EEC) 78/855 concerning mergers of public limited liability companies [1978] O.J. L295/36; Sixth Council Directive (EEC) 82/891 concerning the division of public limited liability companies [1982], O.J. L378/47.

[7] Fourth Council Directive (EEC) 78/660 on the annual accounts of certain types of companies [1978] O.J. L222/11; Seventh Council Directive (EEC) 83/349 on consolidated accounts [1983] O.J. L193/1; see also the amending directives : Council Directive 90/605/EEC [1990] O.J. L317; Council Directive 94/8/EC [1994] O.J. L82 and Council Directive 1999/60/EC [1999] O.J. L162; see finally Eleventh Council Directive (EEC) 89/666 concerning disclosure requirements in respect of branches opened in a Member State by certain types of companies governed by the law of another State [1989] O.J. L395/36.

[8] Twelfth Council Directive (EEC) 89/667 on single-member private limited liability companies [1989] O.J. L395/40.

[9] Proposal for a Fifth Directive (structure, powers and obligations of the organs of the public company) [1972] O.J. C131; amended proposal [1983] O.J. C240, further amended [1991] O.J. C7 and C321. This proposal has finally been withdrawn by the Commission in 2001.

given to the modified (and seriously trimmed) proposals for a European Company from 1991.[10] The respective Commission services have started preparatory work on various subjects, particularly the transfer of a company's seat. Questionnaires as to the future fate of the harmonisation of company law have been sent to Member States; a general debate with Member States experts was organized in 1998 and reports of outside consultants have been requested.[11] However, the overall impression remains that Brussels has become fairly reticent about taking new harmonization initiatives in the company law field.[12] The only new initiative announced by the Commission's Communication of November 1999 on the Strategy for Europe's Internal Market is in essence an initiative for deregulation: proposals are being prepared within the framework of the so-called SLIM exercise to improve and simplify the First and Second Company Law Directives in order to reduce the regulatory burden on business, particularly for small and medium-sized businesses.[13]

C. How to Explain this Striking Change in Aspirations?

A number of reasons can be given.

I. The Intrinsic Difficulties of a Harmonization Process of this Kind

There are difficulties of substance (how to agree on workers' participation for instance) and difficulties of decision-making. The First Directive was decided by six Member States, the Second by nine, the Seventh by 10, the Eleventh by 12 Member States; for the time being 15 Member States are participating in decision-making (although, a qualified majority is sufficient). This reason alone, however, is not sufficient to explain the obvious change of attitude of the Commission in particular. There are other sectors, where objective difficulties for harmonization were no less considerable and the decision-making process is sometimes even more difficult (unanimity required for a Council decision).

---

[10] Amended proposal for a Council Regulation (Statute for a European Company) and amended proposal for a Council Directive (involvement of employees) [1991] O.J. C176. Both instruments were finally adopted in 2001 (Council Regulation (EC) No 2157/2001 of 8 October 2001, on the Statute for a European Company (SE), OJ 2001, L294/4; Council Directive 2001/86/EC of 8 October 2001 supplementing the Statute for a European Company with regard to the involvement of employees, OJ 2001, L194/22.

[11] See Acts of the Conference on Company Law and the Single Market, 15 and 16 December 1997, European Commission 1998.

[12] K.J. Hopt writes in his 1999 article referred to above, n. 4 at 41 : ". . . European Company law harmonization seems to be in a deadlock".

[13] COM (99) 624 final Communication from the Commission The Strategy for Europe's Internal Market, 18.

Nevertheless progress has appeared possible (VAT harmonization for the completion of the internal market, harmonization regarding intellectual property rights: much quicker than a statute for a European Company, a European Trade Mark and a European plant breeders right were able to be introduced).

To give a more complete explanation of the apparent change of attitude in Brussels regarding the harmonization of company law, I think—this is a personal judgment—at least two more reasons should be added:
- the completion of the internal market,
- the quest for subsidiarity.

II. Completion of the Internal Market

The internal market has been completed, without completion of the harmonization of company law. That could give the impression that the one does not need the other. Indeed, most of the legislative programme of the White Paper of 1985 has been realized. Market integration as far as trade in goods and services is concerned is largely a reality (more and more also for the free movement of persons). So, it seems, the internal market can function without further harmonization of company law. The merger boom of the end of the eighties, and the beginning of the nineties which brought about a substantial increase of cross-border investment and cooperation between companies, was apparently not hampered by the incomplete state of company law harmonization. The more recent, massive increase of intra-community crossborder direct investment (its total value almost doubled between 1997 and 1998) and of intra-community merger and take-over operations (total value in the first nine months of 1998 amounts to more than double the value for 1995) would seem to confirm this conclusion. There are no clear signals to the contrary from European business or practising business lawyers (that is not entirely true for the European company). So, in this respect, there seems to be no direct impetus for a completion of the harmonization programme.

It should be added that the general attitude in Brussels towards harmonization has changed. Nowadays there exists a profound scepticism with regard to detailed harmonization. Inspired by the so-called new approach to harmonization in the field of technical standards to trade, and sustained by the case law of the Court in the field of free movement of goods and services, there exists a clear preference for home country control, that is to accept the law of the country of origin (of the product or the service), wherever possible, as *equivalent* to the rules of the country of import. This change of approach makes a case for a detailed, substantive harmonization much more difficult to plead than in the sixties.

Now, to come back to the relationship between the harmonization of company law and the internal market: it follows from the legal base for this harmonization, article 44 para. 2(g) referred to above, that harmonization is only required 'to the necessary extent'. The internal market having being completed, is no *further* company law harmonization required?

That brings me to the old debate on the objectives of this harmonization. It is a lengthy debate, at least in academic writing; there never was a thorough debate between the EC institutions and amongst Member States. However, until now this debate has not been really conclusive. To summarize, three objectives are to be distinguished.

First objective.   this is the one which the founding fathers seem to have had particularly in view; it was also the objective most actively supported by France. Establishing an internal market and granting a right of establishment will open the national markets for foreign companies. That liberalization is unacceptable, if the guarantees given by foreign companies under their company law statute are substantially lower than those of the law of the country where they trade and set up establishments. Dutch company law in the fifties was fairly lenient, more lenient than that of the other five Member States. France feared that the lax Dutch company law would attract massive incorporation by foreign business in the Netherlands, in order to penetrate the common market. For that reason, granting the right of establishment to companies should go together with a harmonization of national company law systems to bring the protection for members and others (creditors) to an equivalent level (see the wording of article 44 para. 2(g)). According to this objective, harmonization of company law is not intended to facilitate the completion of the internal market, it is an entrance fee Member States accepted to pay for market integration. One should add, to prevent misunderstandings or dispel false hopes, that since the fifties Dutch company law has incomparably changed and become much more stringent. An objective indication for that has been the flight of Dutch businesses into foreign company forms, to escape disclosure and capital protection requirements applying to Dutch private companies. This has become sufficiently serious for the Dutch government to initiate legislation in order to impose specific requirements on these pseudo-foreign companies (contrary to the classic incorporation approach followed by the Netherlands with regard to recognition of foreign companies).[14]

The two other objectives, normally ascribed to company law harmonization are closely related to the completion and functioning of the internal market.

Second objective.   No Delaware effect in its Community variant (Delaware effect in U.S. form is not possible, a majority of Member States applying the "siège réel" system): the decision in which Member State to locate investment should not be "perverted" by considerations of company law.

---

[14] *Wet Formeel Buitenlandse Vennootschappen*, 1997, *Staatsblad* 1997, 697.

Third objective. Harmonization should facilitate the functioning and restructuring of international groups of companies based in the EC as well as cross-border mergers, take-overs and transfers of a company's seat. This objective is of course most closely linked to the completion of the internal market.

My conclusion on this point is that in the process of completing the internal market the Council (Member States) and the Commission (the European Parliament is rather absent from the debate) have apparently become less convinced about the need to harmonize company law to accomplish the first two objectives just mentioned. The confrontation with foreign company law systems in the daily practice of market integration has apparently not been really painful or caused real problems because of differences in the level of protection. As far as the so-called Delaware effect is concerned, Member States apparently have not been sufficiently afraid of competition between their company law systems in attracting foreign investments to prefer harmonization by law to harmonization through the market.

The reason for this is also certainly that Member States were able to continue to apply various devices to protect themselves against the import of less strict company statutes either by applying the real seat approach, or by adopting special rules with regard to pseudo-foreign companies. Now it is precisely in this respect that the *Centros* judgment of March 9, 1999 might change this feeling of relative comfort of Member States with regard to the present situation of piecemeal harmonization only (public company) or no harmonization (private company).

III. Subsidiarity

As to a further reason for the slackening pace of company law harmonization subsidiarity needs to be mentioned. Not only has the subsidiarity principle been written into the EC Treaty (article 5), the subsidiarity test is now fully integrated in the decision-making process. Legally, it could be argued that where the Treaty already imposes a company law harmonization with a view to achieving the internal market, a subsidiarity test is superfluous. But that is theory. Ivo Schwartz, some time director of the EC Commission responsible over many years for private law harmonization, including company law, refers to 'die Verbannung der Rechtsangleichung in die Subsidiarität'.[15] And, indeed, subsidiarity has now become part and parcel of the EC decision-making culture. The message is, in plain terms: it is necessary *not* to do what it is not necessary to do. That is to say that the case for harmonization must be really convincing

---

[15] I.E. Schwartz, 'Perspektiven der Angleichung des Privatrechts in der Europäischen Gemeinschaft' [1994] *Zeitschrift für Europäisches Privatrecht* 559.

for the Commission to take an initiative and the Council to decide (the European Parliament is by nature less subsidiarity minded).

D. The Centros Judgment of March 9, 1999

One hesitates to produce another comment on this case. "Half of the experts have already written on Centros, the other half are preparing a contribution", one of them said to me recently.[16] But for our subject an analysis of the judgment is inevitable.

The *Centros* case presented the perfect context to test the consequences of the right of establishment of companies under articles 43 and 48 of the EC Treaty for the pseudo-foreign company. Mr. and Mrs. Bryde, Danish citizens living and working in Denmark had acquired an 'empty' private company, incorporated under English law, which had never traded in the U.K., in order to carry on business in Denmark, and there only. The reason for this operation, as frankly admitted by Mr. and Mrs. Bryde in the main proceedings for the Danish Courts, had been to avoid the capital protection rules under Danish company law for companies of this type, and particularly the requirement as to a minimum capital. For the English private company such a requirement does not exist. Under Danish law foreign companies of this type may do business in Denmark through a branch after they have been registered. However, the Danish authorities refused to register a branch of Centros because Centros was in fact seeking to establish in Denmark, not a branch, but its principal establishment; moreover it intended by doing so to escape the application of the Danish rules on minimum capital. Centros argued that the refusal of registration was incompatible with the EC Treaty: as a company formed in accordance with the law of the U.K. and having its registered office in that Member State it satisfied the conditions of article 48 of the EC Treaty to be able to invoke the right of establishing a branch in another Member State in conformity with article 43 of that Treaty. During the subsequent proceedings in the Danish courts and a preliminary ruling having been requested from the European Court of Justice, also in that Court, the various arguments were produced which, in view of the case-law of the European Court itself, might allow for the denial to the pseudo-foreign company of the benefit of the right of establishment, or at least the restriction of the benefit of that right.

---

[16] See, also for further references, W.-H. Roth, '"Centros": Viel Lärm um Nichts?' [2000] *Zeitschrift für Unternehmens- und Gesellschaftsrecht* 311; E. Wymeersch, 'Centros : A Landmark Decision in European Company Law' in Th. Baums, K.J. Hopt, and N. Horn (eds.), *Festschrift for Richard M. Buxbaum, Corporations, Capital Markets and Business in the Law* (2000); H. De Wulf, 'Centros: vrijheid van vestiging zonder race to the bottom' [1999] *Ondernemingsrecht* 318.

The Danish government argued in the first place that the EC Treaty did not apply at all to the case in hand in the absence of any cross-border element. That argument is not without merit: there is no question of a cross-border movement of economic activity. Also after the business had been brought into Centros, it would have continued to be carried out in Denmark only. However, it already followed from the judgment in the *Segers* case that the European Court would reject this interpretation.[17] The company being lawfully incorporated under English law, it could invoke the right of establishment under article 43 EC in order to set up a branch in Denmark. The Court had no difficulty at all in qualifying the establishment as a branch, following its earlier judgment in the *Segers* case, albeit that the establishment of Centros in Denmark would be its single, and consequently its principal establishment. For that reason also the Danish authorities had refused to register the establishment as a branch.

The distinction between principal (primary) and secondary establishment is legally relevant in so far as each company falling within the scope of article 48 EC can always claim the right of primary establishment, even if it has no activity whatsoever in the Community. However, according to orthodox views,[18] it can only invoke the right of secondary establishment if it has an economic link with the Community ; just as natural persons, which are nationals of a Member State can only do so if they are *established* within the Community. Following this interpretation, Centros would therefore not have been able to invoke Article 43 EC to establish a branch in Denmark because being an 'empty' company, it did not satisfy the conditions of having an economic link with the Community. However, if the establishment of Centros in Denmark were to be considered as its primary establishment, that difficulty would not arise, just as a national of a Member State can always establish himself into another Member State, once this concerns the exercise of his main economic activities. However that may be, the Court confirmed its ruling in the *Segers* case and refused to contest the qualification of a branch in this context. That might not be in conformity with established doctrine, but remains without practical consequences because the condition of an economic link has been implicitly satisfied, the establishment of Centros in Denmark being the main establishment. Incidentally, I would expect the Court to return to the orthodox distinction between primary and secondary establishment with regard to mailbox companies, having only their registered seat in the Community but carrying out all their activities in third countries, if they were to invoke article 43 EC in order to set-up a secondary establishment within a Member State.

---

[17] [1986] E.C.R. I-2375.

[18] Cf. the General Programme for the abolition of existing restrictions on freedom of establishment, O.J. n. 2 of 15 January 1962.

The Danish government argued secondly that the operation envisaged by Centros had to be considered as an abuse of the right of establishment and that the refusal of registration could therefore be justified under the EC Treaty. The concept of abuse of a fundamental freedom is indeed firmly established in the Court's case-law.[19] There would be such abuse in this case because of the admitted purpose of circumventing the Danish rules on minimum capital. The Court rejected this argument in unqualified and principled terms. That is why the *Centros* ruling is so important. The Danish rules in question being rules of company law and not rules concerning the carrying on of certain trades, professions or business, the choice of a less severe, more attractive foreign company statute is in itself perfectly legitimate. "The right to form a company in accordance with the law of a Member State and to set up branches in other Member States is inherent in the exercise, in a single market, of the freedom of establishment guaranteed by the Treaty" (para. 27).[20] Also, the pseudo-foreign company must therefore be considered as a perfectly normal phenomenon within the single market. At least, the fictitious nature of its foreign quality could not be raised to deny the company the benefit of the right of establishment under the EC Treaty. Measures may be taken against abuse or fraudulent conduct but only case by case and on the basis of objective evidence.[21] To prefer a less strict foreign company statute can not in itself be qualified as such.

That brings us to the third and final argument brought forward by the Danish government. Even if the refusal to register a branch of Centros were to be considered as a restriction of the right of establishment, it could be justified on the basis of the exception clause of article 46 of the Treaty or in view of imperative requirements in the general interest as accepted under the Court's case-law. The Danish government referred in that respect to the need to protect creditors, also against the risk of fraudulent bankruptcy due to the insolvency of companies whose initial capitalization was inadequate. The creditor's protection does not figure in the list of general interests referred to in article 46, so that argument fails. However, the Court has indeed accepted within the scope of article 43 itself the possibility to justify restrictions on the right of establishment under a rule of reason but subject to strict conditions. First of all, the measure in question must be applied in a non-discriminatory manner, secondly the general interest pursued must be of an imperative nature, thirdly the measure must be suitable for securing the attainment of the objective pursued, and fourthly it must be proportionate. The Danish measure fails this test. Fortunately, the reasons why have been fairly extensively explained by the Court.

[19] See the case-law referred to in para. 24 of the *Centros* judgment [1999] E.C.R. I-1492.

[20] [1999] E.C.R. I-1493.

[21] See too para. 38 of the *Centros* judgment [1999] E.C.R. I-1496, also *Segers* [1987] E.C.R. 2388, para. 17.

First of all, the condition as to the suitability of the measure has not been met. Had Centros traded in the U.K. the lack of a minimum capital would have been accepted without any difficulty by the Danish authorities (the Court could also have said that in this respect Danish practice discriminates between foreign and pseudo-foreign companies). It is important to note that the Court held the third condition was also not met for another reason: creditors contracting with a foreign company like Centros know that they are dealing with a company governed by foreign law. Moreover, they are protected by the harmonized rules on accounting (Fourth Company Law Directive) and the specific rules of the Eleventh Directive on disclosure in respect of branches established by foreign companies.[22] Apparently, the Court considers the existence of this harmonized body of disclosure rules an important safeguard for the protection of creditors with regard to foreign companies. Could one infer from this that a general, indiscriminate application of a minimum capital requirement with regard to foreign companies like the English private company would also fail the test under the rule of reason? That seems at least arguable. The Court adds that less restrictive measures could have been taken to protect the creditors. On the other hand, measures to protect creditors from fraudulent actions by foreign companies always remain possible in individual cases if concrete indications for an *animus fraudendi* exist. However, a practice of generally refusing to register a branch of a company having its registered office in another Member State can never be justified for that purpose.

The Court has not answered the important question whether in a case like this the EC Treaty would have allowed the registration of a branch of the pseudo-foreign company to be refused by invoking the real seat doctrine, as a conflict rule. And indeed the *Centros* case did not raise that question. Denmark belongs (quite probably, there seems to be some doubt on this) to the minority of Member States applying the incorporation system. Would it be possible for Member States applying the real seat of a company, however defined (central administration, principal establishment, directors' seat) as the connecting factor for determining the company's statute to thwart the exercise of the right of establishment of the pseudo-foreign company by invoking that criterion as a conflict rule? In its Daily Mail judgment of 27 September 1988 the Court ruled that companies as defined by Article 48 of the EC Treaty cannot invoke the right of establishment in order to enforce the transfer of their seat to another Member State if the national law by which they are governed does not allow such a transfer.[23] The Court has arrived at this conclusion by referring to the text of Article 48, which clearly demonstrates that the Treaty accepts the continuing existence of very divergent conflict rules of Member States on company law and that a

---

[22] See above, n. 7.

[23] Case 81/87, [1988] ECR 5483.

harmonization in this respect, which might be possible in itself, has not (yet) been achieved. This seems indeed to imply that the application of national conflict rules for determining a company's statute cannot be opposed by invoking the Treaty rules on the right of establishment.

In an annotation of this judgment I have argued for limiting the consequences of the rule in Daily Mail to situations like the one in the Daily Mail case itself: a restriction to the right of establishment with regard to the *departure* from the Member State of origin because of the application of a conflict rule by that Member State.[24] In my view this reading of the Daily Mail case does full justice to the equal treatment by Article 48 of the variety of conflict rules. In the absence of harmonization Member States are fully entitled to require as a constitutive requirement for the formation of a company that the real seat of the company shall be established within their territory; also that this seat should remain there, were the legal existence of the company not to be endangered.[25] It appears acceptable that the EC right of establishment cannot be invoked to cure a deficiency as to one of the constitutive elements for the existence of a company. However, it would be quite a different matter to allow a Member State to which the real seat would be transferred, to frustrate such exercise of the right of establishment, if the law of incorporation of that company would allow that transfer.

The *Centros* judgment might not have solved this controversy. However, by qualifying the phenomenon of the pseudo-foreign company so explicitly as a legitimate exercise of the right of establishment, it provides in my view new arguments in favour of a restrictive reading of the ruling in *Daily Mail*. A further argument for this could be derived from the willingness of the Court to consider the principal establishment in the case of a pseudo-foreign company as a branch and to define such an exercise of the right of establishment so emphatically as intended by the Treaty provisions on the right of establishment.[26] A strict distinction between principal and secondary establishment would make it easier to condition the exercise of the right of establishment in case of a transfer of the principal establishment in so far as this would be frustrated by a conflict rule of the Member State of establishment. I agree with Wulf-Henning Roth that *Daily Mail* has not been overruled by *Centros*.[27] *Centros* assists me, however, in the restrictive interpretation of *Daily Mail* mentioned above. Indeed, the rationale for the real seat doctrine is very much linked to the objective of preventing abuse. Companies having their centre of gravity in a state should be organized according to the laws of that state. Now, if within the European single market the

---

[24] 1991 *SEW (Tijdschrift voor Europees en economisch recht)*, 72 n 5.

[25] Cf. also the regime applicable to the European Economic Interest Grouping, Regulation (EEC) 2137/85 on the European Economic Interest Grouping (EEIG) [1985] O.J. L124, arts 12 to 14 and the amended proposal for a European Company Regulation [1991] O.J. C176, arts 5 and 5a.

[26] para. 26 of *Centros* [1999] E.C.R. I-1493.

[27] See his article referred to above, n. 16.

pseudo-foreign company cannot be seen as a special case for treatment, different from the real foreign company, much of the basic justification for applying the real seat doctrine seems to fall.

If one were to accept a more generous interpretation of *Daily Mail* as implying a general declaration of immunity of international company law of the Member States from any interference through the Treaty rules on the right of establishment, Denmark, if it had applied the real seat doctrine, could then have refused the registration of Centros by invoking that doctrine. I fail to see why national conflict rules should benefit from a higher degree of protection in relation to the right of establishment than rules of substantive company law. At any rate, new preliminary references on these questions might be expected in the near future, particularly from Germany.

What conclusion may be drawn from this analysis of the *Centros* judgment?

(1) The pseudo-foreign company constitutes a fully legitimate exercise of the right of establishment. Special measures taken by Member States with regard to pseudo-foreign companies which limit their scope to that category of companies, will normally be incompatible with the EC Treaty if they were to restrict ('liable to hinder or make less attractive') the exercise of the right of establishment under the EC Treaty. Their justification under the Treaty is not entirely excluded, at any rate the pseudo-foreign quality of a company can never be invoked as a sufficient ground for justification.

(2) Whether Member States will be allowed to apply part of their own rules of company law to branches of foreign companies falling within the scope of article 48 of the EC Treaty, in order to maintain a higher level of protection of shareholders, workers', creditors' or other third party interests than that provided by the law of incorporation of the foreign company, is uncertain in cases where the application of such rules of the Member State of the branch could be said to cause a restriction to the exercise of the right of establishment.

(3) The application of conflict rules of the Member State of the branch, obliging the foreign company in application of the real seat doctrine, to respect the local company law or to be set-up under the form of a local company, is probably incompatible with the EC Treaty. In other words, the consequences of the *Centros* judgment for the treatment of foreign companies within the framework of the company law system of the host country of a branch, are unclear but potentially far-reaching. One might expect further clarifications of this case law by the European Court in the years to come. If the Court were to follow the lines of thinking just explored, what would then be the consequences for the harmonization activity of the Community?

E. The EC Harmonization of Company Law in the Future

These consequences are highly unpredictable. The aftermath of *Centros* might foster more statute shopping in the EC, more 'Delawarization' because it will be easier to set-up or to move—I leave aside the very important tax aspects—principal establishments to Member States applying the real seat doctrine. Those Member States, seeing their defence against the pseudo-foreign company seriously undermined, might become more interested in harmonization initiatives on Community level. However, it would be highly unlikely to achieve agreement between Member States on a harmonized Community regime as to rules of conflict, making a fundamental choice in favour of either the incorporation or the real seat approach. The contents and fate of the 1968 Convention on the mutual recognition of companies have established an ominous precedent in this respect.

A specific Community regime with regard to pseudo-foreign companies, allowing Member States to impose part of their company law rules on pseudo-foreign companies, would seem to be excluded in the light of the *Centros* judgment. A similar regime, but applying indiscriminately to branches of foreign companies, might be difficult to reconcile with Community law if the Court were to be as strict as *Centros* seems to suggest with regard to the acceptance of the foreign company's statute.

There remains the possibility of a further substantive harmonization for the private company, limited perhaps to some topical issues when levels of protection are substantially different between Member States. Those Member States applying the incorporation system might not be very much interested in such a harmonization. For the other Member States much will depend on the nature of the rules involved, the objectives pursued and the differences of the level of protection between the national company law systems as they exist or are perceived to exist. Answers to these questions will of course vary between Member States. That being so, it would not seem at all sure or even probable that sufficient momentum could be built up for such a harmonization.

As to the free movement of companies in a stricter sense, good cases for harmonization continue to be measures facilitating international mergers, and a transfer of a company's seat maintaining its legal personality. They are objectively required in a single market. What could be the consequences of *Centros* for such measures? Again, free movement as to the possibility to transfer principal establishments to other Member States, that is from Member States applying the incorporation method, might be facilitated (but again not taking into account the tax aspects). That is not necessarily so for companies incorporated in Member States applying the real seat method. Such imbalance might give an impetus to complete—with regard to the transfer of seat to start with—a harmonization for that purpose (provided the moratorium of the persistent conflict on workers' participation rules was first lifted).

All in all, the future of company law harmonization remains highly uncertain. It cannot, however, be excluded that the evolution of the case-law of the European Court of Justice might bring new surprises able to change the present outlook and perspectives for this harmonization. Change could also result from incidents or scandals in Member States putting into question the adequacy of company law rules and with an obvious impact on the single market (harmonization is sometimes also a conjectural affair.)

32

Thou Shalt Not Sow Thy Vineyard with Divers Seeds? The Case Against the Harmonization of Private Law[1]

URIEL PROCACCIA AND UZI SEGAL

Abstract

This chapter argues that inter-jurisdictional legal harmonization ought to be undertaken with great caution. The purpose of rules is to address economic and social problems. Many such problems are regional. To the extent that these problems are different across regions, each region requires a different, not a harmonized, legal solution. The same result is obtained if the "objective" conditions across regions are uniform, but the "subjective" attitude ("preferences") of the population to feasible legal solutions is not. Thus harmonization is called for if and only if both the objective conditions and the subjective preferences are uniform across regions. In the real world, some jurisdictions agree to harmonize their legal regimes even if they suffer a detriment as a result of their acquiescence. It is argued that jurisdictions are prone to adopt this strategy if they are penalized for holding out. The extent of their participation in the harmonization effort is a direct function of the size of the penalty. Harmonized products also suffer from an inordinately large number of *lacunae*. *Lacunae* are generated when harmonizing agencies have enough clout to force jurisdictions to abandon some of their unique legal solutions, but not enough clout to administer universally accepted substitutes. In the final part of the chapter it is argued that whenever harmonization is called for, i.e. whenever both the objective needs and the subjective preferences are similar across jurisdictions, the market provides sufficient incentives for spontaneous uniformity.

Contents

A. Introduction

The European Union is hard at work in a colossal effort to harmonize the separate legal systems of its Member States. Similar efforts are undertaken

---

[1] The first sentence in the title of this Article is taken from Deuteronomy 22:9 (King James Version). We thank Marvin Chirelstein, John Coffee, Miri Gur-Arye, Guy Halfteck, Alon Harel, Lance Liebman, Tommaso Monacelli, and Yuval Procaccia for helpful comments. Guy Halfteck provided invaluable research assistance. The original version of this paper was modified to fit the mould of the other papers in the learned conference whose proceedings gave rise to this volume. We thank the participants of the conference for their insightful comments.

everywhere, both within closely-knit political unions (e.g. the U.S.) and other-wise (devising a new *ius commune* for the global village).[2] There are many distinguishing features among those harmonization projects. But their practi-tioners seem to share at least two implicit assumptions. The first assumption is that legal uniformity across jurisdictions is basically a good thing. The second assumption is that enlightened regulators ought to facilitate harmonization by urging independent legislatures to forgo their diverse legal traditions.

In this short chapter we wish to challenge both assumptions. We claim that neither uniformity nor diversity is globally "better" than the other. In the sim-pler case, where the jurisdictions are "different", we demonstrate that they are often better served by diversity than by uniformity. This result may hold in many important situations regardless of the transaction costs involved in the intro-duction of multiple legal systems. And what if the conditions in some jurisdic-tions are in fact "similar"? In this case we agree that uniformity does dominate diversity. However, similar jurisdictions have an incentive to craft similar legal orders on their own initiative, even without administrative prodding. Moreover, spontaneous uniformity sprouting up from the jurisdictions themselves is likely to generate more complete and more efficient harmonized products than the genre of uniformity resulting from administrative fiat. Thus, one has to proceed warily in promoting harmonization.

The first proposition, that uniformity is often harmful in the case of dissimi-lar jurisdictions, is the subject of the first section. We start out by drawing on the existing literature in forming a theory of similarity. We show that where simi-larity is lacking diversity is normally more attractive than uniformity. This result is often unaltered even if the transaction costs associated with diversity are high. This proposition runs counter to the accepted wisdom that uniformity is justifi-able because it reduces transaction costs.

Given the attractiveness of diversity among dissimilar jurisdictions one may wonder why uniform legal products exist in the first place. We show that although harmonization may not be optimal overall, its attainment serves the particular interests of larger nations. These nations can then exercise their clout over smaller nations and force the latter, to their detriment, to forgo their legal independence. Since the process of harmonization is carried out by harmoniza-tion agencies, the political economy of their mission can be understood only by exploring the nature of their interactive relationship with the affected jurisdic-tions. This exploration reveals that harmonization agencies are often con-strained to craft "incomplete" standardized products, i.e. statutory instruments filled with an inordinately large number of *lacunae*. We propose a novel blue-print for a theory of these legislative voids. We also show that given the expected

[2] See generally, D. Leebron, 'Lying Down with Procrustes: An Analysis of Harmonization Claims' in J. Bhagwati and R. Hudec (eds.), *Fair Trade and Harmonization* (vol. 1 Cambridge 1996) 41.

lacunae-filled nature of harmonized law, it cannot serve its purpose as a device for minimizing the transaction costs, which are commonly associated with diversity.

The second section explains why similar jurisdictions are likely to produce uniform statutory results even without administrative prodding. We start by showing the incentives of independent jurisdictions to craft "efficient" legal products. We first show why this might be the case not only in the well-known case of corporate legislation, but in many other areas of the law too, e.g. *lex mercatoria.* We next proceed to establish that if different jurisdictions are similar, they are likely, in responding to their incentive to craft efficient statutes, to converge to uniform solutions. This proposition dispels the notion that similar jurisdictions may adopt different efficient solutions: Similarity among jurisdictions yields spontaneous similarity of legal products.

B. Dissimilar Jurisdictions

I. Introduction

The general theme of this section is that if jurisdictions are not "similar" they ought to be governed by diverse, rather than by either unified or harmonized legal systems (we take "harmonization" to be a diluted form of "unification"). Let us denote all jurisdictions that are sufficiently similar "duplicate jurisdictions", or "duplicates", and all jurisdictions that are sufficiently dissimilar "alien jurisdictions". We start by defining the concepts of duplicate and alien jurisdictions, and proceed to the assessment of the various propositions that emanate from these concepts.

II. What is "Similarity"?

The best approach to the concept of similarity is by considering its mirror image, *dissimilarity.* Two (or more) jurisdictions are "alien" if either the objective conditions prevailing in them are different, or the subjective tastes of their subjects are different, or both. "Duplicates", then, are non-alien jurisdictions.

1. Objective Dissimilarity

Law is designed to address social problems. Different societies experience different sets of problems. The optimal legal response to different social problems cannot be uniform. The following two illustrations illuminate this proposition.

The first illustration is associated with the name of Harold Demsetz, an important pioneer in this field. Demsetz conducted a study of the development of property rights among Canadian aborigines.[3] His empirical observations revealed the fact that title to land in northern Labrador evolved only recently, as a corollary to the growing scarcity of fur producing animals in world markets. The underlying theory is quite simple. When goods are plentiful, the definition of property rights is wasteful. Society must allocate real resources to assign different entitlements to different claimants and then to enforce the resulting entitlement structure. This situation is dramatically reversed with scarcity. If scarce resources are owned in common by the entire human race, each player has an incentive to appropriate for himself the largest portion thereof, lest he be denied his fair share of the pie by the greed of the other players. This in turn may lead to an accelerated depletion of the common resources, known in the literature as "the tragedy of the commons".[4] No individual has an incentive to forgo present consumption in the interest of preserving the common pool, because from each player's perspective the best strategy is to increase consumption while the other players abstain. As long as northern mink could be found in abundance, there was no point in fencing it within private domains. When it became scarce, not fencing it in resulted in accelerated depletion of the common pool, and a land registration system became imperative.[5]

When northern mink was plentiful common ownership was the efficient legal norm. When it became scarce private ownership emerged as the more efficient solution. If in one jurisdiction mink is plentiful and in the other scarce, these two jurisdictions are "alien" and should maintain diverse legal systems. Alien jurisdictions ought to avoid the waste inherent in harmonization.

The northern mink example may strike some readers as too esoteric to shed light on the modern debate. Consider, then, the following (and last) illustration.

All legal systems struggle with the perennial problem of the *bona fide* purchaser without notice. A, the "real" owner of some property (call it a "widget")[6] is denied possession by a thief, who sells it to B, a *bona fide* purchaser without notice. A and B compete for the law's recognition of their respective claims. Given the good faith of both claimants, it is hard to settle this controversy by applying the principles of equity. It feels "right" to settle it on the basis of efficiency considerations. But which solution is more efficient? Standard economic

---

[3] H. Demsetz, 'Toward a Theory of Property Rights' [1967] 57 *American Economic Review* 13.

[4] H.S. Gordon, 'The Economic Theory of a Common-Property Resource: The Fishery' [1954] 62 *Journal of Political Economics* 124. For a general modern overview, see E.L. Ostrom, 'Self-Governance of Common Pool Resources' in P. Newman (ed.) *The New Palgrave Dictionary of Economics and the Law* (vol. 3 New York 1998) 434.

[5] Demsetz's ideas became very popular in more recent contributions to the literature, which far transcend the special case of the Labrador aborigines (as, indeed, was clearly Demsetz's idea as well). See, for example, R. Ellickson, 'Property in Land' [1993] 102 Yale Law Journal 1315.

[6] This "widget" can be any property whatsoever, real estate, personal property, an obligation, an interest *in re aliena*, a negotiable instrument or even cold cash.

analysis suggests that it is best to endow the party whose costs of preventing the harm (in this case, the theft) are higher.[7] To see this, consider what would have happened if the right were bestowed on the other party. In that case the latter would have had no incentive to prevent the harm. The harm would have been prevented by the party for whom it is costlier to fend it off; or, if transaction costs are low enough, the parties would have engaged in a Coasian deal, a costly affair too, to reverse the entitlement structure. The canonical solution, "Give the entitlement to the party with the higher prevention costs", is a neat one. The problem, however, is that in different jurisdictions different parties (A or B) can prevent the harm at lesser cost. Suppose, for instance, that in jurisdiction X the state maintains a readily accessible public record of widgets which indicates to all and sundry who owns them. Suppose that such a record does not exist in jurisdiction Y. In jurisdiction X, A should clearly prevail, because B could find out, at a low cost, that his seller was impersonating the true owner. In jurisdiction Y, by counter-distinction, B should have the upper hand, because he could have prevented the harm only by launching an excessively costly inquiry. The costs of this inquiry would have presumably exceeded A's costs in keeping a close watch on his own property. X and Y, then, are alien jurisdictions. Their interests cannot be served by uniformity.

So much for objective dissimilarity. But dissimilarity can be wholly subjective, too.

2. Subjective Dissimilarity

Subjective dissimilarity stems from the simple fact that different human beings may have different preferences over identical bundles. Had it been otherwise, nobody would ever trade a stallion for a stack of cash; the essence of exchange lies in the heterogeneity of tastes and preferences. This is as true for entire societies as it is true for individual players. Hence one's ability to speak about *social* welfare functions, or, indeed, in the most general terms, about the Social Good.

In this respect law is not different from any other bundle of goods. Historical examples abound. Friedrich von Savigny was, perhaps, the most influential of Continental jurists who believed that law, like language, should emanate directly from the people, from the most deeply rooted cultural tenets of any given society.[8] His lore carried such weight among his contemporaries that the process of

---

[7] R. Posner, *Economic Analysis of Law* 5th edn. (Boston 1998) 91–92; R. Cooter and Th. Ulen, *Law and Economics* 3rd edn. (Reading, Mass 2000) 140–142.

[8] "Every culture as a whole", wrote Savigny, "expresses itself in all its parts and fulfils itself with its spirit. Law (and each of its institutions) carries within itself the spirit from which it originated." F.K. von Savigny, *Of The Vocation of Our Age for Legislation and Jurisprudence* (Heidelberg 1914; A. Hayward, translator, 1831).

codifying German law and confining it, as it were, to a formal act of legislation, was retarded for a full century.[9] The Jewish nation was launched into two millennia of statelessness because it attempted to resist Emperor Hadrian's attempt to annex ancient Judea to the global zone of the Roman *jus commune*.[10] Less heroically, one notes that life under the adversarial, case oriented, pragmatic mills of the Common Law is different from life under the inquisitorial, deductive and high-principled processes of the Civil Law systems. It is hardly surprising that different social groups developed conflicting loyalties to these different bundles.

Now in all micro-economic thinking there is no meaning to rational choice (the selection of efficient solutions) unless one takes into account *both* the objectively available alternatives (the choice set) and the preferences of the actors (the actors may be either individual players or a given society as a whole). Maximizing one's utility (or welfare) on the basis of the choice set alone is analogous to the Zen paradox of applauding a performance by clapping a single palm.

We are now ready to understand the concept of "similarity" as we wish to employ it in this section. Two (or more) legal systems are "duplicates", if they are both objectively and subjectively similar. The systems are "alien" if they are either objectively or subjectively dissimilar. Objective similarity relates to the external conditions that prevail in a given economy, i.e. whether a given brand of goods is plentiful or scarce, or whether or not the state maintains a cheaply accessible record of entitlements to widgets. Subjective similarity relates to resemblance of preferences over identical bundles. A given legal system is "efficient" if it is rational in its strategy of satisfying its own preferences, subject to the constraint of its feasible (objective) conditions. It is easy to realize that if some legal systems are alien (i.e. either their preferences are different or the objective conditions that constrain these preferences are different or both), then there is no unique legal solution that maximizes their welfare. Overall maximization is better served by diversity than by uniformity.

All this is straightforward microeconomics. We turn now to explore some of the more subtle implications.

III. On the Limited Role of Transaction Costs

The obvious response (so it seems) to our rejection of harmonized law for alien jurisdictions is that it ignores the downside of diversity, costs. Many private law

---

[9] On Savigny's loathsome attitude to codification see G.P. Gouch, *History and Historians in the Nineteenth Century* (Ch. IV: Eichhorn, Savigny and Jakob Grimm) 39ff (2nd edn. 1952).

[10] A. Rabello, 'The Ban on Circumcision as a Cause of Bar Kokhba's Rebellion' [1995] 29 *Israel Law Review* 176.

transactions feature trans-national elements. Arguably, subjecting trans-national transactions to the diverse idiosyncrasies of multiple legal systems may simply be too expensive. Although we recognize the added cost of having to cope with numerous legal systems, our main claim, that alien jurisdictions are better served by diversity, remains unbending. Our key assumption in this section is that in an unharmonized world, all relevant national laws can be opted out of. In other words, we assume that the rules of private international law give the parties a *carte blanche* permission to abandon the default rule of their own legal system and to "migrate"—albeit at a cost—to a foreign legal regime. We believe that at least in the realm of private law this "freedom of migration" fairly reflects the existing legal culture in most jurisdictions. We further assume that harmonization destroys the freedom of migration. This is so for two cumulative reasons. First, some harmonized products are mandatory. For instance, the famous European "directives" to the Member States are not mere recommendations. The second, and more important, reason, is that when several jurisdictions repeal their national laws and adopt a single uniform product, the repealed legal orders cannot truthfully be reincorporated by private ordering. Unused legal systems get stale (or suffer a high amortization rate), because they are not litigated in courts, nor brushed up by precedent, nor illuminated by scholarship, nor respond to stimuli and to the changing *mores* of time. As viable alternatives of choice, they are lost. Armed with these assumptions, we turn to the proof of our claim.

1. Case I: Zero Network Externalities

Country A and country B are two alien jurisdictions. Both are assumed to be democratic countries, and their (initially diverse) laws reflect the collective will of the majority of A's subjects to be governed by legal system X and the collective decision of the majority of B's subjects to be governed by legal system Y. Assume, first (we later discard this assumption) that the utility of all subjects depends solely on the legal rules that govern their own behaviour, rather than, inter-personally, on the rules that govern the behaviour of others. In other words, our initial assumption is zero network externalities. We further assume that in the absence of harmonization, individual subjects in either jurisdiction are free to "consume" the legal system of the other country, if they are willing to defray the "migration" costs. Denote these costs as c. It is reasonable to expect that a minority of the subjects of jurisdiction A prefer the legal system of jurisdiction B to their own. Some of them are willing to pay c to obtain the legal order of their choice, while some others find c too prohibitive and are locked into their own legal system. Similarly, a minority of the subjects of jurisdiction B prefers the legal system of jurisdiction A to their own. Some of the latter are willing to pay c to obtain the legal order of their choice, and some are not. Enter a harmonization agency. Suppose that the agency is convinced that X is superior to Y and consequently incorporates it into a uniform law, with full application in both countries. Consider first the effects of the harmonization on the citizens of country A. Some of those subjects will suffer a detriment and none will derive a benefit as a result of the harmonization. The majority of A's subjects preferred X to Y in the first place, and therefore will be indifferent to the change. So will be A's subjects who actually preferred Y to X, but found c too prohibitive and would not have migrated in a world *sans* harmonization. However, the subset of A's subjects who would have migrated (i.e. for whom the benefit of migration exceeded c) would now be stuck with an unwanted legal system and suffer a detriment. Consider now the citizens of B. Some of them will benefit by the change, to be sure. More specifically, the citizens of B who preferred X to Y in the first place, would now be able to consume the system of their choice without having to pay c. But the majority of subjects in B will suffer a detriment, because they preferred Y to X (this is why Y was legislated in B in the first place), but will no longer be permitted to consume the system of their choice.

If we combine the results of the two jurisdictions, it turns out that uniformity is Pareto-inferior in the case of one jurisdiction (A), and detrimental to the majority of citizens in the other (B). This result is interesting, we think, because its robustness does not depend on the magnitude of the costs. Even if migration costs are quite substantial, if the preferences of the subjects are not inter-personal, alien jurisdictions are *always* better served by diversity than by uniformity.

2. Case II: Positive Network Externalities

To be sure, our assumption that the utility of all subjects solely depends on the set of norms applicable to themselves, is an over-simplification. The fact that one's legal system is binding outside of one's own jurisdiction (in other words, it is also practised by others) may well enhance one's own utility. For example, if an importer of goods in A can transact with subjects of B using his own legal system (X) rather than the other country's legal system (Y), because the sellers of the imported goods, like himself, are now using (harmonized) X, the importer's utility may well be enhanced. In other words, harmonization entails network externalities. To the extent that this is true, it is (arguably) no longer sustainable that for the citizens of A, diversity is Pareto-superior to harmonization. In addition, it is no longer safe to assume that the majority of B's subjects will suffer a detriment as a result of the destruction of their preferred system (Y) and its substitution by harmonized X. Their disutility resulting from this undesired substitution will now be mitigated by the salutary effects of network externalities in international trade. The extent of this mitigating effect is largely an empirical question.

With this said, we still feel that the adverse effects of harmonization among alien jurisdictions eclipse its benefits, even in a world with positive network externalities. We base our claim on three cumulative reasons.

Network externalities exist only among network players.   To begin with, network externalities may be relevant to only one subset of rules in any given legal system. Consider, for example, our example concerning the *bona fide* purchaser without notice. The allocation of property rights in this paradigmatic dispute is likely to be, in almost every case, a purely domestic problem. Thus the citizens of jurisdiction A are *not* likely to derive an external benefit if the citizens of jurisdiction B play by the same rules. Or consider any transaction involving some fungible product, which may be obtained everywhere, e.g. a standard insurance policy. If the citizens of A do not have to extend themselves extra-territorially for taking out such a policy, their domestic consumption of the desired coverage is not likely to be affected by network externalities. In other words, *network externalities are relevant (only) for network players*, i.e. for persons involved in transnational transactions.

On the hidden cost of network externalities.   Network externalities are commonly thought of as positive externalities. Consider, for example, a telecommunication network. Obviously, it would be absurd to think of the utility of each consumer as depending only on his own use of the equipment: There is a marked difference between using the telephone and playing solitaire. It is the network participation of the other users, alongside with one's own, which makes each player's participation worthwhile. But telecommunication is only one example of networks. Consider, next, the case of a linguistic network, achievable, for example, by the wholesale abolition of all languages except Esperanto. Just as in the case of a telecommunication network, a language network entails network externalities (any given Esperanto user derives a benefit by the fact that others, like himself, are using the same language). But this benefit is achievable only at a cost. The cost is the dumping of all languages except Esperanto. From a purely economic perspective, this strategy is costly because some players have a preference to use languages other than Esperanto, such that coercing them to use Esperanto reduces their utility.[11] Finally, consider the relevant case, a network of laws. Assume, first, a world *sans* harmonization, and a possible trade between subjects of different jurisdictions. Such players will trade a widget, if its value to the buyer exceeds its value to the seller. Such a sale entails an economic surplus, which the parties can split between them (say, in equal shares). But the economic surplus results not only from the physical properties of the widget, but also from

---

[11] Obviously, the cost may be framed in cultural terms too, but to do that would fall outside the scope of our chapter.

the applicable legal system, and from its compatibility with the preferences of the parties. In seeking to maximize their respective shares of the surplus, the parties will search for and adopt the sales law of the jurisdiction, which maximizes their aggregate utility. If the result of harmonization is to have their sale regulated by any other legal system, their economic surplus will be reduced, and so would the individual utility of each player. The creation of a network of laws, then, generates two opposing effects on the utility of the players. On the one hand, it enhances their utility because other players use the same legal system as they do, whether they prefer it or not. On the other hand, it reduces their utility, because they are now forced to consume a set of laws which they do not prefer. From this vantage point, it seems that even for trans-national players the lure of uniformity is not so clear.

Is the spectre of network externalities real? A substantial number of harmonization efforts have centred on trans-national players. This is, of course, good, because harmonizing purely domestic legal norms seems outright silly[12] (some harmonization efforts seem to have gone astray in these directions). [13] As we noted earlier, it is hard to tell whether in this case, of trans-national players, the salutary network effects of harmonization are greater or less than the costs. But even if we make the assumption that the benefits eclipse the costs, the whole issue seems rather moot, because in actual reality it is hard to believe that a genuine network of laws is a feasible proposition, in spite of all the usual rhetoric in praise of harmonization. To substantiate this claim we develop a (sketchy) theory of harmonized legal products. We show that these products are likely to be ridden with *lacunae*, which allows alien jurisdictions to maintain their substantive legal independence in the teeth of the harmonized product. We conclude that *lacunae*-filled harmonized products cannot be relied on to generate the salutary external effects of efficient networks. We turn now to a fuller exposition of this latter claim.

IV. Why do Alien Jurisdictions Harmonize their Laws?

As far as the domestic aspects of a given legal rule are concerned, alien jurisdictions are better off under diversity than under uniformity. Even where the

---

[12] For example, the 1964 Convention relating to a Uniform Law on the Formation of Contracts for the International Sale of Goods (The Hague); the 1970 International Convention on the Travel Contract (Brussels), or the currently active Unidroit project concerning the Principles of International Commercial Contracts (1994).

[13] For example, the 1955 *Benelux Treaty on compulsory insurance against civil liability in respect of motor vehicles* (although the operation of motor vehicles may sometimes have cross border repercussions, including in matters of insurance). Many of the famous company law directives seem to tackle purely domestic issues too.

international aspects of a given transaction predominate, each jurisdiction prefers that the harmonized product conform to its own legal traditions, rather than to the traditions of it harmonization partners. This is true even if, *ceteris paribus*, harmonization is preferred to diversity. This notion, that each jurisdiction prefers to be bound by a harmonized product that conforms to its own traditions, stems from two cumulative reasons. The first, simple, reason is that its citizens have a substantive (revealed) preference for the contents of their own system (this is why they adopted their unique system in the first place). The second, subtler, reason, is that, as we show in the second section of this chapter, each jurisdiction derives a benefit by applying its home-made rules to foreigners, and suffers a detriment when its own citizens "migrate" to foreign jurisdictional domains.

In spite of each jurisdiction's incentive to stick to its own legal traditions, harmonization is rampant across the globe. This phenomenon calls for a rational explanation. Multiplicity of legal systems allows individuals to migrate among jurisdictions, in quest of the set of laws that best suits their tastes. Our assumption, again, is that each jurisdiction suffers from the migration of its citizens to the legal domain of other countries and benefits from the migration of foreign citizens to its own domain. We further assume that in each (democratic) country the majority of subjects favours its own laws to the laws of foreign jurisdictions, but a (fixed) minority would rather be ruled by some foreign norms. This assumption yields the result that under diversity there is more migration from large to small countries than the other way around (a given percentage of a large country outnumbers the same percentage of a small nation). Consequently, small countries are favoured by diversity and large nations are favoured by uniformity.[14] If large nations retain the clout to force their will on their smaller neighbours, they can be expected to block the migration trail by crafting a mandatory harmonized product. In a world where sheer military violence is out of vogue, we assume that large countries forcefully promulgate harmonized products by imposing a penalty on holdout jurisdictions.[15] If these assumptions hold water, we can demonstrate why harmonized products tend to be incomplete, i.e. to be filled with *lacunae*. The incidence of numerous *lacunae* in

[14] The greatest beneficiary of the freedom of migration among American jurisdictions, for example, is the tiny state of Delaware. The larger states suffer from negative migration effects. Likewise, the corporate law directives on European soil are largely powered by the larger jurisdictions, e.g. Germany, and resisted by smaller jurisdictions (we interpret the U.K. as a "small" jurisdiction, because it uniquely adheres to the principles of the Common Law system, within a continent that bases its numerous legal systems on the common ground of the Civil Law system). Arguably, similar considerations apply to other domains of unification, e.g. currency unification. As these lines are being written, the voters of a small nation, Denmark, decided to reject the Euro and hold their ground with their own national currency.

[15] On the notion of penalizing non-conforming jurisdictions see Leebron, above, n. 2.

harmonized legal products dramatically reduced their usefulness as legal networks, and their ability to generate network externalities disappears.

V. The *Lacunae* Factory

Even the existing theoretical literature has it that harmonized products tend to be incomplete, i.e. to be filled with *lacunae*. It appears that this theoretical prediction is clearly borne out by the evidence. Alan Schwartz and Robert Scott, the two main theorists in this field, contend that incompleteness is a natural corollary of the political economy of private lawmaking, i.e. of crafting harmonized legal products. Harmonization officials, they explain, yield to the incentives of rational maximization. They are charged with the task of unifying diverse legal systems, and the success of their respective careers hinges on their ability to deliver the goods. Even if they are naturally disposed to carry on their responsibilities in the public interest, they have an incentive not to abort the project altogether. Given the reluctance of alien jurisdictions to abandon their legal independence, harmonization officials are constrained to offer them incomplete legal arrangements, which allows the jurisdictions to fill the *lacunae* in conformity with their old traditions.[16]

We find these observations insightful, because they bring to the fore considerations of political economy and identify the link between these considerations and the outcome of incompleteness. In the following lines we wish to augment these considerations and to model, however informally, the interplay between the relevant jurisdictions and the harmonization agency.

Suppose that the harmonization agency (H) is charged with the task of harmonizing the systems of two jurisdictions, A and B. Perhaps H is commissioned to fulfil its mission at the behest of some third jurisdiction, call it T. T is the largest, most influential, jurisdiction in the region, and its objective function is to force the other, smaller, jurisdictions to harmonize their laws in conformity with its own. To empower H to carry out its assignment, it is vested with authority to impose a fine (F) on holdout jurisdictions. If the harmonization project is accepted by both jurisdictions H gets a bonus, which declines, however, with the number of *lacunae* (not much credit can be earned for a harmonized product that does not say much). Each jurisdiction is presumed to be loath to accept the harmonized product and would have been better off without it. However, if conform they must, they prefer that the harmonized product be as filled with *lacunae*

---

[16] A. Schwartz and R. Scott, 'The Political Economy of Private Legislatures' [1995] 143 *University of Pennsylvania Law Review* 595; R. Scott, 'The Uniformity Norm in Commercial Law: A Comparative Analysis of Common Law and Code Methodologies' in J. Kraus and S. Walt (eds.) *The Jurisprudential Foundations of Corporate and Commercial Law*, Cambridge University Press, 2001.

as possible (except where the legal norms of T happen to conform to their own independent traditions; in this case they prefer to have rules rather than *lacunae*). The reason why the small jurisdictions prefer *lacunae* where their legal traditions differ from those of T, is that their judges would be free to interpret ambiguities, at least to a certain extent, in conformity with their previous independent traditions.

If we accept these assumptions, we can predict a few outcomes, that may be summarized in the following four propositions.

Proposition 1

If the harmonization project catches on, it is likely to contain all the legal norms that are common to all the jurisdictions. In this simple case T's objective function, of spreading its own laws across the entire domain of harmonized systems is expected to meet no resistance from either A or B. In this case diversity is Pareto-inferior to uniformity.

Proposition 2

The success of adopting the harmonized product, in whatever form, depends on how onerous is F. If F is (too) slight A and B might be better off forking it out than submitting themselves to the yoke of an unwanted legal system. Only (sufficiently) burdensome fines might persuade them to abandon diversity and to go along with harmonization.

Proposition 3

If H is vested with authority to impose particularly heavy penalties, the harmonized product is likely to be complete, i.e. not to contain *lacunae*. This is because even if the smaller jurisdictions intensely dislike the legal system of T, they might be better off succumbing to it than paying the fine. In this case H has no incentive to settle for a harmonized product *cum lacunae*, because its bonus is inversely related to the number of legislative voids, and its powerful tools of coercion allow it to force an "undamaged" legal product, without any holes in it.

Proposition 4

Finally, if F is sufficiently onerous to ensure passage of the harmonized product, but not quite as onerous as to let H act as a dictator, the number of *lacunae* is predicted to be inversely related to F. Heavier fines will produce fewer ambiguities and lighter fines will generate more ambiguities. Thus empirical observations reporting a high incidence of incomplete legal norms suggest that H is only minimally armed with coercive power. Had H insisted, with the limited means at its disposal, on a more complete harmonized product, the smaller jurisdictions would have rather paid the fine than gone along with harmonization. In this case H optimizes by accepting the reduced bonus for a harmonized product *cum lacunae* rather than by insisting on a complete product and witnessing a total debacle of the whole project (and a total loss of the bonus). Many famous harmonized products conform to the predictions of this last proposition.[17]

Obviously, this general outline is not intended to be more than a rough sketch. In real life, for instance, it might be important whether the harmonization effort depends on a universal participation of every affected jurisdiction (Common Market projects are often of this variety); or that harmonization can take place even where some jurisdictions hold out (American uniform laws belong to that category). If universal participation is required, jurisdictions have an incentive to appear willing to join, as long as they have some assurance that other jurisdictions might not. In such a situation all the jurisdictions will continue to enjoy legal independence, but only the explicit holdouts will foot the bill. Without dwelling on these niceties at this stage, it is clear that fitting the model with some additional nuance and detail may result in modified game-theoretic outcomes.

---

[17] Consider, for example, the remedy of specific performance in trans-national commercial contracts. Given the opposite attitude of Common Law and Civil Law jurisdictions to this remedy, it can be predicted to generate a bone of contention in any harmonization effort. This issue was first tackled by the Unidroit in its highly successful 1964 Convention relating to a Uniform Law on the International Sale of Goods. Article 64 of that document adopts the majority view in Europe upholding specific performance as a regular contract remedy subject to certain qualifications. However, Article 28 provides that "[A] court is not bound to enter a judgement of specific performance unless the court would do so under its own law in respect of similar contracts of sale not governed by [the] Convention". Clearly, there was no apparent reason for Common Law jurisdictions to oppose such a compromising language. With the passage of time, the orthodoxy of Common Law jurisdictions against specific performance mellowed quite a bit, which allowed the Unidroit, some 30 years later, to draft article 7.2.2 of its 1994 Principles of International Commercial Contracts. The new rule, once again, prescribes specific performance as a normal remedy for breach of contract. The need to curry favour with Common Law jurisdictions was no longer as pronounced as in 1964, but nevertheless their needs and preferences were not altogether neglected. Subsection (b) now provides that specific performance may be denied where "performance, or, where relevant, enforcement is unreasonably burdensome or expensive", and subsection (c) provides that the remedy may be denied if "the party entitled to performance may reasonably obtain performance from another source".

C. Similar Jurisdictions

I. Introduction

We turn now to deal with similar jurisdictions, i.e. duplicates. The main thesis in this subchapter is not that duplicates ought to have diverse legal systems. Rather, it is that they can be trusted to craft their own uniform laws as a means of promoting their own best interests. Thus we do not maintain that harmonization among duplicates is not necessary; it is that harmonization *by fiat* isn't; spontaneous, self-interested harmonization does not suffer from the kind of agency problems we identified in the previous chapter and should be viewed as preferable overall. We start by identifying the incentive of independent jurisdictions to opt for efficient legal regimes and conclude our discussion by showing how this effort is likely to lead to spontaneously generated uniform laws.

II. The Incentive to Craft Efficient Rules

Jurisdictions have an incentive to craft efficient legal regimes. It is a well-known fact that the tiny State of Delaware has benefited greatly by capturing the lion's share of the American market for corporate charters. Many commentators, however, interpret this fact as an idiosyncrasy, which affects only corporate law, and only within the American Union. In this section, we wish to dispel this misconception.

1. A Point of Departure: the (Well-known) Case of Delaware

A vast number of large American companies, and many foreign corporations to boot, choose the State of Delaware as their site of incorporation. This choice implies that those companies "buy into" the Delaware law of corporations as the legal system that governs their affairs. In fact, companies are willing to incur the additional cost associated with incorporating far from home *because* this is their only way of "consuming" the laws of Delaware. Why are corporations eager to be governed by this particular statute? Because law matters. Superior legal rules facilitate better corporate governance, which, in turn, yields higher returns for the shareholders. The assumption here is that shareholders are attracted to Delaware corporations for exactly this reason; they simply fare better when they invest their money in a Delaware company than otherwise. Indeed, recent research seems to have put any lingering doubts at rest.[18] Delaware corporations

---

[18] Those doubts emanate from W. Cary's ground-breaking article, 'Federalism and Corporate Law: Reflections Upon Delaware [1974] 83 Yale Law Journal 663, and are echoed in recent writings

tend to do better, on the average, than comparable companies incorporated in other American jurisdictions.[19]

The State of Delaware is a primary beneficiary of its marketing efforts to offer itself as an incorporating haven for out of State enterprises. Besides its clear explicit benefits—incorporation and annual fees account for about 20% of the State revenues—Delaware is able to obtain a large number of tangible and intangible side benefits. Wilmington, an otherwise dormant provincial capital, is turned into a veritable hub of activity. Its bar prospers. A large industry of side players, including lawyers, economists, accountants, bankers, and other traders hum around the edges of the thriving corporate business. Altogether, there can be little doubt that the corporate code is the State's number one export and moneymaking commodity. Nor can it easily be grabbed away by competing industries. Delaware enjoys a first mover advantage in relation to all other jurisdictions, and their numerous efforts to emulate its product usually come to naught. Nevertheless, one notes in passing that many other jurisdictions, fearful of further erosion of their share in the market for corporate charters, craft laws that are strikingly similar to Delaware's.[20] The race between Delaware and its many competitors is, in the final analysis, a race to the top. The story of corporate law across America speaks eloquently of the forces of spontaneous harmonization among duplicates and the futility of bringing it about by administrative prodding.

2. A European Perspective: the (Not Less Well-known) *Centros* Case

European nations differ on the applicable choice of law rule determining corporate governance. Some jurisdictions follow the state of incorporation rule, much like the domestic choice of law rule in the U.S. Some other nations follow the centre of activities (*situs*) rule.[21] According to this latter alternative, corpora-

---

as well, e.g. L. Bebchuk and A. Ferrell, 'Federalism and Corporate Law: The Race to Protect Managers from Takeovers' [1999] 99 Colorado Law Review 1168.

[19] See R. Daines, 'Does Delaware Law Protect Value?' (2001) 62 *Journal of Finance* 25. These empirical results substantiate a long lasting theoretical prediction, dating back to R. Winter's famous article, 'State Law, Shareholder Protection and the Theory of the Corporation' [1977] 6 Journal of Legal Studies 251, and supported by the mainstream of corporate scholars, e.g. R. Romano, 'Law as a Product: Some Pieces of the Incorporation Puzzle' [1985] 1 *Journal of Law, Economics and Organizations* 225.

[20] A prime example is Nevada, which both imitates Delaware's statutory language and mimics its court decisions. This practice prompted Delaware to alert the public to its own superiority, in spite of the marked similarity between its laws and those of its imitators. For a website war between Delaware and its upstart competitors see, the official website of the State of Delaware at www.delaware.gov

[21] Some implications of the centre of activities rule (or the "seat" doctrine, as it sometimes referred to), are delineated in E. Wymeersch, 'Centros: A Landmark Decision in European Company Law' in Th. Baums, K.J. Hopt, and N. Horn (eds.), *Corporations, Capital Markets and Business in the Law, Liber Amicorum Richard M Buxbaum* (London/The Hague 2000).

tions cannot shop for the legal regime of their choice without moving their plant and other activities to the desired location. This rule bestows upon the centre of activities jurisdiction a monopoly power to determine rules of corporate governance, without fear of losing its hold on the market for corporate charters.

The celebrated *Centros*[22] case may mark a turning point from this anti-competitive environment. To be sure, the Court's reasoning in this case is far from being lucid, and seems to rest on technical, rather than on principled grounds. It remains to be seen if future holdings will choose to keep it within the narrow boundaries of relatively unimportant issues (e.g. minimum capital requirements) or to expand it to more significant domains (e.g. co-determination). In view of these doubts, there is very little we can offer in terms of divining the future or analysing the Court's ruling *de lege lata*. Let us, then, confine ourselves to the following two remarks.

First, the theoretical framework of the market for corporate charters in the U.S. and in Europe is not appreciably different. If one believes that American States have an incentive to craft superior legislative products and that corporations, if given the choice, have an incentive to "buy into" them, there is no reason to think that European jurisdictions and European companies should follow a different path. Moreover, if the race in the American market for corporate charters is a "race to the top", there is no reason to fear that in Europe, for some unspecified reason, it might transform itself into a "race to the bottom". If all of this is true, then it seems that the state of incorporation choice of law rule clearly dominates the centre of activities rule, because only the former is compatible with the existence of a market for corporate charters. Hence, *Centros* should be given the broadest possible interpretation. Not only should this achieve an upgrading of European corporate rule-formation, but it will also yield legal harmonization of the spontaneous variety, a much better (and cheaper) breed than coercive legal cloning.

The second comment we wish to make is more like raising an eyebrow than offering an analytical insight. We note with the utmost astonishment that the greatest potential winners of the *Centros* case, the architects of the British corporate system, do not feel elated at their triumph. Rather than encourage foreign incorporations on British soil, the British often frown upon the prospect of foreign companies "clogging up" their registry. One seldom encounters comparable complaints from Delaware officials.

3. The Non Corporate World

Is there a viable market for statutory products outside of the corporate law domain? We do not wish to make a claim that transcends all legal boundaries

---

[22] Case C-212/97 *Centros Ltd v Erhvervs-og Selskabsstyrelsen* [1999] E.C.R. I-1459.

656 Uriel Procaccia and Uzi Segal Chapter 32

(perhaps it is a good idea to have, say, a system of uniform weights and measures). Nor do we object to minimal standards in such matters as human rights or the environment. The following analysis is restricted, then, to *lex mercatoria* broadly defined. In that restricted domain, we feel that the answer to the question is Yes. To see this, we have to consider at least two major hurdles.

a. Difficulty Number One: No Explicit Payoffs for Successful Jurisdictions

Delaware is explicitly rewarded for its entrepreneurial legislation by collecting incorporation and annual fees from all Delaware corporations. The State's ability to tax its corporations is a corollary of the choice of law rule that holds that in order to "buy into" Delaware law, companies need incorporate there.[23] The choice of law rule in commercial matters is different. The parties are free to choose the proper law of the contract whichever their nationality and other relevant links.[24] The chosen country cannot tax this choice, and arguably has a diminished incentive to craft superior laws. However, as we have already seen, Delaware's reward from its superior corporate code is not limited to explicit taxation. Quite as importantly, the code virtually floods the state with commercial activity that would have gone elsewhere if it were not for its attractive features. If the law of contracts in jurisdiction X, for instance, will be universally recognized as more attractive than the law of contract in other jurisdictions, the bar in that jurisdiction will prosper; disputes will be either litigated, or arbitrated, or settled in X; commercial activities in the jurisdiction will flourish. Indeed, it is exactly this interest of every jurisdiction to attract as many users of its legal products as it can, which accounts for the proclivity of large jurisdictions to favour harmonization. They fear that in a world *without* harmonization more subjects will exit its internal legislative market than enter it and they will net a loss.

b. Difficulty Number Two: No Active Capital Markets

Delaware shareholders invest in Delaware corporations because their return on their investment is higher. Delaware law cannot change for the worse because if it does Delaware shareholders will migrate to out of state companies, or else the cost of capital for domestic corporations will be too high. It seems, then, that the role played by capital markets is indispensable for the success story of Delaware

---

[23] R. Leflar, A. McDougal, and R. Felix, *American Conflicts Law* 4th edn. (Charelottesville 1986) s. 14 and 255.

[24] ibid., s. 147.

corporate law.[25] Now, in commercial law settings, capital markets do not play a similar role. The question is what mechanism might replace them in triggering a race to the top in commercial legislation.

We submit that the products market can play this role. Products do not come bare of the contractual arrangements surrounding them. They are composite goods. Suppose, to take a deliberately extreme example, that a given legal system does not enforce executory promises. Buying a product under such a system is tantamount to ignoring the time preferences of the contracting parties.[26] Parties who are not agnostic about this sort of preferences would find such a system inferior to a system, which holds that "every contract executory imports in itself an assumpsit".[27] Other things equal, any jurisdiction insisting on real exchange of goods and services (i.e. not committing itself to the enforcement of "bare" promises) will get quickly deserted by contract law users with non-neutral time preferences.[28] Other examples may be less extreme, but not less convincing. Buying a product under an expectation measure of damages is not like buying the otherwise same product under a reliance measure of damages.[29] If one rule is more efficient overall than the other is, jurisdictions in quest of maximizing the number of their contract law users have an incentive to adopt the efficient rule. None but the fittest will survive. And if several (or all) jurisdictions are duplicates, they will all move to efficient equilibria.

4. Are Multiple Efficient Equilibria Possible?

All duplicate jurisdictions will move, then, to *efficient* equilibria. But is it possible that different duplicates will move to *different efficient* equilibria? If this scenario is possible then unity may be frustrated where it is due, i.e. among duplicates. We submit, though, that this contingency is not very likely.

Without involving the reader in mathematical technicalities we can present this argument in the following simplified form: Commercial and civil law is about dividing societal wealth among rival claimants, under every possible

---

[25] The role of capital markets in the formation of good governance structures was first suggested in R. Winter's seminal article, above, n. 19.

[26] See Cooter and Ulen, above, n. 7, at 184–185.

[27] This quaint language is taken, of course, from the famous *Slade's Case*, where an English court decided, in 1602, that executory contracts ought to be enforced as a matter of principle.

[28] It seems that the Russian legal system is a modern example of an entire legal culture that does not respect the institution of promises. For a general discussion of this phenomenon in the corporate domain, see B. Black and R. Kraakman, 'A Self-Enforcing Model of Corporate Law' [1996] 109 Harvard Law Review 1911.

[29] Only the expectation measure for damages compensates the promisee for the value of the broken promise. Thus, it is the only rule of damages that sanctions a market for promises.

contingency.[30] For example, if a finder (F) finds a banknote in the public domain, and the original owner (O) makes an ownership claim to the same note (these are two arbitrary examples of "contingencies"), then the legal system can confer title either on F or on O, or divide the value of the note (not necessarily in equal parts) between the two claimants. How much would "the legal system" (which is, of course, a euphemism for social preferences within a given society) fork out to each claimant? That would depend on societal preferences. Societies that "like" finders would give the note to F. Societies that "like" owners would give the note to O. Most societies would presumably prefer to either share the proceeds of the note between the two parties or hinge the result on some set of contingencies. If two societies have different preferences, than they are alien jurisdictions, and their laws should not be harmonized. If they are duplicates they have similar preferences and would generate equal results. Or would they? Suppose that two duplicates happen to be indifferent between two possible allocations, which seem equally desired. For example, the two duplicates may be indifferent between giving 60% to F and 40% to O ("solution number 1"), or vice versa, giving 60% to O and 40% to F ("solution number 2"). Is it not possible that one of them might pick (at random) solution number 1 and the other jurisdiction may opt for solution number 2? Indifference between the solutions may generate, according to this line of thought, diversity among duplicates, although they may be better served by uniformity.

Economic theory predicts, however, that this result is not probable. This prediction is based on a standard assumption in micro-economic theory, termed "quasi concavity of the preferences". In non-technical language, it simply means, that if a person (or a society) is indifferent between two solutions, there must be some third solution (an "in-between" solution) that is preferable to both.[31] There is only one solution, which is globally the "best" (and, as we have seen before, players have an incentive to choose it). To get a better intuition of the reasonableness of this assumption (quasi concavity) consider the following example: An individual is invited to choose whether he wants to spend all his (finite) resources on obtaining alimentary provisions (A) or on clothing (C) or on any combination thereof. If his initial endowment is rich with culinary delicacies but he has virtually nothing to wear, he would presumably trade a lot of food to obtain a relatively small quantity of garments. If his initial endowment is rich with clothing but there is not enough food to keep his body and soul in one piece, he would give closets of apparel for a piece of bread. We always attach a greater subjective value to that which we have less of. Now suppose that the

[30] In technical language, we can think of all laws that allocate property rights among different claimants as "convex sets".

[31] A familiar quasi-concave preference structure in the case of individual players is the "indifference curve". Quasi-concave *social* preferences are a more elusive concept, but are also very common.

individual in question is indifferent between spending 80% of his resources on A and 20% on C, or vice versa, 80% on C and 20% on A. Given our assumption (attaching more subjective value to scarce than to plentiful goods) a reasonable interpretation of the indifference is that the first possibility allocates too much of his resources to A and the second possibility not enough resources to A. Obviously, the individual in question could enhance his utility by choosing some middle ground solution, such as allocating 50% of his resources to either commodity.

If quasi concavity holds in the case of duplicate jurisdictions[32] choosing among bundles of property entitlements, the spectre of *different* efficient equilibria is not possible. There is one, and only one, globally optimal solution for all duplicate jurisdictions.

There is little wonder that duplicates engage in spontaneous, uncoerced, harmonization of their respective legal systems (e.g. corporate law in America or the paradigmatic *lex mercatoria* of olden times). But not all jurisdictions are duplicates. The existing differences among the legal systems of the world are still very numerous. It is the alien jurisdictions, not the similar ones, which reject cloning, and enrich the legal culture of this planet with their breathtaking diversity.

---

[32] Once again, we wish to emphasize that quasi concavity is an *assumption*, rather than an empirical necessity.

Part X:

Convergence of Divergence

The Rise of Dispersed Ownership: The Roles of Law and the State in the Separation of Ownership and Control

JOHN C. COFFEE, JR.*

Abstract

Recent commentary has argued that deep and liquid securities markets and a dispersed shareholder base are unlikely to develop in civil law countries and transitional economies for a variety of reasons, including (1) the absence of adequate legal protections for minority shareholders, (2) the inability of dispersed shareholders to hold control or pay an equivalent control premium to that which a prospective controlling shareholder will pay, and (3) the political vulnerability of dispersed shareholder ownership in left-leaning "social democracies". Nonetheless, this chapter finds that significant movement in the direction of dispersed ownership has occurred and is accelerating across Europe.

To understand how dispersed ownership can arise in the absence of the supposed legal and political preconditions, this article reconsiders the appearance of dispersed ownership in the late nineteenth and early twentieth century in the U.S. and the U.K. During this era, the private benefits of control were high, and minority legal protections in the U.S. were notoriously lacking, as the famous Robber Barons of the age bribed judges and legislators and effectively employed regulatory arbitrage to escape even minimal anti-fraud regulation. Nonetheless, strong self-regulatory institutions (most notably, the New York Stock Exchange) and private bonding mechanisms by which leading underwriters pledged their reputational capital by placing directors on the board of sponsored firms enabled the equity market to expand and dispersed ownership to arise. In contrast, in the U.K., the London Stock Exchange for a variety of path-dependent reasons played a far more passive role and did not become an effective self-regulator until much later in the Twentieth Century. Yet, dispersed ownership also arose, although at a slower pace. The lesser role for private self-regulation in the U.K. may have been the consequence of its lesser need for self-regulation as a functional substitute for formal law, given both earlier legislation in the U.K. and lesser exposure to judicial corruption and regulatory arbitrage. Finally, the Paris Bourse over this same period operated as a state-administered monopoly whose stockbrokers were formally considered civil servants. Facing no competition and having little need to enhance its reputational capital, it did not innovate and fell behind the London Stock Exchange. The intrusive role of state regulation, which discouraged private self-regulatory initiatives, appears to have a factor in its competitive failure.

Based on these examples, this chapter argues that "functional convergence" will dominate "formal convergence" and that the principal mechanism of functional convergence may be private self-regulation. However, rather than reject the "law matters" hypothesis,

* The author is grateful for helpful comments from Brian Cheffins, John Langbein, Roberta Romano, and Andrei Schleifer, from my colleagues, Ronald Gilson, Victor Goldberg, Jeffrey Gordon, and Curtis Milhaupt, and from participants at the Yale Law School Raben Lecture. This article originally appeared in Volume 111 of the Yale Law Journal as Coffee, 'The Rise of Dispersed Ownership: The Roles of Law and the State in the Separation of Ownership and Control' [2001] 111 Yale Law Journal 1 and appears here in an amended version, with the permission of the Yale Law Journal.

this chapter suggests that one of the principal advantages of common law legal systems is their decentralized character, which encourages self-regulatory initiatives, whereas in civil law systems the state may monopolize all law-making initiatives. Further, this chapter proposes that legal reforms, while important, are likely to follow, rather than precede, market changes—as happened in both the U.S. and the U.K.. Once however a constituency for liquid and transparent securities market is thus created, it will predictably seek and secure legislation that fills in the enforcement gap that self-regulation leaves. Both in the U.S., the U.K., and Europe today, the growth of securities markets has been largely divorced from politics.

What then are the preconditions for the separation of ownership and control? A critical factor is that public shareholders be able to protect themselves from control acquisitions that make them worse off. During the late Nineteenth Century, this meant protection from stealth raiders who sought to assemble controlling blocks without paying a control premium. In both the U.S. and the U.K., these protections were first developed through private (or semi-private) ordering and then formalized in legislation.

Contents

Tables

A. Introduction

Recent scholarship on comparative corporate governance has produced a puzzle. While Berle and Means had assumed that all large public corporations would mature to an end-stage capital structure characterized by the separation of ownership and control,[1] the contemporary empirical evidence is decidedly to the contrary. Instead of convergence toward a single capital structure, the twentieth century saw the polarization of corporate structure between two rival systems of corporate governance:

(1) *A Dispersed Ownership System*, characterized by strong securities markets, rigorous disclosure standards, and high market transparency, in which the market for corporate control constitutes the ultimate disciplinary mechanism; and

---

[1] A.A. Berle, Jr and G.C. Means, *The Modern Corporation and Private Property* (New York 1932) 5–19.

(2) *A Concentrated Ownership System*, characterized by controlling blockholders, weak securities markets, high private benefits of control, and low disclosure and market transparency standards, with only a modest role played
by the market for corporate control, but with a possible substitutionary
monitoring role played by large banks.[2]

An initial puzzle is whether such a dichotomy can persist in an increasingly
competitive global capital market. Arguably, as markets globalize and corporations having very different governance systems are compelled to compete head
to head (in product, labour, and capital markets), a Darwinian struggle becomes
likely, out of which, in theory, the most efficient form should emerge dominant.
Indeed, some have predicted that such a competition implies an "end to history"
for corporate law.[3] A rival and newer position—hereinafter called the "Path
Dependency Thesis"—postulates instead that institutions evolve along path-
dependent trajectories, which are heavily shaped by initial starting points and
pre-existing conditions.[4] In short, history matters, because it constrains the way
in which institutions can change, and efficiency does not necessarily triumph.

These two rival positions do not, however, state the deeper puzzle. That
puzzle involves the origins of dispersed ownership. The provocative scholarship
of La Porta, Lopez-de-Silanes, Shleifer, and Vishny (LLS&V) has not only
shown the existence of two fundamentally different systems of corporate
governance, but has placed legal variables at centre stage in explaining the persistence of these two systems.[5] LLS&V have boldly argued that civil-law legal

---

[2] The seminal work of La Porta, Lopez-de-Silanes, Shleifer, and Vishny (LLS&V) has established the existence of these rival systems, that they seem to have evolved along distinctive legal trajectories, and that they correlate with significant differences in the legal protections provided to
minority shareholders. R. La Porta et al., 'Corporate Ownership Around the World' [1999] 54
Journal of Finance 471. More recent work in the same vein has shown that the private benefits of control appear to be much higher in French civil law countries than in common law or Scandinavian
countries. T. Nenova, *The Value of Corporate Votes and Control Benefits: A Cross-Country
Analysis (SSRN Electronic Library, Working Paper no. 237,809, 2000), available at* http://papers.
ssrn.com/sol3/paper.taf?abstract_id=237809 .

[3] For representative statements of this position, see F.H. Easterbrook and D.R. Fischel, *The
Economic Structure of Corporate Law* (Cambridge 1991) 4–15; and H. Hansmann and R. Kraakman,
'The End of History for Corporate Law' [2001] 89 Georgetown Law Journal 439.

[4] L.A. Bebchuk and M.J. Roe, 'A Theory of Path Dependence in Corporate Ownership and
Governance' [1999] 52 Stanford Law Review 127; A.N. Licht, 'The Mother of All Path
Dependencies: Toward a Cross-Cultural Theory of Corporate Governance Systems' [2001] 26
Delaware Journal of Corporate Law 147.

[5] R. La Porta et al, 'Law and Finance' [1998] 106 *Journal of Political Economics* 1113 [hereinafter
R. La Porta et al., 'Law and Finance']; R. La Porta et al., 'Legal Determinants of External Finance'
[1997] 52 *Journal of Finance* 1131. For the latest and fullest statement of their position, see R. La
Porta et al., *Investor Protection and Corporate Governance* (2000) (unpublished manuscript, on file
with author). See also Nenova, above, n. 2 (finding significant disparities in the private benefits of
control enjoyed by controlling shareholders depending upon the country of incorporation and the
legal family to which that jurisdiction of incorporation belongs).

systems provide inadequate protections to minority shareholders, and hence dispersed ownership can arise only in a common-law legal environment. To support this conclusion, they assembled a worldwide database that shows that the depth and liquidity of equity markets around the world correlate closely with particular families of legal systems, with common-law systems consistently outperforming civil-law systems.[6]

If LLS&V are correct, the implications of their research seem profoundly pessimistic for parts of the world seeking to develop deeper, more liquid securities markets. In the absence of sweeping legal changes, civil-law countries would seem condemned to concentrated ownership and thin securities markets. Not only might this legal barrier frustrate European efforts to develop a pan-European securities market, but its implications are even more significant and adverse for transitional economies. A growing body of research suggests that an active securities market is an engine for economic growth.[7] Must transitional

---

[6] LLS&V initially conducted an inventory of the laws governing investor protection in 49 countries. Focusing on the corporate law and bankruptcy law of these countries, they next constructed measures of shareholder rights (for example, the presence or absence of "one share, one vote" rules, the existence of remedies available to minority shareholders, and the possibility of proxy voting by mail as opposed to voting in person) and measures of creditor rights (for example, whether creditors are paid first in liquidation, whether managers can unilaterally seek judicial protection from creditors, etc.). R. La Porta et al., 'Law and Finance', above, n. 5. These measures were then combined with measures of the quality of law enforcement in each jurisdiction to create an unprecedented data set quantifying differences in legal rules, and in rule enforcement, around the world. Although they found large differences in the prevailing rules and established that these differences could be grouped into four major legal families—common law, French, German, and Scandinavian civil law—doubt has persisted among legal scholars as to the meaningfulness of the differences observed. Basically, the LLS&V index focuses on six legal variables: (1) proxy voting by mail; (2) the absence of any requirement that shareholders deposit their shares prior to the general shareholders' meeting in order to vote them; (3) cumulative voting; (4) the ability of shareholders to sue their directors or otherwise challenge in court the decisions reached at shareholder meetings; (5) the ability of 10% or less of the shareholders to call an extraordinary shareholders' meeting; and (6) shareholder pre-emptive rights. By no means is it here implied that these rights are unimportant, but they seem to supply only partial and sometimes easily outflanked safeguards, which have little to do with the protection of control and the entitlement to a control premium. As this chapter suggests, dispersed ownership can persist only if the dispersed shareholders have the capacity to block an incoming control seeker from acquiring control without paying a control premium. Indeed, this fear of a premium-less acquisition of control was a major concern in the late nineteenth century well before the appearance of the modern tender offer. See text accompanying nn. 87–88.

[7] E.g. A. Demirgüç-Kunt and V. Maksimovic, 'Law, Finance and Firm Growth' [1998] 53 *Journal of Finance* 2107 (finding that firms in countries with active stock markets were able to obtain greater funds to finance growth); R. Levine and S. Zervos, 'Stock Markets, Banks, and Economic Growth' [1998] 88 *American Economics Review* 537 (relating economic growth to financial development); M. Obstfeld, 'Risk-Taking, Global Diversification and Growth' [1994] 84 *American Economics Review* 1310 (finding that the ability of investors to diversify through markets encourages growth); R.G. Rajan and L. Zingales, 'Financial Dependence and Growth' [1998] 88 *American Economics Review* 559 (finding that industries dependent on external finance are more developed in countries with better protection of external investors).

economies therefore adopt the rules of common-law legal systems (and possibly common-law enforcement techniques) in order to develop their economies? Although a number of transitional countries have in fact begun to adopt U.S. corporate and securities laws, other researchers have warned that attempts to "transplant" law in this fashion have usually failed because the legal rules so adopted are incongruent with local customs and traditions.[8]

Nor are LLS&V alone in predicting the persistence of the current bipolar division of the world into rival systems of dispersed and concentrated ownership. While LLS&V argue that dispersed ownership cannot spread unless fundamental legal reforms protecting minority rights are adopted as a precondition, other recent commentators have advanced entirely independent reasons why dispersed ownership will remain the exception, with concentrated ownership being the rule. Lucian Bebchuk has advanced a "rent-protection" model of share ownership that posits that, when the private benefits of control are high, concentrated ownership will dominate dispersed ownership.[9] The core idea here is that the entrepreneurs taking a firm public will not sell a majority of the firm's voting rights to dispersed shareholders in the public market, because they can obtain a higher price for such a control block from an incoming controlling shareholder or group, who alone can enjoy the private benefits of control.[10] Thus the control holder will sell only a minority interest or will sell control as a block, but will not break up its control block—and hence concentrated ownership will persist.[11]

---

[8] E.g. D. Berkowitz et al., *Economic Development, Legality, and the Transplant Effect* (SSRN Electronic Library, Working Paper no. 183,269, 2000), available at http://papers.ssrn.com/paper.taf?abstract_id=183269.

[9] L. Bebchuk, *A Rent-Protection Theory of Corporate Ownership and Control* (National Bureau of Economic Research, Working Paper no. 7203, 1999), available at http://www.nber.org/papers/7203 ; see also Bebchuk and Roe, above, n. 4 (predicting the persistence of concentrated ownership under certain conditions).

[10] There are several possible answers to Professor Bebchuk's thesis. First, to the extent that the private benefits of control are enjoyed at the expense of the non-controlling shareholders, the controlling shareholder's motive for paying a higher control premium than public shareholders is matched by their expected loss. To the extent that they can solve the coordination costs in organizing to protect themselves from a future controlling shareholder who will divest them of control, public shareholders may be able to match the premium that the large shareholder will pay for control. Secondly, in the case of high-risk investments, the public market affords investors the benefits of diversification, while the incoming controlling shareholder (or any large blockholder) must accept undiversified risk (and may not be willing to do so or may discount the price it offers to reflect this risk). Although this point about undiversified risk suggests that high-tech companies may obtain a higher price from the public market, as they long have on the Nasdaq (including many foreign issuers), it does not deny that the corporate controlling shareholder may often pay a higher premium in anticipation of synergy gains not available to portfolio or retail investors.

[11] Studies of initial public offerings (IPOs) in concentrated securities markets have tended to confirm this prediction: IPOs seldom distribute more than a minority of the firm's voting shares to the market, with the controlling blockholder generally retaining control. For example, one recent study of Swedish IPOs finds that in close to 90% of all privately controlled IPOs, the controlling

Similarly, Mark Roe has offered an entirely independent "political" theory for why strong securities markets are inconsistent with the European political tradition of "social democracy".[12] In his view, social democracies pressure corporate managers to forgo opportunities for profit maximization in order to maintain high employment. Under circumstances that would lead firms in other political environments to downsize their operations because of adverse market conditions, firms in social democracies, he argues, are compelled to expend their shareholders' capital in order to subsidize other constituencies. Public firms are relatively more exposed than private firms, he believes, to the higher managerial agency costs that social democracies impose. As a result, concentrated ownership is a defensive reaction to these pressures; through non-transparent accounting, hidden reserves, and direct supervision of management, large blockholders, he claims, can better resist these political pressures to expend the firm's resources on other constituencies.

In overview, a common denominator runs through the theories of LLS&V, Bebchuk, and Roe: *Ownership and control cannot easily separate when managerial agency costs are high.* Although they disagree about the causes of high agency costs—i.e., weak legal standards versus political pressures that cause firms sometimes to subordinate the interests of shareholders—they implicitly concur that the emergence of deep, liquid markets requires that the agency cost problem first be adequately resolved by state action.

This chapter dissents. Although it does not doubt that "law matters," it finds that a transition toward dispersed ownership is already well advanced and seems likely to continue, even in the short-term absence of legal change. Part I surveys this evidence, which reveals increasing signs of fission within the world of concentrated ownership. Despite the asserted barriers, securities markets are growing across Europe at an extraordinary rate, entrepreneurs in civil-law countries are making use of IPOs at a rate equivalent to that in the common-law world, and the market for corporate control has become truly international. Something is destabilizing the old equilibrium, but how far it will progress remains an open question. Part II then analyses the claim that securities markets require a strong legal foundation that protects the minority shareholder in order to become deep or liquid. Although the association between minority protection and liquidity seems real, Part II will argue that the cause and effect sequence is backwards. Much historical evidence suggests that legal developments have tended to fol-

---

owner did not sell shares and controlled on average 68.5% of the voting power after the IPO. P. Hogfeldt and M. Holmen, *A Law and Finance Analysis of Initial Public Offerings* 3–4 (SSRN Electronic Library, Working Paper no. 236,042, 2000), available at http://papers.ssrn.com/paper.taf?abstract_id=236042 .

[12] M.J. Roe, 'Political Preconditions to Separating Ownership from Control' [2000] 53 Stanford Law Review 539.

low, rather than precede, economic change.[13] Specifically, Part II will examine the early development of the New York Stock Exchange (NYSE) and the London Stock Exchange (LSE), and contrast their experiences with the arrested development of equity securities markets in France and Germany over the same period. Although securities exchanges have existed since the seventeenth century, exchanges primarily traded debt securities up until the mid-nineteenth century. Then, over a relatively brief period and at a time when the private benefits of control were unquestionably high, dispersed ownership arose in both the U.S. and the U.K.—largely in the absence of strong legal protections for minority shareholders, which came afterwards. Viewed in retrospect, this sequence makes obvious political sense: Legal reforms are enacted at the behest of a motivated constituency that will be protected (or at least perceives that it will be protected) by the proposed reforms. Hence, the constituency (here, dispersed public shareholders) must first arise before it can become an effective lobbying force and an instrument of legal change.

But how do liquid markets develop if minority shareholders are systematically exposed to expropriation by controlling shareholders because of inadequate legal protections (as LLS&V conclude they are exposed)? A problem with much recent law and economics commentary on the natural predominance of concentrated ownership has been its historical character. A closer look at the experience of U.S. corporations in the late nineteenth century shows that, even in the absence of adequate minority protections and even in the presence of high private benefits of control, private actors could bond themselves in ways that credibly signalled to the minority shareholders that they would not be exploited. Both through such bonding measures and through self-regulation, as implemented by the NYSE, investors were assured that their investments would neither be expropriated by the firm's founders nor, once ownership had become dispersed, subjected to a low premium take-over by an incoming control seeker. That the U.S. led the way toward dispersed ownership seems best explained not by the state of its nineteenth century corporate law, but by a more basic fact: As a debtor nation facing the need to develop highly capital-intensive industries (e.g., railroads, steel, and electrical power), the U.S. was more dependent upon foreign capital, and it had to strive harder to convince remote foreign investors of the adequacy of the safeguards taken to protect their investments.

---

[13] Stuart Banner has made the interesting argument that, over the last 300 years, most major waves of securities regulation have followed a sustained price collapse on the securities market. S. Banner, 'What Causes New Securities Regulation?: 300 Years of Evidence' [1997] 75 Washington University Law Quarterly 849, 850. It is not surprising that "bubbles" and eventual crashes produce victims and hence a political demand for reform. But perhaps the deeper meaning of this finding is that the reform of securities regulation has not been associated with any broader political movement. Thus this evidence is in tension with Professor Roe's claim that there are "political preconditions" to the growth of securities markets. See Roe, above, n. 12.

Dispersed ownership did not, however, arrive in France or Germany, even though the Paris Bourse was the leading international rival to the LSE during the last quarter of the nineteenth century. Why not? The "political thesis" offered by Roe clearly cannot explain the failure of securities markets to develop in France and Germany during the late nineteenth century, because neither country approached being a social democracy in this era.[14] A possible explanation could be that offered by LLS&V, namely, that French and German law provided insufficient protections for minority shareholders. But the LLS&V explanation has a serious problem: The specific "anti-director" rights that they identify as the central factors distinguishing common-law from civil-law systems strike many legal commentators as only tangentially related to effective legal protection for minority shareholders.[15] The possibility thus surfaces that the observed legal differences identified by LLS&V may serve as a proxy for something deeper.

What, then, is the hidden variable that at least historically distinguished common-law from civil-law systems? Part III suggests that the principal variable accounting for the earlier development of dispersed ownership in the U.S. and the U.K. than in Continental Europe was the early separation of the private sector in the common-law world from the close supervision and control of the central government. In the absence of direct governmental regulation, relatively strong systems of self-regulation arose in the U.S. and the U.K., which were administered by private bodies (most notably, private stock exchanges) that sought to regulate their members' conduct in their mutual self-interest. Although these exchanges may not have been optimal regulators, they were at least entrepreneurial entities that adapted quickly to new conditions and opportunities. In contrast, in France and, to a lesser extent, in Germany, the state intervened constantly in the market, sometimes to protect it and sometimes to chill it, but the degree of paternalistic supervision that was imposed froze the development of continental markets and left little room for enlightened self-regulation.

Viewed in this light, the critical role of law in the separation of ownership and control was not that it fostered minority shareholders (in common-law countries) or abandoned them (in civil-law countries), but rather that the common-

---

[14] For example, no matter how Prince Otto von Bismarck, the leading German statesman and politician of the last half of the nineteenth century, is characterized, he was not a social democrat. See W.J. Mommsen, *Imperial Germany, 1867–1918: Politics, Culture and Society in an Authoritarian State* (R. Deveson translation, London/New York 1995); see also below, nn. 205–207 and accompanying text (discussing this period). Correspondingly, the dominant figure behind French efforts to develop a system of international investment banking in the late nineteenth century was Napoleon III, who was the sponsor of Credit Mobilier, the first major investment bank organized on a corporate basis. See below, nn. 157–159 and accompanying text. His motives were, however, largely statist, rather than economic.

[15] For a description of LLS&V's "anti-director" rights, see above, n. 6.

law world was, for a variety of reasons, more hospitable than the civil-law world to private self-regulatory institutions.[16] If the common law has a more decentralized character that encourages private law-making, while the civil law tends to be more centralized and hostile to private law-making, this difference transcends the field of comparative law and has contemporary relevance for planners and regulators in transitional economies. As will be stressed, it suggests that private action, through bonding and signalling measures, may be the critical first step toward stronger securities markets. This proposed interpretation, which deemphasizes the role of formal law, agrees with LLS&V that it was not coincidental that liquid equity securities markets arose in the U.S. and the U.K., but not in France or Germany, but disagrees with them that the key explanatory variable was the impact of the substantive law on shareholder rights. Because this interpretation focuses less on substantive law, and more on the structure for law making within the broader society, it is not confounded by the special case of the Netherlands, where securities markets first arose in Amsterdam well ahead of London. Although the Netherlands is a civil-law country, the critical fact explaining the early appearance of securities markets there in this chapter's view was that it was, much like England, a pluralistic, decentralized society in which the private sector was relatively autonomous and free from direct state supervision.[17] Moreover, if legal protections of minority shareholders were the indispensable precondition for the growth of securities markets, as LLS&V posit, the successful U.S. experience would seem inexplicable. As will be seen, in the late nineteenth century, U.S. law was characterized by a high level of judicial corruption, was demonstrably vulnerable to regulatory arbitrage (as participants in corporate control battles regularly played one court and one state off against another), and wholly lacked any federal law on securities regulation. Given that the private benefits of control were high and realistic minority protections were weak, the LLS&V model would predict that dispersed ownership could not arise in such an environment. But it did.

That dispersed ownership was able to arise in this era derived in large measure from the ability of private actors to develop functional substitutes for formal law.[18] Over time, the systems of securities regulation in the U.S. and the

[16] This thesis that decentralization encouraged economic growth has been developed on a grander scale by the British historian and anthropologist A. MacFarlane. See generally A. Macfarlane, *The Origins of English Individualism* (Oxford 1978) [hereinafter, Macfarlane, *Origins*]; A. Macfarlane, *The Riddle of the Modern World* (Houndmills/New York 2000) [hereinafter, Macfarlane, *Riddle*]; below, nn. 222–228 and accompanying text.

[17] This same point that the U.K. and the Netherlands had a similar social structure, but different legal origins, has been well made by A. MacFarlane. See Macfarlane, *Riddle*, above, n. 16, at 279–80.

[18] In earlier work, I have distinguished "formal convergence" from "functional convergence." J.C. Coffee, Jr, 'The Future as History: The Prospects for Global Convergence in Corporate Governance and Its Implications' [1999] 93 Northwestern University Law Review 641, 657. Formal

U.K. functionally converged. Only later did legislative changes bring about formal convergence. That functional convergence should precede formal convergence is even more predictable in a rapidly globalizing world in which competitive pressures in the increasingly international capital and product markets compel firms to adapt and penalize those firms that have a higher cost of capital.[19] Thus, Part III predicts that functional convergence may be the principal mechanism by which the separation of ownership and control will come both to Europe and, more slowly, to transitional economies. Specifically, it suggests that some recent developments in Russian corporate governance are functional parallels to the bonding and signalling devices used in the U.S. in the 1870s and 1880s, and that some European stock exchanges are beginning to show today the same activism that the NYSE displayed at the end of the nineteenth century. If it is too much to claim that it is "déjà vu, all over again," the parallels are at least striking.

Finally, Part III challenges the "political thesis" that social democracy and strong securities markets cannot co-exist. Others have also challenged this very ambitious claim, noting that England supplies a strong counter-example of social democracy co-existing with strong securities markets.[20] This chapter will advance a more general objection: Financial institutions—including the much-used example of German universal banks—do not operate as buffers that can protect shareholder interests from social-democratic pressures. Rather, because large financial intermediaries tend to be state controlled (directly or indirectly), they are likely to be more exposed to political pressures to subordinate shareholder interests. Even large blockholders are more visible and exposed than anonymous small shareholders, who themselves can constitute a significant political interest group. As politicians in democracies with dispersed ownership have repeatedly found, political actions that cause (or are perceived to cause) a stock market decline are painful and self-disciplining. Concentrated ownership,

convergence requires multiple jurisdictions to enact common legal rules and practices. Functional convergence can arise, however, because of the use of functional substitutes that look dissimilar but have equivalent effects. Functional convergence can also be achieved as the result of private actions, such as bonding devices or related actions that deliberately limit managerial discretion. For example, a firm in a country with weak legal rules and disclosure standards might deliberately list on the NYSE in order to subject itself voluntarily to its higher disclosure, accounting, and market transparency standards and to the enforcement mechanisms that apply to firms that enter the U.S. market (that is, private class actions and SEC enforcement). Such bonding through cross-listing on a foreign exchange has recently become common and appears to increase the firm's stock price. Ibid., 673–75.

[19] Professors Hansmann and Kraakman emphasise this point at some length, arguing that as a result a norm of shareholder primacy is becoming dominant worldwide. Hansmann and Kraakman, above, n. 3.

[20] E.g. B.R. Cheffins, *Putting Britain on the Roe Map: The Emergence of the Berle-Means Corporation in the United Kingdom* (SSRN Electronic Library, Working Paper no. 218,655, 2000), available at http://papers.ssrn.com/paper.taf?abstract_id=218655 .

then, may survive not because large financial intermediaries are good monitors or politically less vulnerable, but because the status quo favours incumbent interest groups against new entrants who wish to compete. Further, as I have argued elsewhere,[21] institutions seem to prefer liquidity to control. As a result, concentrated ownership is no more a natural state than is dispersed ownership, but is the artefact of a particular set of legal controls and political pressures. More importantly, across Europe today, financial institutions appear on the verge of liberation—and seem delighted at the prospect of being able to liquidate their controlling blocks.

Ultimately, the policy message of this chapter is optimistic. While formidable obstacles may exist to the development of liquid securities markets, both in transitional economies and in civil-law countries, a wholesale transplantation of common-law rules is not necessary. Self-help measures, including exchange self-regulation, can potentially provide functional substitutes that significantly compensate for any deficit in minority protection that the use of civil-law standards entails. This does not mean that substantive law reform is unimportant, or that self-regulation can provide a fully adequate substitute for public law enforcement, but only that adaptive strategies can be designed for nations, individual markets, and individual firms. What is most important for the emergence and survival of dispersed ownership in new legal environments is that public shareholders be able to hold control against the attack of the control seeker who wishes to avoid paying a control premium. As will be seen, the U.S. and the U.K. have developed independent and divergent techniques to address this problem, the former relying on the shareholders' agents (the board of directors) to protect their right to a control premium,[22] and the latter relying on mandated collective action (a shareholder vote).[23] This divergence illustrates a central theme of this

---

[21] J.C. Coffee, Jr, 'Liquidity Versus Control: The Institutional Investor as Corporate Monitor' [1991] 91 Columbia Law Review 1277.

[22] The board of directors' obligation to obtain a control premium for its shareholders before it allows control to pass from public shareholders to a new controlling shareholder is a thread that runs through much Delaware case law. See *Paramount Communications, Inc v. QVC Network Inc,* 637 A.2d 34, 42–45 (Del 1993); *Barkan v. Amsted Indus Inc,* 567 A.2d 1279, 1286 (Del 1989); *Mills Acquisition Co v. Macmillan Inc,* 559 A.2d 1261, 1288 (Del 1988).

[23] In contrast to U.S. law, British law discourages most defensive tactics in corporate control battles, but it does restrict the potential control acquirer's ability to make a coercive, partial bid. Specifically, British take-over law imposes a buyout obligation on the control buyer under which it must offer to buy out the remaining minority shareholders at the same price as it paid to the control seller. See D.A. DeMott, 'Comparative Dimensions of Takeover Regulation' [1987] 65 Washington University Law Quarterly 69, 94. Specifically, under the City Code on Take-Overs and Mergers, which is a self-regulatory code, a tender offer for more than 30% and less than 100% is precluded unless first approved by a majority vote of the shareholders. Ibid. at 93–94. In short, British law and U.S. law both protect the public shareholder's right in some circumstances to share in a control premium, but they use totally divergent approaches, not a unified common-law approach.

chapter. There is not a single common-law solution to the most important problems of corporate law, but rather multiple functional substitutes.

B. The Evidence of Convergence

Attempts to describe an ongoing transition in corporate governance and structure are always vulnerable to the criticism that they rely on anecdotal evidence. By now, however, the available evidence is substantial and involves quantitative as well as qualitative data. For the sake of convenience, the most salient evidence can be grouped under the following four categories. Although the transition is far from complete, the collective weight of the evidence suggests that a new equity culture has received de facto (if not yet formal) acceptance across Europe, with both investors and regulators seeking to encourage its development. That such a transition has occurred in the absence of sweeping legal changes, or any apparent shift within Continental Europe toward common-law legal standards, seems at least mildly inconsistent with the LLS&V thesis.

I. Formal Legal Change

Formal legal change is the area where those adopting a path-dependent perspective have suggested that change would be the slowest and most marginal,[24] because formal legal change generally requires legislative action and can be blocked by political interest groups or strongly motivated minorities (who may have little concern with overall efficiency). Still, even here, significant change is evident.

The clearest evidence relates to the transition economies. Employing a methodology that uses cross-country formalized legal indicators to measure statistically the degree of legal change, Katharina Pistor constructed a database covering 24 transition economies (namely, most of the formerly socialist states in Europe and Eurasia) that tracked the development of shareholder and creditor rights from 1990 through 1998.[25] She concluded: "Despite substantial differ-

---

[24] Bebchuk and Roe properly argue that legal rules are the product of political processes. To the extent that interest groups play a role in such processes, the corporate legal rules that are chosen are likely to reflect the relative strength of the relevant interest groups. Bebchuk and Roe, above, n. 4, 157–58. In particular, controlling shareholders who enjoy substantial private benefits of control in countries characterized by concentrated ownership will wish to maintain the existing legal rules that favour their interests, even if a different ownership structure would be more efficient. Ibid., 158.

Arguably, the data in this section is consistent with the Bebchuk and Roe prediction, because the most rapid and thoroughgoing formal legal changes have occurred in transitional economies, where strongly entrenched interests that were aligned with the existing legal structure did not already exist.

[25] K. Pistor, *Patterns of Legal Change: Shareholder and Creditor Rights in Transition Economies* (EBRD Working Paper no. 49/2000, on file with author).

ences in the initial conditions across countries, there is a strong tendency towards convergence of formal legal rules as the result of extensive legal reforms".[26] She notes, however, that "law reform has been primarily responsive to economic change rather than initiating or leading it".[27] As discussed later, this same pattern appears to be evident in the development of diffused securities markets in both the U.S. and the U.K.

The direction of these changes has been uniformly in the "Anglo-Saxon" direction: "By 1998, legal changes had been introduced that raised the level of investor protection in most transition economies above the level of the civil law systems and brought them within close range of the average for common law countries. . . .".[28]

In overview, this transition seems largely to have involved the outright substitution of common-law rules for civil-law rules, with the total package of legal reforms usually designed by foreign legal advisors (often supplied by the U.S.). Still, because these reforms have been legislatively adopted, this wholesale transplantation seems to indicate that, at least under the pressures faced by transition economies, lawmakers have not felt obliged to maintain continuity with their historical legal systems. Radical legal change is at least sometimes possible.

A possible response to the evidence of sharp discontinuity in the law of transitional economies is that mass privatization programmes in these countries imposed a diffused, Anglo-Saxon structure of share ownership on these countries and so required a corresponding movement to Anglo-Saxon (or common-law) systems of corporate governance and securities regulation. From this perspective, one might argue that no similar rate of legal change should be predicted for those economies in which an insider-dominated system of concentrated ownership already prevailed. In short, if form follows function (that is, if legal rules are determined by the system of corporate governance that pre-exists those rules), then no similar rapid legal transition should necessarily be expected in the Continental economies in which concentrated ownership is still the norm.

The actual picture is, however, more mixed. Rather than individual states modifying their own individual statutes, law reform within the European Community has proceeded largely on the basis of efforts at harmonization.[29] That is, a Company Law Directive will be proposed (after much negotiation) by the European Union's Council of Ministers, and an effort will then be made to secure its ratification by Member States. Although such efforts have regularly succeeded in other private law areas, they have elicited major struggles in the

[26] ibid., 2.

[27] ibid.

[28] ibid., 13.

[29] For an overview of this process, see Coffee, above, n. 18, 667–70. See also U. Geiger, 'Harmonization of Securities Disclosure Rules in the Global Market—A Proposal' [1998] 66 Fordham Law Review 1785 (describing and evaluating efforts at harmonization).

corporate law area. Throughout the 1980s, efforts by the European Union to adopt directives dealing with take-over bid procedures, codetermination, and employee rights all failed amidst considerable ideological controversy about the place of the private corporation in European society.[30] Yet contemporaneously, the European Union adopted a variety of securities-oriented directives intended to integrate disclosure and transparency standards in order to facilitate a pan-European securities market.[31] In short, while the old battles over codetermination and workers' rights continue, little, if any, opposition surfaces to directives intended to develop securities markets or improve disclosure standards. Again, this suggests that at least the goal of liquid securities markets has become a "motherhood issue" with no active opponents.

II. The Structure of Share Ownership

Considerable evidence exists that the traditional system of concentrated ownership is at least marginally weakening across Europe. Data compiled by the Conference Board shows a measurable decline in the stakes held in the 25 largest corporations by banks and non-financial corporations in Germany, France, and Japan.[32] Traditionally, these holders were the allies of the founding families and managements that ran the largest European and Japanese companies. Yet, over just a one-year period between September 30, 1998 and September 30, 1999, these traditional stakeholders unwound their holdings to the following degree:

Table 1. Closely Held Ownership in the 25 Largest Corporations

	September 30, 1998	September 30, 1999
France	33.5%	30.2%
Germany	24.2%	17.8%
Japan	21.2%	14.0%

Of course, a one-year trend may be unrepresentative, and these data do not demonstrate that the shares so unwound necessarily moved into the hands of public investors. Yet, there is also evidence of a substitution effect—that is, the

---

[30] Coffee, above, n. 18, 668–69; A.N. Licht, 'International Diversity in Securities Regulation: Roadblocks on the Way to Convergence' [1998] 20 Cardozo Law Review 227, 239–40.

[31] Geiger, above, n. 29, 1789–90.

[32] C.K. Brancato, 'Corporations Outside U.S. Become More Subject to Investor Demands' [2000] *Corporate Governance Advisor* July–August, at 1.

shares are passing into the hands of more active owners. Thirty-five per cent of the outstanding shares of the forty largest companies on the Paris Bourse are now held by American and British institutional investors.[33] Over this same period, U.S. institutional investors have dramatically increased their investments in foreign equity. The largest 25 U.S. pension fund holders of international equity held $110.8 billion in foreign equities in 1996, $181.1 billion in 1998, and $265.6 billion in September, 1999—a nearly 150% increase in only two years.[34] With this heightened ownership comes, of course, a demand for additional voice.

More importantly, many expect that this rate of change will soon accelerate, at least in some of the largest and most traditional European economies. In Germany, a high capital gains tax locked financial institutions into their elaborate web of cross-shareholdings because any attempt to liquidate these blocks would have been punitively taxed.[35] Yet, effective January 1, 2002, the capital gains tax on such investments will be abolished, and some of the largest German financial institutions have already announced plans to reduce the extent of their cross-shareholdings.[36] The apparent eagerness of German financial institutions to divest themselves of long-held blocks and to scale back non-core assets raises the always-lurking question about how deeply the German system of concentrated ownership was truly entrenched. Professor Roe, among others, has suggested that concentrated ownership (and correspondingly weak securities markets) reflects a strong social and political commitment to a cluster of social values that he calls "social democracy".[37] Yet, if a simple change in the corporate tax laws causes the system to collapse by the mutual consent of those locked into this system of cross-shareholdings, the simpler explanation for concentrated ownership may be that German tax laws either caused this system, or, more likely, enforced its persistence well after competitive forces would otherwise have compelled its dismantling.[38]

---

[33] J. Tagliabue, Resisting Those Ugly Americans [2000] *New York Times* 9 January, § 3 at 10.

[34] Brancato, above, n. 32, 1.

[35] H. Simonian, 'Germany Unbound: Measures To Reduce the Country's Restrictive Tax Burden Have Delighted Many Businesses' [2000] *Financial Times* (London), 10 August, 14.

[36] ibid. (noting plan of Allianz and Munich Re to reduce their cross-holdings).

[37] Roe, above, n. 12, 543.

[38] German scholars have also suggested that the German tax system may be the better explanation for at least the contemporary system of concentrated ownership in Germany. E.g., F. Kübler, 'On Mark Roe, German Codetermination and German Securities Markets' [1999] 5 Columbia Journal of European Law 213, 214–15.

III. The Growth of European Stock Markets

Continental stock markets have long been thin and illiquid. For some, this was arguably a virtue of European corporate governance because it protected corporate managements from the tyranny of a "short-sighted" stock market and instead permitted long-term business planning by corporations in conjunction with their principal stakeholders.[39] Whatever the historical validity of this story, it now seems increasingly dated.

A particularly useful recent study shows that the number of firms listing on European stock changes rose sharply at the end of the 1990s:[40]

Table 2: Evolution of the Number of Stock Exchange Listed Companies

	1990	1993	1996	1999	% Growth (1990–1999)
Network-oriented:					
Belgium	182	159	136	140	−23.1%
France	443	726	686	968	118.5%
Germany	548	568	579	1043	90.3%
Italy	257	242	244	247	−3.9%
Netherlands	222	239	217	233	5.0%
Spain					
Japan (Tokyo)					
Market-oriented:					
United Kingdom	1946	1927	2339	2292	17.8%
United States (NYSE)	1774	1945	2476	2631	48.3%
United States (Nasdaq)	3876	4310	5167	4829	24.6%

---

[39] Some observers wholly disagree with LLS&V and consider concentrated ownership to be more efficient, in part because managers possess information that market participants lack. See E. Berglöf and E.-L. von Thadden, *The Changing Corporate Governance Paradigm: Implications for Transition and Developing Countries* 14 (SSRN Electronic Library, Working Paper no. 183,708, 1999) (noting the "popular view" that "outside investors do not necessarily take into account the long-term interest of the firm"), available at http://papers.ssrn.com/paper.taf?abstract_id=183708 .

[40] C. Van der Elst, *The Equity Markets, Ownership Structures and Control: Towards an International Harmonization?* (2000) (unpublished manuscript, on file with author) [hereinafter, *"Van der Elst Dissertation"*]. This paper is a condensed and preliminary version of a PhD

Although the pattern is far from uniform, listings on the equity market rose rapidly in the late 1990s in France, Germany, and Spain, more rapidly than in the U.S. or the U.K. Elsewhere, the number of listed companies may have declined, possibly because of an international wave of mergers and acquisitions, which is itself a sign of convergence.

Beyond this growth in the number of listed companies, two other statistics reveal even more clearly the suddenly increased role of the equity markets in European economies, a transition that again seems to date only from the latter half of the last decade. First, stock market capitalization as a percentage of GDP skyrocketed in several European countries—indeed, to the point that one or two European countries approach or exceed the same ratios in the U.S. or the U.K. The following selected examples show how long-stable percentages veered suddenly upward at the end of the decade.

Of course, these percentages are subject to greater fluctuation in countries with small populations (such as the Netherlands and Switzerland), and much of the market capitalization in these countries may remain in the hands of a few controlling owners. Nonetheless, the real point is the suddenness of the transition. Essentially, as the European market integrated in the mid-1990s, stock market values soared, both in absolute terms and as a percentage of GDP. Second, while IPOs once characterized only the markets of the U.S. and the U.K., they have become common across Europe. In 1999, Germany saw 168 IPOs, and France saw 75. For the decade, France led with 581 IPOs, Germany followed with 380, and Spain was a close third with 355.[41] The significance of this point bears emphasis because systems of concentrated ownership were thought to lack the institutions necessary to bring new companies directly into the equity market. Instead, new firms were believed to be dependent on bank and debt financing, not equity finance. Yet, by the end of the decade, several European countries were raising more equity through initial public offerings as a percentage of GDP than were either the U.S. or the U.K.[42]

There is a double-edged significance to these findings. On the one hand, by the end of the last decade, the stock market was raising equity capital for European issuers at levels (and percentages of GDP) that were thought to characterize only market-oriented systems of corporate governance (i.e. the U.S. and the U.K.). But on the other hand, this sudden surge in the use of equity finance has been

---

dissertation in Dutch, entitled *Aandeelhoudersstructuren, Aandeelhoudersconcentratie en Controle Van Beursgenoteerde Ondernemingen*. The data set forth in this contribution came from the later dissertation; copies of those tables are on file with the author.

[41] ibid., tbl 3.5.

[42] Van der Elst finds that both the Netherlands and Spain raised significantly more equity capital in IPOs as a percentage of GDP than did the U.S. or the U.K. Ibid., 10. This is not simply an artifact of small GDP size, as in 1999 Germany raised equity capital equal to 1.02% of its GDP through IPOs, while the U.K. raised only 0.6%, and the U.S. raised 1.23%. Ibid.

unaccompanied by any significant increase in the legal protections afforded to minority shareholders. In this sense, both the "path dependency" theorists, who maintain that the stock market cannot grow in social democracies, and the economists (most notably, LLS&V), who maintain that the availability of equity finance depends on minority protections, appear to have been confounded. Neither the "path dependency" claim nor the assertion that "law matters" can draw unambiguous support from this evidence.

It is also clear that new market institutions and structures are appearing. A race has begun to create the first pan-European stock market. Easdaq, which began trading as a pan-European exchange in November 1996, was unable to establish itself as a viable market,[43] but was recently acquired by Nasdaq in a move that will clearly intensify competition.[44] The German Neuer Markt, which serves over 300 listings, has been far more successful.[45] But even its success is now being tested by a worldwide stock market decline following the crash of the Nasdaq in 2000. Between March 2000 and April 2001, price levels on the Neuer Markt proved even more volatile than on the Nasdaq and fell by an estimated 83%.[46] The public response has not been a rejection of the new equity culture, but rather a demand for more regulation and higher listing standards.[47] Thus a familiar pattern—crash, then law—is once again reappearing.

To sum up, the equity culture is still less established in Europe than it is in the U.S., and a much smaller percentage of the general European population owns shares than is the case in the U.S.[48] Nonetheless, the current ownership levels in nations such as Germany probably exceed those in the U.S. in the early twentieth century when dispersed ownership first arrived.[49]

[43] As of mid-2000, Easdaq had only been able to secure some 62 listings. C. Karmin, 'Europe's Easdaq Finds That Success Doesn't Come Easy' [2000] *Wall Street Journal* August 14, C1.

[44] S. Ascarelli, 'Nasdaq Confirms Its Acquisition of Easdaq Stake' [2001] *Wall Street Journal* March 28, C14.

[45] See Karmin, above, n. 43.

[46] S. Ascarelli, 'Europe's Faith in Stocks Gets Put to the Test' [2001] *Wall Street Journal* April 9, C1.

[47] See N. Bondette and A. Kueppers, 'Frustrated Neuer Markt Members Push for Tightening Listing Rules' [2001] *Wall Street Journal* July 11, C12 (noting that even issuers on the Neuer Markt want tighter regulation). For the observation that European investors are not dumping their shares or disinvesting, see Ascarelli, above, n. 46, at C10.

[48] For example, in Germany, it is now estimated that 9.7% of Germans own shares directly and 13.7% own through mutual funds, while in the U.S., roughly 50% of citizens own stocks. Ibid.

[49] While the percentage of Americans who own stocks appears to be around 50%, it was recently much lower. In 1995, 41.1% of U.S. families owned stock directly, and in 1989 that level was only 31.7%. R.W. Jennings et al., *Securities Regulation* 3 8th edn. (New York 1998).

Table 3: Evolution of Market Capitalization as a Percentage of GDP (1990–1999)

	1975	1980	1990	1996	1998	1999
Network–						
Belgium	15%	8%	33%	44%	97.5%	75.4%
France	10%	8%	26%	38%	67.8%	105.3%
Germany	12%	9%	22%	28%	50.6%	68.1%
Italy	5%	6%	14%	21%	47.9%	62.4%
Netherlands	21%	17%	42%	95%	157.6%	177.3%
Spain	—	8%	23%	33%	71.9%	72.6%
Sweden	3%	10%	40%	95%	122.3%	156.3%
Switzerland	30%	42%	69%	136%	259.4%	267.5%
Market–						
United Kingdom	37%	38%	87%	142%	167.3%	198.0%
United States	48%	50%	56%	114%	157.0%	181.1%

IV. The Emergence of an International Market for Corporate Control

In market-centred economies, the market for corporate control is the ultimate disciplinary mechanism, and the hostile take-over, its final guillotine. In contrast, in concentrated ownership systems of corporate governance, the take-over has historically played only a minor role. But, once again, that pattern appears to be changing rapidly. In 1985, 86% of all take-overs involved at least one American party, but in 1999, this percentage fell to only 40%.[50] Over the same time span, the percentage of corporate take-overs involving at least one European party rose from 15% to 43%, and the percentage involving an Asian party rose from approximately 2% to nearly 14%.[51] If one looks instead to the market value of these transactions, take-overs involving a European party have gone from 11% of the world total in 1985 to 47% in 1999.[52] Evidence of this sort has led some scholars to describe the last two years as amounting to the "First International Merger Wave".[53]

---

[50] B. Stokes, 'The M&A Game's Global Field' [2000] *National Journal*, July 15, 2290.

[51] ibid.

[52] B.S. Black, 'The First International Merger Wave (and the Fifth and Last U.S. Wave)' [2000] 54 University of Miami Law Review 799, 801.

[53] ibid., 800.

What is driving this transition? One answer starts with the integration of European currencies into the Euro. A consequence of a single, unified currency has been the growth of a unified European corporate bond market, which tripled in size last year and has thereby ended the dependence of European acquirers on bank financing.[54] Acquirers can now directly access the capital markets, offering debt, equity, or a package of both. To this extent, the growth of the take-over market has been concomitant with the declining role of the universal bank. For some time, the legitimisation of the hostile take-over seemed about to be officially recognized with the scheduled adoption of the Thirteenth Company Law Directive by the European Union. As approved by the European Union's Council of Ministers in mid-2000, that directive required all EU Member States to legislate (over four years) so as to bar most anti-take-over defensive measures after a take-over has been announced.[55] But the Council's action proved not to be the end of the story. An unexpected snag was hit, however, when the European Parliament split evenly on a vote to approve the directive, thereby rejecting the measure.[56] Although this development again demonstrates the continuing ideological dimension in corporate law reform, acceptance of the take-over as a mechanism of corporate governance appears to have arrived at least on a de facto basis within the European business community. Indeed, the passivity of a German labour government in the face of a hostile take-over bid by a British acquirer (Vodafone) for a German target (Mannesmann) in 1999 demonstrated this change in attitude (at least for Germany). Only in a few countries (most notably, the Netherlands and France) does real opposition remain, and even there the objection is more to the foreign character of the bidder, not the use of the take-over device itself. Finally, a common international business culture has at least begun to develop around the use of the take-over. A wave of international mergers between law firms (chiefly between U.S. and British firms as well as British and German firms) appears to have been driven by the perceived need to effect cross-border acquisitions.

[54] See Stokes, above, n. 50, 2291.

[55] After much delay, the Council of Ministers adopted the Thirteenth Company Law Directive in June 2000. See 'European Union Agrees to Common Takeover Rules' [2000] *Financial Times*, June 20, 11; C. Swann, 'The Weak Will Become Prey' [2000] *Financial Times* June 30, 4. The proposed directive did permit shareholders to vote to approve defensive tactics.

[56] The tied vote was 273 for to 273 against, with a number of abstentions. An absolute majority was required for passage. See 'Company Law: Parliament No Vote Shreds Takeover Directive' [2001] *European Report,* July 6. It is anticipated that a revised take-over directive will be submitted by the European Commission to the European Parliament in 2002, but it will have to address newly controversial issues involving "golden shares" (i.e., large blocks of shares retained by the state in privatizations) and voting limitations, and thus the directive may have to be significantly diluted to secure passage. See 'Company Law: Makeover of the Takeover Directive Unlikely Before 2002' [2001] *European Report,* July 14. The sudden increase in the opposition to the take-over directive seems best explained by late-developing anxieties in Germany, where a major sell-off of controlling stakes held by German financial institutions is expected. See above, n. 36 and accompanying text.

V. A Preliminary Evaluation

Why now? The integration of Europe has been in progress for several decades, and the emergence of the transitional economies in the wake of the collapse of the Soviet Union is itself over a decade old. Why have stock markets suddenly surged, take-overs become accepted, and IPOs crested? Both a psychological and a political account seem necessary. Overused as the concept is, a paradigm shift seems in progress.

At the political level, one possible story is that regulators came to sense that economic growth depended on the encouragement of venture capital and high-tech start-up firms. Bank financing for such ventures is generally unavailable and also unattractive to the entrepreneurs. In this light, the success of the Neuer Markt (and other incubator stock markets) was necessary if Europe was not to fall rapidly behind the U.S. From this perspective, policy planners saw at least some transition to a market-centred economy as central to economic growth. Yet, even if this story sounds plausible, regulators have in reality done relatively little to drive the foregoing transition.

The closer one looks at the European evidence, the more viewing law as controlling the structure of finance seems like a simplistic theory of causality; rather, the relationship has been more reciprocal and interactive. The Thirteenth Company Law Directive (known popularly as the "Take-overs Directive") may be a leading case in point. Rather than leading a movement, it seems to be slowly following in the wake of changes that have already received de facto acceptance (at least throughout the corporate community of Europe). Similarly, there is evidence that insider-trading prohibitions have recently been widely adopted around the world, but in the wake of greater depth and diffusion in securities markets.[57]

But what fundamental economic and financial changes could have disturbed the old equilibrium and thereby set in motion processes that eventually produced the new equity culture? Rajan and Zingales have developed strong statistical evidence that openness to trade and the liberalization of cross-border capital flows were the hidden causal forces that have recently spurred financial development in Europe after decades of stagnation.[58] While the U.S. opened up to cross-border capital flows in the mid-1970s, and the U.K. and Japan similarly turned the corner around 1980, the nations of Continental Europe lowered their

---

[57] L. Beny, *A Comparative Empirical Investigation of Agency and Market Theories of Insider Trading* 16 (Harvard Law School, John M. Olin Discussion Paper Series, Working Paper no. 264, 1999), available at http://papers.ssrn.com/paper.taf?abstract_id=193070 .

[58] R.G. Rajan and L. Zingales, *The Great Reversals: The Politics of Financial Development in the 20th Century* 31–35 (National Bureau of Economic Research, Working Paper no. 8178, 2001), available at http://www.nber.org/papers/w8178.

barriers only in the late 1980s.[59] But as they did, market capitalizations soared, and barriers to entry ceased to be politically defended.[60] Equally important and roughly contemporaneous was the independent political decision to privatize formerly state-owned industries. Mass privatization deepened securities markets across Europe and thereby created a constituency that came to desire fairer rules. That constituency is now beginning to pressure for legal changes.

Such a sequence seems predictable. Legal changes may have to await the appearance of a constituency to lobby for them. For example, mass privatization came overnight to the Czech Republic, and its securities market soon crashed, at least in part because of the absence of investor protections. Only then, several years later, were statutory reforms adopted to protect minority shareholders.[61] Pistor has generalized that the same responsive reaction of law to economic change has broadly characterized the adoption of common-law reforms by transitional economies.[62]

Thus, with the recent growth of European securities markets, a constituency for reform (or at least enhancement) of European securities regulation may soon coalesce. What would its objectives be? Once a truly pan-European securities market comes into existence, the next logical step would be the responsive creation of a European SEC to enforce a harmonized system of securities regulation. But such a step requires, first, the unequivocal emergence of a pan-European securities market that is supra-national in character and, second, public dissatisfaction with its performance. The history of both the U.S.'s and the U.K.'s systems of securities regulation, as next discussed, suggests that such a reform program may only succeed once it is scandal driven. Neither the pan-European market nor the requisite scandals have arrived.

VI. The Status of the Insider-dominated Firm

While take-overs have come to Europe, securities markets have deepened, and securities regulation may toughen, these developments should not obscure the still-unchanged status of the insider-dominated firm. Even if ownership concentration has declined across Europe, the difference may be only marginal, as the average free float of German listed companies has been estimated at only 32%, and 89% of all listed companies have a single shareholder controlling more than

---

[59] ibid., 33.

[60] ibid., 33–34.

[61] For an overview of the Czech experience, see J.C. Coffee, Jr, 'Privatization and Corporate Governance: The Lessons from Securities Market Failure' [1999] 25 Journal of Corporations Law 1, 9–10.

[62] See above, nn. 25–28 and accompanying text.

25% of their equity.[63] Although many of these holders seem prepared to sell once the German capital gains tax is abolished on January 1, 2002, the critical question becomes to whom they will sell: to a single purchaser of a controlling block, or to the public market through a secondary offering?

Those who believe that path-dependent forces will limit corporate convergence and preclude the appearance of "Anglo-Saxon" style dispersed ownership make the powerful argument that blockholders will continue to find it more profitable to sell control to new controlling purchasers than to break up the controlling block through a secondary offering.[64] Indeed, precisely this pattern of controlling blocks remaining intact after an initial public offering has long been observed in Scandinavia.[65] But, as discussed below, that pattern can change, and did so relatively quickly in both the U.S. and the U.K.

C. When Does Separation of Ownership and Control Arise?
A Historical Perspective

Most of the participants in the recent debate over corporate convergence have implicitly agreed on one (and possibly only one) theme: deep, liquid securities markets arise only under special conditions. LLS&V have emphasized the legal backdrop: dispersed ownership is possible in their view only when the legal system provides adequate protection for minority shareholders. While stressing a path-dependency perspective, Professor Bebchuk has formulated a model that essentially states the reverse side of this coin: when the private benefits of control are high, dispersed share ownership will be a transient state, and controlling blockholders will eventually reappear.[66] In such an environment, leaving control up for grabs would, he argues, only attract attempts by rivals to seize control and extract the private benefits of control. Hence, the firm's initial owners will not find it in their financial interest to sell a potentially controlling block of shares to the market, but will instead sell only to another incoming controlling blockholder, who will pay more because it can enjoy the private benefits of control. Finally, Professor Roe's view that the separation of ownership and control arises only when certain political preconditions are satisfied also implies that the evolution of deep and liquid securities markets is an exceptional event. In common, all these theories suggest that liquid securities market should not naturally evolve, in the absence of the prior satisfaction of special legal or political preconditions.

---

[63] Swann, above, n. 55.

[64] Bebchuk, above, n. 9.

[65] Högfeldt and Holmén, above, n. 11, 16.

[66] Bebchuk, above, n. 9, 10–12. Obviously, the Bebchuk and LLS&V positions are consistent, although each need not agree fully with the other.

Yet modern history seemingly supplies two counter-examples. Beginning in the last quarter of the nineteenth century and culminating no later than the 1930s in the U.S. and mid-century in the U.K., the largest private businesses in both the U.S. and the U.K. were converted into publicly owned corporations.[67] In the process, control generally passed from families to the market.

Although both the timing and dynamics differed notably between these two countries, one common denominator was shared: Neither country provided strong legal protections for minority shareholders during this period. Moreover, at least during the late nineteenth century in the U.S., the private benefits of control appeared very high—indeed to the point that the exploitation of minority shareholders resembled that which has occurred in Russia and other transitional economies over the last decade. Finally, although one can reasonably debate the precise timing of this transition, dispersed ownership persisted and grew in both countries during periods in which the local political environment arguably satisfied Professor Roe's definition of "social democracy," namely, the U.S. during the New Deal and the U.K. during the Labour governments of the 1940s and 1970s.

How then did these markets evolve? As next discussed, their experiences have less in common than their shared legal institutions or common cultural heritage might suggest. Instead, by very different means, both countries made it possible for corporate control to be held by the market—with the result that a company's initial owners could find it as profitable to sell control to the market as to an incoming controlling shareholder.

I. The U.S. Experience

The growth of public securities markets in the U.S. in the nineteenth century was driven by the enormous capital requirements of its railroads.[68] Railroad finance created a template. The financial infrastructure that their heavy demands for

---

[67] B. Cheffins reports that, as late as the decade of the 1880s, only 5 to 10% of Britain's largest business enterprises were incorporated, and "barely sixty domestic" companies had shares quoted on the LSE. Cheffins, above, n. 20, 15. Yet, by 1907, almost 600 industrial and commercial companies were quoted on the LSE. Ibid. at 16. Clearly, this amounts to a rapid and significant transition.

In the U.S., the pace of this transition was even faster. In the period after the Civil War, U.S. financial markets were clearly less developed than those in London. Yet by 1913, the Pennsylvania Railroad had 86,804 shareholders holding its various classes of stock, the American Telephone & Telegraph Company had 53,737 shareholders, and U.S. Steel, founded in 1901, had 44,398 common shareholders and 77,420 persons holding its preferred stock. R.C. Michie, *The London and New York Stock Exchanges, 1850–1914* (London 1987) 222–23. The financial network that created such a dispersed structure of share ownership in a few short decades is obviously worthy of serious study.

[68] See V.P. Carosso, *Investment Banking in America: A History* (Cambridge 1970) 29 (noting that between 1870 and 1900 railroad "carriers were the largest corporate seekers of funds in the capital markets . . . and as such were the investment bankers' principal customers").

capital created was in turn utilized, with only modest adjustments, to serve the similar financial needs of the steel, automobile, and telephone industries in the early twentieth century. Because the greater geographic distances to be connected in the U.S. implied that the capital costs were necessarily higher than in Europe, financing the railroad industry in the U.S. necessarily required the infusion of foreign capital. An estimated 40% of this capital came from Europe,[69] most of it funnelled through London, which had already developed an expertise in international finance.[70] This constantly increasing demand for capital and the reliance on foreign investors in turn produced two basic innovations that appeared in late nineteenth-century America in order to maximize the reputational capital underlying major stock issuances: (1) a corporate governance system in which investment bankers, originally protecting foreign investors, took seats on the issuer's board both to monitor management and to protect public investors from predatory raiders seeking to acquire control by stealth; and (2) the growth of self-regulation through stock exchange rules.

1. The Role of Investment Bankers

The financial infrastructure that arose in the second half of the nineteenth century in the U.S. was designed to satisfy relatively sophisticated investors in countries that were at the time more financially developed. The first generation of the new American investment bankers consisted in essence of bond salesmen to Europe: August Belmont was widely known as the Rothschilds' agent in the U.S., and even J.P. Morgan himself was the American representative of an Anglo-American investment bank founded by his father with British investment bankers.[71] These firms grew to dominance based on their ability to recruit foreign capital.[72]

---

[69] A.D. Chandler, Jr, *Scale and Scope: The Dynamics of Industrial Capitalism* (Cambridge 1990); S. Engelbourg and L. Bushkoff, *The Man Who Found the Money: John Stewart Kennedy and the Financing of the Western Railroads* (Michigan 1996). Between 1870 and 1900, "foreign investment in the United States more than doubled, increasing from approximately $1.4 billion to $3.3 billion." Carosso, above, n. 68, 30.

[70] See R.C. Michie, *The City of London 72–79* (London 1992) 109–11. Professor Cheffins notes that prior to World War I, British companies accounted for only "one-third of the funds raised on London's Stock Exchange". Cheffins, n. 20, 16. Hence, London was a financial market accustomed to exporting its capital abroad, particularly to Commonwealth countries and projects.

[71] V.C. Carosso, *The Morgans* (Cambridge 1987). For a discussion of August Belmont's role as the American agent of the Rothschilds, see Carosso, n. 68, 9–10.

[72] Many of these firms, including Drexel, Morgan & Co and J.W. Seligman, were founded as private unincorporated banks in the 1860s. The characteristic that "distinguished these firms . . . was their ability to recruit foreign capital." Carosso, n. 68, at 30. For example, one measure of this dependence on foreign capital is the fact that, as late as 1913, 18% of the stock of U.S. Steel, a firm founded by JP Morgan & Co, was still owned by foreign investors. See Michie, n. 67, 56. It seems likely that

As elsewhere, the financial institutions that arose in the U.S. were primarily engaged in the marketing of debt securities. Expanding into equity securities was essentially equivalent to an established merchant adding an additional product line; both the merchant and the investment banker carried their reputational capital with them into the new business. This extension into equity securities probably occurred earlier in the U.S. because of the highly leveraged status of U.S. railroads. Inevitably, there are limits on the degree of leverage that any business firm can tolerate, and the greater capital needs of U.S. railroads thus implied that public equity issuances were necessary. In consequence, public equity markets developed earlier in the U.S. than elsewhere, even though the overall U.S. securities market was substantially smaller than the English market.

Formal corporate governance in these early railroad corporations did little to protect minority shareholders. Not only did control groups quickly form, but in some cases the objective of these blockholders was primarily to manipulate the stock price of their corporation. The story of the epic battle for control of the Erie Railroad—the "Scarlet Lady of Wall Street"—between Commodore Vanderbilt, on one side, and Jay Gould and Daniel Drew, the leading stock manipulators of the era, on the other, has been told many times,[73] but it deserves further consideration in light of the recent debates over comparative corporate governance. At the high point of the "Erie War" in the late 1860s, the Gould/ Drew faction, which controlled the board, essentially prevented Commodore Vanderbilt from buying control of Erie in the open market by selling convertible bonds at heavily discounted prices to their allies, who would convert the bonds into stock in order to dilute Vanderbilt's voting power. Although not as elegant a take-over defence as the poison pill of the late twentieth century, this tactic worked very effectively. Even though Vanderbilt secured judicial injunctions against this tactic (apparently by bribing judges), they were ignored by the Erie control group, who secured rival injunctions from the judges that they bribed. Ultimately, Gould bribed enough members of the New York State Legislature to obtain passage of legislation that legitimized his tactics.

What was the lesson here? Essentially, the Erie control battle illustrated the manner in which regulatory arbitrage, carried to the extreme, could nullify minority legal protections. In the absence of any federal regulatory authority, the contending sides could move from jurisdiction to jurisdiction, seducing courts and legislatures. Even if the Erie battle was an exceptional case, it was

higher percentages of stock in the largest U.S. corporations would have been held by foreign investors as of the end of the nineteenth century and that their investment decisions would have been coordinated, or at least strongly influenced, by their American investment bankers.

[73] For standard accounts, see J. Steele Gordon, *The Scarlet Woman of Wall Street* (New York 1988); and J. Grodinsky, *Jay Gould 1867–1892* (Philadelphia 1957). For a recent and highly relevant review of Gould's manipulative schemes from a corporate law perspective, see E.B. Rock, 'Encountering the Scarlet Woman of Wall Street: Speculative Comments at the End of the Century' [2001] 2 *Theoretical Inquiries in Law* 237.

heavily publicized and presented by at least one prominent contemporary commentator as representative.[74] In less epic battles, the parties probably could not afford the massive transaction costs of corruption on the Erie scale, but the real point is that investors were vulnerable less because of the substantive inadequacy of American corporate law itself than because of the lack of enforcement mechanisms and the prospect of corruption. In truth, substantive corporate law in the U.S. during this era was arguably favourable to the minority shareholder. Most state statutes restricted the issuance of "watered" stock, the derivative suit had been recognized by the Supreme Court as a legal mechanism to protect minority shareholders, and the law of fiduciary duties generally required any corporate official who engaged in a self-dealing transaction with his firm to prove its "intrinsic fairness".[75] But, once the investor had committed his capital, he might discover that the corporation had migrated to another, more permissive jurisdiction or that its founders had amended its certificate of incorporation or caused the legislature to amend the law to give them greater freedom to exploit the public investor.[76] Or, a judge would simply be bribed to accept some pretext for clearly predatory misbehaviour. Because of these risks, some prominent underwriters (including Kuhn, Loeb) refused until the very end of the century to underwrite the common stock of industrial corporations.[77]

The investor who was defrauded in a securities transaction did have legal remedies against the promoters and managers of a company whose stock price had been inflated. By the middle of the nineteenth century, the American case law had established that a cause of action for fraud could be pleaded "where stock had been purchased in reliance on knowing misrepresentations by the issuer's agents as to the stock's value".[78] Both in the U.K. and the U.S., courts had by mid-century also extended fraud liability "to misrepresentations not

---

[74] Charles Francis Adams's famous article, 'A Chapter of Erie', focused on financial chicanery at the Erie Railroad and was probably the first true "muckraking" article, one that founded a literary genre in the late nineteenth and early twentieth centuries. C.F. Adams, 'A Chapter of Erie' [1869] 109 *North American Review* 30. Given Adams's status as a son and grandson of American presidents, his attack naturally had credibility and would have influenced European readers. Thus it seems fair to conclude that Europeans would have perceived themselves to be exposed as minority investors in U.S. companies at this time.

[75] Later, many of these rules were relaxed. For a review of American corporate law at this late nineteenth-century stage, see L.M. Friedman, *A History of American Law* 446–63 (Texas 1973). Harold Marsh has also surveyed the status of the officer and director's fiduciary duty to the corporation during this era and concluded that strong prophylactic rules against self-dealing existed. See H. Marsh, Jr, 'Are Directors Trustees?' [1966] 22 Business Lawyer 35.

[76] Friedman, above, n. 75, 457–59.

[77] See Carosso, above, n. 68, 43–44 (noting that Jacob Schiff of Kuhn, Loeb and others considered such investments to be of dubious value, principally because of the inadequate disclosures made by these corporations).

[78] S. Banner, Anglo-American Securities Regulation 237 (Cambridge 1998).

made specifically to the plaintiffs," but on which they had "relied to their detriment."[79] New York had even criminalized the fraudulent issuance of stock.[80] But before these legal developments can be asserted to supply the legal preconditions to the appearance of liquid securities markets in the U.S. and the U.K., their limitations need to be recognized. First, the law of fraud as of this time applied only to affirmative misrepresentations, not to omissions, and imposed no duty on the seller to disclose information in its possession.[81] Nor could plaintiff shareholders join together to file a class action, which had not yet developed in the U.S. and which remains largely unknown today in the U.K. Hence, given the costs of litigation, the fraudulent promoter probably faced liability as a practical matter only to its larger customers. Next, because the U.S. was a federal system, the enforceability of a judgment against a defendant who had fled the jurisdiction remained a major problem. Finally, there was the problem of judicial corruption. In New York, the home of most securities transactions, many of the most notorious stock promoters, such as Jay Gould, were closely associated with Tammany Hall, the Democratic political machine that selected and often controlled local judges.

Given this uninviting legal environment, which would particularly deter foreign investors who could not easily conduct litigation from across an ocean, investment bankers hoping to interest such investors in the equity securities of U.S. corporations had to find some means by which these corporations and their entrepreneurs could credibly bond their promises. Litigation was simply not the answer for the foreign investor. Although foreign investors might buy debt and equity securities on the reputational capital of merchant bankers like J.P. Morgan, this reliance implied in turn that these agents had to develop a governance structure that enabled them to fulfil their representations to their clients that their investments were safe and sound.

One means to this end was pioneered by J.P. Morgan & Co., namely, placing a partner of the firm on the client's board. Up until World War I, the American investment banking industry was extremely concentrated, and any flotation of more than $10 million invariably was underwritten by one of six firms, of which the largest was J.P. Morgan & Co.[82] Given their market power and the desires of distant investors for a "hands on" representative protecting their interests, it became common in the U.S. (but much less so in the U.K.) for the investment banker to place one or more representatives on the issuer's board. During the last two decades of the nineteenth century, virtually every major U.S. railroad

[79] ibid., 241.

[80] ibid., 242.

[81] ibid., 243.

[82] R.C. Michie, *The London and New York Stock Exchanges, 1850–1914* (London 1987) 226–27.

developed close ties with one or more U.S. investment banking firms, and the practice of partners from investment banks and officers of commercial banks going on the railroad's board became institutionalized.[83]

Recent research by financial economists suggests that these practices were both widespread and created value for investors. One survey of just the financial industry has found that during this period J.P. Morgan & Co. held 23 director-ships in just 13 banks; First National Bank, which worked closely with J.P. Morgan, held 14 directorships in other banks, and National City Bank held 32 such positions in 16 banks and trust companies.[84] More importantly, Professor Bradford De Long has assembled evidence suggesting that the pres-ence of a J.P. Morgan & Co. representative on an issuer's board of directors added approximately 30% to the value of the firm's common stock equity.[85]

But why? Financial economists have theorized that such a representative enabled bankers to monitor the firm's mangers and investment projects, replac-ing those managers that were substandard and rejecting unpromising investment projects.[86] Perhaps, this sometimes happened. Still, the problem with this simple agency cost story is that investment bankers have generally not been viewed as activists in corporate governance, in part because any agent, including an invest-ment banker, who intervenes aggressively in the principal's business risks losing the client. An alternative partial explanation is that investment bankers on the boards of competing firms sometimes served as a mechanism for price collusion (as reformers in the Progressive Era clearly believed).

A simpler and nonexclusive hypothesis may contribute a better explanation: The fundamental agency problem facing public investors in this era was not that their managers would expropriate wealth, but that incoming controlling shareholders would.[87] In a world of still relatively concentrated ownership, shareholders could control managers, but were exposed to any shareholder who achieved majority control. Hence, the presence of a major investment banking firm on the corporation's board offered mutual advantages both to the minority

---

[83] Carosso, above, n. 71, 32–33. It should be noted that one firm (Kuhn, Loeb & Co) character-istically did not place its representatives on the issuer's board. It was seemingly the exception that proved the rule, but it may have limited its clientele to firms that found other means by which to bond their commitments to investors.

[84] C.D. Ramirez, 'Did J.P. Morgan's Men Add Liquidity? Corporate Investment, Cash Flow, and Financial Structure at the Turn of the Twentieth Century' [1995] 50 *Journal of Finance* 661, 665.

[85] J. Bradford De Long, 'Did J.P. Morgan's Men Add Value? An Economist's Perspective on Financial Capitalism' in P. Temin (ed.) *Inside the Business Enterprise* (Chicago 1991) 205.

[86] See ibid.

[87] A single-minded focus on managerial expropriation is probably a legacy of Berle and Means's continuing influence. More recent scholars have argued, however, that investors are more exposed to expropriation by controlling shareholders. E.g. A. Shleifer and R.W. Vishny, 'A Survey of Corporate Governance' [1997] 52 *Journal of Finance* 737.

investors and to the corporate management by protecting both from the prospect of a stealth attack by a corporate raider seeking to acquire control without paying a control premium. That is, while the presence of the investment banker may have also reduced agency costs or prevented "disastrous" price wars, the greater problem at the end of the nineteenth century was the instability of control and the relative inability of public investors to demand and receive a control premium for its transfer. Take-over raids occurred in the nineteenth century,[88] but lacked the visibility of the later tender offer wars of the late twentieth century, precisely because the control seeker did not need to offer publicly to purchase a majority of the issuer's shares at a premium, but instead could assemble a controlling block at low cost by buying secretly in the open market. Because the major investment banking firms were positioned close to the market, they were logically in a position to detect such a raid and to finance a counter bid or design appropriate defensive measures. More importantly, they also spoke for the foreign investors, who were likely to act collectively based on the advice of their American agent.

This explanation of the investment banker's role as a protector of the public shareholder from attempts by speculators to steal a firm's control premium is not merely theoretical, but can be corroborated with actual examples. In the late 1880s, Kidder Peabody, in conjunction with Barings, a British merchant bank, took control of the affairs of the Santa Fe Railroad, which was then teetering on the brink of insolvency, placing three partners on its board. Kidder Peabody did not, however, hold a large equity stake itself, so it devised a complicated voting trust strategy explicitly to defeat a perceived control threat from Jay Gould.[89] Indeed, even the redoubtable J.P. Morgan first made his reputation as a railroad financier when, as a young man in 1869, he coordinated the efforts of the Albany & Susquehanna Railroad to fight off the attempt of Jay Gould and Jim Fisk to take control of that railroad in a battle popularly known as the Susquehanna War.[90] After each side obtained rival injunctions and a pitched battle between small armies hired by both sides proved inconclusive, Morgan resolved matters by negotiating a merger of the Albany & Susquehanna Railroad into the larger Delaware & Hudson, thereby putting the target beyond Gould's reach. Morgan then went on the board of the new entity. However, neither Morgan nor other investment bankers in similar battles during this era sought to take personal

---

[88] See W. Werner and S.T. Smith, *Wall Street 133–40* (New York 1991). Jay Gould, in particular, was noted for conducting proxy fights after buying a substantial block of stock. Often, these contests produced a "greenmail" payment to him, or he would short the stock before announcing the end of his proxy contest. M. Klein, *The Life and Legend of Jay Gould* (New York 1986) 197–205.

[89] See Carosso, above, n. 68, 36–37.

[90] Carosso, above, n. 71, 121–22. For a fuller account, see R. Chernow, *The House of Morgan* (New York 1990) 31–32.

control of the corporations they defended. Their role was rather that of an agent protecting their investors. "Board membership," as Ron Chernow has generalized, "[became] a warning flag to . . . [others] to stay away from a captive company".[91]

As a result, to the extent that public shareholders received protection from predatory raiders seeking to acquire control without paying a premium, public shareholders could afford to pay a higher premium for shares. Correspondingly, the firm's founders benefited from such a relationship because they now could, in effect, sell control to the market, rather than having to retain a control block until a majority purchaser appeared. Moreover, to the extent that the firm's founders remained active in management, they also gained protection from a subsequent disruptive hostile take-over by a robber baron, which would typically have been a coercive partial bid made without a premium.

From a comparative perspective, the most interesting aspect of this hypothesis is that it helps explain why control was not transferred to the market by similar means across Europe. First, financial institutions closely corresponding to the House of Morgan either did not exist outside the U.S., or simply did not wish to accept the risks inherent in underwriting equity securities. Partly, this was because J.P. Morgan & Co. and its very few peers were highly capitalized, specialized institutions that, from the 1890s on, focused on basically two activities: (1) underwriting very large issuances of securities, and (2) arranging mergers and acquisitions. The leading English merchant banks were unwilling (until later in the twentieth century) to engage in Morgan's high-risk underwriting activities, which typically involved buying the entire issue from the company and then reselling it to the market. Instead, English merchant banks largely left this realm to more marginal players, known as "stock promoters", who acted only as agents.[92] For reasons discussed later, English underwriters tended to be smaller in size and thus less able to take such risks. In addition, they did not develop in an equivalent environment in which their client industries had a constantly expanding need for capital that required ever larger flotations.

Second, investment bankers in the U.K. did not represent the same cohesive and substantial fraction of the public shareholders as did an American investment banker serving as agent for the foreign investors in U.S. securities. Not only did foreign investors represent a smaller proportion of the U.K. equity market, but U.K. investment banks, being considerably smaller, would typically represent fewer domestic investors as well.[93]

---

[91] Chernow, above, n. 90, 32.

[92] According to some authorities, British merchant banks did not become interested or heavily involved in underwriting domestic new issues until the 1920s. See D. Kynaston, *The City of London* (London 1999) 135–36.

[93] With entry to the LSE being relatively easy, "there was . . . little incentive for the creation of large firms." Michie, above, n. 82, 256. In contrast, because membership in the NYSE was fixed,

Finally, a third factor that played a role in both the growth of investment banking firms and the rapid appearance of dispersed ownership in the decades just before 1900 was the first great merger wave of 1895 to 1903. Interestingly, the greater scale of this consolidation movement in the U.S., in contrast to that in the U.K., illustrates the significance of legal differences. Historians believe that the merger wave of 1890 to 1905 was driven in large part by the passage of the Sherman Antitrust Act of 1890.[94] That Act prohibited price-fixing and collusion among competitors, thereby outlawing the cartel-like structure that characterized many American industries. But if cartels of conspiring firms were forbidden, competitors could instead employ mergers to create monopolies—at least until this was later also prohibited. In any event, the Sherman Act triggered a wave of horizontal mergers among competitors that, in the process, also diluted existing blockholders and thereby created dispersed ownership. The classic example was the consolidation of some eight competing steel companies into a new firm, U.S. Steel, in 1901. The transaction was engineered by J.P. Morgan and created the largest business corporation in the world. A transaction on such a scale inherently created dispersed ownership, even if each of the corporate participants previously had concentrated ownership, and it also produced a new firm with so heightened a capitalization that it was simply beyond the ambitions of any potential raider, thus making dispersed ownership stable.

In contrast to U.S. courts, British courts appear to have been significantly less aggressive in restricting cartels or prohibiting horizontal price-fixing agreements during this period. Hence, there was a weaker incentive to merge, and larger scale business entities emerged more slowly, while family capitalism survived longer in the U.K.[95] For immediate purposes, however, the relevant point is that the lesser the incentive to merge, the slower the movement toward dispersed ownership. Hence, we encounter an additional reason why dispersed ownership arrived earlier in the U.S., and it has little to do with the relative legal rights of minority shareholders.

---

brokerage firms with a seat on the NYSE grew both in order to exploit their monopoly position and to realise economies of scale that could not be realised in London as a result of restrictions on outside financing and prohibitions on partners in brokerage firms conducting other business. See nn. 105–12 and accompanying text. In short, as the demand for brokerage services increased, the size of firms grew in New York, while the number of firms increased in London. Ibid., 256.

[94] A.D. Chandler, Jr and L. Hannah, both noted business historians, have argued that differing policies toward cartels in the U.S. and Britain help explain the different scale of the turn-of-the-century merger wave in both nations. A.D. Chandler, Jr, *Scale and Scope: The Dynamics of Industrial Capitalism* (London 1990) 288–94; L. Hannah, 'Mergers, Cartels and Concentration: Legal Factors in the U.S. and European Experience' in N. Horn and J. Kocka (eds.) *Law and Formation of the Big Enterprises in the 19th and Early 20th Centuries* (1979) 306, 306–15.

[95] See T. Freyer, 'Legal Restraints on Economic Coordination: Antitrust in Great Britain and the Americas, 1880–1920' in N.R. Lamoreaux & D.M.G. Raff (eds.) *Coordination and Information* (1995) 183, 183–202.

2. The New York Stock Exchange as Guardian of the Public Investor

The active role played by the New York Stock Exchange (NYSE) in American corporate governance has been noted by others,[96] but its path-dependent history has escaped serious attention. Three points merit special emphasis at the outset: First, exchange activism was not the norm elsewhere, and the NYSE's active efforts contrast sharply with the passivity of the London Stock Exchange (LSE) and that of the European bourses generally. Secondly, the NYSE did not possess a de facto monopoly position in trading equity securities as of the late nineteenth century. Predominant as it may have been in debt securities, it ranked well behind other exchanges in the trading of equity securities throughout the late nineteenth century. Prior to 1900, "the Boston Stock Exchange was the principal market for industrial securities",[97] and two Boston investment banking firms—Kidder, Peabody and Lee, Higginson—were the dominant underwriters of equities securities.[98] Thirdly, that the NYSE uniquely became an activist on corporate governance issues and ultimately the champion of the public investor seems directly attributable to its organizational structure and its competitive position.

This last point comes most clearly into focus when we compare the NYSE with the LSE. Between 1850 and 1905, the membership of the LSE rose from 864 to 5,567.[99] In sharp contrast, the membership of the NYSE stayed constant between 1879 and 1914 at 1,100.[100] While admission to the LSE was "cheap and

---

[96] Indeed, the NYSE's leadership role was recognized from early in the last century. Prior to the passage of the federal securities laws in the 1930s, "even the most unrelenting critics of corporate finance lauded the Exchange's listing requirements". J. Seligman, *The Transformation of Wall Street* (New York 1982) 46. Dean Seligman notes that the NYSE's listing requirements were "far more precise than any found in the blue sky laws" and became the model for the subsequently-enacted Schedule A to the Securities Act of 1933. Ibid. Probably the most outspoken critic of Wall Street practices prior to the stock market crash of 1929 was Harvard Professor William Z. Ripley. But even he described the NYSE as "the leading influence in the promotion of adequate corporate disclosure". W.Z. Ripley, *Main Street and Wall Street* (Cambridge 1927) 210, 213–14.

[97] Carosso, above, n. 68, 44.

[98] ibid. The Boston Stock Exchange's early predominance came from its natural leadership position in the underwriting of the New England textile mills; also, some early railroad underwritings—such as those of the Atichison, Topeka and Santa Fe—were effected exclusively in New England, with the railroad's stock being listed only on the Boston Stock Exchange. Ibid., 34.

[99] Michie, above, n. 82, 252. One reason that admission to the LSE was open was that the stockholders of the LSE were distinct from the LSE's member brokers, and they profited from the admission fees paid by new brokers. Thus, the LSE's owners wished to maximize admission fees, while its brokers might have preferred to maximize brokerage commissions.

[100] ibid., 253. The only increase between 1868 and 1914 came in 1879 when the NYSE added 40 seats. Ibid.

easy",[101] entry to the NYSE could only be gained by buying the seat of an existing member. The closed structure of the NYSE gave its members very different incentives, particularly regarding regulation, from those of members of an "open" exchange, such as the LSE. First, the NYSE's restrictions on membership encouraged the growth of large, diversified financial services firms (such as J.P. Morgan & Co.), while the typical British brokerage firm remained small in size, with typically only six to seven partners. Secondly, having paid more to join the NYSE and holding a transferable asset with a substantial market value, a NYSE member had a stronger reason to favour self-regulation that protected the value of its seat; also, larger firms probably enjoyed greater reputational capital and thus had a greater interest in protecting it. Thirdly, the small size of the NYSE implied logistical constraints on the ability of its membership to trade all securities for which a public market might have been made. Necessarily, the NYSE's decision to limit its membership fragmented the U.S. equity market, creating a high quality tier and a lower quality tier that traded elsewhere on an over-the-counter basis. Further encouraging larger and better capitalized firms on the NYSE was another difference in the two exchanges' organizational rules: NYSE member firms could raise capital from outsiders—known as "special partners"—and not all partners in a firm were required to be members of the exchange.[102] In contrast, the LSE required all partners in a firm to be members of the exchange and further prohibited every member from engaging in any other business.[103] The relative freedom enjoyed by NYSE firms in obtaining outside capital resulted not only in larger size, but also in a greater ability to engage in higher risk underwriting activities.

Another key difference between the two exchanges was their positions on the question of competitive versus fixed brokerage commissions. Throughout the late nineteenth century, the NYSE had fixed brokerage commissions, while the LSE did not (at least until just before World War I). Again, this difference reflected the cartel-like organization of the NYSE in comparison to the open market character of the LSE. Because fixed commissions raised the cost of trading, this practice drove trading in lower-volume and lower-price stocks off the NYSE. Competitors could, and did, win the low volume business from the NYSE. But the business that migrated elsewhere consisted disproportionately of lower-price and higher-risk stocks.[104] Consequently, the NYSE quickly made a

---

[101] R.C. Michie, 'Different in Name Only?: The London Stock Exchange and Foreign Bourses, c1850–1914' in R.C. Michie (ed.), *The Development of London as a Financial Centre* (London 2000).

[102] Michie, above, n. 82, 256–57.

[103] ibid.

[104] The NYSE's $\frac{1}{8}$% commission "was considered high by contemporaries, and it encouraged many interested parties to deal with outside brokers or members of other exchanges, where the rates were lower". Ibid. at 259. Moreover, because the rate was charged on par value, it was "particularly onerous on shares with low real value, such as many mining and later industrial securities, and so

virtue of this inevitability, arguing that the low-priced or low-volume stocks that migrated to other trading venues were unsuitable for the public customer. In combination with the fact that the NYSE's small and fixed number of member firms could not logistically handle the trading in all firms that might wish to list on the NYSE, fixed-price commissions led the NYSE to define its role narrowly and limit itself to a high-volume, high quality business. In short, for economic reasons, the NYSE recognized by the mid-nineteenth century that it made sense for it to pursue a strategy of exclusivity.[105] Accordingly, it would deliberately list and trade only large issuers whose high-volume trading could support minimum commissions. Thus, as of 1900, the LSE listed 3,631 different issuers of securities, while the NYSE listed only 1,157.[106] This difference was largely the NYSE's choice, and the product of its decision to reject most listing applications.

A final factor that reinforced the NYSE's preference for listing only large, high quality issuers was its fear that listing high-volatility stocks would invite predictable insolvencies among its members. Such insolvencies could expose the broker's trading partners to similar failure. Repeatedly, in the late nineteenth century, financial panics had caused NYSE member firms to fail and had imposed significant liabilities on the failed firm's trading partners. Because the NYSE, as an essentially closed cartel, had far fewer members than the LSE, it also had more to fear from the failure of any member firm. Hence, to minimize the risk of member failure, the NYSE was far more conservative (and risk averse) about the securities that it would list. For example, it refused to list mining or petroleum companies during this period, because such securities were thought to be especially volatile.[107] The rationale here was less a paternalistic concern for the investor than the fear that mining and petroleum stocks typically experienced volatile price movements (based on discoveries or rumours of discoveries), and a broker holding such stocks was exposed to greater risk in a financial panic. The consequence was that to be listed on the NYSE, a company as of 1900 had to be at least five times larger than its counterpart on the LSE.[108]

From these differences in the organizational structure of the NYSE and the LSE, very different approaches toward self-regulation quickly emerged. From

---

discouraged trading in these on the New York Stock Exchange". Ibid. Typically, lower priced stocks ("penny stocks" in the contemporary parlance) were riskier and more volatile. In the late nineteenth century, some mining and industrial companies used such "small-denomination securities to attract investors." Ibid., 199. But because the NYSE focused on the needs of "substantial investor[s]", it did not attempt to compete for this business. Ibid. At least during the late nineteenth century, however, these more speculative issues were driven off the NYSE less by quality controls than by the impact of the NYSE's high cost commission structure.

[105] ibid., 272.

[106] ibid., 264.

[107] ibid., 198, 273.

[108] ibid., 272.

well before 1900, the NYSE saw itself as the guardian of the financial quality of the issuers listed on it. Perhaps it imposed high listing standards for its own self-interested reasons, but it clearly did regularly reject issuer applications, either because the issuer lacked an adequate earnings track record, had insufficient assets, or was in a high-risk industry. In so doing, the NYSE was also able to distinguish itself from its American competitors and present an image to investors as the most reputable exchange. Indeed, under the NYSE's prodding, the standard of disclosure for public companies was significantly enhanced, and some financial historians date the advent of modern financial reporting from 1900, not from 1933, when the federal securities laws were first adopted.[109] In contrast, the LSE made no similar effort to police its securities market, at least until the period after World War I.[110] The LSE's more laissez-faire approach probably reflected the fact that it faced less competition and that its stockholders profited directly from the admission of additional brokers and issuers.

The NYSE's acceptance of the role of guardian of the public investor probably climaxed in the 1920s with its express, if reluctant, decision to protect the voting rights of the dispersed shareholder by refusing to list nonvoting common stock. Prior to 1900, corporate shares, both common and preferred, typically carried equal voting rights, but beginning shortly after 1900, investment bankers began to develop devices to centralize voting control in a small percentage of the outstanding equity shares, which were typically held by investment banking firms.[111] A number of devices, including dual class stock, voting trusts, and pyramid holding company structures, came into increasingly common use. Indeed, when Berle and Means surveyed the American corporate scene in 1930, they found that, in 21% of the 200 largest corporations, ultimate control was attributable to a legal device.[112] Matters came to a head in 1925, when a few leading corporations made large offerings of nonvoting common stock, with the consequence that investment banking firms, sometimes owning securities representing well under 5% of the firm's market capitalization, held majority voting control.[113] A Harvard professor of political economy, William Ripley, made a

---

[109] See D.F. Hawkins, 'The Development of Modern Financial Reporting Practices Among American Manufacturing Corporations' in R.S. Tedlow and R.R. John, Jr (eds.) *Managing Big Business* (Cambridge 1986) 166–67.

[110] R.C. Michie, *The London Stock Exchange* (London 1999) 115.

[111] This observation was first made by contemporaneous observers who dated the transition to around 1903. See, e.g. W.H.S. Stevens, 'Stockholders' Voting Rights and the Centralization of Voting Control' [1926] 40 *Quarterly Journal of Economics* 353, 355–56; W.H.S. Stevens, 'Voting Rights of Capital Stock and Shareholders' [1938] 11 *Journal of Business* 311 (noting the trend away from equal voting rights).

[112] A.A. Berle and G.C. Means, *The Modern Corporation and Private Property* (revised edn. New York 1991) 109.

[113] The best known incident involved a stock offering by Dodge Brothers Inc, which, with a total market capitalization of $130 million, was controlled by the investment banking firm of Dillon, Read

highly critical speech, attacking this development as ensuring "banker control" of large corporations. The speech received wide press coverage, and the professor was ultimately invited to the White House to explain his concerns to an apparently sympathetic President Coolidge.[114] Although the NYSE sought to keep a low profile throughout the controversy, it saw that nonvoting common stock had become an issue of broad public concern, and early in the following year (1926), it adopted a policy not to list nonvoting common stock or companies that issued such a class of securities.[115] Over time, this policy was broadened to require listed companies not to issue a block of stock carrying sufficient voting power to transfer control without an authorizing shareholder vote.[116] As a result, without intending to champion any movement, the NYSE became identified with mandatory listing conditions that protected "shareholder democracy" and prevented the separation of cash flow rights from voting rights. In the wake of recent economic research finding that the separation of cash flow and voting rights has been the principal technique for expropriation from minority shareholders in Asia,[117] the NYSE's 1926 reform may have had unrecognized significance, not because it barred nonvoting common stock, but because it grew into a normative principle that effectively barred voting trusts and dual class capitalisations from U.S. public markets.[118]

& Co based on less than $2.25 million investment (or less than 2% of all capital invested in the firm). J. Seligman, 'Equal Protection in Shareholder Voting Rights: The One Common Share, One Vote Controversy' [1986] 54 George Washington University Law Review 687, 694.

[114] ibid., 694–96. The controversy surrounding the Dodge Brothers offering and the public outcry over "banker control" based on small minority stakes has been reviewed by numerous commentators. See J.A. Livingston, *The American Stockholder* (New York 1958) 186–87; R. Sobel, *The Big Board* (New York 1965) 236. Professor Ripley went on to generalize his views in a broader populist critique, which was one of the significant influences leading Congress to enact the federal securities laws. W.Z. Ripley, *Main Street and Wall Street* (1927) 86–87 (describing the Dodge offering).

[115] Seligman, above, n. 113, 697; Livingston, n. 114, at 187; Sobel, n. 114, at 236 (reviewing NYSE's 1926 decision not to list such issuers).

[116] Seligman above, n. 113, 689. The NYSE policy barred not only the issuance of a control block, but, as it came to be framed in a bright-line rule, any issuance of common stock carrying more than 18.5% of the firm's voting power without a prior shareholder vote. Ibid.

[117] S. Claessens et al., *The Separation of Ownership and Control in East Asian Corporations* (SSRN Electronic Library, Working Paper no. 206,448, 2000), available at http://papers.ssrn.com/paper.taf?abstract_id=206448; S. Claessens et al., *On Expropriation of Minority Shareholders: Evidence from East Asia*, (SSRN Electronic Library, Working Paper no. 202,390, 2000), available at http://papers.ssrn.com/paper.taf?abstract_id=202390.

[118] Ironically, economic analysis today regards the issuance of nonvoting common stock as essentially innocuous, as the purchasers will pay little for such a security and hence they risk little. More sinister in the view of most recent commentators is the issuance of a high-voting security after common stock has been sold to public investors, because this later issuance dilutes the voting power of outstanding shares. R.J. Gilson, 'Evaluating Dual Class Common Stock: The Relevance of Substitutes' [1987] 73 Vanderbilt Law Review 807, 840–42; J.N. Gordon, 'Ties That Bond: Dual Class Common Stock and the Problem of Shareholder Choice' [1988] 76 California Law Review 3,

The point of this story is not that the NYSE has always behaved as a public-regarding, altruistically motivated entity. Rather, it is that for a variety of path-dependent reasons, the NYSE organized itself as an exclusive, high quality securities market that would list only securities that were suitable for the public investor—while the LSE did not. In the total absence of legal requirements, the NYSE imposed mandatory disclosure obligations on its listed firms and protected shareholder voting rights. Correspondingly, the larger size of U.S. brokerage firms, which again was originally attributable to differences in the organizational rules of the NYSE and the LSE, gave U.S. brokers greater ability to underwrite securities and to develop and pledge their reputational capital to their investor customers. These two developments—the development of a monitoring capacity by the NYSE and the bonding mechanisms first developed by U.S. underwriters to attract foreign capital—constitute the twin pillars that supported the development of a liquid equity securities market in the United States. Such a public market arose more quickly in the U.S. than in the U.K. For example, by 1907 one Wall Street firm already had 22,000 customers,[119] indicating that it was providing services on a mass scale. Yet, the legal framework that today characterizes the U.S. securities markets did not arise until decades later.

II. The British Experience

In contrast to the high listing standards that the NYSE imposed by the late 1800s, the LSE's basic policy was to list any security that was expected to generate business.[120] Only in "rare cases, where something adverse was known about the security and the circumstances surrounding its issue", would a listing application be denied for reasons other than lack of trading interest.[121] Of course, this attitude reflected the natural attitude of an "open" exchange with broad membership: More listings implied more business, and the failure of an occasional brokerage firm (which were characteristically smaller in size) did not constitute as serious a threat to the LSE as it did to the NYSE—in part because the LSE had a considerably deeper capital base.[122] Finally, stock issuances were typically arranged in the U.K. by stock promoters, not the largest merchant banks. These

---

4. Yet, however myopic its original purpose, the NYSE's "one share, one vote" rules served to protect common shareholders from any significant dilution of their voting power.

[119] Michie, above, n. 82, 228.

[120] Michie, above, n. 110, 96.

[121] ibid.

[122] Michie, above, n. 82, 272 (noting that the NYSE's capitalization was one-third that of the LSE).

promoters often had unsavoury reputations and little reputational capital to pledge.[123]

Given the LSE's laissez-faire approach and, indeed, its caveat emptor attitude, it is thus not surprising that the public equity market developed more slowly in the U.K. than in the U.S. Exactly when dispersed ownership arrived in the U.K. is debatable. In 1936, the median proportion of the voting share held by the 20 largest shareholders in the 82 largest non-financial U.K. corporations was approximately 40% (whereas the same ownership level for U.S. corporations was then 28%).[124] Moreover, in 40% of U.K. companies, the twenty largest shareholders held a collective absolute majority.[125] Thus, although share ownership may have been dispersed, the separation of ownership and control had not yet truly occurred. A parallel study based on 1977 data found that the largest 20 shareholders then held between 20% and 29% of the voting stock.[126] Although such a block might still carry control, it is doubtful that the 20 largest shareholders were by this point truly a cohesive group, as institutional investors were now heavily represented in the top 20.[127] Hence, sometime between the late 1930s and the mid-1970s, ownership and control probably separated in most U.K. companies.[128]

The deeper question is not when dispersed ownership arrived, but why it occurred. In the absence of high listing standards or underwriting practices that placed the reputational capital of credible financial intermediaries behind most offerings, why did public investors place trust and confidence in the U.K. market?

Several tentative hypotheses can be advanced. First, less effort may have been expended on self-regulation in the U.K. because judicial corruption and regulatory arbitrage posed less of a threat. In this light, self-regulation is an example

[123] For this common assessment, see W.A. Thomas, *The Finance of British Industry: 1918–1976* (London 1978) 23; and J. Armstrong, 'The Rise and Fall of the Company Promoter and the Financing of British Industry' in J.J. Van Helten and Y. Cassis (eds.), *Capitalism in a Mature Economy* (London 1990) 115, 130–31.

[124] P. Sargant Florence, *The Logic of British and American Industry* (London 1953) 189.

[125] ibid.

[126] J. Scott, *Capitalist Property and Financial Power* (New York 1986) 95. For a review of this literature, see B.S. Black and J.C. Coffee, Jr, 'Hail Britannia?: Institutional Investor Behaviour Under Limited Regulation' [1994] 92 Michigan Law Review 1997, 2029–33.

[127] Ibid., 2030–31 (analysing the list of 20 largest shareholders in Scott's study).

[128] Cambridge University Professor Brian Cheffins opines that "[t]here is some evidence which suggests that the period prior to 1950 was pivotal". Cheffins, above, n. 20, 19. While he is equivocal about 1950, he is, however, more convinced that it arrived before 1970. Leslie Hannah, a British business historian, similarly concludes that the separation of ownership and control was established in Britain by the middle of the twentieth century. L. Hannah, *The Rise of the Corporate Economy* (2nd edn. London 1976) 90–91, 123–24; Cheffins, above, n. 20, 22. These dates precede the appearance of Margaret Thatcher on the political scene and suggest that dispersed ownership arrived during a social democratic era in Britain.

of a functional substitute that arose at least in part to solve the problem of endemic judicial corruption in the U.S. during the late nineteenth century. Again, this is an illustration of functional convergence.

Secondly, the U.K. may have had a more cohesive business community than did the U.S. in this era, with either a stronger normative code or a perceived greater exposure to the loss of reputational capital based on any association with a securities scandal. Either factor could have restrained U.K. managers in the absence of law. Contemporary data show that the private benefits of control differ significantly among countries, even countries belonging to the same legal family.[129] As of the late nineteenth century, there is every reason to believe that in the U.K., the business community in general, and the securities industry in particular, was more socially stratified and class bound than were the same industries in the U.S.

Finally, as next discussed, there were material differences between U.S. and U.K. law in this era, and British law did regulate securities offerings to a greater degree than did U.S. law, from as early as the 1860s. Thus, although U.S. institutions moved more quickly to adopt self-regulatory standards, British mandatory law regulating disclosure was enacted well in advance of similar developments in the U.S. Different paths were followed at different speeds to an approximately equivalent end point. If one looks at the aggregate effect of mandatory law plus self-regulation in both countries, the level of shareholder protection was arguably similar in the U.S. and the U.K. up until the passage of the federal securities laws and the creation of the SEC in the U.S. in the mid-1930s. What Britain did by legislation, the U.S. did by self-regulation. It need not be claimed that the two countries had equivalent protections at equivalent times, but only that both satisfied the minimum standards necessary for dispersed ownership to result. That both could have reached this same level by different means is again an example of functional convergence.

The claim that U.K. law provided superior protections to minority investors may seem surprising and must be qualified, because only the disclosure provisions of U.K. law were more protective than the equivalent standards in the U.S. Outside this context, the contrasts between U.S. corporate law and British company law as of 1900 would seem to have largely favoured the minority shareholders in the U.S. over their British counterparts. Basically, the U.K. shareholder had no appraisal right and only an ineffective derivative action remedy. Worse, the shareholder's rights were subject to the ability of a majority of the shareholders to ratify any conflict of interest transaction and thereby place it

---

[129] J.C. Coffee, Jr, 'Do Norms Matter?': A Cross-Country Examination of the Private Benefits of Control', 149 University of Pennsylvania Law Review 2151 (2001) (citing data showing cross-country disparities in the private benefits of control, including among countries within the common-law family).

beyond judicial review.[130] Worse yet, exculpatory provisions were permitted in the corporate charter that could cancel even the duty of loyalty.[131] In short, U.K. corporate law had not yet comprehensively adopted the standards of minority protection that LLS&V contemplate as the precondition for dispersed ownership.

Still, whatever the status of its substantive corporate law, Britain did lead the U.S. in its statutory regulation of disclosure to investors.[132] A series of stock market scandals in the U.K. in the 1870s had led to two "public enquiries" by Parliament, but had not produced legislation.[133] Then, in 1890, at the very outset of the relevant transitional period for U.K. purposes, Parliament overruled a judicial decision that had narrowly construed the law of fraud by enacting legislation that permitted investors to recover damages if (1) they suffered loss by reason of an untrue statement in a prospectus, and (2) those responsible for its preparation could not prove that they had reasonable grounds to believe that the statement was true.[134] Not until 1933 was U.S. law to reach a similarly pro-investor position when Congress enacted the Securities Act of 1933, which, in section 11, contains a similar standard for prospectuses that was in fact modelled after this 1890 statute.[135] The Companies Act of 1900 supplemented this antifraud standard by specifying what the prospectus offering securities had to disclose.[136] In 1907, the first step toward a mandatory continuing disclosure system was taken with legislation that required publication of an annual balance sheet.[137]

---

[130] For a review of U.K. law in this era, see B.R. Cheffins, *Does Law Matter?: The Separation of Ownership and Control in the United Kingdom* (ESRC Centre for Business Research, University of Cambridge, Working Paper no. 172, 2000), available at http://papers.ssrn.com/paper.taf? abstract_id=245560 . For a notable case from the period, see *North-West Transportation Co v. Beatty* (1887) 12 App. Cas. 589 (PC) (appeal taken from Ontario) (upholding the majority ratification of a self-dealing transaction).

[131] P.L. Davies, *Gower's Principles of Modern Company Law* 6th edn. (London 1997) 611–12.

[132] The history of securities regulation in the U.K. dates back to 1844, when in the Companies Act of 1844 Parliament "enacted the first modern prospectus requirement". L. Loss and J. Seligman, *Securities Regulation* 5 3rd edn. (Boston 1989). However, it was not until the Companies Act of 1867 that "the contents of the prospectus were in any way specified". Ibid., 6. In any event, these provisions were "easily evaded by exacting waivers from subscribers". Ibid. Thus the risk of liability does not appear to have become real until the 1890 legislation. See below, n. 134 and accompanying text. However, beginning with the report of the Lord Davey Committee in 1895, Parliament expressly rejected the norm of caveat emptor and in 1900 mandated in detail the specific contents of the prospectus used to sell securities. Ibid.

[133] See Michie, above, n. 70, 3.

[134] Directors Liability Act, 1890, 53 and 54 Vict, c. 64 (overruling *Derry v. Peak* (1889) 14 App. Cas. 337 (appeal).

[135] Loss and Seligman, above, n. 132, 6–8; Kilbride, 'The British Heritage of Securities Legislation in the United States' [1963] 17 Southwestern Law Journal 258.

[136] Companies Act, 1900, 63 and 64 Vict, c. 48, s. 10(1).

[137] Companies Act, 1907, 7 Edw, c. 50, ss. 19, 21.

Legislation in 1908 addressed (albeit in a limited manner) abuses in the new issue market.[138] Finally, in 1929, legislation obliged the issuer to provide an income statement and related data on current earnings.[139] Rudimentary as these requirements may seem today, they were enacted well ahead of corresponding legislation in the U.S., although they may have been slightly behind practices at the NYSE. As a generalization then, the U.K. seems to have led the U.S. in the area of securities regulation, but lagged behind the U.S. in terms of minority protections in its substantive corporate law. Not until amendments to the Companies Act in 1948 were strong restrictions on self-dealing enacted.

Well before this point, however, the reluctance of the LSE to play any regulatory role in the protection of investors began to change, probably starting shortly after World War I.[140] In 1921, it adopted its first regulations governing the rights of members to deal in or quote a security.[141] During the years between the two World Wars, the LSE's Share and Loan Department began to make inquiries before listing a company into the company's operations and the personnel connected with it. By the 1930s, the LSE's own disclosure requirements for listed companies were more extensive than those set forth in the U.K.'s companies legislation.[142] Still, the LSE did not become a de facto regulator in partnership with the state until after World War II.

The willingness of the LSE to assume a greater regulatory role appears to have been largely scandal-driven. Following a speculative boom in new issues in the 1920s, a major scandal shook the LSE in 1929, when a flamboyant promoter, Charles Hatry, was found to have fraudulently sold counterfeit shares in established companies, intending to buy them back before dividends were declared.[143] The Hatry scandal produced little, if any, legislation, but it did force the LSE to accept some role as a guardian of issuer quality.[144] The LSE became less willing to list what would today be called "penny stocks", or development-stage companies. By the 1950s, the LSE's listing rules had been tightened to require issuers to reveal all material information on an ongoing basis.[145] Still, legislation establishing anything resembling a U.K. counterpart to the SEC did not come until the Financial Services Act of 1986.

---

[138] See F.N. Paish, 'The London New Issue Market' in R.C. Michie (ed.) *The Development of London as a Financial Centre* (London 2000) 22, 24.

[139] Companies Act, 1929, 19 and 20 Geo 5, c. 23, s. 123.

[140] Michie, above, n. 110, 115.

[141] Paish, above, n. 138, 24–25.

[142] See Cheffins, above, n. 130, 24–26.

[143] Michie, above, n. 110, 262–63.

[144] ibid., 268.

[145] See L.C.B. Gower, *The Principles of Modern Company Law* (London 1954) 437.

If the LSE's efforts at self-regulation seem in general to have been laxer than those of the NYSE, there is a later chapter in this self-regulatory story in which the U.K.'s efforts clearly outpaced those in the U.S. Take-over bids first began to appear in the U.K. in the early 1950s, and by late 1959, the first voluntary code of conduct had been drawn up, largely at the request of the Bank of England, to regulate them.[146] While often ineffective, this voluntary code eventually evolved by the late 1960s into the City Take-Over Code and its now well-known Take-Over Panel. In 1972, the Code was revised to require an acquirer to make a mandatory bid for all the target's shares once the acquirer crossed a specified threshold of stock ownership (generally 30%).[147] The effect of this provision was to protect the right of the public shareholder to share in any control premium and to discourage stealth raids that sought to acquire control without the payment of such a premium. The U.K.'s mandatory bid has, of course, now been incorporated into the Thirteenth Directive, but the more relevant point is that it encouraged dispersed ownership by effectively allowing the value of control to be held by public shareholders.

Thus, we come full circle: By a variety of means, including a substantial self-regulatory component, both the U.S. and the U.K. developed legal and institutional mechanisms that enabled dispersed ownership to persist. Generally, these mechanisms followed, rather than preceded, economic changes, but they did protect and facilitate the growth of dispersed ownership. Finally, conspicuously absent from this process was politics. No political party in either country appears actively to have raised the issue of securities market reform (or opposed such reform) as a major issue. Most importantly, if the separation of ownership and control arrived in Britain somewhere between the late 1930s and 1970 (as British historians and academics believe[148]), it occurred at a time when Britain was under a Labour government whose philosophy can be fairly characterized as somewhere between social-democratic and outright socialistic.

III. A Civil-law Contrast: the French Experience

While both the NYSE and the LSE were and remain private bodies, the Paris Bourse has historically been a state-chartered monopoly, run under very close governmental supervision.[149] Far older than either the LSE or the NYSE, it

---

[146] See A. Johnson, *The City Take-Over Code* (London 1980) 19–20.

[147] ibid., 91–92.

[148] See nn. 128–138 and accompanying text.

[149] See, e.g. N.S. Poser, *International Securities Regulation* (Boston 1991) 381–86; T. Schoen, *The French Stock Exchange* (Paris 1995). For a contemporaneous account of the Bourse during the early twentieth century, see W. Parker, *The Paris Bourse and French Finance* (New York, 1919).

traces its origins back to 1141, when Louis VII granted a charter to the Guild of Moneychangers, giving them the sole right to operate on the Great Bridge of Paris.[150] For most of its existence, it fought to preserve this monopoly status, which was formally reconfirmed by Napoleon, who in 1807 gave the exclusive right to the Bourse's stockbrokers (known as *agents de change* or *agents*) to effect transactions in listed securities.[151] A securities transaction off the Bourse was made unlawful, and only an *agent de change* was permitted to transact business on the Bourse.[152] In effect, the Bourse was a publicly administered monopoly, and its *agents de change* had the status of civil servants, who were formally appointed to office by the Minister of Finance after first passing a civil service-like exam.[153] This insulated, monopoly-like status of the Bourse persisted until the late 1980s, when both global competitive pressures (including London's "Big Bang") and a series of scandals forced a wholesale restructuring of the French securities market.[154]

Nonetheless, as of the late nineteenth century, the Paris Bourse was the one potential international rival to the LSE, and it actively traded American railroad securities and later American industrial stocks (such as U.S. Steel). To an even greater extent than London, its market focused on foreign securities, chiefly governmental and railroad bonds.[155] In its competition with the LSE, however, the Bourse was subject to an immense, self-imposed handicap: the Bourse's *agents de change* were permitted to act as commission brokers only and never to function as dealers or principals.[156] To be sure, the LSE also did not permit a member firm to be both a broker and a jobber (that is, a "dealer" in the U.S. par-

---

[150] M.G. Myers, *Paris as a Financial Centre* (1936) 146. For the fullest account of the history of the Paris Bourse, see Vidal, *National Monetary Communcation, The History and Methods of the Paris Bourse*, S Doc no. 61573 (1910).

[151] See Poser, above n. 149, 381. The Paris Bourse was briefly closed during the French Revolution.

[152] ibid. It should be noted that there were a number of regional exchanges in France and a "curb" exchange, but these did not generally compete with the Bourse with regard to securities listed there.

[153] See Myers, above n. 150, 146–47; L.A. Goldman, Note, 'The Modernization of the French Securities Market: Making the SEEC Connection' [1992] 60 Fordham Law Review S227, S231 no. 28.

[154] For a brief overview of this process, see ibid., S230–36.

[155] Myers presents data showing that between 1869 and 1908, foreign securities owned as a percentage of all securities owned in France ranged between 32% (in 1869) and 36% (in 1908), with a decline to 27% between 1880 and 1890 (as a result of France's indemnity obligations arising out of the Franco-Prussian War). Myers, above, n. 153, 136. Between 1908 and 1913 (or just prior to the outbreak of World War I), new issues of foreign securities in France always exceeded (and sometimes more than tripled) new issuance of French securities in France. Ibid. at 138. Myers attributes the popularity of foreign issues to both their higher interest rates and the greater commissions they paid stockbrokers. Ibid., 135–36.

[156] ibid., 146; Parker, above, n. 149, 28.

lance), but it did permit and encourage jobbers to function, and it thereby gained its liquidity from them.

By barring from its trading floor any financial intermediaries who could take positions in stocks in the absence of equilibrating customers' orders, the Paris Bourse thus effectively denied itself liquidity. Partly for this reason, a shadow market, known as the Coulisse, arose to fill this void, but, even though it occasionally threatened the Bourse during this era, it principally served as a market for unlisted securities. Indeed, when in the 1890s the brokers on the Coulisse began to challenge seriously the Bourse's monopoly, the Bourse secured legislation that effectively immunized it from competition.

The Bourse's status as a protected monopoly was by no means unique; rather, it was the standard French pattern. Elsewhere, in the U.S., U.K., and Germany, exchanges competed and the winner became dominant. In France, the government chose the winner. Similarly, the French government chose and chartered the dominant investment-banking house of the era. Perhaps the most important French financial innovation of the nineteenth century was its creation in 1852 of the world's first major corporate investment bank—Sociéte Générale de Crédit Mobilier, which became the template for a series of successor institutions.[157] Designed as an investment bank to promote industrialization, it both advanced promotional loans and underwrote the securities of its clients, and it proved to be an engine of French economic growth for its brief, 15-year existence.[158] But in both the rise and fall of Crédit Mobilier, the French government was deeply implicated. Originally, it was founded under the patronage of Napoleon III, who saw it as a state-controlled rival to the House of Rothschild. But, because it came to rival and infringe the monopoly status of the Bank of France, Crédit Mobilier had envious rivals from its outset (including, of course, the formidable House of Rothschild). Its failure in 1867 came not from a normal financial collapse, but rather from a liquidity crisis occasioned by the government's refusal, prodded by the Bank of France, to allow Crédit Mobilier to issue additional debentures.[159] In short, no institution, however important, truly escaped the government's control.

Similarly, the Bourse was also administered, according to a contemporaneous observer, as a unique "monopoly that operates under the strict and comprehensive

[157] On the rise, fall, and significance of Crédit Mobilier, see R.E. Cameron, *France and the Economic Development of Europe, 1800–1914* (New York 1961) 98–144. The principal innovation in the design of Crédit Mobilier was its capital structure. Most banks obtain most of their capital from depositors, and having short-term liabilities can only safely make short-term loans. Crédit Mobilier attempted to obtain long-term capital by issuing debentures, but never received full governmental permission for the debenture issuances it originally planned. Ibid., 128–31.

[158] ibid., 105–06.

[159] ibid., 128–31.

control of the French Government".[160] Specifically, French law fixed both the commission rates on securities transactions and the number of *agents de change*.[161] In sharp contrast to both the LSE, where the number of seats was unlimited, and the NYSE, where the number of seats was limited but seats could be freely sold, seats on the Bourse were both fixed in number and not freely tradable; rather, seats were usually handed down from father to son. If there was no male heir, the Minister of Finance would typically accept a nomination made in the will of the deceased *agent de change* (or submitted by his executor),[162] but the process of transfer still required that the proposed transferee be an eligible individual, who could have no interest in any commercial enterprise and who had to pass a qualifying exam, before the proposed transferee could be voted upon by the membership and then have his name passed on to the Ministry of Finance.[163] As a result, because (1) the *agents de change* could not serve (or profit) as dealers, (2) no real market in seats existed, and (3) *agents de change* were jointly and severally liable for the business debts of their fellow agents,[164] French stockbrokers remained small and undercapitalized. As much civil servants as economic entrepreneurs, the Bourse's *agents de change* could not develop into securities firms, as could their British and American counterparts. Moreover, limited to a total size of 70 members (each of which could employ no more than six clerks on the trading floor), the Bourse was also logistically constrained.

The important point here is not simply that the Bourse was inefficiently designed or structured, or that it lacked liquidity, but that in a fundamental sense, it lacked true owners who had the incentive to improve or change its structure and rules. Denied the ability to profit as dealers or to transfer their seats freely, the stockbrokers of the Bourse had limited incentives to improve the Bourse's operation or regulation. Indeed, knowing the historic French tendency toward centralization and strong governmental regulation, the ideal of self-regulation may have seemed both alien and infeasible to them—if it were ever considered at all.

In sum, the government regulated all aspects of the Bourse's operation. Even the decision to list securities had to be approved by the Ministry of Finance, and the decision to list a foreign security required the additional approval of the Ministry of Foreign Affairs,[165] which was sometimes withheld.[166] Even more

---

[160] Parker, above n. 149, 28.

[161] In 1898, the number of *agents de change* was raised from 60 to 70 as a move to block the competitive efforts of the Coulissiers. Ibid., 34.

[162] Parker, above, n. 149, 28.

[163] See Myers, above n. 150, 146–47.

[164] ibid.

[165] ibid., 147.

[166] Parker, above, n. 149, 28.

invasive of the Bourse's autonomy was the decision of these ministries to require the Bourse to list foreign securities, a proposal that had been rejected by the Bourse.[167] By the end of the century, as international tensions mounted, a Bourse listing came to be seen by the ministries as a low-cost tool of French foreign policy.[168] Obviously, there was a cost to such a policy, but it fell instead on investors and the financial infrastructure.

Nor did close governmental regulation result in high public esteem for the Bourse. While the NYSE strove to enhance and protect its reputational capital, the reputation of the Bourse among French citizens was, from the nineteenth century on, that of "a place of mystery, or even danger",[169] which Emile Zola attacked and ridiculed in his popular novels.[170] During the early twentieth century, the "flood of foreign issues into France drew criticism", according to one contemporaneous observer, in part "because of the poor quality of many of the securities".[171] Neither the banks that issued securities nor the government exercised "adequate supervision over them",[172] she reports. Yet, at the same time, the "Bourse was under tighter governmental control than were the markets of any other Western European country".[173]

This combination of tight control and poor reputation presents a puzzle. Why did not the government or, at least, the Bourse itself, intervene to exclude low quality issuers? One answer is that neither the banks nor the government had much interest in improved regulation.[174] The banks seldom held the securities they underwrote, but sold them to relatively small and often unsophisticated consumers. The government often had political reasons to list (or reject) foreign securities,[175] and in any event profited handsomely on the taxes to which it subjected such issuances.[176]

This answer still leaves open the question of why the Bourse's own members did not seek to exclude low quality issuers, as the NYSE had done early on and as the LSE eventually did. One hypothesis is that tight governmental supervision plus the limited economic stake of the *agents de change* suffocated any attempt

---

[167] Cameron, above, n. 157, 82.

[168] ibid., 82.

[169] K. Nunes et al., 'French and SEC Securities Regulation: The Search for Transparency and Openness in Decision Making' [1993] 26 Vanderbilt Journal of Transnational Law 217, 219.

[170] e.g., Emile Zola, *L'Argent* (Paris 1891). *L'Argent* detailed the experiences of its young hero in a mysterious investment bank that vaguely resembles Crédit Mobilier.

[171] Myers, above, n. 150, 136–37.

[172] ibid., 137.

[173] Goldman, above, n. 153, S230.

[174] This is the answer given by Myers, above, n. 150, 137.

[175] ibid., 136; see Cameron, above, n. 157, 82.

[176] Myers, above, n. 150, 137.

at proactive self-regulation. As noted earlier, the Bourse's members would not share as fully in the gains from an improved public reputation as would, for example, the NYSE's members, because the Bourse's brokers were more restricted in their ability to profit as owners. But, even beyond this organizational point, there was still a deeper problem that is possibly inherent in the civil law. As one observer wrote in 1919 with particular reference to the Bourse: "The rigid governmental regulation of the Continental bourses is a practice that finds no counterpart in the English-speaking world, where each man is supposed to look out for himself".[177]

To generalize, while common-law countries assumed there was a zone of private activity within which individuals were expected to protect their own interests, no such assumption influenced the civil law, which was inherently and pervasively paternalistic. The underlying reasons for this contrast have been most fully explored by the British historian and anthropologist, Alan MacFarlane, who has explained the rapid rise of industrialization in the U.K. as largely based on the fact that England had much earlier and uniquely evolved into a "highly developed and individualistic market society" characterized by "absolute ownership" of private property and high labour mobility.[178] Never truly feudal, England was, from at least the thirteenth century on, he finds, a land of small property owners in which private contractual relationships were recognized, respected, and enforced by the courts. In short, entrepreneurial activity did not need the blessing of the state or sovereign and was generally not within their legitimate concern.

In contrast, in truly feudal societies, power came from the sovereign, and the sovereign—often aided by a powerful, permanent, and centralized bureaucracy—intervened in and oversaw most matters of consequence. Thus it is symptomatic that the Paris Bourse evolved out of a twelfth-century concession by Louis VII to the Guild of Moneychangers.[179] From these feudal origins came a tradition of close government involvement in all matters of economic consequence, which was precisely the opposite of the English tradition. More to the point, the natural consequence of this intrusive governmental regulation of private economic activity was arguably to stifle innovation and, in particular, any effort at self-regulation. Centralized governmental control also had its natural allies because those regulated could then look to the government for protection from new competitors. Thus the Bourse turned to the government for protection

---

[177] Parker, above, n. 149, 112.

[178] Macfarlane, *Origins*, above, n. 16, 165. According to Macfarlane, an active market in land ownership plus a high degree of economic mobility allowed citizens having no position in the aristocracy to assemble significant wealth in medieval England, which was far less possible in France during the same era. For a fuller consideration of MacFarlane's views, see nn. 222–226 and accompanying text.

[179] See n. 150 and accompanying text.

from its chief competitor, the Coulisse, and generally received it.[180] In turn, given the Bourse's de facto monopoly status, the Bourse lacked the spur of competition to induce it to innovate (at least prior to the appearance of global competition in the 1980s). Yet, even in the face of greater competition, self-regulation might still not have developed during the late nineteenth century. Observers of the French business scene have long noted that "[i]n French business law, everything is proscribed unless explicitly permitted under the country's legal code".[181] Thus, to the extent that the civil law (especially in France) assumed direct governmental control of business activity, it tended to create static entities unlikely to innovate on their own.

In fairness, an important ambiguity surrounds this proposed explanation for the apparent difference in paternalism between common-law and civil law countries. To the extent that the Bourse was a private monopoly, it made economic sense for the government to regulate it more closely than one would regulate a private entity in an open and competitive market; one would not defer lightly to, or encourage, private lawmaking by a monopoly.[182] Potentially, two alternative hypotheses are possible: (1) the civil law inherently discouraged private lawmaking; or (2) having created a private monopoly (perhaps unwisely), French authorities could not defer to it, but instead logically recognized the need to regulate it closely (often, however, with the government's interest in maximizing tax revenues or achieving foreign policy goals overriding investor interests in the determination of actual policies). Still, even if there was a justification for not permitting the Bourse to become a self-regulating body, this justification does not extend to the persistent preference of the French government throughout the late nineteenth century for protecting the monopoly status of the Bourse. Rather than encourage competition, the French approach was to create a centralized monopoly and then regulate it closely.[183] The bottom line consequence was to preclude private self-regulation.

The suffocating impact of close governmental regulation becomes clearest when we contrast the simultaneous development of the Paris Bourse and the NYSE during the nineteenth century. From its inception, the NYSE "operated a miniature legal system, with its own rules governing securities trading and its own mechanism for resolving trade-related disputes".[184] In so doing, the NYSE

---

[180] See nn. 153–157 and accompanying text.

[181] See 'La Grande Boum', *The Economist*, October 1, 1988, at 83.

[182] This thesis is implicit in Vidal's work, although not expressly stated as such. See Vidal, above, n. 150, 8–9.

[183] As discussed below, Professor Alan Macfarlane argues that this structural tendency toward centralization and hierarchical control was the dominant approach in most countries, with only Holland and later England developing a decentralized society that truly encouraged free markets. See nn. 222–227 and accompanying text.

[184] Banner, above, n. 78, 271.

"drew upon a centuries-old Anglo-American tradition of self-regulation by mercantile groups."[185] To be sure, development of this self-regulatory capacity was especially important during the early nineteenth century because the American legal system regarded many of the standard contracts that securities dealers entered into with each other as essentially gambling contracts and would not enforce them.[186] This judicial neglect of (or hostility towards) the securities industry may have been the principal factor that initially compelled the U.S. securities industry to rely on self-regulation. Even so, what is most noteworthy here is that the common-law system could disapprove of an industry's practices (and in truth view them as but amoral gambling), but still tolerate the industry to function without state intervention or supervision.

In any event, if self-regulation on the NYSE was born of necessity, it quickly developed a momentum of its own. The industry soon found that its use could be expanded to achieve other goals, including that of enhancing the NYSE's (and the infant industry's) reputational capital. In contrast, in Europe, where every issue of consequence was regulated by law or needed to be referred to the appropriate ministry for approval, Continental exchanges were not positioned to develop self-regulation as a means of private law-making in their own common interest.

V. The German Experience: Government Intervention that Stunted the Market

If the French experience shows the state creating a securities market as a state monopoly, the German experience reveals the opposite: the state disfavouring the securities market, intervening aggressively, and ultimately stunting its potential growth. Both attitudes—the state as protector and the state as antagonist—are opposite sides of the same civil-law coin in which the state plays favourites and regularly intervenes in private economic decision-making. This presumption of government intervention contrasts sharply with the neutrality and indifference shown by common-law authorities to the growth of securities markets during the late nineteenth century in both the U.S. and the U.K. Ultimately, securities markets appear to have fared better under a regime of benign neglect in the U.S. and the U.K. than under the favouritism or antagonism of France and Germany, respectively.

Historically, the two principal German securities markets trace back to origins well before the founding of the NYSE or the LSE. The Frankfurt Exchange

---

[185] ibid. See also W.C. Jones, 'An Inquiry into the History of the Adjudication of Mercantile Disputes in Great Britain and the United States' [1958] 25 University of Chicago Law Review 445 (discussing this tradition).

[186] Banner, above, n. 78, 271–72.

was founded in 1585 and the Berlin exchange was established in 1685.[187] But, as with other exchanges of the period, they traded debt securities and commodities almost exclusively and were not serious rivals to the London or Paris exchanges prior to German unification in 1871.[188] Throughout this era, the Prussian government intervened periodically in the bond market, usually with a heavy hand. Sometimes, it banned the trading of the bonds of a specific foreign government, and, once, in 1842, it banned "all dealings in foreign bond issues".[189] Two years later, fearing that speculation in railroad stocks had reached a dangerous level, the Prussian finance minister unilaterally declared "all transactions for future delivery null and void".[190]

As in the U.S., the catalyst for the emergence of investment banking as an industry and for the growth of the equity securities market was the enormous need for capital of the German railroad industry.[191] Until the 1850s, those German railroads that were privately organized were financed by underwriting syndicates composed of traditional investment banking partnerships. These partnerships were relatively small and, even when organized as syndicates, found it difficult to underwrite securities in the amounts needed by the rapidly expanding railroad industry. Recognizing that they needed to create larger-scale entities to provide long-term financing for their clients, both the banking industry and their clients lobbied the Prussian government to charter banks organized as joint stock companies, which entities would thus have limited liability.[192]

This goal was, however, repeatedly frustrated by the German crown and its bureaucracy, which feared the creation of large independent banks. The result was a major political collision between, on the one hand, the Prussian aristocracy, whose wealth was largely agriculturally based and who feared further industrialization, and an emerging business and commercial middle class that essentially wished "to practice trade free of government wishes and restrictions".[193] This confrontation came to a head in 1856 when, having been rebuffed in their attempts to found joint stocks banks by the government's refusal to issue charters, certain leading German financiers organized "commandite banks".[194]

---

[187] U.R. Siebel et al. (eds.) *German Capital Market Law* (Munich 1995) 3.

[188] 1871 is the date of the German Imperial Constitution, which reflected the incorporation of the Southern German states into Imperial Germany. For an overview, see Mommsen, n. 14.

[189] E. Friend, Note, 'Stock-Exchange Regulation in Germany' [1908] 16 *Journal of Political Economy* 369, 370. The Prussian Government may have been motivated by the belief that banning foreign bond trading would "preserve a market for its own bonds." Ibid.

[190] ibid. This decree was ultimately overturned by the courts. Ibid.

[191] J.M. Brophy, *Capitalism, Politics, and Railroads in Prussia, 1830–1870* (Columbus (Ohio) 1998) at 87–88.

[192] ibid., 89–106.

[193] ibid., 87.

[194] J.M. Brophy, *Capitalism, Politics, and Railroads in Prussia, 1830–1870*, 89–99.

Commandite firms were substitutes for joint stock corporations and basically resembled limited partnerships or modern-day limited liability companies in that silent partners provided capital but had de facto limited liability by virtue of the fact that their identity was not disclosed to outsiders.[195] The Prussian government perceived the unauthorized formation of these banks to be an act of defiance and drafted a decree declaring commandite banks unlawful. Cooler heads within the Prussian government convinced the crown to relent for fear that an economic panic might result from any attempt to close down these banks.[196] Still, the episode illustrates the limited range given to even the business élite to conduct business operations on a significant scale.

Gradually, the middle class won a series of battles that restricted governmental interference in the market, but they could not conclusively triumph in the larger war.[197] A significant milestone came in 1870, when they obtained free incorporation as of right, and, that same year, Deutsche Bank was founded, followed by Dresdner Bank in 1872.[198] Formed principally to finance heavy industry, these "credit banks" or *Grossbanken*, combined commercial and investment banking; typically, they both purchased a newly capitalized firm's stock, underwrote its debt securities, and made it short-to-medium term bank loans.[199] Although they were modelled after a French prototype, the Société Général de Crédit Mobilier, the *Grossbanken* were distinctive and indeed constituted an institutional breakthrough in one critical respect: They were entirely private and were formed without the German government's direct backing or support. In contrast, Crédit Mobilier was founded under the auspices of Napoleon III and had little distance from the French government.[200] Politically, the *Grossbanken* were "the expression of an assertive middle class",[201] which sought to break free from governmental control. From 1820 onward, "banking freedom" (or "*Bankfreiheit*") was the rallying cry of the German merchant or commercial middle class,[202] and gradually over a half-century, they partially

---

[195] ibid., 90.

[196] ibid., 89.

[197] Probably their first significant victory came in 1860 when the law permitting the government to nullify transactions in any securities was abrogated. Friend, above, n. 189, 370.

[198] J.C. Baker, *The German Stock Market* (1970) 6. The original *Grossbanken* were Schaaffhausensche Bank and Darmstädter Bank, which date back to the early 1850s, ibid., but were created as the result of special political accommodations. Brophy, above, n. 191, 91–92.

[199] For the fullest history of the origins of the German credit banks, see J. Riesser, *The German Great Banks and Their Concentration*, S Doc No. 61–593 3rd edn. (1911). This translation of an earlier German work by a professor at the University of Berlin was prepared for the National Monetary Commission in 1911.

[200] For a review of the founding of Crédit Mobilier and its significance, see R.E. Cameron, *France and the Economic Development of Europe, 1800–1914* (New York 1961) 134–203.

[201] Brophy, above, n. 191, 87.

[202] ibid., 90.

achieved it. In contrast, the same issues never needed to be debated or pursued in the U.S. or the U.K., where the government seldom intervened in economic matters. Still, as of the last quarter of the nineteenth century, the German economy had probably advanced further than the French toward recognition of a true private sector in which major financial projects could be undertaken without state approval or supervision. But the effort to secure a zone of business activity free from state intervention required a constant struggle, because the German state remained committed to active intervention in economic decision-making.

German business history over the remainder of the nineteenth century exemplified this pattern of recurrent state intervention. Although the best known of the *Grossbanken* were founded in the early 1870s, primarily to finance railroad and industrial expansion, the German government succeeded in 1879, after a multi-year struggle, in nationalizing all private railroads.[203] Control over the operation of private railroads had long been a source of friction, and ultimately the state insisted on total control. Although reasonable compensation was paid to stockholders, one cannot easily imagine the British or U.S. governments taking, or even contemplating, similar steps during this era. Later, in the 1890s, the government also severely tightened its regulation of the securities exchanges in a manner that deeply chilled trading and speculation.[204] The point here is not that the conservative German government of Bismarck was hostile to the interests of business; rather, it assumed, in the manner of many civil-law countries, that it was naturally entitled to direct major business policies.

Often, this governmental intervention was benign and supportive of business. The best such example was Bismarck's policy of encouraging the development of the *Grossbanken*. Unlike his predecessors, Bismarck saw the great banks as natural allies in his policy of spurring the development of heavy industry; he envisioned, it was said, a political alliance of "iron and rye"—that is, a political marriage between the new industrial magnates and the landed Junker aristocracy.[205] Yet his policies actually worked to the detriment of the development of securities markets. Essentially, his administration opened the bank window at the German central bank (the *Reichsbank*) for the *Grossbanken* by liberalizing the central bank's discount policy to such a degree that the *Grossbanken* could finance the needs of their client industries largely through debt, thereby diminishing their clients' need to resort to equity financing. The impact of this policy

---

[203] ibid., 169–70.

[204] See nn. 210–219 and accompanying text.

[205] Bismarck is normally credited with brokering such an alliance between heavy industry and the agrarian Junker aristocracy, which came at the expense of other commercial groups. See Brophy, above, n. 191, 170. Of course, low cost loans by the state to the largest banks with the expectation that they would lend to heavy industry could be an important part of this political arrangement. See nn. 209–210 and accompanying text.

was to give virtually unlimited liquidity to the major German private banks.[206] Secure in the knowledge that they could rediscount their loans to corporate clients with the *Reichsbank*, the major German private banks could "lend to the hilt," undeterred by the fear of illiquidity.[207] In contrast, British commercial banks, although they also combined commercial and investment banking operations, were acutely aware that they could not finance long-term loans to corporate borrowers using short-term customer deposits. Nor was the Bank of England willing to extend similarly liberal discounting rights to its major banks; rather, it frequently resorted to credit rationing.[208]

This difference in the behaviour of the central banks in Germany and the U.K. over the last decades of the nineteenth century is critical to an understanding of the thin character of the German equity capital market (and the highly leveraged balance sheets of major German corporations). Had the German government not intervened to encourage liberal lending by its major banks, it seems likely that the growth of German securities markets would have paralleled that of the British market and produced a slow evolution toward dispersed ownership. After all, the *Grossbanken* largely controlled the securities exchanges and profited from securities underwritings. Yet if the central bank in Germany would in effect underwrite loans to major German corporations while the central bank in England would not do the same for its banks, it should be no surprise that heavy industry was financed by debt to a much greater extent in Germany than in the U.K. and that German corporations had less need to raise equity capital in their securities markets. Rationally, there was no reason for a German corporation to seek expensive equity capital when it could receive subsidized loans orchestrated by the state. Finally, because the U.S. in this era did not even have a central bank,[209] there was no possibility that it could encourage its commercial banks to be similarly generous in order to finance industrialization in the U.S.

Beyond simply encouraging risky, promotional lending that made equity financing less necessary or attractive, the German government took far more aggressive steps in the 1890s that effectively stunted the development of its then-growing securities markets. Ironically, the precipitating cause of this tightened regulation was a series of speculative bubbles and manipulations that occurred

---

[206]   R.H. Tilly, 'Germany Banking, 1850–1914: Development Assistance for the Strong' [1986] 15 *Journal of European Economic History* 113, 144–45.

[207]   ibid., 145; see also G. Herrigel, *Industrial Concentrations* (Chicago 1996) 6 (agreeing with Tilly that major German banks pooled scarce capital to subsidize heavy industry).

[208]   Tilly, above, n. 206, 145.

[209]   Andrew Jackson's veto of the Second Bank of the United States resulted in the U.S. being without a central bank to provide bank liquidity throughout the remainder of the nineteenth century.

in the German commodities markets, not in the securities market. In 1888, spec-ulators cornered the coffee market on the Hamburg exchange; in 1889, a dra-matic market break occurred in sugar prices; and in 1891, an attempt to corner the wheat market on the Berlin exchange failed, but resulted in the collapse of several banks and brokerage firms.[210] These events touched off a wave of agrar-ian protests directed against speculators who farmers and their allies saw as responsible for a downward trend in grain prices.[211] Because the German exchanges traded both commodities and securities, reformers began to lobby generally for reform of exchange trading, based on a popular sense that price manipulation was pervasive and that ordinary investors needed to be paternal-istically protected. After a three-year study by a government commission, the Stock Exchange Law of 1896 was enacted to curb these abuses, but an irate legislature went well beyond the commission's original, more cautious propos-als. All told, the process seemed to anticipate the same angry legislative response that later occurred in the U.S., following the crash of 1929, and culminated in the enactment of the federal securities laws in the early 1930s. The difference was that the German legislation effectively eclipsed its market.[212]

Even prior to the 1896 law, the Imperial Stamp Act of 1894 had doubled the tax rate on securities transfers, and this tax rate was further raised in 1900 to triple the pre-1894 rate.[213] Not only did this chill securities trading, it also moved trading off the stock exchanges. This occurred because the major German banks found that they could avoid the tax by internalizing their execution of customer orders. That is, if a German bank bought 10,000 shares and sold 8,000 shares of the same stock, it could net these orders, and pay tax only on the 2,000 share bal-ance. The consequence was to permit the major banks to take business away from the smaller brokers and banks that had a smaller order flow and could not avoid the tax in this fashion.[214] German shareholders quickly learned that they could substantially avoid the tax by leaving their stock in the hands of their bank. The result was to lock in place an already developing system of concen-trated ownership under which German banks would vote the customers' shares as the customers might direct at the annual shareholder meeting, but not disclose the customers' identities. In truth, such a system is not significantly different from the practice of "street name" ownership in the U.S., under which brokers

[210] Baker, above, n. 198, 7; Friend, n. 189, at 371; E. Loeb, 'The German Exchange Act of 1896' [1897] 11 *Quarterly Journal of Economics* 388, 389–91.

[211] Loeb, above, n. 210, at 409–10.

[212] For the conclusion that the German markets were "stunted" by this legislation, see M.J. Roe, 'Some Differences in Corporate Structure in Germany, Japan, and the United States' [1993] 102 Yale Law Journal 1927, 1971 no 142.

[213] Riesser, above, n. 199, 618–19.

[214] ibid., 620–621.

hold securities registered in their names for their customers—except that in Germany this system was enforced by a punitive tax on stock transfer. Even more importantly, to the extent that banks internalized order flow, thus netting stock transfers at the existing market price without entering those orders in the market, the market lost liquidity and priced less efficiently.[215] The 1896 law disrupted trading to an even greater extent by barring transactions on credit for many classes of securities and commodities transactions.[216] The statute also required all "speculators" entering into exchange transactions to register publicly; failure to do so could lead speculative contracts to be declared null and void as gambling transactions.[217] But the Act literally applied only to trading on an exchange. Hence, although designed to curb speculation, the 1896 Act succeeded primarily in driving trading off the exchanges. The upshot was quickly to turn the traditional exchanges into "disorganized markets".[218]

The impact of the 1896 Act was so draconian that it quickly produced a demand for its repeal, even within the trading public that it "protected," and portions of the law were in fact repealed in 1908.[219] But the enhanced transfer tax remained in place, and volume did not return to the German market prior to World War I. The war's aftermath, in turn, triggered a series of economic disasters, including the runaway inflation of the post-World War I era that crippled the German securities markets until the 1990s.

In this light, the disparity between the size of the German equity market and those of the U.S. and the U.K. appears to be less the result of differences in the legal rights accorded shareholders in the countries than the consequence of a strong government policy in Germany designed to curb speculation and to

[215] This phenomenon was recognised contemporaneously. Writing in the first decade of the 1900s, University of Berlin Professor Jacob Riesser described the banks' response to the tax legislation as equivalent to their "taking over the function of the exchange" and resulting in an impairment "of proper price determination." Ibid. at 771–72. More recent historians have doubted that the 1896 securities legislation or the associated increases in securities transfer taxes truly explain the consolidation in German universal banks, which occurred throughout the last two decades of the nineteenth century and accelerated after World War I. See C. Fohlin, *Regulation, Taxation, and the Development of the German Universal Banking System, 1884–1913* (SSRN Electronic Library, Working Paper no. 273,547, 2001), available at http://papers.ssrn.com/sol3/paper.taf?abstract_id =273547. This interpretation notes that banks were usurping the role of the exchanges even prior to the 1896 legislation. Thus, to the extent that this revisionist interpretation is correct, the role of the state in encouraging and subsidizing low-cost loans to heavy industry again seems to outweigh the impact of legal or regulatory changes as the primary explanation for the relative decline of securities markets in Germany.

[216] Baker, above, n. 198, 63. In addition, a last minute legislative rider to the 1896 Act removed from the exchange seven industrial stocks so important that they accounted for 70% of trading at the time. Friend, above, n. 189, 372.

[217] Baker, above, n. 198, 63.

[218] ibid., 65; see Riesser, above, n. 199, 620–22, 720–22.

[219] Baker, above, n. 198, 8.

achieve industrialization through bank finance. Never supportive of securities exchanges, an irate German legislature, reacting to scandals, enacted punitive legislation that virtually closed down the securities markets for a time. Thus, rather than evolving naturally toward concentrated ownership, the German experience—in contrast to those of the U.S. and the U.K.—comprised an initial evolution toward developed securities markets that was interrupted and stunted by regular state intervention. If this capsule history shows how centralized ownership persisted in Germany amidst great industrial expansion, it also shows that this pattern was planned and directed by the state, and not the result of natural Darwinian competition.

VI. A Preliminary Summary

What have we learned from this tour of New York, London, Paris, and Germany? Seemingly, there is a difference between common-law and civil-law jurisdictions, but it does not appear to lie in different legal technologies. Rather, by the late nineteenth century, there was already a private sector in the U.S. and the U.K. into which the state did not normally intrude. In contrast, the state intervened incessantly in the development of securities markets in France and Germany, either to protect the Paris Bourse's monopoly in France or to favour the development of commercial banks in Germany. To be sure, significant differences exist between the French and German experiences. In Germany, private actors emerged and played a greater role, whereas in France the state's monopoly was always zealously protected. But even in Germany, the state ruled with a heavy hand and regulated its securities markets into oblivion.[220]

Within the common-law world, the overriding policy was rather one of benign neglect. Even though the experiences of the NYSE and the LSE diverged, the greater activism of the NYSE seems primarily attributable to non-legal factors, including (1) its greater exposure to competitive pressure in this era; (2) its different organizational structure; (3) its dependence upon foreign capital; and (4) its greater need to develop bonding and monitoring mechanisms, given the vulnerability of U.S. investors to the predations of the Robber Barons and the prevalence of judicial corruption. In short, private bodies, having different incentives, responded differently to the problems before them.

---

[220] That the German Exchange Act of 1896 was scandal-driven does not truly distinguish the German experience from that of the U.S. or the U.K. Both the U.S. and, to a lesser extent, the U.K. had recurrent scandals during this era. Prior to the 1929 crash, the U.S. did not legislate on the national level, while the U.K. did not enact major legislation even in the face of the 1929 crash. Again, this may reveal the strength of the assumption in these common-law countries that the state did not interfere in the private sector.

D. "Does Law Matter" Reconsidered

I. Law and the Decentralized Common-law World

If self-regulation and private self-help measures appear then to have been the principal catalysts for the growth of equity securities markets in the U.S., a tension arises between this finding and the LLS&V thesis that dispersed ownership and liquid markets arise only when minority shareholders are accorded strong legal rights. Nor is this tension new. Indeed, a precisely contrary position to that of LLS&V has long been popular in the law and economics literature on securities regulation. Opponents of the U.S.'s mandatory disclosure system have long argued that the SEC's disclosure requirements were unnecessary and wasteful because market mechanisms had already developed prior to 1933 that were sufficient to satisfy investors' real demand for information.[221] These critics might interpret the foregoing capsule histories as proof that law does not matter and self-sustaining markets can arise and persist spontaneously without law. Such a conclusion seems, however, to over-read the evidence, given the fairly uniform subsequent market histories of these diverse countries. In the U.S., the U.K., and Germany, political pressures emerged early in the development of equity securities markets that eventually resulted in legislative constraints on the private market. These pressures brought legislation in 1896 in Germany, in the 1930s in the U.S., and at varying stages in the U.K., both early and late.

Although the relative success of self-regulation in the U.S. may initially seem inconsistent with the "law matters" hypothesis, much depends on what we count as "law." Stripped to its essentials, the LLS&V hypothesis asserts (or, at least, need assert) only that strong equity markets require strong minority rights. Those minority rights could in principle come from any source (legislative, judicial or self-regulatory), or from a combination of sources. More to the point, the process by which strong legal protections are obtained could logically begin with self-regulation, which creates nascent rights that later are codified into mandatory law. In effect, some firms, in order to market their stock, experiment with new ways of signalling that they will treat minority shareholders fairly. As their efforts succeed in the market, minority shareholders demand that similar stan-

---

[221] This debate, which goes back to the work of George Stigler and George Benston in the 1960s, has been revisited by many commentators. See G.J. Benston, 'Required Disclosure and the Stock Market: An Evaluation of the Securities Exchange Act of 1934' [1973] 63 *American Economics Review* 132; G.J. Stigler, 'Public Regulation of the Securities Markets' [1964] 37 *Journal of Business* 117. But see I. Friend and E.S. Herman, 'The S.E.C. Through a Glass Darkly' [1964] 37 *Journal of Business* 382 (arguing that Stigler's data demonstrates the positive impact of the federal securities laws). For an updated discussion of the impact of the securities laws, see C.J. Simon, 'The Effect of the 1933 Securities Act on Investor Information and the Performance of New Issues' [1989] 79 *American Economics Review* 295, 311–13.

dards be imposed on other public firms, in part to reduce the cost to them of interpreting noisy signals. This sequential interpretation views the role of law in markets as essentially one of imposing market-proven standards on laggard firms.

Such an interpretation leaves open, however, the question of why self-regulation developed in common-law countries and not in civil-law countries. Here, the principal weakness of the LLS&V thesis is its narrow focus on substantive legal rights. Viewing law in effect as only a type of technology, the LLS&V thesis overlooks the possibility that law and legal institutions may have shaped the broader society, not just the rights of minority shareholders. When one's perspective expands to consider this broader context, differences between the common law and the civil law come into clearer focus. The British historian and anthropologist, Alan Macfarlane, has argued that only two European countries, England and Holland, deviated from the pattern of absolutism and increased centralization of authority that characterized post-feudal Europe from the thirteenth to the eighteenth centuries.[222] In both countries, but particularly in England, the absolute authority of the sovereign was constrained by law. In England, in lieu of an absolute monarch assisted by a vast centralized bureaucracy, there occurred a "devolution of power through a complex of often voluntary and honorary power holders such as constables and the justices of the peace".[223] Ecclesiastical power was also confined, and a tradition of religious tolerance arose that further accelerated the movement towards decentralization and diversity. Finally, in place of the caste-like social structure of feudal Europe, a class system arose in which power and wealth tended to depend more on personal achievements. In truth, these conditions probably first crystallized in Holland, but it was a smaller country, surrounded by larger, envious rivals (including England), and its prosperity thus proved short-lived.[224]

Law, of course, was not the only force that produced this environment in which the worlds of political power and economic activity largely separated. But law may have played an important role. While the rest of Europe accepted Roman law during the late Middle Ages, which in turn enhanced the power of the sovereign, England persisted in the development of the common law that it inherited from its Germanic ancestors.[225] As a result, MacFarlane concludes "[t]he English judicial system was confused, unprincipled, inefficient and cumbersome. Yet it somehow protected the citizen against the state better than anywhere else in the world".[226]

[222] Macfarlane, *Riddle,* above, n. 16, 280–85.

[223] ibid., 280.

[224] ibid., 279–80.

[225] ibid., 280.

[226] ibid., 205 (acknowledging that de Tocqueville recognized this capacity of the common-law system).

Why did the English judicial system prove better able than its civil-law counterparts to protect individual rights? Different answers are possible, but the core
of any answer probably involves individuals' greater distance from the sovereign
and their closer identity with the local community around them.[227] Already
decentralized, the English legal system furthered the decentralization of power
elsewhere in society and thereby assisted the growth of a market economy, in
part by referring the inevitable commercial disputes to persons independent of
the sovereign or the bureaucracy under his control.

Decentralization in turn made possible private law making and the growth of
self-regulatory bodies. Ultimately, this in turn facilitated the development of
market-based institutions, such as stock exchanges, and enabled them to adapt
and to gain the trust of their customers. Much in the late nineteenth-century
histories of stock exchanges in the U.S. and the U.K., as contrasted with the histories of similar institutions in France and Germany, confirms this emphasis on
decentralization and the growth of a private sector as the initial precondition.
Most obviously, the fact that true stock exchanges first emerged in Amsterdam
and later London seems neither accidental nor unrelated to the earlier appearance of a pluralistic society. More to the point, what the emerging business class
in Germany most desired during the late nineteenth century was precisely what
the U.S. and the U.K. business classes already had: protection from arbitrary
governmental interventions in the private sector. This desire translates easily
(and in fact did translate in practice) into a powerful belief in the rule of law.[228]
But if German industries that resisted the government were nationalized (as the
private railroads were in 1878–1879) and if the French financial industry never
escaped close governmental control, the British and American entrepreneur of
the same era had no such fears. Nationalization was unthinkable, and close governmental supervision had simply not yet been experienced.

Any attempt to derive basic political differences, such as the earlier separation
of the private sector in common-law countries, from legal differences is necessarily speculative, and the causal influences are probably modest at best. Still, it
does seem plausible to suggest that the common law was more hospitable to private ordering and to the channelling of private disputes to resolution mechanisms outside the boundaries of the state. Historians and civil-law scholars
appear to agree that the civil law inherently tends to codify private law, while the

---

[227] For a more detailed theory of why English judges and the English system were more independent of centralized control than the civil-law system, see E.L. Glaeser and A. Shleifer, *Legal
Origins* (October 19, 2000) (unpublished manuscript, on file with the author).

[228] For example, Professor Brophy, writing of the political desires of the late nineteenth-century
German business elite, observes: "The sole principle consistently upheld by businessmen throughout
this era was perhaps the belief in law, especially as it affected property relations". Brophy, above,
n. 191, 171.

common law rarely does so.[229] Codification naturally adopts bright-line and prophylactic rules that leave less room for flexibility or innovation. Further, codified civil law usually seeks to eliminate all gaps in the law in order to minimize opportunities for judicial discretion.[230] The natural impact of such comprehensive legislation is to crowd out the possibility for local variation, experimentation, or adjustments to changed circumstances. Similarly, in the view of some leading scholars, the civil law is inherently interventionist and "policy-implementing", whereas the common law tends to view its task as "dispute resolving".[231] This more passive, neutral, and indeed laissez-faire approach of the common law seems more tolerant of efforts at private law making and self-regulation.

A more concrete example of the manner in which the common law protected the autonomy of the private sector involves the ease and thoroughness with which it accepted private ordering mechanisms for commercial disputes. In the U.K. and the U.S., commercial disputes seem to have largely migrated from the courts to private arbitration systems by no later than the early eighteenth century.[232] An arbitration statute, enacted in the U.K. in 1697, gave formal recognition to private arbitration awards and required that they be judicially enforced.[233] Even cases that were brought to court were frequently referred to arbitration, and some early U.S. legislation actually made arbitration compulsory for certain types of disputes.[234] The new financial institutions that arose in

[229] For this broad proposition, see A. Von Mehren, *The Civil Law System* (New York 1957) 3 (noting that the "first" difference between the common law and the civil law was that "in the civil law, large areas of private law are codified").

[230] J. Merryman, *The Civil Law Tradition* (Stanford 1969) 30.

[231] M. Damaska, *The Faces of Justice and State Authority* (London 1986). In Professor Damaska's view, "[t]he legal process of a truly activist state is a process organized around the central idea of an official inquiry and is devoted to the implementation of state policy." Ibid., 147. In contrast, common law systems tend to view the judiciary as a coordinate branch of the government, not as a "hierarchical" organ of state policy. Ibid. at 29–46 (distinguishing Continental from the Anglo-American "machinery of justice"). The frequently made distinction between the adversarial process of common-law systems versus the "inquisitorial approach" of civil-law systems reflects and maps onto this deeper distinction between the judiciary as a coordinate branch versus a hierarchical organ. Possibly because of this difference, common-law systems seem to have accepted greater delegation of dispute resolution to private arbitration systems. See Jones, above, n. 185 (tracing the history of arbitration in Anglo-American jurisprudence).

[232] ibid., 458–59. Arbitration procedures appear to have been used in London since 1327. Ibid., 455 no. 56; P.L. Sayre, 'Development of Commercial Arbitration Law' [1928] 37 Yale Law Journal 595, 597–98. Of course, the search for historical antecedents involving specialized commercial tribunals can take one back to the medieval fair (with its specialized courts) and the common-law staple (another specialized court). But as Professor Jones has shown, these institutions had died out by the Tudor period in England. Jones, above, n. 185, 451–52.

[233] ibid., 455.

[234] In 1767, the New York legislature adopted such a compulsory statute for disputes involving merchants' accounts. Ibid., 460.

the U.S. and the U.K. in the eighteenth century were quick to mandate arbitration, in part to keep themselves beyond the oversight of the courts. In 1768, merchants in New York founded the New York Chamber of Commerce and made one of its stated purposes the establishment of an arbitral forum for its members.[235] When the NYSE was founded in 1792, Rule 17 of its Constitution of 1817 mandated compulsory arbitration of all disputes among its members.[236] Virtually all other exchanges and mercantile associations founded in the U.S. during the nineteenth century followed this pattern.[237] Perhaps fear of judicial corruption spurred the aggressive American adoption of arbitration in the nineteenth century, but the original motivation was more simply that private adjudication could outperform public adjudication in terms of speed, cost, and accuracy. While arbitration was not unknown to civil-law jurisdictions, the common-law tradition gave it a more central role, and Anglo-American exchanges placed it at the centre of their constitutional framework. Inherently, the growth of such private law-making institutions kept disputes out of the state's range of vision and thus reduced the opportunities for state intervention.

Nonetheless, this article need not make exaggerated claims for the significance of the differences between the civil law and the common law. Clearly, a decentralized and indeed pluralistic society arose in Holland more or less contemporaneously with corresponding developments in England. Hence, it cannot be argued that the civil-law system precluded the separation of politics from economics or the emergence of a market-oriented private sector. All that might be plausibly asserted is that the common-law tradition was more conducive to the emergence and separation of a private sector and that self-regulation was more feasible once the state had effectively ceded operational control of that sector to private actors.

II. The Sequence of Legal Change: Reinterpreting LLS&V

That equity securities markets could develop in a regime of private self-regulation does not end the story. Many private innovations arise, but do not persist. Moreover, the fact that markets arose in a specific fashion does not imply that this was the only, or even the least costly, means by which to encourage market development. Even though equity markets can arise in the absence of strong minority protections, it hardly follows that they can develop to their full potential in such an environment. In this light, self-regulation seems better viewed as a partial functional substitute for legal institutions, which can work but may still fall well short of optimal efficiency. That self-regulation played the sizable role

[235] Jones, 461.
[236] ibid., 462.
[237] ibid., 462–63 (listing 13 U.S. exchanges or trade associations with similar provisions).

that it did in the U.S. may be primarily attributable to the limitations of the U.S. judicial system in the late nineteenth century (i.e., perceived corruption plus the ability of the antagonists to escape judicial control by pitting one state's judges against those in another state). Had the judicial system been more reliable in this era, the same emphasis might not have been placed on self-regulation or on self-help measures to preclude any need for resort to courts. To suggest this is only to suggest that economic evolution is path-dependent and thus will follow different trajectories in different environments.

Still, the question needs to be squarely faced: What explains the pattern in both the U.S., the U.K., and most other developed economies that fairly comprehensive securities legislation has been enacted after markets have become established?[238] Here, this chapter's answer is that the LLS&V data does fairly suggest that securities markets cannot grow or expand to their full potential under a purely voluntary legal regime. If LLS&V have not shown that common-law legal rules are a precondition to the appearance of equity securities markets, they may have shown that the persistence and growth of such markets are closely correlated with a strong system of regulation that sustains investor confidence. Sooner or later, securities markets predictably encounter crises and experience shocks that result in a loss of investor confidence. As discussed below, the recent experience in Europe and Asia, particularly in the transitional economies, has shown that there are limits to self-regulation, and that markets that are not supported by strong legal institutions can lose credibility during periods of economic stress.[239] Conceivably, a strong system of self-regulation (as in the case of the U.K.'s City Take-Over Code) may prove adequate to this challenge, but the line between self-regulation and indirect governmental regulation is often

[238] I have no doubt that a host of public choice and interest group theories can be offered. However, the focus here is on how to read the significance of the LLS&V data.

[239] For an overview of the experience in the transitional economies of Central Europe following the Asian financial crisis of 1997–1998, see Coffee, above, n. 61. The German Neuer Markt experienced a similar crisis in the wake of the recent worldwide decline in high-tech stock prices. See notes 45–48 and accompanying text. Although the Neuer Markt established very high listing standards, exceeding those of its parent, the Deutsche Borse, it has experienced a series of scandals over the last two years. See A. Kueppers, 'A Busy Bidder in Germany Highlights Flaws in Neuer Markt's Efforts To Challenge Nasdaq' *Wall Street Journal*, 6 August 2001, at C11; J. Ewing, 'The Neuer Markt: Can It Hang On?' *Business Week,* July 30, 2001, at 18. Ultimately, its parent, the Deutsche Borse, determined to close it, but also to replace it with a special listing section, to be called the 'Prime Standard,' on its own exchange. See M. Landler, 'German Technology Stock Market to be Dissolved' N.Y. Times, 27 September 2002, at W-1. Observers have attributed the persistence of these scandals to Germany's chronically weak enforcement of insider trading and anti-manipulation laws; in particular, enforcement of suspected insider trading and manipulation cases detected by Germany's securities regulator is delegated to local criminal authorities and hence rarely results in criminal prosecution. See Kueppers, above. To the extent that this diagnosis is correct, it suggests that self-regulatory bodies necessarily rely to some extent on public enforcement and thus may face an unavoidable shortfall in deterrence when public legal institutions are weak.

difficult to define. Even when a strong private institutional structure arises (as it did in the case of the NYSE), the incentive to continue in such an activist role does not necessarily persist. For example, the NYSE faced far more competition in the nineteenth century than it did in the mid-twentieth century,[240] and in the absence of competition, a self-regulator may have less reason to enforce rules against its own members in order to preserve its reputational capital.

A second general observation is that legislative action seems likely to follow, rather than precede, the appearance of securities markets, in substantial part because a self-conscious constituency of public investors must first arise before there will be political pressure for legislative reform that intrudes upon the market. Phrased differently, the legislature cannot anticipate problems that it has never seen (much as it could not legislate with respect to the Internet before the Internet first appeared).

These observations lead to a proposed re-interpretation of the LLS&V hypothesis that sidesteps the historical flaw in their analysis in order to focus instead on its central truth: *While markets can arise in the absence of a strong, mandatory legal framework, they neither function optimally nor develop to their potential in the absence of mandatory law that seeks to mitigate the risks of crashes.* To focus simply on the fact that equity markets can arise without a legal foundation ignores the other half of the historical record. A "crash-then-law" cycle has characterized the history of securities markets.[241] The historical aim of securities regulation has chiefly been to reduce or mitigate the risks and consequences of such crashes.[242] This assertion that legislative action will generally be necessary because private ordering cannot adequately protect investors (or society generally) from destructive market crashes requires examination from two distinct perspectives: (1) the U.S. experience, and (2) the recent global experience following the Asian and Russian financial crises.

---

[240] The NYSE's principal rival between 1885 and World War I was the Consolidated Stock Exchange, which unlike the Curb Exchange (later the American Stock Exchange) traded securities listed on the NYSE. See Michie, above, n. 82, 204–08. Eventually, the Consolidated Stock Exchange found itself caught between the NYSE and the Curb Exchange and closed, but in its heyday, during the late nineteenth century, it was the low cost rival to the NYSE that successfully competed to attract the small investor and the smaller company.

[241] I borrow this term from Professor Frank Partnoy. F. Partnoy, 'Why Markets Crash and What Law Can Do About It' [2000] 61 University of Pittsburg Law Review 741, 743 no. 11; see also Banner, n. 13, at 850 (finding that all major instances of securities legislation followed market crashes).

[242] For a careful study finding that market crashes are not isolated or aberrant phenomena, but are endemic to markets for deep-seated reasons, see C.P. Kindleberger, *Manias, Panics, and Crashes* (New York 1978). I do not mean to suggest that this goal has necessarily been well pursued by legislatures. The 1896 German Act illustrates counter-productive legislation. But this goal is very different from the goal of improving allocative efficiency or pricing accuracy, which much academic commentary assumes is the only proper rationale for securities regulation.

1. The U.S. Experience

Within the U.S., there has been a long-standing academic debate over the necessity for, and impact of, the federal securities laws.[243] Seeking to disprove the need for legislation, George Stigler, the first and still the most vehement critic of the rationale for the federal securities laws, analysed the impact of the Securities Act of 1933 and found that the variance in the relative price performance of new issues of securities declined by almost half after its passage.[244] Despite this dramatic change, Professor Stigler interpreted this data to mean only that riskier new issues were being excluded as a result of the Securities Act's passage.[245] Subsequent analyses have, however, interpreted this pronounced reduction in price dispersion to mean that greater pricing accuracy resulted.[246] Although the debate will predictably continue, an informed basis exists for believing that the federal securities laws increased pricing accuracy and the amount of meaningful information in the market.[247]

Nonetheless, that may not have been the U.S. Congress's principal concern in 1933. Having heard testimony that fraud and manipulation had been rampant in the securities markets during the 1920s, Congress was intent on strengthening the existing system of enforcement, which it did by creating the SEC and a liberalized system of antifraud liability borrowed in part from the U.K. Although revisionist scholars have recently challenged the logic of this approach, arguing that exchanges are the superior regulator,[248] severe constraints appear to exist on both incentives and ability of a private body (such as a stock exchange) to enforce rules against its member firms and its listed companies.[249] As we have

[243] See above, n. 221.

[244] Stigler, above, n. 221, 120–21.

[245] ibid., 24.

[246] See, e.g. Friend and Herman, above, n. 221, 390–91; see also M.B. Fox, 'Retaining Mandatory Securities Disclosure: Why Issuer Choice Is Not Investor Empowerment' [1999] 85 Vanderbilt Law Review 1335, 1369–80 (finding that federal securities laws increased pricing accuracy).

[247] Fox, above, n. 246, 1376–91. Most recently, new research has asserted that the introduction in the early 1980s of the SEC's mandatory "Management Discussion and Analysis of Financial Condition and Results of Operations" (which disclosures are set forth in Item 303 of Regulation S-K and must be included in all periodic reports filed with the SEC by "reporting companies") significantly improved the accuracy of share pricing in the U.S. equity markets. See A. Durnev, M.B. Fox, R. Morck, and B. Yeung, *Law, Share Price Accuracy and Economic Performance: The New Evidence* (25 June 2001) (unpublished manuscript, on file with author). This is the strongest claim yet, based on statistical evidence, that mandatory disclosure improves the efficiency of securities markets.

[248] P. Mahoney, 'The Exchange as Regulator' [1997] 83 Vanderbilt Law Review 1453. Professor Mahoney agrees, however, that Congress was motivated to legislate by its perception that stock exchanges could not adequately prevent manipulation, in particular by stock pools. Ibid., 1464–65.

[249] For this purpose, securities exchanges and commodities exchanges do not differ substantially, and economic analyses of attempts by commodities exchanges to preclude market manipulation

earlier seen, the LSE did not make a serious effort until probably after World War II. While considerably more aggressive than the LSE as a self-regulator, even the NYSE faced resistance from its listed companies when it sought to upgrade disclosure standards. For example, Merritt Fox has found that, although the NYSE continually upgraded its listing requirements applicable to newly listed firms, it was unable (or unwilling) to apply these new rules to earlier listed firms, which collectively constituted the great majority of the firms traded on the exchange.[250] This is but one example of the enforcement shortfall that is inherent in any self-regulatory system. Such a shortfall is likely for several different reasons: (1) A private body has weak incentives to enforce rules protecting third parties against its own members and clients;[251] (2) a private body has little ability to enforce its rules against non-members; (3) enforcement may be too costly for a private body to undertake on a thoroughgoing basis; and (4) private bodies necessarily lack the investigative tools and punitive sanctions that the state has at its disposal.

This limited enforcement effort should not be surprising. It is not simply a matter of weak incentives, but also of difficulty of proof. Conspiracies by their nature do not reveal themselves to the observer. Only the public enforcer can threaten criminal penalties or truly punitive civil fines, and only public authorities have investigative tools, such as the grand jury, search warrants, and subpoena power, at their disposal. Private regulatory bodies, including the NYSE, have limited incentives to enforce their rules in a manner that restricts trading volume or reduces listings,[252] and have no sanction other than the denial of trading privileges in the case of rule violations by non-members. Yet, non-members may often be the parties most likely to engage in insider trading or

have been both critical and pessimistic. See S. Pirrong, 'The Self-Regulation of Commodity Exchanges: The Case of Market Manipulation' [1995] 38 *Journal of Law and Economics* 141.

[250] See Fox, above, n. 246, 1376–79. This pattern continues today on other exchanges. For example, the *Deutsche Borse* has recently been involved in a much-publicized dispute with one of its better-known listed companies, Porsche AG, because the latter will not provide quarterly financial results. Although the *Deutsche Borse* has as result dropped Porsche from its mid-cap index, it has been unwilling to de-list this prominent and highly profitable issuer. See S. Miller, 'For Porsche Investors, Disclosure Matters Less Than Rocking Results' *Wall Street Journal,* August 13, 2001, at C14 (noting that investors accepted limited disclosure where the company was highly profitable).

[251] Professor Banner has found, for example, that market manipulation was the one context where the NYSE seldom, if ever, enforced its own disciplinary rules. S. Banner, 'The Origin of the New York Stock Exchange, 1791–1860' [1998] 27 Journal of Legal Studies 113, 138–39 (noting that the exchange often did not discipline parties to fictitious sales); see also Werner and Smith, above, n. 88, 32 (noting that the exchange forbade fictitious sales, but perpetrators were seldom punished). For a nearly contemporaneous discussion of the role of stock pools in the 1930s, see Twentieth Century Fund, Inc, *Stock Market Control* (1934) 108–10.

[252] Close students of exchanges have recently made this observation. E.g. Banner, above, n. 251, 138–39; Pirrong, above, n. 249; see also M. Kahan, 'Some Problems with Stock Exchange-Based Securities Regulation' [1997] 83 Vanderbilt Law Review 1509 (doubting that the market for stock exchange listings will be characterized by vigorous competition).

other manipulative practices. In the absence of a public regulatory body, victims would predictably be left to enforce their rights through private litigation, and the high costs of enforcement may dissuade at least the small public investor from relying on such remedies.[253] As a practical matter, the creation of the SEC gave public investors a public guardian to champion their rights—in effect, a public subsidy for the prevention of fraud. Such a subsidy is justifiable if fraud produces externalities, namely, disintermediation by investors who perceive themselves to be unprotected and thus move to safer investments in other markets. The more that stock markets are perceived to be an engine of economic growth,[254] the more that the protection of investor confidence to prevent such disintermediation merits a priority as a public policy goal.

2. The Global Experience

From a global perspective, a modern pattern is evident: As securities markets begin to grow and mature, the host country codifies its law and creates a permanent enforcement and regulatory agency. Between the 1960s and the 1980s, each of the major European countries copied the U.S. in creating a strong regulatory agency that was more or less modelled after the American SEC.[255] Much of this legislation was, of course, crisis- and scandal-driven, but it has not been subsequently cut back. The movement toward stronger regulatory authority has had a decidedly one-way character.

---

[253] This is particularly true in the U.K. where small investors may be deterred by its "loser pays" rule under which the losing side must pay the litigation expenses of the winning side. In the U.S., private enforcement constitutes a greater deterrent threat, principally because of the availability of the class action, which did not develop, however, until the late 1960s.

[254] See n. 7 and accompanying text.

[255] The pattern seems almost uniform. France, traditionally the fourth largest securities market, created the *Commission des Operations de Bourse* (or *COB*) in 1967 and then greatly strengthened its enforcement powers in 1988. Goldman, above, n. 153, S235–37. The latter step was part of a sweeping deregulation of the French market that removed it from the direct control of the French Treasury. Italy created its *Commissione Nazionale per le Societe e la Borse* (*Consob*), or National Commission for Companies and the Stock Exchange, in 1974. P. Del Duca and D. Mortillaro, 'The Maturation of Italy's Response to European Community Law: Electric and Telecommunication Sector Institutional Innovations' [2000] 23 Fordham International Law Journal 536, 576–77. In Britain, the Financial Services Act of 1986 (FSA) created the Securities and Investments Board (SIB), which is in essence an SEC-like administrative agency that supervises a host of self-regulatory agencies. P. Thorpe, 'Regulation of the Futures Market in the United Kingdom' in F. Edwards and H. Patrick (eds.) *Regulating International Financial Markets* (London 1992). Only Germany remains a partial exception to this pattern, because it created in 1994 a weaker agency with only limited oversight powers over the securities exchanges. *German Capital Market Law*, above, n. 187, 8, 13–15 (discussing Federal Supervisory Office for Securities Trading (or BAW), which was created by the Second Financial Market Promotion Act in 1994). The German regulatory structure is currently in transition, however, as a consolidation of agencies is planned.

One crisis stands out above all others. Probably the strongest contemporary evidence that unregulated (or under-regulated) securities markets are vulnerable to crashes and that the severity of these crashes are in large part attributable to weak corporate governance has emerged from the Asian financial crisis of 1997–1998. One important study of the Asian crisis has found that measures of corporate governance, particularly the effectiveness of protections for minority shareholders, explained the extent of the stock market decline in individual countries better than did the standard macroeconomic measures.[256] This unexpected result seems to rest on a behavioural finding: In good times, managers and controlling shareholders do not expropriate wealth from minority shareholders (or at least prudently constrain their rate of expropriation). But, when an adverse shock hits the financial system, the rate of expropriation soars, and the relative market decline will be worst in those countries that have the weakest protections for minority shareholders.[257]

Other studies have found that a high percentage of family ownership characterized those Asian economies that suffered the worst decline and suggested that the high concentration of control rights in these firms exposed minority shareholders to expropriation.[258] Examining the separation of ownership and control in 2,980 East Asian corporations, Claessens, Djankov, and Lang found that more than two-thirds of these firms were controlled by a single shareholder typically through pyramid structures and cross-holdings.[259] Claessens, Djankov, Fan, and Lang concluded that the risk of expropriation of minority shareholders was the "primary" principal-agent problem for public corporations in East Asia.[260]

[256] Simon Johnson et al., 'Corporate Governance in the Asian Financial Crisis' [2000] 58 *Journal of Financial Economics* 141, 142, 171–72.

[257] This study found that three indices of legal institutions—"efficiency of the judiciary," "corruption," and the "rule of law"—were statistically significant in explaining exchange rate collapse, ibid. at 171–72, and the last two also correlated significantly with the extent of stock market decline. Ibid., 181. It also found that "corporate governance variables explain more of the variation in exchange rates and stock market performance during the Asian crisis than do macroeconomic variables." Ibid., 184. Overall, it concluded that "[c]orporate governance can be of first-order importance in determining the extent of macroeconomic problems in crisis situations." Ibid., 185.

[258] E.g. S. Claessens et al., *On Expropriation of Minority Shareholders: Evidence from East Asia* (SSRN Electronic Library, Working Paper No 202,390, 2000), available at http://papers.ssrn.com/paper.taf?abstract_id=202390 [hereinafter Claessens et al., *Expropriation*]; S. Claessens et al., *The Separation of Ownership and Control in East Asian Corporations*, (SSRN Electronic Library, Working Paper no. 206,448, 2000), available at http://papers.ssrn.com/paper.taf?abstract_id =206448 [hereinafter Claessens et al., *Separation of Ownership*].

[259] Claessens et al., *Separation of Ownership*, above, n. 258, 2. In contrast, Japanese firms, they found, were widely held and seldom family-controlled. Ibid. at 3.

[260] Claessens et al., *Expropriation,* above, n. 258, 2–3. They further concluded that such expropriation was chiefly effected through the separation of cash-flow from voting rights. Ibid., 2. In this light, it is noteworthy that the NYSE began to restrict attempts to separate cash flow from voting rights in the 1920s (well before the advent of the SEC) by imposing its "one share, one vote" rule. See nn. 111–118 and accompanying text.

These findings have a "déjà vu, all over again" familiarity for those with knowledge of U.S. corporate governance in the 1920s. During this era, holding companies and investment trusts assembled vast pyramids in which the control rights and cash flow rights of investors became widely separated, and large segments of the utility, railroad, and entertainment industries fell under the control of persons holding relatively modest equity stakes in proportion to the market capitalization of the firms they controlled.[261] Following the 1929 Crash, Congress legislated the levelling of some of these pyramids,[262] and many of the rest collapsed under their own weight. In short, the U.S. experience dovetails with that of Asia: Poor corporate governance can either contribute to or intensify the losses in a market crash, and this danger has been the motive force behind much securities legislation.

III. The Political Theory of Dispersed Ownership

This chapter's account of the rise of dispersed ownership in the U.S. and the U.K. disagrees also with the leading counter-thesis to the LLS&V hypothesis: that politics is the critical determinant and that legal differences simply flow from deeply rooted political values. The fullest and best statement of this position has been by Professor Mark Roe, who argues that because social democracies prefer the interests of other constituencies to those of shareholders, they will pressure corporate managers to subordinate shareholder interests, and only concentrated large shareholders can effectively compel managers to resist these pressures.[263] In a nutshell, he argues that:

> Aligning managers with dispersed shareholders is harder in social democracies than elsewhere: Owners dislike transparent accounting, which would give employees more information than many owners would like them to have, but transparent accounting is necessary for distant securities holders . . . The strong control mechanisms of the hostile take-over and publicly known incentive compensation have been harder or impossible to implement in the social democracies.[264]

---

[261] By 1932, "holding companies had not only obtained control of the great bulk of the nation's electric and gas utilities, but had also extended into such diverse fields as coal mining and retailing, oil foundries, textiles, agriculture, transportation, ice and cold storage, real estate, finance and credit, water, telephone companies, quarries, theatres, amusement parks" and other businesses. L. Loss and J. Seligman, *Securities Regulation* 3rd edn. (New York 1989) 229.

[262] Section 11 of the Public Utility Holding Company Act of 1935 effectively required the liquidation of most holding companies in that industry. Ibid., 234–37.

[263] Roe, above, n. 12.

[264] ibid., 603. Inevitably, this assessment that it is harder to align shareholder and managerial interests in social democracies invites the response: compared to what? Public shareholders would seem to face far greater difficulties in assuring managerial loyalty in the concentrated ownership systems of East Asia, where expropriation of minority shareholders seems the norm. See nn. 256–260 and accompanying text.

Arguably, this assessment is already dated, both because take-overs and transparent accounting have already come to Europe[265] and because the older, post-war corporatist system of industrial relations seems to be changing under the pressure of global competition and the cross-border mobility of capital and labour.[266]

But, even if we ignore these trends, the logic of Roe's thesis that social democracy discourages the separation of ownership and control encounters at least three basic problems. First, its premise that concentrated ownership is a defensive response to pressure from left-leaning social democracies seems doubtful, because it does not account for the presence of concentrated ownership in other countries. The most concentrated share ownership in the world appears to be in Asia,[267] not Europe, and at least some of the East Asian countries in which this form of ownership has reached the highest known levels of concentration seem closer to plutocracies than to democracies.[268] This is the dark side of concentrated ownership; put simply, the separation of cash-flow rights from voting rights can serve as a means by which those controlling the public sector can extend their control over the private sector. At a minimum, the prospect of crony capitalism—that is, closely interlocked political and economic leaderships, each reciprocally assisting the other—ensures that concentrated owners will need to become deeply involved in government in order to protect their positions from existing rivals, new entrants, and political sycophants. To be sure, ownership

---

[265] With regard to the take-over movement in Europe, see nn. 50–56 and accompanying text. Correspondingly, while it is possible that co-determination once discouraged transparent accounting, the inexorable movement toward a pan-European stock market is clearly bringing transparent accounting to Europe. See nn. 46–52 and accompanying text. Listing on Germany's Neuer Markt requires that the listed company comply with international accounting standards, not simply German standards. See V Fuhrmans, 'Playing by the Rules: How Neuer Markt Gets Respect' [2000] *Wall Street Journal*, August 21, 2000, C1; see also nn. 284–86 and accompanying text.

[266] University of Chicago Professor Gary Herrigel has closely studied the German industrial model and reported that the pressure of "international industrial competition" undermined the traditional German system of industrial relations in the 1990s. G. Herrigel, *Industrial Constructions* 275–77 (Chicago 1996). In his view, the traditional model of German industrial relations, which he characterizes as "Social Democratic Modell Deutschland" or "organized capitalism," has already become outdated, with actual labour-management bargaining now occurring on a more decentralised basis, frequently at the plant level. Ibid., 274–75, 281–85. As labour negotiations become localized, rather than national, the prospect of governmental intervention to pressure corporate employers, which seldom occurred even in the past, now recedes even further.

[267] See generally Claessens et al., *Separation of Ownership*, above, n. 258 (reviewing the ownership structure of 2,980 corporations in nine East Asian countries and finding that over two-thirds of the firms are controlled by a single shareholder, with voting rights frequently exceeding cash-flow rights as the result of pyramid structures and cross-holdings).

[268] Claessens, Djankov and Lang report that ownership of approximately 17% of the total market capitalisation in each of Indonesia and the Phillipines can be traced to a single family (the Marcos family in the Phillipines and the Suharto family in Indonesia). Ibid., 3. Indonesia was found to have more than two-thirds of its publicly listed companies controlled by a family if control were equated with ownership of 10% or more of the voting rights. Ibid., 24.

concentration may sometimes be a defensive strategy in a corrupt economy, but this has nothing to do with social democracy, and it implies an incestuous relationship between the dominant shareholders and political leaders.

Secondly, even if we assume that social democracies, however defined, do pressure managers to favour non-shareholder constituencies, it is far from clear that concentrated ownership would be a successful defence strategy. This is particularly true in countries such as Germany, where the largest shareowners are universal banks and other financial intermediaries. Both in Germany and elsewhere, large banks appear to be uniquely subject to governmental influence, not immune from it.[269] In contrast, dispersed shareowners are both anonymous and potentially a powerful political interest group. If, as currently reported,[270] 10% of German citizens own stocks and nearly fourteen percent own mutual funds, this is a constituency that few democratically elected politicians would dare to pressure. Put differently, there is safety in numbers, because it is politically safer for a government to pressure a few large holders than an anonymous herd of small investors. Logically, one does not lightly pressure a mobile corporation, which can re-deploy assets outside the country and whose increasingly international shareholders will expect such a response, but a social-democratic government can pressure large, concentrated shareholders, who often are less mobile and more visible.

In any event, the Roe hypothesis that concentrated ownership is a defence against overreaching by the social-democratic state frames a testable proposition: if concentrated ownership does outperform dispersed ownership in this special political setting, then corporations with concentrated ownership in such countries should exhibit greater profitability than those with dispersed ownership. But the data is precisely to the contrary. A recent study of 361 German corporations between 1991 and 1996 found "a significantly negative impact of ownership concentration on profitability as measured by the return on total assets".[271] Rather than protect shareholders, this study and earlier research have concluded that "concentration of ownership seems to further rent extraction".[272]

---

[269] See nn. 203–209 and accompanying text for a discussion of the traditional dependence of the German universal banks on the Finance Ministry.

[270] Ascarelli, above, n. 46.

[271] See E. Lehmann and J. Weigand, 'Does the Governed Corporation Perform Better? Governance Structures and Corporate Performance in Germany' [2000] 4 *European Finance Review* 157, 190. This finding of lower profitability held true both for quoted and non-quoted German firms and was found to support "the view that large shareholders inflict costs on the firm (e.g. rent extraction, too much monitoring, or infighting)." Ibid., 190.

[272] ibid., 164 (discussing earlier studies). Interestingly, there is some evidence that German firms with highly concentrated ownership "enjoyed higher returns during the 1970s and early 1980s," but this positive impact then eroded or turned negative during the late 1980s and thereafter. Ibid., 165. Lehmann and Weigand conclude that increasing international competition may have reversed the former profitability of ownership concentration. Ibid.

Finally, whatever the strength of the economic logic of this hypothesized relationship between social democracy and ownership structure, its historical foundations are shaky. In both the U.S. and the U.K., politics appears to have played
no more than a negligible role in the rise of dispersed ownership, and concentrated ownership was established in Germany and France by the late nineteenth
century, well before the earliest appearance of a social-democratic government
in either country. In addition, Cambridge Professor Brian Cheffins has found
that the separation of ownership and control in the United Kingdom actually
occurred during a period in which British Labour governments were pursuing
policies that can fairly be called social-democratic.[273] Under the Roe theory,
such a political environment should have produced increasing concentration of
share ownership, but it did not.

More generally, Professor Roe's claim that politics constrained the development of powerful financial intermediaries in the U.S. may read too much into the
limited evidence.[274] His hypothesis ignores that unconstrained institutional
investors in the U.K. closely resemble their American counterparts, even though
no regulatory inhibitions hobbled their growth.[275] Other things being equal, the
simpler model is preferable to the more complex. Here, the simpler model is that
financial institutions greatly value liquidity and hence do not wish to hold large
and illiquid equity stakes in business corporations.[276] Concentrated ownership
therefore occurs when legislative policies encourage it, and our earlier tour of the
French and German experiences suggested that concentrated ownership was
legislatively shaped by such policies.[277]

Finally, Professor Roe's thesis rests on the behavioural premise that large
investors in social-democratic countries seek to avoid the culture of transparency that comes with the development of securities markets, because it would
arguably subject them to even greater expropriation by the state. A problem
with this reasoning, however, is that if concentrated ownership were an important defence mechanism against social democracy, then social democracies
should logically seek to encourage ownership dispersion by, for example,
enhancing transparency. Logically, on Roe's behavioural premise, left-leaning

---

[273] See n. 128 and accompanying text.

[274] For a full statement of the claim, see M.J. Roe, *Strong Managers, Weak Owners: The
Political Roots of American Corporate Finance* (New York 1994).

[275] B.S. Black and J.C. Coffee, Jr, 'Hail Britannia?: Institutional Investor Behaviour Under
Limited Regulation' [1994] 92 Michigan Law Review 1997.

[276] I have argued this "liquidity versus control" thesis at considerable length elsewhere, Coffee,
above, n. 21, and will not elaborate further here. Suffice it to say that banks, as institutions with
short-term liabilities to depositors, have a major problem with making illiquid long-term investments.

[277] The pattern is clearest in Germany where the Finance Ministry subsidized the largest banks
with low-cost loans and in turn encouraged them to lend to heavy industry on a massive scale. See
nn. 205–207 and accompanying text.

governments should favour the development of securities markets in order to gain greater control over the private sector. In principle, one should then observe private investors across Europe opposing the development of securities markets while the left advocates their growth. The reverse is probably closer to the truth, although, in fact, a broad consensus across Europe seems today to support the growth of securities markets.

To sum up, the Roe social-democratic thesis does not explain the origins of concentrated ownership in any country, certainly does not explain its persistence in Asia or much of the Third World, and only explains its survival in Europe if one accepts the debatable premise that a few large owners can better resist governmental pressure than can an anonymous herd of small investors. The better historical and political explanation for the bank-centred system of corporate governance that has dominated Europe until recently is that it maximized state control of the economy.[278] Particularly in times of war and social turmoil during the last century, those in power—whether socialists or fascists—preferred a bank centred system, because large banks were ultimately more subject to state control than were securities markets.[279] That securities markets have developed slowly across Europe thus may well have a political as well as a legal explanation, but that political explanation is that power-seeking nationalists could use

---

[278] For one version of this thesis, see R.G. Rajan and L Zingales, *The Great Reversals: The Politics of Financial Development in the 20th Century* (National Bureau of Economic Research, Working Paper no. 8178, 2001), available at http://papers.ssrn.com/paper.taf?abstract_id=236100. Under their "interest group" theory of financial development, incumbents opposed financial development because it bred competition. This is certainly consistent with the French history and much of the German history. In France, the *Bourse* sought to disable the Coulisse from conducting a rival market. See nn. 152–157 and accompanying text. Similarly, in Germany, the Junker aristocracy long resisted free incorporation and the creation of incorporated banks. See nn. 192–198 and accompanying text.

[279] Rajan and Zingales examine the experiences of several countries during the early to middle twentieth century and find that, while ideologies differed, "the basic outcome did not: the working of financial markets was severely impaired by the intervention of the Government, which assumed a greater direct and indirect role in allocating funds to industry". Ibid.,42. The common denominator, they argue, is that, in the absence of external competition, "the government and the bankers . . . [can] enter into a Faustian pact, with the government restricting entry and inter-bank competition, ostensibly in the interest of the stability of the system, and bankers obeying government diktats about whom to lend to in return for being allowed to be part of the privileged pact". Ibid., 41. The government's goal in protecting banks from competition was to cause "private investment to flow through the banking sector because these flows could be more easily directed to preferred activities than if they went through the arm's length markets where the government had little control". Ibid. This is a powerful theory that applies both to the desires of European governments engaged in an arms race during the late 1930s and Asian governments seeking to control the private sector in the 1990s. Better than Roe's social democracy theory of concentrated ownership, this theory fits the historical evidence. Indeed, although Rajan and Zingales do not discuss nineteenth-century Germany, its experience with the state encouraging the largest banks to subsidize selected industries also is captured by their theory. See nn. 205–207 and accompanying text.

banks as their agents and that banks, once entrenched, had natural reasons to resist the rise of rivals for their business.

Moreover, the idea that the state should control and manage the economy was not a new idea in continental Europe, but rather a continuation of policies and attitudes that dated back to feudal times. In this light, the real division is not between left and right, but between centralized and decentralized. Those countries—most notably the U.K. and the Netherlands—that were the most decentralized and that divorced economic activity from political control were, not surprisingly, the first to develop true securities markets.

IV. Implications for Transitional Economies

If this chapter's assessment is correct that strong self-regulation was the principal catalyst for the appearance of an active and liquid market in equity securities and the arrival of dispersed ownership, then very practical implications follow. Even in countries with weak legal protections for minority shareholders, it may be possible for those firms that are prepared to bond themselves, install credible monitoring controls, and meet higher standards of disclosure to sell stock to dispersed public shareholders at prices exceeding that which a controlling shareholder would pay. Similarly, the void created by weak formal law can be at least partially filled by a functional substitute: strong stock exchange rules or other forms of self-regulation. These claims do not deny the desirability of stronger formal legal rules or the likelihood that shareholder values will be further maximized by such legal changes. But the thrust of this chapter is to suggest that a very real payoff can be obtained from private ordering and credible corporate governance.

Speculative as this prediction may sound, there is already some persuasive empirical evidence to support it. If the U.S. equity market grew and attracted foreign capital, despite the highly publicized predations of the robber barons,[280] it is at least plausible that the same phenomenon could occur in contemporary Russia, where legal institutions appear equally weak or weaker. The available evidence suggests that a similar process is already well underway. Professor Bernard Black has found that firm-specific corporate governance practices do greatly affect the market value of publicly traded Russian companies.[281] Using corporate governance rankings prepared in 1999 by one Russian investment bank, he compared these ratings with a "value ratio" of actual market capitalization to theoretical Western market capitalization for these same firms prepared by another investment bank. The value ratios revealed the high discounts

---

[280] See nn. 73–87 and accompanying text.

[281] See B.S. Black, 'Does Corporate Governance Matter?: A Crude Test Using Russian Data' [2001] 149 University of Pennsylvania Law Review 2131.

that investors applied to these firms, and they showed an enormous variation with some firms trading at only 0.01% of their theoretical Western market value, while others traded at nearly half their Western value. Most importantly, the correlation between the firms' corporate governance rankings and their value ratios was strikingly high and statistically significant.[282] Even small changes in governance rankings produced substantial changes in firm value.[283] The natural inference from this data is that corporate governance matters, but also that private actors can generate credible signals that at least partially satisfy investor demands for adequate governance. Thus, although a legal regime may provide inadequate protections itself, those firms that install a credible corporate governance structure can, through private ordering, achieve a much higher proportion of their potential value in a Western market.[284] Obviously, the implications of this and similar findings are two-sided: much can be done through private action, but full valuation may require Western-style legislation and enforcement.

The other aspect of the nineteenth century American experience that appears to be in the process of being re-enacted today involves stock exchange self-regulation. A century ago, the NYSE adopted rules that were considerably stricter than prevailing local law. Today, the Neuer Markt in Germany appears to be following its example. Created as an intended European rival to Nasdaq with the hope that it could provide a market for high-tech start-up companies, the Neuer Markt has grown from two to 302 listed companies in only three years, with a current aggregate market capitalization of $172 billion.[285] Yet not only does the Neuer Markt have stricter disclosure and listing standards than its own parent, the Deutsche Borse, but it actually prides itself on being the "most regulated market" in Europe.[286] Such a strategy seems identical to that of the NYSE a century earlier: develop reputational capital by pledging to observe requirements far stricter than those required by local law. The Neuer Markt's success has

---

[282] Professor Black found a very robust correlation between the value ratio and the governance ranking that yielded a Pearson *r* equal to .90. Ibid., 2133. He concluded that corporate governance was the "dominant determinant of the value ratio". Ibid., 2143.

[283] In Professor Black's study, a one-standard deviation change in governance ranking predicted an eight-fold increase in firm value. Ibid. at 2133.

[284] A recent study of 495 companies by CLSA Emerging Markets has reached similar conclusions to Professor Black's study. This study found that while the stocks of the 100 largest companies in the sample fell by 8.7% in 2000, the stocks of the 25 companies rated best for corporate governance rose by an average of 3.3%. It concluded that the correlation between good corporate governance and share performance for large companies is "a near perfect fit." P. Day, 'Corporate Governance Can Be Strong Indicator of Stock Performance Within Emerging Markets' *Wall Street Journal,* May 1, 2001, C14.

[285] V. Fuhrmans, *Playing by the Rules: How Neuer Markt Gets Respect, Wall Street Journal,* August 21, 2000, at C1.

[286] ibid. (quoting *Deutsche Börse* Chief Executive Werner Seifert).

already produced attempts to imitate it continents away.[287] The point here is not that law does not matter, but that partial functional substitutes for formal legal requirements are both feasible and spreading.

E. Conclusion

The ongoing debate over common-law versus civil law legal systems may have obscured the greater impact of a hidden variable on the growth of securities markets, namely, the level of state involvement in economic decision-making. Three generalizations emerge from a historical examination of the rise of dispersed ownership:

First, the growth of securities exchanges and the rise of dispersed ownership correlate most closely not with specific legal rules or protections, but with the appearance of a private sector that is relatively free from direct governmental interference. A political economy that was decentralized and pluralistic fostered the growth of securities markets by permitting private entrepreneurs to devise their own techniques with which to make their promises credible. In more centralized economies, the government found it more convenient to use large banks to accomplish its purposes. Thus securities markets first arose in Amsterdam and London—two societies characterized by relative decentralization, but having very different legal systems. This suggests that doctrinal legal differences had only a secondary impact and that the fundamental precondition for the separation of ownership and control was the recognition—both legal and political—of the presumptive autonomy of the private sector. A case can be made that the greater activism and entrepreneurial energy shown by private institutions in the common-law world is at least partially attributable to the common law's greater tolerance for private law-making. But even in the common-law world, the emergence of self-regulation was not automatic. Organizational differences and other path dependent reasons explain why the NYSE moved more quickly than the LSE to protect shareholders and raise listing standards. In the absence of pervasive judicial corruption or regulatory arbitrage, there was less urgency in the U.K. than in the U.S. to develop bonding mechanisms or other protections for minority investors. Add to this the fact that the U.S. was a capital-importing debtor nation, while the U.K. was a

---

[287] Brazil's Novo Mercado is the clearest example. It invited U.S. institutional investors to help it design its listing rules, which forbid the issuance of nonvoting shares and require compliance with U.S. or international accounting standards. Merrill Lynch ranks the new exchange as significantly more protective of minority investors than the main Brazilian exchange. See C. Karmin and J. Karp, 'Brazilian Market Tries Friendly Approach' *Wall Street Journal,* May 10, 2001, C1. Thus, as in the case of the Neuer Markt, the newest exchange must bond itself more.

capital-exporting creditor,[288] and the quicker pace of developments at the NYSE becomes easily understandable.

Perhaps the more striking contrast during the late nineteenth and early twentieth centuries was that between private exchanges (such as the LSE and the NYSE) and the virtual state-run monopoly that was the Paris Bourse. The active role taken by the French government in intruding so deeply into the affairs of the Paris Bourse that the Ministry of Finance had to approve all new listings and transfers of seats seems a paradigm of the kind of state control that could suffocate the development of both self-regulation and innovation. Yet, virtually this same level of government involvement in listing decisions seems evident today in contemporary China.[289] Such state intrusion in the market seems likely to outweigh the impact of legal variables, including the choice between common-law and civil-law rules.

Secondly, to the extent that any political theory can explain the persistence of concentrated ownership, that theory is that it has protected entrenched incumbents from competition and innovation. It was not coincidental that both the NYSE and LSE faced (and ultimately overcame) active competitors in the late nineteenth century, while the competitors of the Paris Bourse were legislatively constrained. Although it cannot be proven that the more decentralized character of common-law legal institutions made inevitable the rise of self-regulatory bodies in the U.S. and the U.K., it is considerably clearer that private monopolies (such as the Paris Bourse) were the product of a centralized state-run economy. To this extent, the French experience suggests a basic reason for the slower growth and evolution of securities markets in civil-law countries: that competition and innovation go hand-in-hand.

More generally, bank-centred economies appear to facilitate government control over the flow of investment, while market-centred economies impede such control.[290] Although real historical examples fit this simpler political theory of concentrated ownership, no concrete evidence in contrast shows that

---

[288] Between 1870 and 1900, foreign investment in the U.S. more than doubled. See Carosso, n. 68, at 30. Correspondingly, capital was flowing from the U.K. to overseas borrowers, as from 1856 to 1913 net overseas assets in the U.K. rose from 9.3% of all assets to 34%. See Michie, n. 82, at 112.

[289] Although China has an active and volatile securities market, "China's government controls the vast majority of the companies whose shares trade on the country's two exchanges, in Shanghai and Shenzhen, and so far, politics has played a larger role than profits in the companies' fates". C.S. Smith, 'Shanghai Exchange Expels a Poorly Performing Stock', *New York Times,* April 25, 2001, W1. Until this year, exchange officials had not enforced listing requirements with respect to "state-owned, politically well-connected enterprises". Ibid. When one such company was de-listed by the Shanghai Exchange after four consecutive years of losses, this precedent merited a story in the *New York Times*, but even that story concluded that stock exchange "enforcement is likely to remain highly politicized, with little clear sign of why some companies are de-listed and others not". Ibid. The French model of politicized exchange regulation may then have a modern analogue.

[290] See nn. 278–279 and accompanying text.

concentrated ownership has served as a protection for shareholders against the re-distributive designs of social-democratic governments. Rather, much contemporary evidence demonstrates that concentrated ownership systems can serve as a means by which powerful families and governments reinforce each other and control economies in some areas of the Third World. Crony capitalism is the dark side of concentrated ownership, and it has simply been ignored by the proponents of political theories of finance.

The rise of dispersed ownership has recently encountered little political opposition, but this may be because the barriers to free trade and cross-border capital flows have already fallen.[291] Some hostility to the growth of securities markets can be dimly discerned in Europe, but it dates back to the late nineteenth century and was most evident at that time in Germany,[292] a country that could not then be called by any stretch of the imagination a social democracy. Correspondingly, the reliance of German firms on bank finance seems to have been state-determined, in large part caused by legislative restrictions on the issuance of securities.[293] The limited amount of legislation that has restricted securities markets in Europe seems to have been less the product of rent-seeking by banks than the moralistic sense of legislators, prodded by scandals, that trading on the stock market was "little better than gambling".[294] No plausible connection is historically discernable, however, between the rise of the social welfare state and the decline of securities markets. Although European securities markets declined in relative size during most of the twentieth century, two world wars that devastated the continent of Europe supply the most sensible explanation for that decline.

Thirdly, the cause and effect sequence posited by the LLS&V thesis may in effect read history backwards. They argue that strong markets require strong mandatory rules as a precondition. Although there is little evidence that strong legal rules encouraged the development of either the New York or London Stock Exchanges (and there is at least some evidence that strong legal rules hindered the growth of the Paris Bourse), the reverse does seem to be true: Strong markets do create a demand for stronger legal rules. Both in the U.S. and the U.K., as liquid securities markets developed and dispersed ownership became prevalent, a new political constituency developed that desired legal rules capable of filling in the inevitable enforcement gaps that self-regulation left. Both the federal secu-

[291] This is essentially the hypothesis that Rajan and Zingales have offered. See nn. 278–280 and accompanying text.

[292] See Michie, above, n. 110, 42 (finding that "German companies were denied the ease of access to finance via security issues that their British counterparts enjoyed").

[293] See nn. 210–219 and accompanying text.

[294] See Michie, above n. 101, 286. This interpretation is, of course, also consistent with Professor Banner's thesis that securities legislation is adopted only in the wake of scandals. See Banner, above, n. 13.

rities laws passed in the 1930s in the U.S. and the Company Act amendments adopted in the late 1940s in the U.K. were a response to this demand (and both were passed by essentially social-democratic administrations seeking to protect public securities markets). More recently, as markets have matured across Europe, similar forces have led to the creation of European parallels to the SEC.[295] In each case, the law appears to be responding to changes in the market, not consciously leading it.

In this light, if private institutional structures played the pivotal role in the rise of dispersed ownership in the U.S. and the U.K., what does this fact portend for the future of corporate governance in Europe and in transitional economies? The good news in this Article is that self-regulation might take hold in Europe and in the transitional economies, even though optimal legislation remains lacking. The bad news is that the mere transplanting of U.S. or U.K. law to transitional economies may not accomplish its intended goals if the government still directs, approves, and vetoes major economic decisions in the private sector. Currently, the state's hand in purely economic decisions such as exchange listings remains easily visible in many countries.[296] Once concentrated ownership degenerates into a "crony capitalization" that unites political and economic power, the role of law is likely to become minimal.

To the extent that a decentralized political economy was the critical precondition that enabled active securities markets to arise in both Holland and England, the appearance of open, competitive markets in transitional economies will be the more telling signal that a real transition has occurred and that capital markets can develop. Even in a legal environment in which investor protection is substandard, the optimist can still hope that private actors may develop private institutions capable of partially filling this legal vacuum, just as they did in the U.S. during the late nineteenth century. Rather than wait for optimal legislation to be enacted, companies in these countries have the practical ability to adopt governance and contractual reforms that will enable them to access Western financial markets or to distinguish themselves credibly from firms in their own markets that remain ready to exploit minority investors. By no means does this imply that stronger legislation protecting minority rights is not desirable, but historically this step has followed, rather than preceded, the initial growth of the equity market.

Today, the most dynamic forces on the European stage are not the various efforts to secure harmonized corporate and securities law, but rather the quieter changes that are currently underway in the markets themselves, including (1) the inexorable movement toward a pan-European stock exchange; (2) the increased activity of securities analysts with regard to European corporations

---

[295] See n. 255 and accompanying text.
[296] See n. 289 and accompanying text.

with minority public ownership;[297] (3) the accelerating convergence in international accounting standards;[298] and (4) the current international wave of mergers and acquisitions. None of these conclusions deny that remedial legislation is desirable in order to establish stronger minority protections, but the U.S.' and the U.K.'s experiences suggest that if private actors can generate credible signals that investor rights will be protected, then an equity market can arise, and in time protective legislation will predictably follow. Indeed, self-regulatory initiatives have already begun to play a critical role in the development of European securities markets, particularly in countries where the prevailing legal rules seem weak.[299]

In this light, the short term is harder to predict than the long term. The crash of the high-tech market in 2001, the American corporate scandals of 2001–2002, and overall economic uncertainty will predictably slow the rise of an "equity culture" in Europe. But it has not been the point of this chapter to predict how quickly institutions will change or a new culture develop. Rather, the central claim has been that the development of securities markets occurs principally through private action, not public action. The historical role of public action—i.e., legislation and regulatory rule-making—has more been to codify and generalize standards that have already begun to appear in the marketplace. This conclusion does not assert that the unbroken development of global securities markets is inevitable, because history clearly shows that governments seeking to control and direct their economies may prefer bank-centered systems of finance to securities markets, which are inherently fickle and unresponsive to governmental influence, and so may act to favor one structure of finance over another. Still, even in the face of governmental resistance, private actors have relevant options, including cross-listing in foreign markets. Hence, for the long-run, continued financial convergence and global equity market development seem safe predictions, with political considerations affecting more the pace, than the direction, of change.

---

[297] On this important theme, see J.J. Chang et al., *Analyst Activity Around the World*, (SSRN Electronic Library, Working Paper no. 204,570, 2000) (finding analysts able to penetrate and restate earnings of companies with concentrated ownership and non-transparent accounting), available at http://papers.ssrn.com/paper.taf?abstract_id=204570 .

[298] See J. Land and M. Lang, *Empirical Evidence on the Evolution of Global Accounting* (SSRN Electronic Library, Working Paper no. 233,602, 2000) (finding strong evidence of such convergence), available at http://papers.ssrn.com/paper.taf?abstract_id=233602.

[299] See nn. 281–286 and accompanying text.

Index